THE ENVIRONMENTAL ETHICS
AND POLICY BOOK

THE ENVIRONMENTAL ETHICS AND POLICY BOOK

Philosophy, Ecology, Economics

Donald VanDeVeer □ Christine Pierce

North Carolina State University

Wadsworth Publishing Company
Belmont, California
A Division of Wadsworth

Philosophy Editor: Kenneth King
Editorial Assistant: Kristina Pappas
Production Editor: The Book Company
Print Buyer: Karen Hunt
Permissions Editor: Robert Kauser
Designer: Cynthia Bogue
Copy Editor: Bob Klingensmith
Cover: Cassandra Chu
Cover Photo: Uniphoto, Inc.
Signing Representative: Charles Delmar
Compositor: Graphic Composition, Inc.
Printer: Arcata Graphics/Fairfield

This book is printed on acid-free recycled paper.

I(T)P ™

International Thomson Publishing
The trademark ITP is used under license

Printed in the United States of America

1 2 3 4 5 6 7 8 9 10—98 97 96 95 94

Library of Congress Cataloging in Publication Data
VanDeVeer, Donald, 1939–
　The environmental ethics and policy book : philosophy, ecology, and economics / Donald VanDeVeer, Christine Pierce.
　　p.　cm.
　Includes bibliographical references.
　ISBN 0-534-21030-9
　1. Human ecology—Moral and ethical aspects.　2. Environmental policy—Moral and ethical aspects.　I. Pierce, Christine.
II. Title.
GF80.V36　1993
179′.1—dc20　　　　　　　　　　　　　　　　　　　93-5289
　　　　　　　　　　　　　　　　　　　　　　　　　CIP

Preface

This text is designed for students in under-graduate, university-level courses[1] who wish to explore in depth questions about *how on earth we ought to live,* e.g., how we can live responsibly with nonhumans and the planet. Although primarily oriented toward questions of ethics that are broadly understood, and approached philosophically, the volume crosses academic disciplines and attends seriously to economic reasoning and its implications for environmental policy issues. It seeks to unearth, to extract for critical attention, the relevant moral or normative presuppositions which underlie policy recommendations, whether they are made, for example, by biologists, ecologists, economists, philosophers, or public officials. Such recommendations are heavily influenced by scientific beliefs; hence the text includes important essays by Stephen Jay Gould, Edward O. Wilson, Norman Myers, Rachel Carson, Garrett Hardin, Stephen Schneider, and others. Although often critical of mainstream economics, the volume includes a variety of views from economists: A. Myrick Freeman, Herman Leonard, Richard Zeckhauser, Herman Daly, Robert Repetto, and Alan Randall. It includes historically important papers or excerpts by various philosophers, historians, and environmentalists, e.g., Peter Singer, Kenneth Goodpaster, Aldo Leopold, and Lynn White, Jr.

[1] We also believe that the volume is well suited for graduate courses when supplemented appropriately.

Some of the key topics are:

- Preserving biodiversity
- Moral relations with nonhumans
- Ethical grounds for decision making
- Relations to the biosphere at large
- The moral standing of ecosystems
- The deep ecology movement
- Ecofeminism
- Third-world criticism of first-world policies
- Principles of interspecific conflict resolution
- Market solutions to problems; efficiency
- Cost-benefit analysis
- Ecological sustainability (an ignored value)
- Measures of economic and ecological health
- Population pressures; reproductive choice
- Intergenerational justice
- The place of private property; the "takings" issue
- The value of forests and wilderness
- The trashing of the planet
- Ozone deterioration
- Global warming; potential catastrophe
- Modes of environmental activism

In the selection of essays, in the Previews that introduce and set in context the 16 subsections, in the six Sidelights designed to touch on related issues, and in the extensive Introduction to Ethical Theory, we have sought to create a volume which:

· Contains a thorough range of views

· Is readable, with down-to-earth examples

· Is scientifically literate and informed

· Is intelligible to curious, intelligent readers

· Ranges from philosophical assumptions to policy

· Explains key terminology and avoids jargon

· Presents diverse views

· Contains the vast majority of materials that instructors desire for courses in environmental ethics or policy

We were duly impressed, and sometimes overwhelmed, by all the knowledge that was or could have been helpful in designing the volume that we wished to create. Our reach sometimes exceeded our grasp. However, we sought to construct a coherent whole from the relevant materials, one which reflects the deepest concerns of citizens of the planet and centers on those of professionals in a variety of fields: biology, forestry, economics, philosophy, and climatology, for example. Indeed we hope that people from diverse fields may talk and listen to each other more. Doing so could initiate a useful form of erosion, the erosion of stereotypes we have about each other, or about other academic disciplines. We believe that this is an urgent matter.

Our work on this volume has heightened our sadness about some of the ways in which we humans are transforming the planet and our fears about what more may happen to it. There is hope for change, but change cannot occur without the adoption of radically different attitudes. Such a transfor-

mation can come to pass if we think through, reexamine, and critically appraise our ethical and empirical beliefs about what we are doing and our effects on the milieu of life in which we exist. Ideas have consequences, especially the "prevailing" ones. However, many of the prevailing ideas are only comforting us about what we are doing as we play roulette with species of ancient lineage and with the biosphere.

We are grateful to many people for their honest feedback about the proposed structure of this volume and for their sometimes detailed comments and criticisms of the evolving contents and writing. Some comments were like vaccinations: they stung but were good for us. Occasionally we disagreed with analyses. However, we very much valued honest responses, of all sorts, and have not the slightest doubt that the book is enormously better than it would have been in the absence of the diverse and extensive responses which we received. Our editor at Wadsworth, Ken King, went to considerable length to ensure that good feedback was made available. We profited from the extensive remarks of Talbot Page and especially those of Anthony Weston, who was patient and instructive. Marvin Soroos, at North Carolina State University, was generous with help on the Bibliography. We also benefitted from the suggestions or assistance of Claudia Card, Robin Attfield, Dale Jamieson, J. Baird Callicott, Eric Katz, Bryan Norton, Mark Sagoff, and Tom Regan. Without our full consent, Beth Timson and Ed Martin took away our pens and enhanced our computer literacy. We were sped along with the typing assistance and bright smile of Wanda McLean. We were delighted that Ann Rives periodically gave us chocolates or otherwise bailed us out. We are further indebted to the many instructors who have used our collection, *People, Penguins, and Plastic Trees: Basic Issues in Environmental Ethics*, the predecessor to this volume. We thank those instructors for their usage and comments, and we welcome responses to this collection.[2]

[2] We can be reached by telephone at 919-515-3214 at North Carolina State University or by FAX at 919-515-7856. Our address is: Department of Philosophy and Religion, Box 8103, North Carolina State University, Raleigh, NC 27695-8103.

We also thank Georgia Brown, Chris Pierce's Siamese cat, who helped develop the section on deep ecology by insisting on reviewing the text whenever that subject was being considered. Finally, any mistakes in the volume are to be blamed on our parents; but for them there would not have been any.

Contents

VI PROBLEMS AND ENVIRONMENTAL POLICIES   370

INTRODUCTION

Don't look back. Something might be
gaining on you.

Satchel Paige

We are simply not very good at recognizing
slowly emerging catastrophes. People seldom
notice the onset of cancer. The first stages of
the death of a lake tend to fall beneath the
threshold of attention. The dying of a forest
may occur slowly and imperceptibly, until
nothing can be done to save it. If we have been
causing the catastrophic warming of the
planet by our industrial activities in the last
two centuries, we may not realize it "for sure"
until tragedy is upon us. And if we have not
properly valued the lives of the hundreds of
thousands, perhaps millions, of species becoming extinct during our, and the next, generation, the products of billions of years of
evolution may be gone because we have chosen, half-wittingly, to play "Russian roulette"
with the planet in the name of profit maximizing, efficiency, "progress," or some other modern "god." To have a clue about "what on
earth we are doing," we need a clear, well-
reasoned basis for deciding how to *evaluate*
what we are doing. The price of our not doing
so is already being paid by virtually all species of living creatures, as well as our own.

For reasons that are made clear in various
parts of this volume, there is much under the
sun that is going awry, or has already done so.
This claim is not entirely uncontroversial.
Why think so? What exactly are we doing to
the planet that we ought not to be doing or
that we ought to be doing differently? There
is much dispute about how to deal appropriately with our nonhuman surroundings: the
other animals, the forests, the air, and the
oceans, for example.

Indeed, one of the fundamental questions
explored in this volume is whether living beings other than humans have a value of their
own, not reducible to their instrumental value
(the value of something as a means to an end)
to human beings. As we shall put the point,
do such beings have "moral standing"? If so,
just what value should we assign to, or recognize in, such beings, and why? Or can we determine what is the "right thing to do" to "nature" or nonhuman entities solely on the basis
of considering the short- or long-term interests of humans of this and/or future generations? These questions, and diverse answers
to them, underlie competing views concerning a host of important issues. The belief that
certain nonhumans do have moral standing
has motivated the formulation of a new "environmental ethic" and a critique of traditional
moral philosophy and economic theory, both
of which historically have assumed that all
and only humans "count" (an assumption labeled "*anthropocentrism*").

In the last decade especially, a further criticism has developed, a criticism of those who,
although they recognize certain nonhumans
as having a kind of inherent worth of their
own, still restrict the bearers of value to individual animals or plants. Some environmental
thinkers believe that such a view cannot account for the value of ecosystems, habitats,
systems of life, indeed the existence of a biodiverse and ecologically sustainable planet. So,
from this critical stance, if we are to formulate
the right view to take about our planet or the
biosphere, we must surrender both the anthropocentric assumption that all and only humans possess inherent worth or value and the
widely held assumption that only *individuals*
have such value. The wrong view on these

matters is not only intellectually indefensible; acting on this view promises to destroy the biosphere, and perhaps more quickly than people realize who are unaware of the current rate of extinction of nonhumans, the connections between modern industrialization as often practiced, and its destructive effects on our global climate.

The development of a comprehensive, reasoned view about how we ought to be dealing with our nonhuman environment may be labeled an "environmental ethic." We would not quarrel with those who wish to speak of an "ecological ethic" or a "moral philosophy of the environment." In the final analysis, this volume is philosophical in the somewhat restricted sense in which professional philosophers use that term, and not in the loose and popular sense in which our university once offered a course in the "philosophy of home decorating." Indeed, the materials presented herein were chosen with the aim of setting out those relevant facts, moral principles, and other considerations which foster the formulation of such an ethic.

Problems about pollution, pesticide use, smog, worries about running out of fossil fuels, and so on are now familiar. However, because of the rapid growth in the human population, our commandeering of remaining animal habitats, the great increase in carbon emissions, the spread of the "cattle culture" (consequent demand for land for grazing and/or growing grain and resulting destruction of the rain forest), we are now bumping up against certain of nature's thresholds for the first time since humans came to exist on this planet. Our activities are more intense; our population has increased to almost six billion. Our impact is greater. Thus, our decisions, our modes of determining policy and designing social institutions, are more important than ever. As a cartoon character used to say, "Time's a wasting."

Successful formulation of a new environmental ethic will require attention to the best science available. For reasons suggested in Part I, "Introduction to Ethical Theory," empirical assumptions will play a crucial role in the formulation and defense of normative or moral conclusions about what we ought to be doing with regard to environmental policies. Indeed, we believe that philosophers, scientists, analysts, and formulators of public policy are doomed to important failures if they follow a different path.

Scientists, like others, are often guided by normative assumptions, however, of which they are only dimly aware and which, hence, often lie hidden.[1] In contrast to some volumes concerned with environmental issues, we tried to give a prominent place to the *unearthing and critical examination of moral principles* which are often invoked either explicitly (openly) or tacitly. Further, one cannot be in a position to decide whether a new ethic, a new "environmental ethic," is needed unless one has an understanding of the leading and dominant points of view up until the last decade or so, at which time they began to come under assault. For those reasons, a somewhat extensive and detailed (to newcomers) review of the leading, competing ethical outlooks is provided in the Introduction to Ethical Theory. A complete first reading may be usefully followed by a rereading of relevant parts as the occasion arises. Some instructors in college or university courses will choose to assign parts of it in a piecemeal fashion. In this regard some of the essays can be read easily and easily understood by the typical advanced undergraduate student. Others are more like a steep curved road and require slow, careful driving, perhaps with a rest stop thrown in as one gets weary of completing the whole trip without a break. Sometimes a guide is crucial.

A word is much in order about how we chose the essays or excerpts and also what led us to order them as we did. First, the range of materials available on the issues discussed herein is extensive. Ideally, a person fully knowledgeable in biology, geology, meteorology, climatology, ethics, political philosophy, forestry, botany, economics, decision theory, *and* a few other domains would make a good editor. This editorial pair failed to qualify in this respect. Still, we refused to "stay on our own turf" as might more proper academicians. No doubt we are, therefore, still unaware of some the best essays deserving consideration. In addition to our own limitations, there is a kind of holistic consideration in choosing essays; we wanted some degree of balance and diversity, not among all views, but among those which we believe deserve a hearing. Sheer lack of space also led to some painful omissions. In some cases the historical influence of an essay led to its inclusion, even if we thought that it was not the most sophisticated or the most illuminating one available; in some cases we opted for essays of high quality which have not been so influential, at least not yet.

We comment now about our ordering of the materials and briefly identify the focal points of the different sections in the seven parts of this volume.

After the initial survey, in Part I, of the leading ethical theories, the vocabulary and ingredients of moral argument, some reflection on the relation of moral and empirical claims, and the relevance of science to normative policy conclusions, we turn in Part II, "Western Religions and Environmental Attitudes," to a limited examination of the influence of the Judeo-Christian tradition on our environmental attitudes and policies over the last 2000 plus years. A focal point concerns historian Lynn White's famous essay which traces some of the historic roots of our current environmental crises to the influence of that tradition. There are also, of course, important secular thinkers who have influenced our environmental attitudes; e.g., the views of Aristotle, Descartes, Bentham, J. S. Mill, Darwin and others emerge elsewhere in this book. Some brief comments on secular influences round out the Preview to Part II.

After the broad sweep of Part II, in large part a matter of intellectual history, Part III, "The Other Animals," focuses on our dealings with those nonhuman entities in "the environment," some of which closely resemble us and some of which are, in fact, loved by humans more than humans love, or care about, other members of their own species. It is tempting to think that if we ought to respect, attribute rights to, or acknowledge duties toward any entities in the not-members-of-our-species category, it would be the animals, or at least some subset of them. So it seems natural to begin one's reflections there.

Part III begins the exploration of just what our stance toward animals should be; which ones are owed duties, if any, and on what grounds?

Part IV, "Constructing an Environmental Ethic," examines the arguments underlying the assumption that we have stringent duties to nonhuman animals (itself a nontraditional view) and *at most* to them. Indeed, this view is attacked or questioned on at least two fronts. First, some claim that it is not merely some set of animals (e.g., those that are sentient or are subjects of a life) to which we owe duties of nonharm (or, for example, respect or aid), but a wider range of entities in the nonhuman environment, for example, all living creatures. Thus, defenders of *"biocentric"* views may attribute a kind of noninstrumental or intrinsic worth both to plants and animals, if not the inanimate parts of the planet which interact in a crucial, life-supporting way with living creatures. *"Biocentric egalitarians"* may attribute "equal inherent worth," in some sense, to all living creatures (not necessarily implying that all merit equal *treatment*). Thus, these philosophers, and others, view "animal liberationists" (such as Peter Singer or Tom Regan) as stopping short in their recognition of beings which possess moral standing (on this latter concept, see the preview to Part III). Another deep source of disagreement is that between those who think that intrinsic value is attributable not to nonhuman *individuals* only (e.g., animals or trees) but rather to certain complexes, for example, to ecosystems or habitats or perhaps to the planet as a whole—and those who take a more "individualist" view of things. The former may discount, or even deny, that individual animals and other entities possess intrinsic value. The latter are often accused of only extending those bounds of moral concern which were defined more narrowly by traditional theories of rights or the theory of utilitarianism (see Part I). Holistically oriented critics, especially, claim that a more radical, new "ethic" is needed which goes beyond extending (compare "extensionist views") moral standing to nonhuman individuals.

If we allow that certain nonhuman entities have moral standing, the nature of conflicts of interest becomes considerably more complicated. Some essays in Part IV struggle with questions about how to resolve such conflicts. Others focus on the views of *"deep ecologists"* who bring their own brand of criticism to traditional anthropocentric orientations as well as dissent from other "environmentalist" views. In recent years some feminists have both defended certain views described as *"ecofeminist"* and explored the question of how feminist concerns mesh or do not mesh with those of certain environmentalists, e.g., those who think that the metaphor "Mother Earth" is useful in exploring questions of environmental policy. Vandana Shiva focuses on the special conflicts for women in "third-world" nations who may be caught between prodevelopment forces and those who call for something other than slash-and-burn approaches to economic growth.

Part V, "Economics, Ethics, and Ecology," focuses in part on the question of whether traditional economic theory incorporates a defensible view of what is intrinsically valuable. Since such theory and standard versions of cost-benefit analysis are normally entirely anthropocentric in outlook, there is much dispute over the use of cost-benefit techniques to decide questions of public policy regarding the environment—since such techniques tend to assign value only on the basis of individual humans' willingness and ability to pay in actual or hypothetical markets. But we may ask whether the value of a rain forest or a species should be equated with its market value during a *particular time slice*.

Two related points concern the extent to which that arch value of modern economics, efficiency, is, in fact, the only value worth promoting; indeed, how important is it to promote it at all given the technical sense assigned to that term in economic theory? Is efficiency well promoted by the marketplace and by the use of some of the standard techniques for recording benefits and losses in national income accounting (e.g., in methods for determining the "gross domestic product")? Sadly, a nation can sometimes squander its important natural assets without this loss showing up much in its national accounting procedures. Given the heroic effort economists make to measure the actual gains and losses related to various social arrangements and, further, the enormous influence economists have in the formulation of public policy, these questions are of great practical and theoretical importance. Section V-C explores some proposed new measures of how a nation is doing, ones with which users try to measure ecological, as well as economic, gains and losses.

Part V also examines a goal whose value was given little attention until recent years: *sustainability* of the ways in which we live. How to define sustainability and why it should be valued, if at all, are discussed. The relation of "economic health" to "ecological health" is also explored.

Part VI, "Problems and Environmental Policies," turns more directly to specific environmental problems and to questions of policy, especially concerns about population pressures and environmental "resources." Ironically, the Earth Summit at Rio de Janeiro in 1992 managed to avoid addressing what is, arguably, the major source of the rapid destruction of the earth's ecosystems and elimination of extraordinary numbers of the earth's species during this era, namely the vast increase in the *population* of the very adaptive, intelligent, and omnivorous species of which we are members. Questions of environmental policy are, thus, closely connected to questions about the desirability of controlling human population growth and the permissibility or obligation to do so. The regular political denial of this problem is, then, a further practical obstacle. Issues concerning the supply of natural resources and places for our wastes, "sources and sinks," are only made more urgent by population increases. One essayist, however, argues that resources are infinite, so we need not worry.

Both certain proposed solutions to some environmental problems and the explanations of some problems are tied to questions about the appropriate distribution of *property rights.* In a famous essay, "The Tragedy of the Commons," Garrett Hardin urges that many of our problems derive from the fact that certain goods are jointly owned or held in common, e.g., the oceans, the air, and certain lands. It is predictable that such "commons" are exploited since it is in the self-interest of anyone to partake of the benefits in question and to pass on the costs to others. But is the remedy to such problems to privatize such commons or to mutually to agree to coercively enforceable restraints—as Hardin suggests?

Perhaps the most important section on policy is Section VI-C on preserving biodiversity. The moral questions about whether we have duties to individual plants and animals, to species, or to entire ecosystems seem all the more urgent given that as we chainsaw and burn our forests, over 70 species become extinct each day, about 27,000 per year. At this moment we are turning the earth into a more sterile, more homogenous place; 20 percent of the earth's species will become extinct in the

next 30 years.[2] Facts about the rates and nature of extinction are well delineated in the essay by E. O. Wilson and in a later section by Norman Myers. Some puzzles about the concept of species and various grounds for preserving or not preserving species are also explored in Section VI-C.

Section VI-D focuses on forests and wilderness. One central point is related to the preservation of biodiversity in view of the fact that old-growth forests, and especially tropical rain forests, constitute the habitats of an astonishingly large number of the world's species. Although the record of the United States in some environmental matters has been, in a number of respects, admirable, there is much criticism of the policy of the U.S. Forest Service and its practice of massive clear-cutting and selling off the trees to logging companies at fees below the actual costs of putting in roads to, and maintaining, the forests. One wonders whether the American people would remain so acquiescent if the Lincoln Memorial, the wall dedicated to the soldiers who died in Viet Nam, the Statue of Liberty, or the Grand Canyon were being sold off for the benefit of private corporations. These matters are discussed by Perri Knize and Bryan Norton.

The final section in Part VI all too briefly touches on some very large issues concerning how we degrade the planet and its ecosystems, sometimes on a global scale. One is the familiar question of what to do to alleviate problems of *pollution.* And what should we do about the extraordinary amount of trash that we generate, often as a result of engrained consumer habits into which we have been socialized? Also important are the large pent-up demands of people in third-world nations; consider the possibility of most of one billion Chinese acquiring refrigerators, cars, televisions, and other goods. In addition to the exploration of these matters, two other selections examine two issues of cosmic importance, and perhaps of a proportion not comparable to that of any humanly induced problem in the history of humankind. One is the thinning of the protective ozone layer, arguably a problem now internationally acknowledged and acted on even if only with partial effectiveness. The other is the problem of global warming due, in part, to humanly generated carbon emissions and the consequent *intensification* of the "greenhouse effect." This latter problem, in the worst case, could make World War II seem like a minor event in terms of the sheer amount of morbidity and mortality that could result. So far, this issue has been largely ignored by the public and most politicians and denied by various corporate interests. The evidence suggests, however, the prospect of events of low to moderate probability occurring which would involve, as we have noted, horrendous losses of both humans and other living things.

In becoming more aware of the way things are, it seems perfectly natural to become more than a bit discouraged about what has happened, and what cannot be halted. After all, much of what is occurring has momentum and cannot be stopped or redirected quickly. Still, things can be done to alter policy, and, in fact, some are being done. The last part—Part VII, "Varieties of Activism"—considers questions about what one might do, assuming that one has done his or her "theoretical homework" and formulated a reasoned view about possible solutions. The options range from making personal changes in one's life-style, minor or major (compare giving up ivory piano keys, real fur from snow leopards, or the use of a car), to lobbying or educating in order to persuade others to change public policy and alter our political and economic institutions, or engaging in serious civil disobedience as have some of the courageous members of Earth First! or the Sea Shepherds.

A final word about the order of the readings. They can be read chronologically, and in some sections we ordered them with that in mind. The reader can move from the simpler to the more complex materials; the order in some sections reflects the difficulty of the content. We gave the heaviest consideration to pedagogical considerations, namely what we determined to be a useful order of investigation, reflection, teaching, and learning (especially the natural rhythms of learning)—and not necessarily learning over a two- or three-day period, but sequences that help to "put things in place" over a long time period (or span of material). For example, in "Preserving Biodiversity," puzzles and arguments about the preservation of species are explored initially; later, the reader is brought full circle in the fact-oriented piece of E. O. Wilson. By then, the reader is better able to consider the current wave of extinctions in a more developed intellectual framework. Then, he or she can perhaps step back and be self-critical, asking whether his or her first thoughts remain belief-worthy, and whether a coherent and defensible view is perhaps close at hand.

NOTES

1. The hideous experimentation of Nazi scientists and physicians on Jews and gypsies constitutes one example. The fudging of data on so-called IQ tests by American scientists during the 1920s and 1930s to support racist and ethnic preconceptions is documented by Stephen Jay Gould in *The Mismeasure of Man*. Government officials and physicians cooperated from the 1930s to the 1960s not to treat, and simply to observe, black men in the southern United States who were infected with syphilis (see James Jones, *Bad Blood*). And the lack of research on the causes and treatment of breast cancer in the United States probably reflects a certain sexist bias inside and outside the scientific professions, in view of the fact that breast cancer affects one out of nine women in the United States. One may hold the *belief* that one has a method which ensures the elimination of bias and irrationality, which, in part, fosters one's unwillingness to look critically and reasonably at certain of one's own inferences or beliefs. The point is, we think, well-supported in the history of science, philosophy, and other disciplines.

2. The figures are due to E. O. Wilson, *The Diversity of Life* (Cambridge, MA: Harvard University Press, 1992).

I

AN INTRODUCTION TO ETHICAL THEORY

The creatures with which we are particularly concerned were, not so long ago, gregarious to a fault, noisy, quarrelsome, arboreal, bossy, sexy, clever, tool-using, with prolonged childhoods and tender regard for their young. One thing led to another, and in a twinkling their descendants had multiplied all over the planet, killed off their rivals, devised world-transforming technologies, and posed a mortal danger to themselves and to the many other beings with whom they share their small home.

Carl Sagan and Ann Druyan[1]

I dislike arguments of any kind. They are always vulgar, and often convincing.

Oscar Wilde

A. MORAL ARGUMENT AND ETHICAL THEORY

1. DISTINGUISHING MORAL AND EMPIRICAL CLAIMS

Determining how we ought to live our "private" lives is hard enough; designing a just and sustainable nation is harder. Designing a just, sustainable, and biodiverse way to live on planet Earth is no mean task; it is not obvious that we members of *Homo sapiens* are up to the challenge—as we bicker during the largest extinction spasm since the last ice age and during massive, human-induced, risky changes in those processes which have hitherto supported life on earth.

Charles Darwin (1809–1882), author of *The Origin of Species*, is one of the most influential thinkers that the planet has ever seen. Since he was a notorious opponent of slavery and was known to heap "abuse" on those who readily took the whip to their horses, it comes as a surprise to read his words, "I want *practice* at mistreating the female sex."[2] The context of his remark is illuminating and exculpatory. He and a few fellow scientists (male) had managed to inflict a long, perhaps tedious, discussion of biological issues on their spouses (female). The context reveals that Darwin had used 'want' in its now archaic sense of 'lack' (to find someone "wanting in common sense" meant that he or she lacked common sense). Darwin, a generous man, did not mean that he desired practice at mistreating females. His remark did not suggest misogyny on his part after all, and our frequent desire to find flaws in great people must wait for another day. What, one might wonder, is the point of this piece of Darwiniana? It is simply that we often talk past each other, or simply do not grasp what someone is asserting unless we pay careful attention to the meaning of the words being used.

To begin our exploration of ethical theory and its relation to environmental issues, we need to reflect on the meaning of key terms such as 'moral,' 'ethical,' and 'empirical.' Ultimately, we want to have some reasonably clear concept of just what environmental ethics is and its role in the larger intellectual scheme of things, assuming that there is a larger scheme of things.

A widespread view is that morality is

1

about certain kinds of behavior, e.g., truth-telling, sexual behavior, or the use of force. But it is difficult to define 'morality' or 'ethics' in terms of kinds of behavior. Let us consider some paradigm (perfectly clear, noncontroversial) examples of moral or ethical claims:

> Rape is wrong.
>
> Child abuse is contrary to one's duty.
>
> We should not let people starve to death.
>
> It is sometimes all right to lie.
>
> Jeffrey Dahmer was an evil man.
>
> Human life is very valuable.

By way of contrast, consider this list of sentences:

> Rape is occurring as one reads this sentence.
>
> Child abuse is absent in the Dominican Republic.
>
> Thousands of people will die in Somalia.
>
> Lying is often motivated by the desire to avoid feeling shame.
>
> Jeffrey Dahmer was an avowed heterosexual.
>
> In 1992 there were over 5.4 billion people on earth.

The claims in the second list are matters of common sense or subject to scientific assessment (probably only the second sentence is false). What they seem to have in common is that they are all claims about the world (or some small aspect of it) and they are claims about the way the world *is*, *was*, or *will be*. Their truth or falsity is not simply a "matter of definition" or something to be ascertained merely from an examination of the meanings of the words (compare: "It's raining or it's not." "Red is a color." "What will be, will be."). We shall label the claims about the world *empirical claims*. Such a use of the term 'empirical' is common practice, but other terms are often used to refer to the same types of claims; e.g.,

'descriptive,' 'contingent,' 'scientific,' 'positive,' and 'factual.' The important point is not to fight over who gets to choose the label, but rather to be clear about what kind of claim we are assessing. As we have characterized them, empirical claims may be true or false; that is, being true is not a necessary feature for a claim to be an empirical claim. By 'factual claim' some mean what we here mean by 'empirical claim'; others use 'factual claim' to mean a true, empirical claim.

Given the above, the following are empirical claims:

> If the invertebrates all died, the species *Homo sapiens* would die out within a year.
>
> Stories about a hole in the ozone layer are, like the story about the Holocaust, concocted to scare decent, hardworking citizens.
>
> It takes about 500 years for an inch of topsoil to accumulate.
>
> Stereotypes about "eggheads" and "nerds" suggest that those who use such terms have a certain prejudice against those who think hard or thoroughly about certain matters.
>
> The earth is about 4.5 billion years old.

Obviously, we cannot ascertain the truth or falsity of many empirical claims without scientific inquiry. Although humans have been on this planet for several million years (and "prehuman hominids" even longer), it is only in the last few "moments" so to speak, namely the last three centuries, that we have acquired certain substantial empirical knowledge about our planet, e.g., some knowledge of its age, of the ice ages, of prior mass extinctions, of atomic structure, of the evolution of life, of the transmission of genes, of continental drift. This is a point of enormous import for making decisions about the environment, one to which we shall return.

Now we are in a better position to inquire how moral or ethical claims differ from empirical ones. What makes a moral or ethical claim a moral or ethical claim? The feature that seems to characterize, and in fact be definitive of, a moral claim is that it is one which is about what someone (a person, a church, a corporation) *ought or ought not to do*—or a claim about the merit or demerit of someone's character.[3] Look once more at the initial set of claims, which seem to include noncontroversial examples of moral claims. Empirical claims are, then, claims about what is, was, or will be the case and whose truth or falsity depends on what did, does, or will happen. In contrast, moral (or "ethical" or "normative") claims are primarily about what ought or ought not to be done (or to have been done).[4] Thus, moral and empirical claims seem to be of logically different sorts. Shortly, we shall consider further the relationship between the two.

Given our functional, but not fastidious, working conception about what is a moral or ethical claim, the following are moral claims:

Children should be eliminated from television advertisements.

White males should be exterminated.

Inefficiency ought to be maximized.

Species' diversity ought to be minimized.

It's all right to torture cats for fun.

Arguably, all of the above claims are unreasonable; so, in saying that a claim is a moral one, we speak only of the *kind* of claim that it is and not of the *assessment* to be made of that claim (notice that the term 'moral' may also be used evaluatively as in 'the moral thing to do'—in which 'moral' is contrasted with 'immoral'). The question of what sort of rational assessment of moral claims may be made is another one to which we shall return.

Our working definition of 'moral claim' remains deficient in one respect. It requires us to say that "keep your elbows off the table when dining" and "it's impermissible to drool when in polite society" are moral claims; our (linguistic) intuitions, however, suggest otherwise. We may wish to preserve some sort of etiquette-versus-morality contrast by recognizing a distinction between comparatively urgent and nonurgent moral claims (classifying claims of etiquette in the latter category). Ultimately, a more thorough account may need to insist that we cannot entirely succeed in explicating the concept of a moral claim without taking into account the kinds of reasons people are prepared to give in defense of their judgments.

If our distinctions are on the right track, a few points of interest emerge. One is that we cannot identify moral claims by their subject matter. We cannot, for example, rightly say that moral claims are always *about* sex, force, killing, or truth-telling. The following may be, and often are, claims about what someone ought to do:

The United States ought to maximize its self-interest.

Japan ought to maximize its self-interest.

We ought not let any species become extinct.

Brazil ought to cut down its tropical forests to provide jobs for poor people.

The Federal Reserve in the United States ought to raise interest rates.

A hysterectomy is contraindicated.

Corporations ought radically to reduce CO_2 production.

In brief, based on the analysis given, a considerable number of claims of intuitively diverse sorts are to be classified as moral or ethical. Indeed, many leading "policy" issues are moral issues; they are questions about what we ought to do, or cease doing. Questions of what public policy ought to be, or of what laws we should or should not have, are moral questions, and they can be thought of as part of moral philosophy (we do not suggest for a moment that they should be explored only by professional moral philosophers). Some important questions in this volume are, then, moral or ethical in nature:

How ought we to treat animals?

Should we have a national biodiversity policy?

What should we do about the holes in the ozone layer?

What should we do about global warming?

What should we do to slow population growth?

What should we do about mass starvation?

Should we eliminate old-growth forests in order to provide jobs?

The last two lists suggest that an issue may be both "medical" *and* "moral," or "economic" *and* "moral," or "biological" *and* "moral," or "political" *and* "moral." There is, then, a kind of remark which ought to be regarded with great suspicion, namely the kind in which an "authority" in one field says in an authoritative tone, "But that is a question of economics" (or "science," or "philosophy," or "law," or "chemistry," or "demography"). Many of these categories are not mutually exclusive, and insights from different fields may be relevant. Claims implying otherwise often perform only the function that saying "shut up" performs; the latter does not normally foster rational inquiry.

The extent to which we routinely engage in moral and other sorts of evaluation is rarely acknowledged. Indeed, many people seem to hold the belief that they rarely, if ever, make moral or ethical judgments. This is surpassing strange. There seem to be at least two reasons for this. First, there are a small number of terms that seem "explicitly moral," namely "right," "wrong," "ought," "duty," "has a right," "wicked," "evil," "irresponsible," "permissible," and so on. It is tempting to think

that in the absence of such language, there is no moral claim being made. But we should consider the many (often apparently empirical) terms that are used in an evaluative manner, indeed to make moral judgments about what ought to be done or, perhaps, what is permissible to do. Consider these claims:

This policy is old-fashioned.

Senator Watt is defending his usual Neanderthal stance.

Your proposal is idiotic.

Where did Baker meet that bimbo?

Not to allow clear-cutting would be inefficient.

Your remark to Lakesha was ugly.

Stop being obsessive.

The economy is anemic.

The U.S. policy on global population control is myopic.

Well, yes, if abortion is legally prohibited, then there will be the side effect that some women will die using coat hangers in attempts to self-abort.

This is not a novel to be tossed aside lightly; it should be thrown with great force.[5]

It is rather evident that these claims are either moral (*or* at least evaluative) claims or clearly imply such. None, of course, uses the explicit moral language we noted earlier. Many terms have both an evaluative and a nonevaluative use; indeed, some began their lives, so to speak, as descriptive or empirical terms but came to be used primarily in an evaluative manner. One example involves the terms 'idiot,' 'imbecile,' and 'moron.' At one time they were adopted by those who believed in the reliability of IQ tests to refer, respectfully, to those thought to have an IQ of 1 to 25, 26 to 50, or 51 to 75. We all know, however, that any fourth grader is evaluating and not describing when he or she says "you're acting like a moron." We also often use the language of medicine (sick, myopic) or aesthetics (ugly) or other terms (beastly, unnatural, primitive, state of the art) to make evaluations.

A second possible, more indirect, reason for the widespread failure to recognize the extent of moral evaluation is found in the fact, as we might put it, that "morality gets a bad rap." The stereotypical image of "the moralist" or "the moralizer" is that of a person who tends to make unreasonable, harsh, moral judgments and is overly ready to use the coercive power of the law to see to it that everyone obeys the judgment. Most of us are rightly appalled by such persons and go to extreme lengths to avoid *appearing* to be like them, e.g., we avoid the use of explicit moral language and comfort ourselves with the notion that we do not even make moral claims. We kick them out the front door and sneak them in the back.

Another, more obscure, reason for refusing to be explicit about our moral judgments we only note in passing. From the 1920s through the 1940s especially, the Logical Positivist movement insisted, most roughly, that *only* empirically testable or verifiable claims were "cognitively meaningful."[6] In brief, it was held that everything else (poetry, moral claims, metaphysics, and religious claims) was either nonsense, the mere expression of emotion, commanding or prescribing, or at least not anything to which rational discrimination was relevant (the frequently invoked, obscure, undefined "fact-versus-mere-opinion" distinction seems to be a cultural by-product, one known to haunt universities and a fair number of writings in the natural and social sciences). If one believed that one could not rationally choose among competing moral claims or that to make them is to speak nonsense, it would be natural to avoid the appearance of engaging in moral decision making. We note two difficulties with the thesis mentioned. It itself is not empirically verifiable; is the thesis nonsense? Second, it seems to imply that the two claims—(a) we ought to

destroy life on earth, and (b) we ought not to destroy life on earth—are equally reasonable, or equally nonsense. On the face of it, such a claim is absurd.

In our view, of course, we make judgments about what people, ourselves included, and governments ought or ought not to do, and of course not all moral claims are equally reasonable. That fact settles nothing; that is where the interesting arguments *begin*, and no one should apologize for exploring them. As Socrates said about 2400 years ago: "We are discussing no small matter, but how we ought to live."[7]

2. JUSTIFICATION, EXPLANATION, PREDICTION, AND DESCRIPTION

There are a small number of intellectual activities in which we engage. They are largely exhausted by listing these categories: moral justification, explanation, prediction, and description. To think more clearly about trying to justify claims about what we ought to do regarding environmental issues, we need to consider the nature of explanation, description, and so on and explore briefly how these activities are related to one another. By so doing, we will better identify the role of moral argument and the respective roles of empirical and moral assumptions. Sometimes we simply want to *describe* the world:

In 1992, two out of three Japanese who were surveyed believed that one could become HIV infected by being bitten by mosquitoes.

Some airplanes purchased by the U.S. military cost almost a billion dollars apiece.

Philosophers can be overbearing.

There are more than 43,000 students at Texas A&M University.

Fourteen years after evidence strongly suggested that CFCs are severely destructive to the ozone layer, the DuPont corporation agreed to stop producing them.

Much of science aims simply at creating a correct *description* of the world (the sample claims above happen to be true); doing so may be revolutionary. Consider, for example, the transforming impact of the establishment of descriptive claims such as these: the earth is not the center of the universe; humans evolved from far more simple forms of life.

Future-tense true descriptions are the sorts of *predictions* at which science aims. Correct prediction is often possible when another scientific aim is achieved, namely, obtaining satisfactory *explanations* of events and processes. One influential, but by no means uncontroversial, view is that satisfactory scientific explanation must fit the "covering-law model," that is, such an explanation must be stated as an argument in which:

> The conclusion is a statement that the event to be explained occurred.
>
> The premises state that certain initial conditions were satisfied and state a scientific law.
>
> The premises are all true.
>
> The argument is valid (the conclusion must be true if the premises are).

A crude example explaining why some water turned to steam is this:

> Under normal conditions of pressure, water, if heated to 100 degrees centigrade, will undergo a change of state and turn to steam.
>
> This water was heated to 100 degrees centigrade.
>
> This water turned to steam when so heated.

This is one simple example of the kind of causal story that is commonly regarded as necessary for giving a scientific explanation of an event; note that it is stated in the form of an argument. Arguments can be assessed in two main ways: (1) by assessing them for validity, and (2) by assessing the plausibility of their premises.

We suggest that the main activities of the sciences fall into the categories of describing, explaining, and predicting. Explaining and predicting, when fleshed out, take the form of making a claim and defending it, i.e., setting out an argument, as noted. These arguments consist of empirical claims of one level of generality or another (or occasional logical truths or tautologies).[8]

There is another activity in which we engage which often *also* takes the form of making a claim and defending it with arguments (reasons). We try to identify justifications for moral judgments in cases of controversy between people and in cases about which we ourselves are morally perplexed.

To *justify a moral claim* is basically to give good reasons for the claim. Often, the claim in question will be to the effect that a certain act is right (or wrong as the case may be) either in the sense of being a duty or in the sense of being permissible. Many actions seem both morally justifiable *and* explainable, e.g., Ivan's giving his dad a birthday present, Maria's going to college, or Michael Jordan's choosing a career in professional basketball.

But to explain and to justify are not the same thing. There may be an explanation of why serial killer Jeffrey Dahmer killed a number of innocent persons and ate some of their bodily parts, but surely there is no moral justification for his doing so (so we insist without here offering any argument). We note that if certain explanations of actions are obtainable, then they also may serve to *excuse* the agents from blame. But to find that an agent is excused from blame for an act is not the same as finding that the act was right, that it was morally justified. For example, a killer may be determined to have been insane at the time of committing a murder; in such a case she or he may be judged not responsible for her or his act and, hence, not to blame. It does not follow that murder is acceptable.

3. MORAL ARGUMENT: THE INTERPLAY OF MORAL AND EMPIRICAL CLAIMS

Many important "environmental controversies" are moral or ethical in nature, questions about what moral agents ought or ought not to do. A *moral agent* is a being capable of reflecting on reasons, weighing them, and deliberately choosing—normally a member of *Homo sapiens*.[9] Positions on these controversies take the form of normative or moral assertions, e.g., we *ought* radically to curtail the practice of eating beef since the cattle culture plays a huge role in the destruction of the rain forests and of the ecological balance of natural habitats around the planet. To give reasons for one's claim is to make statements which can function as premises in an argument (e.g., we ought not to destroy the rain forests, or we ought not to do anything to contribute to global warming). The argument will be a *"moral argument"* since all we shall mean by that expression is an argument with a moral *conclusion*.[10] So, the following is a moral argument:

> Informally stated: that creosote plant shouldn't be destroyed, since it is very valuable.

> More formally and fully stated:

> We ought to go to great lengths to avoid destroying rare living organisms.

> This plant in the Joshua Tree forest in California is an 11,700-year-old creosote bush and is, hence, the world's oldest living organism.

> Thus, we ought not destroy this creosote bush.

So, we have a moral argument; we may also have an argument about public policy, an eco-logical argument, an argument about flora. Is it a good argument? That question is not so simple to answer.[11] We only note that the argument has at least two virtues; its second premise is true and it is *valid* (in the technical sense of being one in which the conclusion *must* be true *if* the premises are). We will further consider how to assess arguments at a later point.

Many scientists and ordinary citizens have concluded that we ought to be acting quite differently from the way we have been with regard to preserving biodiversity, halting destruction of the ozone layer, warding off massive global warming, destroying coral reefs, polluting the air, and trashing the oceans. Many others defend policies which are directly to the contrary. Do these normative or moral conclusions just fall from the sky, just spill out of scientific theories and assumptions, or are they not subject to rational assessment? Let us explore this question.

Since, as we noted earlier, moral and empirical claims seem to be of logically different sorts, it is tempting to think that an observation of 18th century Scottish philosopher David Hume is correct. In a famous passage, after examining the writings of other moral philosophers, Hume noted:

> In every system of morality, which I have hitherto met with, I have always remark'd that the author proceeds for some time in the ordinary way of reasoning, and establishes the being of a God, or makes observations concerning human affairs; when of a sudden I am surpriz'd to find, that instead of the usual copulations of the propositions, *is,* and *is not,* I meet with no proposition that is not connected with an ought, or an ought not. This change is imperceptible; but is, however, of the last consequence. For as this *ought* or *ought not,* expresses some new relation or affirmation, 'tis necessary that it should be observed and explained; and at the same time that a reason should be given, for what seems altogether inconceivable, how this new re-

lation can be a deduction from others, which are entirely different from it.[12]

Hume seems to be asserting that we cannot rightly infer any normative claim from any set of purely empirical premises. Indeed, it seems correct that we cannot validly infer

Rape is wrong (or right).

from

Rape will occur (or did or does).

And we cannot validly infer that:

It is wrong to generate and use leaded gasoline.

from

The use of leaded gasoline causes brain damage among children who are heavily exposed to it.

Most informally stated arguments are, however, *enthymematic* ones; i.e., either the conclusion or one or more of the premises are not explicitly stated. In our last example, the argument *as stated* is invalid: the conclusion does not necessarily follow from the premises.[13] However, we might reasonably presume that the proponent of the argument is making a moral assumption and that when it is added to the original argument, the *revised* argument is valid; the likely assumption may be (something like) that it is wrong to do that which is known to cause nontrivial harm to children. If we were trying to be fastidiously complete, we might also state explicitly another tacit assumption, namely, that to cause brain damage is to cause nontrivial harm.

We are urging two key points about our recent discussion. One is that Hume seems to be correct. No moral conclusion validly follows from a set of purely empirical premises.[14] Many premises are paraded as purely empirical or purely scientific but are, in fact, *value-laden* and are not, thus, subject to Hume's strictures. Here are a few claims which seem to be purely empirical but which may not be:

It is inefficient to install scrubbers on those SO_2-emitting smokestacks.

Lethal Dosage 50 tests impose gratuitous pain on the animal subjects.[15]

Abortion is the murder of a fetus.[16]

Those tree-hugging environmentalists want to halt growth.

These are my children.

Resources are unlimited.

The un-American proposal to limit the size of one's family . . .

Those are weeds.

That nation exceeded its carrying capacity.

In these examples much depends on the interpretation of the key terms 'inefficient,' 'gratuitous,' 'murder,' 'growth,' 'my,' 'resource,' 'un-American,' and so on.

Hume's claim that there is an "is-ought gap" or that there is a gulf between facts and values, as is sometimes said, is controversial. The matter is relevant to other arguments in this volume, e.g., attempts to derive some moral ideal from facts about the natural world (compare: "What's right is what is natural." or "What is right is whatever is conducive to the survival of the fittest." or "Whatever is unnatural is wrong."). It is also relevant to the assessment of various specific arguments, e.g., Japanese representatives at an international conference on whaling arguing that they should be allowed to continue the killings because that is a very ancient practice for Japan. The familiar argument that it is morally permissible for the United States (or China, or Germany, or . . .) to sell large numbers of military weapons to most any developing nation since others will do so if the United States does not also seems to be an invalid inference (the inference of a normative conclusion from a purely empirical premise). One might be tempted to think that if Hume is correct, that there is no sense in which science can be a basis for ethics and that there is no purely scientific ground for normative policy recommendations. Nevertheless, it is clear that empirical suppositions play a *crucial* role in moral argument. Let us explore why. Consider this argument:

(b) If the United States set off its stock of lethal nerve gas weapons, millions, if not billions, of human and other lives would be destroyed.

(c) Hence, the United States ought not to set off its stock of lethal nerve gas weapons.

The argument, as stated, is simply an invalid one.[17] The conclusion does not follow unless we supply a relevant normative assumption. In this *particular* case we may supply one which is not very controversial, e.g., we ought not to do that which would cause the deaths of millions of humans and other beings on earth. As originally stated, the argument above violated Hume's stricture. Consider this argument:

(a) We ought not to do that which would cause the death of millions of human and other lives.

(c) Hence, the United States ought not to set off its stock of lethal nerve gas weapons.

This argument is also one in which the conclusion does not necessarily follow from the premises (and not even with any degree of probability). In brief, one could construct a valid and plausible argument in favor of the conclusion by assuming (a) *and* (b) and inferring (c). Without the crucial empirical assumption, the argument is not valid. So, even if one cannot validly infer moral conclusions from purely empirical premises, empirical claims may still play a crucial role in moral arguments. Since we must often employ scientific inquiry to determine on which empirical assumptions we should rely, it follows that science and ethics are not divorced. Indeed, particular issues in applied ethics cannot be explored without some reliance on good science. Thus, many explorations in environmental

ethics must make good use of the results of biology, botany, chemistry, geology, climatology, marine science, forestry, and so on (both basic and derivative and mixed fields). The two-fold task is to determine which empirical assumptions to make and to determine which moral assumptions to make, i.e., what empirical and moral beliefs we should have or, to put the point another way, which ones are *belief-worthy*. In brief, systematic scientific inquiry and theorizing are necessary to achieve one of these goals, and systematic ethical inquiry and theorizing are necessary to achieve the other. But these tasks are not unusual, esoteric, or merely academic ones. For example, many have pondered the question of whether John F. Kennedy (or Martin Luther King, Jr., or Franklin D. Roosevelt or Eleanor Roosevelt or . . .) engaged in extramarital affairs and, if so, whether he (or they) deserve serious blame for doing so. In other words, familiar discussions involve trying to determine facts and relevant normative principles.[18]

Sometimes, that which seems elusive or controversial is the relevant *moral* principle or assumption. For example, there is much dispute over whether nonhuman animals have rights, and if so, which rights, and so on. We speak of moral rights which may or may not be embodied in the law.[19] Similarly, should we think that human fetuses, or adult humans in permanent vegetative states, have rights? Should we think that above all we should do what is "efficient" (for whom?)? Do we have duties to future generations—of humans, of sentient creatures, of the biota? Is it a wrong or a terrible wrong to *allow* a species (or a subspecies) to become extinct—or cause it to become extinct—even if it is the human immuno-deficiency virus (HIV)? However, there is a great deal of exaggeration about how much distinctly "moral disagreement" there is. Further, we may question the pessimistic assumption that such matters are unassessable, inscrutable, and so on.

In fact, *much so-called moral disagreement is really empirical or scientific disagreement.* Consider some examples. In the mid-1980s some held the normative view that those "with AIDS" (actually only those HIV-infected) ought to be isolated (incarcerated) on islands or in camps (something like this is done in Cuba); others took the contrary view. In *many* cases, however, the parties agreed on the moral principle to be invoked, e.g., we ought to do what is necessary to prevent the further spread of HIV infection. Some believed, though falsely, that HIV is an airborne virus that is spreadable by sneezing, and some correctly denied that empirical assumption. The basis of the specific, normative disagreement was not disagreement over the moral principle but over the facts.

Consider another example. Should the United States spend $18 to $28 dollars per barrel of crude oil imported from the Near East, as opposed to putting that sum into other energy sources? Suppose what seems reasonable—that we agree that the United States, in the absence of other, countervailing moral considerations, ought to purchase oil at the lowest price (this is the relevant normative principle). Suppose there is no competitive energy source in that price range. If (a big 'if,' of course) there are no countervailing considerations, then it seems that the United States should buy at that price. But some people reject that normative conclusion because they reject the empirical assumption that the cost of Near Eastern oil is as we have represented it. They reason that the true cost of that oil ought to include the subsidies provided by the U.S. government to many Near Eastern countries and the tremendous investment in the U.S. military, much of which is aimed at ensuring favorable conditions for U.S. trade with such countries. Some economists estimate that if such costs were factored in, the true cost of that oil to the United States would be closer to $80 to $85 per barrel. There may be other sources of energy that are superior or competitive at that price. Again, we have normative or moral disagreement about what *ought* to be done, but it is rooted in empirical

disagreement (over what *is* the case—pricewise).

Coming to understand just what the facts are can be absolutely transforming. It may provoke a change of attitude, perhaps by altering one's arguments, but sometimes a new perspective seems to occur in a flash, as if a blindfold were removed from one's eyes. For example, one consequence of clear-cutting forests, tropical or otherwise, is the erosion of topsoil. This result may be thought unfortunate, but when one realizes that it takes from 200 to 500 years for 1 inch of topsoil to accumulate, the severity and comparative irreversibility of the effect strikes home. Similarly, when Michael Boskin, the head of the Council of Economic Advisers under former President Bush, was told that global warming might mean that the temperature would be, on average, 3 to 5 degrees centigrade warmer in northern latitudes, he supposedly replied that it often got that much warmer in Washington, D.C., in a single morning.[20] This appears to be a casual discounting of a situation which, were it to occur, *could* involve millions of deaths. Why? First, it is important that the focus be on average surface global temperature and not a one-day, local variation. Second, during the last ice age, when the average temperature was that many degrees cooler, there were massive glaciers in the northern part of the United States, and New York City was underneath about a half mile of ice. So much for the significance of an alteration of a few degrees in the average global temperature. The significance of global warming or global cooling can be properly assessed only if one understands just *what* the facts are (both the harms and benefits which would occur if certain scenarios were to be realized as well as the probabilities of their occurrence). An increase of 3 to 5 degrees centigrade in average temperature would, due to the melting of ice and the consequent rise in ocean levels, put the entire Republic of Maldives under water. Imagine an economist (or anyone else) trying to do a cost-benefit analysis on such matters if she or he had no grasp of climatology and geology. So, in examining and constructing arguments for normative environmental policy conclusions, the facts are crucial.[21]

Deeply held preconceptions often *determine* what we *perceive* to be "the facts" or "the data." They do not just leap onto the table, so to speak, for our examination. For example, in 1985, when the hole in the ozone layer over the Antarctic was discovered, the data supporting such a conclusion were discarded as erroneous; the computer was programmed to disregard data which the programmers assumed to be incredible.[22] Today, philosophers have little influence compared to Aristotle, whose view that the planets were crystalline spheres was still accepted in 1609, when Galileo, looking at the moon through his telescope, declared the moon to be pockmarked. That view also was regarded as incredible. Similarly, when scientist Louis Agassiz concluded in 1837 that rocks and boulders in Switzerland were not put there by a "Great Flood" but were put there by other causes, scientists wedded to the traditional view were furious.[23] The procedures of empirical science do not guarantee the filtering out of deep, *a priori* (apart from all experience or evidence) assumptions or those based on very limited experience or evidence.[24]

4. HARM AND BENEFIT

Most negative moral principles or judgments seem aimed at preventing harm to members of one species, *Homo sapiens.* Compare:

It's wrong to kill.

It's wrong to steal.

It's wrong to break promises.

One ought to get regular medical checkups.

One ought not to smoke.

One ought not to drive 85 miles per hour in school zones.

The point will be addressed further in the Preview to Part III, but almost all traditional moral outlooks and theories suppose that only harm or benefit to *humans* is morally significant—deserving weight in decisions about what ought or ought not to be done (moral or normative decision making). This point is widely taken for granted, but the presupposition is of enormous consequence. Basically, it has meant that we humans have always, with a few notable exceptions, thought and acted as if everything nonhuman, all other forms of life as well as inanimate matter, has no value except its utility to us as a means to an end. We have tended to divide the world into what is consumable (everything nonhuman) and what is not (other members of our species, though even here the lines are sometimes drawn more narrowly, e.g., between those in our nation, our tribe, or our family, and those without). The assumption that all, and only, humans "count" or are valuable in themselves (not just as a means to an end of some other creature) is called *anthropocentrism* (a quasi-technical term in the literature of moral philosophy).[25] To state the anthropocentric view in a second useful manner, let us first define another important term in the literature: To say that a being has *moral standing* is to say that the well-being of that individual (or ecosystem, habitat, or some other entity) is morally relevant for its own sake and not just because it is of value to another individual or group of such. The anthropocentric view, then, is just the view that all and only humans have moral standing. Whether anthropocentrism is just a bald prejudice, or on a par with racism or sexism, is examined in Part III. If it is, traditional moral theories need to be revised or eliminated, along with other theories which seem strongly anthropocentric, namely, standard economic theory, in so far as the latter functions as a normative theory, as well as political philosophy.

Aside from the question of *whose* harm or benefit is morally relevant, the notions of harm and benefit need examining. The notion of harm tends to be analyzed into (1) premature *death* (often premature, permanent cessation of consciousness, whether or not accompanied by permanent cessation of all bodily functions); (2) *pain* (ranging from agony to frustration); and (3) *nonfulfillment of wants* or desires. Those "states of affairs" which we call "bad," or "undesirable," tend to involve one of these three conditions. The expression *frustration of desire* may refer to (2) or (3). What's the difference? One can have one's desires blocked and not fulfilled without knowing that this is the case; e.g., one wants to be loved by one's spouse but is not, and is ignorant of the fact. In contrast, we often experience unpleasant mental states (depression, sorrow, anger, worry, or frustration) because we are aware that we did not get what we wanted (e.g., the job, affection, a raise, attention, recognition, a good grade). It is also worth noting how this "pain" may be the by-product of what we believe and may be rationally assessed, e.g., his jealousy was foolish since it was based on a false belief. If is often said that "what people don't know won't hurt them," but while it may not hurt in sense (2) of 'harm,' it may harm them in sense (3).

Is there a presumption against harming those capable of suffering harm? A number of important matters must be kept in mind. One is that there are different forms and degrees of harm. It is one thing to be vaccinated with a needle and another to be burned alive. Second, it is one thing to discuss whether harm is a bad state of affairs as such and another to discuss the justification of imposing harm on another individual (or collective entity, ecosystem, and so forth).

Special, morally significant considerations arise when we focus on options or policy alternatives which will, foreseeably, cause harm to those subject to them. For example, one may plausibly argue that there is some qualified right of self-defense against individuals who in a blameworthy manner initiate an attack on innocent parties (our law tends to reflect this moral judgment, but these matters are not as simple as some think). Further, there may be significant differences between individual and collective defense. In short, considerations of innocence and noninnocence may rightly influence the answer to the question of when it is justifiable to impose (redundantly, then unconsented to) harm on another person. Other morally relevant considerations may also be involved. For example, many arguments about the justifiability of pollution concern whether or not people have consented to it by, for instance, living in certain areas, taking certain high-risk jobs (say, handling pesticides), or accepting so-called compensating wage differentials attached to their work. A great deal of environmental ethics is concerned with the question of whether it is permissible to impose harm, or the risk of harm, on parts of "the environment" or to what extent we have a duty to avoid doing so.

Situations which are "morally difficult" tend to be ones in which all the alternatives (including doing nothing) involve causing, or allowing, harm to someone. We might call them "conflict situations," and it is often in this context that talk of "moral dilemmas" arises. The situation may be naturally describable as one in which the conflict concerns one harm versus another or, alternatively, a harm versus a benefit. Recall familiar alleged "trade-offs:" farming versus habitat preservation, industrial growth versus the halting of the buildup of greenhouse gases, use of the oceans as sinks for wastes and maintenance of coral reefs and sea life, use of the air as a sink and having air fit to breathe. Some of these conflicts pit human life against human life, human life now versus that of future (human) generations, or human life against that of nonhuman fauna or flora. Sometimes, in cases of conflicts of interest, the parties are readily identifiable, and the nature of the conflict is quite clear; e.g., compare a thief and his or her victim, the killing of an elephant to obtain an ivory tusk, or the killing of a wildebeest to make a flyswatter of its tail. We need to see what makes some environmental cases difficult to think about and resolve. Among the central cases of conflict of interest among humans (the cases we are accustomed to thinking about), we have (imagine a case of assault), two humans, a deliberate, single act causing a clear harm which rises above some threshold of significance, and agreement by all that the recipient possesses *moral standing* (recall the meaning: the well-being of this individual is morally relevant for its own sake and not just because it is of value to another individual).

In contrast, many environmental disputes are complex for a number of reasons: (1) the individuals affected are "nonstandard" (e.g., spotted owls, pandas, krill); (2) rather than individuals, the focus may be on, say, ecosystems; the (3) the individuals may not exist (e.g., future generations); (4) the harm is the *cumulative* result of the acts of many individuals over a long period of time (compare forests dying from air pollution, rivers dying from agricultural runoffs of fertilizer, pesticides, or dioxin from paper mills); and (5) the occurrence of actual harm is a matter of some probability. Consider harm resulting from the existence of stocks of nerve gas, stocks of deadly plutonium, the storage of other forms of toxic wastes, the effects of substantial global warming, and the likely dire consequences to be associated with a probable increase of the world's population to 11 or 12 billion people by the year 2050.

The point of systematic thinking about ethical questions is to help us decide what to do in hard cases.[26] And many of the issues in environmental ethics are hard cases indeed for some of the reasons we just mentioned. The following, however, is not a difficult case. In the spring of 1992 in Durham, North Carolina, a 13-year-old boy brutally beat to death, in about 45 blows with a pipe, an innocent 90-year-old woman in order to get a car for the evening. The morality of that act is not in doubt; it was wrong if anything is. We are not helped in deciding the morality of such acts by ethical theories; rather, we insist that any acceptable theory must yield that moral judgment—barring some extraordinary showing to the contrary.

To emphasize, however, our main point, there is a good deal of perplexity and dispute about certain environmental issues for the reasons we have begun to discuss and which we explore in this volume. In the ongoing, and not so easy, task of assessing the small number of influential and competing ethical theories, it is reasonable to insist that any theory deserving acceptance should have, when combined with relevant, plausible empirical assumptions, a reasonably clear, precise set of implications for what we should do in the hard cases and a clear, coherent rationale as to why. Some philosophers would insist that this last claim is too strong and that all one can reasonably demand is that a theory explain the moral dimensions of why a particular case is, in fact, a morally difficult case to decide. We leave the question open. As a minimum the systematic moral outlook or theory should (1) state whose life, well-being, or integrity morally counts and why; and (2) yield reasonably determinate implications for how the noted "conflict" situations ought to be handled and why. Traditional ethical theories have seemed dogmatic with respect to (1), namely because they are based on an anthropocentric view with little or no rationale for so being. Recent efforts to develop an "environmental ethic" tend to explicitly address (1), but often tend to be less than explicit about (2).

5. THE BEST ETHICAL THEORY

Arguably, the best *scientific* theory with respect to some set of phenomena is not one to which there are no tempting objections or one which offers no difficulty whatsoever in the "handling" of evidence to the contrary. Rather, it is one which is superior to all its competitors in a number of relevant respects. Something similar needs to be said about the concept of the best ethical theory. With embarrassing brevity, we will note some relevant criteria for choosing among competing ethical theories. We do not maintain that all these criteria are noncontroversial.

Any theory consists of a *set of claims*, claims thought to be belief-worthy. Ethical theories will involve one or more normative claims but, explicitly or not, will presuppose certain empirical claims as well; e.g., that human nature is like this or that, that there is or is not freedom of choice, that there is or is not an afterlife, or that some animals are or are not sentient. One criterion of assessment, then, for an ethical theory is simply whether its empirical assumptions are plausible. For example, certain socialist visions of the ideal society suppose the possibility of substantial sharing of resources or products without the use of serious market incentives. They are often thought to be faulty because human beings are not capable of regular, thoroughgoing high levels of altruism toward strangers. In brief, if a normative theory presupposes empirically false assumptions, that seems sufficient reason to reject it. So here is a way in which even a normative theory may be said to be "testable" or "falsifiable." There is an old, not well-defined doctrine that "ought implies can." The slogan is often understood to mean that certain judgments about what people ought to do presuppose the existence of certain capacities (e.g., to choose freely, to act altruistically). The judgment about what ought to be done is implausible if the capacities for doing it do not exist. Again, scientific inquiry may be required to determine whether the capacity exists.

A set of claims is said to be logically *consistent* if and only if they *can* all be true. If a set is *inconsistent*, the statements in the set *cannot* all be true; i.e., at least one will be false. We want any theory to be consistent; otherwise, it will have at least one false assumption. A simple example is the set below, which is inconsistent:

The earth was created in 4004 B.C.

The earth was created 4.5 billion years ago.

It cannot be the case that both statements are true, though they might both be false. It seems reasonable to demand consistency in any theory, ethical or otherwise.

As noted earlier, since we want an ethical theory to guide our decision making in hard cases, we want it to yield reasonably determinate or precise judgments about what is permissible or what is obligatory. Normally a theory will not do this if its basic principle(s) are too vague; the following statements, however wholesome sounding, all seem excessively vague (without further supplementary guidelines):

Do the right thing.

Be good.

Love your neighbor.

Be kind.

Promote happiness.

Look out for number one.

Do no harm.

Leave the world a better place than when you got here.

In contrast, "maximize one's self-interest" or "maximize total net utility" or "do whatever maximizes the gross national product of Japan" all seem more precise and can yield precise conclusions when combined with other relevant assumptions.

Consider next *comprehensiveness* of scope. Other things being equal, it would be nice to have an ethical theory which would provide guidance over a greater range of decision making. Thus we may prefer to have a theory about when it is all right to take any life and not merely a theory about when it is all right to use lethal force in self-defense. A theory about how we ought to live so as to have a just and sustainable mode of life on earth would be one of considerable breadth, one calling for consideration of a great variety of complex moral and scientific matters.

Another widely accepted criterion of the

acceptability of a moral theory is whether the judgments it yields, when combined with suitable empirical assumptions, exhibit *compatibility with our deepest, pretheoretical moral convictions* (ones which are not psychologically suspect).[27] When a normative principle yields a conclusion which seems "radically counterintuitive," there are two choices that can be made (if the empirical premises are beyond criticism). One is to reject the theory and adhere to one's convictions. The other is to surrender one's convictions and accept the theory. Sometimes it seems reasonable to do the latter. A principle which implied that the previously mentioned beating of the 90-year-old woman was all right is extremely uninviting, to put the point mildly. Sometimes principles have surprising implications. For example, "we ought to minimize human suffering" would, if we could painlessly kill everyone instantaneously, imply that we have a duty to wipe out the human race. Further, as George Bernard Shaw pointed out, the implications of acting on the principle "do unto others as you would have them do unto you" have rather harsh (read: counterintuitive) implications when combined with a statement by a sadomasochist of what he or she, the sadomasochist, wants. He or she may enjoy being whipped and.... The worry is about compatibility with one's deepest pretheoretical moral convictions (say, about the moral unacceptability of routine torture of children for purposes of constructing an interesting Saturday evening) and not one's conjectures about whether South American coffee-producing nations ought to pay an ongoing fee to Ethiopia, the country in which coffee originated. Still, one's deepest conviction may be the result of cultural indoctrination *and* rationally suspect. Aristotle (384–322 B.C.) believed that some people were slaves by nature. Many Christian churches in the 19th century defended human slavery as ordained by God. A sincere Nazi might have been shocked at the notion that Jews should *not* be exterminated. Still, our deepest convictions, perhaps especially those of well-informed psychologically healthy persons, must be given weight, but must be continually subjected to scrutiny—lest we accept only those principles which are compatible with our deepest, perhaps irrational, prejudices.[28]

In summary, it is widely and plausibly held that the most acceptable moral outlook will be one which is clear, sufficiently precise, comprehensive, logically consistent, compatible with the best scientific theories and results, and compatible with our deepest, most prejudice-free, specific moral convictions about particular cases. We turn now to a succinct overview of the leading theories.

B. INFLUENTIAL ETHICAL IDEAS AND THEORIES

1. THE EGOISMS

Two "egoisms" (two theses) are commonly distinguished:

1. *Psychological Egoism:* that every human act is motivated by a desire to promote one's self-interest   and

2. *Ethical Egoism:* that each person ought to act in such a manner as to promote (or maximize) her or his self-interest

Note that (1) *seems* to be an empirical thesis and a most sweeping one, namely about every human action, or rather, the motive behind every action. We will not review the arguments pro and con here except to say that defenders of psychological egoism do not deny that people donate blood anonymously, that soldiers jump on grenades to save their buddies, or that people spend years caring for children or for aging parents without overt compensation; rather, defenders try to find reasons to construe each and every one of these cases as involving a self-interested motive, e.g., hope of a reward in the next life. A different story, of course, must be told about atheists. To be less than neutral here, as the defender of the thesis tries to spin his or her web of interpretation about each purported counterexample, one begins to suspect that the thesis is not really an empirical one at all.[29] Still, if Psychological Egoism were true, that fact would be subversive of policy proposals which require for their success that people act altruistically; hence, its relevance to normative questions. We should note that one need not believe that people *always* act altruistically if one rejects Psychological Egoism; one should reject the thesis if one thinks altruistic acts occur, even if not routinely.

This matter, or at least the question of just how extensive our altruistic resources are, arises with regard to whether it is feasible to ask or expect people, or nations, to act altruistically to benefit other species, other nations, or future generations. For example, many nations, such as those which are the habitats of many rare species of plants and animals, ask how they can be expected to function as custodians of those living creatures (and often thereby forego, as a result, the rewards of other uses of these habitats) without receiving compensation. An alternative sometimes is to try to structure markets in such a way that there are adequate incentives of self-interest ("market-based incentives") for nations or individuals to act in an environmentally friendly manner. It is worth observing that we do not *always* think it appropriate to provide market incentives to get people to act in a certain manner; for example, we do not try to provide market-based incentives to get people to refrain from child abuse. Still, we sometimes hear "tough-minded" business people insist that "environmentalists" must provide such incentives (as if that were the only possible motivation).

Ethical Egoism is the thesis that each person ought to promote her or his own interest. It seems noncontroversial to say that we ought to do so up to a point; after all, should not each person seek to feed herself or himself, alleviate or prevent illness to himself or herself, and so on? Often, promotion of one's own interest will require that one act so as to benefit others; e.g., one might take care of one's children to maintain his or her reputation or to have extra farmhands. No one denies that *many* acts that benefit others proceed from actions aimed at promoting self-interest. Ethical Egoism, and similar variants such as those found in the (overly popular) writings of Ayn Rand, may have an understandable appeal to those (such as females or those raised in certain religious families) who have been subjected to messages throughout their lives that it is "selfish" to be concerned about one's own welfare or to fail to "stuff" (repress expression of) one's feelings in order to promote the ostensive well-being of some group, e.g., the family.

Still, the thesis is not merely that one should *sometimes* act in her or his self-interest. That is thin soup indeed. The main objection to the principle is that it is counterintuitive. It advocates placing noninstrumental value on only the well-being and aims of the agent, and in effect no value on anyone else's well-being or aims *except* in so far as promoting them is in the agent's interest (the latter is called placing instrumental value on another's well-being, e.g., as a slaveholder might value a slave's well-being). What could justify this discrimination between Self and Anyone Else? On the face of things, Ethical Egoism is radically at odds with our deepest convictions and with the view that other people (for starters) are not mere commodities or resources to be used or abused according to the agent's slightest whim. There is no evident basis for an environmental ethic emerging from Ethical Egoism except one which says that the universe is to be divided into the Agent and Everything Else, the latter being the environment for the agent, and that the Agent should do whatever he or she wishes to the latter in promoting his or her interest.

2. THE DIVINE COMMAND THEORY

A character in one of Dostoyevsky's novels proclaims that if there is no God, everything is permitted. The suggestion seems to be that there are no duties, no moral constraints at all if there is no God: one may murder, plunder, and make sandwiches of human babies if one wishes. Many think that morality must be "based on" religion, perhaps in the sense that what is right or wrong is, in fact, dependent on what God commands (that is, prescribes, not causes). The approach to moral decision making being proposed, then, involves at least the following assumptions:

1. There is a God.
2. God commands and forbids certain acts.
3. An act is right (or permissible) if and only if God commands it.
4. Humans can sometimes ascertain what it is that God commands or forbids.

Unless all of these claims are deserving of our belief, this theory must be rejected; it is worth observing that scientific results have not been friendly to (1) and (2). And even if (1), (2), and (3) were acceptable, if (4) were false, then this theory would be entirely useless in the quest to figure out how we ought to live. If (1) through (4) were unproblematic, the next assumption needed to arrive at any specific moral conclusion would be one to the effect that God does command some specific act or omission. Many believe that some do know what God commands either through direct divine revelation or through reliable reports of such ("scriptures" of some sort).

There are problems here. There is disagreement about what the scriptures are. And even when there is agreement about what they are, there is disagreement over interpretation. Thomas Aquinas (1222–1274), the most influential writer in the history of the Roman Catholic church, was once asked whether it was all right to kill since, after all, the second commandment allegedly given to Moses by God was not to kill; but in Deut. 22 it is reported that God commanded the Israelites to wipe out an entire tribe of people, including "women, children, and asses." The Thomistic solution was that it is a misunderstanding of Christian morality to think that a crucial part of it is an unqualified prohibition on killing (popular misconceptions to the contrary, including simplifications by those who describe themselves as "prolife"), even the killing of innocent human beings. In other words, on this version of Christianity, *whether an act is right or not depends solely on whether God commands it.*

True believers often have great confidence that God *would not* command anything such as genocide or other acts which we may be sure would be rejected by any right-thinking person—although the ways of God are said to be mysterious and beyond human understanding. Nevertheless, the voice of God has often resembled the norms of the culture or subculture of those reporting it; for example, the "new Testament" urges that women be silent in the churches, slavery is taken for granted, and views are expressed which many today would describe as homophobic. The Hebrew scriptures in places condone war, animal sacrifice, slavery, and brutal punishment ("whoever curses his father or his mother shall be put to death"; Exod. 21:17), and prohibits the taking of (monetary) interest (Deut. 23:19). A person who acted on many of these beliefs today would stand a good chance of being locked up—so great is the distance between a good deal of biblical prescription and ordinary notions of what is permissible and right. None of this is to deny that certain biblical stories hold out ideals which retain their pull, e.g., Jesus' pressing the issue of "who is your neighbor?", the Good Samaritan, and the emphasis on unpretentiousness. Perhaps the "intuitively good parts" make it difficult for many believers to recognize or acknowledge the morally counterintuitive parts, the parts that get ignored, or are claimed to be merely derivative, inessential, superseded, or misinterpretations.

There is another puzzle about the Divine Command Theory, arguably an even deeper one. It is identified in the question of whether an act is right just because God commands it, or does God command it *because* it is (antecedently) right? If the answer is the former, then what is right seems dependent on the arbitrary will of God; if God were to command universal suicide, then it would be right! Is it plausible that such mayhem, or to consider another case, the gassing of Jews by the thousands in the ovens at Auschwitz, could be right *if* God prescribed it? Alternatively, if God commands acts *because* they are right, then they must be right independently of God's so commanding them; it must be *some other feature which makes right acts right*. But if so, perhaps we can figure that out (maybe it's respecting rights, or maximizing the opportunity for all sentient creatures to have a decent life in a manner that is indefinitely sustainable on our planet or . . .) independently of any reference to God's will or any commitment to the metaphysics of the Divine Command Theory.

These difficulties aside, it is clear that possibly billions of people are influenced by religious doctrine (we have focused on only theistic types), and in thinking about environmental issues we may ask whether The Divine Command Theory can be a rational basis for our moral beliefs (we cast a negative vote here). We may also ask whether its overall influence has been for evil or for good. The matter is controversial, and it is explored in more detail in Part II of this book.

It is evident, in a world with a human population of close to six billion, that there is not, and never will be, unanimity on matters of moral principle or even basic science. The intellectual world of many people remains one in which the earth is only a few thousand years old, in which the continents have never moved, in which sinks (places to put what we think of as "waste") and resources are unlimited, in which human life did not evolve from more simple forms, and in which immortal souls have a wonderful life after death. But, fortunately, we need not agree about all those matters in order to agree about many important things. For example, people who hold wildly diverse views about scientific matters, about religious questions, or about basic moral principles *may* totally agree about the morality of certain specific acts, e.g., child abuse, rape, and murder; freedom of thought; and the value of knowledge. So, for example, an ethical egoist, a religious believer, a rights theorist, and a utilitarian, respectively, may agree that poisoning the local water supply is wrong, although they infer that conclusion from quite different principles. This convergence has its limits, of course. We should not assume that agreement of different parties is sufficient to conclude the moral justification of the policy to which there is agreement; for example, some historic defenders of rights *and* some Christians have denied that women have equal moral rights, and we may recall the agreement between Nazi Germany and the (then) Soviet Union to carve up Poland and other East European nations at the beginning of World War II.

3. RIGHTS THEORIES

In English-, and, perhaps, French-speaking nations, especially, we are used to thinking about moral questions in terms of who *has a right* and whether the right is being respected. We may tend to overlook that not all peoples at all times have thought this way (a defender of a rights theory may think, "Well, *too bad* for those who do not; there are also a lot of people who fail to realize that the sun does not revolve around the earth, that humans could not long exist without invertebrates, or that smoking of tobacco enhances the risk of cancer"). Indeed, it appears that a clear notion of "having a right" did not seem to emerge before the late medieval period; so the ethical views of Socrates (470–399 B.C.E.), Plato (427–347 B.C.E.), and Aristotle (384–322 B.C.E.) did not include the concept as we know it. Today, some ridicule talk of "turkey rights" or "the rights of rats," but the idea of "human rights" might have been ridiculed by the ancients.

What is *meant* by "has a right"? Later we will consider possible *grounds for the possession* of rights. To say that an act *is right* and to say that someone *has a right* is to make two different, but not unrelated, claims. Often, to say that an act is right is merely to assert that someone has a duty to perform the act, but that is not an implication of saying that someone has a right to perform an act; e.g., one might have a right to a slice of the "killer chocolate cake" but no duty to take it. We now offer one plausible (slightly fastidious, but not canonical) analysis of 'having a right' and 'having a duty.' To say that

A has a right against *B* (*B* may be another moral agent or many or all such agents) to do *X* (where *X* is some action, e.g., to speak), to enjoy some state (e.g., being in private, living), or to be the recipient of an act of another (e.g., to receive a wage, punitive damages, or attention; use the apartment; not to be coerced)

is to say that

1. It is permissible for *A* to so do, enjoy, or have these things.   and

2. It is impermissible for *B* to prevent, disrupt, or fail to provide these things.

We are trying briefly to offer some clarification of the idea of what it is to possess a right, the moral relation between the right's possessor (or bearer of the right) and others who may be moral agents and who, thus, can deliberately "respect" or "accord" the right. What is

"owed" to the holder of the right will depend on the *content* of the right—what the right is a right to. We may think of some rights as "active rights," that is, rights to *do* things (e.g., use the library, drive the rental car, eat the meal, or take the sneakers from Wal-Mart [one acquired the right if he or she gave the store *the right* to some of his or her money]); some are "passive rights" (e.g., to be left alone). We shall turn to the concept of a duty in a moment, but there is another important distinction to be made, that between negative and positive rights. A right is said to be *negative* if the agent respecting the right morally ought to refrain from acting in a certain manner toward the holder of the right, e.g., a right not to be noncasually touched without one's consent. A right is said to be *positive* if the respecter of the right must act in some positive fashion; e.g., a child is often said to have a right to care (provision of food and shelter) from her or his parents.[30] The relations between friends, family members, and employees and employers, for example, are often spelled out at least partially in terms of rights (though loving relationships are commonly thought to require "going beyond" respecting rights, it does not follow that respect for rights is inessential; compare what goes wrong in cases of child abuse).[31]

Many rights are often, arguably, *packages* of rights. In Section V-B, questions about property are explored. What is involved in having property in something, i.e., a property right? First, it is often thought that the concept of a property right involves the right to *use* what is owned, to *exclude* others from so doing, to *transfer* the right to another (as a gift, or as part of an exchange—what we call trade, sale, or purchase), and sometimes, controversially, to *destroy*.[32] Do people collectively *own* the earth? Do parents own "their" children? Do those with legal property rights to a wetland have a moral right to destroy it—even when to do so would be to wreak serious ecological damage to the surrounding ecosystem and virtually permanent losses to the chain of future generations? Who owns the oceans, the old-growth forests, or nonhuman animals?

It is commonplace to distinguish between moral and legal rights; indeed, slaves in the United States in the early 19th century had few legal rights and possessed many moral rights which, in fact, were not embodied in the racist laws which prevailed. It is worth recalling that the revered "founding fathers" counted a black human being as three-fifths of a person for purposes of distributing electoral votes to the states. Until 1920, women in the United States lacked the legal right to vote (as remains the case in Swiss cantons today), but they surely had the moral right if men did. Given the legal/moral distinction, we may ask whether biotechnological creators of new life forms have special moral rights with respect to such forms and should be allowed to patent (have legal rights to) those forms. One notion is some sort of property rights (the standard kind of right that companies seek), but another might be the sort of rights possessed by guardians. On this issue the reader might consult Christopher Stone's essay "Should Trees Have Standing?" in Section IV-A. In brief many environmental issues, including absolutely fundamental ones, can be couched in terms of the existence of moral rights.

The distinctions we have noted can help us investigate many questions. For example, before deciding whether some entity (say, a human fetus, a comatose adult human, a Maine coon cat, a Norwegian elkhound, an iguana, a giant Sequoia, a coral reef, a logger in the state of Washington, or a philosopher in Vancouver) has a right to life, we need to know exactly *what* the "right to life" is a right to. Perhaps 'right to life' should be construed negatively, as a right not to be killed. If so, it may not be difficult for one to respect another's right to life; one only has to refrain from killing the other person. This may not be too demanding. Alternatively, if the 'right to life' is to be construed positively, as a right to

be supplied with whatever one needs to live, then it will be most burdensome for one to respect another's right to life, assuming that the latter is a creature in possession of such. Indeed, one may need a heart transplant; surely, another person does not *owe* his or hers, albeit the case that it would be quite hospitable of the person to give his or hers. So, it is counterintuitive to think that all people have a *positive* right to life (along the line of interpretation noted here). Whether we believe something has a right to life depends in part on what we *mean* by 'right to life' (thus, the importance of conceptual analysis with complex matters—in moral philosophy, science, or some other area).

We also need some defensible conception of the *grounds for possession* of any particular kind of right. Some rights are thought to be possessed because of a prior act, such as a contract or a gift; e.g., a person has a right to kiss another person because that person has agreed to it; otherwise, not. Some rights are thought to be possessed by certain entities just because the entities are of a certain kind, e.g., because they are human, alive, sentient, or subjects of a life. Any adequate rights theory must address these matters and defend some set of grounds as necessary and/or sufficient for the possession of rights. There is, in fact, extensive literature that does just this.

In this space it is impossible to convey much of the substance of any particular theory of rights. Historically, the works of Thomas Hobbes (1588–1679), John Locke (1632–1704), Jean Jacques Rousseau (1712–1778), and Immanuel Kant (1724–1804) are important. Both Hobbes and Locke asserted that humans have certain basic rights in a "state of nature," that is, in a hypothetical state in which government and law are absent. Locke claimed that people have a right to life, liberty, and property. A central thrust of all rights theories is that bearers of rights have a certain moral standing and that they are owed at least certain forms of treatment. Thus, they are not to be viewed as "mere resources" or as entities whose use is entirely unconstrained by duty. Generally, such theories have a certain egalitarian thrust in that they maintain that all beings within a certain more or less "natural" kind have the same rights (e.g., all persons, all men, all male property owners, all adult male property owners, or all sentient creatures). There is, however, one rub, so to speak. The rights theorists that we just mentioned all seemed to deny rights to any nonhuman; thus, the recent critique of *anthropocentrism* is a radical one, for it calls in question a fundamental assumption of all such theories. These matters receive attention in Parts II, III, and IV especially.

There is little reason to think that all humans, say, have all the same rights. First, if a ground for possessing a right to drive is that one can see, then not everybody can have that right. Second, a distinction is often made between certain *natural rights* (rights one has because one is of a certain natural kind: human, sentient, rational, or simply alive?), such as a right to life or a right not to be tortured, and rights one may have because of some past action, e.g., a right to one's shirt because of a purchase or a gift (often labeled "acquired" or "artificial" rights). Likewise, even if some rights are possessed only by humans (say, a right to vote), it does not follow that all animals are entirely lacking in rights. Popular discussion to the contrary, acknowledgment that certain nonhumans, such as animals, ecosystems, or forests, have rights would not necessarily settle moral disputes. Consider a common distinction, namely the distinction between *absolute* and *presumptive* rights. If by 'absolute right' one means a right upon which it is *always* wrong to infringe, then it is doubtful that any rights (attributed to individuals) are "absolute." For example, we might not unreasonably conclude that it would be right to torture an innocent grandmother (or perhaps the editors) who possesses a right to life *if* that were *the only way* to prevent nuclear war. If fairly serious rights can be justifiably overrid-

den under certain circumstances, then the seeming great gap between rights theories and utilitarian modes of thinking fades seriously; the reader might "file" this basic point and consider it after the upcoming discussion of utilitarianism.

Let's consider a brief comment on the concept of a duty. To say that

A has a duty to B to do X (whether X is an act or an omission),

is to say (roughly) that

it is impermissible for A not to do X on account of B (whether X is an act or an omission).

In our analysis of rights and duties in terms of permissibility, for each right there is one or more correlative duties. But some duties may exist without any particular individual possessing any corresponding rights. Perhaps we have, for example, a duty to be charitable even if no particular individual has a right to our charity. Something similar might be said about a duty of an existing person to help pass on a stock of environmental resources no smaller than that which was passed on to her or him. It was, in fact, the view of Jeremy Bentham, the famous British philosopher and exponent of Utilitarianism (1748–1832), that we have *only* certain duties and that talk about rights (moral, not legal) is "nonsense on stilts." We leave it an open question whether talk of rights is not more than rhetorically useful, and whether all that which we wish to say, morally, can be said in the language of duty.

Most rights theories are "individualistic" in their attribution of rights only to individuals, say humans or animals, but it is not obvious that the bearers of rights *must* be individuals; so those who value collectivities or communities may hope to revise the traditional rights framework. Legal rights are attributed to corporations, states, cities, and so forth. Nevertheless, some philosophers believe that the notion of species' rights is nonsense.[33] Further, rights theories are often criticized as being focused on a selfish stance, on what is mine as a matter of right, on violations of "my rights," and it is claimed that all this contributes to a complaining attitude and a litigious society. Many complaints are misguided; those who insist on respect of rights *need not* defend their own rights, but the rights of, say, sexually abused children, raped women, gay persons who have been discriminated against, blacks, or innocent whites who may have been unfairly treated (say, those poisoned to death in recent years by a North Carolina woman, Blanche Moore). These objections hardly exhaust the list of complaints made against rights theories.

A theory of rights should address the above and other objections. If it allows rights to be overridden under certain circumstances, its defense needs to show why it does not collapse into Utilitarianism or some other consequentialist theory. A rights theory should say what is to be done in the event that rights conflict with one another. It should, as noted, specify the grounds for the possession of rights. The theory should be reasonably clear in terms of its policy implications, and reasons should be given as to why the theory should be preferred over competing theories.

Probably the two most influential ethical outlooks among contemporary moral philosophers are rights theories on the one hand and versions of Utilitarianism on the other. We now turn to the latter. Since Utilitarianism has special importance in current environmental controversies and because, arguably, in its anthropocentric incarnation Utilitarianism underlies mainstream economic theory, we will spend some time examining it.

4. UTILITARIANISM

Although the writings of David Hume (1711–1776) and others were suggestive, it was the work of Jeremy Bentham, especially his *Introduction to the Principles of Morals and Legislation* (1789), which articulated the theory of Utilitarianism. His work and that of one of his disciples, John Stuart Mill (1806–1873), constitute the classic sources of this view. Bentham was a critic of British law and policy and believed that it was a hodgepodge, inconsistent and unprincipled. He sought to identify some rational, principled basis for deciding what should be a matter of law and policy. He reasoned that while many things are good as means to some ends, there is only one state of affairs which can be said to be good for its own sake or intrinsically good and that is the experience of pleasure or happiness. The opposite state is pain, which is intrinsically bad. Having formulated this "theory of the (nonmoral) good," the question "What should we do?" remains. The short answer is: do whatever results in good or has good consequences. Since many acts bring pleasure for some and pain for others, we ought, Bentham thought, do that which will bring about the greatest balance of pleasure over pain, or utility over disutility; indeed, this constitutes the fundamental duty of all individuals and governments as well. Thus, we arrive at the famous *Principle of Utility;* our formulation here will be: what is right (or a duty) is whatever maximizes the total amount of net utility. The principle is sometimes referred to as the Greatest Happiness Principle.

Arguably, this view has revolutionary implications. First, normative theories which suppose that the rightness or wrongness of an act is entirely dependent on the kinds of consequences that an act has are called *consequentialist* theories, and Utilitarianism is a clear example (so is Ethical Egoism). Unlike the thesis of Ethical Egoism, Utilitarianism demands that the good and bad consequences for *everyone* affected by an action be taken into account and given due weight in determining whether the action, among all the alternatives available, will maximize total net utility (or, at least, result in as much net utility as any other available alternative) and, hence, be the right thing to do. So it is not merely the agent's well-being that is significant.

The emphasis on consequences is striking in that consideration of motives seems neglected, and the latter are often thought important. Jesus is alleged to have said that any man who has looked on a woman with lust in his heart has already sinned. A rather high standard, and one which former U.S. President Jimmy Carter confessed to not meeting. A utilitarian might insist that motives may be relevant to judgments of moral character but that they play no direct role in the assessment of actions.

It is tempting to translate talk of 'benefit' as 'utility' and 'harm' or 'cost' as 'disutility.'[34] So it looks as if the Principle of Utility approximates the principle that we should maximize benefits minus costs, though employers of *cost-benefit analysis* usually operate with "dollar" or monetary measures of cost and benefit. Since this procedure is widely used and recommended in deciding questions of public policy, indeed, environmental policy, assessing the adequacy of utilitarianism is closely related to the task of assessing the cost-benefit approach. Both are consequentialist in outlook, and both are maximizing principles. These matters receive attention in Part V.

It is worth observing that although we have lived, in the last two decades, in an era in which appeals to rights are very popular (compare the movement for civil rights, women's rights, and so on), the utilitarians can claim to have a method for deciding between competing policies, a method that is responsive to considerations of welfare and illfare. When it comes to formulating public policy, cost-benefit analysis is the prevalent approach. When it comes to deciding an array of legal questions, we tend to think often in terms of rights. Why this disparity exists is a question deserving consideration.

Utilitarianism is untraditional in that it promises to discard traditional moral rules that we learn, or are supposed to learn, as

children, e.g., tell the truth, keep promises, don't steal, don't kill. This is so because there are cases in which violating these admonitions will maximize utility. For example, it might maximize utility to lie to an Uzi-toting maniac about the whereabouts of schoolchildren he or she wishes to harm. Indeed, utilitarians may say that this example illustrates the intuitive superiority of their theory because rigid adherence to traditional, specific rules leads to radically counterintuitive results. If their defender says, "Well, one must apply them judiciously," the utilitarian can insist that *that* suggestion is either urging arbitrariness or is sneaking utilitarian considerations in the back door after kicking them out the front door. Further, specific principles, such as "keep promises" and "help those in distress," can conflict; in contrast the utilitarian theory avoids this problem of rule-conflict since the theory contains only one rule: maximize total net utility.

Whose utility or disutility, whose welfare or illfare must be taken into account? Surprisingly perhaps, given the virtual omnipresence of anthropocentrism, Bentham and Mill thought that pain and pleasure were an evil and a good, respectively, *to whomever* they occur. Since many animals evidently have both these capacities, it would be arbitrary for a moral agent not to take that into account in deciding which act will maximize utility. So the class of creatures to whom duties are owed is the class of all *sentient* creatures. The term 'sentient' is used in philosophy to refer to any creature capable of experiencing suffering or satisfaction, in whatever forms they may take. Evidence of such capacities tends to be linguistic ("Stop, you're hurting me!"), nonlinguistic behavior ("screams of pain," moaning, writhing), and the presence of physiological traits such as a central nervous system.[35] Which animals or humans are sentient is, thus, an empirical question and subject to scientific investigation. The implications of this theory for our treatment of animals are explored in Part III, especially by Peter Singer. What duties we have with respect to nonsentient life on earth is the focus of much of this volume, but Part IV is especially relevant.

We need to consider a familiar misunderstanding of Utilitarianism and then turn to a leading objection to the theory. The Principle of Utility is normally understood as not being equivalent to a certain bastardized variant of it, namely, the view that what's right is what most people want (what some call "the principle of majority rule").[36] For the moment let us finesse a serious question, namely, whether utility and disutility can be adequately measured so as to have units which can be added or subtracted. Recall that when economists estimate the costs of a particular instance of pollution in terms of dollars, they are attempting to establish some measure of the magnitude of harm or disutility to humans. An agent, in applying the Principle of Utility, attempts to identify alternative actions, say, A, B, and C; next she or he will identify the likely relevant consequences (those involving utility or disutility) to all who will be affected by her or his choice of alternative. To simplify *enormously* and to speak most abstractly, suppose that doing A will involve five bad results (sooner or later; later might be in 50 or 500 years) and three good ones (benefits or utilities of some sort to a sentient creature). Suppose that these numbers represent the magnitude of the bad results: -40, -80, -90, -25, and -70 (so, the sum of the disutilities is -305). Suppose, too, that these numbers represent the magnitudes of the benefits of utilities: $+83$, $+77$, and $+36$ (so, the sum of the utilities is $+196$).[37] The projected total net utility (TNU), then, of the agent's performing alternative A is -109 (subtracting the smaller from the larger). Abstractly that is how the calculation is to be done for each alternative. Suppose that the TNU of option B is $+99$ and that the TNU of C is $+550$.[38] Given these results, act C maximizes TNU, and the utilitarian argument for doing C takes this form:

1. What is right is whatever maximizes TNU.

2. C maximizes TNU.

3. C is right.

Since the argument is valid, one who is skeptical of the conclusion can only question the calculation leading to (2) or find reason to reject the principle, (1).

Note that one of the bad consequences of doing C may be to cause serious harm to one person, say, giving over a known innocent person to terrorists who are certain to torture the individual. Since the utilitarian calculation allows *summing* the harms and benefits, the act which maximizes TNU may include what many of us may be sure is a terrible wrong. It is partly because of actual or hypothetical cases like this that many people find utilitarian, and other maximizing, consequentialist theories, radically counterintuitive. Utilitarianism involves other worries, too. Suppose that a rapist got so much pleasure from raping that his or her pleasure exceeded the sum of the disutilities resulting from the act (is this not *possible*?). If so, the raping might maximize utility. In brief, the very idea that we should count this pleasure as a good and/or assign it positive weight in a calculation of utility is preposterous to many. Perhaps what is morally right should not be thought of as identical with *whatever* maximizes utility.

Concerns about *justice* or fairness have to do with the acceptability of the *distribution* of benefits or burdens among a number of individuals.[39] In certain cases, such as a judge's choosing to mete out radically unequal punishments to two persons equally responsible for the same kind of crime, there is, other things being equal, a clear case of injustice. One standard accusation is that the utilitarian theory ignores morally significant considerations having to do with the distribution of "goods" and "bads." In passing, we note that many environmental disputes concern the distribution of environmental benefits (say, from burning coal) and the distribution of environmental harms (say, pollution in the form of acid rain); one dispute concerns distribution between nations (e.g., U.S. coal-burning plants versus forest damage in Canada); another concerns benefits to the current generation versus losses to later generations (or the reverse). This last matter is labeled a matter of "intergenerational equity." It will receive attention in Part V and more in Parts VI-A, VI-B, and, especially, VI-C.

Three further points regarding distributional issues. First, although utilitarianism includes no principle of distribution as such, it may be that more or less egalitarian social arrangements (say, some limit on inequality of wealth but equality of basic legal rights) are more productive of happiness (at least human happiness) than the alternatives. In short, utilitarianism conjoined with relevant empirical assumptions will have interesting and perhaps intuitively plausible *distributional implications*. This type of concern motivated much of the political efforts of the "19th-century radicals." (Bentham, J. S. Mill, and others; in particular, Mill fought the milieu of his day in opposing the unequal treatment of women. On this topic, see his extraordinary little book *On the Subjection of Women*.)

Second, the *"principle" of declining marginal utility* seems to be a rough but plausible generalization; it says that "consumption" of further successive homogeneous units of certain goods (e.g., gin or ice cream) yields declining amounts of satisfaction or utility. More intelligibly, one's first ice cream serving is very satisfying, the second almost as satisfying, the third not bad, the fourth an effort, the fifth hard work, and the sixth nausea-inducing. Perhaps something similar is true of one's first million dollars, and so on. Although it would involve making a much disputed judgment involving "interpersonal comparison of utility levels," it is credible that the disutility we might cause to Sam Walton (a billionaire) if we took a million dollars from him and gave

it to a poor person would be much less than the increase in utility to that poor individual. If so, the transfer, the reduction in financial inequality, yields a net increase in total utility. Thus, taking into account the principle of declining marginal utility, a utilitarian argument exists in favor of limiting inequalities, even if we agree that the Principle of Utility is not itself a distributional principle.[40]

A third point regarding equality is that at the stage in which judgments of the amount of utility or disutility are involved in different consequences. Bentham insisted that "each is to count as one" and no one more than one. That is, like amounts of utility are to be counted equally whether the subjects of it are friends or foes, relatives or not, compatriots or not, indeed, fellow humans or not. This egalitarian streak is, nevertheless, compatible with the theory's condoning severe inequalities of treatment in the effort to maximize utility.

In view of the serious objections which have been made to the utilitarian theory, many are surprised that it is the preferred view of many professional moral philosophers (who would not be surprised by any objection noted here). In this short space, we can only observe that some difficulties confront all theories (no, we do *not* think that they are all equally serious). The main attraction of rights theories is that they tend to insist that there are moral limits of a rather urgent kind on what one can permissibly do to people (and perhaps other creatures as well); that is, they insist that an act which may, as a contingent matter of fact, maximize the sum of happiness in the world does not serve as a justification for doing some very nasty things to innocent, nonconsenting individuals in the process.[41] But the idea that *any means* leading to the greatest sum total of happiness is all right, much less a duty, seems to countenance many counterintuitive and radical inequalities. Still, rights theories may allow the overriding of rights in extreme cases, and when they do, then they may also condone, counterintuitively, some rather nasty acts. The utilitarian view avoids the rather generous metaphysical assumptions of the Divine Command Theory and its stringent requirement of knowing what God wills. Utilitarians also avoid the extraordinary understanding of moral relevance embodied in Ethical Egoism, namely, that the well-being of those other than the agent is important *only* in so far as it bears on the well-being of the agent.

We need to investigate theories which might suggest maximizing, or perhaps only optimizing, a good such as happiness or desire fulfillment *under constraints,* constraints that when respected ensure that the relevant individuals have decent lives, or at least the opportunity for such, given certain unalterable results of the natural lottery.

5. UTILITARIANISM AND ECONOMIC THEORY

For about 125 years, from the publication of *An Inquiry into the Causes of the Wealth of Nations* in 1776 to the turn of the century, there was a perceived closer connection between economics and moral philosophy. Adam Smith was a friend of David Hume, and taught moral philosophy at the University of Edinburgh in Scotland.[42] To be concerned about how to increase the wealth of individuals or nations is normally to be concerned about how to promote the opportunities and welfare of human beings, their utility. One mark of the work done by economists is their focus on specific empirical questions relevant to choice (exactly what are the effects of rent control, the effects of allowing a free market in drugs, or a 10 percent increase in the minimum wage), while moral philosophers have had more general concerns and have not shied away from the exploration of explicitly normative questions (Mill in his *On the Subjection of Women* [1869] argued that it was the unjust treatment of women that is the proper expla-

nation of their less significant, known, intellectual and artistic contributions historically). It seems fair to say that late 19th-century Western economic theory took a consequentialist, indeed utilitarian, view—that what ought to be done is whatever maximizes, or at least increases, human satisfaction or utility. Hence, the importance of choosing the most *efficient* policies and social/economic arrangements or institutions. This moral assumption, the principle of utility, has become largely covert as economists aspired to be scientists, something which they assumed to be a "value-free" discipline; hence, a certain embarrassment about saying in public that they thought efficiency *valuable,* or valuable *because* it is a means to promote total net utility and that that is what *ought* to be done (the recent posture has been *if* you want to know which is the most efficient policy, we can tell you what it is). This adoption of a posture of moral neutrality, if not indifference, was due in part to their being somewhat intimidated (so it appears) by the challenge of the Logical Positivists, who implied that anyone making normative judgments was thinking or talking nonsense.[43] A similar effect of the positivists seemed to drive philosophers away from any serious examination of specific normative issues for about three decades (from the 1920s to the late 1950s). Since then both groups have been less reluctant to regard such matters as fit subjects of intellectual inquiry.

Economic theorizing has been relentlessly anthropocentric, and the deepest cleavage between it and some moral theories and some environmental critics derives from that source. In cost-benefit analysis, 'cost' and 'benefit' refer, ultimately, in studies by standard economists, to what harms or helps humans alone. As we noted earlier, there are two fundamentally different ways in which the term 'utility' has been understood historically: as simple preference, or *want fulfillment* (whether or not accompanied by some pleasant mental or psychological state), or, alternatively, as a pleasing psychological state, that is, *pleasure*. Since pleasure (and pain) seem to come in amounts, one view is that we can ascertain when individuals experience such, and how much, and we can sum the utilities or disutilities to determine which act maximizes total net utility. Aside from one's own case, many economists and some philosophers became convinced that it is either logically impossible (but why?), or at least practically impossible, to ascertain how much pleasure or pain others experience or to make sensible judgments which compare the pains or pleasures of others to one another; if so, there can be no summing and rational selection of the option which maximizes utility. That path, it is claimed, is a dead end.

The other path that modern economists take is roughly the following one. Construe "utility" as (human) want-fulfillment. Ignore questions about how wants arise and whether they have important cognitive components (consider: *Why* did Sirhan Sirhan want to shoot Robert F. Kennedy?). Make an extreme antipaternalistic assumption that each person (focus on competent adults, thus ignoring one or two billion people) knows better than anyone else what makes him or her better or worse off and chooses accordingly if apprised of relevant information.[44] Avoid as much as possible making choices for others (since it is not, as it is said, possible rationally to make interpersonal utility comparisons and, say, distribute things in a fashion which would maximize utility); let each person decide for himself or herself (by having a market) whether to keep what she or he has (time, money, leisure, and so on) or to make an exchange (purchase, sale).[45] Assume that no one will do so unless he or she will be better off (perhaps acknowledging that there will be rare, masochistic exceptions, and of course, occasional difficulties in gathering information.)[46] Without our trying to state all the as-sumptions economists make, under these conditions with each exchange *at least someone will be better off and no one will be worse off* (at least if there are no "negative externalities," that is, cases in which there are harms caused to individuals not party to [consenting to] the exchange). Now if someone is better off and no one is worse off, we have an increase in total net utility; what has come to be called a "Pareto improvement" has occurred (after the Italian economist and sociologist Vilfredo Pareto [1848–1923]). The postexchange state of affairs is more efficient than the preexchange state (since at least one person is better off and no one is worse off than in the preexchange situation).

Several important points are worth observing at this point in our discussion. First, economists have adopted a definition of 'efficiency' (or its cognates) which may only loosely connect with ordinary usage of the term 'efficient;' compare "more efficient engine." Some situation, A, then, is said to be more *efficient* than another, B, if in A there is at least one person better off in his or her own estimation than in B, and no one is worse off in her or his own estimation. Why, then, is efficiency a good thing? The natural answer would seem to be because it increases utility. Note that there may be acts which increase utility but which fail to make Pareto improvements. For example, we might experiment on some unwilling people to find a cure for AIDS; perhaps the result would maximize total utility. Still, some people would be worse off (they may suffer and die prematurely). One serious objection to the utilitarian view (as we noted earlier) is that it seems to condone doing nasty things to innocent, unconsenting individuals (keep in mind that a rights theory may also do so if it allows for cases of justified infringement of certain rights[47]). In contrast, if we only act according to what we shall dub the Normative Pareto Principle (make *only* Pareto improvements), then that possibly counterintuitive implication is avoided. So the Normative Pareto Principle has its attractions. Two difficulties of utilitarianism are avoided. First, no interpersonal comparisons of utility are made. Second, the principle does not sanction intuitively immoral actions. However, there is a severe difficulty with the notion that much of life could be organized along lines dictated by the Normative Pareto Principle since almost any nontrivial proposal will make some parties worse off. The principle will support virtually no changes; it is a recipe for paralysis outside of certain highly limited contexts.[48] In the larger world, we morally must coerce from time to time, and we cannot do *only* those things that *avoid* making some worse off in their own estimation. It seems as if efficiency *is* a good thing *if* there are no countervailing considerations and *if* we have an appropriate conception of what counts as someone's being better off (surely identifying this with on-balance want-fulfillment will not do) and a justifiable conception of whose well-being matters (surely the answer that it is only the well-being of humans is dubious). So in spite of support for the value of efficiency derivable from the utilitarian theory and partly because of some suspect aspects which the assumption of such value shares with that theory, it is morally problematic to assume that we ought to choose whichever policy is the most efficient one, or that we ought to maximize benefits minus costs, or that these principles should guide us as we try to formulate a sound basis for environmental decision making. Efficiency, like sex, is not nothing, but it is not everything either. These matters are very important, given the undue influence which such principles have had, overtly or covertly, and they will receive further exploration in this book, especially in Part V and Sections IV-C, VI-B, and VI-D. Our main aim here has been to lay out some of the bones of economic thinking, some connections to one influential ethical

theory, to open the door to exploring relations to other moral points of view and, ultimately, to questions of environmental policy.

6. NATURAL LAW THEORY

"Natural law" theory is not as well defined a position as Utilitarianism. It is tempting to speak of this position as a tradition; those who are thought to be representative figures (the Stoics, Aristotle, Aquinas, Grotius [1583–1645], Suarez [1548–1617], and sometimes Kant) share some common features perhaps, but often they simply exhibit resemblances, in the way that members of a family might exhibit physical similarities. Hence, it is not surprising that one contemporary defender of this approach, Alan Donagan, responded to a critique of his view by saying, "What she says is natural law is not what natural law theorists say it is." His general characterization of the theory is that it is "a set of rules or precepts of conduct, constituting a divine law which is binding upon all rational creatures as such, and which in principle can be ascertained by human reason."[49] Except for the reference to divine law, this characterization fits almost any normative ethical theory (e.g., Utilitarianism and Ethical Egoism) in that it only insists that there are normative principles which determine what we ought to do and that these are ascertainable by reason. This abstraction needs fleshing out by stating the specific "precepts of conduct."

Without further defense, we will suggest that there are a small number of features which have been characteristic of, and some arguably definitive of, what has been labeled the natural law tradition from the Stoics to Hugo Grotius and others. We have noted (1) the belief in objective, given norms or principles by which rational beings should guide their conduct. Thus, (2) a contrast is marked between what is merely a matter of convention (e.g., to queue up for a purchase in some cultures) and what is a matter of human law (often called "positive" law historically). There is further a "natural order of things." This last claim seems to be construed both as (3) an empirical claim about the regularity we find in the nexus of causal processes around us, and also as (4) a claim that what is good and right is a direct function of the way things are, in particular the way human beings are (focus on their natural capacities, tendencies, and desires). Given the latter, certain norms are to be found in nature. Indeed, we usually find the assumption that (5) the good of humans (perhaps other creatures as well) is constituted by the realization of these natural strivings or natural tendencies; the "perfection" of such capacities in humans constitutes human flourishing. The (6) discovery of the natural law is ascertainable by the use of reason. As noted, (7) the natural law is often claimed to be an expression of the divine will. A specific instance of this theory will include (8) a list of the natural tendencies, the fulfillment of which constitutes flourishing. Claims (1) through (3) do not much individuate this theory. Developed in one way, feature (7) may render this view a variant of the already discussed Divine Command theory. If, however, the divine will prescribes conduct *because* human nature is as it is, then we have a view more deserving of the label "naturalistic ethic" or "ethic based on nature." But it is not obvious that *any* ethical theory allows no role for facts about human nature.

It is assumptions (4) and (5) which make this view distinctive. A central thrust of this theory, then, is that the world ought to be organized in such a fashion as to foster human flourishing; this feature is supportive, or reflective, of an anthropocentric view, although to the extent that value may be assigned to the fulfillment of *any* natural tendencies (not just human ones), one may find some basis for a biocentric outlook (here understood simply as the view that it is desirable that all living things flourish). Natural law theorists, however, do not seem to take this path. For an example of the biocentric outlook, see the selection by Paul Taylor in Section IV-A.

A serious problem with this view concerns whether we can ascertain natural tendencies. Of whom? The majority? Adult members of our species? Normal (statistically average?) adult members of our species? The need to sift out what is a result of cultural influence is a familiar, persistent difficulty. Suppose we can identify natural tendencies (perhaps by identifying what is statistically typical for adult members of the species, or appropriate subsets); must their fulfillment be assumed to constitute a good?[50] However, the tendency to act self-destructively seems rather natural, as does the tendency to act violently toward others. A defender of natural law might cry "foul" here. There is certainly a good deal of evidence that tendencies toward self- and other destructiveness, although very widespread, are a result of physical and/or emotional deprivation. Further, many evidently important sources of intense satisfaction are found in sexual relations, in challenging work, in intimate give and take with friends and family, and in the exercise of one's talents in various ways; all these activities seem in many ways natural, and one's capacities as a human play a central role in what results in what is, arguably, our good. Still, what follows by way of giving moral guidance to us is either not so obvious, or when implications have been drawn by natural law theorists, are problematic.

In *its* historical development of the natural law doctrine, going back to Aquinas, the Roman Catholic Church has classified sexual relations not between male and female as unnatural and to be condemned. A partial byproduct of this view is the legal prohibition on homosexual acts by consenting adults. Indeed, the view of the Roman Catholic Church is even narrower; what is claimed to be natural is procreation and the desire to procreate. Thus, heterosexual relations not involving the *possibility* of procreation are condemned; e.g., sexual acts not leading to the possibility of conception such as those employing artificial contraceptives, masturbation, or, for that matter, anal intercourse among heterosexuals. In view of the fact that some 10 to 20 million people are projected to die from AIDS in the next decade or two, one would think that the consequence *in part* of not using condoms would weigh heavily in the thinking of those who appeal to an ethic which waves the banner of human flourishing. Something similar might be said about the harmful effects of burgeoning human population—also a partial by-product of the unavailability of contraceptives and the opposition of powerful groups to their becoming more available, e.g., the Roman Catholic Church. Indeed the tendency to ignore weighty, cosmic consequences constitutes an objection to *certain* familiar developments of natural law theory. A broader conception of the nature of human flourishing *within* the natural law framework would lead to a radically different set of moral precepts.[51]

One may object that, after all, natural law theory is *not* a consequentialist view, and one may insist that what one ought to do is what it is natural to do *regardless of the consequences.* Further, Aristotle and Aquinas tend to define 'natural' in terms of the *function* of an object. When one has identified the function of an object *somehow,* then one may assume that it is appropriate to *assess* the behavior of the entity in question according to whether or not it fulfills that function. Thus, if the function of an object is to hammer nails, we may label it "a hammer" and then evaluate it according to whether or not it performs that function or does so well. For it to be a "good hammer" is for it to so function. It is tempting to equate two different things: whether an entity is effective in fulfilling a certain function and whether its so doing is morally good (or failing to do so is morally bad). One may be good

at the function of assassinating and therefore be a good assassin, but not, as a result, be morally good. It is worth noting that it is not wrong to use a hammer as a doorstop, to not use an Uzi to kill, or to use one's mouth to kiss (though its "natural" function is, arguably, to eat with). Sexual activity in which procreation is possible may fulfill one function of sexual activity, but it does not follow that we ought to judge to be wrong or unnatural any activity which does not. From the fact that something *can* fulfill a certain function, it does not follow that it *ought* to do so. Even though a person might make a mighty fine slave, it does not follow that the individual is wrong not to fulfill that function or that his or her "deviating" from so doing is "unnatural" if the latter is construed to mean "wrongful."[52]

We do not wish to suggest that natural law theorists should be saddled with Aristotle's view that some people are "slaves by nature," but there is a question on this view of whether *kinds* of beings have certain identifiable natural ends. For example, in a famous passage, Aristotle said that:

> Plants exist for the sake of animals. . . . all other animals exist for the sake of man, tame animals for the use he can make of them as well as for the food they provide; and as for the wild animals most though not all of these can be used for food or are useful in other ways; clothing and instruments can be made out of them. If we are right in believing that nature makes nothing without some end in view, nothing to no purpose, it must be that nature has made all things specifically for the sake of man.[53]

It is not obvious that the inference in the last sentence would be less invalid, in spite of Aristotle's extraordinary intellectual feats, if 'man' were replaced by 'the HIV.' That aside, can we defend a particular hierarchy of beings on the ground that one group is *useful* to another? Aren't humans quite *useful* to the human immuno-deficiency virus? In effect, the virus makes homes out of us. Can we say, then, that the natural end of some species is to serve others? A similar problem arises with Aristotle's broader hierarchy; he said "animals are to serve human ends, women are to serve the ends of men, and men are to serve the ends of God." This view has had enormous influence historically. It need not be part of a natural law theory, but it has been. The deeper question is whether living things should achieve their *natural ends* (a difficult concept to understand clearly, but one may consider: those outcomes which a being has a natural tendency to achieve), if they have such (perhaps all living things do), or all of them, and whether any of this provides the basis for a moral ideal attractive to rational persons. Behavior is often thought to be good or right because it is natural, but then devotees of this view ought to say what we should make of natural tendencies; for example, toward infanticide, which has been observed among various birds, rodents, lions, African wild dogs, and langurs (and not just among defective offspring).[54] See the Sidelight in Section IV-C called "Do What's Natural, You Say?".

We have called attention to some worries about whether one can *nonarbitrarily* (e.g., "find" them and elaborate good reasons for so doing) determine from nature just what are natural tendencies and, if so, whether one should assume that the good for humans (or others) is constituted by the fulfillment of these tendencies, and whether fulfillment of "unnatural" tendencies must be counted as an evil—something to be either voluntarily avoided, prevented, or punished by the coercive power of the law. Recall Hume's claim that one cannot validly infer normative conclusions from purely empirical premises. Further, one might accuse natural law theory of focusing *too little* on nature, and instead on *some* desires of *some* humans and weaving an ethic around the view that the world should be organized to promote fulfillment of those desires. No doubt we are too skeptical, and

the curious should read those who are believers and who set out sophisticated versions of this view. After all, some worries stated here are only about certain ways of identifying just what are natural human tendencies, and some natural law theorists may draw quite different moral conclusions if they identify natural tendencies differently, or assign positive weight to the fulfillment of nonhuman natural tendencies. No one disputes that the realization of certain human tendencies is sometimes a good and sometimes ought to be fostered; the arguments begin there, not terminate.

7. THE INFLUENCE OF KANT

Our glimpse of influential theories is much like our view of icebergs; we look too quickly and see only a small part.[55] A major implication of the moral view of Immanuel Kant (1724–1804) is that one cannot determine the moral value of an act solely by some sort of assessment of its consequences, i.e., it is anticonsequentialist. Kant claimed that the supreme principle of morality is what he called the Categorical Imperative. It had two "versions," which Kant deemed equivalent. It is not obvious, however, that they are. The first version, in our terms, says that one should *act only on those maxims of one's actions which one can, as a rational being, will to be (or endorse as) a universal law, i.e., obeyed by all moral agents.* Kant seems to give heavy weight to the idea of reciprocity and to the related notion that what is right or a duty for one is a duty for any other relevantly similar moral agent, and that moral principles are not custom-designed for only certain agents. He reasoned that the maxim of one person's deciding not to help another who is in distress is "help others only if it is convenient," but that no rational agent could endorse everyone's acting on that principle since the agent herself or himself might be in need of help on some occasion, thus involving himself or herself in a sort of contradiction of the will. We will not explore whether passing

Kant's "test" for maxims is necessary, sufficient, or merely relevant to a maxim's being defensible. But suppose that a maxim is "let generation X use up environmental resource and let generation Y bear the burden." With one further supposition, that the agent is not allowed to know into which generation he or she is born, an argument may be developed for a duty to use up resources only in sustainable ways or ways that make other generations no worse off.[56]

We have suggested a connection between Kant's theory and environmental questions about whether we have duties to future generations, if so, why, and just what they are. If Kant is right, then "drive a car if it is convenient" might be indefensible since if all obeyed such a maxim (say, about four billion adults), the result would be environmental catastrophe (a scenario not "willable" by a rational person). Of course, one person's driving may have no noticeable effect; so from a consequentialist's point of view, there may be no objection to the maxim. It is of interest, however, that since no rational being could approve of everyone's acting on the rule in question, no one should act according to that rule. Hence we seem to observe a difference between Kant's view and the approach of a consequentialist. This is food for thought about the environment.

Kant's other version of the Categorical Imperative is that we would *never treat a person as a mere means*; by 'person' he seems to mean "rational creature." Indeed there is great stress in Kant's writing on the value of rational beings, beings capable of reflecting on options, on principles, and autonomously deciding for themselves what duty demands. That is, this value is due to the fact that people have the capacity to formulate goals, reflect on values, and so on. Thus, we as such agents owe them a certain respect; generally, for example, we must refrain from causing them harm by acting contrary to their wills. Having a servant need not involve treating the person as a mere

means if, for example, the person consents and is compensated for his or her efforts. If we should never treat a person as a mere means (a most suggestive notion; but what is precluded here—e.g., bad argument, bribery, guilt-tripping, browbeating, insulting, ridiculing, shaming—along with the usual "force and fraud"?), then we may not do so *even if* the result would be maximization of total net utility. On occasion Kant expresses his view in terms of respects for rights. Thus we note a major source of tension between the Kantian approach and the utilitarian approach to deciding moral questions.

Kant's strikingly different attitude toward treatment of those he took to be (all?) nonrational beings ("animals") is found in this passage:

> . . . so far as animals are concerned we have no direct duties. Animals are not self-conscious and are there merely as a means to an end. That end is man. . . . Our duties toward animals are merely indirect duties towards humanity . . . . If he is not to stifle his human feelings, he must practice kindness towards animals, for he who is cruel to animals becomes hard also in his dealings with men. . . . Vivisectionists . . . certainly act cruelly . . . and they can justify their cruelty, since animals must be regarded as man's instruments.[57]

In the same lecture, he claimed that a man who shoots his dog when the dog is no longer useful "does not fail in his duty to the dog," in brief, because there is no duty to the dog. One cannot *wrong* it even if one can *harm* it in Kant's view—for "it cannot judge."[58] Note the importance of cognitive capacities in Kant's view. The question arises as to whether it would then be all right to vivisect profoundly retarded humans—if, in fact, the presence of the capacity to judge is a necessary condition for being owed any duties. Is there a justification for differential treatment of animals and humans when they are on a par with respect to mental capacities and sentience? It may be evident that Kant's thesis about the source of noninstrumental value implies that virtually nothing nonhuman has such value; perhaps strictly speaking Kant would, or should, deny that profoundly retarded humans or the severely senile are owed any direct duties either. If so, then he does not mark the boundary of those possessing moral standing (see the Preview to Part III) in a way coextensive with the bounds around our species. A powerful moral intuition is that there are relevant differences between rocks, cabbages, and giant pandas. With respect to their being owed direct duties, Kant says not. Many today insist that we should not treat sentient nonhumans, for example, as mere means—thus differently deploying Kant's conception. Frequently, the term "animal liberationists" or "defender of animal rights" is used for those who take, roughly, this view (e.g., Peter Singer and Tom Regan, respectively). Some philosophers and others hold that we have duties to all living things ("biocentrists," e.g., Paul Taylor), or to the earth itself (which some tend to view as itself alive, e.g., James Lovelock). The various viewpoints emerge with accompanying arguments, especially in Part III and Part IV.

8. THE IDEA OF A UNIQUE ENVIRONMENTAL ETHIC

Can there be a distinctive "environmental ethic"? The question itself is not clear. If it concerns the possibility of there being an ethic with implications about how we treat the environment, then the answer is that all ethical theories have such implications. We may think the implications of some are intolerable, but that is another matter. Indeed many have thought that the implications of most or all traditional ethical theories with regard to our dealings with the environment are unacceptable and have therefore called for a new, distinct environmental ethic. Whether the new theory will be a revision of some traditional

theoretical framework (John Passmore has defended this possibility[59]) or one which involves a radical jettisoning of all traditional frameworks is an open question. It is difficult to imagine a theory which would not incorporate key features of traditional views; arguably, however, none has appeared. Some incorporate significantly new assumptions; see especially the views of Leopold, Callicott, and Taylor in Part IV-A, and Rolston in Part III.

Serious questions have been raised in recent years about traditional views. The major issue is the attack on anthropocentrism: the assumption that it is the well-being of *all and only* human beings which counts (for its own sake and not merely instrumentally). This matter is explored in Part III and Part IV. Competing views extend moral standing to all sentient beings, to all "subjects of a life," or to all living individuals. A second challenging thesis of recent work is that not only individuals count, but entire ecosystems or biological processes or sets of such. Once one grants moral standing to entities other than humans, a third crucial, seemingly inscrutable, recalcitrant difficulty arises about how to articulate a reasonable, principled way to resolve conflicts between competing interests of very diverse beings or webs of life. Some essays in Parts IV-A, IV-B, and IV-C address this issue. Recent moral positions which urge an extension of moral standing to nonhumans, and especially to *collectivities* ("environmental holist" views as opposed to "individualist" views) of some sort, sometimes seem to offer little guidance about this issue, e.g., rather romantic nostrums about how we humans are one with nature or are mere nodes of consciousness in the sea of life. Analogous *intrahuman* conflict situations are extremely difficult to think through; to add nonhuman interests muddies the ethical waters; but something similar must have occurred to those who, in earlier times, came to the view that women counted, or that blacks counted. Sometimes simplicity is purchased at the price of reasonableness.

An individual might regard one's own skin as the line of division between oneself and "the environment," and this is just what the ethical egoist recommends. To call attention to this point is to remind oneself, or perhaps notice more vividly, that many of the environmental questions which we face are largely (if not solely) questions of a more or less familiar type about how we may, and how we ought to, treat *human beings*. To suggest a crude taxonomy, many of the important questions concern the justification of restrictions on the liberty of persons (or governments, corporations, and the like), questions about justice, and questions about the defensibility of imposing risks on other persons. That is, they are the central questions of recent work in moral and political philosophy. Hence one point we urge is increased integration of environmental ethics and modern moral and political philosophy. For this to occur, people who work in these areas must pay attention to the explorations of others who have often worked in comparative isolation.

Consider some examples. Questions about the defensibility of pollution, or the desirability of auctioning off pollution rights, at once involve issues about the acceptability of imposing risks on others, typically those who have not given informed consent to the risk. Such actions evidently restrict the liberty of others. And the distribution of burdens may occur in such a manner that questions of fairness arise. Frequently spokespersons for the third world complain that countries such as the United States and Germany generate extremely high rates of pollution per capita in comparison to third-world countries. Imagine the pollution we would see if one billion people in China owned one or more cars that ran on fossil fuels. Yet, developed countries insist that nations such as Brazil abstain from cutting tropical forests in order to have more trees to recycle the great carbon output of heavily industrialized nations. The U.S. government has claimed in reply that many of its high-tech products benefit the world, including the less developed nations, thereby compensating for higher pollution rates. These matters raise familiar questions about the extent to which nations ought to respect the sovereignty of other nations. The United States invaded Panama to depose President Noriega; is it permissible for other nations to depose a U.S. President on the ground that he leads a country which is the major contributor to the production of plutonium, nerve gas, and carbon pollution? The question of how, and at what rate, any nation should be using up resources raises the question of what duties current generations have to future ones. This, too, can be thought of as a question of fairness, in part, as well as a question about subjecting others to serious risks.

Complicating matters is an issue which thus far has received no comment herein. It is widely held that each nation should do only what will promote or maximize its own interests. Sometimes, instead of this broad doctrine, the view one finds in, say, the United States is that the United States ought to do whatever will promote its own interest. This view looks like Ethical Egoism on a national scale (we could call it National Ethical Egoism). This view is no obscure doctrine; it is the basis for much foreign policy. It is often associated with the assumption that there are *no* moral relations between nations, no duties, no rights, and that rather the situation is one Hobbes described as a state of nature (the doctrine of so-called *political realism*). Addressing many of the planetary environmental issues is indeed difficult if this (we think absurd) doctrine is accepted. With respect to certain ecological advantages, it might well be better if the world were not organized into numerous nation-states in which national boundaries bear little or no relation to ecotones, the boundaries between roughly identifiable sets of ecosystems (or bioregions). Perhaps it would be easier under such circumstances to avoid habitat deterioration, the massive kill-off of species, the diminishment of biodiversity, population crashes, and decline in the quality of life for humans and others. But we do not start with an undesigned planet, one consisting of raw material to be distributed, or more than five billion people to be assigned to spaces as on the first day of school. We are, for better or worse, up to our sometimes myopic, nationalistic eyeballs in existing political, religious, racial, and ethnic loyalties, with systems of property rights, traditions of sovereignty, and so on. These practices, norms, and institutions often deserve to be radically criticized and altered, but doing so could also be unjust in certain ways, and this fact must also be given weight in proposed solutions. For some otherwise desirable goals, we may not be able morally "to get there from here." But we do not wish to urge any presumption in favor of the status quo. We are suggesting that many traditional questions of *intranational* and *international* justice have important bearings on attempts to identify morally acceptable solutions to the problems we confront. Indeed, they will also affect just how we define or identify those problems.

NOTES

1. Carl Sagan and Ann Druyan, *Shadows of Forgotten Ancestors* (New York: Random House, 1992), p. 3.

2. As quoted in William Irvine, *Apes, Angels, and Victorians* (London: Reader's Union, 1956), p. 49.

3. This is a loose and somewhat formal characterization that in the end will not do; intuitively, "You ought to wear your purple tie" is not a moral claim. Likewise, neither is "If you are going to Montreal, you ought to brush up on your French."

4. A plausible, broader taxonomy might regard moral or normative claims as a subset of evaluative ones. *Evaluative* claims would be understood to include both moral claims but also nonmoral evaluative claims. The latter category would include evaluative claims about objects or states of affairs, e.g., Mrs. Brown has got a lovely daughter, the Musee D'Orsay is exhilarating, Beethoven's Fifth Symphony is sublime, pleasure is good, Koko is one fine animal, or Lake Louise in British Columbia is a joy to the eyes. We will often use 'normative' interchangeably with 'moral' or 'ethical,' but it is frequently used by others as a more generic term such as 'evaluative.'

5. A remark of Dorothy Parker in a book review.

6. This movement consisted largely of a group of philosophers and scientists who wished to rid the world of what they considered nonsense; it is associated with the Vienna Circle and the names of A. J. Ayer, Moritz Schlick, and Rudolph Carnap, among others.

7. As reported by Plato in the *Republic*.

8. Tautologies and logical truths are statements which are true because of their form or simply in virtue of the meaning of the words used, e.g., all bachelors are unmarried, everything which has shape has size, all purple things are colored, eye color is a heritable trait or it is not.

9. However, we note that there may be moral agents who are not humans and that not all humans are moral agents. One should compare, regardless of whether they exist, human infants, profoundly retarded humans, God, angels, E. T., or Koko the gorilla (who signed in American Sign Language "me bite, bad" after biting her trainer one day).

10. This characterization no doubt needs qualification.

11. If one is unfamiliar with certain basic standards used in the assessment of arguments, a logic course can be very helpful.

12. David Hume, from Book III, Part I, Section I of *A Treatise of Human Nature*. Edited by L. A. Selby-Bigge (Oxford: Clarendon Press, 1965), p. 469.

13. We can validly infer "Hilary's car is colored" from the premise "Hilary's care is blue." However, it is invalid to infer that "Hilary's car is blue" *from* the premise "Hilary's car is colored"—*even if* it happens to be true that her car is blue. Valid arguments are "truth-preserving" but *may* not start with true premises. The terms 'valid' and 'invalid' are technical terms as used here.

14. The fact that one cannot validly infer normative conclusions from purely empirical premises in the examples noted would not, of course, show that one can never do so. Many philosophers, "ethical naturalists," think otherwise. On this point one might consult the writings of Phillipa Foot.

15. By design this test for toxicity of substances is not complete until at least half of the test animals die.

16. If 'murder' is used to mean "unlawful killing," the sentence looks empirical, but if what is meant is "wrongful killing," the sentence is being used to make a moral claim.

17. As the term is used technically by mathematicians, philosophers, and logicians, 'invalid' does not *mean*

'bad,' and an invalid argument need not, but may, have a false conclusion. However, invalid arguments are commonly appraised as bad in one respect: their premises fail to support their conclusions in the strongest possible manner. An argument which has this fault may nevertheless happen to have a true conclusion.

18. Compare the remark of Albert Einstein, no artsy antiscientific sort, ". . . we should be on our guard not to overestimate science and scientific methods when it is a question of human problems; and we should not assume that experts are the only ones who have a right to express themselves on questions affecting the organization of society." From *Ideas and Opinions by Albert Einstein* (New York: Crown Publishers, 1954), p. 152.

19. On the moral/legal distinction, recall the view that black persons had moral rights even when in the antebellum period in the United States few such rights were also legally institutionalized.

20. Paul and Anne Ehrlich, *Healing the Planet* (Reading, MA: Addison-Wesley, 1991), p. 85.

21. The best philosophy and the best science get the facts straight; *even if* that is done, reasoning *about* the facts is another matter. We leave it to a well-known scientist to express an opinion about the receptiveness of scientists to philosophical untangling of arguments. To quote Stephen Jay Gould, ". . . I deplore the unwillingness of scientists to explore seriously the logical structure of arguments." And further, "Scientists tend to ignore academic philosophy as an empty pursuit. Surely, any intelligent person can think straight by intuition." Evidently, Gould is speaking ironically in the last sentence. See Stephen Jay Gould, *Ever Since Darwin* (New York: W. W. Norton, 1977), p. 40.

22. Paul and Anne Ehrlich, *op. cit.*, p. 116.

23. For the Galileo example see Jonathan Weiner, *Planet Earth* (Toronto: Bantam Books, 1986), p. 153. Concerning Agassiz, see p. 116.

24. The term 'a priori' means "before or apart from" experience or empirical evidence. An *a priori* assumption may be true; whether it is belief-worthy is another matter.

25. By "anthropocentric grounds" or "anthropocentric values," some may mean simply "human ideals," but among them may be the view, for example, that we ought not inflict pain or premature death on *animals* gratuitously, or even the view that species boundaries are morally without weight. But such a usage of "anthropocentrism" threatens to muddy the conceptual waters. Compare Bryan Norton's characterization and use of "weak anthropocentrism:" Bryan Norton, *Why Preserve Natural Variety?* (Princeton, NJ: Princeton University Press, 1987) pp. 7, 12.

26. Strictly, philosophers normally divide "ethics" as a discipline into *normative* ethics and *metaethics*, and the attempt to figure out the most defensible moral principles, or specifically what we ought to do, is the focus of normative ethics. The focus of metaethics is more abstract; the questions are those *about* ethical claims, e.g., are they rationally decidable, does 'right' refer to some natural property, and so on.

27. On this point one might consult Mary Midgley, "Duties Concerning Islands," reprinted in *People, Penguins, and Plastic Trees*, edited by Donald VanDeVeer and Christine Pierce (Belmont, CA: Wadsworth Publishing, 1986) pp. 156–164.

28. Richard Brandt suggests that it is those convictions surviving cognitive psychotherapy that deserve weight. See his *Theory of the Good and the Right* (New York: Oxford University Press, 1979). One critic has observed that we would regard as suspect any theory of psychotherapy *unless it* accorded with our deepest pretheoretical moral convictions; the reference has evaporated.

29. Rather what is said in defense of the claim seems to support only theses like all acts have motives, people always want to achieve whatever they desire to achieve, or all acts are acts of a self.

30. How to characterize the negative-positive distinction is not straightforward. Refraining from acting may be a kind of effortful action, e.g., braking a car to refrain from hitting another one.

31. See Susan Miller Okin, *Justice, Gender, and the Family* (New York: Basic Books, 1989).

32. We employ suggestions from Frank Stare, "The Concept of Property" (*American Philosophical Quarterly*, Vol. 9, 1972), pp. 200–207.

33. See J. Baird Callicott, "On the Intrinsic Value of Non-Human Species" in *The Preservation of Species*, edited by Bryan Norton (Princeton, NJ: Princeton University Press, 1986), p. 144. Note also Norton's view that appeals to rights ". . . provide no theoretically defensible basis for species preservation." *Ibid.*, p. 275.

34. However, dying prematurely seems to count as a harm or a cost, and it may be painless. So one cannot classify painless dying as a form of disutility (understood as pain of some sort).

35. See Charles Darwin's *The Expression of Emotion in Man and Animals* (Chicago: University of Chicago Press, 1965) for Darwin's focus on bodily and facial expressions as compelling evidence of emotional states in humans *and* animals.

36. If the sum of the utilities of a majority's getting its wants fulfilled is more than offset by the sum of the disutilities of a minority's losing out, then what maximizes total net utility and what most persons want may be contrary paths.

37. We note in passing that in his *Introduction to the Principles of Morals and Legislation* (1789), Bentham addressed the difficulty of measuring pleasure or pain and proposed that intensity, duration, fecundity (the tendency of the feeling to give rise to more of the same kind), and so on should be taken into account.

38. Predicting consequences may be very difficult (compare current worries over whether someone released from jail will steal again or whether global warming by the year 2050 will increase at least 4 degrees centigrade). Probabilities may need to be taken into account; so strictly the calculation is to determine total net *expected* utility.

39. In 1992 it was decided that the captain of the oil tanker *Exxon Valdez* was immune to prosecution for having allowed his ship to run aground. The law is that a captain is immune to prosecution once he reports the event. The rationale for the law is thus utilitarian or consequentialist in nature; it is to encourage captains to report such events, presumably thereby promoting the overall best results. Some utilitarians might draw a different conclusion. Defenders of a retributivist theory of justice may insist that the captain deserved a serious punishment and that it is wrongheaded to look forward to the consequences as a way of determining the correct policy. There are serious worries about fairness here; compare the severe penalties imposed on certain consenting adult homosexual behavior (up to 20 years in jail in North Carolina). In the days of David Hume (18th century), in Great Britain one could be hung for simply disbelieving in the existence of God. This fact tended to discourage publication on certain issues.

40. Economists and philosophers agree, to our knowledge, that there are many Pareto-optimal states of affairs at which one might arrive depending on the initial situation of goods. A Pareto-optimal situation is one in which it is impossible to rearrange things and make someone better off without also making someone worse off; in that respect it is one which is totally "efficient" as economists use that term. The initial or final distribution of goods may or may not be thought of as fair or just. Discerning whether a situation is Pareto-optimal or not, i.e., efficient, does not then address the distributional problem. In an imaginary two-person community consisting of a slave and his "master," it might be

impossible to make one better off without making the other worse off and, thus, the situation would be efficient; all this suggests, of course, that efficiency is not everything. We believe that a theory of justice is required and that only within the constraints required by principles of justice (whatever those constraints might be) is it permissible to pursue efficiency. The principles of justice may, of course, allow an important role for moral rights. Such a theory of efficiency within justice may allow for cost-benefit analysis within the framework of a rights theory. These most succinct, if not obtuse, remarks are meant to be suggestive for further inquiry. The burden would seem to be on philosophers to try to supply the right theory of justice.

41. Maybe we should not go so far as Albert Schweitzer, who purportedly said "happiness is for pigs." No doubt this was Schweitzer's way of discounting the importance of human happiness, but Benthamite utilitarians might give it a different twist (we should care about the happiness of animals as well).

42. Although we would strongly discourage anyone from thinking that ethical issues have any necessary connection with religious ones, Malcolm Gillis cites an essay by E. Mason, who points out that the economics department at Harvard University was dominated by preachers until the 1880s. See Malcolm Ellis, "Economics, Ecology, and Ethics: Mending the Broken Circle of the Tropical Forests" in the excellent volume *The Broken Circle*, edited by F. H. Bormann and Stephen Kellert (New Haven, CT: Yale University Press, 1991), p. 155.

43. We rely here on one of many helpful comments by Talbot Page.

44. The term 'paternalism' or 'paternalistic interference' refers to interference with others in an effort to promote their own good, e.g., taking away car keys from a drunk. One question that arises is whether we can ever know better than the other what is for his or her own good and if so under what circumstances. On this topic see Joel Feinberg, *Harm to Self* (New York: Oxford University Press, 1986) or Donald VanDeVeer, *Paternalistic Intervention* (Princeton, NJ: Princeton University Press, 1986).

45. It is worth reminding ourselves of all the choices that routinely get made for others, e.g., children, the severely retarded, the senile, many medical patients, and animals. And those without funds cannot cast a "dollar vote" in the marketplace.

46. Something like the thesis of psychological egoism (each person always acts out of a desire to promote his or her own interest) usually seems to get as-

sumed about here. On the other hand, if being "better off" simply means getting one's desires satisfied on balance, then one might be "better off" if one commits suicide or is subjected to torture—*if* that is what one wanted, on balance.

47. Still, the rights theory may allow that infringements are justified only under certain rather limited conditions. The utilitarian theory is committed to condoning any and all nasty acts if doing so would indeed maximize utility. A question for any rights theory allowing infringements is whether its grounds for doing so are nonarbitrary.

48. If potential gainers from a transaction *compensated* those who would otherwise be losers (and remained gainers), then interesting alternatives would arise. Generally, economists insist that moving to a situation in which such compensation *could* be made is an improvement (why? because there would be an increase in total net utility?) even if compensation is *not* actually paid. This "potential compensation" variant on the Pareto principle seems nontrivial partly because it seems to condone unjust redistributions (on balance the losers just appear to be wrongfully harmed), as does the principle of utility. So it seems to gain nontriviality at the cost of serious conflict with our pretheoretical convictions.

49. These comments were made at a meeting of the American Philosophical Association in Columbus, Ohio, April 29–May 1, 1982. The paper was entitled "Natural Law and Moral Rights: Comments on a Paper by Christine Pierce."

50. On this matter one might consult the essay by Christopher Boorse, "Concepts of Health," in *Health Care Ethics,* edited by Donald VanDeVeer and Tom Regan (Philadelphia: Temple University Press, 1987).

51. On this point one might examine the work of Joseph Raz or Germain Grisez.

52. It is crucial to notice the frequent slide from purely descriptive uses of 'abnormal' and 'unnatural' (e.g., statistically unusual) to evaluative uses of the same terms.

53. There is no doubt that there are certain natural tendencies. Some hold that these are divinely implanted. Some hold that they are just there and offer no explanation. The prevailing scientific view is, of course, that there is an explanation and that it has to do with which behaviors were advantageous in the competitive process of natural selection. Male robber flies, for example, court female robber flies; this behavior, to which there is a natural tendency, seems to have the advantage of helping the female to recognize the male as something not to be eaten (at least not at that moment).

54. Arthur Fisher, "A New Synthesis Comes of Age," *Mosaic,* Vol. 22, No. 1 (Spring 1991), p. 13.

55. We speak of "influential *theories.*" Perhaps no one has gone to war thinking that she or he is out to defend "a theory," but as we have used the term, the evaluative beliefs of the Nazis led them to war; the Crusades sought to spread a certain doctrine, and Columbus both wanted to find lots of gold for Spain and to Christianize "the natives" in the process. The gospel of free trade, of the classless society, of ethnic purity, and certain Islamic ideals have led to enslavement and to wholesale destruction of species and ecosystems. Somewhere, John Stuart Mill noted that the logic of tyrants is: *since we are right, it is all right to persecute those who disagree.* Prescriptions such as that of one of the church fathers, Tertullian, "love God and do as you as please" are recipes for God knows what, so to speak. Some theories explicitly prohibit the forcible spread of any doctrine, including their own. One might compare Kant's views and Utilitarianism in this respect. If it would maximize utility to forcibly spread the doctrine of Utilitarianism, why not do it—if one accepts the Principle of Utility? In contrast the Kantian notion to never treat a person as a mere means would seem to prohibit the forcible spread of that very notion.

56. In passing, we note that a work of great importance and one with acknowledgment of Kant's influence, John Rawls's *A Theory of Justice,* makes important and inventive use of the idea that principles of justice plausibly may be thought of, in an elaborate thought-experiment, as those principles which would be accepted by rational, "self-interested" persons seeking to determine those principles which would guide their own future interaction, including the design of basic institutions, the distribution of basic goods and opportunities—such deciders being subject to important informational constraints, namely, that they are not allowed to know or to use information by which everyday bargainers seek special advantage; that is, they are supposed to be ignorant of the generation into which they are born (see p. 136 ff.), their race, their nationality, and so on. In effect Kant says: pay attention only to what you can rationally endorse or will, not your actual wants. Similarly, Rawls constructs a decision scenario to give weight to people's impartial wants, not their actual, biased ones. See John Rawls, *A Theory of Justice* (Cambridge, MA: Belknap Press

of Harvard University, 1971). It may be useful to take a course in moral philosophy first, or to take along one's personal philosopher for the trip.

57. Immanuel Kant, "Duties to Animals and Spirits, in *Lectures on Ethics,* translated by Louis Infield (New York: Harper and Row, 1963), pp. 239–241.

58. Most wrongings involve harming, but arguably many do not. On this, see Joel Feinberg, *Harmless Wrongdoing* (Oxford: Oxford University Press, 1988).

59. John Passmore, *Man's Responsibility for Nature* (New York: Scribner's, 1974).

II

WESTERN RELIGIONS AND ENVIRONMENTAL ATTITUDES

PREVIEW

> Whenever I injure life of any kind I must be quite clear as to whether this is necessary or not. I ought never to pass the limits of the unavoidable, even in apparently insignificant cases. The countryman who has mowed down a thousand blossoms in his meadow as fodder for his cows should take care that on the way home he does not, in wanton pastime, switch off the head of a single flower growing on the edge of the road, for in so doing he injures life without being forced to do so by necessity.
>
> *Albert Schweitzer*[1]

> Christ himself shows that to refrain from the killing of animals and the destroying of plants is the height of superstition for, judging that there are no common rights between us and the beasts and trees, he sent the devils into a herd of swine and with a curse withered the tree on which he found no fruit.
>
> *Augustine*[2]

Many systems of ideas and bodies of doctrine have influenced our views on nature. Some are religious; some are secular. We will say a little about secular influences later. However, in this section we will focus on the Judeo-Christian tradition, acknowledging that the category of the religious is overbroad for our purposes because it would include Buddhist, Hindu, and other outlooks.

When we speak, in particular, of Christianity, it is important to distinguish between (1) the historical institution of the Christian church on the one hand, and (2) the logical implications of its doctrine on the other (especially those found in its chosen sacred writings).[3] Lynn White, Jr., in his famous 1967 essay "The Historic Roots of our Ecologic Crisis," discusses Christianity in the former sense, that is, as a historical institution in the Latin West, when he blames Christianity for the part it has played in fostering an attitude of human arrogance toward nature. White says, "No new set of values has been accepted in our society to displace those of Christianity. Hence we shall continue to have a worsening ecologic crisis until we reject the Christian axiom that nature has no reason for existence save to serve man."[4]

White's focus is not on how one *ought* to interpret Biblical texts, but rather on how Biblical texts *have* been interpreted (historically) and how those interpretations have fit together with the emergence of a democratic culture and the growth of science and technology to produce ecologic crisis. The following is a striking example of his thesis: In Antiquity, White reminds us, ". . . every tree, every spring, every stream, every hill had its own . . . guardian spirit."[5] This belief is called *animism*. Christianity destroyed animism . . . and many forests. As White points out, "For nearly 2 millennia Christian missionaries have been chopping down sacred groves, which are idolatrous because they assume spirit in nature."[6] Presumably, the actions of Christians are and were linked to their beliefs that "man [sic] shares, in great measure, God's transcendence of nature."[7] Spirit then, belongs to humans only. By destroying pagan animism, White asserts, ". . . Christianity made it possible to exploit nature in a mood of indifference to the feelings of natural objects."[8] White is saying that people have beliefs and that their beliefs have consequences. Many beliefs that are destructive to the environment stem from what Latin Christians took biblical doctrine to be. It could have been (or could be) otherwise. In "Continuing the Conversation," a paper White wrote in 1973 as a reply to his critics, he says, "Scattered through the Bible, but especially the Old Testament, there are passages that can be read as sustaining the notion of a spiritual democracy of all creatures. The point is that historically they seem seldom or never to have been so interpreted. This should not inhibit anyone from taking a fresh look at them."[9]

In "Continuing the Conversation," White says of his critics: "The most common charge was that I had ignorantly misunderstood the nature of 'man's dominion' and that it is not an arbitrary rule but rather a stewardship of our fellow creatures for which mankind is responsible to God."[10] The relevant biblical passage here is the creation story in Gen. 1:

> "Then God said,
> 'Let us make man in our image, after our likeness; and let them have dominion over the fish of the sea and over the birds of the air, and over the cattle, and over all the earth and over every creeping thing that creeps upon the earth.'
> So God created man in his own image, in the image of God he created them; male and female he created them.
> And God blessed them, and God said to them,
> 'Be fruitful and multiply, and fill the earth and subdue it; and have dominion over the fish of the sea and over the birds of the air, and over every living thing that moves upon the earth.'
> And God said,
> 'Behold I have given you every plant

> yielding seed which is upon the face of all the earth, and every tree with seed in its fruit; you shall have them for food. . . .'"[11]

Whether A. R. Peacocke is representative of White's critics, he does exactly that about which White protests. Peacocke sets out to show that "dominion" really means "leadership," not "exploitation," that man [sic] is to be a steward, not a despot.[12] Peacocke's criticism misses the point of White's thesis—that biblical texts are often open to more than one interpretation and that, historically, for the most part, a particular reading unfavorable to the environment became dogma.

As White's discussion of St. Francis of Assisi (1181–1226) makes clear, there was some difference of opinion about what Christian doctrine was taken to be even in medieval times. Again, the historical point is that it was the views of, for example, Augustine (354–430) and St. Thomas Aquinas (1225–1274) that prevailed, not the views of St. Francis. As White puts it, "The prime miracle of St. Francis is the fact that he did not end up at the stake, as many of his left-wing followers did."

"For God So Loved the World," a following selection, is a sermon preached in Salisbury Cathedral by Andrew Linzey, IFAW Senior Research Fellow, Mansfield College, Oxford, and Special Professor in Theology, University of Nottingham, England. In his piece, Linzey sounds a little like Lynn White, Jr., when he says, "It seems to me that there is no use pretending that all has been well with the Church either in the past, or even now in the present. The very community which should be the cradle of the Gospel of God's Love for the world has only been too good at justifying violence and legitimizing hatred towards the world."[13] His claim that ". . . the record of Christianity has been, and still is, . . . in many respects shameful and second rate"[14] is backed up by interesting detail about various Popes and about Christian practice.

White, also a self-acknowledged "churchman," is hopeful that Westerners will ". . . find a new religion or rethink our old one."[15] Linzey is optimistic: "The same tradition which helped keep slavery alive was the same community that became by and large determined to end it."[16]

The stewardship view is a fairly popular example of recent rethinking. What exactly is this view? Peacocke gives the following characterization:

> Although "dominion" has [a] kingly reference, it is a caring "dominion" exercised under the authority of the Creator, and so it is a more accurate reflection of the meaning of the Genesis myth to say that it describes man as vicegerent, or steward, or manager, or trustee (as of a property, or a charity) as well as exercising the leadership of a king of creation. He is, in the myth, called to tend the earth and its creatures in responsibility to its Creator. He is accountable. He is responsible.[17]

According to the stewardship view, there is a God who expects us to exercise responsibility toward the earth. The earth belongs to God, and members of *Homo sapiens* are commanded to take care of it and the creatures that dwell therein.

A stewardship interpretation may be committed to an acceptance of a traditional private-property view. That is, it may assume that humans should not ruthlessly exploit the earth, *because* the earth belongs to God. If we ought to treat the earth in a responsible and virtuous way, it is not because the earth and its creatures have independent moral standing or inherent worth, but because they are God's property. Another interpretation is possible here if the relevant parts of the Genesis story are read as a directive for humans to look after the goods of the beings and things created by God not insofar as they are God's property, but insofar as they have goods of their own. For example, the text, "And God saw that [the cre-

ation] was good,"[18] may mean that God declared that the earth and the things and beings in it have intrinsic value, that is, a value of their own.[19]

Whether the concept of stewardship is sufficiently democratic to be the substitute for the animism White wants is an interesting question. Philosopher Anthony Weston thinks we could do better. Drawing on a famous statement made by Aldo Leopold (1887–1948), a major environmental thinker whose work we will look at in detail in Section IV-A, Weston says, "No longer are we, like Adam, lords of creation, the reference points of the whole process, but, in Leopold's words, 'plain biotic citizens.' We are not even 'stewards' of the land—even that is too superior a role—but simply coinhabitants of what Leopold called the biotic community."[20]

Stephen Jay Gould, a well-known biologist and geologist, makes an interesting observation about the appropriateness of humans viewing themselves as stewards for a threatened world. Such a view, Gould maintains, is

> . . . rooted in the old sin of pride and exaggerated self-importance. We are one among millions of species, stewards of nothing. By what argument could we, arising just a geological microsecond ago, become responsible for the affairs of a world 4.5 billion years old, teeming with life that has been evolving and diversifying for at least three-quarters of that immense span? Nature does not exist for us, had no idea we were coming, and doesn't give a damn about us.[21]

Just as nature cannot be said to give a damn about us, it must be said that neither do our yet-to-be-born children; still, we can, and often should, care for those who cannot care for us. In addition to religious influences on current environmental attitudes, so there are important secular ones as well. Many of these sources cannot be judged earth-friendly. We sketch a few of them below. In many cases it is difficult to sort out the secular and sacred strands or beliefs.

In ancient Greece there arose a number of intellectual mavericks who refused simply to accept as explanatory legends and stories of the gods being angry at each other (e.g., lightning was Zeus's hurling arrows of fire). These curiosity seekers, or intellectual nonconformists, were labeled "lovers of knowledge or wisdom" (from *philos* and *sophos* in the Greek), that is, "philosophers" (a label which included those today we label as scientists and mathematicians also). Among them was Protagoras, who is famous for his remark that "man is the measure of all things." With the tendency to reject the view that humans are merely the playthings of the gods, there came a focus on the natural powers and importance of human beings. There was certainly an interest in learning about the nonhuman parts of the natural world, but not a strong tendency to assign any particular noninstrumental value to it. As we noted in the Introduction, Aristotle (387–322 B.C.E.), whose views were enormously influential in the West for the next 2000 years, regarded nature as hierarchically arranged, with plants having the purpose of serving animals and animals having the purpose of serving human beings. This view looks like the kind of evaluative pyramid found in the Judeo-Christian tradition without an omniscient, omnipotent Being reigning at the top. Suffice it to say that these secular sources also tend to place the nonhuman at the bottom (or "off the chart") of a great chain of beings. Aristotle's teacher, Plato (427–347 B.C.E.), tended to find the Real (we speak vaguely) in the nonmaterial realm of the perfect forms, rather like the domain of the perfect figures of geometry, in the world of the unchangeable, not in the world of Appearances (that is, among the breathing, changing, copulating, fighting, excreting, decaying, growing creatures of the biosphere).

It was characteristic of the Stoics (4th century B.C.E. and following) to conceive of the body as a tomb (*soma sema* in Greek), as inferior to the mind and a drag on achieving the good or ideal life. This view is, of course, paralleled by the Christian tendency to believe in the survival of a soul without a body, or the belief that one will get a new "spiritual" body in the afterlife, at which time one may be liberated from the "warring in one's members" (see Paul's remarks about this issue and his plea to be delivered from "the body of this death" in Romans 7:23–25), the lust of the flesh or the lack of voluntary control over his sexual organ, a phenomenon which enabled young Augustine to believe in the doctrine of the inheritance of original sin. In any case, this attitude of devaluation of the body, of the wild, of the organic can be found in nonreligious sources as well, although we know of no secular dogma which urged poverty or chastity in the same way as some Christian elements.

During the Renaissance, and the advent of the new sciences in the 14th to the 17th centuries especially, we find an emphasis on mind-body dualism (it and materialism can be found among the ancient philosophers). French philosopher and mathematician (recall Cartesian coordinates) René Descartes (1596–1650) notoriously found animals lacking in minds. He claimed that in spite of "the astuteness and cunning of dogs and foxes," one could explain the acts of all of them "from the constitution of their organs."[22] In Descartes's influential view, all natural beings are mindless except for humans; this empirical claim is typically found in tandem with the evaluative claim that only humans have any intrinsic value or inherent worth.

The rise of modern science tended to contribute to a kind of human euphoria. A new era was at hand; humans could understand the world. Far from being a place filled with demons over which one might lack control, nature was intelligible, governed by natural laws accessible and discoverable in principle by human beings. Humans could overcome natural obstacles, "conquer nature," or later in the New World (after Native Americans discovered Christopher Columbus and his men on their shores) "win the West." Often, nature came to be thought of as more like a machine, something over which one could exert influence for one's own ends. Indeed, Descartes conceived of animals as being like clocks that emitted noises but that were merely automata. With understanding and the power to predict came the power to control, to manipulate, and to dominate. The later works of Galileo and Isaac Newton, for all their merits, certainly encouraged the view of the universe as matter in motion, functioning in ways describable by precise mathematical formulas; the full title of Newton's famous work of 1687 was *Mathematical Principles of Natural Philosophy*.[23] Some philosophers and scientists concluded that humans were no special exception to the rule in this huge, mechanistic, mindless, deterministic universe; they viewed humans as machines that also possessed the illusion of free choice. Generally, however, the view has been, especially to the period of Charles Darwin[24] (and even after), that humans are exceptions, that we are not really "animals" (people tend to reserve the term for nonhumans), not fully determined, and of special value—hence we have a right and perhaps a duty to manage the planet. Thus, religious traditions have no monopoly on this brand of anthropocentrism.

The emergence of industrialization and development of market economies have greatly affected what humans have *done* to the planet. They also have influenced *attitudes* about the planet and what is permissible to do to nonhumans. The influences run in both directions. In the view of the nonhuman as simply a source of goods for human benefit or a sink for human wastes, obstacles to "development" and "growth" are not given any weight in decision making. Humans get used to the cornucopia of products and services that industrial production contributes and the market (or the state in "command" economies) distributes. It is in the self-interest of producers in market economies to generate a diverse and unending stream of desires for their products, even when those products generate social costs that exceed their social benefits. So, although it may be the bread maker's self-interest (and not his or her altruism) which gets us our bread, the so-called invisible hand of which Adam Smith spoke in 1776 will not, unaided by the right sorts of social structures, generate that which is beneficial on balance. The free market also supplies, if enough persons are willing and able to pay for them, slaves, child prostitutes, assassinations, destructive drugs, enough nerve gas to destroy all mammals on the earth, and exquisite devices of torture. The market shapes preferences, and it responds to virtually any existing ones; its role, therefore, in the use and abuse of the biosphere is hardly negligible, and the question about what constraints should be placed on it is a moral question.

The rise of industrial forces and the market system in the West brought both goods and bads. We are *beginning* to notice the bads and their magnitudes. Many of them are like a series of time bombs starting to go off, a few here and a few there: dying lakes and oceans, sick coral reefs, the loss of 70 percent of the world's forests, nuclear wastes for which there are no evident safe depositories, the cascade of extinctions occurring in life forms whose lineage dates back 3.5 billion years, a hole in the ozone layer and the related, increasing risk of cancer as well as destruction of ocean life, and possibly vast devastation due to global warming in the next century. In the final analysis, we recall the line from the Pogo cartoon: "We have met the enemy and he is us."

NOTES

1. "The Ethic of Reverence for Life," from *Civilization and Ethics* in *Animal Rights and Human Obligations*, edited by Tom Regan and Peter Singer (Englewood Cliffs, NJ: Prentice-Hall, 1976), p. 137.

2. Robin Attfield, *The Ethics of Environmental Concern* (Athens: The University of Georgia Press, 2nd edition, 1991), pp. 29–30. For relevant biblical passages, see Matt. 8:28 ff., Mark 5:1–20, Luke 8:26–39 (on swine), and Matt. 21:18–19, and Mark 11:12–14 (on the withered tree).

3. The interest in determining what the scriptures actually prescribe regarding treatment of the nonhuman environment is usually motivated by the belief that they provide a reliable guide to determining God's will; the latter is one of several assumptions that constitute, or supplement, the divine command theory. For discussion, see Section I-B22.

4. Lynn White, Jr., "The Historical Roots of Our Ecologic Crisis," *Science*, p. 1207.

5. Lynn White, Jr., "The Historical Roots of Our Ecologic Crisis," p. 1205.

6. Lynn White, Jr., "The Historical Roots of Our Ecologic Crisis," p. 1206.

7. Lynn White, Jr., "The Historical Roots of Our Ecologic Crisis," p. 1205.

8. Lynn White, Jr., "The Historical Roots of Our Ecologic Crisis," p. 1205.

9. Lynn White, Jr., "Continuing the Conversation," in *Western Man and Environmental Ethics*, edited by Ian Barbour (Reading, MA: Addison-Wesley, 1973), p. 61.

10. Lynn White, Jr., "Continuing the Conversation," p. 60.

11. Gen. 1:26 ff, revised standard version.

12. A. R. Peacocke, *Creation and the World of Science* (Oxford: Oxford University Press, 1979), pp. 281–283. For an extended discussion of the stewardship view, see Robin Attfield, *The Ethics of Environmental Concern* (New York: Columbia University Press), 1983.

13. Andrew Linzey, "For God So Loved the World," *Between the Species*. Vol. 6, No. 1, (Winter 1990), p. 13.

14. Andrew Linzey, "For God So Loved the World," p. 13.

15. Lynn White, Jr., "The Historical Roots," p. 1206.

16. Andrew Linzey, "For God So Loved the World," p. 15.

17. A. R. Peacocke, *Creation and the World of Science*, p. 283.

18. Gen. 1:11 ff (revised standard version).

19. This alternative was suggested to us by a reviewer. We used his words almost exactly. He further observed that Robin Attfield in the closing passage of "The Good of Trees" comes to this interpretation. See *People, Penguins and Plastic Trees*, edited by Donald VanDeVeer and Christine Pierce (Belmont, CA: Wadsworth Publishing Company, 1986).

20. Anthony Weston, *Toward Better Problems: New Perspectives on Abortion, Animal Rights, the Environment, and Justice* (Philadelphia: Temple University Press, 1992), p. 106. Philosopher J. Baird Callicott offers a "plain citizen" interpretation of Genesis. See "Genesis and John Muir," in *Living in the Light of the Creation and the Covenant*, edited by Carol Robb and Carl Casebolt (Maryknoll, NY: Orbis Press, 1991).

21. Stephen Jay Gould, "The Golden Rule—A Proper Scale for Our Environmental Crisis," *Natural History* (September 1990), p. 30.

22. See the selection from Descartes in *Animal Rights and Human Obligations*, edited by Tom Regan and Peter Singer (Englewood Cliffs, NJ: Prentice-Hall, 1976), p. 65.

23. At least until the time of Newton, "scientists" were not called "scientists"; from about the medieval period they were called "natural philosophers," as Newton's title suggests. One would do well to keep this in mind. For a long time intellectual inquiry was not compartmentalized as it is in the contemporary university. Most sciences are less than a few hundred years old as distinct disciplines.

24. *The Origin of Species* was published in 1859.

The Historical Roots of Our Ecologic Crisis

Lynn White, Jr.

A conversation with Aldous Huxley not infrequently put one at the receiving end of an unforgettable monologue. About a year before his lamented death he was discoursing on a favorite topic: Man's unnatural treatment of nature and its sad results. To illustrate his point he told how, during the previous summer, he had returned to a little valley in England where he had spent many happy months

Science, Vol. 155, No. 3767 (March 1967), pp. 1203–1207. © 1967 by the AAAS. Reprinted by permission.

as a child. Once it had been composed of delightful grassy glades; now it was becoming overgrown with unsightly brush because the rabbits that formerly kept such growth under control had largely succumbed to a disease, myxomatosis, that was deliberately introduced by the local farmers to reduce the rabbits' destruction of crops. Being something of a Philistine, I could be silent no longer, even in the interests of great rhetoric. I interrupted to point out that the rabbit itself had been brought as a domestic animal to England in 1176, presumably to improve the protein diet of the peasantry.

All forms of life modify their contexts. The most spectacular and benign instance is doubtless the coral polyp. By serving its own ends, it has created a vast undersea world favorable to thousands of other kinds of animals and plants. Ever since man became a numerous species he has affected his environment notably. The hypothesis that his fire-drive method of hunting created the world's great grasslands and helped to exterminate the monster mammals of the Pleistocene from much of the globe is plausible, if not proved. For 6 millennia at least, the banks of the lower Nile have been a human artifact rather than the swampy African jungle which nature, apart from man, would have made it. The Aswan Dam, flooding 5000 square miles, is only the latest stage in a long process. In many regions terracing or irrigation, overgrazing, the cutting of forests by Romans to build ships to fight Carthaginians or by Crusaders to solve the logistics problems of their expeditions, have profoundly changed some ecologies. Observation that the French landscape falls into two basic types, the open fields of the north and the *bocage* of the south and west, inspired Marc Bloch to undertake his classic study of medieval agricultural methods. Quite unintentionally, changes in human ways often affect nonhuman nature. It has been noted, for example, that the advent of the automobile eliminated huge flocks of sparrows that once fed on the horse manure littering every street.

The history of ecologic change is still so rudimentary that we know little about what really happened, or what the results were. The extinction of the European aurochs as late as 1627 would seem to have been a simple case of overenthusiastic hunting. On more intricate matters it often is impossible to find solid information. For a thousand years or more the Frisians and Hollanders have been pushing back the North Sea, and the process is culminating in our own time in the reclamation of the Zuider Zee. What, if any, species of animals, birds, fish, shore life, or plants have died out in the process? In their epic combat with Neptune have the Netherlanders overlooked ecological values in such a way that the quality of human life in the Netherlands has suffered? I cannot discover that the questions have ever been asked, much less answered.

People, then, have often been a dynamic element in their own environment, but in the present state of historical scholarship we usually do not know exactly when, where, or with what effects man-induced changes came. As we enter the last third of the 20th century, however, concern for the problem of ecologic backlash is mounting feverishly. Natural science, conceived as the effort to understand the nature of things, had flourished in several eras and among several peoples. Similarly there had been an age-old accumulation of technological skills, sometimes growing rapidly, sometimes slowly. But it was not until about four generations ago that Western Europe and North America arranged a marriage between science and technology, a union of the theoretical and the empirical approaches to our natural environment. The emergence in widespread practice of the Baconian creed that scientific knowledge means technological power over nature can scarcely be dated before about 1850, save in the chemical industries, where it is anticipated in the 18th century. Its acceptance as a normal pattern of action may mark the greatest event in human history since the invention of agriculture, and perhaps in nonhuman terrestrial history as well.

Almost at once the new situation forced the crystallization of the novel concept of ecology; indeed, the word *ecology* first appeared in the English language in 1873. Today, less than a century later, the impact of our race upon the environment has so increased in force that it has changed in essence. When the first cannons were fired, in the early 14th century, they affected ecology by sending workers scrambling to the forests and mountains for more potash, sulfur, iron ore, and charcoal, with some resulting erosion and deforestation. Hydrogen bombs are of a different order: a war fought with them might alter the genetics of all life on this planet. By 1285 London had a smog problem arising from the burning of soft coal, but our present combustion of fossil fuels threatens to change the chemistry of the globe's atmosphere as a whole, with consequences which we are only beginning to guess. With the population explosion, the carcinoma of planless urbanism, the now geological deposits of sewage and garbage, surely no creature other than man has ever managed to foul its nest in such short order.

There are many calls to action, but specific proposals, however worthy as individual items, seem too partial, palliative, negative: ban the bomb, tear down the billboards, give the Hindus contraceptives and tell them to eat their sacred cows. The simplest solution to any suspect change is, of course, to stop it, or, better yet, to revert to a romanticized past: make those ugly gasoline stations look like Anne Hathaway's cottage or (in the Far West) like ghost-town saloons. The "wilderness area" mentality invariably advocates deep-freezing an ecology, whether San Gimignano or the High Sierra, as it was before the first Kleenex was dropped. But neither atavism nor prettification will cope with the ecologic crisis of our time.

What shall we do? No one yet knows. Unless we think about fundamentals, our specific measures may produce new backlashes more serious than those they are designed to remedy.

As a beginning we should try to clarify our thinking by looking, in some historical depth, at the presuppositions that underlie modern technology and science. Science was traditionally aristocratic, speculative, intellectual in intent; technology was lower-class, empirical, action-oriented. The quite sudden fusion of these two, towards the middle of the 19th century, is surely related to the slightly prior and contemporary democratic revolutions which, by reducing social barriers, tended to assert a functional unity of brain and hand. Our ecologic crisis is the product of an emerging, entirely novel, democratic culture. The issue is whether a democratized world can survive its own implications. Presumably we cannot unless we rethink our axioms.

The Western Traditions of Technology and Science

One thing is so certain that it seems stupid to verbalize it: both modern technology and modern science are distinctively *Occidental*. Our technology has absorbed elements from all over the world, no-tably from China; yet everywhere today, whether in Japan or in Nigeria, successful technology is Western. Our science is the heir to all the sciences of the past, especially perhaps to the work of the great Islamic scientists of the Middle Ages, who so often outdid the ancient Greeks in skill and perspicacity: al-Rāzī in medicine, for example; or ibn-al-Haytham in optics; or Omar Khay-yám in mathematics. Indeed, not a few works of such geniuses seem to have vanished in the original Arabic and to survive only in medieval Latin translations that helped to lay the foundations for later Western developments. Today, around the globe, all significant science is Western in style and method, whatever the pigmentation or language of the scientists.

A second pair of facts is less well recognized because they result from quite recent historical scholarship. The leadership of the West, both in technology and in science, is far older than the so-called Scientific Revolution of the 17th century or the so-called Industrial Revolution of the 18th century. These terms are in fact outmoded and obscure the true nature of what they try to describe—significant stages in two long and separate developments. By A.D. 1000 at the latest—and perhaps, feebly, as much as 200 years earlier—the West began to apply water power to industrial processes other than milling grain. This was followed in the late 12th century by the harnessing of wind power. From simple beginnings, but with remarkable consistency of style, the West rapidly expanded its skills in the development of power machinery, labor-saving devices, and automation. Those who doubt should contemplate that most monumental achievement in the history of automation: the weight-driven mechanical clock, which appeared in two forms in the early 14th century. Not in craftsmanship but in basic technological capacity, the Latin West of the later Middle Ages far outstripped its elaborate, sophisticated, and esthetically magnificent sister cultures, Byzantium and Islam. In 1444 a great Greek ecclesiastic, Bessarion, who had gone to Italy, wrote a letter to a prince in Greece. He is amazed by the superiority of Western ships, arms, textiles, glass. But above all he is astonished by the spectacle of water-wheels sawing timbers and pumping the bellows of blast furnaces. Clearly, he had seen nothing of the sort in the Near East.

By the end of the 15th century the technological superiority of Europe was such that its small, mutually hostile nations could spill out over all the rest of the world, conquering, looting, and colonizing. The symbol of this technological superiority is the fact that Portugal, one of the weakest states of the Occident, was able to become, and to remain for a century, mistress of the East Indies. And we must remember that the technology of Vasco da Gama and Albuquerque was built by pure empiricism, drawing remarkably little support or inspiration from science.

In the present-day vernacular understanding, modern science is supposed to have begun in 1543, when both Copernicus and Vesalius published their great works. It is no derogation of their accomplishments, however, to point out that such structures as the *Fabrica* and the *De revolutionibus* do not appear overnight. The distinctive Western tradition of science, in fact, began in the late 11th century with a massive movement of translation of Arabic and Greek scientific works into Latin. A few notable books—Theophrastus, for example—escaped the West's avid new appetite for science, but within less than 200 years effectively the entire corpus of Greek and Muslim science was available in Latin, and was being eagerly read and criticized in the new European universities. Out of criticism arose new observation, speculation, and increasing distrust of ancient authorities. By the late 13th century Europe had seized global scientific leadership from the faltering hands of Islam. It would be as absurd to deny the profound originality of Newton, Galileo, or Copernicus as to deny that of the 14th century scholastic scientists like Buridan or Oresme on whose work they built. Before the 11th century, science scarcely existed in the Latin West, even in Roman times. From the 11th century onward, the scientific sector of Occidental culture has increased in a steady crescendo.

Since both our technological and our scientific movements got their start, acquired their character, and achieved world dominance in the Middle Ages, it would seem that we cannot understand their nature or their present impact upon ecology without examining fundamental medieval assumptions and developments.

Medieval View of Man and Nature

Until recently, agriculture has been the chief occupation even in "advanced" societies; hence,

any change in methods of tillage has much importance. Early plows, drawn by two oxen, did not normally turn the sod but merely scratched it. Thus, cross-plowing was needed and fields tended to be squarish. In the fairly light soils and semiarid climates of the Near East and Mediterranean, this worked well. But such a plow was inappropriate to the wet climate and often sticky soils of northern Europe. By the latter part of the 7th century after Christ, however, following obscure beginnings, certain northern peasants were using an entirely new kind of plow, equipped with a vertical knife to cut the line of the furrow, a horizontal share to slice under the sod, and a moldboard to turn it over. The friction of this plow with the soil was so great that it normally required not two but eight oxen. It attacked the land with such violence that cross-plowing was not needed, and fields tended to be shaped in long strips.

In the days of the scratch-plow, fields were distributed generally in units capable of supporting a single family. Subsistence farming was the presupposition. But no peasant owned eight oxen: to use the new and more efficient plow, peasants pooled their oxen to form large plow-teams, originally receiving (it would appear) plowed strips in proportion to their contribution. Thus, distribution of land was based no longer on the needs of a family but, rather, on the capacity of a power machine to till the earth. Man's relation to the soil was profoundly changed. Formerly man had been part of nature; now he was the exploiter of nature. Nowhere else in the world did farmers develop any analogous agricultural implement. Is it coincidence that modern technology, with its ruthlessness toward nature, has so largely been produced by descendants of these peasants of northern Europe?

This same exploitive attitude appears slightly before A.D. 830 in Western illustrated calendars. In older calendars the months were shown as passive personifications. The new Frankish calendars, which set the style for the Middle Ages, are very different: they show men coercing the world around them—plowing, harvesting, chopping trees, butchering pigs. Man and nature are two things, and man is master.

These novelties seem to be in harmony with larger intellectual patterns. What people do about their ecology depends on what they think about themselves in relation to things around them. Human ecology is deeply conditioned by beliefs about our nature and destiny—that is, by religion. To Western eyes this is very evident in, say, India or Ceylon. It is equally true of ourselves and of our medieval ancestors.

The victory of Christianity over paganism was the greatest psychic revolution in the history of our culture. It has become fashionable today to say that, for better or worse, we live in "the post-Christian age." Certainly the forms of our thinking and language have largely ceased to be Christian, but to my eye the substance often remains amazingly akin to that of the past. Our daily habits of action, for example, are dominated by an implicit faith in perpetual progress which was unknown either to Greco-Roman antiquity or to the Orient. It is rooted in, and is indefensible apart from, Judeo-Christian teleology. The fact that Communists share it merely helps to show what can be demonstrated on many other grounds: that Marxism, like Islam, is a Judeo-Christian heresy. We continue today to live, as we have lived for about 1700 years, very largely in the context of Christian axioms.

What did Christianity tell people about their relations with the environment?

While many of the world's mythologies provide stories of creation, Greco-Roman mythology was singularly incoherent in this respect. Like Aristotle, the intellectuals of the ancient West denied that the visible world had had a beginning. Indeed, the idea of a beginning was impossible in the framework of their cyclical notion of time. In sharp contrast, Christianity inherited from Judaism not only a concept of time as nonrepetitive and linear but also a striking story of creation. By gradual stages a loving and all-powerful God had created light and darkness, the heavenly bodies, the earth and all its plants, animals, birds, and fishes. Finally, God had created Adam and, as an afterthought, Eve to keep man from being lonely. Man named all the animals, thus establishing his dominance over them. God planned all of this explicitly for man's benefit and rule: no item in the physical creation had any purpose save to serve man's purposes. And, although man's body is made of clay, he is not simply part of nature: he is made in God's image.

Especially in its Western form, Christianity is the most anthropocentric religion the world has seen. As early as the 2nd century both Tertullian and Saint Irenaeus of Lyons were insisting that when God shaped Adam he was foreshadowing the image of the incarnate Christ, the Second Adam. Man shares, in great measure, God's transcendence of nature. Christianity, in absolute contrast to ancient paganism and Asia's religions (except, perhaps, Zoroastrianism), not only established a dualism of man and nature but also insisted that it is God's will that man exploit nature for his proper ends.

At the level of the common people, this worked out in an interesting way. In antiquity every tree, every spring, every stream, every hill had its own *genius loci*, its guardian spirit. These spirits were accessible to men, but were very unlike men; centaurs, fauns, and mermaids show their ambivalence. Before one cut a tree, mined a mountain, or dammed a brook, it was important to placate the spirit in charge of that particular situation, and to keep it placated. By destroying pagan animism, Christianity made it possible to exploit nature in a mood of indifference to the feelings of natural objects.

It is often said that for animism the Church substituted the cult of saints. True; but the cult of saints is functionally quite different from animism. The saint is not *in* natural objects; he may have special shrines, but his citizenship is in heaven. Moreover, a saint is entirely a man; he can be approached in human terms. In addition to saints, Christianity of course also has angels and demons inherited from Judaism and perhaps, at one remove, from Zoroastrianism. But these were all as mobile as the saints themselves. The spirits *in* natural objects, which formerly had protected nature from man, evaporated. Man's effective monopoly on spirit in this world was confirmed, and the old inhibitions to the exploitation of nature crumbled.

When one speaks in such sweeping terms, a note of caution is in order. Christianity is a complex faith, and its consequences differ in differing contexts. What I have said may well apply to the medieval West, where in fact technology made spectacular advances. But the Greek East, a highly civilized realm of equal Christian devotion, seems to have produced no marked technological innovation after the late 7th century, when Greek fire was invented. The key to the contrast may perhaps be found in a difference in the tonality of piety and thought which students of comparative theology find between the Greek and the Latin Churches. The Greeks believed that sin was intellectual blindness, and that salvation was found in illumination, orthodoxy—that is, clear thinking. The Latins, on the other hand, felt that sin was moral evil, and that salvation was to be found in right conduct. Eastern theology has been intellectualist. Western theology has been voluntarist. The Greek saint contemplates; the Western saint acts. The implications of Christianity for the conquest of nature would emerge more easily in the Western atmosphere.

The Christian dogma of creation, which is found in the first clause of all the Creeds, has another meaning for our comprehension of today's ecologic crisis. By revelation, God had given man the Bible, the Book of Scripture. But since God had made nature, nature also must reveal the divine mentality. The religious study of nature for the better understanding of God was known as natural theology. In the early Church, and always in the Greek East, nature was conceived primarily as a symbolic system through which God speaks to men: the ant is a sermon to sluggards; rising flames are the symbol of the soul's aspiration. This view of nature was essentially artistic rather than scientific. While Byzantium preserved and copied great numbers of ancient Greek scientific texts, science as we conceive it could scarcely flourish in such an ambience.

However, in the Latin West by the early 13th century natural theology was following a very different bent. It was ceasing to be the decoding of the physical symbols of God's communication with man and was becoming the effort to understand God's mind by discovering how his creation operates. The rainbow was no longer simply a symbol of hope first sent to Noah after the Deluge: Robert Grosseteste, Friar Roger Bacon, and Theodoric of Freiberg produced startlingly sophisticated work on the optics of the rainbow, but they did it as a venture in religious understanding. From the 13th century onward, up to and including Leibnitz and Newton, every major scientist, in effect, explained his motivations in religious terms. Indeed, if Galileo had not been so expert an amateur theologian he would have got into far less trouble: the professionals resented his intrusion. And Newton seems to have regarded himself more as a theologian than as a scientist. It was not until the late 18th century that the hypothesis of God became unnecessary to many scientists.

It is often hard for the historian to judge, when men explain why they are doing what they want to do, whether they are offering real reasons or merely culturally acceptable reasons. The consistency with which scientists during the long formative centuries of Western science said that the task and the reward of the scientist was "to think God's thoughts after him" leads one to believe that this was their real motivation. If so, then modern Western science was cast in a matrix of Christian theology. The dynamism of religious devotion, shaped by the Judeo-Christian dogma of creation, gave it impetus.

An Alternative Christian View

We would seem to be headed toward conclusions unpalatable to many Christians. Since both *science* and *technology* are blessed words in our contemporary vocabulary, some may be happy at the notions, first, that, viewed historically, modern science is an extrapolation of natural theology and, second, that modern technology is at least partly to be explained as an Occidental, voluntarist realization of the Christian dogma of man's transcendence of, and rightful mastery over, nature. But, as we now recognize, somewhat over a century ago science and technology—hitherto quite separate activities—joined to give mankind powers which, to judge by many of the ecologic effects, are out of control. If so, Christianity bears a huge burden of guilt.

I personally doubt that disastrous ecologic backlash can be avoided simply by applying to our problems more science and more technology. Our science and technology have grown out of Christian attitudes toward man's relation to nature which are almost universally held not only by Christians and neo-Christians but also by those who fondly regard themselves as post-Christians. Despite Copernicus, all the cosmos rotates around our little globe. Despite Darwin, we are *not*, in our hearts, part of the natural process. We are superior to nature, contemptuous of it, willing to use it for our slightest whim. The newly elected Governor of California, like myself a churchman but less troubled than I, spoke for the Christian tradition when he said (as is alleged), "when you've seen one redwood tree, you've seen them all." To a Christian a tree can be no more than a physical fact. The whole concept of the sacred grove is alien to Christianity and to the ethos of the West. For nearly 2 millennia Christian missionaries have been chopping down sacred groves, which are idolatrous because they assume spirit in nature.

What we do about ecology depends on our ideas of the man-nature relationship. More science and more technology are not going to get us out of the present ecologic crisis until we find a new religion, or rethink our old one. The beatniks, who are the basic revolutionaries of our time, show a sound instinct in their affinity for Zen Buddhism, which conceives of the man-nature relationship as very nearly the mirror image of the Christian view. Zen, however, is as deeply conditioned by Asian history as Christianity is by the experience of the West, and I am dubious of its viability among us.

Possibly we should ponder the greatest radical in Christian history since Christ: Saint Francis of Assisi. The prime miracle of Saint Francis is the fact that he did not end at the stake, as many of his left-wing followers did. He was so clearly heretical that a General of the Franciscan Order, Saint Bonaventura, a great and perceptive Christian, tried to suppress the early accounts of Franciscanism. The key to an understanding of Francis is his belief in the virtue of humility—not merely for the individual but for man as a species. Francis tried to depose man from his monarchy over creation and set up a democracy of all God's creatures. With him the ant is no longer simply a homily for the lazy, flames a sign of the thrust of the soul toward union with God; now they are Brother Ant and Sister Fire, praising the Creator in their own ways as Brother Man does in his.

Later commentators have said that Francis preached to the birds as a rebuke to men who would not listen. The records do not read so: he urged the little birds to praise God, and in spiritual ecstasy they flapped their wings and chirped rejoicing. Legends of saints, especially the Irish saints, had long told of their dealings with animals but always, I believe, to show their human dominance over creatures. With Francis it is different. The land around Gubbio in the Apennines was being ravaged by a fierce wolf. Saint Francis, says the legend, talked to the wolf and persuaded him of the error of his ways. The wolf repented, died in the odor of sanctity, and was buried in consecrated ground.

What Sir Steven Ruciman calls "the Franciscan doctrine of the animal soul" was quickly stamped out. Quite possibly it was in part inspired, con-

sciously or unconsciously, by the belief in reincarnation held by the Cathar heretics who at that time teemed in Italy and southern France, and who presumably had got it originally from India. It is significant that at just the same moment, about 1200, traces of metempsychosis are found also in western Judaism, in the Provençal *Cabbala.* But Francis held neither to transmigration of souls nor to pantheism. His view of nature and of man rested on a unique sort of pan-psychism of all things animate and inanimate, designed for the glorification of their transcendent Creator, who, in the ultimate gesture of cosmic humility, assumed flesh, lay helpless in a manger, and hung dying on a scaffold.

I am not suggesting that many contemporary Americans who are concerned about our ecologic crisis will be either able or willing to counsel with wolves or exhort birds. However, the present increasing disruption of the global environment is the product of a dynamic technology and science which were originating in the Western medieval world against which Saint Francis was rebelling in so original a way. Their growth cannot be understood historically apart from distinctive attitudes toward nature which are deeply grounded in Christian dogma. The fact that most people do not think of these attitudes as Christian is irrelevant. No new set of basic values has been accepted in our society to displace those of Christianity. Hence we shall continue to have a worsening ecologic crisis until we reject the Christian axiom that nature has no reason for existence save to serve man.

The greatest spiritual revolutionary in Western history, Saint Francis, proposed what he thought was an alternative Christian view of nature and man's relation to it: he tried to substitute the idea of the equality of all creatures, including man, for the idea of man's limitless rule of creation. He failed. Both our present science and our present technology are so tinctured with orthodox Christian arrogance toward nature that no solution for our ecologic crisis can be expected from them alone. Since the roots of our trouble are so largely religious, the remedy must also be essentially religious, whether we call it that or not. We must rethink and refeel our nature and destiny. The profoundly religious, but heretical, sense of the primitive Franciscans for the spiritual autonomy of all parts of nature may point a direction. I propose Francis as a patron saint for ecologists.

For God So Loved the World

The Reverend Dr. Andrew Linzey

Imagine a scene. The date is the 18th of April, 1499. The time is sometime in the afternoon. The place is the Abbey of Josaphat, near Chartres. Within this Abbey a trial is taking place. It is a criminal prosecution before the Bailiff of the Abbey. The defendant is charged with having killed an infant. The verdict is announced. The defendant is found guilty. The sentence of the ecclesiastical court is that the defendant should be hanged. Mercifully, unlike other defendants, the fate is only death and not torture or mangulation. And the defendant was hanged by its neck at a public hanging that day in the market square. The defendant, however, was not a human being, but a pig.

What is the point of recounting this grisly, surely altogether extraordinary episode from the 15th century, you may ask? The answer is this: grisly it certainly was, extraordinary it certainly was not. From the 9th to the 19th century we have over 200 written accounts of the criminal prosecution and capital punishment of animals. These trials of animals, pigs, dogs, wolves, locusts, rats, termites, cows, horses and doves inflicted great and terrible suffering. And the important thing to appreciate is that these trials were mainly or wholly religious in character. They drew their inspiration from Christian doctrine, based on a silly biblical fundamentalism—a fundamentalism I'm distressed to say is still with us in some quarters of the Church today. In particular it was St. Thomas Aquinas in his *Summa Theologiae* who held that some animals were satellites of Satan: "instigated by the powers of hell and proper to be cursed?" St. Thomas added: "the anathema then is not to be pronounced against the animals as such, but should be hurled inferentially at the devil who makes use of irrational creatures to our detriment."

Armed with this awful dictum (however originally qualified by St. Thomas) Christians have spent more than 10 centuries anathematizing, cursing and reviling the animal world. The echoes of this violence are found today in our very language. The word 'animal' is a term of abuse, not to men-

tion 'brute,' 'beast' or 'bestial.' How we have libelled the animal world. For myself I cannot but be bemused by the reference in the marriage service of the *Book of Common Prayer* to "brute beasts which hath no understanding." Who are these brute beasts? Most higher mammals seem to know more about life-long monogamy than many human beings.

This low, negative, even hating, attitude towards animals, regarding them as a source of evil, or as instruments of the devil, or regarding them as beings without any moral status, has, sad to say, been the dominant view within Christendom for the largest part of its history. In the 9th century, Pope Stephen IV prepared great quantities of holy water with which to anathematize hordes of locusts. In the 19th century, Pope Pius IX forbade the opening of an animal protection office in Rome on the grounds that humans had duties to other humans, but none to animals. For a clear run of at least 10 centuries the dominant ecclesiastical voice did not even regard animals as worthy of moral concern. We do well to remember that Catholic textbooks still regard animals as morally without status, save when they are deemed human property. Worse than that, they have been frequently classified as things without rights, to be used—as St. Thomas himself wrote—"in any way whatever." If Jesus can weep over Jerusalem we have more than good reason to weep over the sins of Mother Church.

It seems to me that there is no use pretending that all has been well with the Church either in the past, or even now in the present. The very community which should be the cradle of the Gospel of God's Love for the world has only been too good at justifying violence and legitimizing hatred towards the world. Those like myself who have the temerity to preach to Christian and non-Christian alike, must be quite clear that the record of Christianity has been, and still is, on this issue as on many others, in many respects shameful and second rate. Christians are simply too good at forgetting how

Between the Species, Vol. 6, No. 1 (Winter 1990), pp. 12–16. Reprinted by permission.

awful they have been. The fact is that Christians have had enormous difficulties in believing their own Gospel.

And what is this Gospel? It is nothing less than the conviction and experience that God loves the whole world. What we see in Jesus is the revelation of an inclusive, all-embracing, generous Loving. A Loving that washes the feet of the world. A Loving that heals individuals from oppression—physical and spiritual. A Loving that takes sides with the poor, vulnerable, diseased, hated, despised, and outcasts of his day. A Loving that is summed up in his absolute commitment to love at all costs even in extreme suffering and death. As that distinguished former Dean of Salisbury, Sydney Evans, once wrote: "What Jesus did on the Cross was to demonstrate the truth of what he had taught: he showed a quality of love—such that the worst that evil could do to such love was to give such love ever fresh opportunities for loving."

The world we live in is desperate for love. The whole world needs to be loved. When I was young I used to mock the notion of "Gentle Jesus, meek and mild." How wrong I was! For there is great power in humility, strength in gentleness, wisdom in forbearance. We need to listen again to Father Zossima's advice in Dostoyevsky's *The Brothers Karamazov*:

> Brothers, be not afraid of men's sins. Love man even in his sin, for that already bears the semblance of divine love and is the highest love on earth. Love all God's creation, the whole of it and every grain of sand. Love every leaf, every ray of God's light! Love the animals, love the plants, love everything. And if you love everything you will perceive the divine mystery in things. And once you have perceived it, you will begin to comprehend it ceaselessly more and more every day. And you will at last come to love the whole world with an abiding, universal love.

Not all Christians have been happy with this Gospel. While God's love is free, generous and unlimited, we Christians have only been too good at placing limits on Divine Love. St. Thomas Aquinas was a great scholar and saint, but even he believed quite erroneously that God did not love animals for their own sakes, but only in so far as they were of use to human beings. We Christians have at various times made of this Revelation of Unlimited Love its

precise opposite. We have conceived of this Revelation in exclusive terms, exclusive of one group or race: those who were non-Jews, those who are women, those who are coloured, and so on. Not all Christians have seen how the love of God gives each individual human being a unique and equal value. But at least we can say that these issues have been on the agenda of the Churches. Not so with other suffering non-human creatures. What has not been seen is that the love of God is inclusive not only of humans *but also all creatures*. It took Christians many years to realize that we cannot love God and keep humans as slaves. It has taken even longer for Christians to realize that we cannot love God and regard women as second class humans. Now is the time for Christians to realize that we cannot love God and hate his non-human creatures. Christians are people who need to be liberated by the Gospel they preach. Christians cannot love God and be free to hate.

For people, like myself, who are concerned for justice in our dealings with animals there are three things we must learn.

The first is that we must not hate even those who hate animals. "Do not be afraid of men's sins," writes Dostoyevsky. People who work for justice for animals are often disappointed, angry, unhappy people, and more often than not with just cause. It is incredible that we should treat God's creatures with so little love and respect; incredible that we should despoil animal life for fun and amusement; incredible that we should wantonly slaughter; incredible that we should make wild animals captive for entertainment; incredible that we should inflict suffering and pain on farm and laboratory animals. It is spiritually infantile that we should continue to look upon the world as "made for us" and animals simply as means to human ends, as resources, as tools, as machines, indeed simply as things. And yet we must not hate those who hate God's world. By doing so we simply push them further into their own abyss and spiritual darkness. All of us need to be loved, all of us need interior resources to go on loving. And all this is very, very hard especially when we see creatures treated so cruelly that their cause cries to heaven for justice. But we have one real and lasting weapon at our disposal: 'Soulforce.' As Dostoyevsky writes: "Loving humility is a terrible force, the strongest of all . . . (with it we shall) conquer the world." So I don't want to hate anybody, even vivisectors, butchers, trappers, factory farmers and bullfighters. On the contrary I want to love them so much that they will not find time, or have the inclination, to hunt, and kill, and destroy and maim God's good creatures. I refuse to give those who exploit animals another good reason for not believing in a God of love.

Secondly, we must not hate, even the Church. I know that this is very difficult, not least of all because the Church has a lamentable record on animals and, what is more, is still a party to animal cruelty. I say now, and have said privately in the past, to the Church Commissioners that the time has come when in the name of God most loving they must stop allowing factory farming (and also hunting) on their owned lands. Christians, even Church Commissioners, must be signs of the Gospel for which all creatures long. I know that the Church is not always very lovable to say the least. But I also say to you that we shall not advance the cause of animals by hating the Church. On the contrary we must love it so much that it repents of its theological foolishness, its far too frequent humanist arrogance and its complicity in sins against animals. But I say to you that hatred is too great a burden to bear.

I want to give you one example that should give us hope. If we go back in history 200 years or so, we will find intelligent, respectable, conscientious Christians for whom slavery was not a moral issue. If pressed some might have defended slavery as 'progress' as many thought it was. Some might even have taken the view of William Henry Holcombe writing in 1860 that slavery was a natural means of "the Christianization of the dark races." The quite staggering fact to grapple with is that this very same community which in some ways provided the major ideological impetus for the defence of slavery came within an historically short period, 100, perhaps only 50, years to change its mind. The same tradition which helped keep slavery alive was the same community that became by and large determined to end it. So successful has this change been that within this congregation today we shall have difficulty in finding one slave trader, even one individual Christian who thought that the practice was anything other than inimical to the moral demands of the Christian faith. In short, while it is true that Christian churches have been and frequently are awful on the subject of animals, it is just possible, even plausible that given say 50 or 100 years we shall witness among this same community amazing shifts of consciousness as we have witnessed on other moral issues, no less complex or controversial. Christian Churches then have been agents of oppression—that is commonplace—but they can also be agents of liberation.

We do well in this context to remember and honour all those courageous Christians: saints, and seers, theologians and poets, mystics and writers who have championed the cause of animals. The list must include almost two thirds of those canonized saints East and West, not only St. Francis but also St. Martin, Richard of Chichester, Chrysostom, Isaac the Syrian, Bonaventure, and countless others. Poets also like Rosetti, Browning, Carlyle, Longfellow, Hardy, Cowper, and the many others who have led the way in sensitivity to the animal world. And if we are to be grateful for these luminaries, then one name especially must be mentioned, namely Arthur Broome. Few people appreciate that it was this Anglican priest who founded the first animal welfare society in the world, the RSPCA, in 1824. Fewer people appreciate that this Society was the result of Christian inspiration and vision. Even fewer appreciate that this Society was founded specifically on "Christian Faith and Christian Principles." Broome's work was immensely sacrificial. He served the Society as its first secretary; he gave up his London living to work full-time for the Society, he suffered imprisonment for the Society's debts, and finally died in obscurity. The animal movement today would be nowhere if it was not for this one man's courage and Christian faith. Long may his name be honoured among those who work for the cause of animals.

And there are just one or two hints today that Christians are again waking up to the idea that God's creation must not be reviled, anathematized, and treated as evil as in the past.

"[P]reoccupation with humanity will seem distinctly parochial . . . our theology . . . has been distorted by being too man-centered. We need to maintain the value, the preciousness of the human by maintaining the value, the preciousness of the non-human also." These words are not mine. They come from no less a person than the Archbishop of Canterbury, Robert Runcie, speaking in April of this year. He went on:

"For our concept of God forbids the idea of a

cheap creation, of a throwaway universe in which everything is expendable save human existence. The whole universe is a work of love. And nothing which is made in love is cheap. The value, the worth of natural things is not found in Man's view of himself but in the goodness of God who made all things good and precious in his sight . . ." As Barbara Ward used to say, "We have only one earth. Is it not worth our love?" These words may have cost our Archbishop more than we imagine. Let us congratulate him on his testimony and take heart.

The third thing we must learn is that we must not hate one another. It is no use people like me in the animal rights movement—complaining about animal abusers and the churches for their lack of love and compassion—when we so often show so little love and compassion to one another. I can give personal testimony here. I spent 4 years on the ruling council of one of the largest animal welfare societies in this country and 10 or more years later I am still trying to heal the wounds I suffered. The animal movement is the place where we can find as much if not more sin than anywhere else. Jealously, rivalry, misquotation, guile, stupidity, and, worst of all, self-righteousness. We must not fall into this last trap especially. None of us is pure when it comes to animals. We are all involved in animal abuse either through the food we eat, the products we buy, or the taxes we pay. There is no pure land on earth. A clean conscience is a figment of the imagination. I spend some of my time counselling students who suffer from unrelieved feelings of guilt—often inculcated by the Churches—I have no desire to make anyone feel guilty. Guilt is a redundant emotion.

Christians in the animal movement have a unique opportunity. St. Paul speaks of the creation as in a state of childbirth awaiting a new age. Together we have vision of a new age, a new world. A world at peace, a world in which we have begun to make peace with creation. A world in which the Love of God is claimed and championed and through whose Spirit new world possibilities are constantly being opened up for us. What a difference it would make if Christians began to practice

the Gospel of Love they preach. At the very least what we need to do is to encourage and inspire people to live free of injury to animals. All of us, in addition to whatever social vision we may have, need a programme of personal disengagement from injury to animal life.

Let me be personal for a moment. I haven't always been an advocate of animal rights. By no means. When I was young I used to enjoy controlling animals and making them captive. I used to enjoy fishing. I used to eat animals. I had no problems about eating veal. My entry into the animal rights movement coincided with my entry into a slaughterhouse when I was 16 years old. The questions that it raised in my mind have been with me ever since. Recently, during my speaking tour of the United States, I visited another slaughterhouse in the State of Massachusetts. As I stood watching a young pig being slaughtered—'stuck' as they say in the US—I asked myself this question: "What has changed in 26 years when animals are still treated as things?" And soon I had my answer: the owner of the slaughterhouse, despite the fact that I had asked permission in the usual way, turfed me out. I'm not used to being turfed out of places. It was a new experience and a valuable one. For I learnt this one thing: What is changing is that many people, even those intensely involved in the exploitation of animals, many people are not so sure as they once were that what they are doing is right. People are beginning to have a conscience even in the most unlikely places.

When I became intellectually convinced of the case for animal rights, I first thought it one of those important but comparatively minor questions in Christian ethics. I don't think that today. On the contrary, I think the question of how we treat animals one of the BIG questions confronting all humanity: if God loves and cares for this world, shall we learn to live at peace with one another and with this world? In short: Are we to hate the world or are we to love it? "We must love one another or die," wrote W. H. Auden. The truth we also have to learn is this: We must love the world, or we shall perish with it.

III

THE OTHER ANIMALS

PREVIEW

> The lion looked at Alice wearily, "Are you animal, vegetable, or mineral?" he said, yawning at every other word. "Ti's a fabulous monster!" the Unicorn cried out, before Alice could reply.
>
> *Lewis Carroll*

> . . . the mental faculties of man and the lower animals do not differ in kind, although immensely in degree. A difference in degree, however great, does not justify placing man in a distinct kingdom. . . .
>
> *Charles Darwin*

Immanuel Kant thought there is something very special about human beings and that because of this they should never be treated as a mere means; in contrast, in his view it is permissible to so act toward nonhumans, the notable exception probably being any divine being. Other things could be, as we put it today, of great instrumental value, and we may have great duties *regarding* them (e.g., one's *indirect* duty not to destroy a sculpture of Rodin). Are all nonhuman animals like that—of only instrumental value? Are they only of value if and when there is some human around who desires them for some reason or another? Or is it only a very deep-seated prejudice that we learn as children that we have only *direct* duties toward *one species* on the entire planet? And what would we think of such a claim if the word *species* were replaced with the word 'race' or 'sex'? What is the great gulf that should be regarded as the morally relevant difference between humans and other animals—especially between humans and those closest to us in terms of intelligence and psychological capacities? By virtue of possessing what trait or traits does one have that special status of being owed a certain respect or owed certain duties of nonharm? Surely, these are among the most basic questions an environmental ethic must address. We will look carefully at some of the arguments, but first we must clarify some terminology so that we can address a few central questions in a careful manner.

Let us turn to the concept of *moral standing*. Quite apart from the question of whether someone has "legal standing," we commonly think that the interest or well-being of certain things (normally, certain organisms) must be positively weighed in deciding what is permissible to do.[1] Thus, it is morally wrong to kill humans for food when one is hungry. Similarly, it seems wrong to cause premature death to young (human) children to achieve the same goal. (Compare a simple taxonomy of the world: division into edibles and inedibles.) However, most people have few reservations about causing premature death to young nonhuman offspring for culinary purposes. The different outlooks presupposed in these latter differential judgments may be couched in terms of moral standing. Let us stipulate for anything, X,

> X has moral standing if and only if the continued existence of X or its interests in well-being have positive moral weight.[2]

Explicitly or implicitly, one traditional view, often called the "anthropocentric paradigm," answers the basic question

Which things have moral standing?

by proposing that

All and only human beings have moral standing.

This latter view, in effect, assumes that the most defensible answer to another question,

What is the appropriate *criterion of moral standing?*,

is

Membership in *Homo sapiens.*

This proposed criterion has several virtues, one of which is reasonable clarity. However, there are hard cases: does it include human fetal progeny, brain-dead, yet breathing, humans, recently dead humans, anencephalic babies? Also worrisome is what the anthropocentric criterion excludes; based on such a criterion, the well-being of nonhuman animals, nonhuman members or parts of the ecosystem, or even intelligent, "personable," alien beings do not, in themselves, count. If by "natural resource" we mean anything that is not a human being (or part of one), such things are, based on the view under consideration, mere resources to be used to pursue human goals. This pervasive and traditional outlook has come under sharp attack in the last decade—as the following essays demonstrate.

Shortly, we shall return to questions about (1) the implications of the anthropocentric criterion of moral standing, and (2) competing criteria. First, however, it is useful to reflect on the relation of duty to the issue of moral standing. If we could settle the issue of what is the appropriate criterion of moral standing, then, in principle, we could ascertain which things have moral standing (technically, the *extension* of "things with moral standing").

Suppose that these difficult problems were resolved. What would be the implications of recognizing that something has moral standing, that its continued existence or interests in well-being have positive moral weight? A plausible answer is that, if so, then we moral agents (those who have the freedom and rational capacities to be responsible for choices) have a presumptive duty not to terminate, or undermine the interests of, those entities with moral standing. If this is right, matters are clarified somewhat. However, most of the important questions are left to be resolved, for reasons that will become clearer as we proceed.

If something lacks moral standing, its well-being just does not morally count (by definition of "moral standing"). However, if something has moral standing, its well-being does count and is the basis of a presumptive duty to that thing. Presumptive duties, however, can be overridden under certain circumstances. Consider that most of us think that ordinary people have moral standing. Thus, we have a presumptive duty not to kill them—roughly, a duty not to kill them in the absence of morally compelling reasons for doing so. Most people, however, think that some killing in self-defense, or in defense of other innocents against aggressors, is morally justifiable. The contrary view, that we have an "absolute" or "categorical" duty never to kill persons (those paradigmatic beings with moral standing) is held by few (not even those who talk of the sanctity or infinite value of life or all human life) and is hard to defend rationally. The appeal to what most people think is not a compelling consideration. The more basic point is that even with regard to those paradigms of beings with moral standing (persons), there well may be important issues to be decided regarding legitimate treatment of such beings, even if we accept that such beings have moral standing. The moral of this story is twofold:

1. Whether we have a presumptive duty to some entity depends on our settling the dispute over whether it has moral standing.

2. However, even if we settle (1), there is still the issue of just what reasons would justify our thwarting the interests of a being with moral standing.

To stress a point, a *necessary* but not *sufficient* condition of formulating an adequate ethical theory (and, hence, an adequate environmental ethic) is determining the most defensible criterion of moral standing. Beyond that, there are other recalcitrant and challenging issues. The issue of moral standing, however, is more basic. Further, it is the one most neglected because historically very few writers have questioned the anthropocentric position. Like other deeply entrenched assumptions, it often has functioned as a pair of lenses through which we view and conceptualize the environment—and not as an object itself, something to be subjected to philosophical scrutiny.

Let us reflect again on the implications of the anthropocentric viewpoint—and the assumption that all, and only, humans have moral standing. For one with such a view, only the well-being or the lives of humans count. Does this mean that it is all right to burn cats for recreational purposes? Or poison one's privately owned lake? Or blow up a small planet to entertain those with astronomical curiosities? Or fertilize our gardens with the cadavers of those who died natural deaths (and, perhaps, earlier voiced no objection)? Or, *if* I knew that I was the last person on earth, would it be all right for me to trigger (if I could) all the nuclear weapons already in place—when I was ready to say "farewell," of course? After all, according to one view the well-being of all, and only, humans counts! The answer to these questions (except perhaps the last one), according to the anthropocentric view, surely is: not necessarily.

To explain, or call to mind, why not, it is useful to consider further the distinction between (1) duties to something, and (2) duties *regarding* something. If a person has moral standing, then one has a presumptive duty not to harm that person. Suppose that nonliving things lack moral standing—as the anthropocentric paradigm implies. Then a car lacks moral standing. One cannot have duties to it since one can have (direct) duties only to (or toward) entities with moral standing. Still, the anthropocentric view reasonably can account for why it is wrong to destroy another's car without that individual's consent. Were one to do so, it would damage the legitimate interests of a being with moral standing, namely, the owner. Hence, one has duties regarding another's car (for example, not to destroy it) even though its well-being in itself does not count; that is, it lacks moral standing. In principle, then, even though the anthropocentric criterion of moral standing excludes everything nonhuman (mountains, penguins, real or plastic trees, blue whales, and so on) from possessing such standing, humans have certain duties to protect or not harm the nonhuman "furniture of the earth." A key feature, of course, is that according to this view any such duties will obtain only if they are derivative from duties we have toward human beings. Some writers make this (or a similar) point in terms of intrinsic versus extrinsic value. Certain things, human beings (their existence or their well-being), for example, are thought to be valuable in themselves, or intrinsically valuable; hence, certain duties are owed to them. In contrast, other things are thought to lack intrinsic value, and if valuable at all, they are valuable only if valued by beings that are intrinsically valuable. According to such views, duties regarding certain things, or values being assigned to them, are contingent on their being valued by, or being objects whose existence is in the legitimate interest of, beings with moral standing. That certain animals, for example, are extrinsically valuable (so are humans) is noncontroversial. That no duties are owed to animals, that they lack intrinsic value, is not noncontroversial. Similar points may be proposed about mountains, oceans, redwood trees, and marshes. Such claims are among the central sources of contention in environmental ethics.

So far, we have focused on only one proposed criterion of moral standing, albeit a pervasive and influential one: membership in *Homo sapiens*. As several of the selections to follow make clear, other views have been proposed as more defensible. A list of some of the leading views among them would include the following (or some combination):

1. Personhood
2. Potential personhood
3. Rationality
4. Linguistic capacity
5. Sentience
6. Being alive
7. Being an integral part of an ecosystem
8. Being an ecosystem.

Generally, the different criteria will select out different sets of beings (or entities) as possessing moral standing; some of the criteria clearly are more inclusive than others. Those who, like Albert Schweitzer (20th-century Christian physician and talented organist), would try to maneuver a housefly outside rather than kill it may be committed to, or presuppose, Criterion 6. Criterion 7 promises to be even more inclusive since, according to this view, even things that are not alive (for example, a mountain) may be part of an ecosystem. Some people, of course, are inclined toward vitalism, which we understand as asserting that all things are, in some sense, alive. Others would insist that at least the earth's surface and atmosphere, the biosphere, should be thought of as a dynamic, living system—even like a gigantic, somewhat diffuse organism. In recent years, atmospheric chem-

ist James Lovelock, in his book *Gaia*, has argued that the earth's biosphere behaves like "a single organism, even a living creature." This view revives, after a fashion, the predominant ancient conception of the earth as a goddess, as alive and a fitting referent of the expression "sister" or "earth mother" used by both Plato and St. Francis of Assisi.

Some contemporary environmentalists think it no small matter, and indeed of the greatest consequence, that a shift occurred (about the time of Descartes and Newton) in the 17th and 18th centuries from the concept of the earth as alive, as a generous parent, to the concept of its being an object, a wound-up clock to be tinkered with instead of affectionately tended by humans. Evidently, the implications of being alive as the criterion of moral standing will vary depending on what is viewed as being alive. In contrast, as we noted earlier, the famous English utilitarian Jeremy Bentham defended sentience as the criterion of moral standing. Thus, in his view the central question is whether a being can suffer or experience satisfaction—is it sentient? (criterion 5)—not whether it can reason (criterion 3), can use language (criterion 4), or is simply alive (criterion 6). In a possibly ambiguous passage, the famous 17th-century French philosopher and mathematician René Descartes seems to have taken the view that nonhuman animals lack linguistic capacity and, therefore, lack a mental-psychological life. Thus, animals are not sentient. If so, of course, they cannot be caused pain—appearances to the contrary. Hence, there could be no duty not to cause them pain. In Cartesian language they are mere automata; in modern language they are like programmed robots. Thus, if Descartes is right—even if sentience is the most defensible criterion of moral standing—then nonhuman animals cannot have such standing. Some people may side with Descartes in his denial of sentience to (any) animals, but his view seems indefensible. Many animals, after all, exhibit physiological and behavioral responses similar to those of humans and possess developed central nervous systems whose presence is normally sufficient for us to infer the presence of pain and pleasure in others. Darwin considered Cartesian skepticism on this issue irrational.

It is worth noting that the criterion of sentience would not only include certain animals (those that are sentient; contrary to Descartes, we assume many are) but also exclude nonsentient humans. But which humans are not sentient? Possibly the irreversibly comatose, some anencephalic (brainless or partly brainless) babies, first-trimester fetuses, and perhaps those of later fetal stages as well. In any case, the class of sentient creatures certainly does not coincide with the class of members of *Homo sapiens*. At least three reasons may be offered for accepting sentience, as opposed to membership in our species, as the most defensible criterion of moral standing: (1) drawing the line around our own species is entirely arbitrary—much like what, in effect, the racist or sexist does in favoring his or her own race or gender; (2) it is implausible that some humans, for example, the irreversibly comatose, have moral standing; and (3) if suffering is an evil that, in the absence of other morally relevant considerations, ought to be prevented, it is arbitrary to regard only human suffering as an evil. These points are somewhat controversial; we note them here merely to hint at some of the debates that are part of the current reassessment of our dealings with animals. They are discussed in later essays.

Criterion 4, linguistic capacity, has few defenders today. Even if it were the most defensible criterion of moral standing, two implications are of interest. First, it would imply that some very seriously retarded humans lack moral standing. That we have no presumptive duties to such beings is a view that many find repugnant. Second, a plausible case can be made that some nonhuman primates (at least) satisfy this condition—given recent successes in teaching Ameslan

(American Sign Language) to certain gorillas and chimpanzees. Whether certain animals possess linguistic competence is a matter of current dispute, mainly because of a conceptual disagreement over what counts as "possessing a language."

Criterion 3 is somewhat obscure also. What counts as being rational? If rationality is construed in a nonstringent fashion, many animals would likely satisfy the condition (though not rocks, rivers, coral reefs, or ecosystems). If the concept of rationality is construed stringently, it *may* exclude all animals, but it is likely to exclude certain humans as well, for example, the severely retarded. Those who accept the sentience criterion or the anthropocentric one will find this implication intolerable. Some philosophers who regard rationality as the proper criterion (as do some who accept sentience) do not hesitate to conclude that some members of *Homo sapiens* lack moral standing. Others, finding this implication repugnant, seek to avoid it by defending other proposals. According to one variant of the rationality view, if something is a member of a species whose paradigm members (for example, normal adult members) are rational, then any member is classifiable as a rational creature. Thus, although no one would say that a human zygote (fertilized egg) can reason, one philosopher, Alan Donagan, views it as a rational creature, and, hence, deserving of the respect owed to rational creatures. According to this view, of course, possession of the (allegedly) crucial trait, rationality, is not judged as necessary for moral standing.

Donagan's view should be contrasted with various "potentiality principles." Suppose, for example, one were to propose that actual rationality or potential rationality (either trait, or both) is the proper criterion of moral standing. Under this criterion, normal persons, infants, and embryos (maybe zygotes, too) have moral standing. Embryos would have it, of course, because of their potential to become actually rational. Under this criterion, however, an anencephalic infant is not potentially rational, and, thus, lacks moral standing. Under Donagan's criterion, in contrast, it (probably) possesses moral standing. So, Donagan's extension of moral standing (though he does not employ this terminology) to "marginal members" of *Homo sapiens* diverges from potentiality principles.

Some people think that, although neonates or fetuses lack rationality or certain other complex psychological characteristics, they (or most of them) are directly owed certain duties, and, hence, the presupposition that they possess moral standing. Further, it is tempting to think that such standing is possessed because of their prospect of developing into beings who uncontroversially are agreed to have standing, namely, normal persons. Some claim that, although certain adult primates may exhibit "more personality" or have capacities for rational choice not possessed by neonatal humans, a reason for attributing moral standing to such humans, but not to such primates, is that the former have a unique potential that the latter do not. According to this line of thought, membership in *Homo sapiens* as such may not be thought to be the proper criterion of moral standing; rather, it is actual or potential personhood (or rationality according to a variant view). This criterion tends to include virtually all humans (though not the most severely retarded, anencephalic infants, or those in persistent vegetative states), but probably no animals—at least if the facts support the claim that no animal is rational or that none exhibits the requisites of personhood. Such a view contrasts with the anthropocentric criterion; it also allows the possibility that nonhumans (e.g., possible alien creatures; consider "E.T.") possess moral standing.

In spite of the intuitive appeal of regarding a creature's potentiality as morally significant, some deny its relevance. We note one objection here. Suppose that a sufficient con-

dition for possessing moral standing were that an entity, X, possess a certain trait (P), that is, is a person. Let MS stand for "moral standing." Then the supposition is that:

1. For any X, if X has P, then X has MS.

Defenders of the importance of potential personhood seem to assume that:

2. For any X, if X potentially has P, then X has MS.

Opponents of (2) wonder why we should accept (2). Claim (2) does not follow from (1). Nor does (2) follow from the weaker claim (3):

3. For any X, if X potentially has P, then X potentially has MS.

To be less formal, consider some related examples. Although an acorn potentially is an adult oak tree, and adult oak trees are large, acorns are not large. Adult persons, it is commonly held (at least in the Western world), have a moral right to decide whom to marry (or at least whom to refuse to marry); human zygotes are (generally) potential normal adults, but arguably, they lack the right in question. Even though we may agree that a certain morally important trait (for example, having certain rights) is possessed by an entity by virtue of its having certain actual properties (for example, being an adult person), why think that an entity that only has the potential for these properties has the relevant trait? To press the point, infants are potentially adults. Actual adults (normally) have a right to vote. Why attribute such a right to the infant? Its potential adulthood does not seem a good reason. In short, there is a puzzle as to why potential possession of relevant properties is morally significant as opposed to actual possession. Getting clear about these matters is no easy task; here we call attention only to one source of contention. Further inquiry is in order.

Another perspective is worth noting here. One might think that the most stringent duties of all are directly owed to persons (in the psychological as opposed to the biological interpretation), and yet other entities, say, the merely sentient ones, also possess moral standing. Thus, one might think that there is a sort of moral hierarchy of entities; for example, all and only sentient creatures have moral standing, but among those with such standing, the well-being or lives of some morally count more heavily than others. Thus, although there is a presumption against destroying or causing pain to any sentient creature, in certain conflicts of interest between persons and the merely sentient it is all right (or obligatory) to sacrifice the interest of the latter. If a baboon heart or liver can be transplanted to a human to save the latter's life (but the baboon will die), it is, according to this view, proper that the transplant be carried out. Even some staunch advocates of animal liberation or animal rights (for example, Peter Singer or Tom Regan) seem to accept this judgment (see the discussion in the Preview to Section IV-B and the selection from Regan there). Why it should be accepted is, however, a matter of considerable controversy. If one is to include both persons and others (say, the merely sentient) within the moral community—but one is to view some as, in some sense, second-class citizens, serious perplexities arise. Is there a nonarbitrary basis for such differentiations within the set of beings possessing moral standing? If so, what is it? And if rationality, for example, is invoked, will that not suggest that we can, or ought to, discriminate (differentiate) among humans—according to possession (or not) of rationality (or even degrees of rationality)? Further, does such a view open the door to, or commit one to, a policy of invidious discrimination? If not, why not? The question of whether to assign or recognize diverse values to those beings possessing moral standing is developed further in Section IV-B, "Approaches to Conflict Resolution."

In discussing the question of what sorts of entities have moral standing, we have focused on individuals. Some think that the real locus of value is in ecosystems or networks of life and that, at the very least, the focus on lives of individuals is misplaced and wrongheaded. The view of "holists" on this matter does not seem entirely clear, but one possible position (call it Extreme Holism) is that the value of individuals is derivative and dependent on its value to some larger network. Thus, individuals seem replaceable and perhaps of only instrumental value; there is a similar worry about the value of individuals in the view of utilitarians in that the principle of utility would require the elimination of individuals if they could be replaced by others whose existence would contribute more to the total sum of utility. Another possible form of holism (call it Moderate Holism) would hold that both the relevant individuals and the relevant systems possess moral standing; with this latter view the value of the individuals would not be merely derivative.[3]

The first selection, by Alice Walker, makes one reflect on the significance that individual animals often play in our lives and how some may be seen as suffering from losses similar to those which afflict humans.[4] Her story of the horse Blue is a poignant one. Then, we turn to "Animal Liberation," the famous essay by Peter Singer (his later well-known book has the same title) in which he sketches the utilitarian-based case for the view that we have duties at least to all sentient creatures and we are, therefore, unjust in much of our treatment of animals, especially in our imposition of pain (as opposed to death) on them in scientific experiments and in their plight on factory farms. Singer has little to say (as he intended) in that essay about how we should think about ecosystems or questions of preserving biodiversity. From the standpoint of some advocates of an environmental ethic, there is an important distinction to be made between domestic and wild animals. For example, Baird Callicott says that "From the perspective of the land ethic a herd of cattle, sheep, or pigs is as much or more a ruinous blight on the landscape as a fleet of four-wheel drive off-road vehicles."[5] The wild/domestic distinction is not regarded as having any particular significance in the position of Singer, or in that of Tom Regan.

The next selection, by Barry Lopez, which is a change from philosophy as such, focuses on a wild animal. We note, in passing, that some thinkers believe that our duties to wild animals are quite different from those toward domesticated ones. Some people, however, seem to infer that since we domesticated certain animals, we owe them more—since *we made them* incapable of living in the wild. Others seem to conclude that since some animals are domesticated, it is all right to think of them and treat them as if they were just egg, milk, or meat machines. Of course, the voices of profit-maximizers said similar things during the 19th-century slave trade about the domestication of "wild savages." Lopez helps one think about the extraordinary talent of the wolf in surviving in the wild, the way in which the Eskimos, for example, must become more like the wolves in order to survive.

Next, Tom Regan sets out a case for the view that we must radically alter our treatment of animals and that the appropriate view of things is one in which we recognize that (many) animals have rights. In this respect he rejects the assumption that the utilitarian theory provides an acceptable approach to deciding how we ought to treat animals. He calls for a complete halt to scientific experimentation on animals. In Section IV-B we shall return directly to the question of how to resolve conflicts of interest between humans and animals; the conflict between animal welfare and human welfare via scientific experimentation

is one of many examples. The main focus of many "animal liberationists" is on sentient animals; hence, it is useful to think about the little, probably nonsentient, creatures that we so often ignore, ones that, in fact, have at least an enormously instrumental value to the ongoing dynamic of life on earth. E. O. Wilson explains why. Should we think of them as beyond the moral pale—in the sense that they should be judged as lacking moral standing—even if they have enormous value as parts of ecosystems?

NOTES

1. Some people in a country (for example, illegal aliens) may have no legal standing as citizens; that is, they may enjoy none (or few) of the constitutional protections guaranteed to those who enjoy the status of citizens. For certain purposes, at least, they are not owed certain legal duties, and they lack certain legal rights. To have the legal standing of being a citizen, then, is to be regarded as a being whose interests must be positively weighed in governmental decisions about what may be done. The state is thought to have at least a presumptive duty not to disregard or subvert the basic interests (say, in continued life, bodily integrity, or freedom of movement) of one who possesses legal standing. That these interests must be given positive weight in the decision making of others is a point usually implicit in claims that such interest-bearers have rights or that we owe them certain duties.

2. To give positive moral weight to the interests of a being is, roughly, to give those interests favorable and proper weight in one's deciding what one ought to do.

3. We are indebted to one of our reviewers for suggesting this useful distinction.

4. In a more analytic fashion, Mary Midgley, in *Animals: Why They Matter,* calls attention to the fact of our living in communities of mixed species and that for many the presence of animals is like that of kin; we have ongoing relationships with animals. They have names. It is contrary to much of our experience to think of (many of) them as mere commodities, or "crops" to be harvested.

5. J. Baird Callicott, "Animal Liberation: A Triangular Affair," *Environmental Ethics,* Vol. 2, No. 4 (Winter 1980), pp. 311–338.

Am I Blue?

Alice Walker

For about three years my companion and I rented a small house in the country that stood on the edge of a large meadow that appeared to run from the end of our deck straight into the mountains. The mountains, however, were quite far away, and between us and them there was, in fact, a town. It was one of the many pleasant aspects of the house that you never really were aware of this.

It was a house of many windows, low, wide, nearly floor to ceiling in the living room, which faced the meadow, and it was from one of these that I first saw our closest neighbor, a large white horse, cropping grass, flipping its mane, and ambling about—not over the entire meadow, which stretched well out of sight of the house, but over the five or so fenced-in acres that were next to the twenty-odd that we had rented. I soon learned that the horse, whose name was Blue, belonged to a man who lived in another town, but was boarded by our neighbors next door. Occasionally, one of the children, usually a stocky teen-ager, but sometimes a much younger girl or boy, could be seen riding Blue. They would appear in the meadow, climb up on his back, ride furiously for ten or fifteen minutes, then get off, slap Blue on the flanks, and not be seen again for a month or more.

There were many apple trees in our yard, and one by the fence that Blue could almost reach. We were soon in the habit of feeding him apples, which he relished, especially because by the middle of summer the meadow grasses—so green and succulent since January—had dried out from lack of rain, and Blue stumbled about munching the dried stalks half-heartedly. Sometimes he would stand very still just by the apple tree, and when one of us came out he would whinny, snort loudly, or stamp the ground. This meant, of course: I want an apple.

It was quite wonderful to pick a few apples, or collect those that had fallen to the ground overnight, and patiently hold them, one by one, up to his large, toothy mouth. I remained as thrilled as a child by his flexible dark lips, huge, cubelike teeth that crunched the apples, core and all, with such finality, and his high, broad-breasted *enormity*; beside which, I felt small indeed. When I was a child, I used to ride horses, and was especially friendly with one named Nan until the day I was riding and my brother deliberately spooked her and I was thrown, head first, against the trunk of a tree. When I came to, I was in bed and my mother was bending worriedly over me; we silently agreed that perhaps horseback riding was not the safest sport for me. Since then I have walked, and prefer walking to horseback riding—but I had forgotten the depth of feeling one could see in horses' eyes.

I was therefore unprepared for the expression in Blue's. Blue was lonely. Blue was horribly lonely and bored. I was not shocked that this should be the case; five acres to tramp by yourself, endlessly, even in the most beautiful of meadows—and his was—cannot provide many interesting events, and once rainy season turned to dry that was about it. No, I was shocked that I had forgotten that human animals and nonhuman animals can communicate quite well; if we are brought up around animals as children we take this for granted. By the time we are adults we no longer remember. However, the animals have not changed. They are in fact *completed* creations (at least they seem to be, so much more than we) who are not likely *to* change; it is their nature to express themselves. What else are they going to express? And they do. And, generally speaking, they are ignored.

After giving Blue the apples, I would wander back to the house, aware that he was observing me. Were more apples not forthcoming then? Was that to be his sole entertainment for the day? My partner's small son had decided he wanted to learn how to piece a quilt; we worked in silence on our respective squares as I thought . . .

Well, about slavery: about white children, who were raised by black people, who knew their first all-accepting love from black women, and then, when they were twelve or so, were told they must "forget" the deep levels of communication between themselves and "mammy" that they knew. Later they would be able to relate quite calmly, "My old mammy was sold to another good family." "My old mammy was – –." Fill in the blank. Many more years later a white woman would say: "I can't understand these Negroes, these blacks. What do they want? They're so different from us."

And about the Indians, considered to be "like animals" by the "settlers" (a very benign euphemism for what they actually were), who did not understand their description as a compliment.

And about the thousands of American men who marry Japanese, Korean, Filipina, and other non-English-speaking women and of how happy they report they are, *"blissfully,"* until their brides learn to speak English, at which point the marriages tend to fall apart. What then did the men see, when they looked into the eyes of the women they married, before they could speak English? Apparently only their own reflections.

I thought of society's impatience with the young. "Why are they playing the music so loud?" Perhaps the children have listened to much of the music of oppressed people their parents danced to before they were born, with its passionate but soft cries for acceptance and love, and they have wondered why their parents failed to hear.

I do not know how long Blue had inhabited his five beautiful, boring acres before we moved into our house; a year after we had arrived—and had also traveled to other valleys, other cities, other worlds—he was still there.

But then, in our second year at the house, something happened in Blue's life. One morning, looking out the window at the fog that lay like a ribbon over the meadow, I saw another horse, a brown one, at the other end of Blue's field. Blue appeared to be afraid of it, and for several days made no attempt to go near. We went away for a week. When we returned, Blue had decided to make friends and the two horses ambled or galloped along together, and Blue did not come nearly as often to the fence underneath the apple tree.

When he did, bringing his new friend with him, there was a different look in his eyes. A look of independence, of self-possession, of inalienable *horse*ness. His friend eventually became pregnant. For months and months there was, it seemed to me, a mutual feeling between me and the horses of jus-

tice, of peace. I fed apples to them both. The look in Blue's eyes was one of unabashed "this is *it*ness."

It did not, however, last forever. One day, after a visit to the city, I went out to give Blue some apples. He stood waiting, or so I thought, though not beneath the tree. When I shook the tree and jumped back from the shower of apples, he made no move. I carried some over to him. He managed to half-crunch one. The rest he let fall to the ground. I dreaded looking into his eyes—because I had of course noticed that Brown, his partner, had gone—but I did look. If I had been born into slavery, and my partner had been sold or killed, my eyes would have looked like that. The children next door explained that Blue's partner had been "put with him" (the same expression that old people used, I had noticed, when speaking of an ancestor during slavery who had been impregnated by her owner) so that they could mate and she conceive. Since that was accomplished, she had been taken back by her owner, who lived somewhere else.

Will she be back? I asked.

They didn't know.

Blue was like a crazed person. Blue *was*, to me, a crazed person. He galloped furiously, as if he were being ridden, around and around his five beautiful acres. He whinnied until he couldn't. He tore at the ground with his hooves. He butted himself against his single shade tree. He looked always and always toward the road down which his partner had gone. And then, occasionally, when he came up for apples, or I took apples to him, he looked at me. It was a look so piercing, so full of grief, a look so *human*, I almost laughed (I felt too sad to cry) to think there are people who do not know that animals suffer. People like me who have forgotten, and daily forget, all that animals try to tell us. "Everything you do to us will happen you; we are your teachers, as you are ours. We are one lesson" is essentially it, I think. There are those who never once have even considered animals' rights: those who have been taught that animals actually want to be used and abused by us, as small children "love" to be frightened, or women "love" to be mutilated and raped.... They are the great-grandchildren of those who honestly thought, because someone taught them this: "Women can't think," and "niggers can't faint." But most disturbing of all, in Blue's large brown eyes was a new look, more painful than the look of despair:

the look of disgust with human beings, with life; the look of hatred. And it was odd what the look of hatred did. It gave him, for the first time, the look of a beast. And what that meant was that he had put up a barrier within to protect himself from further violence; all the apples in the world wouldn't change that fact.

And so Blue remained, a beautiful part of our landscape, very peaceful to look at from the window, white against the grass. Once a friend came to visit and said, looking out on the soothing view: "And it *would* have to be a *white* horse; the very image of freedom." And I thought, yes, the animals are forced to become for us merely "images" of what they once so beautifully expressed. And we are used to drinking milk from containers showing "contented" cows, whose real lives we want to hear nothing about, eating eggs and drumsticks from "happy" hens, and munching hamburgers advertised by bulls of integrity who seem to command their fate.

As we talked of freedom and justice one day for all, we sat down to steaks. I am eating misery, I thought, as I took the first bite. And spit it out.

Animal Liberation[1]

Peter Singer

I

We are familiar with Black Liberation, Gay Liberation, and a variety of other movements. With Women's Liberation some thought we had come to the end of the road. Discrimination on the basis of sex, it has been said, is the last form of discrimination that is universally accepted and practiced without pretense, even in those liberal circles which have long prided themselves on their freedom from racial discrimination. But one should always be wary of talking of "the last remaining form of discrimination." If we have learned anything from the liberation movements, we should have learned how difficult it is to be aware of the ways in which we discriminate until they are forcefully pointed out to us. A liberation movement demands an expansion of our moral horizons, so that practices that were previously regarded as natural and inevitable are now seen as intolerable.

Animals, Men and Morals is a manifesto for an Animals Liberation movement. The contributers to the book may not all see the issue this way. They are a varied group. Philosophers, ranging from professors to graduate students, make up the largest contingent. There are five of them, including the three editors, and there is also an extract from the unjustly neglected German philosopher with an English name, Leonard Nelson, who died in 1927. There are essays by two novelist/critics, Brigid Brophy and Maureen Duffy, and another by Muriel the Lady Dowding, widow of Dowding of Battle of Britain fame and the founder of "Beauty without Cruelty," a movement that campaigns against the use of animals for furs and cosmetics. The other pieces are by a psychologist, a botanist, a sociologist, and Ruth Harrison, who is probably best described as a professional campaigner for animal welfare.

Whether or not these people, as individuals, would all agree that they are launching a liberation movement for animals, the book as a whole amounts to no less. It is a demand for a complete change in our attitudes to nonhumans. It is a demand that we cease to regard the exploitation of other species as natural and inevitable, and that, instead, we see it as a continuing moral outrage. Patrick Corbett, Professor of Philosophy at Sussex University, captures the spirit of the book in his closing words:

> ... we require now to extend the great principles of liberty, equality and fraternity over the lives of animals. Let animal slavery join human slavery in the graveyard of the past.

The reader is likely to be skeptical. "Animal Liberation" sounds more like a parody of liberation movements than a serious objective. The reader may think: We support the claims of blacks and women for equality because blacks and women really are equal to whites and males—equal in intelligence and in abilities, capacity for leadership, rationality, and so on. Humans and nonhumans obviously are not equal in these respects. Since justice demands only that we treat equals equally, unequal treatment of humans and nonhumans cannot be an injustice.

This is a tempting reply, but a dangerous one. It commits the non-racist and non-sexist to a dogmatic belief that blacks and women really are just as intelligent, able, etc., as whites and males—and no more. Quite possibly this happens to be the case. Certainly attempts to prove that racial or sexual differences in these respects have a genetic origin have not been conclusive. But do we really want to stake our demand for equality on the assumption that there are no genetic differences of this kind between the different races or sexes? Surely the appropriate response to those who claim to have found evidence for such genetic differences is not to stick to the belief that there are no differences, whatever the evidence to the contrary; rather one should be clear that the claim to equality does not depend on IQ. Moral equality is distinct from factual equality. Otherwise it would be nonsense to talk of the equality of human beings, since humans, as individuals, obviously differ in intelligence and almost any ability one cares to name. If possessing greater intelligence does not entitle one human to exploit another, why should it entitle humans to exploit nonhumans?

Jeremy Bentham expressed the essential basis of equality in his famous formula: "Each to count for one and none for more than one." In other words, the interests of every being that has interests are to be taken into account and treated equally with the like interest of any other being. Other moral philosophers, before and after Bentham, have made the same point in different ways. Our concern for others must not depend on whether they possess certain characteristics, though just what that concern involves may, of course, vary according to such characteristics.

Bentham, incidentally, was well aware that the logic of the demand for racial equality did not stop at the equality of humans. He wrote:

> The day *may* come when the rest of the animal creation may acquire those rights which never could have been withholden from them but by the hand of tyranny. The French have already discovered that the blackness of the skin is no

reason why a human being should be abandoned without redress to the caprice of a tormentor. It may one day come to be recognized that the number of the legs, the villosity of the skin, or the termination of the *os sacrum,* are reasons equally insufficient for abandoning a sensitive being to the same fate. What else is it that should trace the insuperable line? Is it the faculty of reason, or perhaps the faculty of discourse? But a full-grown horse or dog is beyond comparison a more rational, as well as more conversable animal, than an infant of a day, or a week, or even a month old. But suppose they were otherwise, what would it avail? The question is not, Can they *reason?* nor Can they *talk?* but, Can they *suffer?*[2]

Surely Bentham was right, If a being suffers, there can be no moral justification for refusing to take that suffering into consideration, and, indeed, to count it equally with the like suffering (if rough comparisons can be made) of any other being.

So the only question is: do animals other than man suffer? Most people agree unhesitatingly that animals like cats and dogs can and do suffer, and this seems also to be assumed by those laws that prohibit wanton cruelty to such animals. Personally, I have no doubt at all about this and find it hard to take seriously the doubts that a few people apparently do have. The editors and contributors of *Animals, Men and Morals* seem to feel the same way, for although the question is raised more than once, doubts are quickly dismissed each time. Nevertheless, because this is such a fundamental point, it is worth asking what grounds we have for attributing suffering to other animals.

It is best to begin by asking what grounds any individual human has for supposing that other humans feel pain. Since pain is a state of consciousness, a "mental event," it can never be directly observed. No observations, whether behavioral signs such as writhing or screaming or physiological or neurological recordings, are observations of pain itself. Pain is something one feels and one can only infer that others are feeling it from various external indications. The fact that only philosophers are ever skeptical about whether other humans feel pain shows that we regard such inference as justifiable in the case of humans.

Is there any reason why the same inference should be unjustifiable for other animals? Nearly all the external signs which lead us to infer pain in other humans can be seen in other species, especially "higher" animals such as mammals and birds. Behavioral signs—writhing, yelping, or other forms of calling, attempts to avoid the source of pain, and many others—are present. We know, too, that these animals are biologically similar in the relevant respects, having nervous systems like ours which can be observed to function as ours do.

So the grounds for inferring that these animals can feel pain are nearly as good as the grounds for inferring other humans do. Only nearly, for there is one behavioral sign that humans have but nonhumans, with the exception of one or two specially raised chimpanzees, do not have. This, of course, is a developed language. As the quotation from Bentham indicates, this has long been regarded as an important distinction between man and other animals. Other animals may communicate with each other, but not in the way we do. Following Chomsky, many people now mark this distinction by saying that only humans communicate in a form that is governed by rules of syntax. (For the purposes of this argument, linguists allow those chimpanzees who have learned a syntactic sign language to rank as honorary humans.) Nevertheless, as Bentham pointed out, this distinction is not relevant to the question of how animals ought to be treated, unless it can be linked to the issue of whether animals suffer.

This link may be attempted in two ways. First, there is a hazy line of philosophical thought, stemming perhaps from some doctrines associated with Wittgenstein, which maintains that we cannot meaningfully attribute states of consciousness to beings without language. I have not seen this argument made explicit in print, though I have come across it in conversation. This position seems to me very implausible, and I doubt that it would be held at all if it were not thought to be a consequence of a broader view of the significance of language. It may be that the use of a public, rule-governed language is a precondition of conceptual thought. It may even be, although personally I doubt it, that we cannot meaningfully speak of a creature having an intention unless that creature can use a language. But states like pain, surely, are more primitive than either of these, and seem to have nothing to do with language.

Indeed, as Jane Goodall points out in her study of chimpanzees, when it comes to the expression of feelings and emotions, humans tend to fall back on nonlinguistic modes of communication which are often found among apes, such as a cheering pat on the back, an exuberant embrace, a clasp of hands, and so on.[3] Michael Peters makes a similar point in his contribution to *Animals, Men and Morals* when he notes that the basic signals we use to convey pain, fear, sexual arousal, and so on are not specific to our species. So there seems to be no reason at all to believe that a creature without language cannot suffer.

The second, and more easily appreciated way of linking language and the existence of pain is to say that the best evidence that we can have that another creature is in pain is when he tells us that he is. This is a distinct line of argument, for it is not being denied that a non-language-user conceivably could suffer, but only that we could know that he is suffering. Still, this line of argument seems to me to fail, and for reasons similar to those just given. "I am in pain" is not the best possible evidence that the speaker is in pain (he might be lying) and it is certainly not the only possible evidence. Behavioral signs and knowledge of the animals' biological similarity to ourselves together provide adequate evidence that animals do suffer. After all, we would not accept linguistic evidence if it contradicted the rest of the evidence. If a man was severely burned, and behaved as if he were in pain, writhing, groaning, being very careful not to let his burned skin touch anything, and so on, but later said he had not been in pain at all, we would be more likely to conclude that he was lying or suffering from amnesia than that he had not been in pain.

Even if there were stronger grounds for refusing to attribute pain to those who do not have a language, the consequences of this refusal might lead us to examine these grounds unusually critically. Human infants, as well as some adults, are unable to use language. Are we to deny that a year-old infant can suffer? If not, how can language be crucial? Of course, most parents can understand the responses of even very young infants better than they understand the responses of other animals, and sometimes infant responses can be understood in the light of later development.

This, however, is just a fact about the relative knowledge we have of our own species and other species, and most of this knowledge is simply derived from closer contact. Those who have studied the behavior of other animals soon learn to understand their responses at least as well as we understand those of an infant. (I am not just referring to Jane Goodall's and other well-known studies of apes. Consider, for example, the degree of understanding achieved by Tinbergen from watching herring gulls.)[4] Just as we can understand infant human behavior in the light of adult human behavior, so we can understand the behavior of other species in the light of our own behavior (and sometimes we can understand our own behavior better in the light of the behavior of other species).

The grounds we have for believing that other mammals and birds suffer are, then, closely analogous to the grounds we have for believing that other humans suffer. It remains to consider how far down the evolutionary scale this analogy holds. Obviously it becomes poorer when we get further away from man. To be more precise would require a detailed examination of all that we know about other forms of life. With fish, reptiles, and other vertebrates the analogy still seems strong, with molluscs like oysters it is much weaker. Insects are more difficult, and it may be that in our present state of knowledge we must be agnostic about whether they are capable of suffering.

If there is no moral justification for ignoring suffering when it occurs, and it does occur in other species, what are we to say of our attitudes toward these other species? Richard Ryder, one of the contributors of *Animals, Men and Morals,* uses the term "speciesism" to describe the belief that we are entitled to treat members of other species in a way in which it would be wrong to treat members of our own species. The term is not euphonious, but it neatly makes the analogy with racism. The nonracist would do well to bear the analogy in mind when he is inclined to defend human behavior toward nonhumans. "Shouldn't we worry about improving the lot of our own species before we concern ourselves with other species?" he may ask. If we substitute "race" for "species" we shall see that the question is better not asked. "Is a vegetarian diet nutritionally adequate?" resembles the slave-owner's claim that he and the whole economy of the South would be ruined without slave labor. There is even a parallel with skeptical doubts about whether animals suffer, for some defenders of slavery professed to doubt whether blacks really suffer in the way that whites do.

I do not want to give the impression, however,

that the case for Animal Liberation is based on the analogy with racism and no more. On the contrary, *Animals, Men and Morals* describes the various ways in which humans exploit nonhumans, and several contributors consider the defenses that have been offered, including the defense of meat-eating mentioned in the last paragraph. Sometimes the rebuttals are scornfully dismissive, rather than carefully designed to convince the detached critic. This may be a fault, but it is a fault that is inevitable, given the kind of book this is. The issue is not one on which one can remain detached. As the editors state in their Introduction:

> Once the full force of moral assessment has been made explicit there can be no rational excuse left for killing animals, be they killed for food, science, or sheer personal indulgence. We have not assembled this book to provide the reader with yet another manual on how to make brutalities less brutal. Compromise, in the traditional sense of the term, is simple unthinking weakness when one considers the actual reasons for our crude relationships with the other animals.

The point is that on this issue there are few critics who are genuinely detached. People who eat pieces of slaughtered nonhumans every day find it hard to believe that they are doing wrong; and they also find it hard to imagine what else they could eat. So for those who do not place nonhumans beyond the pale of morality, there comes a stage when further argument seems pointless, a stage at which one can only accuse one's opponent of hypocrisy and reach for the sort of sociological account of our practices and the way we defend them that is attempted by David Wood in his contribution to this book. On the other hand, to those unconvinced by the arguments, and unable to accept that they are rationalizing their dietary preferences and their fear of being thought peculiar, such sociological explanations can only seem insultingly arrogant.

II

The logic of speciesism is most apparent in the practice of experimenting on nonhumans in order to benefit humans. This is because the issue is rarely obscured by allegations that nonhumans are so different from humans that we cannot know anything about whether they suffer. The defender of vivisection cannot use this argument because he needs to stress the similarities between man and other animals in order to justify the usefulness to the former of experiments on the latter. The researcher who makes rats choose between starvation and electric shocks to see if they develop ulcers (they do) does so because he knows that the rat has a nervous system very similar to man's, and presumably feels an electric shock in a similar way.

Richard Ryder's restrained account of experiments on animals made me angrier with my fellow men than anything else in this book. Ryder, a clinical psychologist by profession, himself experimented on animals before he came to hold the view he puts forward in his essay. Experimenting on animals is now a large industry, both academic and commercial. In 1969, more than 5 million experiments were performed in Britain, the vast majority without anesthetic (though how many of these involved pain is not known). There are no accurate US figures, since there is no federal law on the subject, and in many cases no state law either. Estimates vary from 20 million to 200 million. Ryder suggests that 80 million may be the best guess. We tend to think that this is all for vital medical research, but of course it is not. Huge numbers of animals are used in university departments from Forestry to Psychology, and even more are used for commercial purposes, to test whether cosmetics can cause skin damage, or shampoos eye damage, or to test food additives or laxatives or sleeping pills or anything else.

A standard test for foodstuffs is the "LD50." The object of this test is to find the dosage level at which 50 percent of the test animals will die. This means that nearly all of them will become very sick before finally succumbing or surviving. When the substance is a harmless one, it may be necessary to force huge doses down the animals, until in some cases sheer volume or concentration causes death.

Ryder gives a selection of experiments, taken from recent scientific journals. I will quote two, not for the sake of indulging in gory details, but in order to give an idea of what normal researchers think they may legitimately do to other species. The point is not that the individual researchers are cruel men, but that they are behaving in a way that is allowed by our speciesist attitudes. As Ryder

points out, even if only 1 percent of the experiments involve severe pain, that is 50,000 experiments in Britain each year, or nearly 150 every day (and about fifteen times as many in the United States, if Ryder's guess is right). Here then are two experiments:

O. S. Ray and R. J. Barrett of Pittsburgh gave electric shocks to the feet of 1,042 mice. They then caused convulsions by giving more intense shocks through cup-shaped electrodes applied to the animals' eyes or through pressure spring clips attached to their ears. Unfortunately some of the mice who "successfully completed Day One training were found sick or dead prior to testing on Day Two." [*Journal of Comparative and Physiological Psychology*, 1969, Vol. 67, pp. 110–116]

At the National Institute for Medical Research, Mill Hill, London, W. Feldberg and S. L. Sherwood injected chemicals into the brains of cats—"with a number of widely different substances, recurrent patterns of reaction were obtained. Retching, vomiting, defaecation, increased salivation and greatly accelerated respiration leading to panting were common features." . . .

The injection into the brain of a large dose of Tubocuraine caused the cat to jump "from the table to the floor and then straight into its cage, where it started calling more and more noisily whilst moving about restlessly and jerkily . . . finally the cat fell with legs and neck flexed, jerking in rapid clonic movements, the condition being that of a major [epileptic] convulsion . . . within a few seconds the cat got up, ran for a few yards at high speed and fell in another fit. The whole process was repeated several times within the next ten minutes, during which the cat lost faeces and foamed at the mouth."

This animal finally died thirty-five minutes after the brain injection. [*Journal of Physiology*, 1954, Vol. 123, pp. 148–167]

There is nothing secret about these experiments. One has only to open any recent volume of a learned journal, such as the *Journal of Comparative and Physiological Psychology*, to find full descriptions of experiments of this sort, together with the results obtained—results that are frequently trivial and obvious. The experiments are often supported by public funds.

It is a significant indication of the level of acceptability of these practices that, although these experiments are taking place at this moment on university campuses throughout the country, there has, so far as I know, not been the slightest protest from the student movement. Students have been rightly concerned that their universities should not discriminate on grounds of race or sex, and that they should not serve the purposes of the military or big business. Speciesism continues undisturbed, and many students participate in it. There may be a few qualms at first, but since everyone regards it as normal, and it may even be a required part of a course, the student soon becomes hardened and, dismissing his earlier feelings as "mere sentiment," comes to regard animals as statistics rather than sentient beings with interests that warrant consideration.

Argument about vivisection has often missed the point because it has been put in absolutist terms: would the abolitionist be prepared to let thousands die if they could be saved by experimenting on a single animal? The way to reply to this purely hypothetical question is to pose another: Would the experimenter be prepared to experiment on a human orphan under six months old, if it were the only way to save many lives? (I say "orphan" to avoid the complication of parental feelings, although in doing so I am being overfair to the experimenter, since the nonhuman subjects of experiments are not orphans.) A negative answer to this question indicates that the experimenter's readiness to use nonhumans is simple discrimination, for adult apes, cats, mice, and other mammals are more conscious of what is happening to them, more self-directing, and, so far as we can tell, just as sensitive to pain as a human infant. There is no characteristic that human infants possess that adult mammals do not have to the same or a higher degree.

(It might be possible to hold that what makes it wrong to experiment on a human infant is that the infant will in time develop into more than the nonhuman, but one would then, to be consistent, have to oppose abortion, and perhaps contraception, too, for the fetus and the egg and sperm have the same potential as the infant. Moreover, one would still have no reason for experimenting on a nonhuman rather than a human with brain damage severe enough to make it impossible for him to rise above infant level.)

The experimenter, then, shows a bias for his own species whenever he carries out an experiment on a nonhuman for a purpose that he would not think justified him in using a human being at an equal or lower level of sentience, awareness, ability to be self-directing, etc. No one familiar with the kind of results yielded by these experiments can have the slightest doubt that if this bias were eliminated the number of experiments performed would be zero or very close to it.

III

If it is vivisection that shows the logic of speciesism most clearly, it is the use of other species for food that is at the heart of our attitudes toward them. Most of *Animals, Men and Morals* is an attack on meat-eating—an attack which is based solely on concern for nonhumans, without reference to arguments derived from considerations of ecology, macrobiotics, health, or religion.

The idea that nonhumans are utilities, means to our ends, pervades our thought. Even conservationists who are concerned about the slaughter of wild fowl but not about the vastly greater slaughter of chickens for our tables are thinking in this way—they are worried about what we would lose if there were less wildlife. Stanley Godlovitch, pursuing the Marxist idea that our thinking is formed by the activities we undertake in satisfying our needs, suggests that man's first classification of his environment was into Edibles and Inedibles. Most animals came into the first category, and there they have remained.

Man may always have killed other species for food, but he has never exploited them so ruthlessly as he does today. Farming has succumbed to business methods, the objective being to get the highest possible ratio of output (meat, eggs, milk) to input (fodder, labor costs, etc.). Ruth Harrison's essay "On Factory Farming" gives an account of some aspects of modern methods, and of the unsuccessful British campaign for effective controls, a campaign which was sparked off by her *Animal Machines* (Stuart: London, 1964).

Her article is in no way a substitute for her earlier book. This is a pity since, as she says "Farm produce is still associated with mental pictures of animals browsing in the fields, . . . of hens having a last forage before going to roost. . . ." Yet neither in her article nor elsewhere in *Animals, Men and Morals* is this false image replaced by a clear idea of the nature and extent of factory farming. We learn of this only indirectly, when we hear of the code of reform proposed by an advisory committee set up by the British government.

Among the proposals, which the government refused to implement on the grounds that they were too idealistic, were: *"Any animal should at least have room to turn around freely."*

Factory farm animals need liberation in the most literal sense. Veal calves are kept in stalls five feet by two feet. They are usually slaughtered when about four months old, and have been too big to turn in their stalls for at least a month. Intensive beef herds, kept in stalls only proportionately larger for much longer periods, account for a growing percentage of beef production. Sows are often similarly confined when pregnant, which, because of artificial methods of increasing fertility, can be most of the time. Animals confined in this way do not waste food by exercising, nor do they develop unpalatable muscle.

"A dry bedded area should be provided for all stock." Intensively kept animals usually have to stand and sleep on slatted floors without straw, because this makes cleaning easier.

"Palatable roughage must be readily available to all calves after one week of age." In order to produce the pale veal housewives are said to prefer, calves are fed on an all-liquid diet until slaughter, even though they are long past the age at which they would normally eat grass. They develop a craving for roughage, evidenced by attempts to gnaw wood from their stalls. (For the same reason, their diet is deficient in iron.)

"Battery cages for poultry should be large enough for a bird to be able to stretch one wing at a time." Under current British practice, a cage for four or five laying hens has a floor area of twenty inches by eighteen inches, scarcely larger than a double page of the *New York Review of Books*. In this space, on a sloping wire floor (sloping so the eggs roll down, wire so the dung drops through) the birds live for a year or eighteen months while artificial lighting and temperature conditions combine with drugs in their food to squeeze the maximum number of eggs out of them. Table birds are also sometimes kept in cages. More often they are reared in sheds, no less crowded. Under these conditions all the birds' natural activities are frustrated, and they develop "vices" such as pecking each other to death. To pre-

vent this, beaks are often cut off, and the sheds kept dark.

How many of those who support factory farming by buying its produce know anything about the way it is produced? How many have heard something about it, but are reluctant to check up for fear that it will make them uncomfortable? To nonspeciesists, the typical consumer's mixture of ignorance, reluctance to find out the truth, and vague belief that nothing really bad could be allowed seems analogous to the attitudes of "decent Germans" to the death camps.

There are, of course, some defenders of factory farming. Their arguments are considered, though again rather sketchily, by John Harris. Among the most common: "Since they have never known anything else, they don't suffer." This argument will not be put by anyone who knows anything about animal behavior, since he will know that not all behavior has to be learned. Chickens attempt to stretch wings, walk around, scratch, and even dust-bathe or build a nest, even though they have never lived under conditions that allowed these activities. Calves can suffer from maternal deprivation no matter at what age they were taken from their mothers. "We need these intensive methods to provide protein for a growing population." As ecologists and famine relief organizations know, we can produce far more protein per acre if we grow the right vegetable crop, soy beans for instance, than if we use the land to grow crops to be converted into protein by animals who use nearly 90 percent of the protein themselves, even when unable to exercise.

There will be many readers of this book who will agree that factory farming involves an unjustifiable degree of exploitation of sentient creatures, and yet will want to say that there is nothing wrong with rearing animals for food, provided it is done "humanely." These people are saying, in effect, that although we should not cause animals to suffer, there is nothing wrong with killing them.

There are two possible replies to this view. One is to attempt to show that this combination of attitudes is absurd. Roslind Godlovitch takes this course in her essay, which is an examination of some common attitudes to animals. She argues that from the combination of "animal suffering is to be avoided" and "there is nothing wrong with killing animals" it follows that all animal life ought to be exterminated (since all sentient creatures will suffer to some degree at some point in their lives). Euthanasia is a contentious issue only because we place some value on living. If we did not, the least amount of suffering would justify it. Accordingly, if we deny that we have a duty to exterminate all animal life, we must concede that we are placing some value on animal life.

This argument seems to me valid, although one could still reply that the value of animal life is to be derived from the pleasures that life can have for them, so that, provided their lives have a balance of pleasure over pain, we are justified in rearing them. But this would imply that we ought to produce animals and let them live as pleasantly as possible, without suffering.

At this point, one can make the second of the two possible replies to the view that rearing and killing animals for food is all right so long as it is done humanely. This second reply is that so long as we think that a nonhuman may be killed simply so that a human can satisfy his taste for meat, we are still thinking of nonhumans as means rather than as ends in themselves. The factory farm is nothing more than the application of technology to this concept. Even traditional methods involve castration, the separation of mothers and their young, the breaking up of herds, branding or ear-punching, and of course transportation to the abattoirs and the final moments of terror when the animal smells blood and senses danger. If we were to try rearing animals so that they lived and died without suffering, we should find that to do so on anything like the scale of today's meat industry would be a sheer impossibility. Meat would become the prerogative of the rich.

I have been able to discuss only some of the contributions to this book, saying nothing about, for instance, the essays on killing for furs and for sport. Nor have I considered all the detailed questions that need to be asked once we start thinking about other species in the radically different way presented by this book. What, for instance, are we to do about genuine conflicts of interest like rats biting slum children? I am not sure of the answer, but the essential point is just that we *do* see this as a conflict of interests, that we recognize that rats have interests too. Then we may begin to think about other ways of resolving the conflict—perhaps by leaving out rat baits that sterilize the rats instead of killing them.

I have not discussed such problems because they are side issues compared with the exploitation of other species for food and for experimental purposes. On these central matters, I hope that I have said enough to show that this book, despite its flaws, is a challenge to every human to recognize his attitudes to nonhumans as a form of prejudice no less objectionable than racism or sexism. It is a challenge that demands not just a change of attitudes, but a change in our way of life, for it requires us to become vegetarians.

Can a purely moral demand of this kind succeed? The odds are certainly against it. The book holds out no inducements. It does not tell us that we will become healthier, or enjoy life more, if we cease exploiting animals. Animal Liberation will require greater altruism on the part of mankind than any other liberation movement, since animals are incapable of demanding it for themselves, or of protesting against their exploitation by votes, demonstrations, or bombs. Is man capable of such genuine altruism? Who knows? If this book does have a significant effect, however, it will be a vindication of all those who have believed that man has within himself the potential for more than cruelty and selfishness.

Notes

1. This article originally appeared as a book review of *Animals, Men and Morals*, edited by Stanley and Roslind Godlovitch and John Harris.
2. *The Principles of Morals and Legislation*, Ch. XVII, Sec. 1, footnote to paragraph 4. (Italics in original.)
3. Jane van Lawick-Goodall, *In the Shadow of Man* (Houghton Mifflin, 1971), p. 225.
4. N. Tinbergen, *The Herring Gull's World* (New York: Basic Books, 1961).

On Wolves

Barry Lopez

The Nunamiut are a seminomadic hunting society who lead lives similar to wolves'. They eat almost the same foods—caribou, some sheep and moose, berries, not much vegetable matter. The harsh environment requires of them both the same stamina, alertness, cooperativeness, self-assurance, and, possibly, sense of humor to survive. They often hunt caribou in the same way, anticipating caribou movement patterns and waiting at likely spots to ambush them.

Hunting in this country is hard and Eskimos respect a good hunter. In all the time he spent with them, Stephenson never heard Nunamiut say anything degrading or contemptuous about a wolf. They admire his skill as a hunter because they know how hard it is to secure game. In the collective years of tribal memory there are very few stories about wolves that starved to death. The Nunamiut, on the other hand, have starved to death. Some of them alive today have gone for a month or more on only scraps of dried meat, pieces of caribou hide, and water. It is neither a mystery, nor surprising to anyone but a white man who no longer hunts for his food, that the Nunamiut admire the wolf and emulate his ways. In the land they share, hunting among the same caribou herds, hunting as the wolf does has proved to be the most reliable way to put meat in your belly.

I would like to suggest that there is a correspondence between the worlds of these two hunters about which the reader should be both open-minded and critical. I will not try to prove that primitive hunting societies were socially or psychologically organized like wolves that lived in the same environment, though this may be close to the truth. What I am saying is this: we do not know very much at all about animals. We cannot understand them except in terms of our own needs and experiences. And to approach them solely in terms of the Western imagination is, really, to deny the animal. It behooves us to visit with a people with whom we share a planet and an interest in wolves but who themselves come from a different time-space and who, so far as we know, are very much closer to the wolf than we will ever be.

*

What, if anything, does this correspondence mean? I think it can mean almost everything if you are trying to fathom wolves.

It became clear to me one evening in a single question.

An old Nunamiut man was asked who, at the end of his life, knew more about the mountains and foothills of the Brooks Range near Anaktuvuk, an old man or an old wolf? Where and when to hunt, how to survive a blizzard or a year when the caribou didn't come? After a pause the man said, "The same. They know the same." The remark has special meaning for what it implies about wolves. It comes from a man who has had to negotiate in polar darkness and in whiteouts, when the world surrounding him was entirely without the one thing indispensable to a Western navigator—an edge. Anthropologist Edmund Carpenter has written of the extraordinary ability of polar Eskimos like the Aivilik to find their way about in a world that is often without horizon or actual points or objects for reference. What the Aivilik perceive is relationships, clusters of information that include what type of snow is underfoot, the direction and sound (against a parka ruff) of wind, any smells in the air, the contour of the landscape, the movement of animals, and so on. By constantly processing this information, the Aivilik knows where he is and where he is going. By implication, the Eskimo suggests that *the wolf does something similar.*

James Gibson, in a book called *The Perception of the Visual World*, wrote of not just one but thirteen kinds of depth perception. Most of us remain oblivious to such distinctions. We don't need them. The Eskimo does; if he is not aware of such things, he will not find his way home.

What Gibson and Carpenter together suggest is this: he who reads the landscape without the aid of maps as a matter of habit becomes as sophisticated of eye as it is popular to believe the bat is sophisticated of ear. The Eskimo, in other words, probably sees in a way that is more analogous to the way the wolf sees than Western man's way of seeing is.

If you are trying to fathom wolves, it is important to know how they might see. Maybe they see like Eskimos. And we can converse with Eskimos.

Recall the question asked of the old man. Who, at the end, knows more about the land—an old man or an old wolf?

*

Amaguk is like Nunamiut. He doesn't hunt when the weather is bad. He likes to play. He works hard to get food for his family. His hair starts to get white when he is old. Young wolves, just like Nunamiut, run around in shallow melt ponds scaring the ducks.

And Amaguk is tough, living at fifty below zero, through blizzards, for months without caribou. Like Nunamiut. Maybe tougher. And Amaguk is smart. He sets up ambushes for caribou. He sleeps high up on the ridges when there are humans around. He brings his pups to a kill but won't let them stay there alone. Grizzly bears. Young wolves do a lot of foolish things. Get killed.

Amaguk used to kill Nunamiut sometimes. Now Nunamiut can reach out and kill Amaguk from a distance with a rifle. Now Amaguk leaves Nunamiut alone.

Times change.

Amaguk and Nunamiut like caribou meat, know the good places for caribou hunting. Where ground squirrels are good. Where to get raspberries. A good place for getting away from mosquitoes. Where lupine blooms first in May. Where that big rock is that looks like achlack, the grizzly bear. Where the creeks are still running in August . . .

After a pause the old man looks up and say, "The same."

*

What aligns wolf and primitive hunter more strongly than anything else is that to live each must hunt and kill animals. In an area where both men and wolves hunt, they tend to hunt the same sorts of game. Given the same terrain, weather, food storage problems, and the fact that they are hunting the same prey, they tend to hunt in similar ways. The differences between them have more to do with the fact that one moves around on two feet and kills with such extensions of himself as bullets and arrows.

The Naskapi, a seminomadic hunting people of northeastern Canada, live out a hard life in a bleak and almost barren landscape. For centuries they· have hunted the same caribou herds the wolves have. I would like to turn to them now to illustrate some deeper ways in which wolf and human hunters are alike.

Here is the anthropologist Georg Henriksen writing about Naskapi hunters:

"On snowshoes, the hunters quickly shuffle away from camp carrying their rifles over their shoulders. The Naskapi walk at a fast and steady pace, keeping up the same speed hour after hour. When from a hilltop the men spot caribou some miles in the distance they set off at a brisk pace alternating between putting on their snowshoes when moving in deep snow, and removing them and hanging them over their rifle barrels as soon as they reach a hard and icy surface. No words are spoken. Half running, every man takes the wind, weather and every feature of the terrain into account and relates it to the position of the caribou. Suddenly one of the men stops and crouches, whistling low to the other men. He has seen the herd. Without a word the men scatter in different directions. No strategy is verbalized, but each man has made up his mind about the way in which the herd can best be tackled. Seeing the other men choose their directions, he acts accordingly."

Approach, observation, conservation of energy, and attack—it could not be more wolflike.

It is said of the wolf that he is a deliberate hunter, that he does not wander aimlessly around the landscape but knows pretty well where prey animals are, even when he can't see them. John Kelsall, a Canadian wildlife biologist, has seen wolves shortcutting cross-country in the taiga to intercept caribou two days ahead of them with almost pinpoint accuracy.

Again, Henriksen says of the Naskapi:

"The hunting grounds of the Naskapi do not teem with caribou. The Naskapi have to search for the animals, moving their camps and hunting over a wide range of country. In this search, they use their knowledge of the country and experience with the animals and their behavior under different circumstances. They take into account features of the terrain such as how hilly it is and whether it is forested or barren. They must consider the snow and ice conditions and relate them to the feeding and moving patterns of the caribou. They have theories about how other animals and insects such as wolves and warble flies affect the behavior of caribou. For example, when no caribou are found in an area where it was reckoned there would be plenty, they explain this by the presence of wolves. They said the caribou probably fled into the forest where the deep snow would keep the wolves at a distance.

"They make use of this knowledge and do not decide randomly where to search for caribou."

It does not require two men, any more than it takes two wolves, to kill one caribou, but the Naskapi are social hunters anyway. Even when they hunt alone they are social hunters, because whatever meat they get is shared. The social fabric of the Naskapi tribe is the result of an acknowledgment of dependence on each other for food. The young, the old, the sick, they cannot hunt. The social system of the Naskapi bestows prestige on the successful hunter; that is what is exchanged for meat. Each man hunts as he chooses, calling on personal skills, but with a single, overriding goal: to secure food. The individual ego is therefore both nurtured and submerged. A man's skills are praised, his food is eaten, his pride is reinforced.

I think a similar sense of social pressure and interdependence operates to hold a wolf pack together. Old wolves and young pups can eat only because the middle-aged wolves are good hunters. During rendezvous season the wolf, hungry himself, having eaten at the kill, returns home from ten miles away with a haunch of meat in his mouth. And he is besieged with as much affection as the successful Naskapi hunter is by *his* family. In this, perhaps more than anything else, we find a basis for alpha wolves—the hunters, whose prowess is encouraged for the sake of survival. Pack survival. . . .

*

I think, as the twentieth century comes to a close, that we are coming to an understanding of animals different from the one that has guided us for the past three hundred years. We have begun to see again, as our primitive ancestors did, that animals are neither imperfect imitations of men nor machines that can be described entirely in terms of endocrine secretions and neural impulses. Like us, they are genetically variable, and both the species and the individual are capable of unprecedented behavior. They are like us in the sense that we can

figuratively talk of them as beings some of whose forms, movements, activities, and social organizations are analogous, but they are no more literally like us than are trees. To paraphrase Henry Beston, they move in another universe, as complete as we are, both of us caught at a moment in mid-evolution.

I do not think it possible to define completely the sort of animals men require in order to live. They are always changing and are different for different peoples. Nor do I think it possible that science can by itself produce the animal entire. The range of the human mind, the scale and depth of the metaphors the mind is capable of manufacturing as it grapples with the universe, stand in stunning contrast to the belief that there is only one reality, which is man's, or worse, that only one culture among the many on earth possesses the truth.

To allow mystery, which is to say to yourself, "There could be more, there could be things we don't understand," is not to damn knowledge. It is to take a wider view. It is to permit yourself an extraordinary freedom: someone else does not have to be wrong in order that you may be right.

In the Western world, in the biological sciences, we have an extraordinary tool for discovery of knowledge about animals, together with a system for its classification; and through the existence of journals and libraries we have a system for its dissemination. But if we are going to learn more about animals—real knowledge, not more facts—we are going to have to get out into the woods. We are going to have to pay more attention to free-ranging as opposed to penned animals, which will require an unfamiliar patience. And we are going to have to find ways in which single, startling incidents in animal behavior, now discarded in the winnowing process of science's data assembly, can be preserved, can somehow be incorporated. And we are going to have to find a way, not necessarily to esteem, but at least not to despise intuition in the scientific process, for it is, as Kepler and Darwin and Einstein have said, the key.

The English philosopher Alfred North Whitehead, writing about human inquiry into the nature of the universe, said that in simply discussing the issues, the merest hint of dogmatic certainty is an exhibition of folly. This tolerance for mystery invigorates the imagination; and it is the imagination that gives shape to the universe.

The Case for Animal Rights

Tom Regan

I regard myself as an advocate of animal rights—as a part of the animal rights movement. That movement, as I conceive it, is committed to a number of goals, including:

1. the total abolition of the use of animals in science
2. the total dissolution of commercial animal agriculture
3. and the total elimination of commercial and sport hunting and trapping.

There are, I know, people who profess to believe in animal rights who do not avow these goals. Factory farming, they say, is wrong—violates animals' rights—but traditional animal agriculture is all right. Toxicity tests of cosmetics on animals violates their rights; but not important medical research—cancer research, for example. The clubbing of baby seals is abhorrent; but not the harvesting of adult seals. I used to think I understood this reasoning. Not any more. You don't change unjust institutions by tidying them up.

What's wrong—what's fundamentally wrong—with the way animals are treated isn't the details that vary from case to case. It's the whole system. The forlornness of the veal calf is pathetic—heart wrenching; the pulsing pain of the chimp with electrodes planted deep in her brain is repulsive; the slow, torturous death of the raccoon caught in the leg hold trap, agonizing. But what is fundamentally wrong isn't the pain, isn't the suffering, isn't the deprivation. These compound what's wrong. Sometimes—often—they make it much worse. But they are not the fundamental wrong.

The fundamental wrong is the system that allows us to view animals as *our resources*, here for us—to be eaten, or surgically manipulated, or put in our cross hairs for sport or money. Once we accept this view of animals—as our resources—the rest is as predictable as it is regrettable. Why worry about their loneliness, their pain, their death? Since animals exist for us, here to benefit us in one way or another, what harms them really doesn't matter—or matters only if it starts to bother us, makes us feel a trifle uneasy when we eat our veal scampi, for example. So, yes, let us get veal calves out of solitary confinement, give them more space, a little straw, a few companions. But let us keep our veal scampi.

But a little straw, more space, and a few companions don't eliminate—don't even touch—the fundamental wrong, the wrong that attaches to our viewing and treating these animals as our resources. A veal calf killed to be eaten after living in close confinement is viewed and treated in this way: but so, too, is another who is raised (as they say) "more humanely." To right the fundamental wrong of our treatment of farm animals requires more than making rearing methods "more human"—requires something quite different—requires the total dissolution of commercial animal agriculture.

How we do this—whether we do this, or as in the case of animals in science, whether and how we abolish their use—these are to a large extent political questions. People must change their beliefs before they change their habits. Enough people, especially those elected to public office, must believe in change—must want it—before we will have laws that protect the rights of animals. This process of change is very complicated, very demanding, very exhausting, calling for the efforts of many hands—in education, publicity, political organization and activity, down to the licking of envelopes and stamps. As a trained and practicing philosopher the sort of contribution I can make is limited, but, I like to think important. The currency of philosophy is ideas—their meaning and rational foundation—not the nuts and bolts of the legislative process, say, or the mechanics of community organization. That's what I have been exploring over the past ten years or so in my essays and talks and, more recently, in my book, *The Case for Animal Rights*.[1] I believe the major conclusions I reach in that book are true because they are supported by

In Defense of Animals, edited by Peter Singer. (Oxford: Basil Blackwell, Inc., 1985), pp. 13–26. Reprinted by permission.

the weight of the best arguments. I believe the idea of animal rights has reason, not just emotion, on its side.

In the space I have at my disposal here I can only sketch, in the barest outlines, some of the main features of the book. Its main themes—and we should not be surprised by this—involve asking and answering deep foundational moral questions, questions about what morality is, how it should be understood, what is the best moral theory all considered. I hope I can convey something of the shape I think this theory is. The attempt to do this will be—to use a word a friendly critic once used to describe my work—cerebral. In fact I was told by this person that my work is "too cerebral." But this is misleading. My feelings about how animals sometimes are treated are just as deep and just as strong as those of my more volatile compatriots. Philosophers do—to use the jargon of the day—have a right side to their brains. If it's the left side we contribute—or mainly should—that's because what talents we have reside there.

How to proceed? We begin by asking how the moral status of animals has been understood by thinkers who deny that animals have rights. Then we test the mettle of their ideas by seeing how well they stand up under the heat of fair criticism. If we start our thinking in this way we soon find that some people believe that we have no duties directly to animals—that we owe nothing *to them*—that we can do nothing that *wrongs them*. Rather, we can do wrong acts that involve animals, and so we have duties regarding them, though none to them. Such views may be called indirect duty views. By way of illustration:

Suppose your neighbor kicks your dog. Then your neighbor has done something wrong. But not to your dog. The wrong that has been done is a wrong to you. After all, it is wrong to upset people, and your neighbor's kicking your dog upsets you. So you are the one who is wronged, not your dog. Or again: by kicking your dog your neighbor damages your property. And since it is wrong to damage another person's property, your neighbor has done something wrong—to you, of course, not to your dog. Your neighbor no more wrongs your dog than your car would be wronged if the windshield were smashed. Your neighbor's duties involving your dog are indirect duties to you. More generally, all of our duties regarding animals are indirect duties to one another—to humanity.

How could someone try to justify such a view? One could say that your dog doesn't feel anything and so isn't hurt by your neighbor's kick, doesn't care about the pain since none is felt, is as unaware of anything as your windshield. Someone could say this but no rational person will since, among other considerations, such a view will commit one who holds it to the position that no human being feels pain either—that human beings also don't care about what happens to them. A second possibility is that though both humans and your dog are hurt when kicked, it is only human pain that matters. But, again, no rational person can believe this. Pain is pain wheresoever it occurs. If your neighbor's causing you pain is wrong because of the pain that is caused, we cannot rationally ignore or dismiss the moral relevance of the pain your dog feels.

Philosophers who hold indirect duty views— and many still do—have come to understand that they must avoid the two defects just noted—avoid, that is, both the view that animals don't feel anything as well as the idea that only human pain can be morally relevant. Among such thinkers the sort of view now favored is one or another form of what is called *contractarianism*.

Here, very crudely, is the root idea: morality consists of a set of rules that individuals voluntarily agree to abide by—as we do when we sign a contract (hence the name: contractarianism). Those who understand and accept the terms of the contract are covered directly—have rights created by, and recognized and protected in, the contract. And these contractors can also have protection spelled out for others who, though they lack the ability to understand morality and so cannot sign the contract themselves, are loved or cherished by those who can. Thus young children, for example, are unable to sign and lack rights. But they are protected by the contract nonetheless because of the sentimental interests of others, most notably their parents. So we have, then, duties involving these children, duties regarding them, but no duties to them. Our duties in their case are indirect duties to other human beings, usually their parents.

As for animals, since they cannot understand the contract, they obviously cannot sign; and since they cannot sign, they have no rights. Like children, however, some animals are the objects of the sentimental interest of others. You, for example, love your dog . . . or cat. So these animals—those enough people care about: companion animals, whales, baby seals, the American bald eagle—these animals, though they lack rights themselves, will be protected because of the sentimental interests of people. I have, then, according to contractarianism, no duty directly to your dog or any other animal, not even the duty not to cause them pain or suffering; my duty not to hurt them is a duty I have to those people who care about what happens to them. As for other animals, where no or little sentimental interest is present—farm animals, for example, or laboratory rats—what duties we have grow weaker and weaker, perhaps to the vanishing point. The pain and death they endure, though real, are not wrong if no one cares about them.

Contractarianism could be a hard view to refute when it comes to the moral status of animals if it was an adequate theoretical approach to the moral status of human beings. It is not adequate in this latter respect, however, which makes the question of its adequacy in the former—regarding animals—utterly moot. For consider: morality, according to the (crude) contractarian position before us, consists of rules people agree to abide by. What people? Well, enough to make a difference—enough, that is, so that collectively they have the power to enforce the rules that are drawn up in the contract. That is very well and good for the signatories—but not so good for anyone who is not asked to sign. And there is nothing in contractarianism of the sort we are discussing that guarantees or requires that everyone will have a chance to participate equitably in framing the rules of morality. The result is that this approach to ethics could sanction the most blatant forms of social, economic, moral, and political injustice, ranging from a repressive caste system to systematic racial or sexual discrimination. Might, on this theory, does make right. Let those who are the victims of injustice suffer as they will. It matters not so long as no one else—no contractor, or too few of them—cares about it. Such a theory takes one's moral breath away . . . as if, for example, there is nothing wrong with apartheid in South Africa if too few white South Africans are upset by it. A theory with so little to recommend it at the level of the ethics of our treatment of our fellow humans cannot have anything more to recommend it when it comes to the ethics of how we treat our fellow animals.

The version of contractarianism just examined is, as I have noted, a crude variety, and in fairness to those of a contractarian persuasion it must be noted that much more refined, subtle, and ingenious varieties are possible. For example, John Rawls, in his *A Theory of Justice,* sets forth a version of contractarianism that forces the contractors to ignore the accidental features of being a human being—for example, whether one is white or black, male or female, a genius or of modest intellect. Only by ignoring such features, Rawls believes, can we insure that the principles of justice contractors would agree upon are not based on bias or prejudice. Despite the improvement a view such as Rawls's shows over the cruder forms of contractarianism, it remains deficient: it systematically denies that we have direct duties to those human beings who do not have a sense of justice—young children, for instance, and many mentally retarded humans. And yet it seems reasonably certain that, were we to torture a young child or a retarded elder, we would be doing something that wrongs them, not something that is wrong if (and only if) other humans with a sense of justice are upset. And since this is true in the case of these humans, we cannot rationally deny the same in the case of animals.

Indirect duty views, then, including the best among them, fail to command our rational assent. Whatever ethical theory we rationally should accept, therefore, it must at least recognize that we have some duties directly to animals, just as we have some duties directly to each other. The next two theories I'll sketch attempt to meet this requirement.

The first I call the cruelty-kindness view. Simply stated, this view says that we have a direct duty to be kind to animals and a direct duty not to be cruel to them. Despite the familiar, reassuring ring of these ideas, I do not believe this view offers an adequate theory. To make this clearer, consider kindness. A kind person acts from a certain kind of motive—compassion or concern, for example. And that is a virtue. But there is no guarantee that a kind act is a right act. If I am a generous racist, for example, I will be inclined to act kindly toward members of my own race, favoring their interests above others. My kindness would be real and, so far as it goes, good. But I trust it is too obvious to require comment that my kind acts may not be above moral reproach—may, in fact, be positively wrong because rooted in injustice. So kindness, notwithstanding its status as a virtue to be encouraged, simply will not cancel the weight of a theory of right action.

Cruelty fares no better. People or their acts are cruel if they display either a lack of sympathy for or, worse, the presence of enjoyment in, seeing another suffer. Cruelty in all its guises *is* a bad thing—*is* a tragic human failing. But just as a person's being motivated by kindness does not guarantee that they do what is right, so the absence of cruelty does not assure that they avoid doing what is wrong. Many people who perform abortions, for example, are not cruel, sadistic people. But that fact about their character and motivation does not settle the terribly difficult question about the morality of abortion. The case is no different when we examine the ethics of our treatment of animals. So, yes, let us be for kindness and against cruelty. But let us not suppose that being for the one and against the other answers questions about moral right and wrong.

Some people think the theory we are looking for is utilitarianism. A utilitarian accepts two moral principles. The first is a principle of equality: everyone's interests count, and similar interests must be counted as having similar weight or importance. White or black, male or female, American or Iranian, human or animal: everyone's pain or frustration matter and matter equally with the like pain or frustration of anyone else. The second principle a utilitarian accepts is the principle of utility: do that act that will bring about the best balance of satisfaction over frustration for everyone affected by the outcome.

As a utilitarian, then, here is how I am to approach the task of deciding what I morally ought to do: I must ask who will be affected if I choose to do one thing rather than another, how much each individual will be affected, and where the best results are most likely to lie—which option, in other words, is most likely to bring about the best results, the best balance of satisfaction over frustration. That option, whatever it may be, is the one I ought to choose. That is where my moral duty lies.

The great appeal of utilitarianism rests with its uncompromising *egalitarianism:* everyone's interests count and count equally with the like interests of everyone else. The kind of odious discrimination some forms of contractarianism can justify—discrimination based on race or sex, for example—seems disallowed in principle by utilitarianism, as is speciesism—systematic discrimination based on species membership.

The sort of equality we find in utilitarianism,

however, is not the sort an advocate of animal or human rights should have in mind. Utilitarianism has no room for the equal moral rights of different individuals because it has no room for their equal inherent value or worth. What has value for the utilitarian is the satisfaction of an individual's interests, not the individual whose interests they are. A universe in which you satisfy your desire for water, food, and warmth, is, other things being equal, better than a universe in which these desires are frustrated. And the same is true in the case of an animal with similar desires. But neither you nor the animal have any value in your own right. Only your feelings do.

Here is an analogy to help make the philosophical point clearer: a cup contains different liquids—sometimes sweet, sometimes bitter, sometimes a mix of the two. What has value are the liquids: the sweeter the better, the bitter the worse. The cup—the container—has no value. It's what goes into it, not what they go into, that has value. For the utilitarian, you and I are like the cup; we have no value as individuals and thus no equal value. What has value is what goes into us, what we serve as receptacles for; our feelings of satisfaction have positive value, our feelings of frustration have negative value.

Serious problems arise for utilitarianism when we remind ourselves that it enjoins us to bring about the best consequences. What does this mean? it doesn't mean the best consequences for me alone, or for my family or friends, or any other person taken individually. No, what we must do is, roughly, as follows: we must add up—somehow!—the separate satisfactions and frustrations of everyone likely to be affected by our choice, the satisfactions in one column, the frustrations in the other. We must total each column for each of the options before us. That is what it means to say the theory is aggregative. And then we must choose that option which is most likely to bring about the best balance of totaled satisfactions over totaled frustrations. Whatever act would lead to this outcome is the one we morally ought to perform—is where our moral duty lies. And that act quite clearly might not be the same one that would bring about the best results for me personally, or my family or friends, or a lab animal. The best aggregated consequences for everyone concerned are not necessarily the best for each individual.

That utilitarianism is an aggregative theory—that different individual's satisfactions or frustrations are added, or summed, or totaled—is the key objection to this theory. My Aunt Bea is old, inactive, a cranky, sour person, though not physically ill. She prefers to go on living. She is also rather rich. I could make a fortune if I could get my hands on her money, money she intends to give me in any event, after she dies, but which she refuses to give me now. In order to avoid a huge tax bite, I plan to donate a handsome sum of my profits to a local children's hospital. Many, many children will benefit from my generosity, and much joy will be brought to their parents, relatives, and friends. If I don't get the money rather soon, all these ambitions will come to naught. The once-in-a-life-time-opportunity to make a real killing will be gone. Why, then, not really kill my Aunt Bea? Oh, of course I *might* get caught. But I'm no fool and, besides, her doctor can be counted on to cooperate (he has an eye for the same investment and I happen to know a good deal about his shady past). The deed can be done . . . professionally, shall we say. There is *very* little chance of getting caught. And as for my conscience being guilt ridden, I am a resourceful sort of fellow and will take more than sufficient comfort—as I lie on the beach at Acapulco—in contemplating the joy and health I have brought to so many others.

Suppose Aunt Bea is killed and the rest of the story comes out as told. Would I have done anything wrong? Anything immoral? One would have thought that I had. But not according to utilitarianism. Since what I did brought about the best balance of totaled satisfaction over frustration for all those affected by the outcome, what I did was not wrong. Indeed, in killing Aunt Bea the physician and I did what duty required.

This same kind of argument can be repeated in all sorts of cases, illustrating, time after time, how the utilitarian's position leads to results that impartial people find morally callous. It *is* wrong to kill my Aunt Bea in the name of bringing about the best results for others. A good end does not justify an evil means. Any adequate moral theory will have to explain why this is so. Utilitarianism fails in this respect and so cannot be the theory we seek.

What to do? Where to begin anew? The place to begin, I think, is with the utilitarian's view of the value of the individual—or, rather, lack of value. In its place suppose we consider that you and I, for example, do have value as individuals—what we'll call *inherent value*. To say we have such value is to say that we are something more than, something different from, mere receptacles. Moreover, to insure that we do not pave the way for such injustices as slavery or sexual discrimination, we must believe that all who have inherent value have it equally, regardless of their sex, race, religion, birthplace, and so on. Similarly to be discarded as irrelevant are one's talents or skills, intelligence and wealth, personality or pathology, whether one is loved and admired—or despised and loathed. The genius and the retarded child, the prince and the pauper, the brain surgeon and the fruit vendor, Mother Theresa and the most unscrupulous used car salesman—all have inherent value, all possess it equally, and all have an equal right to be treated with respect, to be treated in ways that do not reduce them to the status of things, as if they exist as resources for others. My value as an individual is independent of my usefulness to you. Yours is not dependent on your usefulness to me. For either of us to treat the other in ways that fail to show respect for the other's independent value is to act immorally—is to violate the individual's rights.

Some of the rational virtues of this view—what I call the rights view—should be evident. Unlike (crude) contractarianism, for example, the rights view *in principle* denies the moral tolerability of any and all forms of racial, sexual, or social discrimination; and unlike utilitarianism, this view *in principle* denies that we can justify good results by using evil means that violate an individual's rights—denies, for example, that it would be moral to kill my Aunt Bea to harvest beneficial consequences for others. That would be to sanction the disrespectful treatment of the individual in the name of the social good, something the rights view will not—categorically will not—ever allow.

The rights view—or so I believe—is rationally the most satisfactory moral theory. It surpasses all other theories in the degree to which it illuminates and explains the foundation of our duties to one another—the domain of human morality. On this score, it has the best reasons, the best arguments, on its side. Of course, if it were possible to show that only human beings are included within its scope, then a person like myself, who believes in animal rights, would be obliged to look elsewhere than to the rights view.

But attempts to limit its scope to humans only can be shown to be rationally defective. Animals, it is true, lack many of the abilities humans possess. They can't read, do higher mathematics, build a bookcase, or make *baba ghanoush*. Neither can many human beings, however, and yet we don't say—and shouldn't say—that they (these humans) therefore have less inherent value, less of a right to be treated with respect, than do others. It is the *similarities* between those human beings who most clearly, most noncontroversially have such value—the people reading this, for example—it is our similarities, not our differences that matter most. And the really crucial, the basic similarity is simply this; we are each of us the experiencing subject of a life, each of us a conscious creature having an individual welfare that has importance to us whatever our usefulness to others. We want and prefer things; believe and feel things; recall and expect things. And all these dimensions of our life, including our pleasure and pain, our enjoyment and suffering, our satisfaction and frustration, our continued existence or our untimely death—all make a difference to the quality of our life as lived, as experienced by us as individuals. As the same is true of those animals who concern us (those who are eaten and trapped, for example), they, too, must be viewed as the experiencing subjects of a life with inherent value of their own.

There are some who resist the idea that animals have inherent value. "Only humans have such value," they profess. How might this narrow view be defended? Shall we say that only humans have the requisite intelligence, or autonomy, or reason? But there are many, many humans who will fail to meet these standards and yet who are reasonably viewed as having value above and beyond their usefulness to others. Shall we claim that only humans belong to the right species—the species *Homo sapiens?* But this is blatant speciesism. Will it be said, then, that all—and only—humans have immortal souls? Then our opponents more than have their work cut out for them. I am myself not ill-disposed to there being immortal souls. Personally, I profoundly hope I have one. But I would not want to rest my position on a controversial ethical issue on the even more controversial question

about who or what has an immortal soul. That is to dig one's hole deeper, not climb out. Rationally, it is better to resolve moral issues without making more controversial assumptions than are needed. The question of who has inherent value is such a question, one that is more rationally resolved without the introduction of the idea of immortal souls than by its use.

Well, perhaps some will say that animals have some inherent value, only *less* than we do. Once again, however, attempts to defend this view can be shown to lack rational justification. What could be the basis of our having more inherent value than animals? Will it be their lack of reason, or autonomy, or intellect? Only if we are willing to make the same judgment in the case of humans who are similarly deficient. But it is not true that such humans—the retarded child, for example, or the mentally deranged—have less inherent value than you or I. Neither, then, can we rationally sustain the view that animals like them in being the experiencing subjects of a life have less inherent value. *All* who have inherent value have it *equally,* whether they be human animals or not.

Inherent value, then, belongs equally to those who are the experiencing subjects of a life. Whether it belongs to others—to rocks and rivers, trees and glaciers, for example—we do not know. And may never know. But neither do we need to know, if we are to make the case for animal rights. We do not need to know how many people, for example, are eligible to vote in the next presidential election before we can know whether I am. Similarly, we do not need to know *how many* individuals have inherent value before we can know that some do. When it comes to the case for animal rights, then what we need to know is whether the animals who, in our culture are routinely eaten, hunted, and used in our laboratories, for example, are like us in being subjects of a life. And we *do* know this. We do *know* that many—literally, billions and billions—of these animals are the subjects of a life in the sense explained and so have inherent value if we do. And since, in order to have the best theory of our duties to one another, we must recognize our equal inherent value, as individuals, reason—not sentiment, not emotion—reason compels us to recognize the equal inherent value of these animals. And, with this, their equal right to be treated with respect.

That, *very* roughly, is the shape and feel of the case for animal rights. Most of the details of the supporting argument are missing. They are to be found in the book I alluded to earlier. Here, the details go begging and I must in closing, limit myself to four final points.

The first is how the theory that underlies the case for animal rights shows that the animal rights movement is a part of, not antagonistic to, the human rights movement. The theory that rationally grounds the rights of animals also grounds the rights of humans. Thus are those involved in the animal rights movement partners in the struggle to secure respect for human rights—the rights of women, for example, or minorities and workers. The animal rights movement is cut from the same moral cloth as these.

Second, having set out the broad outlines of the rights view, I can now say why its implications for farming and science, for example, are both clear and uncompromising. In the case of using animals in science, the rights view is categorically abolitionist. Lab animals are not our tasters; we are not their kings. Because these animals are treated—routinely, systematically—as if their value is reducible to their usefulness to others, they are routinely, systematically treated with a lack of respect, and thus are their rights routinely, systematically violated. This is just as true when they are used in trivial, duplicative, unnecessary or unwise research as it is when they are used in studies that hold out real promise of human benefits. We can't justify harming or killing a human being (my Aunt Bea, for example) just for these sorts of reasons. Neither can we do so even in the case of so lowly a creature as a laboratory rat. It is not just refinement or reduction that are called for, not just larger, cleaner cages, not just more generous use of anaesthetic or the elimination of multiple surgery, not just tidying up the system. It is replacement—completely. The best we can do when it comes to using animals in science is—not to use them. That is where our duty lies, according to the rights view.

As for commercial animal agriculture, the rights view takes a similar abolitionist position. The fundamental moral wrong here is not that animals are kept in stressful close confinement, or in isolation, or that they have their pain and suffering, their needs and preferences ignored or discounted.

All these *are* wrong, of course, but they are not the fundamental wrong. They are symptoms and effects of the deeper, systematic wrong that allows these animals to be viewed and treated as lacking independent value, as resources for us—as, indeed, a renewable resource. Giving farm animals more space, more natural environments, more companions does not right the fundamental wrong, any more than giving lab animals more anaesthesia or bigger, clearer cages would right the fundamental wrong in their case. Nothing less than the total dissolution of commercial animal agriculture will do this, just as, for similar reasons I won't develop at length here, morality requires nothing less than the total elimination of commercial and sport hunting and trapping. The rights view's implications, then, as I have said, are clear—and are uncompromising.

My last two points are about philosophy—my profession. It is most obviously, no substitute for political action. The words I have written here and in other places by themselves don't change a thing. It is what we do with the thoughts the words express—our acts, our deeds—that change things. All that philosophy can do, and all I have attempted, is to offer a vision of what our deeds could aim at. And the why. But not the how.

Finally, I am reminded of my thoughtful critic, the one I mentioned earlier, who chastised me for being "too cerebral." Well, cerebral I have been: indirect duty views, utilitarianism, contractarianism—hardly the stuff deep passions are made of. I am also reminded, however, of the image another friend once set before me—the image of the ballerina as expressive of disciplined passion. Long hours of sweat and toil, of loneliness and practice, of doubt and fatigue; that is the discipline of her craft. But the passion is there, too; the fierce drive to excel, to speak through her body, to do it right, to pierce our minds. That is the image of philosophy I would leave with you; not "too cerebral," but *disciplined passion*. Of the discipline, enough has been seen. As for the passion:

There are times, and these are not infrequent, when tears come to my eyes when I see, or read, or hear of the wretched plight of animals in the hands of humans. Their pain, their suffering, their loneliness, their innocence, their death. Anger. Rage. Pity. Sorrow. Disgust. The whole creation groans under the weight of the evil we humans visit upon these mute, powerless creatures. It *is* our heart, not just our head, that calls for an end, that demands of us that we overcome, for them, the habits and forces behind their systematic oppression. All great movements, it is written, go through three stages: ridicule, discussion, adoption. It is the realization of this third stage—adoption—that demands both our passion and our discipline, our heart and our head. The fate of animals is in our hands. God grant we are equal to the task.

Note

1. Tom Regan, *The Case For Animal Rights* (Berkeley: University of California Press. 1983).

The Little Things That Run the World*

Edward O. Wilson

On the occasion of the opening of the remarkable new invertebrate exhibit of the National Zoological Park, let me say a word on behalf of these little things that run the world. To start, there are vastly more kinds of invertebrates than of vertebrates. At the present time, on the basis of the tabulation that I have just completed (from the literature and with the help of specialists), I estimate that a total of 42,580 vertebrate species have been described, of which 6,300 are reptiles, 9,040 are birds, and 4,000 are mammals. In contrast, 990,000 species of invertebrates have been described, of which 290,000 alone are beetles—seven times the number of all the vertebrates together. Recent estimates have placed the number of invertebrates on the earth as high as 30 million, again mostly beetles—although many other taxonomically comparable groups of insects and other invertebrates also greatly outnumber vertebrates.

We don't know with certainty why invertebrates are so diverse, but a commonly held opinion is that the key trait is their small size. Their niches are correspondingly small, and they can therefore divide up the environment into many more little domains where specialists can coexist. One of my favorite examples of such specialists living in microniches are the mites that live on the bodies of army ants: one kind is found only on the mandibles of the soldier caste, where it sits and feeds from the mouth of its host; another kind is found only on the hind foot of the soldier caste, where it sucks blood for a living; and so on through various bizarre configurations.

Another possible cause of invertebrate diversity is the greater antiquity of these little animals, giving them more time to explore and fill the environment. The first invertebrates appeared well back into Precambrian times, at least 600 million years ago. Most invertebrate phyla were flourishing before the vertebrates arrived on the scene, some 500 million years ago.

Invertebrates also rule the earth by virtue of sheer body mass. For example, in tropical rain forest near Manaus, in the Brazilian Amazon, each hectare (or 2.5 acres) contains a few dozen birds and mammals but well over one billion invertebrates, of which the vast majority are not beetles this time but mites and springtails. There are about 200 kilograms dry weight of animal tissue in a hectare, of which 93 percent consists of invertebrates. The ants and termites alone compose one-third of this biomass. So when you walk through a tropical forest, or most other terrestrial habitats for that matter, or snorkel above a coral reef or some other marine or aquatic environment, vertebrates may catch your eye most of the time—biologists would say that your search image is for large animals—but you are visiting a primarily invertebrate world.

It is a common misconception that vertebrates are the movers and shakers of the world, tearing the vegetation down, cutting paths through the forest, and consuming most of the energy. That may

Address given at the opening of the invertebrate exhibit, National Zoological Park, Washington, D.C., on May 7, 1987.

Conservation Biology, Vol. 1, No. 4 (December 1987), pp. 344–346. Reprinted by permission of Blackwell Scientific Publications, Inc., and the Society for Conservation Biology.

be true in a few ecosystems such as the grasslands of Africa with their great herds of herbivorous mammals. It has certainly become true in the last few centuries in the case of our own species, which now appropriates in one form or other as much as 50 percent of the solar energy captured by plants. That circumstance is what makes us so dangerous to the fragile environment of the world. But it is otherwise more nearly true in most parts of the world of the invertebrates rather than the nonhuman vertebrates. The leafcutter ants, for example, rather than deer, or rodents, or birds, are the principal consumers of vegetation in Central and South America. A single colony contains over two million workers. It sends out columns of foragers a hundred meters or more in all directions to cut forest leaves, flower parts, and succulent stems. Each day a typical mature colony collects about 50 kilograms of this fresh vegetation, more than the average cow. Inside the nest, the ants shape the material into intricate sponge-like bodies on which they grow a symbiotic fungus. The fungus thrives as it breaks down and consumes the cellulose, while the ants thrive by eating the fungus.

The leafcutting ants excavate vertical galleries and living chambers as deep as 5 meters into the soil. They and other kinds of ants, as well as bacteria, fungi, termites, and mites, process most of the dead vegetation and return its nutrients to the plants to keep the great tropical forests alive.

Much the same situation exists in other parts of the world. The coral reefs are built out of the bodies of coelenterates. The most abundant animals of the open sea are copepods, tiny crustaceans forming part of the plankton. The mud of the deep sea is home to a vast array of mollusks, crustaceans, and other small creatures that subsist on the fragments of wood and dead animals that drift down from the lighted areas above, and on each other.

The truth is that we need invertebrates but they don't need us. If human beings were to disappear tomorrow, the world would go on with little change. Gaia, the totality of life on earth, would set about healing itself and return to the rich environmental states of a few thousand years ago. But if invertebrates were to disappear, I doubt that the human species could last more than a few months. Most of the fishes, amphibians, birds, and mammals would crash to extinction about the same time. Next would go the bulk of the flowering plants and with them the physical structure of the majority of the forests and other terrestrial habitats of the world. The earth would rot. As dead vegetation piled up and dried out, narrowing and closing the channels of the nutrient cycles, other complex forms of vegetation would die off, and with them the last remnants of the vertebrates. The remaining fungi, after enjoying a population explosion of stupendous proportions, would also perish. Within a few decades the world would return to the state of a billion years ago, composed primarily of bacteria, algae, and a few other very simple multicellular plants.

If humanity depends so completely on these little creatures that run the earth, they also provide us with an endless source of scientific exploration and naturalistic wonder. When you scoop up a double handful of earth almost anywhere except the most barren deserts, you will find thousands of invertebrate animals, ranging in size from clearly visible to microscopic, from ants and springtails to tardigrades and rotifers. The biology of most of the species you hold is unknown: we have only the vaguest idea of what they eat, what eats them, and the details of their life cycle, and probably nothing at all about their biochemistry and genetics. Some of the species might even lack scientific names. We have little concept of how important any of them are to our existence. Their study would certainly teach us new principles of science to the benefit of humanity. Each one is fascinating in its own right. If human beings were not so impressed by size alone, they would consider an ant more wonderful than a rhinoceros.

New emphasis should be placed on the conservation of invertebrates. Their staggering abundance and diversity should not lead us to think that they are indestructible. On the contrary, their species are just as subject to extinction due to human interference as are those of birds and mammals. When a valley in Peru or an island in the Pacific is stripped of the last of its native vegetation, the result is likely to be the extinction of several kinds of birds and some dozen of plant species. Of that tragedy we are painfully aware, but what is not perceived is that hundreds of invertebrate species will also vanish.

The conservation movement is at last beginning to take recognition of the potential loss of invertebrate diversity. The International Union for the Conservation of Nature has an ongoing invertebrate program that has already published a Red Data Book of threatened and endangered species—although this catalog is obviously still woefully incomplete. The Xerces Society, named after an extinct California butterfly, was created in 1971 to further the protection of butterflies and other invertebrates. These two programs are designed to complement the much larger organized efforts of other organizations on behalf of vertebrates and plants. They will help to expand programs to encompass entire ecosystems instead of just selected star species. The new invertebrate exhibition of the National Zoological Park is one of the most promising means for raising public appreciation of invertebrates, and I hope such exhibits will come routinely to include rare and endangered species identified prominently as such.

Several themes can be profitably pursued in the new field of invertebrate conservation:

- It needs to be repeatedly stressed that invertebrates as a whole are even more important in the maintenance of ecosystems than are vertebrates.

- Reserves for invertebrate conservation are practicable and relatively inexpensive. Many species can be maintained in large, breeding populations in areas too small to sustain viable populations of vertebrates. A 10-ha plot is likely to be enough to sustain a butterfly or crustacean species indefinitely. The same is true for at least some plant species. Consequently, even if just a tiny remnant of natural habitat exists, and its native vertebrates have vanished, it is still worth setting aside for the plants and invertebrates it will save.

- The *ex situ* preservation of invertebrate species is also very cost-effective. A single pair of rare mammals typically costs hundreds or thousands of dollars yearly to maintain in a zoo (and worth every penny!). At the same time, large numbers of beautiful tree snails, butterflies, and other endangered invertebrates can be cultured in the laboratory, often in conjunction with public exhibits and educational programs, for the same price.

- It will be useful to concentrate biological research and public education on star species when these are available in threatened habitats, in the manner that has proved so successful in vertebrate conservation. Examples of such species include the tree snails of Moorea, Hawaii, and the Florida Keys; the Prairie sphinx moth of the Central States; the birdwing butterflies of New Guinea; and the metallic blue and golden ants of Cuba.

- We need to launch a major effort to measure biodiversity, to create a complete inventory of all the species of organisms on Earth, and to assess their importance for the environment and humanity. Our museums, zoological parks, and arboreta deserve far more support than they are getting—for the future of our children.

A hundred years ago few people thought of saving any kind of animal or plant. The circle of concern has expanded steadily since, and it is just now beginning to encompass the invertebrates. For reasons that have to do with almost every facet of human welfare, we should welcome this new development.

Sidelight: Parachuting Cats and Interconnectedness

One need not believe that we are "all one," or that there are not significant differences between people and their environments, to recognize the incredible mutual interdependence among many living creatures or between systems of life. Indeed, much contemporary discussion is flawed by the tacit assumption that there is much less dependence than, in fact, exists.

It is frequently tempting to ask, "What does that have to do with me?" "So what; what difference does that make?" Paul and Anne Ehrlich tell of the spraying of DDT in Borneo in order to kill houseflies. Someone must have thought that the costs and benefits made doing so worthwhile. Leading animal rights theorists do not attribute rights to houseflies.[1] The gecko lizards ate the houseflies and died. Then house cats ate the dying lizards, and there were fewer house cats. Rats found the situation more agreeable, but they brought bubonic plague. And humans did not find this situation at all agreeable. In short, the houseflies were part of a food chain and the disturbance of that chain had a profound impact on some members of *Homo sapiens*. To try to remedy the problem, the government of Borneo parachuted cats into the area. We often leap at technological solutions without careful estimation of the long-term, possibly unknown, effects of their adoption. There is no need for one to be either protechnology or antitechnology. Some innovations are wonderful, as far as we can tell, but some turn out to be a witches' brew. In many cases there is certainly no evil intent on the part of the inventors or developers of technology. In the best of cases, a scientist wishes to make life better for all; the worst cases are marked by recklessness or out and out indifference to the well-being of others, mixed perhaps with a measure of self-deception. In many cases what generated risky or extremely risky consequences were the collective actions of millions of people who sought to carry on, or achieve, a happy existence. The creation of CFCs (chlorofluorocarbons), for example, was part of an effort to find effective means of cooling, and their use in refrigerators and automobile air-conditioning systems improved the lives of millions. The goal was admirable. The means seemed perfectly innocent, indeed a brilliant solution and another occasion to salute the "wonders" of modern science. And the developers could make a profit. The situation seemed, like many others, to involve no losers. But then we began to learn the effects of CFCs on the ozone layer. This layer of ozone is about 12 to 20 miles up in the stratosphere and protects life from the harmful effects of certain ultraviolet rays of the sun (the UV-B rays). Aside from their capacity to alter genetic material deep within human cells and cause skin cancer (in Australia, with greater exposure to these rays, two out of three people get some form of this cancer), these rays seem to have harmful effects on phytoplankton, tiny creatures that tend to inhabit the upper few feet of the ocean. It is just here that one tends to engage in the knee-jerk reaction "so what?" or "who cares?" We must think about the fact that small fish survive on a diet of phytoplankton, and larger fish and other forms of sea life survive by eating the smaller ones. We make no final estimate of the prospective danger that we and other forms of life may face, but millions and millions of people depend on the existence of sea creatures. Nevertheless, the introduction of CFCs (whose effects in eroding the ozone layer will be felt throughout the 21st century even if their production is phased out by 1995) may have catastrophic consequences beyond those associated with cancer and cataracts— largely because of our ignorance, our lack of caution, and our bravado in our ability to manipulate nature. Similarly, we produced dangerous amounts of nuclear wastes on the assumption that our political leaders and world-class scientists would devise a means of dealing with them at some point. In poker they say that one should not bid to an inside straight.

Note

1. For example, Tom Regan in *The Case for Animal Rights* holds that at least animals which are "subjects of a life" have rights (for starters, mammals over one year of age). He leaves it an open question whether other creatures do.

Beyond Ethics by Extension*

Holmes Rolston III

Environmental ethics stretches classical ethics to the breaking point. All ethics seeks an appropriate respect for life. But we do not need just a humanistic ethic applied to the environment as we have needed one for business, law, medicine, technology, international development, or nuclear disarmament. Respect for life does demand an ethic concerned about human welfare, an ethic like the others and now applied to the environment. But environmental ethics in a deeper sense stands on a frontier, as radically theoretical as it is applied. It alone asks whether there can be nonhuman objects of duty.

Neither theory nor practice elsewhere needs values outside of human subjects, but environmental ethics must be more biologically objective—nonanthropocentric. It challenges the separation of science and ethics, trying to reform a science that finds nature value-free and an ethics that assumes that only humans count morally. Environmental ethics seeks to escape relativism in ethics, to discover a way past culturally based ethics. However much our world views, ethics included, are embedded in our cultural heritages, and thereby theory-laden and value-laden, all of us know that a natural world exists apart from human cultures. Humans interact with nature. Environmental ethics is the only ethics that breaks out of culture. It has to evaluate nature, both wild nature and the nature that mixes with culture, and to judge duty thereby. After accepting environmental ethics, you will no longer be the humanist you once were.

Environmental ethics requires risk. It explores poorly charted terrain, where one can easily get lost. One must hazard the kind of insight that first looks like foolishness. Some people approach environmental ethics with a smile—expecting chicken liberation and rights for rocks, misplaced concern for chipmunks and daisies. Elsewhere, they think, ethicists deal with sober concerns: medical ethics, business ethics, justice in public affairs, questions of life and death and of peace and war. But the questions here are no less serious: The degradation of the environment poses as great a threat to life as nuclear war, and a more probable tragedy.

Higher Animals

Logically and psychologically, the best and easiest breakthrough past the traditional boundaries of interhuman ethics is made when confronting higher animals. Animals defend their lives; they have a good of their own and suffer pains and pleasures like ourselves. Human moral concern should at least cross over into the domain of animal experience. This boundary crossing is also dangerous because if made only psychologically and not biologically, the would-be environmental ethicist may be too disoriented to travel further. The promised environmental ethics will degenerate into a mammalian ethics. We certainly need an ethic for animals, but that is only one level of concern in a comprehensive environmental ethics.

One might expect classical ethics to have sifted well an ethics for animals. Our ancestors did not think about endangered species, ecosystems, acid rain, or the ozone layer, but they lived in closer association with wild and domestic animals than we do. Hunters track wounded deer; ranchers who let their horses starve are prosecuted. Still, until recently, the scientific, humanistic centuries since the so-called Enlightenment have not been sensitive ones for animals, owing to the Cartesian legacy. Animals were mindless, living matter; biology has been mechanistic. Even psychology, rather than defending animal experience, has been behaviorist.

*The title is due to the editors; it refers to the first portion of Rolston's essay "Environmental Ethics: Values in and Duties to the Natural World." The latter portion is reprinted in this volume as well under the title "Why Species Matter" in Part VI-C, "Preserving Biodiversity." Readers may wish to pursue it straight through.

"Environmental Ethics: Values in and Duties to the Natural World," by Holmes Rolston III, in *Ecology, Economics, Ethics: The Broken Circle*, edited by F. Herbert Bormann and Stephen R. Kellert (New Haven: Yale University Press, 1991), pp. 73–82. Reprinted by permission.

Philosophy has protested little, concerned instead with locating values in human experiences at the same time that it dispirited and devalued nature. Across several centuries of hard science and humanistic ethics there has been little compassion for animals.

The progress of science itself smeared the human-nonhuman boundary line. Animal anatomy, biochemistry, cognition, perception, experience, behavior, and evolutionary history are kin to our own. Animals have no immortal souls, but then persons may not either, or beings with souls may not be the only kind that count morally. Ethical progress further smeared the boundary. Sensual pleasures are a good thing; ethics should be egalitarian, nonarbitrary, nondiscriminatory. There are ample scientific grounds that animals enjoy pleasures and suffer pains; and ethically there are no grounds to value these sensations in humans and not in animals. So there has been a vigorous reassessment of human duties to sentient life. The world cheered in the fall of 1988 when humans rescued two whales from winter ice.

"Respect their right to life": A sign in Rocky Mountain National Park enjoins humans not to harass bighorn sheep. "The question is not, Can they reason, nor Can they talk? but, Can they suffer?" wrote Jeremy Bentham (1948 [1789]), insisting that animal welfare counts too. The Park Service sign and Bentham's question increase sensitivity by extending rights and hedonist goods to animals. The gain is a vital breakthrough past humans, and the first lesson in environmental ethics has been learned. But the risk is a moral extension that expands rights as far as mammals and not much further, a psychologically based ethic that counts only felt experience. We respect life in our nonhuman but near-human animal cousins, a semianthropic and still quite subjective ethics. Justice remains a concern for just-us subjects. There has, in fact, not been much of a theoretical breakthrough, no paradigm shift.

Lacking that, we are left with anomaly and conceptual strain. When we try to use culturally extended rights and psychologically based utilities to protect the flora or even the insentient fauna, to protect endangered species or ecosystems, we can only stammer. Indeed, we get lost trying to protect bighorns, because, in the wild, cougars are not respecting the rights or utilities of the sheep they slay,

and, in culture, humans slay sheep and eat them regularly, while humans have every right not to be eaten by either humans or cougars. There are no rights in the wild, and nature is indifferent to the welfare of particular animals. A bison fell through the ice into a river in Yellowstone Park; the environmental ethic there, letting nature take its course, forbade would-be rescuers from either saving or killing the suffering animal to put it out of its misery. A drowning human would have been saved at once. Perhaps it was a mistake to save those whales.

The ethics by extension now seems too nondiscriminating; we are unable to separate an ethics for humans from an ethics for wildlife. To treat wild animals with compassion learned in culture does not appreciate their wildness. Man, said Socrates, is the political animal; humans maximally are what they are in culture, where the natural selection pressures (impressively productive in ecosystems) are relaxed without detriment to the species *Homo sapiens,* and indeed with great benefit to its member persons. Wild animals cannot enter culture; they do not have that capacity. They cannot acquire language at sufficient levels to take part in culture; they cannot make their clothing or build fires, much less read books or receive an education. Animals can, by human adoption, receive some of the protections of culture, which happens when we domesticate them, but neither pets nor food animals enter the culture that shelters them.

Worse, such cultural protection can work to their detriment; their wildness is made over into a human artifact as food or pet animal. A cow does not have the integrity of a deer, or a poodle that of a wolf. Culture is a good thing for humans but often a bad thing for animals. Their biology and ecology—neither justice nor charity, nor rights nor welfare—provide the benchmark for an ethics.

Culture does make a relevant ethical difference, and environmental ethics has different criteria from interhuman ethics. Can they talk? and, Can they reason?—indicating cultural capacities—are relevant questions; not just, Can they suffer? *Equality* is a positive word in ethics, *discriminatory* a pejorative one. On the other hand, simplistic reduction is a failing in the philosophy of science and epistemology; to be "discriminating" is desirable in logic and value theory. Something about treating humans as equals with bighorns and cougars seems to "reduce" humans to merely animal levels of value, a "no more than" counterpart in ethics of the "nothing but" fallacy often met in science. Humans are "nothing but" naked apes. Something about treating sheep and cougars as the equals of humans seems to elevate them unnaturally and not to value them for what they are. There is something insufficiently discriminating in such judgments; they are species-blind in a bad sense, blind to the real differences between species, valuational differences that do count morally. To the contrary, a discriminating ethicist will insist on preserving the differing richness of valuational complexity, wherever found. Compassionate respect for life in its suffering is only part of the analysis.

Two tests of discrimination are pains and diet. It might be thought that pain is a bad thing, whether in nature or culture. Perhaps when dealing with humans in culture, additional levels of value and utility must be protected by conferring rights that do not exist in the wild, but meanwhile we should at least minimize animal suffering. That is indeed a worthy imperative in culture where animals are removed from nature and bred, but it may be misguided where animals remain in ecosystems. When the bighorn sheep of Yellowstone caught pinkeye, they were blinded, injured, and starving as a result, and three hundred of them, more than half the herd, perished. Wildlife veterinarians wanted to treat the disease, as they would have in any domestic herd, and as they did with Colorado bighorns infected with an introduced lungworm, but the Yellowstone ethicists left the animals to suffer, seemingly not respecting their life.

Had those ethicists no mercy? They knew rather that, although intrinsic pain is a bad thing whether in humans or in sheep, pain in ecosystems is instrumental pain, through which the sheep are naturally selected for a more satisfactory adaptive fit. Pain in a medically skilled culture is pointless, once the alarm to health is sounded, but pain operates functionally in bighorns in their niche, even after it becomes no longer in the interests of the pained individual. To have interfered in the interests of the blinded sheep would have weakened the species. Even the question, Can they suffer? is not as simple as Bentham thought. What we ought to do depends on what is. The *is* of nature differs significantly from the *is* of culture, even when similar suffering is present in both.

At this point some ethicists will insist that at least in culture we can minimize animal pain, and that will constrain our diet. There is predation in nature; humans evolved as omnivores. But humans, the only moral animals, should refuse to participate in the meat-eating phase of their ecology, just as they refuse to play the game merely by the rules of natural selection. Humans do not look to the behavior of the wild animals as an ethical guide in other matters (marriage, truth telling, promise keeping, justice, charity). Why should they justify their dietary habits by watching what animals do?

But the difference is that these other matters are affairs of culture; these are person-to-person events, not events at all in spontaneous nature. By contrast, eating is omnipresent in wild nature; humans eat because they are in nature, not because they are in culture. Eating animals is not an event between persons but a human-to-animal event; and the rules for this act come from the ecosystems in which humans evolved and have no duty to remake. Humans, then, can model their dietary habits from their ecosystems, though they cannot and should not so model their interpersonal justice or charity. When eating, they ought to minimize animal suffering, but they have no duty to revise trophic pyramids whether in nature or culture. The boundary between animals and humans has not been rubbed out after all; only what was a boundary line has been smeared into a boundary zone. We have discovered that animals count morally, though we have not yet solved the challenge of how to count them.

Animals enjoy psychological lives, subjective experiences, the satisfaction of felt interests—intrinsic values that count morally when humans encounter them. But the pains, pleasures, interests, and welfare of individual animals are only one of the considerations in a more complex environmental ethics that cannot be reached by conferring rights on them or by a hedonist calculus, however far extended. We have to travel further into a more biologically based ethics.

Organisms

If we are to respect all life, we have still another boundary to cross, from zoology to botany, from sentient to insentient life. In Yosemite National Park for almost a century humans entertained themselves by driving through a tunnel cut in a giant sequoia. Two decades ago the Wawona tree, weakened by the cut, blew down in a storm. People said, "Cut us another drive-through sequoia." The Yosemite environmental ethic, deepening over the years, answered, "No. You ought not to mutilate majestic sequoias for amusement. Respect their life." Indeed, some ethicists count the value of redwoods so highly that they will spike redwoods, lest they be cut. In the Rawah Wilderness in alpine Colorado, old signs read, "Please leave the flowers for others to enjoy." When the signs rotted out, new signs urged a less humanist ethic: "Let the flowers live!"

But trees and flowers cannot care, so why should we? We are not considering animals that are close kin, nor can they suffer or experience anything. Plants are not valuers with preferences that can be satisfied or frustrated. It seems odd to assert that plants need our sympathy, odd to ask that we should consider their point of view. They have no subjective life, only objective life.

Perhaps the questions are wrong, because they are coming out of the old paradigm. We are at a critical divide. That is why I earlier warned that environmental ethicists who seek only to extend a humanistic ethic to mammalian cousins will get lost. Seeing no moral landmarks, those ethicists may turn back to more familiar terrain. Afraid of the naturalistic fallacy, they will say that people should enjoy letting flowers live or that it is silly to cut drive-through sequoias, that it is aesthetically more excellent for humans to appreciate both for what they are. But these ethically conservative reasons really do not understand what biological conservation is in the deepest sense.

It takes ethical courage to go on, to move past a hedonistic, humanistic logic to a bio-logic. Pains, pleasures, and psychological experience will no further be useful categories, but—lest some think that from here on I as a philosopher become illogical and lose all ethical sense—let us orient ourselves by extending logical, propositional, cognitive, and normative categories into biology. Nothing matters to a tree, but much is vital to it.

An organism is a spontaneous, self-maintaining system, sustaining and reproducing itself, executing its program, making a way through the world, checking against performance by means of responsive capacities with which to measure success. It can reckon with vicissitudes, opportunities, and adversities that the world presents. Something more than physical causes, even when less than sentience, is operating within every organism. There is information superintending the causes; without it, the organism would collapse into a sand heap. This information is a modern equivalent of what Aristotle called formal and final causes; it gives the organisms a telos, or end, a kind of (nonfelt) goal. Organisms have ends, although not always ends in view.

All this cargo is carried by the DNA, essentially a linguistic molecule. By a serial reading of the DNA, a polypeptide chain is synthesized, such that its sequential structure determines the bioform into which it will fold. Ever-lengthening chains are organized into genes, as ever-longer sentences are organized into paragraphs and chapters. Diverse proteins, lipids, carbohydrates, enzymes—all the life structures—are written into the genetic library. The DNA is thus a logical set, not less than a biological set, and is informed as well as formed. Organisms use a sort of symbolic logic, using these molecular shapes as symbols of life. The novel resourcefulness lies in the epistemic content conserved, developed, and thrown forward to make biological resources out of the physicochemical sources. This executive steering core is cybernetic—partly a special kind of cause-and-effect system and partly something more. It is partly a historical information system discovering and evaluating ends so as to map and make a way through the world, and partly a system of significances attached to operations, pursuits, and resources. In this sense, the genome is a set of conservation molecules.

The genetic set is really a propositional set—to choose a provocative term—recalling that the Latin *propositum* is an assertion, a set task, a theme, a plan, a proposal, a project, as well as a cognitive statement. From this, it is also a motivational set, unlike human books, because these life motifs are set to drive the movement from genotypic potential to phenotypic expression. Given a chance, these molecules seek organic self-expression. They thus proclaim a lifeway; and with this an organism, unlike an inert rock, claims the environment as source and sink, from which to abstract energy and materials and into which to excrete them. It takes advantage of its environment. Life thus arises out of earthen sources (as do rocks), but life (unlike rocks) turns back on its sources to make resources out of them. An acorn becomes an oak; the oak stands on its own.

So far we have only description. We begin to pass to value when we recognize that the genetic set is a normative set; it distinguishes between what is and what ought to be. This does not mean that the organism is a moral system, for there are no moral agents in nature; but the organism is an axiological, evaluative system. So the oak grows, reproduces, repairs its wounds, and resists death. The physical state that the organism seeks, idealized in its programmatic form, is a valued state. Value is present in this achievement. *Vital* seems a better word here than *biological*. We are dealing not simply with another individual defending its solitary life but with an individual having situated fitness in an ecosystem. Still, we want to affirm that the living individual, taken as a point-experience in the web of interconnected life, is per se an intrinsic value.

A life is defended for what it is in itself, without necessary further contributory reference, although, given the structure of all ecosystems, such lives necessarily do have further contributory reference. The organism has something it is conserving, something for which it is standing: its life. Though organisms must fit into their niche, they have their own standards. They promote their own realization, at the same time that they track an environment. They have a technique, a know-how. Every organism has a good of its kind; it defends its own kind as a good kind. In that sense, as soon as one knows what a giant sequoia tree is, one knows the biological identity that is sought and conserved.

There seems no reason why such own-standing normative organisms are not morally significant. A moral agent deciding his or her behavior ought to take account of the consequences for other evaluative systems. Within the community of moral agents, one has not merely to ask whether x is a normative system but also, because the norms are at personal option, to judge the norm. But within the biotic community, organisms are amoral normative systems, and there are no cases in which an organism seeks a good of its own that is morally reprehensible. The distinction between having a good of its kind and being a good kind vanishes, so far as any faulting of the organism if concerned. To this extent, everything with a good of its kind is a good kind and thereby has intrinsic value.

One might say that an organism is a bad organism if, during the course of pressing its normative expression, it upsets the ecosystem or causes widespread disease. Remember, though, that an organism cannot be a good kind without situated environmental fitness. By natural selection the kind of goods to which it is genetically programmed must mesh with its ecosystemic role. In spite of the ecosystem as a perpetual contest of goods in dialectic and exchange, it is difficult to say that any organism is a bad kind in this instrumental sense either. The misfits are extinct, or soon will be. In spontaneous nature any species that preys upon, parasitizes, competes with, or crowds another will be a bad kind from the narrow perspective of its victim or competitor.

But if we enlarge that perspective, we typically have difficulty in saying that any species is a bad kind overall in the ecosystem. An "enemy" may even be good for the "victimized" species, though harmful to indivdual members of it, as when predation keeps the deer herd healthy. Beyond this, the "bad kinds" typically play useful roles in population control, in symbiotic relationships, or in providing opportunities for other species. The *Chlamydia* microbe is a bad kind from the perspective of the bighorns, but when one thing dies, something else lives. After the pinkeye outbreak among the bighorns, the golden eagle population in Yellowstone flourished, preying on the bighorn carcasses. For the eagles, *Chlamydia* is a good kind instrumentally.

Some biologist-philosophers will say that even though an organism evolves to have a situated environmental fitness, not all such situations are good arrangements; some can be clumsy or bad. True, the vicissitudes of historical evolution do sometimes result in ecological webs that are suboptimal solutions within the biologically limited possibilities and powers of interacting organisms. Still, such systems have been selected over millennia for functional stability, and at least the burden of proof is on a human evaluator to say why any natural kind is a bad kind and ought not to call forth admiring respect. Something may be a good kind intrinsically but a bad kind instrumentally in the system; such cases will be anomalous however, with selection pressures against them. These assertions about good kinds do not say that things are perfect kinds or that there can be no better ones, only that natural kinds are good kinds until proven otherwise.

In fact, what is almost invariably meant by a bad kind is an organism that is instrumentally bad when judged form the viewpoint of human interests, often with the further complication that human interests have disrupted natural systems. *Bad* as so used is an anthropocentric word; there is nothing at all biological or ecological about it, and so it has no force in evaluating objective nature, however much humanistic force it may sometimes have.

A vital ethic respects all life, not just animal pains and pleasures, much less just human preferences. The old signs in the Rawah Wilderness— "Please leave the flowers for others to enjoy"— were application signs using an old, ethically conservative, humanistic ethic. The new ones invite a change of reference frame—a wilder ethic that is more logical because it is more biological, a radical ethic that goes down to the roots of life, that really is conservative because it understands biological conservation at depths. What the injunction "Let the flowers live!" means is this: "Daisies, marsh marigolds, geraniums, and larkspurs are evaluative systems that conserve goods of their kind and, in the absence of evidence to the contrary, are good kinds. There are trails here by which you may enjoy these flowers. Is there any reason why your human interests should not also conserve these good kinds?" A drive-through sequoia causes no suffering; it is not cruel. But it is callous and insensitive to the wonder of life.

IV

CONSTRUCTING AN ⸻⸻⸻⸻⸻⸻⸻⸻⸻⸻ ENVIRONMENTAL ETHIC

A. The Broader, Biotic Community ⸻⸻⸻⸻⸻⸻⸻⸻⸻⸻⸻⸻

PREVIEW

> On reflection, I find it as odd to think that the plants have value only for the happiness of the dusky-footed woodrats as to think that the dusky-footed wood-rats have value only for the happiness of humans.[1]
>
> *John Rodman*

> Cows scream louder than carrots.[2]
>
> *Alan Watts (explaining why he is a vegetarian)*

We begin Part IV with a discussion of the 19th-century environmental movements in the United States called conservationism and preservationism. These movements were in-fluential in the thinking of major environmen-tal writers such as Aldo Leopold. Moreover, contemporary philosophers such as J. Baird Callicott, Bryan G. Norton, and Anthony Wes-ton employ the terms "conservationism" and "preservationism" in their work. To under-stand what they are talking about, we need some historical background.

The first essay in Part IV is N. Scott Mo-maday's "Native American Attitudes to the Environment." Momaday, a Native American, writes about American Indian attitudes toward the land. In particular, he discusses ethical or appropriate attitudes toward it. Na-tive Americans have much to teach others about how to relate to land in ways other than the domination of it. Anthony Weston ad-dresses the issue nicely: "We need to think of

the earth itself in a different way: not as an infinite waste sink, and not as a collection of resources fortuitously provided for our use, but as a complex system with its own integrity and dynamics, far more intricate than we un-derstand or perhaps *can* understand, but still the system within which we live and on which we necessarily and utterly depend. We must learn a new kind of respect."[3]

If being more mindful of, and attentive to, the way we interact with and depend on na-ture is, as Weston claims, the minimum re-quired by an environmental ethic, what else is required? For answers, we examine "the land ethic," deep ecology, social ecology, and eco-feminism. In this larger discussion in Section IV-A, we read works by legal theorist Christo-pher Stone, philosophers Kenneth Goodpaster and Paul Taylor, and the originator of the land ethic, Aldo Leopold. They raise such ques-tions as the following: Is sentience the correct standard for determining who or what has moral standing or inherent value? Do trees have rights? Do wildflowers have inherent value? Are ecosystems, rather than the indi-viduals who make up such systems, the real sources of inherent value? Even though Leo-pold is chronologically earlier than Goodpas-ter, Stone, and Taylor, some believe that his ideas are more of a radical departure from tra-ditional humanistic ethics than those of Good-paster, Stone, and Taylor.[4] So our classification in this part is based on the logical progression of ideas rather than historical order. J. Baird

Callicott and Eric Katz, who follow Leopold in our order, interpret and/or defend important aspects of Leopold's land ethic.

Historical Movements

The conservation movement had scientific roots. Some of its leaders, like Gifford Pinchot (1865–1914), came from different fields of study, such as forestry. The emphasis of the movement was on wise management of resources over a long period of time.

Pinchot favored commercial development of the U.S. forest reserves for present and future American citizens. In his book, *The Fight for Conservation*, he maintained the following:

> The first great fact about conservation is that it stands for development. There has been a fundamental misconception that conservation means nothing but the husbanding of resources for future generations. There could be no more serious mistake. Conservation does mean provision for the future, but it means also and first of all the recognition of the right of the present generation to the fullest necessary use of all the resources with which this country is so abundantly blessed. Conservation demands the welfare of this generation first, and afterward the welfare of the generations to follow. The first principle of conservation is development, the use of the natural resources now existing on this continent for the benefit of the people who live here now.[5]

Pinchot further emphasized that forest resources should not fall into the hands of the powerful few, corporations, for example, but should be used to make homes for all American citizens. Pinchot, who in 1905 became head of the newly established U.S. Forest Service, once told the Society of American Foresters, "The object of our forest policy is not to preserve the forests because they are beautiful ... or because they are refuges for the wild creatures of the wilderness ... but ... the

making of prosperous homes.[6] As a spokesperson for the conservationist movement and a supporter of Theodore Roosevelt's policies, he said, "If we succeed, there will exist upon this continent a sane, strong people, living through the centuries in a land subdued and controlled for the service of the people, its rightful masters, owned by the many and not by the few."[7]

Pinchot was opposed by the preservationist movement, headed by John Muir (1838–1914), the founder of the Sierra Club. Muir wanted to preserve the wilderness for aesthetic and spiritual reasons:

> Watch the sunbeams over the forest awakening the flowers, feeding them every one, warming, reviving the myriads of the air, setting countless wings in motion—making diamonds of dewdrops, lakes, painting the spray of falls in rainbow colors. Enjoy the great night like a day, hinting the eternal and imperishable in nature amid the transient and material.[8]

For Muir, nature provides an experience of the sacred or holy. The experience is not simply one of inspiration, but one of recognition of the divine in nature. As Muir once reported his experience of a stroll in the woods: "How beautiful and fresh and Godful the world began to appear."[9]

One famous example of the opposition between the conservationists and the preservationists is the controversy over the Hetch Hetchy Valley in California. Muir and his followers fought for the protection of the Hetch Hetchy Valley in Yosemite National Park. The city of San Francisco wanted to dam the area, thus flooding the park, and construct a reservoir. Pinchot, whose colleagues contemptuously referred to the preservationists as "nature lovers," threw his support behind James R. Garfield, Secretary of the Interior, who approved the city's request to build a dam. Both Pinchot and Muir brought pressure to bear on President Theodore Roosevelt who, in the end, supported Pinchot.

Despite their differences, it can be argued that both traditions, conservationism and preservationism, were anthropocentric. If so, whether Hetch Hetchy Valley is used as a water supply for human beings or as a source of peak experiences for humans, its value lies in human use.[10] Nonetheless, one can find in the writings of John Muir the idea that nature has value independent of human beings: "Rocks have a kind of life not so different from ours as we imagine. Anyhow their material beauty is only a veil covering spiritual beauty—a divine incarnation—instonation."[11] Although this independent value may not be independent of a pantheistic view of nature, it is nevertheless independent of human beings.[12] As such, Muir and his followers influenced Aldo Leopold and later advocates of the land ethic such as J. Baird Callicott and advocates of the rights of trees such as Christopher Stone. Callicott claims that nature has value in itself or for its own sake, that we should value nature in much the same way as parents value their children. Stone argues that trees and streams should be able to sue in court (or have guardians sue on their behalf) for their own injuries. One of the tasks of this section is to investigate the various grounds for attempting to establish the independent value of nature.

The Contemporary Discussion

Christopher Stone, a law professor at the University of Southern California, wrote an important treatise entitled *Should Trees Have Standing?* Stone sees the history of moral development as an extension of the scope of our moral concern to more and more beings and entities as we progressively are able to identify or empathize with them. Originally, according to Stone, "each man had regard only for himself and those of a very narrow circle around him."[13] As we have seen, the circle that Aristotle drew was very small indeed. What

we have done, says Stone, is to view many beings and entities in the world as less than persons, and indeed as objects or things in the world that exist only for the use of people. Our law increasingly has reflected a shift from this view by "making persons of children . . . prisoners, aliens, women (especially of the married variety), the insane, Blacks, foetuses, and Indians."[14] Many authors in this volume argue against the notion that nature exists solely for the use of human beings. Some believe that such a denial points the way to expanding the circle of right-holders to include environmental "objects" such as trees and streams.

Stone suggests that as we become more sensitive, we add more and more previously rightless entities to the list of persons. His remarks on sensitivity and empathy raise questions about the role of rational argument in ethics. On what basis is the law "making persons"? In Stone's view, it is only when we perceive nature as like us that we will be able to generate the love and empathy for the environment that in turn will enable us to attribute rights to it. Does such a thesis imply that rights should be attributed to all things cute and cuddly? Suppose we identify with human fetuses. Do they have rights on that account? Must E.T. be rightless if we do not empathize with him (it)? Is there anything in the universe we will not add to the list of persons assuming we can empathize with it? Should our capacities for empathy be a determining factor in ascertaining what sorts of things possess rights? Suppose some cannot identify with Jews, Gypsies, or people of another color?

Justice William O. Douglas, in the U.S. Supreme Court case *Sierra* v. *Morton*, 1972, cited Stone's book in support of his dissenting opinion that "Contemporary public concern for protecting nature's ecological equilibrium should lead to the conferral of standing upon environmental objects to sue for their own preservation."[15] In this landmark case, the Sierra Club tried to prevent Walt Disney Enterprises, Inc., from building a ski resort in the Mineral King Valley adjacent to Sequoia National Park. The case was not decided on the relative merits of ski resorts versus natural beauty. Rather, it was decided on the issue of standing to sue. "Whether a party has a sufficient stake in an otherwise justiciable controversy to obtain judicial resolution of that controversy is what traditionally has been referred to as the question of standing to sue."[16] The law requires that the party seeking review must itself have suffered an injury or itself have been adversely affected. The Court decided in favor of Disney and against the Sierra Club. After all, it is hard to say that the Sierra Club's members suffered an injury simply because others like to ski. Mineral King Valley might have received legal consideration if trees and streams had standing to sue for their own preservation and/or injury. Much of Stone's essay is a plea for a liberalized domain of *legal* standing. Since trees cannot initiate proceedings on their own behalf, Stone recommends a guardianship approach similar to the one we have now with respect to incompetent human beings, e.g., the profoundly retarded and young children. Incompetent humans have legal rights even if they are unable to claim them for themselves, e.g., rights to proper medical treatment.

As recently as June 12, 1992, in *Lujan* v. *Defenders of Wildlife,* the U.S. Supreme Court decided an important environmental case on the basis of the standing to sue doctrine articulated in *Sierra* v. *Morton.* As a result, the Court did not address substantive environmental issues such as alleged violations of the Endangered Species Act of 1973 by U.S.-funded agency projects in foreign countries and whether the Endangered Species Act applies only within the borders of the United States.

In 1978, the Carter administration issued a regulation saying that the Endangered Species Act did apply to American projects abroad. In 1983, Ronald Reagan's Secretary of the Inte-

rior, James Watt, reversed that policy. Several environmental groups sought to challenge the policy continued by George Bush's Secretary of the Interior, Manuel Lujan. Two members of the Defenders of Wildlife, Joyce Kelly and Amy Skilbred, submitted affidavits claiming that certain federally supported projects threatened an endangered Egyptian crocodile and the Asian elephant and leopard in Sri Lanka. The information in the affidavits was based on Kelly and Skilbred's professional interest in the areas and their visits to the sites of the federal projects.

The Court said, "We shall assume for the sake of argument that these affidavits contain facts showing that certain agency-funded projects threatened listed species.... They plainly contain no facts, however, showing how damage to the species will produce 'imminent' injury to Mss. Kelly and Skilbred."[17] In making their case that Kelly and Skilbred were not injured, the Court weighed heavily the fact that the environmentalists were unable to say exactly when they would return to the areas. Despite the fact that a civil war was going on in Sri Lanka, thus hampering one plaintiff's ability to be precise about her future plans to return to the area, the Court demanded detail on future conduct.

In *Lujan,* the Court admitted that "... when the plaintiff is not himself the object of the government action or inaction he challenges, standing is not precluded, but it is ordinarily 'substantially more difficult' to establish."[18] In Stone's view, the crocodiles, elephants, and leopards should have been the plaintiffs in this case, but, of course, they do not have standing to sue. In our efforts to think hard about how to achieve better environmental policies in the United States, we need to consider whether changing the standing to sue doctrine will bring about significant gains.

In a move similar to Peter Singer's claim that species membership as such is irrelevant to moral standing, Kenneth Goodpaster rejects sentience as the criterion that must be met in order for a being (or entity) to count for something morally speaking. Singer believes that the species one happens to be, like the race or the sex one happens to be, is an arbitrary characteristic that has no moral significance. What matters, in his view, is whether a being can suffer. But Goodpaster, like the deep ecologists, and others such as Paul Taylor, thinks that seeing sentience as all important is as arbitrary as claiming the same for membership in *Homo sapiens*. Goodpaster says: "Nothing short of the condition of *being alive* seems to me to be a plausible and nonarbitrary criterion [of moral considerability]."[19] He adds: ". . . this criterion, if taken seriously, could admit of application to . . . the biosystem itself."[20] In making this claim, Goodpaster seems to be moving in the direction of what is called ethical holism.

Roughly speaking, *holism* is the view that the biosphere as an interconnected whole has moral standing. Such a view is often attributed to Aldo Leopold and is explicitly endorsed by his intellectual descendant, J. Baird Callicott. Paul Taylor's views must be distinguished from those of the holists. Taylor describes his view as *biocentric egalitarianism.* According to Taylor, all living beings have equal inherent worth in that each living being is a goal-directed system pursuing its own good.[21] Respect for nature is respect for these pursuits. However, Taylor's biocentric ethic, in contrast to Callicott, is individualistic and not holistic. In Taylor's view, according to reviewer T. L. S. Sprigge, "Total eco-systems only matter because individuals find their good within them; there is no over-all value of the whole, since the whole (it is claimed) is pursuing no good of its own."[22]

Taylor, as Sprigge points out, is prepared to push his individualistic biocentrism pretty far. For example, it is just as important that nonconscious individuals such as plants achieve their goals as it is that a conscious individual should.[23] Plants do not have to be

conscious in order to be valued for their own sake or in order to be as valuable as human beings. Taylor says: "[t]he killing of a wildflower, then, when taken in and of itself, is just as wrong, other-things-being-equal, as the killing of a human."[24]

Aldo Leopold (1887–1948) is a major figure in the emergence of contemporary ecological/environmental ethics. His ethical views, often referred to as "the land ethic," are found mainly in his book *A Sand County Almanac*. In this influential work, Leopold tells the story of Odysseus who, after returning from the wars of Troy, hanged a dozen female slaves whom he suspected of misconduct. Because Odysseus thought of slaves as mere property, his concept of ethical obligation did not extend to them. He felt that he could dispose of them as he wished. Leopold draws an analogy between the former status of slaves and the current status of land. Land, Leopold argues, should not be viewed as property. His "land ethic" extends moral concern to "soils, waters, plants, and animals, or collectively: the land."[25] Land in Leopold's view is not a commodity that belongs to us, but a community to which we belong.[26] Elsewhere, Leopold refers to the land as an "organism." As might be expected, some expositors of Leopold have emphasized the "community" model and others the "organism" model. Eric Katz, in his essay "Organism, Community, and the 'Substitution Problem,'" investigates the merits of each model, defending the metaphor of community on the grounds that only it represents the importance of individuals within a holistic framework that is committed to the importance of the whole. If he is correct, organicist versions of holism are indefensible.

A study of Leopold's work raises a host of important questions. Leopold advocated a harmonious relationship with the land. The land ethic, he said, "changes the role of *Homo sapiens* from conqueror of the land-community to plain member and citizen of it. It implies respect for his fellow-members, and also respect for the community as such."[27] But what does this respect entail? Respect for land, in his view, does not mean leaving it alone, since Leopold believed that we can alter it for the better. "The swampy forests of Caesar's Gaul were utterly changed by human use—for the better. Moses' land of milk and honey was utterly changed—for the worse."[28] In Leopold's view, a harmonious, as opposed to an exploitative, relationship with nature does not imply that humans will refrain from killing animals. As John Rodman characterizes Leopold's view, "it would be pretentious to talk of a land ethic until we have . . . shot a wolf (once) and looked into its eyes as it died."[29]

Callicott, in his essay, "The Conceptual Foundations of the Land Ethic," reads Leopold as intending to extend moral standing to things that are not themselves individual humans or animals. This, according to Callicott, is what is new and radical about Leopold's land ethic. "[The] standard modern model of ethical theory provides no possibility whatever for the moral consideration of wholes— of threatened *populations* of animals and plants, or of endemic, rare, or endangered *species*, or of biotic *communities*, or most expansively, of the *biosphere* in its totality. . . ."[30] Callicott emphasizes Leopold's call for "respect for the community as such" in the famous characterization of the land ethic (quoted above) where human beings are said to be plain members and citizens of the earth.

Not everyone agrees with Callicott that Leopold intended to attribute moral standing to the biosphere as a whole. Bryan Norton, for example, says the following: "That Leopold saw new and grave responsibilities limiting human activities in the modern world of bulldozers and concrete is without question. But whether he saw these obligations as deriving from sources outside of, and independent of, human affairs seems to me doubtful."[31] Although both Callicott and Norton characterize Leopold's view as "holistic," the two could not

be further apart on the issue of whether the biosphere as a whole has moral standing or intrinsic value and whether Leopold claimed that it does. The difference is this: By "holism," Norton means ". . . the interests of the human species interpenetrate those of the living Earth. . . ."[32]

It might be helpful to contrast Norton's view of holism with our earlier characterization. Earlier, we said that holism is the view that the biosphere as an interconnected whole has moral standing. For Norton, holism is the view that the biosphere is an interconnected whole. As individuals we are part of a larger system and we should value the system, but we value the system from the viewpoint of individuals rather than claiming that the system is the source of independent value.[33] Norton rejects the following dilemma: ". . . either nature is saved for future consumptive purposes or it is saved for itself. . . . this reasoning ignores human, nonconsumptive motives for protecting natural ecosystems."[34]

Calling Leopold an "uncompromising preservationist," Norton goes on to claim that preservationism is characterized by ". . . the exclusion of disruptive human activities from specified areas"[35] for the purpose of preventing overexploitation and in turn ecological breakdown. "On the grandest scale, [preservationists] pursue . . . the setting aside of large, pristine tracts where the struggle to survive can continue untrammelled by human interference, or as nearly so as possible."[36] In Norton's view, whether preservationists are motivated by anthropocentrism or nonanthropocentrism matters little. Nonanthropocentrism, Norton says, ". . . is sufficient, but not necessary, to support preservationism. The preservationist perspective requires no more than a concern for long-term effects of pervasive management on biological diversity."[37]

The disagreement between integrator of perspectives, Bryan Norton on the one hand, and Callicott and his followers on the other, runs deep. Norton is something of a pragmatist and would probably agree with the following assessment of Leopold's work by Anthony Weston: Leopold is ". . . not offering an ethical *theory*, [but] only a provisional statement of *some* of the values that ought to find their place in an ecologically intelligent land-use policy."[38] The values to which Weston refers are integrity, stability, and beauty—the ones expressed in Leopold's famous maxim: "A thing is right when it tends to preserve the integrity, stability, and beauty of the biotic community. It is wrong when it tends otherwise."[39] Callicott characterizes Leopold's maxim as the "'summary moral maxim' of the land ethic."[40] For Callicott, Leopold is not simply suggesting some intelligent land-use values; he is asserting a fundamental, if not ultimate, ethical principle which is part of a larger ethical theory, the land ethic.

Callicott's approach to the land ethic has developed over a long period of time. In 1980, he wrote his provocative "Animal Liberation: A Triangular Affair" in which he argued that animal liberation with its emphasis of the importance of individuals and environmental ethics with its holistic emphasis are based on incompatible philosophies. In the article, he referred to Leopold's maxim as ". . . the categorical imperative or principle precept of the land ethic."[41] It expresses ". . . the idea that the good of the biotic *community* is the ultimate measure of the moral value, the rightness or wrongness of actions."[42] Callicott interpreted Leopold's maxim as implying that concern for the biotic system should take precedence over a more traditional concern for individuals. "The land ethic manifestly does not accord equal moral worth to each and every member of the biotic community; the moral worth of individuals (including, N.B., human individuals) is relative, to be assessed in accordance with the particular relation of each to the collective entity which Leopold called 'land.'"[43]

Claims like the above, ones that seem to imply that individual animals may be sacrificed for ecological reasons or that humans

might be killed for obstructing a sustainable future, prompted Tom Regan to accuse advocates of the land ethic of environmental fascism—a charge Callicott alludes to in "The Conceptual Foundations of the Land Ethic." Regan says:

> The implications of [Leopold's maxim] include the clear prospect that the individual may be sacrificed for the greater biotic good. . . . It is difficult to see how the notion of rights of the individual could find a home within a view that . . . might be fairly dubbed "environmental fascism." . . . The rights view cannot abide this position . . . because it denies the propriety of deciding what should be done to individuals who have rights by appeal to aggregative considerations, including, therefore, computations about what will or will not maximally "contribute to the integrity, stability, and beauty of the biotic community." Individual rights are not to be outweighed by such considerations. . . . Environmental fascism and the rights view are like oil and water: they don't mix.[44]

Callicott now repudiates many of the views he expressed in "Animal Liberation: A Triangular Affair." His article "Animal Liberation and Environmental Ethics: Back Together Again"[45] is his major effort at reconciliation; however, some such effort can be seen in an essay reprinted herein, "The Conceptual Foundations of the Land Ethic." Following Mary Midgley, Callicott talks about ever-widening circles of kinship which eventually embrace the land. However, ". . . the land ethic . . . neither replaces nor overrides . . . inner social circles to which we belong. . . ."[46] In fact, ". . . as a general rule, the duties correlative to the inner social circles to which we belong eclipse those correlative to the rings farther from the heartwood when conflicts arise."[47]

Once it has been claimed that not only human beings and many nonhuman animals have moral standing, but plants, soils, rivers, and trees (either individually or collectively) do as well, the issue of how to settle conflicts of interest between and among such beings and entities arises. Callicott has addressed this issue in "The Conceptual Foundations of the Land Ethic." Elsewhere, Taylor and other philosophers have taken up this issue. The discussion of it continues in the next section (IV-B) on approaches to conflicts.

NOTES

1. John Rodman, "The Liberation of Nature," *Inquiry*, v. 20 (Spring 1977), 84.

2. Bryan G. Norton, *Toward Unity Among Environmentalists*. New York: Oxford University Press, 1991, p. 224.

3. Anthony Weston, *Toward Better Problems: New Perspectives on Abortion, Animal Rights, the Environment, and Justice*. Philadelphia: Temple University Press, 1992, p. 105.

4. J. Baird Callicott, in correspondence.

5. Gifford Pinchot, *The Fight for Conservation*. Seattle: University of Washington Press, 1910, pp. 42–43.

6. Samuel P. Hays, *Conservation and the Gospel of Efficiency: The Progressive Conservation Movement, 1890–1920*, Cambridge, MA: Harvard University Press, 1959, pp. 41–42.

7. Gifford Pinchot, *The Fight for Conservation*, p. 27.

8. John Muir, *To Yosemite and Beyond, Writings from the Years 1863 to 1875*, edited by Robert Engberg and Donald Wesling. Madison: University of Wisconsin Press, 1980, p. 113.

9. John Muir, *To Yosemite and Beyond*, p. 27.

10. Samuel Hays makes a similar point when he says that the crux of the controversy was over two public uses of the area: water supply and recreation. *Conservation and the Gospel of Efficiency*, p. 193.

11. John Muir, *To Yosemite and Beyond*, p. 113.

12. John Rodman suggests this in "Four Forms of Ecological Consciousness Reconsidered," *Ethics and the Environment*, edited by Donald Scherer and Thomas Attig. Englewood Cliffs, NJ: Prentice-Hall, 1983, p. 85.

13. Christopher Stone, *Should Trees Have Standing? Toward Legal Rights for Natural Objects*, Los Altos, CA: William Kaufmann, Inc., 1974, p. 3.

14. Christopher Stone, *Should Trees Have Standing?*, p. 4.

15. *Sierra* v. *Morton*, 70-34, April 19, 1972.

16. *Sierra* v. *Morton*, quoted in Stone, p. 62.

17. *Manuel Lujan, Jr., Secretary of the Interior, Petitioner* v. *Defenders of Wildlife, et al.*, June 12, 1992, *The United States Law Week*, Vol. 60, No. 48 (June 9, 1992), 4498.

18. *Lujan*, p. 4497.

19. Kenneth E. Goodpaster, "On Being Morally Considerable," *Ethics and the Environment*, edited by Donald Scherer and Thomas Attig. Englewood Cliffs, NJ: Prentice-Hall, 1983, p. 31.

20. Kenneth E. Goodpaster, "On Being Morally Considerable," p. 31.

21. Tom Regan challenges Taylor's species egalitarianism by arguing that Taylor has made an improper inference from the "equal *independence* of the good of individual living beings" to the "equal *inherent* worth" of such beings. Tom Regan, "Less Is More: Some Remarks on Paul Taylor's *Respect for Nature*," unpublished paper presented at Brooklyn College, 1987, p. 13.

22. T. L. S. Sprigge, "Some Recent Positions in Environmental Ethics Examined," *Inquiry*, Vol. 34, No. 1 (March 1991), 117.

23. This remark is a paraphrase of a point made by Sprigge in "Some Recent Positions in Environmental Ethics Examined," 116.

24. Paul Taylor, "In Defense of Biocentrism," *Environmental Ethics* 5 (1983), p. 242, quoted in Sprigge, p. 116.

25. Aldo Leopold, *A Sand County Almanac*. New York: Ballantine Books, 1970, p. 239.

26. Aldo Leopold, *A Sand County Almanac*, p. xxviii.

27. Aldo Leopold, *A Sand County Almanac*, p. 240.

28. Aldo Leopold, "The Conservation Ethic," *Journal of Forestry*, 31 (1993), p. 636.

29. John Rodman, "The Liberation of Nature," *Inquiry*, 20 (1977), 110.

30. J. Baird Callicott, "The Conceptual Foundations of the Land Ethic," *Companion to A Sand County Almanac: Interpretive and Critical Essays*, edited by J. Baird Callicott. Madison: University of Wisconsin Press, 1987, pp. 197–198.

31. Bryan G. Norton, *Toward Unity Among Environmentalists*. New York: Oxford University Press, 1991, p. 57.

32. Bryan G. Norton, "Conservation and Preservation: A Conceptual Rehabilitation," *Environmental Ethics*, Vol. 8 (Fall 1986), 220.

33. This point is a paraphrase of a remark made by Norton in a review of J. Baird Callicott's *In Defense of the Land Ethic: Essays in Environmental Philosophy*, *Environmental Ethics*, Vol. 13, No. 2 (Summer 1991), p. 182.

34. Bryan G. Norton, "Conservation and Preservation," 208.

35 Bryan G. Norton, "Conservation and Preservation," 201.

36 Bryan G. Norton, "Conservation and Preservation," 218.

37 Bryan G. Norton, "Conservation and Preservation," 214.

38 Anthony Weston, *Toward Better Problems*, p. 121.

39 Aldo Leopold, *A Sand County Almanac*, p. 262.

40 J. Baird Callicott, "Conceptual Foundations of the Land Ethic," p. 196.

41 J. Baird Callicott, "Animal Liberation: A Triangular Affair," in *People, Penguins and Plastic Trees*, edited by Donald VanDeVeer and Christine Pierce. Bel-

mont, CA: Wadsworth Publishing Company, 1986, p. 188.

42 J. Baird Callicott, "Animal Liberation: A Triangular Affair," p. 188.

43 J. Baird Callicott, "Animal Liberation, A Triangular Affair," p. 192.

44 Tom Regan, *The Case for Animal Rights*. Berkeley: University of California Press, 1983, pp. 361–362.

45 J. Baird Callicott, editor, *In Defense of the Land Ethic: Essays in Environmental Philosophy*. Albany: State University of New York Press, 1989.

46 J. Baird Callicott, "The Conceptual Foundations of the Land Ethic," pp. 207, 208.

47 J. Baird Callicott, "The Conceptual Foundations of the Land Ethic," p. 208.

Native American Attitudes to the Environment

N. Scott Momaday

The first thing to say about the native American perspective on environmental ethics is that there is a great deal to be said. I don't think that anyone has clearly understood yet how the Indian conceives of himself in relation to the landscape. We have formulated certain generalities about that relationship, and the generalities have served a purpose, but they have been rather too general. For example, take the idea that the Indian reveres the earth, thinks of it as the place of his origin, and thinks of the sky also in a personal way. These statements are true. But they can also be misleading because they don't indicate anything about the nature of the relationship, which is, I think, an intricate thing in itself.

I have done much thinking about the "Indian worldview," as it is sometimes called. And I have had some personal experience of Indian religion and Indian societies within the framework of a worldview. Sometime ago I wrote an essay entitled "An American Land Ethic" in which I tried to talk in certain ways about this idea of a native American attitude toward the landscape. And in that essay I

made certain observations. I tried to express the notion first that the native American ethic with respect to the physical world is a matter of reciprocal appropriation: appropriations in which man invests himself in the landscape, and at the same time incorporates the landscape into his own most fundamental experience. That suggests a dichotomy, or a paradox, and I think it is a paradox. It is difficult to understand a relationship which is defined in these terms, and yet I don't know how better to define it.

Secondly, this appropriation is primarily a matter of the imagination. The appropriation is realized through an act of the imagination which is moral and kind. I mean to say that we are all, I suppose, at the most fundamental level what we imagine ourselves to be. And this is certainly true of the American Indian. If you want a definition, you would not go, I hope, to the stereotype which has burdened the American Indian for many years. He is not that befeathered spectacle who is always chasing John Wayne across the silver screen. Rather, he is someone who thinks of himself in a particular

Note: This paper was adapted from transcriptions of oral remarks Professor Momaday made on this subject, informally, during a discussion with faculty and students.

way and his idea comprehends his relationship to the physical world, among other things. He imagines himself in terms of that relationship and others. And it is that act of the imagination, that moral act of the imagination, which I think constitutes his understanding of the physical world.

Thirdly, this imagining, this understanding of the relationship between man and the landscape, or man and the physical world, man and nature, proceeds from a racial or cultural experience. I think his attitude toward the landscape has been formulated over a long period of time, and the length of time itself suggests an evolutionary process perhaps instead of a purely rational and decisive experience. Now I am not sure that you can understand me on this point; perhaps I should elaborate. I mean that the Indian has determined himself in his imagination over a period of untold generations. His racial memory is an essential part of his understanding. He understands himself more clearly than perhaps other people, given his situation in time and space. His heritage has always been rather closely focused, centered upon the landscape as a particular reality. Beyond this, the native American has a particular investment in vision and in the idea of vision. You are familiar with the term "vision quest" for example. This is another essential idea to the Indian worldview, particularly that view as it is expressed among the cultures of the Plains Indians. This is significant. I think we should not lose the force of the idea of seeing something or envisioning something in a particular way. I happen to think that there are two visions in particular with reference to man and his relationship to the natural world. One is physical and the other is imaginative. And we all deal in one way or another with these visions simultaneously. If I can try to find an analogy, it's rather like looking through the viewfinder of a camera, the viewfinder which is based upon the principle of the split image. And it is a matter of trying to align the two planes of that particular view. This can be used as an example of how we look at the world around us. We see it with the physical eye. We see it as it appears to us, in one dimension of reality. But we also see it with the eye of the mind. It seems to me that the Indian has achieved a particularly effective alignment of those two planes of vision. He perceives the landscape in both ways. He realizes a whole image from the

possibilities within his reach. The moral implications of this are very far-reaching. Here is where we get into the consideration of religion and religious ideas and ideals.

There is another way in which I think one can very profitably and accurately think of the Indian in relation to the landscape and in terms of his idea of that relationship. This is to center on such a word as *appropriate*. The idea of "appropriateness" is central to the Indian experience of the natural world. It is a fundamental idea within his philosophy. I recall the story told to me some years ago by a friend, who is not himself a Navajo, but was married for a time to a Navajo girl and lived with her family in southern Utah. And he said that he had been told this story and was passing it on to me. There was a man living in a remote place on the Navajo reservation who had lost his job and was having a difficult time making ends meet. He had a wife and several children. As a matter of fact, his wife was expecting another child. One day a friend came to visit him and perceived that his situation was bad. The friend said to him "Look, I see that you're in tight straits, I see you have many mouths to feed, that you have no wood and that there is very little food in your larder. But one thing puzzles me. I know you're a hunter, and I know, too, there are deer in the mountains very close at hand. Tell me, why don't you kill a deer so that you and your family might have fresh meat to eat?" And after a time the man replied, "No, it is inappropriate that I should take life just now when I am expecting the gift of life."

The implications of that idea, and the way in which the concept of appropriateness lies at the center of that little parable is a central consideration within the Indian world. You cannot understand how the Indian thinks of himself in relation to the world around him unless you understand his conception of what is appropriate; particularly what is morally appropriate within the context of that relationship.

Question: Could you probe a little deeper into what lies behind the idea of appropriate or inappropriate behavior regarding the natural world. Is it a religious element? Is it biological or a matter of survival? How would you characterize what makes an action appropriate or inappropriate?

Momaday: It is certainly a fair question but I'm not sure that I have the answer to it. I suspect that whatever it is that makes for the idea of appropriateness is a very complex thing in itself. Many things constitute the idea of appropriateness. Basically, I think it is a moral idea as opposed to a religious one. It is a basic understanding of right within the framework of relationships, and, within the framework of that relationship I was talking about a moment ago, between man and the physical world. That which is appropriate within this context is that which is *natural.* This another key word. My father used to tell me of an old man who has lived a whole life. I have often thought of this image. The old man used to come to my grandfather's house periodically to pay visits, and my father has very vivid recollections of this man whom I never knew. But his name was Chaney. Father says that Chaney would come to the house and he would make himself perfectly at home. He would be passing by going from one place to another, exercising his ethnic prerogative for nomadism. But he would make my grandfather's house a kind of resting place. He stayed there on many occasions. My father says that every morning when Chaney was there as a guest he would get up in the first light, paint his face, go outside, face the east, and bring the sun out of the horizon. Then he would pray. He would pray aloud to the rising sun. He did that because it was appropriate that he should do that. He understood. Or perhaps I should say that in terms of his own understanding, the sun was the origin of his strength. He understood the sun, within a more formal religious context, similar to the way someone else understands the presence of a deity. And in the face of that recognition, he acted naturally or appropriately. Through the medium of prayer, he returned some of his strength to the sun. He did this everyday. It was a part of his daily life. It was as natural and appropriate to him as anything could be. There is in the Indian worldview this kind of understanding of what is and what is not appropriate. It isn't a matter of intellection. It is respect for the understanding of one's heritage. It is a kind of racial memory and it has its origin beyond any sort of historical experience. It reaches back to the dawn of time.

Question: When talking about vision, you said that the Indians saw things physically and also with the eye of the mind, I think this is the way you put it. You also said that this was a whole image, and that it had certain moral implications. Would you elaborate further?

Momaday: I think there are different ways of seeing things. I myself am particularly interested in literature, and in the traditions of various peoples, the Indians in particular. I understand something of how this works within the context of literature. For example, in the nineteenth century in America, there were poets who were trying very hard to see nature and to write about it. This is one kind of vision. They succeeded in different ways, some succeeding more than others. They succeeded in seeing what was really there on the vision plain of the natural world and they translated that vision, or that perception of the natural world, into poetry. Many of them had a kind of scientific training. Their observations were trained through the study of botany, astronomy, or zoology, etc. This refers, of course, to one kind of vision.

But, obviously, this is not the sort of view of the landscape which characterizes the Indian world. His view rather is of a different and more imaginative kind. It is a more comprehensive view. When the native American looks at nature, it isn't with the idea of training a glass upon it, or pushing it away so that he can focus upon it from a distance. In his mind, nature is not something apart from him. He conceives of it, rather, as an element in which he exists. He has existence within that element, much in the same way we think of having existence within the element of air. It would be unimaginable for him to think of it in the way the nineteenth century "nature poets" thought of looking at nature and writing about it. They employed a kind of "esthetic distance," as it is sometimes called. This idea would be alien to the Indian. This is what I meant by trying to make the distinction between two sides of a split image.

Question: So then, presumably in moral terms, the Indian would say that a person should not harm nature because it's something in which one participates oneself.

Momaday: This is one aspect of it. There is this moral aspect, and it refers to perfect alignment. The appropriation of both images into the one reality is what the Indian is concerned to do: to see what is really there, but also to see what is *really* there.

This reminds me of another story. It is very brief. It was told to me by the same fellow who told me about the man who did not kill the deer. (To take a certain liberty with the title of a novel that I know well.) He told me that while he himself was living in southern Utah with his wife's family, he became very ill. He contracted pneumonia. There was no doctor, no physician nearby. But there was a medicine man close at hand. The family called in a diagnostician (the traditional thing to do), who came and said that my friend was suffering from a particular malady whose cure would be the red-ant ceremony. So a man who is very well versed in that ceremony, a seer, a kind of specialist in the red-ant ceremony, came in and administered it to my friend. Soon after that my friend recovered com-

pletely. Not long after this he was talking to his father-in-law, and he was very curious about what had taken place. He said, "I wonder about the red-ant ceremony. Why is it that the diagnostician prescribed that particular ceremony for me?" His father-in-law looked at him and said, "Well, it was obvious to him that there were red ants in your system, and so we had to call in a seer to take the red ants out of your system." At this point, my friend became very incredulous, and said, "Yes, but surely you don't mean that there were red ants inside of me." His father-in-law looked at him for a moment, then said, "Not ants, but ants." Unless you understand this distinction, you might have difficulty understanding something about the Indian view of the natural world.

On Being Morally Considerable

Kenneth E. Goodpaster

> A thing is right when it tends to preserve the integrity, stability, and beauty of the biotic community. It is wrong when it tends otherwise.
>
> —Aldo Leopold

What follows is a preliminary inquiry into a question which needs more elaborate treatment than an essay can provide. The question can be and has been addressed in different rhetorical formats, but perhaps G. J. Warnock's formulation of it[1] is the best to start with:

> Let us consider the question to whom principles of morality apply from, so to speak, the other end—from the standpoint not of the agent, but of the "patient." What, we may ask here, is the condition of moral *relevance?* What is the condition of having a claim to be *considered,* by rational agents to whom moral principles apply? (148)

*

Modern moral philosophy has taken ethical egoism as its principal foil for developing what can fairly be called a *humanistic* perspective on value

and obligation. That is, both Kantian and Humean approaches to ethics tend to view the philosophical challenge as that of providing an epistemological and motivational generalization of an agent's natural self-interested concern. Because of this preoccupation with moral "take-off," however, too little critical thought has been devoted to the flight and its destination. One result might be a certain feeling of impotence in the minds of many moral philosophers when faced with the sorts of issues . . . that question the breadth of the moral enterprise more than its departure point. To be sure, questions of conservation, preservation of the environment, and technology assessment *can* be approached simply as application questions, e.g., "How shall we evaluate the alternatives available to us instrumentally in relation to humanistic satisfactions?" But there is something distressingly uncritical in this way of framing such issues—distressingly uncritical in the way that deciding foreign policy solely in terms of "the national interest" is uncritical. Or at least, so I think.

It seems to me that we should not only won-

Kenneth E. Goodpaster in *The Journal of Philosophy,* Vol. LXXV, No. 6 (June 1978), pp. 308–325 (with deletions). Reprinted by permission.

der about, but actually follow "the road not taken into the wood." Neither rationality nor the capacity to experience pleasure and pain seem to me necessary (even though they may be sufficient) conditions on moral considerability. And only our hedonistic and concentric forms of ethical reflection keep us from acknowledging this fact. Nothing short of the condition of *being alive* seems to me to be a plausible and nonarbitrary criterion. What is more, this criterion, if taken seriously, could admit of application to entities and systems of entities heretofore unimagined as claimants on our moral attention (such as the biosystem itself). Some may be inclined to take such implications as a *reductio* of the move "beyond humanism." I am beginning to be persuaded, however, that such implications may provide both a meaningful ethical vision and the hope of a more adequate action guide for the long-term future. Paradigms are crucial components in knowledge—but they can conceal as much as they reveal. Our paradigms of moral considerability are individual persons and their joys and sorrows. I want to venture the belief that the universe of moral consideration is more complex than these paradigms allow.

*

My strategy, now that my cards are on the table, will be to spell out a few rules of the game . . . and then to examine the "hands" of several respected philosophers whose arguments seem to count against casting the moral net as widely as I am inclined to. . . . In concluding . . . I will discuss several objections and touch on further questions needing attention.

The first (of four) distinctions that must be kept clear in addressing our question has already been alluded to. It is that between moral *rights* and moral *considerability*. My inclination is to construe the notion of rights as more specific than that of considerability, largely to avoid what seem to be unnecessary complications over the requirements for something's being an appropriate "bearer of rights." The concept of rights is used in wider and narrower senses, of course. Some authors (indeed, one whom we shall consider later in this paper) use it as roughly synonymous with Warnock's notion of "moral relevance." Others believe that being a bearer of rights involves the satisfaction of much more demanding requirements. The sentiments of

John Passmore[2] are probably typical of this narrower view:

> The idea of "rights" is simply not applicable to what is non-human. . . . It is one thing to say that it is wrong to treat animals cruelly, quite another to say that animals have rights (116/7).

I doubt whether it is so clear that the class of rights-bearers is or ought to be restricted to human beings, but I propose to suspend this question entirely by framing the discussion in terms of the notion of moral considerability (following Warnock), except in contexts where there is reason to think the widest sense of "rights" is at work. Whether beings who deserve moral consideration in themselves, not simply by reason of their utility to human beings, also possess moral *rights* in some narrow sense is a question which will, therefore, remain open here—and it is a question the answer to which need not be determined in advance.

A second distinction is that between what might be called a *criterion of moral considerability* and a *criterion of moral significance*. The former represents the central quarry here, while the latter, which might easily get confused with the former, aims at governing *comparative* judgments of moral "weight" in cases of conflict. Whether a tree, say, deserves any moral consideration is a question that must be kept separate from the question of whether trees deserve more or less consideration than dogs, or dogs than human persons. We should not expect that the criterion for having "moral standing" at all will be the same as the criterion for adjudicating competing claims to priority among beings that merit that standing. In fact, it may well be an insufficient appreciation of this distinction which leads some to a preoccupation with rights in dealing with morality. I suspect that the real force of attributions of "rights" derives from comparative contexts, contexts in which moral considerability is presupposed and the issue of strength is crucial. Eventually, of course, the priority issues have to be dealt with for an operational ethical account—this much I have already acknowledged—but in the interests of clarity, I set them aside for now.

Another important distinction, the third, turns on the difference between questions of intelligibility and questions of normative substance. An adequate treatment of this difficult and complicated division would take us far afield,[3] but a few remarks are in order. It is tempting to assume, with Joel Feinberg,[4] that we can neatly separate such questions as

1. What sorts of beings can (logically) be *said* to deserve moral consideration?

from questions like

2. What sorts of beings do, as a matter of "ethical fact" deserve moral consideration?

But our confidence in the separation here wanes (perhaps more quickly than in other philosophical contexts where the conceptual/substantive distinction arises) when we reflect upon the apparent *flexibility* of our metamoral beliefs. One might argue plausibly, for example, that there were times and societies in which the moral standing of blacks was, as a matter of *conceptual analysis,* deniable. Examples could be multiplied to include women, children, fetuses, and various other instances of what might be called "metamoral disenfranchisement." I suspect that the lesson to be learned here is that, as William Frankena has pointed out,[5] metaethics is, and has always been, a partially normative discipline. Whether we are to take this to mean that it is really impossible ever to engage in morally neutral conceptual analysis in ethics is, of course, another question. In any case, it appears that, with respect to the issue at hand, keeping (1) and (2) apart will be difficult. At the very least, I think, we must be wary of arguments that purport to answer (2) *solely* on the basis of "ordinary language"–style answers to (1).

Though the focus of the present inquiry is more normative than conceptual [hence aimed more at (2) than at (1)], it remains what I called a "framework" inquiry nonetheless, since it prescinds from the question of relative weights (moral significance) of moral considerability claims.

Moreover—and this brings us to the fourth and last distinction—there is another respect in which the present inquiry involves framework questions rather than questions of application. There is clearly a sense in which we are subject to *thresholds* of moral sensitivity just as we are subject to thresholds of cognitive or perceptual sensitivity. Beyond such thresholds we are "morally blind" or suffer disintegrative consequences analogous to

"information overload" in a computer. . . . Let us, then, say that the moral considerability of X is *operative* for an agent A if and only if the thorough acknowledgment of X by A is psychologically (and in general, causally) possible for A. If the moral considerability of X is defensible on all grounds independent of operativity, we shall say that it is *regulative.* An agent may, for example, have an obligation to grant regulative considerability to all living things, but be able psychologically and in terms of his own nutrition to grant operative consideration to a much smaller class of things (though note that capacities in this regard differ among persons and change over time).

Using all these distinctions, and the rough and ready terminology that they yield, we can now state the issue in (1) as a concern for a relatively substantive (vs. purely logical) criterion of moral considerability (vs. moral significance) of a regulative (vs. operative) sort. As far as I can see, X's being a living thing is both necessary and sufficient for moral considerability so understood, whatever may be the case for the moral *rights* that rational agents should acknowledge. Let us begin with Warnock's own answer to the question, now that the question has been clarified somewhat. In setting out his answer, Warnock argues (in my view, persuasively) against two more restrictive candidates. The first, what might be called the *Kantian principle,* amounts to little more than a reflection of the requirements of moral *agency* onto those of moral considerability:

3. For X to deserve moral consideration from A, X must be a rational human person.

Observing that such a criterion of considerability eliminates children and mentally handicapped adults, among others, Warnock dismisses it as intolerably narrow.

The second candidate, actually a more generous variant of the first, sets the limits of moral considerability by disjoining "potentiality":

4. For all A, X deserves moral consideration from A if and only if X is a rational human person or is a potential rational human person.

Warnock's reply to this suggestion is also persuasive. Infants and imbeciles are no doubt potentially rational, but this does not appear to be the reason why we should not maltreat them. And we would not say that an imbecile reasonably judged to be incurable would thereby reasonably be taken to have no moral claims (151). In short, it seems arbitrary to draw the boundary of moral *considerability* around rational human beings (actual or potential), however plausible it might be to draw the boundary of moral *responsibility* there.[6]

Warnock then settles upon his own solution. The basis of moral claims, he says, may be put as follows:

> . . . just as liability to be judged as a moral agent follows from one's general capability of alleviating, by moral action, the ills of the predicament, and is for that reason confined to rational beings, so the condition of being a proper "beneficiary" of moral action is the capability of *suffering* the ills of the predicament—and for that reason is not confined to rational beings, nor even to potential members of that class (151).

The criterion of moral considerability then, is located in the *capacity to suffer:*

5. For all *A, X* deserves moral consideration from *A* if and only if *X* is capable of suffering pain (or experiencing enjoyment).

And the defense involves appeal to what Warnock considers to be (analytically) the *object* of the moral enterprise: amelioration of "the predicament."

*

W. K. Frankena, in a recent paper,[7] joins forces:

> Like Warnock, I believe that there are right and wrong ways to treat infants, animals, imbeciles, and idiots even if or even though (as the case may be) they are not persons or human beings—just because they are capable of pleasure and suffering, and not just because their lives happen to have some value to or for those who clearly are persons or human beings.

And Peter Singer[8] writes:

> If a being is not capable of suffering, or of experiencing enjoyment or happiness, there is nothing to be taken into account. This is why the limit of sentience (using the term as a convenient, if not strictly accurate, shorthand for the capacity to suffer or experience enjoyment or happiness) is the only defensible boundary of concern for the interests of others (154).

. . . although I acknowledge and even applaud the conviction expressed by these philosophers that the capacity to suffer (or perhaps better, *sentience*) is sufficient for moral considerability, I fail to understand their reasons for thinking such a criterion necessary. To be sure, there are hints at reasons in each case. Warnock implies that nonsentient beings could not be proper "beneficiaries" of moral action. Singer seems to think that beyond sentience "there is nothing to take into account." And Frankena suggests that nonsentient beings simply do not provide us with moral reasons for respecting them unless it be potentiality for sentience.[9] Yet it is so clear that there *is* something to take into account, something that is not merely "potential sentience" and which surely does qualify beings as beneficiaries and capable of harm—namely, *life*—that the hints provided seem to me to fall short of good reasons.

Biologically, it appears that sentience is an adaptive characteristic of living organisms that provides them with a better capacity to anticipate, and so avoid, threats to life. This at least suggests, though of course it does not prove, that the capacities to suffer and to enjoy are ancillary to something more important rather than tickets to considerability in their own right. In the words of one perceptive scientific observer:

> If we view pleasure as rooted in our sensory physiology, it is not difficult to see that our neurophysiological equipment must have evolved via variation and selective retention in such a way as to record a positive signal to adaptationally satisfactory conditions. . . . The pleasure signal is only an evolutionarily derived indicator, not the goal itself. It is the applause which signals a job well done, but not the actual completion of the job.[10]

Nor is it absurd to imagine that evolution might have resulted (indeed might still result?) in beings whose capacities to maintain, protect, and advance their lives did not depend upon mechanisms of pain and pleasure at all.

*

Joel Feinberg (51) offers what may be the clearest and most explicit case for a restrictive criterion on moral considerability (restrictive with respect to life). . . .

*

The central thesis defended by Feinberg is that a being cannot intelligibly be said to possess moral rights (read: deserve moral consideration) unless that being satisfies the "interest principle," and that only the subclass of humans and higher animals among living beings satisfies this principle:

> . . . the sorts of beings who can have rights are precisely those who have (or can have) interests. I have come to this tentative conclusion for two reasons: (1) because a rightholder must be capable of being represented and it is impossible to represent a being that has no interests, and (2) because a rightholder must be capable of being a beneficiary in his own person, and a being without interests is a being that is incapable of being harmed or benefited, having no good or "sake" of its own. (51)

Implicit in this passage are the following two arguments, interpreted in terms of moral considerability:

(A1) Only beings who can be represented can deserve moral consideration.

Only beings who have (or can have) interests can be represented.

Therefore, only beings who have (or can have) interests can deserve moral consideration.

(A2) Only beings capable of being beneficiaries can deserve moral consideration.

Only beings who have (or can have) interests are capable of being beneficiaries.

Therefore, only beings who have (or can have) interests can deserve moral consideration.

I suspect that these two arguments are at work between the lines in Warnock, Frankena, and Singer, though of course one can never be sure. In any case, I propose to consider them as the best defense of the sentience criterion in recent literature.

I am prepared to grant, with some reservations, the first premises in each of these obviously valid arguments. The second premises, though, are *both* importantly equivocal. To claim that only beings who have (or can have) interests can be represented might mean that "mere things" cannot be represented because they have nothing to represent, no "interests" as opposed to "usefulness" to defend or protect. Similarly, to claim that only beings who have (or can have) interests are capable of being beneficiaries might mean that "mere things"

are incapable of being benefited or harmed—they have no "well-being" to be sought or acknowledged by rational moral agents. So construed, Feinberg seems to be right; but he also seems to be committed to allowing any *living* thing the status of moral considerability. For as he himself admits, even plants

> . . . are not "mere things"; they are vital objects with inherited biological propensities determining their natural growth. Moreover we do say that certain conditions are "good" or "bad" for plants, thereby suggesting that plants, unlike rocks, are capable of having a "good." (51)

But Feinberg pretty clearly wants to draw the nets tighter than this—and he does so by interpreting the notion of "interests" in the two second premises more narrowly. The contrast term he favors is not "mere things" but "mindless creatures." And he makes this move by insisting that "interests" logically presuppose *desires* or *wants* or *aims,* the equipment for which is not possessed by plants (nor, we might add, by many animals or even some humans?).

But why should we accept this shift in strength of the criterion? In doing so, we clearly abandon one sense in which living organisms like plants do have interests that can be represented. There is no absurdity in imagining the representation of the needs of a tree for sun and water in the face of a proposal to cut it down or pave its immediate radius for a parking lot. We might of course, on reflection, decide to go ahead and cut it down or do the paving, but there is hardly an intelligibility problem about representing the tree's interest in our deciding not to. In the face of their obvious tendencies to maintain and heal themselves, it is very difficult to reject the idea of interests on the part of trees (and plants generally) in remaining alive.[11]

Nor will it do to suggest, as Feinberg does, that the needs (interests) of living things like trees are not really their own but implicitly *ours:* "Plants may need things in order to discharge their functions, but their functions are assigned by human interests, not their own." (54) As if it were human interests that assigned to trees the tasks of growth or maintenance! The interests at stake are clearly those of the living things themselves, not simply those of the owners or users or other human persons involved. Indeed, there is a suggestion in this passage that, to be capable of being represented, an organism must *matter* to human beings somehow—a suggestion whose implications for human rights (disenfranchisement) let alone the rights of animals (inconsistently for Feinberg, I think)—are grim.

The truth seems to be that the "interests" that nonsentient beings share with sentient beings (over and against "mere things") are far more plausible as criteria of *considerability* than the "interests" that sentient beings share (over and against "mindless creatures"). This is not to say that interests construed in the latter way are morally irrelevant—for they may play a role as criteria of moral *significance*—but it is to say that psychological or hedonic capacities seem unnecessarily sophisticated when it comes to locating the minimal conditions for something's deserving to be valued for its own sake. Surprisingly, Feinberg's own reflections on "mere things" appear to support this very point:

> . . . mere things have no conative life: no conscious wishes, desires, and hopes; or urges and impulses; or unconscious drives, aims, and goals; or latent tendencies, direction of growth, and natural fulfillments. Interests must be compounded somehow out of conations; hence mere things have no interests (49).

Together with the acknowledgment, quoted earlier, that plants, for example, are not "mere things," such observations seem to undermine the interest principle in its more restrictive form. I conclude, with appropriate caution, that the interest principle either grows to fit what we might call a "life principle" or requires an arbitrary stipulation of psychological capacities (for desires, wants, etc.) which are neither warranted by (A1) and (A2) nor independently plausible.

*

Let us now turn to several objections that might be thought to render a "life principle" of moral considerability untenable quite independently of the adequacy or inadequacy of the sentience or interest principle.

*

(O1) Consideration of life can serve as a criterion only to the degree that life itself can be given a precise definition; and it can't.

(R1) I fail to see why a criterion of moral considerability must be strictly decidable in order to

be tenable. Surely rationality, potential rationality, sentience, and the capacity for or possession of interests fare no better here. Moreover, there do seem to be empirically respectable accounts of the nature of living beings available which are not intolerably vague or open-textured:

> The typifying mark of a living system . . . appears to be its persistent state of low entropy, sustained by metabolic processes for accumulating energy, and maintained in equilibrium with its environment by homeostatic feedback processes.[12]

Granting the need for certain further qualifications, a definition such as this strikes me as not only plausible in its own right, but ethically illuminating, since it suggests that the core of moral concern lies in respect for self-sustaining organization and integration in the face of pressures toward high entropy.

(O2) If life, as understood in the previous response, is really taken as the key to moral considerability, then it is possible that larger systems besides our ordinarily understood "linear" extrapolations from human beings (e.g., animals, plants, etc.) might satisfy the conditions, such as the biosystem as a whole. This surely would be a *reductio* of the life principle.

(R2) At best, it would be a *reductio* of the life principle in this form or without qualification. But it seems to me that such (perhaps surprising) implications, if true, should be taken seriously. There is some evidence that the biosystem as a whole exhibits behavior approximating to the definition sketched above,[13] and I see no reason to deny it moral considerability on that account. Why should the universe of moral considerability map neatly onto our medium-sized framework of organisms?

(O3) There are severe epistemological problems about imputing interests, benefits, harms, etc., to nonsentient beings. What is it for a tree to have needs?

(R3) I am not convinced that the epistemological problems are more severe in this context than they would be in numerous others which the objector would probably not find problematic. Christopher Stone has put this point nicely:

> I am sure I can judge with more certainty and meaningfulness whether and when my lawn wants (needs) water than the Attorney General can judge whether and when the United States

wants (needs) to take an appeal from an adverse judgment by a lower court. The lawn tells me that it wants water by a certain dryness of the blades and soil—immediately obvious to the touch—the appearance of bald spots, yellowing, and a lack of springiness after being walked on; how does "the United States" communicate to the Attorney General? (24).

We make decisions in the interests of others or on behalf of others every day—"others" whose wants are far less verifiable than those of most living creatures.

(O4) Whatever the force of the previous objections, the clearest and most decisive refutation of the principle of respect for life is that one cannot *live* according to it, nor is there any indication in nature that we were intended to. We must eat, experiment to gain knowledge, protect ourselves from predation (macroscopic and microscopic), and in general deal with the overwhelming complexities of the moral life while remaining psychologically intact. To take seriously the criterion of considerability being defended, all these things must be seen as somehow morally wrong.

(R4) This objection . . . can be met, I think, by recalling the distinction made earlier between regulative and operative moral consideration. It seems to me that there clearly are limits to the operational character of respect for living things. We must eat, and usually this involves killing (though not always). We must have knowledge, and sometimes this involves experimentation with living things and killing (though not always). We must protect ourselves from predation and disease, and sometimes this involves killing (though not always). The regulative character of the moral consideration due to all living things asks, as far as I can see, for sensitivity and awareness, not for suicide (psychic or otherwise). But it is not vacuous, in that it does provide a *ceteris paribus* encouragement in the direction of nutritional, scientific, and medical practices of a genuinely life-respecting sort.

As for the implicit claim, in the objection, that since nature doesn't respect life, we needn't, there are two rejoinders. The first is that the premise is not so clearly true. Gratuitous killing in nature is rare indeed. The second, and more important, response is that the issue at hand has to do with the appropriate moral demands to be made on rational moral agents, not on beings who are not rational moral agents. Besides, this objection would tell equally against *any* criterion of moral considerability so far as I can see, if the suggestion is that nature is amoral.

Notes

1. *The Object of Morality* (New York: Methuen, 1971); parenthetical page references to Warnock will be to this book.
2. *Man's Responsibility for Nature* (New York: Scribner's, 1974).
3. Cf. R. M. Hare, "The Argument from Received Opinion," in *Essays on Philosophical Method* (New York: Macmillan, 1971), p. 117.
4. "The Rights of Animals and Unborn Generations," in Blackstone, *Philosophy and Environmental Crisis* (Athens: University of Georgia, 1974), p. 43; parenthetical page references to Feinberg will be to this paper.
5. "On Saying the Ethical Thing," in Goodpaster, ed., *Perspectives on Morality* (Notre Dame, IN: Notre Dame University Press, 1976), pp. 107–24.
6. Actually, it seems to me that we ought not to draw the boundary of moral responsibility just here. See my "Morality and Organizations," in *Proceedings of the Second National Conference on Business Ethics* (Waltham, MA: Bentley College, 1978).
7. "Ethics and the Environment," in K. E. Goodpaster and K. M. Sayre, eds., *Ethics and Problems of the 21st Century* (Notre Dame, IN: Notre Dame University Press, 1978).
8. "All Animals Are Equal," in Tom Regan and Peter Singer, *Animal Rights and Human Obligations* (Englewood Cliffs, NJ: Prentice-Hall, 1976), p. 316.
9. "I can see no reason, from the moral point of view, why we should respect something that is alive but has no conscious sentiency and so can experience no pleasure or pain, joy or suffering, unless perhaps it is potentially a consciously sentient being, as in the case of a fetus. Why, if leaves and trees have no capacity to feel pleasure or to suffer, should I tear no leaf from a tree? Why should I respect its location any more than that of a stone in my driveway, if no benefit or harm comes to any person or sentient being by my moving it?" ("Ethics and the Environment.")
10. Mark W. Lipsey, "Value Science and Developing Society," paper delivered to the Society for Religion in Higher Education, Institute on Society, Technology and Values (July 15–August 4, 1973), p. 11.
11. See Albert Szent-Gyorgyi, *The Living State* (New York: Academic Press, 1972), esp. chap. vi, "Vegetable Defense Systems."

12. K. M. Sayre, *Cybernetics and the Philosophy of Mind* (New York: Humanities, 1976), p. 91.

13. See J. Lovelock and S. Epton, "The Quest for Gaia," *The New Scientist*, 65:935 (February 6, 1975): 304–09.

Should Trees Have Standing?—Toward Legal Rights for Natural Objects

Christopher D. Stone

Introduction: The Unthinkable

In *Descent of Man,* Darwin observes that the history of man's moral development has been a continual extension in the objects of his "social instincts and sympathies." Originally each man had regard only for himself and those of a very narrow circle about him; later, he came to regard more and more "not only the welfare, but the happiness of all his fellow-men"; then "his sympathies became more tender and widely diffused, extending to men of all races, to the imbecile, maimed, and other useless members of society, and finally to the lower animals. . . ."[1]

The history of the law suggests a parallel development. Perhaps there never was a pure Hobbesian state of nature, in which no "rights" existed except in the vacant sense of each man's "right to self-defense." But it is not unlikely that so far as the earliest "families" (including extended kinship groups and clans) were concerned, everyone outside the family was suspect, alien, rightless.[2] And even within the family, persons we presently regard as the natural holders of at least some rights had none. Take, for example, children. We know something of the early rights-status of children from the widespread practice of infanticide–especially of the deformed and female.[3] (Senicide,[4] as among the North American Indians, was the corresponding rightlessness of the aged.)[5] Maine tells us that as late as the Patria Potestas of the Romans, the father had *jus vitae necisque*—the power of life and death—over his children. A fortiori, Maine writes, he had power of "uncontrolled corporal chastisement; he can modify their personal condition at pleasure; he can give a wife to his son; he can give

his daughter in marriage; he can divorce his children of either sex; he can transfer them to another family by adoption; and he can sell them." The child was less than a person: an object, a thing.[6]

The legal rights of children have long since been recognized in principle, and are still expanding in practice. Witness, just within recent time, *In re Gault,*[7] guaranteeing basic constitutional protections to juvenile defendants, and the Voting Rights Act of 1970.[8] We have been making persons of children although they were not, in law, always so. And we have done the same, albeit imperfectly some would say, with prisoners,[9] aliens, women (especially of the married variety), the insane,[10] Blacks, foetuses,[11] and Indians.

Nor is it only matter in human form that has come to be recognized as the possessor of rights. The world of the lawyer is peopled with inanimate right-holders: trusts, corporations, joint ventures, municipalities, Subchapter R partnerships,[12] and nation-states, to mention just a few. Ships, still referred to by courts in the feminine gender, have long had an independent jural life, often with striking consequences.[13] We have become so accustomed to the idea of a corporation having "its" own rights, and being a "person" and "citizen" for so many statutory and constitutional purposes, that we forget how jarring the notion was to early jurists. "That invisible, intangible and artificial being, that mere legal entity" Chief Justice Marshall wrote of the corporation in *Bank of the United States v. Deveaux*[14]—could a suit be brought in *its* name? Ten years later, in the *Dartmouth College* case,[15] he was still refusing to let pass unnoticed the wonder of an entity "existing only in contemplation of law."[16] Yet, long before Marshall worried over the personi-

Source: *Should Trees Have Standing?—Toward Legal Rights for Natural Objects,* by Christopher D. Stone (Portola Valley, CA: Tioga Publishing Company, 1974), pp. 3–18, 24, 27–33, 45–46, 48–54. Reprinted by permission.

fying of the modern corporation, the best medieval legal scholars had spent hundreds of years struggling with the notion of the legal nature of those great public "corporate bodies," the Church and the State. How could they exist in law, as entities transcending the living Pope and King? It was clear how a king could bind *himself*—on his honor—by a treaty. But when the king died, what was it that was burdened with the obligations of, and claimed the rights under, the treaty *his* tangible hand had signed? The medieval mind saw (what we have lost our capacity to see)[17] how *unthinkable* it was, and worked out the most elaborate conceits and fallacies to serve as anthropomorphic flesh for the Universal Church and the Universal Empire.[18]

It is this note of the *unthinkable* that I want to dwell upon for a moment. Throughout legal history, each successive extension of rights to some new entity has been, theretofore, a bit unthinkable. We are inclined to suppose the rightlessness of rightless "things" to be a decree of Nature, not a legal convention acting in support of some status quo. It is thus that we defer considering the choices involved in all their moral, social, and economic dimensions. And so the United States Supreme Court could straight-facedly tell us in *Dred Scott* that Blacks had been denied the rights of citizenship "as a subordinate and inferior class of beings, who had been subjugated by the dominant race. . . ."[19] In the nineteenth century, the highest court in California explained that Chinese had not the right to testify against white men in criminal matters because they were "a race of people whom nature has marked as inferior, and who are incapable of progress or intellectual development beyond a certain point . . . between whom and ourselves nature has placed an impassable difference."[20] The popular conception of the Jew in the 13th Century contributed to a law which treated them as "men *ferae naturae,* protected by a quasi-forest law. Like the roe and the deer, they form an order apart."[21] Recall, too, that it was not so long ago that the foetus was "like the roe and the deer." In an early suit attempting to establish a wrongful death action on behalf of a negligently killed foetus (now widely accepted practice), Holmes, then on the Massachusetts Supreme Court, seems to have thought it simply inconceivable "that a man might owe a civil duty and incur a conditional prospective liability in tort to one not yet in being."[22] The first woman in Wisconsin who thought she might have a right to practice law was told that she did not, in the following terms:

> The law of nature destines and qualifies the female sex for the bearing and nurture of the children of our race and for the custody of the homes of the world. . . . [A]ll life-long callings of women, inconsistent with these radical and sacred duties of their sex, as is the profession of the law, are departures from the order of nature; and when voluntary, treason against it. . . . The peculiar qualities of womanhood, its gentle graces, its quick sensibility, its tender susceptibility, its purity, its delicacy, its emotional impulses, its subordination of hard reason to sympathetic feeling, are surely not qualifications for forensic strife. Nature has tempered woman as little for the juridical conflicts of the court room, as for the physical conflicts of the battle field. . . . [23]

The fact is, the each time there is a movement to confer rights onto some new "entity," the proposal is bound to sound odd or frightening or laughable. This is partly because until the rightless thing receives its rights, we cannot see it as anything but a *thing* for the use of "us"—those who are holding rights at the time.[24] In this vein, what is striking about the Wisconsin case above is that the court, for all its talk about women, so clearly was never able to see women as they are (and might become). All it could see was the popular "idealized" version of *an object it needed.* Such is the way the slave South looked upon the Black.[25] There is something of a seamless web involved: there will be resistance to giving the thing "rights" until it can be seen and valued for itself; yet, it is hard to see it and value it for itself until we can bring ourselves to give it "rights"—which is almost inevitably going to sound inconceivable to a large group of people.

The reason for this little discourse on the unthinkable, the reader must know by now, if only from the title of the paper. I am quite seriously proposing that we give legal rights to forests, oceans, rivers and other so-called "natural objects" in the environment—indeed, to the natural environment as a whole.

As strange as such a notion may sound, it is neither fanciful nor devoid of operational content. In fact, I do not think it would be a misdescription of recent developments in the law to say that we are already on the verge of assigning some such rights, although we have not faced up to what we are doing in those particular terms.[26] We should do so now, and begin to explore the implications such a notion would hold.

Toward Rights for the Environment

Now, to say that the natural environment should have rights is not to say anything as silly as that no one should be allowed to cut down a tree. We say human beings have rights, but—at least as of the time of this writing—they can be executed. Corporations have rights, but they cannot plead the fifth amendment; *In re Gault* gave 15-year-olds certain rights in juvenile proceedings, but it did not give them the right to vote. Thus, to say that the environment should have rights is not to say that it should have every right we can imagine, or even the same body of rights as human beings have. Nor is it to say that everything in the environment should have the same rights as every other thing in the environment.

What the granting of rights does involve has two sides to it. The first involves what might be called the legal-operational aspects; the second, the psychic and socio-psychic aspects. I shall deal with these aspects in turn.

The Legal-Operational Aspects

What It Means to Be a Holder of Legal Rights

There is, so far as I know, no generally accepted standard for how one ought to use the term "legal rights." Let me indicate how I shall be using it in this piece.

First and most obviously, if the term is to have any content at all, an entity cannot be said to hold a legal right unless and until *some public authoritative body* is prepared to give *some amount of review* to actions that are colorably inconsistent with that "right." For example, if a student can be expelled from a university and cannot get any public official, even a judge or administrative agent at the lowest level, either (i) to require the university to justify its actions (if only to the extent of filling out an affidavit alleging that the expulsion "was not wholly arbitrary and capricious") or (ii) to compel the uni-

versity to accord the student some procedural safeguards (a hearing, right to counsel, right to have notice of charges), then the minimum requirements for saying that the student has a legal right to his education do not exist.[27]

But for a thing to be *a holder of legal rights,* something more is needed than that some authoritative body will review the actions and processes of those who threaten it. As I shall use the term, "holder of legal rights," each of three additional criteria must be satisfied. All three, one will observe, go towards making a thing *count* jurally—to have a legally recognized worth and dignity in its own right, and not merely to serve as a means to benefit "us" (whoever the contemporary group of rights-holders may be). They are, first, that the thing can institute legal actions *at its behest;* second, that in determining the granting of legal relief, the court must take *injury to it* into account; and, third, that relief must run to the *benefit of it.* . . .

The Rightlessness of Natural Objects at Common Law

Consider, for example, the common law's posture toward the pollution of a stream. True, courts have always been able, in some circumstances, to issue orders that will stop the pollution. . . . But the stream itself is fundamentally rightless, with implications that deserve careful reconsideration.

The first sense in which the stream is not a rights-holder has to do with standing. The stream itself has none. So far as the common law is concerned, there is in general no way to challenge the polluter's actions save at the behest of a lower riparian—another human being—able to show an invasion of *his* rights. This conception of the riparian as the holder of the right to bring suit has more than theoretical interest. The lower riparians may simply not care about the pollution. They themselves may be polluting, and not wish to stir up legal waters. They may be economically dependent on their polluting neighbor. And, of course, when they discount the value of winning by the costs of bringing suit and the chances of success, the action may not seem worth undertaking. Consider, for example, that while the polluter might be injuring 100 downstream riparians $10,000 a year *in the aggregate,* each riparian separately might be suffering injury only to the extent of $100—possibly not enough for any one of them to want to press suit by himself, or even to go to the trouble and cost of securing co-plaintiffs to make it worth everyone's while. This hesitance will be especially likely when the potential plaintiffs consider the burdens the law puts in their way:[28] proving, e.g., specific damages, the "unreasonableness" of defendant's use of the water, the fact that practicable means of abatement exist, and overcoming difficulties raised by issues such as joint causality, right to pollute by prescription, and so forth. Even in states which, like California, sought to overcome these difficulties by empowering the attorney general to sue for abatement of pollution in limited instances, the power has been sparingly invoked and, when invoked, narrowly construed by the courts.[29]

The second sense in which the common law denies "rights" to natural objects has to do with the way in which the merits are decided in those cases in which someone is competent and willing to establish standing. At its more primitive levels, the system protected the "rights" of the property-owning human with minimal weighing of any values: *"Cujus est solum, ejus est usque ad coelum et ad infernos."*[30] Today we have come more and more to make balances—but only such as will adjust the economic best interests of identifiable humans. For example, continuing with the case of streams, there are commentators who speak of a "general rule" that "a riparian owner is legally entitled to have the stream flow by his land with its quality unimpaired" and observe that "an upper owner has, prima facie, no right to pollute the water."[31] Such a doctrine, if strictly invoked, would protect the stream absolutely whenever a suit was brought; but obviously, to look around us, the law does not work that way. Almost everywhere there are doctrinal qualifications on riparian "rights" to an unpolluted stream.[32] Although these rules vary from jurisdiction to jurisdiction, and upon whether one is suing for an equitable injunction or for damages, what they all have in common is some sort of balancing. Whether under language of "reasonable use," "reasonable methods of use," "balance of convenience" or "the public interest doctrine," what the courts are balancing, with varying degrees of directness, are the economic hardships on the upper riparian (or dependent community) of abating the pollution vis-à-vis the economic hardships of continued pollution on the lower riparians. What does not weigh in the balance is the damage to the stream, its fish

and turtles and "lower" life. So long as the natural environment itself is rightless, these are not matters for judicial cognizance. Thus, we find the highest court of Pennsylvania refusing to stop a coal company from discharging polluted mine water into a tributary of the Lackawana River because a plaintiff's "grievance is for a mere personal inconvenience; and . . . mere private personal inconveniences . . . must yield to the necessities of a great public industry, which although in the hands of a private corporation, subserves a great public interest."[33] The stream itself is lost sight of in "a quantitative compromise between *two* conflicting interests."[34]

The third way in which the common law makes natural objects rightless has to do with who is regarded as the beneficiary of a favorable judgment. Here, too, it makes a considerable difference that it is not the natural object that counts in its own right. To illustrate this point, let me begin by observing that it makes perfectly good sense to speak of, and ascertain, the legal damage to a natural object, if only in the sense of "making it whole" with respect to the most obvious factors. The costs of making a forest whole, for example, would include the costs of reseeding, repairing watersheds, restocking wildlife—the sorts of costs the Forest Service undergoes after a fire. Making a polluted stream whole would include the costs of restocking with fish, water-fowl, and other animal and vegetable life, dredging, washing out impurities, establishing natural and/or artificial aerating agents, and so forth. Now, what is important to note is that, under our present system, even if a plaintiff riparian wins a water pollution suit for damages, no money goes to the benefit of the stream itself to repair *its* damages. This omission has the further effect that, at most, the law confronts a polluter with what it takes to make the plaintiff riparians whole; this may be far less than the damages to the stream, but not so much so as to force the polluter to desist. For example, it is easy to imagine a polluter whose activities damage a stream to the extent of $10,000 annually, although the aggregate damage to all the riparian plaintiffs who come into the suit is only $3000. If $3000 is less than the cost to the polluter of shutting down, or making the requisite technological changes, he might prefer to pay off the damages (i.e., the legally cognizable damages) and continue to pollute the stream. Similarly, even if the jurisdiction issues an injunction at the plaintiffs' behest (rather than to order payment of damages), there is nothing to stop the plaintiffs from "selling out" the stream, i.e., agreeing to dissolve or not enforce the injunction at some price (in the example above, somewhere between plaintiffs' damages—$3000—and defendants' next best economic alternative). Indeed, I take it this is exactly what Learned Hand had in mind in an opinion in which, after issuing an anti-pollution injunction, he suggests that the defendant "make its peace with the plaintiff as best it can."[35] What is meant is a peace between *them*, and not amongst them and the river.

I ought to make clear at this point that the common law as it affects streams and rivers, which I have been using as an example so far, is not exactly the same as the law affecting other environmental objects. Indeed, one would be hard pressed to say that there was a "typical" environmental object, so far as its treatment at the hands of the law is concerned. There are some differences in the law applicable to all the various resources that are held in common: rivers, lakes, oceans, dunes, air, streams (surface and subterranean), beaches, and so forth. And there is an even greater difference as between these traditional communal resources on the one hand, and natural objects on traditionally private land, e.g., the pond on the farmer's field, or the stand of trees on the suburbanite's lawn.

On the other hand, although there be these differences which would make it fatuous to generalize about a law of the natural environment, most of these differences simply underscore the points made in the instance of rivers and streams. None of the natural objects, whether held in common or situated on private land, has any of the three criteria of a rights-holder. They have no standing in their own right; their unique damages do not count in determining outcome; and they are not the beneficiaries of awards. In such fashion, these objects have traditionally been regarded by the common law, and even by all but the most recent legislation, as objects for man to conquer and master and use—in such a way as the law once looked upon "man's" relationships to African Negroes. Even where special measures have been taken to conserve them, as by seasons on game and limits on timber cutting, the dominant motive has been to conserve them *for us*—for the greatest good of the

greatest number of human beings. Conservationists, so far as I am aware, are generally reluctant to maintain otherwise.[36] As the name implies, they want to conserve and guarantee *our* consumption and *our* enjoyment of these other living things. In their own right, natural objects have counted for little, in law as in popular movements.

As I mentioned at the outset, however, the rightlessness of the natural environment can and should change; it already shows some signs of doing so.

Toward Having Standing in Its Own Right

It is not inevitable, nor is it wise, that natural objects should have no rights to seek redress in their own behalf. It is no answer to say that streams and forests cannot have standing because streams and forest cannot speak. Corporations cannot speak either; nor can states, estates; infants, incompetents, municipalities or universities. Lawyers speak for them, as they customarily do for the ordinary citizen with legal problems. One ought, I think, to handle the legal problems of natural objects as one does the problems of legal incompetents—human beings who have become vegetable. If a human being shows signs of becoming senile and has affairs that he is de jure incompetent to manage, those concerned with his well-being make such a showing to the court, and someone is designated by the court with the authority to manage the incompetent's affairs. The guardian (or "conservator" or "committee"—the terminology varies) then represents the incompetent in his legal affairs. Courts make similar appointments when a corporation has become "incompetent"—they appoint a trustee in bankruptcy or reorganization to oversee its affairs and speak for it in court when that becomes necessary.

On a parity of reasoning, we should have a system in which, when a friend of a natural object perceives it to be endangered, he can apply to a court for the creation of a guardianship. Perhaps we already have the machinery to do so. California law, for example, defines an incompetent as "any person, whether insane or not, who by reason of old age, disease, weakness of mind, or other cause, is unable, unassisted, properly to manage and take care of himself or his property, and by reason thereof is likely to be deceived or imposed upon by artful or designing persons."[37] Of course, to urge a court that an endangered river is "a person" under this provision will call for lawyers as bold and imaginative as those who convinced the Supreme Court that a railroad corporation was a "person" under the fourteenth amendment, a constitutional provision theretofore generally thought of as designed to secure the rights of freedmen.[38] . . .

The guardianship approach, however, is apt to raise . . . [the following objection]: a committee or guardian could not judge the needs of the river or forest in its charge; indeed, the very concept of "needs," it might be said, could be used here only in the most metaphorical way. . . .

. . . Natural objects *can* communicate their wants (needs) to us, and in ways that are not terribly ambiguous. I am sure I can judge with more certainty and meaningfulness whether and when my lawn wants (needs) water, than the Attorney General can judge whether and when the United States wants (needs) to take an appeal from an adverse judgment by a lower court. The lawn tells me that it wants water by a certain dryness of the blades and soil—immediately obvious to the touch—the appearance of bald spots, yellowing, and a lack of springiness after being walked on; how does "the United States" communicate to the Attorney General? For similar reasons, the guardian-attorney for a smog-endangered stand of pines could venture with more confidence that his client wants the smog stopped, than the directors of a corporation can assert that "the corporation" wants dividends declared. We make decisions on behalf of, and in the purported interests of, others every day; these "others" are often creatures whose wants are far less verifiable, and even far more metaphysical in conception, than the wants of rivers, trees, and land. . . .

The argument for "personifying" the environment, from the point of damage calculations, can best be demonstrated from the welfare economics position. Every well-working legal-economic system should be so structured as to confront each of us with the full costs that our activities are imposing on society. Ideally, a paper mill, in deciding what to produce—and where, and by what methods—ought to be forced to take into account not only the lumber, acid, and labor that its production "takes" from other uses in the society, but also what costs alternative production plans will impose on

society through pollution. The legal system, through the law of contracts and the criminal law, for example, makes the mill confront the costs of the first group of demands. When, for example, the company's purchasing agent orders 1000 drums of acid from the Z Company, the Z Company can bind the mill to pay for them, and thereby reimburse the society for what the mill is removing from alternative uses.

Unfortunately, so far as the pollution costs are concerned, the allocative ideal begins to break down, because the traditional legal institutions have a more difficult time "catching" and confronting us with the full social costs of our activities. In the lakeside mill example, major riparian interests might bring an action, forcing a court to weigh *their* aggregate losses against the costs to the mill of installing the anti-pollution device. But many other interests—and I am speaking for the moment of recognized homocentric interests—are too fragmented and perhaps "too remote" causally to warrant securing representation and pressing for recovery: the people who own summer homes and motels, the man who sells fishing tackle and bait, the man who rents rowboats. There is no reason not to allow the lake to prove damages to them as the prima facie measure of damages to it. *By doing so, we in effect make the natural object, through its guardian, a jural entity competent to gather up these fragmented and otherwise unrepresented damage claims, and press them before the court even where, for legal or practical reasons, they are not going to be pressed by traditional class action plaintiffs.* Indeed, one way—the homocentric way—to view what I am proposing so far, is to view the guardian of the natural object as the guardian of unborn generations, as well as of the otherwise unrepresented, but distantly injured, contemporary humans.[39] By making the lake itself the focus of these damages, and "incorporating" it so to speak, the legal system can effectively take proof upon, and confront the mill with, a larger and more representative measure of the damages its pollution causes.

So far, I do not suppose that my economist friends (unremittant human chauvinists, every one of them!) will have any large quarrel in principle with the concept. Many will view it as a *trompe l'oeil* that comes down, at best, to effectuate the goals of the paragon class action, or the paragon water pollution control district. Where we are apt to part company is here—I propose going beyond gathering up the loose ends of what most people would presently recognize as economically valid damages. The guardian would urge before the court injuries not presently cognizable—the death of eagles and inedible crabs, the suffering of sea lions, the loss from the face of the earth of species of commercially valueless birds, the disappearance of a wilderness area. One might, of course, speak of the damages involved as "damages" to us humans, and indeed, the widespread growth of environmental groups shows that human beings do feel these losses. But they are not, at present, economically measurable losses: how can they have a monetary value for the guardian to prove in court?

The answer for me is simple. Wherever it carves out "property" rights, the legal system is engaged in the process of *creating* monetary worth. One's literary works would have minimal monetary value if anyone could copy them at will. Their economic value to the author is a product of the law of copyright; the person who copies a copyrighted book has to bear a cost to the copyright-holder because the law says he must. Similarly, it is through the law of torts that we have made a "right" of— and guaranteed an economically meaningful value to—privacy. (The value we place on gold—a yellow inanimate dirt—is not simply a function of supply and demand—wilderness areas are scarce and pretty too—, but results from the actions of the legal systems of the world, which have institutionalized that value; they have even done a remarkable jog of stabilizing the price). I am proposing we do the same with eagles and wilderness areas as we do with copyrighted works, patented inventions, and privacy: *make* the violation of rights in them to be a cost by declaring the "pirating" of them to be the invasion of a property interest.[40] If we do so, the net social costs the polluter would be confronted with would include not only the extended homocentric costs of his pollution (explained above) but also costs to the environment *per se*.

How, though, would these costs be calculated? When we protect an invention, we can at least speak of a fair market value for it, by reference to which damages can be computed. But the lost environmental "values" of which we are now speaking are by definition over and above those that the market is prepared to bid for: they are priceless.

One possible measure of damages, suggested

earlier, would be the cost of making the environment whole, just as, when a man is injured in an automobile accident, we impose upon the responsible party the injured man's medical expenses. Comparable expenses to a polluted river would be the costs of dredging, restocking with fish, and so forth. It is on the basis of such costs as these, I assume, that we get the figure of $1 billion as the cost of saving Lake Erie.[41] As an ideal, I think this is a good guide applicable in many environmental situations. It is by no means free from difficulties, however.

One problem with computing damages on the basis of making the environment whole is that, if understood most literally, it is tantamount to asking for a "freeze" on environmental quality, even at the costs (and there will be costs) of preserving "useless" objects. Such a "freeze" is not inconceivable to me as a general goal, especially considering that, even by the most immediately discernible homocentric interests, in so many areas we ought to be cleaning up and not merely preserving the environmental status quo. In fact, there is presently strong sentiment in the Congress for a total elimination of all river pollutants by 1985,[42] notwithstanding that such a decision would impose quite large direct and indirect costs on us all. Here one is inclined to recall the instructions of Judge Hays, in remanding Consolidated Edison's Storm King application to the Federal Power Commission in *Scenic Hudson:*

> The Commission's renewed proceedings must include as a basic concern the preservation of natural beauty and of natural historic shrines, keeping in mind that, in our affluent society, the cost of a project is only one of several factors to be considered.[43]

Nevertheless, whatever the merits of such a goal in principle, there are many cases in which the social price tag of putting it into effect are going to seem too high to accept. Consider, for example, an oceanside nuclear generator that could produce low cost electricity for a million homes at a savings of $1 a year per home, spare us the air pollution that comes of burning fossil fuels, but which through a slight heating effect threatened to kill off a rare species of temperature-sensitive sea urchins; suppose further that technological improvements adequate to reduce the temperature to present environmental quality would expend the entire one million dollars in anticipated fuel savings. Are we prepared to tax ourselves $1,000,000 a year on behalf of the sea urchins? In comparable problems under the present law of damages, we work out practicable compromises by abandoning restoration costs and calling upon fair market value. For example, if an automobile is so severely damaged that the cost of bringing the car to its original state by repair is greater than the fair market value, we would allow the responsible tortfeasor to pay the fair market value only. Or if a human being suffers the loss of an arm (as we might conceive of the ocean having irreparably lost the sea urchins), we can fall back on the capitalization of reduced earning power (and pain and suffering) to measure the damages. But what is the fair market value of sea urchins? How can we capitalize their loss to the ocean, independent of any commercial value they may have to someone else?

One answer is that the problem can sometimes be sidestepped quite satisfactorily. In the sea urchin example, one compromise solution would be to impose on the nuclear generator the costs of making the ocean whole somewhere else, in some other way, e.g., reestablishing a sea urchin colony elsewhere, or making a somehow comparable contribution.[44] In the debate over the laying of the trans-Alaskan pipeline, the builders are apparently prepared to meet conservationists' objections half-way by re-establishing wildlife away from the pipeline, so far as is feasible.[45]

But even if damage calculations have to be made, one ought to recognize that the measurement of damages is rarely a simple report of economic facts about "the market," whether we are valuing the loss of a foot, a foetus, or a work of fine art. Decisions of this sort are always hard, but not impossible. We have increasingly taken (human) pain and suffering into account in reckoning damages, not because we think we can ascertain them as objective "facts" about the universe, but because, even in view of all the room for disagreement, we come up with a better society by making rude estimates of them than by ignoring them.[46] We can make such estimates in regard to environmental losses fully aware that what we are really doing is making implicit normative judgments (as with pain and suffering)—laying down rules as to what the society is going to "value" rather than reporting market evaluations. In making such normative estimates decision-makers would not go wrong if they

estimated on the "high side," putting the burden of trimming the figure down on the immediate human interests present. All burdens of proof should reflect common experience; our experience in environmental matters has been a continual discovery that our acts have caused more long-range damage than we were able to appreciate at the outset.

To what extent the decision-maker should factor in costs such as the pain and suffering of animals and other sentient natural objects, I cannot say; although I am prepared to do so in principle.[47] Given the conjectural nature of the "estimates" in all events, and the roughness of the "balance of conveniences" procedure where that is involved, the practice would be of more interest from the socio-psychic point of view, discussed below, than from the legal-operational.

The Psychic and Socio-Psychic Aspects

. . . The strongest case can be made from the perspective of human advantage for conferring rights on the environment. Scientists have been warning of the crises the earth and all humans on it face if we do not change our ways—radically—and these crises make the lost "recreational use" of rivers seem absolutely trivial. The earth's very atmosphere is threatened with frightening possibilities: absorption of sunlight, upon which the entire life cycle depends, may be diminished; the oceans may warm (increasing the "greenhouse effect" of the atmosphere), melting the polar ice caps, and destroying our great coastal cities; the portion of the atmosphere that shields us from dangerous radiation may be destroyed. Testifying before Congress, sea explorer Jacques Cousteau predicted that the oceans (to which we dreamily look to feed our booming populations) are headed toward their own death: "The cycle of life is intricately tied up with the cycle of water . . . the water system has to remain alive if we are to remain alive on earth."[48] We are depleting our energy and our food sources at a rate that takes little account of the needs even of humans now living.

These problems will not be solved easily; they very likely can be solved, if at all, only through a willingness to suspend the rate of increase in the standard of living (by present values) of the earth's "advanced" nations, and by stabilizing the total human population. For some of us this will involve forfeiting material comforts; for others it will involve abandoning the hope someday to obtain comforts long envied. For all of us it will involve giving up the right to have as many offspring as we might wish. Such a program is not impossible of realization, however. Many of our so-called "material comforts" are not only in excess of, but are probably in opposition to, basic biological needs. Further, the "costs" to the advanced nations is not as large as would appear from Gross National Product figures. G.N.P. reflects social gain (of a sort) without discounting for the social *cost* of that gain, *e.g.,* the losses through depletion of resources, pollution, and so forth. As has well been shown, as societies become more and more "advanced," their real marginal gains become less and less for each additional dollar of G.N.P.[49] Thus, to give up "human progress" would not be as costly as might appear on first blush.

Nonetheless, such far-reaching social changes are going to involve us in a serious reconsideration of our consciousness toward the environment. . . .

A radical new conception of man's relationship to the rest of nature would not only be a step toward solving the material planetary problems; there are strong reasons for such a changed consciousness from the point of making us far better humans. If we only stop for a moment and look at the underlying human qualities that our present attitudes toward property and nature draw upon and reinforce, we have to be struck by how stultifying of our own personal growth and satisfaction they can become when they take rein of us. Hegel, in "justifying" private property, unwittingly reflects the tone and quality of some of the needs that are played upon:

> A person has as his substantive end the right of putting his will into any and every thing and thereby making it his, because it has no such end in itself and derives its destiny and soul from his will. This is the absolute right of appropriation which man has over all "things."[50]

What is it within us that gives us this need not just to satisfy basic biological wants, but to extend our wills over things, to objectify them, to make them ours, to manipulate them, to keep them at a psychic distance? Can it all be explained on "rational" bases? Should we not be suspect of such needs within us, cautious as to why we wish to gratify

them? When I first read that passage of Hegel, I immediately thought not only of the emotional contrast with Spinoza, but of the passage in Carson McCuller's *A Tree, A Rock, A Cloud,* in which an old derelict has collared a twelve year old boy in a streetcar cafe. The old man asks whether the boy knows "how love should be begun?"

The old man leaned closer and whispered:

> "A tree. A rock. A cloud."
>
> . . .
>
> "The weather was like this in Portland," he said. "At the time my science was begun. I meditated and I started very cautious. I would pick up something from the street and take it home with me. I bought a goldfish and I concentrated on the goldfish and I loved it. I graduated from one thing to another. Day by day I was getting this technique. . . .
>
> . . .
>
> . . . "For six years now I have gone around by myself and built up my science. And now I am a master. Son. I can love anything. No longer do I have to think about it even. I see a street full of people and a beautiful light comes in me. I watch a bird in the sky. Or I meet a traveler on the road. Everything, Son. And anybody. All stranger and all loved! Do you realize what a science like mine can mean?"[51]

To be able to get away from the view that Nature is a collection of useful senseless objects is, as McCullers' "madman" suggests, deeply involved in the development of our abilities to love—or, if that is putting it too strongly, to be able to reach a heightened awareness of our own, and others' capacities in their mutual interplay. To do so, we have to give up some psychic investment in our sense of separateness and specialness in the universe. And this, in turn, is hard giving indeed, because it involves us in a flight backwards, into earlier stages of civilization and childhood in which we had to trust (and perhaps fear) our environment, for we had not then the power to master it. Yet, in doing so, we—as persons—gradually free ourselves of needs for supportive illusions. Is not this one of the triumphs for "us" of our giving legal rights to (or acknowledging the legal rights of) the Blacks and women? . . .

. . . A few years ago the pollution of streams was thought of only as a problem of smelly, unsightly, unpotable water *i.e.,* to us. Now we are beginning to discover that pollution is a process that destroys wonderously subtle balances of life within the water, and as between the water and its banks. This heightened awareness enlarges our sense of the dangers to us. But it also enlarges our empathy. We are not only developing the scientific capacity, but we are cultivating the personal capacities *within us* to recognize more and more the ways in which nature—like the woman, the Black, the Indian and the Alien—is like us (and we will also become more able realistically to define, confront, live with, and admire the ways in which we are all different).

The time may be on hand when these sentiments, and the early stirrings of the laws, can be coalesced into radical new theory or myth—felt as well as intellectualized—of man's relationships to the rest of nature. I do not mean "myth" in a demeaning sense of the term, but in the sense in which, at different times in history, our social "facts" and relationships have been comprehended and integrated by reference to the "myths" that we are co-signers of a social contract, that the Pope is God's agent, and that all men are created equal. Pantheism, Shinto and Tao all have myths to offer. But they are all, each in its own fashion, quaint, primitive and archaic. What is needed is a myth that can fit our growing body of knowledge of geophysics, biology and the cosmos. In this vein, I do not think it too remote that we may come to regard the Earth, as some have suggested, as one organism, of which Mankind is a functional part—the mind, perhaps: different from the rest of nature, but different as a man's brain is from his lungs.

> . . . As I see it, the Earth is only one organized "field" of activities—and so is the *human person*—but these activities take place at various levels, in different "spheres" of being and realms of consciousness. The lithosphere is not the biosphere, and the latter not the . . . ionosphere. The Earth is not *only* a material mass. Consciousness is not only "human"; it exists at animal and vegetable levels, and most likely must be latent, or operating in some form, in the molecule and the atom; and all these diverse and in a sense hierarchical modes of activity and consciousness should be seen integrated in and perhaps transcended by an all-encompassing and "eonic" planetary Consciousness.
>
> . . . .
>
> Mankind's function within the Earth-organism is to extract from the activities of all other operative systems within this organism

the type of consciousness which we call "reflective" or "self" consciousness—or, we may also say to *mentalize* and give meaning, value, and "name" to all that takes place anywhere within the Earth-field. . . . [52]

As radical as such a consciousness may sound today, all the dominant changes we see about us point in its direction. Consider just the impact of space travel, of world-wide mass media, of increasing scientific discoveries about the interrelatedness of all life processes. Is it any wonder that the term "spaceship earth" has so captured the popular imagination? The problems we have to confront are increasingly the world-wide crises of a global organism: not pollution of a stream, but pollution of the atmosphere and of the ocean. Increasingly, the death that occupies each human's imagination is not his own, but that of the entire life cycle of the planet earth, to which each of us is as but a cell to a body.

To shift from such a lofty fancy as the planetarization of consciousness to the operation of our municipal legal system is to come down to earth hard. Before the forces that are at work, our highest court is but a frail and feeble—a distinctly human—institution. Yet, the Court may be at its best not in its work of handing down decrees, but at the very task that is called for: of summoning up from the human spirit the kindest and most generous and worthy ideas that abound there, giving them shape and reality and legitimacy. Witness the School Desegregation Cases which, more importantly than to integrate the schools (assuming they did), awakened us to moral needs which, when made visible, could not be denied. And so here, too, in the case of the environment, the Supreme Court may find itself in a position to award "rights" in a way that will contribute to a change in popular consciousness. It would be a modest move, to be sure, but one in furtherance of a large goal: the future of the planet as we know it.

How far we are from such a state of affairs, where the law treats "environmental objects" as holders of legal rights, I cannot say. But there is certainly intriguing language in one of Justice Black's last dissents, regarding the Texas Highway Department's plan to run a six-lane expressway through a San Antonio Park.[53] Complaining of the Court's refusal to stay the plan, Black observed that "after today's decision, the people of San Antonio and the birds and animals that make their home in the park will share their quiet retreat with an ugly, smelly stream of traffic. . . . Trees, shrubs, and flowers will be mowed down."[54] Elsewhere he speaks of the "burial of public parks," of segments of a highway which "devour parkland," and of the park's heartland.[55] Was he, at the end of his great career, on the verge of saying—just saying—that "nature has 'rights' on its own account"? Would it be so hard to do?

Notes

1. C. Darwin, *Descent of Man*, 119, 120–21 (2d ed. 1874). *See also* R. Waelder, *Progress and Revolution* 39 et seq. (1967).

2. *See* Darwin, *supra* note 1, at 113–14.

3. *See* Darwin, *supra* note 1, at 113. *See also* E. Westermarck, 1 *The Origin and Development of the Moral Ideas* 406–12 (1912).

4. There does not appear to be a word "gericide" or "geronticide" to designate the killing of the aged. "Senicide" is as close as the *Oxford English Dictionary* comes, although, as it indicates, the word is rare. 9 *Oxford English Dictionary*, 454 (1933).

5. *See* Darwin, *supra* note 1, at 386–93. Westermarck, *supra* note 3, at 387–89, observes that where the killing of the aged and infirm is practiced, it is often supported by humanitarian justification; this, however, is a far cry from saying that the killing is *requested* by the victim as his right.

6. H. Maine, *Ancient Law* 153 (Pollock ed. 1930).

7. 387 U.S. 1 (1967).

8. 42 U.S.C. §§ 1973 et seq. (1970).

9. *See Landman* v. *Royster*, 40 U.S.L.W. 2256 (E.D. Va., Oct. 30, 1971).

10. *But See* T. Szasz, *Law, Liberty and Psychiatry* (1963).

11. *See* note 22. The trend toward liberalized abortion can be seen either as a legislative tendency back in the direction of rightlessness for the foetus—or toward increasing rights of women. This inconsistency is not unique in the law of course; it is simply support for Hohfeld's scheme that the "jural opposite" of someone's right is someone else's "noright." W. Hohfeld, *Fundamental Legal Conceptions* (1923) . . .

12. Int. Rev. Code of 1954, § 1361 (repealed by Pub. L. No. 89-389, effective Jan. 1, 1969).

13. For example, *see United States* v. *Cargo of the Brig Malek Adhel*, 43 U.S. (2 How.) 210 (1844). There, a ship had been seized and used by pirates. All this was done without the knowledge or consent of the owners of the ship. After the ship had been captured, the United States condemned and sold the "offending vessel." The owners objected. In denying release to the owners, Justice Story cited Chief Justice Marshall from an earlier case: "This is not a proceeding against the owner; it is a proceeding against the vessel for an offense committed by the vessel; which is not the less an offense . . . because it was committed without the authority and against the will of the owner." 43 U.S. at 234, quoting from *United States* v. *Schooner Little Charles*, 26 F. Cas. 979 (No. 15,612) (C.C.D. Va. 1818).

14. 9 U.S. (5 Cranch) 61, 86 (1809).

15. *Trustees of Dartmouth College* v. *Woodward*, 17 U.S. (4 Wheat.) 518 (1819).

16. *Id.* at 636.

17. Consider, for example, that the claim of the United States to the naval station at Guantanamo Bay, at $2000-a-year rental, is based upon a treaty signed in 1903 by José Montes for the President of Cuba and a minister representing Theodore Roosevelt; it was subsequently ratified by two-thirds of a Senate no member of which is living today. Lease [from Cuba] of Certain Areas for Naval or Coaling Stations, July 2, 1903, T.S. No. 426; C. Bevans, 6 *Treaties and Other International Agreements of the United States 1776–1949*, at 1120 (U.S. Dep't. of State Pub. 8549, 1971).

18. O. Gierke, *Political Theories of the Middle Age* (Maitland transl. 1927), especially at 22–30. . . .

19. *Dred Scott* v. *Sandford*, 60 U.S. (19 How.) 396, 404–05 (1856). . . .

20. *People* v. *Hall*, 4 Cal. 399, 405 (1854). . . .

21. Schechter, *The Rightlessness of Mediaeval English Jewry*, 45 Jewish Q. Rev. 121, 135 (1954) quoting from M. Bateson, *Medieval England* 139 (1904). . . .

22. *Dietrich* v. *Inhabitants of Northampton*, 138 Mass. 14, 16 (1884).

23. In re Goddell, 39 Wics. 232, 245 (1875). The court continued with the following "clincher":

    And when counsel was arguing for this lady that the word, person, in sec. 32, ch. 119 [respecting those qualified to practice law], necessarily includes females, her presence made it impossible to suggest to him as *reductio ad absurdum* of his position, that the same construction of the same word . . . would subject woman to prosecution for the paternity of a bastard, and . . . prosecution for rape.

    Id. at 246.

    The relationship between our attitudes toward woman, on the one hand, and, on the other, the more central concern of this article—land—is captured in an unguarded aside of our colleague, Curt

Berger: "... after all, land, like woman, was meant to be possessed...." *Land Ownership and Use*, 139 (1968).

24. Thus it was that the Founding Fathers could speak of the inalienable rights of all men, and yet maintain a society that was, by modern standards, without the most basic rights for Blacks, Indians, children and women. There was no hypocrisy; emotionally, no one *felt* that these other things were men.

25. The second thought streaming from ... the older South [is] the sincere and passionate belief that somewhere between men and cattle, God created a *tertium quid*, and called it a Negro–a clownish, simple creature, at times even lovable within its limitations, but straitly foreordained to walk within the Veil. W. E. B. DuBois, *The Souls of Black Folk* 89 (1924).

26. The statement in text is not quite true; *cf.* Murphy, *Has Nature Any Right to Life?*, 22 Hast. L. J. 467 (1971). An Irish court, passing upon the validity of a testamentary trust to the benefit of someone's dogs, observed in dictum that "'lives' means lives of human beings, not of animals or trees in California." *Kelly* v. *Dillon*, 1932 Ir. R. 255, 261. (The intended gift over on the death of the last surviving dog was held void for remoteness, the court refusing "to enter into the question of a dog's expectation of life," although prepared to observe that "in point of fact neighbor's [sic] dogs and cats are unpleasantly long-lived...." *Id.* at 260–61).

27. *See Dixon* v. *Alabama State Bd. of Educ.*, 294 F.2d 150 (5th Cir.), *cert. denied*, 368 U.S. 930 (1961).

28. The law in a suit for injunctive relief is commonly easier on the plaintiff than in a suit for damages. *See* J. Gould, *Law of Waters* § 206 (1883).

29. However, in 1970 California amended its Water Quality Act to make it easier for the Attorney General to obtain relief, e.g., one must no longer allege irreparable injury in a suit for an injunction. Cal. Water Code § 13350(b) (West 1971).

30. To whomsoever the soil belongs, he owns also to the sky and to the depths. *See* W. Blackstone, 2 Commentaries *18.

31. *See* Note, *Statutory Treatment of Industrial Stream Pollution*, 24 Geo. Wash. L. Rev. 302, 306 (1955); H. Farnham, 2 Law of Waters and Water Rights § 461 (1904); Gould, *supra* note 32, at § 204.

32. For example, courts have upheld a right to pollute by prescription, *Mississippi Mills Co.* v. *Smith*, 69 Miss. 299, 11 So. 26 (1882), and by easement, *Luama* v. *Bunker Hill & Sullivan Mining & Concentrating Co.*, 41 F.2d 358 (9th Cir. 1930).

33. *Pennsylvania Coal Co.* v. *Sanderson*, 113 Pa. 126, 149, 6 A. 453, 459 (1886).

34. Hand, J. in *Smith* v. *Staso Milling Co.*, 18 F.2d 736, 738 (2d Cir. 1927) (emphasis added). *See also Harrisonville* v. *Dickey Clay Co.*, 289 U.S. 334 (1933) (Brandeis, J.).

35. *Smith* v. *Staso*, 18 F.2d 736, 738 (2d Cir. 1927).

36. By contrast, for example, with humane societies.

37. Cal. Prob. Code § 1460 (West Supp. 1971)....

38. *Santa Clara County* v. *Southern Pac. R.R.*, 118 U.S. 394 (1886).

39. *Cf.* Golding, *Ethical Issues in Biological Engineering*, 15 U.C.L.A. L. Rev. 443, 451–63 (1968).

40. Of course, in the instance of copyright and patent protection, the creation of the "property right" can be more directly justified on homocentric grounds.

41. *See* Schrag, *Life on a Dying Lake*, in The Politics of Neglect 167, at 173 (R. Meek & J. Straayer eds. 1971).

42. On November 2, 1971, the Senate, by a vote of 86–0, passed and sent to the House the proposed Federal Water Pollution Control Act Amendments of 1971, 117 Cong. Rec. S17464 (daily ed. Nov. 2, 1971). Sections 101(a) and (a)(1) of the bill declare it to be "national policy that, consistent with the provisions of this Act—(1) the discharge of pollutants into the navigable waters be eliminated by 1985." S.2770, 92d Cong., 1st Sess., 117 Cong. Rec. S17464 (daily ed. Nov. 2, 1971).

43. 354 F.2d 608, 624 (2d Cir. 1965).

44. Again, there is a problem involving what we conceive to be the injured entity.

45. *New York Times*, Jan. 14, 1971, § 1, col. 2, and at 74, col. 7.

46. Courts have not been reluctant to award damages for the destruction of heirlooms, literary manuscripts or other property having no ascertainable market value. In *Willard* v. *Valley Gas Fuel Co.*, 171 Cal. 9, 151 Pac. 286 (1915), it was held that the measure of damages for the negligent destruction of a rare old book written by one of plaintiff's ancestors was the amount which would compensate the owner for all detriment including sentimental loss proximately caused by such destruction....

47. It is not easy to dismiss the idea of "lower" life having consciousness and feeling pain, especially since it is so difficult to know what these terms mean even as applied to humans. *See* Austin, *Other Minds*, in *Logic and Language* 342 (S. Flew ed. 1965); Schopenhauer, *On the Will in Nature*, in *Two Essays by Arthur Schopenhauer* 193, 281–304 (1889). Some experiments on plant sensitivity—of varying de-

grees of extravagance in their claims—include Lawrence, *Plants Have Feelings, Too . . .* , Organic Gardening & Farming 64 (April 1971); Woodlief, Royster & Huang, *Effect of Random Noise on Plant Growth*, 46.J. Acoustical Soc. Am. 481 (1969); Backster, *Evidence of a Primary Perception in Plant Life*, 10 Int'l J. Parapsychology 250 (1968).

48. Cousteau, *The Oceans: No Time to Lose*, L.A. Times, Oct. 24, 1971, § (opinion), at 1, col. 4.

49. *See* J. Harte & R. Socolow, Patient Earth (1971).

50. G. Hegel, Hegel's Philosophy of Right, 41 (T. Knox transl. 1945).

51. C. McCullers, *The Ballad of the Sad Cafe and Other Stories* 150–51 (1958).

52. D. Rudhyar, Directives for New Life 21—23 (1971).

53. 136. *San Antonio Conservation Soc'y v. Texas Highway Dep't, cert. denied*, 400 U.S. 968 (1970) (Black, J. dissenting to denial of certiorari).

54. *Id.* at 969.

55. *Id.* at 971.

The Ethics of Respect for Nature

Paul W. Taylor

I. Human-centered and Life-centered Systems of Environmental Ethics

In this paper I show how the taking of a certain ultimate moral attitude toward nature, which I call "respect for nature," has a central place in the foundations of a life-centered system of environmental ethics. I hold that a set of moral norms (both standards of character and rules of conduct) governing human treatment of the natural world is a rationally grounded set if and only if, first, commitment to those norms is a practical entailment of adopting the attitude of respect for nature as an ultimate moral attitude, and second, the adopting of that attitude on the part of all rational agents can itself be justified. When the basic characteristics of the attitude of respect for nature are made clear, it will be seen that a life-centered system of environmental ethics need not be holistic or organicist in its conception of the kinds of entities that are deemed the appropriate objects of moral concern and consideration. Nor does such a system require that the concepts of ecological homeostasis, equilibrium, and integrity provide us with normative principles from which could be derived (with the addition of factual knowledge) our obligations with regard to natural ecosystems. The "balance of nature" is not itself a moral norm, however important may be the role it plays in our general outlook on the natural world that underlies the attitude of respect for nature. I argue that finally it is the good (well-being,

welfare) of individual organisms, considered as entities having inherent worth, that determines our moral relations with the Earth's wild communities of life.

In designating the theory to be set forth as life-centered, I intend to contrast it with all anthropocentric views. According to the latter, human actions affecting the natural environment and its nonhuman inhabitants are right (or wrong) by either of two criteria: they have consequences which are favorable (or unfavorable) to human well-being, or they are consistent (or inconsistent) with the system of norms that protect and implement human rights. From this human-centered standpoint it is to humans and only to humans that all duties are ultimately owed. We may have responsibilities *with regard to* the natural ecosystems and biotic communities of our planet, but these responsibilities are in every case based on the contingent fact that our treatment of those ecosystems and communities of life can further the realization of human values and/or human rights. We have no obligation to promote or protect the good of nonhuman living things, independently of this contingent fact.

A life-centered system of environmental ethics is opposed to human-centered ones precisely on this point. From the perspective of a life-centered theory, we have prima facie moral obligations that are owed to wild plants and animals themselves as members of the Earth's biotic community. We are morally bound (other things being equal) to protect or promote their good for *their* sake. Our duties to

Environmental Ethics, Vol. 3 (Fall 1981), pp. 197–218. Reprinted by permission.

respect the integrity of natural ecosystems, to preserve endangered species, and to avoid environmental pollution stem from the fact that these are ways in which we can help make it possible for wild species populations to achieve and maintain a healthy existence in a natural state. Such obligations are due those living things out of recognition of their inherent worth. They are entirely additional to and independent of the obligations we owe to our fellow humans. Although many of the actions that fulfill one set of obligations will also fulfill the other, two different grounds of obligation are involved. Their well-being, as well as human well-being, is something to be realized *as an end in itself.*

If we were to accept a life-centered theory of environmental ethics, a profound reordering of our moral universe would take place. We would begin to look at the whole of the Earth's biosphere in a new light. Our duties with respect to the "world" of nature would be seen as making prima facie claims upon us to be balanced against our duties with respect to the "world" of human civilization. We could no longer simply take the human point of view and consider the effects of our actions exclusively from the perspective of our own good.

II. The Good of a Being and the Concept of Inherent Worth

What would justify acceptance of a life-centered system of ethical principles? In order to answer this it is first necessary to make clear the fundamental moral attitude that underlies and makes intelligible the commitment to live by such a system. It is then necessary to examine the considerations that would justify any rational agent's adopting that moral attitude.

Two concepts are essential to the taking of a moral attitude of the sort in question. A being which does not "have" these concepts, that is, which is unable to grasp their meaning and conditions of applicability, cannot be said to have the attitude as part of its moral outlook. These concepts are, first, that of the good (well-being, welfare) of a living thing, and second, the idea of an entity possessing inherent worth. I examine each concept in turn.

1. Every organism, species population, and community of life has a good of its own which moral agents can intentionally further or damage

by their actions. To say that an entity has a good of its own is simply to say that, without reference to any *other* entity, it can be benefited or harmed. One can act in its overall interest, and environmental conditions can be good for it (advantageous to it) or bad for it (disadvantageous to it). What is good for an entity is what "does it good" in the sense of enhancing or preserving its life and well-being. What is bad for an entity is something that is detrimental to its life and well-being.[1]

We can think of the good of an individual non-human organism as consisting in the full development of its biological powers. Its good is realized to the extent that it is strong and healthy. It possesses whatever capacities it needs for successfully coping with its environment and so preserving its existence throughout the various stages of the normal life cycle of its species. The good of a population or community of such individuals consists in the population or community maintaining itself from generation to generation as a coherent system of genetically and ecologically related organisms whose average good is at an optimum level for the given environment. (Here *average good* means that the degree of realization of the good of *individual organisms* in the population or community is, on average, greater than would be the case under any other ecologically functioning order of interrelations among those species populations in the given ecosystem.)

The idea of a being having a good of its own, as I understand it, does not entail that the being must have interests or take an interest in what affects its life for better or for worse. We can act in a being's interest or contrary to its interest without its being interested in what we are doing to it in the sense of wanting or not wanting us to do it. It may, indeed, be wholly unaware that favorable and unfavorable events are taking place in its life. I take it that trees, for example, have no knowledge or desires or feelings. Yet it is undoubtedly the case that trees can be harmed or benefited by our actions. We can crush their roots by running a bulldozer too close to them. We can see to it that they get adequate nourishment and moisture by fertilizing and watering the soil around them. Thus we can help or hinder them in the realization of their good. It is the good of trees themselves that is thereby affected. We can similarly act so as to further the good of an entire tree population of a certain species (say, all the redwood trees in a California valley) or the good of a whole community of plant life in a given wilderness area, just as we can do harm to such a population or community.

When construed in this way, the concept of a being's good is not coextensive with sentience or the capacity for feeling pain. William Frankena has argued for a general theory of environmental ethics in which the ground of a creature's being worthy of moral consideration is its sentience. I have offered some criticisms of this view elsewhere, but the full refutation of such a position, it seems to me, finally depends on the positive reasons for accepting a life-centered theory of the kind I am defending in this essay.[2]

It should be noted further that I am leaving open the question of whether machines—in particular, those which are not only goal-directed, but also self-regulating—can properly be said to have a good of their own.[3] Since I am concerned only with human treatment of wild organisms, species populations, and communities of life as they occur in our planet's natural ecosystems, it is to those entities alone that the concept "having a good of its own" will here be applied. I am not denying that other living things, whose genetic origin and environmental conditions have been produced, controlled, and manipulated by humans for human ends, do have a good of their own in the same sense as do wild plants and animals. It is not my purpose in this essay, however, to set out or defend the principles that should guide our conduct with regard to their good. It is only insofar as their production and use by humans have good or ill effects upon natural ecosystems and their wild inhabitants that the ethics of respect for nature comes into play.

2. The second concept essential to the moral attitude of respect for nature is the idea of inherent worth. We take that attitude toward wild living things (individuals, species populations, or whole biotic communities) when and only when we regard them as entities possessing inherent worth. Indeed, it is only because they are conceived in this way that moral agents can think of themselves as having validly binding duties, obligations, and responsibilities that are *owed* to them as their *due*. I am not at this juncture arguing why they *should* be so regarded; I consider it at length below. But so regarding them is a presupposition of our taking the attitude of respect toward them and accord-

ingly understanding ourselves as bearing certain moral relations to them. This can be shown as follows:

What does it mean to regard an entity that has a good of its own as possessing inherent worth? Two general principles are involved: the principle of moral consideration and the principle of intrinsic value.

According to the principle of moral consideration, wild living things are deserving of the concern and consideration of all moral agents simply in virtue of their being members of the Earth's community of life. From the moral point of view their good must be taken into account whenever it is affected for better or worse by the conduct of rational agents. This holds no matter what species the creature belongs to. The good of each is to be accorded some value and so acknowledged as having some weight in the deliberations of all rational agents. Of course, it may be necessary for such agents to act in ways contrary to the good of this or that particular organism or group of organisms in order to further the good of others, including the good of humans. But the principle of moral consideration prescribes that, with respect to each being an entity having its own good, every individual is deserving of consideration.

The principle of intrinsic value states that, regardless of what kind of entity it is in other respects, if it is a member of the Earth's community of life, the realization of its good is something *intrinsically* valuable. This means that its good is prima facie worthy of being preserved or promoted as an end in itself and for the sake of the entity whose good it is. Insofar as we regard any organism, species population, or life community as an entity having inherent worth, we believe that it must never be treated as if it were a mere object or thing whose entire value lies in being instrumental to the good of some other entity. The well-being of each is judged to have value in and of itself.

Combining these two principles, we can now define what it means for a living thing or group of living things to possess inherent worth. To say that it possesses inherent worth is to say that its good is deserving of the concern and consideration of all moral agents, and that the realization of its good has intrinsic value, to be pursued as an end in itself and for the sake of the entity whose good it is.

The duties owed to wild organisms, species

populations, and communities of life in the Earth's natural ecosystems are grounded on their inherent worth. When rational, autonomous agents regard such entities as possessing inherent worth, they place intrinsic value on the realization of their good and so hold themselves responsible for performing actions that will have this effect and for refraining from actions having the contrary effect.

III. The Attitude of Respect for Nature

Why should moral agents regard wild living things in the natural world as possessing inherent worth? To answer this question we must first take into account the fact that, when rational, autonomous agents subscribe to the principles of moral consideration and intrinsic value and so conceive of wild living things as having that kind of worth, such agents are *adopting a certain ultimate moral attitude toward the natural world.* This is the attitude I call "respect for nature." It parallels the attitude of respect for persons in human ethics. When we adopt the attitude of respect for persons as the proper (fitting, appropriate) attitude to take toward all persons as persons, we consider the fulfillment of the basic interests of each individual to have intrinsic value. We thereby make a moral commitment to live a certain kind of life in relation to other persons. We place ourselves under the direction of a system of standards and rules that we consider validly binding on all moral agents as such.[4]

Similarly, when we adopt the attitude of respect for nature as an ultimate moral attitude we make a commitment to live by certain normative principles. These principles constitute the rules of conduct and standards of character that are to govern our treatment of the natural world. This is, first, an *ultimate* commitment because it is not derived from any higher norm. The attitude of respect for nature is not grounded on some other, more general, or more fundamental attitude. It sets the total framework for our responsibilities toward the natural world. It can be justified, as I show below, but its justification cannot consist in referring to a more general attitude or a more basic normative principle.

Second, the commitment is a *moral* one because it is understood to be a disinterested matter of principle. It is this feature that distinguishes the attitude of respect for nature from the set of feelings and dispositions that comprise the love of nature. The latter stems from one's personal interest in and response to the natural world. Like the affectionate feelings we have toward certain individual human beings, one's love of nature is nothing more than the particular way one feels about the natural environment and its wild inhabitants. And just as our love for an individual person differs from our respect for all persons as such (whether we happen to love them or not), so love of nature differs from respect for nature. Respect for nature is an attitude we believe all moral agents ought to have simply as moral agents, regardless of whether or not they also love nature. Indeed, we have not truly taken the attitude of respect for nature ourselves unless we believe this. To put it in a Kantian way, to adopt the attitude of respect for nature is to take a stance that one wills it to be a universal law for all rational beings. It is to hold that stance categorically, as being validly applicable to every moral agent without exception, irrespective of whatever personal feelings toward nature such an agent might have or might lack.

Although the attitude of respect for nature is in this case a disinterested and universalizable attitude, anyone who does adopt it has certain steady, more or less permanent dispositions. These dispositions, which are themselves to be considered disinterested and universalizable, comprise three interlocking sets: dispositions to seek certain ends, dispositions to carry on one's practical reasoning and deliberation in a certain way, and dispositions to have certain feelings. We may accordingly analyze the attitude of respect for nature into the following components. (a) The disposition to aim at, and to take steps to bring about, as final and disinterested ends, the promoting and protecting of the good of organisms, species populations, and life communities in natural ecosystems. (These ends are "final" in not being pursued as means to further ends. They are "disinterested" in being independent of the self-interest of the agent.) (b) The disposition to consider actions that tend to realize those ends to be prima facie obligatory *because* they have that tendency. (c) The disposition to experience positive and negative feelings toward states of affairs in the world *because* they are favorable or unfavorable to the good of organisms, species populations, and life communities in natural ecosystems.

The logical connection between the attitude of respect for nature and the duties of a life-centered system of environmental ethics can now be made clear. Insofar as one sincerely takes that attitude and so has the three sets of dispositions, one will at the same time be disposed to comply with certain rules of duty (such as nonmaleficence and noninterference) and with standards of character (such as fairness and benevolence) that determine the obligations and virtues of moral agents with regard to the Earth's wild living things. We can say that the actions one performs and the character traits one develops in fulfilling these moral requirements are the way one *expresses* or *embodies* the attitude in one's conduct and character. In his famous essay, "Justice as Fairness," John Rawls describes the rules of the duties of human morality (such as fidelity, gratitude, honesty, and justice) as "forms of conduct in which recognition of others as persons is manifested."[5] I hold that the rules of duty governing our treatment of the natural world and its inhabitants are forms of conduct in which the attitude of respect for nature is manifested.

IV. The Justifiability of the Attitude of Respect for Nature

I return to the question posed earlier, which has not yet been answered: why *should* moral agents regard wild living things as possessing inherent worth? I now argue that the only way we can answer this question is by showing how adopting the attitude of respect for nature is justified for all moral agents. Let us suppose that we were able to establish that there are good reasons for adopting the attitude, reasons which are intersubjectively valid for every rational agent. If there are such reasons, they would justify anyone's having the three sets of dispositions mentioned above as constituting what it means to have the attitude. Since these include the disposition to promote or protect the good of wild living things as a disinterested and ultimate end, as well as the disposition to perform actions for the reason that they tend to realize that end, we see that such dispositions commit a person to the principles of moral consideration and intrinsic value. To be disposed to further, as an end in itself, the good of any entity in nature just because it is that kind of entity, is to be disposed to give consideration to *every* such entity and to place in-

trinsic value on the realization of its good. Insofar as we subscribe to these two principles we regard living things as possessing inherent worth. Subscribing to the principle is what it *means* to so regard them. To justify the attitude of respect for nature, then, is to justify commitment to these principles and thereby to justify regarding wild creatures as possessing inherent worth.

We must keep in mind that inherent worth is not some mysterious sort of objective property belonging to living things that can be discovered by empirical observation or scientific investigation. To ascribe inherent worth to an entity is not to describe it by citing some feature discernible by sense perception or inferable by inductive reasoning. Nor is there a logically necessary connection between the concept of a being having a good of its own and the concept of inherent worth. We do not contradict ourselves by asserting that an entity that has a good of its own lacks inherent worth. In order to show that such an entity "has" inherent worth we must give good reasons for ascribing that kind of value to it (placing that kind of value upon it, conceiving of it to be valuable in that way). Although it is humans (persons, valuers) who must do the valuing, for the ethics of respect for nature, the value so ascribed is not a human value. That is to say, it is not a value derived from considerations regarding human well-being or human rights. It is a value that is ascribed to nonhuman animals and plants themselves, independently of their relationship to what humans judge to be conducive to their own good.

Whatever reasons, then, justify our taking the attitude of respect for nature as defined above are also reasons that show why we *should* regard the living things of the natural world as possessing inherent worth. We saw earlier that, since the attitude is an ultimate one, it cannot be derived from a more fundamental attitude nor shown to be a special case of a more general one. On what sort of grounds, then, can it be established?

The attitude we take toward living things in the natural world depends on the way we look at them, on what kind of beings we conceive them to be, and on how we understand the relations we bear to them. Underlying and supporting our attitude is a certain *belief system* that constitutes a particular world view or outlook on nature and the place of human life in it. To give good reasons for adopting the attitude of respect for nature, then, we must first articulate the belief system which underlies and supports that attitude. If it appears that the belief system is internally coherent and well-ordered, and if, as far as we can now tell, it is consistent with all known scientific truths relevant to our knowledge of the object of the attitude (which in this case includes the whole set of the Earth's natural ecosystems and their communities of life), then there remains the task of indicating why scientifically informed and rational thinkers with a developed capacity of reality awareness can find it acceptable as a way of conceiving of the natural world and our place in it. To the extent we can do this we provide at least a reasonable argument for accepting the belief system and the ultimate moral attitude it supports.

I do not hold that such a belief system can be *proven* to be true, either inductively or deductively. As we shall see, not all of its components can be stated in the form of empirically verifiable propositions. Nor is its internal order governed by purely logical relationships. But the system as a whole, I contend, constitutes a coherent, unified, and rationally acceptable "picture" or "map" of a total world. By examining each of its main components and seeing how they fit together, we obtain a scientifically informed and well-ordered conception of nature and the place of humans in it.

This belief system underlying the attitude of respect for nature I call (for want of a better name) "the biocentric outlook on nature." Since it is not wholly analyzable into empirically confirmable assertions, it should not be thought of as simply a compendium of the biological sciences concerning our planet's ecosystems. It might best be described as a philosophical world view, to distinguish it from a scientific theory or explanatory system. However, one of its major tenets is the great lesson we have learned from the science of ecology: the interdependence of all living things in an organically unified order whose balance and stability are necessary conditions for the realization of the good of its constituent biotic communities.

Before turning to an account of the main components of the biocentric outlook, it is convenient here to set forth the overall structure of my theory of environmental ethics as it has now emerged. The ethics of respect for nature is made up of three basic elements: a belief system, an ultimate moral attitude, and a set of rules of duty and standards of character. These elements are connected with each other in the following manner. The belief system provides a certain outlook on nature which supports and makes intelligible an autonomous agent's adopting, as an ultimate moral attitude, the attitude of respect for nature. It supports and makes intelligible the attitude in the sense that, when an autonomous agent understands its moral relations to the natural world in terms of this outlook, it recognizes the attitude of respect to be the only *suitable* or *fitting* attitude to take toward all wild forms of life in the Earth's biosphere. Living things are now viewed as *the appropriate objects of the attitude of respect* and are accordingly regarded as entities possessing inherent worth. One then places intrinsic value on the promotion and protection of their good. As a consequence of this, one makes a moral commitment to abide by a set of rules of duty and to fulfill (as far as one can by one's own efforts) certain standards of good character. Given one's adoption of the attitude of respect, one makes that moral commitment because one considers those rules and standards to be validly binding on all moral agents. They are seen as embodying forms of conduct and character structures in which the attitude of respect for nature is manifested.

This three-part complex which internally orders the ethics of respect for nature is symmetrical with a theory of human ethics grounded on respect for persons. Such a theory includes, first, a conception of oneself and others as persons, that is, as centers of autonomous choice. Second, there is the attitude of respect for persons as persons. When this is adopted as an ultimate moral attitude it involves the disposition to treat every person as having inherent worth or "human dignity." Every human being, just in virtue of her or his humanity, is understood to be worthy of moral consideration, and intrinsic value is placed on the autonomy and well-being of each. This is what Kant meant by conceiving of persons as ends in themselves. Third, there is an ethical system of duties which are acknowledged to be owed by everyone to everyone. These duties are forms of conduct in which public recognition is given to each individual's inherent worth as a person.

This structural framework for a theory of human ethics is meant to leave open the issue of consequentialism (utilitarianism) versus nonconsequentialism (deontology). That issue concerns the particular kind of system of rules defining the duties of moral agents toward persons. Similarly, I am leaving open in this paper the question of what particular kind of system of rules defines our duties with respect to the natural world.

V. The Biocentric Outlook on Nature

The biocentric outlook on nature has four main components. (1) Humans are thought of as members of the Earth's community of life, holding that membership on the same terms as apply to all the nonhuman members. (2) The Earth's natural ecosystems as a totality are seen as a complex web of interconnected elements, with the sound biological functioning of each being dependent on the sound biological functioning of the others. (This is the component referred to above as the great lesson that the science of ecology has taught us.) (3) Each individual organism is conceived of as a teleological center of life, pursuing its own good in its own way. (4) Whether we are concerned with standards of merit or with the concept of inherent worth, the claim that humans by their very nature are superior to other species is a groundless claim and, in the light of elements (1), (2), and (3) above, must be rejected as nothing more than an irrational bias in our own favor.

The conjunction of these four ideas constitutes the biocentric outlook on nature. In the remainder of this paper I give a brief account of the first three components, followed by a more detailed analysis of the fourth. I then conclude by indicating how this outlook provides a way of justifying the attitude of respect for nature.

VI. Humans as Members of the Earth's Community of Life

We share with other species a common relationship to the Earth. In accepting the biocentric outlook we take the fact of our being an animal species to be a fundamental feature of our existence. We consider it an essential aspect of "the human condition." We do not deny the differences between ourselves and other species, but we keep in the forefront of our consciousness the fact that in relation to our planet's natural ecosystems we are but one species population among many. Thus we ac-

knowledge our origin in the very same evolutionary process that gave rise to all other species and we recognize ourselves to be confronted with similar environmental challenges to those that confront them. The laws of genetics, of natural selection, and of adaptation apply equally to all of us as biological creatures. In this light we consider ourselves as one with them, not set apart from them. We, as well as they, must face certain basic conditions of existence that impose requirements on us for our survival and well-being. Each animal and plant is like us in having a good of its own. Although our human good (what is of true value in human life, including the exercise of individual autonomy in choosing our own particular value systems) is not like the good of a nonhuman animal or plant, it can no more be realized than their good can without the biological necessities for survival and physical health.

When we look at ourselves from the evolutionary point of view, we see that not only are we very recent arrivals on Earth, but that our emergence as a new species on the planet was originally an event of no particular importance to the entire scheme of things. The Earth was teeming with life long before we appeared. Putting the point metaphorically, we are relative newcomers, entering a home that has been the residence of others for hundreds of millions of years, a home that must now be shared by all of us together.

The comparative brevity of human life on Earth may be vividly depicted by imagining the geological time scale in spatial terms. Suppose we start with algae, which have been around for at least 600 million years. (The earliest protozoa actually predated this by several *billion* years.) If the time that algae have been here were represented by the length of a football field (300 feet), then the period during which sharks have been swimming in the world's oceans and spiders have been spinning their webs would occupy three quarters of the length of the field; reptiles would show up at about the center of the field; mammals would cover the last third of the field; hominids (mammals of the family *Hominidae*) the last two feet; and the species *Homo sapiens* the last six inches.

Whether this newcomer is able to survive as long as other species remains to be seen. But there is surely something presumptuous about the way humans look down on the "lower" animals, especially those that have become extinct. We consider the dinosaurs, for example, to be biological failures, though they existed on our planet for 65 million years. One writer has made the point with beautiful simplicity:

> We sometimes speak of the dinosaurs as failures; there will be time enough for that judgment when we have lasted even for one tenth as long. . . .[6]

The possibility of the extinction of the human species, a possibility which starkly confronts us in the contemporary world, makes us aware of another respect in which we should not consider ourselves privileged beings in relation to other species. This is the fact that the well-being of humans is dependent upon the ecological soundness and health of many plant and animal communities, while their soundness and health does not in the least depend upon human well-being. Indeed, from their standpoint the very existence of humans is quite unnecessary. Every last man, woman, and child could disappear from the face of the Earth without any significant detrimental consequence for the good of wild animals and plants. On the contrary, many of them would be greatly benefited. The destruction of their habitats by human "developments" would cease. The poisoning and polluting of their environment would come to an end. The Earth's land, air, and water would no longer be subject to the degradation they are now undergoing as the result of large-scale technology and uncontrolled population growth. Life communities in natural ecosystems would gradually return to their former healthy state. Tropical forests, for example, would again be able to make their full contribution to a life-sustaining atmosphere for the whole planet. The rivers, lakes, and oceans of the world would (perhaps) eventually become clean again. Spilled oil, plastic trash, and even radioactive waste might finally, after many centuries, cease doing their terrible work. Ecosystems would return to their proper balance, suffering only the disruptions of natural events such as volcanic eruptions and glaciation. From these the community of life could recover, as it has so often done in the past. But the ecological disasters now perpetrated on it by humans—disasters from which it might never recover—these it would no longer have to endure.

If, then, the total, final, absolute extermination of our species (by our own hands?) should take place and if we should not carry all the others with us into oblivion, not only would the Earth's community of life continue to exist, but in all probability its well-being would be enhanced. Our presence, in short, is not needed. If we were to take the standpoint of the community and give voice to its true interest, the ending of our 6-inch epoch would most likely be greeted with a hearty "Good riddance!"

VII. The Natural World as an Organic System

To accept the biocentric outlook and regard ourselves and our place in the world from its perspective is to see the whole natural order of the Earth's biosphere as a complex but unified web of interconnected organisms, objects, and events. The ecological relationships between any community of living things and their environment form an organic whole of functionally independent parts. Each ecosystem is a small universe itself in which the interactions of its various species populations comprise an intricately woven network of cause-effect relations. Such dynamic but at the same time relatively stable structures as food chains, predator-prey relations, and plant succession in a forest are self-regulating, energy-recycling mechanisms that preserve the equilibrium of the whole.

As far as the well-being of wild animals and plants is concerned, this ecological equilibrium must not be destroyed. The same holds true of the well-being of humans. When one views the realm of nature from the perspective of the biocentric outlook, one never forgets that in the long run the integrity of the entire biosphere of our planet is essential to the realization of the good of its constituent communities of life, both human and nonhuman.

Although the importance of this idea cannot be overemphasized, it is by now so familiar and so widely acknowledged that I shall not further elaborate on it here. However, I do wish to point out that this "holistic" view of the Earth's ecological systems does not itself constitute a moral norm. It is a factual aspect of biological reality, to be understood as a set of causal connections in ordinary empirical terms. Its significance for humans is the same as its significance for nonhumans, namely, in setting basic conditions for the realization of the good of living things. Its ethical implications for our treatment of the natural environment lie entirely in the fact that our *knowledge* of these causal connections is an essential *means* to fulfilling the aims we set for ourselves in adopting the attitude of respect for nature. In addition, its theoretical implications for the ethics of respect for nature lie in the fact that it (along with the other elements of the biocentric outlook) makes the adopting of that attitude a rational and intelligible thing to do.

VIII. Individual Organisms as Teleological Centers of Life

As our knowledge of living things increases, as we come to a deeper understanding of their life cycles, their interactions with other organisms, and the manifold ways in which they adjust to the environment, we become more fully aware of how each of them is carrying out its biological functions according to the laws of its species-specific nature. But besides this, our increasing knowledge and understanding also develop in us a sharpened awareness of the uniqueness of each individual organism. Scientists who have made careful studies of particular plants and animals, whether in the field or in laboratories, have often acquired a knowledge of their subjects as identifiable individuals. Close observation over extended periods of time has led them to an appreciation of the unique "personalities" of their subjects. Sometimes a scientist may come to take a special interest in a particular animal or plant, all the while remaining strictly objective in the gathering and recording of data. Nonscientists may likewise experience this development of interest when, as amateur naturalists, they make accurate observations over sustained periods of close acquaintance with an individual organism. As one becomes more and more familiar with the organism and its behavior, one becomes fully sensitive to the particular way it is living out its life cycle. One may become fascinated by it and even experience some involvement with its good and bad fortunes (that is, with the occurrence of environmental conditions favorable or unfavorable to the realization of its good). The organism comes to mean something to one as a unique, irreplaceable individual. The final culmination of this process is the achievement of a genuine understanding of its point of view and, with that understanding, an ability to "take" that point of view. *Conceiving of it as a center of life, one is able to look at the world from its perspective.*

This development from objective knowledge to the recognition of individuality, and from the recognition of individuality to full awareness of an organism's standpoint, is a process of heightening our consciousness of what it means to be an individual living thing. We grasp the particularity of the organism as a teleological center of life, striving to preserve itself and to realize its own good in its own unique way.

It is to be noted that we need not be falsely anthropomorphizing when we conceive of individual plants and animals in this manner. Understanding them as teleological centers of life does not necessitate "reading into" them human characteristics. We need not, for example, consider them to have consciousness. Some of them may be aware of the world around them and others may not. Nor need we deny that different kinds and levels of awareness are exemplified when consciousness in some form is present. But conscious or not, all are equally teleological centers of life in the sense that each is a unified system of goal-oriented activities directed toward their preservation and well-being.

When considered from an ethical point of view, a teleological center of life is an entity whose "world" can be viewed from the perspective of *its* life. In looking at the world from that perspective we recognize objects and events occurring in its life as being beneficent, maleficent, or indifferent. The first are occurrences which increase its powers to preserve its existence and realize its good. The second decrease or destroy those powers. The third have neither of these effects on the entity. With regard to our human role as moral agents, we can conceive of a teleological center of life as a being whose standpoint we can take in making judgments about what events in the world are good or evil, desirable or undesirable. In making those judgments it is what promotes or protects the being's own good, not what benefits moral agents themselves, that sets the standard of evaluation. Such judgments can be made about anything that happens to the entity which is favorable or unfavorable in relation to its good. As was pointed out earlier, the entity itself need not have any (conscious) *interest* in what is happening to it for such judgments to be meaningful and true.

It is precisely judgments of this sort that we

are disposed to make when we take the attitude of respect for nature. In adopting that attitude those judgments are given weight as reasons for action in our practical deliberation. They become morally relevant facts in the guidance of our conduct.

IX. The Denial of Human Superiority

This fourth component of the biocentric outlook on nature is the single most important idea in establishing the justifiability of the attitude of respect for nature. Its central role is due to the special relationship it bears to the first three components of the outlook. This relationship will be brought out after the concept of human superiority is examined and analyzed.[7]

In what sense are humans alleged to be superior to other animals? We are different from them in having certain capacities that they lack. But why should these capacities be a mark of superiority? From what point of view are they judged to be signs of superiority and what sense of superiority is meant? After all, various nonhuman species have capacities that humans lack. There is the speed of a cheetah, the vision of an eagle, the agility of a monkey. Why should not these be taken as signs of *their* superiority over humans?

One answer that comes immediately to mind is that these capacities are not as *valuable* as the human capacities that are claimed to make us superior. Such uniquely human characteristics as rational thought, aesthetic creativity, autonomy and self-determination, and moral freedom, it might be held, have a higher value than the capacities found in other species. Yet we must ask: valuable to whom, and on what grounds?

The human characteristics mentioned are all valuable to humans. They are essential to the preservation and enrichment of our civilization and culture. Clearly it is from the human standpoint that they are being judged to be desirable and good. It is not difficult here to recognize a begging of the question. Humans are claiming human superiority from a strictly human point of view, that is, from a point of view in which the good of humans is taken as the standard of judgment. All we need to do is to look at the capacities of nonhuman animals (or plants, for that matter) from the standpoint of *their* good to find a contrary judgment of superiority. The speed of the cheetah, for example, is a sign of

its superiority to humans when considered from the standpoint of the good of its species. If it were as slow a runner as a human, it would not be able to survive. And so for all the other abilities of nonhumans which further their good but which are lacking in humans. In each case the claim to human superiority would be rejected from a nonhuman standpoint.

When superiority assertions are interpreted in this way, they are based on judgments of *merit*. To judge the merits of a person or an organism one must apply grading or ranking standards to it. (As I show below, this distinguishes judgments of merit from judgments of inherent worth.) Empirical investigation then determines whether it has the "good-making properties" (merits) in virtue of which it fulfills the standards being applied. In the case of humans, merits may be either moral or nonmoral. We can judge one person to be better than (superior to) another from the moral point of view by applying certain standards to their character and conduct. Similarly, we can appeal to nonmoral criteria in judging someone to be an excellent piano player, a fair cook, a poor tennis player, and so on. Different social purposes and roles are implicit in the making of such judgments, providing the frame of reference for the choice of standards by which the nonmoral merits of people are determined. Ultimately such purposes and roles stem from a society's way of life as a whole. Now a society's way of life may be thought of as the cultural form given to the realization of human values. Whether moral or nonmoral standards are being applied, then, all judgments of people's merits finally depend on human values. All are made from an exclusively human standpoint.

The question that naturally arises at this juncture is: why should standards that are based on human values be assumed to be the only valid criteria of merit and hence the only true signs of superiority? This question is especially pressing when humans are being judged superior in merit to nonhumans. It is true that a human being may be a better mathematician than a monkey, but the monkey may be a better tree climber than a human being. If we humans value mathematics more than tree climbing, that is because our conception of civilized life makes the development of mathematical ability more desirable than the ability to climb trees. But is it not unreasonable to judge nonhumans by the values of human civilization, rather than by values connected with what it is for a member of *that* species to live a good life? If all living things have a good of their own, it at least makes sense to judge the merits of nonhumans by standards derived from *their* good. To use only standards based on human values is already to commit oneself to holding that humans are superior to nonhumans, which is the point in question.

A further logical flaw arises in connection with the widely held conviction that humans are *morally* superior beings because they possess, while others lack, the capacities of a moral agent (free will, accountability, deliberation, judgment, practical reason). This view rests on a conceptual confusion. As far as moral standards are concerned, only beings that have the capacities of a moral agent can properly be judged to be *either* moral (morally good) *or* immoral (morally deficient). Moral standards are simply not applicable to beings that lack such capacities. Animals and plants cannot therefore be said to be morally inferior in merit to humans. Since the only beings that can have moral merits *or be deficient in such merits* are moral agents, it is conceptually incoherent to judge humans as superior to nonhumans on the ground that humans have moral capacities while nonhumans don't.

Up to this point I have been interpreting the claim that humans are superior to other living things as a grading or ranking judgment regarding their comparative merits. There is, however, another way of understanding the idea of human superiority. According to this interpretation, humans are superior to nonhumans not as regards their merits but as regards their inherent worth. Thus the claim of human superiority is to be understood as asserting that all humans, simply in virtue of their humanity, have *a greater inherent worth* than other living things.

The inherent worth of an entity does not depend on its merits.[8] To consider something as possessing inherent worth, we have seen, is to place intrinsic value on the realization of its good. This is done regardless of whatever particular merits it might have or might lack, as judged by a set of grading or ranking standards. In human affairs, we are all familiar with the principle that one's worth as a person does not vary with one's merits or lack of merits. The same can hold true of animals and plants. To regard such entities as possessing inherent worth entails disregarding their merits and de-

ficiencies, whether they are being judged from a human standpoint or from the standpoint of their own species.

The idea of one entity having more merit than another, and so being superior to it in merit, makes perfectly good sense. Merit is a grading or ranking concept, and judgments of comparative merit are based on the different degrees to which things satisfy a given standard. But what can it mean to talk about one thing being superior to another in inherent worth? In order to get at what is being asserted in such a claim it is helpful first to look at the social origin of the concept of degrees of inherent worth.

The idea that humans can possess different degrees of inherent worth originated in societies having rigid class structures. Before the rise of modern democracies with their egalitarian outlook, one's membership in a hereditary class determined one's social status. People in the upper classes were looked up to, while those in the lower classes were looked down upon. In such a society one's social superiors and social inferiors were clearly defined and easily recognized.

Two aspects of these class-structured societies are especially relevant to the idea of degrees of inherent worth. First, those born into the upper classes were deemed more worthy of respect than those born into the lower orders. Second, the superior worth of upper class people had nothing to do with their merits nor did the inferior worth of those in the lower classes rest on their lack of merits. One's superiority or inferiority entirely derived from a social position one was born into. The modern concept of a meritocracy simply did not apply. One could not advance into a higher class by any sort of moral or nonmoral achievement. Similarly, an aristocrat held his title and all the privileges that went with it just because he was the eldest son of a titled nobleman. Unlike the bestowing of knighthood in contemporary Great Britain, one did not earn membership in the nobility by meritorious conduct.

We who live in modern democracies no longer believe in such hereditary social distinctions. Indeed, we would wholeheartedly condemn them on moral grounds as being fundamentally unjust. We have come to think of class systems as a paradigm of social injustice, it being a central principle of the democratic way of life that among humans there are no superiors and no inferiors. Thus we have rejected the whole conceptual framework in which people are judged to have different degrees of inherent worth. That idea is incompatible with our notion of human equality based on the doctrine that all humans, simply in virtue of their humanity, have the same inherent worth. (The belief in universal human rights is one form that this egalitarianism takes.)

The vast majority of people in modern democracies, however, do not maintain an egalitarian outlook when it comes to comparing human beings with other living things. Most people consider our own species to be superior to all other species and this superiority is understood to be a matter of inherent worth, not merit. There may exist thoroughly vicious and depraved humans who lack all merit. Yet because they are human they are thought to belong to a higher class of entities than any plant or animal. That one is born into the species *Homo sapiens* entitles one to have lordship over those who are one's inferiors, namely, those born into other species. The parallel with hereditary social classes is very close. Implicit in this view is a hierarchical conception of nature according to which an organism has a position of superiority or inferiority in the Earth's community of life simply on the basis of its genetic background. The "lower" orders of life are looked down upon and it is considered perfectly proper that they serve the interests of those belonging to the highest order, namely humans. The intrinsic value we place on the well-being of our fellow humans reflects our recognition of their rightful position as our equals. No such intrinsic value is to be placed on the good of other animals, unless we choose to do so out of fondness or affection for them. But their well-being imposes no moral requirement on us. In this respect there is an absolute difference in moral status between ourselves and them.

This is the structure of concepts and beliefs that people are committed to insofar as they regard humans to be superior in inherent worth to all other species. I now wish to argue that this structure of concepts and beliefs is completely groundless. If we accept the first three components of the biocentric outlook and from that perspective look at the major philosophical traditions which have supported that structure, we find it to be at bottom nothing more than the expression of an irrational bias in our own favor. The philosophical traditions themselves rest on very questionable assumptions or else simply beg the question. I briefly consider three of the main traditions to substantiate the point. These are classical Greek humanism, Cartesian dualism, and the Judeo-Christian concept of the Great Chain of Being.

The inherent superiority of humans over other species was implicit in the Greek definition of man as a rational animal. Our animal nature was identified with "brute" desires that need the order and restraint of reason to rule them (just as reason is the special virtue of those who rule in the ideal state). Rationality was then seen to be the key to our superiority over animals. It enables us to live on a higher plane and endows us with a nobility and worth that other creatures lack. This familiar way of comparing humans with other species is deeply ingrained in our Western philosophical outlook. The point to consider here is that this view does not actually provide an argument *for* human superiority but rather makes explicit the framework of thought that is implicitly used by those who think of humans as inherently superior to nonhumans. The Greeks who held that humans, in virtue of their rational capacities, have a kind of worth greater than that of any nonrational being, never looked at rationality as but one capacity of living things among many others. But when we consider rationality from the standpoint of the first three elements of the ecological outlook, we see that its value lies in its importance for *human* life. Other creatures achieve their species-specific good without the need of rationality, although they often make use of capacities that humans lack. So the humanistic outlook of classical Greek thought does not give us a neutral (nonquestion-begging) ground on which to construct a scale of degrees of inherent worth possessed by different species of living things.

The second tradition, centering on the Cartesian dualism of soul and body, also fails to justify the claim to human superiority. That superiority is supposed to derive from the fact that we have souls while animals do not. Animals are mere automata and lack the divine element that makes us spiritual beings. I won't go into the now familiar criticisms of this two-substance view. I only add the point that, even if humans are composed of an immaterial, unextended soul and a material, extended body, this in itself is not a reason to deem them of greater worth than entities that are only bodies.

Why is a soul substance a thing that adds value to its possessor? Unless some theological reasoning is offered here (which many, including myself, would find unacceptable on epistemological grounds), no logical connection is evident. An immaterial something which thinks is better than a material something which does not think only if thinking itself has value, either intrinsically or instrumentally. Now it is intrinsically valuable to humans alone, who value it as an end in itself, and it is instrumentally valuable to those who benefit from it, namely humans.

For animals that neither enjoy thinking for its own sake nor need it for living the kind of life for which they are best adapted, it has no value. Even if "thinking" is broadened to include all forms of consciousness, there are still many living things that can do without it and yet live what is for their species a good life. The anthropocentricity underlying the claim to human superiority runs throughout Cartesian dualism.

A third major source of the idea of human superiority is the Judeo-Christian concept of the Great Chain of Being. Humans are superior to animals and plants because their Creator has given them a higher place on the chain. It begins with God at the top, and then moves to the angels, who are lower than God but higher than humans, then to humans, positioned between the angels and the beasts (partaking of the nature of both), and then on down to the lower levels occupied by nonhuman animals, plants, and finally inanimate objects. Humans, being "made in God's image," are inherently superior to animals and plants by virtue of their being closer (in their essential nature) to God.

The metaphysical and epistemological difficulties with this conception of a hierarchy of entities are, in my mind, insuperable. Without entering into this matter here, I only point out that if we are unwilling to accept the metaphysics of traditional Judaism and Christianity, we are again left without good reasons for holding to the claim of inherent human superiority.

The foregoing considerations (and others like them) leave us with but one ground for the assertion that a human being, regardless of merit, is a higher kind of entity than any other living thing. This is the mere fact of the genetic makeup of the species *Homo sapiens*. But this is surely irrational and arbitrary. Why should the arrangement of genes of a certain type be a mark of superior value,

especially when this fact about an organism is taken by itself, unrelated to any other aspect of its life? We might just as well refer to any other genetic makeup as a ground of superior value. Clearly we are confronted here with a wholly arbitrary claim that can only be explained as an irrational bias in our own favor.

That the claim is nothing more than a deep-seated prejudice is brought home to us when we look at our relation to other species in the light of the first three elements of biocentric outlook. Those elements taken conjointly give us a certain overall view of the natural world and of the place of humans in it. When we take this view we come to understand other living things, their environmental conditions, and their ecological relationships in such a way as to awake in us a deep sense of our kinship with them as fellow members of the Earth's community of life. Humans and nonhumans alike are viewed together as integral parts of one unified whole in which all living things are functionally interrelated. Finally, when our awareness focuses on the individual lives of plants and animals, each is seen to share with us the characteristic of being a teleological center of life striving to realize its own good in its own unique way.

As this entire belief system becomes part of the conceptual framework through which we understand and perceive the world, we come to see ourselves as bearing a certain moral relation to nonhuman forms of life. Our ethical role in nature takes on a new significance. We begin to look at other species as we look at ourselves, seeing them as beings which have a good they are striving to realize just as we have a good we are striving to realize. We accordingly develop the disposition to view the world from the standpoint of their good as well as from the standpoint of our own good. Now if the groundlessness of the claim that humans are inherently superior to other species were brought clearly before our minds, we would not remain intellectually neutral toward that claim but would reject it as being fundamentally at variance with our total world outlook. In the absence of any good reasons for holding it, the assertion of human superiority would then appear simply as the expression of an irrational and self-serving prejudice that favors one particular species over several million others.

Rejecting the notion of human superiority entails its positive counterpart: the doctrine of species impartiality. One who accepts that doctrine regards all living things as possessing inherent worth—the *same* inherent worth, since no one species has been shown to be either "higher" or "lower" than any other. Now we saw earlier that, insofar as one thinks of a living thing as possessing inherent worth, one considers it to be the appropriate object of the attitude of respect and believes that attitude to be the only fitting or suitable one for all moral agents to take toward it.

Here, then, is the key to understanding how the attitude of respect is rooted in the biocentric outlook on nature. The basic connection is made through the denial of human superiority. Once we reject the claim that humans are superior either in merit or in worth to other living things, we are ready to adopt the attitude of respect. The denial of human superiority is itself the result of taking the perspective on nature built into the first three elements of the biocentric outlook.

Now the first three elements of the biocentric outlook, it seems clear, would be found acceptable to any rational and scientifically informed thinker who is fully "open" to the reality of the lives of nonhuman organisms. Without denying our distinctively human characteristics, such a thinker can acknowledge the fundamental respects in which we are members of the Earth's community of life and in which the biological conditions necessary for the realization of our human values are inextricably linked with the whole system of nature. In addition, the conception of individual living things as teleological centers of life simply articulates how a scientifically informed thinker comes to understand them as the result of increasingly careful and detailed observations. Thus, the biocentric outlook recommends itself as an acceptable system of concepts and beliefs to anyone who is clear-minded, unbiased, and factually enlightened, and who has a developed capacity of reality awareness with regard to the lives of individual organisms. This, I submit, is as good a reason for making the moral commitment involved in adopting the attitude of respect for nature as any theory of environmental ethics could possibly have.

X. Moral Rights and the Matter of Competing Claims

I have not asserted anywhere in the foregoing account that animals or plants have moral rights. This omission was deliberate. I do not think that the reference class of the concept, bearer of moral rights, should be extended to include nonhuman living things. My reasons for taking this position, however, go beyond the scope of this paper. I believe I have been able to accomplish many of the same ends which those who ascribe rights to animals or plants wish to accomplish. There is no reason, moreover, why plants and animals, including whole species populations and life communities, cannot be accorded *legal* rights under my theory. To grant them legal protection could be interpreted as giving them legal entitlement to be protected, and this, in fact, would be a means by which a society that subscribed to the ethics of respect for nature could give public recognition to their inherent worth.

There remains the problem of competing claims, even when wild plants and animals are not thought of as bearers of moral rights. If we accept the biocentric outlook and accordingly adopt the attitude of respect for nature as our ultimate moral attitude, how do we resolve conflicts that arise from our respect for persons in the domain of human ethics and our respect for nature in the domain of environmental ethics? This is a question that cannot adequately be dealt with here. My main purpose in this paper has been to try to establish a base point from which we can start working toward a solution to the problem. I have shown why we cannot just begin with an initial presumption in favor of the interests of our own species. It is after all within our power as moral beings to place limits on human population and technology with the deliberate intention of sharing the Earth's bounty with other species. That such sharing is an ideal difficult to realize even in an approximate way does not take away its claim to our deepest moral commitment.

Notes

1. The conceptual links between an entity *having* a good, something being good *for* it, and events doing good *to* it are examined by G. H. Von Wright in *The Varieties of Goodness* (New York: Humanities Press, 1963), chaps. 3 and 5.

2. See W. K. Frankena, "Ethics and the Environment," in K. E. Goodpaster and K. M. Sayre, eds., *Ethics and Problems of the 21st Century* (Notre Dame, IN: University of Notre Dame Press, 1979), pp. 3–20. I critically examine Frankena's views in "Frankena on Environmental Ethics," *Monist,* forthcoming.

3. In the light of considerations set forth in Daniel

Dennett's *Brainstorms: Philosophical Essays on Mind and Psychology* (Montgomery, VT: Bradford Books, 1978), it is advisable to leave this question unsettled at this time. When machines are developed that function in the way our brains do, we may well come to deem them proper subjects of moral consideration.

4. I have analyzed the nature of this commitment of human ethics in "On Taking the Moral Point of View," *Midwest Studies in Philosophy*, Vol. 3, *Studies in Ethical Theory* (1978), pp. 35–61.

5. John Rawls, "Justice As Fairness," *Philosophical Review* 67 (1958): 183.

6. Stephen R. L. Clark, *The Moral Status of Animals* (Oxford: Clarendon Press, 1977), p. 112.

7. My criticisms of the dogma of human superiority gain independent support from a carefully reasoned essay by R. and V. Routley showing the many logical weaknesses in arguments for human-centered theories of environmental ethics. R. and V. Routley, "Against the Inevitability of Human Chauvinism," in K. E. Goodpaster and K. M. Sayre, eds., *Ethics and Problems of the 21st Century* (Notre Dame, IN: University of Notre Dame Press, 1979), pp. 36–59.

8. For this way of distinguishing between merit and inherent worth, I am indebted to Gregory Vlastos, "Justice and Equality," in R. Brandt, ed., *Social Justice* (Englewood Cliffs, NJ: Prentice-Hall, 1962), pp. 31–72.

The Land Ethic

Aldo Leopold

When godlike Odysseus returned from the wars in Troy, he hanged all on one rope a dozen slave-girls of his household whom he suspected of misbehavior during his absence.

This hanging involved no question of propriety. The girls were property. The disposal of property was then, as now, a matter of expediency, not of right and wrong.

Concepts of right and wrong were not lacking from Odysseus' Greece: witness the fidelity of his wife through the long years before at last his black-prowed galleys clove the wine-dark seas for home. The ethical structure of that day covered wives, but had not yet been extended to human chattels. During the three thousand years which have since elapsed, ethical criteria have been extended to many fields of conduct, with corresponding shrinkages in those judged by expediency only.

The Ethical Sequence

This extension of ethics, so far studied only by philosophers, is actually a process in ecological evolution. Its sequences may be described in ecological as well as in philosophical terms. An ethic, ecologically, is a limitation on freedom of action in the struggle for existence. An ethic, philosophically, is a differentiation of social from antisocial conduct. These are two definitions of one thing. The thing has its origin in the tendency of interdependent individuals or groups to evolve modes of cooperation. The ecologist calls these symbioses. Politics and economics are advanced symbioses in which the original free-for-all competition has been replaced, in part, by cooperative mechanisms with an ethical content.

The complexity of cooperative mechanisms has increased with population density, and with the efficiency of tools. It was simpler, for example, to define the anti-social uses of sticks and stones in the days of the mastodons than of bullets and billboards in the age of motors.

The first ethics dealt with the relation between individuals; the Mosaic Decalogue is an example. Later accretions dealt with the relation between the individual and society. The Golden Rule tries to integrate the individual to society; democracy to integrate social organization to the individual.

There is as yet no ethic dealing with man's relation to land and to the animals and plants which grow upon it. Land, like Odysseus' slave-girls, is still property. The land-relation is still strictly economic, entailing privileges but not obligations.

The extension of ethics to this third element in human environment is, if I read the evidence correctly, an evolutionary possibility and an ecological necessity. It is the third step in a sequence. The first two have already been taken. Individual thinkers since the days of Ezekiel and Isaiah have asserted that the despoliation of land is not only inexpedient but wrong. Society, however, has not yet affirmed their belief. I regard the present conservation movement as the embryo of such an affirmation.

An ethic may be regarded as a mode of guidance for meeting ecological situations so new or intricate, or involving such deferred reactions, that the path of social expediency is not discernible to the average individual. Animal instincts are modes of guidance for the individual in meeting such situations. Ethics are possibly a kind of community instinct in-the-making.

The Community Concept

All ethics so far evolved rest upon a single premise: that the individual is a member of a community of interdependent parts. His instincts prompt him to compete for his place in the community, but his ethics prompt him also to cooperate (perhaps in order that there may be a place to compete for).

The land ethic simply enlarges the boundaries of the community to include soils, waters, plants, and animals, or collectively: the land.

This sounds simple: do we not already sing our love for and obligation to the land of the free and the home of the brave? Yes, but just what and whom do we love? Certainly not the soil, which we are sending helter-skelter downriver. Certainly not the waters, which we assume have no function except to turn turbines, float barges, and carry off sewage. Certainly not the plants, of which we exterminate whole communities without batting an eye. Certainly not the animals, of which we have already extirpated many of the largest and most beautiful species. A land ethic of course cannot prevent the alteration, management, and use of these "resources," but it does affirm their right to continued existence, and, at least in spots, their continued existence in a natural state.

In short, a land ethic changes the role of *Homo*

sapiens from conqueror of the land-community to plain member and citizen of it. It implies respect for his fellow-members, and also respect for the community as such.

In human history, we have learned (I hope) that the conqueror role is eventually self-defeating. Why? Because it is implicit in such a role that the conqueror knows, *ex cathedra,* just what makes the community clock tick, and just what and who is valuable, and what and who is worthless, in community life. It always turns out that he knows neither, and this is why his conquests eventually defeat themselves.

In the biotic community, a parallel situation exists. Abraham knew exactly what the land was for: it was to drip milk and honey into Abraham's mouth. At the present moment, the assurance with which we regard this assumption is inverse to the degree of our education.

The ordinary citizen today assumes that science knows what makes the community clock tick; the scientist is equally sure that he does not. He knows that the biotic mechanism is so complex that its workings may never be fully understood.

That man is, in fact, only a member of a biotic team is shown by an ecological interpretation of history. Many historical events, hitherto explained solely in terms of human enterprise, were actually biotic interactions between people and land. The characteristics of the land determined the facts quite as potently as the characteristics of the men who lived on it.

Consider, for example, the settlement of the Mississippi valley. In the years following the Revolution, three groups were contending for its control: the native Indian, the French and English traders, and the American settlers. Historians wonder what would have happened if the English at Detroit had thrown a little more weight into the Indian side of those tipsy scales which decided the outcome of the colonial migration into the cane-lands of Kentucky. It is time now to ponder the fact that the cane-lands, when subjected to the particular mixture of forces represented by the cow, plow, fire, and axe of the pioneer, became bluegrass. What if the plant succession inherent in this dark and bloody ground had, under the impact of these forces, given us some worthless sedge, shrub, or weed? Would Boone and Kenton have held out? Would there have been any overflow into Ohio, Indiana, Illinois, and

Missouri? Any Louisiana Purchase? Any transcontinental union of new states? Any Civil War?

Kentucky was one sentence in the drama of history. We are commonly told what the human actors in this drama tried to do, but we are seldom told that their success, or the lack of it, hung in large degree on the reaction of particular soils to the impact of the particular forces exerted by their occupancy. In the case of Kentucky, we do not even know where the bluegrass came from—whether it is a native species, or a stowaway from Europe.

Contrast the cane-lands with what hindsight tells us about the Southwest, where the pioneers were equally brave, resourceful, and persevering. The impact of the occupancy here brought no bluegrass, or other plant fitted to withstand the bumps and buffetings of hard use. This region, when grazed by livestock, reverted through a series of more and more worthless grasses, shrubs, and weeds to a condition of unstable equilibrium. Each recession of plant types bred erosion; each increment to erosion bred a further recession of plants. The result today is a progressive and mutual deterioration, not only of plants and soils, but of the animal community subsisting thereon. The early settlers did not expect this: on the ciénegas of New Mexico some even cut ditches to hasten it. So subtle has been its progress that few residents of the region are aware of it. It is quite invisible to the tourist who finds this wrecked landscape colorful and charming (as indeed it is, but it bears scant resemblance to what it was in 1848).

This same landscape was 'developed' once before, but with quite different results. The Pueblo Indians settled the Southwest in pre-Columbian times, but they happened *not* to be equipped with range livestock. Their civilization expired, but not because their land expired.

In India, regions devoid of any sod-forming grass have been settled, apparently without wrecking the land, by the simple expedient of carrying the grass to the cow, rather than vice versa. (Was this the result of some deep wisdom, or was it just good luck? I do not know.)

In short, the plant succession steered the course of history; the pioneer simply demonstrated, for good or ill, what successions inhered in the land. Is history taught in this spirit? It will be, once the concept of land as a community really penetrates our intellectual life.

The Ecological Conscience

Conservation is a state of harmony between men and land. Despite nearly a century of propaganda, conservation still proceeds at a snail's pace; progress still consists largely of letterhead pieties and convention oratory. On the back forty we still slip two steps backward for each forward stride.

The usual answer to this dilemma is "more conservation education." No one will debate this, but is it certain that only the *volume* of education needs stepping up? Is something lacking in the *content* as well?

It is difficult to give a fair summary of its content in brief form, but as I understand it, the content is substantially this: obey the law, vote right, join some organizations, and practice what conservation is profitable on your own land; the government will do the rest.

Is not this formula too easy to accomplish anything worthwhile? It defines no right or wrong, assigns no obligation, calls for no sacrifice, implies no change in the current philosophy of values. In respect of land-use, it urges only enlightened self-interest. Just how far will such education take us? An example will perhaps yield a partial answer.

By 1930 it had become clear to all except the ecologically blind that southwestern Wisconsin's topsoil was slipping seaward. In 1933 the farmers were told that if they would adopt certain remedial practices for five years, the public would donate CCC labor to install them, plus the necessary machinery and materials. The offer was widely accepted, but the practices were widely forgotten when the five-year contract period was up. The farmers continued only those practices that yielded an immediate and visible economic gain for themselves.

This led to the idea that maybe farmers would learn more quickly if they themselves wrote the rules. Accordingly the Wisconsin Legislature in 1937 passed the Soil Conservation District Law. This said to farmers, in effect: *We, the public, will furnish you free technical service and loan you specialized machinery, if you will write your own rules for land-use. Each county may write its own rules, and these will have the force of* law. Nearly all the counties promptly organized to accept the proffered help, but after a decade of operation, *no county has yet written a single rule.* There has been visible progress in such practices as strip-cropping, pasture renovation, and soil liming, but none in fencing woodlots against grazing, and none in excluding plow and cow from steep slopes. The farmers, in short, have selected those remedial practices which were profitable anyhow, and ignored those which were profitable to the community, but not clearly profitable to themselves.

When one asks why no rules have been written, one is told that the community is not yet ready to support them; education must precede rules. But the education actually in progress makes no mention of obligations to land over and above those dictated by self-interest. The net result is that we have more education but less soil, fewer healthy woods, and as many floods as in 1937.

The puzzling aspect of such situations is that the existence of obligations over and above self-interest is taken for granted in such rural community enterprise as the betterment of roads, schools, churches, and baseball teams. Their existence is not taken for granted, nor as yet seriously discussed, in bettering the behavior of the water that falls on the land, or in the preserving of the beauty or diversity of the farm landscape. Land-use ethics are still governed wholly by economic self-interest, just as social ethics were a century ago.

To sum up: we asked the farmer to do what he conveniently could to save his soil, and he has done just that, and only that. The farmer who clears the woods off a 75 per cent slope, turns his cows into the clearing, and dumps its rainfall, rocks, and soil into the community creek, is still (if otherwise decent) a respected member of society. If he puts lime on his fields and plants his crops on contour, he is still entitled to all the privileges and emoluments of his Soil Conservation District. The District is a beautiful piece of social machinery, but it is coughing along on two cylinders because we have been too timid, and too anxious for quick success, to tell the farmer the true magnitude of his obligations. Obligations have no meaning without conscience, and the problem we face is the extension of the social conscience from people to land.

No important change in ethics was ever accomplished without an internal change in our intellectual emphasis, loyalties, affections, and convictions. The proof that conservation has not yet touched these foundations of conduct lies in the fact that philosophy and religion have not yet heard of it. In our attempt to make conservation easy, we have made it trivial.

Substitutes for a Land Ethic

When the logic of history hungers for bread and we hand out a stone, we are at pains to explain how much the stone resembles bread. I now describe some of the stones which serve in lieu of a land ethic.

One basic weakness in a conservation system based wholly on economic motives is that most members of the land community have no economic value. Wildflowers and songbirds are examples. Of the 22,000 higher plants and animals native to Wisconsin, it is doubtful whether more than 5 percent can be sold, fed, eaten, or otherwise put to economic use. Yet these creatures are members of the biotic community, and if (as I believe) its stability depends on its integrity, they are entitled to continuance.

When one of these non-economic categories is threatened, and if we happen to love it, we invent subterfuges to give it economic importance. At the beginning of the century songbirds were supposed to be disappearing. Ornithologists jumped to the rescue with some distinctly shaky evidence to the effect that insects would eat us up if birds failed to control them. The evidence had to be economic in order to be valid.

It is painful to read these circumlocutions today. We have no land ethic yet, but we have at least drawn nearer the point of admitting that birds should continue as a matter of biotic right, regardless of the presence or absence of economic advantage to us.

A parallel situation exists in respect of predatory mammals, raptorial birds, and fish-eating birds. Time was when biologists somewhat overworked the evidence that these creatures preserve the health of game by killing weaklings, or that they control rodents for the farmer, or that they prey only on "worthless" species. Here again, the evidence had to be economic in order to be valid. It is only in recent years that we hear the more honest argument that predators are members of the community, and that no special interest has the right to exterminate them for the sake of a benefit, real or fancied, to itself. Unfortunately this enlightened view is still in the talk stage. In the field the extermination of predators goes merrily on: witness the impending erasure of the timber wolf by fiat of Congress, the Conservation Bureaus, and many state legislatures.

Some species of trees have been "read out of the party" by economics-minded foresters because they grow too slowly, or have too low a sale value to pay as timber crops: white cedar, tamarack, cypress, beech, and hemlock are examples. In Europe, where forestry is ecologically more advanced, the non-commercial tree species are recognized as members of the native forest community, to be preserved as such, within reason. Moreover some (like beech) have been found to have a valuable function in building up soil fertility. The interdependence of the forest and its constituent tree species, ground flora, and fauna is taken for granted.

Lack of economic value is sometimes a character not only of species or groups, but of entire biotic communities: marshes, bogs, dunes, and "deserts" are examples. Our formula in such cases is to relegate their conservation to government as refuges, monuments, or parks. The difficulty is that these communities are usually interspersed with more valuable private lands; the government cannot possibly own or control such scattered parcels. The net effect is that we have relegated some of them to ultimate extinction over large areas. If the private owner were ecologically minded, he would be proud to be the custodian of a reasonable proportion of such areas, which add diversity and beauty to his farm and to his community.

In some instances, the assumed lack of profit in these "waste" areas has proved to be wrong, but only after most of them had been done away with. The present scramble to reflood muskrat marshes is a case in point.

There is a clear tendency in American conservation to relegate to government all necessary jobs that private landowners fail to perform. Government ownership, operation, subsidy, or regulation is now widely prevalent in forestry, range management, soil and watershed management, park and wilderness conservation, fisheries management, and migratory bird management, with more to come. Most of this growth in governmental conservation is proper and logical, some of it is inevitable. That I imply no disapproval of it is implicit in the fact that I have spent most of my life working for it. Nevertheless the question arises: What is the ultimate magnitude of the enterprise? Will the tax base carry its eventual ramifications? At what point will governmental conservation, like the mastodon, become handicapped by its own dimensions? The answer, if there is any, seems to be in a land ethic, or some other force which assigns more obligation to the private landowner.

Industrial landowners and users, especially lumbermen and stockmen, are inclined to wail long and loudly about the extension of government ownership and regulation to land, but (with notable exceptions) they show little disposition to develop the only visible alternative: the voluntary practice of conservation on their own lands.

When the private landowner is asked to perform some unprofitable act for the good of the community, he today assents only with outstretched palm. If the act costs him cash this is fair and proper, but when it costs only forethought, openmindedness, or time, the issue is at least debatable. The overwhelming growth of land-use subsidies in recent years must be ascribed, in large part, to the government's own agencies for conservation education: the land bureaus, the agricultural colleges, and the extension services. As far as I can detect, no ethical obligation toward land is taught in these institutions.

To sum up: a system of conservation based solely on economic self-interest is hopelessly lopsided. It tends to ignore, and thus eventually to eliminate, many elements in the land community that lack commercial value, but that are (as far as we know) essential to its healthy functioning. It assumes, falsely, I think, that the economic parts of the biotic clock will function without the uneconomic parts. It tends to relegate to government many functions eventually too large, too complex, or too widely dispersed to be performed by government.

An ethical obligation on the part of the private owner is the only visible remedy for these situations.

The Land Pyramid

An ethic to supplement and guide the economic relation to land presupposes the existence of some mental image of land as a biotic mechanism. We can be ethical only in relation to something we can see, feel, understand, love, or otherwise have faith in.

The image commonly employed in conservation education is "the balance of nature." For reasons too lengthy to detail here, this figure of speech fails to describe accurately what little we know about the land mechanism. A much truer image is the one employed in ecology: the biotic pyramid. I shall first sketch the pyramid as a symbol of land, and later develop some of its implications in terms of land-use.

Plants absorb energy from the sun. This energy flows through a circuit called the biota, which may be represented by a pyramid consisting of layers. The bottom layer is the soil. A plant layer rests on the soil, an insect layer on the plants, a bird and rodent layer on the insects, and so on up through various animal groups to the apex layer, which consists of the larger carnivores.

The species of a layer are alike not in where they came from, or in what they look like, but rather in what they eat. Each successive layer depends on those below it for food and often for other services, and each in turn furnishes food and services to those above. Proceeding upward, each successive layer decreases in numerical abundance. Thus, for every carnivore there are hundreds of his prey, thousands of their prey, millions of insects, uncountable plants. The pyramidal form of the system reflects this numerical progression from apex to base. Man shares an intermediate layer with the bears, raccoons, and squirrels which eat both meat and vegetables.

The lines of dependency for food and other services are called food chains. Thus soil-oak-deer-Indian is a chain that has now been largely converted to soil-corn-cow-farmer. Each species, including ourselves, is a link in many chains. The deer eats a hundred plants other than oak, and the cow a hundred plants other than corn. Both, then, are links in a hundred chains. The pyramid is a tangle of chains so complex as to seem disorderly, yet the stability of the system proves it to be a highly organized structure. Its functioning depends on the cooperation and competition of its diverse parts.

In the beginning, the pyramid of life was low and squat; the food chains short and simple. Evolution has added layer after layer, link after link. Man is one of thousands of accretions to the height and complexity of the pyramid. Science has given us many doubts, but it has given us at least one certainty: the trend of evolution is to elaborate and diversify the biota.

Land, then, is not merely soil; it is a fountain of energy flowing through a circuit of soils, plants, and animals. Food chains are the living channels which conduct energy upward; death and decay return it to the soil. The circuit is not closed; some energy is dissipated in decay, some is added by absorption from the air, some is stored in soils, peats, and long-lived forests; but it is a sustained circuit, like a slowly augmented revolving fund of life. There is always a net loss by downhill wash, but this is normally small and offset by the decay of rocks. It is deposited in the ocean and, in the course of geological time, raised to form new lands and new pyramids.

The velocity and character of the upward flow of energy depend on the complex structure of the plant and animal community, much as the upward flow of sap in a tree depends on its complex cellular organization. Without this complexity, normal circulation would presumably not occur. Structure means the characteristic numbers, as well as the characteristic kinds and functions, of the component species. This interdependence between the complex structure of the land and its smooth functioning as an energy unit is one of its basic attributes.

When a change occurs in one part of the circuit, many other parts must adjust themselves to it. Change does not necessarily obstruct or divert the flow of energy; evolution is a long series of self-induced changes, the net result of which has been to elaborate the flow mechanism and to lengthen the circuit. Evolutionary changes, however, are usually slow and local. Man's invention of tools has enabled him to make changes of unprecedented violence, rapidity, and scope.

One change is in the composition of floras and faunas. The larger predators are lopped off the apex of the pyramid; food chains, for the first time in history, become shorter rather than longer. Domesticated species from other lands are substituted for wild ones, and wild ones are moved to new habitats. In this worldwide pooling of faunas and floras, some species get out of bounds as pests and diseases, others are extinguished. Such effects are seldom intended or foreseen; they represent unpredicted and often untraceable readjustments in the structure. Agricultural science is largely a race between the emergence of new pests and the emergence of new techniques for their control.

Another change touches the flow of energy through plants and animals and its return to the soil. Fertility is the ability of soil to receive, store, and release energy. Agriculture, by overdrafts on the soil, or by too radical a substitution of domestic for native species in the superstructure, may derange the channels of flow or deplete storage. Soils depleted of their storage, or of the organic matter which anchors it, wash away faster than they form. This is erosion.

Waters, like soil, are part of the energy circuit. Industry, by polluting waters or obstructing them with dams, may exclude the plants and animals necessary to keep energy in circulation.

Transportation brings about another basic change: the plants or animals grown in one region are now consumed and returned to the soil in another. Transportation taps the energy stored in rocks, and in the air, and uses it elsewhere; thus we fertilize the garden with nitrogen gleaned by the guano birds from the fishes of seas on the other side of the Equator. Thus the formerly localized and self-contained circuits are pooled on a worldwide scale.

The process of altering the pyramid for human occupation releases stored energy, and this often gives rise, during the pioneering period, to a deceptive exuberance of plant and animal life, both wild and tame. These releases of biotic capital tend to becloud or postpone the penalties of violence.

This thumbnail sketch of land as an energy circuit conveys three basic ideas:

1. That land is not merely soil.

2. That the native plants and animals kept the energy circuit open; others may or may not.

3. That man-made changes are of a different order than evolutionary changes, and have effects more comprehensive than is intended or foreseen.

These ideas, collectively, raise two basic issues: Can the land adjust itself to the new order? Can the desired alterations be accomplished with less violence?

Biotas seem to differ in their capacity to sustain violent conversion. Western Europe, for example, carries a far different pyramid than Caesar found there. Some large animals are lost; swampy forests have become meadows or plowland; many new plants and animals are introduced, some of which escape as pests; the remaining natives are greatly changed in distribution and abundance. Yet the soil is still there and, with the help of imported nutrients, still fertile; the waters flow normally; the new structure seems to function and to persist. There is no visible stoppage or derangement of the circuit.

Western Europe, then, has a resistant biota. Its inner processes are tough, elastic, resistant to strain. No matter how violent the alterations, the pyramid, so far, has developed some new *modus vivendi* which preserves its habitability for man, and for most of the other natives.

Japan seems to present another instance of radical conversion without disorganization.

Most other civilized regions, and some as yet barely touched by civilization, display various stages of disorganization, varying from initial symptoms to advanced wastage. In Asia Minor and North Africa diagnosis is confused by climatic changes, which may have been either the cause or the effect of advanced wastage. In the United States the degree of disorganization varies locally; it is worst in the Southwest, the Ozarks, and parts of the South, and least in New England and the Northwest. Better land-uses may still arrest it in the less advanced regions. In parts of Mexico, South America, South Africa, and Australia a violent and accelerating wastage is in progress, but I cannot assess the prospects.

This almost world-wide display of disorganization in the land seems to be similar to disease in an animal, except that it never culminates in complete disorganization or death. The land recovers, but at some reduced level of complexity, and with a reduced carrying capacity for people, plants, and animals. Many biotas currently regarded as 'lands of opportunity' are in fact already subsisting on exploitative agriculture, i.e., they have already exceeded their sustained carrying capacity. Most of South America is overpopulated in this sense.

In arid regions we attempt to offset the process of wastage by reclamation, but it is only too evident that the prospective longevity of reclamation projects is often short. In our own West, the best of them may not last a century.

The combined evidence of history and ecology seems to support one general deduction: the less violent the man-made changes, the greater the probability of successful readjustment in the pyramid. Violence, in turn, varies with human population density; a dense population requires a more violent conversion. In this respect, North America has a better chance for permanence than Europe, if she can contrive to limit her density.

This deduction runs counter to our current philosophy, which assumes that because a small increase in density enriched human life, that an indefinite increase will enrich it indefinitely. Ecology knows of no density relationship that holds for indefinitely wide limits. All gains from density are subject to a law of diminishing returns.

Whatever may be the equation for men and land, it is improbable that we as yet know all its terms. Recent discoveries in mineral and vitamin nutrition reveal unsuspected dependencies in the up-circuit: incredibly minute quantities of certain substances determine the value of soils to plants, of plants to animals. What of the down-circuit? What of the vanishing species, the preservation of which we now regard as an esthetic luxury? They helped build the soil; in what unsuspected ways may they be essential to its maintenance? Professor Weaver proposes that we use prairie flowers to reflocculate the wasting soils of the dust bowl; who knows for what purpose cranes and condors, otters and grizzlies may some day be used?

Land Health and the A-B Cleavage

A land ethic, then, reflects the existence of an ecological conscience, and this in turn reflects a conviction of individual responsibility for the health of the land. Health is the capacity of the land for self-renewal. Conservation is our effort to understand and preserve this capacity.

Conservationists are notorious for their dissensions. Superficially these seem to add up to mere confusion, but a more careful scrutiny reveals a single plane of cleavage common to many specialized fields. In each field one group (A) regards the land as soil, and its function as commodity-production; another group (B) regards the land as a biota, and its function as something broader. How much broader is admittedly in a state of doubt and confusion.

In my own field, forestry, group A is quite content to grow trees like cabbages, with cellulose as the basic forest commodity. It feels no inhibition against violence; its ideology is agronomic. Group B, on the other hand, sees forestry as fundamen-

tally different from agronomy because it employs natural species, and manages a natural environment rather than creating an artificial one. Group B prefers natural reproduction on principle. It worries on biotic as well as economic grounds about the loss of species like chestnut, and the threatened loss of the white pines. It worries about a whole series of secondary forest functions: wildlife, recreation, watersheds, wilderness areas. To my mind, Group B feels the stirrings of an ecological conscience.

In the wildlife field, a parallel cleavage exists. For Group A the basic commodities are sport and meat; the yardsticks of production are ciphers of take in pheasants and trout. Artificial propagation is acceptable as a permanent as well as a temporary recourse—if its unit costs permit. Group B, on the other hand, worries about a whole series of biotic side-issues. What is the cost in predators of producing a game crop? Should we have further recourse to exotics? How can management restore the shrinking species, like prairie grouse, already hopeless as shootable game? How can management restore the threatened rarities, like trumpeter swan and whooping crane? Can management principles be extended to wildflowers? Here again it is clear to me that we have the same A-B cleavage as in forestry.

In the larger field of agriculture I am less competent to speak, but there seem to be somewhat parallel cleavages. Scientific agriculture was actively developing before ecology was born, hence a slower penetration of ecological concepts might be expected. Moreover the farmer, by the very nature of his techniques, must modify the biota more radically than the forester or the wildlife manager. Nevertheless, there are many discontents in agriculture which seem to add up to a new vision of 'biotic farming.'

Perhaps the most important of these is the new evidence that poundage or tonnage is no measure of the food-value of farm crops; the products of fertile soil may be qualitatively as well as quantitatively superior. We can bolster poundage from depleted soils by pouring on imported fertility, but we are not necessarily bolstering food-value. The possible ultimate ramifications of this idea are so immense that I must leave their exposition to abler pens.

The discontent that labels itself 'organic farming,' while bearing some of the earmarks of a cult, is nevertheless biotic in its direction, particularly in its insistence on the importance of soil flora and fauna.

The ecological fundamentals of agriculture are just as poorly known to the public as in other fields of land-use. For example, few educated people realize that the marvelous advances in technique made during recent decades are improvements in the pump, rather than the well. Acre for acre, they have barely sufficed to offset the sinking level of fertility.

In all of these cleavages, we see repeated the same basic paradoxes: man the conqueror *versus* man the biotic citizen; science the sharpener of his sword *versus* science the searchlight on his universe; land the slave and servant *versus* land the collective organism. Robinson's injunction to Tristram may well be applied, at this juncture, to *Homo sapiens* as a species in geological time:

> Whether you will or not
> You are a King, Tristram, for you are one
> Of the time-tested few that leave the world,
> When they are gone, not the same place it was.
> Mark what you leave.

The Outlook

It is inconceivable to me that an ethical relation to land can exist without love, respect, and admiration for land, and a high regard for its value. By value, I of course mean something far broader than mere economic value; I mean value in the philosophical sense.

Perhaps the most serious obstacle impeding the evolution of a land ethic is the fact that our educational and economic system is headed away from, rather than toward, an intense consciousness of land. Your true modern is separated from the land by many middlemen, and by innumerable physical gadgets. He has no vital relation to it; to him it is the space between cities on which crops grow. Turn him loose for a day on the land, and if the spot does not happen to be a golf links or a "scenic" area, he is bored stiff. If crops could be raised by hydroponics instead of farming, it would suit him very well. Synthetic substitutes for wood, leather, wool, and other natural land products suit him better than the originals. In short, land is something he has "outgrown."

Almost equally serious as an obstacle to a land ethic is the attitude of the farmer for whom the land is still an adversary, or a taskmaster that keeps him in slavery. Theoretically, the mechanization of farming ought to cut the farmer's chains, but whether it really does is debatable.

One of the requisites for an ecological comprehension of land is an understanding of ecology, and this is by no means co-extensive with "education"; in fact, much higher education seems deliberately to avoid ecological concepts. An understanding of ecology does not necessarily originate in courses bearing ecological labels; it is quite as likely to be labeled geography, botany, agronomy, history, or economics. This is as it should be, but whatever the label, ecological training is scarce.

The case for a land ethic would appear hopeless but for the minority which is in obvious revolt against these "modern" trends.

The "key-log" which must be moved to release the evolutionary process for an ethic is simply this: quit thinking about decent land-use as solely an economic problem. Examine each question in terms of what is ethically and esthetically right, as well as what is economically expedient. A thing is right when it tends to preserve the integrity, stability, and beauty of the biotic community. It is wrong when it tends otherwise.

It of course goes without saying that economic feasibility limits the tether of what can or cannot be done for land. It always has and it always will. The fallacy the economic determinists have tied around our collective neck, and which we now need to cast off, is the belief that economics determines *all* land-use. This is simply not true. An innumerable host of actions and attitudes, comprising perhaps the bulk of all land relations, is determined by the land-users' tastes and predilections, rather than by his purse. The bulk of all land relations hinges on investments of time, forethought, skill, and faith rather than on investments of cash. As a land-user thinketh, so is he.

I have purposely presented the land ethic as a product of social evolution because nothing so important as an ethic is ever "written." Only the most superficial student of history supposes that Moses "wrote" the Decalogue; it evolved in the minds of a thinking community, and Moses wrote a tentative summary of it for a "seminar." I say tentative because evolution never stops.

The evolution of a land ethic is an intellectual as well as emotional process. Conservation is paved with good intentions which prove to be futile, or even dangerous, because they are devoid of critical understanding either of the land, or of economic land-use. I think it is a truism that as the ethical frontier advances from the individual to the community, its intellectual content increases.

The mechanism of operation is the same for any ethic: social approbation for right actions: social disapproval for wrong actions.

By and large, our present problem is one of attitudes and implements. We are remodeling the Alhambra with a steam-shovel, and we are proud of our yardage. We shall hardly relinquish the shovel, which after all has many good points, but we are in need of gentler and more objective criteria for its successful use.

The Conceptual Foundations of the Land Ethic _____

J. Baird Callicott

As Wallace Stegner observes, *A Sand County Almanac* is considered "almost a holy book in conservation circles," and Aldo Leopold a prophet, "an American Isaiah." And as Curt Meine points out, "The Land Ethic" is the climactic essay of *Sand County*, "the upshot of 'The Upshot.'"[1] One might, therefore, fairly say that the recommendation and justification of moral obligations on the part of people to nature is what the prophetic *A Sand County Almanac* is all about. . . .

Here I first examine and elaborate the compactly expressed abstract elements of the land ethic and expose the "logic" which binds them into a proper, but revolutionary, moral theory. I then discuss the controversial features of the land ethic and defend them against actual and potential criticism. I hope to show that the land ethic cannot be ignored as merely the groundless emotive exhortations of a moonstruck conservationist or dismissed as entailing wildly untoward practical consequences. It poses, rather, a serious intellectual challenge to business-as-usual moral philosophy.

"The Land Ethic" opens with a charming and poetic evocation of Homer's Greece, the point of which is to suggest that today land is just as routinely and remorsely enslaved as human beings then were. A panoramic glance backward to our most distant cultural origins, Leopold suggests, reveals a slow but steady moral development over three millennia. More of our relationships and activities ("fields of conduct") have fallen under the aegis of moral principles ("ethical criteria") as civilization has grown and matured. If moral growth and development continue, as not only a synoptic review of history, but recent past experience suggest that it will, future generations will censure today's casual and universal environmental bondage as today we censure the casual and universal human bondage of three thousand years ago.

A cynically inclined critic might scoff at Leopold's sanguine portrayal of human history. Slavery survived as an institution in the "civilized" West, more particularly in the morally self-congratulatory United States, until a mere generation before Leopold's own birth. And Western history from imperial Athens and Rome to the Spanish Inquisition and the Third Reich has been a disgraceful series of wars, persecutions, tyrannies, pogroms, and other atrocities.

The history of moral practice, however, is not identical with the history of moral consciousness. Morality is not descriptive; it is prescriptive or normative. In light of this distinction, it is clear that today, despite rising rates of violent crime in the United States and institutional abuses of human rights in Iran, Chile, Ethiopia, Guatemala, South Africa, and many other places, and despite persistent organized social injustice and oppression in still others, moral consciousness is expanding more rapidly now than ever before. Civil rights, human rights, women's liberation, children's liberation, animal liberation, etc., all indicate, as expressions of

Companion to A Sand County Almanac: Interpretive and Critical Essays, edited by J. Baird Callicott. Madison: University of Wisconsin Press, 1987, pp. 186–214. Reprinted by permission.

newly emergent moral ideals, that ethical consciousness (as distinct from practice) has if anything recently accelerated—thus confirming Leopold's historical observation.

Leopold next points out that "this extension of ethics, so far studied only by philosophers"—and, therefore, the implication is clear, not very satisfactorily studied—"is actually a process in ecological evolution" (202).* What Leopold is saying here, simply, is that we may understand the history of ethics, fancifully alluded to by means of the Odysseus vignette, in biological as well as philosophical terms. From a biological point of view, an ethic is "a limitation on freedom of action in the struggle for existence" (202).

I had this passage in mind when I remarked that Leopold manages to convey a whole network of ideas in a couple of phrases. The phrase "struggle for existence" unmistakably calls to mind Darwinian evolution as the conceptual context in which a biological account of the origin and development of ethics must ultimately be located. And at once it points up a paradox: Given the unremitting competitive "struggle for existence" how could "limitations on freedom of action" ever have been conserved and spread through a population of *Homo sapiens* or their evolutionary progenitors?

For a biological account of ethics, as Harvard social entomologist Edward O. Wilson has recently written, "the central theoretical problem . . . [is] how can altruism [elaborately articulated as morality or ethics in the human species], which by definition reduces personal fitness, possibly evolve by natural selection?" [2] According to modern sociobiology, the answer lies in kinship. But according to Darwin—who had tackled this problem himself "exclusively from the side of natural history" in *The Descent of Man*—the answer lies in society.[3] And it was Darwin's classical account (and its divers variations), from the side of natural history, which informed Leopold's thinking in the late 1940s.

Let me put the problem in perspective. How, we are asking, did ethics originate and, once in existence, grow in scope and complexity?

The oldest answer in living human memory is theological. God (or the gods) imposes morality on people. And God (or the gods) sanctions it. A most vivid and graphic example of this kind of account occurs in the Bible when Moses goes up on Mount Sinai to receive the Ten Commandments directly from God. That text also clearly illustrates the divine sanctions (plagues, pestilences, droughts, military defeats, etc.) for moral disobedience. Ongoing revelation of the divine will, of course, as handily and as simply explains subsequent moral growth and development.

Western philosophy, on the other hand, is almost unanimous in the opinion that the origin of ethics in human experience has somehow to do with human reason. Reason figures centrally and pivotally in the "social contract theory" of the origin and nature of morals in all its ancient, modern, and contemporary expressions from Protagoras, to Hobbes, to Rawls. Reason is the wellspring of virtue, according to both Plato and Aristotle, and of categorical imperatives, according to Kant. In short, the weight of Western philosophy inclines to the view that we are moral beings because we are rational beings. The ongoing sophistication of reason and the progressive illumination it sheds upon the good and the right explain "the ethical sequence," the historical growth and development of morality, noticed by Leopold.

An evolutionary natural historian, however, cannot be satisfied with either of these general accounts of the origin and development of ethics. The idea that God gave morals to man is ruled out in principle—as any supernatural explanation of a natural phenomenon is ruled out in principle in natural science. And while morality might *in principle* be a function of human reason (as, say, mathematical calculation clearly is), to suppose that it is so *in fact* would be to put the cart before the horse. Reason appears to be a delicate, variable, and recently emerged faculty. It cannot, under any circumstances, be supposed to have evolved in the absence of complex linguistic capabilities which depend, in turn, for their evolution upon a highly developed social matrix. But we cannot have become social beings unless we assumed limitations on freedom of action in the struggle for existence. Hence we must have become ethical before we became rational.

Darwin, probably in consequence of reflections somewhat like these, turned to a minority tradition of modern philosophy for a moral psychol-

*Page references are to Aldo Leopold's *A Sand County Almanac with Sketches Here and There* (New York: Oxford University Press, 1949).

ogy consistent with and useful to a general evolutionary account of ethical phenomena. A century earlier, Scottish philosophers David Hume and Adam Smith had argued that ethics rest upon feelings or "sentiments"—which, to be sure, may be both amplified and informed by reason.[4] And since in the animal kingdom feelings or sentiments are arguably far more common or widespread than reason, they would be a far more likely starting point for an evolutionary account of the origin and growth of ethics.

Darwin's account, to which Leopold unmistakably (if elliptically) alludes in "The Land Ethic," begins with the parental and filial affections common, perhaps, to all mammals.[5] Bonds of affection and sympathy between parents and offspring permitted the formation of small, closely kin social groups, Darwin argued. Should the parental and filial affections bonding family members chance to extend to less closely related individuals, that would permit an enlargement of the family group. And should the newly extended community more successfully defend itself and/or more efficiently provision itself, the inclusive fitness of its members severally would be increased, Darwin reasoned. Thus, the more diffuse familial affections, which Darwin (echoing Hume and Smith) calls the "social sentiments," would be spread throughout a population.[6]

Morality, properly speaking—i.e., morality as opposed to mere altruistic instinct—requires, in Darwin's terms, "intellectual powers" sufficient to recall the past and imagine the future, "the power of language" sufficient to express "common opinion," and "habituation" to patterns of behavior deemed, by common opinion, to be socially acceptable and beneficial.[7] Even so, ethics proper, in Darwin's account, remains firmly rooted in moral feelings or social sentiments which were—no less than physical faculties, he expressly avers—naturally selected, by the advantages for survival and especially for successful reproduction, afforded by society.[8]

The protosociobiological perspective on ethical phenomena, to which Leopold as a natural historian was heir, leads him to a generalization which is remarkably explicit in his condensed and often merely resonant rendering of Darwin's more deliberate and extended paradigm: Since "the thing [ethics] has its origin in the tendency of interdependent individuals or groups to evolve modes of co-operation, . . . all ethics so far evolved rest upon a single premise: that the individual is a member of a community of interdependent parts" (202–3).

Hence, we may expect to find that the scope and specific content of ethics will reflect both the perceived boundaries and actual structure or organization of a cooperative community or society. *Ethics and society or community are correlative.* This single, simple principle constitutes a powerful tool for the analysis of moral natural history, for the anticipation of future moral development (including, ultimately, the land ethic), and for systematically deriving the specific precepts, the prescriptions and proscriptions, of an emergent and culturally unprecedented ethic like a land or environmental ethic.

Anthropological studies of ethics reveal that, in fact, the boundaries of the moral community are generally coextensive with the perceived boundaries of society.[9] And the peculiar (and, from the urbane point of view, sometimes inverted) representation of virtue and vice in tribal society—the virtue, for example, of sharing to the point of personal destitution and the vice of privacy and private property—reflects and fosters the life way of tribal peoples.[10] Darwin, in his leisurely, anecdotal discussion, paints a vivid picture of the intensity, peculiarity, and sharp circumscription of "savage" mores: "A savage will risk his life to save that of a member of the same community, but will be wholly indifferent about a stranger."[11] As Darwin portrays them, tribes-people are at once paragons of virtue "within the limits of the same tribe" and enthusiastic thieves, manslaughterers, and torturers without.[12]

For purposes of more effective defense against common enemies, or because of increased population density, or in response to innovations in subsistence methods and technologies, or for some mix of these or other forces, human societies have grown in extent or scope and changed in form or structure. Nations—like the Iroquois nation or the Sioux nation—came into being upon the merger of previously separate and mutually hostile tribes. Animals and plants were domesticated and erstwhile hunter-gatherers became herders and farmers. Permanent habitations were established. Trade, craft, and (later) industry flourished. With each change in society came corresponding and correlative changes in ethics. The moral community expanded to become coextensive with the newly drawn boundaries of societies and the representation of virtue and vice, right and wrong, good and evil, changed to accommodate, foster, and preserve the economic and institutional organization of emergent social orders.

Today we are witnessing the painful birth of a human super-community, global in scope. Modern transportation and communication technologies, international economic interdependencies, international economic entities, and nuclear arms have brought into being a "global village." It has not yet become fully formed and it is at tension—a very dangerous tension—with its predecessor, the nation-state. Its eventual institutional structure, a global federalism or whatever it may turn out to be, is, at this point, completely unpredictable. Interestingly, however, a corresponding global human ethic—the "human rights" ethic, as it is popularly called—has been more definitely articulated.

Most educated people today pay lip service at least to the ethical precept that all members of the human species, regardless of race, creed, or national origin, are endowed with certain fundamental rights which it is wrong not to respect. According to the evolutionary scenario set out by Darwin, the contemporary moral ideal of human rights is a response to a perception—however vague and indefinite—that mankind worldwide is united into one society, one community—however indeterminate or yet institutionally unorganized. As Darwin presciently wrote:

> As man advances in civilization, and small tribes are united into larger communities, the simplest reason would tell each individual that he ought to extend his social instincts and sympathies to all the members of the same nation, though personally unknown to him. This point being once reached, there is only an artificial barrier to prevent his sympathies extending to the men of all nations and races. If, indeed, such men are separated from him by great differences of appearance or habits, experience unfortunately shows us how long it is, before we look at them as our fellow-creatures.[13]

According to Leopold, the next step in this sequence beyond the still incomplete ethic of universal humanity, a step that is clearly discernible on the horizon, is the land ethic. The "community concept" has, so far, propelled the development of ethics from the savage clan to the family of man. "The land ethic simply enlarges the boundary of the community to include soils, waters, plants, and animals, or collectively: the land" (204).

As the foreword to *Sand County* makes plain, the overarching thematic principle of the book is the inculcation of the idea—through narrative description, discursive exposition, abstractive generalization, and occasional preachment—"that land is a community" (viii). The community concept is "the basic concept of ecology" (viii). Once land is popularly perceived as a biotic community—as it is professionally perceived in ecology—a correlative land ethic will emerge in the collective cultural consciousness.

Although anticipated as far back as the mid-eighteenth century—in the notion of an "economy of nature"—the concept of the biotic community was more fully and deliberately developed as a working model or paradigm for ecology by Charles Elton in the 1920s.[14] The natural world is organized as an intricate corporate society in which plants and animals occupy "niches," or as Elton alternatively called them, "roles" or "professions," in the economy of nature.[15] As in a feudal community, little or no socioeconomic mobility (upward or otherwise) exists in the biotic community. One is born to one's trade.

Human society, Leopold argues, is founded, in large part, upon mutual security and economic interdependency and preserved only by limitations on freedom of action in the struggle for existence—that is, by ethical constraints. Since the biotic community exhibits, as modern ecology reveals, an analogous structure, it too can be preserved, given the newly amplified impact of "mechanized man," only by analogous limitations on freedom of action—that is, by a land ethic (viii). A land ethic, furthermore, is not only "an ecological necessity," but an "evolutionary possibility" because a moral response to the natural environment—Darwin's social sympathies, sentiments, and instincts translated and codified into a body of principles and precepts—would be automatically triggered in human beings by ecology's social representation of nature (203).

Therefore, the key to the emergence of a land ethic is, simply, universal ecological literacy.

The land ethic rests upon three scientific cornerstones: (1) evolutionary and (2) ecological biology set in a background of (3) Copernican astronomy. Evolutionary theory provides the conceptual link between ethics and social organization and development. It provides a sense of "kinship with fellow-creatures" as well, "fellow-voyagers" with us in the "odyssey of evolution" (109). It establishes a diachronic link between people and nonhuman nature.

Ecological theory provides a synchronic link— the community concept—a sense of social integration of human and nonhuman nature. Human beings, plants, animals, soils, and waters are "all interlocked in one humming community of cooperations and competitions, one biota." [16] The simplest reason, to paraphrase Darwin, should, therefore, tell each individual that he or she ought to extend his or her social instincts and sympathies to all the members of the biotic community though different from him or her in appearance or habits.

And although Leopold never directly mentions it in *A Sand County Almanac*, the Copernican perspective, the perception of the Earth as "a small planet" in an immense and utterly hostile universe beyond, contributes, perhaps subconsciously, but nevertheless very powerfully, to our sense of kinship, community, and interdependence with fellow denizens of the Earth household. It scales the Earth down to something like a cozy island paradise in a desert ocean.

Here in outline, then, are the conceptual and logical foundations of the land ethic: Its conceptual elements are a Copernican cosmology, a Darwinian protosociobiological natural history of ethics, Darwinian ties of kinship among all forms of life on Earth, and an Eltonian model of the structure of biocenoses all overlaid on a Humean-Smithian moral psychology. Its logic is that natural selection has endowed human beings with an affective moral response to perceived bonds of kinship and community membership and identity; that today the natural environment, the land, is represented as a community, the biotic community; and that, therefore, an environmental or land ethic is both possible—the biopsychological and cognitive conditions are in place—and necessary, since human beings collectively have acquired the power to destroy the integrity, diversity, and stability of the environing and supporting economy of nature. In the remainder of this essay I discuss special features and problems of the land ethic germane to moral philosophy.

The most salient feature of Leopold's land ethic is its provision of what Kenneth Goodpaster has carefully called "moral considerability" for the biotic community per se, not just for fellow members of the biotic community:[17]

> In short, a land ethic changes the role of *Homo sapiens* from conquerer of the land-community to plain member and citizen of it. It implies respect for his fellow-members, *and also respect for the community as such.* (204, emphasis added)

The land ethic, thus, has a holistic as well as an individualistic cast.

Indeed, as "The Land Ethic" develops, the focus of moral concern shifts gradually away from plants, animals, soils, and waters severally to the biotic community collectively. Toward the middle, in the subsection called Substitutes for a Land Ethic, Leopold invokes the "biotic rights" of *species*—as the context indicates—of wildflowers, songbirds, and predators. In The Outlook, the climatic section of "The Land Ethic," nonhuman natural entities, first appearing as fellow members, then considered in profile as species, are not so much as mentioned in what might be called the "summary moral maxim" of the land ethic: "A thing is right when it tends to preserve the integrity, stability, and beauty of the biotic community. It is wrong when it tends otherwise" (224–25).

By this measure of right and wrong, not only would it be wrong for a farmer, in the interest of higher profits, to clear the woods off a 75 percent slope, turn his cows into the clearing, and dump its rainfall, rocks, and soil into the community creek, it would also be wrong for the federal fish and wildlife agency, in the interest of individual animal welfare, to permit populations of deer, rabbits, feral burros, or whatever to increase unchecked and, thus to threaten the integrity, stability, and beauty of the biotic communities of which they are members. The land ethic not only provides moral considerability for the biotic community per se, but ethical consideration of its individual members is preempted by concern for the preservation of the integrity, stability, and beauty of the biotic community. The land ethic, thus, not only has a holistic aspect; it is holistic with a vengeance.

The holism of the land ethic, more than any other feature, sets it apart from the predominant paradigm of modern moral philosophy. It is, therefore, the feature of the land ethic which requires the most patient theoretical analysis and the most sensitive practical interpretation.

As Kenneth Goodpaster pointed out, mainstream modern ethical philosophy has taken egoism as its point of departure and reached a wider circle of moral entitlement by a process of generalization:[18] I am sure that *I*, the enveloped ego, am intrinsically or inherently valuable and thus that *my* interests ought to be considered, taken into account, by "others" when their actions may substantively affect *me*. My own claim to moral consideration, according to the conventional wisdom, ultimately rests upon a psychological capacity—rationality or sentiency were the classical candidates of Kant and Bentham, respectively—which is arguably valuable in itself and which thus qualifies *me* for moral standing.[19] However, then I am forced grudgingly to grant the same moral consideration I demand from others, on this basis, to those others who can also claim to possess the same general psychological characteristic.

A *criterion* of moral value and consideration is thus identified. Goodpaster convincingly argues that mainstream modern moral theory is based, when all the learned dust has settled, on this simple paradigm of ethical justification and logic exemplified by the Benthamic and Kantian prototypes.[20] If the criterion of moral value and consideration is pushed low enough—as it is in Bentham's criterion of sentiency—a wide variety of animals are admitted to moral entitlement.[21] If the criterion of moral value and consideration is pushed lower still—as it is in Albert Schweitzer's reverence-for-life ethic—all minimally conative things (plants as well as animals) would be extended moral consideration.[22] The contemporary animal liberation/rights, and reverence-for-life/life-principle ethics are, at bottom, simply direct applications of the modern classical paradigm of moral argument. But this standard modern model of ethical theory provides no possibility whatever for the moral consideration of wholes—of threatened *populations* of animals and plants, or of endemic, rare, or endangered *species*, or of biotic *communities*, or most expansively, of the *biosphere* in its totality—since wholes per se have no psychological experience of any kind.[23] Because mainstream mod-

ern moral theory has been "psychocentric," it has been radically and intractably individualistic or "atomistic" in its fundamental theoretical orientation.

Hume, Smith, and Darwin diverged from the prevailing theoretical model by recognizing that altruism is as fundamental and autochthonous in human nature as is egoism. According to their analysis, moral value is not identified with a natural quality objectively present in morally considerable beings—as reason and/or sentiency is objectively present in people and/or animals—it is, as it were, projected by valuing subjects.[24]

Hume and Darwin, furthermore, recognize inborn moral sentiments which have society as such as their natural object. Hume insists that "we must renounce the theory which accounts for every moral sentiment by the principle of self-love. We must adopt a more *public affection* and allow that the *interests of society* are not, *even on their own account,* entirely indifferent to us."[25] And Darwin, somewhat ironically (since "Darwinian evolution" very often means natural selection operating exclusively with respect to individuals), sometimes writes as if morality had no other object than the commonweal, the welfare of the community as a corporate entity:

> We have now seen that actions are regarded by savages, and were probably so regarded by primeval man, as good or bad, solely as they obviously affect the welfare of the tribe,—not that of the species, nor that of individual members of the tribe. This conclusion agrees well with the belief that the so-called moral sense is aboriginally derived from social instincts, for both relate at first exclusively to the community.[26]

Theoretically then, the biotic community owns what Leopold, in the lead paragraph of The Outlook, calls "value in the philosophical sense"—i.e., direct moral considerability—because it is a newly discovered proper object of a specially evolved "public affection" or "moral sense" which all psychologically normal human beings have inherited from a long line of ancestral social primates (223).[27]

In the land ethic, as in all earlier stages of social-ethical evolution, there exists a tension between the good of the community as a whole and the "rights" of its individual members considered severally. While The Ethical Sequence section of "The Land Ethic" clearly evokes Darwin's classical biosocial account of the origin and extension of morals, Leopold is actually more explicitly concerned, in that section, with the interplay between the holistic and individualistic moral sentiments— sympathy and fellow-feeling on the one hand, and public affection for the commonweal on the other:

> The first ethics dealt with the relation between individuals; the Mosaic Decalogue is an example. Later accretions dealt with the relation between the individual and society. The Golden Rule tries to integrate the individual to society; democracy to integrate social organization to the individual. (202–3)

Actually, it is doubtful that the first ethics dealt with the relation between individuals and not at all with the relation between the individual and society. (This, along with the remark that ethics replaced an "original free-for-all competition," suggests that Leopold's Darwinian line of thought has been uncritically tainted with Hobbesean elements. [202]. Of course, Hobbes's "state of nature," in which there prevailed a war of each against all, is absurd from an evolutionary point of view.) A century of ethnographic studies seems to confirm, rather, Darwin's conjecture that the relative weight of the holistic component is greater in tribal ethics—the tribal ethic of the Hebrews recorded in the Old Testament constitutes a vivid case in point— than in more recent accretions. The Golden Rule, on the other hand, does not mention, in any of its formulations, society per se. Rather, its primary concern seems to be "others," i.e., other human individuals. Democracy, with its stress on individual liberties and rights, seems to further rather than countervail the individualistic thrust of the Golden Rule.

In any case, the conceptual foundations of the land ethic provide a well-formed, self-consistent theoretical basis for including both fellow members of the biotic community and the biotic community itself (considered as a corporate entity) within the purview of morals. The preemptive emphasis, however, on the welfare of the community as a whole, in Leopold's articulation of the land ethic, while certainly *consistent* with its Humean-Darwinian theoretical foundations, is not *determined* by them alone. The overriding holism of the land ethic results, rather, more from the way our moral sensibilities are informed by ecology.

Ecological thought, historically, has tended to be holistic in outlook.[28] Ecology is the study of the *relationships* of organisms to one another and to the elemental environment. These relationships bind the *relata*—plants, animals, soils, and waters—into a seamless fabric. The ontological primacy of objects and the ontological subordination of relationships, characteristic of classical Western science, is, in fact, reversed in ecology.[29] Ecological relationships determine the nature of organisms rather than the other way around. A species is what it is because it has adapted to a niche in the ecosystem. The whole, the system itself, thus, literally and quite straightforwardly shapes and forms its component parts.

Antedating Charles Elton's community model of ecology was F. E. Clements' and S. A. Forbes' organism model.[30] Plants and animals, soils and waters, according to this paradigm, are integrated into one superorganism. Species are, as it were, its organs; specimens its cells. Although Elton's community paradigm (later modified, as we shall see, by Arthur Tansley's ecosystem idea) is the principal and morally fertile ecological concept of "The Land Ethic," the more radically holistic superorganism paradigm of Clements and Forbes resonates in "The Land Ethic" as an audible overtone. In the peroration of Land Health and the A-B Cleavage, for example, which immediately precedes The Outlook, Leopold insists that

> in all of these cleavages, we see repeated the same basic paradoxes: man the conqueror *versus* man the biotic citizen; science the sharpener of his sword *versus* science the searchlight on his universe; land the slave and servant *versus* land the collective organism. (223)

And on more than one occasion Leopold, in the latter quarter of "The Land Ethic," talks about the "health" and "disease" of the land—terms which are at once descriptive and normative and which, taken literally, characterize only organisms proper.

In an early essay, "Some Fundamentals of Conservation in the Southwest," Leopold speculatively flirted with the intensely holistic superorganism model of the environment as a paradigm pregnant with moral implications:

> It is at least not impossible to regard the earth's parts—soil, mountains, rivers, atmosphere, etc—as organs or parts of organs, of *a coordinated whole*, each part with a definite function. And if we could see *this whole, as a whole,* through a great period of time, we

might perceive not only organs with coordinated functions, but possibly also that process of consumption and replacement which in biology we call metabolism, or growth. In such a case we would have all the visible attributes of a living thing, which we do not realize to be such because it is too big, and its life processes too slow. And there would also follow that invisible attribute—a soul or consciousness—which . . . many philosophers of all ages ascribe to all living things and aggregates thereof, including the "dead" earth.

Possibly in our intuitive perceptions, which may be truer than our science and less impeded by words than our philosophies, we realize the indivisibility of the earth—its soil, mountains, rivers, forests, climate, plants, and animals—and *respect it collectively* not only as a useful servant but as a living being, vastly less alive than ourselves, but vastly greater than ourselves in time and space. . . . Philosophy, then, suggests one reason why we cannot destroy the earth with moral impunity; namely, that the "dead" earth is an organism possessing a certain kind and degree of life, which we intuitively respect as such.[31]

Had Leopold retained this overall theoretical approach in "The Land Ethic," the land ethic would doubtless have enjoyed more critical attention from philosophers. The moral foundations of a land or, as he might then have called it, "earth" ethic, would rest upon the hypothesis that the Earth is alive and ensouled—possessing inherent psychological characteristics, logically parallel to reason and sentiency. This notion of a conative whole Earth could plausibly have served as a general criterion of intrinsic worth and moral considerability, in the familiar format of mainstream moral thought.

Part of the reason, therefore, that "The Land Ethic" emphasizes more and more the integrity, stability, and beauty of the environment as a whole, and less and less the "biotic right" of individual plants and animals to life, liberty, and the pursuit of happiness, is that the superorganism ecological paradigm invites one, much more than does the community paradigm, to hypostatize, to reify the whole, and to subordinate its individual members.

In any case, as we see, rereading "The Land Ethic" in light of "Some Fundamentals," the whole Earth organism image of nature is vestigially present in Leopold's later thinking. Leopold may have abandoned the "earth ethic" because ecology had

abandoned the organism analogy, in favor of the community analogy, as a working theoretical paradigm. And the community model was more suitably given moral implications by the social/sentimental ethical natural history of Hume and Darwin.

Meanwhile, the biotic community ecological paradigm itself had acquired, by the late thirties and forties, a more holistic cast of its own. In 1935 British ecologist Arthur Tansley pointed out that from the perspective of physics the "currency" of the "economy of nature" is energy.[32] Tansley suggested that Elton's qualitative and descriptive food chains, food webs, trophic niches, and biosocial professions could be quantitatively expressed by means of a thermodynamic flow model. It is Tansley's state-of-the-art thermodynamic paradigm of the environment that Leopold explicitly sets out as a "mental image of land" in relation to which "we can be ethical" (214). And it is the ecosystemic model of land which informs the cardinal practical precepts of the land ethic.

The Land Pyramid is the pivotal section of "The Land Ethic"—the section which effects a complete transition from concern for "fellow-members" to the "community as such." It is also its longest and most technical section. A description of the "ecosystem" (Tansley's deliberately nonmetaphorical term) begins with the sun. Solar energy "flows through a circuit called the biota" (215). It enters the biota through the leaves of green plants and courses through plant-eating animals, and then on to omnivores and carnivores. At last the tiny fraction of solar energy converted to biomass by green plants remaining in the corpse of a predator, animal feces, plant detritus, or other dead organic material is garnered by decomposers— worms, fungi, and bacteria. They recycle the participating elements and degrade into entropic equilibrium any remaining energy. According to this paradigm

> land, then, is not merely soil; it is a fountain of energy flowing through a circuit of soils, plants, and animals. Food chains are the living channels which conduct energy upward; death and decay return it to the soil. The circuit is not closed; . . . but it is a sustained circuit, like a slowly augmented revolving fund of life. (216)

In this exceedingly abstract (albeit poetically expressed) model of nature, process precedes substance and energy is more fundamental than matter. Individual plants and animals become less autonomous beings than ephemeral structures in a patterned flux of energy. According to Yale biophysicist Harold Morowitz,

> viewed from the point of view of modern [ecology], each living thing ... is a dissipative structure, that is it does not endure in and of itself but only as a result of the continual flow of energy in the system. An example might be instructive. Consider a vortex in a stream of flowing water. The vortex is a structure made of an ever-changing group of water molecules. It does not exist as an entity in the classical Western sense; it exists only because of the flow of water through the stream. In the same sense, the structures out of which biological entities are made are transient, unstable entities with constantly changing molecules, dependent on a constant flow of energy from food in order to maintain form and structure.... From this point of view the reality of individuals is problematic because they do not exist per se but only as local perturbations in this universal energy flow.[33]

Though less bluntly stated and made more palatable by the unfailing charm of his prose, Leopold's proffered mental image of land is just as expansive, systemic, and distanced as Morowitz'. The maintenance of "the complex structure of the land and its smooth functioning as an energy unit" emerges in The Land Pyramid as the *summum bonum* of the land ethic (216).

From this good Leopold derives several practical principles slightly less general, and therefore more substantive, than the summary moral maxim of the land ethic distilled in The Outlook. "The trend of evolution [not its "goal," since evolution is ateleological] is to elaborate and diversify the biota" (216). Hence, among our cardinal duties is the duty to preserve what species we can, especially those at the apex of the pyramid—the top carnivores. "In the beginning, the pyramid of life was low and squat; the food chains short and simple. Evolution has added layer after layer, link after link" (215–16). Human activities today, especially those, like systematic deforestation in the tropics, resulting in abrupt massive extinctions of species, are in effect "devolutionary"; they flatten the biotic pyramid; they choke off some of the channels and gorge others (those which terminate in our own species).[34]

The land ethic does not enshrine the ecological status quo and devalue the dynamic dimension of nature. Leopold explains that "evolution is a long series of self-induced changes, the net result of which has been to elaborate the flow mechanism and to lengthen the circuit. Evolutionary changes, however, are usually slow and local. Man's invention of tools has enabled him to make changes of unprecedented violence, rapidity, and scope" (216–17). "Natural" species extinction, i.e., species extinction in the normal course of evolution, occurs when a species is replaced by competitive exclusion or evolves into another form.[35] Normally speciation outpaces extinction. Mankind inherited a richer, more diverse world than had ever existed before in the 3.5 billion-year odyssey of life on Earth.[36] What is wrong with anthropogenic species extirpation and extinction is the *rate* at which it is occurring and the *result*: biological impoverishment instead of enrichment.

Leopold goes on here to condemn, in terms of its impact on the ecosystem, "the world-wide pooling of faunas and floras," i.e., the indiscriminate introduction of exotic and domestic species and the dislocation of native and endemic species; mining the soil for its stored biotic energy, leading ultimately to diminished fertility and to erosion; and polluting and damming water courses (217).

According to the land ethic, therefore: Thou shalt not extirpate or render species extinct; thou shalt exercise great caution in introducing exotic and domestic species into local ecosystems, in extracting energy from the soil and releasing it into the biota, and in damming or polluting water courses; and thou shalt be especially solicitous of predatory birds and mammals. Here in brief are the express moral precepts of the land ethic. They are all explicitly informed—not to say derived—from the energy circuit model of the environment.

The living channels—"food chains"—through which energy courses are composed of individual plants and animals. A central, stark fact lies at the heart of ecological processes: Energy, the currency of the economy nature, passes from one organism to another, not from hand to hand, like coined money, but, so to speak, from stomach to stomach. Eating *and being eaten,* living *and dying* are what make the biotic community hum.

The precepts of the land ethic, like those of all previous accretions, reflect and reinforce the structure of the community to which it is correlative.

Trophic asymmetries constitute the kernel of the biotic community. It seems unjust, unfair. But that is how the economy of nature is organized (and has been for thousands of millions of years). The land ethic, thus, affirms as good, and strives to preserve, the very inequities in nature whose social counterparts in human communities are condemned as bad and would be eradicated by familiar social ethics, especially by the more recent Christian and secular egalitarian exemplars. A "right to life" for individual members is not consistent with the structure of the biotic community and hence is not mandated by the land ethic. This disparity between the land ethic and its more familiar social precedents contributes to the apparent devaluation of individual *members* of the biotic community and augments and reinforces the tendency of the land ethic, driven by the systemic vision of ecology, toward a more holistic or community-per-se orientation.

Of the few moral philosophers who have given the land ethic a moment's serious thought, most have regarded it with horror because of its emphasis on the good of the community and its deemphasis on the welfare of individual members of the community. Not only are other sentient creatures members of the biotic community and subordinate to its integrity, beauty, and stability; so are *we*. Thus, if it is not only morally permissible, from the point of view of the land ethic, but morally required, that members of certain species be abandoned to predation and other vicissitudes of wild life or even deliberately culled (as in the case of alert and sentient whitetail deer) for the sake of the integrity, stability, and beauty of the biotic community, how can we consistently exempt ourselves from a similar draconian regime? We too are only "plain members and citizens" of the biotic community. And our global population is growing unchecked. According to William Aiken, from the point of view of the land ethic, therefore, "massive human diebacks would be good. It is our duty to cause them. It is our species' duty, relative to the whole, to eliminate 90 percent of our numbers." Thus, according to Tom Regan, the land ethic is a clear case of "environmental fascism."[37]

Of course Leopold never intended the land ethic to have either inhumane or antihumanitarian implications or consequences. But whether he intended them or not, a logically consistent deduction from the theoretical premises of the land ethic might force such untoward conclusions. And given their magnitude and monstrosity, these derivations would constitute a *reductio ad absurdum* of the whole land ethic enterprise and entrench and reinforce our current human chauvinism and moral alienation from nature. If this is what membership in the biotic community entails, then all but the most radical misanthropes would surely want to opt out.

The land ethic, happily, implies neither inhumane nor inhuman consequences. That some philosophers think it must follows more from their own theoretical presuppositions than from the theoretical elements of the land ethic itself. Conventional modern ethical theory rests moral entitlement, as I earlier pointed out, on a criterion or qualification. If a candidate meets the criterion—rationality or sentiency are the most commonly posited—he, she, or it is entitled to equal moral standing with others who possess the same qualification in equal degree. Hence, reasoning in this philosophically orthodox way, and forcing Leopold's theory to conform: if human beings are, with other animals, plants, soils, and waters, equally members of the biotic community, and if community membership is the criterion of equal moral consideration, then not only do animals, plants, soils, and waters have equal (highly attenuated) "rights," but human beings are equally subject to the same subordination of individual welfare and rights in respect to the good of the community as a whole.

But the land ethic, as I have been at pains to point out, is heir to a line of moral analysis different from that institutionalized in contemporary moral philosophy. From the biosocial evolutionary analysis of ethics upon which Leopold builds the land ethic, it (the land ethic) neither replaces nor overrides previous accretions. Prior moral sensibilities and obligations attendant upon and correlative to prior strata of social involvement remain operative and preemptive.

Being citizens of the United States, or the United Kingdom, or the Soviet Union, or Venezuela, or some other nation-state, and therefore having national obligations and patriotic duties, does not mean that we are not also members of smaller communities or social groups—cities or townships, neighborhoods, and families—or that we are relieved of the peculiar moral responsibilities attendant upon and correlative to these memberships as well. Similarly, our recognition of the biotic community and our immersion in it does not imply that we do not also remain members of the human community—the "family of man" or "global village"—or that we are relieved of the attendant and correlative moral responsibilities of that membership, among them to respect universal human rights and uphold the principles of individual human worth and dignity. The biosocial development of morality does not grow in extent like an expanding balloon, leaving no trace of its previous boundaries, so much as like the circumference of a tree.[38] Each emergent, and larger, social unit is layered over the more primitive, and intimate, ones.

Moreover, as a general rule, the duties correlative to the inner social circles to which we belong eclipse those correlative to the rings farther from the heartwood when conflicts arise. Consider our moral revulsion when zealous ideological nationalists encourage children to turn their parents in to the authorities if their parents should dissent from the political or economic doctrines of the ruling party. A zealous environmentalist who advocated visiting war, famine, or pestilence on human populations (those existing somewhere else, of course) in the name of the integrity, beauty, and stability of the biotic community would be similarly perverse. Family obligations in general come before nationalistic duties and humanitarian obligations in general come before environmental duties. The land ethic, therefore, is not draconian or fascist. It does not cancel human morality. The land ethic may, however, as with any new accretion, demand choices which affect, in turn, the demands of the more interior social-ethical circles. Taxes and the military draft may conflict with family-level obligations. While the land ethic, certainly, does not cancel human morality, neither does it leave it unaffected.

Nor is the land ethic inhumane. Nonhuman fellow members of the biotic community have no "human rights," because they are not, by definition, members of the human community. As fellow members of the biotic community, however, they deserve respect.

How exactly to express or manifest respect, while at the same time abandoning our fellow members of the biotic community to their several fates or even actively consuming them for our own needs (and wants), or deliberately making them

casualties of wildlife management for ecological integrity, is a difficult and delicate question.

Fortunately, American Indian and other traditional patterns of human-nature interaction provide rich and detailed models. Algonkian woodland peoples, for instance, represented animals, plants, birds, waters, and minerals as other-than-human persons engaged in reciprocal, mutually beneficial socioeconomic intercourse with human beings.[39] Tokens of payment, together with expressions of apology, were routinely offered to the beings whom it was necessary for these Indians to exploit. Care not to waste the usable parts, and care in the disposal of unusable animal and plant remains, were also an aspect of the respectful, albeit necessarily consumptive, Algonkian relationship with fellow members of the land community. As I have more fully argued elsewhere, the Algonkian portrayal of human-nature relationships is, indeed, although certainly different in specifics, identical in abstract form to that recommended by Leopold in the land ethic.[40] . . .

Today, two processes internal to civilization are bringing us to a recognition that our renunciation of our biotic citizenship was a mistaken self-deception. Evolutionary science and ecological science, which certainly are products of modern civilization now supplanting the anthropomorphic and anthropocentric myths of earlier civilized generations, have rediscovered our integration with the biotic community. And the negative feedback received from modern civilization's technological impact upon nature—pollution, biological impoverishment, etc.—forcefully reminds us that mankind never really has, despite past assumptions to the contrary, existed apart from the environing biotic community.

This reminder of our recent rediscovery of our biotic citizenship brings us face to face with the paradox posed by Peter Fritzell:[41] Either we are plain members and citizens of the biotic community, on a par with other creatures, or we are not. If we are, then we have no moral obligations to our fellow members or to the community per se because, as understood from a modern scientific perspective, nature and natural phenomena are amoral. Wolves and alligators do no wrong in killing and eating deer and dogs (respectively). Elephants cannot be blamed for bulldozing acacia trees and generally wreaking havoc in their natural habitats. If human beings are natural beings, then human behavior, however destructive, is natural behavior and is as blameless, from a natural point of view, as any other behavioral phenomenon exhibited by other natural beings. On the other hand, we are moral beings, the implication seems clear, precisely to the extent that we are civilized, that we have removed ourselves from nature. We are more than natural beings; we are metanatural—not to say, "supernatural"—beings. But then our moral community is limited to only those beings who share our transcendence of nature, i.e., to human beings (and perhaps to pets who have joined our civilized community as surrogate persons) and to the human community. Hence, have it either way—we are members of the biotic community or we are not—a land or environmental ethic is aborted by either choice.

But nature is *not* amoral. The tacit assumption that we are deliberating, choice-making ethical beings only to the extent that we are metanatural, civilized beings, generates this dilemma. The biosocial analysis of human moral behavior, in which the land ethic is grounded, is designed precisely to show that in fact intelligent moral behavior *is* natural behavior. Hence, we are moral beings not in spite of, but in accordance with, nature. To the extent that nature has produced at least one ethical species, *Homo sapiens,* nature is not amoral.

Alligators, wolves, and elephants are not subject to reciprocal interspecies duties or land ethical obligations themselves because they are incapable of conceiving and/or assuming them. Alligators, as mostly solitary, entrepreneurial reptiles, have no apparent moral sentiments or social instincts whatever. And while wolves and elephants certainly do have social instincts and at least protomoral sentiments, as their social behavior amply indicates, their conception or imagination of community appears to be less culturally plastic than ours and less amenable to cognitive information. Thus, while we might regard them as ethical beings, they are not able, as we are, to form the concept of a universal biotic community, and hence conceive an all-inclusive, holistic land ethic.

The paradox of the land ethic, elaborately noticed by Fritzell, may be cast more generally still in more conventional philosophical terms: Is the land ethic prudential or deontological? Is the land ethic, in other words, a matter of enlightened (collective,

human) self-interest, or does it genuinely admit nonhuman natural entities and nature as a whole to true moral standing?

The conceptual foundations of the land ethic, as I have here set them out, and much of Leopold's hortatory rhetoric, would certainly indicate that the land ethic is deontological (or duty oriented) rather than prudential. In the section significantly titled The Ecological Conscience, Leopold complains that the then-current conservation philosophy is inadequate because "it defines no right or wrong, assigns no obligations, calls for no sacrifice, implies no change in the current philosophy of values. In respect of land-use, it urges *only* enlightened self-interest" (207–8, emphasis added). Clearly, Leopold himself thinks that the land ethic goes beyond prudence. In this section he disparages mere "self-interest" two more times, and concludes that "obligations have no meaning without conscience, and the problem we face is the extension of the social conscience from people to land" (209).

In the next section, Substitutes for a Land Ethic, he mentions rights twice—the "biotic right" of birds to continuance and the absence of a right on the part of human special interest to exterminate predators.

Finally, the first sentences of The Outlook read: "It is inconceivable to me that an ethical relation to land can exist without love, respect, and admiration for land, and a high regard for its value. By value, I of course mean something far broader than mere economic value; I mean value in the philosophical sense" (223). By "value in the philosophical sense," Leopold can only mean what philosophers more technically call "intrinsic value" or "inherent worth."[42] Something that has intrinsic value or inherent worth is valuable in and of itself, not because of what it can do for us. "Obligation," "sacrifice," "conscience," "respect," the ascription of rights, and intrinsic value—all of these are consistently opposed to self-interest and seem to indicate decisively that the land ethic is of the deontological type.

Some philosophers, however, have seen it differently. Scott Lehmann, for example, writes,

> Although Leopold claims for communities of plants and animals a "right to continued existence," his argument is homocentric, appealing to the human stake in preservation. Basically it is an argument from enlightened

self-interest, where the self in question is not an individual human being but humanity—present and future—as a whole. . . .[43]

Lehmann's claim has some merits, even though it flies in the face of Leopold's express commitments. Leopold does frequently lapse into the language of (collective, long-range, human) self-interest. Early on, for example, he remarks, "in human history, we have learned (I hope) that the conqueror role is eventually *self*-defeating" (204, emphasis added). And later, of the 95 percent of Wisconsin's species which cannot be "sold, fed, eaten, or otherwise put to economic use," Leopold reminds us that "these creatures are members of the biotic community, and if (as I believe) its stability depends on its integrity, they are entitled to continuance" (210). The implication is clear: the economic 5 percent cannot survive if a significant portion of the uneconomic 95 percent are extirpated; nor may *we*, it goes without saying, survive without these "resources."

Leopold, in fact, seems to be consciously aware of this moral paradox. Consistent with the biosocial foundations of his theory, he expresses it in sociological terms:

An ethic may be regarded as a mode of guidance for meeting ecological situations so new or intricate, or involving such deferred reactions, that the path of social expediency is not discernible to the average individual. Animal instincts are modes of guidance for the individual in meeting such situations. Ethics are possibly a kind of community instinct in-the-making. (203)

From an objective, descriptive sociological point of view, ethics evolve because they contribute to the inclusive fitness of their carriers (or, more reductively still, to the multiplication of their carriers' genes); they are expedient. However, the path to self-interest (or to the self-interest of the selfish gene) is not discernible to the participating individuals (nor, certainly, to their genes). Hence, ethics are grounded in instinctive feeling—love, sympathy, respect—not in self-conscious calculating intelligence. Somewhat like the paradox of hedonism—the notion that one cannot achieve happiness if one directly pursues happiness per se and not other things—one can only secure self-interest by putting the interests of others on a par with one's own (in this case long-range collective ·human self-

interest and the interest of other forms of life and of the biotic community per se).

So, is the land ethic deontological or prudential, after all? It is both—self-consistently both—depending upon point of view. From the inside, from the lived, felt point of view of the community member with evolved moral sensibilities, it is deontological. It involves an affective-cognitive posture of genuine love, respect, admiration, obligation, self-sacrifice, conscience, duty, and the ascription of intrinsic value and biotic rights. From the outside, from the objective and analytic scientific point of view, it is prudential. "There is no other way for land to survive the impact of mechanized man," nor, therefore, for mechanized man to survive his own impact upon the land (viii).

Notes

1. Wallace Stegner, "The Legacy of Aldo Leopold"; Curt Meine, "Building 'The Land Ethic'."; both in this volume. The oft-repeated characterization of Leopold as a prophet appears traceable to Roberts Mann, "Aldo Leopold: Priest and Prophet," *American Forests* 60, no. 8 (August 1954): 23, 42–43; it was picked up, apparently, by Ernest Swift, "Aldo Leopold: Wisconsin's Conservationist Prophet," *Wisconsin Tales and Trails* 2, no. 2 (September 1961): 2–5; Roderick Nash institutionalized it in his chapter, "Aldo Leopold: Prophet," in *Wilderness and the American Mind* (New Haven: Yale University Press, 1967; revised edition, 1982).

2. Edward O. Wilson, *Sociobiology: The New Synthesis* (Cambridge: Harvard University Press, 1975), 3. See also W. D. Hamilton, "The Genetical Theory of Social Behavior," *Journal of Theoretical Biology* 7 (1964): 1–52.

3. Charles R. Darwin, *The Descent of Man and Selection in Relation to Sex.* (New York: J. A. Hill and Company, 1904). The quoted phrase occurs on p. 97.

4. See Adam Smith, *Theory of the Moral Sentiments* (London and Edinburgh: A Millar, A. Kinkaid, and J. Bell, 1759) and David Hume, *An Enquiry Concerning the Principles of Morals* (Oxford: The Clarendon Press, 1777; first published in 1751). Darwin cites both works in the key fourth chapter of *Descent* (pp. 106 and 109, respectively).

5. Darwin, *Descent*, p. 98 ff.

6. Ibid., p. 105 f.

7. Ibid., p. 113 ff.

8. Ibid., p. 105.

9. See, for example, Elman R. Service, *Primitive Social*

Organization: An Evolutionary Perspective (New York: Random House, 1962).

10. See Marshall Sahlins, *Stone Age Economics* (Chicago: Aldine Atherton, 1972).

11. Darwin, *Descent*, p. III.

12. Ibid., p. 117 ff. The quoted phrase occurs on p. 118.

13. Ibid., p. 124.

14. See Donald Worster, *Nature's Economy: The Roots of Ecology* (San Francisco: Sierra Club Books, 1977).

15. Charles Elton, *Animal Ecology* (New York: Macmillan, 1927).

16. Aldo Leopold, *Round River* (New York: Oxford University Press, 1953), 148.

17. Kenneth Goodpaster, "On Being Morally Considerable," *Journal of Philosophy* 22 (1978): 308–25. Goodpaster wisely avoids the term *rights*, defined so strictly albeit so variously by philosophers, and used so loosely by nonphilosophers.

18. Kenneth Goodpaster, "From Egoism to Environmentalism" in *Ethics and Problems of the 21st Century*, ed. K. E. Goodpaster and K. M. Sayre (Notre Dame, IN: University of Notre Dame Press, 1979), pp. 21–35.

19. See Immanuel Kant, *Foundations of the Metaphysics of Morals* (New York: Bobbs-Merrill, 1959; first published in 1785); and Jeremy Bentham, *An Introduction to the Principles of Morals and Legislation*, new edition (Oxford: The Clarendon Press, 1823).

20. Goodpaster, "Egoism to Environmentalism." Actually Goodpaster regards Hume and Kant as the co-fountainheads of this sort of moral philosophy. But Hume does not reason in this way. For Hume, the other-oriented sentiments are as primitive as self-love.

21. See Peter Singer, *Animal Liberation: A New Ethics for Our Treatment of Animals* (New York: Avon Books, 1975) for animal liberation; and see Tom Regan, *All That Dwell Therein: Animal Rights and Environmental Ethics* (Berkeley: University of California Press, 1982) for animal rights.

22. See Albert Schweitzer, *Philosophy of Civilization: Civilization and Ethics*, trans. John Naish (London: A. & C. Black, 1923). For a fuller discussion, see J. Baird Callicott, "On the Intrinsic Value of Non-human Species," in *The Preservation of Species*, ed. Bryan Norton (Princeton: Princeton University Press, 1986), pp. 138–72.

23. Peter Singer and Tom Regan are both proud of this circumstance and consider it a virtue. See Peter Singer, "Not for Humans Only: The Place of Non-humans in Environmental Issues" in *Ethics and Problems of the 21st Century*, pp. 191–206; and Tom Regan, "Ethical Vegetarianism and Commercial

Animal Farming" in *Contemporary Moral Problems*, ed. James E. White (St. Paul, MN: West Publishing Co., 1985), pp. 279–94.

24. See J. Baird Callicott, "Hume's Is/Ought Dichotomy and the Relation of Ecology to Leopold's Land Ethic," *Environmental Ethics* 4 (1982): 163–74, and "Non-anthropocentric Value Theory and Environmental Ethics," *American Philosophical Quarterly* 21 (1984): 299–309, for an elaboration.

25. Hume, *Enquiry*, p. 219.

26. Darwin, *Descent*, p. 120.

27. I have elsewhere argued that "value in the philosophical sense" means "intrinsic" or "inherent" value. See J. Baird Callicott, "The Philosophical Value of Wildlife," in *Valuing Wildlife: Economic and Social Values of Wildlife*, ed. Daniel J. Decker and Gary Goff (Boulder, CO: Westview Press, 1986), pp. 214–221.

28. See Worster, *Nature's Economy.*

29. See J. Baird Callicott, "The Metaphysical Implications of Ecology," *Environmental Ethics* 8 (1986): 300–315, for an elaboration of this point.

30. Robert P. McIntosh, *The Background of Ecology: Concept and Theory* (Cambridge: Cambridge University Press, 1985).

31. Aldo Leopold, "Some Fundamentals of Conservation in the Southwest," *Environmental Ethics* I (1979): 139–40, emphasis added.

32. Arthur Tansley, "The Use and Abuse of Vegetational Concepts and Terms, *Ecology* 16 (1935): 292–303.

33. Harold J. Morowitz, "Biology as a Cosmological Science," *Main Currents in Modern Thought* 28 (1972): 156.

34. I borrow the term "devolution" from Austin Meredith, "Devolution," *Journal of Theoretical Biology* 96 (1982): 49–65.

35. Holmes Rolston III, "Duties to Endangered Species," *Bioscience* 35 (1985): 718–26. See also Geerat Vermeij, "The Biology of Human-Caused Extinction," in Norton, *Preservation of Species*, pp. 28–49.

36. See D. M. Raup and J. J. Sepkoski, Jr., "Mass Extinctions in the Marine Fossil Record," *Science* 215 (1982): 1501–3.

37. William Aiken, "Ethical Issues in Agriculture," in *Earthbound: New Introductory Essays in Environmental Ethics*, ed. Tom Regan (New York: Random House, 1984), p. 269. Tom Regan, *The Case for Animal Rights* (Berkeley: University of California Press, 1983) p. 262, and "Ethical Vegetarianism," 291. See also Eliott Sober, "Philosophical Problems for Environmentalism," in Norton, *Preservation of Species*, pp. 173–94.

38. I owe the tree-ring analogy to Richard and Val Routley (now Sylvan and Plumwood, respectively), "Human Chauvinism and Environmental Ethics," in *Environmental Philosophy*, ed. D. Mannison, M.
McRobbie, and R. Routley (Canberra: Department
of Philosophy, Research School of the Social Sciences, Australian National University, 1980), pp.
96–189. A good illustration of the balloon analogy
may be found in Peter Singer, *The Expanding Circle:
Ethics and Sociobiology* (New York: Farrar, Straus and
Giroux, 1983).

39. For an elaboration see Thomas W. Overholt and J.
Baird Callicott, *Clothed-in-Fur and Other Tales: An In-
troduction to an Ojibwa World View* (Washington, DC:
University Press of America, 1982).

40. J. Baird Callicott, "Traditional American Indian and
Western European Attitudes Toward Nature: An
Overview," *Environmental Ethics* 4 (1982): 163–74.

41. Peter Fritzell, "The Conflicts of Ecological Conscience," in *Companion to A Sand County Almanac*,
ed. J. Baird Callicott (Madison: University of Wisconsin Press, 1987).

42. See Worster, *Nature's Economy*.

43. Scott Lehmann, "Do Wildernesses Have Rights?"
Environmental Ethics 3 (1981), 131.

Organism, Community, and the "Substitution Problem"

Eric Katz

I. Introduction

In this essay I examine two basic holistic models of natural systems—organism and community—in order to determine their significance in the
formation of an environmental ethic. To develop a
convincing, working environmental ethic it is necessary to have a model of the natural environment
that is both ecologically and ethically sound. Further, any such model used by philosophers and decision makers must be compatible with current scientific theories concerning ecological systems.[1]
Finally, this model must be in accord with basic ethical presumptions regarding environmental policy.
An environmental ethic must not violate *basic* environmentalist attitudes.[2]

I suggest here that an environmental ethic
based on a holistic model of nature as an organism
is unconvincing or unworkable in the light of basic
principles or attitudes of environmentalists, that an
environmental ethic based on a model of a natural
community is in accord with basic environmentalist attitudes, and thus that a community model will
be more acceptable to environmentalists and ethical
decision makers.

One preliminary warning is in order: I am not
directly concerned with any metaethical justification of an environmental ethic, nor do I claim to
present any such justification. What interests me is
the actual practical operation of an environmental
ethic. I want to see if the principles, concepts, and
models used in an environmental ethic actually
agree with basic intuitions about environmental
policy. Obviously, I realize that my intuitions about
environmental policy may not be in accord with the
intuitions of others; thus, I have tried to present
clear cases through which environmentalists of different backgrounds can reach agreement.

II. Leopold's Double Holistic Vision

The holistic orientation of environmental ethics has led to the use of two models of nature—
organism and community. It has often been noted
that a truly *environmental* or *ecological* ethic cannot
be exclusively based on either (a) the interests of
the human population or (b) the interests of individual natural entities.[3] Instead, advocates of an environmental ethic must adopt a holistic or "total
field" view of natural systems, in which individual
natural entities and humans are "conceived as
nodes in a biotic web of intrinsically related parts."[4]
In an environmental ethic the ecological *system* or
the natural environment becomes morally considerable. Don E. Marietta, Jr. writes: "The basic con-

Environmental Ethics, Vol. 7 (Fall 1985), pp. 241–256. Reprinted by permission of the author.

cept behind an ecological ethic is that morally acceptable treatment of the environment is that which does not upset the integrity of the ecosystem as it is seen in a diversity of life forms existing in a dynamic and complex but stable interdependency." [5] The *interdependency* is what counts. The system as a whole—and not merely the individuals in the system—is of primary moral significance. A theory of environmental ethics, thus, takes seriously Aldo Leopold's maxim of moral action: "A thing is right when it tends to preserve the integrity, stability, and beauty of the biotic community. It is wrong when it tends otherwise." [6]

Leopold's maxim is a good place to begin a review of the concepts of organism and community because, despite his use of the term *biotic community,* there is a definite ambivalence in his vision of an environmental ethic, or what he calls the "land ethic." A section of his essay, subtitled "The Community Concept," begins with a straightforward statement about the importance of the idea of community in *any* ethical system: "All ethics so far evolved rest upon a single premise: that the individual is a member of a community with interdependent parts." This premise is also the basis of an environmental ethic because "the land ethic simply enlarges the boundaries of the community to include soils, waters, plants, and animals, or collectively: the land." [7] The source of moral obligations, duties, and rules is the community, extended now to include the entities in the natural world, although human society and individual human beings also remain part of this natural and moral community. "A land ethic changes the role of *Homo sapiens* from conqueror of the land-community to plain member and citizen of it. It implies respect for his fellow-members and also respect for the community as such." [8] Thus, an environmental ethic enlarges the traditional model of a human community as the basis of moral principles. Humanity is part of a broader unit of moral concern and relevance, a broader source of moral value and obligation: humanity is part of the "land," the natural system conceived as a community of interdependent parts.

Leopold, however, does not steadfastly maintain this community model of the land. He also conceives of the land as an organism, modelled after a living individual. For Leopold, an environmental ethic "presupposes the existence of some mental image of land as a biotic mechanism." The reason is that "we can be ethical only in relation to something we can see, feel, understand, love, or otherwise have faith in." [9] Leopold apparently believed that it is impossible to be ethical toward an abstraction, and that nature conceived as a communal system is such an abstraction. If, on the other hand, the natural system is conceived as one biotic entity, it becomes easier to care for its continued life or health, to respect its interests, and to consider it as morally worthwhile. Thus, Leopold describes the "land" as a biotic pyramid, a highly complex organizational structure of various kinds of living and nonliving natural entities. These entities are organized in such a way as to transfer energy throughout the system, "a fountain of energy flowing through a circuit of soils, plants, and animals." [10] Although the land, a biotic pyramid, is a collection of individual entities, it is similar to an individual organism in responding to outside stimuli, adapting to varying conditions, and maintaining its "health" and energy. Leopold also describes it as "a sustained circuit, like a slowly augmented revolving fund of life." [11] It is a "collective organism." [12]

It is true that this image of the natural environment as an organism or a biotic mechanism is only a subordinate theme in "The Land Ethic." The idea of land as a new member in an ever broadening moral community is clearly the dominant theme of the essay. Yet, Leopold sometimes thought of the natural environment as a kind of living organism, similar in structure to an individual animal or plant. In an essay published after his death (but written some twenty-five years before "The Land Ethic"), Leopold wrote that "in our intuitive perceptions ... we realize the indivisibility of the earth—its soil, mountains, rivers, forests, climate, plants, and animals, and respect it collectively not only as a useful servant but as a living being, vastly less alive than ourselves in degree, but vastly greater than ourselves in time and space. . . ." [13] This organic conception of the natural environment as a vast living being was an integral aspect of Leopold's vision; it was indispensable to his development of a primitive environmental ethic. [14]

It is not my purpose in this essay to trace the development of Leopold's thought concerning the establishment of an environmental ethic. Nevertheless, the fact that Leopold used two different models or metaphors in describing the land ethic shows that even in the work of one influential author there can be various kinds of *holistic* accounts of the natural environment. This kind of equivocation can cause problems, moreover, once the implications of the model are brought to bear on ethics. As I show in the following sections, the models of organism and community as applied to natural systems are quite different and yield different and incompatible moral conclusions.

III. Individual Autonomy in Holistic Systems

The crucial difference between the concepts of community and organism as applied to ecological systems lies in the *autonomy* of the individual parts within the holistic system. The model of community implies that there is some autonomy for the individual *members* of the community, while the model of organism implies that the *parts* are not independent beings. Even the terminology is revealing, for each individual in a community can be called a *member* because it exists both in its own right and as a functioning unit of a community. In contrast, the parts within an organism lack the autonomous existence and value of an individual in a community—they are *parts*, nothing more; they are not members, not individuals, but units or elements in an organic whole.

A comparison of a typical organic whole—a human body—and a typical community—a university—clearly demonstrates the distinction. The muscles, liver, the blood, and other parts of the human body are not independent beings with lives or value apart from their organic function. Their existence is due to the continuous functioning of the organic whole of which they are a part. Although various organs of a human body can be removed and transferred to another human body, the organic part is not an independent being in its own right. Organs are not organisms. If an organ is not transferred fairly quickly into another human body—i.e., a similar organic whole—its existence will come to an end.

In a community such as a university, however, the individual members—students, faculty, buildings, laboratory equipment, library materials—have an existence and value both in themselves and as functioning parts in the community. For this collection of entities to function as a university, of course, all the parts must play their roles: students must attend classes, faculty members must teach and do research, the library must update and organize its collections. Yet, all these parts of the university have an autonomous existence that can be separated from their functions in the university system. Members are not organs. Students and faculty have interests that transcend their roles as members of the university. In part, they have lives that are based on *other* communities: a student may have an outside job; a faculty member may also be a scoutmaster. Moreover, they have interests that are valuable outside of a communal context. A student jogs; a professor gambles at the race track. Even the nonliving elements of the university need not be parts of the university to be meaningfully employed. The buildings might be used after school hours by groups not affiliated with the university; the library books bring knowledge to individuals outside the school. In sum, the various entities that make up the university community are not *merely* parts of a holistic system; each has an independent existence. In an organic system, however, the elements are merely parts of the organic whole; each lacks a meaningful independent existence.

The natural ecosystem is more similar to a community like the university than to an organic system like a human body. It is difficult to conceive of humans, plants, and inanimate natural objects as mere parts of one large organism. Although these autonomous entities do participate in an ecological system, they also have independent lives and functions. In addition to the role the entities in an ecological system play in maintaining the natural order, they also perform functions on their own. Evolutionary theory teaches that all species strive for their own survival, but in doing so they contribute to the functioning of the natural system. Bees are attracted to flowering plants for nectar, food for the bees, and as a result, they pollinate plant species, insuring their survival. Natural individuals live and act for and in themselves and as members of a communal system. They pursue their own interests while serving in roles in the community. It is not at all clear that organs in an organism do this.

In addition, consider how individuals can be removed from one particular ecosystem and placed in a different ecosystem. They can be introduced into systems where they do not occur naturally—

as "exotics"—and still thrive. They can even be removed from a "natural" ecosystem completely and placed in a zoo. In contrast, the parts of an organism cannot transcend their natural organic role. Organs can be transplanted, but unlike the introduction of exotic species, the organ must be transplanted into a nearly identical organism—they cannot "live" on their own. The ability of natural individual organisms in an ecosystem to be moved (and to move on their own) into new environments shows that they are not simply parts of an organism—they are independent individuals which operate in a flexible system of communal harmony.

An organic model of natural ecosystems is therefore misconceived. J. Baird Callicott, for example, claims that one can differentiate three "orders" of "organic wholes": single cell organisms, second-order multicell organisms (with "limbs, various organs, myriad cells"), and "biocoenoses," third-order organic wholes such as the natural environment that are "a unified system of integrally related parts."[15] Nothing is gained from this terminology, for it blurs the clear distinction between individual organic bodies and ecological systems composed of individual organic bodies. There are some genuine analogies in the relationship between Callicott's first and second-order organic wholes and his second and third-orders: a second-order organic whole is made up of many individual cells, first-order organic wholes; and a third-order organic whole (an ecosystem) is made up of many individual second-order wholes. However, the degree of autonomy in the lives of the individuals in the system is an important disanalogy. The cells that make up a "second-order organism" are not autonomous individuals sharing and creating a common environment, but rather elements of a complex, unified entity. In comparison, the so-called third-order organic whole is not really an organic whole—i.e., an organism—at all. It is a collection of autonomous individuals that function as a system.

Apparently, Callicott and other environmental philosophers[16] conceive or speak of the natural environment or a particular ecosystem as an organic whole in order to emphasize ecological interdependency. As a corrective measure for the common anthropocentric belief that humans exist beyond the realm of natural processes, this organic model may be acceptable—but eventually the organism model

overemphasizes the *dependency* of the individuals in the system. I am not denying that there is a dependency. However, the value of natural entities should not be based solely on their dependent functioning in the holistic system.[17]

What I have said so far does not show that the community model of the natural environment is better or more plausible than the organism model. I have merely relied on the intuitive appeal of relevant comparisons. I now argue (1) that the organic model leads to moral conclusions that are incompatible with basic environmentalist positions and (2) that the community model is superior, since it does not lead to problematic moral conclusions. As a first step in my argument, I introduce the concepts of intrinsic and instrumental value and examine the relationship between these two kinds of value and the concepts of organism and community.

IV. Intrinsic and Instrumental Value

An entity has intrinsic value if the entity has value in itself, without regard to other entities, without regard to its effects on other entities. The intrinsic value of an entity is based on its own independent properties. To have intrinsic value it need not have any relationship with another entity; its value, after all, is intrinsic to it.[18] An entity has instrumental value if the value of the entity is a result of some function or use to which it is put. While the function of an entity may depend on its independent, intrinsic properties, the value of the entity is derived from its functional purpose and not its intrinsic properties. It is an instrument to be utilized in some fashion, and nothing more: the effect it has on other entities is the criterion of its value.

In an important sense, then, instrumental value is directly contrary to intrinsic value. An entity valued intrinsically requires no relationships with any other entities. An entity valued instrumentally is dependent on the existence of other entities and the functional relationships between it and these other entities. Instrumental value is not intrinsic but extrinsic. It is a result of interdependent relationships that exist between entities. It is the value an entity has *for* other entities.

Conceived in this manner, these two kinds of value are related to the concepts of organism and community in significant ways. Instrumental value bears a marked similarity to the way in which the parts of an *organism* are related to the whole. Organic parts have no independent value—their value is derived from the entire functioning whole, the organism. The liver, muscles, and blood in a human body are important for what they do *for* the organic whole. They are not valuable in themselves, i.e., intrinsically, but only instrumentally in that they perform functions for other entities. Thus, the parts of the organism have value as *parts* of a system, just as an entity with instrumental value only possesses value through its functional relations with other entities. In a community system, on the other hand, the members have independent existence and value. They may have communal value (i.e., functional value for the community), but they also maintain independent status and value in (conceptual) isolation from the rest of the community. Thus, because a member of a community can be considered as an autonomous individual, it is similar to an entity with intrinsic value; it possesses some value in itself without regard to other entities.

Of course, individual entities possess both kinds of value in different situations and contexts. A member of a community has intrinsic value in itself and instrumental value as a functioning part of a system. As an individual human being, a university student possesses personal characteristics that give him intrinsic value. As a student this individual also serves a function that is valuable for the community of which he is a member: he attends classes, interacts with the faculty, and uses the facilities of the campus. In contrast, it is more difficult to see how parts of an organism can have intrinsic value, for they derive their value only from the role they play as part of a larger organic system. A human liver, in general, has merely instrumental value as a functioning part of an organism.[19]

In sum, the model of community permits the consideration of both intrinsic and instrumental value to a greater extent than the model of organism. Since an organism is primarily concerned with the functions of interdependent parts, it emphasizes instrumental value. A community, on the other hand, which is composed of autonomous members interacting toward a common goal, allows for both kinds of value. The ability of the community model to deal with both, I contend, makes it a better foundation for an environmental ethic than the model of organism. As I show in the next section, the emphasis on instrumental value in the organic model violates the spirit of environmentalism.

V. Intrinsic Value and the Substitution Problem

Other important analyses of the *holistic* structure of an environmental ethic have failed to stress the significance of intrinsic value.[20] In an oft quoted passage, for example, Paul Shepard writes:

> Ecological thinking . . . requires a kind of vision across boundaries. The epidermis of the skin is ecologically like a pond surface or a forest soil, not a shell so much as a delicate interpenetration. It reveals the self ennobled and extended . . . as part of the landscape and the ecosystem, because the beauty and complexity of nature are continuous with ourselves . . . [w]e must affirm that the world is a being, a part of our own body.[21]

Shepard's metaphor that the natural world is part of my body, and similarly, that my body is part of the organic structure of the natural world, is clearly an organic conception. This concentration on the organic unity of the entities in the natural environment results in an emphasis on the instrumental value of entities in the organic system instead of on the intrinsic value of the entities in themselves. Even Holmes Rolston, who is sympathetic to both kinds of value, argues that when one considers natural systems the idea of intrinsic value tends to blur or fade into the idea of instrumental value: the idea that an entity can be evaluated " 'for what it is in itself' . . . becomes problematic in a holistic web." The concept of intrinsic value ignores "relatedness and externality." [22] Within a natural system, "things do not have their separate natures merely in and for themselves, but they face outward and co-fit into broader natures." [23] This "fit into broader natures" is the instrumental value that an entity has; its significance is determined by its effects on the external entities with which it is related, not merely on its own "separate nature," its own individual properties and intrinsic status.

The emphasis on the organic model for natural systems—with the resulting overemphasis on instrumental value—leads to a particular interpretation of the primary rule of action in an environmental ethic: the good for the natural system as a whole is the primary consideration. Callicott interprets Leopold's maxim—"A thing is right when it tends to preserve the integrity, stability, and beauty of the biotic community"—to mean that "the effect upon ecological systems is the decisive factor in the determination of the ethical quality of action."[24] This concern for systemic good tends to downgrade or even to ignore the intrinsic value of individual entities. Thus, Callicott criticizes the advocates of animal rights for focusing on the intrinsic evil of pain. He argues that it is not a proper consideration in the treatment of animals in natural ecological systems. Even if pain were an intrinsic evil, it is irrelevant from the point of view of systemic good. "Pain and pleasure seem to have nothing at all to do with good and evil if our appraisal is taken from the vantage point of ecological biology."[25] Pain and pleasure are intrinsically related to an entity in itself; they contribute nothing directly to the overall functioning of the natural system. The existence of intrinsic values in individuals, moreover, can be ignored in the evaluation of the overall good for the natural system, since the instrumental functional value of entities contributing to systemic well-being is given ethical priority. What is evil for individuals might be, and often is, a systemic functional good, and in this sense is acceptable.

This organic model of the natural environment and its overemphasis on instrumental value leads to an unacceptable conclusion involving a serious moral problem which I call "the substitution problem." If an entity in a system is valued for its instrumental function and not its intrinsic value, then it can be replaced by a substitute entity as long as the function it performs remains undisturbed. In other words, if an entity is considered valuable because of its functional role in the system, then what is really important is the role, and if an adequate substitute can be found, then the entity itself can be destroyed or replaced without loss of value. None of the overall good of the system is lost. As long as the system is maintained, the precise character or intrinsic worth of the particular individuals performing its functions is irrelevant.

The substitution problem arises as a result of human action in the environment. It is ethically significant only as a consequence of human activity. There is nothing problematic about substitutions or modifications that result from natural evolutionary processes. Since only human beings—and human institutions—are moral *agents*, only their actions can be considered to be morally correct or not. Although nature and its inhabitants may be conceived of as moral patients—the recipients of moral considerability—it is meaningless to attribute moral responsibility to nonrational beings and systems. Thus, the substitution problem involves the "artificial" replacement of one natural entity or species with something else—usually a different natural entity or species—that performs the function of the original entity.

Although there are no perfect or "pure" cases of the substitution problem, in which one species or entity is substituted for another with no other changes in the natural system, this kind of substitution is a logical possibility, and provides the basis for a useful thought experiment. From time to time, something like the substitution problem occurs in nature, since ecological competition concerns the conflict of species over particular ecological niches in the system. One species drives out another with little or no change in the overall functioning of the natural environment. The ecological niche is filled by a different species which assumes the role of its defeated competitor. The natural system is maintained unchanged. Our human knowledge of ecology might eventually reach the point where nonnatural substitutions of natural species could also be made with little or no damage to the natural system. While these substitutions are morally acceptable policies of action in accordance with any organic model, they clearly violate the spirit of environmentalism, for destroying and replacing a natural entity is not what environmental protection is all about.

There are related examples of the problem that are not merely theoretical. Lilly-Marlene Russow and John Passmore, for example, each discuss the possibility of modifying an existing ecosystem by increasing its diversity. Russow is interested in criticizing any environmental ethic that is based on a holistic principle such as the overall good of the natural community. This kind of argument seems to allow "changes which do not affect the system, or which result in the substitution of a richer, more complex system for one that is more primitive or less evolved."[26] The institution of "changes which do not affect the system" is quite similar to the "substitution problem." The idea of creating more complex systems is simply another version of the problem. Russow cites the introduction of new species in isolated areas (such as New Zealand and Australia) that replace the indigenous species and create a new, workable ecosystem.[27] An environmental ethic based on the good of the natural ecosystem cannot prohibit this modification of nature, provided we know with certainty that the new ecosystem will be successful, and that the life of the natural entities in the system will continue in a normal or improved state. But surely there is something wrong with this kind of modification.

Passmore considers whether ecological diversity can be a moral criterion. Should the enrichment of an ecosystem by human action be given more weight in moral decisions? Passmore—arguing from an admittedly human-centered perspective—notes that increasing or decreasing species diversity can be either good or bad depending on the factual circumstances. Although environmentalists are usually concerned about the loss of diversity caused by the extinction of species, not all such extinctions are considered moral evils. The elimination of the small-pox virus, for example, was not condemned as a loss of ecological diversity.[28] Passmore considers the possibility of eradicating disease-bearing mosquitoes if this could be achieved without any ecological damage to the rest of the ecosystem.[29] In such a situation, the preservation of a mosquito species just for the sake of diversity appears to be a mistake. Similarly, the addition of species, increasing diversity, can either be correct or incorrect. Passmore cites the introduction of the elm and oak in Britain, where the increased diversity led to a more beneficial and stable environment.[30] Depending on the circumstances, therefore, the increase or decrease in diversity can have good or bad consequences for an ecological system. Thus, an environmental ethic cannot blindly employ the principle of diversity for adjudicating cases. Passmore concludes that "there is no general argument from a principle of diversity to preservationist conclusions."[31]

Granting that the overall system is not harmed, why do certain kinds of cases involving diversity strike an environmentalist as inappropriate? Why is the elimination of a thriving species or the artificial diversification of an ecosystem considered bad? The answer involves the ideas of identity, integrity, or intrinsic value applied to individual organisms and species. This set of ideas provides the key to understanding the "substitution problem." Artificial diversification of a natural system violates the "naturalness" of the system. It alters the system in a way that is not the outgrowth of natural evolutionary change. In a sense it imposes a human ideal on the operations of a nonhuman natural system. Passmore, for example, also thinks that a wilderness without flies would be better than a wilderness with flies. A hypothetical wilderness experience without bug bites would be more pleasurable and just as (spiritually) enriching as the wilderness experience as it actually is today.[32] Nevertheless, there is something terribly wrong with this kind of modification. The best way I can express this is to say that human modifications harm the intrinsic value of the entities contained within natural systems. Individuals within natural systems have intrinsic value (among other reasons) by virtue of their existence in the *natural* world. Forcing these entities to conform to a human ideal, a human value, or what nature ought to be, would harm this intrinsic value. Thus, the modification of natural systems—even when the result is an increase in systemic well-being—is a violation of the intrinsic value of natural entities.

In other words, what I am suggesting is that *part* of what we mean by the intrinsic value of natural entities is their source or origin—what caused them to be what they are. A natural entity possesses intrinsic value to some extent because it is *natural*, an entity that arose through processes that are not artificially human. This "naturalness" is one of the properties that gives it its value. Robert Elliot makes this same point about natural entities by comparing them to works of art. A technically perfect reproduction of a work of art lacks the value that the original has because of its "causal genesis."[33] Art reproductions are, in fact, a fine analogue to instances of the substitution problem. A technically perfect art reproduction *functions* as well as the original; what it lacks is the intrinsic value of the original, because it is a copy, a fake, a forgery; it is not the product of the original artist's creative process. The same is true for natural entities: a technically adequate functional substitute, because it is not an outgrowth of the original natural processes of the system, does not possess the same intrinsic value as the original entity.

Moreover, the violation of individuals' intrinsic value ultimately affects the integrity or value of the system as a whole. When the individuals are changed as substitutions are made, the system becomes different. Consider a case involving a human system. A school administrator wants to increase the overall reading level of his school. Rather than hire more remedial reading tutors, he simply transfers into his district several dozen students who are much better than average readers. To make room for these students, he suspends some of his worst students for a semester. Something is wrong with this "artificial substitution" of individuals. Although the reading scores go up, although the system is improved, there has been a violation of individual and systemic intrinsic value and integrity.

Finally, consider the preservation of rare and endangered species. Russow notes that the preservation of rare species—particularly those that have been removed almost entirely from their natural habitats—cannot be justified by an appeal to ecological well-being, to the functional value these individuals provide the ecosystem.[34] Such individuals are no longer really part of an ecological system. They have no instrumental value, since the ecological system seems to function quite well without them.[35] Thus, if they are to be preserved or protected, as environmentalist policies universally dictate, it must be because of their intrinsic value. What makes this conclusion interesting is that cases of rare and endangered species can be considered to be instances of the substitution problem, so to speak, in midstream. A species becoming extinct was once a functional member of the natural system; because it occupied an ecological niche in the system, it had instrumental value. Its present endangered state is a result of some kind of substitution—either it lost an evolutionary-biological battle with a more competitive species that is replacing it or it has been displaced by artificial human modifications of the environment. The fact that the completion of the substitution process— extinction—is viewed by environmentalists as a wrong to be prevented shows clearly that the intrinsic value of species is a prime consideration in environmental decision making.

At the core of the "substitution problem" lies the idea of intrinsic value in a natural system. To take a well functioning ecological system and replace one entity or species with another, to substitute one element of a system for another, to increase or decrease the diversity of the ecological structure, to fail to prevent or even to aid the extinction of the species—all these actions compromise the intrinsic value of the entities in the system. An environmentally conscious moral decision maker cannot merely consider the instrumental value, the functional operation of the entities in the ecological system; he must also consider the integrity and identity of the entities in the system, i.e., their intrinsic value.

VI. Conclusion

Consideration of the substitution problem suggests that the community model of the natural environment is superior to the organic model as the guiding metaphor of an environmental ethic. If an environmental ethic uses the model of organism, it will be unable to account for the intrinsic value of the individuals in the system, and will fall prey to the substitution problem. Because an organic model overemphasizes the functional dependency of all the entities in the system, it can only consider the instrumental value that the parts of the organism have for the whole. The substitution of one part for another, one natural entity or species for another, will be morally and environmentally acceptable, as long as the overall functioning of the organic system continues.

An environmental ethic that considers the natural environment to be a community of autonomous but interdependent entities can, however, contain both instrumental and intrinsic value. It can consider both the contribution each member makes to the system and its independent existence and value. The consideration of both kinds of value enables a community-based environmental ethic to avoid the consequences of the substitution problem. Such an ethic will be able to explain why a functionally appropriate substitute for a natural entity (or species) is environmentally and ethically incorrect. The substitution of one entity for another violates the intrinsic value of the entity—ultimately, it violates the integrity of the system—despite the maintenance of the functional value of the system. Because the community model is flexible enough to consider both instrumental and intrinsic value, it does not violate environmentalist principles by permitting substitutions.

Let me conclude with the words of Leopold: "A land ethic changes the role of *Homo sapiens* from conqueror of the land-community to plain member and citizen of it. It implies respect for his fellow-members and also respect for the community as such."[36] We must take Leopold quite seriously on this point. An environmental ethic must take into account the good for the community as a whole, and the good for each and every member of the community as an individual. The community model of nature can do this, and thus it results in a modification of a *purely holistic* ideal. A practical and meaningful environmental ethic thus requires a definite formula for the balancing of instrumental and intrinsic value criteria relative to *individuals* in a *system*. This is a task that remains to be done; but it cannot even be considered from the organic holistic perspective.[37]

Notes

1. I do not mean to raise the spectre of the fact/value problem. This problem is pervasive throughout the literature on environmental ethics, and I cannot address it here. See E. M. Adams, "Ecology and Value Theory," *Southern Journal of Philosophy* 10 (1972): 3–6; Thomas B. Colwell, Jr., "The Balance of Nature: A Ground for Human Value," *Main Currents in Modern Thought* 26 (1969): 46–52; Holmes Rolston III, "Is There an Ecological Ethic?" *Ethics* 85 (1975): 93–109, and "Are Values in Nature Subjective or Objective?" *Environmental Ethics* 4 (1982): 125–51, and J. Baird Callicott, "Hume's *Is/Ought* Dichotomy and the Relation of Ecology to Leopold's Land Ethic," *Environmental Ethics* 4 (1982): 163–74. What I am saying here is much simpler. A workable environmental ethic cannot violate scientific laws about the operation of ecological systems. An environmental ethic that prescribed pollution (scientifically described) would be absurd.

2. I mean *basic* attitudes. Obviously, there are many different kinds of environmentalists, with different ideas about the use and preservation of the natural environment. I make no dogmatic assumptions about what constitutes an environmentalist. I do assume, however, that the careful use and protection of natural resources, the control of pollution, and the preservation of endangered species are the broad heart of the position. In this light, the differences between Garret Hardin, Barry Commoner,

David Brower, and Edward Abbey—to name just a few—are matters of degree.

3. This literature is too vast to be noted completely. For the general character of an environmental ethic, see Rolston and Colwell in note 1. See also Don E. Marietta, Jr., "The Interrelationship of Ecological Science and Environmental Ethics," *Environmental Ethics* 1 (1979): 195–207, and J. Baird Callicott, "Animal Liberation: A Triangular Affair," *Environmental Ethics* 2 (1980), 311–38. An environmental ethic cannot be based on human interests because of the contingent relationship between human interests and the welfare of the natural environment. For a discussion of this point see Martin H. Krieger, "What's Wrong with Plastic Trees?" *Science* 179 (1973): 446–55; Laurence H. Tribe, "Ways Not to Think About Plastic Trees," *Yale Law Journal* 83 (1974): 1315–48; Mark Sagoff, "On Preserving the Natural Environment," *Yale Law Journal* 84 (1974): 205–67, and "Do We Need a Land Use Ethic?" *Environmental Ethics* 3 (1981): 293–308; Christopher Stone, *Should Trees Have Standing? Towards Legal Rights for Natural Objects* (Los Altos, CA: William Kaufmann, 1974); William Godfrey-Smith, "The Value of Wilderness," *Environmental Ethics* 1 (1979), 308–19; and my "Utilitarianism and Preservation," *Environmental Ethics* 1 (1979): 357–64. An environmental ethic cannot be based on the interests of individual natural beings because many natural entities worth preserving are not clearly the possessors of interests. These nonliving and nonsentient beings acquire moral standing through membership in a holistic system. See Kenneth E. Goodpaster, "On Being Morally Considerable," *The Journal of Philosophy* 75 (1978): 308–25, and "From Egoism to Environmentalism," in *Ethics and Problems of the 21st Century*, ed. K. E. Goodpaster and K. M. Sayre (Notre Dame, IN: University of Notre Dame Press, 1979), pp. 21–35; Bryan G. Norton, "Environmental Ethics and Nonhuman Rights," *Environmental Ethics* 4 (1982): 17–36; and my "Is There a Place for Animals in the Moral Consideration of Nature?" *Ethics and Animals* 4 (1983): 74–87.

4. Godfrey-Smith, "Value of Wilderness," p. 316. He cites Arne Naess, "The Shallow and the Deep, Long-Range Ecology Movement: A Summary," *Inquiry* 16 (1973): 95–100.

5. Marietta, "Ecological Science and Environmental Ethics, p. 197.

6. Aldo Leopold, "The Land Ethic," in *A Sand County Almanac* (New York: Ballantine, 1970), p. 262.

7. Ibid., p. 239.

8. Ibid., p. 240.

9. Ibid., p. 251.

10. Ibid., p. 253.

11. Ibid., p. 253. The full discussion is on pp. 251–61.

12. Ibid., p. 261.

13. Aldo Leopold, "Some Fundamentals of Conservation in the Southwest," *Environmental Ethics* 1 (1979): 140.

14. "... a rereading of 'The Land Ethic' in the light of 'Some Fundamentals' reveals that Leopold did not entirely abandon the organic analogy in favor of the community analogy." Callicott, "Animal Liberation," p. 322, note 26.

15. Ibid., p. 321, and note 25.

16. See, for example, Paul Shepard, "Ecology and Man—A Viewpoint," in *The Subversive Science*, ed. Paul Shepard and Daniel McKinley (Boston: Houghton Mifflin, 1969), pp. 2–3. Shepard is discussed below in the text.

17. In reviewing an earlier version of this paper, Callicott was severely critical of the preceding section of the argument. As a means of making the argument clearer, I will attempt a brief summary of Callicott's criticisms and an answer to them. Callicott has two major complaints regarding my contrast of the models of organism and community, and the subsequent comparison of community and natural ecosystems. First, he claims that I misrepresent the model of organism by focusing on the parts of an organism as organs rather than cells. If we consider a "cellular model" of organism, the parts of the organism gain a substantial amount of autonomy. Cells can be more easily transferred than organs. Now I agree that the cells in an organism are more autonomous than organs—but this only makes the "cellular-model" of organism more akin to a community model. As I see it, Callicott's cellular view of organic parts is simply another form of community, and it gains its plausibility from its affinity with a communal model. Second, Callicott claims that my argument is only plausible because I have limited my discussion to "micro" holistic systems—a university instead of society *per se*, a natural ecosystem instead of the global biosphere. An organ cannot exist outside an organism; a person cannot exist outside of all society; a natural entity cannot exist outside the global biosphere. These "macro" comparisons suggest to Callicott an organic approach. Yet, even on this large scale there are differences. An organic part must be transplanted into a nearly identical being—a human liver into a human body. But a social individual can be transferred into many different kinds of society.

Although a twentieth-century social being might perish if cut off from all society, he might still survive in an assortment of social frameworks: with Bedouins, monks in Tibet, the elite in Hollywood, or even a family of baboons. Members of a community—unlike organic parts—have a greater freedom to move and change their systemic places. This freedom is their autonomy, their difference from organic parts. Finally, it is my intuition that the "larger" these models get the more implausible both of them seem to be. The entire biosphere is neither one organism nor one community. To consider it to be either seems to result in a vague generalization—similar to the "brotherhood of man"—that does nothing to advance environmental ethics.

18. I exclude from consideration the relationship between the entity and the perceiver of value (i.e., the consciousness aware of the intrinsic value). Although consciousness *may* be necessary for the existence of value (I leave this question open and do not address it here), it is still the case that consciousness can value an entity for what it is in itself, intrinsically. Note also that I am not arguing that intrinsic value is a psychological state of an individual, as a Benthamite would. I do not know what intrinsic value is, and I do not specifically define it here. The precise characterization of intrinsic value awaits further study. All that I claim is that intrinsic value, whatever it is, is based on the entity's own properties. See for more discussion, Andrew Brennan, "The Moral Standing of Natural Objects," *Environmental Ethics* 6 (1984): 35–56, and the references in note 20 below.

19. One might want to argue that a human liver is aesthetically beautiful, and that if beauty is an intrinsic value, that the liver thus possesses intrinsic value. But I think this kind of example is far-fetched. Although *any* existing thing could have intrinsic value based on its own individual properties, the predominant value associated with organic parts is instrumental value.

20. Those that do stress intrinsic value (for example, Tom Regan, "The Nature and Possibility of an Environmental Ethic," *Environmental Ethics* 3 [1981]: 19–34, and Lilly-Marlene Russow, "Why Do Species Matter?" *Environmental Ethics* 3 [1981]: 101–12) tend to abandon the holistic conceptions of an environmental ethic.

21. Shepard, "Ecology and Man," pp. 2–3.

22. Rolston, "Are Values in Nature Subjective or Objective," p. 146.

23. Ibid., p. 147. See also Holmes Rolston III, "Values Gone Wild?" *Inquiry* 26 (1983): 181–207, for a fur-

ther discussion of the blending of intrinsic and instrumental value.

24. Callicott, "Animal Liberation," p. 320.
25. Ibid., p. 332.
26. Russow, "Why Do Species Matter?" p. 107.
27. Ibid., p. 108.
28. But see David Ehrenfeld, *The Arrogance of Humanism* (New York: Oxford, 1978), pp. 207–11, where he does condemn this loss. The implication of my essay is that the loss of the smallpox virus would be a moral wrong, for it is a loss of intrinsic value.
29. John Passmore, *Man's Responsibility for Nature* (New York: Scribner's, 1974), p. 119.
30. Ibid., p. 120.
31. Ibid., p. 121.
32. Ibid., p. 107. Passmore writes: "But it is not at all clear that to sustain this [wilderness] experience the wild country needs to be a wilderness in the full sense of the word: were it, for example, to be purged of flies, I, for one, would not find the refreshment diminished. It is much easier to state a case for the preservation of humanised wildernesses as places of recreation than for the preservation of wildernesses proper."
33. Compare Robert Elliot, "Faking Nature," *Inquiry* 25 (1982): 81–93. Elliot considers the "forgery" of natural ecological systems in an analogy with art works.
34. Russow, "Why Do Species Matter?" p. 107. For another discussion of the difficulty in justifying the preservation of rare species, see Alastair S. Gunn, "Why Should We Care about Rare Species?" *Environmental Ethics* 2 (1980): 17–37. Gunn demonstrates the impossibility of utilitarian (i.e., instrumental) arguments for preservation of rare species, and suggests the importance of intrinsic value.
35. Note that I am not discussing rare endangered species that are biologically important to an ecosystem. There are obvious reasons for preserving those kinds of endangered species. What interests me is why we should preserve species that are *not* biologically important.
36. Leopold, "The Land Ethic," p. 240.
37. I have attempted to balance the communal (instrumental) and the individual (intrinsic) moral criteria in an environmental ethic in "Is There a Place for Animals in the Moral Consideration of Nature?" See also Evelyn B. Pluhar, "Two Conceptions of an Environmental Ethic and Their Implications," *Ethics and Animals* 4 (1983): 110–27.

B. APPROACHES TO CONFLICT RESOLUTION

PREVIEW

The moral side constraints upon what we may do, I claim, reflect the fact of our separate existences. They reflect the fact that no moral balancing act can take place among us; there is no moral outweighing of one of our lives by others so as to lead to a greater overall *social* good. There is no justified sacrifice of some of us for others.

Robert Nozick[1] (in speaking of intrahuman relationships)

. . . I think there is nothing more rational, nothing more sensible than trying to keep in mind what Aldo Leopold called the first rule of intelligent tinkering: *save all the pieces.* We aren't saving all the pieces. Species and whole habitats are being destroyed at a rate unparalleled in the Earth's history. It is as if we are going through a complicated Swiss watch with a bulldozer right now.

Dave Foreman[2]

At least two fundamental questions must be answered in order to develop a reasoned environmental ethic from which one may be able to derive policy conclusions. One concerns the matter of what is the appropriate criterion of moral standing, a matter that is discussed extensively in the Preview to Part III. A reasoned answer to this question will determine one's view about the range of things which possess moral standing, that is, the range of entities to which presumptive duties are owed and which possess intrinsic value (or some close counterpart). The range of entities which may be thought to possess moral standing may vary enormously; on different views it includes all and only humans, all and only sentient creatures, all subjects of a life and perhaps only them, all living individuals, possibly all and only ecosystems, perhaps all ecosystems and all living beings, possibly the earth itself—or some combination of the above. The list is not intended to be exhaustive.

The second fundamental question is how we should resolve conflicts of interest among beings (or systems of life). It is reasonable to think that the more entities that are recognized as having moral standing, or the more types of entities possessing moral standing, then the more difficult it will be to figure out how to resolve conflicts of interest among such entities. Hence, it will be more difficult to reasonably answer the second fundamental question and to identify plausible principles of conflict adjudication, or, if one prefers, *priority principles*. We confront another philosophical perplexity. Without suggesting any easy way around the problem, we should recall the parallel, out-and-out difficulty we have trying to figure out how to resolve conflicts of interest of an *intraspecies* sort, e.g., among humans, not only in practice but also at the level of principle. Arguably, the development of law, its common and conceptually messy way of recognizing various rights of various degrees of urgency, various interests of different degrees of weight, principles identifying different kinds of suspect treatment of different classes, acceptable and unacceptable ways of breaking contracts, and acceptable and unacceptable forms of compensation for harm done, are all attempts to identify and institutionalize a highly complex, but morally permissible, manner of adjudicating conflicts of interests. (We do not suggest, however, that this is the only function of the law.) *Interspecific* conflicts of interest among a wider range of beings, not just humans, promise to be even more difficult. The proper response would seem to be *c'est la vie*, and let us rise to the challenge. Analogously, one could imagine a

certain theoretical regret felt at one time by those who felt forced to extend the bounds (which they recognized) of moral standing to beings previously excluded, e.g., slaves, thus having to acknowledge a more complex moral and intellectual world.[3] Simplicity is not the only attribute a theory should have.

One of the difficulties of some recent work in environmental ethics is that, while the range of entities (we do not use "entities" in such a fashion as to exclude reference to what some would describe as communities, systems, or complex organisms, including "individual beings") defended as possessing moral standing has expanded, little has been said of a principled nature; frequently, however, sides have been taken on how to resolve particular conflicts. We will examine an example in a moment.

The conflicts, without attempting to formulate any set of mutually exclusive and jointly exhaustive set of categories, are of frighteningly diverse types. For example, depending on what, in fact, has moral standing, conflicts may be between baboons and humans (imagine transpecies organ transplants or experiments on chimpanzees to try to find a vaccine or cure for HIV infection), between trees or forests and certain humans (recall the dispute over the clear-cutting of old-growth forests and preserving jobs, for a few years at least, for loggers), between flora and fauna (mountain goats, an "alien" species in Olympic National Park in the state of Washington, are a threat to much plant life there), between corporate interests in obtaining disposal sites for toxic wastes (the plan in mid-1992 of one Swedish company to ship them to Somalia) and the well-being of humans and ecosystems in and around those sites, and between ship owners who (want to) dump wastes into the oceans and the health of fishes and coral reefs.

Admonitions to love the planet, care for all living things, realize that we are all part of the great biotic web, do unto others as we would like them to do unto us, respect nature, recognize the earth as one with us or part of our larger selves, not disrupt natural processes, care for future generations—all these admonitions *unsupplemented* by further principles seem entirely unable to guide decision making about what sort of trade-offs we should make when confronted by alternatives which involve imposing costs on certain beings or systems possessing moral standing. Historically, the trade-offs we have chosen, by and large, have favored a subset of *Homo sapiens,* especially those existing at the time of the choice—commonly those whom we have regarded as compatriots, those already wealthy, and perhaps those thought to be of the "appropriate" race or gender as well.

One of the attractions of utilitarianism is that it offers us a principle for deciding what to do when whatever one does will cause harmful consequences to some beings thought to possess moral standing, e.g., all sentient individuals in the view of Jeremy Bentham, John Stuart Mill, and contemporary utilitarian Peter Singer. Singer believes that we must give *equal consideration to equal interests* in carrying out the utilitarian calculus (alternatively, the like interests of humans and animals should be given equal weight). Elsewhere in this volume we have elaborated some of the objections to the utilitarian approach; see Sections I-B-4 and I-B-5 in the Introduction to Ethical Theory and also the essays by Tom Regan, Kenneth Goodpaster, and Paul Taylor in earlier sections of this volume, and by Bryan Norton in Section VI-C.

The essay and two book excerpts which follow are efforts to focus more specifically on identifying principled and defensible ways of resolving certain conflicts of interest. The explorations took place over a span of about a dozen years. Even if it is not possible to discover a "decision procedure" to resolve such matters, it seems worth the effort to try to formulate the most reasonable views, to assess the defenses and objections, and to see whether we have attained some degree of clarity.[4]

Before commenting on the three selections, we will briefly note some of the perplexities confronting such a task. First, what are the relevant relata (the entities related; here, the parties to the conflict of interest) in the conflict of interest? It is natural to think of conflicts between individual animals, humans, and/or plants, but one might consider the possibility that this view reflects some individualist bias; but are collectivities, biotic communities, or systems of more than instrumental value apart from the valuable individuals which are nodes, so to speak, in the web of which we speak? Second, if we agree that entities other than humans have moral standing, much will depend on which criterion of moral standing we adopt. In Paul Taylor's view, all teleological centers of life have value and, hence, the range of morally significant conflicts of interest is, in his view, far more complex than in some others' views. So a related question is whether any defensible position must be "species blind" or exhibit "species impartiality."

There is a basis in the selections of both Regan and VanDeVeer for giving different moral weight to different interests (e.g., an interest in studying history or attending the opera), possession of which typically and commonly, if not invariably, systematically diverges from one species to another. The reader can contemplate whether such posi- tions avoid the charge of "speciesism" or avoid a label which has come to be for many a pejorative term, namely, *mere extensionism.*[5] Regan's position allows that under certain conditions it is permissible to sacrifice a thousand or a million horses rather than take the life of a single human. This view may come as a surprise to those who caricature his view or assume that any defender of "animal rights" must be opposed to most, if not all, cases of seriously harming any animal. We leave it to the reader to observe how and whether this conclusion is compatible with giving respect to all "subjects of a life." Regan's position leaves open whether those who are *not* subjects of a life have, in our terminology, moral standing or are owed any direct duties. Its implication regarding those who are not subjects of a life (e.g., most animals, all plants, any ecosystem not containing subjects of a life) is that their value is wholly instrumental, barring some newly articulated principles.[6]

If one does not decide how to resolve conflicts of interest on the basis of the species identity of the possessors of the interests in question, what else is morally relevant? We literally preview here, in rather succinct fashion, some possibilities. The essays to follow make an effort to systematize many of these considerations.

If we assume that an interest in not suffering is possessed by any being capable of suffering, then the amount or *magnitude of suffering* to be avoided by a favorable resolution is a relevant variable. The stream of dissatisfaction which a being may suffer evidently varies from one being to another. Being the loser in a conflict of interest may also leave a being *disabled* and in a position of having to forego future satisfactions or fulfillment; this factor may or may not attend pain. Further, and arguably, the *disvalue of death* varies from being to being since what is foregone as a result of death will vary depending on the beings in question. Consider Mozart and a weeping fig tree, or perhaps Madonna and a giant redwood (we leave it to the reader to contrive a scenario in which these pairs of entities are in a conflict of interest). The intrinsic value of the mental experiences of Madonna and the redwood tree no doubt vary, with the prize going to Madonna (the tree not having any so far as we know). However, in Paul Taylor's view "all living things, human and nonhuman, have the same inherent worth."[7] If this is true, what follows? We leave the matter to the reader's assessment of Taylor's discussion of priority principles.

Apart from experienced suffering or goods foregone, one might focus on the *number* of wrongs done. Suppose one must choose between harming A by amount S or, alternatively, B and C by one half S each. Thus, one will cause the same total amount of harm either way; it is unavoidable, alas. We assume that the first option involves wronging one individual and that the second involves two wrongs. Should one choose the first option? Regan's essay gives some weight to the relevance of the number of wrongs done and the moral acceptability of summing up harms as a step toward determining what is morally permissible. This latter point is a deep source of dispute between utilitarians and the critics of utilitarianism.

No doubt we believe that the life of an oyster is less rich than the life of most politicians. Does it follow that humans have a right to subordinate or somehow exploit the oyster (after all, how would you like to be eaten, and some say that we should do unto others . . .), or another being with a less rich psychological existence? If one answers affirmatively, is one committed to the view that it is all right for the normal person to subordinate the seriously retarded person, other things being equal? Does bright make right? Do traits which we may think fail to justify *intraspecific* differential treatment ("discrimination" in one sense) justify *interspecific* differential treatment? VanDeVeer insists on not ignoring differences in the psychological capacities of the beings in question. And is having lesser psychological capacity a sufficient, or only a necessary, condition of being justifiably given the short end of the stick (if relevant at all)? Alternatively, is any view credible which implies that under some circumstances, the life of an oyster should be valued on a par with that of a normal human? What about a chimpanzee and a human? What about a chimpanzee and an anencephalic human baby?

What if we could save the life of a rare white tiger from Siberia by transplanting an organ from a rightfully convicted mass murderer, on the order of Jeffrey Dahmer, in an operation which would kill the mass murderer? This example brings up the question of the weight to be given to innocence or the lack of it on the part of one party involved in a conflict of interest. Robert Nozick distinguishes between innocent and noninnocent attackers.[8] A genuinely psychotic human or a rabid dog may serve as an example of the former. We often think it permissible to use violence, perhaps lethal, on a noninnocent aggressor who attacks us. Virtually all animals lack the capacity for functioning as moral agents and, hence, are not *morally responsible* for harms they cause; hence, they are not to blame for attacks they make and, thus, are innocent. Whether a being (innocent or not) has initiated an attack and whether that being is innocent seem to be morally relevant considerations in deciding how one ought to resolve a conflict of interest between the being and another. We note, then, a consideration about the *moral relevance of prior acts,* a consideration about the history or genesis of the conflict of interest. If we take away or destroy someone's food, say, a farmer's crops, we have attacked him or her; analogously, humans are often the initiators of aggression toward animals, e.g., by destroying their habitats or food sources.

VanDeVeer, Taylor, and Regan all give some weight to the innocent/noninnocent distinction; Taylor also assigns moral significance to the existence of prior wrongs and duties to *compensate* in the decision as to how to resolve a conflict of interest.

We have spoken here of conflicts of interest. We have not, however, assumed that any being *has a right* to whatever is in its interest. After all, it might be in your interest (for now, conducive to your well-being) if all your friends committed themselves to form a Be Nice to—(fill in your name here) Club and donated 10 to 20 percent of their annual incomes to promoting your well-being. But it is doubtful that you have *a right* to such or should complain of a rights violation if they fail to do so. Still, rights and interests no doubt have some important relation to one another. We flag the question here.

VanDeVeer's essay articulates the deeply entrenched intuition that the interests of beings which possess moral standing must be regarded as of diverse moral significance and further that even the most basic interests of different beings (say, the interest in the continued life of a mouse and the same interest of a human) may not deserve equal moral weight in decisions about how to treat them or how to resolve conflicts of interest between them. Paul Taylor claims that we should not put any serious weight on such pretheoretical moral intuitions, as he makes clear in his later selection. Whether one should accept a theory, no matter how counterintuitive it is, we leave for the reader to consider.[9]

VanDeVeer sorts out cases of conflicts of interest by, for starters, distinguishing between the basic and nonbasic interests of a being. An animal's or a human's interest in avoiding serious suffering, and in having basic nutritional needs satisfied, are basic interests. An interest in not getting drenched during a storm is nonbasic. Humans' interests in owning an exotic bird, in having ivory piano keys, in watching a nuclear explosion, in wearing musk perfume, or in shooting a wolf for pleasure are nonbasic; in fact, they are peripheral. One can sort human-animal conflicts into categories, the two most striking of which are (1) those between basic human and basic animal (or plant) interests, and (2) those between nonbasic human and basic animal (or plant) interests.

Let's consider one of many possible examples. In 1992 the U.S. Supreme Court began to address a case in which a Hialeah, Florida, priest of the Santeria religion and his congregation claimed the right to exercise their religious beliefs, ones which included the sacrifice of thousands of animals, including chickens, goats, turtles, and doves.[10] These practices were, of course, common in the era of the Hebrew scriptures (the "Old Testament" among Christians), and we also note in passing the conception of Jesus as the "sacrificial lamb" whose death was thought necessary to placate a god who required such. This is one of many cases in which basic animal interests are at stake, and we leave it open as to how essential the human ones are; of course, if one says that it is a basic interest to carry out any or all of one's religious beliefs, then it is not clear why the door is not opened to human sacrifice as well since some religions require it.

VanDeVeer formulates several principles which we might use to guide our decision making in these and other cases. In the end he defends the one he calls "Two-Factor Egalitarianism," which he claims is not speciesist but which also avoids a kind of fantastic, out-of-control egalitarianism, which, we have it on good authority, he is tempted to attribute to Taylor's view.

How VanDeVeer's rather individualist orientation in that essay would be modified to take into account the powerful presumptive value of biodiversity and healthy ecosystems remains an open question for him; we have this on good authority as well. But neither he nor anyone else needs to assume that all the morally important questions about "the environment" are reducible to properly resolving conflicts of interest among entities possessing moral standing. Indeed, the question arises for any theory that has an individualist orientation; we follow tradition here in leaving obscure what is meant by "individualist orientation." This tradition has been raised to a fine art, especially by those who are critics of some undefined enemy they refer to as "individualism." In one sense, utilitarianism is "individualist" in regarding the mental states or the want-fulfillment of individuals as the good to be promoted; still, the principle of utility allows, and indeed may require, the ruthless elimination of certain individuals for the sake of certain communities. So, on the face of it, would certain holist views and the views (ap-

parent principles) of certain "deep ecologists" who in the name of preserving the planet, or habitats, or ecosystems, seem to be content that doing so may require the elimination of individuals with moral standing (the reason, no doubt, that Tom Regan charged such doctrines with being committed to some sort of "environmental fascism"). We now comment on the selection from his book.

Regan maintains that "all *subjects of a life*" (*not*, be it noted, *all* animals) have *equal inherent worth* or value. So he is not committed to the view that the life of a fish and, say, that of the University of Texas's Homecoming Queen are of equal inherent worth—at least on the assumption that the fish is not the subject of a life (and that the Queen is). In Regan's view, to qualify as a subject of a life, an entity must be sentient, be self-conscious, and have a sense of itself as existing over time; the focus of his book *The Case for Animal Rights*, in defense of his view, is on mammals over 1 year of age—a long way from a defense of animal rights for all animals. Still to be addressed is the question of whether we should believe that *all* subjects of a life have lives of equal inherent value, for believing so commits one to holding the view, most likely, that one's child and a pig have the same inherent value. Given this view, how should one handle trade-off cases? Should one decide to transplant a pig's liver to one's child if it is needed, or the other way around, and should one make that decision by flipping a coin? Regan addresses certain "conflict cases" by proposing and defending two principles. Each principle is a "mouthful," and it takes some active reflection to understand the structure of both. Examining them in the context of the excerpt will be most useful. The first, *the Miniride Principle*, says, crudely put here, that when all one's options involve harming innocent parties in a *comparable* way, one ought to override the rights of the few rather than the rights of the many; thus, minimize the overriding of rights. If all one's options involve harming some and some would be harmed in ways much worse than others, one should override the rights of the many if choosing the alternative would make the few worse off than any of the many would be if the other option were chosen (this is labeled the *Worse-Off Principle*). Again, our version of Regan's view is succinct and lacks details. As Regan admits, in an imaginary case, in the absence of "special considerations," in which one had to choose between preserving the lives of a million horses and that of one healthy human, if the death of the human would be a worse harm than the death of any one of the million horses, then one ought to choose the death of the million horses. An interesting result for a vigorously argued defense of "animal rights."

Holists will probably oppose the focus on individual animals. Further, it is of interest that worries about endangered species and the promotion of biodiversity appear in no crucial way in the statement of the miniride and worse-off principles. But we should observe that the principles address the conflict problem explicitly, unlike the vague romanticized pronouncements we occasionally hear. What Regan has in mind in attaching the qualifying rider to both principles, namely, "special considerations aside," is not entirely clear. Correlative to his defense of these principles is an attack on the "minimize harm" principle, a principle which seems to be a negative version of the principle of utility (contrast: maximize utility). In any case, examining their implications for various conflict cases is of interest and may force us to consider further whether we believe that certain sets of beings have *equal* inherent value and, if they do, what sorts of constraints on discriminatory policies are in order.

Paul Taylor sets out five principles to resolve conflicts of interest, principles which he believes to be impartial between species and which he allows will not enable one to neatly resolve conflicts when confronted with hard cases:

1. Principle of self-defense
2. Principle of proportionality
3. Principle of minimum wrong
4. Principle of distributive justice
5. Principle of restitutive justice

The five principles attempt to capture the relevance of many of the considerations which we noted earlier. Taylor defends different principles as relevant to different sorts of conflicts, and he is quite deliberately focused on a world which includes flora, and not just fauna. Whether his position is any less individualistic than Regan's or VanDeVeer's is a matter of interest. His position seems to be that we have duties only to living individuals, and not to a group as such or a system of living entities. The reader can look closely at Taylor's remarks. Also of interest is the question as to what anyone has in mind when he or she says that we have duties to a biotic web or ecosystem *over and above* duties to the individuals which to a large extent constitute it.

Taylor's last four principles are intended to apply to conflicts of interest between organisms whose existence is "harmless to humans" or whose "harmfulness can reasonably be avoided." It is worth observing that some weight is given here to the concept of reasonable avoidability. We may wonder about the criterion to be employed. What sort of calculation is acceptable? Is it a utilitarian one? Should we consult the considered judgment of rational and informed people and, if so, is this not a kind of refined intuitionism which Taylor seems to dismiss elsewhere?

Taylor, like Regan, asserts that under certain conditions it is morally necessary to minimize the number of wrongs done as opposed to summing the harms of the various alternatives and then choosing the one which minimizes the total amount. One may sympathize with attempts to avoid the seemingly horrendous implications of utilitarianism under certain conditions. There is, however, a worrisome implication, or so it would seem, about a minimize-wrongs principle, especially if one, like Taylor, recognizes moral standing for all living things. There are millions of micro-organisms in an average shovel of healthy soil. Is incinerating that soil for scientific purposes permissible (thus killing millions of "wild animals" and perhaps plants, each of which in Taylor's view has the same inherent worth as one's child)? We do not try to nail down conclusions here, but only provoke questions. The existence of microorganisms may pose difficulties for Taylor since the interest in continued existence seems basic for any one of them. Nevertheless, we may misread Taylor; it is worth observing that his is a subtle, thorough attempt to construct a nonconsequentialist environmental ethic. The resources for handling the above objections may be found in his theory.

It is common to distinguish between what is *in* someone's interests and what the person is interested in (roughly, what he or she wants). For example, it may be in one's interest not to have unprotected sexual intercourse, but one may desire not to use condoms or other contraceptives. Even within the category of what is in one person's interest, one should distinguish between legitimate and illegitimate interests. It might be in one's interest to be the recipient of multiple organ transplants from one's "personal banker," yet it does not follow that it is permissible to take them without the banker's consent. Taylor notes that some human interests may be incompatible with maintaining a respect for nature; hence, they are in a sense illegitimate, and conflicts ought not to be resolved in their favor. We "flag" the questions of whether there may be basic, but illegitimate, interests and if so how to identify them.

There is a dilemma in Taylor's position that arises from his conviction that "all living things have the *same* inherent worth." Either his priority principles will reflect this radical egalitarianism or they will not. If they do reflect it, the implications may be radically

counterintuitive in a manner that cannot be ignored. For example, if we allow that a mouse has a basic interest in not dying prematurely and that a human has a similar interest, then why not flip a coin in deciding which shall live (try to imagine a case in which a poison gas can be diverted only by indirect means from one underground cavern to another after a cave-in; the mouse is in one room, and the human in the other; there is no happy third alternative). If Taylor's principles allow coin-flipping, many of us will find this troublesome. If the principles do not, we shall want to examine how it is that impartial principles allow favoring the human (or the mouse) and how this result is compatible with the assumption of equal inherent worth.

There is much to be said for trying to foster a world in which fewer *conflicts of interests arise in the first place.* Indeed, many crises have arisen simply because our human population is wildly out of control and because we as a species are running amok, acting as if our sources and sinks are unlimited and as if we are the only animals of value on the planet; indeed many people are offended at the very idea that they themselves are animals who have evolved like others from much simpler organisms and that they are only occupants of the planet in the last twinkling of the geological eye. So we must also think globally, about millennia and not months, and assess the value of planetary patterns of biodiversity, of morally relevant relational properties, and how to understand the notion of ecological health—and not just focus on admittedly significant, but ground-level, passing, conflicts of interest. An adequate environmental ethic must do both.

NOTES

1. Robert Nozick, Anarchy, State, and Utopia (New York: Basic Books, 1973), p. 33.

2. Murray Bookchin and Dave Foreman, *Defending the Earth* (Boston: South End Press, 1991), p. 45.

3. The practice of slavery is a good example of how a

conflict of interest may, in fact, *get* resolved. Our question, rather, is how such conflicts *ought to be* resolved or ought to have been resolved.

4. The term 'decision procedure' is defined as a procedure that is designed to answer a question by carrying out a finite series of steps, all of which are specified by precise rules and as a result of which one gets an answer one way or the other.

5. The term 'extensionism' is used to refer to attempts to take the frameworks of traditional ethical theories, such as utilitarianism or rights theories, and apply them to a broader range of beings than those to which the theories originally were applied (or to do so more rigorously). The broader range was a result of adopting a more inclusive criterion of moral standing. Critics claim that this is not satisfactory and, hence, speak of "mere extensionism." However, this pejorative labeling needs defending.

6. We say "most animals" since the vast majority are invertebrates and microorganisms. It is worth observing again that when Regan focuses on those he classifies as "subjects of a life," he focuses on the narrow category of mammals over 1 year of age.

7. Terminology can vary somewhat. Some philosophers attribute a certain noninstrumental value to certain individuals; some use "intrinsic value" here, and some use "inherent worth." Some, such as Regan, tend to use "intrinsic value" only for certain mental states. *Caveat emptor.*

8. Robert Nozick, *Anarchy, State, and Utopia.* (New York: Basic Books, 1974), pp. 34–35.

9. The reader may wish to review the discussion in the Introduction to Ethical Theory of criteria for the acceptability of a moral theory and in particular the discussion of the relevance of moral "intuitions" or pretheoretical moral convictions. There is a problem about the possibility of their being tainted by ignorance or prejudice.

10. See the account "Chicken on Every Altar" in *Newsweek* (November 9, 1992), 79.

Interspecific Justice

Donald VanDeVeer

I have never committed an axe-murder, bludgeoned fellow-humans to death, nor eaten any of their babies. Even though I would not think of setting fire to cats (though I am not at all fond of them), I have most of my adult life paid people to axe-murder and bludgeon to death a considerable variety of creatures, some of whom were babies, so that I might eat them; they were, in fact, tasty. That this description applied to my actions or that there were moral questions about these practices is something to which I was largely oblivious until reading Peter Singer's essay 'Animal Liberation' several years ago.[1]

The effect of Singer's early essay was sometimes—and in my case—to shake one from his 'dogmatic slumbers'. However, before the uptake could secure itself, Singer lost some hard-won credibility near the end of his essay by stating:

> What, for instance, are we to do about genuine conflicts of interest like rats biting slum children? I am not sure of the answer, but the essential point is just that we *do* see this as a conflict of interests, that we recognize that rats have interests too.[2]

To be fair, Singer does *not* say or suggest that the interests of rats ought to be weighed equally, but his willingness to consider that there might be a serious moral question here no doubt struck some readers as a *reductio* of his position. A further factor in such a reaction may be that there is naturally a powerful *desire* to believe that one is not party to morally outrageous practices and that arguments which suggest as much 'must' be fallacious. This less than reflective reaction may have occurred, I speculate, with many initial encounters with Singer's essay.

In that essay and more explicitly in Singer's book by the same title, there is a simple, tempting argument in favor of the view that humans have some duties toward animals; one possible reconstruction is this:

1. All or virtually all human beings are sentient creatures.

2. Many animals are sentient creatures.

3. Moral agents have a duty not to cause suffering to sentient creatures.

Inquiry, Vol. 22, No. 1–2 (Summer 1979), 55–70. Reprinted by permission of the publisher.

4. So, moral agents have a duty to refrain from causing suffering to (sentient) humans and (sentient) animals.

5. The interests of *all* sentient creatures (in not suffering) must be given equal consideration.

6. So, the imposition of suffering on animals (an overriding of the duty mentioned in (4)) would have to be justified by grounds of the same moral weight as those which would be necessary to justify the imposition of suffering on humans.[3]

The argument seems plausible, and some of its premises are incontrovertible. Singer's strong and specific admonitions (e.g. to become a vegetarian) in his radical critique of almost universal current practices affecting animals appeal to this argument and to further assumptions about (a) the actual effects of existing practices on animals (e.g. experimentation, raising animals for food and other products), (b) judgments about the painfulness or disability of these practices for the animals involved, and (c) the falsity of the claim that certain human satisfactions are obtainable only by harming or killing animals. The first four claims of my reconstruction of Singer's argument are reasonable. What is meant, in (5), by giving the interests of all sentient creatures 'equal consideration' is less clear. Does it mean 'taking into account' all such interests? Does this mean giving *equal* moral *weight* to like interests? If not, will (6) follow? Further, since killing may be performed painlessly the constraint on causing animals suffering (even if [6] is conceded) cannot yield an adequate basis for deciding on the legitimacy of killing animals if it is done painlessly. It is not my purpose to dwell on Singer's argument in any direct way, although I shall survey some principles which proffer answers to some of the above questions. Of the views to be considered, one emerges which is reasonable and in some important ways stands in agreement with *Animal Liberation*. At points, however, it delineates a competing view on the question of how we may legitimately treat animals. While I shall allude on occasion to the views of those who have taken a stand on these matters in recent literature, e.g. Peter Singer and Tom Regan, I conceive my task as a more constructive than critical one, and I shall try to sketch some of the features which I think must be incorporated in an adequate theory. Since I will

focus on conflicts of interests between humans and animals and the question of a just resolution of competing morally relevant claims, one might describe what is needed as a theory of interspecific justice.[4] Questions about the treatment of animals, like questions about non-paradigm humans (e.g. Homo sapiens fetuses) are hard cases, and even if the suggestions posed here are correct, they will fall short of a fully adequate account. Indeed, it seems to me that the formulation of an adequate theoretical basis for the legitimate treatment of animals is no simple task and cannot be done simply by extending, in any straightforward way, principles widely accepted or thought to be uncontroversial. It is not surprising that some of the recalcitrant problems confronting the formulation of an adequate theory of justice with regard to humans have parallels in attempts to formulate an adequate theory of interspecific justice.

I. Interests and Conflicts of Interests

Of those animals capable of suffering we may assume that they have at least one interest, namely, in not suffering. By this assumption I do not mean that they are interested in not suffering (though they may be) but, roughly, that it is *in their interest* not to suffer. This last claim means that it is not conducive to an animal's well-being to suffer— whether or not the animal is capable of 'consciously' wanting not to suffer. Further, the claim that it is not in the interest of an animal to suffer is, I think, a strong presumptive one. While pain *per se* is undesirable, it may be in the interest of animals to suffer *on balance* for the sake of a certain beneficial result—as in the painful removal of a gangrenous leg by surgery—as it is also for human beings. While the concept of an action's being in the interest of a creature is not transparently clear, it is contingently and commonly in the interest of a being not to suffer, although there are exceptions when it is in its over-all interest to do so. Since it is possible to cause death painlessly, an animal in whose interest it is not to suffer *may* not be such that it is in its interest not to die. However, I shall simply assume that *generally* when it is in some creature's interest not to suffer it is also in its interest not to die (and, hence, not to be killed). Let us assume, then,— somewhat more strongly than our earlier (3)—that moral agents have a duty, *ceteris paribus*, not to cause suffering to those animals which can suffer and a duty, *ceteris paribus*, not to cause animals to die. On this view there are many common practices which are not in the interests of many animals, and there is a presumptive duty not to engage in certain practices, namely, any which cause suffering or death to *those* animals in whose interest it is not to suffer or not to die. The troublesome and difficult question which arises, once one is convinced that both human beings (or many) and animals (or many) have at least some morally relevant interests, concerns how to *weigh* their respective interests in general and how to adjudicate *conflicts of interest* which arise between humans and animals. What we crucially need, to advance the current reconsideration of our treatment of animals, is an identification and assessment of principles which provide a basis for comparatively weighing such interests. We may be guided here by the standard method of testing principles by checking their implications against our deepest and strongest pre-theoretical convictions about specific cases ('intuitions' in *one* sense of the term), and also by how well such principles cohere with other defensible principles, in particular, how well principles advocating interspecific discriminations (weightings of respective interests) seem to be consistent with parallel and defensible intraspecific discriminations.[5]

II. Principles of Adjudicating Conflicts of Interests

Singer characterizes views which advocate a certain preferential weighing of human interests over that of animals as 'speciesist'.[6] He claims:

If a being suffers there can be no moral justification for refusing to take that suffering into consideration. No matter what the nature of the being, the principle of equality requires that its suffering be counted equally with the like suffering—in so far as rough comparisons can be made—of any other being.

*

The racist violates the principle of equality by giving greater weight to the interests of members of his own race when there is a clash between their interests and the interests of those of another race. The sexist violates the principle of equality by favoring the interests of his own sex. Similarly the speciesist allows the in-

terests of his own species to override the greater interests of members of other species. The pattern is identical in each case.[7]

The quoted passage does not distinguish some relevantly different principles which may be aptly classified as speciesist views and not all of which are equally tempting. I shall identify three forms of speciesism and two non-speciesist views which I shall dub Two Factor Egalitarianism and Species Egalitarianism respectively; the first three principles may be entitled 'speciesist' because they all advocate a heavier weighting of human interests over that of animals or do not concede that animals have any interests at all. The fourth principle also weights human interests more heavily but only when certain contingent conditions are satisfied; for reasons mentioned later, it would be misleading to label it a speciesist view. I list the names of the principles here, and consider each in turn:

1. Radical Speciesism
2. Extreme Speciesism
3. Interest Sensitive Speciesism
4. Two Factor Egalitarianism
5. Species Egalitarianism

In turning to Radical Speciesism we consider the only one of the five principles to be identified which in fact is incompatible with the premises of the mentioned argument appealing to animal suffering.

Radical Speciesism

Radical Speciesism is the view that:

It is morally permissible, *ceteris paribus*, to treat animals in any fashion one chooses.

One ground for this claim is the view that there is no *intrinsic* feature of any animal *per se* in virtue of which there is any moral constraint on how it may be treated. I speak of 'intrinsic feature' because the radical speciesist may allow that a given animal ought not to be harmed because of its relational trait, e.g. it is Smith's pet. This view is similar to the by now familiar view of Descartes's that animals were mere automata, extended things which neither think nor are sentient. With the further assumption that only thinking or sentient things are such that something may be in their interests, it follows that animals have no interests. So, it could not be the case that the interest of any animal outweighs that of any human being. There seem to be no premises which are both strong enough to entail Radical Speciesism (RS) and plausible. The Cartesian assumption is a strong one but not at all tempting. I shall not explore it. That many animals can and do suffer intensely is quite obvious. The anti-Cartesian arguments may be found elsewhere; in general, they are the arguments against extreme scepticism about Other Minds. Since many animals can suffer, the Cartesian assumption is evidently an untenable view. I include it for purposes of contrast and completeness. The reader may wish to examine the more patient discussions in Singer's book.[8]

What are the moral implications of Radical Speciesism? On RS there is no presumption at all, based on the effects *on the animal,* against putting live puppies in one's oven, and heating them in order to watch them squirm or convulse or fall over; the reader can imagine other 'perverse' experiments. The important issue here is simply put. Can animals (some) suffer? If so, it is, in general, in their interest not to suffer and moral agents have a presumptive duty to avoid causing such suffering. Hence, we must judge, if we acknowledge that animals suffer, that RS is mistaken or that the *ceteris paribus* clause is rarely satisfied.

It may be noted that Singer characterizes the 'speciesist' as allowing 'the interests of his own species to override the greater interests of members of other species' (see earlier quotation). While such unequal weighting of interests seems to be an objectionable feature of other principles which I have dubbed speciesist, it is worth observing that the Cartesian elaboration which may be associated with Radical Speciesism (as part of the ground for the latter) is not speciesist on Singer's criterion, for RS in its Cartesian elaboration does not weigh interests *unequally;* it simply concedes no interests at all to animals.

Those forms of speciesism which allow that animals have interests and which are compatible with the statements constituting the Suffering Argument are those remaining to be considered. They may all be regarded as principles purporting to guide action in cases of *conflicts of interests.* In examining such cases it is desirable to focus, when possible, on cases where the existence of animals is no threat to humans (e.g. not on cases of animals at-

tacking humans) and, when possible, on 'normal' before extreme or bizarre situations.

Extreme Speciesism

To distinguish two further forms of speciesism we must suppose that there is a difference between the basic and peripheral interests of a being. It would be difficult to elaborate such a distinction in a precise manner or offer a full-fledged defense of it. It is clear, however, that in the absence of certain sorts of goods many creatures cannot function in ways common to their species; they do not function in a 'minimally adequate' way, for example, in the absence of food, water, oxygen or the presence of prolonged, intense pain. We may say that it is in a creature's *basic* interest to have (not have) such things. In contrast there are goods such that in their absence it is true only that the creature does not thrive and which are, then, not in its basic interest (e.g. toys for my dog). This distinction is admittedly vague but it is not empty. Its application must, in part, depend on contextual matters. Given such a distinction, Extreme Speciesism is the view that:

When there is a conflict of interests between an animal and a human being, it is morally permissible, *ceteris paribus,* so to act that a basic interest of the animal is subordinated for the sake of promoting even a peripheral interest of a human being.

Extreme Speciesism (ES) proffers a different theoretical basis for actions affecting animals from Radical Speciesism when RS is linked to Cartesian assumptions, but, as stated, RS and ES will, in practice, sanction the same policies when there is, in fact, a requisite conflict of interests. When there is not, ES allows (is compatible with) acting to promote an animal interest, e.g. the interest in not suffering. As stated, however, ES would not prohibit puppy cooking and cat-torturing as long as such acts promote some peripheral (or basic) human interest. In the end, perhaps, much may depend on *how* peripheral the human interest one is considering is or further discriminations of that sort. Nevertheless, unless we wish to defend the moral permissibility of recreational puppy cooking and like acts, ES must be rejected as well as RS. On ES the kind or level of animal interest involved in a conflict of interests is, in effect, unimportant and need not be considered; this is not true of the next form of speciesism to be considered.

Interest Sensitive Speciesism

Interest Sensitive Speciesism (ISS) is the view that:

When there is a conflict of interests between an animal and a human being, it is morally permissible, *ceteris paribus,* so to act that an interest of the animal is subordinated for the sake of promoting a *like* interest of a human being (or a more basic one) but one may not subordinate a *basic* interest of an animal for the sake of promoting a *peripheral* human interest.

On this principle what is permissible depends importantly on whether or not the conflicting interests are basic or not; it is, thus, 'interest sensitive'. This principle sanctions a wide range of treatment preferential to human beings. For example, in a life raft case where the raft is overloaded and about to go under and either I or my dog will die (not both) before rescue, ISS permits me to sacrifice my dog if I so choose. In cases of conflict of *like* interests it is permissible, *ceteris paribus,* to subordinate that of the animal. Anti-speciesist principles which do *not* yield this result are hard to defend. Unlike RS and ES, which also yield this result, ISS does *not* permit puppy cooking or cat torturing for the pleasure of watching them squirm. This fact immediately makes ISS a more viable contender for the appellation, 'justifiable form of speciesism'.

While ISS clearly permits an evident discrimination in favor of human interests while not, in effect, assigning infinite weight to the latter, it will strike many as giving *insufficient* weight to human interests. For, on ISS, if it is in a bird's interest not to be incarcerated (as in a cage) and this interest is more basic than a hedonistic interest of a human owner in keeping it there, then such acts are impermissible since they would subordinate a basic animal interest in order to promote a peripheral human one. Suppose that having musk perfume, leather wearing apparel or luggage, fur rugs, ivory piano keys, or animal derived glue are not necessary to promote basic human interests. If so, then ISS would entail that killing animals for these purposes would (supposing that doing so violates a basic interest of these animals in continuing to live),

ceteris paribus, be impermissible. Given the mentioned suppositions some would judge ISS as 'too strong' even though it plausibly prohibits cat torturing to promote sadistic pleasure. I leave the question of whether ISS is 'too strong' or 'too weak' open here. There is a more basic objection to ISS, namely, that it omits consideration of another factor which is morally relevant in adjudicating conflicts of interests.

The objection calls attention, in part, to the enormous diversity *among* animals whose basic interest may conflict with some human interest. In this regard, the use of the expression 'speciesism' tends to suggest, perhaps, that we are only dealing with two groups and, hence, encourages formulating principles which suggest the permissibility of some sort of subordination of the interests of members of one group to the interests of members of the other.[9] This perspective reflects our tendency, Jonathan Swift to the contrary, to divide the animal world into the human and non-human or, analogously, into the inedible and the edible.[10] We ought not to forget that there are estimated to be about 1.5 million species and about 10,000 new ones discovered each year.[11] Significant differences *among* non-human species may become ignored with Interest Sensitive Speciesism. If it is in the interest of both an oyster and a chimpanzee not to be killed, ISS only requires that one consider the fact that the interest is in each case a basic and not a peripheral one. However, it is most tempting to think that while both interests are basic, the interest of the chimpanzee is of greater moral weight than that of the oyster, a judgment analogous to the one about the same-level or 'like' interests of my dog and myself in my life raft case. If so, then a principle purporting to be a reasonable guide to weighting the interests of members of different species must take account of something other than whether the interests in question are 'like' or 'unlike'. Such a consideration provides a basis for another principle, one to which we may now turn.

Two Factor Egalitarianism

It is necessary, to formulate our next principle, to recognize interests that are not basic in the sense suggested earlier yet not frivolous. I shall call such interests 'serious interests'. A rough criterion for serious interests would be that something is in a being's serious interest if and only if, though it can survive without it, it is difficult or costly (to its well-being) to do so. Hence, it may in the serious interest of a lonely child to have a pet or in the serious interest of an eagle to be able to fly. Serious interests are not *as* peripheral as Jones's interest in watching cockfights. It would be less messy if interests did not exhibit degrees of importance to their possessors; unfortunately, they do. This is also true of the other factor considered by the next principle, the factor of psychological capacities.

Two Factor Egalitarianism can now be formulated; it holds that

When there is an interspecies conflict of interests between two beings, *A* and *B,* it is morally permissible, *ceteris paribus:*

(1) to sacrifice the interest of *A* to promote a like interest of *B* if *A* lacks significant psychological capacities possessed by *B,*

(2) to sacrifice a basic interest of *A* to promote a serious interest of *B* if *A* substantially lacks significant psychological capacities possessed by *B,*

(3) to sacrifice the peripheral interest to promote the more basic interest if the beings are similar with respect to psychological capacity (regardless of who possesses the interests).[12]

On TFE the subordination of basic animal interests (say, in living or not suffering) may be subordinated if the animal is (significantly) psychologically 'inferior' to the human in question. 'Psychological' is intended to include the 'mental.' Let us conjecture about the implications of TFE; I leave certain assumptions tacit. On TFE killing oysters or (most kinds of) fish for food for human survival would be permissible; killing them only for the human pleasure of doing so would not be. On this view *certain* forms of hunting (recreational killing) would seem to be immoral. Similarly certain rodeo activities and bull-fighting would not be justified. The killing of seals for food by an Eskimo would be justified; the killing (and radical deprivation and suffering) of veal calves by people in agriculturally affluent areas may be wrong.[13] TFE allows the sacrifice of my dog in our life raft case. Many of these implications are plausible. In general, TFE permits scientific experiments on animals where the promised utility for humans and/or animals is very con-

siderable but not otherwise; recent criticisms suggest that a small proportion of the millions of experiments regularly performed can be so categorized.[14] It appears, then, on TFE as well as with some other speciesist principles, that fairly *simple* generalizations about the morality of hunting, killing animals for food, and experiments on animals are unreasonable. This feature of course parallels the difficulties with familiar simple generalizations about when it is permissible to kill or experiment on humans; this consideration is not unfavorable to TFE.

So far I have neglected what will strike the traditionally minded as an unfortunate and 'radical' implication of TFE. On TFE if there is a conflict of interests between a human permanently and (seriously) psychologically incapacitated by illness, injury, or senility and, on the other hand, an animal with similar or superior psychological capacities (self-awareness, capacity for purposive action, diverse emotions, affection, devotion, and so on), then the more peripheral interest must be subordinated, and the peripheral interest *may* be that of the human being. If the animal is sufficiently developed psychologically, then even a serious interest of a no more capacitated human should not take precedence over the basic interests of the animal. An example where an 'under-capacity' human is involved might be this. Suppose, contrary to fact, that an infant with Tay-Sachs disease could be saved from imminent death by a kidney transplant from a healthy chimpanzee at the expense of the chimpanzee's life; TFE prohibits this way of adjudicating the conflict of interests.[15] This case would be, at best, a statistically unusual one, and is mentioned in the attempt to get clearer about principles which have implications concerning other almost universal practices, e.g. raising and killing animals for certain human purposes. An important general characteristic of TFE is that not *any* interest of *any* human morally outweighs *any* interest of *any* animal, such a consideration seems a desideratum of any acceptable principle. TFE attempts to take into account both the kind of interests at stake and also psychological traits of the beings in question.

If the core of speciesism is the belief that it is permissible to give preferential treatment to humans over animals *just because* the former are human beings, then TFE is not a speciesist view. Being a member of Homo sapiens *per se* is not assumed to justify preferential treatment of humans over animals. It is a matter of fact as to whether a given human being will match or exceed a given animal in terms of psychological capacity; usually humans will. However, TFE allows that if there were, for example, beings physiologically like apes except for large brains and more complicated central nervous systems who had intellectual and emotional lives more developed than mature humans, then in a conflict of *like* interests the interests of these ape-looking persons should take precedence.[16]

We shall return (in Section IV) to further examination of TFE. First, I shall describe a final principle purporting to adjudicate interspecific conflicts of interest. Then I shall turn to the challenge posed by those who are sharply opposed to much of our preferential treatment of humans, with the larger aim of seeing whether any principle proposed here meets the challenge and provides a satisfactory basis for justifying certain preferential treatment of humans over animals.

Species Egalitarianism

In contrast to principles which permit the subordination of animal interests in *a priori* fashion (radical speciesism) or do so in practice even when like interests are being considered (extreme speciesism), is a view which is distinctly anti-speciesist, one I label Species Egalitarianism:

When there is a conflict of interests between an animal and a human being it is morally permissible, *ceteris paribus*, to subordinate the more peripheral to the more basic interest and not otherwise; facts not relevant to how basic the interests are, are not morally relevant to resolving this conflict.

SE is a one factor (level of interests) principle in contrast to TFE. Like TFE it plausibly denies that any interest of any human outweighs any interest of any animal. In fact it suggests, in a radical way, that species identification of the possessors of the interests is irrelevant except in so far as this might bear on a non-evaluative description of the interests in question.

It is tempting to call this view 'radical egalitarianism' because it allows, like Interest Sensitive Speciesism, no weight to the many impressive and (seemingly) morally relevant psychological differences among species. On this view it is not 'where

you are on the evolutionary scale' or what psychological capacities you have but only how fundamental your interest is which counts. This view is unacceptable. That we should, for example, equally weigh the interest in not being killed of an oyster, earthworm, or fruitfly with that of a like interest of a human being, is an implication in virtue of which we can summarily judge, I submit, that SE indeed reduces to an absurdity. While Radical and Extreme Speciesism both give undue weight to human interests over that of animals, Species Egalitarianism swings to the opposite error of giving too little. Part of the attraction of the former views may in fact derive from the blatant ignoring of relevant differences which occurs with SE and the assumption that there are no plausible alternative positions. In view of reasons discussed to this point the least counterintuitive principle appears to be Two Factor Egalitarianism, or possibly some variant of it. Before elaborating on such a view and considering objections to it, it will be useful to consider more thoroughly the challenge posed by those who are critical of current policies toward radically differential treatment of animals and humans. After doing so we will be in a better position to determine whether TFE is acceptable as it is, whether it requires revision, or whether it should be relegated to the wasteland of tempting but, in the end, irrational proposals.

III. The Challenge of the Critics

It has been argued by Tom Regan that the radically differential treatment that we extend toward animals as opposed to human beings cannot be justified unless 'we are given some morally relevant difference that characterizes all humans, but no animals'—one that would, in other words, justify the different sorts of duties and/or rights which we commonly assume we have toward the two groups, or attribute to the two groups, respectively.[17] It is tempting to believe (as Regan allows), however, that not all animals have interests, e.g. protozoa. While protozoa, I shall assume, are not *sentient*, perhaps we should allow, to the contrary, that even for protozoa something may be in their interest, e.g., conducive to their well-being. If so, possession of some (at least one) interest will not serve as a difference, possibly a morally relevant one, between all human beings on the one hand and all animals on the other. A feature that *is* possessed by humans but not, however, by all animals is sentience. This feature, since it *is* possessed by many animals, will not, however, satisfy Regan's requirement that we be given 'some morally relevant difference that characterizes *all* humans, but *no* animals' (my italics). Such a feature will not, then, serve as a justification, or part of a justification, for radically differential treatment of all humans on the one hand and *all* animals on the other. The presence or absence of sentience is, however, a morally relevant trait, and it *will* serve to justify, or as part of a justification of, differential treatment of sentient creatures on the one hand and non-sentient creatures on the other, e.g. the subordination of certain animals (non-sentient ones) for the sake of the well-being of others (sentient humans and sentient non-humans). Hence, *some* differential treatment of humans on the one hand and *some* animals on the other is, *ceteris paribus,* justifiable, I believe, without satisfying the stringent requirement that there is 'some morally relevant difference that characterizes all humans, but no animals'. This conclusion serves to undermine certain arguments prohibiting radically differential treatment of non-sentient animals. The conclusion is, however, a very weak one. For most differential treatment of humans and animals which is controversial involves differential treatment *within* the class of sentient creatures. The challenge posed by critics of established practices toward animals, such as Tom Regan and, possibly, Peter Singer, is more reasonably posed in the following way: to justify radically differential treatment of creatures *all of whom are sentient* it is necessary to identify a morally relevant difference between those who receive preferential treatment and those who do not. Further, any such morally relevant difference must be sufficiently significant to justify the specific differential treatment in question.[18] Of the views previously considered the only one not subject to decisive objections (considered to this point) which also proposes a basis for subordinating the interests of animals when there is a conflict of like interests between humans and sentient animals, is Two Factor Egalitarianism. It, thus, *purports* to provide the requisite morally relevant difference which would serve to justify some, at least, of the radically differential treatment of humans and animals, treatment which is not merely the kind involved in extending preferential treatment to humans over *non-sentient* animals. TFE is, then, of special interest and, in view of current disputes, not uncontroversial. Let us examine it in more detail.

IV. Two Factor Egalitarianism Explored

Two Factor Egalitarianism assumes the relevance of two matters: (1) level or importance of interests to each being in a conflict of interests, and (2) the psychological capacities of the parties whose interests conflict. It is worth considering further the rationale for assuming their relevance. First, consider the importance of the respective interests. In familiar infelicitous situations where a conflict of interests can be resolved only by sacrificing the interest of one party, a plausible principle would seem to be that there is a *presumption* in favor of maximizing utility or at least choosing an alternative which will minimize net disutility.[19] Given our initial crude distinction between basic and peripheral interests we can classify four basic types of conflicts of interests between, to oversimplify, a human and an animal:

	human interest	animal interest
1.	basic	basic
2.	basic	peripheral
3.	peripheral	basic
4.	peripheral	peripheral

The following examples illustrate (roughly) the above conflicts, e.g. (1) my life versus my dog's in the life raft case, (2) giving up my career to move to a climate where my dog will be happier, (3) my obtaining a new flyswatter by killing a wildebeest (for its tail), (4) my spending for a new wallet for myself or spending for a toy for my dog. If we suppose that the non-satisfaction of a basic interest yields a greater disutility than the non-satisfaction of a peripheral interest and if the conflict of interests in (2) and (3) is resolved by sacrificing the basic to the peripheral interest, it is tempting to suppose that there is a net loss of aggregate utility. Giving the interests of the animal no weight in calculating utilities in (2) or (3) is speciesism with a vengeance. That tack is an obvious target of current critics of many standard ways in which animals are treated and ways in which their interests are evaluated (if indeed recognized at all). For an example of the latter, to the criticism that DDT usage damages penguins, one writer states

> My criteria are oriented to people, not penguins. Damage to penguins . . . is . . . simply irrelevant . . . Penguins are important because people enjoy seeing them walk about rocks . . . I have no interest in preserving penguins for their own sake . . . it is the only tenable starting place for analysis . . . First, no other position corresponds to the way most people really think and act . . . [20]

On the principle that utility ought to be maximized in adjudicating conflicts of interests, peripheral interests ought to be subordinated to basic ones. Such a principle seems to underlie Interest Sensitive Speciesism. For reasons mentioned earlier such a view is problematic, e.g. if it is in any animal's basic interest to live then killing cockroaches for the sake of a certain convenience to humans would be prohibited. On the assumption that satisfaction (or nonsatisfaction) of like interests involves promotion (or non-attainment) of like utilities and the assumption that we should maximize aggregate utility, it is not clear how to resolve conflicts of types (1) and (4). Recall the case of my dog and myself in the overloaded life raft. The conflict is between basic interests; one has to go overboard (assume drowning is then inevitable) so that the other may live. If promoting my dog's interest will promote the same utility as promoting my own, the principle of maximizing utility will fail to require what, intuitively, seems permissible, namely, that I sadly do away with my canine friend.[21]

It is reasonable to believe, however, that in the life raft example the disutilities of my dying and my dog's dying are not really equal, even though the case seems correctly describable as one where a *basic* interest of mine is in conflict with an *equally basic* interest of my dog. But would not the assignment of different utilities to *like interests* be arbitrary—a giving of greater *weight* to interests of my own species over like interests of members of other species—and, hence, in some sense, 'speciesist'? The more important question, labels aside, is whether a case can be made for giving *greater weight* to my own interest in such a case as opposed to my dog's.[22] In general, is there a justification for weighting human interests more heavily than *comparable* or *like* interests of animals in cases of con-

flicts of interests and, thus, justifying the extension of differential treatment toward animals in certain cases where it would not be justified if extended to (most) other humans (e.g. it may be worth comparing a life raft case like the one discussed except that the conflict is between the reader and myself)?[23] Two Factor Egalitarianism assumes an affirmative answer to this question. The basis for doing so is *not* simply that human interests are, after all, *human* interests and necessarily deserving of more weight than comparable or like interests of animals. The ground is rather that the interests of beings with more complex psychological capacities deserve greater weight than those with lesser capacities—up to a point. Let us call this the Weighting Principle.[24] What may be said in defense of the Weighting Principle? I am not sure that an adequate defense can be proposed, but let us consider some possible attempts. It might be proposed that humans are typically subject to certain kinds of suffering that animals are not. For example, humans are typically capable of suffering from the dread of impending disaster (e.g. death from terminal cancer) in a way that animals are not (e.g. a turkey will not be wary of impending Thanksgiving events). This fact, however, may only show that a given type of act (e.g. death sentence) may cause unequal disutilities to an animal and a human. However, the *same amount* of suffering may be imposed on a human and an animal on a given occasion. Would there be any reason for assigning different disutilities to the two acts respectively? There may be if we take into account not just the comparative amounts of suffering on *that* occasion but consequent suffering over time, a factor affected by life span and the capacity to remember. Suppose it were true that the pain experienced by a steer upon being castrated and the pain experienced by a woman who was raped were of the 'same amount'.[25] The steer would not suffer from the memory of such an experience in the way that women continue to suffer from the trauma of rape, e.g. 'reliving' of the experience in dreams, and so on. What such an example suggests is that in cases where a basic interest (e.g. an interest in not being subjected to serious bodily harm) is violated, the different disutilities to the animal and human may be obscured by focusing on the fact that a 'basic interest' was violated in *both* cases. The long term disutilities of each individual may be radically different, and whether this is so is very much a function of the psychological capacities of the beings involved. That the *interests* of a human and an animal are 'like or comparable' seems no sure guide to the comparative amounts of harm done in such cases. Hence, in conflicts of *like* interests between humans and animals (basic–basic, or peripheral–peripheral) it may be important to focus on the less obvious and long term disutilities which may accrue in not promoting the interest; focusing on 'levels of interest' may fail to take into account matters of importance.

Another and, I believe, overlooked consideration which may be used in defense of the Weighting Principle concerns the economist's notion of 'opportunity cost'. Generally, in employing one's capital or one's efforts in achieving one goal, the cost of doing so can be thought of as the opportunities thereby forgone, goods and satisfactions that may not be obtained but which could have been if one's capital or efforts were employed in other ways. Most of my examples have focused on cases of inflicting pain or deprivation rather than death. The notion of opportunity cost is a useful one in trying to assign some weight to the imposition of death upon a human or an animal—as well as to weighting the imposition of pain or deprivation upon an animal or a human. Suppose that a group of rabbits is used in testing possibly toxic drugs and that the test is of the LD-50 type, where it is built into the experimental design that the experiment is complete only when fifty percent of the rabbits die (thus, Lethal Dosage—fifty percent).[26] Imagine a comparable test on a group of retarded human beings. Why are we inclined to think that if either experiment (but not both) is justified it must be the one involving rabbits? It need not be, I believe, because we think the suffering of rabbits has no weight. Neither must it be because we would deny that like interests are involved in the two cases. The psychological capabilities of even retarded human beings, such as those suffering from Downs Syndrome, are, however, far greater than those of rabbits. Even with the predictable shorter than normal life span for Downs Syndrome persons, the opportunities for a satisfying life for the retarded which would be forgone in the event of death are enormously greater than those of rabbits—or even, to take a 'less favorable' case—those of typical non-human primates. Generally, though not necessarily nor in every case, the prospects of

satisfaction are qualitatively and quantitatively greater for human beings than for animals. And this fact, this morally relevant fact, is a function of the psychological complexity of the beings in question. Further, it is clear that membership in the species Homo sapiens is no *a priori* guarantee of the existence of greater psychological capacity to experience satisfaction than that which may be possessed by beings of other species. The more basic point is that, generally, the opportunity cost of dying for humans and for animals at comparable ages, barring abnormalities, is vastly greater for the former. The harm, then, of killing in the former case is much greater than in the latter. From the fact, *if it were a fact*, that nothing could be more important to a given human than preservation of his life and that nothing could be more important to a given animal than preservation of its life, it does not follow that the disvalue of the loss of life in the two cases is equal.[27] For reasons mentioned, the discounting of the value of the preservation of the lives of many animals seems reasonable. A principle such as Two Factor Egalitarianism, based in part, then, on the Weighting Principle, is not unreasonable, and need not appeal to species membership *per se* as a basis for assigning unequal weights to like interests of animals and humans, respectively.

The extent of discounting the interests of a being, or more generally—weighting its interests— will, on this view, depend on the psychological complexities of the being in question. There is no reason, except to have practical presumptions, to make, *a priori*, generalizations about the capacities of all humans, all animals, all primates, or all chimpanzees. Non-trivial variations in capacity occur in any such group.

The importance of forgone satisfactions, as I have observed in passing, is a function not only of psychological capacity but of life span. The fact that the merciful letting die of quite aged humans with terminal diseases seems more acceptable than failure to extend analogous life preserving treatment to young adult humans, may reflect an implicit acceptance of the view that the opportunity cost of death is morally relevant and, in fact, a relevant difference in the two cases just mentioned.[28] In that respect, more familiar judgments about the comparative value of preserving human lives suggest that the emphasis here on opportunity cost accords with reflective moral judgments that are made with regard to differential treatment among human beings. Similarly, the general acceptance of allowing seriously defective infants to expire may assume the plausibility of attending to psychological capacity as part of the determination of the value of promoting or sacrificing a basic interest—such as the interest in the preservation of life.

If Two Factor Egalitarianism is correct, and for the reasons mentioned, it will *sometimes* be permissible to do what Singer regards as an arbitrary prejudice, namely, for the speciesist (or any human) to 'allow the interests of his own species to override the greater interests of members of other species'. The unfortunate implication of Singer's claim that this is impermissible is that it prohibits killing a minimally sentient non-human creature for the sake of a 'lesser human interest' in cases where the human's psychological capacities are distinctly more complex. TFE is not anthropocentric in the way that a view is if it regards species membership in Homo sapiens as relevant *per se*. The latter assumption is what Singer takes to be invidious and arbitrary about views he labels speciesist. On this point Singer is right. If Singer, or others, were to claim that TFE is also invidious and arbitrary in its 'psychocentric' emphasis, reasons need to be stated other than that it takes species membership *per se* as relevant; for it does not.

V. Some Persistent Difficulties

To this point I have argued that among the widely divergent proposals considered (Radical Speciesism, etc.), Two Factor Egalitarianism best accords with both matters of fact and considered and not unreasonable pre-theoretical convictions about how we ought to resolve conflicts of interests between humans and animals. Thus, it seems the most plausible among the five positions considered. I have further suggested an answer (or part of one) to the basic challenge posed by critics of our treatment of animals (as I would pose it): to justify radically differential treatment of creatures all of whom are sentient it is necessary to identify a morally relevant difference between those who receive preferential treatment and those who do not. The difference proposed is psychological complexity in so far as that bears on the capacity of the entity to live a satisfying life; further, to the extent that the

entity lacks capacities necessary for such, it is reasonable to discount its interests. The thorny question of what counts as a reasonable discounting I have not tried to settle. I have further argued that TFE avoids the counter-intuitive implications of Singer's principle of equality which requires (of *any* being) 'that its suffering be counted equally with the like suffering—in so far as rough comparisons can be made—of any other being'. As I understand the principle it focuses on actual suffering and not also on forgone satisfactions. Further, TFE avoids the charge of taking species membership *per se* as a morally relevant difference serving to justify interspecific differential treatment. If the argument so far is correct (perhaps even, approximately correct), TFE stands as the most reasonable approach.

Nevertheless, TFE is subject to a number of objections not yet considered, some of which are obvious and some of which are not. Most evident, the principle is vague. There is no precise way of determining which interests are basic, which serious, and which are more peripheral or how to rank interests precisely. Similarly, no adequate account has been offered of how to determine levels of psychological complexity. I will not dwell on these problems. If they are relevant (I believe they are) we must do the best we can; perhaps these difficulties are *no more* difficult than those faced in analogous problems of intraspecies conflicts of interests. These difficulties do not strike me as *decisive* ones; in any case I do not pursue them here.

TFE is, I believe, more troubling in another respect. In regarding level of psychological complexity as morally important (rather than, say, possession or lack of fur, feathers, a tail, or claws) it may require or allow that the interests of human beings need not be assigned equal weight where it is the case that there are significant empirical differences among humans in terms of psychological capacity. If an implication exists that the interests of dull, psychologically less complicated humans (the retarded? the senile? the brain damaged?) need not be counted as much as that of other humans (in the process of coming to some all-things-considered moral judgment about acts affecting them and perhaps others), it will be tempting to judge that accepting TFE would commit one to sanctioning intraspecific injustices—perhaps on the conviction that 'all human beings are of equal intrinsic worth' or convictions which appear to demand that the like interests of all human beings must be assigned equal moral weight initially regardless of final specific moral judgments. The worry is, generally, that a tempting basis for making *interspecific discrimination* entails possibly counter-intuitive results with regard to *intraspecific* discriminations.

Is there any way of reasonably weighting interests based on the psychological capacities of interest holders which will not commit one who does so to policies of intraspecific (human) discrimination of an objectionable sort. A simple principle—give greater weight to the interests of a being with greater psychological capacity than one with less, proportionately—may indeed lead to objectionable discrimination. But a plausible weighting principle need not look like this. We may well regard it as an arbitrary and unjustified extension of differential treatment to offer, other things being equal, to finance the college education of one of our children with an 'I.Q.' of 140 but to refuse to do so for another with an 'I.Q.' of 120. Possession of a capacity beyond a certain degree may not count as a morally relevant difference. Beyond a certain threshold point it may. It might not be unjustified to refuse such support for a Downs Syndrome child. Suppose we adopt a bright chimpanzee and a quite retarded Downs Syndrome child. Would it be permissible to torture either? Intuitively: no. Would it be permissible to extend differential treatment to them regarding the provision of educational opportunities? Intuitively, one would think so. My more general point is that differences in psychological capacity may, up to a point, not justify differential treatment. Beyond a certain point they may, and whether they do may depend in part on the kind of differential treatment we are considering and what difference it might make to the prospective satisfactions or dissatisfactions of the beings considered. For example, virtually all human beings are capable of understanding promises and forming expectations of their being kept. Wide variations in psychological capacity exist alongside this particular capacity. These variations may provide no reason for justifying differing presumptions about the importance of promise-keeping for these humans. It is not evident that any non-human is capable of understanding promises, although some certainly seem to form expectations.[29]

To clarify, a weighting principle may recognize threshold points. Possession of certain capacities

(e.g. intelligence) above a certain point may preclude certain forms of differential treatment. Below a certain point it may not. These assumptions may justify certain forms of interspecific discrimination. They also may serve to justify *certain* forms of intraspecific discrimination (among humans), e.g. treating differently an anencephalic infant, a Downs Syndrome infant, and a normal infant.[30] Because of the recognition of the importance of threshold considerations it is not obvious that a weighting principle, if applied, would lead to *objectionable* forms of intraspecific discrimination. So, the genuine worry about such a consequence does not evidently disqualify TFE (or some variant on it), which presupposes a weighting principle, from consideration. If so, more needs to be said, but I shall make no attempt to say it here (at least partly because it is beyond *my* capacity).

For the reasons discussed TFE seems more adequate than other proposals about how we ought to treat animals—in spite of its deficiencies. Some of its deficiencies may be remedied by a more specific, determinate statement of a variant on TFE. Further, supplementary principles are needed to elaborate and defend distinctions among levels of interests, as well as an elaboration of which psychological capacities are relevant or which sets of such capacities are relevant (and relevant to different forms of proposed differential treatment). That such supplementary assumptions are necessary complicates what may be called, appropriately, a theory of interspecific justice. That such a theory would be complicated may be disappointing; most of us hope for and value simplicity in a theory. TFE is not itself complicated, from one standpoint. It explicitly recognizes only two considerations as morally relevant in adjudicating interspecific conflicts of interests (levels of interests and psychological complexity of the beings). As noted, however, these considerations need more complicated elaboration and defense. Given the difficulties commonly acknowledged today in formulating and defending principles of justice for human interaction, it should not be surprising that plausible principles for just interspecific interactions turn out to be not readily or easily formulated.

In testing the proposed principles I have depended considerably on what I take to be thoughtful pre-theoretic convictions about how specific conflicts ought to be or may permissibly be resolved. Some may claim that this approach is wrong-headed at the outset, but I will leave it to others to say why. More likely, some will claim that the convictions invoked are a by-product of prejudice or are uniquely mine. I do not find this obvious, and I have tried to show that distinctions among levels of interests are supposed by those who take a somewhat different view of these matters, e.g., Peter Singer. I have also indicated how some limited weighting of interests is presupposed in what appears to be reasonable albeit differential treatment of human beings. If the admittedly incomplete account presented here is approximately correct, then certain general criteria are available for assessing which sorts of subordination of animal interests are justifiable and which are not. That some subordination of animal interests is, in general, acceptable and that some is not is evident. The important and more practical task of ascertaining which is which remains. In general, the implications of the position defended here will, I think, neither sanction many common dealings with animals nor lend support to some of the sweeping condemnations of preferential treatment set out by recent critics. But a more moderate position on the proper treatment of animals must, I think, side with recent critics in judging much of the prevailing wholesale disregard of the basic interests of higher animals as unconscionable.[31]

Notes

1. Peter Singer's essay 'Animal Liberation' appeared in *The New York Review of Books* (April 5, 1973), pp. 10–15.

2. Ibid., p. 15.

3. Later references will be to Singer's book, *Animal Liberation*. Avon Books, New York 1977. In that book Singer emphasizes that his primary moral assumption is 'the principle of equality' which does not require identical treatment of but 'equal consideration' of beings with interests (pp. 3, 6). Further, beings with interests are only those with a capacity for suffering and enjoyment (p. 8). Recognizing complexities about killing, as opposed to the imposition of pain, he claims that 'the conclusions that are argued for in this book flow from the principle of minimizing suffering alone' (p. 22). Given this last emphasis and Singer's rejection of any necessity to couch his position in terms of animal rights (see Peter Singer, 'The Fable of the Fox and the Unliberated Animals', *Ethics*, Vol. 88, No. 2 [January

1978], p. 122), I have chosen to reconstruct his argument as above.

4. The parallel with current theories of justice 'for' human beings, theories which attempt to adjudicate conflicting interests, is evident.

5. Of course, the radical subordination of certain *human* interests (those of 'natural slaves') seemed intuitively innocent and natural to Aristotle, and, as J. S. Mill noted in *The Subjection of Women*, it is a standard mark of a deeply held prejudice that it seem perfectly *natural* to the one who holds it. There is always the danger of accepting only those principles which are compatible with our prejudices.

6. For aesthetic reasons I would prefer use of 'speciesism', but to avoid multiplication of variants I adhere to the current use of 'speciesism'.

7. Singer, op. cit., pp. 8–9.

8. Ibid., pp. 9–15.

9. It is worth noting a dissimilarity between racism or sexism on the one hand and speciesism on the other, namely, that in the former cases those whose interests are subordinated are biologically 'homogeneous' with their subordinators but not in the latter case.

10. See Stanley Godlovitch, 'Utilities' in *Animals, Men, and Morals*, Taplinger Publishing Company, New York 1972, p. 181.

11. A. J. Cain, *Animal Species and Their Evolution*, Harper & Row, New York 1960.

12. It would be plausible to add: (4) to use a fair (e.g. random) procedure to decide whose interest should be sacrificed if the beings are psychologically similar and the interests are like. But see the (here unincorporated) consideration in Note 19.

13. See Singer, op. cit., pp. 122–8.

14. Ibid., Ch. 2.

15. The Tay-Sachs infant will die 'soon' anyway, typically by the age of five or six years and will suffer in the interim. Its interest in continuing to exist may, then, be less basic than that of the healthy chimpanzee in continuing to live. The capacities of the infant may not exceed those of the chimpanzee at the time supposed.

16. See the intriguing fictionalized thought-experiment in Desmond Stewart's "The Limits of Trooghaft" in Tom Regan and Peter Singer (Eds.), *Animal Rights and Human Obligations*, Prentice Hall, Englewood Cliffs, New Jersey 1976, pp. 238–45.

17. Tom Regan, 'The Moral Basis of Vegetarianism', *Canadian Journal of Philosophy*, Vol. 5, No. 2 (October 1975), pp. 181–214.

18. Without this qualification (sufficiently . . .), someone might argue that since there is a morally relevant difference between those who commit traffic violations and those who do not, it is justified to extend capital punishment to the former but not the latter.

19. I have so far deliberately ignored a complicating factor which seems relevant, namely, how a conflict of interest arises. A fuller account of things should consider this; I make no such attempt here. To elaborate, however, conflicts of interests sometimes arise only because one party *wants* what another has, and resolution of such a conflict *may not* be a matter of balancing legitimate claims. There may be a conflict of interests between my neighbor and myself since I want his new car, or between a rapist and his victim. Many of the conflicts of interests between humans and animals are generated by human desires to do what is harmful to animals; we eat them more than they eat us.

20. William F. Baxter, *People or Penguins: The Case for Optimal Pollution,* Columbia University Press, New York 1974, p. 5.

21. Considering utilities or disutilities to others would likely weight the case in favor of my preservation—solely on grounds of maximizing aggregate utility. But we can imagine cases where this would not be so; in any case I exclude such considerations above by assumption.

22. The relation between having rights and having interests is not clear. It is doubtful that having interests is sufficient for having rights (on this see the discussions by myself and James Rachels in Tom Regan and Peter Singer's anthology, *Animal Rights and Human Obligations,* Prentice Hall, Englewood Cliffs, New Jersey 1976, pp. 205–32). More plausible is the claim that any entity having rights must also have interests. If so, at least many entities having interests also have rights. If the interests of rightholders are regarded as very important, according those interests may be thought to be sufficiently important to override the *interests* of others—or, and this seems not insignificant—the *rights* of others (who have not only interests but rights). For example, Lawrence Haworth, who defends the view that some non-humans have rights, maintains that when the latter rights conflict with 'worthy human interests . . . then it is in general reasonable to give preference to these human concerns and violate . . . the rights of nonhumans'. See Lawrence Haworth, 'Rights, Wrongs, and Animals'. *Ethics.* Vol. 88, No. 2 (January 1978), p. 100.

    So *even if* it is allowed that some animals have *rights,* the *weightings* of the respective interests in in- terspecific conflicts of interests are important and may affect our ultimate 'on balance' judgments concerning justified violations (or justified infringements) of rights. Hence, my aims in the text are not, I think, irrelevant *even if* it is shown that animals have rights (short of being unqualifiedly 'absolute').

23. Again, I simplify. Assume that neither of us owns the boat, has a special duty to sacrifice for the other, consents to die, or agrees to 'draw straws'.

24. The notion of psychological complexity needs further elaboration. I do have in mind complexity bearing on capacity to experience satisfaction and dissatisfaction. After all there might be a type of psychological complexity *not* conducive to a greater capacity to experience satisfaction. Suppose a micro-computer could be implanted in a turkey so that it became an excellent chess player but in other respects remained turkey-like, e.g., still did not worry about the prospect of Thanksgiving rituals.

25. I am, of course, by-passing all sorts of difficulties about the possibility of having a cardinal measure of utility and making 'interbeing' comparisons of utilities.

26. On this type of test, see Peter Singer, op. cit., p. 48.

27. While the death of an animal or a human results in its forgoing *all* the potential satisfactions either could have, still the quantity of such satisfactions would typically be different for each. Hence it is reasonable to conclude that the disvalue of the death of a normal animal is less than the disvalue of the death of a normal human (at similar stages in typical life spans) even though the death of each involves a total loss of their respective potential satisfactions. The difference in disvalues is partly a function of whatever differences there are in respective psychological capacities.

28. Compare the absence of capacities in aged humans due to their waning, their absence in defective humans, and their absence in young normal animals. Absence of capacities may be a result of natural decline, injury, disease, or one's genetic lot.

29. Who would not feel some sense of betrayal when an aged dog eagerly gets in the car for a ride but does not know that it is being taken to be put to death (commonly: 'to sleep')? Further, it will not surprise me if communications with non-human primates, in Ameslan, provide evidence of a capacity for understanding promises or, indeed, a sense of regret or remorse.

30. It does not seem to me that one should shrink from the view that *some* weighting of human interests and, hence, *some* differential treatment of humans is justi-

fied. There is great danger that I shall be misunderstood here—as approving in some degree the sorts of unequal consideration intrinsic to repulsive doctrines commonly labeled racist, sexist, or Nazi-like. Respect for persons requires respecting their interests but not, I think, giving equal weight to them.

31. With regard to various facets of this essay I have benefited from discussions with my colleagues, W. R. Carter, Robert Hoffman, Harold Levin, Tom Regan, and Alan Sparer—as well as the writings of both Tom Regan and Peter Singer. Any or all are, of course, entitled to complain that I did not benefit enough.

The Miniride and Worse-Off Principles

Tom Regan

One way to decide whether and when it is permissible to harm those who are innocent is as follows: What we must do is act so as to minimize the total aggregate of harm of the innocent (*the minimize harm principle*). Thus, whenever we find ourselves in a situation where all of the options at hand will produce some harm to those who are innocent, we must choose that option that will result in the least total sum of harm.

The minimize harm principle runs afoul of our considered beliefs. Imagine this prevention case. We may harm A quite radically, *or* we may harm a thousand others in a modest way, *or* we may do nothing, in which case both A and the thousand will be harmed as described. Suppose we could place numerical values on the harms in question. A's harm equals, say, -125; the aggregate of the thousand, each of whom will be harmed at a value of -1, is $-1,000$; and the aggregate of both, then, is $-1,125$. All are innocent. Which alternative ought we to choose? If we are to decide these matters on the basis recommended by the minimize harm principle, what we ought to do is harm A. And that seems grossly unfair. The quality of his life, after all, would be in a shambles, if we chose that option, whereas the welfare of the others, considered as individuals, would only be modestly diminished. What we ought to do is spare A gross harm and spread the harm around by choosing the second option.

Now, if that is what we ought to do, we must resist the minimize harm principle. But because appeals to our considered beliefs are controversial, one would like to be able to invalidate this principle without making such appeals. Taurek's* argument against the possibility of aggregating harms can be understood (it is not clear that he intended it in this way) as an attempt to unseat that principle without appealing to our intuitions. If harms *cannot* be aggregated, then we have solid reasons to reject the minimize harm principle.

But it is possible to reject this principle without accepting Taurek's arguments for doing so and without merely appealing to our considered beliefs. The grounds for rejecting it are to be found by working out the implications of the respect principle and the postulate of inherent value on which it rests. The minimize harm principle is a consequentialist principle, one that instructs us to act so as to avoid the worst consequences, where "the worst consequences" are understood as the greatest sum of harm done to all the innocents affected by the outcome. To accept the minimize harm principle thus is to assume that moral agents or patients *are mere receptacles after all*, not of, say, pleasures and pains, but of harms and benefits, so that the harm done to any one individual can be more than compensated for by the greater sum of harm that is thereby spared others. The rights view refuses to regard moral agents and patients in this

*The reference is to an essay by John Taurek, "Should the Numbers Count?" in *Philosophy and Public Affairs* (Volume 6, Number 4), pp. 293–216. Taurek's essay explores the question of whether the number of lives to be saved is a morally decisive factor in cases in which not all lives can be saved and the number which can be saved depends on which alternative one takes; he argues that one need not always save the largest number.

The Case for Animal Rights, by Tom Regan (Berkeley: University of California Press, 1983), pp. 301–312. Reprinted by permission. © 1983 The Regents of the University of California.

way. Individuals who have inherent values are *not to be viewed as mere receptacles of anything* and so may never be treated in ways that assume that they are. To treat them so is to fail to treat them with that respect to which, as possessors of inherent value, they are entitled as a matter of strict justice, treatment to which they have a basic moral right. The fundamental error of the minimize harm principle, then, is not that it assumes that the separate harms of different individuals can be aggregated (they can, Taurek's objections to the contrary notwithstanding) *or* that it has implications that clash with our considered beliefs (though it does). Its fundamental error lies in assuming that moral agents and patients are mere receptacles of value, having no distinctive value in their own right. *That is why* this principle has implications that fail to match our considered beliefs.

To reject the minimize harm principle is not enough. If the rights view is to have any claim on our rational assent, it must be able to provide guidance in precisely those sorts of cases where one might be tempted to rely on the minimize harm principle—prevention cases, that is, where, for example, we are required to choose between harming the few or harming the many who are innocent. The rights view recognizes two principles that apply to such cases, both of which are derivable from the respect principle. To prepare the grounds for this derivation requires recalling some of the results of the earlier analysis of harm. . . .

Comparable Harm

In that earlier analysis a distinction was drawn between those harms that are inflictions and those that are deprivations. Harms that are deprivations deny an individual opportunities for doing what will bring satisfaction, when it is in that individual's interest to do this. Harms that are inflictions diminish the quality of an individual's life, not just if or as they deprive that individual of opportunities for satisfaction, though they usually will do this, but because they detract directly from the individual's overall welfare. Debilitating suffering is the paradigm of a harm that is an infliction; harms that are deprivations include limitations on one's autonomy. Whatever the category, not all harms are equal. An untimely death, for example, is a prima facie greater harm than a temporary loss of free-

dom, and it is a prima facie greater harm because it marks a prima facie greater loss. But harms can be unequal not only when the same individual is harmed in different ways; they may also be unequal when different individuals are harmed in the same way. The untimely death of a woman in the prime of her life is prima facie a greater harm than the death of her senile mother. Though both lose their life, the magnitude of the loss, and thus the harm, suffered by the younger woman is prima facie greater.

It is a virtue of the earlier discussion of harm that it allows us to make distinctions between the magnitude or severity of harms. A related virtue is that it enables us to give content to the notion of comparable harm. Two harms are comparable when they detract equally from an individual's welfare, or from the welfare of two or more individuals. For example, separate episodes of suffering of a certain kind and intensity are comparable harms if they cause an equal diminution in the welfare of the same individual at different times, or in two different individuals at the same or different times. And death is a comparable harm if the loss of opportunities it marks are equal in any two cases. Because of individual variability, however, some things that harm some may not harm others or may not harm them equally. In the case of physical pain, for example, some people can endure more than others, and some people who suffer can in time come to see this as "a blessing in disguise," while others have their lives shattered as a result. We cannot, therefore, automatically assume that prima facie harms of the same kind will necessarily constitute comparable harm in any two cases. What we *may* assume is that there is a strong presumption that they will. Other things being equal, that is, it is reasonable to assume that like harms have like effects—that is, detract equally from individual welfare and so are to be counted as comparable. Moreover, there is a limit to how much harm suffered by someone may be morally attributable to others. If you have grown accustomed to walking through a neighboring field on your way to work, and if I purchase the field and fence it, thereby requiring you to walk around it, which in turn requires that you rise earlier and take longer to go to work, then you are no doubt inconvenienced by what I do and, let us agree, prima facie harmed by it. But *how much you make* of this modest inconvenience is your affair, not mine. If you are driven to distraction by the extra time, lose sleep over it, divorce your wife, and burn down my house, ruining your career and spending time in prison in the bargain, then it is preposterous to hold *me* morally responsible for the heavy dose of harm that has fallen your way. My decision to erect the fence is *causally* linked to your downfall, and I must take moral responsibility for making the decision I've made; but it does not follow that I should be held accountable for your making a greater harm out of a lesser one. When, therefore, the rights view speaks of harming individuals in prima facie comparable ways and of the agent's having to take responsibility for doing this, it does not imply that the agent must also take responsibility for another's making that harm, as a result of his own volition, into something greater than it is.

The Miniride Principle

By making use of the notion of comparable harm, the rights view can formulate two principles that can be appealed to in order to make decisions in prevention cases. The first principle (*the minimize overriding principle,* or *the miniride principle*) states the following:

> Special considerations aside, when we must choose between overriding the rights of many who are innocent or the rights of few who are innocent, and when each affected individual will be harmed in a prima facie comparable way,[1] then we ought to choose to override the rights of the few in preference to overriding the rights of the many.

This principle is derivable from the respect principle. This latter principle entails that all moral agents and patients are directly owed the prima facie duty not to be harmed . . . and that all those who are owed this duty have an equally valid claim, and thus an equal prima facie moral right, against being harmed. . . . Now, *precisely because* this right is equal, no one individual's right can count for any more than any other's, when the harm that might befall either is prima facie comparable. Thus, A's right cannot count for more than B's, or C's, or D's. However, when we are faced with choosing between options, one of which will harm A, the other of which will harm B, C, and D, and the third of which will harm them all, and when the foresee-

able harm involved for each individual is prima facie comparable, then numbers count. *Precisely because* each is to count for one, no one for more than one, we cannot count choosing to override the rights of B, C, and D as neither better nor worse than choosing to override A's right alone. Three are more than one, and when the four individuals have an equal prima facie right not to be harmed, when the harm they face is prima facie comparable, and when there are no special considerations at hand, then showing equal respect for the equal rights of the individuals involved requires that we override the right of A (the few) rather than the rights of the many (B, C, D). To choose to override the rights of the many in this case would be to override an equal right three times (i.e., in the case of three different individuals) when we could choose to override such a right only once, and *that* cannot be consistent with showing equal respect for the equal rights of all the individuals involved.

To favor overriding the rights of the few in no way contravenes the requirement that each is to count for one, no one for more than one; on the contrary, special considerations apart, to choose to override the rights of the many rather than those of the few would be to count A's right for more than one—that is, as being equal to overriding the rights of three relevantly similar individuals. Accordingly, because we must not allow any one individual a greater voice in the determination of what ought to be done than any other relevantly similar individual, what we ought to do in prevention cases of the sort under consideration is choose to override the rights of the fewest innocents rather than override the rights of the many. And since this is precisely what the miniride principle enjoins, that principle is derivable from the respect principle.

Two objections to this derivation can be anticipated. Since A's right is equal to B's, and to C's, and to D's, it might be claimed, then A's right must be equal to the rights of A, B, and C taken together. Therefore, this objection contends, to favor doing what will harm A in preference to what will harm B, C, and D is not to let each count for one, no one more for one. The reply to this objection is in some ways reminiscent of earlier criticisms lodged against Taurek. The essential point is a simple one. There is no aggregate individual—no composite of B, C, and D—who has a right not to be harmed, and this for the quite simple reason that there is no aggregate individual in the first place. There are only the separate, distinct individuals—B, C, D—and each of these individuals has a right equal to the right of A. What we are faced with, then, is having to choose not between overriding A's right *or* overriding the equal right of this composite individual, but between overriding A's right or overriding the equal rights of three other, separate, distinct individuals. To treat the three as one—as if they constituted a single, conglomerate individual, with the same (equal) right as A—not only is not required in order to give significance to the idea that each individual has an individual right not to be harmed but is also contrary to the requirement to treat each of the affected individuals equally.

The second objection takes a different tack. It claims that the miniride principle is at odds with the respect principle because it allows us to treat the few who are innocent merely as receptacles, something the respect principle will not tolerate. Since by choosing to override A's right we thereby prevent a much greater aggregate of harm befalling B, C, and D, it is claimed, to allow A's right to be overriden is to imply that A's losses are not as bad as this aggregate, which is why A's right may be overriden. And this, so this objection urges, is to treat A as a mere receptacle in just the same way and for just the same reasons as A is treated as a mere receptacle according to the minimize harm principle—a principle which, it was argued in the above, must be rejected if one accepts the respect principle. Thus, if one accepts the respect principle, one must reject the miniride principle.

This objection confuses considerations about the foreseeable consequences of acting in compliance with the miniride principle with the rights view's grounds for accepting this principle. It is true that the aggregate of harm that will result when the rights of the few who are innocent are overridden in preference to those of the many is foreseeably less bad (i.e., constitutes a less aggregate sum of harm) than that that would result if the rights of the many were overridden in preference to those of the few. But the reason for choosing the former option, according to the rights view, is not that the aggregated consequences of making this choice would be better (i.e., less bad); that *would* be to view the individuals involved as mere receptacles. The reason the rights view gives for choosing to override the rights of the few is that this is what we must do if we are to show equal respect for the equal inherent value, *and* the equal prima facie rights, of the individuals involved. It is, in a word, not the aggregate consequences for all affected by the outcome that matter; it is respect for the equality of the involved individuals that does.

The miniride principle illuminates why, on the rights view, we ought to act to save the fifty miners rather than the one. Earlier discussions of that example tacitly assumed that the harm each of the miners would suffer, if he died, is comparable to the harm that any other miner would suffer. That is a reasonable assumption to make, given that their losses are prima facie comparable. This much granted, and assuming that no special considerations are at hand, the miniride principle requires doing what must be done to save the many even if this means overriding the rights of the few. And it requires this not because the aggregate of the harms that would result from this choice would be less bad than if we chose to act otherwise; it requires this because this is the choice we must make if we are to show equal respect for the inherent value of the individuals involved and if we are to count their equal rights equally.

The Worse-off Principle

The fundamental difference between the rights view and the minimize harm principle comes into sharper focus when we turn to consider prevention cases where harms are not comparable. Recall the earlier prevention case where we are called upon to choose between harming A quite radically (−125), or harming a thousand individuals modestly (−1 each), or doing nothing. If the only consideration relevant to deciding such cases is to minimize the number of rights that are overriden, then what we ought to do is harm A, since one individual is fewer than a thousand and a thousand-and-one. But the miniride principle does not enjoin us *simply* to minimize the number of rights that are overridden; it enjoins us to do this on the assumption that, special considerations aside, the harms faced by all the innocents *are prima facie comparable*. In the example just given, however, the harms are not prima facie comparable. The harm A faces greatly exceeds the harm faced by any one of the thousand, and the aggregate of the harm that would befall the thousand harms no one individual and thus cannot be construed as constituting harm that is comparable to (or more than comparable to) the harm that would befall A. The minimize harm principle would require choosing the option that harms A. The miniride principle, since it applies *only* in prevention cases where harms are prima facie comparable, cannot be relied on in cases, such as this one, where the harm all the innocents face is not prima facie comparable. The rights view thus requires a second principle, distinct from but consistent with the miniride principle, and one that is distinct from and not reducible to the minimize harm principle. The following principle (*the worse-off principle*) meets these requirements. (The following formulation is given in terms of "the rights of the many" and "the rights of the few." However, unequal numbers [the few, the many] are not essential to the worse-off principle; it applies in cases where we must choose between harming one innocent *or* harming another. . . It also applies when we act to prevent ourselves from being made worse-off. . . .)

> Special considerations aside, when we must decide to override the rights of the many or the rights of the few who are innocent, and when the harm faced by the few would make them worse-off than any of the many would be if any other option were chosen, then we ought to override the rights of the many.

Unlike the miniride principle, the worse-off principle applies to the type of prevention case illustrated by the example at hand, and unlike the minimize harm principle the worse-off principle would not sanction overriding A's right because doing so brought about a lesser aggregate of harm. The worse-off principle sanctions overriding the rights of the thousand even though each is innocent and even though, by overriding their individual rights, we override the right of a thousand innocent individuals not to be harmed in preference to overriding the right of one individual. In this kind of case, in short, numbers don't count.

The worse-off principle, like the miniride principle, is derivable from the respect principle. Notice, first, that the respect principle cannot allow harming A on the grounds that the thousand will be spared *a greater aggregate amount* of harm. To suppose that the harm done to A can be justified in this way is to treat A as a mere receptacle—is to assume, that is, that A's losses can be outweighed by the sum of the losses of the others. The respect principle will not allow this. If we are to treat A with the respect A is due as a matter of strict jus-

tice, we cannot simply sum A's losses and then compare them with the aggregate total of the losses of the thousand except at the price of ignoring the distinctive kind of value (inherent value) A has. The approach to decision making affirmed by the minimize harm principle is denied by the respect principle. Appeal to the respect principle will not justify choosing an option that makes the few individuals involved worse-off than any other involved individual would be, if any other option were chosen.

Appeal to the respect principle justifies overriding the rights of the many in prevention cases of the type at hand. This is shown by considering a simple case first. To say that two individuals, M and N, have an equal right not to be harmed, based on the equal respect each is owed, does not imply that each and every harm either may suffer is equally harmful. Other things being equal, M's death is a greater harm than N's migraine. If we are to show equal respect for the value and rights of individuals, therefore, we cannot count a lesser harm to N as equal to or greater than a greater harm to M. To show equal respect for the equal rights of the two, one must count their equal harms equally, not their unequal harms equally, a requirement that entails, other things being equal in prevention cases, that M's right override N's when the harm done to M would be greater if one choice were made than the harm done to N would be if another option were chosen. To assess the matter otherwise—to flip a coin or to override M's right—would be to give to N *more* than N is due. *Precisely because* M and N are *equal* in inherent value, *because* the two have an *equal* prima facie right not to be harmed, and *because* the harm M faces is *greater* than the harm N faces, equal respect for the two requires that we not choose to override M's right but choose to override N's instead.

Now, adding numbers makes no difference in such a case. If, as in our earlier example, A would be made worse-off than any one of the thousand individuals if we chose to harm A and spare the others, then aggregating the harms of the thousand can make no difference. No one *else* is harmed by summing the harms of the thousand; there is, that is, no aggregate individual whose harm can be placed at −1,000 and who can be viewed as having a right not to be harmed that justifiably overrides A's. There are just the thousand, each one of whom will be harmed less than A will and no one of whom will be made worse-off than A would be, if we chose to harm A. For *each* of the thousand, then, A's right overrides his, just as, in the previous paragraph, M's right justifiably overrides N's. *It is the magnitude of the harm done to A and each individual member of the thousand, not the sum of A's harm compared with the sum of the thousands', that determines whose right overrides whose.* Since, *ex hypothesi*, the harm done to A would be greater than that done to, and would make A worse-off than, any other involved individual, respect for the equal rights and value of all those involved requires overriding the rights of the many rather than the right of the individual. In the absence of special considerations, and assuming the few who are innocent would be made worse-off than any of the many who are innocent if we chose to override the rights of the few, the respect principle requires that we override the rights of the many. And since this is what the worse-off principle requires, that principle is derivable from the respect principle.

An objection to this derivation and to the earlier derivation of the miniride principle argues that the rights view is inconsistent. On the one hand, the rights view denies the moral relevance of consequences, as witness its steady attack on utilitarianism and its rejection of the minimize harm principle; and yet, on the other hand, it relies on the notion of comparable harm and invokes considerations about who will be harmed most, as witness its miniride and worse-off principles. And this, so this objection goes, is inconsistent.

This objection is a product of confusion. What the rights view denies is that moral right and wrong can be determined *merely* by determining which alternative act or, as in the case of rule utilitarianism, the adoption of which rules, will bring about "the best" aggregate consequences for all those affected by the outcome, even when "the best" consequences are "the least bad," as, according to the minimize harm principle, they are. The rights view rejects any and all consequentialist theories because any and all assume that consequences and consequences alone determine moral right, wrong, and duty. . . . But the rights view does not hold that considerations about consequences are *morally irrelevant;* in particular, it does not claim that we can dispense with such considerations in determining *how much* those directly involved will be harmed. However, to insist on the relevance of such considerations is not the same as, and does

not entail, the belief that *aggregating* consequences for all those affected by the outcome determines moral right, wrong, and duty. Consequences are relevant because we cannot fix the magnitude of harm for those directly involved without attention to them. Even so, the moral relevance of these consequences is parasitic on moral principles whose validity is *not* argued for on the grounds that their adoption will bring about better consequences for all those affected by the outcome (utilitarianism), or for those individuals who enter into certain agreements (rational egoism). The validity of the respect principle and those principles derivable from it—the harm principle . . . and the miniride and the worse-off principles . . . —rests on the postulate of inherent value, *not* on the principle of utility, *or* on the agreements reached by rational egoists, *or* on any other consequentialist ethical principle. Indeed, to insist, as the rights view does, that considerations about *how much each* of those directly involved will be harmed are *relevant* considerations in prevention cases is precisely what one would expect and should require of a view that advocates *the equal rights of the individuals* involved. How else are we to show equal respect toward each of these individuals except by considering how well their *individual* prima facie right not to be harmed stacks up against the equal prima facie right of the other individuals involved? And how are we to determine this without considering which of those individuals directly involved will be harmed, how much each will be harmed, and so forth? To insist on the relevance of these considerations is simply to insist on the necessity of treating all those directly involved with the equal respect they are due. What we must not do—what would be contrary to the letter and the spirit of the rights view—is to sanction overriding an individual's right *merely* on the grounds that this brings about a better aggregate balance of good over evil for all those affected by the outcome. That would be to authorize treating those who have inherent value merely as a means to this collective goal, and that is prohibited, given the rights view, since it is to treat right-bearers as if they were mere receptacles. Mistaken the rights view may be—only future challenges can decide this—but certainly it is not mistaken because it is inconsistent, at least not for the reasons alleged.

The rights view is antagonistic to utilitarianism, even to those utilitarians, such as Mill, who are not acrimonious to appeals to moral rights; it is, in some respects, sympathetic to Taurek's position, especially in denying, in concert with him, the validity of the minimize harm principle. But one can deny the validity of that principle without denying that harms can be aggregated and without denying that "the numbers" ever count. The miniride and worse-off principles provide an alternative basis to Taurek's position of denying the minimize harm principle and the general utilitarian inclination with which that principle is naturally allied,[2] an alternative that is decidedly nonutilitarian and can only mistakenly be regarded as consequentialist. Moreover, these principles, for the reasons given above, are not independent or disconnected principles—not "self-evident moral axioms," not "self-evident moral laws," not "self-evident moral absolutes." They are principles that can be derived from a still more fundamental principle (the respect principle), a principle that itself can be defended by means of argument rather than by appeals to what is claimed to be "self-evident." None of these principles, including miniride and worse-off, are ad hoc devices tailor-made to fit some favored set of considered beliefs. To dispute the rights view just on these grounds would be as unfair as it would be unfounded.

Notes

1. In saying that the harms are prima facie comparable it is assumed that no one individual would be made worse-off than any other. Cases where someone, or some number, would be made worse-off are discussed below.

2. I must confess that I have not always been clear about this myself, since on more than one occasion I have stated or implied that individual rights can be justifiably overriden by appeal to the minimize harm principle. On this, see, for example, my "Animal Rights, Human Wrongs," *Environmental Ethics* (Summer 1980); reprinted in Regan, *All That Dwell Therein* (see chap. 3, n. 6) and in *Ethics and Animals,* ed. Harlan Miller and William Williams (Clifton, N.J.: Humana Press, 1982).

Priority Principles

Paul W. Taylor

... We must ... try to find priority principles for resolving conflicts between humans and nonhumans which do not assign greater inherent worth to humans, but consider all parties as having the same worth. The principles, in other words, must be consistent with the fundamental requirement of *species-impartiality*. For only then can there be genuine fairness in the resolution of such conflicts.

Five Priority Principles for the Fair Resolution of Conflicting Claims

I now consider in depth five such principles, to be designated as follows:

a. The principle of self-defense.

b. The principle of proportionality.

c. The principle of minimum wrong.

d. The principle of distributive justice.

e. The principle of restitutive justice.

Although I believe these five principles cover all the major ways of adjudicating fairly among competing claims arising from clashes between the duties of human ethics and those of environmental ethics, I must emphasize at the outset that they do not yield a neat solution to every possible conflict situation. Each principle represents one cluster of morally relevant considerations one must take into account, and these considerations can serve as rough guides in reaching decisions about what duties outweigh others. But the principles do not function as premises in a deductive argument. We cannot deduce from them, along with the facts of the case, a true conclusion expressible in a normative statement about what ought to be done, all things considered. We should strive to make our decisions on the basis of relevant considerations, and the relevance of a consideration is determined by the application of the principles. To the extent we are successful in this case we can have some confidence in the fairness of our judgment. Nevertheless, there will always be a degree of uncertainty, and our minds should accordingly be open to the possibility that we have made a mistake. We must remain ready to revise our judgment, not only in the light of new factual information but also on the basis of further critical reflection concerning the precise meaning of a principle and the conditions of its proper application.

Using these five principles as normative guides in our decision making will not enable us to avoid the "hard cases." (The same holds true for conflicts of duties *within* human ethics or environmental ethics.) These are the cases where the competing claims are so complex and so powerful on both sides that no solution by reference to the principles alone can be reached. These inevitable gaps in our decision-making procedure, however, need not mean that we must then become arbitrary in our choice of what to do. We must take another step in seeking a fair resolution of the conflict. This step involves appealing to *the ethical ideal* that underlies and inspires (defines the "spirit" of) the whole structure of priority relations contained in the five principles and their conditions of applicability. I shall analyze and explain what this ethical ideal is after discussing the five principles. It provides a comprehensive vision of the place of human values in the larger world of the natural order of living things. We might designate it "an ideal harmony between nature and human civilization." It is this vision of a "best possible world" that expresses the spirit behind the letter of the five principles, that unifies them and interrelates them in a coherent manner, and that gives them their overall point and purpose. It is in the light of this ethical ideal that all the hard cases must finally be resolved. Thus a fair resolution to a problem of competing claims, even when not wholly determined by one of the principles, is a decision that fits coherently into the overall vision of human civilization and nature that underlies and unifies the five principles.

Putting aside consideration of this ethical ideal until later, I shall now consider the five priority principles in the order given in the foregoing list.

The Principle of Self-Defense

The principle of self-defense states that it is permissible for moral agents to protect themselves against dangerous or harmful organisms by destroying them. This holds, however, only when moral agents, using reasonable care, cannot avoid being exposed to such organisms and cannot prevent them from doing serious damage to the environmental conditions that make it possible for moral agents to exist and function as moral agents. Furthermore, the principle does not allow the use of just any means of self-protection, but only those means that will do the least possible harm to the organisms consistent with the purpose of preserving the existence and functioning of moral agents. There must be no available alternative that is known to be equally effective but to cause less harm to the "attacking" organisms.

The principle of self-defense permits actions that are absolutely required for maintaining the very existence of moral agents and for enabling them to exercise the capacities of moral agency. It does not permit actions that involve the destruction of organisms when those actions simply promote the interests or values which moral agents may have as persons. Self-defense is defense against *harmful* and *dangerous* organisms, and a harmful or dangerous organism in this context is understood to be one whose activities threaten the life or basic health of those entities which need normally functioning bodies to exist as moral agents.

There is a close parallel here with the principle of self-defense as it is found in the domain of human ethics. If we have a moral right to life it follows that we also have a moral right to protect ourselves, by forceful means if necessary, when our lives are threatened by others. But this does not mean we are permitted to use force against others merely to further our own ends and values. It should be noted that even when the attacker is an innocent human being, as would be the case where an insane man is going berserk and will harm us unless we use force to stop him, our right of self-defense makes it permissible to protect ourselves against him to the point of killing him if there is no other way to avoid being killed ourselves. Thus the parallel with self-defense in environmental ethics against nonhuman animals and plants holds. The fact that the "attackers" are morally innocent does not invalidate the principle.

The full meaning of this priority principle and the grounds on which it rests can be brought out by considering the following three points.

(i) The principle of self-defense does not justify harming creatures that do not harm us unless doing so is a practical necessity arising from a situation where we cannot separate harmless organisms from the harmful ones against which we are defending ourselves. In this respect we shall see that the principle of self-defense differs from the second, third, and fourth principles to be considered. In certain situations to which these other principles apply, harm may have to be done to at least some harmless creatures even when this is not a matter of protecting ourselves from harm.

(ii) Despite what might at first appear to be a bias in favor of humans over other species, the principle of self-defense is actually consistent with the requirement of species-impartiality. It does not allow moral agents to further the interests of any organism because it belongs to one species rather than another. In particular, humans are not given an advantage simply on the basis of their humanity.

There are two considerations that support this claim to species neutrality. In the first place the principle of self-defense is formulated in such a way as to be species-blind. The statement of the principle refers only to moral agents and organisms (of whatever species) that are not moral agents. No mention is made of humans and nonhumans. Of course, in discussing various aspects and implications of the principle, one ordinarily refers to humans defending themselves against nonhumans as typical of situations in which the principle applies to the practical circumstances of life. Strictly speaking, however, no reference to any species need be made. The fact that (most) humans are moral agents and (most) nonhumans are not is a contingent truth which the principle does not take to be morally relevant. Moral agents are permitted to defend themselves against harmful or dangerous organisms that are not moral agents. This is all the principle of self-defense allows. If there happen to be nonhuman moral agents whose existence as moral agents is endangered by the actions of humans who are not moral agents (such as the insane and the severely retarded), then the principle states that it is permissible for the nonhumans in question to kill those humans who endanger them, if this is required for the preservation of the nonhumans'

status as moral agents and there is no alternative way to protect themselves.

The second consideration that supports the species-impartiality of the principle is that the principle is fully consistent with the idea that all living things, human and nonhuman alike, have the same inherent worth. It is helpful here to refer once again to the principle of self-defense in the domain of human ethics. Our right to use force against another human being who assaults us does not imply that we have greater inherent worth than the attacker. It only means that we can rightfully use a "least evil" means to preserve our own existence. Indeed, out of respect for the personhood of the other we are duty-bound to do him or her no greater harm than is absolutely needed for our defense.

Equality of worth between aggressor and defender in human ethics is shown in our willingness to make the principle of self-defense universal. From a moral point of view we would judge it right for another to defend herself or himself against ourselves if *we* were the aggressor. This idea of reversibility (if it is right for A to do X to B it is right for B to do X to A) entails the equal worth of agent and subject. For any person may be in the role of subject and any may be in the role of agent, without change in the justifiability of acts of self-defense.

In the case of self-defense against animals and plants, however, the universalizability and reversibility tests are inapplicable, since animals and plants cannot take the role of moral agents, though they can be in the position of moral subjects. What they do to us is neither right nor wrong, because their activities are not within the range of moral standards or rules. Still, the permissibility of our defense against them does not imply they are inferior in worth to us, as we can see from the following considerations. When we have a firm sense of our own worth we place intrinsic value on our existence as persons. Out of self-respect we judge our personhood to be something worthy of being preserved. At the same time we believe that we are not inferior in worth to animals or plants. Now if we were to refrain from defending ourselves against them and so allow them to kill us, we would be sacrificing our very existence to them. To *require* such a sacrifice as a moral duty could only be justified on the ground that they have greater inherent worth than we do. Assuming that we have no good reasons for accepting that ground, we may conclude that there is no validly binding duty on our part to sacrifice ourselves to them. It is therefore morally permissible for us to defend ourselves against them, even though they are equal to us in inherent worth.

(iii) The third point has to do with the unavoidability of actions taken under the principle. With regard to the parallel case in the domain of human ethics, we are permitted to use force against another in defense of our life only when we cannot avoid the other's attack or escape from the situation. If someone threatens us and we can safely get out of the way, we should do so. For the analogous case of resolving competing claims by reference to the principle of self-defense, we should make every reasonable effort to avoid situations where nonhuman organisms will be likely to harm us, and we should keep ourselves strong and healthy so that there is less need to destroy other creatures whose activities would endanger us in a weak condition. Finally, before the harming of nonhuman organisms can be permitted on grounds of self-defense, it must be the case that reasonable precautions have been taken by moral agents to guard against known circumstances where disease, poisoning, or other biologically caused dangers are apt to be present.

The reason for these restrictions and qualifications is that all living things, whether harmful or harmless to humans, possess inherent worth and so are the appropriate objects of the attitude of respect. To kill or otherwise harm such creatures is always something morally bad in itself and can only be justified if we have no feasible alternative. At the same time we must have a valid moral reason for doing so, and a moral reason sufficiently weighty to override the prima facie reason against doing so. Self-defense, when understood as an act absolutely required to preserve the very existence of a moral agent, can be such an overriding reason. It is only under these conditions that the principle of self-defense applies.[1]

The Principle of Proportionality

Before considering in detail each of the four remaining priority principles, it is well to look at the way they are interrelated. First, all four principles apply to situations where the nonhuman organisms involved are *harmless*. If left alone their activities would not endanger or threaten human life and health. Thus all four principles apply to cases

of conflict between humans and nonhumans that are not covered by the principle of self-defense.

Next we must make a distinction between basic and nonbasic interests.[2] Using this distinction, the arrangement of the four principles can be set out as follows. The principles of proportionality and minimum wrong apply to cases in which there is a conflict between the *basic* interests of animals or plants and the *nonbasic* interests of humans. The principle of distributive justice, on the other hand, covers conflicts where the interests of all parties involved are *basic*. Finally, the principle of restitutive justice applies only where, in the past, either the principle of minimum wrong or that of distributive justice has been used. Each of those principles creates situations where some form of compensation or reparation must be made to nonhuman organisms, and thus the idea of restitution becomes applicable.

What differentiates basic from nonbasic interests? To answer this it is necessary first to define what is meant by the term "interests" and then specify criteria for determining whether interests are basic or nonbasic. In our present context it will be convenient if we speak of those events and conditions in the lives of organisms that are conducive to the realization of their good as furthering, promoting, or advancing their interests. Events and conditions detrimental to the realization of their good will be described as being adverse to, opposed to, or unfavorable to their interests. I shall also use the term "interests" to refer to whatever objects or events serve to preserve or protect to some degree or other the good of a living thing. Whether or not an organism likes or dislikes anything, feels pleasure or pain, has any conscious desires, aims, or goals, cares about or is concerned with what happens to it, and whether or not it is even conscious at all, I shall here speak of its interests in this way.

In considering how interests can be classified as basic and nonbasic, we must take into account the fact that the interests of an organism can be of different degrees of comparative importance to it. One of its interests is of greater importance to it than another, either if the occurrence of the first makes a more substantial contribution to the realization of its good than the second, or if the occurrence of the first is a necessary condition for the preservation of its existence while the occurrence of the second is not. We might say that one interest is of greater importance than another to the extent that the nonfulfillment of the first will constitute a more serious deprivation or loss than the nonfulfillment of the second. The most important interests are those whose fulfillment is needed by an organism if it is to remain alive.

It is possible for us to make judgments of the comparative importance of interests of nonhuman animals and plants because, once we become factually enlightened about what protects or promotes their good, we can *take their standpoint* and judge what is, from their point of view, an important or unimportant event in their lives as far as their overall well-being is concerned. Thus we are able to make a reasonable estimate of how seriously they would be harmed or deprived of something good if a certain condition were absent from their lives.

What counts as a serious harm or deprivation will, of course, depend on the kind of organism concerned. If each organism has a good of its own, so that it makes sense to speak of its faring well or poorly to the extent that it is able or unable to live a life fitted for its species-specific nature, then we may consider a serious harm or deprivation as being whatever severely impairs its ability to live such a life or makes it totally unable to do so.

In the case of humans a serious harm or deprivation will be whatever takes away or greatly reduces their powers of rationality and autonomy, including conditions of mental or physical incapacity that make it impossible for them to live a meaningful life. Since properly functioning organs and the soundness and health of other components of one's body are essential to human well-being, whatever injures these parts of one's body is a harm. The seriousness of the harm depends on the extent and permanence of damage done to those parts and on their contribution to the ability of the organism as a whole to function in a healthy way. With regard to the psychological aspects of a human being, a serious harm will include anything that causes insanity, severe emotional disorder, or mental retardation of a kind that prevents the development or exercise of the basic powers of rationality and autonomy.

I might note that with reference to humans, basic interests are what rational and factually enlightened people would value as an essential part of their very existence as *persons*. They are what people need if they are going to be able to pursue those goals and purposes that make life meaningful and worthwhile. Thus for human persons their basic interests are those interests which, when morally legitimate, they have a *right* to have fulfilled. . . . We do not have a right to whatever will make us happy or contribute to the realization of our value system; we do have a right to the necessary conditions for the maintenance and development of our personhood. These conditions include subsistence and security ("the right to life"), autonomy, and liberty. A violation of people's moral rights is the worst thing that can happen to them, since it deprives them of what is essential to their being able to live a meaningful and worthwhile life. And since the fundamental, necessary conditions for such a life are the same for everyone, our human rights have to do with universal values or primary goods. They are the entitlement we all have as persons to what makes us persons and preserves our existence as persons.

In contrast with these universal values or primary goods that constitute our basic interests, our non-basic interests are the particular ends we consider worth seeking and the means we consider best for achieving them that make up our individual value systems. The nonbasic interests of humans thus vary from person to person, while their basic interests are common to all.

This discussion of basic and non-basic interests has been presented to introduce the second and third priority principles on our list, proportionality and minimum wrong. Both principles employ the distinction between basic and nonbasic interests, so it was necessary to clarify this distinction before examining them.

The principles apply to two different kinds of conflicts among competing claims. In both cases we are dealing with situations in which the *basic* interests of animals and plants conflict with the *nonbasic* interests of humans. But each principle applies to a different type of nonbasic human interests. In order to differentiate between these types, we must consider various ways in which the nonbasic interests of humans are related to the attitude of respect for nature.

First, there are nonbasic human interests which are *intrinsically incompatible with* the attitude of respect for nature. The pursuit of these interests would be given up by anyone who had respect for nature since the kind of actions and intentions involved in satisfying them directly embody or express an exploitative attitude toward nature. Such an attitude is incompatible with that of respect because it means that one considers wild creatures to have merely instrumental value for human ends. To satisfy nonbasic interests of this first kind is to deny the inherent worth of animals and plants in natural ecosystems. Examples of such interests and of actions performed to satisfy them are the following (all actually occur in the contemporary world):

> Slaughtering elephants so the ivory of their tusks can be used to carve items for the tourist trade.
>
> Killing rhinoceroses so that their horns can be used as dagger handles.
>
> Picking rare wildflowers, such as orchids and cactuses, for one's private collection.
>
> Capturing tropical birds, for sale as caged pets.
>
> Trapping and killing reptiles, such as snakes, crocodiles, alligators, and turtles, for their skins and shells to be used in making expensive shoes, handbags, and other "fashion" products.
>
> Hunting and killing rare wild mammals, such as leopards and jaguars, for the luxury fur trade.
>
> All hunting and fishing which is done as an enjoyable pastime (whether or not the animals killed are eaten), when such activities are not necessary to meet the basic interests of humans. This includes all sport hunting and recreational fishing.

The ends and purposes of these practices and the human interests that motivate them are inherently incompatible with the attitude of respect for nature in the following sense. If we consider the various practices along with their central purposes as representing a certain human attitude toward nature, this attitude can only be described as exploitative. Those who participate in such activities with the aim of accomplishing the various purposes that motivate and direct them, as well as those who enjoy or consume the products while knowing the methods by which they were obtained, cannot be said to have genuine respect for nature. For all such practices treat wild creatures as mere instruments to human ends, thus denying

their inherent worth. Wild animals and plants are being valued only as a source of human pleasure or as things that can be manipulated and used to bring about human pleasure.

It is important to realize that the human interests that underlie these practices are nonbasic. Even when hunters and fishermen eat what they have killed, this is incidental to the central purpose and governing aim of their sport. (I am not at this point considering the very different case of subsistence hunting and fishing, where such activities are not done as enjoyable pastimes but out of necessity.) That eating what they kill is a matter of pleasure and hence serves only a nonbasic interest is shown by the fact that they would continue to hunt or fish even if, for some reason of health or convenience, they did not eat the mammal, bird, or fish they killed. They are not hunting or fishing in order to have enough food to live.

With reference to this and to all the other examples given, it should be noted that none of the actions violate human rights. Indeed, if we stay within the boundaries of human ethics alone, people have a moral right to do such things, since they have a freedom-right to pursue without interference their legitimate interests and, within those boundaries, an interest is "legitimate" if its pursuit does not involve doing any wrong *to another human being*.

It is only when the principles of environmental ethics are applied to such actions that the exercise of freedom-rights in these cases must be weighed against the demands of the ethics of respect for nature. We then find that the practices in question are wrong, *all things considered*. For if they were judged permissible, the basic interests of animals and plants would be assigned a lower value or importance than the nonbasic interests of humans, which no one who had the attitude of respect for nature (as well as the attitude of respect for persons) would find acceptable. After all, a human being can still live a good life even if he or she does not own caged wild birds, wear apparel made from furs and reptile skins, collect rare wildflowers, engage in hunting and fishing as recreational pastimes, buy ivory carvings, or use horn dagger handles. But every one of these practices treats wild animals and plants as if their very existence is something having no value at all, other than as means to the satisfaction of human preferences.

Let us now consider another type of nonbasic human interest that can come into conflict with the basic interests of wild animals and plants. These are human interests which, in contrast with those just considered, are not *in themselves* incompatible with respect for nature. Nevertheless, the pursuit of these interests has *consequences* that are undesirable from the perspective of respect for nature and should therefore be avoided if possible. Sometimes the nonbasic human interests concerned will not be valued highly enough to outweigh the bad consequences of fulfilling them. In that case a person who has respect for nature would willingly forgo the pursuit of those interests. Other times the interests will be so highly valued that even those who genuinely respect nature will not be willing to forgo the pursuit of the interests. In the latter case, although having and pursuing the interests do not embody or express the attitude of respect for nature, neither do they embody or express a purely exploitative attitude toward nature. Wild animals and plants are not being used or consumed as mere means to human ends, though the consequences of actions in which the interests are pursued are such that wild creatures suffer harm. Examples of non-basic interests of this type are:

Building an art museum or library where natural habitat must be destroyed.

Constructing an airport, railroad, harbor, or highway involving the serious disturbance of a natural ecosystem.

Replacing a native forest with a timber plantation.

Damming a free-flowing river for a hydroelectric power project.

Landscaping a natural woodland in making a public park.

Whether people who have true respect for nature would give up the activities involved in these situations depends on the value they place on the various interests being furthered. This in turn would depend on people's total systems of value and on what alternatives were available—in particular, whether substitutes less damaging to the environment could be found and whether some or all of the interests could be satisfied in other ways.

Let us recapitulate this classification of non-basic human interests, since it is crucial to the examination of the priority principles I will consider below. First there are interests that directly express an exploitative attitude toward nature; actions taken to satisfy such interests are intrinsically incompatible with respect for nature. Second, there are interests that do not exemplify in themselves an exploitative attitude toward nature, but in many practical circumstances the means taken to satisfy those interests bring about effects on the natural world which, in the eyes of those who have respect for nature, are to be avoided whenever possible. Among this second class of interests are those which are not important enough to (not so highly valued by) a person to make the gains of their pursuit outweigh the undesirable consequences for wildlife. Others are such that their value does outweigh the undesirable consequences, even when such weight is assigned by one who has full respect for nature.

This classification bears on the two priority principles we are now about to consider: the principle of proportionality and that of minimum wrong. Each of the two kinds of non-basic human interests mentioned above determines the range of application of one of these principles. The principle of proportionality applies to situations of conflict between the basic interests of wild animals and plants and those nonbasic human interests that are intrinsically incompatible with respect for nature. The principle of minimum wrong, on the other hand, applies to conflicts between the basic interests of wild animals and plants and those non-basic human interests that are so highly valued that even a person who has respect for nature would not be willing to abstain from pursuing them, knowing that the pursuit of such interests will bring about conditions detrimental to the natural world.

. . . [Figure 1] schematically represents the relations among the five priority principles and their ranges of application.

Putting aside consideration of the principle of minimum wrong until later, I shall now discuss that of proportionality. The central idea of the principle of proportionality is that, in a conflict between human values and the good of (harmless) wild animals and plants, greater weight is to be given to basic than to nonbasic interests, no matter what species, human or other, the competing claims arise from. Within its proper range of application the principle prohibits us from allowing nonbasic in-

WILD ANIMALS AND PLANTS	Harmful to Humans	Harmless to Humans (Or: their harmfulness can reasonably be avoided)		
		Basic Interests		*Basic Interests*
...in conflict with...		...in conflict with...		...in conflict with...
		Nonbasic interests		*Basic interests*
HUMANS		Intrinsically incompatible with respect for nature	Intrinsically compatible with respect for nature, but extrinsically detrimental to wildlife and natural ecosystems	
PRIORITY PRINCIPLES	*(1) Self-defense*	*(2) Proportionality*	*(3) Minimum wrong*	*(4) Distributive justice*
			...when (3) or (4) have been applied... *(5) Restitutive justice*	

Figure 1 Relations among the five priority principles and their ranges of application

terests to override basic ones, even if the nonbasic interests are those of humans and the basic are those of animals and plants.[3]

The conditions of applicability of this principle are that the human interests concerned are non-basic ones that are intrinsically incompatible with the attitude of respect for nature, that the competing claims arise from the basic interests of wild animals and/or plants, and that these animals and plants are harmless to humans (self-defense is not in question). Examples of conflicts of the relevant sort were given earlier. It should be noted that such practices as recreational fishing and hunting and buying luxury furs made from the pelts of wild creatures are actually accepted by millions of people as morally permissible. This fact merely shows the unquestioned, total anthropocentricity of their outlook on nature and their attitude toward wild creatures. It is clear, however, that from the standpoint of the life-centered system of environmental ethics defended in this book, such practices are to be condemned as being fundamentally ex-

ploitative of beings who have as much inherent worth as those who exploit them.

The Principle of Minimum Wrong

The principle of minimum wrong applies to situations in which (i) the basic interests of animals and plants are unavoidably in competition with nonbasic interests of humans; (ii) the human interests in question are *not* intrinsically incompatible with respect for nature; (iii) actions needed to satisfy those interests, however, are detrimental to the basic interests of animals and plants; and (iv) the human interests involved are so important that rational and factually informed people who have genuine respect for nature are not willing to relinquish the pursuit of those interests even when they take into account the undesirable consequences for wildlife.

Examples of such situations were given earlier: building a library or art museum where natural habitat must be destroyed; constructing an airport, railroad, harbor, or highway involving serious disturbance of a natural ecosystem; damming a river for a hydroelectric power project; replacing a wilderness forest with a timber plantation; landscaping a natural woodland to make a public park. The problem of priority in these situations is this: How can we tell when it is morally permissible for humans to pursue their nonbasic interests when doing so adversely affects the basic interests of wild animals and plants?

It is true here as it was in the case of the principle of proportionality that human ethics *alone* permits actions (such as destroying wildlife habitat in order to build an art museum) that further nonbasic human interests at the expense of the basic interests of other living things. This is because humans have a freedom-right to pursue their legitimate interests, where an interest is legitimate when its pursuit does not involve wrongdoing *to other humans.* But as soon as the principles of environmental ethics are brought in, what people have a right to do with regard to other persons is no longer the decisive question. The well-being of other living things must be taken into consideration.

Now, fulfilling the nonbasic interests of humans in our present case is held to be so important that, even for those who have the attitude of respect for nature, such fulfillment is deemed to be worth the cost of harming wildlife. What is the basis for this special importance? The answer lies, first, in the role such interests play in the overall view of civilized life that rational and informed people tend to adopt autonomously as part of their total world outlook. Secondly, the special value given to these interests stems from the central place they occupy in people's rational conception of their own true good. The first point concerns the cultural or social aspect of the valued interests—more specifically, the importance of their contribution to human civilization seen from a broad historical perspective. The second concerns the relation of the valued interests to an individual's view of the kind of life which, given one's circumstances and capacities, is most worth living.

With regard to the first point, the interests in question are considered by the people as essential to a whole society's maintaining a high level of culture, when judged from the shared standards of its common way of life as it has developed throughout its history. The judgment of contribution to a high level of culture, I assume here, is being made by persons who are fully rational and enlightened. Not only the endeavor to create meritorious works and make worthwhile discoveries in the intellectual and aesthetic dimensions of human culture will be included among these valued interests, but also the legal, political, and economic systems needed for the community's steady advancement toward a high level of civilized life. Thus the goals and practices that form the core of a rational and informed conception of a community's highest values will be interests that carry great weight when they compete with the (basic) interests of the Earth's nonhuman inhabitants, even in the minds of people who regard those inhabitants as possessing an inherent worth equal to that of humans themselves. Using the concepts of intrinsic value and inherent value introduced earlier in this book, we might say that the system of *intrinsically valued ends* shared by a whole society as the focus of its way of life, along with those human creations and productions that are judged as *supremely inherently valuable* by rational and enlightened members of the society, determine the set of human interests that are to be weighed against the interests of animals and plants in the situations of conflict to which the principle of minimum wrong is applicable. Within the framework of a given culture's way of life when we see it from the perspective of its history, taking into account the *meaning* its history has for the people of that culture, we can make a rational and informed judgment of the kind of civilization that is, within that framework and from that perspective, most worthy of being preserved. The human values, intrinsic and inherent, whose realization is central to that conception of civilization are the values that must be compared in importance with the undesirability of destroying wildlife habitat and natural ecosystems, when that is an unavoidable consequence of realizing those values.

Similarly, when certain human interests are seen to lie at the center of a rational person's system of autonomously chosen ends, thus functioning as the unifying framework for a total conception of an individual's own true good, the value placed on such interests may be given greater weight by the person than the undesirable effects on the natural world the pursuit of those interests might have, even when the person has adopted the attitude of respect for nature.

We have so far dealt with the kinds of conflict to which the principle of minimum wrong applies. It is now time to make clear the content of the principle. The principle states that, when rational, informed, and autonomous persons *who have adopted the attitude of respect for nature* are nevertheless unwilling to forgo the two sorts of values mentioned above, even though they are aware that the consequences of pursuing those values will involve harm to wild animals and plants, it is permissible for them to pursue those values only so long as doing so involves fewer wrongs (violations of duties) than any alternative way of pursuing those values.

This principle sets certain moral constraints on the pursuit of the two types of human values we are concerned with here. In the case of social institutions and practices basic to a community's realization of a high level of civilization, the principle requires that the particular institutions and practices of a community are such that they result in the least wrong being done to the natural world. Here "least wrong" means the lowest number of violations of the rule of nonmaleficence in the ethical system of respect for nature. This lowest number of wrongdoings assumes that there are no alternative institutions and practices which could be used by the community to accomplish the same social ends but which would involve still fewer instances of wrongdoing to wild living things in natural ecosystems.

Concerning the second type of human value, the principle of minimum wrong lays down the requirement that actions taken by individuals in the pursuit of ends that lie at the core of their rational conceptions of their true good must be such that no alternative ways of achieving those ends produce fewer wrongs to wild living things. As before, the key test for moral permissibility is that certain nonbasic interests of humans may be furthered only under the condition of minimizing wrongs done to nonhumans in natural ecosystems.

Is this principle consistent with the idea that wild animals and plants have inherent worth? To answer this we must take into account the difference between a utilitarian calculation of consequences and a deontological or nonconsequential view of minimizing wrongdoings.[4] According to a utilitarian ethical system there is always a duty, when harm must be done to some in bringing benefits to others, to do that action (or follow that rule) which produces the least amount of harm when weighed against the benefits. One simply calculates the best consequences, as measured by quantities of intrinsic value and disvalue. The principle of minimum wrong, on the other hand, does not consider the beings that are benefited or harmed as so many "containers" of intrinsic value or disvalue. They are beings to which are owed prima facie duties. We owe the duty of nonmaleficence, for example, to both humans and nonhumans alike. Each being has inherent worth as an individual and must accordingly be treated with respect, regardless of what species it belongs to. An action that brings harm to any one such being constitutes a prima facie wrong from which moral agents have a duty to refrain. To harm several such beings is not merely to bring about a certain amount of intrinsic disvalue in the world, to be balanced against whatever value might also be produced. It is to commit a number of violations of duty, corresponding to the number of creatures harmed.

Suppose, then, that one alternative way for humans to pursue their interests in situations of the sort we are here concerned with brings harm to a certain number of living things, while another way to pursue the same interests involves harm done to a smaller number of living things. If we were to choose the first alternative we would be knowingly performing more wrong actions than if we chose the second. It is not the aggregate amount of disvalue or harm that is relevant here, but the number of cases in which one fails to carry out one's duty to another being. Each entity that is harmed is thereby treated unjustly and so is wronged. Because the duty of nonmaleficence is owed to each individual organism, it would be morally unjustified to harm a larger number of organisms than a smaller number. If a particular act of a certain kind is wrong because it is of that kind, then more wrongs are committed when more particular acts of that kind are done. This is the central consideration that underlies the principle of minimum wrong.

In the light of this consideration we can now see why in general it is worse to harm a species-population than an individual organism, and still worse to harm a biotic community as a whole. We cannot do harm to a species-population without doing harm to a great many of the organisms that make up the population; harming one species-population is not simply doing wrong to one moral subject. Many such subjects, each having the same inherent worth, will also be wronged, namely all the members of the population that are killed or injured. Similarly, by damaging or destroying the ecological balance and integrity on which the well-being of an entire biotic community depends, harm is done to many of the species-populations that constitute the community. A great number of instances of violations of duty are thus involved.

This way of looking at the principle of minimum wrong does not entail a holistic or organicist view of environmental ethics, such as Aldo Leopold's "Land Ethic" or Holmes Rolston's "Ecological Ethic."[5]

The holistic view was critically discussed in Chapter Three in connection with the second component of the biocentric outlook (the natural world as a system of interdependence). What is relevant in the present context is the role that humans should play in relation to the natural world. According to the holistic view, the basic criterion for right action is the tendency of the action to preserve ecological integrity in the natural environment in which the action takes place. From this perspective one begins with the premises that human life is but one component of the Earth's total ecosystem and that ecological integrity has value in itself. One then argues that the proper moral role of humans on Earth is to function in a biologically sound way in relation to the planet's biosphere. Humans are seen to occupy a certain ecological niche and accordingly should govern their conduct so as to maintain a healthy relationship with the world-wide ecosystem of which they are a part. Such a holistic view includes no conception of moral agents having duties that are owed to individual organisms, each of which is regarded as possessing inherent worth.

In contrast with this, the principle of minimum wrong presupposes that each living thing deserves moral consideration. Since each has inherent worth, a prima facie wrong is done when any one of them is harmed. It is true that a greater wrong is done when a whole species-population or biotic community is harmed. This is not because the group *as such* has a greater claim-to-be-respected

than the individual, but because harming the group necessarily involves harming many individuals. Therefore, whenever we are in circumstances to which the principle of minimum wrong applies we are knowingly committing acts that are prima facie wrong. Only if we perform the fewest such acts available to us are we justified in what we do to living things. Our primary obligation in such situations is to choose the alternative which involves the least number of harm-causing acts.

There is, however, a further obligation that is binding upon us in these situations. This obligation must be fulfilled if we are to act consistently with the attitude of respect for nature. It is the duty entailed by the principle of species-impartiality between humans and nonhumans. Since we are aiming at a fair resolution of conflicting claims, whenever we cause harm to animals and plants in the pursuit of our human values, some recognition must be given to the fact that our treatment of them is prima facie wrong. This recognition is expressed in practical terms by our accepting the moral requirement to make restitution for the injustices we have committed. Even though we may have acted in accordance with the principle of minimum wrong, at least some creatures possessing inherent worth equal to our own have been unjustly treated. As a way of restoring the balance of justice between ourselves and them, some form of compensation must be provided for wild animals and plants. Only when that has been done can the actions we have performed in accordance with the principle of minimum wrong also satisfy the criterion of species-impartiality and so be morally justified, all things considered. (I shall discuss this further in connection with the principle of restitutive justice.)

The moral constraints imposed by the principle of minimum wrong are fully acceptable to the very beings whose actions are so constrained. For they are the agents who have adopted the attitude of respect for nature and who view their relation to the natural world from the perspective of the biocentric outlook. Thus they are disposed to *want* to minimize wrongs done to wild creatures while they pursue ends whose value is so great to them that they are unwilling to give them up. Their respect for nature is not diminished or weakened by their valuing of those ends. So they will readily acknowledge their obligation to adopt the principle of minimum wrong as setting valid moral restrictions upon their own decision and conduct. The principle, in other words, will be one to which they voluntarily subscribe and which they follow as their own normative guide. . . .

Notes

1. For this account of self-defense as a moral principle, I am indebted to Charles Fried, *Right and Wrong*, (Cambridge, Mass.: Harvard University Press, 1978), pp. 42–53.

2. In one of the few systematic studies of priority principles holding between humans and nonhumans, Donald VanDeVeer argues that the distinction between basic and "peripheral" (nonbasic) interests, which applies to all species that can be said to have interests, is a morally relevant difference; see VanDeVeer, "Interspecific Justice," *Inquiry* 22/1–2 (Summer 1979): 55–79. VanDeVeer would not, however, be likely to accept any of the priority principles I set out since he considers the psychological capacity to live a satisfying life a ground for counting the interests of beings possessing that capacity to be of greater weight than the equally basic interests of beings lacking it. His main reason for opposing pure egalitarianism among species seems to be that such a view is counterintuitive, being incompatible with "our deepest and strongest pre-theoretical convictions about specific cases" (p. 58; see also pp. 66 and 76). For reasons given in Chapter One [of Paul W. Taylor's *Respect for Nature: A Theory of Environmental Ethics*], I do not consider any appeal to pre-theoretical convictions, however deeply held, to be philosophically relevant.

   VanDeVeer's position has recently been defended, with certain qualifications, by Robin Attfield in *The Ethics of Environmental Concern* (New York: Columbia University Press, 1983), chapter 9. Attfield holds that ". . . varying degrees of *intrinsic* value attach to lives in which different capacities are realized" (Attfield's italics, p. 176). This is a view similar to that of Louis G. Lombardi, which I critically examined in Chapter Three. Attfield's arguments, unlike Lombardi's, are marred by a failure to distinguish the concept of intrinsic value from that of inherent worth. The utilitarianism Attfield espouses is not seen to be logically incompatible with the principle that each organism has inherent worth as an individual, a principle he also appears to hold. The incompatibility of these two ideas has been clearly explained by Tom Regan in *The Case for Animal Rights,* chapters 7 and 8. See also note 4, below.

3. My principle of proportionality is similar to Tom Regan's "Worse-off Principle," differing mainly from it in that the "Worse-off Principle" is stated in terms of rights and is restricted to conflicts between humans and only those animals that satisfy what Regan calls "the subject-of-a-life criterion." These are animals that ". . . have beliefs and desires; perception, memory, and a sense of the future, including their own future; an emotional life together with feelings of pleasure and pain; preference and welfare interests; the ability to initiate action in pursuit of their desires and goals; a psychophysical identity over time; and an individual welfare in the sense that their experiental life fares well or ill for them, logically independently of their utility for others and logically independently of their being the object of anyone else's interests" (*The Case for Animal Rights*, p. 243). The "Worse-off Principle" is set forth and discussed by Regan on pp. 307–312 of his book.

4. The distinction between a utilitarian calculation of least bad consequences and a nonconsequential principle of minimizing violations of duty has been propounded and carefully examined by Tom Regan in *The Case for Animal Rights*, section 8.9, "Should the Numbers Count?" and section 8.10, "The Miniride and Worse-Off Principles" (pp. 297–312). Regan's work in this area, to which I am indebted, makes an original and significant contribution to human ethics as well as to our understanding of the moral relations between humans and animals.

5. Aldo Leopold, "The Land Ethic," in *A Sand County Almanac* (New York: Oxford University Press, 1949), pp. 201–26; Holmes Rolston III, "Is There an Ecological Ethic?" *Ethics* 85/2 (January 1975): 93–109. See also Chapter Three, note 5 [in Taylor's *Respect for Nature: A Theory of Environmental Ethics*].

C. DEEP ECOLOGY AND SOCIAL ECOLOGY

PREVIEW

Now I see the secret of the making of the best persons. It is to grow in the open air, and then to eat and sleep with the earth.

Walt Whitman, Leaves of Grass

I think it pisses God off if you walk by the color purple in a field and don't notice it.[1]

Alice Walker

The term "deep ecology" was coined by the Norwegian philosopher Arne Naess in his "The Shallow and the Deep, Long-Range Ecology Movement. A Summary."[2] Deep ecology, in what Warwick Fox calls the "formal" sense, refers to a level of questioning that is fundamental. In an interview with Bill Devall and George Sessions reprinted in this section, Naess states, "The essence of deep ecology is to ask deeper questions. The adjective 'deep' stresses that we ask why and how, where others do not."[3] Again, he maintains, "... the deep ecological movement tries to clarify the fundamental presuppositions underlying our economic approach in terms of value priorities, philosophy, religion. In the shallow movement, argument comes to halt long before this."[4] The deep-shallow distinction has come under fire as "... pejorative ... smug, self-congratulatory, self-righteous, or holier-than-thou ... [and] patronizing. ..."[5] Nevertheless, neither Naess nor his followers (for the most part) have abandoned the phrase.

Presumably, Fox labels this construal of 'deep ecology'—asking deeper questions—as "formal" because it refers only to a depth of questioning and not to the content of any answers to these questions. However, "deep ecology" must mean more than this if only because those who call themselves "deep ecologists" typically do have substantive views that can be characterized as nonanthropocentric or ecocentric. The eight-point program arrived at by Naess and Sessions in 1984 and delineated by Devall and Sessions in this section is a representative list of such substantive claims. Moreover, according to Devall and Sessions, deep ecology subscribes to two fundamental or ultimate norms: *biocentric egalitarianism* and *Self-realization.* Fox singles out the idea of Self-realization as central to his views and renames his development of the idea "transpersonal ecology."

Biocentric egalitarianism is the claim that all living things are of equal moral worth or equal intrinsic value. It is important to recognize that "life" here is being used in a very broad sense to include, for example, "... rivers (watersheds), landscapes, ecosystems."[6] A central idea here is that humans are in nature. Humans are not "... above or outside of nature."[7] Deep ecology challenges the human centeredness of the dominant Western world view.

Arne Naess has the following to say about biospherical egalitarianism:

> The ecological field-worker acquires a deep-seated respect ... for ways and forms of life. He reaches ... a kind of understanding that others reserve for fellow men and for a narrow section of ways and forms of life. To the ecological field-worker, the equal right to live and blossom is an intuitively clear and obvious value axiom. Its restriction to humans is an anthropocentrism with detrimental effects upon the life quality of humans themselves. This quality depends in part upon the deep pleasure and satisfaction we receive from close partnership with other forms of life. The attempt to ignore our dependence and to establish a master-slave role has contributed to the alienation of man from himself.[8]

Carolyn Merchant, in her discussion of deep ecology, suggests that there is a connection between our world view and our attitude toward the earth. Of the deep ecologists, she says, "Modesty and humility and an awe of evolution take precedence over an assertion of power over the biosphere."[9] Changing our attitude toward nature, according to some, is mainly what deep ecology is about. For example, Eric Katz says, "Deep Ecology, its advocates argue, is not an attempt to discover 'intrinsic value' or to develop universal moral rules, but a re-shaping and re-direction of human consciousness."[10] In a review of Devall and Sessions's *Deep Ecology: Living as if Nature Mattered*, Evelyn M. Hurwich expresses pleasure at the prospect that concepts like 'biocentric equality' and 'Self-realization' ". . . may serve to develop ecological consciousness . . . an experiential and uniquely personal process of discovery," but she is frustrated because these phrases and concepts do ". . . not help move us forward as a global society faced by critical issues that require choices made between varying and often conflicting . . . values."[11] Hurwich continues: "Until an ecological basis is articulated by which competing vital interests can be weighed and evaluated, it cannot be expected that any meaningful decisionmaking process will evolve out of the deep ecology movement."[12] It may be true that deep ecologists do not formulate specific trade-off principles of the type Hurwich and others desire; nonetheless, in fairness to Naess, he addresses questions about conflict.

In "Self-realization in Mixed Communities of Humans, Bears, Sheep, and Wolves," Naess says, "the interaction between the members of the community is not systematically codified."[13] He calls his approach . . . *a posteriori*. . . .[14] *A posteriori* is a latin phrase used especially by philosophers when they refer to knowledge obtained by experience rather than by reason alone. So, Naess means here that the way to achieve the well-being of the members of the community is not by applying previously adopted rules es-

tablished by reason, but by experiencing the problems and character of individual bears. In listening to Arne Naess talk about bears, it seems as if the bears are "Fred" and "Esther"—folks we know:

> Bears and humans live in overlapping territories in southern Norway. Conflicts arise because some bears develop a habit of killing sheep. No sheep-owner thinks that all bears in his area should be killed. The cultural pattern is such that bears are considered to have a right to live and flourish. They are considered to have a value in themselves. The problem is one of co-existence with humans and with sheep.
>
> When sheep are killed in southern Norway and a bear seems to have been responsible, an expert is called in. He investigates closely the way the sheep has been killed and notes all the signs of the presence of the bear. Knowing the various habits of practically all the bears of the area—even if he has not actually seen them—he is generally able to tell not only whether a bear has been there, but also which bear.
>
> The sheep-owner is paid an indemnity if the expert arrives at the conclusion that a bear is responsible. If that bear has been guilty of similar "crimes," a verdict may be reached that it has forfeited its right to existence. An expert bear-hunter is given licence to kill it, but if he does not succeed, a whole team of hunters is mobilized. (Somewhat inexplicably, bears are able under such circumstances to hide for years, which is deeply embarrassing as well as mystifying for the hunters.)
>
> Many factors are considered before a bear is condemned to death. What is his or her total record of misdeeds? How many sheep have been killed? Does he or she mainly kill to eat, or does he or she maim or hurt sheep without eating? Is particular cruelty shown? Is it a bear mother who will probably influence her cubs in a bad way? Did the sheep enter

the heart of the bear area or did the bear stray far into established sheep territory?[15]

Whatever guidelines are used by Naess emerge from the situation in which bears, wolves, sheep, and people find themselves. For a more abstract principled or rule-orientated approach to conflict resolution by a biocentric egalitarian, the reader may examine the views of Paul Taylor in Section IV-B.

Self-realization is the remaining ultimate norm of deep ecology to be considered. "We underestimate ourselves," says Naess, if we ". . . confuse [self] with the narrow ego."[16] In a fairly sophisticated summary of the notion, Naess says that Self-realization "in its absolute maximum is . . . the mature experience of oneness in diversity. . . . The minimum is the self-realization by more or less consistent egoism—by the narrowest experience of what constitutes one's self and a maximum of alienation. As empirical beings we dwell somewhere in between, but increased maturity involves increase of the wideness of the self."[17] We develop a wider Self, according to Naess, by a process of identification. Sometimes, Naess talks as though identification is a psychological process, something like empathy or solidarity, by which we establish connection with other life forms. For example, he says, "Identification is a spontaneous, nonrational, but not irrational, process in which *the interest or interests of another being are reacted to as our own interest or interests*."[18] At other times, when speaking of identification, he seems to be talking about what is real (metaphysics or ontology) or what we can know (epistemology). For example, Naess says, "In the shallow ecological movement, intense and wide identification is described and explained psychologically. In the deep movement [mysticism] is at least taken seriously: reality consists of wholes which we cut down rather than of isolated items which we put together."[19] Eric Katz maintains that in ". . . the most complete expression of the philosophy of deep ecology,

[Naess] makes clear that deep ecology is much less a theory of ethics than a theory of ontology and epistemology."[20] Naess, in our view, leans heavily on Hindu metaphysics. Note that in the selection reprinted here he says, "As a student and admirer since 1930 of Gandhi's nonviolent direct action, I am inevitably influenced by his metaphysics. . . ."[21] However, it is also true that Naess's view has implications for ethics even if his "deep ecology" ("ecosophy," as he would prefer) is not, in his view, properly called ethics.

Both the concept of Self-realization and its ethical implications are analyzed by Val Plumwood in her essay, "Nature, Self, and Gender: Feminism, Environmental Philosophy, and the Critique of Rationalism" in Section IV-D. Here we note one ethical implication of the Self-realization doctrine. As Plumwood explains, "The motivation for the expansion of self is to allow the self to operate on the fuel of self-interest. . . . This is apparent from [Fox's] claim that 'in this light . . . ecological resistance is simply another name for self-defense.'"[22] These consequences for ethics are also apparent in the following remark by Naess: ". . . *if your self in the wide sense embraces another being, you need no moral exhortation to show care. You care for yourself without feeling any moral pressure to do it—unless you have succumbed to a neurosis of some kind, developed self-destructive tendencies, or hate yourself."[23] Another commentator's remarks are also illustrative here:

> Indeed, I consider that this shift [to an emphasis on our "capacity to identify with the larger collective of all beings"] is essential to our survival at this point in history precisely because it can serve in lieu of morality and because moralizing is so ineffective. . . . It would not occur to me, for example, to exhort you to refrain from cutting off your leg. That wouldn't occur to me or to you, because your leg is part of you. Well, so are the trees in the Amazon Basin; they are our external

lungs. We are gradually discovering that we are our world.[24]

"... [I]n environmental affairs," Naess says, "we should primarily try to influence people toward beautiful acts by finding ways to work on their inclinations rather than their morals."[25] Naess borrows the phrase "beautiful action" from philosopher Immanuel Kant. Naess notes in the selection reprinted here that for Kant, a moral act is one done out of duty, not inclination. Indeed, acts done from inclination, according to Kant, are suspect from a moral point of view even if we do the right thing. Doing the right thing from inclination Naess calls—and claims that Kant does too—a beautiful action. Naess wants to dispense with moral actions in favor of beautiful ones. Recall what he said above about "no moral exhortation," no "moral pressure." Bill Devall talks about not "imposing environmental ethics"; instead, "... we will naturally respect, love, honor, and protect that which is our self."[26] Still, it is worth observing how many people are "naturally" self-destructive! Elsewhere, Arne Naess has said, "The history of cruelty [inflicted] in the name of morals has convinced me that increase in identification might achieve what moralizing cannot: beautiful actions."[27]

Dave Foreman, who represents the activist wing of deep ecology, and Murray Bookchin, a socialist critic of deep ecology, seek common ground in the final selection in this section. A severe and irreverent critic of deep ecology, Murray Bookchin has for many years chided deep ecologists for caring only about wilderness preservation and little or nothing about social justice. In a similar vein, Ramachandra Guha, in his essay, "Radical American Environmentalism and Wilderness Preservation: A Third World Critique" (in Section VI-D), reprimands deep ecologists like Foreman for failing to see how the social consequences of an exclusive focus on wilderness might be different for different countries. What is of particular interest in the dialogue between Bookchin and Foreman is that Bookchin is talking about the importance of wilderness and Foreman is talking about the irresponsibility of corporations—just the reverse of positions they are known to defend. In the light of his being criticized on many fronts, it is noteworthy to hear Foreman talk about his experiences with the FBI and how being arrested for his activities in conjunction with Earth First! (a radical environmental organization) raised his political consciousness.

NOTES

1. Alice Walker, *The Color Purple*. New York: Pocket Books, 1982, p. 203.
2. Arne Naess, "The Shallow and the Deep, Long-Range Ecology Movement. A Summary," *Inquiry*, Vol. 16, No. 1 (Spring 1973). This piece is a summary of an introductory lecture at the third World Future Research Conference, Bucharest, September 3–10, 1972.
3. Arne Naess, "Interview with Naess," in *Deep Ecology: Living as if Nature Mattered* by Bill Devall and George Sessions (Salt Lake City, UT: Peregrine Smith Books, 1985), p. 74.
4. Arne Naess, "The Deep Ecological Movement: Some Philosophical Aspects," *Philosophical Inquiry*, Vol 8, No. 1–2, 1986, 22.
5. Warwick Fox, *Toward a Transpersonal Ecology* (Boston: Shambhala Publications, Inc., 1990), pp. 112–123.
6. Bill Devall and George Sessions, *Deep Ecology: Living as if Nature Mattered* (Salt Lake City, UT: Peregrine Smith Books, 1985), p. 71.
7. Bill Devall, "The Deep Ecology Movement," *Natural Resources Journal*, Vol. 20, No. 2 (April 1980), 303.
8. Arne Naess, "The Shallow and the Deep, Long-Range Ecology Movement. A Summary," 95–96.
9. Carolyn Merchant, *Radical Ecology: The Search for a Livable World*. New York: Routledge, 1992, p. 87.
10. Eric Katz, "Ethics and Philosophy of the Environment: A Brief Review of the Major Literature," *Environmental History Review*, Vol. 15, No 2 (1991), 84.
11. Evelyn M. Hurwich, Review of *Deep Ecology: Living as if Nature Mattered* by Bill Devall and George Sessions (Salt Lake City, UT: Peregrine Smith Books,

1985), in *Ecology Law Quarterly*, Vol. 13 (1986), 770–771.

12. Evelyn M. Hurwich, review of *Deep Ecology*, p. 771. See also Bryan G. Norton's discussion of deep ecology in his book *Toward Unity Among Environmentalists* (New York: Oxford University Press, 1991).

13. Arne Naess, "Self-realization in Mixed Communities of Humans, Bears, Sheep, and Wolves," *Inquiry*, Vol. 22, No. 1–2 (Summer 1979), 238.

14. Arne Naess, "Self-realization in Mixed Communities of Humans, Bears, Sheep, and Wolves," p. 238.

15. Arne Naess, "Self-realization in Mixed Communities of Humans, Bears, Sheep, and Wolves," p. 237.

16. Arne Naess, "Self Realization: An Ecological Approach to Being in the World," in *Thinking Like a Mountain: Towards a Council of All Beings*, edited by John Seed, Joanna Macy, Pat Fleming, and Arne Naess (Philadelphia: New Society Publishers, 1988), p. 19.

17. Arne Naess, "Identification as a Source of Deep Ecological Attitudes," in *Radical Environmentalism: Philosophy and Tactics*, edited by Peter C. List (Belmont, CA: Wadsworth Publishing Company, 1993), p. 28.

18. Arne Naess, "Identification as a Source of Deep Ecological Attitudes," in *Radical Environmentalism*, p. 29.

19. Arne Naess, "Identification as a Source of Deep Ecological Attitudes," in *Radical Environmentalism*, p. 30.

20. Eric Katz, "Ethics and Philosophy of the Environment: A Brief Review of the Major Literature," p. 85. Katz means by "most complete expression"

Naess's *Ecology, Community and Lifestyle* (New York: Cambridge University Press, 1989).

21. Arne Naess, "Self Realization: An Ecological Approach to Being in the World," p. 24.

22. Val Plumwood, "Nature, Self, and Gender: Feminism, Environmental Philosophy, and the Critique of Rationalism," p. 14. Warwick Fox, "Approaching Deep Ecology: A Response to Richard Sylvan's Critique of Deep Ecology," *Environmental Studies Occasional Paper 20* (Hobart: University of Tasmania Centre for Environmental Studies, 1986), p. 60. See also *Green Rage*, in which the following position is attributed to Arne Naess, Bill Devall, and other deep ecologists: "If our selves belong to a larger self that encompasses the whole biological community in which we dwell, then an attack on the trees, the wolves, the rivers, is an attack upon all of us. Defense of place becomes a form of self-defense, which in most ethical and legal systems would be ample grounds for spiking a tree or ruining a tire." *Green Rage: Radical Environmentalism and the Unmaking of Civilization*, by Christopher Manes (Boston: Little, Brown and Company, 1990), p. 177.

23. Arne Naess, "Self Realization: An Ecological Approach to Being in the World," pp. 26–27.

24. Joanna Macy in *Toward a Transpersonal Ecology* by Warwick Fox, p. 229.

25. Arne Naess, "Self-Realization: An Ecological Approach to Being in the World," p. 28.

26. Bill Devall, *Simple in Means, Rich in Ends: Practicing Deep Ecology* (Salt Lake City, UT: Peregrine Smith Books, 1988), p. 43.

27. Arne Naess, "Identification as a Source of Deep Ecological Attitudes," in *Radical Environmentalism*, p. 32.

Deep Ecology

Bill Devall and George Sessions

The term *deep ecology* was coined by Arne Naess in his 1973 article, "The Shallow and the Deep, Long-Range Ecology Movements."[1] Naess was attempting to describe the deeper, more spiritual approach to nature exemplified in the writings of Aldo Leopold and Rachel Carson. He thought that this deeper approach resulted from a more sensitive openness to ourselves and nonhuman life around us. The essence of deep ecology is to keep asking more searching questions about human life, society, and Nature as in the Western philosophical tradition of Socrates. As examples of this deep questioning, Naess points out "that we ask why and how, where others do not. For instance, ecology

Deep Ecology: Living as if Nature Mattered, by Bill Devall and George Sessions. (Layton, UT: Peregrine Smith Books, 1985), pp. 65–73. Reprinted by permission of the publisher.

as a science does not ask what kind of a society would be the best for maintaining a particular ecosystem—that is considered a question for value theory, for politics, for ethics." Thus deep ecology goes beyond the so-called factual scientific level to the level of self and Earth wisdom.

Deep ecology goes beyond a limited piecemeal shallow approach to environmental problems and attempts to articulate a comprehensive religious and philosophical worldview. The foundations of deep ecology are the basic intuitions and experiencing of ourselves and Nature which comprise ecological consciousness. Certain outlooks on politics and public policy flow naturally from this consciousness. And in the context of this book, we discuss the minority tradition as the type of community most conducive both to cultivating ecological consciousness and to asking the basic questions of values and ethics addressed in these pages.

Many of these questions are perennial philosophical and religious questions faced by humans in all cultures over the ages. What does it mean to be a unique human individual? How can the individual self maintain and increase its uniqueness while also being an inseparable aspect of the whole system wherein there are no sharp breaks between self and the *other*? An ecological perspective, in this deeper sense, results in what Theodore Roszak calls "an awakening of wholes greater than the sum of their parts. In spirit, the discipline is contemplative and therapeutic." [2]

Ecological consciousness and deep ecology are in sharp contrast with the dominant worldview of technocratic-industrial societies which regards humans as isolated and fundamentally separate from the rest of Nature, as superior to, and in charge of, the rest of creation. But the view of humans as separate and superior to the rest of Nature is only part of larger cultural patterns. For thousands of years, Western culture has become increasingly obsessed with the idea of *dominance:* with dominance of humans over nonhuman Nature, masculine over the feminine, wealthy and powerful over the poor, with the dominance of the West over non-Western cultures. Deep ecological consciousness allows us to see through these erroneous and dangerous illusions.

For deep ecology, the study of our place in the Earth household includes the study of ourselves as part of the organic whole. Going beyond a narrowly materialist scientific understanding of reality, the spiritual and the material aspects of reality fuse together. While the leading intellectuals of the dominant worldview have tended to view religion as "just superstition," and have looked upon ancient spiritual practice and enlightenment, such as found in Zen Buddhism, as essentially subjective, the search for deep ecological consciousness is the search for a more objective consciousness and state of being through an active deep questioning and meditative process and way of life.

Many people have asked these deeper questions and cultivated ecological consciousness within the context of different spiritual traditions—Christianity, Taoism, Buddhism, and Native American rituals, for example. While differing greatly in other regards, many in these traditions agree with the basic principles of deep ecology.

Warwick Fox, an Australian philosopher, has succinctly expressed the central intuition of deep ecology: "It is the idea that we can make no firm ontological divide in the field of existence: That there is no bifurcation in reality between the human and the non-human realms . . . to the extent that we perceive boundaries, we fall short of deep ecological consciousness." [3]

From this most basic insight or characteristic of deep ecological consciousness, Arne Naess has developed two *ultimate norms* or intuitions which are themselves not derivable from other principles or intuitions. They are arrived at by the deep-questioning process and reveal the importance of moving to the philosophical and religious level of wisdom. They cannot be validated, of course, by the methodology of modern science based on its usual mechanistic assumptions and its very narrow definition of data. These ultimate norms are *self-realization* and *biocentric equality*.

I. Self-Realization

In keeping with the spiritual traditions of many of the world's religions, the deep ecology norm of self-realization goes beyond the modern Western *self* which is defined as an isolated ego striving primarily for hedonistic gratification or for a narrow sense of individual salvation in this life or the next. This socially programmed sense of the narrow self or social self dislocates us, and leaves us prey to whatever fad or fashion is prevalent in our society or social reference group. We are thus robbed of beginning the search for our unique spiritual/biological personhood. Spiritual growth, or unfolding, begins when we cease to understand or see ourselves as isolated and narrow competing egos and begin to identify with other humans from our family and friends to, eventually, our species. But the deep ecology sense of self requires a further maturity and growth, an identification which goes beyond humanity to include the nonhuman world. We must see beyond our narrow contemporary cultural assumptions and values, and the conventional wisdom of our time and place, and this is best achieved by the meditative deep questioning process. Only in this way can we hope to attain full mature personhood and uniqueness.

A nurturing nondominating society can help in the "real work" of becoming a whole person. The "real work" can be summarized symbolically as the realization of "self-in-Self" where "Self" stands for organic wholeness. This process of the full unfolding of the self can also be summarized by the phrase, "No one is saved until we are all saved," where the phrase "one" includes not only me, an individual human, but all humans, whales, grizzly bears, whole rain forest ecosystems, mountains and rivers, the tiniest microbes in the soil, and so on.

II. Biocentric Equality

The intuition of biocentric equality is that all things in the biosphere have an equal right to live and blossom and to reach their own individual forms of unfolding and self-realization within the larger Self-realization. This basic intuition is that all organisms and entities in the ecosphere, as parts of the interrelated whole, are equal in intrinsic worth. Naess suggests that biocentric equality as an intuition is true in principle, although in the process of living, all species use each other as food, shelter, etc. Mutual predation is a biological fact of life, and many of the world's religions have struggled with the spiritual implications of this. Some animal liberationists who attempt to side-step this problem by advocating vegetarianism are forced to say that the entire plant kingdom including rain forests have no right to their own existence. This evasion flies in the face of the basic intuition of equality.[4] Aldo Leopold expressed this intuition when he said humans are "plain citizens" of the biotic community, not lord and master over all other species.

Biocentric equality is intimately related to the all-inclusive Self-realization in the sense that if we harm the rest of Nature then we are harming ourselves. There are no boundaries and everything is interrelated. But insofar as we perceive things as individual organisms or entities, the insight draws us to respect all human and non-human individuals in their own right as parts of the whole without feeling the need to set up hierarchies of species with humans at the top.

The practical implications of this intuition or norm suggest that we should live with minimum rather than maximum impact on other species and on the Earth in general. Thus we see another aspect of our guiding principle: "simple in means, rich in ends.". . .

A fuller discussion of the biocentric norm as it unfolds itself in practice begins with the realization that we, as individual humans, and as communities of humans, have vital needs which go beyond such basics as food, water, and shelter to include love, play, creative expression, intimate relationships with a particular landscape (or Nature taken in its entirety) as well as intimate relationships with other humans, and the vital need for spiritual growth, for becoming a mature human being.

Our vital material needs are probably more simple than many realize. In technocratic-industrial societies there is overwhelming propaganda and advertising which encourages false needs and destructive desires designed to foster increased production and consumption of goods. Most of this actually diverts us from facing reality in an objective way and from beginning the "real work" of spiritual growth and maturity.

Many people who do not see themselves as supporters of deep ecology nevertheless recognize an overriding vital human need for a healthy and high-quality natural environment for humans, if not for all life, with minimum intrusion of toxic waste, nuclear radiation from human enterprises, minimum acid rain and smog, and enough free flowing wilderness so humans can get in touch with their sources, the natural rhythms and the flow of time and place.

Drawing from the minority tradition and from the wisdom of many who have offered the insight of interconnectedness, we recognize that deep ecologists can offer suggestions for gaining maturity and encouraging the processes of harmony with nature, but that there is no grand solution which is guaranteed to save us from ourselves.

The ultimate norms of deep ecology suggest a

Dominant Worldview	Deep Ecology
Dominance over Nature	Harmony with Nature
Natural environment as resource for humans	All nature has intrinsic worth/biospecies equality
Material/economic growth for growing human population	Elegantly simple material needs (material goals serving the larger goal of self-realization)
Belief in ample resource reserves	Earth "supplies" limited
High technological progress and solutions	Appropriate technology; nondominating science
Consumerism	Doing with enough/recycling
National/centralized community	Minority tradition/bioregion

Figure 1   The contrast between the dominant world view and deep ecology

view of the nature of reality and our place as an individual (many in the one) in the larger scheme of things. They cannot be fully grasped intellectually but are ultimately experiential. . . .

As a brief summary of our position thus far, Figure 1 summarizes the contrast between the dominant world view and deep ecology.

III. Basic Principles of Deep Ecology

In April 1984, during the advent of spring and John Muir's birthday, George Sessions and Arne Naess summarized fifteen years of thinking on the principles of deep ecology while camping in Death Valley, California. In this great and special place, they articulated these principles in a literal, somewhat neutral way, hoping that they would be understood and accepted by persons coming from different philosophical and religious positions.

Readers are encouraged to elaborate their own versions of deep ecology, clarify key concepts and think through the consequences of acting from these principles.

Basic Principles

1. The well-being and flourishing of human and nonhuman Life on earth have value in themselves (synonyms: intrinsic value, inherent

value). These values are independent of the usefulness of the non-human world for human purposes.

2. Richness and diversity of life forms contribute to the realization of these values and are also values in themselves.

3. Humans have no right to reduce this richness and diversity except to satisfy *vital* needs.

4. The flourishing of human life and cultures is compatible with a substantial decrease of the human population. The flourishing of non-human life requires such a decrease.

5. Present human interference with the non-human world is excessive, and the situation is rapidly worsening.

6. Policies must therefore be changed. These policies affect basic economic, technological, and ideological structures. The resulting state of affairs will be deeply different from the present.

7. The ideological change is mainly that of appreciating *life quality* (dwelling in situations of inherent value) rather than adhering to an increasingly higher standard of living. There will be a profound awareness of the difference between big and great.

8. Those who subscribe to the foregoing points have an obligation directly or indirectly to try to implement the necessary changes.

Naess and Sessions Provide Comments on the Basic Principles

RE (1). This formulation refers to the biosphere, or more accurately, to the ecosphere as a whole. This includes individuals, species, populations, habitat, as well as human and nonhuman cultures. From our current knowledge of all-pervasive intimate relationships, this implies a fundamental deep concern and respect. Ecological processes of the planet should, on the whole, remain intact. "The world environment should remain 'natural'" (Gary Snyder).

The term "life" is used here in a more comprehensive nontechnical way to refer also to what biologists classify as "nonliving"; rivers (watersheds), landscapes, ecosystems. For supporters of deep ecology, slogans such as "Let the river live" illustrate this broader usage so common in most cultures.

Inherent value as used in (1) is common in

deep ecology literature. ("The presence of inherent value in a natural object is independent of any awareness, interest, or appreciation of it by a conscious being.")[5]

RE (2). More technically, this is a formulation concerning diversity and complexity. From an ecological standpoint, complexity and symbiosis are conditions for maximizing diversity. So-called simple, lower, or primitive species of plants and animals contribute essentially to the richness and diversity of life. They have value in themselves and are not merely steps toward the so-called higher or rational life forms. The second principle presupposes that life itself, as a process over evolutionary time, implies an increase of diversity and richness. The refusal to acknowledge that some life forms have greater or lesser intrinsic value than others (see points 1 and 2) runs counter to the formulations of some ecological philosophers and New Age writers.

Complexity, as referred to here, is different from complication. Urban life may be more complicated than life in a natural setting without being more complex in the sense of multifaceted quality.

RE (3). The term "vital need" is left deliberately vague to allow for considerable latitude in judgment. Differences in climate and related factors, together with differences in the structures of societies as they now exist, need to be considered (for some Eskimos, snow-mobiles are necessary today to satisfy vital needs).

People in the materially richest countries cannot be expected to reduce their excessive interference with the nonhuman world to a moderate level overnight. The stabilization and reduction of the human population will take time. Interim strategies need to be developed. But this in no way excuses the present complacency—the extreme seriousness of our current situation must first be realized. But the longer we wait the more drastic will be the measures needed. Until deep changes are made, substantial decreases in richness and diversity are liable to occur: the rate of extinction of species will be ten to one hundred times greater than any other period of earth history.

RE (4). The United Nations Fund for Population Activities in their State of World Population Report (1984) said that high human population growth rates (over 2.0 percent annum) in many developing countries "were diminishing the quality of life for many millions of people." During the decade 1974–1984, the world population grew by nearly 800 million—more than the size of India. "And we will be adding about one Bangladesh (population 93 million) per annum between now and the year 2000."

The report noted that "The growth rate of the human population has declined for the first time in human history. But at the same time, the number of people being added to the human population is bigger than at any time in history because the population base is larger."

Most of the nations in the developing world (including India and China) have as their official government policy the goal of reducing the rate of human population increase, but there are debates over the types of measures to take (contraception, abortion, etc.) consistent with human rights and feasibility.

The report concludes that if all governments set specific population targets as public policy to help alleviate poverty and advance the quality of life, the current situation could be improved.

As many ecologists have pointed out, it is also absolutely crucial to curb population growth in the so-called developed (i.e., overdeveloped) industrial societies. Given the tremendous rate of consumption and waste production of individuals in these societies, they represent a much greater threat and impact on the biosphere per capita than individuals in Second and Third World countries.

RE (5). This formulation is mild. For a realistic assessment of the situation, see the unabbreviated version of the IUCN's *World Conservation Strategy*. There are other works to be highly recommended, such as Gerald Barney's *Global 2000 Report to the President of the United States*.

The slogan of "noninterference" does not imply that humans should not modify some ecosystems as do other species. Humans have modified the earth and will probably continue to do so. At issue is the nature and extent of such interference.

The fight to preserve and extend areas of wilderness or near-wilderness should continue and should focus on the general ecological functions of these areas (one such function: large wilderness areas are required in the biosphere to allow for continued evolutionary speciation of animals and plants). Most present designated wilderness areas and game preserves are not large enough to allow for such speciation.

RE (6). Economic growth as conceived and implemented today by the industrial states is incompatible with (1)–(5). There is only a faint resemblance between ideal sustainable forms of economic growth and present policies of the industrial societies. And "sustainable" still means "sustainable in relation to humans."

Present ideology tends to value things because they are scarce and because they have a commodity value. There is prestige in vast consumption and waste (to mention only several relevant factors).

Whereas "self-determination," "local community," and "think globally, act locally," will remain key terms in the ecology of human societies, nevertheless the implementation of deep changes requires increasingly global action—action across borders.

Governments in Third World countries (with the exception of Costa Rica and a few others) are uninterested in deep ecological issues. When the governments of industrial societies try to promote ecological measures through Third World governments, practically nothing is accomplished (e.g., with problems of desertification). Given this situation, support for global action through nongovernmental international organizations becomes increasingly important. Many of these organizations are able to act globally "from grassroots to grassroots," thus avoiding negative governmental interference.

Cultural diversity today requires advanced technology, that is, techniques that advance the basic goals of each culture. So-called soft, intermediate, and alternative technologies are steps in this direction.

RE (7). Some economists criticize the term "quality of life" because it is supposed to be vague. But on closer inspection, what they consider to be vague is actually the nonquantitative nature of the term. One cannot quantify adequately what is important for the quality of life as discussed here, and there is no need to do so.

RE (8). There is ample room for different opinions about priorities: what should be done first, what next? What is most urgent? What is clearly necessary as opposed to what is highly desirable but not absolutely pressing?

Notes

1. Arne Naess, "The Shallow and The Deep, Long-Range Ecology Movements: A Summary," *Inquiry* 16 (Oslo, 1973), pp. 95–100.

2. Theodore Roszak, *Where the Wasteland Ends* (New York: Anchor, 1972).

3. Warwick Fox, "The Intuition of Deep Ecology" (Paper presented at the Ecology and Philosophy Conference, Australian National University, September, 1983). To appear in *The Ecologist* (England, Fall 1984).

4. Tom Regan, *The Case for Animal Rights* (New York: Random House, 1983). For excellent critiques of the animal rights movement, see John Rodman, "The Liberation of Nature?" *Inquiry* 20 (Oslo, 1977). J. Baird Callicott, "Animal Liberation," *Environmental Ethics* 2, 4 (1980); see also John Rodman, "Four Forms of Ecological Consciousness Reconsidered" in T. Attig and D. Scherer, eds., *Ethics and the Environment* (Englewood Cliffs, NJ: Prentice-Hall, 1983).

5. Tom Regan, "The Nature and Possibility of an Environmental Ethic," *Environmental Ethics* 3 (1981), pp. 19–34.

Interview with Arne Naess

Bill Devall and George Sessions

The following excerpts are from an interview with Arne Naess conducted at the Zen Center of Los Angeles in April 1982. It was originally published as an interview in *Ten Directions*.[1] In the interview, Naess further discusses the major perspective of deep ecology. . . .

"The essence of deep ecology is to ask deeper questions. The adjective 'deep' stresses that we ask why and how, where others do not. For instance, ecology as a science does not ask what kind of a society would be the best for maintaining a particular ecosystem—that is considered a question for

Deep Ecology: Living as if Nature Mattered, by Bill Devall and George Sessions (Layton, UT: Peregrine Smith Books, 1985), pp. 74–76. Reprinted by permission of the publisher.

value theory, for politics, for ethics. As long as ecologists keep narrowly to their science, they do not ask such questions. What we need today is a tremendous expansion of ecological thinking in what I call ecosophy. *Sophy* comes from the Greek term *sophia*, 'wisdom,' which relates to ethics, norms, rules, and practice. Ecosophy, or deep ecology, then, involves a shift from science to wisdom.

"For example, we need to ask questions like, Why do we think that economic growth and high levels of consumption are so important? The conventional answer would be to point to the economic consequences of not having economic growth. But in deep ecology, we ask whether the present society fulfills basic human needs like love and security and access to nature, and, in so doing, we question our society's underlying assumptions. We ask which society, which education, which form of religion, is beneficial for all life on the planet as a whole, and then we ask further what we need to do in order to make the necessary changes. We are not limited to a scientific approach; we have an obligation to verbalize a total view.

"Of course, total views may differ. Buddhism, for example, provides a fitting background or context for deep ecology, certain Christian groups have formed platforms of action in favor of deep ecology, and I myself have worked out my own philosophy, which I call ecosophy. In general, however, people do not question deeply enough to explicate or make clear a total view. If they did, most would agree with saving the planet from the destruction that's in progress. A total view, such as deep ecology, can provide a single motivating force for all the activities and movements aimed at saving the planet from human exploitation and domination.

". . . It's easier for deep ecologists than for others because we have certain fundamental values, a fundamental view of what's meaningful in life, what's worth maintaining, which makes it completely clear that we're opposed to further development for the sake of increased domination and an increased standard of living. The material standard of living should be drastically reduced and the quality of life, in the sense of basic satisfaction in the depths of one's heart or soul, should be maintained or increased. This view is intuitive, as are all important views, in the sense that it can't be proven. As Aristotle said, it shows a lack of education to try to prove everything, because you have to have

a starting point. You can't prove the methodology of science, you can't prove logic, because logic presupposes fundamental premises.

"All the sciences are fragmentary and incomplete in relation to basic rules and norms, so it's very shallow to think that science can solve our problems. Without basic norms, there is no science.

". . . People can then oppose nuclear power without having to read thick books and without knowing the myriad facts that are used in newspapers and periodicals. And they must also find others who feel the same and form circles of friends who give one another confidence and support in living in a way that the majority find ridiculous, naive, stupid and simplistic. But in order to do that, one must already have enough self-confidence to follow one's intuition—a quality very much lacking in broad sections of the populace. Most people follow the trends and advertisements and become philosophical and ethical cripples.

"There is a basic intuition in deep ecology that we have no right to destroy other living beings without sufficient reason. Another norm is that, with maturity, human beings will experience joy when other life forms experience joy, and sorrow when other life forms experience sorrow. Not only will we feel sad when our brother or a dog or a cat feels sad, but we will grieve when living beings, including landscapes, are destroyed. In our civilization, we have vast means of destruction at our disposal but extremely little maturity in our feelings. Only a very narrow range of feelings have interested most human beings until now.

"For deep ecology, there is a core democracy in the biosphere. . . . In deep ecology, we have the goal not only of stabilizing human population but also of reducing it to a sustainable minimum without revolution or dictatorship. I should think we must have no more than 100 million people if we are to have the variety of cultures we had one hundred years ago. Because we need the conservation of human cultures, just as we need the conservation of animal species.

". . . Self-realization is the realization of the potentialities of life. Organisms that differ from each other in three ways give us less diversity than organisms that differ from each other in one hundred ways. Therefore, the self-realization we experience when we identify with the universe is heightened by an increase in the number of ways in which individuals, societies, and even species and life forms realize themselves. The greater the diversity, then, the greater the self-realization. This seeming duality between individuals and the totality is encompassed by what I call the Self and the Chinese call the Tao. Most people in deep ecology have had the feeling—usually, but not always, in nature—that they are connected with something greater than their ego, greater than their name, their family, their special attributes as an individual—a feeling that is often called oceanic because many have it on the ocean. Without that identification, one is not easily drawn to become involved in deep ecology. . . .

". . . Insofar as these deep feelings are religious, deep ecology has a religious component, and those people who have done the most to make societies aware of the destructive way in which we live in relation to natural settings have had such religious feelings. Rachel Carson, for example, says that we *cannot* do what we do, we have no religious or ethical justification for behaving as we do toward nature. . . . She is saying that we are simply not per-mitted to behave in that way. Some will say that nature is not man's property, it's the property of God; others will say it in other ways. The main point is that deep ecology has a religious component, fundamental intuitions that everyone must cultivate if he or she is to have a life based on values and not function like a computer.

". . . To maximize self-realization—and I don't mean self as ego but self in a broader sense—we need maximum diversity and maximum symbiosis. . . . Diversity, then, is a fundamental norm and a common delight. As deep ecologists, we take a natural delight in diversity, as long as it does not include crude, intrusive forms, like Nazi culture, that are destructive to others."

Notes

1. Stephen Bodian, "Simple in Means, Rich in Ends: A Conversation with Arne Naess," *Ten Directions.* California: Institute for Transcultural Studies, Zen Center of Los Angeles (Summer/Fall 1982).

Self Realization: An Ecological Approach to Being in the World

Arne Naess

For at least 2500 years, humankind has struggled with basic questions about who we are, what we are heading for, what kind of reality we are part of. Two thousand five hundred years is a short period in the lifetime of a species, and still less in the lifetime of the Earth, on whose surface we belong as mobile parts.

What I am going to say more or less in my own way, may roughly be condensed into the following six points:

1. We underestimate ourselves. I emphasize *self.* We tend to confuse it with the narrow ego.

2. Human nature is such that with sufficient all-sided maturity we cannot avoid "identifying" ourselves with all living beings, beautiful or ugly, big or small, sentient or not. I will elucidate my concept of identifying later.

3. Traditionally, the *maturity of the self* develops through three stages—from ego to social self, and from social self to metaphysical self. In this conception of the process nature—our home, our immediate environment, where we belong as children, and our identification with living human beings—is largely ignored. I therefore tentatively introduce the concept of an *ecological self.* We may be in, of and for nature from our very beginning. Society and human relations are important, but our self is richer in its constitutive relations. These relations are not only relations we have with humans and the human community, but with the larger community of all living beings.

4. The joy and meaning of life is enhanced through increased self-realization, through the fulfillment of each being's potential. Whatever

Thinking Like a Mountain: Towards a Council of All Beings, by John Seed, Joanna Macy, Pat Fleming, and Arne Naess (Philadelphia: New Society Publishers, 1988), pp. 19–30. Reprinted by permission of the publisher.

the differences between beings, increased self-realization implies broadening and deepening of the *self*.

5. Because of an inescapable process of identification with others, with growing maturity, the self is widened and deepened. We "see ourself in others." Self-realization is hindered if the self-realization of others, with whom we identify, is hindered. Love of ourself will labor to overcome this obstacle by assisting in the self-realization of others according to the formula "live and let live." Thus, all that can be achieved by altruism—the dutiful, *moral* consideration of others—can be achieved—and much more—through widening and deepening ourself. Following Immanuel Kant's critique, we then act *beautifully* but neither morally nor immorally.

6. The challenge of today is to save the planet from further devastation which violates both the enlightened self-interest of humans and nonhumans, and decreases the potential of joyful existence for all.

*

The simplest answer to who or what I am is to point to my body, using my finger. But clearly I cannot identify my self or even my ego with my body. For example, compare:

I know Mr. Smith.	with	My body knows Mr. Smith.
I like poetry.		My body likes poetry.
The only difference		The only difference
between us is that		between our bodies is that
you are a Presbyterian		your body is Presbyterian
and I am a Baptist.		whereas mine is Baptist.

In the above sentences we cannot substitute "my body" for "I" nor can we substitute "my mind" or "my mind and body" for "I." But this of course does not tell us what the ego or self is.

Several thousand years of philosophical, psychological and social-psychological discourse has not brought us any stable conception of the "I," ego, or the self. In modern psychotherapy these notions play an indispensable role, but the practical goal of therapy does not necessitate philosophical clarification of the terms. For our purposes, it is important to remind ourselves what strange and marvelous phenomena we are dealing with. They are extremely close to each of us. Perhaps the very nearness of these objects of reflection and discourse adds to our difficulties. I shall only offer a

single sentence resembling a definition of the ecological self. The ecological self of a person is that with which this person identifies.

This key sentence (rather than definition) about the self, shifts the burden of clarification from the term *self* to that of *identification* or more accurately, the *process of identification*.

What would be a paradigmatic situation of identification? It is a situation in which identification elicits intense empathy. My standard example has to do with a nonhuman being I met 40 years ago. I looked through an old-fashioned microscope at the dramatic meeting of two drops of different chemicals. A flea jumped from a lemming strolling along the table and landed in the middle of the acid chemicals. To save it was impossible. It took many minutes for the flea to die. Its movements were dreadfully expressive. What I felt was, naturally, a painful compassion and empathy. But the empathy was *not* basic. What *was* basic was the process of identification, that "I see myself in the flea." If I was alienated from the flea, not seeing intuitively anything resembling myself, the death struggle would have left me indifferent. So there must be identification in order for there to be compassion and, among humans, solidarity.

One of the authors contributing admirably to clarification of the study of self is Erich Fromm:

> The doctrine that love for oneself is identical with *selfishness* and an alternative to love for others has pervaded theology, philosophy, and popular thought; the same doctrine has been rationalized in scientific language in Freud's theory of narcissism. Freud's concept presupposes a fixed amount of libido. In the infant, all of the libido has the child's own person as its objective, the stage of *primary narcissism* as Freud calls it. During the individual's development, the libido is shifted from one's own person toward other objects. If a person is blocked in his *object-relationships* the libido is withdrawn from the objects and returned to his or her own person; this is called *secondary narcissism*. According to Freud, the more love I turn toward the outside world the less love is left for myself, and vice versa. He thus describes the phenomenon of love as an impoverishment of one's self-love because all libido is turned to an object outside oneself.[1]

Fromm, however, disagrees with Freud's analysis. He concerned himself solely with love of humans, but as "ecosophers" we find the notions of "care, respect, responsibility, knowledge" applicable to living beings in the wide sense.

> Love of others and love of ourselves are not alternatives. On the contrary, an attitude of love toward themselves will be found in all those who are capable of loving others. Love, in principle, is indivisible as far as the connection between *objects* and one's own self is concerned. Genuine love is an expression of productiveness and implies care, respect, responsibility, and knowledge. It is not an *effect* in the sense of being effected by somebody, but an active striving for the growth and happiness of the loved person, rooted in one's own capacity to love.[2]

Fromm is very instructive about unselfishness—diametrically opposite to selfishness, but still based upon alienation and a narrow perception of self. What he says applies also to persons experiencing sacrifice of themselves.

The nature of unselfishness becomes particularly apparent in its effect on others and most frequently, in our culture, in the effect the "unselfish" mother has on her children. She believes that by her unselfishness her children will experience what it means to be loved and in turn to learn what it means to love. The effect of her unselfishness, however, does not at all correspond to her expectations. The children do not show the happiness of persons who are convinced that they are loved; they are anxious, tense, afraid of the mother's disapproval, and anxious to live up to her expectations. Usually, they are affected by their mother's hidden hostility against life, which they sense rather than recognize, and eventually become imbued with it themselves:

> If one has a chance to study the effect of a mother with genuine self-love, one can see that there is nothing more conducive to giving a child the experience of what love, joy, and happiness are than being loved by a mother who loves herself.[3]

From the viewpoint of ecophilosophy, the point is this: We need environmental ethics, but when people feel they unselfishly give up, even sacrifice, their interest in order to show love for nature, this is probably in the long run a treacherous basis for ecology. Through broader identification, they may come to see their own interest served by environmental protection, through genuine self-love, love of a widened and deepened self.

*

As a student and admirer since 1930 of Gandhi's nonviolent direct action, I am inevitably influenced by his metaphysics which furnished him tremendously powerful motivation to keep on going until his death. His supreme aim, as he saw it, was not only India's *political* liberation. He led crusades against extreme poverty, caste suppression, and against terror in the name of religion. These crusades were necessary, but the liberation of the individual human being was his highest end. Hearing Gandhi's description of his ultimate goal may sound strange to many of us.

> What I want to achieve—what I have been striving and pining to achieve these thirty years—is self-realization, to see God face to face, to attain *Moksha* (Liberation). I live and move and have my being in pursuit of that goal. All that I do by way of speaking and writing, and all my ventures in the political field, are directed to this same end.[4]

This sounds individualistic to the Western mind, a common misunderstanding. If the self Gandhi is speaking about were the ego or the "narrow" self (*jiva*) of egocentric interest, of narrow ego gratifications, why then work for the poor? For him it is the supreme or universal Self—the *atman*—that is to be realized. Paradoxically, it seems, he tries to reach self-realization through *selfless action*, that is, through reduction of the dominance of the narrow self or ego. Through the wider Self every living being is connected intimately, and from this intimacy follows the capacity of *identification* and as its natural consequences, the practice of nonviolence. No moralizing is necessary, just as we do not require moralizing to make us breathe. We need to cultivate our insight, to quote Gandhi again: "The rock-bottom foundation of the technique for achieving the power of nonviolence is belief in the essential oneness of all life."

Historically we have seen how ecological preservation is nonviolent at its very core. Gandhi notes:

> I believe in *advaita* (non-duality), I believe in the essential unity of man and, for that matter, of all that lives. Therefore I believe that if one man gains spirituality, the whole world gains with him and, if one man fails, the whole world fails to that extent.[5]

Some people might consider Gandhi extreme in his personal consideration for the self-realization of living beings other than humans. He traveled with a goat to satisfy his need for milk. This was part of a nonviolent witness against certain cruel features in the Hindu way of milking cows. Furthermore, some European companions who lived with Gandhi in his ashram were taken aback that he let snakes, scorpions and spiders move unhindered into their bedrooms—animals fulfilling their lives. He even prohibited people from having a stock of medicines against poisonous bites. He believed in the possibility of satisfactory coexistence and he proved right. There were no accidents. Ashram people would naturally look into their shoes for scorpions before putting them on. Even when moving over the floor in darkness one could easily avoid trampling on one's fellow beings. Thus, Gandhi recognized a basic, common right to live and blossom, to self-realization applicable to any being having interests or needs. Gandhi made manifest the internal relation between self-realization, nonviolence and what is sometimes called biospherical egalitarianism.

In the environment in which I grew up, I heard that what is important in life is to *be* somebody—usually implying to outdo others, to be victorious in comparison of abilities. This conception of the meaning and goal of life is especially dangerous today in the context of vast international economic competition. The law of supply and demand of separate, isolatable "goods and services" independent of real needs, must not be made to reign over increasing areas of our lives. The ability to cooperate, to work with people, to make them feel good *pays* of course in a fiercely individualist society, and high positions may require it. These virtues are often subordinated to the career, to the basic norms of narrow ego fulfillment, not to a self-realization worth the name. To identify self-realization with ego indicates a vast underestimation of the human self.

According to a usual translation of Pali or Sanskrit, Buddha taught his disciples that the human *mind* should embrace all living things as a mother cares for her son, her only son. For some it is not meaningful or possible for a human *self* to embrace all living things, then the usual translation can remain. We ask only that your *mind* embrace all living beings, and that you maintain an intention to care, feel and act with compassion.

If the Sanskrit word *atman* is translated into English, it is instructive to note that this term has the basic meaning of *self* rather than *mind* or *spirit*,

as you see in translations. The superiority of the translation using the word *self* stems from the consideration that *if* your *self* in the wide sense embraces another being, you need no moral exhortation to show care. You care for yourself without feeling any moral pressure to do it—unless you have succumbed to a neurosis of some kind, developed self-destructive tendencies, or hate yourself.

The Australian ecological feminist Patsy Hallen uses a formula close to that of Buddha: "we are here to embrace rather than conquer the world." Notice that the term *world* is used here rather than *living beings.* I suspect that our thinking need not proceed from the notion of living being to that of the world. If we can conceive of reality or the world we live in as alive in a wide, not easily defined sense then there will be no non-living beings to care for!

If "self-realization" today is associated with life-long narrow ego gratification, isn't it inaccurate to use this term for self-realization in the widely different sense of Gandhi, or less religiously loaded, as a term for the widening and deepening of the self so it embraces all life forms? Perhaps it is. But I think the very popularity of the term makes people listen for a moment and feel safe. In that moment the notion of a greater Self can be introduced, contending that if people equate self-realization with narrow ego fulfillment, they seriously *underestimate* themselves. We are much greater, deeper, more generous and capable of dignity and joy than we think! A wealth of non-competitive joys is open to us!

I have another important reason for inviting people to think in terms of deepening and widening their selves, starting with narrow ego gratification as the crudest, but inescapable starting point. It has to do with the notion usually placed as the opposite of egoism, namely the notion of *altruism*. The Latin term *ego* has as its opposite the *alter*. Altruism implies that *ego* sacrifices its interest in favour of the other, the *alter*. The motivation is primarily that of duty; it is said that we *ought* to love others as strongly as we love ourself.

What humankind is capable of loving from mere duty or more generally from moral exhortation is, unfortunately, very limited. From the Renaissance to the Second World War about four hundred cruel wars have been fought by Christian nations, usually for the flimsiest of reasons. It seems to me that in the future more emphasis has to be given to the conditions which naturally widen and deepen our self. With a sufficiently wide and deep sense of self, ego and alter as opposites are eliminated stage by stage as the distinctions are transcended.

Early in life, the social *self* is sufficiently developed so that we do not prefer to eat a big cake alone. We share the cake with our family and friends. We identify with these people sufficiently to see our joy in their joy, and to see our disappointment in theirs. Now is the time to share with all life on our maltreated earth by deepening our identification with all life-forms, with the ecosystems, and with Gaia, this fabulous, old planet of ours.

The philosopher Immanuel Kant introduced a pair of contrasting concepts which deserve extensive use in our effort to live harmoniously in, for, and of nature: the concept of *moral* act and that of *beautiful* act. Moral acts are acts motivated by the intention to follow moral laws, at whatever cost, that is, to do our moral duty solely out of respect for that duty. Therefore, the supreme indication of our success in performing a pure, moral act is that we do it completely against our inclination, that we hate to do it, but are compelled by our respect for moral law. Kant was deeply awed by two phenomena, "the heaven with its stars above me and the moral law within me."

If we do something we should because of a moral law, but do it out of inclination and with pleasure—what then? If we do what is right because of positive inclination, then, according to Kant, we perform a *beautiful* act. My point is that in environmental affairs we should primarily try to influence people toward beautiful acts by finding ways to work on their inclinations rather than their morals. Unhappily, the extensive moralizing within the ecological movement has given the public the false impression that they are primarily asked to sacrifice, to show more responsibility, more concern, and better morals. As I see it we need the immense variety of sources of joy opened through increased sensitivity toward the richness and diversity of life, through the profound cherishing of free natural landscapes. We all can contribute to this individually, and it is also a question of politics, local and global. Part of the joy stems from the consciousness of our intimate relation to something bigger than our own ego, something which has endured for millions of years and is worth continued life for millions of years. The requisite care flows naturally if the self is widened and deepened so that protection of free nature is felt and conceived of as protection of our very selves.

What I am suggesting is the supremacy of ecological ontology and a higher realism over environmental ethics as a means of invigorating the ecology movement in the years to come. If reality is experienced by the ecological Self, our behavior *naturally* and beautifully follows norms of strict environmental ethics. We certainly need to hear about our ethical shortcomings from time to time, but we change more easily through encouragement and a deepened perception of reality and our own *self*, that is, through a deepened realism. How that is to be brought about is too large a question for me to deal with here. But it will clearly be more a question of community therapy than community science: we must find and develop therapies which heal our relations with the widest community, that of all living beings.

Notes

1. Erich Fromm, "Selfishness, Self-love, and Self-interest," in *The Self: Explorations in Personal Growth,* edited by Clark E. Moustakas (New York: Harper, 1956), p. 58.

2. Ibid., page 59.

3. Gandhi quotations are taken from Arne Naess, *Gandhi and Group Conflict* (Oslo, Norway: Universitetsforlaget, 1974), p. 35 where the metaphysics of self-realization are treated more thoroughly in that work.

4. Ibid.

5. Ibid.

SIDELIGHT: Do What's Natural, You Say?

We live in an age in which some marketing specialists exploit a certain revulsion against the plastic, that is, what is quintessentially artificial, a matter of artifice, or humanmade. Correlatively there is a certain desire to live more naturally. "Natural" fibers and "all-natural" food are increasingly in demand. Indeed, the term 'natural' seems honorific; conversely, the term 'unnatural' is frequently used pejoratively, that is, implying that the thing so labeled is bad or wrong. Is there any rational basis for associating the natural with the right and the unnatural with the wrong? In particular, should we scan the processes of nature to find normative models, i.e., types of behavior that we should emulate? There are indeed subtleties to this topic, which we shall address briefly.

There is a broad sense of "natural" in which anything that happens is part of the nature of the world as we know it. In this sense any action is natural, so none is unnatural. Thus, Jeffrey Dahmer's cannibalizing was natural, as was the mass destruction of Jews and Gypsies by the Nazis, or the mass killing of hundreds of thousands of Japanese by the American bombing of Hiroshima and Nagasaki.

Typically, however, we identify certain actions or events, from the set of all actions or events, by using labels such as 'natural' or 'unnatural'; that is, we contrast some events with others when we say only of some that they are natural or of others that they are unnatural. Thus, by 'natural' we do not normally mean "whatever happens." Although we humans are without question a part of nature, by 'natural' we often mean that which occurs without deliberate human intervention or a by-product of such. Hence, the mass extinction of 65 million years ago, the glaciations of the last Ice Age, the tides, the ocean currents, the revolution of the earth about the sun, volcanic eruptions, typhoons, photosynthesis, or even the striking of the earth by a meteor are, or would be, natural occurrences. Some of these events may be tragic, but there is no obvious connection between the fact that they are natural and their assessment as good or bad. Natural processes are extremely wasteful of life and potential life; in the ejaculation of a male human, enough sperm are produced to inseminate several hundred million eggs; of the offspring produced by a single member of some species only a tiny fraction can survive. This is not what one would expect of a world guided by the Protestant God of "waste not, want not."[1]

Among "unnatural" events, that is, those resulting from human action, are a wildly diverse lot: the expected leaking of plutonium into arctic waters above Norway from a deteriorating, sunken Russian submarine (not to worry: it will cease to be radioactive by the year 26000), the selling of children into prostitution, destruction of 70 percent of the world's forests, the rescue of millions of people from the ravages of disease and injury, the heroic resistance against Nazi and fascist movements, the music of Mozart, the paintings of Seurat, Matisse, or van Gogh, and so on. *All* such behavior is unnatural if by the term one means involving human action or the result of such.

May we turn to animal behavior for inspiration as to how to live (as if we are not animals and as if we are not part of nature)? Let us consider some interesting examples revealed by recent studies of "animal behavior" (some not to be read just before meals perhaps). Among nonhuman animals are many examples of wonderfully cooperative behavior. We find the analogue of monogamy among geese, swans, angelfish, beavers, and soldier beetles. Among owl monkeys males rear the offspring and females search for food.[2] We focus elsewhere. Burying beetle couples prepare the corpses of small animals for their young to eat. When the young are born, the parents eat the numbers down to a size that the food supply can support (perhaps they have read Garrett Hardin on "carrying capacity"); thus, cannibalism gives the surviving youngsters a "head start" so to speak. Or would you rather be a shark, specifically a tiger shark? Of the 100 eggs formed by the shark after mating, the first one to reach the uterus survives by eating all the other embryos and unfertilized eggs as they are released.[3] So among sharks it is perfectly natural to kill off one's "unborn siblings." Are all mothers nourishing? Not among the Emu; they abandon their offspring at the slightest sign of danger.[4]

Some other examples. Two woodpeckers often share a nest, but when one lays an egg the other destroys it (perhaps to destroy the advantage the first one has). This continues until both lay an egg at the same time. A female praying mantis may start chewing off her partner's head while he is still mating. Among Australian red-backed spiders, the male, halfway through the mating process, will jump into the female's jaws and allow himself to be eaten a bit; when he is finished mating, he surrenders for the last time to her waiting fangs. For the Australian red-backed spider, this is doing what comes naturally. The female Ormia fly can detect a male cricket's sounds, drop down on it, and deposit on it a squirming maggot that bores into the cricket and eats it. The mother fly may have an extra incentive to succeed: if she fails, the hungry maggots begin to devour her from the inside out. So, perhaps nature won't do as a guide to family values. Sometimes, it seems, we *ought* to be unnatural. We note in passing that in the Roman Catholic tradition, homosexuality, masturbation, and heterosexual sex without the possibility of procreation are unnatural, and hence, it is implied, morally wrong (recall the discussion of natural law in the Introduction to Ethical Theory). In this regard various instances of homosexual behavior can be found among nonhuman creatures; e.g., bulls, cows, cats, rams, goats, pigs, apes, and lions.[5] Further, homosexual pair bonding has been found among western gulls.[6] A comment by Alfred Kinsey and his co-workers is of interest: ". . . The sexual acts which are demonstrably part of the phylogenetic heritage of any species cannot be classified as acts contrary to nature, biologically unnatural, abnormal, or perverse."[7]

We encounter appeals to the assumption that what is natural is right and the claim that what is unnatural is wrong with regard to questions of sexual behavior, who should be dominant, the acceptability of biotechnology, debates over vegetarianism, and so on. Perhaps enough has been said to discourage ready acceptance of the key normative, often tacit, assumptions noted.

Notes

1. The apt expression is due to David Hull in his introduction to Lamarck's philosophy.

2. Facts about monogamy are derived from a column entitled "The Kinsey Report," by June Reinisch in the *News and Observer* (September 10, 1987) Raleigh, North Carolina.

3. For this discussion we drew on an article from the *New York Times*, "In Some Species, Eating Your Own Is Good Sense" (September 29, 1992), by Carol Kaesuk Yoon.

4. See the review by Rona Cherry of *Females of the Species*, by Bettyann Kevles (Cambridge: Harvard University Press), found in the October 5, 1986, issue of the *New York Times Book Review*.

5. See the reference to the Kinsey studies in the useful article by James Weinrich, "Is Homosexuality Biologically Natural?" in *Homosexuality: Social, Psychological, and Biological Issues.* (Beverly Hills, CA: Sage Publications, 1982), p. 198.

6. Ibid., p. 200.

7. See Weinrich, op. cit., p. 204.

Social Ecology Versus Deep Ecology

Murray Bookchin

Beyond 'Environmentalism'

The environmental movement has travelled a long way beyond those annual "Earth Day" festivals when millions of school kids were ritualistically mobilized to clean up streets and their parents were scolded by Arthur Godfrey, Barry Commoner, and Paul Ehrlich. The movement has gone beyond a na-

ive belief that patchwork reforms and solemn vows by EPA bureaucrats will seriously arrest the insane pace at which we are tearing down the planet.

This shopworn "Earth Day" approach toward "engineering" nature so that we can ravage the Earth with minimal effects on ourselves—an approach that I called "environmentalism"—has shown signs of giving way to a more searching and

Socialist Review, Vol. 88, No. 3 (1988), 11–29. Published by Duke University. Reprinted with permission of the publisher.

radical mentality. Today, the new word in vogue is "ecology"—be it "deep ecology," "human ecology," "biocentric ecology," "anti-humanist ecology," or, to use a term uniquely rich in meaning, "*social* ecology."

Happily, the new relevance of the word "ecology" reveals a growing dissatisfaction with attempts to use our vast ecological problems for cheaply spectacular and politically manipulative ends. Our forests disappear due to mindless cutting and increasing acid rain; the ozone layer thins out from widespread use of fluorocarbons; toxic dumps multiply all over the planet; highly dangerous, often radioactive pollutants enter into our air, water, and food chains. These innumerable hazards threaten the integrity of life itself, raising far more basic issues than can be resolved by "Earth Day" cleanups and faint-hearted changes in environmental laws.

For good reason, more and more people are trying to go beyond the vapid "environmentalism" of the early 1970s and toward an *ecological* approach: one that is rooted in an ecological philosophy, ethics, sensibility, image of nature, and, ultimately, an ecological movement that will transform our domineering market society into a nonhierarchical cooperative one that will live in harmony with nature, because its members live in harmony with each other. They are beginning to sense that there is a tie-in between the way people deal with each other as social beings—men with women, old with young, rich with poor, white with people of color, first world with third, elites with "masses"—and the way they deal with nature.

The questions that now face us are: what do we really mean by an *ecological* approach? What is a *coherent* ecological philosophy, ethics, and movement? How can the answers to these questions and many others *fit together* so that they form a meaningful and creative whole? If we are not to repeat all the mistakes of the early seventies with their hoopla about "population control," their latent anti-feminism, elitism, arrogance, and ugly authoritarian tendencies, so we must honestly and seriously appraise the new tendencies that today go under the name of one or another form of "ecology."

Two Conflicting Tendencies

Let us agree from the outset that the word "ecology" is no magic term that unlocks the real secret of our abuse of nature. It is a word that can be as easily abused, distorted, and tainted as words like "democracy" and "freedom." Nor does the word "ecology" put us all—whoever "we" may be—in the same boat against environmentalists who are simply trying to make a rotten society work by dressing it in green leaves and colorful flowers, while ignoring the deep-seated *roots* of our ecological problems.

It is time to face the fact that there are differences within the so-called "ecology movement" of the present time that are as serious as those between the "environmentalism" and "ecologism" of the early seventies. There are barely disguised racists, survivalists, macho Daniel Boones, and outright social reactionaries who use the word "ecology" to express their views, just as there are deeply concerned naturalists, communitarians, social radicals, and feminists who use the word "ecology" to express theirs.

The differences between these two tendencies in the so-called "ecology movement" consist not only in quarrels over theory, sensibility, and ethics. They have far-reaching *practical* and *political* consequences on the way we view nature, "humanity," and ecology. Most significantly, they concern how we propose to *change* society and by what *means.*

The greatest differences that are emerging within the so-called "ecology movement" of our day are between a vague, formless, often self-contradictory ideology called "deep ecology" and a socially oriented body of ideas best termed "social ecology." Deep ecology has parachuted into our midst quite recently from the Sunbelt's bizarre mix of Hollywood and Disneyland, spiced with homilies from Taoism, Buddhism, spiritualism, reborn Christianity, and, in some cases, eco-fascism. Social ecology, on the other hand, draws its inspiration from such radical decentralist thinkers as Peter Kropotkin, William Morris, and Paul Goodman, among many others who have challenged society's vast hierarchical, sexist, class-ruled, statist, and militaristic apparatus.

Bluntly speaking, deep ecology, despite all its social rhetoric, has no real sense that our ecological problems have their roots in society and in social problems. It preaches a gospel of a kind of "original sin" that accuses a vague species called "humanity"—as though people of color were equatable with whites, women with men, the third world with the first, the poor with the rich, and the exploited with their exploiters. This vague, undifferentiated humanity is seen as an ugly "anthropocentric" thing—presumably a malignant product of natural evolution—that is "overpopulating" the planet, "devouring" its resources, destroying its wildlife and the biosphere. It assumes that some vague domain called "nature" stands opposed to a constellation of non-natural things called "human beings," with their "technology," "minds," "society," and so on. Formulated largely by privileged white male academics, deep ecology has brought sincere naturalists like Paul Shepard into the same company with patently anti-humanist and macho mountain-men like David Foreman, who writes in *Earth First!*—a Tucson-based journal that styles itself as the voice of a wilderness-oriented movement of the same name—that "humanity" is a cancer in the world of life.

It is easy to forget that this same kind of crude eco-brutalism led Hitler to fashion theories of blood and soil that led to the transport of millions of people to murder camps like Auschwitz. The same eco-brutalism now reappears a half-century later among self-professed deep ecologists who believe that famines are nature's "population control" and immigration into the US should be restricted in order to preserve "our" ecological resources.

Simply Living, an Australian periodical, published this sort of eco-brutalism as part of a laudatory interview of David Foreman by Professor Bill Devall, co-author of *Deep Ecology,* the manifesto of the deep ecology movement. Foreman, who exuberantly expressed his commitment to deep ecology, frankly informs Devall that

> When I tell people how the worst thing we could do in Ethiopia is to give aid—the best thing would be to just let nature seek its own balance, to let the people there just starve—they think this is monstrous. . . . Likewise, letting the USA be an overflow valve for problems in Latin America is not solving a thing. It's just putting more pressure on the resources we have in the USA.

One could reasonably ask what it means for "nature to seek its own balance" in a part of the world where agribusiness, colonialism, and exploitation have ravaged a once culturally and ecologically stable area like East Africa. And who is this all-American "our" that owns the "resources we

have in the USA"? Is it the ordinary people who are driven by sheer need to cut timber, mine ores, operate nuclear power plants? Or are they the giant corporations that are not only wrecking the good old USA, but have produced the main problems in Latin America that are sending Indian folk across the Rio Grande? As an ex-Washington lobbyist and political huckster, David Foreman need not be expected to answer these subtle questions in a radical way. But what is truly surprising is the reaction—more precisely, the *lack* of any reaction—which marked Professor Devall's behavior. Indeed, the interview was notable for his almost reverential introduction and description of Foreman.

What Is "Deep Ecology"?

Deep ecology is enough of a "black hole" of half-digested and ill-formed ideas that a man like Foreman can easily express utterly vicious notions and still sound like a fiery pro-ecology radical. The very words "deep ecology" clue us into the fact that we are not dealing with a body of clear ideas, but with an ideological toxic dump. Does it make sense, for example, to counterpose "deep ecology" with "superficial ecology" as though the word "ecology" were applicable to *everything* that involves environmental issues? Does it not completely degrade the rich meaning of the word "ecology" to append words like "shallow" and "deep" to it? Arne Naess, the pontiff of deep ecology—who, together with George Sessions and Bill Devall, inflicted this vocabulary upon us—have taken a pregnant word—ecology—and stripped it of any inner meaning and integrity by designating the most pedestrian environmentalists as "ecologists," albeit "shallow" ones, in contrast to their notion of "deep."

This is not an example of mere wordplay. It tells us something about the mindset that exists among these "deep" thinkers. To parody the word "shallow" and "deep ecology" is to show not only the absurdity of this terminology but to reveal the superficiality of its inventors. In fact, this kind of absurdity tells us more than we realize about the confusion Naess-Sessions-Devall, not to mention eco-brutalists like Foreman, have introduced into the current ecology movement. Indeed, this trio relies very heavily on the ease with which people forget the history of the ecology movement, the way in which the wheel is reinvented every few years by newly arrived individuals who, well-meaning as they may be, often accept a crude version of highly developed ideas that appeared earlier in a richer context and tradition of ideas. At worst, they shatter such contexts and traditions, picking out tasty pieces that become utterly distorted in a new, utterly alien framework. No regard is paid by such "deep thinkers" to the fact that *the new context in which an idea is placed may utterly change the meaning of the idea itself.* German "National Socialism" was militantly "anti-capitalist." But its "anti-capitalism" was placed in a strongly racist, imperialist, and seemingly "naturalist" context which extolled wilderness, a crude biologism, and anti-rationalism—features one finds in latent or explicit form in Sessions' and Devall's *Deep Ecology.*[1]

Neither Naess, Sessions, nor Devall have written a single line about decentralization, a nonhierarchical society, democracy, small-scale communities, local autonomy, mutual aid, communalism, and tolerance that was not already conceived in painstaking detail and brilliant contextualization by Peter Kropotkin a century ago. But what the boys from Ecotopia do is to totally recontextualize the framework of these ideas, bringing in personalities and notions that basically change their radical libertarian thrust. *Deep Ecology* mingles Woody Guthrie, a Communist Party centralist who no more believed in decentralization than Stalin, with Paul Goodman, an anarchist who would have been mortified to be placed in the same tradition with Guthrie. In philosophy, the book also intermingles Spinoza, a Jew in spirit if not in religious commitment, with Heidegger, a former member of the Nazi party in spirit as well as ideological affiliation—all in the name of a vague word called "process philosophy." Almost opportunistic in their use of catch-words and what Orwell called "doublespeak," "process philosophy" makes it possible for Sessions-Devall to add Alfred North Whitehead to their list of ideological ancestors because he called his ideas "processual."

One could go on indefinitely describing this sloppy admixture of "ancestors," philosophical traditions, social pedigrees, and religions that often have nothing in common with each other and, properly conceived, are commonly in sharp opposition with each other. Thus, a reactionary like Thomas Malthus and the tradition he spawned is celebrated with the same enthusiasm in *Deep Ecology* as Henry Thoreau, a radical libertarian who fostered a highly humanistic tradition. Eclecticism would be too mild a word for this kind of hodgepodge, one that seems shrewdly calculated to embrace everyone under the rubric of deep ecology who is prepared to reduce ecology to a religion rather than a systematic and critical body of ideas. This kind of "ecological" thinking surfaces in an appendix to the Devall-Sessions book, called *Ecosophy T,* by Arne Naess, who regales us with flow diagrams and corporate-type tables of organization that have more in common with logical positivist forms of exposition (Naess, in fact, was an acolyte of this school of thought for years) than anything that could be truly called organic philosophy.

If we look beyond the spiritual eco-babble and examine the *context* in which demands like decentralization, small-scale communities, local autonomy, mutual aid, communalism, and tolerance are placed, the blurred images that Sessions and Devall create come into clearer focus. These demands are not intrinsically ecological or emancipatory. Few societies were more decentralized than European feudalism, which was structured around small-scale communities, mutual aid, and the communal use of land. Local autonomy was highly prized, and autarchy formed the economic key to feudal communities. Yet few societies were more hierarchical. The manorial economy of the Middle Ages placed a high premium on autarchy or "self-sufficiency" and spirituality. Yet oppression was often intolerable and the great mass of people who belonged to that society lived in utter subjugation by their "betters" and the nobility.

If "nature-worship," with its bouquet of wood sprites, animistic fetishes, fertility rites and other such ceremonies, paves the way to an ecological sensibility and society, then it would be hard to understand how ancient Egypt, with its animal deities and all-presiding goddesses, managed to become one of the most hierarchical and oppressive societies in the ancient world. The Nile River, which provided the "life-giving" waters of the valley, was used in a highly ecological manner. Yet the entire society was structured around the oppression of millions of serfs by opulent nobles, such that one wonders how notions of spirituality can be given priority over the need for a critical evaluation of social structures.

Even if one grants the need for a new sensibility and outlook—a point that has been made repeatedly in the literature of social ecology—one can look behind even this limited context of deep ecology to a still broader context. The love affair of deep ecology with Malthusian doctrines, a spirituality that emphasizes self-effacement, a flirtation with a *super*naturalism that stands in flat contradiction to the refreshing naturalism that ecology has introduced into social theory, a crude positivism in the spirit of Naess—all work against a truly organic dialectic so needed to understand *development*. We shall see that all the bumper-sticker demands like decentralization, small-scale communities, local autonomy, mutual aid, communalism, tolerance, and even an avowed opposition to hierarchy, go awry when we place them in the larger context of anti-humanism and "biocentrism" that mark the authentic ideological infrastructure of deep ecology.

The Art of Evading Society

The seeming ideological "tolerance" and pluralism which deep ecology celebrates has a sinister function of its own. It not only reduces richly nuanced ideas and conflicting traditions to their lowest common denominator; it legitimates extremely primitivistic and reactionary notions in the company of authentically radical contexts and traditions.

Deep ecology reduces people from social beings to a simple species—to zoological entities that are interchangeable with bears, bisons, deer, or, for that matter, fruit flies and microbes. The fact that people can consciously change themselves and society, indeed enhance that natural world in a free ecological society, is dismissed as "humanism." Deep ecology essentially ignores the social nature of humanity and the social origins of the ecological crises.

This "zoologization" of human beings and of society yields sinister results. The role of capitalism with its competitive "grow or die" market economy—an economy that would devour the biosphere whether there were 10 billion people on the planet or 10 million—is simply vaporized into a vapid spiritualism. Taoist and Buddhist pieties replace the need for social and economic analysis, and self-indulgent encounter groups replace the

need for political organization and action. Above all, deep ecologists explain the destruction of human beings in terms of the same "natural laws" that are said to govern the population vicissitudes of lemmings. The fact that major reductions of populations would not diminish levels of production and the destruction of the biosphere in a capitalist economy totally eludes Devall, Sessions, and their followers.

In failing to emphasize the unique characteristics of human societies and to give full due to the self-reflective role of human consciousness, deep ecologists essentially evade the *social* roots of the ecological crisis. Deep ecology contains no history of the emergence of society out of nature, a crucial development that brings social theory into organic contact with ecological theory. It presents no explanation of—indeed, it reveals no interest in—the emergence of hierarchy out of society, of classes out of hierarchy, of the state out of classes—in short, the highly graded social as well as ideological developments which are at the roots of the ecological problem.

Instead, we not only lose sight of the social differences that fragment "humanity" into a host of human beings—men and women, ethnic groups, oppressors and oppressed—we lose sight of the individual self in an unending flow of eco-babble that preaches the "realization of self-in-Self where the 'Self' stands for organic wholeness." More of the same cosmic eco-babble appears when we are informed that the "phrase 'one' includes not only men, an individual human, but all humans, grizzly bears, whole rain forest ecosystems, mountains and rivers, the tiniest microbes in the soil, and so on."

On Selfhood and Viruses

Such flippant abstractions of human individuality are extremely dangerous. Historically, a "Self" that absorbs all real existential selves has been used from time immemorial to absorb individual uniqueness and freedom into a supreme "Individual" who heads the state, churches of various sorts, adoring congregations, and spellbound constituencies. The purpose is the same, no matter how much such a "Self" is dressed up in ecological, naturalistic, and "biocentric" attributes. The Paleolithic shaman, in reindeer skins and horns, is the predecessor of the Pharaoh, the Buddha, and, in more recent times, of Hitler, Stalin, and Mussolini.

That the egotistical, greedy, and soloist bourgeois "self" has always been a repellent being goes without saying, and deep ecology as put forth by Devall and Sessions makes the most of it. But is there not a free, independently minded, ecologically concerned, idealistic self with a unique personality that can think of itself as different from "whales, grizzly bears, whole rain forest ecosystems (no less!), mountains and rivers, the tiniest microbes in the soil, and so on"? Is it not indispensable, in fact, for the individual self to disengage itself from a Pharonic "Self," discover its own capacities and uniqueness, and acquire a sense of personality, of self-control and self-direction—all traits indispensable for the achievement of *freedom*? Here, one can imagine Heidegger grimacing with satisfaction at the sight of this self-effacing and passive personality so yielding that it can easily be shaped, distorted, and manipulated by a new "ecological" state machinery with a supreme "Self" at its head. And this all in the name of a "biocentric equality" that is slowly reworked as it has been so often in history, into a social hierarchy. From Shaman to Monarch, from Priest or Priestess to Dictator, our warped social development has been marked by "nature worshippers" and their ritual Supreme Ones who produced unfinished individuals at best or deindividuated the "self-in-Self" at worst, often in the name of the "Great Connected Whole" (to use *exactly* the language of the Chinese ruling classes who kept their peasantry in abject servitude, as Leon E. Stover points out in his *The Cultural Ecology of Chinese Civilization*).

What makes this eco-babble especially dangerous today is that we are already living in a period of massive de-individuation. This is not because deep ecology or Taoism is making any serious inroads into our own cultural ecology, but because the mass media, the commodity culture, and a market society are "reconnecting" us into an increasingly depersonalized "whole" whose essence is passivity and a chronic vulnerability to economic and political manipulation. It is not an excess of "selfhood" from which we are suffering, but rather the surrender of personality to the security and control of corporations, centralized government, and the military. If "selfhood" is identified with a grasping, "anthropocentric," and devouring personality, these traits are to be found not so much among ordinary people, who basically sense they have no control over their destinies, but among the giant corporations and state leaders who are not only plundering the planet, but also robbing from women, people of color, and the underprivileged. It is not deindividuation that the oppressed of the world require, but *re*individuation that will transform them into active agents in the task of remaking society and arresting the growing totalitarianism that threatens to homogenize us all into a Western version of the "Great Connected Whole."

We are also confronted with the delicious "and so on" that follows the "tiniest microbes in the soil" with which our deep ecologists identify the "Self." Taking their argument to its logical extreme, one might ask: why stop with the "tiniest microbes in the soil" and ignore the leprosy microbe, the viruses that give us smallpox, polio, and, more recently, AIDS? Are they, too, not part of "all organisms and entities in the ecosphere ... of the interrelated whole ... equal in intrinsic worth ... ," as Devall and Sessions remind us in their effluvium of eco-babble? Naess, Devall, and Sessions rescue themselves by introducing a number of highly debatable qualifiers:

> The slogan of 'noninterference' does not imply that humans should not modify some ecosystems as do other species. Humans have modified the Earth and will probably continue to do so. At issue is the nature and extent of such interference.

One does not leave the muck of deep ecology without having mud all over one's feet. Exactly *who* is to decide the "nature" of human "interference" in nature and the "extent" to which it can be done? What are "some" of the ecosystems we can modify and which ones are not subject to human "interference"? Here, again, we encounter the key problem that deep ecology poses for serious, ecologically concerned people: the *social* bases of our ecological problems and the role of the human species in the evolutionary scheme of things.

Implicit in deep ecology is the notion that a "Humanity" exists that accurses the natural world; that individual selfhood must be transformed into a cosmic "Selfhood" that essentially transcends the person and his or her uniqueness. Even nature is not spared from a kind of static, prepositional logic that is cultivated by the logical positivists. "Nature," in deep ecology and David Foreman's interpretation of it, becomes a kind of scenic view, a spectacle to be admired around the campfire. It is not viewed as an *evolutionary* development that is cumulative and *includes* the human species.

The problems deep ecology and biocentricity raise have not gone unnoticed in the more thoughtful press in England. During a discussion of "biocentric ethics" in *The New Scientist* 69 (1976), for example, Bernard Dixon observed that no "logical line can be drawn" between the conservation of whales, gentians, and flamingoes on the one hand and the extinction of pathogenic microbes like the smallpox virus. At which point David Ehrenfeld, in his *Arrogance of Humanism*,[2]—a work that is so selective and tendentious in its use of quotations that it should validly be renamed "The Arrogance of Ignorance"—cutely observes that the smallpox virus is "an endangered species." One wonders what to do about the AIDS virus if a vaccine or therapy should threaten its "survival"? Further, given the passion for perpetuating the "ecosystem" of every species, one wonders how smallpox and AIDS viruses should be preserved? In test tubes? Laboratory cultures? Or, to be truly "ecological," in their "native habitat," the human body? In which case, idealistic acolytes of deep ecology should be invited to offer their own bloodstreams in the interests of "biocentric equality." Certainly, "if nature should be permitted to take its course"—as Foreman advises for Ethiopians and Indian peasants—plagues, famines, suffering, wars, and perhaps even lethal asteroids of the kind that exterminated the great reptiles of the Mesozoic should not be kept from defacing the purity of "first nature" by the intervention of human ingenuity and—yes!—*technology*. With so much absurdity to unscramble, one can indeed get heady, almost dizzy, with a sense of polemical intoxication.

At root, the eclecticism which turns deep ecology into a goulash of notions and moods is insufferably reformist and surprisingly environmentalist—all its condemnations of "superficial ecology" aside. Are you, perhaps, a mild-mannered liberal? Then do not fear: Devall and Sessions give a patronizing nod to "reform legislation," "coalitions," "protests," the "women's movement" (this earns all of ten lines in their "Minority Tradition and Direct Action" essay), "working in the Christian tradition," "questioning technology" (a hammering re-

mark, if there ever was one), "working in Green politics" (which faction, the "fundies" or the "realos"?). In short, everything can be expected in so "cosmic" a philosophy. Anything seems to pass through deep ecology's donut hole: anarchism at one extreme and eco-fascism at the other. Like the fast food emporiums that make up our culture, deep ecology is the fast food of quasi-radical environmentalists.

Despite its pretense of "radicality," deep ecology is more "New Age" and "Aquarian" than the environmentalist movements it denounces under those names. Indeed, the extent to which deep ecology accommodates itself to some of the worst features of the "dominant view" it professes to reject is seen with extraordinary clarity in one of its most fundamental and repeatedly asserted demands—namely, that the world's population must be drastically reduced, according to one of its devotees, to 500 million. If deep ecologists have even the faintest knowledge of the "population theorists" Devall and Sessions invoke with admiration—notably, Thomas Malthus, William Vogt, and Paul Ehrlich—then they would be obliged to add: by measures that are virtually eco-fascist. This specter clearly looms before us in Devall's and Sessions' sinister remark: ". . . the longer we wait [for population control], the more drastic will be the measures needed."

The "Deep" Malthusians

Devall and Sessions often write with smug assurance on issues they know virtually nothing about. This is most notably the case in the so-called "population debate," a debate that has raged for over two hundred years and more and involves explosive political and social issues that have pitted the most reactionary elements in English and American society against authentic radicals. In fact, the eco-babble which Devall and Sessions dump on us in only two paragraphs would require a full-sized volume of careful analysis to unravel.

Devall and Sessions hail Thomas Malthus (1766–1854) as a prophet whose warning "that human population growth would exponentially outstrip food production . . . was ignored by the rising tide of industrial/technological optimism." First of all, Thomas Malthus was not a prophet; he was an apologist for the misery that the Industrial Revolution was inflicting on the English peasantry and working classes. His utterly fallacious argument that population increases exponentially while food supplies increase arithmetically was not ignored by England's ruling classes; it was taken to heart and even incorporated into social Darwinism as an explanation of why oppression was a necessary feature of society and why the rich, the white imperialists, and the privileged were the "fittest" who were equipped to "survive"—needless to say, at the expense of the impoverished many. Written and directed in great part as an attack upon the liberatory vision of William Godwin, Malthus' mean-spirited *Essay on the Principle of Population* tried to demonstrate that hunger, poverty, disease, and premature death are *inevitable* precisely because population and food supply increase at different rates. Hence war, famines, and plagues (Malthus later added "moral restraint") were necessary to keep population down—needless to say, among the "lower orders of society," whom he singles out as the chief offenders of his inexorable population "laws."[3] Malthus, in effect, became the ideologue par excellence for the land-grabbing English nobility in its effort to dispossess the peasantry of their traditional common lands and for the English capitalists to work children, women, and men to death in the newly emergent "industrial/technological" factory system.

Malthusianism contributed in great part to that meanness of spirit that Charles Dickens captured in his famous novels, *Oliver Twist* and *Hard Times*. The doctrine, its author, and its overstuffed wealthy beneficiaries were bitterly fought by the great English anarchist, William Godwin, the pioneering socialist, Robert Owen, and the emerging Chartist movement of English workers in the early 19th century. However, Malthusianism was naively picked up by Charles Darwin to explain his theory of "natural selection." It then became the bedrock theory for the new *social* Darwinism, so very much in vogue in the late nineteenth and early twentieth centuries, which saw society as a "jungle" in which only the "fit" (usually, the rich and white) could "survive" at the expense of the "unfit" (usually, the poor and people of color). Malthus, in effect, had provided an ideology that justified class domination, racism, the degradation of women, and, ultimately, British imperialism.

Malthusianism was not only revived in Hitler's Third Reich; it also reemerged in the late 1940s, following the discoveries of antibiotics to control infectious diseases. Riding on the tide of the new Pax Americana after World War II, William F. Vogt and a whole bouquet of neo-Malthusians were to challenge the use of the new antibiotic discoveries to control disease and prevent death—as usual, mainly in Asia, Africa, and Latin America. Again, a new "population debate" erupted, with the Rockefeller interests and large corporate sharks aligning themselves with the neo-Malthusians, and caring people of every sort aligning themselves with third world theorists like Josua de Castro, who wrote damning, highly informed critiques of this new version of misanthropy.

Zero Population Growth fanatics in the early seventies literally polluted the environmental movement with demands for a government bureau to "control" population, advancing the infamous "triage" ethic, according to which various "underdeveloped" countries would be granted or refused aid on the basis of their compliance to population control measures. In *Food First*, Francis Moore Lappe and Joseph Collins have done a superb job in showing how hunger has its origins not in "natural" shortages of food or population growth, but in social and cultural dislocations. (It is notable that Devall and Sessions do *not* list this excellent book in their bibliography.) The book has to be read to understand the reactionary implications of deep ecology's demographic positions.

Demography is a highly ambiguous and ideologically charged social discipline that cannot be reduced to a mere numbers game in biological reproduction. Human beings are not fruit flies (the species which the neo-Malthusians love to cite). Their reproductive behavior is profoundly conditioned by cultural values, standards of living, social traditions, gender relations, religious beliefs, sociopolitical conflicts, and various socio-political expectations. Smash up a stable, precapitalist culture and throw its people off the land into city slums, and, due to demoralization, population may soar rather than decline. As Gandhi told the British, imperialism left India's wretched poor and homeless with little more in life than the immediate gratification provided by sex and an understandably numbed sense of personal, much less social, responsibility. Reduce women to mere reproductive factories and population rates will explode.

Conversely, provide people with decent lives, education, a sense of creative meaning in life, and, above all, expand the role of women in society—and population growth begins to stabilize and population rates even reverse their direction. Nothing more clearly reveals deep ecology's crude, often reactionary, and certainly superficial ideological framework—all its decentralist, antihierarchical, and "radical" rhetoric aside—than its suffocating "biological" treatment of the population issue and its inclusion of Malthus, Vogt, and Ehrlich in its firmament of prophets.

Not surprisingly, the *Earth First!* newsletter, whose editor professes to be an enthusiastic deep ecologist, carried an article titled "Population and AIDS" which advanced the obscene argument that AIDS is desirable as a means of population control. This was no spoof. It was earnestly argued and carefully reasoned in a Paleolithic sort of way. Not only will AIDS claim large numbers of lives, asserts the author (who hides under the pseudonym of "Miss Ann Thropy," a form of black humor that could also pass as an example of macho-male arrogance), but it "may cause a breakdown in technology (read: human food supply) and its export which could also decrease human population." These people feed on human disasters, suffering, and misery, preferably in third world countries where AIDS is by far a more monstrous problem than elsewhere.

We have little reason to doubt that this mentality is perfectly consistent with the "more drastic . . . measures" Devall and Sessions believe we will have to explore. Nor is it inconsistent with Malthus and Vogt that we should make no effort to find a cure for this disease which may do so much to depopulate the world. "Biocentric democracy," I assume, should call for nothing less than a "hands-off" policy on the AIDS virus and perhaps equally lethal pathogens that appear in the human species.

What Is Social Ecology?

Social ecology is neither "deep," "tall," "fat," nor "thick." It is *social*. It does not fall back on incantations, sutras, flow diagrams or spiritual vagaries. It is avowedly *rational*. It does not try to regale metaphorical forms of spiritual mechanism and crude biologism with Taoist, Buddhist, Christian, or shamanistic eco-babble. It is a coherent form of

naturalism that looks to *evolution* and the *biosphere,* not to deities in the sky or under the earth for quasi-religious and supernaturalistic explanations of natural and social phenomena.

Philosophically, social ecology stems from a solid organismic tradition in Western philosophy, beginning with Heraclitus, the near-evolutionary dialectic of Aristotle and Hegel, and the critical approach of the famous Frankfurt School—particularly its devastating critique of logical positivism (which surfaces in Naess repeatedly) and the primitivistic mysticism of Heidegger (which pops up all over the place in deep ecology's literature).

Socially, it is revolutionary, not merely "radical." It critically unmasks the entire evolution of hierarchy in all its forms, including neo-Malthusian elitism, the eco-brutalism of David Foreman, the anti-humanism of David Ehrenfeld and "Miss Ann Thropy," and the latent racism, first-world arrogance, and Yuppie nihilism of postmodernistic spiritualism. It is rooted in the profound eco-anarchistic analyses of Peter Kropotkin, the radical economic insights of Karl Marx, the emancipatory promise of the revolutionary Enlightenment as articulated by the great encyclopedist, Denis Diderot, the *Enrages* of the French Revolution, the revolutionary feminist ideals of Louise Michel and Emma Goldman, the communitarian visions of Paul Goodman and E. A. Gutkind, and the various eco-revolutionary manifestoes of the early 1960s.

Politically, it is *green*—radically green. It takes its stand with the left-wing tendencies in the German Greens and extra-parliamentary street movements of European cities; with the American radical ecofeminist movement; with the demands for a new politics based on citizens' initiatives, neighborhood assemblies, and New England's tradition of town-meetings; with non-aligned anti-imperialist movements at home and abroad; with the struggle by people of color for complete freedom from the domination of privileged whites and from the superpowers.

Morally, it is *humanistic* in the high Renaissance meaning of the term, not the degraded meaning of "humanism" that has been imparted to the world by David Foreman, David Ehrenfeld, and a salad of academic deep ecologists. Humanism from its inception has meant a shift in vision from the skies to the earth, from superstition to reason, from deities to people—who are no less products of natural evolution than grizzly bears and whales. Social ecology accepts neither a "biocentricity" that essentially denies or degrades the uniqueness of human beings, human subjectivity, rationality, aesthetic sensibility, and the ethical potentiality of humanity, nor an "anthropocentricity" that confers on the privileged few the right to plunder the world of life, including human life. Indeed, it opposes "centricity" of *any* kind as a new word for hierarchy and domination—be it that of nature by a mystical "Man" or the domination of people by an equally mystical "Nature." It firmly denies that nature is a static, scenic view which Mountain Men like a Foreman survey from a peak in Nevada or a picture window that spoiled yuppies view from their ticky-tacky country homes. To social ecology, nature *is* natural *evolution*, not a cosmic arrangement of beings frozen in a moment of eternity to be abjectly revered, adored, and worshipped like Gods and Goddesses in a realm of "*super*nature." Natural evolution is nature in the very real sense that it is composed of atoms, molecules that have evolved into amino acids, proteins, unicellular organisms, genetic codes, invertebrates and vertebrates, amphibia, reptiles, mammals, primates, and human beings—all, in a cumulative thrust toward ever-greater complexity, ever-greater subjectivity, and finally, an ever-greater capacity for conceptual thought, symbolic communication, and self-consciousness.

This marvel we call "Nature" has produced a marvel we call homo sapiens—"thinking man"—and, more significantly for the development of society, "thinking woman," whose primeval domestic domain provided the arena for the origins of a caring society, human empathy, love, and idealistic commitment. The human species, in effect, is no less a product of natural evolution and differentiation than blue-green algae. To degrade the human species in the name of "anti-humanism," to deny people their uniqueness as thinking beings with an unprecedented gift for conceptual thought, is to deny the rich fecundity of natural evolution itself. To separate human beings and society from nature is to dualize and truncate nature itself, to diminish the meaning and thrust of natural evolution in the name of a "biocentricity" that spends more time disporting itself with mantras, deities, and supernature than with the realities of the biosphere and the role of society in ecological problems.

Accordingly, social ecology does not try to hide its critical and reconstructive thrust in metaphors. It calls "technological/industrial" society *capitalism*—a word which places the onus for our ecological problems on the *living* sources and *social* relationships that produce them, not on a cutesy "Third Wave" abstraction which buries these sources in technics, a technical "mentality," or perhaps the technicians who work on machines. It sees the domination of women not simply as a "spiritual" problem that can be resolved by rituals, incantations, and shamannesses, important as ritual may be in solidarizing women into a unique community of people, but in the long, highly graded, and subtly nuanced development of hierarchy, which long preceded the development of classes. Nor does it ignore class, ethnic differences, imperialism, and oppression by creating a grab-bag called "Humanity" that is placed in opposition to a mystified "Nature," divested of all development.

All of which brings us as social ecologists to an issue that seems to be totally alien to the crude concerns of deep ecology: natural evolution has conferred on human beings the capacity to form a "second" or cultural nature out of "first" or primeval nature. Natural evolution has not only provided humans with the *ability*, but also the *necessity* to be purposive interveners into "first nature," to consciously *change* "first nature" by means of a highly institutionalized form of community we call "society." It is not alien to natural evolution that a species called human beings have emerged over the billions of years who are capable of thinking in a sophisticated way. Nor is it alien for human beings to develop a highly sophisticated form of symbolic communication which a new kind of community—institutionalized, guided by thought rather than by instinct alone, and ever-changing—has emerged called "society."

Taken together, all of these human traits—intellectual, communicative, and social—have not only emerged from natural evolution and are inherently human; they can also be placed at the *service* of natural evolution to consciously increase biotic diversity, diminish suffering, foster the further evolution of new and ecologically valuable life-forms, reduce the impact of disastrous accidents or the harsh effects of mere change.

Whether this species, gifted by the creativity of natural evolution, can play the role of a nature rendered self-conscious or cut against the grain of natural evolution by simplifying the biosphere, polluting it, and undermining the cumulative results of organic evolution is above all a *social* problem. The primary question ecology faces today is whether an ecologically oriented society can be created out of the present anti-ecological one.

Unless there is a resolute attempt to fully anchor ecological dislocations in social dislocations; to challenge the vested corporate and political interests we should properly call *capitalism;* to analyze, explore, and attack hierarchy as a *reality,* not only as a sensibility; to recognize the material needs of the poor and of third world people; to function politically, and not simply as a religious cult; to give the human species and mind their due in natural evolution, rather than regard them as "cancers" in the biosphere; to examine economies as well as "souls," and freedom instead of scholastic arguments about the "rights" of pathogenic viruses—unless, in short, North American Greens and the ecology movement shift their focus toward a *social ecology* and let deep ecology sink into the pit it has created for us, the ecology movement will become another ugly wart on the skin of society.

What we must do, today, is return to *nature,* conceived in all its fecundity, richness of potentialities, and subjectivity—not to *super*nature with its shamans, priests, priestesses, and fanciful deities that are merely anthropomorphic extensions and distortions of the "Human" as all-embracing divinities. And what we must "enchant" is not only an abstract image of "Nature" *that often reflects our own systems of power, hierarchy, and domination*—but rather human beings, the human mind, and the human spirit.

Notes

1. Unless otherwise indicated, all future references and quotes come from Bill Devall and George Sessions, *Deep Ecology* (Layton, UT: Gibbs M. Smith, 1985), a book which has essentially become the bible of the "movement" that bears its name.

2. David Ehrenfeld, *The Arrogance of Humanism* (New York: The Modern Library, 1978) pp. 207–211.

3. Chapter five of his *Essay,* which, for all its "concern" over the misery of the "lower classes," inveighs against the poor laws and argues that the "pressures of distress on this part of the community is an evil so deeply seated that no human ingenuity can reach it." Thomas Malthus, *On Population* (New York: The Modern Library), p. 34.

Searching for Agreement: A Dialogue Between Murray Bookchin and Dave Foreman

BOOKCHIN: Some of the greatest moments in my life have been hiking deep into forest areas in winter alone, where if I so much as sprained my ankle I would freeze to death. My greatest regret now that I am 70 and suffer from a severe case of osteoarthritis is that I can no longer hike in the wilderness. Today, I have to be a more distant admirer. I would physically stand shoulder to shoulder with everyone in Earth First! to defend wild areas if I could. On this score, there is no opposition between Dave Foreman and myself, none whatsoever!

Our society has got to learn to live in peace with the planet, with the rest of the biosphere. We are in complete agreement on this fundamental point. We now live under the constant threat that the world of life will be irrevocably undermined by a society gone mad in its need to grow—replacing the organic by the inorganic, soil by concrete, forest by barren earth, and the diversity of life-forms by simplified ecosystems; in short, by turning back the evolutionary clock to an earlier, more inorganic, mineralized world that is incapable of supporting complex life-forms of any kind, including the human species. The entire world of life, including those few but wonderful wild places that remain, must be protected. Indeed, wild areas must be expanded. Dave and I have no disagreement on this.

I also agree that we need to promote a rational solution to the human population problem. The

Defending the Earth: A Dialogue Between Murray Bookchin and Dave Foreman, edited by Steve Chase (Boston: South End Press, 1991), pp. 29–34, 43–45, 49–53, 57–61. Reprinted by permission of the publisher.

world's human population needs to be brought into a workable equilibrium with the "carrying capacity" of the planet. Sooner or later, the mindless proliferation of human beings will have to be dealt with. It is absolutely essential, however, that we first clearly identify what we mean by terms like "overpopulation" and "carrying capacity."

This is where the thinking of some deep ecologists frightens me. We need an understanding of the problem that has nothing to do with gas chambers and racism. I know what it means to face the brunt of a "population control" program. All my relatives in Europe are dead. They were murdered in the Nazi Holocaust. They were slaughtered in the name of a "population problem." For Hitler, the world would be overpopulated if just one Jew was left alive.

I've never believed that people in Earth First! are fascists. I am afraid, however, of certain positions and statements, the tendency of which remind me of things I heard fifty years ago when there was a world-wide fascist movement that used "naturalistic" Malthusian arguments to justify racist population control policies. This abuse of the "overpopulation" issue is not just a distant historical issue, either. The abuse of the population issue is ongoing. Just look at what the Rockefeller crowd is trying to do in the Third World. It is a remarkably dangerous question which has to be carefully and rationally discussed if we are to resist racism, sexism, and genocide. Even deep ecologists like Warwick Fox agree that it is "monstrous" to talk of AIDS as a population control measure or, in the name of "letting nature seek its balance," refusing to aid starving children in Ethiopia.[1]

So I ask all of you, everyone in the ecology movement, to please be careful about the population problem. This is a hot issue; a very hot issue. Don't kid yourselves about the objectives of many of those who talk of population control. I went through the 1930s. We paid the price of sixty million lives back then as the result of a racist, imperialist war and mass extermination policy. This sort of thing is not radical ecology. We have to explore this matter carefully and respect the very reasonable fears of women and people of color who have been victimized by population control programs in the past. We have to explore what a humane and ecologically sound solution is. It is important that we unscramble what constitutes the social aspects

of the problem from the purely biological ones and to understand how these two aspects of the problem interact with each other. Please, let us be careful. Can we agree on this?

Let me move on to another concern. The ultimate moral appeal of Earth First! is that it urges us to safeguard the natural world from our ecologically destructive societies, that is, in some sense, from ourselves. But, I have to ask, who is this "us" from which the living world has to be protected? This, too, is an important question. Is it "humanity?" Is it the human "species" *per se*? Is it people, as such? Or is it our particular society, our particular civilization, with its hierarchical social relations which pit men against women, privileged whites against people of color, elites against masses, employers against workers, the first world against the third world, and, ultimately, a cancerlike "grow or die" industrial capitalist economic system against the natural world and other life-forms? Is this not the social root of the popular belief that nature is a mere object of social domination, valuable only as a "resource?"

All too often we are told by liberal environmentalists, and not a few deep ecologists, that it is "we" as a species or, at least, "we" as an amalgam of "anthropocentric" individuals that are responsible for the breakdown of the web of life. I remember an "environmental" presentation staged by the Museum of Natural History in New York during the 1970s in which the public was exposed to a long series of exhibits, each depicting examples of pollution and ecological disruption. The exhibit which closed the presentation carried a startling sign, "The Most Dangerous Animal on Earth." It consisted simply of a huge mirror which reflected back the person who stood in front of it. I remember a black child standing in front of that mirror while a white school teacher tried to explain the message which this arrogant exhibit tried to convey. Mind you, there was no exhibit of corporate boards of directors planning to deforest a mountainside or of government officials acting in collusion with them.

One of the problems with this asocial, "species-centered" way of thinking, of course, is that it blames the victim. Let's face it, when you say a black kid in Harlem is as much to blame for the ecological crisis as the president of Exxon, you are letting one off the hook and slandering the other. Such talk by environmentalists makes grassroots coalition-building next to impossible. Oppressed people know that humanity is hierarchically organized around complicated divisions that are ignored only at their peril. Black people know this well when they confront whites. The poor know this well when they confront the wealthy. The Third World knows it well when it confronts the First World. Women know it well when they confront patriarchal males. The radical ecology movement needs to know it too.

All this loose talk of "we" masks the reality of social power and social institutions. It masks the fact that the social forces that are tearing down the planet are the same social forces which threaten to degrade women, people of color, workers, and ordinary citizens. It masks the fact that there is a historical connection between the way people deal with each other as social beings and the way they treat the rest of nature. It masks the fact that our ecological problems are fundamentally social problems requiring fundamental social change. That is what I mean by social ecology. It makes a big difference in how societies relate to the natural world whether people live in cooperative, nonhierarchical, and decentralized communities or in hierarchical, class-ridden, and authoritarian mass societies. Similarly, the ecological impact of human reason, science, and technology depends enormously on the type of society in which these forces are shaped and employed.

Perhaps the biggest question that all wings of the radical ecology movement must satisfactorily answer is just what do we mean by "nature." If we are committed to defending nature, it is important to clearly understand what we mean by this. Is nature, the real world, essentially the remnants of the earth's prehuman and pristine biosphere that has now been vastly reduced and poisoned by the "alien" presence of the human species? Is nature what we see when we look out on an unpeopled vista from a mountain? Is it a cosmic arrangement of beings frozen in a moment of eternity to be abjectly revered, adored, and untouched by human intervention? Or is nature much broader in meaning? Is nature an evolutionary process which is cumulative and which *includes* human beings?

The ecology movement will get nowhere unless it understands that the human species is no less a product of natural evolution than blue-green algae, whales, and bears. To conceptually separate human beings and society from nature by viewing humanity as an inherently unnatural force in the world leads, philosophically, either to an anti-nature "anthropocentrism" or a misanthropic aversion to the human species. Let's face it, such misanthropy does surface within certain ecological circles. Even Arne Naess admits that many deep ecologists "talk as if they look upon humans as intruders in wonderful nature."[2]

We are part of nature, a product of a long evolutionary journey. To some degree, we carry the ancient oceans in our blood. To a very large degree we go through a kind of biological evolution as fetuses. It is not alien to natural evolution that a species called human beings has emerged over billions of years which is capable of thinking in sophisticated ways. Our brains and nervous systems did not suddenly spring into existence without long antecedents in natural history. That which we most prize as integral to our humanity—our extraordinary capacity to think on complex conceptual levels—can be traced back to the nerve network of primitive invertebrates, the ganglia of a mollusk, the spinal cord of a fish, the brain of an amphibian, and the cerebral cortex of a primate.

We need to understand that the human species has evolved as a remarkably creative and social life form that is organized to create a place for itself in the natural world, not only to adapt to the rest of nature. The human species, its different societies, and its enormous powers to alter the environment were not invented by a group of ideologues called "humanists" who decided that nature was "made" to serve humanity and its needs. Humanity's distinct powers have emerged out of eons of evolutionary development and out of centuries of cultural development. These remarkable powers present us, however, with an enormous moral responsibility. We can contribute to the diversity, fecundity, and richness of the natural world—what I call "first nature"—more consciously, perhaps, than any other animal. Or, our societies—"second nature"—can exploit the whole web of life and tear down the planet in a rapacious, cancerous manner.

The future that awaits the world of life ultimately depends upon what kind of society or "second nature" we create. This probably affects, more than any other single factor, how we interact with and intervene in biological or "first nature." And make no mistake about it, the future of "first nature," the primary concern of conservationists, is dependent on the results of this interaction. The central problem we face today is that the social evolution of "second nature" has taken a wrong turn. Society is poisoned. It has been poisoned for thousands of years, from before the Bronze Age. It has been warped by rule by elders, by patriarchy, by warriors, by hierarchies of all sorts which have led now to the current situation of a world threatened by competitive, nuclear-armed, nation-states and a phenomenally destructive corporate capitalist system in the West and an equally ecologically destructive, though now crumbling, bureaucratic state capitalist system in the East.

We need to create an ecologically oriented society out of the present anti-ecological one. If we can change the direction of our civilization's social evolution, human beings can assist in the creation of a truly "free nature," where all of our human traits—intellectual, communicative, and social— are placed at the service of natural evolution to consciously increase biotic diversity, diminish suffering, foster the further evolution of new and ecologically valuable life-forms, and reduce the impact of disastrous accidents or the harsh effects of harmful change. Our species, gifted by the creativity of natural evolution itself, could play the role of nature rendered self-conscious. . . .

FOREMAN: . . . I must say, however, that for all my intellectual understanding of imperialism, it was directly encountering the repressive power of the FBI and doing a little time in federal custody that really brought home to me the reality of peoples' suffering throughout the world. Personally experiencing a little of the repressive power of the state has a tendency, I think, to create a lot more sympathy for oppressed groups around the world. I certainly have a more visceral appreciation for peoples' suffering these days since the FBI visited me.

From my viewpoint, the FBI effort against me began at about five in the morning on May 30, 1989. A Doberman down the street started barking, so I put my ear plugs in. About two hours later, my wife went to answer the door as it was about to be broken down and opened it up to six men standing there with drawn .357 Magnums and wearing bulletproof vests. They flashed badges at her and pushed her out of the way. They then started running down the hall to our bedroom—they somehow already knew right where it was.

At this point, I vaguely began to come awake as I heard an unfamiliar but authoritative voice yelling my name. I opened up my eyes, still with my ear plugs in, disoriented. May in Tucson is very hot, and I didn't have anything on. And I woke up and there were three guys with bulletproof vests and drawn .357 Magnums standing around the bed. That kind of alarm clock doesn't have a snooze button; you can't go back to sleep for another five minutes. At first I thought, am I on *Candid Camera*? But I realized very quickly that these guys were serious.

I then started thinking about some of the FBI attacks on the Black Panthers, like the FBI/Chicago Police murder of Fred Hampton, who was shot in his apartment while he lay asleep in bed. I fully expected bullets to start coming my way. But being a nice, middle-class honky male, they can't get away with that stuff quite as easily as they could with Fred, or with all the native people on the Pine Ridge Reservation back in the early 70s. So they just dragged me out of bed. They let me put on a pair of shorts, and they hauled me outside.

I did not know what I was being arrested for until six hours later, when I saw a magistrate. Essentially what had happened, we found out, was that the FBI had spent three years and two million dollars trying to frame a bunch of people in Earth First! for trying to create a conspiracy to damage government property. We now know for a fact that the FBI infiltrated Earth First! groups across the country with informers and agent-provocateurs seeking to entrap people into illegal activities. They have amassed 500 hours of tape recordings of our meetings, our personal conversations, and our phone calls. They have also broken into our houses and offices and tried to intimidate numerous ecology activists in several states by agent interrogations and grand jury investigations.

My supposed co-conspirators, three unarmed activists who were arrested by some 50 armed FBI agents on foot, on horseback, and in two helicopters while standing at the base of a power line tower in the desert, were arrested the day before me. Mind you, these three environmentalists were driven to the site by an undercover FBI agent who had infiltrated Earth First!. The whole escapade was largely his idea. He was the only one talking about explosives. I, of course, was nowhere near the "scene" but I was still described by the FBI as "the financier, the leader, the guru to get all this going." I was likened to a "mafia boss" and the other three defendants were described as my "munchkins."

I had only met the FBI infiltrator a couple of times before and very briefly. I couldn't even remember his last name. We had never planned to do anything together. But that doesn't matter to the FBI. Back in the 1970s, the FBI issued a memo to all their field offices telling them that when you are trying to break up a dissident group, don't worry if you have any evidence or facts. Just go in, make a big arrest, make wild charges, have a press conference, and that's what the media's going to pick up. That's the news story. The damage to the group is done. . . .

Before I close, let me just say that I agree with Murray that the warped social evolution of our civilization has left us with a very weird way of looking at reality. I agree a lot with Dave Ehrenfeld, who characterizes the dominant philosophy of the modern world as being one where human beings are the measure of all value; where we think that we can solve all problems, either through technological means or through sociological means; where we believe that all resources are either infinite or have infinite substitutes; and where we believe that human civilization will continue to progress and will exist forever. And to me, that is stark, raving insanity . . . [3]

*

I come from the wide open spaces of New Mexico. I haven't come from the urban centers of the East where the left tradition is so much stronger than in the Southwest. The left tradition is not something I understand that well. Leftists often talk a little different language than me. That doesn't mean we have to fight; it just means we start out emphasizing different things.

I actually think we have a lot to learn from each other. I don't necessarily consider myself a leftist. I don't want to tar that movement with my association, for one thing. But I do have a great deal of sympathy for these movements and I continue to learn from my sometimes clumsy dance with the left.

When we formed Earth First! in 1980, we consciously tried to learn from the strategy and tactics of a number of left social movements. The Wobblies were certainly one group we were drawn to. I even published a Little Green songbook, taking after the Little Red songbook of the IWW. I've talked to Utah Phillips and some old Wobblies; I am really attracted to a lot of what they have to say.

In a place like Oregon, where we are seeing huge multinational corporations essentially practicing a policy of cutting and leaving, a good dose of leftist, anti-capitalist analysis can help us understand the situation. These companies, in their obsession for profit, don't give a damn about community stability or employment. They plan to leave in ten years after they have used up the Northwest forests. They have the capital to move somewhere where they can grow pine trees like corn in Iowa.

I totally agree that we need to get the big money out of the forests and make room for small worker-owned operations. I made such a proposal for the Pacific Northwest four or five years ago. My proposal was to prohibit any logging in the national forests except by small locally-owned companies, preferably worker-owned companies. Furthermore, the plan would have required a certain number of jobs per million board feet both in the woods and in the mills. Right now we are cutting as much timber from the national forests as ever, but the employment, the number of people doing that, is about half of what it used to be. And the reason is automation, because the big companies can make more money that way.

Right now we are cutting something like eleven to twelve billion board feet of timber from the national forests every year, but the large timber companies are sending something like ten billion board feet of barely milled logs to Japan every year. In other words, nearly the entire output of the national forests is going unmilled, unprocessed to Japan. The companies are exporting jobs along with the trees. So, if you want to understand this situation, you need an analysis of multinational capitalism, an analysis of capital mobility and its effects on our communities.

One of my biggest complaints about the workers up in the Pacific Northwest is that most of them aren't "class conscious." That's a big problem. Too many workers blame environmentalists for costing them their jobs. But who is costing them their jobs? It's not the conservation movement to protect the old growth forest that is wiping out jobs in the Pacific Northwest, it's the greed of the multinationals.

We could easily have more employment, more community stability in the Pacific Northwest without cutting any more old-growth forest. But how do you get that across to a lot of workers who have bought into the mentality that the companies have put out for them: that the environmental movement is against them, and that if they're good, if they're obedient, if they resist us, everything will be fine?

The history of the Wobblies and other left-wing union movements undoubtedly has a lot to teach us about organizing with workers. On the other hand, I have some big problems with how the left tends to romanticize workers and only see them as victims. The loggers are victims of an unjust economic system, yes, but that should not absolve them for everything they do. It does not follow from the huge guilt of the capitalists that all workers are blameless for the destruction of the natural world. I think we need to face the fact that industrial workers, by and large, share some of the blame for the Earth's ongoing destruction.

I want workers to resist more, to become a lot more militant and not be such eager and willing slaves to the big companies or believe all of their propaganda all the time. Too many workers buy into the worldview of their masters that the Earth is a smorgasbord of resources for the taking. Indeed, sometimes it is the hardy swain, the sturdy yeoman from the bumpkin proletariat so celebrated in Wobbly lore who holds the most violent and destructive attitudes towards the natural world (and towards those who would defend it). I don't think it is wise to put the working class, or any oppressed group, on a pedestal and make them immune from questioning or criticism.

My biggest problem with the left, of course, is that it has so little appreciation for natural systems and for wilderness and wildlife. Our society, our civilization, has no divine mandate or right to pave, conquer, control, develop, use or exploit every square inch of this planet. At best, the left, if it pays any attention to ecology at all, does so in order to protect a watershed for downstream use by agriculture, industry, and homes. It does so to provide a good place to clean the cobwebs out of our minds after a long week in the auto factory or over the VDT. It does so because it preserves resource extraction options for future generations of humans or because some unknown plant living in the wild may hold a cure for cancer. It does so because nature is instrumentally valuable to human beings. The vast majority of leftists today are still unable to see the natural world as part of the circle of life that deserves direct moral consideration quite apart from any real or imagined instrumental value to human civilization.

Most leftists are for ecological goals such as preserving wilderness and biological diversity only to the extent that we can achieve such goals without negatively affecting the material "standard of living" of any group of human beings. The Earth is always second, never first, in their thinking. This makes many leftists unreliable allies in ecological struggles. The simple fact is that what appears to be in the short-term interest of human beings as a whole—or a select group of human beings or of individual human beings—is sometimes detrimental to the short-term or long-term health of the biosphere (and often even to the actual long-term welfare of human beings). The left, to the extent that it refuses to push for human beings to adjust their way of life to be compatible with the planetary community of life, is part of the problem rather than part of the solution to the ecological crisis.

This is perhaps clearest in most of the left's refusal to admit that there is a human population crisis and that we need to lower human population over the long run. The left puts down all issues of resource scarcity to maldistribution and the venality of multinational corporations. There is much truth in this, of course. There is an unconscionable maldistribution of wealth and the basic necessities of life among human beings that must be overcome. However, even if the problem of equitable distribution was solved, the existence of five billion, seven billion, or eleven billion human beings converting the natural world into material goods and food puts the long-term sustainability of human society into question. Much of the left doesn't understand this simple ecological fact.

Some do, of course. The greens have made the sustainability of human society the cornerstone of their political vision. Yet, from my perspective, this isn't enough. For me, the problem is not just to figure out how to level off human population at a level that can be biologically sustained at equitable levels of consumption. I believe that the ecological community is not just valuable for what it can provide human beings. Other beings, both animal and plant, and even so-called inanimate objects such as rivers, mountains, and wilderness habitats are inherently valuable and live for their own sake, not just for the convenience of the human species. If we are serious, then, about creating an ecological society, we will need to find humane ways to arrive at a global population level that is compatible with the flourishing of bears, tigers, elephants, rainforests, and other wilderness areas, as well as human beings.

This will undoubtedly require us to lower our current population level which, even if we succeed at overcoming poverty and maldistribution, would probably continue to devastate the native diversity of the biosphere which has been evolving for three and a half billion years. I subscribe to the deep ecology principle that "the flourishing of human life and cultures is compatible with a substantial decrease of the human population and that the flourishing of nonhuman life requires such a decrease."[4]. . .

BOOKCHIN: . . . [m]ost leftists who do take an interest in environmental issues do so for purely utilitarian reasons. Such leftists assume that our concern for nature rests solely on our self-interest, rather than on a feeling for the community of life of which we are part, albeit in a very unique and distinctive way. This is a crassly instrumental approach that reflects a serious derangement of our ethical sensibilities. Given such an argument, our ethical relationship with nature is neither better nor worse than the success with which we plunder the natural world without harming ourselves.

I fundamentally reject this idea. Social ecology is a left libertarian perspective that does not subscribe to this pernicious notion. Social ecologists call instead for the creation of a genuinely ecological society and the development of an ecological sensibility that deeply respects the natural world and the creative thrust of natural evolution. We are not interested in undermining the natural world and evolution even if we could find "workable" or "adequate" synthetic or mechanical substitutes for existing life-forms and ecological relationships.

Social ecologists argue, based on considerable anthropological evidence, that the modern view of nature as a hostile, stingy "other" grows historically out of a projection of warped, hierarchical social relations onto the rest of the natural world. Clearly, in non-hierarchical, organic, tribal societies, nature is usually viewed as a fecund source of life and well-being. Indeed, it is seen as a community to which humanity belongs. This yields a very different environmental ethic than today's stratified and hierarchical societies. It explains why social ecologists continually stress the need to reharmonize social relationships as a fundamental part of resolving the ecological crisis in any deep, long-lasting way. It is an essential element in restoring a complementary ethical relationship with the non-human world.

And let's be very clear about one thing. We are not simply talking about ending class exploitation, as most Marxists demand, as important as that is. We are talking about uprooting *all* forms of hierarchy and domination, in all spheres of social life. Of course, the immediate source of the ecological crisis is capitalism, but, to this, social ecologists add a deeper problem at the heart of our civilization— the existence of hierarchies and of a hierarchical mentality or culture that preceded the emergence of economic classes and exploitation. The early radical feminists in the 1970s who first raised the issue of patriarchy clearly understood this. We have much to learn from feminism's and social ecology's anti-hierarchical perspective. We need to search into institutionalized systems of coercion, command, and obedience that exist today and which preceded the emergence of economic classes. Hierarchy is not necessarily economically motivated. We must look beyond economic forms of exploitation into cultural forms of domination that exist in the family, between generations, sexes, racial and ethnic groups, in all institutions of political, economic, and social management, and very significantly in the way we experience reality as a whole, including nature and non-human life-forms.

I believe that the color of radicalism today is not red, but green. I can even understand, given the ecological illiteracy of so much of the conventional left, why many green activists describe themselves as "neither left or right." Initially, I wanted to work with this slogan. I didn't know whether we were "in front," as this slogan contends, but I at least wanted to move on to something new, something barely anticipated by the conventional left. Indeed, few have been as uncompromising in their criticism of the conventional socialist "paradigm" as I have been.

However, as time has passed, I have come to see that it is very important that we consciously develop a left green perspective. While the green movement is right to reject a mere variant of conventional left orthodoxy dressed up in a few new environmental metaphors, it is a huge mistake, I think, to fail to consciously draw on left libertarian and populist traditions, particularly eco-anarchism. When greens reject their affinity with these left traditions, they cut themselves off from an important source of insight, wisdom, and social experience.

Today, for example, the U.S. green movement cannot even bring itself to say with one voice that it is opposed to capitalism. Indeed, some locals of the U.S. Green Committees of Correspondence are made up of moderate Republicans and liberal Democrats who talk of "truly free markets," "green capitalism," and "green consumerism" as a sufficient means for controlling the policies of multinational corporations. They talk about running workshops for corporate managers to encourage them to adopt an ecologically sound business ethics. A left libertarian green perspective cuts through this shallow, reformist, and very naive thinking.

The radical left tradition is unequivocally anti-capitalist. A key lesson greens can learn from a left libertarian ecological perspective is that corporate capitalism is *inherently* anti-ecological. Sooner or later, a market economy whose very law of life is structured around competition and accumulation—a system based on the dictum "grow or die"—must of necessity tear down the planet, all moral and cultural factors aside. This problem is systemic, not just ethical. Multinational, corporate capitalism is a cancer in the biosphere, rapaciously undermining the work of eons of natural evolution and the bases for complex life forms on this planet. The ecology movement will get nowhere if it doesn't directly face this fact. To its credit, Earth First! has done better than most ecology groups in understanding this point.

Furthermore, I believe that the lack of a well-developed, left libertarian green perspective has made too many people in the ecology and feminist movements vulnerable to a "counter-enlightenment" mood that is increasingly gaining ground in Western culture generally. While the growing denigration of the Enlightenment values of humanism, naturalism, reason, science, and technology is certainly understandable in light of how these human ideals have been warped by a cancerous patricentric, racist, capitalist, and bureaucratic society, their uncritical rejection of the Enlightenment's valid achievements ultimately ends up by throwing out the baby with the bath water.

That our society has warped the best Enlightenment ideals, reducing reason to a harsh industrial rationalism focused on efficiency rather than an ethically inspired intellectuality; that it uses science to quantify the world and divide thought against feeling; that it uses technology to exploit nature, including *human* nature, should not negate the value of the underlying Enlightenment ideals. We have much to learn from the solid organismic tradition in Western philosophy, beginning with Heraclitus, and running through the near-evolutionary dialectic of Aristotle, Diderot, and Hegel. We have much to learn from the profound eco-anarchistic analyses of Peter Kropotkin, and, yes, the radical economic insights of Karl Marx, the revolutionary humanist, anti-sexist views of Louise Michel and Emma Goldman, and the communitarian visions of Paul Goodman, E. A. Gutkind, and Lewis Mumford.

The new anti-Enlightenment mood, which declares all these thinkers irrelevant or worse, scares the hell out of me. It is potentially quite dangerous. Anti-rational, anti-humanist, supernatural, parochial, and atavistic moods are a frightening foundation on which to build a movement for a new society. Such perspectives can lead all too easily to the extremes of political fanaticism or a passive social quietism. They can easily become reactionary, cold, and cruel.

I saw this happen in the 1930s. That is why I say that eco-fascism is a real possibility within our movement today. That is why I have criticized several of the misanthropic statements that have been published in *Earth First!*; why I have denounced those few Earth First!ers who stand around campfires and chant "Down With Human Beings"; and why I have expressed dismay over the fact that extreme statements on AIDS, immigration, and famine by some Earth First!ers went unchallenged for so long by deep ecology philosophers such as George Sessions, Bill Devall, and Arne Naess. I agree with Dave that we should respect diversity within our movement, but we should not mistake diversity for outright contradiction. Such views are, at best, unnecessary and, at worst, counterproductive to very dangerous.

Is there really no role in our movement for a humanist ethics? Is there really no role for reason? Is there really no role for an ecologically sound technology that can meet basic material needs with a minimum of arduous toil, leaving people time and energy for direct democratic governance, an intimate social life, an appreciation of nature, and fulfilling cultural pursuits? Is there no role for natural science? Is there no role for an appreciation of a universal human interest? Is it really ecological to go around putting humanity down? Do we really have to replace naturalism with the new supernaturalisms that are now coming into vogue?

Certainly Dave is right that a sense of wonder and the marvelous have a major place beside the rational human spirit. However, let us not permit a celebration of these ways of experiencing the world to degenerate, as happens all too frequently these days, into anti-rationalism. Let us not allow the celebration of nature as an end-in-itself to degenerate into a misanthropic antihumanism. Let us not permit an appreciation of the spiritual traditions of tribal peoples to degenerate into a reactionary, supernaturalist, anti-scientific, anti-technology perspective that calls for the complete "unmaking of civilization" and the valorization of hunting/gathering societies as the only legitimate way of life.

Notes

1. Warwick Fox, "The Deep Ecology-Ecofeminism Debate and Its Parallels," *Environmental Ethics*, No. 11 (1989), note 38.

2. Arne Naess, "Finding Common Ground," *Green Synthesis*, No. 30 (March 1989), 9.

3. For a full presentation of Ehrenfeld's critical view of humanism, see David Ehrenfeld, *The Arrogance of Humanism* (New York: Oxford University Press, 1978).

4. Arne Naess, *Ecology, Community and Lifestyle* (New York: Cambridge University Press, 1989), 29.

D. Ecofeminism

PREVIEW

[Ecofeminism] has asked important questions no one else has thought to pose.

Jan Clausen[1]

There is now a growing awareness that the Western philosophical tradition which has identified, on the one hand, maleness with the sphere of rationality, and on the other hand, femaleness with the sphere of nature, has provided one of the main intellectual bases for the domination of women in Western culture.

Val Plumwood[2]

Ecological feminism, says Karen J. Warren, "is the position that there are important connections—historical, symbolic, theoretical—between the domination of women and the domination of nonhuman nature."[3] Warren argues that ". . . the conceptual connections between the dual dominations of women and nature are located in an oppressive patriarchal conceptual framework characterized by a logic of domination."[4] What Warren implies by her claim that there is a logic of domination that extends to both women and nature is that there is a need for feminism to become ecological feminism and for environmental ethics to become distinctively feminist. Warren concludes: "A re-conceiving and re-visioning of both feminism and environmental ethics is, I think, the power and the promise of ecofeminism."[5]

Crucial to the logic of domination is the assumption that in situations of diversity, differences (real or alleged) such as those between humans and rocks or men and women, are interpreted as moral hierarchies. For example, it is thought that humans are better than rocks and that men are better than women in some moral sense of "better." This assumption, plus the further assumption that moral superiority justifies subordination, transforms talk about diversity—or, for that matter, superiority or hierarchies—into a logic of domination. As Warren puts it so nicely, ". . . without a logic of domination, a description of similarities and differences would be just that—a description of similarities and differences."[6] In a very important observation, she says, "Contrary to what many feminists and ecofeminists have said or suggested, there may be nothing inherently problematic about 'hierarchical thinking' or even 'value hierarchical thinking' in contexts other than contexts of oppression."[7] Warren ties her insights regarding diversity to Marilyn Frye's distinction between "arrogant perception" and "loving perception"[8] in a way that further illuminates Frye's original creative discussion.

In a new collection on ecofeminism,[9] Greta Gaard is critical of Warren's omission of concern for animals in her, Warren's, "The Power and the Promise of Ecological Feminism." Gaard says, "[Warren] leaves no space for addressing animals and how humans should interact with them. In fact . . . [her] conclusion romanticizes the slaughter of an animal."[10] Gaard seems to take the position that the narrative in question can be used to justify deer-slaying in the Lakota culture, but not to justify factory farming and meat-eating in America. However, the narrative seems open to criticism regardless of cultural context for reasons stated by Gaard herself, namely, that the four-legged can hardly be said to have offered itself to the humans given that it was shot in the hind quarters. Although it seems doubtful that Warren intends to justify meat-eating in the United States via this narrative,

speciesism is conspicuously absent from her list of systems of oppression, which include sexism, racism, classism, ageism, and heterosexism.[11] Since the feminist mantra of "race, class, and gender" has for years excluded sexualities, despite reminders and protests, at least one can say for Warren that she shows more concern for diversity than have many feminists in the recent past.

Warren's view that the oppressions of women and nature are connected is shared by Val Plumwood, Vandana Shiva, and Victoria Davion—the other authors represented in this section. Plumwood sees rationalism as ". . . the key to the connected oppressions . . . in the West."[12] She begins with a critique of rationalism and universalistic ethics as found in Paul Taylor and Tom Regan. Universalization in ethics is a purely formal approach to procedures that requires consistency, insisting that people not make exceptions for themselves. As a formal process, universalization in ethics makes statements that do not contain content in the usual narrative sense; that is, universalization in ethics delineates some abstract content, such as the notion of equality, with some criteria of relevant similarities rather than describing a condition of the world.[13] It should come as no surprise, then, that Plumwood says, "This view of morality [is] . . . oppositional to the personal, the particular, and the emotional. . . . Special relationships . . . are treated by universalistic positions as at best morally irrelevant and at worst a positive hindrance to the moral life. . . ."[14]

In her essay, Plumwood develops a ". . . relational account of self, which clearly recognizes the distinctiveness of nature but also our relationship and continuity with it."[15] Her position is opposed to both rationalism and deep ecology. Unsurprisingly, she takes the view that rationalism, which brought us the human/nature dualism in the first place, is in no position to provide an account of a decent relationship between humans and nature.

Deep ecology, however, has tried to heal the human/nature bifurcation. Read how Robert Sessions explains what he believes is at the core of deep ecology:

> Modern humans have lost touch with nature and thus with their own natures— we no longer feel the rhythms of nature within ourselves, we have split ourselves from the world (dualism), and we live at a distance (alienation) from what is natural, leaving us fearful (insecure) and able to deal with the world only on our own terms (control). . . . the basic strategy deep ecologists recommend for ending the domination of nature is to somehow reverse this dualism, to join together what humans have split asunder.[16]

Plumwood's quarrel is not with the end of deep ecology, but with the accounts of self designed to reconcile humans and nature given by particular deep ecologists such as Arne Naess, John Seed, and Warwick Fox. All of these accounts, according to Plumwood, come up short. She labels them (1) the indistinguishability account; (2) the expanded self; and (3) the transpersonal self.

Let us focus on one very important difference between Plumwood's notion of "self-in-relationship" and the deep ecology ideas of "self as other" (the indistinguishability account) and the expanded self. These deep ecology ideas do not recognize the distinctness and independence of the other (in this case, the earth). On the indistinguishability account, self and nature are completely merged; there are no boundaries between them. Plumwood quotes Seed: "'I am protecting the rain forest' develops to 'I am part of the rain forest protecting myself. I am that part of the rain forest recently emerged into thinking.'"[17] The self as expanded is not so much a self identical with the other but a self that widens its interests or concerns. Plumwood's overriding concern in this whole discussion is that ". . . the widening of interest is obtained at the expense of failure to recognize

unambiguously the distinctness and independence of the other."[18] Again, ". . . we need to recognize not only our continuity with the natural world but also its distinctness and independence from us and the distinctness of the needs of things in nature from ours."[19] In espousing this view, Plumwood is rejecting the idea that good relationships (between humans and/or between humans and the earth) are of the type in which the self completely merges with the other. She is arguing against relationships of fusion which entail the loss of self boundaries and have rightly been characterized by Plumwood and others as exemplifying "a feminine ideal."[20]

Plumwood's concerns show up again in a recent piece she wrote on the image of Gaia and the repopularization of the notion of Mother Nature:

> Admittedly, Lovelock's message is that we need to become aware of Gaia and to recognize what she does for us. But the approach remains that of enlightened instrumentalism rather than of recognition of the natural world as a being-for-itself with needs of its own, to be respected for its own sake. Using familiar concepts of motherhood may tempt us to uses of the Gaia concept which are even more problematic: it does not matter if we don't wash our dishes and throw our dirty linen on the floor because Gaia, a sort of super housekeeping goddess operating with whiter than white homeostatic detergent, will clean it all up for us. In this form the concept not only backgrounds the feminine/natural but denies the need for any reciprocal human responsibilities towards Gaia. Such a Gaia might have the trappings of a goddess but is really conceived of a sort of superservant.[21]

Plumwood's account of the "self-in-relationship," which is critical of both masculine "separation" and feminine "merger" views of the self,[22] is in harmony with Victoria Davion's conception of a feminist approach.

Davion argues that "... a truly feminist perspective cannot embrace either the feminine or the masculine uncritically, as a truly feminist perspective requires a critique of gender roles, and this critique must include masculinity *and* femininity."[23] Davion renames as ecofeminine a number of purported ecofeminist views that critique masculinity, but fail to do the same in the case of femininity. To push the point, ecofeminine views see the problem as the devaluation of the feminine role, whereas Davion says that feminists should be highly critical and suspicious of the feminine role in part because the feminine role is both inextricable from, and senseless without, its counterpart, the masculine role. So, it would be unlikely that the one role would have damaging effects for those who play it, but the other role would not. Moreover, says Davion, "A vital tradition in feminist critique has long argued that gender roles cannot exist without domination and subordination."[24] In sum, feminists, according to Davion, see gender roles as the problem, not the undervaluing of the feminine role.

Vandana Shiva's work, equally at home here or under the category of economics, analyzes and makes explicit certain value commitments underlying a number of important Western economic notions such as development, productivity, and poverty. As an ecofeminist, Shiva comes under fire from Victoria Davion for suggesting that "... what is missing from the western patriarchal perspective is the 'feminine principle.'"[25] Davion, however, finds Shiva's arguments on development and poverty convincing, talk about femininity and gender complementarity aside.

Western development in third-world countries, according to Shiva, "... destroys wholesome and sustainable lifestyles and creates real material poverty, or misery, by the denial of survival needs themselves through the diversion of resources to resource intensive commodity production."[26] The point is that the resources needed to produce commodities such as cash crops for a market economy are resources that are *already being used* by third-world people for purposes of sustenance. As Shiva says, "The needs of the Amazonian tribes are more than satisfied by the rich rainforest; their poverty begins with its destruction."[27] Although third-world men as well as women suffer from the devastation of their environment, women are more the losers because they, as the primary producers of food, water, and fuel, have lost their livelihood; their knowledge and practices have been undermined. Moreover, unsurprisingly, they have virtually no access, and certainly less access than do men, to land ownership, technology, employment for wages, and small business loans should they have any desire to convert to a Western life-style. The frustration over the loss of forests can be heard in the voice of Hima Devi, a member of the woman-led Chipko ("tree-hugging") movement when she says to her audiences:

> My sisters are busy harvesting the Kharif crop. They are busy in winnowing. I have come to you with their message. Stop cutting trees. There are no trees even for birds to perch on. Birds flock to our crops and eat them. What will we eat? The firewood is disappearing: how will we cook?[28]

Shiva calls Western-type development "maldevelopment" because it results in real poverty (the denial of survival needs) while, ironically, trying to eliminate culturally perceived poverty. By describing subsistence economies as situations of poverty, those who favor market economies can present themselves as rescuing third-world countries from poverty. In so doing, Shiva says, they mask the need to argue the case that market economies are superior to subsistence economies. Indeed, the Western ploy is to deny that subsistence economies count as economies at all. The work done for the sake of sustenance is not "productive." And if the work done by many women in the Western world is not considered "productive," or worth anything from an economic point of view, it is easy to see how woman-based subsistence economies can be viewed as not "productive." Shiva sums it up in one of her apt subtitles: "development as a new project of Western patriarchy."

NOTES

1. Jan Clausen, "Rethinking the World," *The Nation* (September 23, 1991), 346.

2. Val Plumwood, "Women, Humanity and Nature," *Radical Philosophy,* Vol. 48 (Spring 1988), 16.

3. Karen J. Warren, "Abstract," "The Power and the Promise of Ecological Feminism," *Environmental Ethics,* Vol. 12, No. 2 (Summer 1990), 125.

4. Warren, "Abstract," p. 125.

5. Karen J. Warren, "The Power and the Promise of Ecological Feminism," *Environmental Ethics,* Vol. 12, No. 2 (Summer 1990), 125.

6. Warren, 129.

7. Warren, 128.

8. Marilyn Frye, *The Politics of Reality* (Trumansburg, NY: The Crossing Press, 1983), pp. 66–72.

9. *Ecofeminism: Women, Animals, Nature,* edited by Greta Gaard (Philadelphia: Temple University Press, 1992).

10. Greta Gaard, "Ecofeminism and Native American Cultures: Pushing the Limits of Cultural Imperialism?," in *Ecofeminsm: Women, Animals, Nature,* edited by Greta Gaard (Philadelphia: Temple University Press, 1992, p. 296).

11. Warren does include "naturism," i.e., the oppression of nature, in her discussion. She may mean this to include animals.

12. Val Plumwood, "Abstract," "Nature, Self, and Gender: Feminism, Environmental Philosophy, and the Critique of Rationalism," *Hypatia,* Vol. 6, No. 1 (Spring 1991), 3.

13. These remarks on the topic of universalization in ethics were made by Christine Pierce, "Postmodernism and Other Skepticisms," *Feminist Ethics,* edited by Claudia Card (Lawrence: University Press of Kansas, 1991), p. 64.

14. Val Plumwood, "Nature, Self, and Gender: Feminism, Environmental Philosophy, and the Critique of Rationalism," *Hypatia,* Vol. 6, No. 1 (Spring 1991), 6–7.

15. Plumwood, "Nature, Self, and Gender," 20.

16. Robert Sessions, "Deep Ecology Versus Ecofeminism: Healthy Differences or Incompatible Philosophies?" *Hypatia,* Vol. 6, No. 1 (Spring 1991), 95–96.

17. Plumwood, "Nature, Self, and Gender," 12. John Seed, "Beyond Anthropocentrism," in *Thinking Like a Mountain: Towards a Council of All Beings,* edited by John Seed, Joanna Macy, Pat Fleming, and Arne Naess (Philadelphia: New Society Publishers, 1988), p. 36.

18. Plumwood, "Nature, Self, and Gender," 15.

19. Plumwood, "Nature, Self, and Gender," 13.

20. Plumwood, "Nature, Self, and Gender," 13.

21. Val Plumwood, "Conversations with Gaia," in *APA Newsletters,* Vol. 91, No. 1 (Spring 1992), 63.

22. Val Plumwood, "Nature, Self, and Gender," 20.

23. Victoria Davion, "How Feminist Is Ecofeminism?" in *Ecological Feminism,* edited by Karen J. Warren (London: Routledge, forthcoming) 288–289 this volume.

24. Victoria Davion, "How Feminist Is Ecofeminism?," 292 this volume.

25. Victoria Davion, "How Feminist Is Ecofeminism?," 292 this volume.

26. Vandana Shiva, "Development, Ecology and Women," in *Staying Alive: Women, Ecology and Development* (London: Zed Books Ltd., 1988), p. 10.

27. Vandana Shiva, "Development, Ecology and Women," 12.

28. Vandana Shiva, "Development, Ecology and Women," 74–75.

Nature, Self, and Gender: Feminism, Environmental Philosophy, and the Critique of Rationalism

Val Plumwood

Environmental philosophy has recently been criticized on a number of counts by feminist philosophers. I want to develop further some of this critique and to suggest that much of the issue turns on the failure of environmental philosophy to engage properly with the rationalist tradition, which has been inimical to both women and nature. Damaging assumptions from this tradition have been employed in attempting to formulate a new environmental philosophy that often makes use of or embeds itself within rationalist philosophical frameworks that are not only biased from a gender perspective, but have claimed a negative role for nature as well.

In sections I. through IV. I argue that current mainstream brands of environmental philosophy, both those based in ethics and those based in deep ecology, suffer from this problem, that neither has an adequate historical analysis, and that both continue to rely implicitly upon rationalist-inspired accounts of the self that have been a large part of the problem. In sections V. and VI. I show how the critique of rationalism offers an understanding of a range of key broader issues that environmental philosophy has tended to neglect or treat in too narrow a way. Among these issues are those connected with concepts of the human self and with instrumentalism.

I. Rationalism and the Ethical Approach

The ethical approach aims to center a new view of nature in ethics, especially universalizing ethics or in some extension of human ethics. This approach has been criticized from a feminist perspective by a number of recent authors (especially Cheney 1987, 1989). I partly agree with and partly disagree with these criticisms; that is, I think that the emphasis on ethics as the central part (or even

the whole) of the problem is misplaced, and that although ethics (and especially the ethics of noninstrumental value) has a role, the particular ethical approaches that have been adopted are problematic and unsuitable. I shall illustrate this claim by a brief discussion of two recent books: Paul Taylor's *Respect for Nature* (1986) and Tom Regan's *The Case for Animal Rights* (1986). Both works are significant, and indeed impressive, contributions to their respective areas.

Paul Taylor's book is a detailed working out of an ethical position that rejects the standard and widespread Western treatment of nature as instrumental to human interests and instead takes living things, as teleological centers of life, to be worthy of respect in their own right. Taylor aims to defend a biocentric (life-centered) ethical theory in which a person's true human self includes his or her biological nature (Taylor 1986, 44), but he attempts to embed this within a Kantian ethical framework that makes strong use of the reason/emotion dichotomy. Thus we are assured that the attitude of respect is a moral one because it is universalizing and disinterested, "that is, each moral agent who sincerely has the attitude advocates its universal adoption by all other agents, regardless of whether they are so inclined and regardless of their fondness or lack of fondness for particular individuals" (41). The essential features of morality having been established as distance from emotion and "particular fondness," morality is then seen as the domain of reason and its touchstone, belief. Having carefully distinguished the "valuational, conative, practical, and affective dimensions of the attitude of respect," Taylor goes on to pick out the essentially cognitive "valuational" aspect as central and basic to all the others: "It is *because* moral agents look at animals and plants in this way that they are disposed to pursue the aforementioned ends and purposes" (82) and, similarly, to have the relevant emo-

Hypatia vol. 6, no. 1 (Spring 1991), 3–27. Reprinted by permission of the author.

tions and affective attitudes. The latter must be held at an appropriate distance and not allowed to get the upper hand at any point. Taylor claims that actions do not express moral respect unless they are done as a matter of moral principle conceived as ethically obligatory and pursued disinterestedly and not through inclination, solely or even primarily:

> If one seeks that end solely or primarily from inclination, the attitude being expressed is not moral respect but personal affection or love. . . . It is not that respect for nature *precludes* feelings of care and concern for living things. One may, as a matter of simple kindness, not want to harm them. But the fact that one is so motivated does not itself indicate the presence of a moral attitude of respect. Having the desire to preserve or protect the good of wild animals and plants for their sake is neither contrary to, nor evidence of, respect for nature. It is only if the person who has the desire understands that the actions fulfilling it would be obligatory even in the absence of the desire, that the person has genuine respect for nature. (85–86)

There is good reason to reject as self-indulgent the "kindness" approach that reduces respect and morality in the protection of animals to the satisfaction of the carer's own feelings. Respect for others involves treating them as worthy of consideration for their own sake and not just as an instrument for the carer's satisfaction, and there is a sense in which such "kindness" is not genuine care or respect for the other. But Taylor is doing much more than this—he is treating care, viewed as "inclination" or "desire," as irrelevant to morality. Respect for nature on this account becomes an essentially *cognitive* matter (that of a person believing something to have "inherent worth" and then acting from an understanding of ethical principles as universal).

The account draws on the familiar view of reason and emotion as sharply separated and opposed, and of "desire," caring, and love as merely "personal" and "particular" as opposed to the universality and impartiality of understanding and of "feminine" emotions as essentially unreliable, untrustworthy, and morally irrelevant, an inferior domain to be dominated by a superior, disinterested (and of course masculine) reason. This sort of rationalist account of the place of emotions has come in

for a great deal of well-deserved criticism recently, both for its implicit gender bias and its philosophical inadequacy, especially its dualism and its construal of public reason as sharply differentiated from and controlling private emotion (see, for example, Benhabib 1987; Blum 1980; Gilligan 1982, 1987; Lloyd 1983a and 1983b).

A further major problem in its use in this context is the inconsistency of employing, in the service of constructing an allegedly biocentric ethical theory, a framework that has itself played such a major role in creating a dualistic account of the genuine human self as essentially rational and as sharply discontinuous from the merely emotional, the merely bodily, and the merely animal elements. For emotions and the private sphere with which they are associated have been treated as sharply differentiated and inferior as part of a pattern in which they are seen as linked to the sphere of nature, not the realm of reason.

And it is not only women but also the earth's wild living things that have been denied possession of a reason thus construed along masculine and oppositional lines and which contrasts not only with the "feminine" emotions but also with the physical and the animal. Much of the problem (both for women and nature) lies in rationalist or rationalist-derived conceptions of the self and of what is essential and valuable in the human makeup. It is in the name of such a reason that these other things—the feminine, the emotional, the merely bodily or the merely animal, and the natural world itself—have most often been denied their virtue and been accorded an inferior and merely instrumental position. Thomas Aquinas states this problematic positions succinctly: "the intellectual nature is alone requisite for its own sake in the universe, and all others for its sake" (Thomas Aquinas 1976, 56). And it is precisely reason so construed that is usually taken to characterize the authentically human and to create the supposedly sharp separation, cleavage, or discontinuity between all humans and the nonhuman world, and the similar cleavage within the human self. The supremacy accorded an oppositionally construed reason is the key to the anthropocentrism of the Western tradition. The Kantian-rationalist framework, then, is hardly the area in which to search for a solution. Its use, in a way that perpetuates the supremacy of reason and its opposition to contrast areas, in the service of constructing a supposedly biocentric ethic is a matter for astonishment.

Ethical universalization and abstraction are both closely associated with accounts of the self in terms of rational egoism. Universalization is explicitly seen in both the Kantian and the Rawlsian framework as needed to hold in check natural self-interest; it is the moral complement to the account of the self as "disembodied and disembedded," as the autonomous self of liberal theory, the rational egoist of market theory, the falsely differentiated self of object-relations theory (Benhabib 1987; Poole 1984, 1985). In the same vein, the broadening of the scope of moral concern along with the according of rights to the natural world has been seen by influential environmental philosophers (Leopold 1949, 201–2) as the final step in a process of increasing moral abstraction and generalization, part of the move away from the merely particular—*my* self, *my* family, *my* tribe—the discarding of the merely personal and, by implication, the merely selfish. This is viewed as moral progress, increasingly civilized as it moves further away from primitive selfishness. Nature is the last area to be included in this march away from the unbridled natural egoism of the particular and its close ally, the emotional. Moral progress is marked by increasing adherence to moral rules and a movement away from the supposedly natural (in human nature), and the completion of its empire is, paradoxically, the extension of its domain of adherence to abstract moral rules to nature itself.

On such a view, the particular and the emotional are seen as the enemy of the rational, as corrupting, capricious, and self-interested. And if the "moral emotions" are set aside as irrelevant or suspect, as merely subjective or personal, we can only base morality on the rules of abstract reason, on the justice and rights of the impersonal public sphere.

This view of morality as based on a concept of reason as oppositional to the personal, the particular, and the emotional has been assumed in the framework of much recent environmental ethics. But as a number of feminist critics of the masculine model of moral life and of moral abstraction have pointed out (Blum 1980, Nicholson 1983), this increasing abstraction is not necessarily an improvement. The opposition between the care and concern for particular others and generalized moral concern is associated with a sharp division between public (masculine) and private (feminine) realms. Thus it is part of the set of dualistic contrasts in which the problem of the Western treatment of nature is rooted. And the opposition between care for particular others and general moral concern is a false one. There *can* be opposition between particularity and generality of concern, as when concern for particular others is accompanied by *exclusion* of others from care or chauvinistic attitudes toward them (Blum 1980, 80), but this does not automatically happen, and emphasis on oppositional cases obscures the frequent cases where they work together—and in which care for particular others is essential to a more generalized morality. Special relationships, which are treated by universalizing positions as at best morally irrelevant and at worst a positive hindrance to the moral life, are thus mistreated. For as Blum (1980, 78–83) stresses, special relationships form the basis for much of our moral life and concern, and it could hardly be otherwise. With nature, as with the human sphere, the capacity to care, to experience sympathy, understanding, and sensitivity to the situation and fate of particular others, and to take responsibility for others is an index of our moral being. Special relationship with, care for, or empathy with particular aspects of nature as experiences rather than with nature as abstraction are essential to provide a depth and type of concern that is not otherwise possible. Care and responsibility for particular animals, trees, and rivers that are known well, loved, and appropriately connected to the self are an important basis for acquiring a wider, more generalized concern. (As we shall see, this failure to deal adequately with particularity is a problem for deep ecology as well.)

Concern for nature, then, should not be viewed as the completion of a process of (masculine) universalization, moral abstraction, and disconnection, discarding the self, emotions, and special ties (all, of course, associated with the private sphere and femininity). Environmental ethics has for the most part placed itself uncritically in such a framework, although it is one that is extended with particular difficulty to the natural world. Perhaps the kindest thing that can be said about the framework of ethical universalization is that it is seriously incomplete and fails to capture the most important elements of respect, which are not reducible to or based on duty or obligation any more than the most important elements of friendship are, but which are rather an expression of a certain kind of selfhood and a certain kind of relation between self and other.

II. Rationalism, Rights, and Ethics

An extension to nature of the standard concepts of morality is also the aim of Tom Regan's *The Case for Animal Rights* (1986). This is the most impressive, thorough, and solidly argued book in the area of animal ethics, with excellent chapters on topics such as animal intentionality. But the key concept upon which this account of moral concern for animals is based is that of rights, which requires strong individual separation of rights-holders and is set in a framework of human community and legality. Its extension to the natural world raises a host of problems (Midgley 1983, 61–64). Even in the case of individual higher animals for which Regan uses this concept of rights, the approach is problematic. His concept of rights is based on Mill's notion that, if a being has a right to something not only should he or she (or it) have that thing but others are obliged to intervene to secure it. The application of this concept of rights to individual wild living animals appears to give humans almost limitless obligations to intervene massively in all sorts of far reaching and conflicting ways in natural cycles to secure the rights of a bewildering variety of beings. In the case of the wolf and the sheep, an example discussed by Regan, it is unclear whether humans should intervene to protect the sheep's rights or to avoid doing so in order not to violate the wolf's right to its natural food.

Regan attempts to meet this objection by claiming that since the wolf is not itself a moral agent (although it is a moral patient), it cannot violate the sheep's rights not to suffer a painful and violent death (Regan 1986, 285). But the defense is unconvincing, because even if we concede that the wolf is not a moral agent, it still does not follow that on a rights view we are not obliged to intervene. From the fact that the wolf is not a moral agent it only follows that it is not *responsible* for violating the sheep's rights, not that they are not vio-

lated or that others do not have an obligation (according to the rights view) to intervene. If the wolf were attacking a human baby, it would hardly do as a defense in that case to claim that one did not have a duty to intervene because the wolf was not a moral agent. But on Regan's view the baby and the sheep do have something like the same rights. So we do have a duty, it seems, (on the rights view) to intervene to protect the sheep—leaving us where with the wolf?

The concept of rights seems to produce absurd consequences and is impossible to apply in the context of predators in a natural ecosystem, as opposed to a particular human social context in which claimants are part of a reciprocal social community and conflict cases either few or settleable according to some agreed-on principles. All this seems to me to tell against the concept of rights as the correct one for the general task of dealing with animals in the natural environment (as opposed, of course, to domestic animals in a basically humanized environment).[1]

Rights seem to have acquired an exaggerated importance as part of the prestige of the public sphere and the masculine, and the emphasis on separation and autonomy, on reason and abstraction. A more promising approach for an ethics of nature, and also one much more in line with the current directions in feminism, would be to remove rights from the center of the moral stage and pay more attention to some other, less dualistic, moral concepts such as respect, sympathy, care, concern, compassion, gratitude, friendship, and responsibility (Cook 1977, 118–9). These concepts, because of their dualistic construal as feminine and their consignment to the private sphere as subjective and emotional, have been treated as peripheral and given far less importance than they deserve for several reasons. First, rationalism and the prestige of reason and the public sphere have influenced not only the concept of what morality is (as Taylor explicates it, for example, as essentially a rational and cognitive act of understanding that certain actions are ethically obligatory) but of what is *central* to it or what count as moral concepts. Second, concepts such as respect, care, concern, and so on are resistant to analysis along lines of a dualistic reason/emotion dichotomy, and their construal along these lines has involved confusion and distortion (Blum

1980). They *are* moral "feelings" but they involve reason, behavior and emotion in ways that do not seem separable. Rationalist-inspired ethical concepts are highly ethnocentric and cannot account adequately for the views of many indigenous peoples, and the attempted application of these rationalist concepts to their positions tends to lead to the view that they lack a real ethical framework (Plumwood 1990). These alternative concepts seem better able to apply to the views of such peoples, whose ethic of respect, care and responsibility for land is often based on special relationships with particular areas of land via links to kin (Neidjie, 1985, 1989). Finally these concepts, which allow for particularity and mostly do not require reciprocity, are precisely the sorts of concepts feminist philosophers have argued should have a more significant place in ethics at the expense of abstract, male-stream concepts from the public sphere such as rights and justice (Gilligan 1982, 1987; Benhabib 1987). The ethic of care and responsibility they have articulated seems to extend much less problematically to the nonhuman world than do the impersonal concepts which are currently seen as central, and it also seems capable of providing an excellent basis for the noninstrumental treatment of nature many environmental philosophers have now called for. Such an approach treats ethical relations as an expression of self-in-relationship (Gilligan 1987, 24) rather than as the discarding, containment, or generalization of a self viewed as self-interested and non-relational, as in the conventional ethics of universalization.[2] As I argue later, there are important connections between this relational account of the self and the rejection of instrumentalism.

It is not that we need to abandon ethics or dispense with the universalized ethical approach entirely, although we do need to reassess the centrality of ethics in environmental philosophy.[3] What is needed is not so much the abandonment of ethics as a different and richer understanding of it (and, as I argue later, a richer understanding of environmental philosophy generally than is provided by ethics), one that gives an important place to ethical concepts owing to emotionality and particularity and that abandons the exclusive focus on the universal and the abstract associated with the non-relational self and the dualistic and oppositional accounts of the reason/emotion and universal/particular contrasts as given in rationalist accounts of ethics.

III. The Discontinuity Problem

The problem is not just one of restriction *in* ethics but also of restriction *to* ethics. Most mainstream environmental philosophers continue to view environmental philosophy as mainly concerned with ethics. For example, instrumentalism is generally viewed by mainstream environmental philosophers as a problem in ethics, and its solution is seen as setting up some sort of theory of intrinsic value. This neglects a key aspect of the overall problem that is concerned with the definition of the human self as separate from nature, the connection between this and the instrumental view of nature, and broader *political* aspects of the critique of instrumentalism.

One key aspect of the Western view of nature, which the ethical stance neglects completely, is the view of nature as sharply discontinuous or ontologically divided from the human sphere. This leads to a view of humans as apart from or "outside of" nature, usually as masters or external controllers of it. Attempts to reject this view often speak alternatively of humans as "part of nature" but rarely distinguish this position from the obvious claim that human fate is interconnected with that of the biosphere, that humans are subject to natural laws. But on the divided-self theory it is the essentially or authentically human part of the self, and in that sense the human realm proper, that is outside nature, not the human as a physical phenomenon. The view of humans as outside of and alien to nature seems to be especially strongly a Western one, although not confined to the West. There are many other cultures which do not hold it, which stress what connects us to nature as genuinely human virtues, which emphasize continuity and not dissimilarity.[4]

As ecofeminism points out, Western thought has given us a strong human/nature dualism that is part of the set of interrelated dualisms of mind/body, reason/nature, reason/emotion, masculine/feminine and has important interconnected features with these other dualisms.[5] This dualism has been especially stressed in the rationalist tradition. In this dualism what is characteristically and authentically human is defined against or in opposition to what is taken to be natural, nature, or the physical or biological realm. This takes various forms. For example, the characterization of the genuinely, properly, characteristically, or authentically human, or of human virtue, in polarized terms to exclude what is taken to be characteristic of the natural is what John Rodman (1980) has called "the Differential Imperative" in which what is virtuous in the human is taken to be what maximizes distance from the merely natural. The maintenance of sharp dichotomy and polarization is achieved by the rejection and denial of what links humans to the animal. What is taken to be authentically and characteristically human, defining of the human, as well as the ideal for which humans should strive is *not* to be found in what is shared with the natural and animal (e.g., the body, sexuality, reproduction, emotionality, the senses, agency) but in what is thought to separate and distinguish them—especially reason and its offshoots. Hence humanity is defined not as part of nature (perhaps a special part) but as separate from and in opposition to it. Thus the relation of humans to nature is treated as an oppositional and value dualism.

The process closely parallels the formation of other dualisms, such as masculine/feminine, reason/emotion, and spirit/body criticized in feminist thought (see, for example, Ruether 1975, Griffin 1978, Griscom 1981, King 1981, Lloyd 1983, Jaggar 1983) but this parallel logic is not the only connection between human/nature dualism and masculine/feminine dualism. Moreover, this exclusion of the natural from the concept of the properly human is not the only dualism involved, because what is involved in the construction of this dualistic conception of the human is the rejection of those parts of the human character identified as feminine—also identified as less than fully human—giving the masculine conception of what it is to be human. Masculinity can be linked to this exclusionary and polarized conception of the human, via the desire to exclude and distance from the feminine and the nonhuman. The features that are taken as characteristic of humankind and as where its special virtues lie, are those such as rationality, freedom, and transcendence of nature (all traditionally viewed as masculine), which are viewed as not shared with nature. Humanity is defined oppositionally to both nature and the feminine.

The upshot is a deeply entrenched view of the genuine or ideal human self as not including features shared with nature, and as defined *against* or in *opposition to* the nonhuman realm, so that the human sphere and that of nature cannot significantly overlap. Nature is sharply divided from the human, is alien and usually hostile and inferior. Furthermore, this kind of human self can only have certain kinds of accidental or contingent connections to the realm of nature. I shall call this the discontinuity problem or thesis and I argue later that it plays a key role with respect to other elements of the problem.

IV. Rationalism and Deep Ecology

Although the discontinuity problem is generally neglected by the ethical stance, a significant exception to its neglect within environmental philosophy seems to be found in deep ecology, which is also critical of the location of the problem within ethics.[6] Furthermore, deep ecology also seems initially to be more likely to be compatible with a feminist philosophical framework, emphasizing as it does connections with the self, connectedness, and merger. Nevertheless, there are severe tensions between deep ecology and a feminist perspective. Deep ecology has not satisfactorily identified the key elements in the traditional framework or observed their connections to rationalism. As a result, it fails to reject adequately rationalist assumptions and indeed often seems to provide its own versions of universalization, the discarding of particular connections, and rationalist accounts of self.

Deep ecology locates the key problem area in human-nature relations in the separation of humans and nature, and it provides a solution for this in terms of the "identification" of self with nature. "Identification" is usually left deliberately vague, and corresponding accounts of self are various and shifting and not always compatible.[7] There seem to be at least three different accounts of self involved—indistinguishability, expansion of self, and transcendence of self—and practitioners appear to feel free to move among them at will. As I shall show, all are unsatisfactory from both a feminist perspective and from that of obtaining a satisfactory environmental philosophy, and the appeal of deep ecology rests largely on the failure to distinguish them.

A. The Indistinguishability Account

The indistinguishability account rejects boundaries between self and nature. Humans are said to be just one strand in the biotic web, not the source and ground of all value and the discontinuity thesis is, it seems, firmly rejected. Warwick Fox describes the central intuition of deep ecology as follows: "We can make no firm ontological divide in the field of existence . . . there is no bifurcation in reality between the human and nonhuman realms. . . . to the extent that we perceive boundaries, we fall short of deep ecological consciousness" (Fox 1984, 7). But much more is involved here than the rejection of discontinuity, for deep ecology goes on to replace the human-in-environment image by a holistic or gestalt view that "dissolves not only the human-in-environment concept, but every compact-thing-in-milieu concept"—except when talking at a superficial level of communication (Fox 1984, 1). Deep ecology involves a cosmology of "unbroken wholeness which denies the classical idea of the analyzability of the world into separately and independently existing parts."[8] It is strongly attracted to a variety of mystical traditions and to the Perennial Philosophy, in which the self is merged with the other—"the other is none other than yourself." As John Seed puts it: "I am protecting the rain forest" develops into "I am part of the rain forest protecting myself. I am that part of the rain forest recently emerged into thinking" (Seed et al. 1988, 36).

There are severe problems with these claims, arising not so much from the orientation to the concept of self (which seems to me important and correct) or from the mystical character of the insights themselves as from the indistinguishability metaphysics which is proposed as their basis. It is not merely that the identification process of which deep ecologists speak seems to stand in need of much more clarification, but that it does the wrong thing. The problem, in the sort of account I have given, is the discontinuity between humans and nature that emerges as part of the overall set of Western dualisms. Deep ecology proposes to heal this division by a "unifying process," a metaphysics that insists that everything is really part of and indistinguishable from everything else. This is not

only to employ overly powerful tools but ones that do the wrong job, for the origins of the particular opposition involved in the human/nature dualism remain unaddressed and unanalyzed. The real basis of the discontinuity lies in the concept of an authentic human being, in what is taken to be valuable in human character, society, and culture, as what is distinct from what is taken to be natural. The sources of and remedies for this remain unaddressed in deep ecology. Deep ecology has confused dualism and atomism and then mistakenly taken indistinguishability to follow from the rejection of atomism. The confusion is clear in Fox, who proceeds immediately from the ambiguous claim that there is no "bifurcation in reality between the human and nonhuman realms" (which could be taken as a rejection of human discontinuity from nature) to the conclusion that what is needed is that we embrace an indistinguishability metaphysics of unbroken wholeness in the whole of reality. But the problem must be addressed in terms of this specific dualism and its connections. Instead deep ecology proposes the obliteration of all distinction.

Thus, deep ecology's solution to removing this discontinuity by obliterating *all* division is far too powerful. In its overgenerality it fails to provide a genuine basis for an environmental ethics of the kind sought, for the view of humans as metaphysically unified with the cosmic whole will be equally true whatever relation humans stand in with nature—the situation of exploitation of nature exemplifies such unity equally as well as a conserver situation and the human self is just as indistinguishable from the bulldozer and Coca-Cola bottle as the rocks or the rain forest. What John Seed seems to have in mind here is that once one has realized that one is indistinguishable from the rain forest, its needs would become one's own. But there is nothing to guarantee this—one could equally well take one's own needs for its.

This points to a further problem with the indistinguishability thesis, that we need to recognize not only our human continuity with the natural world but also its distinctness and independence from us and the distinctness of the needs of things in nature from ours. The indistinguishability account does not allow for this, although it is a very important part of respect for nature and of conservation strategy.

The dangers of accounts of the self that involve self-merger appear in feminist contexts as well, where they are sometimes appealed to as the alternative to masculine-defined autonomy as disconnection from others. As Jean Grimshaw writes of the related thesis of the indistinctness of persons (the acceptance of the loss of self-boundaries as a feminine ideal): "It is important not merely because certain forms of symbiosis or 'connection' with others can lead to damaging failures of personal development, but because care for others, understanding of them, are only possible if one can adequately distinguish oneself *from* others. If I see myself as 'indistinct' from you, or you as not having your own being that is not merged with mine, then I cannot preserve a real sense of your well-being as opposed to mine. Care and understanding require the sort of distance that is needed in order not to see the other as a projection of self, or self as a continuation of the other" (Grimshaw 1986, 182–3).

These points seem to me to apply to caring for other species and for the natural world as much as they do to caring for our own species. But just as dualism is confused with atomism, so holistic self-merger is taken to be the only alternative to egoistic accounts of the self as without essential connection to others or to nature. Fortunately, this is a false choice;[9] as I argue below, nonholistic but relational accounts of the self, as developed in some feminist and social philosophy, enable a rejection of dualism, including human/nature dualism, without denying the independence or distinguishability of the other. To the extent that deep ecology is identified with the indistinguishability thesis, it does not provide an adequate basis for a philosophy of nature.

B. The Expanded Self

In fairness to deep ecology it should be noted that it tends to vacillate between mystical indistinguishability and the other accounts of self, between the holistic self and the expanded self. Vacillation occurs often by way of slipperiness as to what is meant by identification of self with the other, a key notion in deep ecology. This slipperiness reflects the confusion of dualism and atomism previously noted but also seems to reflect a desire to retain the mystical appeal of indistinguishability while avoiding its many difficulties. Where "identification" means not "identity" but something more like "empathy," identification with other beings can lead to an expanded self. According to Arne Naess, "The self is as comprehensive as the totality of our identifications. . . . Our Self is that with which we

identify."[10] This larger self (or Self, to deep ecologists) is something for which we should strive "insofar as it is in our power to do so" (Fox 1986, 13–19), and according to Fox we should also strive to make it as large as possible. But this expanded self is not the result of a critique of egoism; rather, it is an enlargement and an extension of egoism.[11] It does not question the structures of possessive egoism and self-interest; rather, it tries to allow for a wider set of interests by an expansion of self. The motivation for the expansion of self is to allow for a wider set of concerns while continuing to allow the self to operate on the fuel of self-interest (or Self-interest). This is apparent from the claim that "in this light . . . ecological resistance is simply another name for self defense" (Fox 1986, 60). Fox quotes with approval John Livingstone's statement: "When I say that the fate of the sea turtle or the tiger or the gibbon is mine, I mean it. All that is in my universe is not merely mine; it is *me*. And I shall defend myself. I shall defend myself not only against overt aggression but also against gratuitous insult" (Fox 1986, 60).

Deep ecology does not question the structures of rational egoism and continues to subscribe to two of the main tenets of the egoist framework—that human nature is egoistic and that the alternative to egoism is self-sacrifice.[12] Given these assumptions about egoism, the obvious way to obtain some sort of human interest in defending nature is through the expanded Self operating in the interests of nature but also along the familiar lines of self-interest.[13] The expanded-self strategy might initially seem to be just another pretentious and obscure way of saying that humans empathize with nature. But the strategy of transferring the structures of egoism is highly problematic, for the widening of interest is obtained at the expense of failing to recognise unambiguously the distinctness and independence of the other.[14] Others are recognized morally only to the extent that they are incorporated into the self, and their difference denied (Warren 1990). And the failure to critique egoism and the disembedded, nonrelational self means a failure to draw connections with other contemporary critiques.

C. The Transcended or Transpersonal Self

To the extent that the expanded Self requires that we detach from the particular concerns of the self (a relinquishment that despite its natural difficulty we should struggle to attain), expansion of self to Self also tends to lead into the third position, the transcendence or overcoming of self. Thus Fox urges us to strive for *impartial* identification with *all* particulars, the cosmos, discarding our identifications with our own particular concerns, personal emotions, and attachments (Fox 1990, 12). Fox presents here the deep ecology version of universalization, with the familiar emphasis on the personal and the particular as corrupting and self-interested—"the cause of possessiveness, war and ecological destruction" (1990, 12).

This treatment of particularity, the devaluation of an identity tied to particular parts of the natural world as opposed to an abstractly conceived whole, the cosmos, reflects the rationalistic preoccupation with the universal and its account of ethical life as oppositional to the particular. The analogy in human terms of impersonal love of the cosmos is the view of morality as based on universal principles or the impersonal and abstract "love of man." Thus Fox (1990, 12) reiterates (as if it were unproblematic) the view of particular attachments as ethically suspect and as oppositional to genuine, impartial "identification," which necessarily falls short with all particulars.

Because this "transpersonal" identification is so indiscriminate and intent on denying particular meanings, it cannot allow for the deep and highly particularistic attachment to place that has motivated both the passion of many modern conservationists and the love of many indigenous peoples for their land (which deep ecology inconsistently tries to treat as a model). This is based not on a vague, bloodless, and abstract cosmological concern but on the formation of identity, social and personal, in relation to particular areas of land, yielding ties often as special and powerful as those to kin, and which are equally expressed in very specific and local responsibilities of care.[15] This emerges clearly in the statements of many indigenous peoples, such as in the moving words of Cecilia Blacktooth explaining why her people would not surrender their land:

> You ask us to think what place we like next best to this place where we always lived. You see the graveyard there? There are our fathers and our grandfathers. You see that Eagle-nest mountain and that Rabbit-hole mountain? When God made them, He gave us this place. We have always been here. We do not care for

any other place. . . . We have always lived here. We would rather die here. Our fathers did. We cannot leave them. Our children were born here—how can we go away? If you give us the best place in the world, it is not so good as this. . . . This is our home. . . . We cannot live any where else. We were born here and our fathers are buried here. . . . We want this place and no other. . . . (McLuhan 1979, 28)

In inferiorizing such particular, emotional, and kinship-based attachments, deep ecology gives us another variant on the superiority of reason and the inferiority of its contrasts, failing to grasp yet again the role of reason and incompletely critiquing its influence. To obtain a more adequate account than that offered by mainstream ethics and deep ecology it seems that we must move toward the sort of ethics feminist theory has suggested, which can allow for both continuity and difference and for ties to nature which are expressive of the rich, caring relationships of kinship and friendship rather than increasing abstraction and detachment from relationship.[16]

V. The Problem in Terms of the Critique of Rationalism

I now show how the problem of the inferiorization of nature appears if it is viewed from the perspective of the critique of rationalism and seen as part of the general problem of revaluing and reintegrating what rationalist culture has split apart, denied, and devalued. Such an account shifts the focus away from the preoccupations of both mainstream ethical approaches and deep ecology, and although it does retain an emphasis on the account of the self as central, it gives a different account from that offered by deep ecology. In section VI. I conclude by arguing that one of the effects of this shift in focus is to make connections with other critiques, especially feminism, central rather than peripheral or accidental, as they are currently viewed by deep ecologists in particular.

First, what is missing from the accounts of both the ethical philosophers and the deep ecologists is an understanding of the problem of discontinuity as created by a dualism linked to a network of related dualisms. Here I believe a good deal can be learned from the critique of dualism feminist philosophy has developed and from the understanding of the mechanisms of dualisms ecofeminists have produced. A dualistically construed dichotomy typically polarizes difference and minimizes shared characteristics, construes difference along lines of superiority/inferiority, and views the inferior side as a means to the higher ends of the superior side (the instrumental thesis). Because its nature is defined oppositionally, the task of the superior side, that in which it realizes itself and expresses its true nature, is to separate from, dominate, and control the lower side. This has happened both with the human/nature division and with other related dualisms such as masculine/feminine, reason/body, and reason/emotion. Challenging these dualisms involves not just a reevaluation of superiority/inferiority and a higher status for the underside of the dualisms (in this case nature) but also a reexamination and reconceptualizing of the dualistically construed categories themselves. So in the case of the human/nature dualism it is not just a question of improving the status of nature, moral or otherwise, while everything else remains the same, but of reexamining and reconceptualizing the concept of the human, and also the concept of the contrasting class of nature. For the concept of the human, of what it is to be fully and authentically human, and of what is genuinely human in the set of characteristics typical humans possess, has been defined oppositionally, by *exclusion* of what is associated with the inferior natural sphere in very much the way that Lloyd (1983), for example, has shown in the case of the categories of masculine and feminine, and of reason and its contrasts. Humans have both biological and mental characteristics, but the mental rather than the biological have been taken to be characteristic of the human and to give what is "fully and authentically" human. The term "human" is, of course, not merely descriptive here but very much an evaluative term setting out an ideal: it is what is essential or worthwhile in the human that excludes the natural. It is not necessarily denied that humans have some material or animal component—rather, it is seen in this framework as alien or inessential to them, not part of their fully or truly human nature. The human essence is often seen as lying in maximizing control over the natural sphere (both within and without) and in qualities such as rationality, freedom, and transcendence of the material sphere. These qualities are also identified as masculine, and hence the *oppositional* model of the human

coincides or converges with a masculine model, in which the characteristics attributed are those of the masculine ideal.

Part of a strategy for challenging this human/nature dualism, then, would involve recognition of these excluded qualities—split off, denied, or construed as alien, or comprehended as the sphere of supposedly *inferior* humans such as women and blacks—as equally and fully human. This would provide a basis for the recognition of *continuities* with the natural world. Thus reproductivity, sensuality, emotionality would be taken to be as fully and authentically human qualities as the capacity for abstract planning and calculation. This proceeds from the assumption that one basis for discontinuity and alienation from nature is alienation from those qualities which provide continuity with nature in ourselves.

This connection between the rationalist account of nature within and nature without has powerful repercussions. So part of what is involved is a challenge to the centrality and dominance of the rational in the account of the human self. Such a challenge would have far-reaching implications for what is valuable in human society and culture, and it connects with the challenge to the cultural legacy of rationalism made by other critiques of rationalism such as feminism, and by critiques of technocracy, bureaucracy, and instrumentalism.

What is involved here is a reconceptualization of the human side of the human/nature dualism, to free it from the legacy of rationalism. Also in need of reconceptualization is the underside of this dualism, the concept of nature, which is construed in polarized terms as bereft of qualities appropriated to the human side, as passive and lacking in agency and teleology, as pure materiality, pure body, or pure mechanism. So what is called for here is the development of alternatives to mechanistic ways of viewing the world, which are also part of the legacy of rationalism.

VI. Instrumentalism and the Self

There are two parts to the restructuring of the human self in relation to nature—reconceptualizing the human and reconceptualizing the self, and especially its possibilities of relating to nature in other than instrumental ways. Here the critique of the egoistic self of liberal individualism by both feminist and social philosophers, as well as the critique of instrumental reason, offers a rich set of connections and insights on which to draw. In the case of both of these parts what is involved is the rejection of basically masculine models, that is, of humanity and of the self.

Instrumentalism has been identified as a major problem by the ethical approach in environmental philosophy but treated in a rather impoverished way, as simply the problem of establishing the inherent worth of nature.[17] Connection has not been made to the broader account that draws on the critique of instrumental reason. This broader account reveals both its links with the discontinuity problem and its connection with the account of the self. A closer look at this further critique gives an indication of how we might develop an account that enables us to stress continuity without drowning in a sea of indistinguishability.

We might notice first the strong connections between discontinuity (the polarization condition of dualism) and instrumentalism—the view that the excluded sphere is appropriately treated as a means to the ends of the higher sphere or group, that its value lies in its usefulness to the privileged group that is, in contrast, worthwhile or significant in itself. Second, it is important to maintain a strong distinction and maximize distance between the sphere of means and that of ends to avoid breaking down the sharp boundaries required by hierarchy. Third, it helps if the sphere treated instrumentally is seen as lacking ends of its own (as in views of nature and women as passive), for then others can be imposed upon it without problem. There are also major connections that come through the account of the self which accompanies both views.

The self that complements the instrumental treatment of the other is one that stresses sharply defined ego boundaries, distinctness, autonomy, and separation from others—that is defined *against* others, and lacks essential connections to them. This corresponds to object/relations account of the masculine self associated with the work of Nancy Chodorow (1979, 1985) and also to the self-interested individual presupposed in market theory (Poole 1985, 1990).[18] This self uses both other humans and the world generally as a means to its egoistic satisfaction, which is assumed to be the satisfaction of interests in which others play no es-

sential role. If we try to specify these interests, they would make no essential reference to the welfare of others, except to the extent that these are useful to serve predetermined ends. Others as means are interchangeable if they produce equivalent satisfactions—anything which conduces to that end is as valuable, other things being equal, as anything else which equally conduces to that end. The interests of such an individual, that of the individual of market theory and of the masculine self as theorized by Chodorow, are defined as essentially independent of or disconnected from those of other people, and his or her transactions with the world at large consist of various attempts to get satisfaction for these predetermined private interests. Others are a "resource," and the interests of others connect with the interests of such autonomous selves only accidentally or contingently. They are not valued for themselves but for their effects in producing gratification. This kind of instrumental picture, so obviously a misdescription in the case of relations to other humans, is precisely still the normal Western model of what our relations to nature should be.

Now this kind of instrumental, disembedded account of the relation of self to others has been extensively criticized in the area of political theory from a variety of quarters, including feminist theory, in the critique of liberalism, and in environmental philosophy (Benhabib 1987; Benhabib and Cornell 1987; Benjamin 1985; Chodorow 1985; Gilligan 1982, 1987; Grimshaw 1986; Jagger 1983; Miller 1978; Plumwood 1980; Poole 1984, 1985, 1990; Warren 1990). It has been objected that this account does not give an accurate picture of the human self—that humans are social and connected in a way such an account does not recognize. People do have interests that make *essential* and not merely accidental or contingent reference to those of others, for example, when a mother wishes for her child's recovery, the child's flourishing is an essential *part* of her flourishing, and similarly with close others and indeed for others more widely ("social others"). But, the objection continues, this gives a misleading picture of the world, one that omits or impoverishes a whole significant dimension of human experience, a dimension which provides important insight into gender difference, without which we cannot give an adequate picture of what it is to be human. Instead we must see human beings and their interests as *essentially* related and interdependent. As Karen Warren notes, "Relationships are not something extrinsic to who we are, not an 'add on' feature of human nature; they play an essential role in shaping what it is to be human" (Warren 1990, 143). That people's interests are relational does not imply a holistic view of them—that they are merged or indistinguishable. Although some of the mother's interests entail satisfaction of the child's interests, they are not identical or even necessarily similar. There is overlap, but the relation is one of intentional inclusion (her interest is *that* the child should thrive, that certain of the child's key interests are satisfied) rather than accidental overlap.

This view of self-in-relationship is, I think, a good candidate for the richer account of self deep ecologists have sought and for which they have mistaken holistic accounts. It is an account that avoids atomism but that enables a recognition of interdependence and relationship without falling into the problems of indistinguishability, that acknowledges both continuity and difference, and that breaks the culturally posed false dichotomy of egoism and altruism of interests;[19] it bypasses both masculine "separation" and traditional-feminine "merger" accounts of the self. It can also provide an appropriate foundation for an ethic of connectedness and caring for others, as argued by Gilligan (1982, 1987) and Miller (1978).

Thus it is unnecessary to adopt any of the stratagems of deep ecology—the indistinguishable self, the expanded self, or the transpersonal self—in order to provide an alternative to anthropocentrism or human self-interest. This can be better done through the relational account of self, which clearly recognizes the distinctness of nature but also our relationship and continuity with it. On this relational account, respect for the other results neither from the containment of self nor from a transcendence of self, but is an *expression* of self in relationship, not egoistic self as merged with the other but self as embedded in a network of essential relationships with distinct others.

The relational account of self can usefully be applied to the case of human relations with nature and to place. The standard Western view of the relation of the self to the nonhuman is that it is always *accidentally* related, and hence the nonhuman can be used as a means to the self-contained ends of human beings. Pieces of land are real estate,

readily interchangeable as equivalent means to the end of human satisfaction; no place is more than "a stage along life's way, a launching pad for higher flights and wider orbits than your own" (Berman 1982, 327). But, of course, we do not all think this way, and instances of contrary behavior would no doubt be more common if their possibility were not denied and distorted by both theoretical and social construction. But other cultures have recognized such essential connection of self to country clearly enough, and many indigenous voices from the past and present speak of the grief and pain in loss of their land, to which they are as essentially connected as to any human other. When Aboriginal people, for example, speak of the land as part of them, "like brother and mother" (Neidjie 1985, 51; 1989, 4, 146), this is, I think, one of their meanings. If instrumentalism is impoverishing and distorting as an account of our relations to other human beings, it is equally so as a guiding principle in our relations to nature and to place.[20]

But to show that the self can be essentially related to nature is by no means to show that it normally would be, especially in modern Western culture. What is culturally viewed as alien and inferior, as not worthy of respect or respectful knowledge, is not something to which such essential connection can easily be made. Here the three parts of the problem—the conception of the human, the conception of the self, and the conception of nature—connect again. And normally such essential relation would involve particularity, through connection to and friendship for *particular* places, forests, animals, to which one is particularly strongly related or attached and toward which one has specific and meaningful, not merely abstract, responsibilities of care.

One of the effects of viewing the problem as arising especially in the context of rationalism is to provide a rich set of connections with other critiques; it makes the connection between the critique of anthropocentrism and various other critiques that also engage critically with rationalism, such as feminism and critical theory, much more important—indeed essential—to the understanding of each. The problem of the Western account of the human/nature relation is seen in the context of the other related sets of dualisms; they are linked through their definitions as the underside of the various contrasts of reason. Since much of the strength and persistence of these dualisms derives from their connections and their ability to mirror, confirm, and support one another, critiques of anthropocentrism that fail to take account of these connections have missed an essential and not merely additional feature.

Anthropocentrism and androcentrism in particular are linked by the rationalist conception of the human self as masculine and by the account of authentically human characteristics as centered around rationality and the exclusion of its contrasts (especially characteristics regarded as feminine, animal, or natural) as less human. This provides a different and richer account of the notion of anthropocentrism, now conceived by deep ecology (Fox 1990, 5) in terms of the notion of equality, which is both excessively narrow and difficult to articulate in any precise or convincing way in a context where needs are so different. The perception of the connection as at best accidental is a feature of some recent critiques of ecofeminism, for example, the discussion of Fox (1990) and Eckersley (1989) on the relation of feminism and environmental philosophy. Fox misses entirely the main thrust of the ecofeminist account of environmental philosophy and the critique of deep ecology which results or which is advanced in the ecofeminist literature, which is that it has failed to observe the way in which anthropocentrism and androcentrism are linked.[21] It is a consequence of my arguments here that this critique needs broadening–deep ecology has failed to observe (and often even goes out of its way to deny) connections with a number of other critiques, not just feminism, for example, but also socialism, especially in the forms that mount a critique of rationalism and of modernity. The failure to observe such connections is the result of an inadequate historical analysis and understanding of the way in which the inferiorization of both women and nature is grounded in rationalism, and the connections of both to the inferiorizing of the body, hierarchical concepts of labor, and disembedded and individualist accounts of the self.

Instead of addressing the real concerns of ecofeminism in terms of connection, Fox takes ecofeminism as aiming to replace concern with anthropocentrism by concern with androcentrism.[22] This would have the effect of making ecofeminism a reductionist position which takes women's oppression as the basic form and attempts to reduce all

other forms to it. This position is a straw woman;[23] the effect of ecofeminism is not to absorb or sacrifice the critique of anthropocentrism, but to deepen and enrich it.

Notes

An earlier version of this paper was read at the Women in Philosophy Conference in Canberra, July, 1989. The author would like to thank Jim Cheney and Karen Warren for comments on an earlier draft.

1. Regan, of course, as part of the animal rights movement, is mainly concerned not with wild animals but with domestic animals as they appear in the context and support of human society and culture, although he does not indicate any qualification in moral treatment. Nevertheless, there may be an important moral boundary here, for natural ecosystems cannot be organized along the lines of justice, fairness and rights, and it would be absurd to try to impose such a social order upon them via intervention in these systems. This does not mean, of course, that humans can do anything in such a situation, just that certain kinds of intervention are not in order. But these kinds of intervention may be in order in the case of human social systems and in the case of animals that have already been brought into these social systems through human intervention, and the concept of rights and of social responsibility may have far more application here. This would mean that the domestic/wild distinction would demarcate an important moral boundary in terms of duties of intervention, although neither Regan (1986) nor Taylor (1986) comes to grips with this problem. In the case of Taylor's "wild living things" rights seem less important than respect for independence and autonomy, and the prima facie obligation may be nonintervention.

2. If the Kantian universalizing perspective is based on self-containment, its major contemporary alternative, that of John Rawls, is based on a "definitional identity" in which the "other" can be considered to the extent that it is not recognized as truly different, as genuinely other (Benhabib 1987, 165).

3. Contra Cheney, who appears to advocate the abandonment of all general ethical concepts and the adoption of a "contextual" ethics based in pure particularity and emotionality. We do need both to reintegrate the personal and particular and reevaluate more positively its role, but overcoming moral dualism will not simply amount to an affirmation of the personal in the moral sphere. To embrace pure particularity and emotionality is implicitly to accept

the dualistic construction of these as oppositional to a rationalist ethics and to attempt to reverse value. In general this reactive response is an inadequate way to deal with such dualisms. And rules themselves, as Grimshaw (1986, 209) points out, are not incompatible with recognition of special relationships and responsibility to particular others. Rules themselves are not the problem, and hence it is not necessary to move to a ruleless ethics; rather it is rules that demand the discarding of the personal, the emotional, and the particular and which aim at self-containment.

4. For example, Bill Neidjie's words "This ground and this earth / like brother and mother" (Neidjie 1985, 46) may be interpreted as an affirmation of such kinship or continuity. (See also Neidjie 1985, 53, 61, 62, 77, 81, 82, 88).

5. The logic of dualism and the masculinity of the concept of humanity are discussed in Plumwood (1986, 1988) and Warren (1987, 1989).

6. Nonetheless, deep ecology's approach to ethics is, like much else, doubtfully consistent, variable, and shifting. Thus, although Arne Naess (1974, 1984, 1988) calls for recognition of the intrinsic value of nature, he also tends to treat "the maxim of self-realization" as *substituting for* and obviating an ethical account of care and respect for nature (Naess 1988, 20, 86), placing the entire emphasis on phenomenology. In more recent work, however, the emphasis seems to have quietly shifted back again from holistic intuition to a broad and extremely vague "biocentric egalitarianism" which places the center once again in ethics and enjoins an ethic of maximum expansion of Self (Fox 1990).

7. Other critics of deep ecology, such as Sylvan (1985) and Cheney (1987), have also suggested that it shifts between different and incompatible versions. Ecofeminist critics of deep ecology have included Salleh (1984), Kheel (1985), Biehl (1987), and Warren (1990).

8. Arne Naess, quoted in Fox (1982, 3, 10).

9. This is argued in Plumwood (1980), where a relational account of self developed in the context of an anarchist theory is applied to relations with nature. Part of the problem lies in the terminology of "holism" itself, which is used in highly variable and ambiguous ways, sometimes carrying commitment to indistinguishability and sometimes meaning only "nonatomistic."

10. Arne Naess, quoted in Fox (1986, 54).

11. As noted by Cheney (1989, 293–325).

12. Thus John Seed says: "Naess wrote that when most people think about conservation, they think about sacrifice. This is a treacherous basis for conservation, because most people aren't capable of working for anything except their own self-interest. . . . Naess argued that we need to find ways to extend our identity into nature. Once that happens, being out in front of bulldozers or whatever becomes no more of a sacrifice than moving your foot if you notice that someone's just about to strike it with an axe" (Seed 1989).

13. This denial of the alterity of the other is also the route taken by J. Baird Callicott, who indeed asserts that "The principle of axiological complementarity posits an essential unity between self and world and establishes the problematic intrinsic value of nature in relation to the axiologically privileged value of self" (1985, 275). Given the impoverishment of Humean theory in the area of relations (and, hence, its inability to conceive a self-in-relationship whose connections to others are not merely contingent but essential), Callicott has little alternative to this direction of development.

14. Grimshaw (1986, 182). See also the excellent discussion in Warren (1990, 136–38) of the importance of recognition and respect for the other's difference; Blum (1980, 75); and Benhabib (1987, 166).

15. This traditional model of land relationship is closely linked to that of bioregionalism, whose strategy is to engage people in greater knowledge and care for the local areas that have meaning for them and where they can most easily evolve a caring and responsible life-style. The feat of "impartial identification with all particulars" is, beyond the seeking of individual enlightenment, strategically empty. Because it cares "impartially" for everything it can, in practice, care for nothing.

16. Thus some ecofeminists, such as Cheney (1987, 1989) and Warren (1990), have been led to the development of alternative accounts of ethics and ethical theory building and the development of distinctively ecofeminist ethics.

17. Although the emphasis of early work in this area (for example, Plumwood 1975) was mainly directed toward showing that a respectful, noninstrumental view of nature was logically viable since that was widely disputed, it is certainly well past time to move beyond that. Although there is now wider support for a respectful, noninstrumental position, it remains controversial; see, for example, Thompson (1990) and Plumwood (1991).

18. Poole (1984) has also shown how this kind of self is presupposed in the Kantian moral picture, where desire or inclination is essentially self-directed and is held in check by reason (acting in the interests of universality).

19. In the sense of altruism, in which one's own interests are neglected in favor of another's, essentially relational interests are neither egoistic nor altruistic.

20. On rationalism and place see Edward Relph (1976, 1981).

21. Fox (1990, 12), in claiming gender neutrality for cosmologically based identification and treating issues of gender as irrelevant to the issue, ignores the historical scholarship linking conceptions of gender and conceptions of morality via the division between public and private spheres (for example, Lloyd [1984] and Nicholson [1983]). To the extent that the ecofeminist thesis is not an essentialist one linking *sex* to emotionality and particularity or to nature but one linking social and historical conceptions of *gender* to conceptions of morality and rationality, it is not refuted by examples of women who buy a universalizing view or who drive bulldozers, or by Mrs. Thatcher. Fox's argument here involves a sex/gender confusion. On the sex/gender distinction see Plumwood (1989, 2–11).

22. Thus Fox (1990) throughout his discussion, like Zimmerman (1987, 37), takes "the ecofeminist charge against deep ecology" to be that "androcentrism is 'the real root' of ecological destruction" (1990, 14), so that "there is no need to worry about any form of human domination other than androcentrism" (1990, 18). Warren (1990, 144) tellingly discusses Fox's claim that "feminist" is redundant as an addition to a deep ecological ethic.

23. This reductionist position has a few representatives in the literature (perhaps Andrée Collard [1988], and Sally Miller Gearhart [1982]), but cannot be taken as representative of the main body of ecofeminist work. Fox, I believe, is right to resist such a reduction and to insist on the noneliminability of the form of oppression the critique of anthropocentrism is concerned with, but the conclusion that the critiques are unrelated does not follow. Critiques and the different kinds of oppression they correspond to can be distinguishable but, like individuals themselves, still related in essential and not merely accidental ways. The choice between merger (reductive elimination) and disconnection (isolation) of critiques is the same false dichotomy that inspires the false contrasts of holism and atomism, and of self as merged, lacking boundaries, versus self as isolated atom, lacking essential connection to others.

References

Benhabib, Seyla. 1987. The generalised and the concrete other. In *Women and moral theory*, 154–77. E. Kittay and D. Meyers, eds. Totowa, N.J.: Rowman and Allenheld.

Benhabib, Seyla, and Drucilla Cornell, eds. 1987. *Feminism as critique*. Minneapolis: University of Minnesota Press; Cambridge: Polity Press.

Benjamin, Jessica. 1985. The bonds of love: Rational violence and erotic domination. In *The future of difference*. H. Eisenstein and A. Jardine, eds. New Brunswick: Rutgers University Press.

Berman, Marshall. 1982. *All that is solid melts into air: The experience of modernity*. New York: Simon & Schuster; London: Penguin.

Biehl, Janet. 1987. It's deep, but is it broad? An ecofeminist looks at deep ecology. *Kick It Over* special supplement (Winter).

Blum, Lawrence A. 1980. *Friendship, altruism and morality*. Boston and London: Routledge & Kegan Paul.

Callicott, J. Baird. 1985. Intrinsic value, quantum theory, and environmental ethics. *Environmental Ethics* 7:261–62.

Cheney, Jim. 1987. Ecofeminism and deep ecology. *Environmental Ethics* 9:115–145.

———. 1989. The neo-stoicism of radical environmentalism. *Environmental Ethics* 11:293–325.

Chodorow, Nancy. 1979. *The reproduction of mothering*. Berkeley: University of California Press.

———. 1985. Gender, relation and difference in psychoanalytic perspective. In *The future of difference*, 3–19. H. Eisenstein and A. Jardine, eds. New Brunswick: Rutgers University Press.

Collard, Andrée. 1988. *Rape of the wild: Man's violence against animals and the earth*. Bloomington: Indiana University Press; London: The Woman's Press.

Cook, Francis. 1977. *Hua-Yen Buddhism: The jewel net of Indra*. University Park: Pennsylvania State University Press. 118–119.

Eckersley, Robyn. 1989. Divining evolution: The ecological ethics of Murray Bookchin. *Environmental Ethics* 11:99–116.

Fox, Warwick. 1982. The intuition of deep ecology. Paper presented at Environment, Ethics and Ecology Conference, Canberra. Also published under the title Deep ecology: A new philosophy of our time? *The Ecologist* 14 (1984): 194–200.

———. 1986. Approaching deep ecology: A response to Richard Sylvan's critique of deep ecology. Environmental Studies Occasional Paper 20. Hobart: University of Tasmania Centre for Environmental Studies.

———. 1989. The deep ecology-ecofeminism debate and its parallels. *Environmental Ethics* 11:5–25.

———. 1990. *Towards a transpersonal ecology: Developing new foundations for environmentalism*. Boston: Shambala.

Gearhart, Sally Miller. 1982. The Future—if there is one—is female. In *Reweaving the web of life*, 266–285. P. McAllister, ed. Philadelphia and Santa Cruz: New Society Publishers.

Gilligan, Carol. 1982. *In a different voice*. Cambridge: Harvard University Press.

———. 1987. Moral orientation and moral development. In *Women and moral theory,* 19–33. E. Kittay and D. Meyers, eds. Totowa, N.J.: Rowman and Allenheld.

Griffin, Susan. 1978. *Woman and nature: The roaring inside her.* New York: Harper and Row.

Grimshaw, Jean. 1986. *Philosophy and feminist thinking.* Minneapolis: University of Minnesota Press. Also published as *Feminist philosophers.* Brighton: Wheatsheaf.

Griscom, Joan L. 1981. On healing the nature/history split in feminist thought. *Heresies* 4(1):4–9.

Jaggar, Alison. 1983. *Feminist politics and human nature.* Totowa, N.J.: Rowman & Allenheld; Brighton: Harvester.

Kheel, Marti. 1985. The liberation of nature: A circular affair. *Environmental Ethics* 7: 135–49.

King, Ynestra. 1981. Feminism and revolt. *Heresies* 4(1):12–16.

———. 1989. The ecology of feminism and the feminism of ecology. In *Healing the wounds.* J. Plant, ed., Philadelphia and Santa Cruz: New Society Publishers.

Leopold, Aldo. 1949. *A Sand County almanac,* 201–2. Oxford and New York: Oxford University Press.

Lloyd, Genevieve. 1983a. Public reason and private passion. *Metaphilosophy* 14:308–26.

———. 1983b. Reason, gender and morality in the history of philosophy. *Social Research* 50(3):490–513.

———. 1984. *The man of reason.* London: Methuen.

McLuhan, T. C., ed. 1973. *Touch the earth.* London: Abacus.

Miller, Jean Baker. 1976, 1978. *Toward a new psychology of women.* Boston: Beacon Press; London: Pelican.

Midgley, Mary. 1983. *Animals and why they matter.* Athens: University of Georgia Press; London: Penguin.

Naess, Arne. 1973. The shallow and the deep, long-range ecology movement: A summary. *Inquiry* 16:95–100.

———. 1986. Intrinsic value: Will the defenders of nature please rise. In *Conservation Biology.* M. Soule, ed. Sunderland, MA: Sinauer Associates.

———. 1988. *Ecology, community and lifestyle.* Cambridge: Cambridge University Press.

Neidjie, Bill. 1985. *Kakadu man.* With S. Davis and A. Fox. Canberra: Mybrood P/L.

Neidjie, Bill and Keith Taylor, eds. 1989. *Story about feeling.* Wyndham: Magabala Books.

Nicholson, Linda J. 1983. Women, morality and history. *Social Research* 50(3):514–36.

Plumwood, Val. 1975. Critical notice of Passmore's *Man's responsibility for nature. Australasian Journal of Philosophy* 53(2):171–85.

———. 1980. Social theories, self-management and environmental problems. In *Environmental Philosophy,* 217–332. D. Mannison, M. McRobbie, and R. Routley eds. Canberra: ANU Department of Philosophy Monograph Series RSSS.

———. 1986. Ecofeminism: an overview and discussion of positions and arguments. In *Women and philosophy,* Supplement to vol. 64 *Australasian Journal of Philosophy* (June 1986):120–38.

———. 1988, 1990. Women, humanity and nature. *Radical Philosophy* 48:6–24. Reprinted in *Feminism, socialism and philosophy: a radical philosophy reader.* S. Sayers, ed. London: Routledge.

———. 1989. Do we need a sex/gender distinction? *Radical Philosophy* 51:2–11.

———. 1990. Plato and the bush. *Meanjin* 49(3):524–36.

———. 1991. Ethics and instrumentalism: A Response to Janna Thompson. *Environmental Ethics.* Forthcoming.

Poole, Ross. 1984. Reason, self-interest and "commercial society": The social content of Kantian morality. *Critical Philosophy* 1:24–46.

———. 1985. Morality, masculinity and the market. *Radical Philosophy* 39:16–23.

———. 1990. Modernity, rationality and "the masculine." In *Femininity/Masculinity and representation.* T. Threadgold and A. Cranny-Francis, eds. Sydney: George Allen and Unwin, 1990.

Regan, Tom. 1986. *The case for animal rights.* Berkeley: University of California Press.

Relph, Edward. 1976. *Place and placelessness.* London: Pion.

———. 1981. *Rational landscapes and humanistic geography.* London: Croom Helm.

Rodman, John. 1980. Paradigm change in political science. *American Behavioural Scientist* 24(1):54–55.

Ruether, Rosemary Radford. 1975. *New woman new earth.* Minneapolis: Seabury Press.

Salleh, Ariel. 1984. deeper than deep ecology. *Environmental Ethics* 6:339–45.

Seed, John. 1989. Interviewed by Pat Stone. *Mother Earth News* (May/June).

Seed, John, Joanna Macy, Pat Fleming, and Arne Naess. 1988. *Thinking like a mountain: Towards a council of all beings* Philadelphia and Santa Cruz: New Society Publishers.

Sylvan, Richard. 1985. A critique of deep ecology. *Radical Philosophy* 40 and 41.

Taylor, Paul. 1986. *Respect for nature.* Princeton: Princeton University Press.

Thomas Aquinas. 1976. *Summa contra Gentiles.* Bk. 3, Pt. 2, chap. 62. Quoted in *Animal rights and human obligations,* 56. T. Regan and P. Singer, eds. Englewood Cliffs, N.J.: Prentice Hall.

Thompson, Janna. 1990. A refutation of environmental ethics. *Environmental Ethics* 12(2):147–60.

Warren, Karen J. 1987. Feminism and ecology: Making connections. *Environmental Ethics* 9:17–18.

———. 1990. The power and promise of ecological feminism. *Environmental Ethics* 12(2):121–46.

Zimmerman, Michael E. 1987. Feminism, deep ecology, and environmental ethics. *Environmental Ethics* 9.

The Power and the Promise of Ecological Feminism

*Karen J. Warren**

Introduction

Ecological feminism (ecofeminism) has begun to receive a fair amount of attention lately as an alternative feminism and environmental ethic.[1] Since Francoise d'Eaubonne introduced the term *ecofeminisme* in 1974 to bring attention to women's potential for bringing about an ecological revolution,[2] the term has been used in a variety of ways. As I use the term in this paper, ecological feminism is the position that there are important connections—historical, experiential, symbolic, theoretical—between the domination of women and the domination of nature, an understanding of which is crucial to both feminism and environmental ethics. I argue that the promise and power of ecological feminism is that *it provides a distinctive framework both for reconceiving feminism and for developing an environmental ethic which takes seriously connections between the domination of women and the domination of nature.* I do so by discussing the nature of a feminist ethic and the ways in which ecofeminism provides a feminist and environmental ethic. I conclude that any feminist theory *and* any environmental ethic which fails to take seriously the twin and interconnected dominations of women and nature is at best incomplete and at worst simply inadequate.

Feminism, Ecological Feminism, and Conceptual Frameworks

Whatever else it is, feminism is at least the movement to end sexist oppression. It involves the elimination of any and all factors that contribute to the continued and systematic domination or subordination of women. While feminists disagree about the nature of and solutions to the subordination of women, all feminists agree that sexist oppression exists, is wrong, and must be abolished.

A "feminist issue" is any issue that contributes in some way to understanding the oppression of women. Equal rights, comparable pay for comparable work, and food production are feminist issues wherever and whenever an understanding of them contributes to an understanding of the continued exploitation or subjugation of women. Carrying water and searching for firewood are feminist issues wherever and whenever women's primary responsibility for these tasks contributes to their lack of full participation in decision making, income producing, or high status positions engaged in by men. What counts as a feminist issue, then, depends largely on context, particularly the historical and material conditions of women's lives.

Environmental degradation and exploitation are feminist issues because an understanding of them contributes to an understanding of the oppression of women. In India, for example, both deforestation and reforestation through the introduction of a monoculture species tree (e.g., eucalyptus) intended for commercial production are feminist issues because the loss of indigenous forests and multiple species of trees has drastically affected rural Indian women's ability to maintain a subsistence household. Indigenous forests provide a variety of trees for food, fuel, fodder, household utensils, dyes, medicines, and income-generating uses, while monoculture-species forests do not.[3] Although I do not argue for this claim here, a look at the global impact of environmental degradation on women's lives suggests important respects in which environmental degradation is a feminist issue.

Feminist philosophers claim that some of the most important feminist issues are *conceptual* ones: these issues concern how one conceptualizes such mainstay philosophical notions as reason and rationality, ethics, and what it is to be human. Ecofeminists extend this feminist philosophical concern to nature. They argue that, ultimately, some of the most important connections between the domination of women and the domination of nature are

Environmental Ethics, Vol. 12, No. 2 (Summer 1990), 125–146. Reprinted by permission of the author and publisher.

conceptual. To see this, consider the nature of conceptual frameworks.

A *conceptual framework* is a set of *basic* beliefs, values, attitudes, and assumptions which shape and reflect how one views oneself and one's world. It is a socially constructed lens through which we perceive ourselves and others. It is affected by such factors as gender, race, class, age, affectional orientation, nationality, and religious background.

Some conceptual frameworks are oppressive. An *oppressive conceptual framework* is one that explains, justifies, and maintains relationships of domination and subordination. When an oppressive conceptual framework is *patriarchal,* it explains, justifies, and maintains the subordination of women by men.

I have argued elsewhere that there are three significant features of oppressive conceptual frameworks: (1) value-hierarchical thinking, i.e., "up-down" thinking which places higher value, status, or prestige on what is "up" rather than on what is "down"; (2) value dualisms, i.e., disjunctive pairs in which the disjuncts are seen as oppositional (rather than as complementary) and exclusive (rather than as inclusive), and which place higher value (status, prestige) on one disjunct rather than the other (e.g., dualisms which give higher value or status to that which has historically been identified as "mind," "reason," and "male" than to that which has historically been identified as "body," "emotion," and "female"); and (3) logic of domination, i.e., a structure of argumentation which leads to a justification of subordination.[4]

The third feature of oppressive conceptual frameworks is the most significant. A logic of domination is not *just* a logical structure. It also involves a substantive value system, since an ethical premise is needed to permit or sanction the "just" subordination of that which is subordinate. This justification typically is given on grounds of some alleged characteristic (e.g., rationality) which the dominant (e.g., men) have and the subordinate (e.g., women) lack.

Contrary to what many feminists and ecofeminists have said or suggested, there may be nothing *inherently* problematic about "hierarchical thinking" or even "value-hierarchical thinking" in contexts other than contexts of oppression. Hierarchical thinking is important in daily living for classifying data, comparing information, and organizing material. Taxonomies (e.g., plant taxonomies) and biological nomenclature seem to require *some* form of "hierarchical thinking." Even "value-hierarchical thinking" may be quite acceptable in certain contexts. (The same may be said of "value dualisms" in nonoppressive contexts.) For example, suppose it is true that what is unique about humans is our conscious capacity to radically reshape our social environments (or "societies"), as Murray Bookchin suggests.[5] Then one could truthfully say that humans are better equipped to radically reshape their environments than are rocks or plants—a "value-hierarchical" way of speaking.

The problem is not simply *that* value-hierarchical thinking and value dualisms are used, but *the way* in which each has been used in *oppressive conceptual frameworks* to establish inferiority and to justify subordination.[6] It is the logic of domination, *coupled with* value-hierarchical thinking and value dualisms, which "justifies" subordination. What is explanatorily basic, then, about the nature of oppressive conceptual frameworks is the logic of domination.

For ecofeminism, that a logic of domination is explanatorily basic is important for at least three reasons. First, without a logic of domination, a description of similarities and differences would be just that—a description of similarities and differences. Consider the claim, "Humans are different from plants and rocks in that humans can (and plants and rocks cannot) consciously and radically reshape the communities in which they live; humans are similar to plants and rocks in that they are both members of an ecological community." Even if humans are "better" than plants and rocks with respect to the conscious ability of humans to radically transform communities, one does not *thereby* get any *morally* relevant distinction between humans and nonhumans, or an argument for the domination of plants and rocks by humans. To get *those* conclusions one needs to add at least two powerful assumptions, viz., (A2) and (A4) in argument A below:

(A1) Humans do, and plants and rocks do not, have the capacity to consciously and radically change the community in which they live.

(A2) Whatever has the capacity to consciously and

radically change the community in which it lives is morally superior to whatever lacks this capacity.

(A3) Thus, humans are morally superior to plants and rocks.

(A4) For any X and Y, if X is morally superior to Y, then X is morally justified in subordinating Y.

(A5) Thus, humans are morally justified in subordinating plants and rocks.

Without the two assumptions that *humans are morally superior* to (at least some) nonhumans, (A2), and that *superiority justifies subordination*, (A4), all one has is some difference between humans and some nonhumans. This is true *even if* that difference is given in terms of superiority. Thus, it is the logic of domination, (A4), which is the bottom line in ecofeminist discussions of oppression.

Second, ecofeminists argue that, at least in Western societies, the oppressive conceptual framework which sanctions the twin dominations of women and nature is a patriarchal one characterized by all three features of an oppressive conceptual framework. Many ecofeminists claim that, historically, within at least the dominant Western culture, a patriarchal conceptual framework has sanctioned the following argument B:

(B1) Women are identified with nature and the realm of the physical; men are identified with the "human" and the realm of the mental.

(B2) Whatever is identified with nature and the realm of the physical is inferior to ("below") whatever is identified with the "human" and the realm of the mental; or, conversely, the latter is superior to ("above") the former.

(B3) Thus, women are inferior to ("below") men; or, conversely, men are superior to ("above") women.

(B4) For any X and Y, if X is superior to Y, then X is justified in subordinating Y.

(B5) Thus, men are justified in subordinating women.

If sound, argument B establishes *patriarchy,* i.e., the conclusion given at (B5) that the systematic domination of women by men is justified. But according to ecofeminists, (B5) is justified by just those three features of an oppressive conceptual framework identified earlier: value-hierarchical thinking, the assumption at (B2); value dualisms, the assumed dualism of the mental and the physical at (B1) and the assumed inferiority of the physical vis-à-vis the mental at (B2); and a logic of domination, the assumption at (B4), the same as the previous premise (A4). Hence, according to ecofeminists, insofar as an oppressive patriarchal conceptual framework has functioned historically (within at least dominant Western culture) to sanction the twin dominations of women and nature (argument B), both argument B and the patriarchal conceptual framework, from whence it comes, ought to be rejected.

Of course, the preceding does not identify which premises of B are false. What is the status of premises (B1) and (B2)? Most, if not all, feminists claim that (B1), and many ecofeminists claim that (B2), have been assumed or asserted within the dominant Western philosophical and intellectual tradition.[7] As such, these feminists assert, as a matter of historical fact, that the dominant Western philosophical tradition has assumed the truth of (B1) and (B2). Ecofeminists, however, either deny (B2) or do not affirm (B2). Furthermore, because some ecofeminists are anxious to deny any ahistorical identification of women with nature, some ecofeminists deny (B1) when (B1) is used to support anything other than a strictly historical claim about what has been asserted or assumed to be true within patriarchal culture—e.g., when (B1) is used to assert that women properly are identified with the realm of nature and the physical.[8] Thus, from an ecofeminist perspective, (B1) and (B2) are properly viewed as problematic though historically sanctioned claims: they are problematic precisely because of the way they have functioned historically in a patriarchal conceptual framework and culture to sanction the dominations of women and nature.

What *all* ecofeminists agree about, then, is the way in which *the logic of domination* has functioned historically within patriarchy to sustain and justify the twin dominations of women and nature.[9] Since *all* feminists (and not just ecofeminists) oppose patriarchy, the conclusion given at (B5), all feminists (including ecofeminists) must oppose at least the logic of domination, premise (B4), on which argument B rests—whatever the truth-value status of (B1) and (B2) *outside of* a patriarchal context.

That *all* feminists must oppose the logic of domination shows the breadth and depth of the ecofeminist critique of B: it is a critique not only of the three assumptions on which this argument for the domination of women and nature rests, viz., the assumptions at (B1), (B2), and (B4); it is also a critique of patriarchal conceptual frameworks generally, i.e., of those oppressive conceptual frameworks which put men "up" and women "down," allege some way in which women are morally inferior to men, and use that alleged difference to justify the subordination of women by men. Therefore, ecofeminism is necessary to *any* feminist critique of patriarchy, and, hence, necessary to feminism (a point I discuss again later).

Third, ecofeminism clarifies why the logic of domination, and any conceptual framework which gives rise to it, must be abolished in order both to make possible a meaningful notion of difference which does not breed domination and to prevent feminism from becoming a "support" movement based primarily on shared experiences. In contemporary society, there is no one "woman's voice," no *woman* (or *human*) *simpliciter*: every woman (or human) is a woman (or human) of some race, class, age, affectional orientation, marital status, regional or national background, and so forth. Because there are no "monolithic experiences" that all women share, feminism must be a "solidarity movement" based on shared beliefs and interests rather than a "unity in sameness" movement based on shared experiences and shared victimization.[10] In the words of Maria Lugones, "Unity—not to be confused with solidarity—is understood as conceptually tied to domination."[11]

Ecofeminists insist that the sort of logic of domination used to justify the domination of humans by gender, racial or ethnic, or class status is also used to justify the domination of nature. Because eliminating a logic of domination is part of a feminist critique—whether a critique of patriarchy, white supremacist culture, or imperialism—ecofeminists insist that *naturism* is properly viewed as an integral part of any feminist solidarity movement to end sexist oppression and the logic of domination which conceptually grounds it.

Ecofeminism Reconceives Feminism

The discussion so far has focused on some of the oppressive conceptual features of patriarchy. As I use the phrase, the "logic of traditional feminism" refers to the location of the conceptual roots of sexist oppression, at least in Western societies, in an oppressive patriarchal conceptual framework characterized by a logic of domination. Insofar as other systems of oppression (e.g., racism, classism, ageism, heterosexism) are also conceptually maintained by a logic of domination, appeal to the logic of traditional feminism ultimately locates the basic conceptual interconnections among *all* systems of oppression in the logic of domination. It thereby explains at a *conceptual* level why the eradication of sexist oppression requires the eradication of the other forms of oppression.[12] It is by clarifying this conceptual connection between systems of oppression that a movement to end sexist oppression—traditionally the special turf of feminist theory and practice—leads to a reconceiving of feminism as *a movement to end all forms of oppression*.

Suppose one agrees that the logic of traditional feminism requires the expansion of feminism to include other social systems of domination (e.g., racism and classism). What warrants the inclusion of nature in these "social systems of domination"? Why must the logic of traditional feminism include the abolition of "naturism" (i.e., the domination or oppression of nonhuman nature) among the "isms" feminism must confront? The conceptual justification for expanding feminism to include ecofeminism is twofold. One basis has already been suggested: by showing that the conceptual connections between the dual dominations of women and nature are located in an oppressive and, at least in Western societies, patriarchal conceptual framework characterized by a logic of domination, ecofeminism explains how and why feminism, conceived as a movement to end sexist oppression, must be expanded and reconceived as also a movement to end naturism. This is made explicit by the following argument C:

(C1) Feminism is a movement to end sexism.

(C2) But Sexism is conceptually linked with naturism (through an oppressive conceptual framework characterized by a logic of domination).

(C3) Thus, Feminism is (also) a movement to end naturism.

Because, ultimately, these connections between sexism and naturism are conceptual—embedded in an oppressive conceptual framework—the logic of traditional feminism leads to the embrace of ecological feminism.[13]

The other justification for reconceiving feminism to include ecofeminism has to do with the concepts of gender and nature. Just as conceptions of gender are socially constructed, so are conceptions of nature. Of course, the claim that women and nature are social constructions does not require anyone to deny that there are actual humans and actual trees, rivers, and plants. It simply implies that *how* women and nature are conceived is a matter of historical and social reality. These conceptions vary cross-culturally and by historical time period. As a result, any discussion of the "oppression or domination of nature" involves reference to historically specific forms of social domination of nonhuman nature by humans, just as discussion of the "domination of women" refers to historically specific forms of social domination of women by men. Although I do not argue for it here, an ecofeminist defense of the historical connections between the dominations of women and of nature, claims (B1) and (B2) in argument B, involves showing that within patriarchy the feminization of nature and the naturalization of women have been crucial to the historically successful subordinations of both.[14]

If ecofeminism promises to reconceive traditional feminism in ways which include naturism as a legitimate feminist issue, does ecofeminism also promise to reconceive environmental ethics in ways which are feminist? I think so. This is the subject of the remainder of the paper.

Climbing from Ecofeminism to Environmental Ethics

Many feminists and some environmental ethicists have begun to explore the use of first-person narrative as a way of raising philosophically germane issues in ethics often lost or underplayed in mainstream philosophical ethics. Why is this so? What is it about narrative which makes it a significant resource for theory and practice in feminism and environmental ethics? Even if appeal to first-person narrative is a helpful literary device for describing ineffable experience or a legitimate social science methodology for documenting personal and social history, how is first-person narrative a valuable vehicle of argumentation for ethical decision making and theory building? One fruitful way to begin answering these questions is to ask them of a particular first-person narrative.

Consider the following first-person narrative about rock climbing:

For my very first rock climbing experience, I chose a somewhat private spot, away from other climbers and on-lookers. After studying "the chimney," I focused all my energy on making it to the top. I climbed with intense determination, using whatever strength and skills I had to accomplish this challenging feat. By midway I was exhausted and anxious. I couldn't see what to do next—where to put my hands or feet. Growing increasingly more weary as I clung somewhat desperately to the rock, I made a move. It didn't work. I fell. There I was, dangling midair above the rocky ground below, frightened but terribly relieved that the belay rope had held me. I knew I was safe. I took a look up at the climb that remained. I was determined to make it to the top. With renewed confidence and concentration, I finished the climb to the top.

On my second day of climbing, I rappelled down about 200 feet from the top of the Palisades at Lake Superior to just a few feet above the water level. I could see no one—not my belayer, not the other climbers, no one. I unhooked slowly from the rappel rope and took a deep cleansing breath. I looked all around me—really looked—and listened. I heard a cacophony of voices—birds, trickles of water on the rock before me, waves lapping against the rocks below. I closed my eyes and began to feel the rock with my hands—the cracks and crannies, the raised lichen and mosses, the almost imperceptible nubs that might provide a resting place for my fingers and toes when I began to climb. At that moment I was bathed in serenity. I began to talk to the rock in an almost inaudible, child-like way, as if the rock were my friend. I felt an overwhelming sense of gratitude for what it offered me—a chance to know myself and the rock differently, to appreciate unforeseen miracles like the tiny flowers growing in the even tinier cracks in the rock's surface, and to come to know a sense of *being in relationship* with the natural environment. It felt as if the rock and I were silent conversational partners in a longstanding friendship. I realized then that I had come to care about this cliff which was so different from me, so unmovable and invincible, independent and seemingly indifferent to my presence. I wanted to be with the rock as I climbed. Gone was the determination to conquer the rock, to forcefully impose my will on it; I wanted simply to work respectfully with the rock as I climbed. And as I climbed, that is what I felt. I felt myself *caring* for this rock and feeling thankful that climbing provided the opportunity for me to know it and myself in this new way.

There are at least four reasons why use of such a first-person narrative is important to feminism and environmental ethics. First, such a narrative gives voice to a felt sensitivity often lacking in traditional analytical ethical discourse, viz., a sensitivity to conceiving of oneself as fundamentally "in relationship with" others, including the nonhuman environment. It is a modality which *takes relationships themselves seriously*. It thereby stands in contrast to a strictly reductionist modality that takes relationships seriously only or primarily because of the nature of the *relators* or parties to those relationships (e.g., relators conceived as moral agents, right holders, interest carriers, or sentient beings). In the rock-climbing narrative above, it is the climber's relationship with the rock she climbs which takes on special significance—which is itself a locus of value—in addition to whatever moral status or moral considerability she or the rock or any other parties to the relationship may also have.[15]

Second, such a first-person narrative gives expression to a variety of ethical attitudes and behaviors often overlooked or underplayed in mainstream Western ethics, e.g., the difference in attitudes and behaviors toward a rock when one is "making it to the top" and when one thinks of oneself as "friends with" or "caring about" the rock one climbs.[16] These different attitudes and behaviors suggest an ethically germane contrast between two different types of relationship humans or climbers may have toward a rock: an imposed conqueror-type relationship, and an emergent caring-type relationship. This contrast grows out of, and is faithful to, felt, lived experience.

The difference between conquering and caring attitudes and behaviors in relation to the natural environment provides a third reason why the use of first-person narrative is important to feminism and environmental ethics: it provides a way of conceiving of ethics and ethical meaning as *emerging out of* particular situations moral agents find themselves in, rather than as being *imposed on* those situations (e.g., as a derivation or instantiation of some predetermined abstract principle or rule). This emergent feature of narrative centralizes the importance of *voice*. When a multiplicity of cross-cultural *voices* are centralized, narrative is able to give expression to a range of attitudes, values, beliefs, and behaviors which may be overlooked or silenced by imposed ethical meaning and theory. As a reflection of and on felt, lived experiences, the use of narrative in ethics provides a stance from which ethical discourse can be held accountable to the historical, material, and social realities in which moral subjects find themselves.

Lastly, and for our purposes perhaps most importantly, the use of narrative has argumentative significance. Jim Cheney calls attention to this feature of narrative when he claims, "To contextualize ethical deliberation is, in some sense, to provide a narrative or story, from which the solution to the ethical dilemma emerges as the fitting conclusion."[17] Narrative has argumentative force by suggesting *what counts* as an appropriate conclusion to an ethical situation. One ethical conclusion suggested by the climbing narrative is that what counts as a proper ethical attitude toward mountains and rocks is an attitude of respect and care (whatever that turns out to be or involve), not one of domination and conquest.

In an essay entitled "In and Out of Harm's Way: Arrogance and Love," feminist philosopher Marilyn Frye distinguishes between "arrogant" and "loving" perception as one way of getting at this difference in the ethical attitudes of care and conquest.[18] Frye writes:

> The loving eye is a contrary of the arrogant eye.
> The loving eye knows the independence of the other. It is the eye of a seer who knows that nature is indifferent. It is the eye of one who knows that to know the seen, one must consult something other than one's own will and interests and fears and imagination. One

must look at the thing. One must look and listen and check and question.

The loving eye is one that pays a certain sort of attention. This attention can require a discipline but *not* a self-denial. The discipline is one of self-knowledge, knowledge of the scope and boundary of the self. . . . In particular, it is a matter of being able to tell one's own interests from those of others and of knowing where one's self leaves off and another begins. . . .

The loving eye does not make the object of perception into something edible, does not try to assimilate it, does not reduce it to the size of the seer's desire, fear and imagination, and hence does not have to simplify. It knows the complexity of the other as something which will forever present new things to be known. The science of the loving eye would favor The Complexity Theory of Truth [in contrast to The Simplicity Theory of Truth] and presuppose The Endless Interestingness of the Universe.[19]

According to Frye, the loving eye is not an invasive, coercive eye which annexes others to itself, but one which "knows the complexity of the other as something which will forever present new things to be known."

When one climbs a rock as a conqueror, one climbs with an arrogant eye. When one climbs with a loving eye, one constantly "must look and listen and check and question." One recognizes the rock as something very different, something perhaps totally indifferent to one's own presence, and finds in that difference joyous occasion for celebration. One knows "the boundary of the self," where the self—the "I," the climber—leaves off and the rock begins. There is no fusion of two into one, but a complement of two entities *acknowledged* as separate, different, independent, *yet in relationship;* they are in relationship *if only* because the loving eye is perceiving it, responding to it, noticing it, attending to it.

An ecofeminist perspective about both women and nature involves this shift in attitude from "arrogant perception" to "loving perception" of the nonhuman world. Arrogant perception of nonhumans by humans presupposes and maintains *sameness* in such a way that it expands the moral community to those beings who are thought to resemble (be like, similar to, or the same as) humans in some

morally significant way. Any environmental movement or ethic based on arrogant perception builds a moral hierarchy of beings and assumes some common denominator of moral considerability in virtue of which like beings deserve similar treatment or moral consideration and unlike beings do not. Such environmental ethics are or generate a "unity in sameness." In contrast, "loving perception" presupposes and maintains *difference*—a distinction between the self and other, between human and at least some nonhumans—in such a way that perception of the other as other *is* an expression of love for one who/which is recognized at the outset as independent, dissimilar, different. As Maria Lugones says, in loving perception, "Love is seen not as fusion and erasure of difference but as incompatible with them."[20] "Unity in sameness" alone is an *erasure of difference.*

"Loving perception" of the nonhuman natural world is an attempt to understand what it means *for humans* to care about the nonhuman world, a world *acknowledged* as being independent, different, perhaps even indifferent to humans. Humans *are* different from rocks in important ways, even if they are also both members of some ecological community. A moral community based on loving perception of oneself *in relationship with* a rock, or with the natural environment as a whole, is one which acknowledges and respects difference, whatever "sameness" also exists.[21] The limits of loving perception are determined only by the limits of one's (e.g., a person's , a community's) ability to respond lovingly (or with appropriate care, trust, or friendship)—whether it is to other humans or to the nonhuman world and elements of it.[22]

If what I have said so far is correct, then there are very different ways to climb a mountain and *how* one climbs it and *how* one narrates the experience of climbing it matter ethically. If one climbs with "arrogant perception," with an attitude of "conquer and control," one keeps intact the very sorts of thinking that characterize a logic of domination and an oppressive conceptual framework. Since the oppressive conceptual framework which sanctions the domination of nature is a patriarchal one, one also thereby keeps intact, even if unwittingly, a patriarchal conceptual framework. Because the dismantling of patriarchal conceptual frameworks is a feminist issue, *how* one climbs a mountain and *how* one narrates—or tells the story—

about the experience of climbing also are *feminist issues*. In this way, ecofeminism makes visible why, at a conceptual level, environmental ethics is a feminist issue. I turn now to a consideration of ecofeminism as a distinctively feminist and environmental ethic.

Ecofeminism as a Feminist and Environmental Ethic

A feminist ethic involves a twofold commitment to critique male bias in ethics wherever it occurs, and to develop ethics which are not male-biased. Sometimes this involves articulation of values (e.g., values of care, appropriate trust, kinship, friendship) often lost or underplayed in mainstream ethics.[23] Sometimes it involves engaging in theory building by pioneering in new directions or by revamping old theories in gender sensitive ways. What makes the critiques of old theories or conceptualizations of new ones "feminist" is that they emerge out of sex-gender analyses and reflect whatever those analyses reveal about gendered experience and gendered social reality.

As I conceive feminist ethics in the pre-feminist present, it rejects attempts to conceive of ethical theory in terms of necessary and sufficient conditions, because it assumes that there is no essence (in the sense of some transhistorical, universal, absolute abstraction) of feminist ethics. While attempts to formulate joint necessary and sufficient conditions of a feminist ethic are unfruitful, nonetheless, there are some necessary conditions, what I prefer to call "boundary conditions," of a feminist ethic. These boundary conditions clarify some of the minimal conditions of a feminist ethic without suggesting that feminist ethics has some ahistorical essence. They are like the boundaries of a quilt or collage. They delimit the territory of the piece without dictating what the interior, the design, the actual pattern of the piece looks like. Because the actual design of the quilt emerges from the multiplicity of voices of women in a cross-cultural context, the design will change over time. It is not something static.

What are some of the boundary conditions of a feminist ethic? First, nothing can become part of a feminist ethic—can be part of the quilt—that promotes sexism, racism, classism, or any other "isms" of social domination. Of course, people may dis-

agree about what counts as a sexist act, racist attitude, classist behavior. What counts as sexism, racism, or classism may vary cross-culturally. Still, because a feminist ethic aims at eliminating sexism and sexist bias, and (as I have already shown) sexism is intimately connected in conceptualization and in practice to racism, classism, and naturism, a feminist ethic must be anti-sexist, anti-racist, anti-classist, anti-naturist and opposed to any "ism" which presupposes or advances a logic of domination.

Second, a feminist ethic is a *contextualist* ethic. A contextualist ethic is one which sees ethical discourse and practice as emerging from the voices of people located in different historical circumstances. A contextualist ethic is properly viewed as a *collage* or *mosaic*, a *tapestry* of voices that emerges out of felt experiences. Like any collage or mosaic, the point is not to have *one picture* based on a unity of voices, but a *pattern* which emerges out of the very different voices of people located in different circumstances. When a contextualist ethic is *feminist*, it gives central place to the voices of women.

Third, since a feminist ethic gives central significance to the diversity of women's voices, a feminist ethic must be structurally pluralistic rather than unitary or reductionistic. It rejects the assumption that there is "one voice" in terms of which ethical values, beliefs, attitudes, and conduct can be assessed.

Fourth, a feminist ethic reconceives ethical theory as theory in process which will change over time. Like all theory, a feminist ethic is based on some generalizations.[24] Nevertheless, the generalizations associated with it are themselves a pattern of voices within which the different voices emerging out of concrete and alternative descriptions of ethical situations have meaning. The coherence of a feminist theory so conceived is given within a historical and conceptual context, i.e., within a set of historical, socioeconomic circumstances (including circumstances of race, class, age, and affectional orientation) and within a set of basic beliefs, values, attitudes, and assumptions about the world.

Fifth, because a feminist ethic is contextualist, structurally pluralistic, and "in-process," one way to evaluate the claims of a feminist ethic is in terms of their *inclusiveness*: those claims (voices, patterns of voices) are morally and epistemologically favored (preferred, better, less partial, less biased) which are more inclusive of the felt experiences and perspectives of oppressed persons. The condition of inclusiveness requires and ensures that the diverse voices of women (as oppressed persons) will be given legitimacy in ethical theory building. It thereby helps to minimize empirical bias, e.g., bias rising from faulty or false generalizations based on stereotyping, too small a sample size, or a skewed sample. It does so by ensuring that any generalizations which are made about ethics and ethical decision making include—indeed cohere with—the patterned voices of women.[25]

Sixth, a feminist ethic makes no attempt to provide an "objective" point of view, since it assumes that in contemporary culture there really is no such point of view. As such, it does not claim to be "unbiased" in the sense of "value-neutral" or "objective." However, it does assume that whatever bias it has as an ethic centralizing the voices of oppressed persons is a *better bias*—"better" because it is more inclusive and therefore less partial—than those which exclude those voices.[26]

Seventh, a feminist ethic provides a central place for values typically unnoticed, underplayed, or misrepresented in traditional ethics, e.g., values of care, love, friendship, and appropriate trust.[27] Again, it need not do this at the exclusion of considerations of rights, rules, or utility. There may be many contexts in which talk of rights or of utility is useful or appropriate. For instance, in contracts or property relationships, talk of rights may be useful and appropriate. In deciding what is cost-effective or advantageous to the most people, talk of utility may be useful and appropriate. In a feminist *qua* contextualist ethic, whether or not such talk is useful or appropriate depends on the context; *other values* (e.g., values of care, trust, friendship) are *not* viewed as reducible to or captured solely in terms of such talk.[28]

Eighth, a feminist ethic also involves a reconception of what it is to be human and what it is for humans to engage in ethical decision making, since it rejects as either meaningless or currently untenable any gender-free or gender-neutral description of humans, ethics, and ethical decision making. It thereby rejects what Alison Jaggar calls "abstract individualism," i.e., the position that it is possible to identify a human essence or human nature that exists independently of any particular historical context.[29] Humans and human moral conduct are

properly understood essentially (and not merely accidentally) in terms of networks or webs of historical and concrete relationships.

All the props are now in place for seeing how ecofeminism provides the framework for a distinctively feminist and environmental ethic. It is a feminism that critiques male bias wherever it occurs in ethics (including environmental ethics) and aims at providing an ethic (including an environmental ethic) which is not male biased—and it does so in a way that satisfies the preliminary boundary conditions of a feminist ethic.

First, ecofeminism is quintessentially anti-naturist. Its anti-naturism consists in the rejection of any way of thinking about or acting toward non-human nature that reflects a logic, values, or attitude of domination. Its anti-naturist, anti-sexist, anti-racist, anti-classist (and so forth, for all other "isms" of social domination) stance forms the outer boundary of the quilt: nothing gets on the quilt which is naturist, sexist, racist, classist, and so forth.

Second, ecofeminism is a contextualist ethic. It involves a shift *from* a conception of ethics as primarily a matter of rights, rules, or principles predetermined and applied in specific cases to entities viewed as competitors in the contest of moral standing, *to* a conception of ethics as growing out of what Jim Cheney calls "defining relationships," i.e., relationships conceived in some sense as defining who one is.[30] As a contextualist ethic, it is not that rights, or rules, or principles are *not* relevant or important. Clearly they are in certain contexts and for certain purposes.[31] It is just that what *makes* them relevant or important is that those to whom they apply are entities *in relationship with* others.

Ecofeminism also involves an ethical shift *from* granting moral consideration to nonhumans *exclusively* on the grounds of some similarity they share with humans (e.g., rationality, interests, moral agency, sentiency, right-holder status) *to* "a highly contextual account to see clearly what a human being is and what the nonhuman world might be, morally speaking, *for* human beings."[32] For an ecofeminist, *how* a moral agent is in relationship to another becomes of central significance, not simply *that* a moral agent is a moral agent or is bound by rights, duties, virtue, or utility to act in a certain way.

Third, ecofeminism is structurally pluralistic

in that it presupposes and maintains difference—difference among humans as well as between humans and at least some elements of nonhuman nature. Thus, while ecofeminism denies the "nature/culture" split, it affirms that humans are both members of an ecological community (in some respects) and different from it (in other respects). Ecofeminism's attention to relationships and community is not, therefore, an erasure of difference but a respectful acknowledgement of it.

Fourth, ecofeminism reconceives theory as theory in process. It focuses on patterns of meaning which emerge, for instance, from the storytelling and first-person narratives of women (and others) who deplore the twin dominations of women and nature. The use of narrative is one way to ensure that the content of the ethic—the pattern of the quilt—may/will change over time, as the historical and material realities of women's lives change and as more is learned about women-nature connections and the destruction of the nonhuman world.[33]

Fifth, ecofeminism is inclusivist. It emerges from the voices of women who experience the harmful domination of nature and the way that domination is tied to their domination as women. It emerges from listening to the voices of indigenous peoples such as Native Americans who have been dislocated from their land and have witnessed the attendant undermining of such values as appropriate reciprocity, sharing, and kinship that characterize traditional Indian culture. It emerges from listening to voices of those who, like Nathan Hare, critique traditional approaches to environmental ethics as white and bourgeois, and as failing to address issues of "black ecology" and the "ecology" of the inner city and urban spaces.[34] It also emerges out of the voices of Chipko women who see the destruction of "earth, soil, and water" as intimately connected with their own inability to survive economically.[35] With its emphasis on inclusivity and difference, ecofeminism provides a framework for recognizing that what counts as ecology and what counts as appropriate conduct toward both human and nonhuman environments is largely a matter of context.

Sixth, as a feminism, ecofeminism makes no attempt to provide an "objective" point of view. It is a social ecology. It recognizes the twin dominations of women and nature as social problems rooted both in very concrete, historical, socioeconomic circumstances and in oppressive patriarchal conceptual frameworks which maintain and sanction these circumstances.

Seventh, ecofeminism makes a central place for values of care, love, friendship, trust, and appropriate reciprocity—values that presuppose that our relationships to others are central to our understanding of who we are.[36] It thereby gives voice to the sensitivity that in climbing a mountain, one is doing something in relationship with an "other," an "other" whom one can come to care about and treat respectfully.

Lastly, an ecofeminist ethic involves a reconception of what it means to be human, and in what human ethical behavior consists. Ecofeminism denies abstract individualism. Humans are who we are in large part by virtue of the historical and social contexts and the relationships we are in, including our relationships with nonhuman nature. Relationships are not something extrinsic to who we are, not an "add on" feature of human nature; they play an essential role in shaping what it is to be human. Relationships of humans to the nonhuman environment are, in part, constitutive of what it is to be a human.

By making visible the interconnections among the dominations of women and nature, ecofeminism shows that both are feminist issues and that explicit acknowledgment of both is vital to any responsible environmental ethic. Feminism *must* embrace ecological feminism if it is to end the domination of women because the domination of women is tied conceptually and historically to the domination of nature.

A responsible environmental ethic also *must* embrace feminism. Otherwise, even the seemingly most revolutionary, liberational, and holistic ecological ethic will fail to take seriously the interconnected dominations of nature and women that are so much a part of the historical legacy and conceptual framework that sanctions the exploitation of nonhuman nature. Failure to make visible these interconnected, twin dominations results in an inaccurate account of how it is that nature has been and continues to be dominated and exploited and produces an environmental ethic that lacks the depth necessary to be truly *inclusive* of the realities of persons who at least in dominant Western culture have been intimately tied with that exploitation, viz., women. Whatever else can be said in favor of such holistic ethics, a failure to make visible ecofeminist insights into the common denominators of the twin oppressions of women and nature is to perpetuate, rather than overcome, the source of that oppression.

This last point deserves further attention. It may be objected that as long as the end result is "the same"—the development of an environmental ethic which does not emerge out of or reinforce an oppressive conceptual framework—it does not matter whether that ethic (or the ethic endorsed in getting there) is feminist or not. Hence, it simply is *not* the case that any adequate environmental ethic must be feminist. My argument, in contrast, has been that it *does* matter, and for three important reasons. First, there is the scholarly issue of accurately representing historical reality, and that, ecofeminists claim, requires acknowledging the historical feminization of nature and naturalization of women as part of the exploitation of nature. Second, I have shown that the conceptual connections between the domination of women and the domination of nature are located in an oppressive and, at least in Western societies, patriarchal conceptual framework characterized by a logic of domination. Thus, I have shown that failure to notice the nature of this connection leaves at best an incomplete, inaccurate, and partial account of what is required of a conceptually adequate environmental ethic. An ethic which *does not* acknowledge this is simply *not* the same as one that does, whatever else the similarities between them. Third, the claim that, in contemporary culture, one can have an adequate environmental ethic which is *not* feminist assumes that, in contemporary culture, the label *feminist* does not add anything crucial to the nature or description of environmental ethics. I have shown that at least in contemporary culture this is false, for the word *feminist* currently helps to clarify just *how* the domination of nature is conceptually linked to patriarchy and, hence, how the liberation of nature is conceptually linked to the termination of patriarchy. Thus, because it has critical bite in contemporary culture, it serves as an important reminder that in contemporary sex-gendered, raced, classed, and naturist culture, an unlabeled position functions as a privileged and "unmarked" position. That is, without the addition of the word *feminist*, one presents environmental ethics as if it has no bias, including male-gender bias, which is just what ecofeminists deny: failure to notice the connections between the twin oppressions of women and nature *is* male-gender bias.

One of the goals of feminism is the eradication of all oppressive sex-gender (and related race, class, age, affectional preference) categories and the creation of a world in which *difference does not breed domination*—say, the world of 4001. If in 4001 an "adequate environmental ethic" is a "feminist environmental ethic," the word *feminist* may then be redundant and unnecessary. However, this is *not* 4001, and in terms of the current historical and conceptual reality the dominations of nature and of women are intimately connected. Failure to notice or make visible that connection in 1990 perpetuates the mistaken (and privileged) view that "environmental ethics" is *not* a feminist issue, and that *feminist* adds nothing to environmental ethics.[37]

Conclusion

I have argued in this paper that ecofeminism provides a framework for a distinctively feminist and environmental ethic. Ecofeminism grows out of the felt and theorized about connections between the domination of women and the domination of nature. As a contextualist ethic, ecofeminism refocuses environmental ethics on what nature might mean, morally speaking, *for* humans, and on how the relational attitudes of humans to others—humans as well as nonhumans—sculpt both what it is to be human and the nature and ground of human responsibilities to the nonhuman environment. Part of what this refocusing does is to take seriously the voices of women and other oppressed persons in the construction of that ethic.

A Sioux elder once told me a story about his son. He sent his seven-year-old son to live with the child's grandparents on a Sioux reservation so that he could "learn the Indian ways." Part of what the grandparents taught the son was how to hunt the four leggeds of the forest. As I heard the story, the boy was taught, "to shoot your four-legged brother in his hind area, slowing it down but not killing it. Then, take the four legged's head in your hands, and look into his eyes. The eyes are where all the suffering is. Look into your brother's eyes and feel his pain. Then, take your knife and cut the four-legged under his chin, here, on his neck, so that he dies quickly. And as you do, ask your brother, the four-legged, for forgiveness for what you do. Offer also a prayer of thanks to your four-legged kin for offering his body to you just now, when you need food to eat and clothing to wear. And promise the four-legged that you will put yourself back into the earth when you die, to become nourishment for the earth, and for the sister flowers, and for the brother deer. It is appropriate that you should offer this blessing for the four-legged and, in due time, reciprocate in turn with your body in this way, as the four-legged gives life to you for your survival." As I reflect upon that story, I am struck by the power of the environmental ethic that grows out of and takes seriously narrative, context, and such values and relational attitudes as care, loving perception, and appropriate reciprocity, and doing what is appropriate in a given situation—however that notion of appropriateness eventually gets filled out. I am also struck by what one is able to see, once one begins to explore some of the historical and conceptual connections between the dominations of women and of nature. A *re-conceiving* and *re-visioning* of both feminism and environmental ethics, is, I think, the power and promise of ecofeminism.

Notes

*Earlier versions of this paper were presented at the American Philosophical Association Meeting in New York City, December 1987, and at the University of Massachusetts, April 1988. The author wishes to thank the following people for their helpful comments and support: Bob Ackerman, Kim Brown, Jim Cheney, Mahmoud El-Kati, Eric Katz, Michael Keenan, Ruthanne Kurth-Schai, Greta Gaard, Roxanne Gudeman, Alison Jaggar, H. Warren Jones, Gareth Matthews, Michael McCall, Patrick Murphy, Bruce Nordstrom, Nancy Shea, Nancy Tuana, Bob Weinstock-Collins, Henry West, and the anonymous referees of *Environmental Ethics*.

1. Explicit ecological feminist literature includes works from a variety of scholarly perspectives and sources. Some of these works are Leonie Caldecott and Stephanie Leland, eds., *Reclaim the Earth: Women Speak Out for Life on Earth* (London: The Women's Press, 1983); Jim Cheney, "Eco-Feminism and Deep Ecology," *Environmental Ethics* 9 (1987): 115–45; Andrée Collard with Joyce Contrucci, *Rape of the Wild: Man's Violence against Animals and the Earth* (Bloomington: Indiana University Press, 1988); Katherine Davies, "Historical Associations:

Women and the Natural World," *Women & Environments* 9, no. 2 (Spring 1987): 4–6; Sharon Doubiago, "Deeper Than Deep Ecology: Men Must Become Feminists," in *The New Catalyst Quarterly*, no. 10 (Winter 1987/88): 10–11; Brian Easlea, *Science and Sexual Oppression: Patriarchy's Confrontation with Women and Nature* (London: Weidenfeld & Nicholson, 1981); Elizabeth Dodson Gray, *Green Paradise Lost* (Wellesley, MA: Roundtable Press, 1979); Susan Griffin, *Women and Nature: The Roaring Inside Her* (San Francisco: Harper and Row, 1978); Joan L. Griscom, "On Healing the Nature/History Split in Feminist Thought," in *Heresies #13: Feminism and Ecology* 4, no. 1 (1981): 4–9; Ynestra King, "The Ecology of Feminism and the Feminism of Ecology," in *Healing Our Wounds: The Power of Ecological Feminism*, ed. Judith Plant (Boston: New Society Publishers, 1989), pp. 18–28; "The Eco-feminist Imperative," in *Reclaim the Earth*, ed. Caldecott and Leland (London: The Women's Press, 1983), pp. 12–16; "Feminism and the Revolt of Nature," in *Heresies #13: Feminism and Ecology* 4, no. 1 (1981), 12–16, and "What Is Ecofeminism?" *The Nation*, 12 December 1987; Marti Kheel, "Animal Liberation Is a Feminist Issue," *The New Catalyst Quarterly*, no. 10 (Winter 1987–88): 8–9; Carolyn Merchant, *The Death of Nature: Women, Ecology and the Scientific Revolution* (San Francisco: Harper and Row, 1980); Patrick Murphy, ed., "Feminism, Ecology, and the Future of the Humanities," special issue of *Studies in the Humanities* 15, no. 2 (December 1988); Abby Peterson and Carolyn Merchant, "'Peace with the Earth': Women and the Environmental Movement in Sweden," *Women's Studies International Forum* 9, no. 5–6. (1986): 465–79; Judith Plant, "Searching for Common Ground: Ecofeminism and Bioregionalism," in *The New Catalyst Quarterly*, no. 10 (Winter 1987/88): 6–7; Judith Plant, ed., *Healing Our Wounds: The Power of Ecological Feminism*, (Boston: New Society Publishers, 1989); Val Plumwood, "Ecofeminism: An Overview and Discussion of Positions and Arguments," *Australasian Journal of Philosophy*, Supplement to vol. 64 (June 1986): 120–37; Rosemary Radford Ruether, *New Woman/New Earth: Sexist Ideologies & Human Liberation* (New York: Seabury Press, 1975); Kirkpatrick Sale, "Ecofeminism—A New Perspective," *The Nation*, 26 September 1987, 302–05; Ariel Kay Salleh, "Deeper Than Deep Ecology: The Eco-Feminist Connection," *Environmental Ethics* 6 (1984): 339–45, and "Epistemology and the Metaphors of Production: An Eco-Feminist Reading of Critical Theory," in *Studies in the Humanities* 15 (1988): 130–39; Vandana Shiva, *Staying Alive: Women, Ecology and Development* (London: Zed Books, 1988); Charlene Spretnak, "Ecofeminism: Our Roots and Flowering," *The*

Elmswood Newsletter, Winter Solstice 1988; Karen J. Warren, "Feminism and Ecology: Making Connections," *Environmental Ethics* 9 (1987): 3–21; "Toward an Ecofeminist Ethic," *Studies in the Humanities* 15 (1988): 140–156; Miriam Wyman, "Explorations of Ecofeminism," *Women & Environments* (Spring 1987): 6–7; Iris Young, "'Feminism and Ecology' and 'Women and Life on Earth: Eco-Feminism in the 80s'," *Environmental Ethics* 5 (1983): 173–80; Michael Zimmerman, "Feminism, Deep Ecology, and Environmental Ethics," *Environmental Ethics* 9 (1987): 21–44.

2. Francoise d'Eaubonne, *Le Feminisme ou la Mort* (Paris: Pierre Horay, 1974), pp. 213–52.

3. I discuss this in my paper, "Toward an Ecofeminist Ethic."

4. The account offered here is a revision of the account given earlier in my paper "Feminism and Ecology: Making Connections." I have changed the account to be about "oppressive" rather than strictly "patriarchal" conceptual frameworks in order to leave open the possibility that there may be some patriarchal conceptual frameworks (e.g., in non-Western cultures) which are *not* properly characterized as based on value dualisms.

5. Murray Bookchin, "Social Ecology Versus 'Deep Ecology'," in *Green Perspectives: Newsletter of the Green Program Project*, no. 4–5 (Summer 1987): 9.

6. It may be that in contemporary Western society, which is so thoroughly structured by categories of gender, race, class, age, and affectional orientation, that there simply is no meaningful notion of "value-hierarchical thinking" which does not function in an oppressive context. For purposes of this paper, I leave that question open.

7. Many feminists who argue for the historical point that claims (B1) and (B2) have been asserted or assumed to be true within the dominant Western philosophical tradition do so by discussion of that tradition's conceptions of reason, rationality, and science. For a sampling of the sorts of claims made within that context, see "Reason, Rationality, and Gender," ed. Nancy Tuana and Karen J. Warren, a special issue of the American Philosophical Association's *Newsletter on Feminism and Philosophy* 88, no. 2 (March 1989): 17–71. Ecofeminists who claim that (B2) has been assumed to be true within the dominant Western philosophical tradition include Gray, *Green Paradise Lost;* Griffin, *Woman and Nature: The Roaring Inside Her;* Merchant, *The Death of Nature;* Ruether, *New Woman/New Earth.* For a discussion of some of these ecofeminist historical accounts, see Plumwood, "Ecofeminism." While I agree that the historical connections between the domination of women and the domination of nature is a crucial one, I do not argue for that claim here.

8. Ecofeminists who deny (B1) when (B1) is offered as anything other than a true, descriptive, historical claim about patriarchal culture often do so on grounds that an objectionable sort of biological determinism, or at least harmful female sex-gender stereotypes, underlie (B1). For a discussion of this "split" among those ecofeminists ("nature feminists") who assert and those ecofeminists ("social feminists") who deny (B1) as anything other than a true historical claim about how women are described in patriarchal culture, see Griscom, "On Healing the Nature/History Split."

9. I make no attempt here to defend the historically sanctioned truth of these premises.

10. See, e.g., bell hooks, *Feminist Theory: From Margin to Center* (Boston: South End Press, 1984), pp. 51–52.

11. Maria Lugones, "Playfulness, 'World-Travelling,' and Loving Perception," *Hypatia* 2, no. 2 (Summer 1987): 3.

12. At an *experiential* level, some women are "women of color," poor, old, lesbian, Jewish, and physically challenged. Thus, if feminism is going to liberate these women, it also needs to end the racism, classism, heterosexism, anti-Semitism, and discrimination against the handicapped that is constitutive of their oppression as black, or Latina, or poor, or older, or lesbian, or Jewish, or physically challenged women.

13. This same sort of reasoning shows that feminism is also a movement to end racism, classism, age-ism, heterosexism and other "isms" which are based in oppressive conceptual frameworks characterized by a logic of domination. However, there is an important caveat: ecofeminism is *not* compatible with all feminisms and all environmentalisms. For a discussion of this point, see my article, "Feminism and Ecology: Making Connections." What it *is* compatible with is the minimal condition characterization of feminism as a movement to end sexism that is accepted by all contemporary feminisms (liberal, traditional Marxist, radical, socialist, Blacks and non-Western).

14. See, e.g., Gray, *Green Paradise Lost;* Griffin, *Women and Nature;* Merchant, *The Death of Nature;* and Ruether, *New Woman/New Earth.*

15. Suppose, as I think is the case, that a necessary condition for the existence of a moral relationship is that at least one party to the relationship is a moral being (leaving open for our purposes what counts as a "moral being"). If this is so, then the *Mona Lisa* cannot properly be said to have or stand in a moral

relationship with the wall on which she hangs, and a wolf cannot have or properly be said to have or stand in a moral relationship with a moose. Such a necessary-condition account leaves open the question whether *both* parties to the relationship must be moral beings. My point here is simply that however one resolves *that* question, recognition of the relationships themselves as a locus of value is a recognition of a source of value that is different from and not reducible to the values of the "moral beings" in those relationships.

16. It is interesting to note that the image of being friends with the Earth is one which cytogeneticist Barbara McClintock uses when she describes the importance of having "a feeling for the organism," "listening to the material [in this case the corn plant]," in one's work as a scientist. See Evelyn Fox Keller, "Women, Science, and Popular Mythology," in *Machina Ex Dea: Feminist Perspectives on Technology,* ed. Joan Rothschild (New York: Pergamon Press, 1983), and Evelyn Fox Keller, *A Feeling for the Organism: The Life and Work of Barbara McClintock* (San Francisco: W. H. Freeman, 1983).

17. Cheney, "Eco-Feminism and Deep Ecology," 144.

18. Marilyn Frye, "In and Out of Harm's Way: Arrogance and Love," *The Politics of Reality* (Trumansburg, New York: The Crossing Press, 1983), pp. 66–72.

19. Ibid., pp. 75–76.

20. Maria Lugones, "Playfulness," p. 3.

21. Cheney makes a similar point in "Eco-Feminism and Deep Ecology," p. 140.

22. Ibid., p. 138.

23. This account of a feminist ethic draws on my paper "Toward an Ecofeminist Ethic."

24. Marilyn Frye makes this point in her illuminating paper, "The Possibility of Feminist Theory," read at the American Philosophical Association Central Division Meetings in Chicago, 29 April–1 May 1986. My discussion of feminist theory is inspired largely by that paper and by Kathryn Addelson's paper "Moral Revolution," in *Women and Values: Reading in Recent Feminist Philosophy,* ed. Marilyn Pearsall (Belmont, CA: Wadsworth Publishing Co., 1986) pp. 291–309.

25. Notice that the standard of inclusiveness does not exclude the voices of men. It is just that those voices must cohere with the voices of women.

26. For a more in-depth discussion of the notions of impartiality and bias, see my paper, "Critical Thinking and Feminism," *Informal Logic* 10, no. 1 (Winter 1988):31–44.

27. The burgeoning literature on these values is noteworthy. See, e.g., Carol Gilligan, *In a Different Voice: Psychological Theories and Women's Development* (Cambridge: Harvard University Press, 1982); *Mapping the Moral Domain: A Contribution of Women's Thinking to Psychological Theory and Education,* ed. Carol Gilligan, Janie Victoria Ward, and Jill McLean Taylor, with Betty Bardige (Cambridge: Harvard University Press, 1988); Nel Noddings, *Caring: A Feminine Approach to Ethics and Moral Education* (Berkeley: University of California Press, 1984); Maria Lugones and Elizabeth V. Spelman, "Have We Got a Theory for You! Feminist Theory, Cultural Imperialism, and the Women's Voice," *Women's Studies International Forum* 6 (1983): 573–81; Maria Lugones, "Playfulness"; Annette C. Baier, "What Do Women Want in a Moral Theory?" *Nous* 19 (1985): 53–63.

28. Jim Cheney would claim that our fundamental relationships to one another as moral agents are not as moral agents to rights-holders, and that whatever rights a person properly may be said to have are relationally defined rights, not rights possessed by atomistic individuals conceived as Robinson Crusoes who do not exist essentially in relation to others. On this view, even rights talk itself is properly conceived as growing out of a relational ethic, not vice versa.

29. Alison Jaggar, *Feminist Politics and Human Nature* (Totowa, NJ: Rowman and Allanheld, 1980), pp. 42–44.

30. Henry West has pointed out that the expression "defining relations" is ambiguous. According to West, "the 'defining' as Cheney uses it is an adjective, not a principle—it is not that ethics defines relationships; it is that ethics grows out of conceiving of the relationships that one is in as defining what the individual is."

31. For example, in relationships involving contracts or promises, those relationships might be correctly described as that of moral agent to rights holders. In relationships involving mere property, those relationships might be correctly described as that of moral agent to objects having only instrumental value, "relationships of instrumentality." In comments on an earlier draft of this paper, West suggested that possessive individualism, for instance, might be recast in such a way that an individual is defined by his or her property relationships.

32. Cheney, "Eco-Feminism and Deep Ecology," p. 144.

33. One might object that such permission for change opens the door for environmental exploitation. This is not the case. An ecofeminist ethic is anti-naturist. Hence, the unjust domination and exploitation of

nature is a "boundary condition" of the ethic; no such actions are sanctioned or justified on ecofeminist grounds. What it *does* leave open is some leeway about what counts as domination and exploitation. This, I think, is a strength of the ethic, not a weakness, since it acknowledges that *that* issue cannot be resolved in any practical way in the abstract, independent of a historical and social context.

34. Nathan Hare, "Black Ecology," in *Environmental Ethics*, ed. K. S. Shrader-Frechette (Pacific Grove, CA: Boxwood Press, 1981), pp. 229–36.

35. For an ecofeminist discussion of the Chipko movement, see my "Toward an Ecofeminist Ethic," and Shiva's *Staying Alive*.

36. See Cheney, "Eco-Feminism and Deep Ecology," p. 122.

37. I offer the same sort of reply to critics of ecofeminism such as Warwick Fox who suggest that for the sort of ecofeminism I defend, the word *feminist*

does not add anything significant to environmental ethics and, consequently, that an ecofeminist like myself might as well call herself a deep ecologist. He asks: "Why doesn't she just call it [i.e., Warren's vision of a transformative feminism] deep ecology? Why specifically attach the label *feminist* to it . . . ?" (Warwick Fox, "The Deep Ecology-Ecofeminism Debate and Its Parallels," *Environmental Ethics* 11, no. 1 [1989]: 14, n.22). Whatever the important similarities between deep ecology and ecofeminism (or, specifically, my verson of ecofeminism)—and, indeed, there are many—it is precisely my point here that the word *feminist* does add something significant to the conception of environmental ethics, and that any environmental ethic (including deep ecology) that fails to make explicit the different kinds of interconnections among the domination of nature and the domination of women will be, from a feminist (and ecofeminist) perspective such as mine, inadequate.

Development, Ecology, and Women

Vandana Shiva

Development as a New Project of Western Patriarchy

'Development' was to have been a post-colonial project, a choice for accepting a model of progress in which the entire world remade itself on the model of the colonising modern west, without having to undergo the subjugation and exploitation that colonialism entailed. The assumption was that western style progress was possible for all. Development, as the improved well-being of all, was thus equated with the westernisation of economic categories—of needs, of productivity, of growth. Concepts and categories about economic development and natural resource utilisation that had emerged in the specific context of industrialisation and capitalist growth in a centre of colonial power, were raised to the level of universal assumptions and applicability in the entirely different context of basic needs satisfaction for the people of the newly independent Third World countries. Yet, as Rosa

Luxemberg has pointed out, early industrial development in western Europe necessitated the permanent occupation of the colonies by the colonial powers and the destruction of the local 'natural economy.'[1] According to her, colonialism is a constant necessary condition for capitalist growth: without colonies, capital accumulation would grind to a halt. 'Development' as capital accumulation and the commercialisation of the economy for the generation of 'surplus' and profits thus involved the reproduction not merely of a particular form of creation of wealth, but also of the associated creation of poverty and dispossession. A replication of economic development based on commercialisation of resource use for commodity production in the newly independent countries created the internal colonies.[2] Development was thus reduced to a continuation of the process of colonisation; it became an extension of the project of wealth creation in modern western patriarchy's economic vision, which was based on the exploita-

Staying Alive, by Vandana Shiva (London: Zed Books Ltd., 1988), pp. 1–13. Reprinted by permission of the publisher.

tion or exclusion of women (of the west and non-west), on the exploitation and degradation of nature, and on the exploitation and erosion of other cultures. 'Development' could not but entail destruction for women, nature and subjugated cultures, which is why, throughout the Third World, women, peasants and tribals are struggling for liberation from 'development' just as they earlier struggled for liberation from colonialism.

The UN Decade for Women was based on the assumption that the improvement of women's economic position would automatically flow from an expansion and diffusion of the development process. Yet, by the end of the Decade, it was becoming clear that development itself was the problem. Insufficient and inadequate 'participation' in 'development' was not the cause for women's increasing underdevelopment; it was, rather, their enforced but asymmetric participation in it, by which they bore the costs but were excluded from the benefits, that was responsible. Development exclusivity and dispossession aggravated and deepened the colonial processes of ecological degradation and the loss of political control over nature's sustenance base. Economic growth was a new colonialism, draining resources away from those who needed them most. The discontinuity lay in the fact that it was now new national elites, not colonial powers, that masterminded the exploitation on grounds of 'national interest' and growing GNPs, and it was accomplished with more powerful technologies of appropriation and destruction.

Ester Boserup[3] has documented how women's impoverishment increased during colonial rule; those rulers who had spent a few centuries in subjugating and crippling their own women into de-skilled, de-intellectualised appendages, disfavoured the women of the colonies on matters of access to land, technology and employment. The economic and political processes of colonial underdevelopment bore the clear mark of modern western patriarchy, and while large numbers of women and men were impoverished by these processes, women tended to lose more. The privatisation of land for revenue generation displaced women more critically, eroding their traditional land-use rights. The expansion of cash crops undermined food production, and women were often left with meagre resources to feed and care for children, the aged and the infirm, when men migrated or were conscripted into forced labour by the colonisers. As a collective document by women activists, organisers and researchers stated at the end of the UN Decade for Women, 'The almost uniform conclusion of the Decade's research is that with a few exceptions, women's relative access to economic resources, incomes and employment has worsened, their burden of work has increased, and their relative and even absolute health, nutritional and educational status has declined.'[4]

The displacement of women from productive activity by the expansion of development was rooted largely in the manner in which development projects appropriated or destroyed the natural resource base for the production of sustenance and survival. It destroyed women's productivity both by removing land, water, and forests from their management and control, as well as through the ecological destruction of soil, water and vegetation systems so that nature's productivity and renewability were impaired. While gender subordination and patriarchy are the oldest of oppressions, they have taken on new and more violent forms through the project of development. Patriarchal categories which understand destruction as 'production' and regeneration of life as 'passivity' have generated a crisis of survival. Passivity, as an assumed category of the 'nature' of nature and of women, denies the activity of nature and life. Fragmentation and uniformity as assumed categories of progress and development destroy the living forces which arise from relationships within the "web of life" and the diversity in the elements and patterns of these relationships.

The economic biases and values against nature, women and indigenous peoples are captured in this typical analysis of the "unproductiveness" of traditional natural societies:

> Production is achieved through human and animal, rather than mechanical, power. Most agriculture is unproductive; human or animal manure may be used but chemical fertilisers and pesticides are unknown. . . . For the masses, these conditions mean poverty.[5]

The assumptions are evident: nature is unproductive; organic agriculture based on nature's cycles of renewability spells poverty; women and tribal and peasant societies embedded in nature are similarly unproductive, not because it has been demonstrated that in cooperation they produce *less* goods and services for needs, but because it is assumed that 'production' takes place only when mediated by technologies for commodity production, even when such technologies destroy life. A stable and clean river is not a productive resource in this view: it needs to be 'developed' with dams in order to become so. Women, sharing the river as a commons to satisfy the water needs of their families and society are not involved in productive labour: when substituted by the engineering man, water management and water use become productive activities. Natural forests remain unproductive till they are developed into monoculture plantations of commercial species. Development thus, is equivalent to maldevelopment, a development bereft of the feminine, the conservation, the ecological principle. The neglect of nature's work in renewing herself, and women's work in producing sustenance in the form of basic, vital needs is an essential part of the paradigm of maldevelopment, which sees all work that does not produce profits and capital as non or unproductive work. As Maria Mies[6] has pointed out, this concept of surplus has a patriarchal bias because, from the point of view of nature and women, it is not based on material surplus produced *over and above* the requirements of the community: it is stolen and appropriated through violent modes from nature (who needs a share of her produce to reproduce herself) and from women (who need a share of nature's produce to produce sustenance and ensure survival).

From the perspective of Third World women, productivity is a measure of producing life and sustenance; that this kind of productivity has been rendered invisible does not reduce its centrality to survival—it merely reflects the domination of modern patriarchal economic categories which see only profits, not life.

Maldevelopment as the Death of the Feminine Principle

In this analysis, maldevelopment becomes a new source of male-female inequality. 'Modernisation' has been associated with the introduction of new forms of dominance. Alice Schlegel[7] has shown that under conditions of subsistence, the interdependence and complementarity of the separate male and female domains of work is the characteristic mode, based on diversity, not inequality.

Maldevelopment militates against this equality in diversity, and superimposes the ideologically constructed category of western technological man as a uniform measure of the worth of classes, cultures and genders. Dominant modes of perception based on reductionism, duality and linearity are unable to cope with equality in diversity, with forms and activities that are significant and valid, even though different. The reductionist mind superimposes the roles and forms of power of western male-oriented concepts on women, all non-western peoples and even on nature, rendering all three 'deficient,' and in need of 'development.' Diversity, and unity and harmony in diversity, become epistemologically unattainable in the context of maldevelopment, which then becomes synonymous with women's underdevelopment (increasing sexist domination), and nature's depletion (deepening ecological crises). Commodities have grown, but nature has shrunk. The poverty crisis of the South arises from the growing scarcity of water, food, fodder, and fuel, associated with increasing maldevelopment and ecological destruction. This poverty crisis touches women most severely, first because they are the poorest among the poor, and then because, with nature, they are the primary sustainers of society.

Maldevelopment is the violation of the integrity of organic, interconnected and interdependent systems, that sets in motion a process of exploitation, inequality, injustice and violence. It is blind to the fact that a recognition of nature's harmony and action to maintain it are preconditions for distributive justice. This is why Mahatma Gandhi said, 'There is enough in the world for everyone's need, but not for some people's greed.'

Maldevelopment is maldevelopment in thought and action. In practice, this fragmented, reductionist, dualist perspective violates the integrity and harmony of man in nature, and the harmony between men and women. It ruptures the cooperative unity of masculine and feminine, and places man, shorn of the feminine principle, above nature and women, and separated from both. The violence to nature as symptomatised by the ecological crisis, and the violence to women, as symptomatised by their subjugation and exploitation, arise from this subjugation of the feminine principle. I want to argue that what is currently called development is essentially maldevelopment, based on the introduction or accentuation of the domination of man over nature and women. In it, both are viewed as the 'other,' the passive nonself. Activity, productivity, creativity which were associated with the feminine principle are expropriated as qualities of nature and women, and transformed into the exclusive qualities of man. Nature and women are turned into passive objects, to be used and exploited for the uncontrolled and uncontrollable desires of alienated man. From being the creators and sustainers of life, nature and women are reduced to being 'resources' in the fragmented, anti-life model of maldevelopment.

Two Kinds of Growth, Two Kinds of Productivity

Maldevelopment is usually called 'economic growth,' measured by the Gross National Product. Porritt, a leading ecologist, has this to say of GNP:

> *Gross* National Product—for once a word is being used correctly. Even conventional economists admit that the hey-day of GNP is over, for the simple reason that as a measure of progress, it's more or less useless. GNP measures the lot, all the goods and services produced in the money economy. Many of these goods and services are not beneficial to people, but rather a measure of just how much is going wrong; increased spending on crime, on pollution, on the many human casualties of our society, increased spending because of waste or planned obsolescence, increased spending because of growing bureaucracies: it's all counted.[8]

The problem with GNP is that it measures some costs as benefits (e.g., pollution control) and fails to measure other costs completely. Among these hidden costs are the new burdens created by ecological devastation, costs that are invariably heavier for women, both in the North and South. It is hardly surprising, therefore, that as GNP rises, it does not necessarily mean that either wealth or welfare increase proportionately. I would argue that GNP is becoming, increasingly, a measure of how real wealth—the wealth of nature and that produced by women for sustaining life—is rapidly decreasing. When commodity production as the prime economic activity is introduced as development, it destroys the potential of nature and women to produce life and goods and services for basic needs. More commodities and more cash mean less life—in nature (through ecological destruction) and in society (through denial of basic needs). Women are devalued first, because their work cooperates with nature's processes, and second, because work which satisfies needs and ensures sustenance is devalued in general. Precisely because more growth in maldevelopment has meant less sustenance of life and life-support systems, it is now imperative to recover the feminine principle as the basis for development which conserves and is ecological. Feminism as ecology, and ecology as the revival of Prakriti, the source of all life, become the decentred powers of political and economic transformation and restructuring.

This involves, first, a recognition that categories of 'productivity' and growth which have been taken to be positive, progressive and universal are, in reality, restricted patriarchal categories. When viewed from the point of view of nature's productivity and growth, and women's production of sustenance, they are found to be ecologically destructive and a source of gender inequality. It is no accident that the modern, efficient and productive technologies created within the context of growth in market economic terms are associated with heavy ecological costs, borne largely by women. The resource and energy intensive production processes they give rise to demand ever increasing resource withdrawals from the ecosystem. These withdrawals disrupt essential ecological processes and convert renewable resources into nonrenewable ones. A forest, for example, provides inexhaustible supplies of diverse biomass over time if its capital stock is maintained and it is harvested on a sustained yield basis. The heavy and uncontrolled demand for industrial and commercial wood, however, requires the continuous overfelling of trees which exceeds the regenerative capacity of the forest ecosystem, and eventually converts the forests into nonrenewable resources. Women's work in the collection of water, fodder and fuel is thus rendered more energy and time-consuming. (In Garhwal, for example, I have seen women who originally collected fodder and fuel in a few hours, now travelling long distances by truck to collect grass and leaves in a task that might take up to two days.) Sometimes the damage to nature's intrinsic regenerative capacity is impaired not by overexploitation of a particular resource but, indirectly, by damage caused to other related natural resources through ecological processes. Thus, the excessive overfelling of trees in the catchment areas of streams and rivers destroys not only forest resources, but also renewable supplies of water, through hydrological destabilisation. Resource-intensive industries disrupt essential ecological processes not only by their excessive demands for raw material, but by their pollution of air and water and soil. Often such destruction is caused by the resource demands of non-vital industrial products. In spite of severe ecological crises, this paradigm continues to operate because for the North and for the elites of the South, resources continue to be available, even now. The lack of recognition of nature's processes for survival *as factors in the process of economic development* shrouds the political issues arising from resource transfer and resource destruction, and creates an ideological weapon for increased control over natural resources in the conventionally employed notion of productivity. All other costs of the economic process consequently become invisible. The forces which contribute to the increased 'productivity' of a modern farmer or factory worker, for instance, come from the increased use of natural resources. Lovins has described this as the amount of 'slave' labour presently at work in the world.[9] According to him each person on earth, on an average, possesses the equivalent of about 50 slaves, each working a 40 hour week. Man's global energy conversion from all sources (wood, fossil fuel, hydroelectric power, nuclear) is currently approximately 8×10^{12} watts. This is more than 20 times the energy content of the food necessary to feed the present world population at the FAO standard diet of 3,600 cal/day. The 'productivity' of the western male compared to women or Third World peasants is not intrinsically superior; it is based on inequalities in the distribution of this "slave" labour. The average inhabitant of the USA for example has 250 times more 'slaves' than the average Nigerian. 'If Americans were short of 249 of those 250 'slaves', one wonders how efficient they would prove themselves to be?'

It is these resource and energy intensive processes of production which divert resources away from survival, and hence from women. What patriarchy sees as productive work is, in ecological terms, highly destructive production. The second

law of thermodynamics predicts that resource intensive and resource wasteful economic development must become a threat to the survival of the human species in the long run. Political struggles based on ecology in industrially advanced countries are rooted in this conflict between *long term survival options* and *short term over-production and over-consumption*. Political struggles of women, peasants and tribals based on ecology in countries like India are far more acute and urgent since they are rooted in the *immediate threat to the options for survival* for the vast majority of the people, *posed by resource intensive and resource wasteful economic growth* for the benefit of a minority.

In the market economy, the organising principle for natural resource use is the maximisation of profits and capital accumulation. Nature and human needs are managed through market mechanisms. Demands for natural resources are restricted to those demands registering on the market; the ideology of development is in large part based on a vision of bringing all natural resources into the market economy for commodity production. When these resources are already being used by nature to maintain her production of renewable resources and by women for sustenance and livelihood, their diversion to the market economy generates a scarcity condition for ecological stability and creates new forms of poverty for women.

Two Kinds of Poverty

In a book entitled *Poverty: The Wealth of the People*[10] an African writer draws a distinction between poverty as subsistence, and misery as deprivation. It is useful to separate a cultural conception of subsistence living as poverty from the material experience of poverty that is a result of dispossession and deprivation. Culturally perceived poverty need not be real material poverty: subsistence economies which satisfy basic needs through self-provisioning are not poor in the sense of being deprived. Yet the ideology of development declares them so because they do not participate overwhelmingly in the market economy, and do not consume commodities produced for and distributed through the market *even though they might be satisfying those needs through self-provisioning mechanisms*. People are perceived as poor if they eat millets (grown by women) rather than commercially produced and distributed processed foods sold by global agri-business. They are seen as poor if they live in self-built housing made from natural material like bamboo and mud rather than in cement houses. They are seen as poor if they wear handmade garments of natural fibre rather than synthetics. Subsistence, as culturally perceived poverty, does not necessarily imply a low physical quality of life. On the contrary, millets are nutritionally far superior to processed foods, houses built with local materials are far superior, being better adapted to the local climate and ecology, natural fibres are preferable to man-made fibres in most cases, and certainly more affordable. This cultural perception of prudent subsistence living as poverty has provided the legitimisation for the development process as a poverty removal project. As a culturally biased project it destroys wholesome and sustainable lifestyles and creates real material poverty, or misery, by the denial of survival needs themselves, through the diversion of resources to resource intensive commodity production. Cash crop production and food processing take land and water resources away from sustenance needs, and exclude increasingly large numbers of people from their entitlements to food. 'The inexorable processes of agriculture-industrialisation and internationalisation are probably responsible for more hungry people than either cruel or unusual whims of nature. There are several reasons why the high-technology-export-crop model increases hunger. Scarce land, credit, water, and technology are preempted for the export market. Most hungry people are not affected by the market at all. . . . The profits flow to corporations that have no interest in feeding hungry people without money.'[11]

The Ethiopian famine is in part an example of the creation of real poverty by development aimed at removing culturally perceived poverty. The displacement of nomadic Afars from their traditional pastureland in Awash Valley by commercial agriculture (financed by foreign companies) led to their struggle for survival in the fragile uplands which degraded the ecosystem and led to the starvation of cattle and the nomads.[12] The market economy conflicted with the survival economy in the Valley, thus creating a conflict between the survival economy and nature's economy in the uplands. At no point has the global marketing of agricultural commodities been assessed against the background of the new conditions of scarcity and poverty that it

has induced. This new poverty moreover, is no longer cultural and relative: it is absolute, threatening the very survival of millions on this planet.

The economic system based on the patriarchal concept of productivity was created for the very specific historical and political phenomenon of colonialism. In it, the input for which efficiency of use had to be maximised in the production centres of Europe, was industrial labour. For colonial interest therefore, it was rational to improve the labour resource *even at the cost of wasteful use of nature's wealth.* This rationalisation has, however, been illegitimately universalised to all contexts and interest groups and, on the plea of increasing productivity, labour reducing technologies have been introduced in situations where labour is abundant and cheap, and resource demanding technologies have been introduced where resources are scarce and already fully utilised for the production of sustenance. Traditional economies with a stable ecology have shared with industrially advanced affluent economies the ability to use natural resources to satisfy basic vital needs. The former differ from the latter in two essential ways: first, the same needs are satisfied in industrial societies through longer technological chains requiring higher energy and resource inputs and excluding large numbers without purchasing power; and second, affluence generates new and artificial needs requiring the increased production of industrial goods and services. Traditional economies are not advanced in the matter of non-vital needs satisfaction, but as far as the satisfaction of basic and vital needs is concerned, they are often what Marshall Sahlins has called 'the original affluent society.' The needs of the Amazonian tribes are more than satisfied by the rich rainforest; their poverty begins with its destruction. The story is the same for the Gonds of Bastar in India or the Penans of Sarawak in Malaysia.

Thus are economies based on indigenous technologies viewed as 'backward' and 'unproductive.' Poverty, as the denial of basic needs, is not necessarily associated with the existence of traditional technologies, and its removal is not necessarily an outcome of the growth of modern ones. On the contrary, the destruction of ecologically sound traditional technologies, often created and used by women, along with the destruction of their material base, is generally believed to be responsible for the 'feminisation' of poverty in societies which have had to bear the costs of resource destruction.

The contemporary poverty of the Afar nomad is not rooted in the inadequacies of traditional nomadic life, but in the *diversion of the productive pastureland of the Awash Valley*. The erosion of the resource base for survival is increasingly being caused by the demand for resources by the market economy, dominated by global forces. The creation of inequality through economic activity which is ecologically disruptive arises in two ways: first, inequalities in the distribution of privileges make for unequal access to natural resources—these include privileges of both a political and economic nature. Second, resource intensive production processes have access to subsidized raw material on which a substantial number of people, especially from the less privileged economic groups, depend for their survival. The consumption of such industrial raw material is determined purely by market forces, and not by considerations of the social or ecological requirements placed on them. The costs of resource destruction are externalized and unequally divided among various economic groups in society, but are borne largely by women and those who satisfy their basic material needs directly from nature, simply because they have no purchasing power to register their demands on the goods and services provided by the modern production system. Gustavo Esteva has called development a permanent war waged by its promoters and suffered by its victims.[13]

The paradox and crisis of development arises from the mistaken identification of culturally perceived poverty with real material poverty, and the mistaken identification of the growth of commodity production as better satisfaction of basic needs. In actual fact, there is less water, less fertile soil, less genetic wealth as a result of the development process. Since these natural resources are the basis of nature's economy and women's survival economy, their scarcity is impoverishing women and marginalized peoples in an unprecedented manner. Their new impoverishment lies in the fact that resources which supported their survival were absorbed into the market economy while they themselves were excluded and displaced by it.

The old assumption that with the development process the availability of goods and services will automatically be increased and poverty will be removed, is now under serious challenge from women's ecology movements in the Third World, even while it continues to guide development thinking in centers of patriarchal power. Survival is based on the assumption of the sanctity of life; maldevelopment is based on the assumption of the sacredness of 'development.' Gustavo Esteva asserts that the sacredness of development has to be refuted because it threatens survival itself. 'My people are tired of development,' he says, 'they just want to live.'[14]

The recovery of the feminine principle allows a transcendence and transformation of these patriarchal foundations of maldevelopment. It allows a redefinition of growth and productivity as categories linked to the production, not the destruction, of life. It is thus simultaneously an ecological and a feminist political project which legitimises the way of knowing and being that create wealth by enhancing life and diversity, and which delegitimises the knowledge and practice of a culture of death as the basis for capital accumulation.

Notes

1. Rosa Luxemberg, *The Accumulation of Capital*, London: Routledge and Kegan Paul, 1951.

2. An elaboration of how 'development' transfers resources from the poor to the well-endowed is contained in J. Bandyopadhyay and V. Shiva, 'Political Economy of Technological Polarisations' in *Economic and Political Weekly*, Vol. XVIII, 1982, pp. 1827–32; and J. Bandyopadhyay and V. Shiva, 'Political Economy of Ecology Movements,' in *Economic and Political Weekly*, forthcoming.

3. Ester Boserup, *Women's Role in Economic Development*, London: Allen and Unwin, 1970.

4. DAWN, *Development Crisis and Alternative Visions: Third World Women's Perspectives*, Bergen: Christian Michelsen Institute, 1985, p. 21.

5. M. George Foster, *Traditional Societies and Technological Change*, Delhi: Allied Publishers, 1973.

6. Maria Mies, *Patriarchy and Accumulation on a World Scale*, London: Zed Books, 1986.

7. Alice Schlegel (ed.), *Sexual Stratification: A Cross-Cultural Study*, New York: Columbia University Press, 1977.

8. Jonathan Porritt, *Seeing Green*, Oxford: Blackwell, 1984.

9. A. Lovins, cited in S. R. Eyre, *The Real Wealth of Nations*, London: Edward Arnold, 1978.

10. R. Bahro, *From Red to Green*, London: Verso, 1984, p. 211.

11. R. J. Barnet, *The Lean Years*, London: Abacus, 1981, p. 171.

12. U. P. Koehn, 'African Approaches to Environmental Stress: A Focus on Ethiopia and Nigeria,' in R. N. Barrett (ed.), *International Dimensions of the Environmental Crisis.* Boulder, CO: Westview, 1982, pp. 253–89.

13. Gustavo Esteva, 'Regenerating People's Space,' in

S. N. Mendlowitz and R. B. J. Walker, *Towards a Just World Peace: Perspectives from Social Movements.* London: Butterworths and Committee for a Just World Peace, 1987.

14. G. Esteva, Remarks made at a conference of the Society for International Development, Rome, 1985.

How Feminist Is Ecofeminism?

Victoria Davion

I. Introduction

This paper explores some doubts I have regarding ecofeminism, a relatively new movement attempting to bring feminist insights to environmental ethics.[1] Although there are a variety of different ecofeminist positions, ecofeminists agree that there is an important link between the domination of women and the domination of nature, and that an understanding of one is aided by an understanding of the other. Ecofeminists argue that any environmental ethic that fails to recognize important conceptual ties between the domination of women and the domination of nature cannot provide an adequate understanding of either.[2] Therefore, ecofeminists argue that a feminist perspective contributes to a fuller understanding of the domination of nature by human beings, and is necessary for the generation of a deeper environmental ethic.

My project is not to question this thesis; I agree with it. My project is to explore whether much of what is currently called "ecofeminist" is actually feminist. I will argue that at least some of the ideas coming from thinkers identifying themselves as ecofeminists are, in very important ways, *not* feminist. Because these ideas are not feminist, they cannot be ecofeminist. The ideas I shall explore glorify the feminine uncritically and suggest that embracing a feminine perspective will help humans solve

the ecological crisis. I will argue that a truly feminist perspective cannot embrace either the feminine or the masculine uncritically, as a truly feminist perspective requires a critique of gender roles, and this critique must include masculinity *and* femininity. While the views I have in mind critique masculinity, they fail to do the same in the case of femininity. I shall, therefore, argue that these views are better understood as *ecofeminine*, as they do not embrace a feminist perspective.[3] Before turning to this task, I shall discuss what I find to be an extremely useful ecofeminist approach in section II. In section III I shall argue that views which *uncritically* embrace masculinity or femininity are, in crucial ways, not feminist. With this conceptual framework in place, I shall discuss five *ecofeminine* views in section IV. Finally, I shall suggest some positive directions for ecofeminism in the concluding section.

II. Important Ecofeminist Insights

Ecofeminists agree that the domination of nature by human beings comes from a patriarchal world view, the same world view that justifies the domination of women. Because both dominations come from the same world view, the movement to stop devaluing nature should, in consistency, include a movement against the domination

Ecological Feminism, edited by Karen J. Warren. New York: Routledge, Chapman & Hall, Inc., forthcoming. Reprinted by permission of the author.

I owe special thanks to Karen J. Warren, whose help in reading earlier drafts of this work has resulted in substantive conceptual changes that have improved the piece greatly, and have also contributed to my understanding of the complexity and importance of various ecofeminist perspectives. An updated version of this piece is scheduled to appear in *Ecological Feminist Philosophies*, edited by Karen Warren, Routledge and Chapman Hall, Spring 1994. I would also like to thank Chris Cuomo and Claudia Card for their helpful suggestions.

of women, i.e., should incorporate a feminist perspective.

In her recent article, "The Power and the Promise of Ecological Feminism," Karen Warren explores some major conceptual connections between the domination of women by men and the domination of nature by humans. She argues that both depend on the "logic of domination." This logic makes use of premises about differences between human beings and the rest of nature, along with a premise that asserts that these differences allow human beings to dominate non-humans. She offers the following example:

(A1) Humans do, . . . plants do not, have the capacity to consciously . . . change the community in which they live.

(A2) Whatever has [this] capacity . . . is morally superior to whatever [doesn't have] it.

(A3) . . . Humans are morally superior to plants and rocks.

(A4) For any X and Y, if X is morally superior to Y, then X is morally justified in subordinating Y.

(A5) . . . Humans are morally justified in subordinating plants and rocks.[4]

This argument incorporates what Warren refers to as an oppressive conceptual framework. Features of such a framework include hierarchical thinking, value dualisms, and the logic of domination. Such a framework includes the idea that particular characteristics of individuals place them either above or below each other in moral hierarchies, and the assumption that whatever is above something else in the hierarchy has the moral right to dominate that which is below it. These features combine to create a world view that offers a justification for human domination of nature. Thus, Warren shows how a particular logic is involved in justifying the domination of nature by humans, and makes explicit just what that logic is.

Warren maintains that the same logic allows for the sexist domination of women under patriarchy by way of the association of women with nature. She sketches the argument as follows:

(B1) Women are identified with nature and the realm of the physical; men are identified with the "human" and the realm of the mental.

(B2) Whatever is identified with nature and the realm of the physical is inferior to ("below") whatever is identified with the "human" and the realm of the mental. . . .

(B3) Thus, women are inferior to . . . men. . . .

(B4) For any X and Y, if X is superior to Y, then X is justified in subordinating Y.

(B5) . . . Men are justified in subordinating women.[5]

As I said earlier, I agree with the ecofeminist argument that there are links between the domination of women under patriarchy and the domination of nature. Noticing these links allows us to recognize that the domination of nature by humans and the sexist domination of women by men rely on the same general framework. Thus, the overthrowing of this framework is fundamental to both projects and, therefore, the projects are conceptually linked. This important insight shows that environmentalists and feminists should be allies, and makes explicit what it is we must work against. It represents a very important ecofeminist contribution to both movements. If one grants conceptual links between the domination of nature and the domination of women, it follows that a movement that is not feminist will yield at best a superficial understanding of the domination of nature.

III. Feminism

Feminism pays attention to women. Although there are many different kinds of feminism, virtually all feminists agree that sexist oppression is wrong, and therefore seek to overthrow patriarchy in its various forms. Thus, for an analysis to be feminist, it must include an analysis of sex and gender. It must look for the various ways that sexist oppression damages women, and seek alternatives to them. In looking at *how* patriarchy damages women, a feminist analysis must look closely at the roles women play in various patriarchies, the *feminine* roles. In so far as these roles are damaging (to those who play them), they must be viewed with suspicion. If feminists fail to assert that at least some of the roles assigned to women under patriarchy are damaging, we fail to assert the very premise that makes feminism, the overthrowing of patriarchy, important. For, if sexist oppression is not damaging to women, women have no reason to resist it. If it does cause damage, we should expect to see this damage in feminine roles. Thus, ecofeminist solutions which assert that feminine roles can provide an answer to the ecological crisis, without first examining how these roles are damaging to those who play them, lose the conceptual underpinnings of feminism in this assertion.

Before continuing, I want to be clear about what it is I am *not* doing here. I am not claiming that there can be only one truly feminist perspective. There are many different kinds of feminism, including radical feminism, marxist feminism, cultural feminism, and so forth. I am not attempting to distinguish between these approaches here. In my view, all of these can be feminist approaches as long as they have a critical analysis of sex and gender. It is the *uncritical* acceptance of various aspects of sex and gender that concerns me.

In what follows I will examine five ecofeminist views which fail to critically examine femininity in its various forms. Each of them suggests that a more "feminine" perspective on the environment will help solve the ecological crisis. Some suggest that we can overthrow patriarchy by having men become more "feminine," without considering that femininity may be a product of patriarchy itself. Because they all fail to consider that feminine perspectives are most likely damaged, and fail to explore just what this damage might be, they fail to explore the possible negative aspects of bringing more "feminine" perspectives to environmental ethics. In addition, several of these views imply that there is something that is THE feminine role, that the feminine perspective is a unified perspective. However, if feminism is to be understood as a movement for the liberation of all women, we must understand that there is no one feminine voice. Rather, there are many different feminine voices, many "feminine" perspectives. Therefore, views which uncritically embrace feminine sides of gender dichotomies are not feminist, and when these views are linked with ecological perspectives they are better understood as *ecofeminine*. They are, in fact, dangerous views from a genuinely feminist perspective.

IV. Five Ecofeminine Views

Although there are significant differences in each of the five views I will discuss, each glorifies

the feminine uncritically, and therefore none are truly feminist on my understanding of feminism as committed to a critique of gender reality.

The first position I shall examine is presented by Ariel Kay Salleh in "Deeper Than Deep Ecology: The Ecofeminist Connection." She says the following about women's lived experience under patriarchy:

> . . . if women's lived experience were recognized as meaningful and were given legitimation in our culture, it would provide an immediate "living" social basis for alternative consciousness which the deep ecologist is trying to formulate and introduce as an abstract ethical construct. Women already, to borrow Devall's turn of phrase, "flow with the system of nature."[6]

According to Salleh, we do not need abstract ethical constructs to help create a consciousness of our connection with the rest of nature; women already have it. What we need to do is to recognize the value of women's experiences, something which patriarchal societies fail to do.

Salleh claims that while the masculine sense of self-worth in our culture has become entrenched in scientific habits of thought:

> Women, on the other hand, socialized as they are for a multiplicity of contingent tasks and practical labor functions in the home and out, do not experience the inhibiting constraints of status validation to the same extent. The traditional feminine role runs counter to the exploitative technical rationality which currently is the requisite masculine norm. In place of the disdain that the feminine role receives from all quarters, "the separate reality" of this role could well be taken seriously by ecologists and reexamined as a legitimate source of alternative values. As Snyder suggests, men should try out roles which are not highly valued in society, and one might add, particularly this one, for herein lies the basis of a genuinely grounded and nurturant environmentalism.[7]

Thus, the problem, according to Salleh, is that "the traditional feminine role" is devalued. Salleh does not tell us exactly what "the traditional feminine role" is. However, she does imply that women under patriarchy are socialized into it. It is a woman's role under conditions of sexual oppression. She suggests that this role can provide the basis for a genuinely grounded and nurturant environmental ethic. However, the arguments supplied to back this up leave out some important facts about domination and submission that feminists must attend to. According to Salleh, because of the way women are socialized, we ". . . do not experience the inhibiting constraints of status validation to the same extent." However, in many contemporary societies the particular ways in which women seek validation are part of the feminine role. Validation-seeking is often bound up with physical attractiveness. It is shown in contemporary American society by such things as the cosmetic industry, the increasing number of women opting for "elective" cosmetic surgery, and by the number of women with eating disorders. Women may demonstrate the quest for social validation differently both from men and from each other, but it is certainly a part of many feminine roles. And the industries supported by women playing out feminine roles are often responsible for gross environmental damage. The damage to the ozone layer that is done by aerosol cans used to package hairsprays is one example, the cruel testing of cosmetics on animals is another. Finally, we must never forget the extent to which women have dominated other women and men through assertion of status conferred by other things such as race and class. Thus, I think it is false to say that women, in our playing out feminine roles, do not seek status validation, and are more concerned with the environment.

I find the reference to "the separate reality" of women disturbing as well. First, this implies that all women share the same reality. However, an important part of the history of feminist thought has been the lessons white middle class feminists have learned from being called on our racism and classism as we attempted to speak for all women. Because of this, sensitivity to such differences has come to be central to feminist projects. Many feminists now realize that if we want feminism to be more than just a movement for the liberation of a particular group of women, if we wish it to be a movement for the liberation of all women, we must accept and address that there may be no unified experience of femininity or womanhood. There are very deep differences among us. The assumption that there is a separate reality occupied by all women must be examined and argued for, rather than simply assumed.

Another aspect of the "separate reality" claim

I find troubling involves the idea that women's reality is separate from men's. In some very important ways, women don't live in a reality separate from men's. Men and women living under conditions of sexist oppression live in a world inhabited by oppressors as well as by the oppressed. The reality of oppressed women is intimately connected to that of the oppressors. Women oppressed under a particular patriarchy may share experiences as members of the same group. However, to say that these experiences constitute a separate reality is not only to ignore some of the differences that other aspects of oppression may bring to the situation (such as race or class oppression), but also to ignore the connections *to* oppressors that make women's oppression possible. Femininity makes sense only in relation to masculinity and vice versa. In an important sense there is no separate reality because patriarchy *is* part of reality, and this is the problem.

The idea that men could adopt the feminine role as a start to changing their attitude implies that the feminine role can be understood without its masculine counterpart. However, because the traditional feminine role is the role of the dominated under conditions of sexist oppression, it makes no sense for it to exist independently of the masculine role. The role of the dominated requires that of the dominator. And, if we must seek a society without domination and subordination as part of the solution to the present ecological crisis, this idea cannot be part of that solution.

These considerations lead me to the conclusion that "the feminine role" is unlikely to provide genuine grounding for anything other than the oppression of women. However, even if this role can provide something more, before we assume that it can, it is important to think about the origins of this role, the possible damaging effects of playing it, and whether it makes sense to abstract it from patriarchy in the first place. We must look critically at femininity in its various forms.

A second so-called "ecofeminist" approach glorifies the feminine as a *principle* rather than a *gender role*. In *Development as a New Project of Western Patriarchy*, Vandana Shiva discusses the concept of "development" from the perspective of western patriarchy. She concludes that this so-called "development" actually breeds poverty in the areas that are "developed," and, therefore, it is really maldevelopment. Her argument for this is convincing. However, her discussion of the problem includes the idea of gender complementarity as a good thing and the idea that what is missing from the western patriarchal perspective is the "feminine principle." The following quotation is taken from her article:

> The western development model based on the neglect of nature's work and women's work has become a source of deprivation of basic needs.
>
> In practice this reductionist, dualist perspective gives rise to the violation of the integrity and harmony between men and women. It ruptures the cooperative unity of the masculine and feminine, and puts men, deprived of the feminine principle above and thus separated from nature and women. The violence to nature as symptomized by the current ecological crisis, and the violence to women as symptomized by women's subjugation and exploitation arise from the subjugation of the feminine principle.[8]

Shiva doesn't supply a definition of the feminine principle. However, she associates it with conservation and nurturing. She states of the western patriarchal concept of development, "Such development becomes maldevelopment—deprived of the feminine, the conserving, the ecological principle."[9]

This analysis implies several things which I believe must be questioned. One is natural gender complementarity. The suggestion is that gender roles aren't the problem, but that rather, the devaluation of the feminine role causes trouble. However, this must be shown rather than assumed. A vital tradition in feminist critique has long argued that gender roles cannot exist without domination and subordination. It is dangerous for feminists to assume that there is something "natural" or good in gender complementarity. References to the integrity and harmony between men and women, the idea that the western patriarchal concept of development ". . . ruptures the cooperative unity between the masculine and the feminine" presuppose that there is some "natural" way for the sexes to relate to each other, that there is a "natural" division of labor, and that problems emerge from the devaluation of the feminine side. To simply accept gender complementarity without exploring questions it raises is to ignore feminist literature claiming that gender roles are part of *the means of* domination and subordination in patriarchy. It thus

ignores questions of gender central to feminist analysis.

Shiva refers to the feminist principle as if there is *a* principle that is feminine. It isn't clear what is meant by this. However, as in Salleh's analysis discussed previously, there is an assumption that the feminine is one thing, and that it has something to offer in solving the ecological crisis. Again my response is that we must remember that the feminine may be shaped by patriarchy, that it is not necessarily an independent category but may be a cluster of various traits emerging out of oppression. There is great danger in abstracting it from patriarchy, and a great danger in assuming it is one thing, given the importance of differences among women.

A third approach within ecofeminist literature which I believe is ecofemin*ine* rather than ecofemin*ist* assumes women have some special understanding of nature but is not clear about the source of this special understanding. Thus far, I have discussed only the views of *women* ecofeminists. However, a number of men also are now identifying with ecofeminism. In "How to Cure a Frontal Lobotomy" Brian Swimme says the following in praise of women's intuition, using Starhawk as an example:

> Starhawk intuits effortlessly what remained beyond the group of the scientists. Our universe is quite clearly a great swelling and birthing event, but why was this hidden from the very discoverers of the primeval birth? The further truth of the universe was closed to them because central regions of the mind were closed. . . . This sentience is awake in Starhawk because of her life as a woman, as one who has the power to give birth herself, and because of her work as a scholar. . . . Women are beings who know from the inside out what it is like to weave the earth into a new human being. Given that experience and the congruent sensitivities seething within body and mind, it would be utterly shocking if ecofeminists did not bring forth meanings to the scientific data that were hidden from the scientists themselves.[10]

Swimme claims that there is some truth to the idea that the earth is a birthing process, but that this truth can only be seen, in fact, effortlessly intuited by women. Swimme seems unsure whether this epistemic privilege is the result of biology, socialization, or both. He refers both to Starhawk's life as a woman, and to the fact that she is a being who can give birth. Perhaps Swimme wants to deny any distinction between biology and socialization as an untenable dualism. However, if Swimme has reasons for leaving the source of this epistemic privilege vague, he doesn't state them. The source of this so-called privilege is of vital importance to any feminist analysis. If this special understanding is the result of oppression, we should expect it to be skewed. Even if it is not skewed, we must ask whether there are other ways to get it. This is a crucial question because if there is no other way to get it, we risk saying that women's oppression is necessary to create the opportunity to gain knowledge needed to solve the ecological crisis. Once again, crucial questions concerning sex and gender are left vague, and women's roles under patriarchy are glorified.[11]

Along with literature assuming that the feminine offers an understanding of human connection to the earth comes literature praising Goddess worship. Much of this literature suggests that cultures that worshiped the Goddess instead of God, cultures in which the feminine was valued, were *peaceful* cultures in which human connection to nonhuman nature was understood. The next position I shall discuss is an example of this. In "The Gaia Tradition and the Partnership Future" Raine Eisler discusses societies that worshiped the Goddess and argues that they were more like the kind of society we need today to solve the ecological crisis. She says:

> Prehistoric societies worshiped the Goddess of nature and spirituality, our great Mother, the giver of life and creator of us all. But even more fascinating is that these ancient societies were structured very much like the more peaceful and just society we are now trying to construct.
>
> In short, they were societies which had what we today call an ecological consciousness: the awareness that the Earth must be treated with reverence and respect. And this reverence for life-giving and life-sustained powers of the Earth was rooted in a social structure where women and "feminine" values such as caring, compassion, and non-violence were not subordinate to men and the so-called masculine values of conquest and domination. Rather, the

life-giving powers incarnated in women's bodies were given the highest social value.[12]

Eisler calls upon us to value these so-called "feminine values" once more:

> Let us reaffirm our ancient covenant, our sacred bond with our Mother, the Goddess of nature and spirituality. Let us renounce the worship of angry gods wielding thunderbolts or swords. Let us once again honor the chalice, the ancient symbol of the power to create and enhance life—and let us understand that this power is not woman's alone but also man's.[13]

Thus, Eisler, like several others discussed here, claims that the problem lies in the devaluing of what she calls "feminine values." By reaffirming such values we can better form the ecological conscience needed to deal with our destructive tendencies.

There is nothing problematic in examining history for ideas to help solve current problems. Eisler's work is interesting and instructive. However, once again I have problems with the use of the gender terms "masculine" and "feminine" in her analysis. My worries in this case stem from the context within which this work is written: this sort of historical work can easily be taken as a glorification of the feminine.

Eisler uses the terms *masculine* and *feminine* to refer to kinds of values in her analysis. She maintains that traits now associated with the term 'feminine' were highly valued during the time period she discusses. However, whether we should refer to these values as feminine is problematic. If patriarchy is necessary for femininity as we now understand it, then if these ancient cultures were not patriarchal or descended from patriarchies, they could not have feminine gender roles. It may be true that some of the respected values in those cultures are devalued in our culture, and that they are considered feminine now. This is very different from asserting that there was anything "feminine" that was respected. Eisler, however, refers to "feminine" values without questioning what it means to call anything "feminine" in a nonpatriarchal culture. Thus, she implies that femininity can exist without patriarchy, a dangerous assumption indeed.

The final view I shall discuss is offered by Marti Kheel in "Ecofeminism and Deep Ecology," and discusses the importance of connection. Kheel argues that ecofeminists and deep ecologists have very different perspectives regarding the kinds of connection to be endorsed in an ecological ethic. Many deep ecologists support developing a sense of oneself that is expanded to include all of nature.[14] They argue that the concept of the self as a static individual with clear ego boundaries is a major factor in the ecological crisis. However, many deep ecologists believe that this sense of self can be developed through activities that involve killing. Hunting is often praised in the literature. Kheel quotes philosopher/biologist Randall Eaton to exemplify this way of thinking.

> To hunt is to experience extreme oneness with nature. . . . The hunter imitates his prey to the point of identity. . . . hunting connects a man completely with the earth more deeply and profoundly than any other human enterprise.[15]

This experience of connection is not the type that ecofeminists should support, according to Kheel. She suggests that the way women feel a sense of connection is very different.

> It is out of women's unique, felt sense of connection to the natural world that an ecofeminist philosophy must be forged. Identification may, in fact, enter into this philosophy, but only to the extent that it flows from an *existing* connection with individual lives. Individual beings must not be used in a kind of psychological instrumentalism to help establish a *feeling* of connection that in fact does not exist. Our sense of oneness with nature must be connected with concrete, loving actions.[16]

If Kheel is right, much more needs to be said. Not all women feel connected to nature. Some men may feel this more than many women. More importantly, in order to decide what kinds of connections are valuable, and in order to distinguish real connection from a feeling of connection that does not exist, we need to examine various kinds of connection. We should not assume that (a) all women feel this connection with nature or (b) that the connections women do feel are healthy. In doing this, we fail once again to recognize important differences between women, and uncritically glorify women's experiences without critically examining them.

V. Conclusion

Ecofeminism raises interesting questions in spite of the failure of some ecofeminists to critically examine gender roles before incorporating them wholesale as part of solutions to the environmental crisis. Ecofeminists such as Karen Warren have shown how the logic of domination is at work in both the domination of nature by humans, and the domination of women by men under various forms of patriarchy. In so doing, they have shown that the fights to end both are linked conceptually and therefore politically. This insight helps us to see that feminists and environmentalists are allies in a greater fight to end the logic of domination. Hence, I believe the next important task facing ecofeminists is that of generating alternative ways of thinking, ways that are not contaminated by the logic of domination. An understanding of how the logic of domination works on the conceptual level places ecofeminists in an excellent position to do this.

Notes

1. This term was first used by Francoise d'Eaubonne in "Feminism or Death," in *New French Feminisms: An Anthology,* edited by Elaine Marks and Isabelle de Courtivron. Amherst: University of Massachusetts Press, 1980. For a useful overview of ecofeminist philosophy, see Karen J. Warren, "Feminism and the Environment: An Overview of the Issues," APA Newsletter on *Feminism and Philosophy* (Fall 1991). Also, for another critique of ecofeminism see Janet Biehl, *Rethinking Ecofeminist Politics* (Boston: South End Press, 1991). Although Biehl makes some similar criticisms in this work, she does not examine the work of individual ecofeminists in detail.

2. This position is explicitly argued in Karen J. Warren, "The Power and the Promise of Ecological Feminism." *Environmental Ethics* 12 (2) (1990), 125–146.

3. The term *ecofeminine* was suggested to me by Lorena Sax. My argument will not presuppose that there is only one way that ideas can be feminist, or that there is only one type of feminism. There are many. Thus, for example, I am not distinguishing between radical feminism and marxist feminism here. Rather, I am making a general claim that all types of feminism *must* include a critical look at gender.

4. Warren, 129. Please note, Warren does not support this argument, and does not argue that (A1) is true. This is merely an example of how the logic of domination works.

5. Warren, 130. Again, it is important to note that Warren does not support this argument, and does not argue in favor of any of its premises. Instead, she

uses it as an example of the logic of domination at work.

6. Ariel Kay Salleh, "Deeper Than Deep Ecology: The Ecofeminist Connection," *Environmental Ethics* (6) 1 (1984), 340.

7. Salleh, 342.

8. Vandana Shiva, "Development as a New Project of Western Patriarchy," in *Reweaving the World: The Emergence of Ecofeminism*, edited by Irene Diamond and Gloria Feman Orenstein (San Francisco: Sierra Club Books, 1990), p. 193.

9. Shiva, p. 191. The word *development* appears in quotation marks to indicate Shiva's position that what is called development is in reality not development at all.

10. Brian Swimme, "How to Cure a Frontal Lobotomy," in *Reweaving the World: The Emergence of Ecofeminism*, p. 19.

11. For an interesting discussion of epistemic privilege, see Uma Narayan, "Working Together Across Difference: Some Considerations on Emotions and Political Practice," *Hypatia: A Journal of Feminist Philosophy* (3) 2 (1988), 31–47.

12. Raine Eisler, "The Gaia Tradition and the Partnership Future," in *Reweaving the World: The Emergence of Ecofeminism*, pp. 23–24.

13. Eisler, p. 34.

14. For an excellent critique of this position see Val Plumwood, "Nature, Self, and Gender: Feminism, Environmental Philosophy, and the Critique of Rationalism," *Hypatia: A Journal of Feminist Philosophy* (6) 1 (1991), 3–27.

15. Marti Kheel, "Ecofeminism and Deep Ecology," in *Reweaving the World: The Emergence of Ecofeminism*, p. 131.

16. Kheel, p. 137.

V

ECONOMICS, ETHICS, AND ECOLOGY

A. LETTING THE MARKET DECIDE

PREVIEW

Many people probably share the sentiments of two writers who, in commenting on the despoliation of "our natural heritage" and the poisoning of the environment with the use of pesticides, stated that "although, it is obvious that what we are doing is wrong, it is by no means obvious what would be right."[1] Indeed, the perplexities are deep. There is disagreement about whether certain practices are wrong, what proper policies would be, and, importantly, the grounds for deciding such matters. As noted in the Introduction to Ethical Theory and in Part III, one source of dispute concerns what sorts of things have moral standing. Even if that difficult question were resolved, there are other sources of perplexity. Although the following suggestion deserves critical reflection and continued reassessment, one way of categorizing competing approaches to deciding an important range of environmental disputes is to divide them crudely into (1) those that assume that the mechanism of the marketplace is the proper means of determining both the allocation of resources to different productive uses and the distribution of benefits and burdens across the relevant populations, and (2) those which assume that these matters should not be left much, or at all, to the contingencies of the marketplace (that is, certain matters should be decided politically and certain protections or constraints on the market must be politically enforced in order to avoid certain failures or abuses to which unconstrained markets lead).

We need to think about the effects of the market mechanism on the environment and assess the arguments for claiming that the environmental effects of the market mechanism are tolerable or desirable. Markets, of course, existed long before economists or ecologists did. A major source of defense of the desirability of the market mechanism comes, however, from economists. For this reason and because economists, more than any other group of social scientists, have explored environmental issues in considerable detail, it is important to identify and examine some fundamental strands in economic theory and also to see how economists tend to approach particular current problems, e.g., pollution, species extinction, or the question of whether we should save for the sake of future generations. "Economic reasoning," indeed the economic point of view, is extremely influential in policy making and, for a number of reasons, inviting. Shortly, we shall note a number of objections to orthodox economic theory; first, however, we should make it quite clear that economists deserve special praise for paying careful attention to consequences and to related trade-offs. In short, the "economic approach" is sensitive to particular facts, it is specific, and it suggests a method for resolving questions of trade-offs between competing and valued ends. The economic approach seems, then, "practical," "hardnosed," and "realistic," and its use of precise, formal modes of quantification and calculation is alluring.

In recent years there has developed a more concentrated effort to identify the points of agreement and disagreement between economic theory, ethical theory, and the outlooks of ecologists. This effort (of which some essays in this volume are examples) promises to be an important and revealing one for developing an adequate view of our environment and a reasonable approach to setting policy on environmental matters. Here, we have room to touch on only a few central matters.

On the one hand, markets seem terribly useful. They provide us (or many of us) with all sorts of goods, including decent shelter, nutrition, medical care, and transportation—some "items" that few fail to value. In a decentralized fashion, without the (maligned) "government bureaucrats" deciding for the rest of us, the market allocates resources to myriad productive functions and provides a mode for distributing benefits (as well as the burdens of work, risk-taking, and so on). That the market mechanism produces all sorts of wonderful results is not subverted by the disdain we may rightly feel for certain insipid, tasteless, or defective products that it also generates. Sometimes, one person's junk is another's treasure; sometimes, it is just another's junk as well.

The main defense of the market mechanism appeals to the value of efficiency; it can be characterized as follows. In the best, perhaps idealized, case, two parties, for example, are mature, have settled preferences, are well informed, and with no undue pressure or misrepresentation agree to exchange goods or services. Perhaps one agrees to paint the other's house in exchange for an old car. One values the car more than the labor-effort the other must make, and the other values having her house painted more than the car. After the exchange, both are better off. Other things being equal, the welfare of each is enhanced, and their respective utility levels are raised. Thus, the sum of (their) utilities is increased; alternatively, even if utilities cannot be summed (there is a dispute about this issue, and many economists since the 1930s "ordinalist" revolution deny the possibility), we may conclude

that overall utility has increased if the judgment of all the affected parties is affirmative (and credible). The pretrade situation was one in which at least one of the two could be better off and no one worse off. It was, in the technical sense in which economists use the term, an *inefficient situation*. The posttrade situation is more efficient. Someone has become better off, and no one is worse off. Is efficiency valuable in itself? The answer from orthodox economic theory is no; rather, moving toward more efficient arrangements is viewed as desirable because to do so is to increase the total utility or welfare (to take a step toward "maximization of total net expected utility" to put matters more carefully). To understand the argument for adopting or perpetuating the use of the market mechanism, it is crucial to note these assumptions—ones that too often are in the background and that, hence, frequently escape scrutiny and moral appraisal.

To highlight some crucial assumptions and to emphasize which values or principles are being treated as basic, or alternatively, as derivative ones, it is useful to set out certain elements of economic reasoning more explicitly and systematically. Typically, what is implicit is the anthropocentric view that all and only humans morally count; thus, only benefits (utilities) or harms (disutilities) to humans have weight in evaluating actions or policies. For example, consider this representative remark:

> To assert that there is a pollution problem or an environmental problem is to assert, at least implicitly, that one or more resources is not being used so as to maximize human satisfactions.[2]

Thus, what is *conceptually to count* (for example) as pollution, directly or indirectly, must involve harm to humans; if penguins are poisoned by an industrial chemical but no humans (now or in the future?) are affected, that is not "pollution" (or, at least, morally significant pollution). Representative of this view are the remarks of William Baxter (from the later selection "People or Penguins"):

> My criteria are oriented to people, not penguins. Damage to penguins, or sugar pines, or geological marvels is, without more, simply irrelevant. One must . . . say: Penguins are important because people enjoy seeing them walk about rocks. . . .

> I reject the proposition that we ought to respect the "balance of nature" or to "preserve the environment" unless the reason for doing so, express or implied, is the benefit of man. Every man is entitled to his own definition of Walden Pond, but there is no definition that has any moral superiority over another, except by reference to the selfish needs of the human race.[3]

To make an important point briefly, if the anthropocentric assumption embodied in orthodox economic theory is indefensible, then the theory as it stands is unacceptable—as would be a theory that regarded only benefits and harms to white people as having moral significance. A theory that is not anthropocentric will be a theoretically more complex one. But simplicity is not the sole determinant of rationality.

The modern economic approach also assumes and accepts (however inexplicitly) a distribution of legally protected property rights. Often, there are further implicit assumptions. For example, human beings can be owners but cannot be owned. Any nonhuman can be owned. This view reflects the anthropocentric criterion of moral standing. Legal property in an object X is best understood as possession of a package of rights over what is owned, often a right to use X, to exclude others from doing so, to authorize others to use X, to be compensated for unauthorized uses, and, sometimes, to destroy X if one wishes. There is a moral question whether anyone should have a legal right to kill (or torture) his

or her animals. The "it's my property to do with as I please" mentality implies an affirmative answer. The main point here, however, is just that orthodox economists typically assume the moral legitimacy of *some* set of well-defined property rights. (On these matters see Section VI-B, "From the Commons to Property.") Further, it is assumed that these rights will foster certain sorts of exchanges, for example, voluntary, nonfraudulent ones between competent persons. Thus, the core of the market mechanism, exchanges of goods or services (actually rights to such), is understood to occur against the background of morally acceptable *norms and institutions;* the latter constitute "the rules of the game" as it were.

Many economists often insist that they engage in *value-free* inquiry, that they are impotent (as economists) to say whether the rules are good or right. Some deny that evaluative claims are rationally decidable or are any more than expressions of emotion. For example, McKenzie and Tullock claim that "the approach of the economist is amoral" and that "as economists we cannot say what is 'just' or 'fair.'"[4] Paul Heyne and Thomas Johnson maintain that "we do not have any (means) of resolving ethical disagreements, they are ultimately judgments of value . . . and cannot finally be proved or disproved."[5] These stances are questionable (and have been explored systematically and in detail in the philosophical literature for years), but many economists seem oblivious to this fact, and to the fact that their own implicit or explicit commitment to the value of the market mechanism or to efficiency or to maximizing utility (or aggregate human want-satisfaction) suggests, to the contrary, that the discipline of economics (in so far as it purports not merely to *explain* or *predict* human behavior) rests, in part, on evaluative assumptions.[6] One who thought that only benefits or harms to penguins were significant would be making an important evaluative assumption. So also does one who says, "Aryans count; Jews do not." The question, rather, would seem to be which view is rationally superior; we simply cannot avoid evaluations.

The concept of efficiency, and its assumed high value (or possibly, overriding value), is so central in economic approaches to environmental matters that we should dissect it more thoroughly. To do so requires a bit of technical terminology; one would be helpless in trying to assess the economic approach without mastery of a few concepts.

In ordinary (nontechnical) talk, there is a tendency to use *efficient* as an honorific term; thus, if *X* is efficient, *X* is thought to be good (in a respect). Conversely, if *X* is inefficient, *X* is thought to be bad (in a respect). *Given* such usage, it seems perverse to question or oppose the efficient course, and unobjectionable or "nice" to urge efficient policies. All this can mislead us, however. The term *efficient* has a technical sense in economics; further, we should distinguish (1) what it *means* to say that some state of affairs is efficient, and (2) whether efficiency is a valuable goal that we ought to pursue. And importantly, is efficiency valuable in itself or only as a means? First, we have noted, in so many words, that a standard implicit assumption is, not surprisingly, that efficiency is understood as *efficiency for humans*. Modern factory farms that raise veal calves may be quite efficient for humans, but hardly so, let us assume, for the calves.[7] Let us return to (1). The standard *criterion of efficiency* that is employed is called the *Pareto criterion* (after the early 20th-century economist-sociologist Vilfredo Pareto). If a situation in which parties possess various goods is such that at least one party could be better off (in that party's own estimation) *without* making anyone worse off, the situation is said to be inefficient (or not maximally efficient). A "*Pareto improvement*" could be made; that is, at least one party could be better off without worsening another's situation. In our earlier tale, in which one individual got another's car and the other got her house painted, a Pareto

improvement was made. Voluntary exchanges are thought to generate Pareto improvements, that is, to increase efficiency. If a situation is one in which it is not possible for anyone to become better off without worsening another's circumstance, it is said to be *Pareto-optimal* (or maximally efficient).[8] As noted before, the core idea is that in a more efficient situation the total welfare of the relevant parties is greater than in the less efficient one even if one is not able to say by how much. Moving toward more efficient circumstances *seems* desirable since it moves things closer to maximum utility. If, in fact, the sketched mechanism is the best means of maximizing welfares or achieving ever-increasing improvements, that fact seems to be a strong reason to employ it. Thus, the market is often defended on grounds that it best maximizes utility (quite apart from, or in addition to, appeals to implementation of, or respecting, some sort of human right to choose). Although we may give three cheers for markets as we commonly encounter them, critical reflection may make us wonder whether they deserve three, or even two. Much depends on how much we should value utility maximization, or efficiency as a means of fostering it—whether voluntary exchanges invariably or usually increase efficiency, and to what extent exchanges really are voluntary when elements of misrepresentation are often present.[9]

It is easy to overlook some crucial points. We may have serious moral reservations about even maximally efficient situations. For example, suppose that *X* is a master and *Y* is *X*'s slave. There may be no way to alter this arrangement so that one can be better off and no one worse off. That is, it may be Pareto optimal or maximally efficient. The criterion focuses on a given situation and prospective departures from it, not on how it came about. As noted, a distribution of goods between master and slave may be Pareto-optimal or maximally efficient (in the Paretian sense), but morally indefensible. In short it seems absurd to believe that whatever is efficient is right or permissible. If so, then we must conclude that although efficiency is desirable, it only is desirable *other things being equal*.

In the exchange of an old car for the painting of a house, there was a gain from trade—both parties were better off, and aggregate welfare increased. In applying the Pareto criterion, economists typically assume that the proper way of determining whether the parties to the transaction are better off is to solicit the judgments of the parties themselves (usually posttrade). Several comments are relevant here, and all of them may reduce one's enthusiasm for thinking that the market is invariably the proper vehicle (or an effective one) to enhance social (human) welfare. First, in idealized models, the traders may possess "complete information." In fact, actual traders are ignorant to a degree (sometimes victimized by self-interested, or profit-maximizing, individuals or corporations). We may *believe*, prior to trading, that acquiring a widget (a product often discussed in economics texts, but hard to find) and foregoing some money may improve our lot. On getting the widget, the car, the meal, or the compact disc, we often regard ourselves as worse off. In fact, voluntary exchanges do not always (often?) yield a Pareto improvement over the preexchange situation, because one party *is* worse off postexchange. This point tends to be overlooked or discounted by some ostensibly empirical scientists.

To avoid, so it would seem, this awkward result of observing what actually happens with some actual transactions, some economists seem to *stipulatively define* "voluntary exchange" as one an individual would engage in if and only if beneficial to that individual. Thus, with this conceptual sleight of hand, it becomes analytically true (roughly, true by definition) that "all voluntary exchanges benefit the parties who engage in them." But then this use of 'voluntary exchange' does not mean what most of us mean by the expression.

A brief comment may provide food for thought. We desire things *under-a-description* (at least often). Thus, Oedipus wanted to marry Jocasta. He got "what he wanted." Was he better off? He did not want to marry his mother, but since Jocasta was his mother, he also got what, in one sense, he did *not* want. The economists' model of human psychology and choice seems too simple in not attending sufficiently to complexities that result from the existence of multiple true descriptions of what one wants, self-deception, ambivalence, weakness of will, subconscious motivation, and so on.

Another feature of the market mechanism concerns *who* participates in market transactions, either small or large. It is worth observing that only those who are *willing and able* to pay have access to markets, that is, can participate in market transactions. It may not be far wrong to estimate that of the world's (almost) 6 billion members of *Homo sapiens*, at least a billion or so are unable to cast, or are radically hindered from casting, an effective vote in the economic marketplace, e.g., the extremely poor, the very young, the severely retarded, the seriously (mentally) disturbed. Nonhumans are not the only ones who have no say about the distribution of benefits and burdens generated by market transactions; a large number of existing humans are also voiceless in this way—not to mention future generations.

For the reasons mentioned, it is doubtful that voluntary, "informed" exchanges invariably benefit *existing human* participants in those exchanges. Even if they did, much of the world's population effectively is excluded from participation in market transactions. In spite of the incautious praise heaped upon capitalism by some ideologues, the proper assessment of markets (and especially commercial practices and environmental effects) must involve consideration of the alternatives to a given market system. Large questions of political philosophy and economics arise that cannot be explored here. However, there are two basic alternatives to a comparatively unconstrained market system. If a given system seems intolerable in some respect, it may be possible to add a new constraint to it in order to remedy the problem. This is the alternative of *setting appropriate constraints* on the market. Thus, if we judge that blood (or bodily parts, or babies) ought not to be bought and sold (to the highest bidder?), we can legally prohibit the practice—and let the distribution be determined by nonmarket procedures. Similarly, if we judge that a corporation's self-interest in a good reputation is not an adequate safeguard to prevent it from selling defective products or polluting the environment, we can require governmental testing and set stringent liability rules that function as disincentives to corporate distribution of dangerous products or polluting. Defenders of the market are fond of pointing out that it is not the baker's altruism but his self-interest that makes bread available for purchase. This is no doubt true, but this same motive also can lead to industrial spying, theft of trade secrets, corporate bribery, and "coverups" of dangerous products.

We have noted some important criticisms of letting the market mechanism determine allocation and distribution questions. The alleged efficiency of the market process seems a means to maximizing utility. Utility maximization is hardly an uncontroversial goal. There are powerful philosophical arguments in favor of the view that maximizing utility allows or *requires* unjust distributions of benefits and burdens. As we have noted, to assume the value of maximizing only human utility is to beg the question against antianthropocentric counterarguments. Further, even if those difficulties were not serious, there are reasons (as noted) to doubt that all (most?) voluntary participants in market exchanges are better off as a result. If they are not, there may be no net increase in efficiency or total utility. We have observed also that much of the world's population is disenfranchised from casting an effective monetary vote in the market decision process.

In this brief survey of moral and other worries about the market, we have omitted a concern that economists rightly and increasingly have stressed in recent decades: that many parties who are not participants to voluntary, informed exchanges are made worse off as a result of the exchanges. These are what are called *negative externalities*. The focus here is on the generation of unconsented-to harms to some individuals, "costs" generated for which compensation is not paid. Thus, much pollution of the air or water is a prime example of negative externalities. Because only some of the costs to all parties are borne by the "private parties," the "social costs" exceed the "private costs." It is commonly held that if external costs only could be "internalized" (borne by those who seek to benefit from activities that generate them), there would be no problem (no moral complaint?). Thus, it is claimed that we *ought* to prevent or minimize externalities (some economists might be uncomfortable with this blatantly normative mode of speaking). How can we do that? To oversimplify, three basic alternatives present themselves: (1) persuade people or corporations or nations not to generate externalities, that is, appeal to voluntary self-restraint; (2) coerce by attaching criminal penalties to violations of publicly set standards; or (3A) coerce by attaching "taxes" or charges to each additional unit of pollution emitted beyond a certain amount—or (3B) coerce by requiring possession of legal rights to pollute and possibly allowing trading in such rights. Many economists have a sufficiently low estimate of human nature so as to dismiss (1) rather quickly. A less than rosy estimate is surely correct even if one regards the picture of people embodied in *homo economicus* (roughly the assumption of psychological egoism and the earlier mentioned simplifications regarding motives) as a nontrivial misrepresentation of human nature.

The current debate between defenders of (2) and (3) is important, intriguing, and embodies noteworthy psychological and moral assumptions. Once more, the focus on *unconsented-to harm to others* is viewed anthropocentrically. Only harms to humans count. The English hunter W. D. M. Bell is reported to have killed 1011 elephants in his lifetime.[7] This slaughter, if involving no unconsented-to harm to humans, fails to count as an externality needing any internalizing—according to the orthodox economic view. The term *social costs* means costs to human society. An obvious question is whether a cost-benefit accounting can be thought thorough when "costs to nonhumans" are either tacitly treated as nonsensical or recognized but treated as irrelevant. These matters will be taken up in the next section.

It should not go unnoticed that many economists would object to labeling negative externalities as "instances of market failure." Instead, they would maintain that unconsented-to harms ("negative externalities," "overexploitation of resources," "pollution," and so on) result from the *failure to have a market*. As some have argued, the solution is to allow property rights in "resources." The "tragedy of the commons" is that "goods" that are unowned (except "owned by all") get misused in one fashion or another. Since "chunks" of air or water rarely can be partitioned off so that particular individuals have a right to them, such persons may have little (self-interest) incentive to preserve, respect, or ration consumption of such things. According to the view being considered, it is better to allow the market to operate more broadly (by creating a more extensive distribution of property rights) than to restrict the market's scope of operation. Having been somewhat negative about much in economic theory in these introductory remarks, we leave it to the reader to critically appraise this proposal—as well as the criticisms we have set forth.

The first selection to follow, by William

Baxter, expresses, in no uncertain terms, an anthropocentric approach to environmental trade-offs. As Baxter states, "Damage to penguins, or sugar pines, or geological marvels is, without more, simply irrelevant." Baxter optimistically believes that what is good for people, often, at least, is good for the environment. One might question whether "maximize human satisfaction" underlies Baxter's economic viewpoint. A more qualified, more cautious, and more sophisticated effort at setting out fundamental, theoretic assumptions of modern economics (such as Pareto considerations) and applying them to environmental questions (for example, what to do about pollution) is found in A. Myrick Freeman's essay. It is not easy reading, but it is a rich summary and deserves careful study. Part of a critique of "the economic viewpoint" is set out in Mark Sagoff's essay. Sagoff calls attention to where market decision making (or "the cult of Pareto optimality") has led us. He is not enamored of the resulting gas stations, tract developments, strip mines, pizza stands, beach condos, and snowmobiles in the mountains. Importantly, he questions the tendency of economists to view citizens' expressions of *ideals* (such as "we ought to preserve dolphins") as just another consumer *preference or desire*—as just another consumer vote in the economic marketplace—to be taken seriously only if backed by the willingness and ability to pay.

NOTES

1. Robert and Nancy Dorfman, eds. *Economics and the Environment* (New York: W. W. Norton & Company, 1972), p. XIX.
2. William Baxter, *People or Penguins: The Case for Optimal Pollution* (New York: Columbia University Press, 1974), p. 17.
3. William Baxter, *People or Penguins*, p. 5.
4. Richard B. McKenzie and Gordon Tullock, *The New World of Economics* (Homewood, IL: Richard D. Irwin, 1978), p. 7.
5. Paul Heyne and Thomas Johnson, *Toward Economic*

Understanding (Chicago: Science Research Associates, 1976), p. 767.

6. It is worth noting that moral and political philosophers and those who work in environmental ethics in particular, have some things to learn from economists. There are many hard choices to make, and much work has been done by economists in game theory, decision theory, and examination of slippery issues surrounding the notions of efficiency and utility that are of importance to virtually any environmental policy question. For example, the important idea of choosing behind a veil of ignorance, one which has been put to such creative use by John Rawls in his *A Theory of Justice*, could have been found in the work of economist John Harsanyi in the early 1950s; we do not know whether Rawls was, in fact, influenced by Harsanyi on this point.

7. See Peter Singer, *Animal Liberation* (New York: Avon Books, 1975).

8. There may be *many* Pareto-optimal situations, and some may be, on the face of things, unjust and have been arrived at in an unjust manner.

9. Recently, for example, General Electric has offered an electric light bulb advertised as replacing a 100-watt bulb and saving money; the deal sounds attractive until one examines the fine print and learns that the "replacement" is simply a 90-watt bulb that yields less light.

10. Bell's act is reported in Cleveland Amory, *Man Kind?* (New York: Dell Publishing Co., 1974), p. 30.

People or Penguins

William Baxter

I start with the modest proposition that, in dealing with pollution, or indeed with any problem, it is helpful to know what one is attempting to accomplish. Agreement on how and whether to pursue a particular objective, such as pollution control, is not possible unless some more general objective has been identified and stated with reasonable precision. We talk loosely of having clean air and clean water, of preserving our wilderness areas, and so forth. But none of these is a sufficiently general objective: each is more accurately viewed as a means rather than as an end.

With regard to clean air, for example, one may ask, "how clean?" and "what does clean mean?" It is even reasonable to ask, "why have clean air?" Each of these questions is an implicit demand that a more general community goal be stated—a goal sufficiently general in its scope and enjoying sufficiently general assent among the community of actors that such "why" questions no longer seem admissible with respect to that goal.

If, for example, one states as a goal the proposition that "every person should be free to do whatever he wishes in contexts where his actions do not interfere with the interests of other human beings," the speaker is unlikely to be met with a response of "why." The goal may be criticized as uncertain in its implications or difficult to implement, but it is so basic a tenet of our civilization—it reflects a cultural value so broadly shared, at least in the abstract—that the question "why" is seen as impertinent or imponderable or both.

I do not mean to suggest that everyone would agree with the "spheres of freedom" objective just stated. Still less do I mean to suggest that a society could subscribe to four or five such general objectives that would be adequate in their coverage to serve as testing criteria by which all other disagreements might be measured. One difficulty in the attempt to construct such a list is that each new goal added will conflict, in certain applications, with each prior goal listed; and thus each goal serves as a limited qualification on prior goals.

Without any expectation of obtaining unanimous consent to them, let me set forth four goals that I generally use as ultimate testing criteria in attempting to frame solutions to problems of human organization. My position regarding pollution stems from these four criteria. If the criteria appeal to you and any part of what appears hereafter does

People or Penguins: The Case for Optimal Pollution, William F. Baxter, 1974. © Columbia University Press, New York. Reprinted by permission of the publisher.

not, our disagreement will have a helpful focus: which of us is correct, analytically, in supposing that his position on pollution would better serve these general goals. If the criteria do not seem acceptable to you, then it is to be expected that our more particular judgments will differ, and the task will then be yours to identify the basic set of criteria upon which your particular judgments rest.

My criteria are as follows:

1. The spheres of freedom criterion stated above.

2. Waste is a bad thing. The dominant feature of human existence is scarcity—our available resources, our aggregate labors, and our skill in employing both have always been, and will continue for some time to be, inadequate to yield to every man all the tangible and intangible satisfactions he would like to have. Hence, none of those resources, or labors, or skills, should be wasted—that is, employed so as to yield less than they might yield in human satisfactions.

3. Every human being should be regarded as an end rather than as a means to be used for the betterment of another. Each should be afforded dignity and regarded as having an absolute claim to an evenhanded application of such rules as the community may adopt for its governance.

4. Both the incentive and the opportunity to improve his share of satisfactions should be preserved to every individual. Preservation of incentive is dictated by the "no-waste" criterion and enjoins against the continuous, totally egalitarian redistribution of satisfactions, or wealth; but subject to that constraint, everyone should receive, by continuous redistribution if necessary, some minimal share of aggregate wealth so as to avoid a level of privation from which the opportunity to improve his situation becomes illusory.

The relationship of these highly general goals to the more specific environmental issues at hand may not be readily apparent, and I am not yet ready to demonstrate their pervasive implications. But let me give one indication of their implications. Recently scientists have informed us that use of DDT in food production is causing damage to the penguin population. For the present purposes let

us accept that assertion as an indisputable scientific fact. The scientific fact is often asserted as if the correct implication—that we must stop agricultural use of DDT—followed from the mere statement of the fact of penguin damage. But plainly it does not follow if my criteria are employed.

My criteria are oriented to people, not penguins. Damage to penguins, or sugar pines, or geological marvels is, without more, simply irrelevant. One must go further, by my criteria, and say: Penguins are important because people enjoy seeing them walk about rocks; and furthermore, the well-being of people would be less impaired by halting use of DDT than by giving up penguins. In short, my observations about environmental problems will be people-oriented, as are my criteria. I have no interest in preserving penguins for their own sake.

It may be said by way of objection to this position, that it is very selfish of people to act as if each person represented one unit of importance and nothing else was of any importance. It is undeniably selfish. Nevertheless I think it is the only tenable starting place for analysis for several reasons. First, no other position corresponds to the way most people really think and act—i.e., corresponds to reality.

Second, this attitude does not portend any massive destruction of nonhuman flora and fauna, for people depend on them in many obvious ways, and they will be preserved because and to the degree that humans do depend on them.

Third, what is good for humans is, in many respects, good for penguins and pine trees—clean air for example. So that humans are, in these respects, surrogates for plant and animal life.

Fourth, I do not know how we could administer any other system. Our decisions are either private or collective. Insofar as Mr. Jones is free to act privately, he may give such preferences as he wishes to other forms of life: he may feed birds in winter and do with less himself, and he may even decline to resist an advancing polar bear on the ground that the bear's appetite is more important than those portions of himself that the bear may choose to eat. In short my basic premise does not rule out private altruism to competing life-forms. It does rule out, however, Mr. Jones' inclination to feed Mr. Smith to the bear, however hungry the bear, however despicable Mr. Smith.

Insofar as we act collectively on the other hand, only humans can be afforded an opportunity to participate in the collective decisions. Penguins cannot vote now and are unlikely subjects for the franchise—pine trees more unlikely still. Again each individual is free to cast his vote so as to benefit sugar pines if that is his inclination. But many of the more extreme assertions that one hears from some conservationists amount to tacit assertions that they are specially appointed representatives of sugar pines, and hence that their preferences should be weighted more heavily than the preferences of other humans who do not enjoy equal rapport with "nature." The simplistic assertion that agricultural use of DDT must stop at once because it is harmful to penguins is of that type.

Fifth, if polar bears or pine trees or penguins, like men, are to be regarded as ends rather than means, if they are to count in our calculus of social organization, someone must tell me how much each one counts, and someone must tell me how these life-forms are to be permitted to express their preferences, for I do not know either answer. If the answer is that certain people are to hold their proxies, then I want to know how those proxy-holders are to be selected: self-appointment does not seem workable to me.

Sixth, and by way of summary of all the foregoing, let me point out that the set of environmental issues under discussion—although they raise very complex technical questions of how to achieve any objective—ultimately raise a normative question: what *ought* we to do? Questions of *ought* are unique to the human mind and world—they are meaningless as applied to a nonhuman situation.

I reject the proposition that we *ought* to respect the "balance of nature" or to "preserve the environment" unless the reason for doing so, express or implied, is the benefit of man.

I reject the idea that there is a "right" or "morally correct" state of nature to which we should return. The word "nature" has no normative connotation. Was it "right" or "wrong" for the earth's crust to heave in contortion and create mountains and seas? Was it "right" for the first amphibian to crawl up out of the primordial ooze? Was it "wrong" for plants to reproduce themselves and alter the atmospheric composition in favor of oxygen? For animals to alter the atmosphere in favor of carbon dioxide both by breathing oxygen and eating plants?

No answers can be given to these questions because they are meaningless questions.

All this may seem obvious to the point of being tedious, but much of the present controversy over environment and pollution rests on tacit normative assumptions about just such nonnormative phenomena: that it is "wrong" to impair penguins with DDT, but not to slaughter cattle for prime rib roasts. That it is wrong to kill stands of sugar pines with industrial fumes, but not to cut sugar pines and build housing for the poor. Every man is entitled to his own preferred definition of Walden Pond, but there is no definition that has any moral superiority over another, except by reference to the selfish needs of the human race.

From the fact that there is no normative definition of the natural state, it follows that there is no normative definition of clean air or pure water—hence no definition of polluted air—or of pollution—except by reference to the needs of man. The "right" composition of the atmosphere is one which has some dust in it and some lead in it and some hydrogen sulfide in it—just those amounts that attend a sensibly organized society thoughtfully and knowledgeably pursuing the greatest possible satisfaction for its human members.

The first and most fundamental step toward solution of our environmental problems is a clear recognition that our objective is not pure air or water but rather some optimal state of pollution. That step immediately suggests the question: How do we define and attain the level of pollution that will yield the maximum possible amount of human satisfaction?

Low levels of pollution contribute to human satisfaction but so do food and shelter and education and music. To attain ever lower levels of pollution, we must pay the cost of having less of these other things. I contrast that view of the cost of pollution control with the more popular statement that pollution control will "cost" very large numbers of dollars. The popular statement is true in some senses, false in others; sorting out the true and false senses is of some importance. The first step in that sorting process is to achieve a clear understanding of the difference between dollars and resources. Resources are the wealth of our nation; dollars are merely claim checks upon those resources. Resources are of vital importance; dollars are comparatively trivial.

Four categories of resources are sufficient for our purposes: At any given time a nation, or a planet if you prefer, has a stock of labor, of technological skill, of capital goods, and of natural resources (such as mineral deposits, timber, water, land, etc.). These resources can be used in various combinations to yield goods and services of all kinds—in some limited quantity. The quantity will be larger if they are combined efficiently, smaller if combined inefficiently. But in either event the resource stock is limited, the goods and services that they can be made to yield are limited; even the most efficient use of them will yield less than our population, in the aggregate, would like to have.

If one considers building a new dam, it is appropriate to say that it will be costly in the sense that it will require x hours of labor, y tons of steel and concrete, and z amount of capital goods. If these resources are devoted to the dam, then they cannot be used to build hospitals, fishing rods, schools, or electric can openers. That is the meaningful sense in which the dam is costly.

Quite apart from the very important question of how wisely we can combine our resources to produce goods and services is the very different question of how they get distributed—who gets how many goods? Dollars constitute the claim checks which are distributed among people and which control their share of national output. Dollars are nearly valueless pieces of paper except to the extent that they do represent claim checks to some fraction of the output of goods and services. Viewed as claim checks, all the dollars outstanding during any period of time are worth, in the aggregate, the goods and services that are available to be claimed with them during that period—neither more nor less.

It is far easier to increase the supply of dollars than to increase the production of goods and services—printing dollars is easy. But printing more dollars doesn't help because each dollar then simply becomes a claim to fewer goods, i.e., becomes worth less.

The point is this: many people fall into error upon hearing the statement that the decision to build a dam, or to clean up a river, will cost $X million. It is regrettably easy to say: "It's only money. This is a wealthy country, and we have lots of money." But you cannot build a dam or clean a river with $X million—unless you also have a

match, you can't even make a fire. One builds a dam or cleans a river by diverting labor and steel and trucks and factories from making one kind of goods to making another. The cost in dollars is merely a shorthand way of describing the extent of the diversion necessary. If we build a dam for $X million, then we must recognize that we will have $X million less housing and food and medical care and electric can openers as a result.

Similarly, the costs of controlling pollution are best expressed in terms of the other goods we will have to give up to do the job. This is not to say the job should not be done. Badly as we need more housing, more medical care, and more can openers, and more symphony orchestras, we could do with somewhat less of them, in my judgment at least, in exchange for somewhat cleaner air and rivers. But that is the nature of the trade-off, and analysis of the problem is advanced if that unpleasant reality is kept in mind. Once the trade-off relationship is clearly perceived, it is possible to state in a very general way what the optimal level of pollution is. I would state it as follows:

> People enjoy watching penguins. They enjoy relatively clean air and smog-free vistas. Their health is improved by relatively clean water and air. Each of these benefits is a type of good or service. As a society we would be well advised to give up one washing machine if the resources that would have gone into that washing machine can yield greater human satisfaction when diverted into pollution control. We should give up one hospital if the resources thereby freed would yield more human satisfaction when devoted to elimination of noise in our cities. And so on, trade-off by trade-off, we should divert our productive capacities from the production of existing goods and services to the production of a cleaner, quieter, more pastoral nation up to—and no further than—the point at which we value more highly the next washing machine or hospital that we would have to do without than we value the next unit of environmental improvement that the diverted resources would create.

> Now this proposition seems to me unassailable but so general and abstract as to be unhelpful—at least unadministerable in the form stated. It assumes we can measure in some way the incremental units of human satisfaction yielded by very different types of goods. The proposition must remain a pious abstrac-

tion until I can explain how this measurement process can occur. In subsequent chapters I will attempt to show that we can do this—in some contexts with great precision and in other contexts only by rough approximation.

But I insist that the proposition stated describes the result for which we should be striving—and again, that it is always useful to know what your target is even if your weapons are too crude to score a bull's-eye.

The Ethical Basis of the Economic View of the Environment

A. Myrick Freeman III

I. Introduction

At least in some circles, economists' recommendations for a policy concerning pollution and other environmental problems are regarded with a good deal of skepticism and perhaps even distrust.[1] For example, when we suggest that economic factors such as cost should be taken into account in setting ambient air quality standards, we are told that it is wrong to put a price on human life or beauty. And when we argue that placing a tax or charge on the emissions of pollutants would be more effective than the present regulatory approach, we are told that this would simply create "licenses to pollute" and pollution is wrong.

I am not sure how much of this type of reaction stems from a misunderstanding or lack of familiarity with the arguments for the economists' policy recommendations, and how much is due to a rejection of the premises, analysis, and value judgments on which these recommendations are based. And I will not attempt to answer this question here. Rather, I will limit myself to making clear the rationale for some of our recommendations concerning policy and the value judgments on which they are based.

To the economist, the environment is a scarce resource which contributes to human welfare. The economic problem of the environment is a small part of the overall economic problem: how to manage our activities so as to meet our material needs and wants in the face of scarcity. The economists' recommendations concerning the environment flow out of our analysis of the overall economic problem. It will be useful to begin with a brief review of the principal conclusions of economic reasoning concerning the allocation of scarce resources to essentially unlimited needs and wants. After reviewing some basic economic principles and the criteria that economists have used in the evaluation of alternative economic outcomes, I will explain the economic view of the environment and some of the major policy recommendations which follow from that view. I will conclude by identifying some of the major questions and possible sources of disagreement about the validity and usefulness of economic reasoning as a way of looking at environmental problems.

II. Some Basic Economics

We begin with the basic premises that the purpose of economic activity is to increase the well-being of the individuals who make up the society, and that each individual is the best judge of how well off he or she is in a given situation. To give this premise some operational content, we assume that each individual has preferences over alternative bundles of economic goods and services. In other words, the individual can rank all of the alternative combinations of goods and services he can consume from most preferred to least preferred. Of course there may be ties in this ranking.[2] We assume that individuals act so as to obtain the most preferred (to them) bundles given the constraints imposed by technology and the availability of the means of production.

These preferences of individuals are assumed

Center for the Study of Values and Social Policy at the University of Colorado at Boulder (1983). Reprinted by permission of the author.

to have two properties which are important for our purposes: substitutability among the components of bundles, and the absence of limits on wants. Substitutability simply means that preferences are not lexicographic. Consider a consumption bundle labeled A with specified quantities of food, clothing, shelter, and so forth. Now consider alternative bundle B which contains 10 percent less clothing and the same quantities of all other goods. Since B contains less clothing, it is less desirable to the individual. In other words, bundle A is preferred to bundle B. But substitutability means that it is possible to alter the composition of bundle B by increasing the quantities of one or more of the other goods in the bundle to the point where the individual will consider A and B as equally preferred. That is to say, the individual can be compensated for the loss of some quantity of one good by increases in the quantities of one or more of the other goods. The value of the lost clothing to this individual can be expressed in terms of the quantities of the other goods which must be added to the bundle to substitute for it. This principle is the basis of the economic theory of value. In a market economy where all goods and services can be bought and sold at given prices in markets, the necessary amount of substitution can be expressed in money terms.

The significance of the substitution principle for the economic view of the environment should be apparent. If the substitution principle applies to good things that are derived from a clean environment, then it is possible to put a price on those things. The price is the money value of the quantities of other goods that must be substituted to compensate for the loss of the environmental good. Whether the substitution principle applies to those things derived from the environment is essentially an empirical question about human behavior. It is possible to think of examples that violate the substitution principle. The slogan printed on all license plates issued in New Hampshire ("Live Free or Die") shows a lexicographic preference for freedom. If the statement is believed, there is no quantity of material goods that can compensate for the loss of freedom. It is not clear that all individuals have lexicographic preferences for freedom. And the question for our purpose is whether there are similar examples in the realm of environmental goods.

By unlimited wants, I mean that for any conceivable bundle A, it is possible to describe another bundle B with larger quantities of one or more goods such that an individual would prefer B to A. Is this property plausible? It is possible to imagine some upper limit on the gross consumption of food as measured by calories or weight. But quality and variety are also goods over which individuals have preferences. And it may always be possible to conceive of a bundle containing a more exotic dish or one with more careful preparation with higher quality ingredients. Again, whether this property is plausible is an empirical question about human behavior. But its significance for anti-growth arguments is apparent.

Much of economic theory is concerned with understanding how individuals with given preferences interact as they seek to attain the highest level of satisfaction. Many societies have developed systems of markets for guiding this interaction; and historically the bulk of economists' effort has gone to the study of market systems. In part this can be explained by the historic fact that economics as a separate discipline emerged during a period of rapid industrialization, economic change, and growth in the extent of the market system. But it is also true that as early as Adam Smith's time, it was recognized that a freely functioning market system had significant advantages over alternative means of organizing and coordinating economic activity. Even in more primitive societies, markets facilitate exchange whereby an individual can attain a more preferred bundle by giving up less preferred goods in exchange for more preferred goods. And in more developed economies, markets also facilitate the specialization of productive activities and the realization of economies of scale in production.

A market system can be said to have advantages only in terms of some criterion and in comparison with some alternative set of economic institutions. It is time now to make the criterion explicit. The criterion is economic efficiency, or after the man who first developed the concept in formal terms, Pareto Optimality. An economy has reached a state of economic efficiency if it is not possible to rearrange production and consumption activity so as to make at least one person better off except by making one or more other individuals worse off. To put it differently, an economy is in an inefficient position if it is possible to raise at least one individual to a more preferred consumption bundle while hurting no one. If an economy is in an inefficient position, it is possible to achieve a sort of "free lunch" in the form of an improvement for at least one individual *at no cost* to anyone.

One of the fundamental conclusions of economic reasoning is that given certain conditions a market system will always reach a position of economic efficiency. The conditions are that: (*a*) all goods that matter to individuals (that is, all goods over which individuals have preference orderings) must be capable of being bought and sold in markets; and (*b*) all such markets must be perfectly competitive in the sense that there are large numbers of both buyers and sellers no one of which has any influence over market price.[3] The extensiveness and competitiveness of markets are sufficient to assure that economic efficiency in the allocation of resources will be achieved. This conclusion provides much of the intellectual rationale for *laissez faire* capitalism as well as the justification for many forms of government intervention in the market, for example, anti-monopoly policies, the regulation of the prices charged by monopolies such as electric utilities, and, as we shall see, the control of pollution.

The ideal of efficiency and the perfectly competitive market economy which guarantees its attainment acts as a yardstick by which the performance of real world economies can be measured. If there is monopoly power in a market, the yardstick shows that there is a shortfall in the performance of the economy. It would be possible by eliminating monopoly and restoring perfect competition to the market to increase output in such a way that no one would be made worse off and at least one person would be made better off. How monopoly power is to be eliminated without making at least the monopolist worse off is a difficult question in practice. But I will return to this point below.

The ideal of perfect competition and economic efficiency is a powerful one. But it is not without its limitations. Perhaps the most important of these is that there is no single, unique Pareto Optimum position. Rather there is an infinite number of alternative Pareto Optimums, each different from the others in the way in which it distributes economic well-being among the members of the society.

A society in which one individual owned all of the capital, land, and resources could achieve a Pareto Optimum position. It would likely be one in which all but one of the individuals lived in relative poverty. But it would not be possible to make any of the workers better off without making the rich person worse off. This Pareto Optimum position would be quite different from the Pareto Optimum which would be achieved by an economy in which each individual owned equal shares of the land, capital, and so forth. Which Pareto Optimum position is attained by an economy depends upon the initial distribution of the entitlements to receive income from the ownership of factor inputs such as land and capital. Each conceivable distribution of rights of ownership has associated with it a different Pareto Optimum. And each Pareto Optimum position represents the best that can be done for the members of society *conditioned* upon acceptance of the initial distribution of entitlements. Since the ranking of different Pareto Optimums requires the comparison of alternative distributions of well-being, it is inherently an ethical question. There is nothing more that economic reasoning can contribute to this issue.

III. Policy Evaluation

Given the fact that the real world economy is characterized by many market imperfections and failures and that for a variety of reasons it is not possible to create the perfect, all encompassing market system of the Pareto ideal, we must consider piecemeal efforts to make things better at the margin. The question is: what criterion should be used to evaluate policy proposals which would alter the outcomes of existing market processes?

The Pareto Criterion says to accept only those policies that benefit some people while harming no one. In other words, this criterion rules out any policy which imposes costs on any individual, no matter how small the cost and no matter how large the benefits to any other members of the society. This is a very stringent criterion in practice. There are very few policy proposals which do not impose some costs on some members of the society. For example, a policy to curb pollution reduces the incomes and welfares of those who find it more profitable to pollute than to control their waste. The Pareto Criterion is not widely accepted by economists as a guide to policy. And it plays no role in what might be called "mainstream" environmental economics.[4]

The most widely accepted criterion asks whether the aggregate of the gains to those made better off measured in money terms is greater than the money value of the losses of those made worse off. If the gains exceed the losses, the policy is accepted by this criterion. The gains and losses are to be measured in terms of each individual's willingness-to-pay to receive the gains or to prevent the policy-imposed losses. Thus this criterion draws on the substitutability principle discussed earlier. If the gains or losses came in the form of goods over which individuals have lexicographic preferences, this criterion could not be utilized.

This criterion is justified on ethical grounds by observing that if the gains outweigh the losses, it would be possible for the gainers to compensate fully the losers with money payments and still themselves be better off with the policy. Thus if the compensation were actually paid, there would be no losers, only gainers. This criterion is sometimes referred to as the potential compensation criterion. This criterion is the basis of the benefit-cost analysis of public policy. Benefits are the money values of the gains to individuals and costs are the money values of the losses to individuals. If benefits exceed costs, the gainers could potentially compensate the losers.

There are two observations concerning the potential compensation criterion. First, the criterion is silent on the question of whether compensation should be paid or not. If society decides that compensation shall always be paid, compensation becomes a mechanism for assuring that there are never any losers and that all adopted policies pass the Pareto Criterion. On the other hand, if society decides that compensation should never be paid, the potential compensation criterion becomes a modern form of utilitarianism in which the aggregate of utilities is measured by the sum of the money values of all goods consumed by all individuals. Finally, society may decide that whether compensation should be paid or not depends upon the identity and relative deservingness of the gainers and losers. If this is the case, then society must adopt some basis for determining relative deservingness, that is, some ethical rule concerning the justness of creating gains and imposing losses on individuals.

The second observation concerns the measurement of gains and losses in money terms. Willing-ness to pay for a good is constrained by ability to pay. Economic theory shows that an individual's willingness to pay for a good depends on his income and that for most goods, higher income means higher willingness to pay, other things equal. As a consequence, the potential compensation criterion has a tendency to give greater weight to the preferences of those individuals with higher incomes. As a practical matter there are reasons to doubt that this bias is quantitatively significant in most cases. But the question is often raised when benefit-cost analysis is applied to environmental goods. And it is well to keep this point in mind.

IV. Environmental Economics

The environment is a resource which yields a variety of valuable services to individuals in their roles as consumers and producers. The environment is the source of the basic means of life support—clean air and clean water. It provides the means for growing food. It is a source of minerals and other raw materials. It can be used for recreation. It is the source of visual amenities. And it can be used as a place to deposit the wastes from production and consumption activities. The economic problem of the environment is that it is a scarce resource. It cannot be called upon to provide all of the desired quantities of all of the services at the same time. Greater use of one type of environmental service usually means that less of some other type of service is available. Thus the use of the environment involves trade-offs. And the environment must be managed as an economic resource. But unlike other resources such as land, labor, or capital, the market does not perform well in allocating the environment to its highest valued uses. This is primarily because individuals do not have effective property rights in units of the environment.

For example, if a firm wishes to use one hour of labor time in production, it must find an individual who is willing to provide one hour of labor and it must pay that individual an amount at least equal to the value to the individual of that time in an alternative use. If a voluntary exchange of labor for money takes place, it is presumed that neither party is made worse off, and it is likely that both parties benefit from the exchange. Otherwise they would not have agreed to it. But if a firm wishes to dump a ton of sulfur dioxide into the atmosphere, it is under no obligation to determine whose health or whose view might be impaired by this use of the environment and to obtain their voluntary agreement through the payment of money. Thus firms need not take into account the costs imposed on others by their uses of the environment. Because there is no market for environmental services, the decentralized decision making of individuals and firms will result in a misallocation of environmental resources. The market fails. And the economy does not achieve a Pareto Optimum allocation.

Where markets have failed, economists have made two kinds of suggestions for dealing with market failure. The first is to see if markets can be established through the creation of legally transferable property rights in certain environmental services. If such property rights can be created, then markets can assume their proper role in achieving an efficient allocation of environmental services. Because of the indivisible nature of many aspects of the environment, for example, the urban air shed, there is limited scope for this solution. The second approach is to use various forms of government regulations, taxes, and subsidies to create incentives which replicate the incentives and outcomes that a perfectly functioning market would produce. Activities under this approach could include the setting of ambient air quality standards, placing limits on discharges from individual polluters, imposing taxes on pollution, and so forth. In the next section, I take up several specific applications of this approach to dealing with the environment in an economically rational manner.

V. Applications

Environment Quality Standards

An environmental quality standard is a legally established minimum level of cleanliness or maximum level of pollution in some part of the environment, for example, an urban air shed or a specific portion of a river. A standard, once established, can be the basis for enforcement actions against a polluter whose discharges cause the standard to be violated. The principle of Pareto Optimality provides a basis for determining at what level an environmental quality standard should be set. In general, Pareto Optimality requires that each good be pro-

vided at the level for which the marginal willingness to pay for the good (the maximum amount that an individual would be willing to give up to get one more unit of the good) is just equal to the cost of providing one more unit of the good (its marginal cost).

Consider for example an environment which is badly polluted because of existing industrial activity. Consider making successive one-unit improvements in some measure of environment quality. For the first unit, individuals' marginal willingnesses to pay for a small improvement are likely to be high. The cost of the first unit of clean-up is likely to be low. The difference between them is a net benefit. Further increases in cleanliness bring further net benefits as long as the marginal willingness to pay is greater than the marginal cost. But as the environment gets cleaner, the willingness to pay for additional units of cleanliness decreases, while the additional cost of further cleanliness rises. At that point where the marginal willingness to pay just equals the marginal cost, the net benefit of further cleanliness is zero, and the total benefits of environmental improvement are at a maximum. This is the point at which the environmental quality standard should be set, if economic reasoning is followed.

There are two points to make about this approach to standard setting. First, an environmental quality standard set by this rule will almost never call for complete elimination of pollution. As the worst of the pollution is cleaned up, the willingness to pay for additional cleanliness will be decreasing, while the extra cost of further clean-up will be increasing. The extra cost of going from 95 percent clean-up to 100 percent clean-up may often be several times larger than the total cost of obtaining the first 95 percent clean-up. And it will seldom be worth it in terms of willingness to pay. Several economists have argued that the air quality standards for ozone that were first established in 1971 were too stringent in terms of the relationship between benefits and costs. If this is true, then the resources devoted to controlling ozone could be put to better use in some other economic activity. Many economists have urged Congress to require that costs be compared with benefits in the setting of ambient air quality standards.

The second point is that the logic of benefit-cost analysis does not require that those who benefit pay for those benefits or that those who ultimately bear the cost of meeting a standard be compensated for those costs. It is true that if standards are set so as to maximize the net benefits, then the gainers could fully compensate the losers and still come out ahead. But when beneficiaries do not compensate losers, there is a political asymmetry. Those who benefit call for ever more strict standards and clean-up, because they obtain the gross benefits and bear none of the costs, while those who must control pollution call for less strict standards.

Charging for Pollution

One way to explain the existence of pollution is in terms of the incentives faced by firms and others whose activities generate waste products. Each unit of pollution discharged imposes costs or damages on other individuals. But typically the dischargers are not required to compensate the losers for these costs. Thus there is no economic incentive for the discharger to take those costs into account. This is the essence of the market failure argument.

If it is impractical to establish a private market in rights to clean air, it may be possible to create a pseudo-market by government regulation. Suppose that the government imposed a charge or tax on each unit of pollution discharged and set the tax equal to the money value of the damage that pollution caused to others. Then each discharger would compare the tax cost of discharging a unit of pollution with the cost of controlling or preventing that discharge. As long as the cost of control were less than the tax or charge, the firm would prevent the discharge. In fact it would control pollution back to the point where its marginal cost of control was just equal to the marginal tax and by indirection equal to the marginal damage the pollution would cause. The properly set tax or charge would cause the firm to undertake on its own accord the optimum amount of pollution control. By replicating a market incentive, the government regulation would bring about an efficient allocation of resources.

Since the firm would likely find that some level of discharges would be more preferred to a zero discharge level, it would be paying taxes to the government equal to the damages caused by the remaining discharges. In principle, the government could use the tax revenues to compensate those who are damaged by the remaining discharges.

Risk and the Value of Life

Because some forms of pollution are harmful to human health and may increase mortality, economists have had to confront the question of the economic value of life. It turns out that the "value of life" is an unfortunate phrase which does not really reflect the true nature of the question at hand. This is because pollutants do not single out and kill readily identifiable people. Rather, they result in usually small increases in the *probability* of death to exposed *groups* of individuals. So what is really at issue is the economic value of reductions in the risk of death. This is a manageable question and one on which we have some evidence.

People in their daily lives make a variety of choices that involve trading off changes in the risk of death with other economic goods whose values we can measure in money terms. For example, some people travel to work in cars rather than by bus or by walking because of the increased convenience and lower travel time, even though they increase the risk of dying prematurely. Also, some people accept jobs with known higher risks of accidental death because those jobs pay higher wages. The "value" of saving a life can be calculated from information on individuals' trade-offs between risk and money.

Suppose there were a thousand people each of whom has a probability of .004 of dying during this next year. Suppose an environmental change would reduce that probability to .003, a change of .001. Let us ask each individual to state his or her maximum willingness to pay for that reduction in risk. Suppose for simplicity that each person states the same willingness to pay, $100. The total willingness to pay of the group is $100,000. If the policy is adopted, there will on average be one less death during this next year, ($.001 \times 1000$). The total willingness to pay for a change that results in one fewer deaths is $100,000. This is the "value of life" that is revealed from individual preferences. Efforts to estimate the value of life from data on wage premiums for risky jobs have led to values in the range of $500,000 to $5 million.

If an economic approach is to be used in setting standards for toxic chemicals, hazardous air pollutants, and so forth, then some measure of the value of reductions in risk must be the basis for computing the benefits of pollution control. There are immense practical difficulties in providing accurate, refined estimates of this value. But these are not my concern here. Rather I am concerned with the ethical issues of even attempting to employ this approach to environmental decision making.

I think that the principal ethical issue here is compensation. Suppose that a standard has been set for an air pollutant such that even with the standard being met the population has a higher probability of death than if the pollutant were fully controlled. The standard was presumably set at this level because the cost of eliminating the remaining risk exceeded the individuals' willingness to pay to eliminate the risk. Many people would argue that the risk should be reduced to zero regardless of cost. After all, some people are being placed at risk while others are benefiting by avoiding the cost of controlling pollution. But suppose the population is compensated for bearing this risk with money from, for example, a charge on the polluting substance. Is there then any reason to argue for reducing pollution to zero? If the pollution were reduced to zero and the compensation withdrawn, the people at risk would be no better off in their own eyes than they are with the pollution and compensation. But some people would be made worse off because of the additional costs of eliminating the pollution.[5]

Future Generations

Some environmental decisions impose risks on future generations in order to achieve present benefits. In standard benefit-cost analysis based on the economic efficiency criterion, a social rate of discount is used to weight benefits and costs occurring at different points in time.[6] There have been long debates about the appropriateness of applying a discount rate to effects on future generations. It is argued that ethically unacceptable damage imposed on future generations may be made to appear acceptably small, from today's perspective, by discounting.

Consider the case where this generation wishes to do something which will yield benefits today worth \$B. This act will also set in motion some physical process which will cause \$D of damages 100,000 years from now. Assume that the events are certain and that the values of benefits

and damages based on individual preferences can be accurately measured.

In brief, the argument against discounting is: at any reasonable (nonzero) discount rate, r, the present value of damages

$$\$P = \frac{\$D}{(1 + r)^{100,000}}$$

will be trivial and almost certainly will be outweighed by present benefits. The implication of discounting is that we care virtually nothing about the damages that we inflict on future generations provided that they are postponed sufficiently far into the future. Therefore, the argument goes, we should discard the discounting procedure. Instead, since the real issue is intergenerational equity, a zero discount rate should be used. This would represent the most appropriate value judgment about the relative weights to be attached to the consumption of present and future generations.

I believe this argument is confused. Certainly, the problem is equity; but that has nothing to do with discounting. Rather, the equity question revolves around the distinction between actual and potential compensation.

In order to separate the compensation and discounting issues, consider a project for which both benefits and costs are realized today. Whenever benefits are greater than costs, the efficiency criterion says that the project should be undertaken, even if the benefits and costs accrue to different groups. This is because there is at least the *possibility* of compensation. Whether compensation should be paid or not is a value judgment hinging on equity considerations.

Now consider the intergenerational case. If \$B is greater than \$P (the discounted present value of future damages), the project is worthwhile and should be undertaken if the objective is economic efficiency. If the trivial sum of \$P is set aside now at interest, it will grow to

$$(1 + r)^{100,000}\$P$$

which of course is the same as \$D and therefore by definition will just compensate the future generation for the damages our actions will have imposed on them. If actual compensation is provided for, no one, present or future, will be made worse off, and some will benefit.

Some may wish to adhere to the principle that

compensation should *always* be paid. The principle would apply to losers in the present as well as future generations. The discount rate would help them to calculate the amount to be set aside for future payment. Others may wish to say that whether compensation should be paid or not depends on the relative positions of potential gainers and losers. Finally some will choose to ignore the compensation question entirely. But no matter how they resolve the compensation question, they should discount future damages.

Ecological Effects

Suppose that an accidental spill of a toxic chemical or crude oil wipes out the population of some marine organism in a certain area. What is the economic value of this damage? If the organism is a fish that is sought by sports or commercial fishermen, then there are standard economic techniques for determining the willingness to pay for or value of fish in the water. If the organism is part of the food chain which supports a commercially valuable fishery, then it is also possible, at least conceptually, to establish the biological link between the organism and the economic system. The value of the organism is based on its contribution to maintaining the stock of the commercially valued fish. But if there is no link between the organism and human production or consumption activity, there is no basis for establishing an economic value. Those species that lie completely outside of the economic system also are beyond the reach of the economic rubric for establishing value.

Some people have suggested alternative bases for establishing values, for example, cost of replacing the organisms, or cost of replacing biological functions such as photosynthesis and nitrogen fixation. But if those functions have no economic value to man, for example, because there are substitute organisms to perform them, then we would not be willing to pay the full cost of replacement. And this signifies that the economic value is less, perhaps much less, than replacement cost.

Rather than introduce some arbitrary or biased method for imputing a value to such organisms, I prefer to be honest about the limitations of the economic approach to determining values. This means that we should acknowledge that certain ecological effects are not commensurable with economic effects measured in dollars. Where trade-offs between noncom-mensurable magnitudes are involved, choices must be made through the political system.

VI. Conclusions

The argument for the adoption of the economists' point of view concerning environmental policy can be summarized as follows. Given the premises about individual preferences and the value judgment that satisfying these preferences should be the objective of policy, the adoption of the economists' recommendations concerning environmental policy will always lead to a potential Pareto improvement, that is, it will always be possible through taxes and compensating payments to make sure that at least some people are better off and that no one loses. Society could choose not to make these compensating payments; but this choice should be on the basis of some ethical judgment concerning the deservingness of the gainers and losers from the policy.

It might be helpful at this point to review and summarize these premises and value judgments so that they might be in the focus of discussion:

1. Should individual preferences matter? If not individual preferences, then whose preferences should matter? What about ecological effects that have no perceptible effect on human welfare, that is, that lie outside of the set of things over which individuals have preferences?

2. Does the substitution principle hold for environmental services? Or are individuals' preferences for environmental goods lexicographic? This is an empirical question. Economists have developed a substantial body of evidence that people are willing to make trade-offs between environmental goods such as recreation, visual amenities, and healthful air and other economic goods.

3. Are preferences characterized by unlimited wants? This is also an empirical question. But I think that most economists would agree that if there are such limits, we have not begun to approach them for the vast bulk of the citizens of this world. A related question is whether it should be the objective of economic activity to satisfy wants without limits? But this question is more closely related to question (1) concerning the role of individual preferences.

4. Is achieving an efficient allocation of resources that important? Or, as Kelman (1981) has argued, should we be willing to accept less economic efficiency in order to preserve the idea that environmental values are in some sense superior to economic values? An affirmative answer to the latter question implies a lexicographic preference system and a rejection of the substitution principle for environmental goods.

5. Should compensation always be paid? Paid sometimes? Never? This is an ethical question. But as I have indicated, I think it plays a central role in judging the ethical implications of economists' environmental policy recommendations. Not only is there the question of whether compensation should be paid, but also the question of who should be compensated. For example, should compensation be paid to those who are damaged by the optimal level of pollution? Or should compensation be paid to those who lose because of the imposition of pollution control requirements?

References

Freeman, A. Myrick, III. "Equity, Efficiency, and Discounting: The Reasons for Discounting Intergenerational Effects," *Futures* (October, 1977), 375–376.

Kelman, Steven. "Economists and the Environmental Muddle," *The Public Interest* 641 (Summer, 1981), 106–123.

Peacock, Alan T., and Charles K. Rowley. *Welfare Economics: A Liberal Restatement*, London, M. Robertson, 1975.

Notes

1. For some empirical evidence in support of this assertion, see Kelman (1981).

2. This is equivalent to saying that the individual has a utility function which assigns utility numbers to all possible consumption bundles. More preferred bundles have higher utility numbers.

3. There are other more technical conditions which need not concern us here.

4. For a different view of the Pareto Criterion and public policy, see Peacock and Rowley (1975).

5. In discussions of the use of risk-benefit analysis in policy making, the distinction is sometimes made between voluntary and involuntary risk. The argument being made is that involuntary risks are somehow worse. But I think that this misses the point. The real distinction is between compensated and uncompensated risk. A compensated risk is one, by the definition of compensation, that the individual would bear voluntarily.

6. The following argument is based on Freeman (1977).

At the Shrine of Our Lady of Fàtima, or Why Political Questions Are Not All Economic

Mark Sagoff

Lewiston, New York, a well-to-do community near Buffalo, is the site of the Lake Ontario Ordinance Works, where the federal government, years ago, disposed of the residues of the Manhattan Project. These radioactive wastes are buried but are not forgotten by the residents, who say that when the wind is southerly radon gas blows through the town. Several parents at a recent conference I attended there described their terror on learning that cases of leukemia had been found among area children. They feared for their own lives as well. At the other sides of the table, officials from New York State and from local corporations replied that these fears were ungrounded. People who smoke, they said, take greater risks than people who live close to waste disposal sites. One speaker talked in terms of "rational methodologies of decisionmaking." This aggravated the parents' rage and frustration.

The speaker suggested that the townspeople, were they to make their decision in a free market, would choose to live near the hazardous waste facility, if they knew the scientific facts. He told me later they were irrational—he said, "neurotic"—because they refused to recognize or to act upon their

Arizona Law Review, Vol. 23, 1283–1298. Copyright © 1981 by the Arizona Board of Regents. Reprinted by permission.

own interests. The residents of Lewiston were unimpressed with his analysis of their "willingness to pay" to avoid this risk or that. They did not see what risk-benefit analysis had to do with the issues they raised.

If you take the Military Highway (as I did) from Buffalo to Lewiston, you will pass through a formidable wasteland. Landfills stretch in all directions, where enormous trucks—tiny in that landscape—incessantly deposit sludge which great bulldozers, like yellow ants, then push into the ground. These machines are the only signs of life, for in the miasma that hangs in the air, no birds, not even scavengers, are seen. Along colossal power lines which criss-cross this dismal land, the dynamos at Niagara send electric power south, where factories have fled, leaving their remains to decay. To drive along this road is to feel, oddly, the mystery and awe one experiences in the presence of so much power and decadence.

Henry Adams had a similar response to the dynamos on display at the Paris Exposition of 1900. To him "the dynamo became a symbol of infinity."[1] To Adams, the dynamo functioned as the modern equivalent of the Virgin, that is, as the center and focus of power. "Before the end, one began to pray to it; inherited instinct taught the natural expression of man before silent and infinite force."[2]

Adams asks in his essay "The Dynamo and the Virgin" how the products of modern industrial civilization will compare with those of the religious culture of the Middle Ages. If he could see the landfills and hazardous waste facilities bordering the power stations and honeymoon hotels of Niagara Falls he would know the answer. He would understand what happens when efficiency replaces infinity as the central conception of value. The dynamos at Niagara will not produce another Mont-Saint-Michel. "All the steam in the world," Adams wrote, "could not, like the Virgin, build Chartres."[3]

At the Shrine of Our Lady of Fàtima, on a plateau north of the Military Highway, a larger than life sculpture of Mary looks into the chemical air. The original of this shrine stands in central Portugal, where in May, 1917, three children said they saw a Lady, brighter than the sun, raised on a cloud in an evergreen tree.[4] Five months later, on a wet and chilly October day, the Lady again appeared, this time before a large crowd. Some who were skeptical did not see the miracle. Others in the crowd reported, however, that "the sun appeared and seemed to tremble, rotate violently and fall, dancing over the heads of the throng. . . ."[5]

The Shrine was empty when I visited it. The cult of Our Lady of Fàtima, I imagine, has only a few devotees. The cult of Pareto optimality, however, has many. Where some people see only environmental devastation, its devotees perceive efficiency, utility, and the maximization of wealth. They see the satisfaction of wants. They envision the good life. As I looked over the smudged and ruined terrain I tried to share that vision. I hoped that Our Lady of Fàtima, worker of miracles, might serve, at least for the moment, as the Patroness of cost-benefit analysis. I thought of all the wants and needs that are satisfied in a landscape of honeymoon cottages, commercial strips, and dumps for hazardous waste. I saw the miracle of efficiency. The prospect, however, looked only darker in that light.

I

This essay concerns the economic decisions we make about the environment. It also concerns our political decisions about the environment. Some people have suggested that ideally these should be the same, that all environmental problems are problems in distribution. According to this view there is an environmental problem only when some resource is not allocated in equitable and efficient ways.[6]

This approach to environmental policy is pitched entirely at the level of the consumer. It is his or her values that count, and the measure of these values is the individual's willingness to pay. The problem of justice or fairness in society becomes, then, the problem of distributing goods and services so that more people get more of what they want to buy. A condo on the beach. A snowmobile for the mountains. A tank full of gas. A day of labor. The only values we have, on this view, are those which a market can price.[7]

How much do you value open space, a stand of trees, an "unspoiled" landscape? Fifty dollars? A hundred? A thousand? This is one way to measure value. You could compare the amount consumers would pay for a townhouse or coal or a landfill and the amount they would pay to preserve an area in its "natural" state. If users would pay more for the land with the house, the coal mine, or the landfill, than without—less construction and other costs of development—then the efficient thing to do is to improve the land and thus increase its value. That is why we have so many tract developments. And pizza stands. And gas stations. And strip mines. And landfills. How much did you spend last year to preserve open space? How much for pizza and gas? "In principle, the ultimate measure of environmental quality," as one basic text assures us, "is the value people place on these . . . services or their *willingness to pay*." [8]

Willingness to pay. What is wrong with that? The rub is this: not all of us think of ourselves simply as *consumers*. Many of us regard ourselves *as citizens* as well. We act as consumers to get what we want *for ourselves*. We act as citizens to achieve what we think is right or best *for the community*. The question arises, then, whether what we want for ourselves individually as consumers is consistent with the goals we would set for ourselves collectively as citizens. Would I vote for the sort of things I shop for? Are my preferences as a consumer consistent with my judgments as a citizen?

They are not. I am schizophrenic. Last year, I fixed a couple of tickets and was happy to do so since I saved fifty dollars. Yet, at election time, I helped to vote the corrupt judge out of office. I speed on the highway; yet I want the police to enforce laws against speeding. I used to buy mixers in returnable bottles—but who can bother to return them? I buy only disposables now, but, to soothe my conscience, I urge my state senator to outlaw one-way containers. I love my car; I hate the bus. Yet I vote for candidates who promise to tax gasoline to pay for public transportation. I send my dues to the Sierra Club to protect areas in Alaska I shall never visit. And I support the work of the American League to Abolish Capital Punishment although, personally, I have nothing to gain one way or the other. (When I hang, I will hang myself.) And of course I applaud the Endangered Species Act, although I have no earthly use for the Colorado squawfish or the Indiana bat. I support almost any political cause that I think will defeat my consumer interests. This is because I have contempt for—although I act upon—those interests. I have an "Ecology Now" sticker on a car that leaks oil everywhere it's parked.

The distinction between consumer and citizen preferences has long vexed the theory of public finance. Should the public economy serve the same goals as the household economy? May it serve, instead, goals emerging from our association as citizens? The question asks if we may collectively strive for and achieve only those items we individually compete for and consume. Should we aspire, instead, to public goals we may legislate as a nation?

The problem, insofar as it concerns public finance, is stated as follows by R. A. Musgrave, who reports a conversation he had with Gerhard Colm.

> He [Colm] holds that the individual voter dealing with political issues has a frame of reference quite distinct from that which underlies his allocation of income as a consumer. In the latter situation the voter acts as a private individual determined by self-interest and deals with his personal wants; in the former, he acts as a political being guided by his image of a good society. The two, Colm holds, are different things.[9]

Are these two different things? Stephen Marglin suggests that they are. He writes:

> The preferences that govern one's unilateral market actions no longer govern his actions when the form of reference is shifted from the market to the political arena. The Economic Man and the Citizen are for all intents and purposes two different individuals. It is not a question, therefore, of rejecting individual . . . preference maps; it is, rather, that market and political preference maps are inconsistent.[10]

Marglin observes that if this is true, social choices optimal under one set of preferences will not be optimal under another. What, then, is the meaning of "optimality"? He notices that if we take a person's true preferences to be those expressed in the market, we may, then, neglect or reject the preferences that person reveals in advocating a political cause or position. "One might argue on welfare grounds," Marglin speculates, "for authoritarian rejection of individuals' politically revealed preferences in favor of their market-revealed preferences!"

II

On February 19, 1981, President Reagan published Executive Order 12,291 requiring all administrative agencies and departments to support every new major regulation with a cost-benefit analysis establishing that the benefits of the regulation to society outweigh its costs.[11] The Order directs the Office of Management and Budget (OMB) to review every such regulation on the basis of the adequacy of the cost-benefit analysis supporting it. This is a departure from tradition. Traditionally, regulations have been reviewed not by OMB but by the courts on the basis of their relation not to cost-benefit analysis but to authorizing legislation.

A month earlier, in January 1981, the Supreme Court heard lawyers for the American Textile Manufacturers Institute argue against a proposed Occupational Safety and Health Administration (OSHA) regulation which would have severely restricted the acceptable levels of cotton dust in textile plants.[12] The lawyers for industry argued that the benefits of the regulation would not equal the costs. The lawyers for the government contended that the law required the tough standard. OSHA, acting consistently with Executive Order 12,291, asked the Court not to decide the cotton dust case, in order to give the agency time to complete the cost-benefit analysis required by the textile industry. The Court declined to accept OSHA's request and handed down its opinion on June 17, 1981.[13]

The Supreme Court, in a 5–3 decision, found that the actions of regulatory agencies which conform to the OSHA law need not be supported by cost-benefit analysis. In addition, the Court asserted that Congress in writing a statute, rather than the agencies in applying it, has the primary responsibility for balancing benefits and costs. The Court said:

> When Congress passed the Occupational Health and Safety Act in 1970, it chose to place preeminent value on assuring employees a safe and healthful working environment, limited only by the feasibility of achieving such an environment. We must measure the validity of the Secretary's actions against the requirements of that Act.[14]

The opinion upheld the finding of the Appeals Court that "Congress itself struck the balance between costs and benefits in the mandate to the agency."[15]

The Appeals Court opinion in *American Textile Manufacturers* vs. *Donovan* supports the principle that legislatures are not necessarily bound to a particular conception of regulatory policy. Agencies that apply the law, therefore, may not need to justify on cost-benefit grounds the standards they set. These standards may conflict with the goal of efficiency and still express our political will as a nation. That is, they may reflect not the personal choices of self-interested individuals, but the collective judgments we make on historical, cultural, aesthetic, moral, and ideological grounds.

The appeal of the Reagan Administration to cost-benefit analysis, however, may arise more from political than economic considerations. The intention, seen in the most favorable light, may not be to replace political or ideological goals with economic ones but to make economic goals more apparent in regulation. This is not to say that Congress should function to reveal a collective willingness-to-pay just as markets reveal an individual willingness-to-pay. It is to suggest that Congress should do more to balance economic with ideological, aesthetic, and moral goals. To think that environmental or worker safety policy can be based exclusively on aspiration for a "natural" and "safe" world is as foolish as to hold that environmental law can be reduced to cost-benefit accounting. The more we move to one extreme, as I found in Lewiston, the more likely we are to hear from the other.

III

The labor unions won an important political victory when Congress passed the Occupational Safety and Health Act of 1970.[16] That Act, among other things, severely restricts worker exposure to toxic substances. It instructs the Secretary of Labor to set "the standard which most adequately assures, to the extent feasible . . . that no employee will suffer material impairment of health or functional capacity even if such employee has regular exposure to the hazard . . . for the period of his working life."[17]

Pursuant to this law, the Secretary of Labor, in 1977, reduced from ten to one part per million (ppm) the permissible ambient exposure level for benzene, a carcinogen for which no safe threshold is known. The American Petroleum Institute thereupon challenged the new standard in court.[18] It argued, with much evidence in its favor, that the benefits (to workers) of the one ppm standard did not equal the costs (to industry). The standard, therefore, did not appear to be a rational response to a market failure in that it did not strike an efficient balance between the interests of workers in safety and the interests of industry and consumers in keeping prices down.

The Secretary of Labor defended the tough safety standard on the ground that the law demanded it. An efficient standard might have required safety until it cost industry more to prevent a risk than it cost workers to accept it. Had Congress adopted this vision of public policy—one which can be found in many economics texts[19]—it would have treated workers not as ends-in-themselves but as means for the production of overall utility. And this, as the Secretary saw it, was what Congress refused to do.

The United States Court of Appeals for the Fifth Circuit agreed with the American Petroleum Institute and invalidated the one ppm benzene standard.[20] On July 2, 1980, the Supreme Court affirmed remanding the benzene standard back to OSHA for revision.[21] The narrowly based Supreme Court decision was divided over the role economic considerations should play in judicial review. Justice Marshall, joined in dissent by three other justices, argued that the Court had undone on the basis of its own theory of regulatory policy an act of Congress inconsistent with that theory. He concluded that the plurality decision of the Court "requires the American worker to return to the political arena to win a victory that he won before in 1970."[22]

To reject cost-benefit analysis, as Justice Marshall would, as a basis for public policy making is not necessarily to reject cost-effectiveness analysis, which is an altogether different thing. "Cost-benefit analysis," one commentator points out, "is used by the decision maker to establish societal goals as well as the means for achieving these goals, whereas cost-effectiveness analysis only compares alternative means for achieving 'given' goals."[23] Justice Marshall's dissent objects to those who would make efficiency the goal of public policy. It does not necessarily object to those who would accomplish as efficiently as possible the goals Congress sets.[24]

IV

When efficiency is the criterion of public safety and health, one tends to conceive of social relations on the model of a market, ignoring competing visions of what we as a society should be like. Yet it is obvious that there are competing conceptions of how we should relate to one another. There are some who believe, on principle, that worker safety and environmental quality ought to be protected only insofar as the benefits of protection balance the costs. On the other hand, people argue, also on principle, that neither worker safety nor environmental quality should be treated merely as a commodity, to be traded at the margin for other commodities, but should be valued for its own sake. The conflict between these two principles is logical or moral, to be resolved by argument or debate. The question whether cost-benefit analysis should play a decisive role in policymaking is not to be decided by cost-benefit analysis. A contradiction between principles—between contending visions of the good society—cannot be settled by asking how much partisans are willing to pay for their beliefs.

The role of the *legislator*, the political role, may be more important to the individual than the role of *consumer*. The person, in other words, is not to be treated as merely a bundle of preferences to be juggled in cost-benefit analyses. The individual is to be respected as an advocate of ideas which are to be judged in relation to the reasons for them. If health and environmental statutes reflect a vision of society as something other than a market by requiring protections beyond what are efficient, then this may express not legislative ineptitude but legislative responsiveness to public values. To deny this vision because it is economically inefficient is simply to replace it with another vision. It is to insist that the ideas of the citizen be sacrificed to the psychology of the consumer.

We hear on all sides that government is routinized, mechanical, entrenched, and bureaucratized; the jargon alone is enough to dissuade the most mettlesome meddler. Who can make a difference? It is plain that for many of us the idea of a national political community has an abstract and suppositious quality. We have only our private conceptions of the good, if no way exists to arrive at a public one. This is only to note the continuation, in our time, of the trend Benjamin Constant described in the essay *De la Liberte des Anciens Comparee a Celle des Modernes*.[25] Constant observes that the modern world, as opposed to the ancient, emphasizes civil over political liberties, the rights of privacy and property over those of community and participation. "Lost in the multitude," Constant writes, "the individual rarely perceives the influence that he exercises," and, therefore, must be content with "the peaceful enjoyment of private independence."[26] The individual asks only to be protected by laws common to all in his pursuit of his own self-interest. The citizen has been replaced by the consumer; the tradition of Rousseau has been supplanted by that of Locke and Mill.

Nowhere are the rights of the moderns, particularly the rights of privacy and property, less helpful than in the area of the natural environment. Here the values we wish to protect—cultural, historical, aesthetic, and moral—are public values; they depend not so much upon what each person wants individually as upon what he or she believes we stand for collectively. We refuse to regard worker health and safety as commodities; we regulate hazards as a matter of right. Likewise, we refuse to treat environmental resources simply as public goods in the economist's sense. Instead, we prevent significant deterioration of air quality not only as a matter of individual self-interest but also as a matter of collective self-respect. How shall we balance efficiency against moral, cultural, and aesthetic values in policy for the workplace and the environment? No better way has been devised to do this than by legislative debate ending in a vote. This is not the same thing as a cost-benefit analysis terminating in a bottom line.

V

It is the characteristic of cost-benefit analysis that it treats all value judgments other than those made on its behalf as nothing but statements of preference, attitude, or emotion, insofar as they are value judgments. The cost-benefit analyst regards as true the judgment that we should maximize efficiency or wealth. The analyst believes that this view can be backed by reasons;[27] the analyst does not regard it as a preference or want for which he or she must be willing to pay. The cost-benefit analyst, however, tends to treat all other normative views and recommendations as if they were nothing but subjective reports of mental states. The analyst supposes in all such cases that "this is right" and "this is what we ought to do" are equivalent to "I want this" and "this is what I prefer." Value judgments

are beyond criticism if, indeed, they are nothing but expressions of personal preference; they are incorrigible since every person is in the best position to know what he or she wants. All valuation, according to this approach, happens *in foro interno*; debate *in foro publico* has no point. On this approach, the reasons that people give for their views, unless these people are welfare economists, do not count; what counts is how much they are willing to pay to satisfy their wants. Those who are willing to pay the most, for all intents and purposes, have the right view; theirs is the more informed opinion, the better aesthetic judgment, and the deeper moral insight.

The assumption that valuation is subjective, that judgments of good and evil are nothing but expressions of desire and aversion, is not unique to economic theory.[28] There are psychotherapists—Carl Rogers is an example—who likewise deny the objectivity or cognitivity of valuation.[29] For Rogers, there is only one criterion of worth: it lies in "the subjective world of the individual. Only he knows it fully."[30] The therapist shows his or her client that a "value system is not necessarily something imposed from without, but is something experienced."[31] Therapy succeeds when the client "perceives himself in such a way that no self-experience can be discriminated as more or less worthy of positive self-regard than any other. . . ."[32] The client then "tends to place the basis of standards within himself, recognizing that the 'goodness' or 'badness' of any experience or perceptual object is not something inherent in that object, but is a value placed in it by himself."[33]

Rogers points out that "some clients make strenuous efforts to have the therapist exercise the valuing function, so as to provide them with guides for action."[34] The therapist, however, "consistently keeps the locus of evaluation with the client."[35] As long as the therapist refuses to "exercise the valuing function" and as long as he or she practices an "unconditional positive regard"[36] for all the affective states of the client, then the therapist remains neutral among the client's values or "sensory and visceral experiences."[37] The role of the therapist is legitimate, Rogers suggests, because of this value neutrality. The therapist accepts all felt preferences as valid and imposes none on the client.

Economists likewise argue that their role as policymakers is legitimate because they are neutral among competing values in the client society. The political economist, according to James Buchanan, "is or should be ethically neutral: the indicated results are influenced by his own value scale only insofar as this reflects his membership in a larger group."[38] The economist might be most confident of the impartiality of his or her policy recommendations if he or she could derive them formally or mathematically from individual preferences. If theoretical difficulties make such a social welfare function impossible,[39] however, the next best thing, to preserve neutrality, is to let markets function to transform individual preference orderings into a collective ordering of social states. The analyst is able then to base policy on preferences that exist in society and are not necessarily his own.

Economists have used this impartial approach to offer solutions to many outstanding social problems, for example, the controversy over abortion. An economist argues that "there is an optimal number of abortions, just as there is an optimal level of pollution, or purity. . . . Those who oppose abortion could eliminate it entirely, if their intensity of feeling were so strong as to lead to payments that were greater at the margin than the price anyone would pay to have an abortion."[40] Likewise economists, in order to determine whether the war in Vietnam was justified, have estimated the willingness to pay of those who demonstrated against it.[41] Likewise it should be possible, following the same line of reasoning, to decide whether Creationism should be taught in the public schools, whether black and white people should be segregated, whether the death penalty should be enforced, and whether the square root of six is three. All of these questions depend upon how much people are willing to pay for their subjective preferences or wants—or none of them do. This is the beauty of cost-benefit analysis: no matter how relevant or irrelevant, wise or stupid, informed or uninformed, responsible or silly, defensible or indefensible wants may be, the analyst is able to derive a policy from them—a policy which is legitimate because, in theory, it treats all of these preferences as equally valid and good.

VI

Consider, by way of contrast, a Kantian conception of value.[42] The individual, for Kant, is a judge of values, not a mere haver of wants, and the individual judges not for himself or herself merely, but as a member of a relevant community or group. The central idea in a Kantian approach to ethics is that some values are more reasonable than others and therefore have a better claim upon the assent of members of the community as such.[43] The world of obligation, like the world of mathematics or the world of empirical fact, is intersubjective, it is public not private, so that objective standards of argument and criticism apply. Kant recognizes that values, like beliefs, are subjective states of mind, but he points out that like beliefs they have an objective content as well; therefore they are either correct or mistaken. Thus Kant discusses valuation in the context not of psychology but of cognition. He believes that a person who makes a value judgment—or a policy recommendation—claims to know what is *right* and not just what is *preferred*. A value judgment is like an empirical or theoretical judgment in that it claims to be *true*, not merely to be *felt*.

We have, then, two approaches to public policy before us. The first, the approach associated with normative versions of welfare economics, asserts that the only policy recommendation that can or need be defended on objective grounds is efficiency or wealth-maximization. Every policy decision after that depends only on the preponderance of feeling or preference, as expressed in willingness to pay. The Kantian approach, on the other hand, assumes that many policy recommendations other than that one may be justified or refuted on objective grounds. It would concede that the approach of welfare economics applies adequately to some questions, e.g., those which ordinary consumer markets typically settle. How many yo-yos should be produced as compared to how many frisbees? Shall pens have black ink or blue? Matters such as these are so trivial it is plain that markets should handle them. It does not follow, however, that we should adopt a market or quasi-market approach to every public question.

A market or quasi-market approach to arithmetic, for example, is plainly inadequate. No matter how much people are willing to pay, three will never be the square root of six. Similarly, segregation is a national curse and the fact that we are willing to pay for it does not make it better but only makes us worse. Similarly, the case for abortion must stand on the merits; it cannot be priced at the margin. Similarly, the war in Vietnam was a moral debacle and this can be determined without shadow-pricing the willingness to pay of those who demonstrated against it. Similarly, we do not decide to execute murderers by asking how much bleeding hearts are willing to pay to see a person pardoned and how much hard hearts are willing to pay to see him hanged. Our failures to make the right decisions in these matters are failures in arithmetic, failures in wisdom, failures in taste, failures in morality—but not market failures. There are no relevant markets to have failed. What separates these questions from those for which markets are appropriate is this. They involve matters of knowledge, wisdom, morality, and taste that admit of better or worse, right or wrong, true or false—and these concepts differ from that of economic optimality. Surely environmental questions—the protection of wilderness, habitats, water, land, and air as well as policy toward environmental safety and health—involve moral and aesthetic principles and not just economic ones. This is consistent, of course, with cost-effectiveness and with a sensible recognition of economic constraints.

The neutrality of the economist, like the neutrality of Rogers' therapist, is legitimate if private preferences or subjective wants are the only values in question. A person should be left free to choose the color of his or her necktie or necklace—but we cannot justify a theory of public policy or private therapy on that basis. If the patient seeks moral advice or tries to find reasons to justify a choice, the therapist, according to Rogers' model, would remind him or her to trust his visceral and sensory experiences. The result of this is to deny the individual status as a cognitive being capable of responding intelligently to reasons; it reduces him or her to a bundle of affective states. What Rogers' therapist does to the patient the cost-benefit analyst does to society as a whole. The analyst is neutral among our "values"—having first imposed a theory of what value is. This is a theory that is impartial among values and for that reason fails to treat the persons who have them with respect or concern. It does not treat them even as persons but only as locations at which wants may be found. And thus we may conclude that the neutrality of economics is not a basis for its legitimacy. We recognize it as an indifference toward value—an indifference so deep, so studied, and so assured that at first one hesitates to call it by its right name.

VII

The residents of Lewiston at the conference I attended demanded to know the truth about the dangers that confronted them and the reasons for these dangers. They wanted to be convinced that the sacrifice asked of them was legitimate even if it served interests other than their own. One official from a large chemical company dumping wastes in the area told them, in reply, that corporations were people and that people could talk to people about their feelings, interests, and needs. This sent a shiver through the audience. Like Joseph K. in *The Trial*,[44] the residents of Lewiston asked for an explanation, justice, and truth, and they were told that their wants would be taken care of. They demanded to know the reasons for what was continually happening to them. They were given a personalized response instead.

This response, that corporations are "just people serving people" is consistent with a particular view of power. This is the view that identified power with the ability to get what one wants as an individual, that is, to satisfy one's personal preferences. When people in official positions in corporations or in the government put aside their personal interests, it would follow that they put aside their power as well. Their neutrality then justifies them in directing the resources of society in ways they determine to be best. This managerial role serves not their own interests but those of their clients. Cost-benefit analysis may be seen as a pervasive form of this paternalism. Behind this paternalism, as William Simon observes of the lawyer-client relationship, lies a theory of value that tends to personalize power. "It resists understanding power as a product of class, property, or institutions and collapses power into the personal needs and dispositions of the individuals who command and obey."[45] Once the economist, the therapist, the lawyer, or the manager abjures his own interests and acts wholly on behalf of client individuals, he appears to have no power of his own and thus justifiably manipulates and controls everything. "From this perspective it becomes difficult to distinguish the powerful from the powerless. In every case, both the exercise of power and submission to it are portrayed as a matter of personal accommodation and adjustment."[46]

The key to the personal interest or emotive theory of value, as one commentator has rightly said, "is the fact that emotivism entails the obliteration of any genuine distinction between manipulative and nonmanipulative social relations."[47] The reason is that once the effective self is made the source of all value, the public self cannot participate in the exercise of power. As Philip Reiff remarks, "the public world is constituted as one vast stranger who appears at inconvenient times and makes demands viewed as purely external and therefore with no power to elicit a moral response."[48] There is no way to distinguish tyranny from the legitimate authority that public values and public law create.[49]

"At the rate of progress since 1900," Henry Adams speculates in his *Education*, "every American who lived into the year 2000 would know how to control unlimited power."[50] Adams thought that the Dynamo would organize and release as much energy as the Virgin. Yet in the 1980s, the citizens of Lewiston, surrounded by dynamos, high tension lines, and nuclear wastes, are powerless. They do not know how to criticize power, resist power, or justify power—for to do so depends on making distinctions between good and evil, right and wrong, innocence and guilt, justice and injustice, truth and lies. These distinctions cannot be made out and have no significance within an emotive or psychological theory of value. To adopt this theory is to imagine society as a market in which individuals trade voluntarily and without coercion. No individual, no belief, no faith has authority over them. To have power to act as a nation, however, we must be able to act, at least at times, on a public philosophy, conviction, or faith. We cannot replace with economic analysis the moral function of public law. The antinomianism of cost-benefit analysis is not enough.

Notes

1. H. Adams, *The Education of Henry Adams* 380 (1970, 1961).

2. *Id.*

3. *Id.* at 388.

4. For an account, see J. Pelletier, *The Sun Danced at Fatima* (1951).

5. *New Catholic Encyclopedia* 856 (1967).

6. See, e.g., W. Baxter, *People or Penguins: The Case for Optimal Pollution*, chap. 1 (1974). See generally

A. Freeman III, R. Haveman, and A. Kneese, *The Economics of Environmental Policy* (1973).

7. R. Posner puts this point well in discussing wealth maximization as an ethical concept. "The only kind of preference that counts in a system of wealth-maximization," he writes, "is . . . one that is backed up by money—in other words, that is registered in a market." Posner, "Utilitarianism, Economics, and Legal Theory," 8 *J. Legal Stud.* 119 (1979).

8. Freeman et al., note 6 *supra* at 23.

9. R. Musgrave, *The Theory of Public Finance* 87–88 (1959).

10. Marglin, "The Social Rate of Discount and the Optimal Rate of Investment," 77 *Q. J. of Econ.* 98 (1963).

11. See 46 *Fed. Reg. 13193* (February 19, 1981). The Order specifies that the cost-benefit requirement shall apply "to the extent permitted by law."

12. *American Textile Mfgrs. Inst. v. Bingham*, 617 F.2d 636 (D.C. Cir. 1979) *cert.* granted *sub nom.* [1980]; *American Textile Mfgrs. v. Marshall*, 49 U.S.L.W. 3208.

13. *Textile Mfgrs. v. Donovan*, 101 S.Ct. 2478 (1981).

14. *Id.* U.S.L.W. (1981), 4733–34.

15. *Ibid.*, 4726–29.

16. Pub. L. No. 91-596, 84 Stat. 1596 (codified at 29 U.S.C. 651-78) (1970).

17. 29 U.S.C., 655(b) (5).

18. *American Petroleum Institute v. Marshall*, 581 F.2d 493 (1978) (5th Cir.), aff'd 100 S. Ct. 2844 (1980).

19. See, e.g., R. Posner, *Economic Analysis of Law*, parts I, II (1972, 1973). In *The Costs of Accidents* (1970), G. Calabresi argues that accident law balances two goals, "efficiency" and "equality" or "justice."

20. 581 F.2d 493 (1978).

21. 100 S.Ct. 2844 (1980).

22. *Id.* at 2903.

23. M. Baram, "Cost-Benefit Analysis: An Inadequate Basis for Health, Safety and Environmental Regulatory Decision Making," 8 *Ecological Law Quarterly* 473 (1980).

24. See 49 U.S.L.W. 4724–29 for this reasoning applied in the cotton dust case.

25. *De la Liberte des Anciens Comparee a Celle des Modernes* (1819).

26. *Oeuvres Politiques de Benjamin Constant*, ed. C. Luandre 269 (Paris, 1874); quoted in S. Wolin, *Politics and Vision* 281 (1960).

27. There are arguments that whatever reasons may be given are no good. See, e.g., Dworkin, "Why Efficiency?" 8 *Hofstra L. Rev.* 563 (1980); Dworkin, "Is Wealth a Value?" 9 *J. Legal Stud.* 191 (1980); Kennedy, "Cost-Benefit Analysis of Entitlement Prob-

lems: A Critique" 33 *Stan. L. Rev.* 387 (1980); Rizzo, "The Mirage of Efficiency" 8 *Hofstra L. Rev.* 641 (1980); Sagoff, "Economic Theory and Environmental Law" 79 *Mich L. Rev. 1393* (1981).

28. This is the emotive theory of value. For the classic statement, see C. Stevenson, *Ethics and Language,* chaps. 1, 2 (1944). For criticism, see Blanshard, "The New Subjectivism in Ethics" 9 *Philosophy and Phenomenological Research* 504 (1949). For a statement of the related interest theory of value, see E. Westermarck, *Ethical Relativity* chaps. 3, 4, 5 (1932); R. Perry, *General Theory of Value* (1926). For criticisms of subjectivism in ethics and a case for the objective theory presupposed here, see generally, P. Edwards, *The Logic of Moral Discourse* (1955) and W. Ross, *The Right and the Good* (1930).

29. My account is based on C. Rogers, *On Becoming a Person* (1961); C. Rogers, *Client Centered Therapy* (1965); and Rogers, "A Theory of Therapy, Personality, and Interpersonal Relationships, as Developed in the Client Centered Framework" 3 *Psychology: A Study of a Science* 184 (S. Koch ed., 1959). For a similar account used as a critique of the lawyer-client relation, see Simon, "Homo Psychologious: Notes on a New Legal Formalism" 32 *Stan. L. Rev.* 487 (1980).

30. Rogers, note 29 *supra* at 210.

31. C. Rogers, *Client Centered Therapy* 150 (1965).

32. Rogers, note 29 *supra* at 208.

33. Rogers, note 31 *supra* at 139.

34. *Id.* at 150.

35. *Id.*

36. Rogers, note 29 *supra* at 208.

37. *Id.* at 523–24.

38. Buchanan, "Positive Economics, Welfare Econom-

ics, and Political Economy" 2 *J. L. and Econ.* 124, 127 (1959).

39. K. Arrow, *Social Choice and Individual Values* i–v (2d ed., 1963).

40. H. Macaulay and B. Yandle, *Environmental Use and the Market* 120–21 (1978).

41. Cicchetti, Freeman, Haveman, and Knetsch, "On the Economics of Mass Demonstrations: A Case Study of the November 1969 March on Washington," 61 *Am. Econ. Rev.* 719 (1971).

42. I. Kant, *Foundations of the Metaphysics of Morals* (R. Wolff, ed., L. Beck trans., 1969). I follow the interpretation of Kantian ethics of W. Sellars, *Science and Metaphysics,* chap. VII (1968) and Sellars, "On Reasoning about Values" 17 *Am. Phil. Q.* 81 (1980).

43. See A. Macintyre, *After Virtue* 22 (1981).

44. F. Kafka, *The Trial* (rev. ed. trans. 1957). Simon (note 29 *supra*) at 524 applies this analogy to the lawyer-client relationship.

45. Simon, note 29 *supra* at 495.

46. *Id.*

47. Macintyre, note 43 *supra* at 22.

48. P. Reiff, *The Triumph of the Therapeutic: Uses of Faith after Freud* 52 (1966).

49. That public law regimes inevitably lead to tyranny seems to be the conclusion of H. Arendt, *The Human Condition* (1958); K. Popper, *The Open Society and Its Enemies* (1966); L. Strauss, *Natural Right and History* (1953). For an important criticism of this conclusion in these authors, see Holmes, "Aristippus in and out of Athens" 73 *Am. Pol. Sci. Rev.* 113 (1979).

50. H. Adams, note 1 *supra* at 476.

B. COST-BENEFIT ANALYSIS

PREVIEW

As noted earlier, it is widely agreed that markets as they exist are thought to fail in various respects. Unowned, or "commonly held," resources are overused or "exploited." Some goods, such as fossil fuels, clean air, or water, are thought to be used up too quickly or in the wrong manner. Burdens are imposed on parties who do not consent to them (hence, "negative externalities"). It is often held that government intervention in certain cases is appropriate, e.g., prohibiting certain activities by

regulation (and perhaps criminal penalties) or placing charges on certain activities (e.g., through licensing or effluent charges). In some cases a government agency decides whether to undertake a project such as building a dam. If the aggregate costs were to exceed the aggregate benefit, it would be foolish to proceed. It is reasonable to claim that (a) if a policy is adopted, then the costs must not exceed the benefits. We should distinguish this claim and the following two claims from one another: (b) if a policy, *P*, ought to be carried out for whatever are the relevant reasons, *P* should be carried out in the way that maximizes benefits-minus-costs, and (c) if a policy, P, maximizes benefits minus costs, then P ought to be carried out (call this the *maximization principle*). The major controversy surrounds (c). Specifically, those who argue for the adoption of a particular policy (such as flooding a valley and building a dam) may do so as follows:

1. We (or a governmental agency) ought to do whatever maximizes benefits-minus costs.

2. Policy P maximizes benefits-minus-costs. Hence,

3. We ought to carry out P.

Two basic questions are (1) why should we do whatever maximizes benefits-minus-costs, and (2) is it ever possible to know or reasonably believe of some (or any) policy that it maximizes benefits-minus-costs. Further, in a given case is it reasonable to believe that a particular policy does so? The essays that follow explore these matters (for example, the proper way to think about, and deal with, pollution) and in some cases how they bear on a particular dispute.

Here we begin to lay out the Pandora's box of puzzles that arise when one sets out to identify and reassess what is presupposed by the sort of normative cost-benefit approach identified above (whose core is [c] that the policy that maximizes benefits-minus-costs is right and, therefore, ought to be adopted). What seems at first only a simple truism like "don't be wasteful" is not so at all; rather, the presuppositions are many, hard to unearth, entrenched, and extremely influential.

The concepts of cost and benefit are not as straightforward as is often implied. What is to count as a cost? A number of possibilities come to mind: premature death, injury, pain, (felt) frustration of preferences, or nonfulfillment of preferences. Such suggestions may focus only on costs to humans. There are reasons to reject such anthropocentrism. Should

we not include what economists (and many others) almost invariably exclude, such as pain or premature death to animals, or destruction of a river or forest if there is no nontrivial loss to humans? Analogously, what is to count as a benefit? Is pure life prolongation of humans a benefit (eternal life *as such* might be boring!)? Are all instances of human preference satisfaction to be weighed positively in a cost-benefit calculation? There is a tendency to equate "benefit," "good," "welfare," "satisfaction," "utility," and "preference fulfillment," but should we regard the fulfillment of "antisocial preferences" (such as sadistic, envious, jealous ones) as a benefit? As noted earlier, should not preferences be "laundered"?

Orthodox economists, perhaps in an excess of antipaternalism, antimoralism, or uncritical acceptance of moral subjectivism (an instance of egalitarianism run amok), tend not to pass judgment on existing preferences—acting as if all preferences had an equal right to be fulfilled (but consider a hunter's intense preference to maximize his or her kill of baby seals or whales, a Serbian soldier's desire to rape Bosnian women, or a resentful heterosexual marine's desire to bash gay soldiers). If one says that some preferences do not *deserve* satisfaction (or that their fulfillment has no positive moral weight), then evaluation enters at a fundamental level, and it is inappropriate to proclaim value neutrality for any such economic theory (even if it does not insist on cardinal measures of utility). However, any theory advocating unqualified want-fulfillment seems morally problematic for the reasons discussed.

Similarly, in many cases little is said about the *relation between beliefs and preferences* (as if preferences were like itches unconnected with cognition). However, it is clear that one's preferences are heavily dependent (sometimes causally and sometimes conceptually) on one's beliefs. Compare preferences for and against slavery, polygamy, the use of DDT, the killing of whales, or Oedipus's preference for

Jocasta when he believed, and when he did not believe, Jocasta to be his mother. If preferences (such as for destroying all Jews, keeping women barefoot and pregnant, "nuking" the latest enemy) are based on irrational beliefs (Jews are vermin; women rightly are property of males—God's designated "helpmates" for men; retaliation by the enemy would be minor), it is not at all clear why satisfaction of such preferences is a benefit to be weighed positively in some cost-benefit calculations. Thus, aside from the fact that only effects on humans are given weight in the calculations, it seems doubtful that all instances of preference fulfillment should be conceptualized as benefits. If so, why maximize them? Further, it is not obvious that all harms to humans ("costs") can be viewed as frustration of wants. When urban children suffer brain damage (and consequent retardation) from exposure to lead (from our use of leaded gasoline), what preference of the child is frustrated? Suppose the child is only a year old. If acid rain destroys many of our forests, is there no cost if and when people do not care, and we come to prefer plastic trees (as a result of indoctrination or not missing what we never experienced)?

A different, competing analysis of welfare/illfare, benefit/cost, gain/loss is presented in terms of promoting or subverting the *interests* of a person or other organism— in terms of what is *in the interest* of, or subversive of, a being. When one takes into account children, the comatose, or the severely retarded—as philosophers and social theorists sometimes forget to do, it is especially clear that *what people want* and *what is in their interest* only overlap. Those who identify benefit with want satisfaction need to give reasons for rejecting a competing analysis of benefit. The person on the street probably believes that cost-benefit techniques are aimed at promoting welfare, but arguably want satisfaction and the promotion of welfare are not the same thing.

Even if it were unproblematic that benefit equals want satisfaction, it is questionable whether all benefits (so understood) can be identified and measured. There is no established market in some goods. Thus, economists infer by indirect means how much people ("consumers") "value" a good or a service ('value' in economics often means 'prefer' in English). There are two main approaches to determining value: (a) determine which packages of goods people are willing and able to pay for if there is a market for them, and (b) ask people direct or indirect questions. Consider (a) first. What people are *willing* to pay is, in part, a function of how much they are *able* to pay. If willingness to pay for safety devices in a car is the criterion, then one may believe that the rich value their lives more than the poor value theirs. Should we believe as much? Suppose Jones is out of work and starving on Monday and then takes a highly risky job on Tuesday (washing windows on the fifth floor). He may "demand" only a modest premium to compensate for the extra risk to his life (suppose he could have had the first-floor job for a slightly smaller salary). Should we infer that the value of Jones's life is small— or that he does not value it much? According to another approach, the value (or "economic value"?) of a person's life is equivalent to his or her foregone earnings. Perhaps this is a suitable criterion for determining how much compensation should be made to a person's estate when that person is wrongfully killed. As a measure of the value of that person's life or the amount of money that should be spent to prevent premature death, a monetary measure seems dubious. Happenstance affects earnings (as do preferences for leisure time and moral convictions). Would Shaquille O'Neal's life be worth less if there were no market for basketball players? Is a ditchdigger's life at age 21 worth less than that of a 21-year-old computer wizard?

Years ago the Ford motor company did a cost-benefit analysis on the policy of adding certain devices to its cars in order to prevent the gas tanks from rupturing. One of the prospective benefits was saving a certain number of lives. How valuable is one life? Can a life rationally be assigned a monetary value? Ford figured $200,000 (for 1971!) as the cost of a death. Presumably, this figure largely reflects costs to others; only $10,000 of the amount was designated as the cost (value?) of the victim's pain and suffering. Why not $50,000 or $100,000? Is the benefit of preserving a life equal to the cost of avoiding the death (which is assumed to be a function of wages forgone)? Of course, the figure that is assigned here directly affects the outcome of the cost-benefit calculation and the ultimate policy determination. We note here the obvious questions that arise about the reasonableness of assigning monetary values to certain "goods and bads." There are important questions about the way "cost" and "benefit" are conceptualized, problems in attempting to identify all the costs and benefits, and difficulties in rationally assigning a monetary measure to many costs and benefits—even when one takes an anthropocentric approach. Avoiding complexities, however, can have a high price. Our cost-benefit calculations would be comparatively simpler if we did not count the well-being of children or the severely retarded.

THE MATTER OF CONSENT

In law and in common sense, whether another (voluntarily and knowingly) consents to the imposition of a "harm" is thought morally significant in deciding on the permissibility or desirability of generating the harm. The surgeon and the mugger may make similar "incisions," perhaps with similar results, but we view the unconsented-to cutting as wrong, and the one to which there is consent as acceptable. It is striking that, in some discussions defending cost-benefit analysis (in contrast, see the Leonard and Zeckhauser selection), little attention is paid to whether those who are harmed, or subjected to risks, consent or not. It is clear that (more or less) voluntary smoking results in great harms (on average and in the aggregate) to smokers. A cost-benefit analysis of smoking (or alcohol usage) might (we conjecture) suggest strongly that the practice fails to maximize benefits-minus-costs. It is natural to wonder, however, whether the burdens on the smokers (aside from associated "indirect" burdens on non-smokers) should be counted as a cost in a cost-benefit calculation. At the least, we raise the question of whether *imposed* costs and *voluntarily absorbed* costs should be viewed similarly. As the issue is often discussed elsewhere, this distinction tends to be ignored.

THE MAXIMIZATION PRINCIPLE

Although an analyst may purport to identify only costs and benefits (and, thus, remain "untainted" by ethical commitments) and not subscribe to the maximization principle (we ought to do whatever maximizes benefits-minus-costs), further questions arise for anyone who accepts the (normative) maximization principle. If the prior difficulties cannot be overcome, the principle may be inapplicable. Also, the principle seems subject to the well-known difficulties with the principle of utility; on one construal "maximize benefits-minus-costs" is just the principle of utility. (Except that the classic utilitarians Jeremy Bentham and John Stuart Mill were not anthropocentric in their conception of "cost" and "benefit." Both explicitly maintained that the suffering of animals must be given weight in deciding what to do.) The main objection to be noted here concerns whether a policy of maximizing the balance of benefits over costs is defensible when it gives no direct weight to how those benefits and costs are *distributed* among the relevant population.

The policy that maximizes benefits-minus-costs may make some individuals worse off. Thus, adopting the policy may not be an efficient step in the sense of making a Pareto improvement (see the preceding Preview for an explanation). The gains to the "winners," however, may outweigh the losses to the losers. If so, it would be *possible* in principle for the gainers to *compensate* the losers—thus, making the latter "nonlosers" (no worse off). The costs of making the transfer (information costs, and so on) may make full compensation impossible. If, however, full compensation were made, a Pareto improvement would occur, there would be no losers on balance, and an injustice could not be claimed, namely, that some suffered an unconsented to, on balance, harm. (Note, however, that some might be relatively, if not absolutely, worse off—on one "objective" measure, at least.) Some economists and others, however, believe a "potential compensation principle" (or potential Pareto criterion) is satisfactory: The results of a policy must make full compensation *possible*, but the compensation need not be paid. This view is puzzling. To accept the potential compensation principle is to set aside an intuitively attractive feature of the strict Pareto principle (that no one will lose), one that sidesteps important moral objections based on considerations of justice. If salesperson *A* "steals" salesperson *B*'s $5,000 car, and as a result earns an extra $50,000 a year, perhaps *A* could compensate *B* for his or her losses. If *A* does not, *B* has ground for serious moral complaint. We do not pursue the point here, but there may be ground for complaint *even if* compensation is made (assuming it can be).

To maximize benefits-minus-costs without compensating losers looks suspiciously like merely maximizing total net utility. Uncompensated losses look like "market failures" or negative externalities. A supposed attraction of cost-benefit analysis is that it helps to eliminate or reduce such externalities. Pure maximization policies (regardless of what is to be maximized, e.g., GNP, utility, wealth, or benefits-minus-costs) seem to give no direct weight to concerns about how benefits and costs are distributed. This seems morally intolerable.

Perhaps, however, a coupling (somehow) of cost-benefit analysis and principles of just distribution may be more attractive. If so, one may have to surrender the unqualified maximization principle. Further, one may have to drop the pervasive metaethical assumption seemingly made by many environmental economists that "the proper use of environmental resources is more a matter of economics than of morals."[1] This last assumption is plausible only if one accepts the maximization principle and the assumption that one can measure all the relevant benefits and costs. These claims cannot, however, be decided without careful inquiry.

Matters are not all this simple, of course. The claims that some "environmentalists," philosophers, and scientists have proposed as guidelines for use in making environmental decisions (maxims such as "nature knows best," "a thing is right when it tends to preserve the integrity, stability, and beauty of the biotic community," "maximize utility" [again], "preserve endangered species," "everything has a right to exist") seem to be too vague and indeterminate to be analytic truisms, or otherwise objectionable. The essays that follow address the attractions of efficiency and cost-benefit considerations—as well as the persistent reservations about their use (especially as grounds for *policy selection*—as opposed to their use to foster cheap implementation of an already selected policy such as *cost-effectiveness*).

To speak at length of these matters is not to talk directly of rain forests, blue whales, acid rain, marshlands, or estuaries; rather, it is to explore grounds for choices that will determine the destiny of such entities as well as that of humans. If one is concerned with the fate of our planet, to ignore such matters is to choose to be a naive environmentalist.

In the first selection that follows, Steven Kelman, apart from considering questions about the anthropocentric nature of cost-benefit analysis, argues that a policy might be right even if it does *not* maximize benefits-minus-costs. Further, he questions the attempt to assign monetary values to nonmarketed benefits and costs. In short, Kelman's critique is important and provocative. Herman Leonard and Richard Zeckhauser then respond to some of the current criticisms of cost-benefit analysis. In particular they argue that such analysis is sensitive to distributional effects and need not be arbitrary in the assignment of monetary values. Their conflict with Kelman's view is not always direct, but the two essays are instructive.

NOTE

1. Robert and Nancy Dorfman, eds. *Economics of the Environment* (New York: W. W. Norton Company, 1972), p. XL.

Cost Benefit Analysis: An Ethical Critique

Steven Kelman

At the broadest and vaguest level, cost-benefit analysis may be regarded simply as systematic thinking about decision-making. Who can oppose, economists sometimes ask, efforts to think in a systematic way about the consequences of different courses of action? The alternative, it would appear, is unexamined decision-making. But defining cost-benefit analysis so simply leaves it with few implications for actual regulatory decision-making. Presumably, therefore, those who urge regulators to make greater use of the technique have a more extensive prescription in mind. I assume here that their prescription includes the following views:

1. There exists a strong presumption that an act should not be undertaken unless its benefits outweigh its costs.

2. In order to determine whether benefits outweigh costs, it is desirable to attempt to express all benefits and costs in a common scale or denominator, so that they can be compared with each other, even when some benefits and costs are not traded on markets and hence have no established dollar values.

3. Getting decision-makers to make more use of cost-benefit techniques is important enough to warrant both the expense required to gather the data for improved cost-benefit estimation and the political efforts needed to give the activity higher priority compared to other activities, also valuable in and of themselves.

My focus is on cost-benefit analysis as applied to environmental, safety, and health regulation. In that context, I examine each of the above propositions from the perspective of formal ethical theory, that is, the study of what actions it is morally right to undertake. My conclusions are:

1. In areas of environmental, safety, and health regulation, there may be many instances where a certain decision might be right even though its benefits do not outweigh its costs.

2. There are good reasons to oppose efforts to put dollar values on nonmarketed benefits and costs.

3. Given the relative frequency of occasions in the areas of environmental, safety, and health regulation where one would not wish to use a benefits-outweigh-costs test as a decision rule, and given the reasons to oppose the monetizing of nonmarketed benefits or costs that is a

Regulation (Jan., Feb. 1981), pp. 74–82. Reprinted by permission of the American Enterprise Institute for Public Policy Research, Washington, DC.

prerequisite for cost-benefit analysis, it is not justifiable to devote major resources to the generation of data for cost-benefit calculations or to undertake efforts to "spread the gospel" of cost-benefit analysis further.

I

How do we decide whether a given action is morally right or wrong and hence, assuming the desire to act morally, why it should be undertaken or refrained from? Like the Molière character who spoke prose without knowing it, economists who advocate use of cost-benefit analysis for public decisions are philosophers without knowing it: the answer given by cost-benefit analysis, that actions should be undertaken so as to maximize net benefits, represents one of the classic answers given by moral philosophers—that given by utilitarians. To determine whether an action is right or wrong, utilitarians tote up all the positive consequences of the action in terms of human satisfaction. The act that maximizes attainment of satisfaction under the circumstances is the right act. That the economists' answer is also the answer of one school of philosophers should not be surprising. Early on, economics was a branch of moral philosophy, and only later did it become an independent discipline.

Before proceeding further, the subtlety of the utilitarian position should be noted. The positive and negative consequences of an act for satisfaction may go beyond the act's immediate consequences. A facile version of utilitarianism would give moral sanction to a lie, for instance, if the satisfaction of an individual attained by telling the lie was greater than the suffering imposed on the lie's victim. Few utilitarians would agree. Most of them would add to the list of negative consequences the effect of the one lie on the tendency of the person who lies to tell other lies, even in instances when the lying produced less satisfaction for him than dissatisfaction for others. They would also add the negative effects of the lie on the general level of social regard for truth-telling, which has many consequences for future utility. A further consequence may be added as well. It is sometimes said that we should include in a utilitarian calculation the feeling of dissatisfaction produced in the liar (and perhaps in others) because, by telling a lie, one has "done the wrong thing." Correspondingly, in this view, among the

positive consequences to be weighed into a utilitarian calculation of truth-telling is satisfaction arising from "doing the right thing." This view rests on an error, however, because it *assumes* what it is the purpose of the calculation to *determine*—that telling the truth in the instance in question is indeed the right thing to do. Economists are likely to object to this point, arguing that no feeling ought "arbitrarily" to be excluded from a complete cost-benefit calculation, including a feeling of dissatisfaction at doing the wrong thing. Indeed, the economists' cost-benefit calculations would, at least ideally, include such feelings. Note the difference between the economist's and the philosopher's cost-benefit calculations, however. The economist may choose to include feelings of dissatisfaction in his cost-benefit calculation, but what happens if somebody asks the economist, "Why is it right to evaluate an action on the basis of a cost-benefit test?" If an answer is to be given to that question (which does not normally preoccupy economists but which does concern both philosophers and the rest of us who need to be persuaded that cost-benefit analysis is right), then the circularity problem reemerges. And there is also another difficulty with counting feelings of dissatisfaction at doing the wrong thing in a cost-benefit calculation. It leads to the perverse result that under certain circumstances a lie, for example, might be morally right if the individual contemplating the lie felt no compunction about lying and morally wrong only if the individual felt such a compunction!

This error is revealing, however, because it begins to suggest a critique of utilitarianism. Utilitarianism is an important and powerful moral doctrine. But it is probably a minority position among contemporary moral philosophers. It is amazing that economists can proceed in unanimous endorsement of cost-benefit analysis as if unaware that their conceptual framework is highly controversial in the discipline from which it arose—moral philosophy.

Let us explore the critique of utilitarianism. The logical error discussed before appears to suggest that we have a notion of certain things being right or wrong that *predates* our calculation of costs and benefits. Imagine the case of an old man in Nazi Germany who is hostile to the regime. He is wondering whether he should speak out against Hitler. If he speaks out, he will lose his pension.

And his action will have done nothing to increase the chances that the Nazi regime will be overthrown: he is regarded as somewhat eccentric by those around him, and nobody has ever consulted his views on political questions. Recall that one cannot add to the benefits of speaking out any satisfaction from doing "the right thing," because the purpose of the exercise is to determine whether speaking out *is* the right thing. How would the utilitarian calculation go? The benefits of the old man's speaking out would, as the example is presented, be nil, while the costs would be his loss of his pension. So the costs of the action would outweigh the benefits. By the utilitarians' cost-benefit calculation, it would be *morally wrong* for the man to speak out.

To those who believe that it would not be morally wrong for the old man to speak out in Nazi Germany, utilitarianism is insufficient as a moral view. We believe that some acts whose costs are greater than their benefits may be morally right and, contrariwise, some acts whose benefits are greater than their costs may be morally wrong.

This does not mean that the question whether benefits are greater than costs is morally irrelevant. Few would claim such. Indeed, for a broad range of individual and social decisions, whether an act's benefits outweigh its costs is a sufficient question to ask. But not for all such decisions. These may involve situations where certain duties—duties not to lie, break promises, or kill, for example—make an act wrong, even if it would result in an excess of benefits over costs. Or they may involve instances where people's rights are at stake. We would not permit rape even if it could be demonstrated that the rapist derived enormous happiness from his act, while the victim experienced only minor displeasure. We do not do cost-benefit analyses of freedom of speech or trial by jury. The Bill of Rights was not RARGed.[1] As the United Steelworkers noted in a comment on the Occupational Safety and Health Administration's economic analysis of its proposed rule to reduce worker exposure to carcinogenic coke-oven emissions, the Emancipation Proclamation was not subjected to an inflationary impact statement. The notion of human rights involves the idea that people may make certain claims to be allowed to act in certain ways or to be treated in certain ways, even if the sum of benefits achieved thereby does not outweigh the sum of costs. It is this view that underlies the statement that "workers have a right to a safe and healthy work place" and the expectation that OSHA's decisions will reflect that judgment.

In the most convincing versions of nonutilitarian ethics, various duties or rights are not absolute. But each has a *prima facie* moral validity so that, if duties or rights do not conflict, the morally right act is the act that reflects a duty or respects a right. If duties or rights do conflict, a moral judgment, based on conscious deliberation, must be made. Since one of the duties non-utilitarian philosophers enumerate is the duty of beneficence (the duty to maximize happiness), which in effect incorporates all of utilitarianism by reference, a non-utilitarian who is faced with conflicts between the results of cost-benefit analysis and non-utility-based considerations will need to undertake such deliberation. But in that deliberation, additional elements, which cannot be reduced to a question of whether benefits outweigh costs, have been introduced. Indeed, depending on the moral importance we attach to the right or duty involved, cost-benefit questions may, within wide ranges, become irrelevant to the outcome of the moral judgment.

In addition to questions involving duties and rights, there is a final sort of question where, in my view, the issue of whether benefits outweigh costs should not govern moral judgment. I noted earlier that, for the common run of questions facing individuals and societies, it is possible to begin and end our judgment simply by finding out if the benefits of the contemplated act outweigh the costs. This very fact means that one way to show the great importance, or value, attached to an area is to say that decisions involving the area should not be determined by cost-benefit calculations. This applies, I think, to the view many environmentalists have of decisions involving our natural environment. When officials are deciding what level of pollution will harm certain vulnerable people—such as asthmatics or the elderly—while not harming others, one issue involved may be the right of those people not to be sacrificed on the altar of somewhat higher living standards for the rest of us. But more broadly than this, many environmentalists fear that subjecting decisions about clean air or water to the cost-benefit tests that determine the general run of decisions removes those matters from the realm of specially valued things.

II

In order for cost-benefit calculations to be performed the way they are supposed to be, all costs and benefits must be expressed in a common measure, typically dollars, including things not normally bought and sold on markets, and to which dollar prices are therefore not attached. The most dramatic example of such things is human life itself; but many of the other benefits achieved or preserved by environmental policy—such as peace and quiet, fresh-smelling air, swimmable rivers, spectacular vistas—are not traded on markets either.

Economists who do cost-benefit analysis regard the quest after dollar values for non-market things as a difficult challenge—but one to be met with relish. They have tried to develop methods for imputing a person's "willingness to pay" for such things, their approach generally involving a search for bundled goods that *are* traded on markets and that vary as to whether they include a feature that is, *by itself*, not marketed. Thus, fresh air is not marketed, but houses in different parts of Los Angeles that are similar except for the degree of smog are. Peace and quiet is not marketed, but similar houses inside and outside airport flight paths are. The risk of death is not marketed, but similar jobs that have different levels of risk are. Economists have produced many often ingenious efforts to impute dollar prices to non-marketed things by observing the premiums accorded homes in clean air areas over similar homes in dirty areas or the premiums paid for risky jobs over similar nonrisky jobs.

These ingenious efforts are subject to criticism on a number of technical grounds. It may be difficult to control for all the dimensions of quality other than the presence or absence of the non-marketed thing. More important, in a world where people have different preferences and are subject to different constraints as they make their choices, the dollar value imputed to the non-market things that most people would wish to avoid will be lower than otherwise, because people with unusually weak aversion to those things or unusually strong constraints on their choices will be willing to take the bundled good in question at less of a discount than the average person. Thus, to use the property value discount of homes near airports as a measure of people's willingness to pay for quiet means to accept as a proxy for the rest of us the behavior of those least sensitive to noise, of airport employees (who value the convenience of a near-airport location) or of others who are susceptible to an agent's assurances that "it's not so bad." To use the wage premiums accorded hazardous work as a measure of the value of life means to accept as proxies for the rest of us the choices of people who do not have many choices or who are exceptional risk-seekers.

A second problem is that the attempts of economists to measure people's willingness to pay for non-marketed things assume that there is no difference between the price a person would require for *giving up* something to which he has a preexisting right and the price he would pay to *gain* something to which he enjoys no right. Thus, the analysis assumes no difference between how much a homeowner would need to be paid in order to give up an unobstructed mountain view that he already enjoys and how much he would be willing to pay to get an obstruction moved once it is already in place. Available evidence suggests that most people would insist on being paid far more to assent to a worsening of their situation than they would be willing to pay to improve their situation. The difference arises from such factors as being accustomed to and psychologically attached to that which one believes one enjoys by right. But this creates a circularity problem for any attempt to use cost-benefit analysis to determine *whether* to assign to, say, the homeowner the right to an unobstructed mountain view. For willingness to pay will be different depending on whether the right is assigned initially or not. The value judgment about whether to assign the right must, thus, be made first. (In order to set an upper bound on the value of the benefit, one might hypothetically assign the right to the person and determine how much he would need to be paid to give it up.)

Third, the efforts of economists to impute willingness to pay invariably involve bundled goods exchanged in *private* transactions. Those who use figures garnered from such analysis to provide guidance for *public* decisions assume no difference between how people value certain things in private individual transactions and how they would wish those same things to be valued in public collective decisions. In making such assumptions, economists insidiously slip into their analysis an important and controversial value judgment, growing naturally out of the highly individualistic micro-economic tradition—namely, the view that there should be no difference between private behavior and the behavior we display in public social life. An alternative view—one that enjoys, I would suggest, wide resonance among citizens—would be that public, social decisions provide an opportunity to give certain things a higher valuation than we choose, for one reason or another, to give them in our private activities.

Thus, opponents of stricter regulation of health risks often argue that we show by our daily risk-taking behavior that we do not value life infinitely, and therefore our public decisions should not reflect the high value of life that proponents of strict regulation propose. However, an alternative view is equally plausible. Precisely because we fail, for whatever reasons, to give life-saving the value in everyday personal decisions that we in some general terms believe we should give it, we may wish our social decisions to provide us the occasion to display the reverence for life that we espouse but do not always show. By this view, people do not have fixed unambiguous "preferences" to which they give expression through private activities and which therefore should be given expression in public decisions. Rather, they may have what they themselves regard as "higher" and "lower" preferences. The latter may come to the fore in private decisions, but people may want the former to come to the fore in public decisions. They may sometimes display racial prejudice, but support antidiscrimination laws. They may buy a certain product after seeing a seductive ad, but be skeptical enough of advertising to want the government to keep a close eye on it. In such cases, the use of private behavior to impute the values that should be entered for public decisions, as is done by using willingness to pay in private transactions, commits grievous offense against a view of the behavior of the citizen that is deeply engrained in our democratic tradition. It is a view that denudes politics of any independent role in society, reducing it to a mechanistic, mimicking recalculation based on private behavior.

Finally, one may oppose the effort to place prices on a non-market thing and hence in effect incorporate it into the market system out of a fear that the very act of doing so will reduce the thing's perceived value. To place a price on the benefit may, in other words, reduce the value of that benefit.

Cost-benefit analysis thus may be like the thermometer that, when placed in a liquid to be measured, itself changes the liquid's temperature.

Examples of the perceived cheapening of a thing's value by the very act of buying and selling it abound in everyday life and language. The disgust that accompanies the idea of buying and selling human beings is based on the sense that this would dramatically diminish human worth. Epithets such as "he prostituted himself," applied as linguistic analogies to people who have sold something, reflect the view that certain things should not be sold because doing so diminishes their value. Praise that is bought is worth little, even to the person buying it. A true anecdote is told of an economist who retired to another university community and complained that he was having difficulty making friends. The laconic response of a critical colleague—"If you want a friend why don't you buy yourself one"—illustrates in a pithy way the intuition that, for some things, the very act of placing a price on them reduces their perceived value.

The first reason that pricing something decreases its perceived value is that, in many circumstances, non-market exchange is associated with the production of certain values not associated with market exchange. These may include spontaneity and various other feelings that come from personal relationships. If a good becomes less associated with the production of positively valued feelings because of market exchange, the perceived value of the good declines to the extent that those feelings are valued. This can be seen clearly in instances where a thing may be transferred both by market and by non-market mechanisms. The willingness to pay for sex bought from a prostitute is less than the perceived value of the sex consummating love. (Imagine the reaction if a practitioner of cost-benefit analysis computed the benefits of sex based on the price of prostitute services.)

Furthermore, if one values in a general sense the existence of a non-market sector because of its connection with the production of certain valued feelings, then one ascribes added value to any non-marketed good simply as a repository of values represented by the non-market sector one wishes to preserve. This seems certainly to be the case for things in nature, such as pristine streams or undisturbed forests: for many people who value them, part of their value comes from their position as repositories of values the non-market sector represents.

The second way in which placing a market price on a thing decreases its perceived value is by removing the possibility of proclaiming that the thing is "not for sale," since things on the market by definition are for sale. The very statement that something is not for sale affirms, enhances, and protects a thing's value in a number of ways. To begin with, the statement is a way of showing that a thing is valued for its own sake, whereas selling a thing for money demonstrates that it was valued only instrumentally. Furthermore, to say that something cannot be transferred in that way places it in the exceptional category—which requires the person interested in obtaining that thing to be able to offer something else that is exceptional, rather than allowing him the easier alternative of obtaining the thing for money that could have been obtained in an infinity of ways. This enhances its value. If I am willing to say "You're a really kind person" to whoever pays me to do so, my praise loses the value that attaches to it from being exchangeable only for an act of kindness.

In addition, if we have already decided we value something highly, one way of stamping it with a cachet affirming its high value is to announce that it is "not for sale." Such an announcement does more, however, than just reflect a pre-existing high valuation. It signals a thing's distinctive value to others and helps us persuade them to value the thing more highly than they otherwise might. It also expresses our resolution to safeguard that distinctive value. To state that something is not for sale is thus also a source of value for that thing, since if a thing's value is easy to affirm or protect, it will be worth more than an otherwise similar thing without such attributes.

If we proclaim that something is not for sale, we make a once-and-for-all judgment of its special value. When something is priced, the issue of its perceived value is constantly coming up, as a standing invitation to reconsider that original judgment. Were people constantly faced with questions such as "how much money could get you to give up your freedom of speech?" or "how much would you sell your vote for if you could?", the perceived value of the freedom to speak or the right to vote would soon become devastated as, in moments of

weakness, people started saying "maybe it's not worth *so much* after all." Better not to be faced with the constant questioning in the first place. Something similar did in fact occur when the slogan "better red than dead" was launched by some pacifists during the Cold War. Critics pointed out that the very posing of this stark choice—in effect, "would you *really* be willing to give up your life in exchange for not living under communism?"—reduced the value people attached to freedom and thus diminished resistance to attacks on freedom.

Finally, of some things valued very highly it is stated that they are "priceless" or that they have "infinite value." Such expressions are reserved for a subset of things not for sale, such as life or health. Economists tend to scoff at talk of pricelessness. For them, saying that something is priceless is to state a willingness to trade off an infinite quantity of all other goods for one unit of the priceless good, a situation that empirically appears highly unlikely. For most people, however, the word "priceless" is pregnant with meaning. Its value-affirming and value-protecting functions cannot be bestowed on expressions that merely denote a determinate, albeit high, valuation. John Kennedy in his inaugural address proclaimed that the nation was ready to "pay any price [and] bear any burden . . . to assure the survival and the success of liberty." Had he said instead that we were willing to "pay a high price" or "bear a large burden" for liberty, the statement would have rung hollow.

III

An objection that advocates of cost-benefit analysis might well make to the preceding argument should be considered. I noted earlier that, in cases where various non-utility-based duties or rights conflict with the maximization of utility, it is necessary to make a deliberative judgment about what act is finally right. I also argued earlier that the search for commensurability might not always be a desirable one, that the attempt to go beyond expressing benefits in terms of (say) lives saved and costs in terms of dollars is not something devoutly to be wished.

In situations involving things that are not expressed in a common measure, advocates of cost-benefit analysis argue that people making judgments "in effect" perform cost-benefit calculations anyway. If government regulators promulgate a regulation that saves 100 lives at a cost of $1 billion, they are "in effect" valuing a life at (a minimum of) $10 million, whether or not they say that they are willing to place a dollar value on a human life. Since, in this view, cost-benefit analysis "in effect" is inevitable, it might as well be made specific.

This argument misconstrues the real difference in the reasoning processes involved. In cost-benefit analysis, equivalencies are established *in advance* as one of the raw materials for the calculation. One determines costs and benefits, one determines equivalencies (to be able to put various costs and benefits into a common measure), and then one sets to toting things up—waiting, as it were, with bated breath for the results of the calculation to come out. The outcome is determined by the arithmetic; if the outcome is a close call or if one is not good at long division, one does not know how it will turn out until the calculation is finished. In the kind of deliberative judgment that is performed without a common measure, no establishment of equivalencies occurs in advance. Equivalencies are not aids to the decision process. In fact, the decision-maker might not even be aware of what the "in effect" equivalencies were, at least before they are revealed to him afterwards by someone pointing out what he had "in effect" done. The decision-maker would see himself as simply having made a deliberative judgment; the "in effect" equivalency number did not play a causal role in the decision but at most merely reflects it. Given this, the argument against making the process explicit is the one discussed earlier in the discussion of problems with putting specific values on things that are not normally quantified—that the very act of doing so may serve to reduce the value of those things.

My own judgment is that modest efforts to assess levels of benefits and costs are justified, although I do not believe that government agencies ought to sponsor efforts to put dollar prices on non-market things. I also do not believe that the cry for more cost-benefit analysis in regulation is, on the whole, justified. If regulatory officials were so insensitive about regulatory costs that they did not provide acceptable raw material for deliberative judgments (even if not of a strictly cost-benefit nature), my conclusion might be different. But a good deal of research into costs and benefits already occurs—actually, far more in the U.S. regulatory process than in that of any other industrial society. The danger now would seem to come more from the other side.

Note

1. The Regulatory Analysis Review Group (RARG) was created by President Carter to improve the cost-benefit analysis of regulatory policy. It was subsequently disbanded by President Reagan. (editors' note)

Cost-Benefit Analysis Defended

Herman B. Leonard and Richard J. Zeckhauser

Cost-benefit analysis, particularly as applied to public decisions involving risks to life and health, has not been notably popular. A number of setbacks—Three Mile Island is perhaps the most memorable—have called into question the reliability of analytic approaches to risk issues. We believe that the current low reputation of cost-benefit analysis is unjustified, and that a close examination of the objections most frequently raised against the method will show that it deserves wider public support.

Society does not and indeed could not require the explicit consent of every affected individual in order to implement public decisions that impose costs or risks. The transactions costs of assembling unanimous consent would be prohibitive, leading to paralysis in the status quo. Moreover, any system that required unanimous consent would create in-

The newsletter, *QQ: Report from the Center for Philosophy and Public Policy* at the University of Maryland at College Park, Maryland, Vol. 3, No. 3 (Summer 1983), pp. 6–9. Reprinted by permission.

centives for individuals to misrepresent their beliefs so as to secure compensation or to prevent the imposition of relatively small costs on them even if the benefits to others might be great.

If actual individual consent is an impractically strong standard to require of centralized decisions, how should such decisions be made? Our test for a proposed public decision is whether the net benefits of the action are positive. The same criterion is frequently phrased: Will those favored by the decision gain enough that they would have a net benefit even if they fully compensated those hurt by the decision? Applying this criterion to all possible actions, we discover that the chosen alternative should be the one for which benefits most exceed costs. We believe that the benefit-cost criterion is a useful way of defining "hypothetical consent" for centralized decisions affecting individuals with widely divergent interests: hypothetically, if compensation could be paid, all would agree to the decision offering the highest net benefits. We turn now to objections commonly raised against this approach.

Compensation and Hypothetical Consent

An immediate problem with the pure cost-benefit criterion is that it does not require the actual payment of compensation to those on whom a given decision imposes net costs. Our standard for public decision-making does not require that losers be compensated, but only that they *could* be if a perfect system of transfers existed. But unless those harmed by a decision are *actually* compensated, they will get little solace from the fact that someone is reaping a surplus in which they could have shared.

To this we make two replies. First, it is typically infeasible to design a compensation system that ensures that all individuals will be net winners. The transactions costs involved in such a system would often be so high as to make the project as a whole a net loss. But it may not even be desirable to construct full compensation systems, since losers will generally have an incentive under such systems to overstate their anticipated losses in order to secure greater compensation.

Second, the problem of compensation is probably smaller in practice than in principle. Society

tends to compensate large losses where possible or to avoid imposing large losses when adequate compensation is not practical. Moreover, compensation is sometimes overpaid; having made allowances *ex ante* for imposing risks, society still chooses sometimes to pay additional compensation *ex post* to those who actually suffer losses.

Libertarians raise one additional argument about the ethical basis of a system that does not require full compensation to losers. They argue that a public decision process that imposes uncompensated losses constitutes an illegal taking of property by the state and should not be tolerated. This objection, however strongly grounded ethically, would lead to an untenable position for society by unduly constraining public decisions to rest with the status quo.

Attention to Distribution

Two distinct types of distributional issue are relevant in cost-benefit analysis. First, we can be concerned about the losers in a particular decision, whoever they may be. Second, we can be concerned with the transfers between income classes (or other defined groups) engendered by a given project. If costs are imposed differentially on groups that are generally disadvantaged, should the decision criterion include special consideration of their interests? This question is closely intertwined with the issue of compensation, because it is often alleged that the uncompensated costs of projects evaluated by cost-benefit criteria frequently fall on those who are disadvantaged to start with.

These objections have little to do with cost-benefit analysis as a method. We see no reason why any widely agreed upon notion of equity, or weighting of different individuals' interests, cannot in principle be built into the cost-benefit decision framework. It is merely a matter of defining carefully what is meant by a benefit or a cost. If, in society's view, benefits (or costs) to some individuals are more valuable (costly) than those to others, this can be reflected in the construction of the decision criterion.

But although distribution concerns could be systematically included in cost-benefit analyses, it is not always—or even generally—a good idea to do so. Taxes and direct expenditures represent a far more efficient means of effecting redistribution than virtually any other public program; we would strongly prefer to rely on one consistent comprehensive tax and expenditure package for redistribution than on attempts to redistribute within every project.

First, if distributional issues are considered everywhere, they will probably not be adequately, carefully, and correctly treated anywhere. Many critics of cost-benefit analysis believe that project-based distributional analysis would create a net addition to society's total redistributive effort; we suggest that is likely, instead, to be only an inefficient substitution.

Second, treating distributional concerns within each project can only lead to transfers within the group affected by a project, often only a small subset of the community. For example, unisex rating of auto insurance redistributes only among drivers. Cross-subsidization of medical costs affects only those who need medical services. Why should not the larger society share the burden of redistribution?

Third, the view that distributional considerations should be treated project-by-project reflects a presumption that on average they do not balance out—that is, that some groups systematically lose more often than others. If it were found that some groups were severely and systematically disadvantaged by the application of cost-benefit analyses that ignore distributional concerns, we would favor redressing the balance. We do not believe this is generally the case.

Sensitive Social Values

Cost-benefit analysis, it is frequently alleged, does a disservice to society because it cannot treat important social values with appropriate sensitivity. We believe that this view does a disservice to society by unduly constraining the use of a reasonable and helpful method for organizing the debate about public decisions. We are not claiming that every important social value can be represented effectively within the confines of cost-benefit analysis. Some values will never fit in a cost-benefit framework and will have to be treated as "additional considerations" in coming to a final decision. Some, such as the inviolability of human life, may simply be binding constraints that cannot be traded off to obtain other gains. Nor can we carry

out a cost-benefit analysis to decide which values should be included and which treated separately— this decision will always have to be made in some other manner.

These considerations do not invalidate cost-benefit analysis, but merely illustrate that more is at stake than just dollar measures of costs and benefits. We would, however, make two observations. First, we must be very careful that only genuinely important and relevant social values be permitted to outweigh the findings of an analysis. Second, social values that frequently stand in the way of important efficiency gains have a way of breaking down and being replaced over time, so that in the long run society manages to accommodate itself to some form of cost-benefit criterion. If nuclear power were 1000 times more dangerous for its employees but 10 times less expensive than it is, we might feel that ethical considerations were respected and the national interest well served if we had rotating cadres of nuclear power employees serving short terms in high-risk positions, much as members of the armed services do. In like fashion, we have fire-fighters risk their lives; universal sprinkler systems would be less dangerous, but more costly. Such policies reflect an accommodation to the costs as a recognition of the benefits.

Measurability

Another objection frequently raised against cost-benefit analysis is that some costs and benefits tend to be ignored because they are much more difficult to measure than others. The long-term environmental impacts of large projects are frequently cited as an example. Cost-benefit analysis is charged with being systematically biased toward consideration of the quantifiable aspects of decisions.

This is unquestionably true: cost-benefit analysis is *designed* as a method of quantification, so it surely is better able to deal with more quantifiable aspects of the issues it confronts. But this limitation is in itself ethically neutral unless it can be shown that the quantifiable considerations systematically push decisions in a particular direction. Its detractors must show that the errors of cost-benefit analysis are systematically unjust or inefficient— for example, that it frequently helps the rich at the expense of the poor, or despoils the environment to the benefit of industry, or vice versa. We have not seen any carefully researched evidence to support such assertions.

We take some comfort in the fact that cost-benefit analysis is sometimes accused of being biased toward development projects and sometimes of being biased against them. Cost-benefit analyses have foiled conservation efforts in national forests—perhaps they systematically weight the future too little. But they have also squelched clearly silly projects designed to bring "economic development" to Alaska—and the developers argued that the analysis gave insufficient weight to the "unquantifiable" value of future industrialization.

In our experience, cost-benefit analysis is often a tool of the "outs"—those not currently in control of the political process. Those who have the political power to back the projects they support often have little need of analyses. By contrast, analysis can be an effective tool for those who are otherwise not strongly empowered politically.

Analyzing Risks

Even those who accept the ethical propriety of cost-benefit analysis of decisions involving transfers of money or other tangible economic costs and benefits sometimes feel that the principles do not extend to analyzing decisions involving the imposition of risks. We believe that such applications constitute a *particularly* important area in which cost-benefit analysis can be of value. The very difficulties of reaching appropriate decisions where risks are involved make it all the more vital to employ the soundest methods available, both ethically and practically.

Historically, cost-benefit analysis has been applied widely to the imposition and regulation of risks, in particular to risks of health loss or bodily harm. The cost-benefit approach is particularly valuable here, for several reasons. Few health risks can be exchanged on a voluntary basis. Their magnitude is difficult to measure. Even if they could be accurately measured, individuals have difficulty interpreting probabilities or gauging how they would feel should the harm eventuate. Compounding these problems of valuation are difficulties in contract, since risks are rarely conveyed singly between one individual and another.

The problem of risks conveyed in the absence of contractual approval has been addressed for centuries through the law of torts, which is designed to provide compensation after a harm has been received. If only a low-probability risk is involved, it is often efficient to wait to see whether a harm occurs, for in the overwhelming majority of circumstances transactions costs will be avoided. This approach also limits debate over the magnitude of a potential harm that has not yet eventuated. The creator of the risk has the incentive to gauge accurately, for he is the one who must pay if harm does occur.

While in principle it provides efficient results, the torts approach encounters at least four difficulties when applied to many of the risks that are encountered in a modern technological society. The option of declaring bankruptcy allows the responsible party to avoid paying and so to impose risks that it should not impose. Causality is often difficult to assign for misfortunes that may have alternative or multiple (and synergistically related) causes. Did the individual contract lung cancer from air pollution or from his own smoking, or both? Furthermore, the traditional torts requirement that individuals be made whole cannot be met in many instances (death, loss of a limb). Finally, paying compensation after the fact may also produce inappropriate incentives, and hence be inefficient. Workers who can be more or less careful around dangerous machinery, for example, are likely to be more careful if they will not be compensated for losing an appendage.

Our normal market and legal system tends to break down when substantial health risks are imposed on a relatively large population. These are, therefore, precisely the situations in which the cost-benefit approach is and should be called into play. Cost-benefit analysis is typically used in just those situations where our normal risk decision processes run into difficulty. We should therefore not expect it to lead to outcomes that are as satisfactory as those that evolve when ordinary market and private contractual trade are employed. But we should be able to expect better outcomes than we would achieve by muddling through unsystematically.

We have defended cost-benefit analysis as the most practical of ethically defensible methods and the most ethical of practically usable methods for conducting public decision-making. It cannot substitute for—nor can it adequately encompass, analyze, or consider—the sensitive application of social values. Thus it cannot be made the final arbiter of public decisions. But it does add a useful structure to public debate, and it does enable us to quantify some of the quantifiable aspects of public decisions. Our defense parallels Winston Churchill's argument for democracy: it is not perfect, but it is better than the alternatives.

SIDELIGHT: Cost-Benefit Analysis: Tool for All Seasons?

Although the White House taping system installed by former president Richard Nixon was dismantled in July 1973 after its existence became publicly known, most offices in the White House still have their own tape machines used for a variety of purposes. Quite by accident in March 1980, one of these machines was left on "Record" and picked up a conversation that was recently transcribed. A reliable source forwarded a copy of that transcript to Alan B. Morrison, director of the Public Citizen Litigation Group in Washington, D.C., who has provided *Legal Times* with the following account.

To get his mind off his work, a tired Zbigniew Brzezinski strolled into the office of Charles Schultze, chairman of President Carter's Council of Economic Advisors. Schultze was out, but one of his deputies, Gary Greene Eyeshades, was there. Brzezinski flopped down and began to talk.

"This Iranian situation is driving me crazy. No one's in charge. They tell you one thing one day, another the next, and a third the day after. The Revolutionary Council contradicts Ghotbzadeh, Bani-Sadr is countered by the students, and no one knows what Khomeini is thinking. How did we ever get into this mess?"

"The problem," responded Eyeshades, "is that your analysis at the beginning was faulty. Everyone was talking about politics, foreign relations, national defense, and oil. Those considerations are marginal. What you needed was a good cost-benefit analysis."

"What does that have to do with anything," snapped the national security advisor. "You economists think you have the answers to everything. This is diplomacy, power politics. It doesn't have anything to do with a cost-benefit analysis. If those things are useful at all, they only work for a few special kinds of problems."

"Not so," rejoined Eyeshades, sensing that he had Brzezinski's attention. "Defense has been using these since MacNamara's days to decide on weapons systems. Business uses them to buy new equipment, and we have been urging EPA to use them on toxic substances, DOT on highway safety, and HEW on regs to make life easier for the handicapped. The principle is well established; it would just have to be modified a little here."

Now Brzezinski's interest was perked. "OK, Mr. Economist. Let's see how you would have gone about it last November."

"It's really rather simple," said Eyeshades, taking out his yellow pad, drawing a line down the middle, and labeling one side "costs" and the other "benefits." "What we do is assign dollar figures to each variable and then see where the arithmetic leaves us. In this case, the only benefit we really want is to get back the hostages, putting us back to where we started. What we do here is compare the costs associated with each option and then pick the least expensive.

"The first option was to try a raid like the Israelis did at Entebbe, or Ford with the Mayaguez. I've been talking to people at DOD, and they say they could do it with 250 troops, four airplanes, some bombs, etc. In short, not a big operation. Now assuming the worst case and we lose all 250 men plus the hostages, what has it cost us?"

"Wait a minute, you can't do that. Those are American lives."

"Why not, we do it all the time. Seat belts and air bags save 10,000 lives a year, but we decided that question largely on cost. Coal mine accidents kill thousands a year, and we decided how much safety we can afford. Even controls on air pollution or cancerous chemicals in the workplace are determined by cost-benefit analyses. Why should this be any different?"

"How do you decide how to value human life?" queried Brzezinski.

"That's a cinch. Lawyers have figured a way in wrongful death cases. It's based primarily on earnings and life expectancy. And besides, in most cases, there will be no survivors, so there won't be any pain and suffering, which really run up the cost.

"And another thing, how do you suppose businesses decide whether to take a defective product off the market. They use a cost-benefit analysis."

"What about other costs?" retorted Brzezinski. "The ayatollah may throw us out, cut off our oil, deny us defense outposts. What do you say to that?"

"Well, we'll factor them in, too. I don't deny they are somewhat harder to calculate, but it's not impossible. After all, assigning dollars to anti-discrimination policies hasn't stood in the way of applying a cost-benefit analysis there, has it?"

Now Brzezinski was getting a little troubled. "The whole idea makes me nervous, deciding to sacrifice people just because of numbers."

Eyeshades quickly countered with two points. "First, let me say if you find our numbers on the value of Iran as an ally, for example, to be too low, you can simply change them."

"Hold on," interrupted Brzezinski. "How can you change the numbers? I thought this was supposed to be a precise, scientific way to solve the insoluble."

"Why not? We do it all the time. The cost-benefit analysis is only a tool in the hands of the decision-maker, not the answer to his prayers."

"But that's not the way you economists advertise it," replied Brzezinski. "You talk about cost-benefit analyses as though they were the answer to every question every bureaucrat has ever had."

"You don't expect us to downplay our own expertise, do you? Besides, a little puffing never hurt anyone."

"What's your second point?" queried Brzezinski.

"We haven't started figuring out the cost of the other options. You can't make up your mind about policy choices until we add up the costs of the alternatives, like loss of U.S. prestige, added defense cost to make us appear tough, the time the president and the senior staff spend worrying about Iran, all the travel of Secretary Vance, and lots of other things.

"Take my word for it. Cost-benefit analysis takes the agony out of decision-making. Now, you just make yourself comfortable while I get out my calculator. We should have this problem licked in no time. While we're at it, anything else been bothering you?"

"Well," said Brzezinski, "we're having a devil of a time with the manpower levels for the army, navy, and air force for the next five years. . . ."

C. ECOLOGICAL SUSTAINABILITY

PREVIEW

[T]he ideas of economists and political philosophers, both when they are right and when they are wrong, are more powerful than is commonly understood. Indeed the world is ruled by little else. Practical men, who believe themselves to be quite exempt from any intellectual influence, are usually the slaves of some defunct economist.

J. M. Keynes

"Progress," as defined by modern economics, is destroying the very natural systems upon which we depend for health and prosperity.

Sandra Postel

Mainstream economic theory has tended to proceed as if human societies constitute a system which is open at both ends. At one end there is an infinite supply of "resources" (at least if one allows for unending discoveries of adequate substitutes for certain materials which, it may be acknowledged, literally will run out, e.g., nonrenewable fossil fuels generated over the earth's 4.5-billion-year history). We have, in effect, already noted the evaluative dimension of 'resource' since the question of moral standing determines in large part what we will classify as "food." Thus, cannibals may not run out of "resources" as quickly as others. At the other end of our envisioned system is an outlet to a sink, a place where you can get rid of the things that you do not want, that are harmful, or otherwise in the way. These things we tend to call wastes, toxic wastes, trash, garbage, or pollutants. These terms, we too seldom acknowledge, are quasi-evaluative terms; we apply them to certain entities only because of certain normative standards to which we adhere. In the right place X is "fertilizer," and in the wrong place X is just "merde" as the French would call it. With the emergence of significant amounts of oxygen on the planet in the distant past, anerobic organisms encountered a "poisonous gas." However, the point here is the tendency of most people and much economic theory, until quite recently, to assume that, or act as if, sinks are in virtually infinite supply also.

If resources are in infinite supply and sinks are in infinite supply, then the task of an efficient economy, some seem to think, is simply to optimize the rate of throughput in the process of producing items that satisfy human wants. The objects wanted, we have noted, range from millions of Malcolm X caps, Elvis dolls, and plastic replicas of Jesus to artificial limbs and life-saving drugs. The views of economists have been split. Many have considered wants as given and applaud a system which effectively supplies them no matter what their *content*. There may be a certain reluctance here to embrace the view that we are *ever* in the position of knowing better than another whether what he or she wants is for his or her own good or whether we are ever in a good position to question whether someone's

wants are self-destructive or fail to reflect the person's all-things-considered judgment. Some people seem to hold the view that a want cannot be rationally appraised since wants are like involuntary sensations, something that just happen to people, over which they have no voluntary control, and which are not cognitive in nature (unless they are desires to have things which are means to ends, in which case the wanter's beliefs may be subject to cognitive appraisal). Some economists, and many philosophers, oppose the idea that any sort of want-fulfillment can, and should, be identified with the "intrinsic good," with "utility," or as something whose production should be thought of in itself as right-making (although not necessarily right-making on balance when all relevant matters are considered). On this latter view preferences need to be "laundered." For example, the fulfillment of the torturer's desire to torture should not count one whit toward a moral justification of the act of torturing. Thus, in trying to repair or revise utilitarianism, some wish to exclude from any positive counting in the utilitarian calculus what utilitarian-economist John Harsanyi has labeled the "fulfillment of antisocial preferences." How can one discriminate between antisocial and the other types of preferences? There is a deep problem here.[1]

Let us not lose sight of the forest for looking at the trees. What does all this have to do with the market and with sustainability? The market is a device which takes sources, produces objects or services to fulfill human wants, and discards most of the residue (some is recycled) into sinks. It is worth recalling that among the sinks are humans and most animals and plants since we and they breathe the air which contains the lead and drink the water which contains the heavy metals. So this "production machine" (we do not question that it is in many respects enormously beneficial) often passes on costs to those other than those who benefit from their generation.

As a related matter, what is a sink or an acceptable sink? If we regard various nonhumans, or for that matter all living things as having inherent value or worth, then arguably the dumping of certain wastes into animal habitats is also morally problematic. To put the matter differently, what we view as (acceptable) sinks depends on our suppositions regarding what sorts of things have moral standing. What counts as a sink, then, is partly an evaluative matter and is not "strictly an economic" or "strictly a scientific" question. We have already observed that for similar reasons what counts as a (an acceptable) source is also partly an evaluative issue. It is fair to say that philosophers and economists by and large have not addressed these issues and have simply made tacit anthropocentric assumptions. Today, this practice is beginning to change with the emergence of "green economic theory," ecological economics, and nonanthropocentric environmental philosophy."[2]

Indeed, as we scrutinize certain key concepts employed in our judgments about progress, improvement, and so on, it is becoming clearer that many are ambiguous, value laden in ways which we have not previously recognized, and tend to grease the path to conceptual confusion and, hence, to problematic or disastrous policy conclusions. An urgent task, we believe, is to deepen our conceptual scrutiny and to sort out the relationships of the various associated evaluative assumptions. It may be that some principles of fairness mandate achieving ecological sustainability. We will return to this point later.

In the same vein it is usually thought that growth, progress, development, wealth, productivity, and more rather than fewer choices are all "good things." However, what do we mean by such terms? By what standards are they to be deemed good? Are they always good, for everyone, or just sometimes good? And if they are good, do we succeed in measuring them properly? Is a higher employment rate always better? We judge the health of our national economy by calculating increases in the Gross National Product or the Net National Product. There are reasons to be skeptical about the assumption that our collective (human) well-being increases with all positive changes in the GNP. The following essays elaborate on this point. Philosophers have done a fair amount of work investigating the notion of the good of (individual) persons (the relation of happiness to health, to rational choice, and to enhanced autonomy, for example). What they (we) have paid less attention to is the material or the economic criteria for judging the well-being of a society, community, or nation, especially when those criteria should be ecologically enlightened and not lead us to false assurances about long-term human, nonhuman, or planetary well-being.[3]

We briefly comment further on some of these fundamental notions. People frequently say that they are "pro-growth," and since 'growth' tends to be a term of positive valuation, we seldom hear people say that they are "antigrowth."[4] But who is in favor of the growth of cancer, rape, racism, slavery, or torture; growth as such is not necessarily a good. What of growth of an individual's wealth? How it is obtained would seem to be a relevant question. Has it occurred by enslavement, by a kidnapping and ransom, by blackmail? Or more to the point of environmental ethics, has it occurred by passing on the risk of radioactive emissions of plutonium to however many generations might live over the next 24,000 years, or by profits from a steel mill which caused the acidification of a lake? Some wealth is obtained by morally and legally wrongful means, some by means legal but in a manner that is ecologically subversive, e.g., a manner which is not ecologically sustainable. The burning of the rain forests in Brazil comes to mind; farmers there clear the land in this manner to farm on poor soil, but they generate erosion, flooding, loss of species of ancient lineage, and a diminishment of the capacity of the planet to recycle carbon emissions. Just what sort of growth or development is morally acceptable? Is there a type which does not result in "stagnation" (however that term is to be defined) and which does not involve our species selling our planet down the intergalactic river—not to mention future generations of people?

It is worth observing that 'growth' and 'development' are not used only in a technical sense. In ordinary conversation their meanings do not stand in sharp contrast to one another, but some writers wish to contrast growth and development. Economist Herman Daly does so in his essay. One can stipulate that the terms have clearly contrasting meanings, but we should be aware that this is a deviation from ordinary usage and that other writers may use the terms in a nontechnical way or stipulate their meaning in a different manner. The more important question concerns what kind of social improvements can be achieved when society lives in an ecologically sustainable way, regardless of how we linguistically mark the distinction. If we can achieve this, we *might* call it "development without growth."

Some sources are renewable indefinitely, e.g., the energy from the sun. Some are finite, e.g., fossil fuels (such as oil or coal), clean water, and clean air (we note that normative standards are involved in the determination of what is "clean"). Some sinks are finite; our landfills can take only so much discarded material. Many lakes are dying, and children in parts of Poland are taken into caves for part of each day to allow them to breathe clean air. Obviously, what is finite cannot be consumed forever. Our use of fossil fuels at a rate which exceeds their replenishment cannot be sustained; once we spend all the "capital," there will be no "income" off of which to live—no matter how high the GNP soars in the meantime. At that point we can only ask the "high priests of infinite resources" (e.g., Herman Kahn or Julian Simon; see Section VI-A) to pray for another "technological fix." Occasionally, we get fixes, but even they seem to be finite, or they are not available when we need them. For example, a technological patching of the hole in the ozone layer does not appear to be imminent. It is doubtful that anyone factored in as part of the production costs of certain chlorofluorocarbons the resulting increase in incidences of skin cancer in the Southern hemisphere. The atmosphere, indeed the skin of millions of humans and nonhumans, is being treated as an acceptable sink.

It is not obvious how best to characterize the ideal of sustainability or even to define 'sustainability.' We might consider the following, however, as a useful *initial* working definition:

> A practice is ecologically sustainable if its indefinite continuation would not diminish the stock of natural and capital resources now available.

Let us call the above the *rough definition of ecological sustainability,* or RES. For the RES to be useful, we need to clarify what counts as a capital stock and what counts as a natural resource. Buildings and human-made tools are usually counted as capital, but what about the current arsenals of nuclear weapons and the frightening stocks of nerve gas the United States and other nations possess? If we count these as capital, we may not wish to advocate ecological sustainability as it is defined in the RES. We note here only a few considerations relevant to revising our definition. Should fetal cell tissue count as a natural resource, or as capital? Is this tissue instrumentally valuable in helping people with Parkinson's disease or Alzheimer's? How are we to regard human body parts (e.g., hearts, lungs, livers, corneas)? Reflection on this matter suggests that there may be hidden normative assumptions in judgments about what we count as part of *usable* stock. An easier problem, perhaps, is that we may not wish to construe nondiminishment literally; for example, given the advent of substitutable materials such as fiberglass, we would be foolish to insist on no diminishment of the amount of existing copper wire. But why should we accept ecological sustainability (sensibly formulated) as an ideal? The answer depends on whether we have duties to future generations of humans, nonhumans, and/or the nested ecosystems which constitute the biosphere. In particular, is it not a matter (at least in part) of fairness that we do not use up all, or disproportionate parts of, the available sources and sinks? The value of ecological sustainability is derived in part (or wholly) from a moral principle that requires fair sharing of the earth's resources with others, where 'others' does not refer only to humans or to existing beings. A complete environmental ethic would clarify this issue.

Indeed, one may wish to refine the RES further. Perhaps a more useful characterization would be in terms of nondiminishment of the *capacities* for future generations to live in a manner that is not inferior to that of the average person today. Although this revision has attractions, which we will not list, the reader should find its difficulties quickly. Some of them may be surmountable.

It is clear that if we humans are to live in an ecologically sustainable manner, we are going to have to redesign many of our institutions and practices and to alter our ways of thinking at a fundamental level. We are going to have to figure out what constraints on our ways of living are appropriate. We may find, however, that our lives improve even if our incomes do not rise, for many of our unsustainable practices already impose heavy costs on many of us. Perhaps we should begin our reconsiderations at an even more fundamental level, namely, thinking in terms of *sustaining whatever is of value*. This may include ways of life, traditions, cultures, and communities as well as clean air, clean water, renewable energy, and a biodiverse planet. Ecological sustainability is, however, even more basic since

it is the precondition of good living for any randomly chosen generation.

In the first essay that follows, Herman Daly criticizes the tendency of mainstream economic theory to ignore the environmental costs of pursuing boundless growth, and to live as if we inhabit a world of boundless sinks and sources. The bull of the well-known Merrill Lynch television commercials, a bull which knows "no boundaries," serves as a useful metaphor for Daly. The next essay, by William Ruckelshaus, former head of the U.S. Environmental Protection Agency, focuses on the difficulty of bringing about political change to achieve the goal of allowing "growth and development" to take place. He compares the magnitude of change he believes is necessary to that of the agricultural revolution of the late Neolithic period and the Industrial Revolution of the past two centuries. Ruckelshaus defends the use of market-based incentives, in part, and governmental modifications of the market to reflect environmental costs in order to move toward a sustainable way of living.

The essay by Bruce Hannon touches on a concept of increasing importance, the notion of *ecological health*. In some respects the model of an organism's health seems a useful one to get a clearer sense of the condition of our planet and how to *evaluate* its condition. We measure our socioeconomic health in a number of ways: estimates of the Gross National Product or Net National Product, the employment rate, the inflation rate, the national debt, morbidity and mortality statistics, among them. Most of our measures tend to ignore ecologically important factors such as the depletion of fossil fuels; the subversion of ecosystems; the increased risk of extinction of, or actual extinction of, species; the increasing dangers of the growing hole in the ozone layer, and the evidence of increasing risk from an intensification of global warming. Hannon explores using our indexes of economic health to measure ecological health.[5]

To those who are unaware of the extent to

which our standard indexes of economic health or improvement fail to register serious environmental degradation, Robert Repetto's investigation "Earth in the Balance Sheet" may have the impact of a cold shower. The brighter side is that with the development of more appropriate measures, nations may become more aware of "what on earth they are doing," develop new measures, and cease treating the nonhuman world as being of little consequence, a mere static backdrop to human activities.

NOTES

1. One serious problem is the identification and defense of a criterion by which one could distinguish "social" from "antisocial" preferences. Should one not count as utility or a good the satisfaction of resentful, envious, or jealous desires? There are objections to this and similar proposals. Is satisfaction of one's resentment of a mass murderer a bad thing? Even if one did find a defensible theoretical criterion, the attempt to implement such a criterion looks staggeringly difficult and enormously complicates the application of a revised principle of utility.

2. There is now a journal entitled *Ecological Economics* and also a recent volume, *Ecological Economics: The Science and Management of Sustainability,* edited by Robert Costanza (New York: Columbia University Press, 1991).

3. In the last decade or so, some moral and political philosophers have begun to shift away from what they see as an individualist bias of modern liberalism; they are often labeled "communitarians," e.g., Michael Sandel, Alasdair McIntyre, and Charles Taylor. Generally, their theories have been purely anthropocentric, and the communities of which they speak have lacked any noticeable ecological dimension. Of course, there is a long history of philosophical attempts to identify and defend a conception of the ideal society, from Plato's *Republic* to John Rawls's *A Theory of Justice.* These great works have also tended to be anthropocentric in outlook.

4. Analogously, critics of the "prolife" position on abortion do not wish to be cast as "antilife."

5. In thinking about the notion of ecological health, one might examine the essay by Eric Katz, 'Organism, Community and the "Substitution" Problem' found in Section IV-A. Further, we mention the volume *Ecosystem Health* edited by Robert Costanza, Bryan G. Norton, and Benjamin D. Haskell (Washington, DC: Island Press, 1992), in which Hannon's essay originally appeared.

Boundless Bull

Herman E. Daly*

If you want to know what is wrong with the American economy it is not enough to go to graduate school, read books, and study statistical trends—you also have to watch TV. Not the Sunday morning talking-head shows or even documentaries, and especially not the network news, but the really serious stuff—the commercials. For instance, the most penetrating insight into the American economy by far is contained in the image of the bull that trots unimpeded through countless Merrill Lynch commercials.

*The views presented here are those of the author and should in no way be attributed to the World Bank.

One such ad opens with a bull trotting along a beach. He is a very powerful animal—nothing is likely to stop him. And since the beach is empty as far as the eye can see, there is nothing that could even slow him down. A chorus in the background intones: "to . . . know . . . no . . . boundaries. . . ." The bull trots off into the sunset.

Abruptly the scene shifts. The bull is now trotting across a bridge that spans a deep gorge. There are no bicycles, cars or eighteen-wheel trucks on the bridge, so again the bull is alone in an empty and unobstructed world. The chasm, which might have proved a barrier to the bull, who after all is

Learning to Listen to the Land, edited by Bill Withers (Washington, DC: Island Press, 1991), pp. 233–238.

not a mountain goat, is conveniently spanned by an empty bridge.

Next the bull finds himself in a forest of giant redwoods, looking just a bit lost as he tramples the underbrush. The camera zooms up the trunk of a giant redwood whose top disappears into the shimmering sun. The chorus chirps on about a "world with no boundaries."

Finally, we see the bull silhouetted against a burgundy sunset, standing in solitary majesty atop a mesa overlooking a great empty southwestern desert. The silhouette clearly outlines the animal's genitalia, making it obvious even to city slickers that this is a bull, not a cow. Fadeout. The bull cult of ancient Crete and the Indus Valley, in which the bull god symbolized the virile principle of generation and invincible force, is alive and well on Wall Street.

The message is clear: Merrill Lynch wants to put you into an individualistic, macho, world without limits—the U.S. economy. The bull, of course, also symbolizes rising stock prices and unlimited optimism, which is ultimately based on this vision of an empty world where strong, solitary individuals have free reign. This vision is what is most fundamentally wrong with the American economy. In addition to TV commercials it can be found in politicians' speeches, in economic textbooks, and between the ears of most economists and business journalists.

No bigger lie can be imagined. The world is not empty; it is full! Even where it is empty of people it is full of other things. In California it is so full that people shoot each other because freeway space is scarce. A few years ago they were shooting each other because gasoline was scarce. Reducing the gasoline shortage just aggravated the space shortage on the freeways.

Many species are driven to extinction each year due to takeover of their "empty" habitat. Indigenous peoples are relocated to make way for dams and highways through "empty" jungles. The "empty" atmosphere is dangerously full of carbon dioxide and pollutants that fall as acid rain.

Unlike Merrill Lynch's bull, most do not trot freely along empty beaches. Most are castrated and live their short lives as steers imprisoned in crowded, stinking feed lots. Like the steers, we too live in a world of imploding fullness. The bonds of community, both moral and biophysical, are stretched, or rather compressed, to the breaking point. We have a massive foreign trade deficit, a domestic federal deficit, unemployment, declining real wages, and inflation. Large accumulated debts, both foreign and domestic, are being used to finance consumption, not investment. Foreign ownership of the U.S. economy is increasing, and soon domestic control over national economic life will decrease.

Why does Merrill Lynch (and the media and academia and the politicians) regale us with this "boundless bull"? Do they believe it? Why do they want you to believe it, or at least to be influenced by it at a subconscious level? Because what they are selling is growth, and growth requires empty space to grow into. Solitary bulls don't have to share the world with other creatures, and neither do you! Growth means that what you get from your bullish investments does not come at anyone else's expense. In a world with no boundaries, the poor can get richer while the rich get richer even faster. Our politicians find the boundless bull cult irresistible.

The boundless bull of unlimited growth appears in economics textbooks with less colorful imagery but greater precision. Economists abstract from natural resources because they do not consider them scarce, or because they think that they can be perfectly substituted by man-made capital. The natural world either puts no obstacles in the bull's path or, if an obstacle like the chasm appears, capital (the bridge) effectively removes it.

Economics textbooks also assume that wants are unlimited. Merrill Lynch's boundless bull is always on the move. What if, like Ferdinand, he were to just sit, smell the flowers, and be content with the world as it is without trampling it underfoot? That would not do. If you are selling continual growth, then you have to sell continual, restless, trotting dissatisfaction with the world as it is, as well as the notion that it has no boundaries.

This pre-analytic vision colors the analysis even of good economists, and many people never get beyond the boundless bull scenario. Certainly the media have not. Would it be asking too much of the media to do what professional economists have failed to do? Probably so, but all disciplines badly need external critics, and in the universities disciplines do not criticize each other. Even philosophy, which historically was the critic of the separate disciplines, has abdicated that role. Who is left? Economist Joan Robinson put it well many years ago when she noted that economists have run off to hide in thickets of algebra and left the really serious problems of economic policy to be handled by journalists. Is it to the media that we must turn for disciplinary criticism, for new analytic thinking about the economy? The thought does not inspire confidence. But in the land of the blind the one-eyed man is king. If journalists are to criticize the disciplinary orthodoxy of economic growth, they will need both the energy provided by moral outrage and the clarity of thought provided by some basic analytic distinctions.

Moral outrage should result from the dawning realization that we are destroying the capacity of the Earth to support life and counting it as progress, or at best as the inevitable cost of progress. "Progress" evidently means converting as much as possible of Creation into ourselves and our furniture. "Ourselves" means, concretely, the unjust combination of overpopulated slums and overconsuming suburbs. Since we do not have the courage to face up to sharing and population control as the solution to injustice, we pretend that further growth will make the poor better off instead of simply making the rich richer. The wholesale extinctions of other species, and some primitive cultures within our own species, are not reckoned as costs. The intrinsic value of other species, their own capacity to enjoy life, is not admitted at all in economics, and their instrumental value as providers of ecological life-support services to humans is only dimly perceived. Costs and benefits to future humans are routinely discounted at 10 percent, meaning that each dollar of cost or benefit fifty years in the future is valued at less than a penny today.

But just getting angry is not sufficient. Doing something requires clear thinking, and clear thinking requires calling different things by different names. The most important analytic distinction comes straight from the dictionary definitions of growth and development. "To grow" means to increase in size by the accretion or assimilation of material. "Growth" therefore means a quantitative increase in the scale of the physical dimensions of the economy. "To develop" means to expand or realize the potentialities of; to bring gradually to a fuller, greater, or better state. "Development" therefore means the qualitative improvement in the structure, design, and composition of the physical stocks of wealth that results from greater knowledge, both of technique and of purpose. A growing economy is getting bigger; a developing economy is getting better. An economy can therefore develop without growing, or grow without developing. A steady-state economy is one that does not grow, but is free to develop. It is not static—births replace deaths and production replaces depreciation, so that stocks of wealth and people are continually renewed and even improved, although neither is growing. Consider a steady-state library. Its stock of books is constant but not static. As a book becomes worn out or obsolete it is replaced by a new or better one. The quality of the library improves, but its physical stock of books does not grow. The library develops without growing. Likewise the economy's physical stock of people and artifacts can develop without growing.

The advantage of defining growth in terms of change in physical scale of the economy is that it forces us to think about the effects of a change in scale and directs attention to the concept of an ecologically sustainable scale, or perhaps even of an optimal scale. The scale of the economy is the product of population times per capita resource use—i.e., the total flow of resources—a flow that might conceivably be ecologically unsustainable, especially in a finite world that is not empty.

The notion of an optimal scale for an activity is the very heart of microeconomics. For every activity, be it eating ice cream or making shoes, there is a cost function and a benefit function, and the rule is to increase the scale of the activity up to the point where rising marginal cost equals falling marginal benefit—i.e., to where the desire for another ice cream is equal to the desire to keep the money for something else, or the extra cost of making another pair of shoes is just equal to the extra revenue from selling the shoes. Yet for the macro level, the aggregate of all microeconomic activities (shoe making, ice cream eating, and everything else), there is no concept of an optimal scale. The notion that the macro economy could become too large relative to the ecosystem is simply absent from macroeconomic theory. The macro economy is supposed to grow forever. Since GNP adds costs and benefits together instead of comparing them at the margin, we have no macro level accounting by which an optimal scale could be identified. Beyond a certain scale growth begins to destroy more values than it creates—economic growth gives way to an era of anti-economic growth. But GNP keeps rising, giving us no clue as to whether we have passed that critical point!

The apt image for the U.S. economy, then, is not the boundless bull on the empty beach, but the proverbial bull in the china shop. The boundless bull is too big and clumsy relative to its delicate environment. Why must it keep growing when it is already destroying more than its extra mass is worth?

Because: (1) We fail to distinguish growth from development, and we classify all scale expansion as "economic growth" without even recognizing the possibility of "anti-economic growth"—i.e., growth that costs us more than it is worth at the margin; (2) we refuse to fight poverty by redistribution and sharing, or by controlling our own numbers, leaving "economic" growth as the only acceptable cure for poverty. But once we are beyond the optimal scale and growth makes us poorer rather than richer, even that reason becomes absurd. Sharing, population control, and true qualitative development are difficult. They are also collective virtues that for the most part cannot be attained by individual action and that do not easily give rise to increased opportunities for private profit. The boundless bull is much easier to sell, and profitable at least to some while the illusion lasts. But further growth has become destructive of community, the environment, and the common good. If the media could help economists and politicians to see that, or at least to entertain the possibility that such a thing might be true, they will have rendered a service far greater than all the reporting of statistics on GNP growth, Dow Jones indexes, and junk bond prices from now until the end of time.

Toward a Sustainable World

William D. Ruckelshaus

The difficulty of converting scientific findings into political action is a function of the uncertainty of the science and the pain generated by the action. Given the current uncertainties surrounding just one aspect of the global environmental crisis—the predicted rise in greenhouse gases—and the enormous technological and social effort that will be required to control that rise, it is fair to say that responding successfully to the multifaceted crisis will be a difficult political enterprise. It means trying to get a substantial proportion of the world's people to change their behavior in order to (possibly) avert threats that will otherwise (probably) affect a world most of them will not be alive to see.

The models that predict climatic change, for example, are subject to varying interpretations as to the timing, distribution and severity of the changes in store. Also, whereas models may convince scientists, who understand their assumptions and limitations, as a rule projections make poor politics. It is hard for people—hard even for the groups of people who constitute governments—to change in response to dangers that may not arise for a long time or that just might not happen at all. . . .

Insurance is the way people ordinarily deal with potentially serious contingencies, and it is appropriate here as well. People consider it prudent to pay insurance premiums so that if catastrophe strikes, they or their survivors will be better off than if there had been no insurance. The analogy is clear. Current resources foregone or spent to prevent the buildup of greenhouse gases are a kind of premium. Moreover, as long as we are going to pay premiums, we might as well pay them in ways that will yield dividends in the form of greater efficiency, improved human health or more widely distributed prosperity. If we turn out to be wrong on greenhouse warming or ozone depletion, we still retain the dividend benefits. In any case, no one complains to the insurance company when disaster does not strike.

That is the argument for some immediate, modest actions. We can hope that if shortages or problems arise, there will turn out to be a technological fix or set of fixes, or that technology and the normal workings of the market will combine to solve the problem by product substitution. Already, for example, new refrigerants that do not have the atmospheric effects of the chlorofluorocarbons are being introduced; perhaps a cheap and nonpolluting source of energy will be discovered.

It is comforting to imagine that we might arrive at a more secure tomorrow with little strain, to suppose with Dickens's Mr. Micawber that something will turn up. Imagining is harmless, but counting on such a rescue is not. We need to face up to the fact that something enormous may be happening to our world. Our species may be pushing up against some immovable limits on the combustion of fossil fuels and damage to ecosystems. We must at least consider the possibility that, besides those modest adjustments for the sake of prudence, we may have to prepare for far more dramatic changes, changes that will begin to shape a sustainable world economy and society.

Sustainability is the nascent doctrine that economic growth and development must take place, and be maintained over time, within the limits set by ecology in the broadest sense—by the interrelations of human beings and their works, the biosphere and the physical and chemical laws that govern it. The doctrine of sustainability holds too that the spread of a reasonable level of prosperity and security to the less developed nations is essential to protecting ecological balance and hence essential to the continued prosperity of the wealthy nations. It follows that environmental protection and economic development are complementary rather than antagonistic processes.

Can we move nations and people in the direction of sustainability? Such a move would be a modification of society comparable in scale to only two other changes: the agricultural revolution of the late Neolithic and the Industrial Revolution of the past two centuries. Those revolutions were gradual, spontaneous, and largely unconscious. This one will have to be a fully conscious operation, guided by the best foresight that science can provide—foresight pushed to its limit. If we actually do it, the undertaking will be absolutely unique in humanity's stay on the earth.

The shape of this undertaking cannot be clearly seen from where we now stand. The conventional image is that of a crossroads: a forced choice of one direction or another that determines the future for some appreciable period. But this does not at all capture the complexity of the current situation. A more appropriate image would be that of a canoeist shooting the rapids: survival depends on continually responding to information by correct steering. In this case the information is supplied by science and economic events; the steering is the work of policy, both governmental and private.

Taking control of the future therefore means tightening the connection between science and policy. We need to understand where the rocks are in time to steer around them. Yet we will not devote the appropriate level of resources to science or accept the policies mandated by science unless we do something else. We have to understand that we are all in the same canoe and that steering toward sustainability is necessary.

Sustainability was the original economy of our species. Preindustrial peoples lived sustainably because they had to; if they did not, if they expanded their populations beyond the available resource base, then sooner or later they starved or had to migrate. The sustainability of their way of life was maintained by a particular consciousness regarding nature: the people were spiritually connected to the animals and plants on which they subsisted; they were part of the landscape, or of nature, not set apart as masters.

The era of this "original sustainability" eventually came to an end. The development of cities and the maintenance of urban populations called for intensive agriculture yielding a surplus. As a population grows, it requires an expansion of production, either by conquest or colonization or improved technique. A different consciousness, also embodied in a structure of myth, sustains this mode of life. The earth and its creatures are considered the property of humankind, a gift from the supernatural. Man stands outside of nature, which is a passive playing field that he dominates, controls and manipulates. Eventually, with industrialization, even the past is colonized: the forests of the Carboniferous are mined to support ever-expanding populations. Advanced technology gives impetus to the basic assumption that there is essentially no limit to humanity's power over nature.

This consciousness, this condition of "transitional unsustainability," is dominant today. It has two forms. In the underdeveloped, industrializing world, it is represented by the drive to develop at any environmental cost. It includes the wholesale destruction of forests, the replacement of sustainable agriculture by cash crops, the attendant exploitation of vulnerable lands by people such cash cropping forces off good land and the creation of industrial centers that are also centers of environmental pollution.

In the industrialized world, unsustainable development has generated wealth and relative comfort for about one fifth of humankind, and among the populations of the industrialized nations the consciousness supporting the unsustainable economy is nearly universal. With a few important exceptions, the environmental-protection movement in those nations, despite its major achievements in passing legislation and mandating pollution-control measures, has not had a substantial effect on the lives of most people. Environmentalism has been ameliorative and corrective—not a restructuring force. It is encompassed within the consciousness of unsustainability.

Although we cannot return to the sustainable economy of our distant ancestors, in principle there is no reason why we cannot create a sustainability consciousness suitable to the modern era. Such a consciousness would include the following beliefs:

1. *The human species is part of nature. Its existence depends on its ability to draw sustenance from a finite natural world; its continuance depends on its ability to abstain from destroying the natural systems that regenerate this world.* This seems to be the major lesson of the current environmental situation as well as being a direct corollary of the second law of thermodynamics.

2. *Economic activity must account for the environmental costs of production.* Environmental regulation has made a start here, albeit a small one. The market has not even begun to be mobilized to preserve the environment; as a consequence an increasing amount of the "wealth" we create is in a sense stolen from our descendants.

3. *The maintenance of a livable global environment depends on the sustainable development of the entire human family.* If 80 percent of the members of our species are poor, we can not hope to live in a world at peace; if the poor nations attempt to improve their lot by the methods we rich have pioneered, the result will eventually be world ecological damage.

This consciousness will not be attained simply because the arguments for change are good or because the alternatives are unpleasant. Nor will exhortation suffice. The central lesson of realistic policy making is that most individuals and organizations change when it is in their interest to change, either because they derive some benefit from changing or because they incur sanctions when they do not—and the shorter the time between change (or failure to change) and benefit (or sanction), the better. This is not mere cynicism. Although people will struggle and suffer for long periods to achieve a goal, it is not reasonable to expect people or organizations to work against their immediate interests for very long—particularly in a democratic system, where what they perceive to be their interests are so important in guiding the government.

To change interests, three things are required. First, a clear set of values consistent with the consciousness of sustainability must be articulated by leaders in both the public and the private sectors. Next, motivations need to be established that will support the values. Finally, institutions must be developed that will effectively apply the motivations. The first is relatively easy, the second much harder and the third perhaps hardest of all.

Values similar to those I described above have indeed been articulated by political leaders throughout the world. In the past year the president and the secretary of state of the U.S., the leader of the Soviet Union, the prime minister of Great Britain and the presidents of France and Brazil have all made major environmental statements. In July the leaders of the Group of Seven major industrialized nations called for "the early adoption, worldwide, of policies based on sustainable development." Most industrialized nations have a structure of national environmental law that to at least some extent reflects such values, and there is even a small set of international conventions that begin to do the same thing.

Mere acceptance of a changed value structure, although it is a prerequisite, does not generate the required change in consciousness, nor does it change the environment. Although diplomats and lawyers may argue passionately over the form of words, talk is not action. In the U.S., which has a set of environmental statutes second to none in their stringency, and where for the past 15 years poll after poll has recorded the American people's desire for increased environmental protection, the majority of the population participates in the industrialized world's most wasteful and most polluting style of life. The values are there; the appropriate motivations and institutions are patently inadequate or nonexistent.

The difficulties of moving from stated values to actual motivations and institutions stem from basic characteristics of the major industrialized nations—the nations that must, because of their economic strength, preeminence as polluters, and dominant share of the world's resources, take the lead in any changing of the present order. These nations are market-system democracies. The difficulties, ironically, are inherent in the free-market economic system on the one hand and in democracy on the other.

The economic problem is the familiar one of externalities: the environmental cost of producing a good or service is not accounted for in the price paid for it. As the economist Kenneth E. Boulding has put it: "All of nature's systems are closed loops, while economic activities are linear and assume inexhaustible resources and 'sinks' in which to throw away our refuse." In willful ignorance, and in violation of the core principle of capitalism, we often refuse to treat environmental resources as capital. We spend them as income and are as befuddled as any profligate heir when our checks start to bounce.

Such "commons" as the atmosphere, the seas, fisheries and goods in public ownership are particularly vulnerable to being overspent in this way, treated as either inexhaustible resources or bottomless sinks. The reason is that the incremental benefit to each user accrues exclusively to that user, and in the short term it is a gain. The environmental degradation is spread out among all users and is apparent only in the long term, when the resource shows signs of severe stress or collapse. Some years ago the biologist Garrett Hardin called this the tragedy of the commons.

The way to avoid the tragedy of the commons—to make people pay the full cost of a resource use—is to close the loops in economic systems. The general failure to do this in the industrialized world is related to the second problem, the problem of action in a democracy. Modifying the market to reflect environmental costs is necessarily a function of government. Those adversely affected by such modifications, although they may be a tiny minority of the population, often have disproportionate influence on public policy. In general, the much injured minority proves to be a more formidable lobbyist than the slightly benefited majority.

The Clean Air Act of 1970 in the U.S., arguably the most expensive and far-reaching environmental legislation in the world, is a case in point. Parts of the act were designed not so much to cleanse the air as to protect the jobs of coal miners in high-sulfur coal regions. Utilities and other high-volume consumers were not allowed to substitute low-sulfur coal to meet regulatory requirements but instead had to install scrubbing devices.

Although the act expired seven years ago, Congress found it extraordinarily difficult to develop a revision, largely because of another set of contrary interests involving acid rain. The generalized national interest in reducing the environmental damage attributable to this long-range pollution had to overcome the resistance of both high-sulfur-coal mining interests and the Midwestern utilities that would incur major expenses if they were forced to control sulfur emissions. The problem of conflicting interests is exacerbated by the distance between major sources of acid rain and the regions that suffer the most damage. It is accentuated when the pollution crosses state and national boundaries: elected representatives are less likely to countenance short-term adverse effects on their constituents when the immediate beneficiaries are nonconstituents.

The question, then, is whether the industrial democracies will be able to overcome political constraints on bending the market system toward long-term sustainability. History provides some cause for optimism: a number of contingencies have led nations to accept short-term burdens in order to meet a long-term goal.

War is the obvious example. Things considered politically or economically impossible can be accomplished in a remarkably short time, given the belief that national survival is at stake. World War II mobilized the U.S. population, changed work patterns, manipulated and controlled the price and supply of goods and reorganized the nation's industrial plant.

Another example is the Marshall Plan for reconstructing Europe after World War II. In 1947 the U.S. spent nearly 3 percent of its gross domestic product on this huge set of projects. Although the impetus for the plan came from fear that Soviet influence would expand into Western Europe, the plan did establish a precedent for massive investment in increasing the prosperity of foreign nations.

There are other examples. Feudalism was abandoned in Japan, as was slavery in the U.S., in the 19th century; this century has seen the retreat of imperialism and the creation of the European Economic Community. In each case important interests gave way to new national goals.

If it is possible to change, how do we begin to motivate change? Clearly, government policy must lead the way, since market prices of commodities typically do not reflect the environmental costs of extracting and replacing them, nor do the prices of energy from fossil fuels reflect the risks of climatic change. Pricing policy is the most direct means of ensuring that the full environmental cost of goods and services is accounted for. When government owns a resource, or supplies it directly, the price charged can be made to reflect the true cost of the product. The market will adjust to this as it does to true scarcity: by product substitution and conservation.

Environmental regulation should be refocused to mobilize rather than suppress the ingenuity and creativity of industry. For example, additional gains in pollution control should be sought not simply by increasing the stringency or technical specificity of command-and-control regulation but also by implementing incentive-based systems. Such systems magnify public-sector decisions by tens of thousands of individual and corporate decisions. To be sure, incentive systems are not a panacea. For some environmental problems, such as the use of unacceptably dangerous chemicals, definitive regulatory measures will always be required. Effective policies will include a mixture of incentive-based and regulatory approaches.

Yet market-based approaches will be a necessary part of any attempt to reduce the greenhouse effect. Here the most attractive options involve the encouragement of energy efficiency. Improving efficiency meets the double-benefit standard of insurance: it is good in itself, and it combats global warming by reducing carbon dioxide emissions. If the world were to improve energy efficiency by 2 percent a year, the global average temperature could be kept within one degree Celsius of present levels. Many industrialized nations have maintained a rate of improvement close to that over the past 15 years.

Promoting energy efficiency is also relatively painless. The U.S. reduced the energy intensity of its domestic product by 23 percent between 1973 and 1985 without much notice. Substantial improvement in efficiency is available even with existing technology. Something as simple as bringing all U.S. buildings up to the best world standards could save enormous amounts of energy. Right now more energy passes through the windows of buildings in the U.S. than flows through the Alaska pipeline.

Efficiency gains may nevertheless have to be promoted by special market incentives, because energy prices tend to lag behind increases in income. A "climate protection" tax of $1 per million Btu's on coal and 60 cents per million Btu's on oil is an example of such an incentive. It would raise gasoline prices by 11 cents a gallon and the cost of electricity an average of 10 percent, and it would yield $53 billion annually.

Direct regulation by the setting of standards is cumbersome, but it may be necessary when implicit market signals are not effective. Examples are the mileage standards set in the U.S. for automobiles and the efficiency standards for appliances that were adopted in 1986. The appliance standards will save $28 billion in energy costs by the year 2000 and keep 342 million tons of carbon out of the atmosphere.

Over the long term it is likely that some form of emissions-trading program will be necessary—and on a much larger scale than has been the case heretofore. (Indeed, the President's new Clean Air Act proposal includes a strengthened system of tradeable permits.) In such a program all major emitters of pollutants would be issued permits specifying an allowable emission level. Firms that decide to reduce emissions below the specified level—for example, by investing in efficiency—could sell their excess "pollution rights" to other firms. Those that find it prohibitively costly to retrofit old plants or build new ones could buy such rights or could close down their least efficient plants and sell the unneeded rights.

Another kind of emissions trading might reduce the impact of carbon dioxide emissions. Companies responsible for new greenhouse-gas emissions could be required to offset them by improving overall efficiency or closing down plants, or by planting or preserving forests that would help absorb the emissions. Once the system is established, progress toward further reduction of emissions would be achieved by progressively cranking down the total allowable levels of various pollutants, on both a national and a permit-by-permit basis.

The kinds of programs I have just described will need to be supported by research providing a scientific basis for new environmental-protection strategies. Research into safe, nonpolluting energy sources and more energy-efficient technologies would seem to be particularly good bets. An example: in the mid-1970's the U.S. Department of Energy developed a number of improved-efficiency technologies at a cost of $16 million; among them were a design for compact fluorescent lamps that could replace incandescent bulbs, and window coatings that save energy during both heating and cooling seasons. At current rates of implementation, the new technologies should generate $63 billion in energy savings by the year 2010.

The motivation of change toward sustainability will have to go far beyond the reduction of pollution and waste in the developed countries, and it cannot be left entirely to the environmental agencies in those countries. The agencies whose goals are economic development, exploitation of resources, and international trade—and indeed foreign policy in general—must also adopt sustainable development as a central goal. This is a formidable challenge, for it touches the heart of numerous special interests. Considerable political skill will be required to achieve for environmental protection the policy preeminence that only economic issues and national security (in the military sense) have commanded.

But it is in relations with the developing world that the industrialized nations will face their greatest challenges. Aid is both an answer and a perpetual problem. Total official development assistance from the developed to the developing world stands at around $35 billion a year. This is not much money. The annual foreign-aid expenditure of the U.S. alone would be $127 billion if it spent the same proportion of its gross national product on foreign aid as it did during the peak years of the Marshall Plan.

There is no point, of course, in even thinking about the adequacy of aid to the undeveloped nations until the debt issue is resolved. The World Bank has reported that in 1988 the 17 most indebted countries paid the industrialized nations and multilateral agencies $31.1 billion more than they received in aid. This obviously cannot go on. Debt-for-nature swapping has taken place between such major lenders as Citicorp and a number of countries in South America: the bank forgives loans in exchange for the placing of land in conservation areas or parks. This is admirable, but it will not in itself solve the problem. Basic international trading relations will have to be redesigned in order to eliminate, among other things, the ill effects on the undeveloped world of agricultural subsidies and tariff barriers in the industrialized world.

A prosperous rural society based on sustainable agriculture must be the prelude to future development in much of the developing world, and governments there will have to focus on what motivates people to live in an environmentally responsible manner. Farmers will not grow crops when governments subsidize urban populations by keeping prices to farmers low. People will not stop having too many children if the labor of children is the only economic asset they have. Farmers will not improve the land if they do not own it; it is clear that land-tenure reform will have to be instituted.

Negative sanctions against abusing the environment are also missing throughout much of the undeveloped world; to help remedy this situation, substantial amounts of foreign aid could be focused directly on improving the status of the environmental ministries in developing nations. These ministries are typically impoverished and ineffective, particularly in comparison with their countries' economic-development and military ministries. To cite one small example: the game wardens of Tanzania receive an annual salary equivalent to the price paid to poachers for two elephant tusks—one reason the nation has lost two-thirds of its elephant population to the ivory trade in the past decade.

To articulate the values and devise the motivations favoring a sustainable world economy, existing institutions will need to change and new ones will have to be established. These will be difficult tasks, because institutions are powerful to the extent that they support powerful interests—which usually implies support of the status quo.

The important international institutions in today's world are those concerned with money, with trade, and with national defense. Those who despair of environmental concerns ever reaching a comparable level of importance should remember that current institutions (for example, NATO, the World Bank, multinational corporations) have fairly short histories. They were formed out of pressing concerns about acquiring and expanding wealth and maintaining national sovereignty. If concern for the environment becomes comparably pressing, comparable institutions will be developed.

To further this goal, three things are wanted. The first is money. The annual budget of the United Nations Environment Program (UNEP) is $30 million, a derisory amount considering its responsibilities. If nations are serious about sustainability, they will provide this central environmental organization with serious money, preferably money derived from an independent source in order to reduce its political vulnerability. A tax on certain uses of common world resources has been suggested as a means to this end.

The second thing wanted is information. We require strong international institutions to collect, analyze and report on environmental trends and risks. The Earthwatch program run by the UNEP is

a beginning, but there is need for an authoritative source of scientific information and advice that is independent of national governments. There are many nongovernmental or quasi-governmental organizations capable of filling this role; they need to be pulled together into a cooperative network. We need a global institution capable of answering questions of global importance.

The third thing wanted is integration of effort. The world cannot afford a multiplication of conflicting efforts to solve common problems. On the aid front in particular, this can be tragically absurd: Africa alone is currently served by 82 international donors and more than 1,700 private organizations. In 1980, in the tiny African nation Burkina Faso (population about eight million) 340 independent aid projects were under way. We need to form and strengthen coordinating institutions that combine the separate strengths of nongovernmental organizations, international bodies, and industrial groups and to focus their efforts on specific problems.

Finally, in creating the consciousness of advanced sustainability, we shall have to redefine our concepts of political and economic feasibility. These concepts are, after all, simply human constructs; they were different in the past, and they will surely change in the future. But the earth is real, and we are obliged by the fact of our utter dependence on it to listen more closely than we have to its messages.

Note

Ruckelshaus acknowledges the major contribution of Michael A. Gruber, a senior policy analyst at the E.P.A., in the preparation of his article.

Measures of Economic and Ecological Health _____

Bruce Hannon

To my unreasoned envy, economists have an organizing device for their professional activities upon which they nearly all agree. Most economists agree that the total consumption in an economy

should be maximized (Sagoff 1988). Of course, there are restraints on the growth of the consumption rate such as the supply rates of labor and natural resources. So the constrained rate of growth of

Ecosystem Health: New Goals for Environmental Management, edited by Robert Costanza, Bryan G. Norton, and Benjamin D. Haskell (Washington, DC: Island Press, 1992), pp. 207–222. Reprinted by permission of the publisher.

consumption approaches the "golden" level when full employment is nearly reached, profits are being maximized by resource holders, and the rate of technical progress is steady. The growth rate is thus limited by the birth rate, the rate of discovery of new natural resources, and the rate of technical progress. All three rates are usually taken as given. They have forged this wonderfully consistent story of how the economy works (or should work) over the last century. Economists contend over the means to achieve maximum rates of consumption, but they agree on the general goal. By virtue of the detail behind the total consumption number, economists are able to argue rather consistently about the effects that certain proposed changes will have on this total.

I envy the economists even though I know that their story is incorrect. Their story does not count the environmental and social calamity that our focus on consumption has caused. The costs of this calamity should be counted into the costs of production, say the economists: these costs are simply externalities whose costs must be internalized. But what is the cost of a forest gone or a community disbanded? Who is there to remember and to count these costs and who will "put" them into the cost of someone else's production?

Nevertheless, the focus of the economists on a single goal to which they largely agree should be very instructive to ecologists. That focus has bathed them in public appreciation and professional success. They claim that this goal is the measure of economic health. It is my purpose here to show ecologists how they too can devise a somewhat similar measure of ecosystem health, but one that avoids some of the more blatant pitfalls of the economic analog.

If you ask ecosystem managers about the goal toward which they manage the system under their control, they might say that they strive to stabilize the system with the least human input possible. This is their measure of ecosystem health. They could measure the principal stocks in that ecosystem and consider their management a success if these stocks would cycle through the same levels in years in which the main external inputs (such as rain) are at typical levels and return to these cycles after an unusual year of inputs. Or they might say that they manage their systems to maximize duck or bass or deer or tree production for the special interests supporting their agencies' programs. Or they might manage their systems to conform to the aesthetic ideals of the foundation that pays their salaries. The system managers might also be ecological historians who wish to restore their systems to their ideas of what these systems were like in prehuman times.

In the broadest sense, these are all measures of ecosystem health. But there are possibly several, if not many, stable states for an ecosystem depending at least on the level and kind of management input (see, for example, May 1977 and Schaeffer 1990.) The management of an ecosystem to maximize the production of a single species is liable to end up sacrificing other species and bring the system to an unstable state. Management for aesthetic reasons is a fickle master as these reasons change when the controlling people die or grow tired of their view. The ecological historians usually cannot determine what the original system was really like and thus sometimes resort to trying to restore the system to the earliest recorded form. If they wish to restore river ecosystems to their original forms but have only anecdotal evidence, for example, they may strive to restore the river to the form they see in the earliest aerial photos (earliest possible: 1930s).

Ecologists need a consistent focus for their idea of ecosystem health, a focus on which most of them come to agree. They must work to achieve consensus on that focus and embed that goal in national and local policymaking. I want to propose a candidate for that goal. It is fashioned after the economist's view of the economic system with an attempt to avoid its pitfalls.

Economic Health Measures

Economists refer to the total consumption of the nation by the general term of "national output" or, in the terms of this essay, "net output." The net output of a modern economy is somewhat arbitrarily but officially defined as the amount of personal and government consumption (cars, food, highways, defense, and so forth), plus the amount of net export of goods and services, plus the amount of new capital formed (investment for expansion and replacement), plus any changes in the inventory of goods, all in a given time period. When taken as an annual sum, this amount is called the gross national product or GNP. The GNP is a flow, not a stock, and it is measured in dollars per year.[1]

All the physical units of things we bought as consumers, the things bought by the government, the exported goods (such as computers) less the imported goods (such as oil), the amount of new capital stock purchased (such as machinery and buildings), the increases in the inventory stocks (such as mined coal), for example, less the decreases of these sorts of stocks (such as unsold cars), are multiplied by their respective prices. This multiplication converts the diverse types of these physical things into a single unit of measure and they can be added together to form the GNP (Peterson 1962).

There is an alternative definition of the same number. The GNP is also the sum of all salaries and wages, plus the sum of all taxes paid, plus the sum of all profits, dividends, and interest payments, plus the total depreciation of capital stocks. When these items are in equivalent monetary units, they too can be added together to give the same dollar value as the GNP. This list is sometimes referred to as the "value added," or in our terms the "net input" to the economy.

So the economists view the economic system as having a set of net inputs and a set of net outputs, the total dollar value of each being equal. They recognize that the value of the input of steel to auto production and the total value of the output of autos are not meaningful measures of the aggregate behavior of the economy. For example, only the value of the steel sold for export or directly to consumers should be counted in the determination of overall economic activity. The dollar value of the steel used by autos will be incorporated into the value of autos. Not all autos are sold to consumers. Some autos are sold to other industries, and the value of those autos is incorporated into the value of the output of the purchasing industries. Therefore, the net output is made up of these net values to the defined targets, and the net inputs are the payments required to obtain the services of the agents who are defined as the net output consumers.

If the GNP is high, inflation fears aside, the economy is thought of as being more *healthy* than when the GNP is low or negative. The GNP's value (or changes in its value) is related to the amount of overall employment and total capital expansion.

These connections are part of the basis on which economic and social welfare policy decisions are made at the national level.

There is a school of thought in economics which argues that only such macropolicy should be made: the details of the needed changes at the corporate and individual level should be worked out by market interactions. A contending school proposes that more government concern should be directed at the corporate and individual levels. The GNP might be growing while segments of the population are losing their jobs, even though total employment is rising. The economy must also be regulated at the detailed level. The economic positivists contend with the regulators. No doubt both schools have something to contribute, but my point is that the whole question of an appropriate measure of economic health is somewhat unsettled. Both schools would probably argue that GNP growth is at least a necessary, if not sufficient, condition for a healthy economy, much to the frustration of many environmentalists.

Every item sold in the economy has a distribution of unit values or prices in any given period. The variation of prices depends largely on how tightly the item is defined ("automobiles" vs. "Ford Escort, two door, smallest available engine"). Price changes in an economy are not generally thought of as measures of economic health. In some cases, however, changes in prices that are unrelated to changes in the nature of the product, termed "inflation" or "deflation," are thought of as health measures. Inflation is thought to be controllable from a central authority (the Federal Reserve) by control of the supply of money (the interbank loan rate, the money printing rate, and so on). Price control is largely achieved through indirect control of the discount rate: the interbank premium charged by lenders. Trends in the discount rate, the time value of money, are thought of in some sense as indicative of economic health. Inflation and deflation are thought by economists to be accurately reflected in the discount rate, along with consumer impatience and uncertainty.

Through various optimization models, used in conjunction with the structure and detail mentioned above, economists are able to make predictions about the effect that certain proposed actions will have on the GNP. Most economists who follow such approaches agree on the nature of the approach. Usually, controversy is confined to the accuracy of the parameters used in such an analysis. Economic policy can arise by rough consensus among economists over the nature and impact of various proposals. Such consensus allows them to agree on recommendations to those who manage the political forces in the nation. Such recommendations may not be accepted for a variety of reasons, including the reason that the analysis was not sufficiently inclusive of certain social or ecological factors. The economists then try to correct their analytic approach and evaluate the criticisms. This process has been going on for more than a century, and today economists as a profession have a major influence on policymaking around the world. A basic reason for this success is their agreement on a single unifying measure of economic health, one that is underpinned by an explanatory and predictive body of economic theory which is being constantly applied, challenged, and refined.

Nevertheless, there have been many criticisms of the GNP measure of economic health. (See, for example, American Academy of Political Science 1967; Nordhaus and Tobin 1972; Zolotas 1981; Daly and Cobb 1989.) I recount here the few that seem to highlight the major problems.

If a homemaker becomes a member of the industrial-commercial work force, the new salary becomes part of the GNP. This is an appropriate event if the new job is created in response to a needed expansion of the work force. But suppose that the new salary is spent on home and child care workers, jobs that the former homemaker was doing without pay. These wages then become part of the GNP. Both before and after the new employment, the same jobs were being done at the home site, but now the GNP has grown.

Health care expenditures are also included in the GNP. Suppose that an expanded need for health care comes from exposure to pollutants that have increased chronic disease. Job attendance would drop, but assume that the cost of production would not increase. Assume further that the decreased workplace attendance is not severe enough to result in decreased wages. The resulting effect is an increase in GNP associated with pollution-bred disease, not a desirable outcome. In fact, we are saying that decreased human health equates to increased (or unchanged) economic health. Increases in crime result in increased local law enforcement

expenditures that increase the GNP, provided that the needed increase in taxes does not reduce personal consumption to an offsetting degree. The result may be GNP growth proportional to a growth in the crime rate. Or take this final example: the decrease in the stocks of finite natural resources due to consumption rates that exceed discovery rates, such as those for oil, iron ore, and fertile soil, are not included in the GNP. Yet these resource inventory changes are very similar to the standard measures that are part of the GNP.

Daly and Cobb (1989) provide the most modern set of corrections to the GNP, including income inequities, ownership of capital, and environmental damage to cultural and natural stocks. The problem becomes one of finding an objective measuring scale for these concepts. From the standard GNP definition, one can see that an attempt is made to include the depreciation of capital in the net input and in the net output of the economy. The replacement capital is easy to include with relative accuracy in the net output or GNP. It is an unspecified part of the gross investment for the economy. But the actual number included in the net input is the depreciated capital as reported by business. This number includes estimates of financial depreciation (perhaps due to a newly invented machine that produces a less costly product) and dollar values of depreciation that are allowed by specific legislation (to help offset taxes or production costs). These measures may be somewhat unrelated to the physical depreciation, the desired addition to the net input measure.

Is the definition of the GNP a thoroughly good one? No. But the usual conclusion is that the definition could be mended to count a little more here and a little less there, resulting in a meaningful indicator of economic health. Yet there are more general criticisms. The economic basis for the GNP is consumption: more consumption is equated to an increase in economic health. Even if natural resources were infinitely abundant and pollution were not a problem, is there no limit to the possible improvement in economic health? We might try to define an optimal limit to per capita consumption, with restraints on the inequality of distribution across the population. Would there then be no limit on how many people should participate in the economy? Does per capita space become the limiting factor on the growth of total economic health?

These questions seem unanswerable because we see our destiny in our own hands, under our own control. We assume that an attitude of continued economic growth is an appropriate policy aim and, because we are in control of Spaceship Earth, we will know when to shift to a more appropriate goal. But there clearly are such things as finite natural resources, and limited and unjust distribution of income and space—things apparently, to some extent, beyond our control. Can we look to the ecologists to find more appropriate measures of economic health?

Ecosystem Health Measures

The control of the economy is a subjective enterprise because the generally accepted measures of economic health are ultimately subjective. When we look at another system, the ecosystem, one that we tend to observe from outside, can we in fact measure that system's health less subjectively? The measures of the economic system cited earlier can be used as a guide. Imperfect as it seems, the economic system measures are the result of a great deal of effort over centuries by some of the best minds in economics. Perhaps a measure of ecosystem health can be found that, by reverse analogy, will reduce the subjectivity of the measures of economic health. As outside observers of the ecosystem, we might assign more objectivity to any conclusions we reach from our observations.

A more difficult problem lies with the ecologists. To gain consensus on a measure of ecological health, they must assume that an ecosystem somehow behaves as though it has a goal or an optimal state. At some reasonable level of aggregation, the ecosystem has what seems to be a preferred state, just as the human body seems to have. Disturbances ("disease") are short-term perturbations that the system tries to eliminate and then return to its optimal state. This assumption alone would require a very great leap—too subjective a move for many ecologists. But I see no alternative to it. If we do not accept the idea of a goal or accept at least the possibility, we are open to the accusation that ecologists are arrogant with regard to nature and can manipulate its processes for the will of humankind without risk of ultimate failure. Dismissal of the possibility of the actual existence of such a goal is unscientific. We must assume first that there

is some internal goal for the development of an ecosystem, some description of optimal health. Through a combination of theory and experimentation on specific ecosystems, we should be able to discern if the growth of an ecosystem conforms to predictions based on hypotheses about the goals of growth. Eventually we should be able to describe the existence and nature of any internal goals.[2] If we can describe those goals, we then have a basis that most ecologists would likely agree is the management basis for ecosystems. In an effort to capture the general system experience of economists and demonstrate the utility of a single ecosystem goal or health measure, I now propose the ecological equivalent of the GNP. (Similar measures proposed by others are discussed later.)

The components of an ecosystem—producers, herbivores, carnivores, decomposers, and the like—can be arranged into an economic-like accounting framework (Hannon, Costanza, and Ulanowicz 1991) with interconnecting flows: herbivores eat producers, carnivores eat herbivores. All components give off heat in the process of using their inputs, and the producers absorb sunlight (among other abiotic substances). A net input and a net output can be defined for an ecosystem. Based on these net flows, a set of system-wide indicators or ecosystem "prices" can be derived (Hannon, Costanza, and Herendeen 1986). The concept of discount rates can also be defined for the ecosystem (Hannon 1984). The end result of such an approach is a view of the ecological system that is parallel to the economist's view of the economic system. Such congruency is useful if the two systems are ever going to be meaningfully combined into the same framework.

The first step in deriving a measure of ecosystem health is to define precisely what is meant by net ecosystem output. These net outputs should include the net exports of biomass and any abiotic substances, and the gross additions to stocks. But what is the ecological parallel to personal and government consumption? Return to the economic framework for a moment. Imagine an isolated economy at steady state. The imports and exports are zero and gross capital formation is entirely used to replace worn-out capital. Suppose further that inventory changes are negligible. The only contributions to the GNP would then be the consumption by people and government and the rate of capital replacement. Some have argued that consumers and government are simply producing-consuming sectors in the production economy, similar to any other industrial-commercial sector (Costanza 1980; Costanza and Herendeen 1984). Consumers supply labor and use housing, food, clothing, transportation, education, and so forth to do so. Governments consume in order to direct and control. Technically, these two sectors can be considered part of the industrial exchange pattern and removed from direct involvement in the GNP measure. In our closed steady-state economy, the only GNP measure would then be the capital replacement rate.

With the consumption sectors removed from the net output, some of the earlier criticisms of the GNP measure would vanish. Crime, health care, and homemaker's labor are considered costs of production of household or government services. By analogy, this reduced GNP definition can be matched in the net output definition for an ecosystem. We have no reason to put any particular species or trophic level in the special position of being a component of net output. To the now "objective" human observer, no species or trophic level seems more important than another. The ecosystem net output for a given period can, therefore, be defined as the net exports and the gross changes in each of the stocks. For the closed steady-state ecosystem, the only net output is the replacement rate of the stocks, making up the losses caused by metabolism and decomposition. This replacement rate is exactly analogous to the capital replacement rate used by economists.

Analogous to the net inputs to the economy (wages, taxes, profits, and so on) is a list of net inputs to the ecosystem. Think of these net ecosystem inputs as necessary for the production of the ecosystem's net output. Among the various forms of net input to a particular ecosystem, such as nitrogen, phosphorus, or sunlight, one of them is generally limiting the size of the system. Assume that the limiting net input is sunlight. With the list of absorbed sunlight quantities, a set of ecosystem sunlight "prices" can be calculated. This set of prices can be multiplied with the associated terms in the net output. The now commensurate result can be summed to give an evaluated net output of the ecosystem under study. This evaluated output is analogous to the redefined GNP: it captures all the activities in the ecosystem, in a weighted man-

ner, and gathers them into a single number. That number—the gross ecosystem product (GEP)—is a viable candidate for aggregate ecosystem health. But the GEP is not a wholly adequate measure, for the GEP, like the GNP, cannot increase forever. We will return to this problem later.

As an application of this ecosystem health measure, the ecosystem input (GEP) was evaluated for two tidal marshes. One of the marshes existed under natural conditions; the other was elevated on average 6°C by the waste heat from an electricity-generating station (Hannon 1985). The net output was evaluated for seventeen biotic sectors of both marshes in terms of absorbed sunlight energy. The evaluated net output of the heated marsh was 33 percent lower than the same measure for the natural marsh. This comparison of systems, however, is the only one of its kind. The comparison is based on a detailed exchange between all the components in the companion marsh ecosystems, a rare combination of ecoscience and research support. This study demonstrates the manner in which the GEP indicates ecosystem health: both marshes are probably close to the steady-state, but the unheated one has a higher GEP. This comparison also reiterates the fact that my favorite measure of ecosystem and economic health is based directly on system flows, not on stocks.

We turn now to other measures of ecosystem health. David J. Rapport (1984) gives five indicators of ecosystem stress: rapid nutrient loss, decline in primary productivity, diminishing size distribution and diversity, and system retrogression (toward early stages). He notes that, in general, such system-wide indicators appear late in the breakdown process and that species-directed fieldwork is needed to provide early warnings (as in the case of Herring Gulls and DDT). These indicators have the advantage that data for them can be easily obtained, but they lack the utility of a single quantitative measure. To varying degrees, the evaluated net output measure captures the ecosystem changes of which Rapport speaks.

James R. Karr (1991) has defined the Index of Biotic Integrity (IBI), which is the sum of the "scores" given each of 12 measurable attributes for an ecosystem. The independence of the various attributes and the completeness of the set of twelve is not seriously questioned. The relative weightings given the attributes are somewhat arbitrary, however, especially if some of them are interrelated. Such measures, based on good intention and sound ecological judgment, may have as their chief asset the fact that they can be easily measured. But the same fate awaits them as has undercut the additional measures proposed for the GNP—that is, the quantitative arbitrariness of each attribute sinks it into controversy.

The ecological health measures of Rapport and Karr are useful in rating or comparing ecosystems. The rated set of ecosystems can augment environmental policy by showing which streams, for example, should be left alone and which might require pollution control. This *a posteriori* form of reasoning, however, does not allow one to indicate the probable outcome of a proposed change to an ecosystem. For such predictive purposes, a model of the ecosystem is needed, preferably dynamic and most likely nonlinear. The first predictive modeling steps, however, can be taken with comparative statics (Hannon and Joiris 1989). The economists have struggled for a long time to provide such a model for economic forecasting. Ecologists are still centered on the idea of an empirical set of ecosystem indicators.

Conclusion

Rapport's view of size diminishment and reversion to a juvenile state are effects that are also captured in the time-value measures of a dynamic system. Ulanowicz and Hannon (1987) point out that the "discount" or "interest" rate of an ecological system captures both the average metabolic rate and the average specific energy content for the living members of the system. Hannon (1990) argues that this rate is both the average and marginal rate of specific metabolism[3] for the living elements in a steady-state ecosystem. He further argues that the steady-state evaluation would reveal the lowest discount rate ever experienced in the development of that ecosystem. It is well known that larger species have smaller specific metabolic rates compared to the physically smaller species. One very general way that the average metabolic rate of an ecosystem becomes smaller is for large individuals to displace the smaller ones.

Climax species seem to have been selected as the least maintenance-requiring in order to store the most order in the climax ecosystem. If this size

shift is assumed to be a goal of the system, an additional constraint on the gross ecosystem product measure is required. The GEP should increase continually but less and less rapidly until it becomes steady. At that point, the system has the largest GEP and the smallest discount rate possible. The combined requirement ensures that the low entropy retained in the system is maximized. If the principal low-entropy input to the ecosystem is sunlight, the optimal system would be storing the most converted sunlight possible.

Thus, we have two indicators of ecosystem health: increasing net output of the ecosystem (GEP), albeit at slower and slower rates, and a decreasing aggregate discount rate. We have no good ecosystem measure of the discount rate, however, except perhaps at the climax or steady state. But some constraint on the GEP is needed, for it clearly cannot increase forever. The decreasing discount rate concept does tell us that the maturing ecosystem will need increasing amounts of biomass whose unit or specific metabolism is increasingly lower. This is usually the case with the introduction of species with larger members, as Rapport has noted. Therefore, if the larger species are disappearing from an ecosystem, its measured discount rate would be rising.

The flow of low entropy from the external environment puts a cap on the size and therefore the GEP for the aggregate ecosystem.[4] How does such a view translate back to evaluation of the economic system? Were it not for our discoveries of metallic ores and the stored energy in fossil and nuclear fuels, identical rules would apply for the optimal growth and ultimate climax level of the economic system. But profitable access to vast quantities of stored low entropy allows the economic system to grow well beyond its agrarian bounds. The GNP, by the standard or by any of the modified measures, is much larger than it would have been without the discovery and use of these vast stores.[5] The average GNP per capita and the total population are both likely to exceed the agrarian bounds. The ecosystem GEP is diminished by the GNP. The GNP and the GEP are competing measures until we can somehow learn to incorporate the economy into the ecological framework.

Are we faced with two indicators of economic health? One indicator is based on continued GNP growth. To use this measure, the known low-entropy stores of the earth must be increased. The net growth in the stores of proved low-entropy energy reserves (discovery rate greater than consumption rate) is then the best short-term indicator of economic health. In the long run, these reserves will be reduced to levels that are not economical to extract. Then the economy will tend toward the agrarian bound—but from above, rather than from below. We will be required to reduce our GNP per capita and probably our population to comply with the solar constraint. Such a change is unprecedented in recorded world history, except perhaps for Ireland. The change would be accompanied by a trauma proportional to the difference between the present level of population and GNP, the ones set by the solar constraint and the time available for the transition. What are the GNP and population level for the agrarian world? The difference between these calculated limits and the current values is a second long-term economic measure of health.

We may rest content with the idea of the incompatibility of the economic and the ecological systems and their GNP and GEP "health" measures described here. The economic system's description with its prices and production measures seems pertinent to human purposes, but ecological processes may be proceeding toward a different and as yet unknown goal.

We may want to push the concept further and try to combine these two net output measures in a single indicator of system health. It has been suggested (Isard 1968; Daly 1968; Hannon et al. 1991) that it is possible to place all economic and ecological transactions in the same matrix or accounting framework. Such a framework would contain the intereconomic and the interecological transactions. It would also have to contain all the important transactions between the economic and ecological systems. The net inputs and outputs of the combined system must be in consistent units of measure. This requirement simply means that the units of measure for each row of the transactions (from the row of steel production to the column of auto production, for example) must be the same (say dollars). The requirement of identical units of measure for all the exchanges in a given row means that the inputs to the ecosystem of pollution by the steel industry (say SO_2) must be collected in a special column, the row version of which is the tons of SO_2

absorbed by the various parts of the ecosystem. Likewise, the inputs to the economic system must be measured in consistent units. The wood, for example, harvested from the nation's forests and used in the various manufacturing industries and in the ecological system could be measured in tons of carbon.

To make the net output of the combined system sum to a single meaningful number, a set of system-wide prices must be devised. As we saw with the ecological system, to calculate this set of prices, we must first decide on the limiting net input to the combined system. Is it labor or energy, for example? If such a critical input can be identified, the system-wide prices can be calculated and multiplied times the net outputs, changing each of the net output entries into commensurate units. The sum of these converted net outputs is the evaluated net output of the combined system. It is a single measure of the "health" of the combined system. It is a measure that would show the net effect of pure economic growth combined with ecological decline: the combined measure may reveal a decline while the economic measure shows an increase.

One of the problems with this combined net output approach is data. We simply do not know all the ways in which the economy has an impact on the ecosystem (such as the effect of organic chemical air releases on fish) nor all the ways in which the ecosystem provides free services to the economy (such as wind-dispersed pollution). Thus, a combined calculation would probably never be complete. But any step toward combining the two systems, such that the net outputs can be joined in a common measure of system health, is a step in the right direction.

References

American Academy of Political Science. 1967. "Social Goals and Indicators for American Society." *Annals*, Vols. 371, 373.

Costanza, R. 1980. "Embodied Energy and Economic Valuation." *Science* 210:1219–1224.

Costanza, R., and R. Herendeen. 1984. "Embodied Energy and Economic Value in the United States Economy: 1963, 1967 and 1972." *Resources and Energy* 6:129–164.

Daly, H. 1968. "Economics as a Life Science." *Journal of Political Economy* 76:392–401.

Daly, H., and J. Cobb. 1989. *For the Common Good.* Boston: Beacon Press.

Hannon, B. 1984. "Discounting in Ecosystems." In A. M. Jansson (ed.), *Integration of Economy and Ecology—An Outlook of the Eighties.* Stockholm: University of Stockholm.

———. 1985. "Ecosystem Flow Analysis." *Canadian Bulletin of Fisheries and Aquatic Sciences* 213:97–118.

———. 1990. "Biological Time Value." *Mathematical Bioscience.* 100:115–140.

Hannon, B., and C. Joiris. 1989. "A Seasonal Analysis of the Southern North Sea Ecosystem." *Ecology* 70(6):1916–1934.

Hannon, B., R. Costanza, and R. Ulanowicz. 1991. "A General Accounting Framework for Ecological Systems: A Functional Taxonomy for Connectivist Ecology." *Theoretical Population Biology* 40: 78–104.

Hannon, B., R. Costanza, and R. Herendeen. 1986. "Measures of Cost and Value in Ecosystems." *Journal of Environmental Economics and Management* 13:391–401.

Isard, W. 1968. "Some Notes on the Linkage of the Ecologic and Economic System." *Regional Science Association Papers* 22:85–96.

Karr, J. 1991. "Biological Integrity: A Long-Neglected Aspect of Water Resource Management." *Ecological Applications* 1(1):66–84.

May, R. 1977. "Thresholds and Breakpoints in Ecosystems with a Multiplicity of Stable States." *Nature* 269:471–477.

Nordhaus, W., and J. Tobin. 1972. "Is Growth Obsolete?" In *Economic Growth.* National Bureau of Economic Research General Series, no. 96E, New York: Columbia University Press.

Peterson, W. 1962. *Income, Employment and Economic Growth.* New York: Norton.

Rapport, D. 1984. "The Interface of Economics and Ecology." In A. M. Jansson (ed.), *Integration of Economy and Ecology—An Outlook for the Eighties.* Stockholm: University of Stockholm.

Sagoff, M. 1988. *The Economy of the Earth.* New York: Cambridge University Press.

Schaeffer, M. 1990. "Multiplicity of Stable States in Fresh Water Systems." *Hydrobiologica* 200–201:475–486.

Ulanowicz, R., and B. Hannon. 1987. "Life and the Production of Entropy." Proceedings of the Royal Society of London, B 232:181–192.

Zolotas, X. 1981. *Economic Growth and Declining Social Welfare.* New York: New York University Press.

Notes

1. We could consider the value of a country's wealth as a measure of its economic health. Wealth is a stock, however, and terribly hard to measure accurately. Since the physical basis for wealth is largely unmarketed on a regular basis, only vague evaluation can be made.

2. I do not see such an existence assumption as a problem. Children learn the complex procedure of "pumping" their playground swing while the theory to demonstrate such behavior requires Newtonian mechanics and an understanding of energy principles. Engineers long ago proved that complex beam deflection can be exactly predicted from a theory which says that the beam deflects in such a way as to minimize its internal strain energy—and does so without a single course in differential equations or optimization techniques!

3. The rate of respiration per unit of stock respiring; the units are one/time.

4. Perhaps sunlight absorption is the limiting factor, or perhaps sunlight embodied in water is limiting, as in desert ecosystems. Or maybe the limit is set by the rate of phosphorus extraction as is the case with certain aquatic ecosystems.

5. Gaiaists alert! What purpose would Gaia have in creating the vast organic fossil stores?

Earth in the Balance Sheet ——————————————

Robert Repetto

———————————————————————————————————

Whatever their shortcomings, the national income accounting systems used by governments to assess macroeconomic performance are undoubtedly one of the 20th century's most significant social inventions. Their political and economic impacts can scarcely be overestimated. However inappropriately, they serve to divide the world into "developed" and "developing" countries. In the devel-

Environment, Vol. 34, No. 7 (September 1992), 13–18, 43–45. Reprinted with permission of the Helen Dwight Reid Educational Foundation. Published by Heldref Publications, 1319 Eighteenth St., N.W., Washington, DC 20036-1802. Copyright © 1992.

oped countries, whenever the quarterly gross domestic product (GDP) figures emerge, policymakers stir. Should the latest figure be lower, even marginally, than those of the preceding three months, a recession is declared, the strategies and competence of the federal administration are impugned, and public political debate ensues. In the developing countries, the rate of growth of GDP is the principal measure of economic progress and transformation.

National income accounts have become so much a part of society that it is hard to remember that they have been in use for only 50 years: They were first published in the United States in 1942. It is no coincidence that, during the last half century, governments have taken responsibility for the growth and stability of their economies and have invested enormous amounts of talent and energy in understanding how economies can be better managed.

The aim of national income accounting is to provide an information framework suitable for analyzing the performance of a country's economic system. The current System of National Accounts promoted by the United Nations is a historical artifact, heavily influenced by the theories of the British economist John Maynard Keynes in the 1930s.[1] The system reflects the economic preoccupations of that time: the business cycle and persistent unemployment in industrial economies. Because raw material prices were at an all-time low in the 1930s, Keynesian economists paid little attention to the possibility of natural resource scarcities. Consequently, even today, the contribution that natural resources make to production and economic welfare is hardly acknowledged in national income accounts. Capital formation is assigned a central role in economic growth theories, but natural resources are not treated like other tangible assets in the System of National Accounts.

The result is a dangerous asymmetry in the way people measure and, hence, the way they think about the value of natural resources (see Figure 1). Manmade assets, such as buildings and equipment, are valued as productive capital and are written off against the value of production as they depreciate. Natural resource assets are not so valued: A country could exhaust its mineral resources, cut down its forests, erode its soils, pollute its aquifers, and hunt its wildlife and fisheries to extinction without

affecting its measured national income. It is a bitter irony that the low-income countries most dependent on natural resources for employment, revenues, and foreign exchange earnings are instructed to use a system for national accounting and macroeconomic analysis that almost completely ignores their principal assets.

Shortcomings of the System

The System of National Accounts (SNA) published by the United Nations Statistical Office provides a standard, internationally accepted framework for setting up national income accounts.[2] SNA includes stock accounts that identify assets and liabilities at particular points in time and flow accounts that keep track of transactions during intervals of time. Flow accounts include all transactions of final goods that determine the level of national income, or GDP, including capital formation and depreciation, purchases of goods and services, payments to wage and profit earners, and import payments and export revenues for goods and services. Flows and stocks are linked, in that flows are equal to differences between stocks and stocks are equal to accumulated past flows. With a few specific exceptions, only goods and services exchanged in the market economy are included in national income accounts. This is so because market prices offer a ready way to establish value.

National income accounts have become the basis for almost all macroeconomic analysis, planning, and evaluation. SNA is supposed to be an integrated, comprehensive, and consistent accounting framework; unfortunately, however, it is not. SNA gives inconsistent treatment to the consumption of capital goods and natural resources. The value of capital goods, such as buildings and equipment, declines with use because of physical wear and obsolescence. This gradual decrease in the future production potential of capital stocks is directly integrated into national flow accounts by a depreciation allowance that amortizes the asset's value over its useful lifetime. (Depreciation is the decline in the present value of a future income flow because of an asset's decay or obsolescence.) Depreciation of tangible, reproducible capital is subtracted from GDP in calculations of net domestic product. This subtraction reflects the fact that a nation must invest enough in new capital goods to offset the depreciation of existing assets if the future income-producing ability of the entire capital stock is to be preserved.

The United Nations recommends that countries create balance sheet accounts that include some natural resources, such as tree plantations, and nonrenewable resources, such as agricultural land and subsoil minerals, along with financial assets and stocks of capital goods.[3] Rather than integrate changes in natural resource stocks directly into national flow accounts, however, the United Nations recommends that stock accounts of natural resources flow through separate "satellite" or "reconciliation" accounts.[4]

Logically, if a country's national balance sheets indicate at two points in time that a natural resource, such as the forest, has been depleted, the flow accounts for the intervening years should show a capital consumption or depreciation allowance. If the forests have expanded, the accounts should show a corresponding amount of capital formation. This change would reflect perhaps the most basic identity[5] in all of accounting—namely, that the difference in stocks between two points of time equals the net flow in the intervening period. SNA violates this basic accounting identity.

Reconciliation accounts, or accounts that reconcile apparent differences or discrepancies in other accounts, are, however, a poor substitute solution. They provide a means of recording changes in the value of net assets between successive measurement dates without having to show any effect on the income of the intervening period.[6] Recording these changes in reconciliation accounts is likely to minimize their consideration in national policy analysis.

Ironically, SNA does classify as gross capital formation those expenses incurred in "improving" land for pastures, developing or extending timber-producing areas, or creating infrastructure for the fishing industry. SNA records such actions as contributing to recorded income and investment even though they sometimes destroy the income-producing potential of natural resources through deforestation, soil erosion, and overfishing. This loss of capital—as natural resources are used beyond their capacity to recover—is not recorded in national income and investment accounts. The national accounts thereby create the illusion of income development when, in fact, national wealth is being destroyed. Thus, economic disaster masquerades as progress.

Several misunderstandings underlie this anomalous treatment of natural resources. First, it is a misconception that natural resources are so abundant that they have no marginal value. Whether or not they enter the marketplace directly, natural resources make important contributions to long-term economic productivity and so, strictly speaking, are economic assets. Another misunderstanding underlies the contention that natural resources are free gifts of nature, so that there are no investment costs to be written off. The value of an asset is not its investment cost but, rather, the capitalized present value of its income potential. Many companies valued by the stock market to be worth many billions of dollars have as their principal assets the brilliant ideas and inventions of their founders. The Polaroid camera, the Apple computer, and the Lotus spreadsheet are good examples. These inspired inventions are worth vastly more than any measurable cost their inventors incurred in developing them and, as the products of genius, could also be regarded as free gifts of nature.

The UN Statistical Office justifies its treatment of natural resources on the grounds that natural resources are nonmarketed goods and that their economic values cannot be readily established.[7] This notion also is wrong. Indeed, the United Nations itself provides guidelines for valuing natural resource assets in the stock accounts that could be applied just as well to the flow accounts: The assets' market values are to be used if available; if not, the discounted present value of the stream of rents or net revenues from the asset is to be used instead.[8]

The Scope of Natural Resource Accounting

A growing number of experts have recognized the need to correct SNA's environmental blind spots. Several member nations of the Organization for Economic Cooperation and Development, including Canada, France, the Netherlands, Japan, Norway, and the United States, have proposed or established systems of environmental accounts.[9] Although natural resources take priority in the Norwegian and French systems, the U.S. and Japanese systems have focused on pollution and environmental quality. Canada and the Netherlands have combined elements of both approaches.

Norway and France have established extensive resource-accounting systems to supplement their national income accounts. The Norwegian system includes accounts for such material resources as fossil fuels and other minerals, such biotic resources as forests and fisheries, and such environmental resources as land, water, and air.[10] The accounts are compiled in physical units of measurement, such as cubic meters or tons, and are not integrated with the national income accounts. However, resource accounts, especially those for petroleum and gas, have been expressed in monetary terms for use in macroeconomic planning.

The French natural patrimony accounts are intended as a comprehensive statistical framework to provide authorities with the data they need to monitor changes in "that subsystem of the terrestrial ecosphere that can be quantitatively and qualitatively altered by human activity."[11] Like their Norwegian counterparts, these accounts cover nonrenewable resources, the physical environment, and living organisms. Because material and energy flows to and from economic activities form only a subset of these accounts, they are conceptually much broader than the national income accounts.

Compiling such environmental statistics may well encourage decision makers to consider the impacts of specific policies on national stocks of natural resources. Physical accounting by itself has considerable shortcomings, however. For instance, it does not lend itself to useful aggregation: Aggregating wood from various tree species into a single number of cubic meters obscures wide differences in the economic value of different species. Aggregating mineral reserves into a single number of tons obscures vast differences—caused by grade and recovery costs—in the value of deposits. Yet, maintaining separate physical accounts for particular species or deposits yields a mountain of statistics that is not easily summarized or used. A further problem with physical accounting is that such accounts do not enable economic planners to understand the impact of economic policies on natural resources or, thereby, to integrate resource considerations into economic decisions, which presumably is the main point of the exercise. There is, however, no conflict between accounting in physical and economic units because physical accounts are necessary prerequisites to economic accounts. If measurement of economic depreciation is extended to cover natural resources, physical accounts are inevitable by-products.

The limits to monetary valuation of natural resources are set mainly by the remoteness of the resource in question from the market economy. Some resources, such as minerals, enter the marketplace directly. Others, such as groundwater, contribute to market production and can readily be assigned a monetary value even though they are rarely bought or sold. Still others, such as noncommercial wild species, are quite remote from the marketplace in that they do not contribute directly to production and can be assigned a monetary value only through quite roundabout methods involving many questionable assumptions. Although research into the economic value of resources that are remote from the market is to be encouraged, common sense suggests that highly speculative values should not be included in official accounts.

In industrial countries, where pollution and congestion are mounting while economies are becoming less dependent on agriculture, mining, and other forms of primary production, economists have proposed systems of environmental accounting that go well beyond the scope of natural resource accounting. One approach considers how GDP might be modified by the costs and benefits associated with pollution and its abatement.[12] Other economists have proposed general systems to account for the impacts of economic activities on the environment broadly defined to include all land, water, and atmospheric resources.[13]

To see, for example, how industrial countries are affected by the bizarre anomalies in the current SNA, consider how SNA treats toxic wastes. If toxic substances leak from a dump and pollute soils and aquifers, measured income does not fall despite the possibly severe impairment of vital natural resources. If the government spends millions of dollars to clean up the mess, however, measured income rises (other things being equal) because such government expenditures are considered to be purchases of final goods and services. If industry itself undertakes the cleanup, even under a court order, income does not rise because the same expenditures are considered to be intermediate production costs when they are made by enterprises. If the site is not cleaned up and nearby residents suffer increased medical expenses, measured income again rises because household medical expenses are also defined as final consumption expenditures in the national income accounts.

Clearly, environmental factors should be accounted for more completely. One aspect of environmental accounting—natural resource accounting—attempts to inject some environmental realities into national income accounting, but it excludes transitory environmental externalities, such as air pollution. There are good reasons to focus rather narrowly on accounting for renewable natural resources: The principal natural resources, such as land, timber, and minerals, are already listed under SNA as economic assets, although they are not treated like other tangible capital, and their physical and economic values can be readily established. Demonstrating the enormous costs of natural resource degradation to a national economy is an important first step in establishing the need for revamping national policy. It also helps people recognize the need for further developing environmental accounting methodologies.

Developing countries whose economies are dependent on natural resources are becoming particularly interested in developing an accounting framework that accounts for these assets more adequately. Work is already under way in the Philippines, China, India, Brazil, Chile, Colombia, El Salvador, and other developing countries.[14]

A Case Study of Costa Rica

The debate over natural resource accounting is not academic. Performance evaluations of resource-based economies are often seriously distorted by their failure to account for natural resource depreciation. Building on an earlier study of Indonesia,[15] the World Resources Institute in Washington, D.C., and the Tropical Science Center in San José, Costa Rica, recently completed a study that shows that the depletion of natural resources in Costa Rica threatens the country's long-term economic prospects.[16] The results of this study should demonstrate the feasibility of incorporating depreciation of natural resources into national income accounts.

In Costa Rica, as in many other developing countries, natural resources are the most important economic asset. If sustainably managed, they can generate a perpetual stream of diverse and important economic benefits. Forests, fisheries, agriculture, and mines directly contribute 17 percent of the national income, 28 percent of employment, and 55 percent of export earnings.[17] Yet, the SNA recommended by the United Nations not only ignores the importance of these assets but also treats their destruction as an increase in national income instead of as a loss of wealth. This distortion conceals from the public and policymakers alike the gravity of the economy's deteriorating resource base.

That Costa Rica's natural resources have deteriorated seriously is indisputable. But the loss is not reflected in the national accounts. On the contrary, the net revenues from overexploiting forest, soil, fishery, and water resources are treated by the national accounts as factor income, not as capital consumption. Furthermore, the accounting system defines as a capital investment the conversion of land suitable only for forests into cattle pastures even if cattle ruin the soil and the livestock enterprise is neither ecologically nor economically viable.

More than 60 percent of Costa Rica's territory is suitable only for forests.[18] Everywhere, the slopes are too steep, the rainfall is too heavy, or the soils are too poor for more intensive uses. Yet, at most, only 40 percent of the land remains under forest cover.[19] In contrast, cattle pasture has spread over 35 percent of the land, although only 8 percent of it is suitable for this use.[20] This expansion of the livestock frontier is squandering the country's natural resources and is draining its financial resources as well. Banks are losing 17 billion colones (about $382 million) annually in uncollectible loans to the cattle industry.[21]

If this trend continues, Costa Rica's commercial forests will be exhausted within the next five years, and the country will be forced to import forest products.[22] Thousands of jobs will be lost, and a source of valuable fuelwood, as well as nonwood products and wildlife habitat, will disappear.[23] Meanwhile, where forests once stood, tons of soil wash away every year from dry, stripped, overgrazed pastures.

The current national accounting system for Costa Rica is poor because it does not reflect the economic value of lost natural resources (see Figure 1). The system classifies clearing forests for pasture as investment and simply ignores the loss of forest capital. Like the national accounts, society and

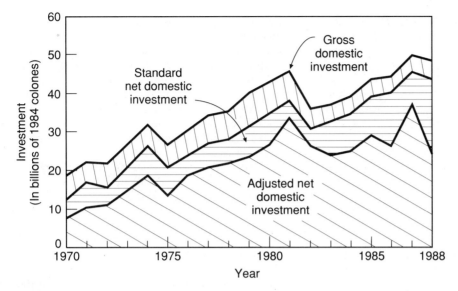

Figure 1 Gross domestic investment and net investment after depreciation of natural and manmade resources.

even forest owners have not recognized that the destruction of a forest today begets a loss of income tomorrow. The results are devastating. Investments in unproductive pasture land are actively promoted by government planners, while the loss of forest capital is shrugged off. If the loss of potential forest income were taken into account, the true net value of conversion would often be negative—a decline in the value of the nation's assets.

The inconsistency is highly misleading. Had the Costa Rican government constructed national balance sheets in 1970 and again in 1989, the calculations would have shown that natural resource assets valued at more than one year's worth of GDP had disappeared during those 20 years.[24] However, in not one of those 20 years did the annual accounts of national income, expenditure, savings, and capital formation reflect that ongoing loss. Instead, the accounts showed only continuing growth in national income and a high rate of capital formation until the economy crashed in the 1980s. The national accounts gave no warning that the basis for continuing growth was being destroyed.

Even after the economic crisis struck, economists labeled it a debt crisis, rather than an environmental crisis. The International Monetary Fund rushed in with programs to stabilize the monetary situation, but nobody spoke of stabilizing the natural resource base.[25] Yet, throughout the previous decade, the depreciation of natural resource assets, as an annual percentage of GDP, dwarfed the balance-

of-payments deficit.[26] The difference was that the balance-of-payments deficit and the accumulation of external liabilities was recorded, obvious, and scrutinized, whereas the loss of domestic assets went unrecorded, unnoticed, and uncorrected. . . .

Recommendations

Natural resources are disappearing with increasing speed, but national policymakers are not yet considering the implications for future economic productivity. The situation can be reversed if corrective environmental and economic policies are adopted. This is unlikely to happen unless leaders are provided with information that genuinely reflects the relationship between economic development and the natural environment and shows how the abuse of natural resources impoverishes the country. Costa Rica's wealth lies in its people, its land, its forests, and the surrounding seas. This study shows that the economic "development" programs carried out to date have sacrificed the last three of these resources to the harm of the first.

The idea of sustainable development, which the World Commission on Environment and Development labored to promote, is undermined by SNA. According to the commission's definition, sustainable development meets the current generation's needs without depriving future generations. Thus, current consumption must match current earnings without depleting a country's productive assets for generating future income. The definition of income commonly recognized by economists encompasses the notion of sustainability. In the standard Hicksian definition, income is the maximum consumption possible in the present period that does not reduce future consumption possibilities. This definition encompasses not only current earnings but also changes in asset positions: Capital gains are a source of income, and capital losses are a reduction in income. The depreciation accounts reflect the fact that, unless the capital stock is maintained and replaced, future consumption possibilities will inevitably decline.

Treating the depletion of natural resource capital as current income, as SNA does, is inconsistent with the Hicksian definition of income and incompatible with sustainable development. Moreover, such treatment gives false signals to policymakers that a dichotomy exists between the economy and the environment and thus leads policymakers to destroy the latter in the name of economic development. It also confuses the depletion of valuable assets with the generation of income and thereby helps validate the idea that rapid economic growth can be achieved and sustained by exploiting the natural resource base. The result can be illusory gains in income and permanent losses in wealth.

A number of steps are warranted to integrate natural resource consumption into the national income accounts. First, in Costa Rica and other resource-dependent developing countries, national accounting systems must be changed so that economic policymakers no longer make misguided decisions based on inadequate and distorted information. Past failures to prevent natural resource degradation have already undermined efforts to develop economies and alleviate poverty. This effect still is not fully recognized by policymakers, however, who act as if natural resources were limitless or as if technology could always replace exhausted or degraded resources. Closer dialogue between policymakers and scientists can help dispel this simplistic view of the natural environment. An economic accounting system that reflects the true condition of natural resources would provide an essential tool for the integrated analysis of environmental and economic policies in every sector of government.

Introducing such an accounting system will require that key international economic institutions—such as the World Bank, the other multilateral development banks, the International Monetary Fund, and the Organization for Economic Cooperation and Development—begin to compile, use, and publish revised estimates of net national product and national income. All such institutions should ready themselves to provide technical assistance to the growing number of national statistical offices that wish to adopt these changes and make such estimates for themselves.

Finally, the United Nations should announce that the distortions in the treatment of natural resources will be removed in the ongoing revisions to SNA. This would be a timely and feasible way to ensure that the process begun at the UN Conference on Environment and Development in Rio de Janeiro in June goes forward with all deliberate speed in coming years. No other single action would go further to raise consciousness about the link between economic growth and the wise use of natural resources.

Notes

1. J. M. Keynes, *General Theory of Employment, Interest, and Money* (New York: Harcourt Brace, 1965). See, also, R. Lekachman, *The Age of Keynes* (New York: Random House, 1966).

2. Readers interested in SNA's evolution might consult the following studies: United Nations, Department of Economic and Social Affairs, "A System of National Accounts," Statistical Papers, series F, no. 2, rev. 3 (New York: United Nations, 1968); UN Statistical Office, "Future Directions for Work on the System of National Accounts" (New York: United Nations, 1975); UN Department of Economic and Social Affairs, "Provisional International Guidelines on the National and Sectoral Balance-Sheet and Reconciliation Accounts of the System of National Accounts," Statistical Papers, series M, no. 60 (New York: United Nations, 1977); UN Statistical Office, "Future Directions for Work on the System of National Accounts," (New York: United Nations, 1979); UN Economic and Social Council, Statistical Commission, "Future Directions for Work on the System of National Accounts" (New York: United Nations, 1980).

3. UN Department of Economic and Social Affairs, 1977, note 2 above.

4. Ibid.

5. *Identity* is a term used in economics to mean a rela-

tionship that is, by definition, true and is described in mathematical terms.

6. UN Department of Economic and Social Affairs, 1977, Note 2 above.

7. UN Statistical Office, 1975, note 2 above.

8. UN Department of Economic and Social Affairs, 1977, note 2 above.

9. For evaluation of these systems, see O. Lone, *Natural Resource Accounting and Budgeting: A Short History of and Some Critical Reflections on the Norwegian Experience 1975–1987* (Paris: Organization for Economic Cooperation and Development, Environmental Directorate, 1987); A. Friend, "Natural Resource Accounting: International Experience" (Paper presented at the Consultative Meeting of the United Nations Environment Programme in Geneva, 23–25 February 1983); and E. Weiller, "The Use of Environmental Accounting for Development Planning" (New York: UNEP, January 1983).

10. For further information, see K. H. Alfsen, T. Bye, and L. Lorentsen, "Natural Resource Accounting and Analysis: The Norwegian Experience 1978–86" (Oslo: Central Bureau of Statistics of Norway, 1987); P. A. Garnasjordet and H. V. Saebo, "A System of Natural Resource Accounts in Norway," in *Information and Natural Resources* (Paris: Organization for Economic Cooperation and Development, 1986); P. Corniere, "Natural Resource Accounts in France: An Example—Inland Water," in *Information and Natural Resources* (Paris: OECD, 1986); Commission Interministerielle des Comptes du Patrimoine Naturel, *Les Comptes du Patrimoine Naturel* (Paris: Institut National de la Statistique et des Études Economiques, 1983); and J. L. Weber, "The French Natural Patrimony Accounts," *Statistical Journal of the United Nations* (ECI 1):419–44.

11. Corniere, note 10 above.

12. O. C. Herfindahl and A. Y. Kneese, "Measuring Social and Economic Change: Benefits and Costs of Environmental Pollution," in M. Moss, ed., *The Measurement of Economic and Social Performance: Studies in Income and Wealth*, no. 38 (New York: National Bureau of Economic Research, 1973); and K.-G. Mäler, "National Accounts and Environmental Resources," *Environmental and Resource Economics* 1, no. 1 (1991):1–16.

13. See R. Eisner, "Extended Accounts for National Income and Product," *Journal of Economic Literature* 26, no. 4 (December 1988):1611–84, for an excellent survey of the approaches taken by Herfindahl and Kneese (see note 11 above) and by others in such works as H. E. Daly, "On Sustainable Development and National Accounts," in D. Collard, D. Pearce, and D. Ulph, eds., *Economics and Sustainable Environ-*ments: Essays in Honour of Richard Lecomber* (New York: Macmillan, 1986); R. Hueting, *New Scarcity and Economic Growth* (Amsterdam: North-Holla Publishing Company, 1980); R. Hueting, "Economic Aspects of Environmental Accounting" (Paper prepared for the Environmental Accounting Workshop organized by UNEP and hosted by the World Bank in Washington, D.C., 5–8 November 1984); H. M. Peskin and J. Peskin, "The Valuation of Nonmarket Activities in Income Accounting," *Review of Income and Wealth* 24 (March 1989): 41–70; and H. M. Peskin, "A National Accounting Framework for Environmental Assets," *Journal of Environmental Economics and Management* 2 (1976):255–62.

14. Information provided at an international workshop on natural resource accounting organized in Vancouver, British Columbia, 5–6 March 1991, by the World Resources Institute.

15. R. Repetto et al., *Wasting Assets: Natural Resources in the National Income Accounts* (Washington, D.C.: World Resources Institute, 1989).

16. R. Repetto et al., *Accounts Overdue: Natural Resource Depreciation in Costa Rica* (Washington, D.C.: World Resources Institute, 1991).

17. Ibid., 2. Values for both income and export earnings are for 1989. Employment values are from 1987.

18. J. A. Tosi, Jr., *Manual para la Determinación de la Capacidad de Uso de las Tierras de Costa Rica* (San José, Costa Rica: Tropical Science Center, 1985).

19. Repetto et al., note 16 above.

20. Suitability in this context implies neither overuse nor underuse of the land, as defined by the land-use capacity system described in Tosi, note 18 above.

21. All economic values that follow are 1984 colones at the exchange rate of 44.53 colones = U.S. $1.00. Banco Central de Costa Rica, *Estadisticas 1950–1985: División Económica* (San José, Costa Rica: BCCR, 1986).

22. Repetto et al., note 16 above.

23. J. F. Rodas, *Diagnostico del Sector Industrial Forestal* (San José, Costa Rica: Editorial Universidad Estato a Distancia, 1985).

24. Repetto et al., note 16 above.

25. Ibid.

26. Ibid. The balance of payments deficit is here defined as the "basic" balance on current account, direct investment, and other long-term capital. The depreciation of natural resource assets is quantified as an annual percentage of GDP.

VI

PROBLEMS AND ENVIRONMENTAL POLICIES

A. HUMAN POPULATION AND PRESSURE ON RESOURCES

PREVIEW

> All the lonely people, where do they all come from. All the lonely people, where do they all belong.
>
> "Eleanor Rigby," *The Beatles*

> It is now quite lawful for a Catholic woman to avoid pregnancy by resort to mathematics, though she is still forbidden to resort to physics and chemistry.
>
> *H. L. Mencken*

About 10,000 years ago there were approximately 5 million human beings on the earth, less than the current population of Rio de Janiero. By the year 1850 the number was about one billion. A few years after World War II, global population had increased to 2.5 billion. In a predecessor of this volume, published in 1986, we spoke of a population of between 4 and 5 billion.[1] As this book goes to press, the number will be close to 6 billion. When a few of today's university students have their earliest grandchildren, there will likely be about 8 billion (near the year 2020 or so). Today's total of close to 6 billion will reach to 11 to 12 billion around 2050 if the current annual rate of increase of 1.7 percent remains constant. Currently, 5 million humans are born every 20 days, about 1 million every four days.[2]

Unlike many animals, we humans have few successful natural predators. A massive nuclear war could be devastating, as could certain other forms of warfare. The spread of AIDS promises to cause premature death to at least 10 to 20 million humans even if a vaccine is found tomorrow. Even though in recent decades there has been an increase in the gross national product of many nations and a significant increase in the total supply of food, the GNP and the amount of food per person have shrunk, the latter due in large part to the rapid increases in population. So even extraordinary technological "advances" have not offset the increased demand for resources. We put "advances" in scare quotes to note that some so-called advances have been, in fact, purchased at a high price to the environment, one which cannot be paid on a sustained basis. Hence, some "advances" have, to put an edge on the matter, simply taken food and water out of the mouths of our grandchildren.

Starvation is not always, or even usually, a by-product of there not being enough food on the planet; it is due to the skewed distribution of food and the radically unequal distribution of wealth or income which makes those who are hungry unable to call forth a response from a market ready to supply those who are willing *and* able to pay for food.[3]

Still, even if current resources were more equally distributed, the prospect of the planet's adding another 6 billion humans in the next century makes dim the hope of relieving absolute destitution and lessening the gap between the nations of the Northern Hemisphere and the Southern. One question, then, concerns what to do about the desperate plight of millions of current and future humans who are, or will be, on a path to premature death and the misery of hunger and nutrition-related diseases.[4] There are difficulties. If global population does not flatten out, will there not be tragedy for all? After all, resources are not infinite. If all the world began to look like the streets of Dacha (or any area of extreme poverty and high population density), is that the inevitable outcome of food sharing and no halt to the increase in global population? So there are some questions:

1. What must we do about the current burgeoning human population?
2. Are resources in fact limited?
3. What must we do about the large number of human beings who are in fact starving to death?
4. In what ways must we think differently about these questions when we take into account the well-being of future generations of humans?
5. In what ways must we think differently about these questions if we do not think that the well-being of all and *only* human beings is important?
6. What is an optimal population for the planet, all morally relevant matters considered?
7. What must we do to limit population size?

In the selections that follow, most of these questions are explored. Garrett Hardin, in a famous essay entitled "The Tragedy of the Commons" (in Section VI-B), has argued that resources (e.g., the oceans) which are "held in common," and, thus, not divided up according to some scheme of property rights, will be "overused" or wrongly exploited. Consider what has happened historically to what is thought of as "unowned" or sometimes "public" property, e.g., the air, many rivers, lakes, the oceans, and outer space. A free good is likely to become an overused good. Without the discipline of having some cost as a means of rationing the use of scarce resources, they will be used inefficiently. On this view it would be a great mistake to supply food at no cost to those nations in which there are a large number of starving persons. Indeed, in Hardin's view, doing so would lead to an even greater tragedy (e.g., a larger population crash) later. So, on this view it is not heroic and not even permissible to supply food; rather, we have a duty not to do so (note the consequentialist train of thought). This view, surprising to many, is spelled out in his essay "Lifeboat Ethics."

An important part of Hardin's argument is that a given nation has a certain "carrying capacity," that is, an ability to support a human population up to a certain point, given its endowment of natural resources, ingenuity, and so on. If a nation exceeds its capacity for very long, there will be a significant gap between the needs of its population and the available resources and, barring an influx of aid, it will suffer from a population dieback. Thus, in his view an even worse harm will occur. However, the judgment that a nation has a carrying capacity of a certain level may not be the straightforward empirical judgment that it appears to be. This critical point is explored in William Aiken's essay 'The "Carrying Capacity" Equivocation.'

According to some philosophers, the lifeboat model provokes us to think of the famine situation as a competitive one in which our choices are severely limited, as one in which we can only think in terms of a simplified and tragic "us and them" model.[5] We need not be driven by this picture of things. We might consider whether we morally ought to take the view of an impartial moral spectator or whether "special relations" deserve weight in the question of who should receive aid (e.g., relationships with friends, relatives, allies), and, indeed, should aid always go to those who are members of our species? In recent years criticism has been levelled at *"impartialist"* theories, utilitarianism being a prime example, on the ground that they do not give appropriate moral weight to the significance of existing loyalties (to friends, family, and so on) in that they require that moral agents be "radically egalitarian" and "treat each equally." A possible upshot is that one ought to give food to (or throw the life raft to, and the like) that individual whose reception of it would maximize utility—even if that means letting the friend die. Some critics believe that any theory with such implications should not be taken seriously. Hardin's view looks to be basically utilitarian in outlook. In thinking about lifeboat situations, we need to remind ourselves that the world is one in which competition *and* cooperation characterize relations between humans and also human-animal interactions. To be fair to Hardin, he holds out the hope of "mutual coercion mutually agreed upon," and this is a form of high-level cooperation.

The extremely important issue of human starvation can be, and commonly has been, discussed independently of attention to the enormous impact human proliferation has had, and is having, on the nonhuman biota of the planet. In a remarkable turn of political events, the Earth Summit which met in Rio in 1992 managed not to have any discussion of human population issues on its official agenda. We are tempted to say that this is a bit like discussing the "greenhouse effect" without discussing carbon emissions, but we shall refrain. From the outset, 77 developing countries wanted to focus on issues other than population increases, for obvious reasons. Without question, a major cause of pollution, the using up of "sources" (fresh water, clean air, a third of the world's forests, other fossil fuels, and so on) and the elimination of "sinks" (places to put wastes), is the leap from 1 billion humans in 1850 to almost 6 billion today. However, the heavy human hand on the nonhuman environment is also a function of the degree of resource consumption *per person.* In the United States and many other "first-world" or developed nations, the population is highly stable. It is not unusual for such developed nations to view with alarm the rate of population growth in certain less developed nations in which population often doubles in only 20 years.[6] This rate cannot be sustained for long without catastrophe. It is tempting to lay blame here and to conclude that the heaviest impact on the planet's environment is generated by the increased numbers of humans in such countries. Once again, things are not so simple. Once again, laying of blame at the feet of others appeals to the desire to be thought innocent and to walk away with "clean hands." However, the environmental impact of one American (on the available sources and sinks) is 50 times that of one citizen of Bangladesh.[7] The amount of carbon emitted into the environment by the activity of the average American is five times the global average.[8] The environmental impact of the average person in other developed countries such as Japan, France, or Canada is very large. Political crosscurrents related to the dual emphasis on population size (and rate of growth) and consumption per person led to an impasse at the Earth Summit in 1992. The final outcome of the negotiations in Brazil is described by one observer in this fashion:

> When, in the final negotiating session, the United States moved to delete all references to consumption in the North, the G-77 retaliated by deleting references to the urgency of slowing population growth. That opened the way for extremely effective lobbying by the Holy See. The fate of the population language was sealed, ironically, by representatives of women. Feminist health groups, along with some women's groups in developing countries and representatives of minority women in the United States have long been antagonistic to population control because they believe it jeopardizes wom-

en's health, is disguised genocide or places blame on women. . . . [9]

The expression "population control" is one, of course, of which we should be wary; it can be used to refer to coercive methods of a more or less extreme sort, ranging from Hitler's "population control" of the Jews and Gypsies, to the massacres of Croats by the Serbs, or to policies of mandatory abortion or mandatory pregnancy. In India in the 1970s thousands of people (males and females) were coercively sterilized.[10] The plight of women in many countries is that of day laborers for the family; they are uneducated and do not understand the nature and function of contraceptions or are not given access to such. Often, they are oppressed by men who disallow their comparatively powerless wives from learning about or using contraception. In many cultures, including our own, a great deal of shame and guilt has been induced over *talking* about, not to mention using, contraceptives; often, Roman Catholic leaders tell those who wish to do so that they are "closing themselves off from God," perhaps dooming themselves to eternal suffering as a result.[11] Dissuading people from using "artificial" contraceptives, or preventing access to them, is, of course, viewed as a "moral victory" by such "leaders." In India one-fourth of the women are so badly off that they die by the time that they are 15 years of age. The low status of those that survive makes it difficult for them to have a voice, to get an education, to gain some autonomy and exercise deliberate choice over their own reproductive capacities. In India some families have to choose between spending money on their daughter's education and spending it on her dowry. If the husband's family believes the wife's dowry is too small, they sometimes engage in the notorious practice of bride-burning, although it is illegal. Under such enormous pressures and frequently taught by their mothers to acquiesce to the wishes of her husband for the sake of a "peaceful" or "happy" marriage, she lives as a passive, powerless, laboring baby producer—with little hope and with little control. When many children die young, the parents often decide that it is necessary to have many children ("gifts of God") since it is not certain that many will live. The ideology that male babies are more valuable than females affects the attitudes of men and women—mothers are often deeply troubled if they have produced only females; the overwhelming majority of abortions in India are of female babies, a form of what some have called "gendericide." Thus, a nasty mixture of poverty, entrenched patriarchal attitudes, ignorance, passivity, prejudice, shame, and institutionalized barriers, sometimes expressive of cultural and religious ideologies, is at the root of the population excess in many poor nations; population control, abstractly speaking, is desirable, but it must address these mentioned difficulties and do so in a just manner.[12] Doing so may require something falling short of "respecting other cultures" (or our own).

The related issues here include, then, earthwide environmental deterioration, sustainability, the availability of birth control and abortion, and others. The ecological dimensions of current population policies and existing human reproductive choices are explored in the essay by Ronnie Zoe Hawkins.

Humans' consumption of the earth is so distressing to many that occasional elements of misanthropy appear. For example, rare "environmentalist" voices express scepticism that AIDS or starvation or war is tragic.[13] Such remarks are spotlighted by very-free market, totally anthropocentric members of the so-called "Wise Use" movement[14] who attack "environmentalists" across the board, with virtually no distinctions, as people who dismiss the value of human beings, as tree-hugging Bambi lovers indifferent to human property rights and to the plight of those who are (claimed to be) losing their jobs because of environmental restrictions (who "put birds, rats, and insects ahead of families and jobs," as Republican candidate for President of the United States Patrick Buchanan said in 1992).[15] Strange to say, but one is reminded of Mao Tse-tung's call for a "war on nature."[16] What to do about the genuine conflicts between legitimate interests is an important and difficult matter. It is addressed in various parts of this volume, especially in Sections IV-C and VI-C. What we believe about what sorts of things possess moral standing will, as discussed earlier in Parts III and IV, directly and profoundly affect the question of which things are possessors of legitimate interests and, hence, how we articulate the nature of the conflict of interests.

Even if we believe that duties are owed only to humans, do we have any duties to future generations of humans? One commentator asserted that we do not since, "after all . . . what have they ever done for us?"[17] But not all duties seem to arise as a matter of reciprocity toward those who have benefitted us. For example, we normally think that we have duties not to harm perfect strangers who have in no way benefitted us, not to mention parental duties toward children from whom parents may never benefit. It is worth noting a distinction made by one philosopher between merely possible people who might exist and those who will exist; call the latter future people.[18] Are they not owed a fair share of the earth's resources and a fair share of the capital stock, comparable in some sense to the share which was part of the world into which we were born? Consider an analogy. Would it be fair for a sibling to take all of a parent's estate and pass on all the debt to his or her sibling? Would it be fair for the prior generation to virtually exhaust most of the planet's sources and sinks and leave the present generation with only the crumbs, so to speak? Could it be all right for us to do so to the next generation? There are some worries here, and they receive attention in Brian Barry's essay "Intergenerational Justice in Energy Policy."

If we are not speaking of existing children, then the future generations do not now exist.

And it is tempting to think that a necessary condition of being owed any duties is that one at least exist! Still, it is a virtual certainty that future people will inherit the world we leave, and it is irrational to believe otherwise. It is also indeterminate as to who will exist and that this fact constitutes a barrier to concluding that we have duties to future generations if we believe that duties can exist only toward determinate individuals. Nevertheless, we have duties to "the poor" or "the homeless" even if we do not know precisely who does or who will constitute the exact members of such groups. To consider one example, this generation and previous ones in the United States have managed, with the able assistance of the U.S. Forest Service and the logging industry, to cut down 90 percent of the old-growth forests.[19] Thus, future generations will grow up in a biologically impoverished world in which it will be difficult or impossible to see and touch and walk among trees 200 to 600 years old, not to mention the associated loss of habitat for other flora and fauna. Also in the last 50 years we have managed to generate enormous amounts of nuclear wastes which will burden future generations for the next 10,000 years. We could reflect on other examples, but we will not. It is tempting to think that the more important questions concern the grounds on which we decide just what we owe future people and, indeed, other future beings with moral standing, and specifically what we must do in this regard. Political systems in which people hold office for a decade or less are not well designed to cope with these problems, because the system includes incentives for politicians to use up resources quickly and pass on the burdens to others to confront later. In short, they are rewarded for acting in this manner. Again, consider the U.S. Forest Service. The problem is no doubt a deeper one, with roots in the prevailing culture. It has been said that no society can be concerned about the future which does not have a sense of the past; in this respect non-Native Americans may have something to learn from Native Americans.

Is there a serious problem of declining or disappearing resources? Can we find alternative materials when existing sources run out? Can we indefinitely find a technological fix for our problems? Some argue that all the worries (or most) about resources drying up are a grand miscalculation, if not a grand hoax. Indeed, such is the view of "technological optimists" or "cornucopians" such as Herman Kahn and Julian Simon (Simon denies that he deserves the label "cornucopian."). Later in this section, Simon defends the view that the supply of natural resources is infinite. Given this view, it is intelligible that Simon holds that "almost equally beyond any doubt, however, an additional person is also a boon."[20] After all, he says, each will pay taxes "and make efforts to beautify the environment."[21] Further, "enabling a potential human being to come into life and to enjoy life is a good thing. . . ."[22] It is at this point that Simon seems to commit the fallacy of inferring that more is better from the assumption that human life is good.[23] Alternatively, he may be claiming, more radically, that all potential human life ought to become actual. Since about one-third of pregnancies spontaneously abort, one wonders whether Simon regrets that the global population is not much larger. It is not clear why he accuses those arguing in favor of a smaller human population, e.g., Paul Ehrlich, as having an absence of respect for human life.[24]

Some predictions of famine and death by Ehrlich and others have been exaggerated. Ehrlich predicted in 1968 in *The Population Bomb* that "The battle to feed all of humanity is now over. In the 1970s and 1980s hundreds of millions of people will starve to death. . . ."[25] Others were more extreme. Ehrlich recently claimed that about 200,000,000 people *have* died of starvation or hunger-related diseases in the last couple of decades.[26] Should we say that the warnings of Ehrlich and others were irrational and to be dismissed because they overestimated the numbers? In comparatively evaluating the magnitude of the human tragedy involved, it is worth recalling the Holocaust, an event which by most accounts involved the deaths of 6 to 15 million people. Still, Simon was correct to insist that technology would allow greater food production than many, including Ehrlich, had estimated. Nevertheless, it seems myopic to focus only on predictions of supply and need over a period of a few decades, although that is expansive compared to the purview of the typical American politician, namely, four to eight years.

Were it true that resources are infinite, it would considerably lessen worries about burgeoning population and sustainability of current patterns of consumption. Were it true, the question of fair distribution or equity might loom as the one important moral issue. There is, admittedly, no doubt that we will continue to discover ways of substituting one material for another as one becomes scarce and costly, e.g., the use of fiber optic cables in place of copper wire. The belief that this will *always* occur without enormous cost to humans or others seems firmly anchored in wish-fulfillment and is largely an article of faith. In contrast, some prospects, e.g., for developing virtually unlimited supplies of energy, are supportable by good reasons. We need not generalize about all resources, and we need not succumb to the psychologically seductive voices which say "don't worry; be happy, and there will be a technological fix in due time."

What is an ideal population size for planet Earth? The question should be addressed in connection with another question explored in this volume, i.e., what size population is *sustainable* indefinitely. (We shall not pursue that point here.) Most people agree, as do we, that the existence of human life is good and that human life is valuable. Some enigmatically say that human life is *infinitely* valuable. But even if it is very valuable, it does *not* follow that the more, the better. This fact is overlooked in many discussions. Certain Roman Catholic bishops have asserted that the earth could support a population of 40 billion. Given the current human predation of the planet, we wonder what transformations of human nature would be required for this scenario to be a realistic one. What argument can be given for urging this or that population size? It is tempting to believe that, given current problems and the stealing from the future that is already under way, we need to scale down the existing population size in permissible ways or at least curtail growth in permissible ways.

There is perplexity here over the implications of the principle of utility. We shall comment succinctly. Given the standard view that we ought to maximize total net utility, it seems that we ought to try to add any probably-happy-on-balance human being. There are worries here about the "total view." Is it plausible that we have a duty to continue adding people who are just barely content until we reduce total utility? Could we adopt a policy whereby we could be confident that this is the likely outcome? It seems doubtful. Further, this kind of discussion by philosophers is admittedly of the sort that is based on the view that only humans matter, with no explicit consideration of ecological balance or sustainability. It is tempting to think that the principle "maximize average utility" is more reasonable than "maximize total utility." However, this principle seems to imply that we ought to eliminate those who are dragging down the average (even if it does not require us to *add* anyone whose utility level would have that undesired effect). One might murder homeless people in their sleep to achieve this end, but surely no utilitarian would, or should, accept this notion. It seems that utilitarians ought to explain why their position does not imply this. If it does not, it may be because the principle of utility has been augmented by other principles, but then it may not be obvi-

ous that the resulting view should be thought of as "utilitarianism."[27] We have here another instance in which it is tempting to say that we ought to foster human (and other) well-being but *only* in certain ways (nonutilitarian philosophers sometimes say that the right precedes the good, i.e., one cannot determine the right as whatever maximizes the good), ways that are simply not indicated by a simple principle urging utility maximization. In general, discussion of what should be the optimal human population size seems a bit like contemplating exactly where to land when one's parachute has failed to open. The basic need is simply to regain control. A fundamental question is whether we should not attempt to promote well-being within certain constraints without trying simply to *maximize* it. Aside from the question of the implications of the principle of utility for population policy, it is clear that any adequate view will have to take into account the *consequences* of alternative policies. To that extent no theory can afford to ignore questions about consequences. So, rights theories must do so as well.

NOTES

1. See Donald VanDeVeer and Christine Pierce, eds., *People, Penguins, and Plastic Trees* (Belmont, CA: Wadsworth Publishing, 1986).

2. Paul and Anne Ehrlich, *Healing the Planet* (Reading, MA: Addison-Wesley Publishing, 1991), pp. 72–73.

3. Amartya Sen has pointed out that lack of access to food among many starving peoples is often a function of their lack of money; when money is supplied, market forces respond with food.

4. In the fall of 1992 some food was being airlifted to Somalia, but matters were so desperate that people there were eating animal skins to survive. Civil war and drought have combined to make one-fifth of its population face imminent starvation; over half suffer from malnutrition. A major airlift began at the end of that year. See "Starving Somalis Eat Animal Skins," in *News and Observer* (August 20, 1992).

5. See Mary Midgley in *Animals and Why They Matter* (Harmondsworth, England: Penguin, Ltd., 1983).

6. In thinking about doubling times, or for that matter

mortgage rates or automobile loans, it is useful to know "the rule of 72." The rate of increase divided into 72 will be the time span it will take for the entity in question to double. So if a population is growing at 2 percent annually, it will double in 36 years. The current rate of increase of the global population is lower than a decade or so ago; it is now about 1.7 percent. Hence, at this rate the doubling time is just over 42 years. A population of 500 million growing at a rate of 4 percent a year would double every 18 years and, hence, quadruple in less than 100 years, and become 2 billion in less than a century.

7. Paul and Anne Ehrlich, op. cit., p. 8.

8. Jonathan Weiner, *The Next One Hundred Years* (New York: Bantam Books, 1991), p. 41.

9. Jessica Matthews, "Rift Is Hampering Real Work on Population Issue," *News and Observer* (April 15, 1990), p. 13A.

10. Some were offered inducements, but the promised benefits were often not delivered.

11. In 1992 a popular singer, Sinead O'Connor, tore up a picture of the Pope on American television. This event offended many and some suggested she needed "spiritual counseling," but this reaction reveals in part a lack of understanding on the part of many as to why the Pope is often not viewed as a source of moral wisdom but a major contributor to environmental tragedy, and, hence, a source of morally evil advice.

12. A powerful film called *The People Bomb*, one which has influenced this paragraph, is available from the television network CNN.

13. Murray Bookchin cites poet Gary Snyder as saying, "Mankind is a locust-blight on the planet" and has cited another environmental writer, under the pseudonym of "Miss Ann Thropy," as welcoming the AIDS epidemic as "a necessary solution" to the "population problem." See *Defending the Earth,* edited by Steve Chase (Boston: South End Press, 1991), p. 123.

14. This movement, a backlash to the "environmental" movement, has Ron Arnold as one spokesman. The movement is supported mostly by those who are bitter about environmental restrictions on their "property rights," restrictions on the "free market," ranchers, various corporate interests, logging companies, and so on. Its views tend to be totally anthropocentric, oriented toward short-term human interests, indeed the interests of some rural Americans and those corporate backers who find common cause.

15. The remark was made at the Republican presidential nominating convention on August 17, 1992.

16. See Ian Barbour, *Technology, Environment and Human Values* (New York: Praeger Publishing), 1980, p. 19.

17. The reference to the author of the remark quoted is lost; however, this sort of position has been expressed by Thomas Schwartz, who has said "we've no obligation extending indefinitely or even terribly far into the future to provide any widespread, continuing benefits to our descendants." See Thomas Schwartz, "Obligations to Posterity" in *Obligations to Future Generations,* edited by R. I. Sikora and Brian Barry (Philadelphia: Temple University Press, 1978), p. 3.

18. The distinction is due to Mary Anne Warren in "Do Potential People Have Rights?" in Sikora and Barry, op. cit., p. 28.

19. Americans are still under what we take to be a harmful delusion, namely, that the U.S. Forest Service carries out the job of protecting the forests. Actually, one of its main functions is to sell off the trees at very low costs to logging companies and to provide roads for logging trucks at the expense of taxpayers. What if the federal government sold off Grand Canyon as one humongous, swell place to dump trash? We are tempted to propose that the U.S. Forest Service be renamed the U.S. Dendrocide Service. In their own defense, the Service points out that they replant trees. This is true; they normally create tree plantations or farms with all the diversity of a Toyota factory, and in a few hundred years someone may get to see how it all turned out—unless they have been replaced by plastic trees.

20. Julian Simon, *The Ultimate Resource* (Princeton: Princeton University Press, 1981), p. 4.

21. Ibid.

22. Ibid., p. 10.

23. It is worth noting that Simon allows himself various evaluative judgments since his official (positivistic) view is that science cannot show that a population size is too large or too small since "such judgments depend upon our values, a matter about which science is silent." See Chapter 23 of his book. It is astonishing how many professionals who are trained in a field commonly labeled a "science" take this positivistic view but go on to defend to the death numerous normative judgments, all the while not admitting it or not ceasing to insist that their view is something more than a preference.

24. Ibid., p. 10. Simon expresses surprise that "Some people even impute feelings to nature, to trees or to animals . . ." (see p. 153). This remark is symptomatic of much economic and philosophical doctrine which, until the last decade or so, has been oblivious to the compelling arguments in favor of regarding many animals as sentient, and, hence, ques-

tioning the purely anthropocentric moral position they presuppose. In a related manner he holds that resources are valuable only when found by humans, gathered and "harnessed for human needs" (see p. 346). And some of us make the mistake of appreciating (hence, valuing) the sunshine, fresh air, and babbling brooks!

25. Ibid., pp. 54–56.

26. Paul and Anne Ehrlich, op. cit., p. 5.

27. For a defense of the utilitarian view against these sorts of objections, see the fine book by Robin Attfield, *The Ethics of Environmental Concern* (New York: Columbia University Press, 1983), Chapter 6.

Lifeboat Ethics

Garrett Hardin

Environmentalists use the metaphor of the earth as a "spaceship" in trying to persuade countries, industries, and people to stop wasting and polluting our natural resources. Since we all share life on this planet, they argue, no single person or institution has the right to destroy, waste, or use more than a fair share of its resources.

But does everyone on earth have an equal right to an equal share of its resources? The spaceship metaphor can be dangerous when used by misguided idealists to justify suicidal policies for sharing our resources through uncontrolled immigration and foreign aid. In their enthusiastic but unrealistic generosity, they confuse the ethics of a spaceship with those of a lifeboat.

A true spaceship would have to be under the control of a captain, since no ship could possibly survive if its course were determined by committee. Spaceship Earth certainly has no captain; the United Nations is merely a toothless tiger, with little power to enforce any policy upon its bickering members.

If we divide the world crudely into rich nations and poor nations, two-thirds of them are desperately poor, and only one third comparatively rich, with the United States the wealthiest of all. Metaphorically, each rich nation can be seen as a lifeboat full of comparatively rich people. In the ocean outside each lifeboat swim the poor of the world, who would like to get in, or at least to share some of the wealth. What should the lifeboat passengers do?

First, we must recognize the limited capacity of any lifeboat. For example, a nation's land has a limited capacity to support a population and as the current energy crisis has shown us, in some ways we have already exceeded the carrying capacity of our land.

Adrift in a Moral Sea.   So here we sit, say 50 people in our lifeboat. To be generous, let us assume it has room for 10 more, making a total capacity of 60. Suppose the 50 of us in the lifeboat see 100 others swimming in the water outside, begging for admission to our boat or for handouts. We have several options: we may be tempted to try to live by the Christian ideal of being "our brother's keeper," or by the Marxist ideal of "to each according to his needs." Since the needs of all in the water are the same, and since they can all be seen as "our brothers," we could take them all into our boat, making a total of 150 in a boat designed for 60. The boat swamps, everyone drowns. Complete justice, complete catastrophe.

Since the boat has an unused excess capacity of 10 more passengers, we could admit just 10 more to it. But which 10 do we let in? How do we choose? Do we pick the best 10, the neediest 10, "first come, first served"? And what do we say to the 90 we exclude? If we do let an extra 10 into our lifeboat, we will have lost our "safety factor," an engineering principle of critical importance. For example, if we don't leave room for excess capacity as a safety factor in our country's agriculture, a new plant disease or a bad change in the weather could have disastrous consequences.

Suppose we decide to preserve our small

safety factor and admit no more to the lifeboat. Our survival is then possible, although we shall have to be constantly on guard against boarding parties.

While this last solution clearly offers the only means of our survival, it is morally abhorrent to many people. Some say they feel guilty about their good luck. My reply is simple: "Get out and yield your place to others." This may solve the problem of the guilt-ridden person's conscience, but it does not change the ethics of the lifeboat. The needy person to whom the guilt-ridden person yields his place will not himself feel guilty about his good luck. If he did, he would not climb aboard. The net result of conscience-stricken people giving up their unjustly held seats is the elimination of that sort of conscience from the lifeboat.

This is the basic metaphor within which we must work out our solutions. Let us now enrich the image, step by step, with substantive additions from the real world, a world that must solve real and pressing problems of overpopulation and hunger.

The harsh ethics of the lifeboat become even harsher when we consider the reproductive differences between the rich nations and the poor nations. The people inside the lifeboats are doubling in numbers every 87 years; those swimming around outside are doubling, on the average, every 35 years, more than twice as fast as the rich. And since the world's resources are dwindling, the difference in prosperity between the rich and the poor can only increase.

As of 1973, the U.S. had a population of 210 million people, who were increasing by 0.8 percent per year. Outside our lifeboat, let us imagine another 210 million people, (say the combined populations of Colombia, Ecuador, Venezuela, Morocco, Pakistan, Thailand, and the Philippines) who are increasing at a rate of 3.3 percent per year. Put differently, the doubling time for this aggregate population is 21 years, compared to 87 years for the U.S.

Multiplying the Rich and the Poor. Now suppose the U.S. agreed to pool its resources with those seven countries, with everyone receiving an equal share. Initially, the ratio of Americans to non-Americans in this model would be one-to-one. But consider what the ratio would be after 87 years, by which time the Americans would have doubled to a population of 420 million. By then, doubling every 21 years, the other group would have swollen to 354 billion. Each American would have to share the available resources with more than eight people.

But, one could argue, this discussion assumes that current population trends will continue, and they may not. Quite so. Most likely the rate of population increase will decline much faster in the U.S. than it will in the other countries, and there does not seem to be much we can do about it. In sharing with "each according to his needs," we must recognize that needs are determined by population size, which is determined by the rate of reproduction, which at present is regarded as a sovereign right of every nation, poor or not. This being so, the philanthropic load created by the sharing ethic of the spaceship can only increase.

The Tragedy of the Commons. The fundamental error of spaceship ethics, and the sharing it requires, is that it leads to what I call "the tragedy of the commons." Under a system of private property, the men who own property recognize their responsibility to care for it, for if they don't they will eventually suffer. A farmer, for instance, will allow no more cattle in a pasture than its carrying capacity justifies. If he overloads it, erosion sets in, weeds take over, and he loses the use of the pasture.

If a pasture becomes a commons open to all, the right of each to use it may not be matched by a corresponding responsibility to protect it. Asking everyone to use it with discretion will hardly do, for the considerate herdsman who refrains from overloading the commons suffers more than a selfish one who says his needs are greater. If everyone would restrain himself, all would be well; but it takes only one less than everyone to ruin a system of voluntary restraint. In a crowded world of less than perfect human beings, mutual ruin is inevitable if there are no controls. This is the tragedy of the commons.

One of the major tasks of education today should be the creation of such an acute awareness of the dangers of the commons that people will recognize its many varieties. For example, the air and water have become polluted because they are treated as commons. Further growth in the population or per-capita conversion of natural resources into pollutants will only make the problem worse. The same holds true for the fish of the oceans. Fishing fleets have nearly disappeared in many parts of the world, technological improvements in the art of fishing are hastening the day of complete ruin. Only the replacement of the system of the commons with a responsible system of control will save the land, air, water and oceanic fisheries.

The World Food Bank.   In recent years there has been a push to create a new commons called a World Food Bank, an international depository of food reserves to which nations would contribute according to their abilities and from which they would draw according to their needs. This humanitarian proposal has received support from many liberal international groups, and from such prominent citizens as Margaret Mead, U.N. Secretary General Kurt Waldheim, and Senators Edward Kennedy and George McGovern.

A world food bank appeals powerfully to our humanitarian impulses. But before we rush ahead with such a plan, let us recognize where the greatest political push comes from, lest we be disillusioned later. Our experience with the "Food for Peace program," or Public Law 480, gives us the answer. This program moved billions of dollars worth of U.S. surplus grain to food-short, population-long countries during the past two decades. But when P.L. 480 first became law, a headline in the business magazine *Forbes* revealed the real power behind it: "Feeding the World's Hungry Millions: How It Will Mean Billions for U.S. Business."

And indeed it did. In the years 1960 to 1970, U.S. taxpayers spent a total of $7.9 billion on the Food for Peace program. Between 1948 and 1970, they also paid an additional $50 billion for other economic-aid programs, some of which went for food and food-producing machinery and technology. Though all U.S. taxpayers were forced to contribute to the cost of P.L. 480, certain special interest groups gained handsomely under the program. Farmers did not have to contribute the grain; the Government, or rather the taxpayers, bought it from them at full market prices. The increased demand raised prices of farm products generally. The manufacturers of farm machinery, fertilizers and pesticides benefited by the farmers' extra efforts to grow more food. Grain elevators profited from storing the surplus until it could be shipped. Railroads made money hauling it to ports, and shipping lines profited from carrying it overseas. The implementation of P.L. 480 required the creation of a vast Government bureaucracy, which then acquired its own vested interest in continuing the program regardless of its merits.

Extracting Dollars.   Those who proposed and defended the Food for Peace program in public rarely mentioned its importance to any of these special interests. The public emphasis was always on its humanitarian effects. The combination of silent selfish interests and highly vocal humanitarian apologists made a powerful and successful lobby for extracting money from taxpayers. We can expect the same lobby to push now for the creation of a World Food Bank.

However great the potential benefit to selfish interests, it should not be a decisive argument against a truly humanitarian program. We must ask if such a program would actually do more good than harm, not only momentarily but also in the long run. Those who propose the food bank usually refer to a current "emergency" or "crisis" in terms of world food supply. But what is an emergency? Although they may be infrequent and sudden, everyone knows that emergencies will occur from time to time. A well-run family, company, organization or country prepares for the likelihood of accidents and emergencies. It expects them, it budgets for them, it saves for them.

Learning the Hard Way.   What happens if some organizations or countries budget for accidents and others do not? If each country is solely responsible for its own well-being, poorly managed ones will suffer. But they can learn from experience. They may mend their ways, and learn to budget for infrequent but certain emergencies. For example, the weather varies from year to year, and periodic crop failures are certain. A wise and competent government saves out of the production of the good years in anticipation of bad years to come. Joseph taught this policy to Pharaoh in Egypt more than 2,000 years ago. Yet the great majority of the governments in the world today do not follow such a policy. They lack either the wisdom or the competence, or both. Should those nations that do manage to put something aside be forced to come to the rescue each time an emergency occurs among the poor nations?

"But it isn't their fault!" Some kind-hearted liberals argue. "How can we blame the poor people who are caught in an emergency? Why must they suffer for the sins of their governments?" The concept of blame is simply not relevant here. The real question is, what are the operational consequences of establishing a world food bank? If it is open to every country every time a need develops, slovenly rulers will not be motivated to take Joseph's advice. Someone will always come to their aid. Some countries will deposit food in the world food bank, and others will withdraw it. There will be almost no overlap. As a result of such solutions to food shortage emergencies, the poor countries will not learn to mend their ways, and will suffer progressively greater emergencies as their populations grow.

Population Control the Crude Way.   On the average, poor countries undergo a 2.5 percent increase in population each year; rich countries, about 0.8 percent. Only rich countries have anything in the way of food reserves set aside, and even they do not have as much as they should. Poor countries have none. If poor countries received no food from the outside, the rate of their population growth would be periodically checked by crop failures and famines. But if they can always draw on a world food bank in time of need, their population can continue to grow unchecked, and so will their "need" for aid. In the short run, a world food bank may diminish that need, but in the long run it actually increases the need without limit.

Without some system of worldwide food sharing, the proportion of people in the rich and poor nations might eventually stabilize. The overpopulated poor countries would decrease in numbers, while the rich countries that had room for more people would increase. But with a well-meaning system of sharing, such as a world food bank, the growth differential between the rich and the poor countries will not only persist, it will increase. Because of the higher rate of population growth in the poor countries of the world, 88 percent of today's children are born poor, and only 12 percent rich. Year by year the ratio becomes worse, as the fast-reproducing poor outnumber the slow-reproducing rich.

A world food bank is thus a commons in disguise. People will have more motivation to draw from it than to add to any common store. The less provident and less able will multiply at the expense of the abler and more provident, bringing eventual ruin upon all who share in the commons. Besides, any system of "sharing" that amounts to foreign aid from the rich nations to the poor nations will carry the taint of charity, which will contribute little to the world peace so devoutly desired by those who support the idea of a world food bank.

As past U.S. foreign-aid programs have amply and depressingly demonstrated, international charity frequently inspires mistrust and antagonism rather than gratitude on the part of the recipient nation [see "What Other Nations Hear When the Eagle Screams," by Kenneth J. and Mary M. Gergen, PT, June].

Chinese Fish and Miracle Rice.   The modern approach to foreign aid stresses the export of technology and advice, rather than money and food. As an ancient Chinese proverb goes: "Give a man a fish and he will eat for a day; teach him how to fish and he will eat for the rest of his days." Acting on this advice, the Rockefeller and Ford Foundations have financed a number of programs for improving agriculture in the hungry nations. Known as the "Green Revolution," these programs have led to the development of "miracle rice" and "miracle wheat," new strains that offer bigger harvests and greater resistance to crop damage. Norman Borlaug, the Nobel Prize winning agronomist who, supported by the Rockefeller Foundation, developed "miracle wheat," is one of the most prominent advocates of a world food bank.

Whether or not the Green Revolution can increase food production as much as its champions claim is a debatable but possibly irrelevant point: Those who support this well-intended humanitarian effort should first consider some of the fundamentals of human ecology. Ironically, one man who did was the late Alan Gregg, a vice president of the Rockefeller Foundation. Two decades ago he expressed strong doubts about the wisdom of such attempts to increase food production. He likened the growth and spread of humanity over the surface of the earth to the spread of cancer in the human body, remarking that "cancerous growths demand food; but, as far as I know, they have never been cured by getting it."

Overloading the Environment. Every human born constitutes a draft on all aspects of the environment: food, air, water, forests, beaches, wildlife, scenery, and solitude. Food can, perhaps, be significantly increased to meet a growing demand. But what about clean beaches, unspoiled forests, and solitude? If we satisfy a growing population's need for food, we necessarily decrease its per capita supply of the other resources needed by men.

India, for example, now has a population of 600 million, which increases by 15 million each year. This population already puts a huge load on a relatively impoverished environment. The country's forests are now only a small fraction of what they were three centuries ago, and floods and erosion continually destroy the insufficient farmland that remains. Every one of the 15 million new lives added to India's population puts an additional burden on the environment, and increases the economic and social costs of crowding. However humanitarian our intent, every Indian life saved through medical or nutritional assistance from abroad diminishes the quality of life for those who remain, and for subsequent generations. If rich countries make it possible, through foreign aid, for 600 million Indians to swell to 1.2 billion in a mere 28 years, as their current growth rate threatens, will future generations of Indians thank us for hastening the destruction of their environment? Will our good intentions be sufficient excuse for the consequences of our actions?

My final example of a commons in action is one for which the public has the least desire for rational discussion—immigration. Anyone who publicly questions the wisdom of current U.S. immigration policy is promptly charged with bigotry, prejudice, ethnocentrism, chauvinism, isolationism or selfishness. Rather than encounter such accusations, one would rather talk about other matters, leaving immigration policy to wallow in the crosscurrents of special interests that take no account of the good of the whole, or the interests of posterity.

Perhaps we still feel guilty about things we said in the past. Two generations ago the popular press frequently referred to Dagos, Wops, Polacks, Chinks and Krauts, in articles about how America was being "overrun" by foreigners of supposedly inferior genetic stock [see "The Politics of Genetic Engineering: Who Decides Who's Defective?" PT,

June]. But because the implied inferiority of foreigners was used then as justification for keeping them out, people now assume that restrictive policies could only be based on such misguided notions. There are other grounds.

A Nation of Immigrants. Just consider the numbers involved. Our Government acknowledges a net inflow of 400,000 immigrants a year. While we have no hard data on the extent of illegal entries, educated guesses put the figure at about 600,000 a year. Since the natural increase (excess of births over deaths) of the resident population now runs about 1.7 million per year, the yearly gain from immigration amounts to at least 19 percent of the total annual increase, and may be as much as 37 percent if we include the estimate for illegal immigrants. Considering the growing use of birth-control devices, the potential effect of educational campaigns by such organizations as Planned Parenthood Federation of America and Zero Population Growth, and the influence of inflation and the housing shortage, the fertility rate of American women may decline so much that immigration could account for all the yearly increase in population. Should we not at least ask if that is what we want?

For the sake of those who worry about whether the "quality" of the average immigrant compares favorably with the quality of the average resident, let us assume that immigrants and native-born citizens are of exactly equal quality, however one defines that term. We will focus here only on quantity; and since our conclusions will depend on nothing else, all charges of bigotry and chauvinism become irrelevant.

Immigration Vs. Food Supply. World food banks *move food to the people,* hastening the exhaustion of the environment of the poor countries. Unrestricted immigration, on the other hand, *moves people to the food,* thus speeding up the destruction of the environment of the rich countries. We can easily understand why poor people should want to make this latter transfer, but why should rich hosts encourage it?

As in the case of foreign-aid programs, immigration receives support from selfish interests and humanitarian impulses. The primary selfish interest in unimpeded immigration is the desire of employers for cheap labor, particularly in industries and trades that offer degrading work. In the past, one wave of foreigners after another was brought into the U.S. to work at wretched jobs for wretched wages. In recent years the Cubans, Puerto Ricans, and Mexicans have had this dubious honor. The interests of the employers of cheap labor mesh well with the guilty silence of the country's liberal intelligentsia. White Anglo-Saxon Protestants are particularly reluctant to call for a closing of the doors to immigration for fear of being called bigots.

But not all countries have such reluctant leadership. Most educated Hawaiians, for example, are keenly aware of the limits of their environment, particularly in terms of population growth. There is only so much room on the islands, and the islanders know it. To Hawaiians, immigrants from the other 49 states present as great a threat as those from other nations. At a recent meeting of Hawaiian government officials in Honolulu, I had the ironic delight of hearing a speaker, who like most of his audience was of Japanese ancestry, ask how the country might practically and constitutionally close its doors to further immigration. One member of the audience countered: "How can we shut the doors now? We have many friends and relatives in Japan that we'd like to bring here some day so that they can enjoy Hawaii too." The Japanese-American speaker smiled sympathetically and answered: "Yes, but we have children now, and someday we'll have grandchildren too. We can bring more people here from Japan only by giving away some of the land that we hope to pass on to our grandchildren some day. What right do we have to do that?"

At this point, I can hear U.S. liberals asking: "How can you justify slamming the door once you're inside? You say that immigrants should be kept out. But aren't we all immigrants, or the descendants of immigrants? If we insist on staying, must we not admit all others?" Our craving for intellectual order leads us to seek and prefer symmetrical rules and morals: a single rule for me and everybody else; the same rule yesterday, today and tomorrow. Justice, we feel, should not change with time and place.

We Americans of non-Indian ancestry can look upon ourselves as the descendants of thieves who are guilty morally, if not legally, of stealing this land from its Indian owners. Should we then give back the land to the now living American descendants of those Indians? However morally or logically sound this proposal may be, I, for one, am unwilling to live by it and I know no one else who is. Besides, the logical consequence would be absurd. Suppose that, intoxicated with a sense of pure justice, we should decide to turn our land over to the Indians. Since all our other wealth has also been derived from the land, wouldn't we be morally obliged to give that back to the Indians too?

Pure Justice Vs. Reality.   Clearly, the concept of pure justice produces an infinite regression to absurdity. Centuries ago, wise men invented statutes of limitations to justify the rejection of such pure justice, in the interest of preventing continual disorder. The law zealously defends property rights, but only relatively recent property rights. Drawing a line after an arbitrary time has elapsed may be unjust, but the alternatives are worse.

We are all the descendants of thieves, and the world's resources are inequitably distributed. But we must begin the journey to tomorrow from the point where we are today. We cannot remake the past. We cannot safely divide the wealth equitably among all peoples so long as people reproduce at different rates. To do so would guarantee that our grandchildren, and everyone else's grandchildren, would have only a ruined world to inhabit.

To be generous with one's own possessions is quite different from being generous with those of posterity. We should call this point to the attention of those who, from a commendable love of justice and equality, would institute a system of the commons, either in the form of a world food bank, or of unrestricted immigration. We must convince them if we wish to save at least some parts of the world from environmental ruin.

Without a true world government to control reproduction and the use of available resources, the sharing ethic of the spaceship is impossible. For the foreseeable future, our survival demands that we govern our actions by the ethics of a lifeboat, harsh though they may be. Posterity will be satisfied with nothing less.

The "Carrying Capacity" Equivocation _____

William Aiken

Offering assistance to innocent persons in need of either a good or a service and assisting them, if they choose to accept the offer, is presumed to be morally permissible.[1] Such action can only be questioned, from a moral point of view, when there is evidence demonstrating that the assistance will result, not in benefit, but in harm. The burden of proof is placed upon those who claim that what is apparently beneficent (assisting the needy) will, in a particular case, turn out to be harmful. In order to show this, a morally relevant difference between the particular case and cases of genuine assistance must be found.

The challenge of demonstration has been accepted by certain Neo-Malthusians and "ecologically oriented ethicists" with respect to offering and rendering food aid to members of certain nation states. They argue that membership in certain nation states disqualifies one from receiving assistance; that although assisting members of these nation states "appears" to be both beneficent and morally permissible, it is, in fact, neither. The morally relevant difference cited involves the notion of "carrying capacity."

The argument used to support this position, which I will call Argument T (since it is sometimes associated with the policy known as "triage") is derived from a maxim in biologist Garrett Hardin's "New Decalogue," that, "Thou shalt not exceed the carrying capacity of any environment."[2] The argument is as follows:

Argument T

1. Every nation has a carrying capacity (that is, the maximum human population which its territory can support without irreparable damage; that is, damage which would result in its diminishing capability to support a population).

2. Some nations threaten to exceed, or have already exceeded, their carrying capacity by increasing their population (either through increased birth rate or decreased death rate).

3. Giving food to starving persons in such a nation will both decrease the death rate (by interfering with the outcome of starvation) and eventually increase the birth rate (those presently saved from death will later procreate) and thus it will either contribute to that nation's exceeding its carrying capacity or it will assist it to further exceed its carrying capacity.

4. Contributing to a nation's exceeding its carrying capacity, or assisting it to exceed this limit further, is morally wrong according to the maxim, "Thou shalt not exceed the carrying capacity of any environment."

5. *Therefore*, giving food to starving persons in nations which threaten to exceed or have already exceeded their carrying capacity is morally wrong (we ought not to do it even if we could do it with little or no cost to ourselves), and so we ought not to assist such persons.[3]

Although generally it may be morally permissible to offer and render assistance, it is not, by Argument T, morally permissible to assist members of some nation states because there is a morally relevant difference between those persons who live in a nation which has exceeded its carrying capacity and those who live in a nation which has not.

The entire framework of Argument T as established in the first premise can be challenged. The selection of nation states as the units of classification appears to be somewhat arbitrary from both a biological perspective and a moral perspective. From the former perspective, populations are examined in relation to their natural ecosystems, but since the natural environments with which populations interact can be smaller or larger than those circumscribed by ecologically irrelevant political boundaries, the adoption of political entities as environmental units requires justification. From the

Social Theory and Practice, Vol. 6, No. 1 (Spring 1980), 1–11. Reprinted by permission of the author and publisher.

moral perspective, it is not clear that the fulfillment of basic human needs should be discussed in terms of *groups* at all—particularly such apparently morally irrelevant groups as those defined by political boundaries. It is not obvious, from a moral point of view, that membership in any geographically defined group could morally disqualify a needy innocent person from receiving assistance. In spite of these difficulties with the entire framework of Argument T, I will not pursue them here, but will rather demonstrate that even granting the questionable framework, Argument T fails to make a convincing case against food assistance because it is a defective argument. It is defective, as I will show, because it rests on an equivocation on the central concept, "carrying capacity."[4]

There is no question that Argument T is very persuasive. It appears to be realistic, sensible, and "hard-headed." Its appeal is due primarily to the apparent empirical basis of the concept *carrying capacity*. In general, this notion has a nice scientific ring to it. The carrying capacity of a vehicle (for example, an elevator, boat, or truck) can be accurately determined by dividing the average size or weight per individual unit into the maximum total space or weight for which the vehicle was designed to safely operate. This limit may be accurately predicted through a calculation of mechanical and physical forces. It is a natural physical limit of the vehicle's capability. Although this "objective physical limit" connotation of "carrying capacity" carries over into the use of the concept in ecological contexts (for example, deer, rabbit, or lemming populations within a specific territorial environment), it is obvious that a natural environment is neither intentionally designed nor inalterably constrained by physical forces to carry only a specific number of units.[5] In an ecological context, the carrying capacity of the environment is approximated by dividing the calculated "living space" required per individual organism (which is primarily determined by assessment of the extent and suitability of the renewable food and water supply available) into the total range of environment under examination. If a given area can support only x number of deer (its carrying capacity), then $x + n$ number of deer will "overgraze" and damage the environment, thereby increasing the living space per individual organism required and thus reducing the

environment's carrying capacity. The determination and prediction of an environment's carrying capacity for animal populations can be made with relative precision (even though it is not as precise as is that of a vehicle's carrying capacity). It, too, is a natural limiting factor of sorts, a "biological fact" about the environment and the species involved. When animal populations reach this limit, the pending crisis of overpopulation can be forestalled by migration or by territorial expansion. Normally, however, this crisis is not forestalled, and starvation and concomitant disease reduce the population to a level which the damaged environment will tolerate—that is, to the new carrying capacity of the damaged environment.

Argument T applies this "biological limit" meaning of carrying capacity to human populations. The specifiable environment whose toleration limits are determined is the territory ruled by a sovereign nation state. By comparing the human population to the nation's available foodstuffs, a carrying capacity for that nation is determined. As in the case of deer, it is implied that if the limit is threatened, then migration, territorial expansion, or death by starvation and disease will restore the population to within the tolerable limits of the nation's environmental carrying capacity. It is the application of the notion of carrying capacity to human populations which generates Argument T with its conclusion that we must not interfere with the effects of starvation.[6]

Like the carrying capacity of a vehicle or a territorial ecosystem, the application of carrying capacity in Argument T has a nice "scientific" ring to it—it is apparently based on hard data, is easily predicted, and is unambiguously determined. But Argument T only gives the appearance of being based on hard facts. When the concept of carrying capacity is applied to human populations within a nation state's territory, it is not a natural fixed ratio of organism to environment. Unlike nonhuman animals, humans have the ability to artificially extend the carrying capacity of their environment.

One method humans use to extend their environment's carrying capacity is to increase agricultural productivity (through technological advances and increased efficiency) and to increase efficiency in storage and transportation. If a given region can produce and preserve more food, it will be able to support more people. Much of the debate surrounding the notion of carrying capacity has focused on the ability of technological advances to keep up with population growth. Supporters of the Green Revolution, algae-based protein advocates, and the "technological optimists" square off against the Neo-Malthusians, the "limits of growth" prophets, and the defenders of "quality" versus mere quantity of life. Although perhaps relevant to an examination of the entire globe's carrying capacity, this debate is irrelevant to the type of application of carrying capacity which Argument T makes, that is, the carrying capacity of a particular nation. No matter how advanced agricultural technology becomes, if a nation cannot afford to buy this technology it is useless to them as a means of providing food for their expanding population. Buying technology, however, is neither an environmental nor a technological matter. It is an economic matter.

This points to the second and most important method which humans use to extend the carrying capacity of their nation's environment: trade and negotiation with other nations who either have advanced agricultural technology to sell or who, because their agricultural productivity exceeds their population's demand, have food to sell. Once trade is introduced into the social environment of humans, a number of additional factors must be examined: national wealth, general productivity and distribution of goods, purchasing power, natural resource development potential, strategic military location, international bargaining power, and so on. Inclusion of these factors alters the notion of carrying capacity. It is no longer merely a biological concept. Now it is determined by a nation's ability not only to produce, but also to trade for the necessary agricultural products and technology required to feed its population. Any country which can afford to purchase these necessary goods has *not* exceeded its carrying capacity. The carrying capacity of a densely populated nation like the Netherlands is much higher than that of the sparsely populated sub-Sahara nations, not because of the amount of indigenous produce per capita, but because of the wealth per capita.

To demonstrate just how far from a "biological fact" the notion of carrying capacity is when applied to nation states, consider the following. If Argument T views human populations in nation states in the same way that non-human populations in territorial regions are viewed, then would it not follow that it would be immoral to *sell* food to any nation which needed it for human consumption? Presumably a nation would not buy food unless its own agricultural productivity was incapable of supporting its population. By selling food for human consumption, we would be assisting that nation (be it Japan or Saudi Arabia) to exceed its carrying capacity which, according to Hardin's maxim, is immoral. But for the advocates of Argument T this is absurd, for they assume that any nation which can buy food or essential agricultural technology has not yet exceeded its carrying capacity. International purchasing power extends a nation's carrying capacity because this is not a biological limit—it is a complex social, economic and political limit. It is not fixed by "nature" but by trade practices (for example, protective tariffs, currency exchange rates, concessionary prices, multinational corporation interests, militarily motivated "loans,") by the international market in terms of who has what to sell (goods, resources, alliances), who wants to buy it, what price you can get for what you have to sell, and by the influence of international interests upon indigenous production and distribution (for example, neo-colonialism with its emphasis upon the mass production of non-food export crops).

It is important to stress the fact that the carrying capacity of a nation is not just a "biological fact" about a population and its environment. If a nation's carrying capacity were a "biological fact," the implicit assumption of Argument T (that a nation's carrying capacity can be determined) would not need justification. However, when the carrying capacity is seen as a socio-economic limit, this assumption must be examined. Can we determine the carrying capacity of a nation, and, if so, are the assumptions which must be made to arrive at this calculation reasonable ones to make? I will divide my discussion into the two cases suggested by Argument T: those nations which have not yet, but threaten to, exceed their carrying capacity, and those nations which have already exceeded their carrying capacity.

In the former case, the determination of carrying capacity of a nation must be predicted, that is, at time t_1 a judgment must be made that at some future time, t_2, the maximum population a nation can withstand will have been reached, and that any further increase in population will exceed the carrying capacity. Such predictions are calculated by assuming the maintenance of all present conditions, projecting the continuation of current trends, and by either reducing all potential variables to constants or eliminating consideration of them by the "other things being equal" assumption. Such predictions are hypothetical in form; that is, if conditions remain unaltered, then the carrying capacity will be reached at time t_2. In dealing with non-human populations, which are incapable of intentional action to alter conditions, effect changes in trends, or actualize options, the truth of the antecedent may be safely assumed. Animals cannot alter their conditions. But such predictions are at least questionable when dealing with human populations, for it is not obvious that the antecedent can be reasonably expected to be true over an extended time period. The multitude of factors which must be taken into account and held to be constant over time is enormous, but the accuracy of the calculation of socio-economic carrying capacity is entirely contingent upon the constancy of these factors. This is not to say that it is impossible to determine a nation's carrying capacity before it is exceeded; only that it is not nearly so simple a matter as is the determination of biological carrying capacity. The longer the range of prediction (the longer time period over which the maintenance of the status quo is assumed), the less likely the antecedent is to be true. Consequently, the accuracy of the determination of carrying capacity upon which Argument T relies is in inverse relation to the length of time covered in the prediction.

It is morally wrong, according to Argument T, to contribute to a nation's exceeding its carrying capacity by giving food aid. The present act of keeping people alive does not in itself increase the population; it merely prevents an anticipated decrease. It would appear then that the immediate effect of food aid does not contribute to a nation's exceeding its carrying capacity; thus, in the "short run," assistance would be permissible. It could be argued, however, that for some nations, the threat of exceeding the carrying capacity is (other things being equal) so severe that preventing any deaths would contribute to a decline in the death rate and, thus,

would contribute to that nation's exceeding its carrying capacity. (But then not only would food aid be prohibited by Argument T, but so, too, would any act which resulted in fewer deaths—for example, trade with that nation in life-preserving commodities such as medical supplies and services, sanitation technology.) It may be that the fewer deaths resulting from assistance do decrease the overall annual death rate, but this must be clearly shown to be the case (for such assistance may only prevent an increase in death rate), and it must be shown that the decreasing death rate will not be offset by other factors (for example, rise in per capita income) which would increase the nation's carrying capacity. In these cases of severe threat, where the prediction of exceeding carrying capacity is a short-range prediction, the relationship of food aid to exceeding carrying capacity is not a direct causal one. Giving assistance "contributes" to that event only in the sense that it is one of many antecedent conditions which, given the entire set of relevant factors, is contingently necessary for the event. So even if a short-range prediction of exceeding carrying capacity were to be made, it could not be immediately inferred that acts of assistance which prevent deaths would "contribute" in a significant way to this event.

But the force of Argument T lies not in short-range predictions. It lies in long-range predictions of the geometric increase in population which results from keeping people alive. As Malthus demonstrated so well, populations multiply geometrically over generations so that, in twenty years, the effect of keeping people alive now will be a sharp increase in total population. So by Argument T, we should refuse to assist now in order to prevent a population increase in twenty years, and thus to avoid contributing to that nation's exceeding its carrying capacity in the next generation. Yet here we must rely upon a long-range prediction of socio-economic carrying capacity which assumes that all current socio-economic factors will remain unaltered for twenty years. It is these predictions which, given the multitude of factors which can change, are questionable. Even if a determination of socio-economic carrying capacity is made and the event of exceeding it is predicted, the status of that prediction will be far below the level of "scientific accuracy" enjoyed by predictions of biological carrying capacity (due to the difference in credibility of the "other things being equal" assumption between human and non-human animals). Given these difficulties in predicting the socio-economic carrying capacity of nations which have not yet exceeded that limit, Argument T is not convincing in its proscription against assisting these nations.

But what about those nations which have *already* exceeded their carrying capacity? Argument T clearly prohibits assisting them. The problems of prediction and determination need not be considered here, for even if a nation's carrying capacity may not be accurately determined in advance of its being exceeded, at least we can know when it has been exceeded by simply observing the fact that large numbers of people in that nation are dying of starvation. Should we not refuse assistance to at least these nations? The strange thing about this criterion (that people are starving in a nation) is that it disregards other potential causes for the starvation such as the economic factors within that nation (for example, production and distribution of wealth, land, and capital ownership, effective social services), the political factors within that nation (for example, expenditure on arms development is given priority over food or population control programs), and the social factors within that nation (for example, the maintenance of an affluent elite at the cost of the impoverished masses). It looks only at the *result* of economic, political, and social arrangements in its judgment of carrying capacity. To ignore these other relevant causes of starvation within a nation merely reduces the statement, "Nation *x* has exceeded its carrying capacity," to the statement, "There is starvation in nation *x*." But then what is the use of this quasi-scientific circumlocution? Why not just assert that we ought not to assist any nation in which starvation is occurring? Why make it sound so objective and so reasonable?

Still there may be some nations in which massive starvation is indeed unavoidable—in which no amount of internal change could avert famine. Surely these should not be given assistance. They are doomed to their fate. Yet even these nations, of what Joseph Fletcher calls the Fifth World, are doomed only by present international market practices.[7] They do not have anything to sell which someone else wants, so their population capacity is very low, dependent entirely upon what their indigenous agricultural productivity can support. They

are forced into the same situation which animal populations are; that is, they are unable to extend their carrying capacity through trade and exchange. It is this group of nations which Argument T zeroes in on and of whom it boldly asserts that, "Thou shalt not assist any nation in which there are starving people who cannot afford to buy food at current market prices," and that, "It is immoral to give people what they cannot afford to buy." Yet it must be repeated again, the carrying capacity of such a nation is not in any way a biological limit, rather it is an economic limit. Its purchasing power determines whether or not its environment's carrying capacity can be extended. If oil is discovered within its territory, the supposed limit on population suddenly bolts upward to whatever extent the oil reserves last. A *nation's* carrying capacity is a by-product of the market—nothing more. It is never merely a biological limit.

In spite of this, Argument T gives the impression that the same notion of carrying capacity which applies to deer and lemmings also applies to humans within a nation state. The maxim, "Thou shalt not exceed the carrying capacity of any environment," suggests the primary biological meaning of the concept. Argument T applies this notion to humans within nation states. In this application there is an ambiguity in the concept since, as I have shown, human populations produce artificial carrying capacities according to socio-economic laws, not biological ones. Two different meanings of the term are simultaneously implied: one means population versus available renewable foodstuffs, the other means population versus international bargaining power. Argument T must either stick to the primary biological meaning of the term and conclude that it is immoral to trade, exchange, sell, or lend food or agricultural assistance to *any* nation which needs it (at which point it becomes an absurd argument), or it must surrender the quasi-scientific connotation of biological carrying capacity and address the economic factors which determine the extent to which a nation can increase its population. By trying to do both, it equivocates on the term and thus renders the argument fallacious. If it were to stick purely to the economic connotation, Argument T would boil down to the claim that it is morally wrong to interfere with the free market and the "natural" consequences which result from lack of interference with that market (*à la* Adam

Smith). In other words, it is immoral to assist a nation which is unsuccessful in trade—a claim which I find to be morally unjustifiable. But because Argument T equivocates between the biological and the socio-economic meanings, it implies that not only can a nation's socio-economic carrying capacity be accurately determined, but that, if that nation exceeds its socio-economic carrying capacity, the same inevitable disaster will occur which occurs when animal populations exceed the biological carrying capacity of their territorial environment; that is, the increased population will deplete the resources and so increase the "living space" per unit required, and consequently increase the concomitant suffering and starvation. Without the equivocation, Argument T would never be seriously considered a *moral* argument. It would be seen for what it is, an attempted moral justification for present world trade practices and allocation of economic goods. Those nations which do not fare well in this arrangement are said to be doomed to suffering and starvation while those who prosper can ease their conscience by the assurance that it would be, after all, immoral to interfere.

By showing that Argument T is defective, I have answered the popular challenge of the Neo-Malthusians and have undercut their claim of exception to the general moral permissibility of benevolence. There may, of course, be other arguments which proscribe assisting the needy in other nations (for example, Lappé and Collins' claim that food aid assistance reinforces unjust social structures and prevents the indigenous power alterations necessary to obtain self-reliance[8]). But, by exposing the confusion in the supposedly "scientific" basis of the Neo-Malthusian arguments, I have at least cleared the way for the debate over the moral permissibility of giving food aid to be waged in its appropriate context—the world of social, political, and economic structures.

Notes

1. In order to respect the autonomy of potential assistees, the possibility of refusing the assistance must be kept open.

2. Garrett Hardin, "Carrying Capacity as an Ethical Concept," in *Lifeboat Ethics: The Moral Dilemmas of World Hunger,* edited by George Lucas and Thomas Ogletree (New York: Harper and Row, 1976), p. 134.

3. Argument T is not Hardin's formulation, but it puts his comments on "situation ethics" into argument form.

4. There are several other ways to attack this argument from within its framework which I will not develop here, for instance: (a) it relies upon the procedure of calculating utility over future generations, thus granting the interests of potential persons the same weight as living persons, and (b) it ignores alternative methods of reducing birth rates to avoid exceeding the carrying capacity of a nation (for example, birth control, demographic transition, alleviating the economic and social need for large families).

5. This is important to remember because no matter how often the "lifeboat" metaphor is used by Hardin and company, an environment simply is not a boat which will "sink" when x number of extra people are added to it.

6. Hardin has anticipated the other two standard population reactions by advocating that the "lifeboat" of the United States close its doors to all immigration and build up its defenses against invasion (to prevent territorial expansion). See Garrett Hardin, "Lifeboat Ethics: The Case Against Helping the Poor," in *World Hunger and Moral Obligation,* edited by William Aiken and Hugh LaFollette (Englewood Cliffs, NJ: Prentice-Hall, 1977), pp. 11–21.

7. Joseph Fletcher, "Give If It Helps But Not If It Hurts," in *World Hunger and Moral Obligation,* p. 108.

8. Frances Moore Lappé and Joseph Collins, *Food First: Beyond the Myth of Scarcity* (Boston: Houghton Mifflin Company, 1977).

Reproductive Choices: The Ecological Dimension

Ronnie Zoe Hawkins

While much has been said about the morality of choosing to abort a human fetus, too little attention has been given to the moral implications, from an ecological perspective, of deciding whether or not to add a new human life to the planet. In this essay I will argue that environmental considerations are relevant to the abortion debate and, conversely, that the abortion dispute ought to enter into a discussion of feminism and the environment. Speaking from a perspective of concern for *life* in a broadly inclusive sense, referring to the diversity of all life-forms on the planet, I will conclude that, when the ecological dimension is added to discussions of reproductive choice, the term "prolife" might most properly undergo a dramatic change in usage.

Environmental Considerations in the Abortion Debate: Population, Poverty, and Environmental Degradation

From a size of less than one billion throughout all our previous history, over the last two centuries the human population has swelled to a present total of between 5 and 6 billion people worldwide and is continuing to expand logarithmically. The median projection for stabilization has recently been upwardly revised to 14 billion people, more than twice the current number, and even this figure incorporates optimistic assumptions about declining growth rates that for the most part are yet to be realized.[1] Estimates of the maximum number of people the planet's resources will support with intensive management vary widely, as do assessments of the quality of life the majority of people will experience.[2] The links between population growth, poverty, and environmental degradation are becoming increasingly well documented, however, the combination frequently producing what is termed a "downward spiral"—a growing number of poor people are forced to make a living on in-

creasingly marginal land, resulting in deforestation, overgrazing, soil erosion, or an assortment of other environmental problems further exacerbating their poverty and often leading them to move on and repeat the process elsewhere.[3] At least 1.2 billion people around the world are presently estimated to be living in absolute poverty, of which about half are thought to be trapped in such a self-reinforcing process of increasing environmental degradation.[4] Unequal access to land and resources, ill-conceived development schemes, local and national politics, and the international economic power structure may all contribute prominently to the maintenance of their poverty, but continued population growth heightens the desperateness of the situation.

While the poor may seek to have large families as a way of coping with their immediate economic conditions, to provide more hands to work and to offer an increased chance that parents will be cared for in their old age, the long-term trade-off parallels that of employing ecologically damaging farming practices because of today's need to eat: tomorrow, the overall needs will be greater, while the resources for meeting them will be proportionally less. Women, bearing a large and growing share of the burden of poverty, are increasingly seeking to limit their family sizes, but all too often, for institutional or social reasons, they are denied access to the means for doing so.[5]

Population, Consumption, and the Toll on Nonhuman Life

Human beings are far from the only victims of the interaction between population growth and environmental degradation, however, and poor people are not the only actors in the ecological tragedy. As more and more land is radically altered to meet growing human needs and its biotic components are converted into resources for human use, nonhuman organisms also are experiencing limita-

APA Newsletters, Vol. 91, No. 1 (Spring 1992), 66–73, plus new additional comments by the author. Reprinted by permission.

tions on their growth, movements, and interactions, deprivation of access to the necessities of life, and frequently loss of life itself. With destruction of habitats and fragmentation of populations, entire species are dwindling and disappearing as a result of human activities. In contrast to natural extinctions, which are relatively rare occurrences that are mitigated by the emergence of new species, anthropogenic or human-caused species extinctions are occurring at several hundred times the natural, background rate and, since they are the result of abrupt and often total destruction of habitats, are not offset by new speciation.[6] The changes are so enormous that scientists working within a "crisis discipline" attempting to stem the massive loss of species from the planet have even begun discussing a possible *end to evolution;* conservation biologist Michael Soulé assesses the situation as follows:

> At best, the planet's macrobiota is entering a kind of pause, an evolutionary lacuna, caused by the human usurpation of the land surface. For the survivors, the pause will last until the human population declines to a biologically tolerable level—a level at which land appropriated by humans is returned to nature, and extinction rates return to the (paleontological) background level.[7]

When we come to grips with the massive scale on which conditions for human and nonhuman life alike are increasingly deteriorating, we must acknowledge that planetary life itself, construed in the larger sense as encompassing all the diverse extant as well as potential future forms arising through the evolutionary process, is faced with a crisis of unprecedented proportions. This crisis is in large part an undeniable if unintended result of the disproportionate expansion in human numbers occurring over very recent time. Perhaps the suddenness of its onset accounts for the relative philosophical neglect it has received heretofore, but continued inattention is no longer acceptable in the face of difficulties that grow more severe with each passing day.

While not overlooking the multiple contributory factors leading to our present predicament, we must clearly define its inescapable biological dimension: the global balance of lifeforms has been changed dramatically, and individual and societal decisions that further increase the human preponderance relative to other forms of life, in aug-

menting the imbalance, serve to aggravate its untoward consequences. And while technological advances may appear to maintain the quality of human life at a much higher carrying capacity than prevailed throughout millennia—at least for certain groups of humans over a finite period of time[8]—the existence and continued evolution of other forms of life, and hence the well-being of life in the larger sense, require a reversal of the present trend and an eventual reduction in the size of the human population.[9]

The Importance of Abortion in Population Limitation

If only for anthropocentric and sometimes even nationalistic or ethnocentric reasons, many people will agree that some form of human population limitation is needed. Often, however, in the industrialized nations the population problem is construed as something "out there," a pressing issue for the poorer nations of the tropics perhaps but of little concern within a wealthy country. Just as frequently, abortion is seen as isolable from the larger picture of population limitation, something quite different from the "acceptable" methods of family planning. But those familiar with the empirical evidence present a somewhat different picture of these issues.

According to the 1992 World Population Data Sheet,[10] the rate of natural increase for the world as a whole is currently 1.7% per year, a growth rate that, if sustained, would result in a doubling of the size of the human population every 41 years.[11] It is true that the "more developed" regions of the world, comprising North America, Europe, Australia, Japan, New Zealand and the former USSR, have a considerably lower annual rate of increase and a longer doubling time overall, 0.5% and 148 years, respectively, as opposed to a growth rate of 2.3% and a doubling time of 30 years for the "lesser developed" regions (excluding China); it must be noted, however, that the United States has one of the highest rates of natural increase of all the industrialized nations, 0.8%, and is currently growing so as to double in size every 89 years—in striking contrast to the common misconception that "zero population growth" has already been achieved in this country.

Even where populations are increasing at a relatively small rate, however, such countries should by no means be considered innocent of the toll being taken on the planet's living systems. Estimates of the consumption of world resources and generation of stress to the global environment have ranged from fifteen to several hundred times as great per capita for citizens of the industrialized nations relative to those of the poorer regions of the world.[12] One group of authors construes population and consumption as intertwined in a *multiplicative* relationship, the total adverse effect of an increase in human numbers in certain regions of the globe thus being greatly amplified, as follows (where '×' indicates the multiplication sign):

> environmental impact = population × consumption of goods per person × environmental impact per quantity of goods consumed[13]

According to this formula, the environmental toll taken by each new human born within the "developed" world will be very much greater than that of one born elsewhere. By the same token, those of us living in the industrialized nations can lower our overall destructive effect on the natural environment both by reducing the amount and nature of our consumption and by reducing the number of us that consume the planet's precious resources.

Projections that foresee the world population leveling off at a total far less than what can be calculated by simply taking today's number through several doubling times (which, at our current rate of growth, yields over forty billion people just past the end of the next century)[14] are dependent in part upon the assumption that the rate of population increase will fall substantially in the less industrialized countries as they undergo the "demographic transition"[15] from a state of high fertility and high mortality to a state where both fertility and mortality rates are low. In the process of making that transition, however, a large gap often develops between the fall in death rate and the decline in birth rate, generating a great increase in absolute numbers before stabilization can be attained. It is at this critical period of time, when smaller family sizes are becoming desirable but contraceptive use is unfamiliar or unavailable, that abortion plays a prominent and necessary role in fertility reduction, with abortion rates later declining as contraceptive use increases.[16] The abortion rates in Japan and in South Korea, for example, countries which underwent

rapid transitions to a low birth rate during this century, rose when fertility was declining most sharply, then fell dramatically as the rate of contraceptive use increased; without abortion, it is estimated that South Korea's birth rate during the transition would have been 22% higher.[17] And since even small changes in the birth rate during this period will result in substantial differences in the size of the reproducing population base and therefore in ultimate population size, abortion has an important role to play in the long-term welfare of many developing nations.

In the industrialized world, too, where each additional "place at life's table" results in consumption of a significantly greater slice of the resource pie, abortion continues to contribute substantially to reducing environmental destruction; termination of over a million and a half undesired pregnancies every year in the United States, for instance, has served to lessen significantly the toll on the global ecosystem, however small a part such concerns may play in an individual woman's decision to choose abortion. Figures for 1986 show that, worldwide, while the total population increased by 82 million, an estimated 54 million abortions were performed, approximately 28 million in "developing" countries and 26 million in the industrialized world; in the preceding year, while the population of the United States grew by 2.2 million, 1.6 million abortions were performed.[18] Abortion, therefore, far from being a minor contributor where population limitation is concerned, is currently serving to reduce the yearly population increase, both in this country and overall, by around 40%. As a backup to contraception, abortion plays a major role in limiting the ecologically damaging effects of continued human population growth in all parts of the globe.

Relevance of the Abortion Issue to Feminist Concerns about the Environment

The above, drawing heavily on empirical material, is intended to illustrate the practical importance of ecological considerations to the abortion debate. Expanding the focus of discussion to include the ecological dimension also serves, as will be shown, to illuminate certain issues of theoretical importance. A certain construal of the emerging position known as *ecofeminism* will be shown to provide additional grounding for a woman's right to choose abortion, while clarifying such an approach to the abortion issue may lead to greater consistency in feminist thinking about the environment.

Women, Nature, Dualism and Domination

While there have been various formulations of ecofeminism, perhaps the dominant theme of ecofeminism as a philosophical position is the recognition of connections existing between the domination of women, the domination of certain groups of human beings by other groups, and the domination of nonhuman animals or of "nature" in general. The common root of such domination is often traced to what has been identified as patriarchal thinking, a type of thinking that has been characterized by various authors as predominantly dualistic, hierarchical, atomistic, abstract, and rationalistic.[19] According to ecofeminist philosopher Karen Warren, underlying all forms of domination is an "oppressive conceptual framework" that sanctions differential power relationships according to a "logic of domination" having its basis in dualism: a dichotomous split is postulated to exist between polar opposites determined by possession or lack of a particular characteristic; one side of the dichotomy is assumed to be morally superior to the other; and this assumption in turn is taken to justify the domination of the side considered inferior by that considered superior.[20] Examples bearing out this analysis abound: mind/body, man/woman, white/black, "developed" society/"undeveloped" society, culture/nature, and human being/nonhuman organism are examples of socially constructed dualisms that, through operation of a logic of domination that assigns unequal value to the two components of each pair and sanctions subjugation of one to the other, can be understood to undergird not only patriarchy but Western (or Northern) imperialism and much ecological destruction as well.

It is claimed by some ecofeminists that women have historically been identified with the physical side of the mind/body dualism and with nature as opposed to culture, and that, through linkage with the "inferior" poles of such traditionally accepted dichotomies, their subordination to men has been reinforced.[21] Many contemporary feminists have rejected these identifications, some recasting liberation in terms of women taking their place alongside men in a separate, nature-transcending realm of the mental or spiritual. In a critical review of the ecofeminist literature, however, Val Plumwood criticizes such a rejection as an incomplete solution to the problem of domination and stresses the need to challenge the dualistic framework itself.[22] She maintains that, since we have heretofore been employing a "basically masculine" model of what it means to be human, a rethinking of the man/woman split must be linked with a reexamination of the mind/body and human/nonhuman dichotomies also, as well as of "the notion of humanity itself."[23]

Dualism and the Abortion Debate

Our conception of what it means to be human is something that lies deep at the heart of the abortion debate, and inspection of some of the underlying assumptions involved provides further support for an ecofeminist critique targeting dualism. Constructed almost entirely within the framework of patriarchal thought, the present "profile" stance is riddled with dualisms. At the social level, for instance, many antiabortion activists reportedly profess a belief in "intrinsic differences" existing between the nature of men and that of women, a belief not shared by their prochoice counterparts.[24] On a more metaphysical plane, the current majority position of Catholic theologians upholds a belief in "ensoulment" occurring at the moment of conception of a human being, a "theory of immediate animation" that is rooted in the Cartesian dichotomy between the mind or soul and the body and that makes the origin of a new human life an abrupt crossing of an absolute threshold.[25] And, clearly, even abortion opponents who would withhold explicit endorsement of the Cartesian view or of strictly separate male and female spheres appear to embrace without reservation the existence of an unbridgeable gap between human life and other forms of life. Without such an assumption, condemnation of the taking of an "innocent life" in "prolife" arguments would have to address issues of meat-eating, animal experimentation, and the destruction of wildlife as well as the aborting of a human fetus.[26]

Does Nature Abhor a Dualism?

Rising to the challenge of Plumwood and others, ecological and other feminists may choose to reject all the dualisms lying at the core of the "pro-life" position, working instead to develop a non-dualistic understanding of humanness and, indeed, of *life* in the broader sense. The traditional view postulating radical differences between men and women has been under siege for some time, of course, and perhaps increasing self-determination of gender roles by individuals will be most effective in loosening the grip of this particular conceptual split on our collective consciousness. The other two sharp divisions mentioned above are, however, also increasingly open to challenge, spurred on in part by developments in the empirical and technological sciences demonstrating that graded differences, not abrupt discontinuities, seem to be the rule rather than the exception in nature.

The controversy surrounding the "abortion pill," mifepristone (RU 486),[27] can, for instance, be interpreted as in part a fight over the need to keep our dichotomies sharp in the face of yet another threat to our time-honored distinctions. An obvious worry to abortion foes is that a medical as well as surgical option will make abortion seem "easier," less traumatic, and perhaps more a matter of "menstrual regulation" than a termination of pregnancy; as a method that can take place in a greater variety of settings and that is less delimited in time than uterine aspiration or curettage, abortion by administration of mifepristone may be somewhat less likely to be perceived as an act that definitively crosses over a line.[28]

In addition, the growing availability of medical abortion as well as the other new reproductive technologies serves to underscore the gradualness of development from the fertilized egg or zygote to the newborn infant—medically recognized as "a continuous process of becoming."[29] Approximately six days are required for the zygote, fertilized in the fallopian tube, to reach a position where it can implant in the lining of the uterus, and another 6 to 8 days are needed for implantation to be completed, with pregnancy, on its medical definition, said to have begun only at this time.[30] While the zygote is recognized as unquestionably "both alive and human" and possessing the potential to develop into an adult human being, this potential is noted to be only "theoretic and statistical," since only about one in three actually succeeds in fulfilling it, a high percentage of conceptions ending in spontaneous abortions that frequently pass unnoticed.[31] Furthermore, since, before implantation, the developing entity has the potential to become either less (through fusion) or more (twinning) than a complete individual, and since its first cellular differentiation involves establishment of what become the placental tissues, it is termed a "preembryo" through the first 14 days after fertilization; the term "embryo" is applied from implantation through the end of the eighth week, during which time the major organ systems are being formed, and the term "fetus" from the second month onward, with the potential being recognized for differentiation in the "status" of the developing entity at various different times along this continuum.[32]

It may be, then, that questions as to whether or not a woman is pregnant or has undergone abortion have answers that are grey rather than black or white. Mifepristone, for instance, has been shown in some experimental studies to be effective in preventing implantation as well as inducing abortion after implantation has taken place, and, thus, can be construed as potentially a contraceptive as well as an abortifacient;[33] making this distinction depends, however, on accepting some such differentiation between the embryo and the preembryo, since the zygote has been formed by the time of action of the agent—as it has by the time of action of other accepted methods of "contraception," including the IUD, progestin implants, and other postcoital methods. In view of the spectrum of time periods during which actions to prevent pregnancy may be undertaken, one of the scientists involved in the development of mifepristone, Etienne-Emile Baulieu, has coined the word "contragestion" (a shortening of "contra-gestation") to emphasize the continuity of the processes at work and of the possibilities for choosing to interrupt them, "stressing the quite natural aspects of fertility and the control thereof."[34]

An understanding of embryological development leads one to an appreciation of another kind of continuity as well, one that speaks against the third type of dualism mentioned earlier, the assumed gap between the human and the non-human. The earliest phases of development are very similar for all vertebrate embryos. By the fifth week after fertilization, for example—three weeks

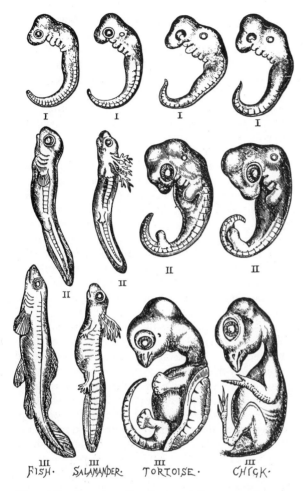

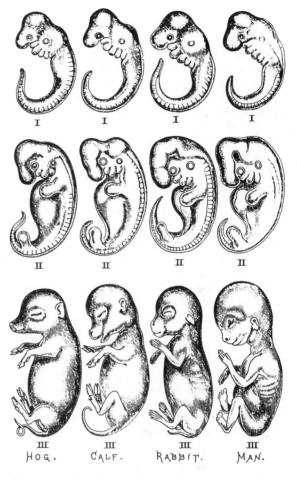

Figure 1 A series of embryos at three comparable and progressive stages of development (marked I, II, III), representing each of the classes of vertebrated animals below the Mammalia. (After Häckel.)

Figure 2 Another series of embryos, also at three comparable and progressive stages of development (marked I, II, III), representing four different divisions of the class Mammalia. (After Häckel).

after a missed period, around the time many women will be discovering their pregnancies and deciding whether or not to continue them—the embryo, about a quarter of an inch in size, shows rather undifferentiated paddle-shaped limb buds, an extremely rudimentary facial structure, and the same kind of skin all vertebrates initially share; it has the type of kidney that is functional in fishes and amphibians and a set of pharyngeal pouches resembling the early stages of the gills formed in these creatures; and, while indeed possessed of a

brain and a beating heart, its early heart is two-chambered, like that of a fish, and its brain at this stage little more than a simple tubular structure that is much the same in developing amphibians, reptiles, birds and mammals.[35] The close resemblance of the developmental sequence among the different vertebrate classes is taken as an indication of a common evolutionary origin, and, indeed, Darwin is said to have considered embryology to provide some of the strongest evidence for his theory of natural selection.[36] (See Figures 1 and 2.)

Furthermore, while the human fetus may be genetically identifiable as human from the time of conception, all life on Earth is remarkably the same in its nucleic-acid basis. Humans and chimpanzees, in particular, are strikingly close in their genetic makeup, with DNA sequences differing by only a little over 1%—so close, in fact, that some taxonomists are proposing that humans and the two chimpanzee species should all share the same genus, *Homo*.[37] And, of perhaps even greater import to philosophers, those who study animal behavior are finding considerable empirical support for attributing mental states such as beliefs and desires to a variety of nonhuman animals, and even the question as to whether chimpanzees and other apes may have their own "theory of mind," the ability to attribute mental states to others, is currently under scrutiny.[38]

Biology thus presents little evidence for a sharp discontinuity between human and nonhuman, offering, instead, virtually overwhelming support for placing human life on a continuum with all other life. It would seem, then, that the burden of proof must fall on those arguing for a sharp division within this spectrum. And if empirical evidence alone falls short of entailing a need for similarity in our moral valuation of other forms of life, it can at the very least be taken as undermining the dualistic assumptions that undergird our currently accepted value hierarchy.[39]

Healing the Splits Is in the Interest of All Life

In rejecting the dualistic thinking rife within our contemporary society, and in particular rejecting a stark division between human and nonhuman life, ecofeminists may draw upon the massive destruction of nonhuman organisms as well as mounting human misery for ample evidence of the need for a reversal of the current population trends among the planet's different species. Such a move shifts the context of the debate away from a pitting of the needs of a certain subset of human beings against those of another (potential) subset and into a domain in which we must at least ask how the consequences of our reproductive choices will affect the needs of all planetary lifeforms.

An antiabortion stance stands as at best narrowly anthropocentric in this regard, at worst falling far short even of anthropocentrism when the long-range interests of humanity are considered.[40] At a more theoretical level, however, without the sharp human/nonhuman dichotomy, the "prolife" position itself collapses, since the assumption of human separateness and superiority makes up its very foundation. If that great moral chasm cannot be defended, then the refusal to weigh human fetal life against other pressing considerations becomes open to question, especially in light of our society's great willingness to take nonhuman life for far more trivial reasons than are likely to underlie the choice of abortion. With a growing body of feminist moral theory developed around frameworks emphasizing continuity, difference without value disparity, relationship, contextual concreteness, and emotional responses such as loving and caring,[41] nondualistic criteria for deciding how, in particular situations, to favor one form of life over another—as all our reproductive choices ultimately do, in consequence of our living on a finite planet—can and must be found.

Abortion has recently received attention as a problematic issue for ecofeminists: it has been viewed as a "masculine" response to unwanted pregnancy that "fails to respect the interconnectedness of all life,"[42] and as a choice that is difficult to reconcile with "an abstract pro-nature stance"[43] that would allow "natural" events such as pregnancy to run their course. As Plumwood maintains, however, there is a need to reconceptualize both the concept of the human and the concept of nature,[44] and part of meeting this challenge will lie in reconceiving ourselves as beings who are part of the natural world and simultaneously beings whose nature is to be active choosers of our own actions, responsible for the effect of those actions on each other and on other lifeforms, including the effects of our own reproductive activities. And at the present time in history, recognition of our connectedness with all other life on the planet reinforces the need for the abortion option. When the interests of life in this larger sense are taken into consideration, the prochoice position is the one most deserving of the adjective "prolife."

Notes

1. See Virginia Abernethy, "Population Growth Curves, False Comfort?" *Population and Environment* 12 (Winter 1990), 97. Paul Demeny, in "The World Demographic Situation," *World Population and U.S.*

Policy: The Choices Ahead, ed. J. Menken (New York: W. W. Norton, 1986), pp. 29–39, presents an examination of population growth curves projected earlier for growth beyond 1985. For three projections making the simple assumption of a fixed growth rate, the "low" rate of 0.5% per year (the average rate of growth in the nineteenth century), yields 8.6 billion people by the end of the twenty-first century, the "medium" rate of 1% per year (the average rate between 1920 and 1950) yields 15.3 billion by that time, and the "high" rate of 1.65% (the rate estimated for 1985—it is somewhat higher now; see note 14) leads to "a world population of over 32 billion people, an outcome implausible on its face" (p. 34); Demeny notes that the assumptions needed to generate the lower figures imply "a discontinuous break from the pre-1985 growth path." "More realistic" extrapolations mesh with earlier growth rates but trace an S-curve showing a progressive leveling off of growth rates over time, though an inflection point in the late 1960s—apparently our only evidence for such an overall leveling off thus far—is "not obvious at a casual glance." A set of three such curves was generated by the U.N., the "low," "medium," and "high" projections yielding populations of 7.4 billion, 8.2 billion, and 9.1 billion, respectively, for the year 2025, with a projected leveling off at about 10.4 billion by 2100 predicted by the World Bank by extending the U.N.'s "medium" projection (the figure that has since been revised upward, as noted). Demeny cautions that "the range of alternative long-term demographic futures is wide, and implications of possible policy choices that may influence the path actually followed are far-reaching" (p. 36). Abernethy is less sanguine in her assessment, noting "an alternate scenario [to the as-yet-unseen slowing of growth] is that rising mortality rates will halt population growth," probably, as in the case of "nonhuman populations that grow beyond the carrying capacity of their environment," in the form of a crash in numbers.

2. Expectations range from the dire predictions of famine and social collapse early in the twenty-first century made in The Limits to Growth, to Donella Meadows et al (New York: Universe Books, 1972), to the wild optimism proclaiming great improvement in life and environmental quality of The Resourceful Earth, by Julian Simon and Herman Kahn (Oxford: Basil Blackwell, 1984). A report by the U.S. National Academy of Sciences in 1969 arrived at a figure of 10 billion as "the upper limit of what an intensively managed world might support with some degree of comfort and choice"; see David Western, "Population, Resources, and Environment in the Twenty-first Century," in Conservation for the Twenty-first Cen-

tury, ed. D. Western and M. C. Pearl (New York: Oxford University Press, 1989), pp. 13–14, for a discussion of the various scenarios within a context of the outlook for wildlife in the coming century, which is generally conceded to be "more uniformly dismal" by all predictors.

3. Alan B. Durning, Poverty and the Environment: Reversing the Downward Spiral, Worldwatch Paper 92 (Washington, DC: Worldwatch Institute, 1989).

4. Ibid., p. 45.

5. Surveys show that 50–60% of couples in Latin America, 60–80% in nonaffluent Asian countries (excluding China), 75% in North Africa and the Middle East, and 90% in sub-Saharan Africa presently use no form of modern birth control. The same research, however, shows that a majority in Latin America and Asia desire to limit their family size, and a growing number do so in the Middle East and Africa, though "the desire to maintain male dominance" on the part of the husband remains a major factor in keeping birth rates in Africa high. See Jodi L. Jacobson, The Global Politics of Abortion, Worldwatch Paper 97 (Washington, DC: Worldwatch Institute, 1990), pp. 22–37.

6. Anthropogenic, or human-caused, extinction must be clearly differentiated from natural extinction, which is "part of the process of replacing less well-adapted gene pools with better adapted ones"; natural extinctions are "rare events on a human time scale," with "few, if any," of the hundreds of vertebrate extinctions incurred over the last several centuries being the result of factors other than human activities, according to Michael Soulé, "What Is Conservation Biology?" Bioscience 35 (1985): 730. The rate of species loss in the present anthropogenic extinction event is "about 400 times that recorded through recent geological time and is accelerating rapidly"; the event is "the most extreme for 65 million years," since the end of the dinosaur era, and it is far more severe with respect to the loss of plant diversity. See Edward O. Wilson, "The Biological Diversity Crisis," Bioscience 35 (1985): 703.

7. Michael Soulé, "Conservation Biology in the Twenty-first Century: Summary and Outlook," in Western and Pearl, p. 303.

8. The carrying capacity is a measure of the number of human beings (or individuals of other species) an environment can sustain over a period of time, usually taken to be the indefinite future—i.e., without causing harm to the environment. It should be noted that "overpopulation" is being defined in recent works not in terms of population density but in terms of the long-term carrying capacity of the region. In The Population Explosion (New York: Simon & Schuster, 1990), Paul and Anne Ehrlich

maintain that an area is overpopulated "when its population can't be maintained without rapidly depleting nonrenewable resources . . . and without degrading the capacity of the environment to support the population," or, "in short, if the long-term carrying capacity of an area is clearly being degraded by its current inhabitants," 38–39. By this definition, virtually all rich and poor nations alike are overpopulated, since virtually all are depleting their resources faster than they can be renewed—the process may be just a little less obvious in the case of the rich nations because they are drawing upon resources that lie largely outside their own boundaries. The Netherlands, for example, often presented as an example of a country with both a high population density and a high standard of living, maintains its 1,031 people per square mile by importing raw materials from around the world, far exceeding the carrying capacity of its own land base.

9. The "deep ecology platform" proposed by philosopher Arne Naess recognizes that, for the "continuing evolution" of, for instance, "mammals defending vast territory," not just a stabilization of the human population but an eventual reduction will be needed; he criticizes traditional discussions that refer only to "'carrying capacity' for humans," not "'carrying capacity for humans and non-humans.'" See Naess, "Sustainable Development and Deep Ecology," in *Ethics of Environment and Development*, ed. J. R. Engel and J. G. Engel (Tucson: University of Arizona Press, 1990), pp. 88–91.

10. Compiled annually by the Population Reference Bureau, Inc., 1875 Connecticut Avenue NW, Suite 520, Washington, DC 20009.

11. The present expansion of the human population is an example of *exponential* growth, the kind of growth that is said to occur when a quantity is increasing by a fixed percentage of its size per interval of time. A simple mathematical relationship holds between the percent growth per unit time and the time it takes for that quantity to double in size: the *doubling time* is equal to 70 divided by the percent growth, or $T_2 = 70/P$. Hence, if the world population is growing by 1.7% per year, its doubling time is 70/1.7 or a little over 41 years. See Albert A. Bartlett, "Forgotten Fundamentals of the Energy Crisis," *Focus* 1 (Winter 1992), 26–40, for a discussion of exponential growth in relation to both population size and resource depletion.

12. F. E. Trainer, in *Abandon Affluence* (London: Zed Books, 1985), estimates the average per capita resource consumption of persons living in the rich nations of the world to be about 15 times that of those living in the poor nations, p. 3; Paul and Anne Ehr-

lich (*National Geographic* 174 [1988], 914–17) estimate that the birth of a baby within the United States will "impose more than a hundred times the stress on the world's resources and environment than a baby born in a developing nation"; and the "Demographic Facts of Life in the U.S.A." fact sheet prepared by Zero Population Growth (Washington, DC, August 1991) maintains that "the average American's energy use is equivalent to the consumption of 3 Japanese, 6 Mexicans, 13 Chinese, 35 Indians, 153 Bangladeshis, or 499 Ethiopians."

13. For a discussion, see Paul R. Ehrlich, Anne H. Ehrlich and John P. Holdren, *Ecoscience: Population, Resources, Environment* (San Francisco: W. H. Freeman and Company, 1977), p. 720. Also see Ehrlich and Ehrlich, *The Population Explosion*, pp. 58–59, where the equation is summarized as Impact = Population $\times$ Affluence $\times$ Technology, or $I = PAT$.

14. If the total world population is 5.42 billion in 1992 and is growing at a rate of 1.7% per year, as per the current World Population Data Sheet, its doubling time is slightly over 41 years, and maintaining this rate of growth through 3 doubling times would yield 10.84 billion in 2033, 21.68 billion in 2074, and 43.36 billion by 2115. See note 1 for an indication of the assumptions made in order to reach projections for leveling off that fall far short of these figures.

15. It should be noted that the theory holding that a "demographic transition" to lower birth rates follows automatically upon economic "development" of a region is controversial in the field of population studies. See, for example, Garrett Hardin, "Mythic Aspects of the Demographic Transition," *Population and Environment* 12 (1990): 41–42.

16. Jacobson, *The Global Politics of Abortion*, p. 23.

17. Ibid.

18. Population Crisis Committee, *Access to Birth Control: A World Assessment*, Population Briefing Paper No. 19 (October 1987), as reported in brief for Population-Environment Balance, et al., as *Amici Curiae* supporting appellees in *Webster* v. *Reproductive Health Services*, Supreme Court of the United States, October Term, 1988. The interest of the *Amici Curiae* preparing the brief, which included the Sierra Club, the Worldwatch Institute and Zero Population Growth among others, was stated to be "the potential detrimental impact on family planning programs both here and abroad of the provision of the Missouri statute at issue that prohibits 'encouraging or counseling a woman to have an abortion not necessary to save her life,'" in light of the fact that "if abortion were not an option, the strains on the environment would be even greater" than they are at present.

19. For characterizations of patriarchal thinking as seen

from an ecofeminist perspective, see Karen J. Warren, "Feminism and Ecology: Making Connections," *Environmental Ethics* 9 (1987): 3–20; Jim Cheney, "Eco-feminism and Deep Ecology," *Environmental Ethics* 9 (1987): 115–145; and Michael E. Zimmerman, "Feminism, Deep Ecology, and Environmental Ethics," *Environmental Ethics* 9 (1987): 21–44.

20. See Karen J. Warren, "The Power and the Promise of Ecological Feminism," *Environmental Ethics* 12 (1990): 125–46, and also Warren, "Feminism and Ecology," above. A conceptual framework is a socially constructed set of assumptions about the nature of the world and ourselves that tends to structure the way we form our beliefs and judgments; its nature is likely to be in large part a result of the characteristics of those involved in its construction, including their gender and other socially relevant variables, but this nature becomes "invisible" to those seeing all things through its coloring lenses. See also Elizabeth Dodson Gray, *Green Paradise Lost* (Wellesley, MA: Roundtable Press, 1981) and *Patriarchy as a Conceptual Trap* (Wellesley, MA: Roundtable Press, 1982).

21. See, for instance, Warren, "The Power and the Promise of Ecological Feminism," 129–31.

22. Val Plumwood, "Ecofeminism: An Overview and Discussion of Positions and Arguments," *Australasian Journal of Philosophy,* Supplement to Vol. 64 (June 1986): 120–37.

23. Ibid., 134.

24. For a thoughtful examination of the contrasting attitudes of "prolife" and "prochoice" women, as expressed in their own words, see Kristin Luker, "Abortion and the Meaning of Life," in *Abortion: Understanding Differences,* ed. S. Callahan and D. Callahan (New York and London: Plenum Press, 1984), pp. 31–45.

25. For a critical discussion of this point, see Joseph F. Donceel, "A Liberal Catholic's View," in *Abortion and Catholicism,* ed. P. B. Jung and T. A. Shannon (New York: Crossroad Publishing Company, 1988), pp. 48–53.

26. The status of nonhuman life has indeed been recognized as problematic for certain approaches to interpretation of the proscription "thou shalt not kill" and for the phrase "the sanctity of life"; see Carol A. Tauer, "Probabilism and the Moral Status of the Early Embryo," in Jung and Shannon, pp. 78–79, and Marjorie Reiley Maguire, "Personhood, Covenant, and Abortion" in the same volume, p. 104.

27. Mifepristone, developed by Roussel-Uclaf under the designation RU 486, is a steroid that blocks the action of progesterone, the hormone essential for the establishment and maintenance of pregnancy. Clinical studies in France and elsewhere have shown mifepristone to be about 95% effective in terminating early pregnancy when given in combination with a prostaglandin; expulsion of uterine contents usually occurs within hours after the administration of the prostaglandin, which is given around 2 days after the mifepristone, and bleeding usually lasts for a little over a week. Possible adverse effects, including excessive bleeding, cramping, abdominal pain and incomplete abortion, indicate a need for medical supervision during the course of treatment but generally have been mild or confined to a small percentage of cases. Mifepristone may also be of benefit for postcoital contraception, induction of labor, and treatment of endometriosis, breast cancer, and premenstrual syndromes, among other conditions. See Etienne-Emile Baulieu, "Contragestion and Other Clinical Applications of RU 486, An Antiprogesterone at the Receptor," *Science* 245 (1989): 1351–56; Louise Silvestre et al., "Voluntary Interruption of Pregnancy with Mifepristone (RU 486) and a Prostaglandin Analogue: A Large-Scale French Experience," *New England Journal of Medicine* 322 (1990): 645–48; "Mifepristone (RU 486)" in *The Medical Letter on Drugs and Therapeutics* 32 (1990): 112–13; Etienne-Emile Baulieu, "Editorial: RU486 and the Early Nineties," *Endocrinology* 127 (1990): 2043–46.

28. See G. W. K. Tang, "A Pilot Study of Acceptability of RU 486 and ONO 802 in a Chinese Population," *Contraception* 44 (1991): 523–32, for an examination of contrasting attitudes toward medical and surgical abortion. Reasons for favoring medical over surgical abortion included its lesser association with injury or trauma to the body, its being "a more natural means to interrupt a pregnancy," and its being akin to "a menstrual regulation," while some negative perceptions were related to the longer time interval required for the medical procedure and a sense of guilt arising from "actively taking part" in the abortion by the act of swallowing the tablets, as opposed to playing a "passive" role in undergoing the surgical procedure.

29. Committee on Ethics of the American Fertility Society, "Ethical Considerations of New Reproductive Technologies," *Fertility and Sterility* 46 Supplement 1 (1986), 26S; a detailed discussion of the early phases of development is presented in chapter 11, "The Biologic Characteristics of the Preembryo," 26S–28S.

30. See Rebecca J. Cook, "Antiprogestin Drugs: Medical and Legal Issues," *Family Planning Perspectives* 21 (1989): 267.

31. Committee on Ethics of the American Fertility Society, *Fertility and Sterility* 46 Supplement 1 (1986), 26S.

32. Ibid.; see also *Fertility and Sterility* 46 Supplement 1 (1986): vii for definition of the preembryo.

33. See E. E. Baulieu and A. Ulmann, "Antiprogesterone Activity of RU 486 and Its Contragestive and Other Applications," *Human Reproduction* 1 (1986): 107–110, and Baulieu, "Contragestion and Other Clinical Applications," above.

34. Baulieu, "Contragestion and Other Clinical Applications," *Science* 245 (1989): 1356.

35. See T. W. Sadler, *Langman's Medical Embryology,* 5th ed. (Baltimore: Williams & Wilkins, 1985), and Scott F. Gilbert, *Developmental Biology,* 2d ed. (Sunderland, MA: Sinauer Associates, Inc., 1988).

36. Gilbert, *Developmental Biology,* p. 154.

37. For a discussion of this point, see Jared Diamond, *The Third Chimpanzee* (New York: HarperCollins, 1992), pp. 19–25.

38. Several recent, detailed explorations of this issue include Richard W. Byrne and Andrew Whiten, eds., *Machiavellian Intelligence: Social Expertise and the Evolution of Intellect in Monkeys, Apes, and Humans* (Oxford: Clarendon Press, 1988); Dorothy L. Cheney and Robert M. Seyfarth, *How Monkeys See the World* (Chicago and London: University of Chicago Press, 1990); Donald R. Griffin, *Animal Minds* (Chicago and London: University of Chicago Press, 1992; Carolyn A. Ristau, ed., *Cognitive Ethology: The Minds of Other Animals* (Hillsdale, NJ: Lawrence Erlbaum Associates, 1991); and Andrew Whiten, ed., *Natural Theories of Mind: Evolution, Development, and Simulation of Everyday Mindreading* (Cambridge, MA: Basil Blackwell, 1991).

39. See James Rachels, *Created from Animals* (Oxford: Oxford University Press, 1990), for an extended discussion of the undermining effect of evolutionary theory on moral claims that assume a value discontinuity between humans and nonhuman animals. Rachels takes aim at the traditional Western concept of "human dignity," which he construes as involving "a sharp contrast between human and non-human life" (p. 86) and maintains that, whereas Darwinism does not entail "that the doctrine of human dignity is false," it "provides reason for doubting the truth of the considerations that support the doctrine," e.g., "that humans are morally special *because* they are made in the image of God, or because they are uniquely rational beings" (p. 97). Using somewhat similar terminology (though not an

evolutionary argument), Peter Singer has criticized "the doctrine of the sanctity of human life," which he takes to mean, similarly, "the idea that there is a radical difference between the value of a human life and the value of the life of some other animal—a difference not merely in degree, but of quality or kind"; see Singer, "Unsanctifying Human Life," in *Philosophy and the Human Condition,* ed. T. L. Beauchamp, W. T. Blackstone, and J. Feinberg (Englewood Cliffs, NJ: Prentice-Hall, 1980), pp. 264–65. The aim of both arguments appears to be one not of lowering the value we place on human life but rather of elevating that which we accord nonhuman life, to "bring our attitudes to human and non-human animals closer together" (Singer, p. 273).

40. Since abortion cannot be separated from its often important role in family planning, discussion of the global problems humanity is facing should also help turn attention to the underlying pronatalist orientation of many "prolife" advocates. Outspoken antiabortionists such as Father Paul Marx, president of Human Life International, a U.S.–based organization acting to further restrict abortion rights in the less industrialized countries, and Judie Brown, president of the American Life Lobby, have gone on record in opposition to contraceptive use as well as abortion; see Jacobson, *The Global Politics of Abortion,* p. 54. Pronatalism is a position that requires a defense on its own merit, distinct from any connection it might exploit to the presumed rights of an unborn fetus. Appeal to "natural law" as a justification for unlimited human procreation in the face of our dramatic departure from the original balance of nature would seem a difficult task.

41. See Carol Gilligan's pioneering work in this area, *In a Different Voice: Psychological Theory and Women's Development* (Cambridge, MA: Harvard University Press, 1982), and, for instance, E. F. Kittay and D. T. Meyers, eds., *Women and Moral Theory* (Savage, MD: Rowman & Littlefield, 1987).

42. Celia Wolf-Devine, "Abortion and the 'Feminine Voice,'" *Public Affairs Quarterly* 3 (1989): 81–97.

43. Patricia Jagentowicz Mills, "Feminism and Ecology: On the Domination of Nature," *Hypatia* 6 (1991): 162–78.

44. See Val Plumwood, "Nature, Self, and Gender: Feminism, Environmental Philosophy, and the Critique of Rationalism," *Hypatia* 6 (1991): 3–27.

Can the Supply of Natural Resources Really Be Infinite? Yes!

Julian Simon

Natural resources are not finite. Yes, you read correctly. This [essay] shows that the supply of natural resources is not finite in any economic sense, which is why their cost can continue to fall in the future.

On the face of it, even to inquire whether natural resources are finite seems like nonsense. Everyone "knows" that resources are finite, from C. P. Snow to Isaac Asimov to as many other persons as you have time to read about in the newspaper. And this belief has led many persons to draw far-reaching conclusions about the future of our world economy and civilization. A prominent example is the *Limits to Growth* group, who open the preface to their 1974 book, a sequel to the *Limits*, as follows.

> Most people acknowledge that the earth is finite. . . . Policy makers generally assume that growth will provide them tomorrow with the resources required to deal with today's problems. . . . Recently, however, concern about the consequences of population growth, increased environmental pollution, and the depletion of fossil fuels has cast doubt upon the belief that continuous growth is either possible or a panacea.[1]

(Note the rhetorical device embedded in the term "acknowledge" in the first sentence of the quotation. That word suggests that the statement is a fact, and that anyone who does not "acknowledge" it is simply refusing to accept or admit it.)

The idea that resources are finite in supply is so pervasive and influential that the President's 1972 Commission on Population Growth and the American Future based its policy recommendations squarely upon this assumption. Right at the beginning of its report the commission asked, "What does this nation stand for and where is it going? At some point in the future, the finite earth will not satisfactorily accommodate more human beings—nor will the United States. . . . It is both proper and in our best interest to participate fully in the worldwide search for the good life, which

must include the eventual stabilization of our numbers."[2]

The assumption of finiteness is responsible for misleading many scientific forecasters because their conclusions follow inexorably from that assumption. From the *Limits to Growth* team again, this time on food: "The world model is based on the fundamental assumption that there is an upper limit to the total amount of food that can be produced annually by the world's agricultural system."[3]

The Theory of Decreasing Natural-Resource Scarcity

We shall begin with a far-out example to see what contrasting possibilities there are. (Such an analysis of far-out examples is a useful and favorite trick of economists and mathematicians.) If there is just one person, Alpha Crusoe, on an island, with a single copper mine on his island, it will be harder to get raw copper next year if Alpha makes a lot of copper pots and bronze tools this year. And if he continues to use his mine, his son Beta Crusoe will have a tougher time getting copper than did his daddy.

Recycling could change the outcome. If Alpha decides in the second year to make new tools to replace the old tools he made in the first year, it will be easier for him to get the necessary copper than it was the first year because he can reuse the copper from the old tools without much new mining. And if Alpha adds fewer new pots and tools from year to year, the proportion of copper that can come from recycling can rise year by year. This could mean a progressive decrease in the cost of obtaining copper with each successive year for this reason alone, even while the total amount of copper in pots and tools increases.

But let us be "conservative" for the moment and ignore the possibility of recycling. Another scenario: If there are two people on the island, Alpha Crusoe and Gamma Defoe, copper will be more scarce for each of them this year than if Alpha lived there alone, unless by cooperative efforts they can devise a more complex but more efficient mining operation—say, one man on the surface and one in the shaft. Or, if there are two fellows this year instead of one, and if copper is therefore harder to get and more scarce, both Alpha and Gamma may spend considerable time looking for new lodes of copper. And they are likely to be successful in their search. This discovery may lower the cost of copper to them somewhat, but on the average the cost will still be higher than if Alpha lived alone on the island.

Alpha and Gamma may follow still other courses of action. Perhaps they will invent better ways of obtaining copper from a given lode, say a better digging tool, or they may develop new materials to substitute for copper, perhaps iron.

The cause of these new discoveries, or the cause of applying ideas that were discovered earlier, is the "shortage" of copper—that is, the increased cost of getting copper. So a "shortage" of copper causes the creation of its own remedy. This has been the key process in the supply and use of natural resources throughout history.

Discovery of an improved mining method or of a substitute product differs, in a manner that affects future generations, from the discovery of a new lode. Even after the discovery of a new lode, on the average it will still be more costly to obtain copper, that is, more costly than if copper had never been used enough to lead to a "shortage." But discoveries of improved mining methods and of substitute products, caused by the shortage of copper, can lead to lower costs of the services people seek from copper. Let's see how.

The key point is that a discovery of a substitute process or product by Alpha or Gamma can benefit innumerable future generations. Alpha and Gamma cannot themselves extract nearly the full benefit from their discovery of iron. (You and I still benefit from the discoveries of the uses of iron and methods of processing it that our ancestors made thousands of years ago.) This benefit to later generations is an example of what economists call an "externality" due to Alpha and Gamma's activities, that is, a result of their discovery that does not affect them directly.

So, if the cost of copper to Alpha and Gamma does not increase, they may not be impelled to develop improved methods and substitutes. If the

cost of getting copper does rise for them, however, they may then bestir themselves to make a new discovery. The discovery may not immediately lower the cost of copper dramatically, and Alpha and Gamma may still not be as well off as if the cost had never risen. But subsequent generations may be better off because their ancestors suffered from increasing cost and "scarcity."

This sequence of events explains how it can be that people have been using cooking pots for thousands of years, as well as using copper for many other purposes, and yet the cost of a pot today is vastly cheaper by any measure than it was 100 or 1,000 or 10,000 years ago.

It is all-important to recognize that discoveries of improved methods and of substitute products are not just luck. They happen in response to "scarcity"—an increase in cost. Even after a discovery is made, there is a good chance that it will not be put into operation until there is need for it due to rising cost. This point is important: Scarcity and technological advance are not two unrelated competitors in a race; rather, each influences the other.

The last major U.S. governmental inquiry into raw materials was the 1952 President's Materials Policy Commission (Paley Commission), organized in response to fears of raw-material shortages during and just after World War II. The Paley Commission's report is distinguished by having some of the right logic, but exactly the wrong predictions, for its twenty-five forecast.

> There is no completely satisfactory way to measure the real costs of materials over the long sweep of our history. But clearly the man-hours required per unit of output declined heavily from 1900 to 1940, thanks especially to improvements in production technology and the heavier use of energy and capital equipment per worker. This long-term decline in real costs is reflected in the downward drift of prices of various groups of materials in relation to the general level of prices in the economy.
>
> [But since 1940 the trend has been] soaring demands, shrinking resources, the consequences pressure toward rising real costs, the risk of wartime shortages, the strong possibility of an arrest or decline in the standard of living we cherish and hope to share.[4]

For the quarter century for which the commission predicted, however, costs declined rather than rose.

The two reasons why the Paley Commission's

cost predictions were topsy-turvy should help keep us from making the same mistakes. First, the commission reasoned from the notion of finiteness and from a static technological analysis.

> A hundred years ago resources seemed limitless and the struggle upward from meager conditions of life was the struggle to create the means and methods of getting those materials into use. In this struggle we have by now succeeded all too well. . . . The nature of the problem can perhaps be successfully oversimplified by saying that the consumption of almost all materials is expanding at compound rates and is thus pressing harder and harder against resources which whatever else they may be doing are not similarly expanding.[5]

The second reason the Paley Commission went wrong is that it looked at the wrong facts. Its report gave too much emphasis to the trends of costs over the short period from 1940 to 1950, which included World War II and therefore was almost inevitably a period of rising costs, instead of examining the longer period from 1900 to 1940, during which the commission knew that "the man-hours required per unit of output declined heavily."[6]

We must not repeat the same mistakes. We should look at cost trends for the longest possible period, rather than focus on a historical blip; the OPEC-led price rise in all resources after 1973 is for us as the temporary 1940–50 wartime reversal was for the Paley Commission. And the long-run trends make it very clear that the costs of materials, and their scarcity, continuously decline with the growth of income and technology.

Resources as Services

As economists or as consumers, we are interested in the particular services that resources yield, not in the resources themselves. Examples of such services are an ability to conduct electricity, an ability to support weight, energy to fuel autos, energy to fuel electrical generators, and food calories.

The supply of a service will depend upon (a) which raw materials can supply that service with the present technology; (b) the availabilities of these materials at various qualities; (c) the costs of extracting and processing them; (d) the amounts needed at the present level of technology to supply the services that we want; (e) the extent to which the previously extracted materials can be recycled; (f) the cost of re-

cycling; (g) the cost of transporting the raw materials and services; and (h) the social and institutional arrangements in force. What is relevant to us is not whether we can find any lead in existing lead mines but whether we can have the services of lead batteries at a reasonable price; it does not matter to us whether this is accomplished by recycling lead, by making batteries last forever, or by replacing lead batteries with another contraption. Similarly, we want intercontinental telephone and television communication, and, as long as we get it, we do not care whether this requires 100,000 tons of copper for cables or just a single quarter-ton communications satellite in space that uses no copper at all.[7]

Let us see how this concept of services is crucial to our understanding of natural resources and the economy. To return to Crusoe's cooking pot, we are interested in a utensil that we can put over the fire and cook with. After iron and aluminum were discovered, quite satisfactory cooking pots, perhaps even better than pots of copper, could be made of these materials. The cost that interests us is the cost of providing the cooking service rather than the cost of copper. If we suppose that copper is used only for pots and that iron is quite satisfactory for the same purpose, as long as we have cheap iron it does not matter if the cost of copper rises sky high. (But in fact that has not happened. As we have seen, the prices of the minerals themselves, as well as the prices of the services they perform, have fallen over the years.)

Are Natural Resources Finite?

Incredible as it may seem at first, the term "finite" is not only inappropriate but is downright misleading when applied to natural resources, from both the practical and philosophical points of view. As with many of the important arguments in this world, the one about "finiteness" is "just semantic." Yet the semantics of resource scarcity muddle public discussion and bring about wrongheaded policy decisions.

The word "finite" originates in mathematics, in which context we all learn it as schoolchildren. But even in mathematics the word's meaning is far from unambiguous. It can have two principal meanings, sometimes with an apparent contradiction between them.[8] For example, the length of a one-inch line is finite in the sense that it is bounded at both ends. But the line within the endpoints contains an infinite number of points; these points can-

consumption has defined size

not be counted, because they have no defined size. Therefore the number of points in that one-inch segment is not finite. Similarly, the quantity of copper that will ever be available to us is not finite, because there is no method (even in principle) of making an appropriate count of it, given the problem of the economic definition of "copper," the possibility of creating copper or its economic equivalent from other materials, and thus the lack of boundaries to the sources from which copper might be drawn.

Consider this quote about potential oil and gas from Sheldon Lambert, an energy forecaster. He begins, "It's like trying to guess the number of beans in a jar without knowing how big the jar is." So far so good. But then he adds, "God is the only one who knows—and even He may not be sure."[9] Of course Lambert is speaking lightly. But the notion that some mind might know the "actual" size of the jar is misleading, because it implies that there is a fixed quantity of standard-sized beans. The quantity of a natural resource that might be available to us—and even more important the quantity of the services that can eventually be rendered to us by that natural resource—can never be known even in principle, just as the number of points in a one-inch line can never be counted even in principle. Even if the "jar" were fixed in size, it might yield ever more "beans." Hence resources are not "finite" in any meaningful sense.

To restate: A satisfactory *operational* definition of the quantity of a natural resource, or of the services we now get from it, is the only sort of definition that is of any use in policy decisions. The definition must tell us about the quantities of a resource (or of a particular service) that we can expect to receive in any particular year to come, at each particular price, conditional on other events that we might reasonably expect to know (such as use of the resource in prior years). And there is no reason to believe that at any given moment in the future the available quantity of any natural resource or service at present prices will be much smaller than it is now, or non-existent. Only such one-of-a-kind resources as an Arthur Rubenstein concert or a Julius Erving basketball game, for which there are no close replacements, will disappear in the future and hence are finite in quantity.

Why do we become hypnotized by the word "finite"? That is an interesting question in psychol-

Circular – trying to predict the future –

ogy, education, and philosophy. A first likely reason is that the word "finite" seems to have a precise and unambiguous meaning in any context, even though it does not. Second, we learn the word in the context of mathematics, where all propositions are tautologous definitions and hence can be shown logically to be true or false (at least in principle). But scientific subjects are empirical rather than definitional, as twentieth-century philosophers have been at great pains to emphasize. Mathematics is not a science in the ordinary sense because it does not deal with facts other than the stuff of mathematics itself, and hence such terms as "finite" do not have the same meaning elsewhere that they do in mathematics.

Third, much of our daily life about which we need to make decisions is countable and finite—our weekly or monthly salaries, the number of gallons of gas in a full tank, the width of the backyard, the number of greeting cards you sent out last year, or those you will send out next year. Since these quantities are finite, why shouldn't the world's total possible salary in the future, or the gasoline in the possible tanks in the future, or the number of cards you ought to send out, also be finite? Though the analogy is appealing, it is not sound. And it is in making this incorrect analogy that we go astray in using the term "finite."

A fourth reason that the term "finite" is not meaningful is that we cannot say with any practical surety where the bounds of a relevant resource system lie, or even if there are any bounds. The bounds for the Crusoes are the shores of their island, and so it was for early man. But then the Crusoes found other islands. Mankind traveled farther and farther in search of resources—finally to the bounds of continents, and then to other continents. When America was opened up, the world, which for Europeans had been bounded by Europe and perhaps by Asia too, was suddenly expanded. Each epoch has seen a shift in the bounds of the relevant resource system. Each time, the old ideas about "limits," and the calculations of "finite resources" within those bounds, were thereby falsified. Now we have begun to explore the sea, which contains amounts of metallic and other resources that dwarf any deposits we know about on land. And we have begun to explore the moon. Why shouldn't the boundaries of the system from which we derive resources continue to expand in such directions, just

as they have expanded in the past? This is one more reason not to regard resources as "finite" in principle.

You may wonder, however, whether "non-renewable" energy resources such as oil, coal, and natural gas differ from the recyclable minerals in such a fashion that the foregoing arguments do not apply. Energy is particularly important because it is the "master resource"; energy is the key constraint on the availability of all other resources. Even so, our energy supply is non-finite, and oil is an important example. (1) The oil potential of a particular well may be measured, and hence is limited (though it is interesting and relevant that as we develop new ways of extracting hard-to-get oil, the economic capacity of a well increases). But the number of wells that will eventually produce oil, and in what quantities, is not known or measurable at present and probably never will be, and hence is not meaningfully finite. (2) Even if we make the unrealistic assumption that the number of potential wells in the earth might be surveyed completely and that we could arrive at a reasonable estimate of the oil that might be obtained with present technology (or even with technology that will be developed in the next 100 years), we still would have to reckon the future possibilities of shale oil and tar sands—a difficult task. (3) But let us assume that we could reckon the oil potential of shale and tar sands. We would then have to reckon the conversion of coal to oil. That, too, might be done; yet we still could not consider the resulting quantity to be "finite" and "limited." (4) Then there is the oil that we might produce not from fossils but from new crops—palm oil, soybean oil, and so on. Clearly, there is no meaningful limit to this source except the sun's energy. The notion of finiteness does not make sense here, either. (5) If we allow for the substitution of nuclear and solar power for oil, since what we really want are the services of oil, not nec-

essarily oil itself, the notion of a limit makes even less sense. (6) Of course the sun may eventually run down. But even if our sun were not as vast as it is, there may well be other suns elsewhere.

About energy from the sun: The assertion that our resources are ultimately finite seems most relevant to energy but yet is actually more misleading with respect to energy than with respect to other resources. When people say that mineral resources are "finite" they are invariably referring to the earth as a boundary, the "spaceship earth," to which we are apparently confined just as astronauts are confined to their spaceship. But the main source of our energy even now is the sun, no matter how you think of the matter. This goes far beyond the fact that the sun was the prior source of the energy locked into the oil and coal we use. The sun is also the source of the energy in the food we eat, and in the trees that we use for many purposes. In coming years, solar energy may be used to heat homes and water in many parts of the world. (Much of Israel's hot water has been heated by solar devices for years, even when the price of oil was much lower than it is now.) And if the prices of conventional energy supplies were to rise considerably higher than they now are, solar energy could be called on for much more of our needs, though this price rise seems unlikely given present technology. And even if the earth were sometime to run out of sources of energy for nuclear processes—a prospect so distant that it is a waste of time to talk about it—there are energy sources on other planets. Hence the notion that the supply of energy is finite because the earth's fossil fuels or even its nuclear fuels are limited is sheer nonsense.

Whether there is an "ultimate" end to all this—that is, whether the energy supply really is "finite" after the sun and all the other planets have been exhausted—is a question so hypothetical that it should be compared with other metaphysical entertainments such as calculating the number of angels that can dance on the head of a pin. As long as we continue to draw energy from the sun, any conclusion about whether energy is "ultimately finite" or not has no bearing upon present policy decisions. . . .

Summary

A conceptual quantity is not finite or infinite in itself. Rather, it is finite or infinite if you make it so—by your own definitions. If you define the subject of discussion suitably, and sufficiently closely so that it can be counted, then it is finite—for example, the money in your wallet or the socks in your top drawer. But without sufficient definition the subject is not finite—for example, the thoughts in your head, the strength of your wish to go to Turkey, your dog's love for you, the number of points in a one-inch line. You can, of course, develop definitions that will make these quantities finite; but that makes it clear that the finiteness inheres in you and in your definitions rather than in the money, love, or one-inch line themselves. There is

no necessity either in logic or in historical trends to suggest that the supply of any given resource is "finite."

Notes

1. Meadows, Dennis L., William W. Behrens III, Donella H. Meadows, Roger F. Naill, Jorgen Randers, and Erich K. O. Zahn. *Dynamics of Growth in a Finite World* (Cambridge, MA: Wright-Allen, 1974), p. vii.
2. U.S., The White House. *Population and the American Future* (New York: Signet, 1972), pp. 2–3.
3. Meadows, et al., p. 265.
4. U.S., The White House. *Resources for the Future.* Four volumes. The President's Materials Policy Commission (Washington, DC: GPO, June, 1952).
5. Ibid., p. 2.
6. Ibid., p. 1.
7. Fuller, Buckminster. *Utopia or Oblivion* (New York: Bantam Press, 1977), p. 45.
8. I appreciate a discussion of this point with Alvin Roth.
9. Sheldon Lambert, quoted in *Newsweek* (June 27, 1977), 71.

SIDELIGHT: The Nuclear Train to the Future

Richard and Val Routley[1]

A long distance country train has just pulled out. The train, which is crowded, carries both passengers and freight. At an early stop in the journey, someone consigns as freight, to a far distant destination, a package which contains a highly toxic and explosive gas. This is packed in a very thin container which, as the consigner is aware, may well not contain the gas for the full distance for which it is consigned, and certainly will not do so if the train should strike any real trouble, for example, if the train should be derailed or involved in a collision, or if some passenger should interfere inadvertently or deliberately with the freight, perhaps trying to steal some of it. All of these sorts of things have happened on some previous journeys. If the container should break the resulting disaster would probably kill at least some of

the people on the train in adjacent carriages, while others could be maimed or poisoned or sooner or later incur serious diseases.

Most of us would roundly condemn such an action. What might the consigner of the parcel say to try to justify it? He might say that it is *not certain* that the gas will escape, or that the world needs his product and it is his duty to supply it, or that in any case he is not responsible for the train or the people on it. These sorts of excuses, however, would normally be seen as ludicrous when set in this context. Unfortunately, similar excuses are often not so seen when the consigner, again a (responsible) businessman, put his workers' health or other peoples' welfare at risk.

Suppose he says that it is his own and others'

And Justice for All: New Introductory Essays in Ethics and Public Policy, edited by Tom Regan and Donald VanDeVeer (Totowa, NJ: Roman and Littlefield, 1982), pp. 116–118. Reprinted by permission of the publisher.

pressing needs which justify his action. The company he controls, which produces the material as a by-product, is in bad financial straits, and could not afford to produce a better container even if it knew how to make one. If the company fails, he and his family will suffer, his employees will lose their jobs and have to look for others, and the whole company town, through loss of spending, will be worse off. The poor and unemployed of the town, whom he would otherwise have been able to help, will suffer especially. Few people would accept such grounds as justification. Even where there are serious risks and costs to oneself or some group for whom one is concerned one is usually considered not to be entitled to simply transfer the heavy burden of those risks and costs onto other uninvolved parties, especially where they arise from one's own, or one's group's chosen life-style.

The matter of nuclear waste has many moral features which resemble the train case. How fitting the analogy is will become apparent as the argument progresses. There is no known proven safe way to package the highly toxic wastes generated by the nuclear plants that will be spread around the world as large-scale nuclear development goes ahead. The waste problem will be much more serious than that generated by the 50 or so reactors in use at present, with each one of the 2000 or so reactors envisaged by the end of the century producing, on average, annual wastes containing 1000 times the radioactivity of the Hiroshima bomb. Much of this waste is extremely toxic. For example, a millionth of a gramme of plutonium is enough to induce a lung cancer. A leak of even a part of the waste material could involve much loss of life, widespread disease and genetic damage, and contamination of immense areas of land. Wastes will include the reactors themselves, which will have to be abandoned after their expected life times of perhaps 40 years, and which, some have estimated, may require 1 ½ million years to reach safe levels of radioactivity.

Nuclear wastes must be kept suitably isolated from the environment for their entire active lifetime. For fission products the required storage period averages a thousand years or so, and for transuranic elements, which include plutonium, there is a half million to a million year storage problem. Serious problems have arisen with both short-term and proposed long-term methods of storage, even

with the comparatively small quantities of waste produced over the last twenty years. Short-term methods of storage require continued human intervention, while proposed longer term methods are subject to both human interference and risk of leakage through non-human factors.

No one with even a slight knowledge of the geological and climatic history of the earth over the last million years, a period whose fluctuations in climate we are only just beginning to gauge and which has seen four Ice Ages, could be confident that a rigorous guarantee of safe storage could be provided for the vast period of time involved. Nor does the history of human affairs over the last 3000 years give ground for confidence in safe storage by methods of requiring human intervention over perhaps a million years. Proposed long-term storage methods such as storage in granite formations or in salt mines, are largely speculative and relatively untested, and have already proved to involve difficulties with attempts made to put them into practice. Even as regards expensive recent proposals for first embedding concentrated wastes in glass and encapsulating the result in multilayered metal containers before rock deposit, simulation models reveal that radioactive material may not remain suitably isolated from human environments. In short, the best present storage proposals carry very real possibilities of irradiating future people and damaging their environment. . . .[2]

The risks imposed on the future by proceeding with nuclear development are, then, *significant*. Perhaps 40,000 generations of future people could be forced to bear significant risks resulting from the provision of the (extravagant) energy use of only a small proportion of the people of 10 generations. . . .

Notes

1. This paper is a condensation of an early version of our 'Nuclear power—ethical, social, and political dimensions' (ESP for short, available from the authors). . . . For help with the condensation we are very considerably indebted to the editors.

In the condensation, we simplify the structure of the argument and suppress underlying political and ideological dimensions (for example, the large measure of responsibility of the USA for spreading nuclear reactors around the world, and thereby in enhancing the chances of nuclear disasters, including nuclear war). We also considerably reduce a heavy load of footnotes and references designed and needed to help make good many of our claims. Further, in order to contain references to a modest length, reference to primary sources has often been replaced by reference through secondary sources. Little difficulty should be encountered however in tracing fuller references through secondary sources or in filling out much important background material from work cited herein. For example, virtually all the data cited in sections I and VII are refer-

enced in Routley. At worst ESP can always be consulted. . . .

2. Naturally the effect on humans is not the only factor that has to be taken into account in arriving at moral assessments. Nuclear radiation, unlike most ethical theories, does not confine its scope to human life and welfare. But since the harm nuclear development may afflict on nonhuman life, for example, can hardly *improve* its case, it suffices if the case against it can be made out solely in terms of its effects on human life in the conventional way.

Intergenerational Justice in Energy Policy

Brian Barry

The problem that I shall address in this [essay] is as follows. How are we to deal with the fact that the energy resources that at present provide the bulk of our supply, namely fossil fuels, are in practical terms nonrenewable? At best they are renewable only over geological time-spans, while we are exhausting them at rates measured in decades, or at most centuries. Is it possible to define a criterion such that, if we meet it, we will be behaving justly toward later generations? In answer I shall define precisely wherein the morally significant problem lies; propose and defend, in outline terms, a solution; and consider several practical problems of interpretation and implementation.

I. The Nature of the Problem

The characteristic of fossil fuels that raises problems of justice between generations is that their quantity is finite. This is, indeed, true of all mineral resources, but fossil fuels are special in two ways. (1) Once a fossil fuel has been used, it cannot be reused: there is no possibility of recycling (which in the case of other mineral resources can be done, if the economic incentives exist), to provide a considerable proportion of what is used in the world economy. And (2), while enormous quantities of most minerals are estimated to be in the top mile of the earth's crust, much of the supply is dif-

ficult and expensive to get at and is located inconveniently in relation to sources of demand. Therefore, winning these minerals will incur steadily increasing costs over a time span measured in centuries.

Of course, as the marginal cost of obtaining a mineral increases, the economic rents that can be realized by those who control the better deposits will also increase. The total cost to consumers will therefore tend to increase more than the total cost of actually extracting, refining, and transporting the minerals. But from the point of view of the world as a whole, this part of the cost is simply a transfer, although it will have distributive implications unless these are neutralized by global policies. The only factor that will make future generations collectively worse off is the additional real cost of minerals. Since at present the total cost of minerals (other than those producing energy) in the world economy is less than 3 percent,[1] it seems clear that, over time, even a doubling or a quadrupling of the real cost of mineral resources could be accommodated without enormous strain.

As far as fossil fuels are concerned, there are already large proved reserves of coal, and there is every reason to believe that there is much more, as well. The immediate impediments to expanding its use are ecological: the damage caused by open-cast mining, and the possible "greenhouse effect" of an

Energy and the Future, edited by Douglas MacLean and Peter G. Brown (Lanham, MD: Rowman and Littlefield, 1983), pp. 15–30. Reprinted by permission of the publisher.

increase in the proportion of carbon dioxide in the atmosphere. (I shall return to these matters in section III). With oil, however, the situation is quite different. It is, of course, dangerous to take too seriously industry estimates of world oil reserves, since these are employed as bargaining counters to obtain better terms from governments, and governments have not yet spent enough on research to be in a position to make entirely independent estimates. But although much of the land surface of the world (let alone the continental shelf) has not yet had a proper geological survey, and although new discoveries, such as the recent Mexican one, are continually being made, almost no one with any degree of expertise will predict that the world can continue to consume oil at the current rate—much less at a continuously increasing rate for centuries.

Of course, tar sands and oil shales do approach the quantities of coal deposits. But even if we waive the ecological problems of processing them, it seems unlikely that any technology will be created that does not make a barrel of oil derived from these sources far more expensive than a barrel of oil from Saudi Arabia or Kuwait, which still costs less than a dollar to pump out and pipe into a tanker. Future generations who relied on such sources for oil in the same amounts as we now use it would, therefore, be worse off than we are, all else remaining the same; that is, if the capital stock and the technology it embodied were what they are now.

Therefore, the context within which energy policy raises issues of fairness toward future generations, while not different in kind, is different in degree from those raised by other nonrenewable resources. What precisely is the problem of fairness? That some natural resources are finite in quantity would not matter if the supply were so huge that we and succeeding generations could use as much of them as necessary and still leave adequate quantities, as easily obtainable and as usefully located as those we now use. It is because that condition does not hold that nonrenewable resources raise a problem of fairness. It is not simply that the more we use, the less they will have—which is a tautology, given the definition of "nonrenewable"—but that the more we use the fewer options they will have, other things being equal. They will not be able to produce as much with the same technology, the same amount of capital, the same amount of

personal effort, or the same degree of environmental degradation as we now can.

We might, of course, say that the only fair thing to do in the circumstances is to pass on the natural resource base that we—the present generation—inherit. But this would exhibit in a more extreme form the same logic as the town council which passed an ordinance to the effect that there should always be at least one taxi waiting at the station to ensure that taxis would be available for arriving passengers. We must come up with a criterion that allows for some exploitation of nonrenewable resources even when that is going to mean that, other things being equal, future generations will be put at a relative disadvantage compared with us.

II. A Solution and Its Defense

Once the problem has been set up in this way, my solution will, I hope, appear quite natural. I propose that future generations are owed compensation in other ways for our reducing their access to easily extracted and conveniently located natural resources. In practice, this entails that the combination of improved technology and increased capital investment should be such as to offset the effects of depletion.

What, precisely, constitutes "offsetting"? There are two possible interpretations. The one that would naturally occur to economists—and not only to economists—would be to define offsetting in terms of utility: we should do whatever is necessary to provide future generations with the same level of utility as they would have had if we had not depleted the natural resources. There are all kinds of difficulties in drawing practical implications from this idea, but the objection that I shall put is pitched at a level of principle and would still be relevant even if all the practical problems could be swept away.

The alternative that I wish to defend is that what constitutes offsetting the depletion of natural resources is the replacement of the productive opportunities we have destroyed by the creation of alternative ones. In other words, when we say that resource depletion makes future generations "worse off" than we are, this should be taken to mean that they will be worse off in terms of productive potential; and it is that loss of productive potential for which justice requires us to compensate. (The notion of productive potential will be explained below.) Questions immediately arise, of course, What is an acceptable "alternative," and what happens if future people have different tastes from ours (as seems a priori very likely)? I shall discuss these and other problems in the next section.

First, I want to offer a general argument for defining the criterion in terms of opportunities rather than utilities.

My answer is that this is true of justice in all contexts, so intergenerational justice is simply an application of the general idea. We therefore need a discussion of the broad thesis rather than one confined to future generations, for the conclusion will surely be stronger for the rather strange case of future generations if it can be shown to be plausible in more familiar cases. To this end, let me return to the alternative interpretation of the criterion of compensation for resource depletion, that it should be defined in terms of utility. This idea stems from a general conception of what should be the subject matter of moral assessment: that, although we perforce distribute rights, opportunities, or material goods rather than utility, the ultimate standard of judgment should be the utility to people that arises from them.

Utilitarianism, understood as the theory that the aggregate amount of utility should be maximized, is the best-known example of a theory that takes utility as the only thing that matters, in the last analysis. Thus, as Sidgwick put it, utilitarianism is concerned with "the distribution of *Happiness*, not the means of happiness."[2] Recently Ted Honderich has advanced a "Principle of Equality," defined not in terms of equal treatment, but in terms of "the qualities of the experience of individuals." The principle is then "that things should be so arranged that we approach as close as we can, which may not be all that close, to equality in satisfaction and distress."[3] Again, Amartya Sen began a recent article by saying: "Usual measures of economic inequality concentrate on income, but frequently one's interest may lie in the inequality of welfare rather than of income as such." And he went on to say that this raises problems not only of "interpersonal comparisons of welfare, but also those arising from differences in nonincome circumstances, e.g., age, the state of one's health, the pattern of love, friendship, concern and hatred surrounding a person."[4]

Of course, it is generally agreed that there are, in practice, severe limits to the extent to which distribution can be individuated so as to take account of the way in which different people either get different amounts of happiness from some baseline amount of the means of happiness, or gain unequal amounts of happiness from the same increments in the means of happiness.

The relevant information is difficult to come by—some would say that the problem is not even well defined. Collecting the information would in any case intrude on personal privacy. The policy would place a premium on dissimulation, as people would try to give the appearance of having a utility function of a kind that would provide them with a large allocation of income or other means of happiness. And the implementation of a program of adapting distribution to individual psychological characteristics would obviously place vast powers in the hands of those doing the allocating—powers to make decisions on a largely discretionary basis, because of the lack of precisely defined objective criteria for establishing the susceptibility of different people to external advantages or disadvantages.

For all these reasons it might be admitted that in practice idiosyncratic differences in the way people convert the means of happiness into happiness itself should be disregarded for purposes of public policy. And it might plausibly be added that the case for disregarding idiosyncrasies becomes overwhelming when we don't know anything definite about the people concerned—as must be the case with people as yet unborn. We could therefore, by invoking ignorance, get from the premise that the ultimate object of distribution is utility to the conclusion that justice between generations should be defined in terms of resources: in the absence of the appropriate information we must fall back on distributing resources without looking beyond resources to utilities. Instead, however, I want to suggest that the whole idea of treating utility as the object of distribution is wrong.

To strip away the practical complications, imagine that by some incredible advance in psychometric technology it became possible to fit people with tiny, tamper-proof "black boxes" implanted under the skin, and that these "black boxes" measured (and somehow could be shown to measure to the satisfaction of anyone with enough training in neurophysiology and electronics) the amount of utility received by the recipient within, say, a period of a year. I don't think that the availability of this kind of publicly verifiable information would eliminate the case against allocating the means of happiness so as to achieve a certain distribution of happiness. For my view is that such information is in principle irrelevant when it comes to determining a just distribution.

Suppose we believe that two people should be paid the same amount: they do the same work equally well, have equal seniority in the same firm, and so on. What this means is that they have an equal claim on the resources of society to do what they like with that chunk of resources. (Taking account of market distortions, we can say that prices do roughly correspond to the real claim on resources at the margin represented by alternative purchases.) Justice consists in their getting an equal crack at society's resources, without any mention of comparative utility. If we discover that one of them gets more fun out of spending his income than does the other, this is no reason for transferring income from the one who derives more utility to the one who derives less. Similarly, if the price of something one of them enjoys goes up (e.g., because of an increased demand for it), this is no reason for increasing his income in compensation. For he had no special claim on the amount of utility he was getting before. All he had a claim on was the share of resources.

The argument as applied to future generations is, then, that we should not hold ourselves responsible for the satisfaction they derive from their opportunities. What is important from the point of view of justice is the range of choice open to them, rather than what they get out of it. But choice of what? The range of choice I have so far discussed has been the range of consumption choices. Broadly speaking, I have been making the case for defining justice in terms of income rather than utility.

But this is not the whole story. For we obviously cannot literally provide people not yet born with income, any more than we can provide them with utility. The question is, in either case, whether we need to predict how much they will actually get, if we do one thing rather than another. Even if this were feasible (which it is not), it would still be beside the point.

The important thing is that we should compensate for the reduction in opportunities to produce brought about by our depleting the supply of natural resources, and that compensation should be defined in terms of productive potential. If we could somehow predict that there would be a general decline in working hours or in the amount of effort people put into work, this would be no reason to say that we must hand over additional productive resources to future generations. This notion of productive potential will be analyzed below. For the present, all we need to grasp is that productive potential is equal in two situations if the same effort would produce the same output.

Two questions follow from this. First, why should future generations be left not worse off (in opportunity terms) than they would have been in the absence of our having depleted the resources? To the second and much more difficult question, I shall not be able to give a wholly satisfactory answer. In order to say that our depletion of resources should not leave future generations with a smaller range of opportunities than they would otherwise have had, we must have some standard on the basis of which we can establish what opportunities they would otherwise have had. What is the appropriate standard?

Let me begin with the first point. The basic argument for an equal claim on natural resources is that none of the usual justifications for an unequal claim—special relationships arising in virtue of past services, promises, etc.—applies here. From an atemporal perspective, no one generation has a better or worse claim than any other to enjoy the earth's resources. In the absence of any powerful argument to the contrary, there would seem to be a strong presumption in favor of arranging things so that, as far as possible, each generation faces the same range of opportunities with respect to natural resources. I must confess that I can see no further positive argument to be made at this point. All I can do is counter what may be arguments on the other side. Is there any way in which the present generation can claim that it is entitled to a larger share of the goods supplied by nature than its successors? If not, then equal shares is the only solution compatible with justice.

The only theory of distributive justice that might appear to have implications inconsistent with the equality of generations is the Lockean one of a "natural right" to appropriate by "mixing one's labor" with natural resources. This might be taken to imply that there is no criterion by which the collective exploitation of natural resources by a generation can be judged, as long as the individualistic requirements of the Lockean theory are met. However, even taking that theory seriously for a moment, we should bear in mind that Locke said that legitimate appropriation was limited by the proviso that "enough and as good" should be left for others. If we interpret "others" to include later generations as well as contemporaries, we get the notion of equality between generations. And Locke's unconvincing attempt to fudge the application of the proviso once people have "consented to the use of money" cannot get a foothold in the intergenerational case, since future generations are obviously in no position to consent to our exploitation of natural resources in a way that fails to leave "as good" for them.

Clearly, if each generation has a equal right to enjoy the productive opportunities provided by natural resources, it does not necessarily follow that compensation for violating that right is acceptable. We all will agree that doing harm is in general not canceled out by doing good, and conversely that doing some good does not license one to do harm, provided it doesn't exceed the amount of good. For example, if you paid for the realignment of a dangerous highway intersection and saved an average of two lives a year, that wouldn't mean that you could shoot one motorist per year and simply reckon on coming out ahead.

Here, however, the example involves gratuitous infliction of harm. In the case of resources and future generations, the crucial feature is that we can't possibly avoid harming them by using up some non-renewable resources, given the existing population level and the technology that has developed to sustain that level. So the choice is not between reducing the resource base for future generations and keeping it intact, but between depletion with compensation and depletion without compensation. The analogy is therefore with the traveler caught in a blizzard who, in order to survive, breaks into somebody's empty weekend cottage, builds a fire, and helps himself to food. Not even Robert Nozick (I think) would deny that this is a legitimate use of another's property without his permission. It will be generally agreed, also, that while the unauthorized taking of another's prop-

erty was entirely justifiable in the circumstances, the traveler is not absolved from making restitution for whatever he damaged or consumed.

The second problem arises in this way. Suppose we say that justice requires us to compensate future generations for depleted resources, so that they have as much productive potential as they would have inherited had the resources not been depleted. To give this criterion any operational significance, we obviously must give some definite content to the notion of the amount of productive potential that future generations would have enjoyed in the absence of resource depletion; or we have no means of deciding what is required by justice in the way of compensation.

We cannot say that "the productive potential that future generations would otherwise have enjoyed" is to be settled by *predicting*. Perhaps, in the absence of resource depletion, we would in fact be inclined to leave future generations with far less productive potential than, as a matter of justice, we ought to leave them with. If we were to leave them an inadequate amount plus an amount calculated to compensate for resource depletion, we would then be behaving unjustly. Conversely, in the absence of resource depletion, maybe we would leave future generations with far more productive potential than is required by justice—whatever that is. In that case, even when resource depletion is taken into account, the same amount would still more than satisfy the requirements of justice.

It is apparent, therefore, that "the productive potential that future generations would otherwise have enjoyed" must be defined in terms of justice. We must understand the following: what future generations would justly have enjoyed in the absence of resource depletion. But how much is that? The answer is critical in determining the whole outcome of our enquiry. To make the most extreme case, suppose we said the only things we owe to future generations are whatever natural resources we inherited plus due compensation (measured in terms of productive capacity) for what we depleted. If we left anything more than a few picks and shovels they would be ahead, since they would then be in a better position to exploit natural resources than if they had to use their bare hands. Anything more than that would go beyond the demands of justice. But human generations do not succeed one another with one generation marching off the stage as another marches on, so self-interest on the part of the living will ensure that far more than that is handed on. However selfishly those alive at any given time behave, they can scarcely avoid passing on to their successors a pretty large capital stock that embodies thousands of years of technological development. Hence, the principle of compensation for the depletion of natural resources could be accepted without the slightest implication that more should be done to protect the interests of future generations than would inevitably be done as a by-product of the pursuit of self-interest by the current generation.

I imagine that few would really want to say that we would be beyond criticism on grounds of justice if we ran down capital and used up natural resources in whatever way best suited us, as long as we left our successors somewhat better equipped than people were in the Stone Age. But it is hard to come up with a clear-cut principle to say exactly how far the bounds of justice extend. I believe, however, that there are some leading ideas which can guide us.

Most of our technology and the capital stock embodying it are not by any stretch of the imagination the sole creation of the present generation; we cannot, therefore, claim exclusive credit for it. The whole process of capital formation presupposes an inheritance of capital and technology. To a considerable extent, then, we can say that, from the standpoint of the current generation, natural resources are not really as sharply distinguished from capital and technology as might at first appear. Both are originally inherited, and, thus, fall outside any special claims based on the present generation's having done something to deserve them. We therefore can make no special claim on our side. But can others (those who did create them) claim that they can endow us with exclusive control over what we inherit? This raises complicated issues.

It seems to me that inherited capital can be looked at from two standpoints, that of the creators and that of the receivers, and that the trick is to give weight to both perspectives. From the side of the recipients, inherited capital is exactly like inherited natural resources—the present generation can claim credit for neither. From the side of the earlier generations, on the other hand, accumulated capital and natural resources that are handed on have different statuses, in that capital is created and natural resources are not. Yet no generation creates from scratch all the capital it hands on. It seems

reasonable to suggest that it should get credit only for the capital it adds.

This, then, gives us a rough basis for proceeding. Let us say that, as a reasonable reconciliation of the two perspectives, each generation's sacrifices (if any) to increase the capital stock it passes on give it a claim to some consideration by the following generation of its objectives in making these sacrifices. Beyond one generation, its specific wishes for the disposition of the increment become progressively less significant as constituting claims on the decisions of the living.

We can now venture a statement of what is required by justice toward future generations. As far as natural resources are concerned, depletion should be compensated for in the sense that later generations should be left no worse off (in terms of productive capacity) than they would have been without the depletion. And how well off they would have been is to be determined by applying the principles that have been worked out above. As a starting point, we may say that the capital stock inherited should be passed on without diminution, but this can be modified somewhat to accommodate the claims of past generations. If we suppose, for example, that the previous generation made sacrifices to permit the present generation a higher standard of living without any expectation that this generation would pass it on, it would seem legitimate for the present generation to pass on slightly less. On the other hand, if one believes that successive past generations made sacrifices in the (no doubt vague) expectation that each generation would pass on more than it inherited, this would constitute a prima facie case for saying that the present generation has a certain obligation to continue with this process. The whole notion of obligations to continue the undertakings of past generations, however, raises difficulties that need further work. I do not think we should go far wrong here if we set it aside and simply say that compensation should be reckoned as what is required to maintain productive potential.

III. Practical Problems

Three practical problems arise in any attempt to apply the conclusions of the abstract discussion so far. The first is whether the compensation criterion can be given a workable significance. The second is where issues of intragenerational distribution fit in. And the third is how to deal with the difficulty that alternative policies have results in the future that are associated with varying degrees of uncertainty.

On the feasibility of the compensation criterion, the apparent problem is this: oil is oil is oil. How do we decide what is adequate compensation for running down the world's reserves of oil? In the most favorable case, it may be possible to compensate in a quite direct way. If we run down the oil by 10 percent but develop technology that makes it possible to extract 10 percent more oil from any given deposit, we have in effect left future generations with as much (exploitable) oil as we found. Or if we develop internal combustion engines that produce more power per gallon of gasoline used, we have made the remaining stock of oil go further, measured in output terms—which is what counts—than it would otherwise have done. And so on.

I do not want to suggest that this will solve all the problems of implementation; where it is not applicable, we have to fall back on the more general idea of maintaining productive capacity. Within limits, which over a long time period may be very wide, it is always possible to substitute capital for raw materials by recycling, cutting down waste, and making things get results by being complicated and well engineered, rather than big and heavy. Energy may appear unamenable to this treatment, since, as I noted at the outset, once it has been used it cannot be recovered. But it can still be economized by a greater expenditure of capital, and the performance of the U.S. economy in recent years has illustrated the way in which, with the right incentives, capital expenditure will be substituted for energy.

The second practical problem is this: What happens when the principles for justice between generations are combined with moral principles governing distribution among people who are contemporaries, whether they live now or in the future? One reason for confronting the question of intragenerational distribution is that there are some who profess impatience with a concern for the interests of unborn generations when there are so many existing people now starving or suffering from preventable malnutrition and disease. I must admit to some sympathy with this impatience. I have a possibly prejudiced idea that one could run

in Marin County more successfully on a platform of doing good things for future generations than of transferring money to poor people now, either domestically or internationally. Being in favor of future generations is somehow more antiseptically apolitical than being in favor of contemporaries, and also, in an odd way, gives an impression of being more high-minded.

If it were really necessary to make a choice between intragenerational and intergenerational justice, it would be a tough one. But in my view there is no such dilemma, because I do not believe that there will turn out to be any inconsistency between the requirements of each. In the absence of a full theory of both, I cannot show this. But I predict that whatever redistribution among contemporaries is required by justice will also be able to observe the constraints that the interests of future generations be protected.

Of course, if citizens and governments in the rich countries are willing to make only token sacrifices to meet the demands of either intragenerational or intergenerational justice, a choice will have to be made. But we ought then to be clear that the necessity for choice arises not from any real incompatibility, but simply from the not unusual phenomenon that people are not prepared to behave justly when it is contrary to their immediate interests, unless they are somehow coerced into doing so. And while poor countries have a certain amount of ability to cause trouble to rich ones, future generations obviously have no way of enforcing a fair deal on the present generation.

It will be apparent that the principles already enunciated for justice among generations may be applied equally well to relations among contemporaries.[5] Thus, the argument that there is no act by which the value of natural resources may be regarded as earned or deserved by whoever happens to find them suggests an equal claim of all contemporaries on that value. Similarly, the idea that inherited capital and technology gradually merge into the "common heritage of mankind" clearly implies a just claim by poor countries on rich ones.

Intragenerational justice would best be met by a combination of a self-balancing, shadow (positive and negative) income tax on countries and a severance tax on the exploitation of natural resources, the proceeds being transferred to resource-poor countries such as India, Bangladesh, or some central African countries. This would, in an admittedly rough and ready way (but no other is to be expected), make tax liability depend on both the special advantages arising from possession of rich natural resources and the more general advantages that make for high per capita income. Intergenerational justice requires, as we have seen, maintenance of capital (with certain modest exceptions) plus the creation of additional technology and capital to compensate for resource depletion. yet this has an intragenerational aspect, too. To say that "the present generation" should pass on certain productive capabilities to "future generations" leaves open the question of how the burdens and the benefits should be distributed among contemporaries, now and in the future. What can be said about this?

It is legitimate for those who form the current generation in a country to make special efforts to provide extra benefits for their own descendants if they choose to do so, since this is more than is called for by justice anyway. This is in effect an intergenerational gift of resources whose disposition the people in that country have a just claim to control. But the mere passing along of the amount of capital inherited draws no credit. And, as I have suggested, the wishes of those who originally made the sacrifices to accumulate it should be regarded as fading out over the course of a few generations. This implies that some of the capital stock should be diffused as claims to special benefits run out, in the same way as patents and copyrights expire with time.

The problem of resource depletion by those living in the country can be divided into two parts: Who should provide the compensation, and who should receive it? I suggest that those countries which consume the largest quantities of nonrenewable natural resources should be responsible for the bulk of the effort to provide the technology and capital formation to substitute for them.

On the other hand, I wish to argue that it would be extremely inequitable if the compensatory technology and capital were passed on for the exclusive benefit of the successors of those in the countries who depleted the natural resources. Since running down any natural resources deprives all future inhabitants of the world of the production from any given combination of capital and labor, the compensation is owed not to descendants of the

current heavy users only, but to all in the future who are disadvantaged by that use—in fact, everybody.

The redistributive case is even stronger than this. For industrial countries have achieved their present prosperity by first using their own natural resources and then, when these began to get scarce, by using those of the rest of the world at relatively low cost to themselves—in the case of oil, for example, for a few cents per gallon through the 1950s and 1960s. In effect, this bonanza has been turned into accumulated capital that is regarded by these countries as their private property to do with as they choose. But it is obviously harder for countries that missed out on this era of cheap resources to undertake a similar course of economic development in the future. (The effect of oil price increases on Indian economic planning is a dramatic illustration, and many others could be offered.) The poor countries, therefore, have been especially disadvantaged because, unlike the rich countries, they have nothing to show for the past depletion of world resources except perhaps in free access to some unpatented technology that was part and parcel of Western development.

The upshot of this discussion is that, generally speaking, the countries with the highest per capita production and the highest use of nonrenewable natural resources (the two are highly correlated) should be making transfers, to meet the requirements of intergenerational justice, to the poor countries. This clearly overlaps with the requirements of purely intragenerational justice that were outlined earlier. An across-the-board international income tax (levied on countries, to be raised through their own domestic tax systems), whether or not supplemented by a severance tax on the extraction of mineral resources, would meet all requirements, as long as part of the proceeds of the tax were devoted to the building up of technology and capital in the recipient countries, and as long as those in the rich countries did not treat payment of the tax as an alternative to accumulating capital domestically to enable their own descendants to offset the effects of resource depletion.

The final problem is that of uncertainty. It cannot be avoided because, in deciding what technologies we ought to develop to compensate future generations for the depletion of resources, we must somehow deal with the fact that the risks and benefits are, to some degree, speculative. Suppose most competent authorities agree that there is a possibility (i.e., it cannot be excluded on the basis of existing scientific knowledge) that some action taken now (e.g., burying nuclear wastes deep underground, releasing fluorocarbons into the atmosphere, or carrying out experiments on recombinant DNA) will have serious and irreversible (or only doubtfully/expensively/gradually reversible) adverse consequences in the long term; and suppose further that either there is disagreement on the likelihood of these adverse consequences coming to pass or agreement on the impossibility, in the present state of knowledge, of quantifying the risk (or some mixture of the two). The question, then, is how we should react to this state of affairs. Should we say that the profound uncertainty makes it unreasonable (or "premature," if one is optimistic about the prospects for finding out more in the future) to decide against taking the action? Or should we say that, in the absence of better information, the possibility of disastrous consequences is a decisive reason for not acting? Ex hypothesi, methods of decision-making that discount alternative outcomes by their probabilities of occurrence are not available here.

The simplest argument for giving the second answer rather than the first is a two-part one: (a) in the case of an individual making a choice that affects only himself, we should regard anyone who acted on the basis of the first alternative as crazy; and (b) when we change the case to one that involves millions of people and extends over many centuries, the same reasoning applies, with increased force.

The best way to establish (a) is by means of an example. Imagine that your dentist were to say: "The only way of saving this tooth is by means of a new procedure. There is every reason to believe that the procedure will succeed in saving the tooth, but it's conceivable that it will kill you. It may be that, however many times it were done, nobody would ever be killed by it. But it can't be ruled out on the basis of anything we currently know about physiology that it's highly lethal. It's not impossible that it has one chance in a hundred of killing you. Since we have no idea of the magnitude of the risks involved, I draw two conclusions: more research is needed, and in the meantime you should undergo the procedure." I predict that not only would you decline his suggestion, but you'd also think he

should have his license withdrawn for professional incompetence.

As far as (b) is concerned, I need only say that there is no prima facie reason for supposing that changing the case so that the numbers involved are larger and extend over a longer time is going to make the choice associated with an uncertain potential for catastrophe more palatable rather than less. If anything, the argument is even strengthened. Let me conclude by offering three considerations.

First, we might ask whether genocide is universally abhorred for no other reason than that it entails killing a large number of individual human beings. Or is it worse to wipe out an entire people than to kill an equal number of individuals scattered throughout the world? One answer might be that genocide is worse because it is the expression of an evil theory—that of racial superiority and inferiority. But genocidal attempts antedated the Nazis (e.g., the "Armenian massacres" and the hunting to extinction of the native populations of Tasmania and California in the nineteenth century), yet those cases were no less terrible.

We can approach what I consider the critical point by discussing what has been called "cultural genocide"—the practice of systematically exterminating the intelligentsia—the professionals, writers, journalists, students, and anyone with an above-average level of education. Those with greater knowledge of history than I can no doubt cite examples going back thousands of years, but the recent examples with which I am familiar are Pakistan (the early stages of the civil war that led to the creation of Bangladesh) and Burundi. (Cambodia may be another case, but I don't know enough to say—maybe nobody does.) These examples of "cultural genocide" seem to me less terrible than the destruction of the entire Bengali or Hutu populations would have been—numbers obviously do make a difference. At the same time, they are, in my view, worse than random killing of the same numbers of the same populations.

My point is that the destruction of cultures is a bad over and above the physical destruction of its bearers. This, then, gives us a reason for holding that destroying a large population is more serious than killing the same number of random individuals. And this in turn is another reason why remote possibilities of catastrophic accidents (e.g., in nuclear reactors) should be treated as especially grave threats, and not simply balanced against the number of deaths from bronchitis or lung cancer that can be associated with the use of fossil fuel as an alternative. One chance in a million per annum of wiping out New York simply is not the same as having ten more people die each year in the United States (or in New York).

Risk may be acceptable if it is accepted voluntarily in the pursuit of something that seems valuable to the person who chooses it. If somebody wishes to risk his or her life gratuitously by rock climbing or white-water canoeing, one might say that there is no case for preventing or discouraging these freely chosen activities. But the risks of, say, nuclear power generation are not at all plausibly construed on that model. The risk cannot be confined to the beneficiaries. We have a public good and a public bad; people who use the electricity get the good, and those who live near the plant get the bad, irrespective of whether they would prefer to do without both. If we were to respond that in the nature of the case consent cannot be obtained from everyone affected before any piece of collective action is undertaken, I would of course agree. But then the question of distributive equity arises. The canoeist gets the risk, and the benefit. But with larger-scale projects, it is unlikely that the risks and the benefits will be distributed to each person in the same proportions. If nuclear plants are located in the country and mainly supply the cities, the rural people get a disproportionate share of the risks, while the city people benefit.

These problems are exacerbated across generations. First, cultural impoverishment is irreversible and continues to impoverish all successive genera-tions. Second, if we do things now that impose risks on future people, there is clearly no way of getting their consent. And, finally, with some examples such as nuclear power plants, the benefits and risks are asymmetrically distributed across time: the benefits disproportionately occur while the plant is producing electricity, and the risks continue in some form for thousands of years, until the radioactivity of the waste decays to a safe level.

Notes

I am grateful to the other participants in the working group on Energy Policy and Future Generations and especially to Miller Spangler, Peter G. Brown, and Douglas MacLean for comments on earlier drafts. I would also like to thank Kenneth Goodpaster, who acted as discussant when a draft of the paper was read at Douglass College, Rutgers University, in October 1980, for raising some difficult questions; and Douglas Rae for written comments.

1 Philip Connelly and Robert Perlman, *The Politics of Scarcity: Resource Conflicts in International Relations* (London: Oxford University Press for the Royal Institute of International Affairs, 1975), p. 10, Table 2.1.

2 Henry Sidgwick, *The Methods of Ethics,* 7th ed. (London: Macmillan & Co., 1907, reprint 1967), p. 47, n. 1.

3 Ted Honderich, *Three Essays on Political Violence* (Oxford: Basil Blackwell, 1976), p. 41.

4 Amartya Sen, "Welfare Inequalities and Rawlsian Axiomatics," *Theory and Decision* 7 (1976): 243–62, esp. p. 243.

5 I have done this at some length in "Humanity and Justice in Global Perspective," *Nomos* 24 (1980): *Ethics, Economics, and the Law.*

B. FROM THE COMMONS TO PROPERTY

PREVIEW

"I wish you wouldn't squeeze so," said the Dormouse, who was sitting next to her. . . . "I can't help it," said Alice very meekly . . . "I'm growing." "You've no right to grow here," said the Dormouse. "Don't talk nonsense," said Alice. . . . "Yes, but I grow at a reasonable pace," said the Dormouse. . . .

Lewis Carroll

Qu'est-ce que la propriété?[1]

Proudhon

There are several key questions to be answered about property rights. The importance of these matters derives in large part from the fact that many people or corporations assert that environmental goals, or constraints advocated in the name of environmental goals, unjustifiably infringe their property rights. Whether this is true depends in part on the nature of property rights, what constitutes them, and a series of other philosophical and legal issues. The deeper questions are about how things ought to be and, hence, are more about moral rights than legal rights (recall Christopher Stone's essay in Section IV-A). The following is a list of some key questions:

1. What does it *mean* to say that someone, *A*, has a property right in something, *X*? If having a property right in something is having a certain set of rights over something, what are those *specific rights?*

2. In hard cases, how can we determine *whether* someone has a property right in something?

3. Related to (2), under what conditions does anything change in status from being unowned to being property? That is, *how* does something become property?

4. Related to (3) *what sorts of things* is it morally impermissible to own or have property rights in? An anthropocentric answer to this question is that all and *only* humans cannot be owned.

5. In regard to respecting someone's rights, what is permissible or impermissible,[2] how do we appropriately weigh the property right in question? Alternatively, what is owed the right-bearer?

As we noted earlier, the concept of having property in something may be understood to mean having some combination of rights with respect to that thing; e.g., a right to *use* it, a right to *exclude* others from doing so, a right to *transfer* what is owned (and the property right), a right to be *compensated* for its use by others (barring the right-bearers's consent to uncompensated use), and, in some cases, a right to *destroy* (compare: "consume") the thing in question.

Debates about whether someone owns, or ought to be able to own, something may be muddled by a failure to clarify which moral and/or legal rights may be at stake. The right

to destroy something and the right to use it indefinitely may be excluded. Consider the rental of a tuxedo or a car. The legal rights inherent in owning a house do not include the right to use it as a brothel, as a laboratory for the manufacture of illegal drugs, or as place to perform torturous experiments on children.

Sometimes, the words 'my' or 'mine' express an ownership relation between an owner and her or his property, and at other times to other relations. Compare "my watch," "my country," "my grandfather." Although many countries have recognized legal property rights in human beings, it seems difficult to believe that one could have moral rights of ownership in another human being. Many of us have probably seen a parent out of control and slapping a small child in a supermarket; it seems more than a conceptual confusion for the parent to defend herself or himself with the claim, "but she's *my* child." The extraordinary and self-righteous indignation of such parents when challenged about their behavior seems to suggest that they literally believe that they have the right do whatever (destructive) thing they believe is necessary (or at least some very destructive actions). When one speaks of "my thumb," she or he may simply be indicating that a certain thumb bears a special relation (e.g., is a part of) to him or her or to "her or his body." The individual may also be suggesting that she or he has the right to decide how (and whether) to use it, e.g., as a bookmark, to plug a hole in the dike, or in an Aztec recipe. Various moral theories suggest a sharp distinction between owners and what is owned or what may be owned. To claim that something has moral standing is to suggest that it is not the sort of thing that can be owned in any full-blown sense, including the right to destroy it for *any* reason.[3] We may want to insist that among things possessing moral standing, there are further important moral distinctions to be made; we may conclude that it is all right to impose a risk of death on certain creatures but not on others, e.g., lab mice as opposed to chimpanzees or gorillas. That is, we may hold that certain rights can be held over some creatures with moral standing, but these matters require some principled criteria which may not be easy to articulate. For example, it seems reasonable to believe that the property rights one could have over what is owned cannot include the prerogative to do anything with or to that entity which would violate one's basic duties to it, duties which may be correlative to the rights possessed by that entity. All this seems truistic, but perhaps a useful truism reminds us that the question of what can be owned, or what sort of ownership rights exist, is a function of the entity's moral standing (or, further, what rights it possesses or what duties it is owed).[4] Our laws reflect only a limited deviation from anthropocentrism here. They have not granted moral standing to all humans, and they usually do not grant any standing to nonhumans. We should recall once more that sometimes property in women or in non-Caucasians has been allowed; one strand of the Hebrew and Christian scriptures permits certain forms of slavery but says that slaves are not to be mistreated.[5] For example, Exodus 21:2 states, "When you buy a Hebrew slave, he shall serve six years, and in the seventh he shall go free, for nothing." Laws against cruelty to animals are a clear recognition of, shall we say, moral limits on the scope of actions compatible with humans having property rights in the animals in question.

The first essay which follows, Garrett Hardin's "The Tragedy of the Commons," was discussed in the Preview to the previous section. We reiterate that in Hardin's view a great deal of environmental harm has occurred because much that is valuable in the natural world has been held in common. Sometimes in such cases there are few effective restraints, or no restraints, on use (tightly knit communities are often exceptions). Without fully reviewing Hardin's reasoning, he believes that possession of commons often leads to "exploitation"

or "overuse" since individuals have little or no disincentive not to withdraw benefits (consume, destroy, and so on) and pass on costs to others. Thus, the way to conserve or preserve nature's goods, or perhaps to use them in a more equitable and sustainable way, is to privatize them. Questions immediately arise about whether it is permissible to grant property rights in ecosystems, or in whichever entities may be thought to have moral standing. Once again, are we speaking of the sort of "property" which is thought to include a right to destroy? Is there any way of distributing private rights to such goods so that as much and as good is left for others?

In short, the proper assessment of Hardin's privatization proposal (or at least some coercive scheme of constraints on usage) depends on certain judgments we make about what counts, or may count, as property, what rights are included in property, and what arguments may be made in favor of adopting that or some alternative scheme of things. It is worth observing that defenders of one institution for exchanging already existing property rights, the marketplace, in fact presuppose certain answers to the above questions. In this respect the market is parasitic on a more basic institution (a system for recognizing the creation of property rights) and answers to more basic questions of an evaluative nature.

With a useful working definition of the concept of property (the essay by Goodin addresses this issue), one then asks how anything becomes property (morally, not legally) in the first place (question 3)? That is, how does anything come to be something over which some individuals come *initially* to have some set of property rights? John Locke (1632–1704) held the view (expressed in an excerpt which follows) that one may make something unowned his or her property by mixing his or her labor with it (a view which influenced Karl Marx's argument about capitalists' stealing value from the workers). So, in Locke's example, if one tills land unused by others and grows crops, the fruit of one's labor belongs by right to that person. Locke also added another condition (often called "the Lockean proviso"): one must "leave as much and as good for others." What counts as "as much and as good" we leave an open question; recall the discussion of sustainability in Part V. Intuitively, Locke has plausibly insisted on a *fairness condition;* one cannot just take as much as one wants. It is worth considering the reasonableness of the "fairness rider," and especially its implications for questions about what we owe future generations. If we owe them as much capital or environmental stock as has been available to us, it would seem to follow that we have serious duties not to destroy access to clean air, not to kill lakes, not to create a mass of toxic wastes (in short, not to diminish the quality and quantity of the sources and sinks which have benefited us), and so on. On these matters, recall the discussions in Part V and Barry's essay in Section VI-A.

In view of important contemporary disputes about the permissibility of "taking" someone's property without his or her consent (e.g., Do certain limitations on the use of property which diminish its market value to the owner constitute an unjustifiable taking of someone's property? Sometimes or always?), we comment here on some much discussed and employed distinctions in contemporary moral philosophy. An "absolute" right may be defined as one which it is always wrong to infringe or override, that is, depriving the right-holder of that to which he or she has a right. If there are such rights, it would be wrong to infringe on them—ever. But, in brief, it is not obvious that any right is absolute. It does not follow, however, that there is no presumption against infringing rights even if no right is absolute (reflect, for example, on a presumed right to life or right not be tortured). Nonabsolute rights are sometimes called presumptive, but, to emphasize a point, a presumptive right may be one that deserves great moral weight and may be the compelling factor in deciding

what ought to be done. So, it is important to decide whether someone *has* a relevant right of some sort and precisely what the *content* of that right is. Still, if a right is not absolute, then infringing it may be all right. Or it may not. If it is, then the bearer of that right may be owed some compensation for the loss resulting from an infringement.

The excerpt from Kristin Schrader-Frechette examines the implications of taking Locke's labor-mixing theory seriously. One worry concerns the number of property rights claims that can be sustained by appeal to it; for example, there are claims to portions of the oceans, the air, and large portions of the land where no serious claim can be made that anyone mixed her or his labor with them. And far from improving their value, claimants have often lessened it; e.g., Italy and Greece dump over 90 percent of their wastes into the Mediterranean. Many more infringements on property rights may deserve rectification than is often admitted by those who take a Lockean view. For example, "acid rain" is a violation of a wide range of property rights; it causes losses of $5 billion a year to the timber industry in Germany alone.[6] And if many Native American peoples mixed their labor appropriately, then there is something amiss in speaking of America as a place of justice for all. Historically, then, what is now de facto property has been gotten by various means: via one's labor, getting there first, usurpation (involving force or fraud) and so on.

Robert Goodin's thorough and analytic essay "Property Rights and Preservationist Duties" deals with a number of the questions we posed earlier. He argues that a right to destroy is not included in property rights as they are typically conceived. In his view, duties of preservation do not necessarily conflict with property rights being properly understood. In so arguing, Goodin addresses the question of how to understand the concept of a property right, the relation of the specific rights which constitute the notion of property, and an issue which we have not yet addressed, namely, what arguments can be made in support of systems of property rights. Goodin sorts such systems into two types: those that view property as a reward for some action, e.g., labor, and those that are utility-based—those that rest the case for a system of property rights on the allegedly beneficial consequences of the system in question (one which may distribute rights independent of desert). Another important issue for environmental ethics concerns what property rights should be institutionalized when there is a risk of the loss of irreplaceable assets. That is, what system of rights is compatible with or best fosters ecologically sound and sustainable ways of life?

In recent years a number of economists have pressed for an economic approach to the analysis of legal questions. They have argued that the ways in which governmental decisions reduce the value of private property must include not only cases in which property owners are literally stripped of their property (as in the case of eminent domain) but also cases in which their property is subjected to regulatory restrictions which may reduce its economic value. A governmental restraint may be placed on the use of property in the name of promoting some public, and perhaps environmental, good, e.g., the preservation of a wetland by not allowing it to be drained for purposes of erecting a condominium development. The imposition of such duties on property owners has been condemned by some on both moral and legal grounds. The legal issue concerns whether such regulation constitutes a violation of the Fifth Amendment of the U.S. Constitution, which provides that "private property [shall not] be taken for public use, without just compensation." An important practical question is whether governments must pay large amounts of compensation to landowners when they "take" property to pursue public, possibly environmental, goods. Mark Sagoff, in "Takings, Just Compensation, and the Environment," defends the view that compensation

need not attend regulation unless it also burdens individuals *unfairly;* hence, questions about "takings" involve not just matters of property rights but also questions of social justice more broadly conceived.

Garrett Hardin pointed out some of the drawbacks of *not* having property rights in certain goods. We have tried to indicate some of the drawbacks of having such systems, or at least the systems which we often encounter (further perspective is provided in the essays by Randall, Ehrenfeld especially, and Wilson in the next section). A major question is whether we can find a system which protects the autonomy of right-bearers as well as such other values as sustainability, the preservation of biodiversity, and fairness to future generations. There is no short *and* intelligent answer to this nor other questions we have noted. A good deal of intellectual work has been done on many of these matters, and the curious reader may wish to investigate them further.[7]

Notes

1. Translation: What is property?
2. For 'permissible act' one may read 'an act one has no duty not to do,' and for 'impermissible' one may read 'an act one has a duty not to do.'
3. In regard to attitudes toward what is legally ownable and the question of what has moral standing, we cannot resist repeating a story told by philosopher J. Baird Callicott. Callicott managed to outrage the dean of a Canadian university's college of agriculture by making remarks critical of industrial approaches to agriculture. The dean replied that he and his fellow "animal scientists" did not consider factory farm animals to be Cartesian automata, but rather "production units." Enough said. See J. Baird Callicott, "La Nature est morte, vive la nature!" in the *Hastings Center Report* (Vol. 22, No. 5), 21.
4. In our view if an entity is owed duties directly or is a possessor of moral rights, then it has moral standing, but an entity may have moral standing without being a possessor of moral rights.
5. See "On the Killing of Nath" in *A Documentary History of Slavery in North America,* edited by Willie Lee Rose (New York: Oxford University Press, 1976), pp. 213–219. On the mixed views of the churches in the 19th century in the United States, see *Slavery*

and Anti-Slavery (New York: Negroe Universities Press, 1968).

6. Paul Ekins, Green Economics (New York: Doubleday Publishing, 1992), p. 15.

7. We mention a few sources: The Realm of Rights, by Judith Thomson (Cambridge, MA: Harvard University Press, 1990); Lawrence Becker, Property Rights:

Philosophic Foundations (London: Routledge and Kegan Paul, 1977); Jeremy Waldron, The Right to Private Property; Richard Epstein, Takings: Private Property and the Power of Eminent Domain (Cambridge, MA: Harvard University Press, 1985); Ellen Frankel Paul, Property Rights and Eminent Domain (New Brunswick, NJ: Transaction Books, 1987).

The Tragedy of the Commons

Garrett Hardin

At the end of a thoughtful article on the future of nuclear war, Wiesner and York[1] concluded that: "Both sides in the arms race are . . . confronted by the dilemma of steadily increasing military power and steadily decreasing national security. *It is our considered professional judgment that this dilemma has no technical solution.* If the great powers continue to look for solutions in the area of science and technology only, the result will be to worsen the situation."

I would like to focus your attention not on the subject of the article (national security in a nuclear world) but on the kind of conclusion they reached, namely that there is no technical solution to the problem. An implicit and almost universal assumption of discussions published in professional and semipopular scientific journals is that the problem under discussion has a technical solution. A technical solution may be defined as one that requires a change only in the techniques of the natural sciences, demanding little or nothing in the way of change in human values or ideas of morality.

In our day (though not in earlier times) technical solutions are always welcome. Because of previous failures in prophecy, it takes courage to assert that a desired technical solution is not possible. Wiesner and York exhibited this courage; publishing in a science journal, they insisted that the solution to the problem was not to be found in the natural sciences. They cautiously qualified their statement with the phrase, "It is our considered professional judgment. . . ." Whether they were

right or not is not the concern of the present article. Rather, the concern here is with the important concept of a class of human problems which can be called "no technical solution problems," and, more specifically, with the identification and discussion of one of these.

It is easy to show that the class is not a null class. Recall the game of tick-tack-toe. Consider the problem, "How can I win the game of tick-tack-toe?" It is well known that I cannot, if I assume (in keeping with the conventions of game theory) that my opponent understands the game perfectly. Put another way, there is no "technical solution" to the problem. I can win only by giving a radical meaning to the word "win." I can hit my opponent over the head; or I can drug him; or I can falsify the records. Every way in which I "win" involves, in some sense, an abandonment of the game, as we intuitively understand it. (I can also, of course, openly abandon the game—refuse to play it. This is what most adults do.)

The class of "no technical solution problems" has members. My thesis is that the "population problem," as conventionally conceived, is a member of this class. How it is conventionally conceived needs some comment. It is fair to say that most people who anguish over the population problem are trying to find a way to avoid the evils of overpopulation without relinquishing any of the privileges they now enjoy. They think that farming the seas or developing new strains of wheat will solve the problem—technologically. I try to show here

The author is professor of biology, University of California, Santa Barbara. This article is based on a presidential address presented before the meeting of the Pacific Division of the American Association for the Advancement of Science at Utah State University, Logan, 25 June 1968.
Science, Vol. 162, No. 3858 (December 1968), 1243–48. Copyright 1968 by the American Association for the Advancement of Science. Reprinted by permission.

that the solution they seek cannot be found. The population problem cannot be solved in a technical way, any more than can the problem of winning the game of tick-tack-toe.

What Shall We Maximize?

Population, as Malthus said, naturally tends to grow "geometrically," or, as we would now say, exponentially. In a finite world this means that the per capita share of the world's goods must steadily decrease. Is ours a finite world?

A fair defense can be put forward for the view that the world is infinite; or that we do not know that it is not. But, in terms of the practical problems that we must face in the next few generations with the foreseeable technology, it is clear that we will greatly increase human misery if we do not, during the immediate future, assume that the world available to the terrestrial human population is finite. "Space" is no escape.[2]

A finite world can support only a finite population; therefore, population growth must eventually equal zero. (The case of perpetual wide fluctuations above and below zero is a trivial variant that need not be discussed.) When this condition is met, what will be the situation of mankind? Specifically, can Bentham's goal of "the greatest good for the greatest number" be realized?

No—for two reasons, each sufficient by itself. The first is a theoretical one. It is not mathematically possible to maximize for two (or more) variables at the same time. This was clearly stated by von Neumann and Morgenstern,[3] but the principle is implicit in the theory of partial differential equations, dating back at least to D'Alembert (1717–1783).

The second reason springs directly from biological facts. To live, any organism must have a source of energy (for example, food). This energy is utilized for two purposes: mere maintenance and work. For man, maintenance of life requires about 1600 kilocalories a day ("maintenance calories"). Anything that he does over and above merely staying alive will be defined as work, and is supported by "work calories" which he takes in. Work calories are used not only for what we call work in common speech; they are also required for all forms of enjoyment, from swimming and automobile racing to playing music and writing poetry. If our goal is to maximize population it is obvious what we must do: We must make the work calories per person approach as close to zero as possible. No gourmet meals, no vacations, no sports, no music, no literature, no art.... I think that everyone will grant, without argument or proof, that maximizing population does not maximize goods. Bentham's goal is impossible.

In reaching this conclusion, I have made the usual assumption that it is the acquisition of energy that is the problem. The appearance of atomic energy has led some to question this assumption. However, given an infinite source of energy, population growth still produces an inescapable problem. The problem of the acquisition of energy is replaced by the problem of its dissipation, as J. H. Fremlin has so wittily shown.[4] The arithmetic signs in the analysis are, as it were, reversed; but Bentham's goal is still unobtainable.

The optimum population is, then, less than the maximum. The difficulty of defining the optimum is enormous; so far as I know, no one has seriously tackled this problem. Reaching an acceptable and stable solution will surely require more than one generation of hard analytical work—and much persuasion.

We want the maximum good per person; but what is good? To one person it is wilderness, to another it is ski lodges for thousands. To one it is estuaries to nourish ducks for hunters to shoot; to another it is factory land. Comparing one good with another is, we usually say, impossible because goods are incommensurable. Incommensurables cannot be compared.

Theoretically this may be true; but in real life incommensurables *are* commensurable. Only a criterion of judgment and a system of weighting are needed. In nature the criterion is survival. Is it better for a species to be small and hideable, or large and powerful? Natural selection commensurates the incommensurables. The compromise achieved depends on a natural weighting of the values of the variables.

Man must imitate this process. There is no doubt that in fact he already does, but unconsciously. It is when the hidden decisions are made explicit that the arguments begin. The problem for the years ahead is to work out an acceptable theory of weighting. Synergistic effects, nonlinear variation, and difficulties in discounting the future make the intellectual problem difficult, but not (in principle) insoluble.

Has any cultural group solved this practical problem at the present time, even on an intuitive level? One simple fact proves that none has: there is no prosperous population in the world today that has, and has had for some time, a growth rate of zero. Any people that has intuitively identified its optimum point will soon reach it, after which its growth rate becomes and remains zero.

Of course, a positive growth rate might be taken as evidence that a population is below its optimum. However, by any reasonable standards, the most rapidly growing populations on earth today are (in general) the most miserable. This association (which need not be invariable) casts doubt on the optimistic assumption that the positive growth rate of a population is evidence that it has yet to reach its optimum.

We can make little progress in working toward optimum population size until we explicitly exorcize the spirit of Adam Smith in the field of practical demography. In economic affairs, *The Wealth of Nations* (1776) popularized the "invisible hand," the idea that an individual who "intends only his own gain," is, as it were, "led by an invisible hand to promote . . . the public interest."[5] Adam Smith did not assert that this was invariably true, and perhaps neither did any of his followers. But he contributed to a dominant tendency of thought that has ever since interfered with positive action based on rational analysis, namely, the tendency to assume that decisions reached individually will, in fact, be the best decisions for an entire society. If this assumption is correct, it justifies the continuance of our present policy of laissez-faire in reproduction. If it is correct, we can assume that men will control their individual fecundity so as to produce the optimum population. If the assumption is not correct, we need to reexamine our individual freedoms to see which ones are defensible.

Tragedy of Freedom in a Commons

The rebuttal to the invisible hand in population control is to be found in a scenario first sketched in a little-known pamphlet[6] in 1833 by a mathematical amateur named William Forster Lloyd (1794–1852). We may well call it "the tragedy of the commons," using the word "tragedy" as the philosopher Whitehead used it[7]: "The essence of dramatic tragedy is not unhappiness. It resides in the solemnity of the remorseless working of things." He then goes on to say, "This inevitableness of destiny can only be illustrated in terms of human life by incidents which in fact involve unhappiness. For it is only by them that the futility of escape can be made evident in the drama."

The tragedy of the commons develops in this way. Picture a pasture open to all. It is to be expected that each herdsman will try to keep as many cattle as possible on the commons. Such an arrangement may work reasonably satisfactorily for centuries because tribal wars, poaching, and disease keep the numbers of both man and beast well below the carrying capacity of the land. Finally, however, comes the day of reckoning, that is, the day when the long-desired goal of social stability becomes a reality. At this point, the inherent logic of the commons remorselessly generates tragedy.

As a rational being, each herdsman seeks to maximize his gain. Explicitly or implicitly, more or less consciously, he asks, "What is the utility *to me* of adding one more animal to my herd?" This utility has one negative and one positive component.

1. The positive component is a function of the increment of one animal. Since the herdsman receives all the proceeds from the sale of the additional animal, the positive utility is nearly +1.

2. The negative component is a function of the additional overgrazing created by one more animal. Since, however, the effects of overgrazing are shared by all the herdsmen, the negative utility for any particular decision-making herdsman is only a fraction of −1.

Adding together the component partial utilities, the rational herdsman concludes that the only sensible course for him to pursue is to add another animal to his herd. And another; and another. . . . But this is the conclusion reached by each and every rational herdsman sharing a commons. Therein is the tragedy. Each man is locked into a system that compels him to increase his herd without limit—in a world that is limited. Ruin is the destination toward which all men rush, each pursuing his own best interest in a society that believes in the freedom of the commons. Freedom in a commons brings ruin to all.

Some would say that this is a platitude. Would that it were! In a sense, it was learned thousands of years ago, but natural selection favors the forces of psychological denial.[8] The individual benefits as an individual from his ability to deny the truth even though society as a whole, of which he is a part, suffers.

Education can counteract the natural tendency to do the wrong thing, but the inexorable succession of generations requires that the basis for this knowledge be constantly refreshed.

A simple incident that occurred a few years ago in Leominster, Massachusetts, shows how perishable the knowledge is. During the Christmas shopping season the parking meters downtown were covered with plastic bags that bore tags reading: "Do not open until after Christmas. Free parking courtesy of the mayor and city council." In other words, facing the prospect of an increased demand for already scarce space, the city fathers reinstituted the system of the commons. (Cynically, we suspect that they gained more votes than they lost by this retrogressive act.)

In an approximate way, the logic of the commons has been understood for a long time, perhaps since the discovery of agriculture or the invention of private property in real estate. But it is understood mostly only in special cases which are not sufficiently generalized. Even at this late date, cattlemen leasing national land on the western ranges demonstrate no more than an ambivalent understanding, in constantly pressuring federal authorities to increase the head count to the point where overgrazing produces erosion and weed-dominance. Likewise, the oceans of the world continue to suffer from the survival of the philosophy of the commons. Maritime nations still respond automatically to the shibboleth of the "freedom of the seas." Professing to believe in the "inexhaustible resources of the oceans," they bring species after species of fish and whales closer to extinction.[9]

The National Parks present another instance of the working out of the tragedy of the commons. At present they are open to all, without limit. The parks themselves are limited in extent—there is only one Yosemite Valley—whereas population seems to grow without limit. The values that visitors seek in the parks are steadily eroded. Plainly,

we must soon cease to treat the parks as commons or they will be of no value to anyone.

What shall we do? We have several options. We might sell them off as private property. We might keep them as public property, but allocate the right to enter them. The allocation might be on the basis of wealth, by the use of an auction system. It might be on the basis of merit, as defined by some agreed upon standards. It might be by lottery. Or it might be on a first-come, first-served basis, administered to long queues. These, I think, are all the reasonable possibilities. They are all objectionable. But we must choose—or acquiesce in the destruction of the commons that we call our National Parks.

Pollution

In a reverse way, the tragedy of the commons reappears in problems of pollution. Here it is not a question of taking something out of the commons, but of putting something in—sewage, or chemical, radioactive, and heat wastes into water; noxious and dangerous fumes into the air; and distracting and unpleasant advertising signs into the line of sight. The calculations of utility are much the same as before. The rational man finds that his share of the cost of the wastes he discharges into the commons is less than the cost of purifying his wastes before releasing them. Since this is true for everyone, we are locked into a system of "fouling our own nest," so long as we behave only as independent, rational, free-enterprisers.

The tragedy of the commons as a food basket is averted by private property, or something formally like it. But the air and waters surrounding us cannot readily be fenced, and so the tragedy of the commons as a cesspool must be prevented by different means, by coercive laws or taxing devices that make it cheaper for the polluter to treat his pollutants than to discharge them untreated. We have not progressed as far with the solution of this problem as we have with the first. Indeed, our particular concept of private property, which deters us from exhausting the positive resources of the earth, favors pollution. The owner of a factory on the bank of a stream—whose property extends to the middle of the stream—often has difficulty seeing why it is not his natural right to muddy the waters flowing past his door. The law, always behind the times, requires elaborate stitching and fitting to adapt it to this newly perceived aspect of the commons.

The pollution problem is a consequence of population. It did not much matter how a lonely American frontiersman disposed of his waste. "Flowing water purifies itself every 10 miles," my grandfather used to say, and the myth was near enough to the truth when he was a boy, for there were not too many people. But as population became denser, the natural chemical and biological recycling processes became overloaded, calling for a redefinition of property rights.

How to Legislate Temperance?

Analysis of the pollution problem as a function of population density uncovers a not generally recognized principle of morality, namely: *the morality of an act is a function of the state of the system at the time it is performed.*[10] Using the commons as a cesspool does not harm the general public under frontier conditions, because there is no public; the same behavior in a metropolis is unbearable. A hundred and fifty years ago a plainsman could kill an American bison, cut out only the tongue for his dinner, and discard the rest of the animal. He was not in any important sense being wasteful. Today, with only a few thousand bison left, we would be appalled at such behavior.

In passing, it is worth noting that the morality of an act cannot be determined from a photograph. One does not know whether a man killing an elephant or setting fire to the grassland is harming others until one knows the total system in which his act appears. "One picture is worth a thousand words," said an ancient Chinese; but it may take 10,000 words to validate it. It is as tempting to ecologist as it is to reformers in general to try to persuade others by way of the photographic shortcut. But the essence of an argument cannot be photographed: it must be presented rationally—in words.

That morality is system-sensitive escaped the attention of most codifiers of ethics in the past. "Thou shalt not . . ." is the form of traditional ethical directives which make no allowance for particular circumstances. The laws of our society follow the pattern of ancient ethics, and therefore are poorly suited to governing a complex, crowded, changeable world. Our epicyclic solution is to augment statutory law with administrative law. Since it is practically impossible to spell out all the conditions under which it is safe to burn trash in the back yard or to run an automobile without smog-control, by law we delegate the details to bureaus. The result is administrative law, which is rightly feared for an ancient reason—*Quis custodiet ipsos custodes?*—"Who shall watch the watchers themselves?" John Adams said that we must have "a government of laws and not men." Bureau administrators, trying to evaluate the morality of acts in the total system, are singularly liable to corruption, producing a government by men, not laws.

Prohibition is easy to legislate (though not necessarily to enforce); but how do we legislate temperance? Experience indicates that it can be accomplished best through the mediation of administrative law. We limit possibilities unnecessarily if we suppose that the sentiment of *Quis custodiet* denies us the use of administrative law. We should rather retain the phrase as a perpetual reminder of fearful dangers we cannot avoid. The great challenge facing us now is to invent the corrective feedbacks that are needed to keep custodians honest. We must find ways to legitimate the needed authority of both the custodians and the corrective feedbacks.

Freedom to Breed Is Intolerable

The tragedy of the commons is involved in population problems in another way. In a world governed solely by the principle of "dog eat dog"—if indeed there ever was such a world—how many children a family had would not be a matter of public concern. Parents who bred too exuberantly would leave fewer descendants, not more, because they would be unable to care adequately for their children. David Lack and others have found that such a negative feedback demonstrably controls the fecundity of birds.[11] But men are not birds, and have not acted like them for millenniums, at least.

If each human family were dependent only on its own resources; *if* the children of improvident parents starved to death; *if,* thus, overbreeding brought its own "punishment" to the germ line—*then* there would be no public interest in controlling the breeding of families. But our society is deeply committed to the welfare state,[12] and, hence, is confronted with another aspect of the tragedy of the commons.

In a welfare state, how shall we deal with the family, the religion, the race, or the class (or indeed any distinguishable and cohesive group) that adopts overbreeding as a policy to secure its own aggrandizement?[13] To couple the concept of freedom to breed with the belief that everyone born has an equal right to the commons is to lock the world into a tragic course of action.

Unfortunately this is just the course of action that is being pursued by the United Nations. In late 1967, some 30 nations agreed to the following:[14]

> The Universal Declaration of Human Rights describes the family as the natural and fundamental unit of society. It follows that any choice and decision with regard to the size of the family must irrevocably rest with the family itself, and cannot be made by anyone else.

It is painful to have to deny categorically the validity of this right; denying it, one feels as uncomfortable as a resident of Salem, Massachusetts, who denied the reality of witches in the 17th century. At the present time, in liberal quarters, something like a taboo acts to inhibit criticism of the United Nations. There is a feeling that the United Nations is "our last and best hope," that we shouldn't find fault with it; we shouldn't play into the hands of the archconservatives. However, let us not forget what Robert Louis Stevenson said: "The truth that is suppressed by friends is the readiest weapon of the enemy." If we love the truth we must openly deny the validity of the Universal Declaration of Human Rights, even though it is promoted by the United Nations. We should also join with Kingsley Davis[15] in attempting to get Planned Parenthood-World Population to see the error of its ways in embracing the same tragic ideal.

Conscience Is Self-Eliminating

It is a mistake to think that we can control the breeding of mankind in the long run by an appeal to conscience. Charles Galton Darwin made this point when he spoke on the centennial of the publication of his grandfather's great book. The argument is straightforward and Darwinian.

People vary. Confronted with appeals to limit breeding, some people will undoubtedly respond to the plea more than others. Those who have more children will produce a larger fraction of the next generation than those with more susceptible consciences. The difference will be accentuated, generation by generation.

In C. G. Darwin's words: "It may well be that it would take hundreds of generations for the progenitive instinct to develop in this way, but if it should do so, nature would have taken her revenge, and the variety *Homo contracipiens* would become extinct and would be replaced by the variety *Homo progenitivus.*"[16]

The argument assumes that conscience or the desire for children (no matter which) is hereditary—but hereditary only in the most general formal sense. The result will be the same whether the attitude is transmitted through germ cells, or exosomatically, to use A. J. Lotka's term. (If one denies the latter possibility as well as the former, then what's the point of education?) The argument has here been stated in the context of the population problem, but it applies equally well to any instance in which society appeals to an individual exploiting a commons to restrain himself for the general good—by means of his conscience. To make such an appeal is to set up a selective system that works toward the elimination of conscience from the race.

Pathogenic Effects of Conscience

The long-term disadvantage of an appeal to conscience should be enough to condemn it; but [it] has serious short-term disadvantages as well. If we ask a man who is exploiting a commons to desist "in the name of conscience," what are we saying to him? What does he hear?—not only at the moment but also in the wee small hours of the night when, half asleep, he remembers not merely the words we used but also the nonverbal communication cues we gave him unawares? Sooner or later, consciously or subconsciously, he senses that he has received two communications, and that they are contradictory: (i) (intended communication) "If you don't do as we ask, we will openly condemn you for not acting like a responsible citizen"; (ii) (the unintended communication) "If you *do* behave as we ask, we will secretly condemn you for a simpleton who can be shamed into standing aside while the rest of us exploit the commons."

Everyman then is caught in what Bateson has

called a "double bind." Bateson and his co-workers have made a plausible case for viewing the double bind as an important causative factor in the genesis of schizophrenia.[17] The double bind may not always be so damaging, but it always endangers the mental health of anyone to whom it is applied. "A bad conscience," said Nietzsche, "is a kind of illness."

To conjure up a conscience in others is tempting to anyone who wishes to extend his control beyond the legal limits. Leaders at the highest level succumb to this temptation. Has any President during the past generation failed to call on labor unions to moderate voluntarily their demands for higher wages, or to steel companies to honor voluntary guidelines on prices? I can recall none. The rhetoric used on such occasions is designed to produce feelings of guilt in noncooperators.

For centuries it was assumed without proof that guilt was a valuable, perhaps even an indispensable, ingredient of the civilized life. Now, in this post-Freudian world, we doubt it.

Paul Goodman speaks from the modern point of view when he says: "No good has ever come from feeling guilty, neither intelligence, policy, nor compassion. The guilty do not pay attention to the object but only to themselves, and not even to their own interests, which might make sense, but to their anxieties."[18]

One does not have to be a professional psychiatrist to see the consequences of anxiety. We in the Western world are just emerging from a dreadful two-centuries-long Dark Ages of Eros that was sustained partly by prohibition laws, but perhaps more effectively by the anxiety-generating mechanisms of education. Alex Comfort has told the story well in *The Anxiety Makers*[19]; it is not a pretty one.

Since proof is difficult, we may even concede that the results of anxiety may sometimes, from certain points of view, be desirable. The larger question we should ask is whether, as a matter of policy, we should ever encourage the use of a technique the tendency (if not the intention) of which is psychologically pathogenic. We hear much talk these days of responsible parenthood; the coupled words are incorporated into the titles of some organizations devoted to birth control. Some people have proposed massive propaganda campaigns to instill responsibility into the nation's (or the world's) breeders. But what is the meaning of the word *responsibility* in this context? Is it not merely a synonym for the word conscience? When we use the word responsibility in the absence of substantial sanctions, are we not trying to browbeat a free man in a commons into acting against his own interest? Responsibility is a verbal counterfeit for a substantial *quid pro quo*. It is an attempt to get something for nothing.

If the word *responsibility* is to be used at all, I suggest that it be in the sense Charles Frankel uses it.[20] "Responsibility," says this philosopher, "is the product of definite social arrangements." Notice that Frankel calls for social arrangements—not propaganda.

Mutual Coercion Mutually Agreed Upon

The social arrangements that produce responsibility are arrangements that create coercion, of some sort. Consider bank-robbing. The man who takes money from a bank acts as if the bank were a commons. How do we prevent such action? Certainly not by trying to control his behavior solely by a verbal appeal to his sense of responsibility. Rather than rely on propaganda, we follow Frankel's lead and insist that a bank is not a commons; we seek the definite social arrangements that will keep it from becoming a commons. That we thereby infringe on the freedom of would-be robbers we neither deny nor regret.

The morality of bank-robbing is particularly easy to understand because we accept complete prohibition of this activity. We are willing to say, "Thou shalt not rob banks," without providing for exceptions. But temperance also can be created by coercion. Taxing is a good coercive device. To keep downtown shoppers temperate in their use of parking space, we introduce parking meters for short periods, and traffic fines for longer ones. We need not actually forbid a citizen to park as long as he wants to; we need merely make it increasingly expensive for him to do so. Not prohibition, but carefully biased options are what we offer him. A Madison Avenue man might call this persuasion; I prefer the greater candor of the word coercion.

Coercion is a dirty word to most liberals now, but it need not forever be so. As with the four-letter words, its dirtiness can be cleansed away by exposure to the light, by saying it over and over without apology or embarrassment. To many, the word coercion implies arbitrary decisions of distant and irresponsible bureaucrats; but this is not a necessary part of its meaning. The only kind of coercion I recommend is mutual coercion, mutually agreed upon by the majority of the people affected.

To say that we mutually agree to coercion is not to say that we are required to enjoy it, or even to pretend we enjoy it. Who enjoys taxes? We all grumble about them. But we accept compulsory taxes because we recognize that voluntary taxes would favor the conscienceless. We institute and (grumblingly) support taxes and other coercive devices to escape the horror of the commons.

An alternative to the commons need not be perfectly just to be preferable. With real estate and other material goods, the alternative we have chosen is the institution of private property coupled with legal inheritance. Is this system perfectly just? As a genetically trained biologist I deny that it is. It seems to me that, if there are to be differences in individual inheritance, legal possession should be perfectly correlated with biological inheritance—that those who are biologically more fit to be the custodians of property and power should legally inherit more. But genetic recombination continually makes a mockery of the doctrine of "like father, like son" implicit in our laws of legal inheritance. An idiot can inherit millions, and a trust fund can keep his estate intact. We must admit that our legal system of private property plus inheritance is unjust—but we put up with it because we are not convinced, at the moment, that anyone has invented a better system. The alternative of the commons is too horrifying to contemplate. Injustice is preferable to total ruin.

It is one of the peculiarities of the warfare between reform and the status quo that it is thoughtlessly governed by a double standard. Whenever a reform measure is proposed it is often defeated when its opponents triumphantly discover a flaw in it. As Kingsley Davis has pointed out,[21] worshippers of the status quo sometimes imply that no reform is possible without unanimous agreement, an implication contrary to historical fact. As nearly as I can make out, automatic rejection of proposed reforms is based on one of two unconscious assumptions: (i) that the status quo is perfect; or (ii) that the choice we face is between reform and no action; if the proposed reform is imperfect, we presumably should take no action at all, while we wait for a perfect proposal.

But we can never do nothing. That which we have done for thousands of years is also action. It also produces evils. Once we are aware that the status quo is action, we can then compare its discoverable advantages and disadvantages with the predicted advantages and disadvantages of the proposed reform, discounting as best we can for our lack of experience. On the basis of such a comparison, we can make a rational decision which will not involve the unworkable assumption that only perfect systems are tolerable.

Recognition of Necessity

Perhaps the simplest summary of this analysis of man's population problems is this: the commons, if justifiable at all, is justifiable only under conditions of low-population density. As the human population has increased, the commons has had to be abandoned in one aspect after another.

First we abandoned the commons in food gathering, enclosing farm land and restricting pastures and hunting and fishing areas. These restrictions are still not complete throughout the world.

Somewhat later we saw that the commons as a place for waste disposal would also have to be abandoned. Restrictions on the disposal of domestic sewage are widely accepted in the Western world; we are still struggling to close the commons to pollution by automobiles, factories, insecticide sprayers, fertilizing operations, and atomic energy installations.

In a still more embryonic state is our recognition of the evils of the commons in matters of pleasure. There is almost no restriction on the propagation of sound waves in the public medium. The shopping public is assaulted with mindless music, without its consent. Our government is paying out billions of dollars to create a supersonic transport which will disturb 50,000 people for every one person who is whisked from coast to coast three hours faster. Advertisers muddy the airwaves of radio and television and pollute the view of travelers. We are a long way from outlawing the commons in matters of pleasure. Is this because our Puritan inheritance makes us view pleasure as something of a sin, and pain (that is, the pollution of advertising) as the sign of virtue?

Every new enclosure of the commons involves the infringement of somebody's personal liberty. Infringements made in the distant past are accepted because no contemporary complains of a loss. It is the newly proposed infringements that we vigorously oppose; cries of "rights" and "freedom" fill the air. But what does "freedom" mean? When men mutually agreed to pass laws against robbing, mankind became more free, not less so. Individuals locked into the logic of the commons are free only to bring on universal ruin; once they see the necessity of mutual coercion, they become free to pursue other goals. I believe it was Hegel who said, "Freedom is the recognition of necessity."

The most important aspect of necessity that we must now recognize is the necessity of abandoning the commons in breeding. No technical solution can rescue us from the misery of overpopulation. Freedom to breed will bring ruin to all. At the moment, to avoid hard decisions many of us are tempted to propagandize for conscience and responsible parenthood. The temptation must be resisted, because an appeal to independently acting consciences selects for the disappearance of all conscience in the long run, and an increase in anxiety in the short.

The only way we can preserve and nurture other and more precious freedoms is by relinquishing the freedom to breed, and that very soon. "Freedom is the recognition of necessity"—and it is the role of education to reveal to all the necessity of abandoning the freedom to breed. Only so, can we put an end to this aspect of the tragedy of the commons.

References

1. J. B. Wiesner and H. F. York, *Sci. Amer.* 211 (No. 4), 27 (1964).

2. G. Hardin, *J. Hered.* 50, 68 (1959); S. von Hoernor, *Science* 137, 18 (1962).

3. J. von Neumann and O. Morgenstern, *Theory of Games and Economic Behavior* (Princeton Univ. Press, Princeton, N.J., 1947), p. 11.

4. J. H. Fremlin, *New Sci.*, No. 415 (1964), p. 285.

5. A. Smith, *The Wealth of Nations* (Modern Library, New York, 1937), p. 423.

6. W. F. Lloyd, *Two Lectures on the Checks to Population* (Oxford Univ. Press, Oxford, England, 1833), reprinted (in part) in *Population, Evolution, and Birth Control*, G. Hardin, Ed. (Freeman, San Francisco, 1964), p. 37.

7. A. N. Whitehead, *Science and The Modern World* (Mentor, New York, 1948), p. 17.

8. G. Hardin, Ed. *Population, Evolution and Birth Control* (Freeman, San Francisco, 1964), p. 56.

9. S. McVay, *Sci. Amer.* 216 (No. 8), 13 (1966).

10. J. Fletcher, *Situation Ethics* (Westminster, Philadelphia, 1966).

11. D. Lack, *The Natural Regulation of Animal Numbers* (Clarendon Press, Oxford, 1954).

12. H. Girvetz, *From Wealth to Welfare* (Stanford Univ. Press, Stanford, Calif., 1950).

13. G. Hardin, *Perspec. Biol. Med. 6,* 366 (1963).

14. U. Thant, *Int. Planned Parenthood News,* No. 168 (February 1968), p. 3.

15. K. Davis, *Science* 158, 730 (1967).

16. S. Tax, Ed., *Evolution after Darwin* (Univ. of Chicago Press, Chicago, 1960), vol. 2, p. 469.

17. G. Bateson, D. D. Jackson, J. Haley, J. Weakland, *Behav. Sci.* 1, 251 (1956).

18. P. Goodman, *New York Rev. Books* 10(8), 22 (23 May 1968).

19. A. Comfort, *The Anxiety Makers* (Nelson, London, 1967).

20. C. Frankel, *The Case for Modern Man* (Harper, New York, 1955), p. 203.

21. J. D. Roslansky, *Genetics and the Future of Man* (Appleton-Century-Crofts, New York, 1966), p. 177.

The Creation of Property

John Locke

Whether we consider natural reason, which tells us that men being once born have a right to their preservation, and consequently to meat and drink and such other things as nature affords for their subsistence; or revelation, which gives us an account of those grants God made of the world to Adam, and to Noah and his sons, 'tis very clear that God, as King David says, Psalm cxv. 16, "has given the earth to the children of men," given it to mankind in common. But this being supposed, it seems to some a very

John Locke, from the second of his two *Treatises of Civil Government.*

great difficulty how anyone should ever come to have a property in anything. I will not content myself to answer that if it be difficult to make out property upon a supposition that God gave the world to Adam and his posterity in common, it is impossible that any man but one universal monarch should have any property upon a supposition that God gave the world to Adam and his heirs in succession, exclusive of all the rest of his posterity. But I shall endeavor to show how men might come to have a property in several parts of that which God gave to mankind in common, and that without any express compact of all the commoners.

God, who hath given the world to men in common, hath also given them reason to make use of it to the best advantage of life and convenience. The earth and all that is therein is given to men for the support and comfort of their being. And though all the fruits it naturally produces, and beasts it feeds, belong to mankind in common, as they are produced by the spontaneous hand of nature; and nobody has originally a private dominion exclusive of the rest of mankind in any of them as they are thus in their natural state; yet being given for the use of men, there must of necessity be a means to appropriate them some way or other before they can be of any use or at all beneficial to any particular man. The fruit or venison which nourishes the wild Indian, who knows no enclosure, and is still a tenant in common, must be his, and so his, i.e., a part of him, that another can no longer have any right to it, before it can do any good for the support of his life.

Though the earth and all inferior creatures be common to all men, yet every man has a property in his own person; this nobody has any right to but himself. The labor of his body and the work of his hands we may say are properly his. Whatsoever, then, he removes out of the state that nature hath provided and left it in, he hath mixed his labor with, and joined it to something that is his own, and thereby makes it his property. It being by him removed from the common state nature placed it in, hath by this labor something annexed to it that excludes the common right of other men. For this labor being the unquestionable property of the laborer, no man but he can have a right to what that is once joined to, at least where there is enough, and as good left in common for others.

He that is nourished by the acorns he picked up under an oak, or the apples he gathered from the trees in the wood, has certainly appropriated them to himself. Nobody can deny but the nourishment is his. I ask, then, When did they begin to be his—when he digested, or when he ate, or when he boiled, or when he brought them home, or when he picked them up? And 'tis plain if the first gathering made them not his, nothing else could. That labor put a distinction between them and common; that added something to them more than nature, the common mother of all, had done, and so they became his private right. And will anyone say he had no right to those acorns or apples he thus appropriated, because he had not the consent of all mankind to make them his? Was it a robbery thus to assume to himself what belonged to all in common? If such a consent as that was necessary, man had starved, notwithstanding the plenty God had given him. We see in commons which remain so by compact that 'tis the taking any part of what is common and removing it out of the state nature leaves it in, which begins the property; without which the common is of no use. And the taking of this or that part does not depend on the express consent of all the commoners. Thus the grass my horse has bit, the turfs my servant has cut, and the ore I have dug in any place where I have a right to them in common with others, become my property without the assignation or consent of anybody. The labor that was mine removing them out of that common state they were in, hath fixed my property in them.

By making an explicit consent of every commoner necessary to anyone's appropriating to himself any part of what is given in common. Children or servants could not cut the meat which their father or master had provided for them in common without assigning to everyone his peculiar part. Though the water running in the fountain be everyone's, yet who can doubt but that in the pitcher is his only who drew it out? His labor hath taken it out of the hands of Nature where it was common, and belonged equally to all her children, and hath thereby appropriated it to himself.

Thus this law of reason makes the deer that Indian's who hath killed it; it is allowed to be his goods who hath bestowed his labor upon it, though, before, it was the common right of everyone. And amongst those who are counted the civilized part of mankind, who have made and multiplied positive laws to determine property, this original law of nature for the beginning of property, in what was before common, still takes place, and by virtue thereof, what fish anyone catches in the ocean, that great and still remaining common of mankind; or what ambergris anyone takes up here is by the labor that removes it out of that common state nature left it in, made his property who takes that pains about it. And even amongst us, the hare that anyone is hunting is thought his who pursues her during the chase. For being a beast that is still looked upon as common, and no man's private possession, whoever has employed so much labor about any of that kind as to find and pursue her has thereby removed her from the state of nature wherein she was common, and hath began a property.

It will perhaps be objected to this, that if gathering the acorns, or other fruits of the earth, etc., makes a right to them, then anyone may engross as much as he will. To which I answer, Not so. The same law of nature that does by this means give us property, does also bound that property too. "God has given us all things richly" (1 Tim. vi. 17), is the voice of reason confirmed by inspiration. But how far has He given it us? To enjoy. As much as anyone can make use of to any advantage of life before it spoils, so much he may by his labor fix a property in; whatever is beyond this, is more than his share, and belongs to others. Nothing was made by God for man to spoil or destroy. And thus considering the plenty of natural provisions there was a long time in the world, and the few spenders, and to how small a part of that provision the industry of one man could extend itself, and engross it to the prejudice of others—especially keeping within the bounds, set by reason, of what might serve for his use—there could be then little room for quarrels or contentions about property so established.

But the chief matter of property being now not the fruits of the earth, and the beasts that subsist on it, but the earth itself, as that which takes in and carries with it all the rest, I think it is plain that property in that, too, is acquired as the former. As much land as a man tills, plants, improves, cultivates, and can use the product of, so much is his property. He by his labor does as it were enclose it from the common. Nor will it invalidate his right to say, everybody else has an equal title to it; and therefore he cannot appropriate, he cannot enclose, without the consent of all his fellow-commoners,

all mankind. God, when He gave the world in common to all mankind, commanded man also to labor, and the penury of his condition required it of him. God and his reason commanded him to subdue the earth, i.e., improve it for the benefit of life, and therein lay out something upon it that was his own, his labor. He that, in obedience to this command of God, subdued, tilled, and sowed any part of it, thereby annexed to it something that was his property, which another had no title to, nor could without injury take from him.

Nor was this appropriation of any parcel of land, by improving it, any prejudice to any other man, since there was still enough and as good left; and more than the yet unprovided could use. So that in effect there was never the less left for others because of his enclosure for himself. For he that leaves as much as another can make use of, does as good as take nothing at all. Nobody could think himself injured by the drinking of another man, though he took a good draught, who had a whole river of the same water left him to quench his thirst; and the case of land and water, where there is enough of both, is perfectly the same.

God gave the world to men in common; but since He gave it them for their benefit, and the greatest conveniences of life they were capable to draw from it, it cannot be supposed He meant that it should always remain common and uncultivated. He gave it to the use of the industrious and rational (and labor was to be his title to it), not to the fancy or covetousness of the quarrelsome and contentious. He that had as good left for his improvement as was already taken up, needed not complain, ought not to meddle with what was already improved by another's labor; if he did, it is plain he desired the benefit of another's pains, which he had no right to, and not the ground which God had given him in common with others to labor on, and whereof there was as good left as that already possessed, and more than he knew what to do with, or his industry could reach to.

It is true, in land that is common in England, or any other country where there is plenty of people under Government, who have money and commerce, no one can enclose or appropriate any part without the consent of all, his fellow-commoners: because this is left common by compact, i.e., by the law of the land, which is not to be violated. And though it be common in respect of some men, it is not so to all mankind: but is the joint property of this country, or this parish. Besides, the remainder, after such enclosure, would not be as good to the rest of the commoners as the whole was, when they could all make use of the whole; whereas in the beginning and first peopling of the great common of the world it was quite otherwise. The law man was under was rather for appropriating. God commanded, and his wants forced him, to labor. That was his property, which could not be taken from him wherever he had fixed it. And hence subduing or cultivating the earth, and having dominion, we see are joined together. The one gave title to the other. So that God, by commanding to subdue, gave authority so far to appropriate. And the condition of human life, which requires labor and materials to work on, necessarily introduces private possessions.

The measure of property nature has well set by the extent of men's labor and the conveniency of life. No man's labor could subdue or appropriate all, nor could his enjoyment consume more than a small part; so that it was impossible for any man, this way, to entrench upon the right of another or acquire to himself a property to the prejudice of his neighbor, who would still have room for as good and as large a possession (after the other had taken out his) as before it was appropriated. Which measure did confine every man's possession to a very modest proportion, and such as might appropriate to himself without injury to anybody in the first ages of the world, when men were more in danger to be lost, by wandering from their company, in the then vast wilderness of the earth than to be straitened for want of room to plant in.

The same measure may be allowed still, without prejudice to anybody, full as the world seems. For, supposing a man or family, in the state they were at first, peopling of the world by the children of Adam or Noah, let him plant in some inland vacant places of America. We shall find that the possessions he could make himself, upon the measures we have given, would not be very large, nor, even to this day, prejudice the rest of mankind or give them reason to complain or think themselves injured by this man's encroachment, though the race of men have now spread themselves to all the corners of the world, and do infinitely exceed the small number was at the beginning. Nay, the extent of ground is of so little value without labor that I have heard it affirmed that in Spain itself a man may be permitted to plough, sow, and reap, without being disturbed, upon land he has no other title to, but only his making use of it. But, on the contrary, the inhabitants think themselves beholden to him who, by his industry on neglected, and consequently waste land, has increased the stock of corn, which they wanted. But be this as it will, which I lay no stress on, this I dare boldly affirm, that the same rule of propriety—viz., that every man should have as much as he could make use of, would hold still in the world, without straitening anybody, since there is land enough in the world to suffice double the inhabitants, had not the invention of money, and the tacit agreement of men to put a value on it, introduced (by consent) larger possessions and a right to them; which. how it has done, I shall by and by show more at large. . . .

Property Rights in Natural Resources

Kristin Shrader-Frechette

Even in terms of classical anthropocentric ethics, our environmental actions are highly questionable. Further, good act-utilitarians, bent on ignoring distributive equity but maximizing the well-being of all persons of all generations, would have to admit that present policies of pollution and resource depletion cannot possibly be justified on the grounds that they optimize the welfare of all persons, especially members of future generations. Similarly, our current views of property rights, al-

The Global Possible: Resources, Development, and the New Century, edited by Robert Repetto (New Haven: Yale University Press, 1985), pp. 115–116. Reprinted by permission of the publisher.

legedly derived from the views of John Locke, are woefully inconsistent with classical criteria for generating and transferring ownership. In fact, if we really accepted some of the claims made by Locke, we would see that it is ethically impossible at the present time to accord humans property rights in natural resources such as land or minerals. Why is this so?

Locke had a labor theory of property. He maintained that whatever a person takes out of the state of nature and mixes his labor with, he makes his own property. He held, further, that people have property rights as much as they "can make use of to any advantage of life before it spoils," but that "whatever is beyond this, is more than his share and belongs to others."[1] The one proviso that Locke made is that there be "as much and as good left in common for others."[2] Locke believed that this proviso could easily be fulfilled, since there were vast lands in the world and relatively few inhabitants,[3] and since he held that labor "puts the greatest part of value upon land, without which it would scarcely be worth anything."[4]

Of course, the crucial point in Locke's theory is whether appropriation of property such as land worsens the situation of others.[5] As long as global population was small and unexplored lands extensive, there was likely to be "enough and as good left in common for others." But it is doubtful that contemporary theorists are correct if they defend Locke's theory of property rights and argue that his proviso can be met. How can one own and use vast amounts of land, oil, or coal, for example, and yet claim that "as much and as good" is left for others?

The whole point of Locke's reasoning is that the earth is given in common to all people, past, present, and future, and that people deserve to have property rights in what has been created by their labor. To the extent that contemporary theorists fail to recognize that one cannot have property rights in what one's labor does not create and in resources when one's ownership does not leave "as much and as good" for others, then to that degree are their allegedly Lockean justifications of private property in natural resources inconsistent with current patterns of ownership. Hence, even on traditional anthropocentric grounds it is not clear that it is ethical for humans to claim to have Lockean property rights over land, water, air, minerals, and other natural resources,[6] when enough and as good will not be left for those to come. But if so, then many of our global problems arise not because our anthropocentric ethics errs but because we do not practice the Lockean ethics we preach. . . .[7]

Notes

1. John Locke, *Second Treatise of Government*, paragraphs 25–31.

2. Ibid., para. 27.

3. Ibid., para. 36.

4. Ibid., para. 43.

5. Robert Nozick, *Anarchy, State, and Utopia* (New York: Basic Books, 1974), pp. 174–76.

6. L. C. Becker, *Property Rights* (London: Routledge and Kegan Paul, 1977), p. 109, presents a similar argument.

7. See John Passmore, *Man's Responsibility for Nature* (New York: Charles Scribner's Sons, 1974), also W. K. Frankena, "Ethics and the Environment," in *Ethics and Problems of the 21st Century*, ed. K. E. Goodpaster and K. M. Sayre (Notre Dame, Ind.: University of Notre Dame Press, 1979), pp. 3–4.

   For Shrader-Frechette's views, see Kristin Shrader-Frechette, "Locke and Limits on Land Ownership," *Journal of the History of Ideas*, v. 54, n. 2 (April 1993), 201–219.

Property Rights and Preservationist Duties

Robert E. Goodin

The 1945 British Labour Government came to power on a programme of securing systematic social control of the means of production. It promptly set about nationalizing coal and steel, the railways, even the hospitals. When it came to farms, though, the government took a different tack. Rather than

Inquiry, Vol. 33, No. 4 (December 1990), 401–414, 417–420, and 422–427. Reprinted by permission of Scandinavian University Press.

taking them formally into public ownership, as with so many other industries, the 1947 Agriculture Act left agricultural land in private ownership and instead merely imposed upon cultivators of it a "duty of good husbandry." Under the terms of that Act, farmers were obliged to cultivate in a responsible manner, with the Minister of Agriculture being given powers to supervise and, ultimately, to sell off lands of those who did not.[1]

Among legal philosophers, that Act has long been regarded as an instance of nationalization-by-other-means.[2] Honoré treats it as a paradigm case of liberal property rights being limited in the larger social interest.[3] The limitation may well be justifiable—but limitation it none the less remains. Similarly, in Epstein's recent book on *Takings*, environmental regulations which circumscribe what people may do with their property are treated as partial takings of private property for public purposes.[4] Those takings may count as justifiable exercises of the police power; but they are takings none the less and, Epstein insists, owners deserve compensation in consequence.

Implicit in all such discussions is a presumption that property rights are necessarily at odds with preservationist duties. If they are, though, it is not only the agricultural policies of Clause 4 socialists that are in jeopardy. The clash would threaten to undermine environmental protection measures quite generally. The central tenet of the conservationist ethic is to "leave it as you found it" in so far as humanly possibly.[5] Such conservationist appeals have undeniable force. Yet if the proposition here in view is correct, always arrayed against them will be the counter-claims of property owners to do what they will with that which is, by rights, their own.

In a way, conservationists need not be overly concerned by that clash of principles. Reconciling a plurality of partially conflicting values and principles is, after all, the workaday task of liberal political theory.[6] And in trading off competing principles for one another, we standardly trade a little of each for a little of the other. So conservationists need not fear that their preferred principles will be utterly swamped by property rights.

There is much merit in that response. To say that property rights are necessarily at odds with preservationist duties is *not* to say that the former will necessarily always prevail over the other in any

such clash. It is important to recall that property rights address just one social value, to be balanced against (and sacrificed to) various other social values as necessary. It is important to emphasize that property rights are in no way sacrosanct, nor are they even necessarily particularly strong in each and every case. It is right to suppose that in any head-on clashes, conservationist principles surely can—and at least sometimes surely should—prevail.

It is important for conservationists to say all that, but it would be wrong for them to stop at that. Doing so would be to make an important concession, and (if the argument of this paper is correct) a quite unnecessary one. What would have been conceded, by those consenting to the proposition that property rights are necessarily in conflict with preservationist duties, is the proposition that we must weigh one against the other on any given occasion. And always weighing property rights into that social balancing inevitably will, at least sometimes, mean that they outweigh preservationist duties.

That is what conservationists would be conceding, in agreeing that there is a necessary trade-off between property rights and preservationist duties. In my view, that concession is quite unnecessary. We would necessarily have to sacrifice preservationist duties in order to honour property rights only if property rights necessarily entailed a right to destroy.[7] They do no such thing, as I hope here to show.

In this paper, I shall be making two quite distinct claims. The first is a 'conceptual compatibility' claim. In Section I, I shall examine the notion of property rights to show that, far from necessarily conflicting with preservationist duties, property rights usually are fully compatible with (and might even entail) them. The right to destroy is usually not part and parcel of the central incidents of the right to property, as ordinarily understood.[8]

Neither is its justification derivative, in any straightforward way, from that of those other more standard incidents of property rights. In Section II, I shall be making a 'justificatory compatibility' claim. There, I examine briefly the broad classes of arguments used to justify property rights to show that, far from necessarily implying a right to destroy, most of them suggest that one has no right to destroy one's property. The one that does imply a right to destroy would require us to limit that right in broadly the same respects as the qualified preservationist duty, carved out in Section I, would demand.

The upshot of all this is simple. If property rights cannot be shown to imply—either analytically or argumentatively—a right to destroy, then there is no necessary trade-off between property rights and preservationist duties. Those who would resist conservationist demands must, therefore, find some grounds other than property rights on which to rest their case.

It is equally important to say at the outset what I will not be attempting to do here. I will not, except very obliquely, be providing any grounds *for* imposing preservationist duties. Why we should want to do that is a larger issue that must be addressed separately. My claim here is merely that, should we find reasons for wanting to do so, there is no legitimate objection based on people's property rights to our doing so. Furthermore, there is no reason to suppose that those preservationist duties, however grounded, will be equally strong with respect to all goods. Even if preservationist duties are given free rein, unencumbered by any necessity to strike a compromise with property rights, it will none the less remain the case that people will still be at liberty to destroy much, perhaps most, of what they own. Much, certainly—most, perhaps—but not all. That is the larger point, for which this argument is a necessary preliminary.

I. The Notion of 'Property Rights'

The modern notion of a 'property right,' as is now widely recognized, is in fact an amalgam of several more specific rights.[9] Lawyers tend to prefer long, ill-sorted lists.[10] Indeed, they sometimes seem to speak as if there is no such thing as 'a' right to property at all, but merely a set of specific rights that we might have with respect to a variety of specific objects.[11]

That way of talking about property may be the one that is most faithful to legal history and practice. But it would preclude us from discussing seriously what might necessarily follow from having a property right at all. Nothing necessarily follows on this account. Everything would just depend upon what rules we happen to impose, and what attendant rights we happen to grant. If there is no analytic core to the notion of property, as this logic suggests, then that is just a matter of what rules law-makers and judges happened to have adopted with respect to any particular set of objects.[12]

If we want to explore the possibility that something might analytically follow from the mere notion of property rights, we will need a more coherent account of property rights than lawyers traditionally provide. The tidiest parsing of the notion of property rights offered to date decomposes them into three principal components: (1) the right to *use* a thing; (2) the right to use it *exclusively*; and (3) the right to *transfer* it at will.[13] To this must, of course, be added various other subsidiary rights and duties (liability rules, for example) that are required for the enforcement of these other rights. And we may also want to add that, for them to have full-blooded property rights, owners must possess these rights in perpetuity.[14] But such caveats aside, this seems a fairly workable characterization of the main incidents of property ownership as we know it in our society.

These more specific rights, which together constitute property rights, are themselves logically separable. There is no compelling reason, logically or practically, for thinking that all of these rights must go together. It is perfectly conceivable that we might have a right of exclusive use without having a right to transfer that right to anyone else.[15] Likewise, it is perfectly conceivable that we might have a right to use something without having a right to use it exclusively; our having a right to use something is not logically incompatible with others having a right to use the same thing when we ourselves are not.[16]

Since all these component rights need not go together as a matter of logic, any argument for property rights incorporating all of them must justify the inclusion of each separately. My own view is that none of the standard arguments are particularly successful in that task. The stronger arguments for property rights justify only a few of those component rights; the full set is justified only by arguments that make the claims of property weaker and hence more easily overridden.

I shall say a little more about that in Section II below. But those are broader issues which are, strictly speaking, beyond the bounds of the present discussion. Instead, the focus here is more narrowly upon the property owner's putative right to destroy that which is his own.

The first thing to notice about this putative right is that no mention of it is contained in the conventional catalogue of the rights that together constitute that complex which we know as property rights. It is not explicitly contained in the shorter list I offered earlier; it is not even explicitly contained, except obliquely and very much in passing, in longer lists that lawyers typically offer. Far from being treated as a distinct component, enumerated separately alongside other components, this right—in so far as it appears at all—tends to be subsumed under one of the others. The first task in assessing claims to a right to destroy, therefore, is to see if it is somehow analytically implicit in one of the other rights of property.

(a) The Right to Transfer and the Right to Destroy

Let us consider first the possibility that the right to destroy might be subsumed under the right to transfer. The only reason to be found in the extant literature for thinking that this might be so goes roughly as follows.[17] First, assimilate the right to transfer to a 'right to alienate' more generally. This is not implausible. After all, it is an essential part of what you do when transferring your property to another that you must sever the bond that links it to you, and in that sense alienate it from yourself. Next, point out that destroying a piece of your property is merely another way of alienating it. Doing that similarly severs the bond linking it to you—here, by eliminating altogether that thing which was formerly linked to you. Finally, spring the trap: if the right to transfer one's property is conceptualized as a right to alienate one's property, then the right to destroy one's property is indeed therefore implicit in that right. Or so the argument would go.[18]

Notice, straightaway, that such an argument proceeds by a flawed piece of reasoning. What the argument so far has succeeded in demonstrating is:

(1) A right to transfer implies a right to alienate.

and

(2) A right to destroy implies a right to alienate.

The conjunction of those two propositions does not, however, entail that:

(3) A right to transfer implies a right to destroy.

To assert that it does would be equivalent to asserting 'if X implies Z and Y implies Z, then X implies Y,' which is plainly a piece of faulty reasoning.

What would be required in order for that third proposition to be warranted would be the converse of proposition (2). We would need a revised version of the second premise, to wit:

(2′) A right to alienate implies a right to destroy.

That new proposition (2′), combined with proposition (1), would indeed yield the desired conclusion (3).

The question is just how reasonable the revised proposition (2′) actually is. The logic underlying that proposition would presumably run something like this. You cannot without limiting my right to transfer my goods restrict the persons to whom, or the conditions under which, I might transfer them. By the same token, you cannot, without limiting my right to alienate my goods more generally, restrict the ways in which I might dispose of them.

It may well be true that whatever reasons we have for giving people a right to alienate something should also provide us with a reason for giving them a right to destroy it. But that would amount to a 'justificatory' linkage, of the sort to be discussed in Section II below. The issue before us at present is the claim of some purely 'conceptual' linkage between the two. The crucial point to be made in that connection is simply that the notion of alienation nowise implies the notion of destruction.

There are a great many things which we are permitted to alienate but which we are prohibited from destroying. Divorce law allows me to sever the bond between my wife and myself. In giving me that right to alienate her from myself, however, the law does not give me the right to destroy her; if I tried, I would rightly be brought up on charges of attempted murder.[19] Or, again, owners of historical buildings which the authorities have placed under a Preservation Order have every right to sell those properties.[20] But to say that they may alienate them in that fashion is not to say that they may burn them to the ground. The issue here is simply the conceptual one: Do those rules, by limiting the right to destroy in such ways, impinge upon the right to alienate? I submit that they do not. And supposing they do not, proposition (2') is proven false.

There are, incidentally, parallel problems with proposition (1) as well. A right to transfer does indeed imply a right to alienate. But that is, strictly speaking, merely a right to alienate *in certain particular ways*—those embraced in the notion of 'transfer.' It is not necessarily an unrestricted right to alienate *tout court*; nor, therefore, is it necessarily a right to alienate-by-destroying. On the contrary, the notion of 'transfer' itself intuitively implies that the thing being transferred does not diminish in the process. We would take a dim view of a bank that, when asked to transfer funds from one account to another, lost half the monies in the process.

(b) The Right to Use and the Right to Destroy

Much more interesting is the derivation purporting to link the right to destroy to the right to use.[21] As a paradigm case of a right merely to use something, consider the case of rented property. (My running example will be that of a rented car.) Of course, no one imagines that people 'own,' in any full sense, property that they merely lease. Precisely because they merely lease or rent it, they have less than the full complement of property rights in that property. They have, for example, no right of transfer; it would be quite illegal for them to try to sell (or, depending on the terms of the contract, perhaps even sublease) property that they merely rent. Still, there is one right that renters do indisputably have—and apparently in its fullest form. That is the right to *use* the property that they have rented.[22] Let us see what follows from that alone.

1. The Right to Abuse. The right to use has, since the earliest commentaries on Roman law, sometimes been phrased as a 'right to use or abuse.'[23] Those in our own day who would oppose the expansive powers of the regulatory state in the name of private property—Richard Epstein, most notably—sometimes appeal explicitly to this older formulation.[24]

When such commentators speak of a 'right to use or abuse,' they suppose that that more expansive formulation merely elucidates what it has always meant to have a 'right to use' in the first place.

Adding that further clause, they suppose, does not in any way alter the original. Since they regard the right to abuse as part and parcel of the right to use in this way, they do not see any need to provide separate arguments for it. They do not see themselves as advocating anything new, but merely as drawing out what has always been implicit in something old and well established.

If pressed for an argument for the right to abuse, they might argue roughly along these lines, however. The right to use something is a right to use it *as you see fit*. To restrict the ways in which you can use something restricts your right to use it; and to deny you the right to abuse something is, in effect, just such a restriction upon how you can use it. Hence, to deny you the right to abuse something is to limit your right to use it.

That is not the way we ordinarily think of a rented car, though. According to our conventional understandings, you have every right to use the car for the period for which you have rented it; and, by and large, you have a right to use it however you please.[25] Your primary obligation as the car's renter is simply to hand it back at the end of the period in as good a condition as that in which you received it.

Here again, the issue is not whether such an obligation is substantively reasonable or unreasonable, justifiable or unjustifiable. That is a matter for discussion in Section II. The issue here is instead the conceptual one: is there anything inherent in the logic of the notion of a right to use that makes that right incompatible, in whole or in part, with a condition being imposed requiring the rightful user not to destroy the thing being used?

The example of the rented car suggests otherwise. The obligation that you return the rented car in the same condition as that in which you received it does not, in and of itself, restrict your right to use or abuse the automobile in any way whatsoever. You could use the auto however you please: transporting yourself to work, your poultry to market, your caravan to the seashore; taking out the engine and using it to operate a hoist, and so forth. The restriction here in view would not be on the *uses* to which you put the car. Rather, it would be upon the *condition* the car is in when it is returned.

What that example points to is, I believe, just this. The right to use and abuse is not strictly equivalent to a right to destroy, because the former refers to a *process* and the latter to an *end-state*. To infer one from the other is to commit an elementary category mistake.

It is perfectly true that we cannot restrict the uses to which people put their own property without restricting their rights in that property. None the less, we may prescribe or proscribe certain end-results that must come about through the use of that property. Their use (and abuse) rights remain unimpaired, just so long as we do not go on to specify how they should go about producing those results. Thus, duties of preservation (that is, denials of the right to destroy) are not necessarily incompatible with the right to use or abuse.

Constraining end-results might, of course, contingently restrain the ways in which property might be used, if it so happens that there is no way to avoid proscribed end-results if the property were used in certain ways. In the case of the rented car, your obligation to hand it back in the same condition in which you received it might thus prevent you from using it for target practice on an artillery range, or from driving it off the end of a jetty to form part of a seawall. But those are merely contingent, not necessary, connections. If you could somehow restore the car perfectly after the howitzers or the barnacles had had a go at it, you would be perfectly at liberty to use the car in those ways.[26] The fact that you are contingently unable to exercise those rights to use the car in that fashion does not change the fact that you have such use rights, any more than the fact that I am contingently unable to play the violin means that I have no right to do so.

2. The Right to Use Up. Another more promising way to link the right to destroy to the right to use is this. Some goods necessarily diminish with use. What destroys these goods is not just abusing them—even merely using them in the ordinary way lessens them. In cases like these, a right to use would, indeed, apparently entail a right to 'use up' such goods.

Consider, again, the example of the rented car. It would make a mockery of the right to use the car to insist that it be returned in exactly the same condition as that in which it was originally hired: the same mileage, the same wear and tear to engine and tyres, etc. Using the car surely entails using up tyre rubber. So too, perhaps, with a Lockean right to use land for cultivation. To cultivate implies to clear and to plough, which in turn necessarily en-

tails destruction of nature as it had previously existed on that patch of land.[27]

Notice, first, however, that the right to 'use up' is a very limited form of the right to destroy. Such destruction or dimunition of the good as is strictly entailed in use is permissible; but nothing in this logic licenses you to destroy wantonly or to diminish unnecessarily.[28] A right to destroy natural habitats for purposes of cultivation does not entail a right to clear more land than you will be able to cultivate. Or, again, with the rented car: your right to use the rented car might entail a right to use up tyre rubber, but that does not constitute permission to squeal the tyres, laying rubber at every stoplight. This limitation on the right to destroy is phrased, in the case of the rented car, as an explicit requirement that the car be returned in the same condition, 'fair wear and tear excepted.'

Notice, next, that even if the strongest form of preservationist duties are incompatible with use rights in such goods, weaker forms of preservationist duties are perfectly compatible. The stronger duty would be one requiring you to leave things exactly as you found them: the *same things*, in the *same state*. With the sorts of goods here under consideration, it is impossible to do that and to have used the goods at all. But there is a weaker sense in which we can leave things as we found them. Where goods of a certain kind are interchangeable with one another, you can leave things exactly as you found them by leaving *different* (albeit *equivalent*) goods in the *same state* as before.

Thus, our duty to return the rented car in the same condition as we received it is in part a duty to leave as much gasoline in the tank. But nobody expects it to be the *same* gasoline as when we hired the car. To insist upon that would preclude our driving the car off the lot at all. It would also be quite unnecessary to insist upon that, though, since one tank of gasoline is much like any other. Or, for another example, leaving a mountain hut you have borrowed exactly as you found it is taken to mean leaving *as much* firewood stacked in the shed, not the *same* firewood stacked there as when you arrived.

The right to use goods that diminish with use is necessarily incompatible only with the stronger form of preservationist duties. The proper formulation of the preservationist duty, in those cases, is the weaker one instead. Something very much like this was clear in Roman law.[29] It has been so more or less continuously ever since.[30] Using things that necessarily diminish with use might be incompatible with preserving those very things, but it is not incompatible with replacing the things used up with others that are in all relevant respects the same.

This presupposes, of course, that there are indeed close substitutes available for those things that we have used up.[31] Sometimes there clearly are. Gasoline, grain, and firewood, at least at one level of analysis, are all straightforward examples. Other times they are not, and the commodities used up are, in some sense or another, irreplaceable. That is at least arguably true of nature in all its forms.[32] Where that is the case, there truly is a trade-off to be faced between use rights and preservationist duties, however weakly they are phrased. I shall return to comment further upon the proper resolution of that trade-off in Section I(b)3(ii) below.

3. The Right (Merely) to Use and the Duty Not to Destroy.

The argument so far has aimed at establishing that preservationist duties are broadly compatible with property rights, that is, that no trade-off between them is usually necessary. That argument has proceeded by showing that there is no 'right to destroy' implicit in any of the standard incidents of property rights. Here I propose to go further still, along these same lines. Not only is there no right to destroy implicit in a right to use. Furthermore, as I shall now show, a 'duty not to destroy' is itself implicit in a *mere* 'right to use.'

This is a strong claim. If it succeeds, the aim of this essay will have been accomplished in a very big way. Not only will it have shown there is no necessary conflict between property rights and preservationist duties; it will have shown the former actually entail the latter. If that stronger claim can be sustained, so much the better. But all that is strictly required to block the property-rights rejoinder to preservationist duties is the weaker claim of compatibilism. For those purposes, the arguments of this section are superfluous. That weaker claim turns entirely on the conjunction of the arguments offered elsewhere together with those of Section II below.

(i) In General. The case for a stronger claim builds on the results established above. There, it

has been shown that other rights involved in the right to property do not imply a right to destroy. That is a separate right, which must be grounded separately and granted separately if it is to exist at all. It does not come along implicitly, as part and parcel of the others.

From that follows the crucial move in my argument for the strong claim: to say merely that you have a right to use something is to say that you have a right *merely to use* it. To say that you have a right to use something, and to say no more than that, constitutes an implicit withholding of permission for you to do more than to use it. The clear implication of saying that you have a right to use it, and saying no more than that, is that you have *no* right to destroy it. To destroy it would clearly be doing something more than merely using it, and that right has been implicitly denied you. Through such reasoning, something rather like a duty to leave things as you found them can be derived from rights (merely) to use the things.

This becomes particularly clear where what is ordinarily only implicit is made explicit. Sometimes it is said, explicitly and emphatically, by a property owner lending you something that 'you have a right *merely to use* this thing.' That constitutes a strong and clear denial of permission to do more than use it. Then, clearly, you would have 'no right' to destroy the thing, and it would be quite wrong for you to do so.

That is what happens with the rented car. You have been granted a right to use it for the period of your rental, and broadly speaking to use it however you like. But you have *merely* the right to use it. You may not sell it, damage it or destroy it.[33] When granting you the right merely to use its car, Hertz was not granting you the right to smash it up, and it says so right on the face of the Rental Agreement. If you have smashed up the car, you have gone beyond your rights and transgressed on those of Hertz, and you therefore owe them compensation for the damage done.[34]

In the case of car rental, this is made explicit in the undertaking you sign, upon accepting the car, to return it in the same condition in which you received it. Whether it was made explicit or not, however, this sort of condition none the less follows logically from the fact that you were merely being given use rights. As has been argued above, the right to destroy is a separate, independent right, not in any way implicit in the right to use or to transfer. If so, then that is a right that must be granted explicitly, over and above any granting of those other rights, if it is to exist at all. The absence of an explicit granting of that 'right to destroy' is tantamount to the implicit withholding of it. The effect, morally, is just the same as if the right had been explicitly withheld.[35]

In the case of the rented car, the emphasis is upon questions of which rights were transferred to the renter in the Rental Agreement. Those conclusions can easily be generalized to property rights more broadly, however. In the case of the rented car, we have seen that we must require independent evidence of a separate transfer of the right to destroy.[36] So, too, must we demand independent moral arguments for a separate right to destroy one's property more generally. Just as the right to destroy the rented car cannot be inferred from the transfer of mere use rights alone, so too the right to destroy one's property more generally cannot be inferred from moral arguments for the right to use, use exclusively or to transfer it, alone.

In the absence of independent evidence of a separate transfer of the right to destroy the rented car, it would seem that the right merely to use it would imply that the renter has no right to destroy it. So, too, with property rights more generally. In the absence of independent moral arguments for a separate right to destroy one's property, it would seem that a right (merely) to use it would imply that the property owner has no right to destroy it.[37]

(ii) In the Case of Irreplaceable, Consumable Commodities. There remains the one case, identified in Section I(b)2 above, in which there truly is a necessary conflict between use rights and preservationist duties. That case is the one involving goods characterized by these two features: (a) the goods diminish with use; and (b) there are no close substitutes for those goods. For one example, consider the case of artists' prints, sketches, and drawings. Museums allow people to view such items, but only for a limited period each day because exposure inevitably causes them to deteriorate. For another example, consider fragile alpine environments: National Park wardens issue a restricted number of permits for people to hike there because of the irreparable damage that people's footsteps inevitably do to those very special areas.

How common or uncommon a conjunction of conditions this might be can, for present purposes,

be left as an open question. The point remains that, wherever it is found, we cannot allow people to use the goods at all without simultaneously allowing them to violate preservationist duties. Conversely, we cannot preserve things as they are without preventing people from using (and hence destroying, or at least diminishing) the goods. There, a trade-off between the two values truly is necessary.

If my argument in Section I(b)3(i) has proven successful, though, the resolution of that trade-off will be clear. There it was argued that rights (merely) to use something entail a duty to preserve, and not to destroy, the thing. If, as in the case here contemplated, we cannot use the thing without destroying it, then we cannot exercise that use right without violating one of the conditions implicitly governing its being granted to us in the first place. It is as if you find your rented car parked in what has, overnight, been turned into a minefield: though you still undoubtedly have the right to use the car, there is no way you can exercise that right without blowing it up, which would contravene one of the conditions upon which the use rights were granted in the first place. Thus it would seem that preservationist duties should, in these cases, have clear primacy. If we have a right (merely) to use something and we cannot use it without destroying it, then we must not use it at all. That is to say, use rights are always bounded by preservationist duties, and in some cases that might mean that in effect there are no use rights at all.

Here, as before, the point is not that it would always and necessarily be wrong to destroy things by using them up. The point is, instead, that the right to destroy must be seen as a separate, independent right, for which separate, independent moral arguments must be given. In the absence of those arguments, the duty to preserve which is implicit in the right (merely) to use will prevent us from availing ourselves of the right to use (and, hence, use up) consumable, irreplaceable assets. Nothing has been said so far to suggest that such arguments cannot be given. (That is the burden of Section II, below.) The only points established so far are that such arguments must be given, and that destruction is impermissible until they are given.

(c) The Right to Exclude and the Right to Destroy

Of the three principal incidents of property rights, there remains merely the right to use exclusively to be considered. The argument of Section I(b) above is that the right to use does not, in and of itself, give rise to a right to destroy. The question now to be considered is whether exclusivity adds anything that might aid in deriving such a right. This possibility is even less well worked out than are the others in the extant literature on property rights. So here we are very much left to our own devices in inventing arguments for ourselves.[38]

In one obvious way, a right to exclude is rather like a right to destroy, in that both would allow the right-holder to deprive others of the enjoyment of the good in question. And the resemblance is all the stronger when, as with a full-blooded property right, the right to exclude is not time-limited (as with a patent) but rather a right to exclude permanently. Destruction is tantamount to permanent exclusion.

All of that is true enough. It is still not of much help in the present context, though. The aim here in view, recall, is to derive a right to destroy from a right to exclude permanently. What we are looking for is therefore an argument that takes the form,

(4) If you have a right to exclude permanently, then you have a right to destroy.

Certainly it is true that if you destroy something then you exclude others permanently from that thing. But that, at most, would be to say:[39]

(5) If you have a right to destroy, then you have a right to exclude permanently.

The argument here in view has simply mistaken proposition (5), which is what is shown by the unobjectionable observation that destruction excludes, for proposition (4), which is what the argument needs to show. The implication simply runs the wrong way to establish what it needs to establish for present purposes. We wanted to show that X implies Y, and all we have shown is that Y implies X.

Still, it might be thought that giving people a right to exclude others permanently from a thing is, in terms of its justification and underlying motivation if not in terms of its pure logic, extensionally equivalent to giving them a right to destroy it. Either way, the thing is unavailable to others and lost to society; whatever *reason* we have for allowing it to be lost to us in one way would lead us to accept its being lost in the other; we ought surely be indif-

ferent between its being lost to us in one way or any other.

But that is not necessarily so, either. We may take pleasure in knowing that the *Mona Lisa* still exists, and experience pain in the prospect of its destruction, even if it has disappeared from the walls of the Louvre into some private collection. Therefore, while we might be prepared to tolerate the disappearance of Leonardo's masterpiece into a private collection (because the purchase price will allow the Louvre to buy and display a great many other masterpieces), we might equally want to insist that the owner not destroy it. It is not motivationally incoherent for us to take this stance. Were we so disposed, we could give the private collector both a right and a duty to enjoy the Mona Lisa exclusively in perpetuity.

Justifications for alternative property regimes are, of course, the proper province of Section II below. The present focus is upon analytic necessity. In those terms, the crucial point is just this. As a purely conceptual matter, certainly it is possible—not logically incoherent—to give someone *both* a right and a duty to use something exclusively in perpetuity. The right to use it exclusively in perpetuity is the right classically associated with property ownership. The duty to do so would amount to a preservationist duty. The fact that the two can, logically, co-exist suffices to show that the right to use exclusively in perpetuity does not necessarily imply a right to destroy. . . .

II. Justifications of Property Rights

Heretofore I have been concerned to show that the right to destroy is a separate right, in no way derivable from any of the other rights that collectively comprise 'property rights' as we know them. The upshot of that discussion is that, if we want to assert a right to destroy, we must argue for it separately—we will not have been arguing for it, implicitly, in the course of arguing for those other aspects of property rights.

Here I shall go on to argue that none of the standard arguments offered for property rights would support an unqualified 'right to destroy.' Many would support instead a duty to preserve. Those arguments for property rights that would endorse a right to destroy would also limit it in roughly the same ways as would be required by the weaker preservationist duties discussed above. Hence, there is a 'justificatory consistency': the same arguments used to justify property also seem to justify preservationist duties, at least of the weaker sort.

Though fleshed out in various different ways, arguments for property rights fall generically into two classes. One is a class of desert-based justifications, the other a class of utility-based justifications.[40] Let us consider each in turn.

(a) Desert-Based Arguments

There are, roughly speaking, two ways to run desert-based arguments for property. The first is the characteristically libertarian approach, deriving rights to external material possessions from one's rights in one's own person. Such rights-based arguments for property always seem to amount to a sort of generalized version of Locke's "mixing" metaphor: (a) you have infused something of yourself into some natural object; (b) it would be wrong to alienate you from (that piece of) yourself; (c) hence, you ought to possess the natural object with which your self is so deeply implicated. For Locke, the 'something of yourself' infused into natural objects was your labour. For Hegel, it was your personality. There are important differences between these versions, of course: one points to a physical fact while the other points to a mental state, and so on. But they are nearly enough the same, at root, to be treated as one for the purposes of the present argument.[41]

One problem with this whole style of argument is that it seems to provide a powerful rationale for some incidents of ownership rights (e.g., the right of exclusive use) but not for others (e.g., the right to transfer). In the above argument sketch, step (b) is crucial. It is essential to explain why, when mixing something that is yours or part of you with something that was not, you come to acquire title to that which was previously unowned rather than merely losing what was previously yours.[42]

To get out the sort of conclusion that this argument requires, we must assume in step (b) that the thing mixed is something that is 'inalienable'—something that it is wrong to separate you from, even as a result of your own voluntary acts in mixing it with something not your own. But if you cannot be allowed to fritter away inalienable bits of

yourself by mixing them with things that are not your own, so too you must not be allowed to trade them away along with goods that are your own. If, morally speaking, it is so important that you not be separated from those aspects of yourself that we are willing to give you property rights in previously unowned things merely to avoid your being separated from them, then by the same token we should be unwilling to let you trade away those aspects of yourself that are inextricably mixed with those things we have allocated to you as private property.

In short, the self-same reasons the mixing metaphor would give us for awarding people rights of exclusive use of something would also serve to indicate the incoherence of our allowing them to transfer that thing to someone else. The self-same considerations that, on the mixing metaphor, militate in favour of a right of exclusive use militate against a right of transfer.

The same argument just given against a right to transfer tells equally strongly, of course, against a right to destroy. If the reason for giving you rights to use, and to use exclusively, certain goods is that you have inalienable bits of yourself vested in them, then we ought not allow you to alienate those bits of yourself by destroying the things on which they are carried. We should not allow that any more than we should allow you to alienate them by trading away the things on which they are carried.

That is just the simplest and most literal understanding of the mixing metaphor. Others might, for example, say that the point of the mixing metaphor is to suggest that, just as your labour cannot be taken from you without your consent, so too can nothing with which it is mixed be taken from you without your consent. On this reading, the point of the mixing metaphor was merely to rule out forced labour and involuntary transfers. But, obviously enough, that would be perfectly consistent with allowing you to transfer the products of your labour voluntarily.

That version of the argument will not be much use, however, in justifying a right to destroy. Saying that you consent to the destruction of the object of your labour is merely to say that no wrong (akin to forced labour) will have been done to you by its destruction. Through your consent, you have waived any objection which *you* might have had to its destruction. That would settle matters morally, however, only if we had some antecedent reason to suppose that yours was the only possible objection. That would, in effect, amount to an assertion that you have an exclusive right to destroy that thing. At that point, though, the argument from consent has ended up asserting what it was designed to prove.

In short, the argument from consent merely serves to show that one objection to destruction is absent. It hardly serves to show what needs to be shown here, which is that all objections are absent—much less that there is any positive justification for allowing people to destroy those things.

Another variation on the mixing theme does strive to provide such a positive justification. On this understanding, the point of the mixing metaphor is to emphasize the way in which you make material objects part of your life's plans and activities. Property rights, on this understanding, become part of your right of autonomy and self-government. How, exactly, those objects fit into your plans and activities is, of course, for you to decide. But one thing you might plan to do with them is to transfer them to others; another is to destroy them. We can have no objection to such transfer or destruction of material resources, in so far as we value your autonomy and self-government and in so far as that transfer/destruction is what your autonomous plans entail.

At this point, though, the pretence that property rights are based on people's moral deserts begins to wear particularly thin. Deserts are predicated upon something good about what people are or what they have done. It is therefore no accident that, in the Lockean version of the story, property rights are predicated upon productive labour. Creating or improving objects of value can obviously count as a meritorious performance, the proper basis of a desert claim. A life plan that involves, in contrast, the intentional, systematic destruction of things is a less obvious candidate for such accolades. A case might still be made, perhaps—especially if destruction is necessary for creation or production or improvement in some other respects. Then, however, what the desert-based argument would give you is not a right to destroy so much as permission to destroy, as a regrettably necessary means to some other worthy end. Again, what we would have is not a positive justification for allowing people to destroy things so much as an argument for excusing such destruction. . . .

(b) Utility-Based Arguments

Utility-based arguments for property are familiar enough. An important subtheme in Locke's *Second Treatise* is that the private appropriation of unowned land is permissible because cultivated land is vastly more productive than uncultivated land—an outcome which, on Locke's account, is pleasing both to God and man.[43] Proto-utilitarians like Hume point to the general social utility of stable expectations in justification of settled rules of property. Later utilitarians point, additionally, to their role in forcing the internalization of externalities, and in that way maximizing social utility.

Some such line seems particularly strong in justifying, at least potentially, all the standard incidents of property rights. In so far as no one can derive utility from something without using it, utility-based reasoning offers a prima-facie justification for use rights; and in so far as one person's utility from using something is undermined by another's also using it, that might (depending on how the utility sums work out) constitute a utility-based argument for a right of exclusive use. Furthermore, in so far as different people derive different amounts of utility from using a thing, utility-based reasoning would provide a prima-facie justification for allowing transfers of those use rights from people who would derive less to those who would derive more utility from that usage.

The weakness of this line of reasoning lies, of course, in its incapacity to generate property rights strong enough to do what their champions most want them to do. Ordinarily, the point of asserting rights is precisely to block (or 'trump') utility-based reasoning. In particular, the principal point of asserting property rights is ordinarily to prevent utilitarian-inspired redistributions of resources based on considerations of the low marginal utility that the rich derive from their superfluous resources, and the high marginal utility that the poor would derive from those resources were they transferred to them instead. If property rights are themselves justified by nothing more than utility-based considerations, however, then they are not different in kind from the sorts of claims that are used to justify such redistributions. That does not guarantee that utility-based arguments for property rights *will* necessarily be overridden, in any particular case. What it does guarantee is that, at least in principle, they always *can* be. Broadly the same sorts of considerations are at work on both sides of the issue. Which prevails is, as ever for utilitarians, just a matter of how the sums come out.

More to the present point, utility-based reasoning also seems incapable, at least on its face, of justifying any general right to destroy things allocated to you to use. Of course, it may not always be worth stopping you from destroying certain sorts of things either. Doing so may cost more than it is worth. Utilitarians may therefore recommend that, as a general principle, the state should not prohibit certain classes of trivial (or, depending on enforcement costs, perhaps not-so-trivial) destruction. But of course a Hohfeldian 'no-power' correlates with a 'liberty,' not with a 'right.' So the most that this argument will yield is a legal liberty, not a right, to destroy—and then only up to a certain point. There is no reason, in such logic, to suppose that utilitarians will ever embrace a general principle licensing destruction on a really grand scale.

The fundamental point remains. The rationale for allocating things to people for their private use is, on the Lockean version of the argument that modern economists often echo, that society thereby gets more use out of those things.[44] Allowing people a right to destroy those things, as well as merely to use them, would offer them the option of curtailing the future usefulness of those things. That hardly looks like a strategy for maximizing their usefulness to society.

There is, of course, a rejoinder available to those who would defend a right to destroy on utility-based premises. The essence of their claim must be this: the utility produced through destroying the thing exceeds the sum-total of utility that might have been produced—now or later—through any alternative use of that thing. That *may* be true at any point in time, as regards any given good. It must be true at *some* point in time, as regards goods that can be used only by being used up.[45]

The trick comes in knowing when, exactly, that is true. Assuming the right to destroy is transferable, then idealized markets (should they ever exist) would tell you. Whoever would derive most utility from destroying the thing would bid most for the right to destroy it. Certain complications arise if the people who would most like the right are not yet born, of course. Notionally, it should be possible even there to hold the right for later sale at higher prices; but you might yourself be dead by

then, and perfectly rational risk-of-death discounting (still more, perfectly irrational 'pure time preference' discounting) would lead you to weigh future utilities much less heavily than present ones in your calculations.[46] In utility-based arguments, that is an unfortunate outcome: a utile is a utile, whenever it arrives. Maybe even that might be overcome, in a really idealized market, by a time-less brokerage firm that makes its profits out of buying from one generation and selling to another. But here the idealization gets simply ridiculous.

Presumably there will always be uncertainty about the future—about both the technologies and the tastes that will be found there. That being so, there will always be a prima-facie case for preserving things, rather than using them up. There is always a chance that something would yield more utility if used later than now. That is captured in the economists' notion of an 'option value.'[47]

If we give people a right to destroy, that would be a right to extinguish the value associated with all future options. In utility-based terms, there must always be a presumption against the destruction of value. Hence, there is a utility-based presumption against the exercise of the right to destroy—which, on the argument here in view, is itself grounded in utility-based reasoning, too.

That is just a presumption, no more. Like all presumptions, this one is capable of being overridden—here, by evidence that the utilities that would definitely be received from destroying the thing exceed the utility of preserving the options.

There are, however, arguments for supposing that that trade-off should be decided in favour of preservationist policies, at least for certain classes of goods. The first, and stronger, of these arguments points to the fact that preserving the option protects us against risks (risks that our tastes or circumstances may change, and, hence, that what we do not want or need today we might want tomorrow). It goes on to argue that, at least with respect to certain classes of goods, it is morally proper or rationally prudent to avoid taking risks. How that class of goods is specified varies, depending on the argument used to establish the immorality or imprudence of risk-taking. Some arguments point to the indispensability of things serving our 'basic needs,' and urge extreme caution in doing anything that might cause us to fall below subsistence thresholds.[48] Another points to the fact that some risks are, by nature, 'collective,' imposing the same level of risk upon everyone in the group; in such circumstances, justice would seem to require that the group respect the most risk-averse member's risk preferences, at least where basic needs are concerned.[49] Yet another argument points to our obligations not to risk defaulting upon our basic moral duties (e.g., it would be wrong to gamble with the family's food budget in a way it would not be with its entertainment budget); and if we do indeed have duties to future generations not to squander their inheritance, but to act instead as responsible trustees of it, then again we would have a reason for preferring the less risky, option-preserving course.[50] However, all of those arguments for preserving options are only as strong as the arguments for avoiding risk. While I am persuaded that some—perhaps all—of those arguments go through, I agree that these are strong, contentious claims, and I would not want to make my case here rely totally upon them.

There is a second, weaker claim that will do almost as well for the purposes at hand. The argument here is that the presumption against exercising a right to destroy is especially strong where irreplaceable assets are concerned, simply because irreplaceability increases something's option value.[51] Imagine two things that are identical in every respect but one, and that one is such as to make the one thing irreplaceable in a way that the other is not. Consider, for example, two mass-produced watches that are perfectly identical, except for the fact that one belonged to your mother and the other did not. Now, even if you do not yourself care about the attribute which the one possesses and the other lacks, someone someday (your grandchildren, for example) might. Preserving for them the option of having their great-grandmother's watch, by not selling it now to a pawnbroker, is therefore particularly valuable, in a way that preserving for them the option of having one of a great number of utterly interchangeable watches would not be. In general, preserving the option of having some irreplaceable object is more valuable than preserving the option of having some object for which there are close substitutes, just because things that are somehow unique and irreplaceable might someday be valued in ways (that is, on account of that unique, irreplaceable, non-repeatable feature) that other objects cannot.[52] That greater option value provides, in turn, a utility-based argument for supposing that the presumption against destruction is particularly strong where irreplaceable objects are concerned.

Strong or weak, it is still only a presumption, of course. In the nature of things, even a strong presumption can be overridden. So even where irreplaceable objects are concerned, the case for not destroying them is not absolutely clinched in utility-based terms. Still, we have gone a long way towards firming it up.

(c) Justifications: Conclusions

The upshot of this survey of justifications for property rights has produced results that, broadly speaking, converge with those produced by the inquiry in Section I into the notion of property rights. Both agree that any general right to destroy that which is our own may properly—and perhaps even must morally—be circumscribed very carefully. From both perspectives, there seem to be reasons to suppose that objects which are completely replaceable may be destroyed in so far as it is strictly necessary to do so in order to make use of them. (That is still perfectly consistent, however, with imposing a weaker preservationist duty to leave adequate substitutes for what has been used up in that process.) From both perspectives, there also seem to be various reasons for supposing that irreplaceable objects deserve strong, special protection.

III. Conclusion

Property rights are legal instantiations of moral ones or of other moral considerations more generally. Only the bold, however, would ever suppose that they are the complete instantiation of all morally relevant considerations for governing .human relationships. There may well be other moral considerations—what exactly they are, when exactly they may be relevant are questions beyond the bounds of this paper—leading us to impose duties of preservation with respect to the very same goods as those over which people are given rights of ownership. The question that this paper has been addressing is whether those considerations are necessarily competing considerations, or whether they can be simultaneously realized. It has been the argument of this paper that they can, indeed, be simultaneously realized: there is no necessary tension between them.

This becomes a practically vexing issue, of course, because the property rights in question have already been legally granted while the preservationist duties are only now being imposed. So it is not, in practice, a question of devising a regime for rendering the two compatible from the start. It is, rather, a question of whether imposing a new preservationist duty now—now that property rights of the traditional sort have already been granted—would infringe people's already-existing property rights. The argument of this paper is, again, that it would not—no more than would a law prohibiting people from driving their cars in newly pedestrianized streets in the city centre deprive them of their property rights in their cars.

Property rights have historically been the refuge of scoundrels. At one time, cruel parents used to appeal to the fact that, after all, they owned their children to license their cruelty.[53] We no longer accept such excuses. Neither, increasingly, are we inclined to accept that the owners of a historic mansion, just because they are the owners, can raze it to build a new office block. My point here has simply been that we need not deny that they have property rights in the mansion altogether (as we did the notion that parents owned their children) in order to underwrite this sentiment.

What I am arguing for, basically, is a trusteeship conception of property, at least with respect to certain sorts of things. What is part of the National Trust and why it should be so is a separate question, beyond the bounds of the present exercise. But on the assumption that there are certain irreplaceable, invaluable assets in whose future we all have a powerful, legitimate interest, we may properly require their owners to use them in such a way that preserves them—without thereby causing them to cease, even in part, to own them. That, in light of current policy debates, is an important finding.[54]

Notes

1. Agriculture Act, 1947, *Public General Acts*, 10 and 11 Geo. 6, ch. 48, secs. 9–21.
2. Though, curiously enough, not among MPs debating the Act or its subsequent partial repeal: none was prepared to assert that the Act violated some "right of *bad* husbandry" deriving from an owner's property rights in the land. See *Hansard's Parliamentary Debates (Commons)*, 5th series, 432 H. C. Deb. (1947), cols. 714–820 and the leading article (i.e., editorial) in the *Times* (London) of 9 June 1947, p. 5. When a subsequent Conservative government finally got around to repealing the offending enforcement mechanisms, it pointedly left the "duty of good husbandry" on the statute books; see Agriculture Act, 1958, *Public General Acts*, 6 & 7 Eliz. 2, ch. 71, sec. 1.
3. A. M. Honoré, "Ownership," *Oxford Essays in Jurisprudence*, ed. by A. G. Guest (Oxford: Clarendon Press, 1961), pp. 107–47 at 146–47 offers among various examples of acts that have partially "displaced the liberal conception of ownership and replaced it by a social conception."
4. Richard Epstein, *Takings: Private Property and the Power of Eminent Domain* (Cambridge, MA.: Harvard University Press, 1985), esp. chs. 5 and 11.
5. See, e.g., the Wilderness Code in the U.S. and the Countryside Code in the U.K. Of course, it is not always possible for us—as individuals or as a society, either—to leave everything *exactly* as we found it. Campers cannot take their footsteps with them when they go or undo their damage to fragile alpine plants. Sometimes the very act of "finding" something itself fundamentally alters it: the first whites to find the Yosemite Valley could not possibly "leave it as they found it," as a valley upon which no whites had previously set eyes.
6. Stephen R. Munzer, *A Theory of Property* (Cambridge: Cambridge University Press, 1990), esp. chs. 1 and 11 defends property rights in terms that are explicitly pluralist in precisely this sense.
7. That is of course a prejudicial way of putting the point. Those arguing for such a right would never phrase it that way, talking instead of a right to "degrade" or to "transform" (with what preservationists might call "destruction" as, at most, an inevitable corollary of such degradation or transformation).
8. "Usually" is a reference ahead to the discussion in section I(b)2 below.
9. William Blackstone, *Commentaries on the Laws of England* (Oxford: Clarendon Press, 1765), bk. 1, ch. 1, sec. 3, characterizes a right of property as consisting "in the free use, enjoyment and disposal of all his acquisitions, without any control or diminution." It is unclear whether he saw those rights as separate or connected.
10. See, e.g., Honoré, "Ownership," op. cit. Following him are: Lawrence C. Becker, *Property Rights: Philosophic Foundations* (London: Routledge & Kegan Paul, 1977), pp. 18–22; Lawrence C. Becker, The

Moral Basis of Property Rights, *Nomos XXII: Property*, ed. by J. R. Pennock and J. W. Chapman (New York: New York University Press, 1980), pp. 190–1; and Munzer, *A Theory of Property*, op. cit., p. 22.

11. Thomas C. Grey, The Disintegration of Property, *Nomos XXII: Property*, pp. 69–85. Even Jeremy Waldron rather speaks in that way at places, both in "What is Private Property?" *Oxford Journal of Legal Studies* 5 (1985), pp. 313–49 and in the version of that article in his *The Right to Private Property* (Oxford: Clarendon Press, 1988), ch. 2.

12. Of course, some rules are better than others, so even on this account there remains much to be done by moral philosophers in guiding law-makers and legislators. But their work would not then be of an analytic kind. Rather, it would lie in assessing justifications for one sort of rule rather than another—a matter to which I shall turn in Section II below.

13. Frank Snare, "The Concept of Property," *American Philosophical Quarterly* 9 (1972), pp. 200–6; C. B. Macpherson, "Human Rights as Property Rights," *Dissent* 24 (1977), pp. 72–77. Far from being "necessary and sufficient conditions" of property, though, these are merely the most salient features upon which basis we ascribe a "family resemblance" between bundles of rights all of which we are prepared to call property rights, as Waldron rightly insists; see his "What Is Private Property?" op. cit., pp. 333–40 and *The Right to Private Property*, op. cit., ch. 2.

14. You have property in your leasehold, to be sure—especially if you can sell it to someone else. But you do not have property, in the full sense, in the things you thereby merely lease for that fixed period.

15. See, e.g., Charles A. Reich, "The New Property," *Yale Law Journal* 73 (1964), pp. 733–87 on publicly granted licenses and franchises: the Reverend Sydney Smith, *Selected Writings*, ed. by W. H. Auden (London: Faber & Faber, 1957), pp. 211–26 on game laws allowing people to eat birds they kill but not to sell them to others; and Max Gluckman, *Politics, Law and Ritual in Tribal Society* (Chicago: Aldine, 1965), ch. 2, on the right, in many primitive societies, to cultivate but not to transfer particular patches of land. While agreeing in principle that the right to use exclusively does not imply a right to transfer, Waldron suggests reasons of a weaker sort for the two tending to travel together; see his "What Is Private Property?" op. cit., pp. 341–3 and *Right to Private Property*, op. cit., pp. 53–55.

16. G. A. Cohen. "Capitalism, Freedom and the Proletariat," *The Idea of Freedom*, edited by Alan Ryan (Ox-

ford: Clarendon Press, 1979), pp. 9–25 at 16–17. Waldron, "What Is Private Property?" pp. 329–330 and *The Right to Private Property*, op. cit., pp. 41–42.

17. In discussion, another has been suggested to me: an unlimited right to transfer something would entitle the owner to transfer the thing to, among others, those who would destroy it; and to prevent destruction of the thing we might sometimes need to prevent transfer to those who would destroy it. That sets the right to transfer and the duty to preserve at odds—but only pragmatically, not analytically, and only as a second-best strategy. Ideally, we would respect both halves of our moral duty, both respecting existing owner X's right to transfer the thing to Y and also enforcing upon Y a duty not to destroy the thing once in his possession. If pragmatically the only way to prevent X from destroying something is to prevent Y from transferring it to him, and if its preservation is sufficiently important to us, we might decide to abridge Y's rights in this way to ensure that X does not violate his duty. But that is akin, of course, to incarcerating X (a potential murderer's mother) to dissuade Y (the potential murderer) from behaving immorally. It would be better, all would agree, to prevent Y's murder without recourse to such morally desperate measures.

18. I ascribe this argument—albeit hesitantly—to Honoré ("Ownership," op. cit., p. 118) and, following him, Becker (*Property Rights*, op. cit., pp. 19–20; cf. "The Moral Basis of Property Rights," op. cit., pp. 191, 216n. 10 and similarly Munzer, *A Theory of Property*, op. cit., p. 22). Very much in passing, they both lump together under a single heading (mysteriously entitled, "the right of capital") both "the power to alienate the thing and the liberty to consume, waste or destroy the whole or part of it." Becker (*Property Rights*, op. cit., p. 20) comments that this, along with the many elements of property rights he discusses, is in and of itself "sufficient" for a property right to exist. But it is nowhere clear, in either Honoré or Becker's discussion, whether "the liberty to consume" and "the liberty to waste or destroy," are to be regarded as two separate elements or one. Hence, the hesitancy of my attribution of this argument to them.

19. Of course divorce laws (in our society, at least) do not allow me to transfer my wife to another, so this example does not speak directly to the issue of whether a right to transfer implies a right to destroy. But remember, the move that was required to tidy the logic of this argument ran it through a right to alienate, with a right to transfer implying a right to alienate implying a right to destroy. It is that latter link—2'—that this counter example

speaks against: while I may well alienate my wife, by divorcing her, I still may not destroy her.

20. Nor indeed, may they sell the house in such a way that the duties arising under the present Preservation Order do not pass to the purchasers.

21. The most explicit formulation is the revised formula Becker offers in "The Moral Basis of Property Rights," op. cit., p. 191: "the right (liberty) to consume or destroy." Again, it is slightly unclear whether this is meant to be two rights or one. But the phrasing here suggests, even more strongly than before, that they are to be regarded as sides of a single coin.

22. Hume says similarly, "A man that hires a horse, tho' but for a day, has as full a right to make use of it for that time, as he whom we call its proprietor has to make use of it any other day; and 'tis evident, that however the use may be bounded in time or degree, the right itself is not susceptible to any such gradation, but is absolute and entire, so far as it extends." David Hume, *A Treatise of Human Nature* (London: John Noon, 1739), bk. 3, pt. 2, sec. 6, subsec. 2.

23. In the Latin formulation, *ius utendi fruendi abutendi*; see Barry Nichols, *An Introduction to Roman Law* (Oxford: Clarendon Press, 1962), p. 154.

24. Epstein, *Takings,* op. cit., p. 59

25. Frequent renters of cars will recall the long list of abuses proscribed in the Rental Agreement that they typically have to sign. But technically that is a list of abuses which will void the rental company's 'damage waiver.' Such abuses will not typically void the Rental Agreement itself. Your right to use the car persists for the duration of the agreed period. All that has changed if you engage in one of the proscribed acts is that you rather than the rental company will now be liable for any ensuing damages. See Betsy Wade, "Taking A Closer Look at those Car Rental Agreements," *St. Louis Post-Dispatch,* 12 July 1987, p. 41.

26. Unless we take so strong a view about the identity conditions pertaining to autos that a repaired car (by virtue of its new parts or altered history) can never be the same car as the one we rented and promised to give back. Ordinarily, however, a weaker view of those identity conditions prevails. So for example a car with the same registration number is regarded as the same car before and after it has been wrecked—which, of course, is why renters must stipulate not only that they want the same car back but furthermore want it back in the same condition.

27. Of course you might be able to recreate the pre-existing state by replanting and restocking, upon expiration of the use rights—just as you might put new tyres on the rented car to replace those you destroyed. But they are not the *same,* in either case, as those you destroyed. In the case of restoration of despoiled lands, especially, the very fact that the environment was (re)created by you fundamentally alters its character as a 'natural' rather than manmade environment. See Robert Elliott, "Faking Nature," *Inquiry* 25 (1982), pp. 81–94 and Robert E. Goodin, "The Ethics of Destroying Irreplaceable Assets," *International Journal of Environmental Studies* 21 (1983), pp. 55–66.

28. Both Jeremy Waldron, *The Right to Private Property,* p. 208 and Andrew Reeve, *Property* (London: Macmillan, 1986), pp. 156–7 emphasize this point in discussing Locke's 'spoilage' limitation. That limitation, however, was justified by Locke himself in narrowly theological terms for which there seem to be no obvious secular equivalents.

29. According to a modern restatement, under Roman law '*Mutuum* . . . was a loan for consumption, not simply for use, i.e., a loan of things, such as money, food and drink, which can ordinarily be used only by being consumed. It accordingly involved a transfer of ownership, and obliged the borrower to return not the thing itself but its equivalent in quantity and quality'; see Nichols, *Introduction to Roman Law,* op. cit., p. 167.

30. Consider Pufendorf's principles governing the loan of consumable commodities,' modelled on those Roman legal principles: 'The ordinary use of such things [as grain, wine, and money] consists in their loss, i.e., I cannot apply them directly to my own uses without consuming them. . . . [Therefore, a loan of consumable commodities (*mutuum*)] differs from the loan of a non-consumable thing (*commodatum*) and that of a thing put out for hire (*Locatum*), for in the last two the very thing lent must be returned, and nothing else can be taken for it without the consent of the creditor. . . . It was expressly stated that I should get back my exact article. But if I receive another's bushel of wheat, e.g., of the same grade as the one which I had lent a person, it is held that I have received what is mine.' Samuel Pufendorf, *On the Law of Nature and Nations,* trans. C. H. and W. A. Oldfather (Oxford: Clarendon Press, 1934; originally published 1688), bk. 5, ch. 7, secs. 2 and 1, respectively.

31. 'Obviously, every *mutuum* must be a loan of a fungible, since the nature of the borrower's obligation presupposes the existence of an equivalent in quality.' But the converse is not necessarily the case: 'many fungibles (e.g., a piece of crockery which is

made in large numbers) are ordinarily used without being consumed,' and hence do not qualify as *mutuum*; Nichols, *Introduction to Roman Law*, op. cit., p. 167, n. 4.

32. That the adjacent valley is a close substitute, in the sense that it is just like the one we have destroyed through strip mining, is irrelevant for these purposes. The point is that, at least in so far as part of what was valuable about that which we destroyed was its naturalness, there is (for reasons rehearsed in note 27) nothing we can do to *produce* a substitute to replace that which we destroyed. But of course 'irreplaceability' is fundamentally a matter of how certain objective facts about the good happen to fit together with our subjective values. That, in turn, makes the description under which something is valued essential in judgments about its irreplaceability. Thus, I regard my grandmother's mass-produced watch as irreplaceable because I value it under the description 'my grandmother's watch' rather than under the description 'a 1957 Timex'; or, again, I regard my home-made table as irreplaceable because I value it under the description of 'a product of my labour' rather than under the description 'a table.' For further analysis of the nature and sources of irreplaceability, see Goodin, 'The Ethics of Destroying Irreplaceable Assets,' op. cit. As regards stocks of natural resources, one way to meet the obligation to 'leave things as you found them' would be to leave a better technology, so your successors could make more effective use of the diminished stocks that remain; such a line is suggested by Brian Barry, 'Intergenerational Justice in Energy Policy,' *Energy and the Future*, ed. by D. MacLean and P. G. Brown (Totowa, NJ: Rowman & Littlefield, 1983), pp. 15–30 and William J. Baumol, 'On the Impossibility of Continuing Expansion of Finite Resources,' *Kyklos* 39 (1986), pp. 167–79.

33. Or, anyway, you may not do so in a way that conflicts with your contractual duty to return the car in the same condition as that in which you received it.

34. Unless you have contracted separately with the rental company for it to waive its right to lodge claims against you for damage—although even there, the 'damage waiver' written into the standard Rental Agreement leaves the renter responsible for intentional damage or damage arising from taking unreasonable risks of various, specified forms (Wade, 'Car Rental Agreements,' op. cit., see note 25).

35. Those worried that too much might be turning here on a mere 'argument from silence' might reflect upon the fact that other, more central incidents of property rights must similarly be transferred explic-

itly if they are to be transferred at all. If someone is so dumbstruck at the sight of his car's being stolen that he fails to shout, 'Stop, thief!' he will not be held to have tacitly consented to the thief's enjoying use rights in his car. The right, if not explicitly granted, is not there at all. Similarly, when it comes to the grounding of rights, if there are no grounds for asserting a right then clearly there can be no such right.

36. Assuming, of course, that the owner himself (a) had a right to destroy the car and (b) had a right to transfer that right.

37. 'No right,' of course, is not necessarily equivalent to saying it would be necessarily wrong to do so. It is merely to say that he cannot excuse his act of destruction by pointing to some right he has to destroy it.

38. Indeed, so far as I can see this possibility has never been canvassed at all in the extant literature. I am indebted to Joe Mintoff, Bruce Coram and, particularly, David Gauthier for helping me think through its implications.

39. 'At most', because saying that 'destroying something excludes others permanently' refers to activities and outcomes, whereas proposition (5) refers to 'rights'. On some arguments, the activities might entail one another without the parallel normative entailment going through as well.

40. These are represented as the only two real runners, even in one of the most comprehensive recent legal-philosophical treatises on property: Munzer's *Theory of Property*, op. cit.

41. See Waldron's *The Right of Private Property*, op. cit., chs. 6 and 10 and Munzer's *Theory of Property*, op. cit, esp. chs. 4 and 5 for extended discussions of models of property rights built upon such premises.

42. The reference here is, of course, to Robert Nozick's famous example in *Anarchy, State and Utopia* (Oxford: Blackwell, 1974), p. 175 of dumping a can of tomato juice which is indisputably yours into the ocean; if there is merit in the 'mixing' metaphor, why do we not say that that gives you title to the ocean? It is a question as vexing for Nozick's theory as Locke's, but one to which he offers not a hint of a reply.

43. Grotius and Pufendorf, wanting to trace the legitimacy of private property to common consent, appeal to the self-same fact to explain why people would have consented to the institution.

44. Harold Demsetz, 'Towards a Theory of Property Rights,' *American Economic Review (Papers and Proceedings)* 57 (1967), pp. 347–59. The Reverend Syd-

ney Smith (*Selected Writings*, p. 212) argued for the Game Laws in similar fashion over a century ago. Though often phrased as an argument about the *protection* of natural resources, this argument is actually one about their *efficient destruction*. Property owners are presumed to have a right to destroy; and it is presumed that they may transfer that right to whomsoever they please, for whatever price they care to set. If all that works out as microeconomists would wish, it leads to the efficient utilization of the resource—which is the utility-based argument to be considered below. What it does not lead to, though, is preservation—contrary to what advocates of this line of analysis sometimes suggest.

45. That is the principle underlying economic discussions of the efficient allocation, and hence consumption, of exhaustible resources; see, e.g., P. S. Dasgupta and G. M. Heal, *Economic Theory and Exhaustible Resources* (Cambridge: Cambridge University Press, 1979).

46. See Robert E. Goodin, 'Discounting Discounting,' *Journal of Public Policy* 2 (1982), pp. 52–72 and Derek Parfit, *Reasons and Persons* (Oxford: Clarendon Press, 1984), pp. 480–6.

47. Kenneth J. Arrow and Anthony C. Fisher, 'Environmental Preservation, Uncertainty and Irreversibility,' *Quarterly Journal of Economics* 88 (1974), pp. 312–19. Robert E. Goodin, *Political Theory and Public Policy* (Chicago: University of Chicago Press 1982), ch. 9.

48. James C. Scott, *The Moral Economy of the Peasant* (New Haven, Conn.: Yale University Press, 1976).

49. Goodin, *Political Theory and Public Policy*, op. cit., pp. 157–61.

50. Brian Barry, 'Intergenerational Justice in Energy Policy' and 'Circumstances of Justice and Future Generations,' in *Obligations to Future Generations*, ed. R. I. Sikora and Brian Barry (Philadelphia, PA.: Temple University Press, 1983), pp. 204–48.

51. Goodin, 'The Ethics of Destroying Irreplaceable Assets,' op. cit.

52. Perhaps at root everything we deem irreplaceable we do so on account of its history, in one way or another. A perfect forgery cannot substitute for the original work of art it imitates, because it has the wrong history: it was created by the wrong hand. A perfect Disneyland replica of the Grand Canyon cannot substitute for the real thing, because in one crucial historical respect it cannot be the same: it was created by people rather than by nature. The simple fact about the watch's history—that it (perhaps almost uniquely) has been handed down through our family for several generations—may be the irreplaceable feature about it that we value. Indeed, even people in very early stages of that chain may value being part of a chain that they expect to stretch far into the future: one of the reasons you especially regret losing your mother's watch is precisely that you had valued it as something to be passed on to your children, and so on down the line.

53. Indeed, in early Roman law the *paterfamilias* enjoyed dominion so strong over his children that he was legally at liberty to put them to death, a rule that only began to change in the second century A.D.: Nichols, *Introduction to Roman Law*, op. cit., p. 67.

54. Earlier versions of this article were read at meetings of the American Political Science Association, the Australasian Association of Philosophy (New Zealand Division), and the Law and Philosophy Seminar, RSSS, Australian National University. I am garteful for comments, then and later, from Charles Bako, Brian Barry, Larry Becker, Keith Campbell, Tom Campbell, Bruce Coram, Debora Friedman, Peter Menzies, Joe Mintoff, David Braddon-Mitchell, David Gauthier, Frank Jackson, Richard Mulgan, Philip Pettit, Andy Reeve, Mark Sagoff, Andrew Sharpe, Jeremy Shearmur, Tom Spragens, Richard Sylvan, and Jeremy Waldron.

Takings, Just Compensation, and the Environment

Mark Sagoff

"The power vested in the American courts of justice of pronouncing a statute to be unconstitutional," Alexis de Tocqueville wrote, "forms one of the most powerful barriers that have ever been devised against the tyranny of political assemblies."[1] Judges apply this power to environmental law in

Upstream/Downstream: Issues in Environmental Ethics, edited by Donald Scherer (Philadelphia: Temple University Press, 1990), pp. 158–79. © 1990 by Temple University Press. Reprinted by permission.

many ways, but especially when they review zoning ordinances and statutes that restrict the uses of property.

Everyone who owns property has the duty, of course, to exercise his or her property rights in ways that respect the similar rights of others. In addition to this basic duty, political assemblies have gone far—perhaps too far—in obliging landowners, for example, to maintain the integrity of landmarks and scenic areas,[2] to refrain from filling wetlands,[3] to preserve open space,[4] to restore mined land to its original contours,[5] to maintain habitat for endangered species,[6] to allow public access to waterways and beaches,[7] to leave minerals in place to support surface structures,[8] and so on.[9] Landowners often ask judges to review these statutes on constitutional grounds.[10]

State and local governments, in general, impose these duties on landowners by regulation rather than by exercising eminent domain. States prefer regulation to condemnation so that they do not have to compensate landowners for the substantial losses in market value that often accompany the duties and restrictions statutes place on them. Governments may attempt to dedicate property to public use, then, not by taking property rights through eminent domain, but by regulating those rights away and, therefore, without compensating owners for the market value of those rights.

Courts are then called on to decide whether a statute that imposes public-spirited duties on property owners complies with the Fifth Amendment of the Constitution, which provides that "private property [shall not] be taken for public use, without just compensation."[11] When courts sustain these statutes and ordinances on constitutional grounds, as they frequently do,[12] local governments gain an important legal weapon for protecting the aesthetic, cultural, historical, and ecological values that often attract people and, therefore, subdividers and developers to a region. If the courts sheathe this legal weapon, however, society may have to kiss these values good-bye, since it can neither afford to exercise eminent domain to purchase the property in question nor can it depend, except in a limited way, on private action in common-law courts to protect these values.

When does a regulatory "taking" of property require the state to pay compensation, and when not? Justice Oliver Wendell Holmes, in a leading case decided in 1922, asserted that "this is a question of degree—and therefore cannot be disposed of by general propositions."[13] The absence of such propositions, that is, the lack of a theory on which to decide cases, has characterized "just compensation" jurisprudence for more than half a century. Commentators generally describe this area of law as a "muddle,"[14] a "crazy quilt,"[15] "unilluminating,"[16] "ad hoc,"[17] "confused,"[18] "baffling,"[19] "mystifying,"[20] and "chaotic."[21] In 1987, Justice John Paul Stevens summarized: "Even the wisest lawyers would have to acknowledge great uncertainty about the scope of this Court's takings jurisprudence."[22]

In recent years, several academic lawyers have analyzed takings law to try to define a theory on which future jurisprudence might be based.[23] Such an analysis could succeed, I think, if it (1) rests on acceptable normative and constitutional principles, and (2) is not so inconsistent with existing case law that it requires a dramatic recission of environmental statutes and ordinances now generally thought to be constitutionally sound.

In this [article], I want to suggest a line of analysis that will satisfy these conditions. I argue that compensation need not attend a regulation that takes property rights unless it also burdens some individuals unfairly to benefit other individuals or the public as a whole. The "takings" question, in other words, may not depend fundamentally on an analysis of property rights; instead, it may depend on a conception of justice.

Pragmatic Versus Theoretical Decision Making

Zoning is ubiquitous. Every state restricts the ways in which property owners can develop their land, especially in sensitive areas such as in flood plains, coastal zones, and agricultural districts. When such a restriction causes the market value of parcels of land to fall, the owners may believe that their land is being dedicated to a public use, for which the public ought to pay. They may then go to court to seek damages under the Fifth Amendment of the Constitution.

In one such case, *Just* v. *Marinette County,* the Supreme Court of Wisconsin upheld a zoning ordinance that prevented owners of a coastal marsh from using landfill on their property and thus from developing it for commercial purposes. The court held that the "takings" clause of the Constitution does not protect an interest, however profitable, in "destroying the natural character of a swamp or a wetland so as to make that location available for human habitation."[24] Citizens have no claim for compensation, the court reasoned, when an ordinance restricts their use of their land "to prevent a harm from the change in the natural character of the citizens' property."[25]

Ellen Frankel Paul, in her timely and well-argued book *Property Rights and Eminent Domain,*[26] points out that decisions such as *Just* strike "at the very heart of the property rights conception—that what is mine may be used by me as I see fit provided only that I not use it in a manner that violates the like right of other owners" (p. 138). Paul notes that by filling in his wetland, Mr. Just did not threaten the rights of others; he merely set about improving the economic utility of his land, just as many others had done up and down the coast.

Paul accepts common law, particularly tort, as the test for determining when a person uses his or her property in a way consistent with the rights of others. As she says, the concept of harm to others that limits the rights of landowners "would have to be comparable to a harm recognized in the tort law" (p. 139). Would filling the wetland cause an injury to anyone sufficient to give him or her standing to sue in common law? What sort of right could anyone assert as a matter of common law to enjoin Mr. Just from filling in his marsh?

Paul argues that nothing in nuisance, tort, or anywhere in common law suggests a basis for such an injunction. For more than a century, the public, for aesthetic, sanitary, economic, and other reasons, encouraged landowners to fill in swamps. Now, the public (for the same reasons) wants to keep remaining wetlands wet. This may be a valid objective; the public may legitimately change its values. Society may correctly believe that it now benefits many localities more from scenic and open space than from condominiums and commercial strips.

The question is whether the state may legitimately force Mr. Just and others like him to provide *gratis* the scenic, ecological, and perhaps moral benefits the public gains from the presence of open and undeveloped land. Should the state instead compensate Mr. Just for his financial loss or, if the government cannot afford to pay, allow him peacefully to develop his wetland?

Richard Epstein, in *Takings: Private Property and the Power of Eminent Domain,* analyzes this case in

the same way. He observes that the plaintiff, by filling in his wetland, might pollute his own property, but he threatens others with no harm cognizable in common law. Epstein argues that "the normal bundle of property rights contains no priority for land in its natural condition; it regards use, including development, as one of the standard incidents of ownership."

By building on their marsh, the plaintiffs do only what their neighbors had already done; no one would have a case against them in common law. Epstein concludes: "Stripped of its rhetoric, *Just* is a condemnation of these property rights, and compensation is thus required."

Ellen Paul's *Property Rights and Eminent Domain* and Richard Epstein's *Takings* endorse a theory of natural property rights, at the heart of which is the principle that people may use their property as they see fit as long as they respect the same rights and liberties of others. Both authors deplore the legal doctrine dominant in "takings" cases for 60 years, since it fails to recognize the existence of "natural" property rights; in fact, it rejects that theory out of hand. In place of this theory, the dominant doctrine, formulated by Justice Holmes, has called for ad hoc, case-by-case decision making, an approach that attempts to determine a fair or just outcome in the circumstances of each suit, without relying or even speculating on a general theory or conception of property rights.

So both Paul and Epstein confront and oppose the pragmatic, case-by-case approach taken by the U.S. Supreme Court and many state courts. They are outraged that these courts routinely uphold legislation that plainly contravenes the theory of natural property rights they espouse. They argue that these courts should overturn their precedents to give legal force to that theory, especially the "core" freedom to do as one wishes with one's property as long as one remains within the constraints of common law. And they find thoroughly offensive the courts' refusal to advance a theory or conception of property—*any* theory—in cases brought under the Fifth Amendment of the Constitution.

Two questions arise, then, that Paul and Epstein must answer. First, is the pragmatic, case-by-case approach unworkable, unfair, or otherwise flawed in itself? In other words, does Paul or Epstein offer telling arguments against current practice per se and, thus, show that it must change to base itself on some theory of property? Or do they condemn it only because it does not accommodate the theory of "natural" property rights they believe to be correct?

Second, let us suppose that the courts reach principled and equitable, if pragmatic, resolutions of "takings" cases. Let us suppose that the principles on which the courts rely, while not unjust or unworkable in themselves, do not recognize but implicitly reject the theory of natural property rights Paul and Epstein espouse. Has this theory such a deep philosophical and constitutional basis that courts should adopt it, even if the pragmatic approach works well enough? The importance of these two books depends on how well they respond to these questions.

What Is Wrong with Current Practice?

The courts now follow a reasonably predictable course in "takings" jurisprudence—although not the one Paul and Epstein recommend. Courts at present view justice in this area as a privative virtue, which is to say, they overturn legislation only if it commits one of a list of specific injustices—for example, if it is intended (or plainly functions) to exclude racial groups from particular localities. Courts ask a series of ad hoc questions: Does the regulation physically remove the owner from the land? or deprive the owner of substantially all reasonable use of it?

Does the regulation fail to advance a legitimate public interest in a way rationally and closely related to the proscribed use? Does the restriction work unfairly to burden a few landowners to benefit a few others? Was the owner prevented from representing his or her interests in the political process? Has the government, through zoning, merely attempted to lower the market value of the land to make it cheaper to condemn?

Courts address "takings" cases with an ad hoc, pragmatic checklist of questions such as these—all of which are well known—reflecting a variety of moral, policy, and equity considerations. These questions go to the fairness and legitimacy of the statutes landowners challenge, but they pay little or no attention to any theory of property rights.

Courts rely on well-known ad hoc principles or rules of thumb, such as those these questions suggest, to determine whether the interests of the

property owner have received a fair shake. The courts also take notice of the political and civil rights of various parties affected by a statute (e.g., the rights of minorities to live where they wish, the rights of individuals to political representation). In "takings" cases, courts mull over questions involving fairness, justice, and personal, civil, and political rights before making their decisions. But in answering these questions, the courts do not address or appear to want or need to address a theory of property rights.

Since lawyers know the kinds of questions the courts will ask—for example, whether a statute is "exclusionary," "extortionary," or "confiscatory"—they nearly always formulate zoning ordinances to survive this kind of review. As a result, the outcome of "takings" or "inverse condemnation" proceedings is generally predictable. Absent some special infirmity in the law (e.g., it may be plainly extortionary), the decisions will go against the plaintiff.

Jurisdictions, then, through zoning and other ordinances, routinely succeed in vastly restricting the otherwise permissible ways landowners might use their land. And a good lawyer will tell aggrieved landowners not to bother to challenge a properly drafted statute because the courts will routinely and predictably uphold it, even though it makes a mockery out of the notion of natural property rights.

As Paul notes, "takings" jurisprudence, which routinely upholds zoning regulations in this way, strikes "at the very heart of the property rights conception." She is right. Should judges take the theory of natural property rights seriously? May they instead properly remain indifferent to that theory and, indeed, to all theorizing about property and property rights?

Professor Paul proposes that the case-by-case, pragmatic, ad hoc decision making that characterizes "takings" jurisprudence "has simply not worked" (p. 188). She offers three arguments to support this contention.

First, Paul proposes that current jurisprudence puts too much power in the hands of politicians, who may next decide, for example, where each citizen will live. "The slippery slope is real, and it is alarming" (p. 192). Paul relies on this "slippery slope" appeal to dispatch what she sees, correctly, as her main opponent, namely, pragmatic modern liberalism. "If liberals are absolutists about any political value, it is certainly not property." Paul adds: "Modern liberalism . . . holds that civil rights can be separated from property rights. For modern liberals like John Dewey, property rights are relatively unimportant. A democratic society can flourish by protecting civil rights while not unduly concerning itself with property rights" (p. 190). Paul fails to provide, however, a single example of the reality of this slippery slope—an instance in which a judge or other public official moved in practice from "takings" precedents to a denial of civil, political, or personal rights. On the contrary, while the U.S. Supreme Court in its "takings" jurisprudence, over the last 60 years, may have kicked property rights into a cocked hat, the same Court has greatly advanced political, civil, and personal rights and liberties against the government. Perhaps Paul believes that the latter rights are connected, logically or empirically, with rights, for example, to develop one's marsh for commercial use. But no argument in her book, or anywhere else, as far as I know, demonstrates such a connection.

The second argument appeals to authority: "Virtually everyone admits that this area of the law is in a chaotic state" (p. 188). The third argument asserts that the pragmatic approach fails "to develop a sound theoretical underpinning for property rights" (p. 185).

These last two arguments are correct as far as they go. Commentators on "takings" jurisprudence, including Supreme Court justices, describe it as chaotic. Yet "takings" doctrine has given predictable results: The property owner will lose unless some special injustice, from an ad hoc but well-known list, has been done. If it is predictable and consistent, how, then, has it failed? People describe it as chaotic—but why should they?

The principal reason Paul, Epstein, and others believe that pragmatic, ad hoc jurisprudence is chaotic, as far as I can tell, is that it is ad hoc and pragmatic. They think it is bad for an important area of constitutional property law to fail to develop a sound theoretical underpinning for property rights. But why? If "takings" jurisprudence relies on an ad hoc, pragmatic list of reasonable concerns, why do judges need to indulge in theorizing? Academics theorize as a condition of getting tenure, of course, but justices already have lifetime terms.

The answer to the question whether the pragmatic, case-by-case approach fails may depend on the answer to the second question, namely, whether a different basis—one residing in deep philosophical principles—can and should be found. "I will

argue that natural rights provides a consistent theory of property rights," Paul says, "and that a theory of property rights is essential for extricating ourselves from this impasse" (p. 188).

Paul Versus Epstein

I want to mention here reasons I believe Paul's *Property Rights and Eminent Domain* is not only an excellent book but is also better argued than Epstein's *Takings*. First, Epstein makes no attempt whatever to show that current jurisprudence has failed in its own terms, that is, failed to provide a workable, predictable resolution of controversies arising under the Fifth Amendment. Instead, Epstein merely reviews a large number of legal decisions, shows that they make mincemeat of the theory of natural property rights, and then rebukes the judges for being such jerks. If you, poor reader, are among the damned who have not seen the divine light of natural property rights theory, Epstein regards you—along with Congress, the courts, state legislatures, municipal authorities, and other sinners—with contempt. Contempt, however, is not argument, and that is the problem with Epstein's treatise.

Paul, on the contrary, does not preach only to the saved. She recognizes that her opponents may favor current jurisprudence for initially plausible reasons, for example, to prevent "irreversible loss of agricultural land, estuaries, wetlands, and open space, and the wasteful consumption of energy" (p. 192). Paul believes that it may be more important for the law to protect natural property rights than to protect nature beyond the limits of tort. Unlike Epstein, she recognizes, however, that the truth of this belief is not self-evident.

Second, Paul clearly recognizes what Epstein only occasionally glimpses, namely, the strict incompatibility and antagonism between utilitarian and libertarian approaches to property rights. The old utilitarians, such as Jeremy Bentham, thought that governments create and protect property rights for purposes of utility maximization; Bentham described talk of natural rights as "nonsense on stilts." When property rights get in the way of the aggregate public interest (as they presumably do in "takings" cases), then it is property rights rather than the general welfare that must give way. Any intellectually honest utilitarian or utility maximizer must agree with Bentham on this point.

Chicago School utilitarians, who would maximize a form of utility Richard Posner calls "wealth," are driven to Bentham's conclusion. They would defend property rights, not as a matter of principle or of basic justice (as Paul would), but only insofar as that policy might promote the efficient allocation of resources. Owing to market failures, bargaining costs, holdouts, and everything else, however, governments may generally achieve greater efficiency through cost-benefit planning than by allowing free exchange. Paul notes correctly that the "wealth-maximization" or "efficiency" view presupposes the communistic fiction that everyone wants the same thing, namely, efficient allocation, and thus it encourages experts to override individual rights to provide it. "It is ironic that a view that sincerely intends to be supportive of individualism and property rights, is actually collectivist, and just as aggregative as utilitarianism" (p. 217).

Paul has replied to Epstein in other places, showing that utilitarian goals, such as wealth maximization, conflict just as thoroughly as any other centralized statist program with a regime of natural property rights.[28] Her discussion of this issue (pp. 212–24), which includes a devastating reply to Posner's conception of *ex ante* compensation, may be the best in the literature.

Epstein, after a wave of the hand to Locke, assumes that every well-socialized individual knows that property rights are natural rights—and he is off and running. Paul, in contrast, recognizes that "the advocates of natural rights did fail to provide a logical, internally consistent, deductive defense of these rights. Bentham certainly has his point" (p. 188). Thus, Paul attempts to argue for the fundamental thesis that Epstein merely assumes, namely, that property rights are natural rights.

She attempts "to supply the natural rights theory of property with such a deductive defense," which, she hopes, will be persuasive to those, like Bentham, "who are highly skeptical of 'metaphysical rights'" (p. 188). How successful, then, is her argument for natural property rights?

The Argument for Natural Property Rights

Paul's argument for natural property rights, although at times hard to follow, seems to depend on two plausible principles. First, following Locke, she reasons that every human being has a natural right

to acquire from the commons such commodities as are necessary to his or her survival. "Man must labor," Paul points out, "in order to attain the rudiments necessary for his survival" (p. 226). Second, following Locke, Paul argues that everyone has a fundamental property right to anything useful that person creates through his or her labor and ingenuity. She asserts "that the person who creates X ought to own X" (p. 232).

While both principles are familiar and plausible, they do not entail anything about compensation in "takings" cases. How does Professor Paul get from a natural right to own what one creates and/or needs for survival to a doctrine about just compensation in "takings" cases? Let us grant that individuals have a natural right to the products they create and/or need in order to survive. How does this show that the government should compensate Mr. Just when an ordinance against certain kinds of development lowers the market value of his land?

While the answer to this question is by no means evident, Paul introduces two further premises. First, she rejects as "artificial" any "distinction between necessities and luxuries" (p. 236). "After all, who is to judge which are goods necessary for survival and which are luxuries?" Paul asks. "Such a task would entail the existence of a godlike omniscience, or else the moral system would hinge on caprice" (p. 234).

Second, Paul emphasizes this principle: "All value is the artifact of some purposive activity on the part of the individual." She continues: "What I am arguing goes one step beyond Locke, who contended, alternately, that nine-tenths or ninety-nine hundredths of the value of any commodity was the handiwork of man rather than nature. *I maintain that 100 percent of the value of a good is the work of human activity*" (p. 230).

Any real estate agent will tell you that there are three determinants of the market value of real property: location, location, and location. None of these depends on the labor, ingenuity, or creativity of the property owner. Henry George adopted his radical views about land tenure in part because he saw the price of property go up tenfold overnight when the government announced its plan to extend the railroad to a section of California. The lucky owners, far from laboring for their survival, were asleep at the time. They woke up to find that the government, by creating a railroad, highway, park, or whatever, had instantly multiplied the price at which they might sell their land.

Paul counters such an objection in advance by writing: "I am not talking about market value (or price) and how it is determined on a free market" (p. 231). She adds, in words that might warm the heart of any defender of current "takings" practice:

> Each person has a perpetual property right in that which he or she has created, that is, in the values produced. Your right, then, is to the object or process itself, and not to the market value or price, which is nothing more than the appraisal in the minds of others, at the margin, of the value to them of your good. The preference orders are beyond your control, and form no part of your entitlement (p. 234).

If Paul is not concerned with market value, then, it seems, she would have little to say on behalf of Mr. Just, who sued for the difference between the price he could get for his land before and after the zoning ordinance. He had made no use of his land—he had invested no labor or ingenuity in processing it—and he still possessed the object itself. The entire value of the land that Mr. Just sued to recover was market value: the value the land would have, as a matter of speculation, if it could be developed for commercial or residential purposes. On Paul's account, then, Mr. Just would have no entitlement to this value, since it is the creation not necessarily of his own action, but of the preferences of others.

All or nearly all zoning ordinances maintain the kind of property right that Paul defends. Statutes and regulations uniformly "grandfather" every existing use that cannot be construed as creating a nuisance. Current "takings" jurisprudence respects the sort of property right a person has to the products of his or her own labor—or at least Paul provides no evidence to the contrary. Accordingly, Paul's interesting defense of property rights seems to support, or at least not to undermine, current pragmatic, ad hoc, case-by-case approaches to "just" compensation under the Fifth Amendment of the Constitution.

Does the Right to Develop Imply a Right to Destroy?

As we have seen, Professor Paul distinguishes between "use value (i.e., the utility of a thing) and market value (or price)" (p. 230). While Paul does

not develop this distinction, there are familiar examples of it. Water and air, for example, have high use values, since life cannot go on without them. Yet air and water are so plentiful in most localities that they have a low market value or price.

Land also has value both as an object of use and an object of exchange and speculation. The use value of a wetland consists, for example, in the many services and benefits it provides to the public. These include its function in the tertiary treatment of wastes, in the control of floods, in providing habitat for fish and wildlife, and so on. Wetlands tend also to be beautiful ecosystems delighting those who experience intelligently the play of natural history, scenic landscapes, and open space.

The market value of a wetland, like that of any real estate, depends principally on its location. In a coastal area, a wetland, once filled in, may provide the site for profitable enterprises, especially if, as in Atlantic City, gambling casinos, massage parlors, bars, and discos can be built. Everyone knows what happened to land values in and around Atlantic City when the government allowed gambling. That is what the market value or price of land is all about.

Now, policy problems arise when the use value of a wetland conflicts with its market value. In order to preserve the uses of the wetland—the ecological and aesthetic values associated with it—we should have to forbid certain kinds of development. In order to maximize the market value of the wetland, however, we should have to develop it in ways that destroy the use value. This is essentially the choice that confronted the *Just* court.

The court may have framed this question in terms of another: Did the owner's destruction of the use value of the wetland—for example, its value as a habitat, aquifer, or whatever—constitute a "noxious" activity that the legislature may prohibit without paying compensation, even though that sort of destruction would not be recognized as a tort in private law? In other words, if legislatures, rather than common-law courts, become the arbiters of what counts as a "nuisance" for purposes of "takings" jurisprudence, the Wisconsin zoning ordinance was perfectly constitutional. If the notion of a nuisance, and therefore the extent of property rights, depend on what may be enjoined at private law, however, the ordinance would not be constitutional. And so the question might amount to this: May legislatures identify and prohibit public nuisances that extend beyond activities that would contravene private rights and therefore be enjoined in common-law courts?

The courts have held that state governments will not run afoul of the Fifth Amendment when they enact measures to protect the public from injurious uses of private property, even when the injuries in question are not cognizable in tort. For example, the U.S. Supreme Court in *Mugler* v. *Kansas* 1887, its first full consideration of regulatory takings, found against the plaintiff, a brewery owner, the value of whose property had been severely diminished when the Kansas legislature prohibited the sale of alcoholic beverages in the state. Justice John Harlan wrote:

> The power which the states have of prohibiting such use by individuals of their property as will be prejudicial to the health, the morals, or the safety of the public, is not . . . burdened with the condition that the state must compensate such individual owners for pecuniary losses they may sustain, by reason of their not being permitted, by a noxious use of their property, to inflict injury upon the community.[29]

It is clear in Harlan's majority opinion that the legislature has the power to declare as "noxious" or "injurious" uses that would not be identified as torts under common law.[30] Although the Supreme Court has held that "the legislature has no right to declare that to be a nuisance which is clearly not so,"[31] it has deferred to legislative findings as long as they met procedural due process requirements. Thus, when states justify regulations on the basis of a colorable "noxious use," the Fifth Amendment has no force beyond what the Fourteenth Amendment also guarantees, namely, that a person shall not be deprived of property without due process of law.[32]

One may surely argue, however, that the legislature should not be the judge of its own case, that is, that some "substantive due process" review is required to determine that the "noxious" use in question does involve a threat to the public health, safety, or welfare. How would this work out with respect to the Wisconsin ordinance? Does the ordinance simply benefit the public at the expense of the landowner? Or does it function to prevent the landowner from enriching himself at the expense of the public?

While it is notoriously hard to identify general principles by which to answer this question, courts have found that restrictions are not compensable when they stop a landowner from "engaging in conduct he ought, as a well-socialized adult, to have recognized as unduly harmful to others."[33] The conception of "undue harm" at work here is drawn not from common law alone but from the wider social and cultural standards of the community.[34] Since these standards change and evolve, "definition and redefinition of the institution of private property is always at stake."[35]

The decision in *Just* builds on this rationale, as one commentator writes, by denying that expectations of profit are legitimate if they "are inconsistent with widely prevailing standards of society."[36] To assume that one has an inherent right to develop one's land (e.g., to fill a marsh) "ignores or distorts an obvious relationship between such activity and interests of the public that have long existed, but that until recently have been taken for granted."[37]

This argument stands on the premise that the central incidents of property—the right to use, to exclude, and to alienate[38]—do not include the right to destroy.[39] Professor Paul correctly attributes this point to Locke. She writes that appropriation from the common is limited by two conditions: "that as much and as good remain in common for the like appropriation of others, and that spoilage must not occur. Indeed, Locke maintains that one's right to land extends not beyond what one can use, so that one does not possess a right to waste" (p. 204).

It is easy to show that a right to use property does not entail a right to destroy it. The right to use a car one has borrowed or hired, for example, does not involve a right to destroy it; similarly, the right to use by consuming food does not entail a right to waste or spoil it. Locke reasons that a person can "heap up" as many resources as he can use or cause to be used economically—"the *exceeding of the bounds of his* just *property* not lying in the largeness of his possession, but in the perishing of anything uselessly in it."[40]

One might reply that the right to use consumables, such as food or fuel, implies a right to "destroy" them, for to use is to consume these things. This reply, however, shows only that the right to use entails a right to use up—not necessarily a right to destroy. The difference between using up provisions and destroying them is too obvious to require examples. Environmental resources of the sort that wetland regulations protect, moreover, are generally not consumable goods but "renewable" services. They are not consumed but conserved through proper use.

Similarly, the right to transfer property does not on its face entail a right to destroy it. Thus the auctioneer has a right to transfer property to the highest bidder, but this does not give him a right to destroy it, even if it is not sold. To be sure, if an item is worthless, the possessor may have a right to toss it out. But the right to destroy does not attach, for that reason, to property that has a high use value. For this reason, courts sometimes impose a "law of waste" to prevent property owners from destroying scarce resources that are of great usefulness to others.[41]

Mr. Just has no valid claim to compensation, according to this argument, because he has no right or entitlement to destroy resources that have become scarce and are of great importance to society. The decision in *Just* is correct, on this view, because a regulation that prevents a landowner from destroying resources by filling a marsh does not take a right from him. He has no right to destroy those resources.

This result seems entirely consistent with a Lockean theory of property rights, which limits property not only to that which can be possessed without waste, as we have seen, but also to that which may be acquired from a commons without creating scarcity. As Locke puts this thought, a person can rightfully acquire an unowned resource from the commons only if there is "enough and as good left in common for others."[42]

The *Just* court argued that an owner may not validly claim compensation when he or she is prevented from "destroying the natural character of a swamp or a wetland ... when the new use ... causes a harm to the general public."[43] The contention may be that the prohibited development would destroy resources that the public owns in common, owing to "the interrelationship of the wetlands, the swamps and the natural environment of shorelands to the purity of the water and to such natural resources as navigation, fishing, and scenic beauty."[44] In the past, an individual may have been free to appropriate these resources without depleting the common unduly, but those times are gone. Mr. Just has come too late to the commons; there is no longer as much and as good for others.

One might argue that this famous Lockean proviso[45] covers aesthetic and ecological resources that belong as organic parts (or even as emergent properties) to larger systems and are destroyed when land is removed from its natural condition. Those who come to the commons early may legitimately appropriate these resources by consuming or destroying them; but when a common resource, such as natural beauty, becomes critically scarce, society may rule against further appropriations because they significantly worsen the social situation from that which would obtain if the proposed "improvements" were not made. As Professor Paul rightly concludes in another place, a natural rights theory that "embraces the Lockean proviso can be utilized to validate environmentalist land use legislation ... without such regulations constituting a compensable takings."[46]

Conclusion

Courts should uphold environmental regulations, such as the Wisconsin ordinance, that prevent landowners from destroying natural resources the public has long enjoyed and in which it has a legitimate interest. The incidents of property include the rights to use, exclude, and transfer, but not the right to destroy. Destruction of resources that implicitly belong to the common, then, constitute a "noxious" use, which is not protected by the Constitution. This approach may leave landowners little protection in the Fifth Amendment that they do not find in the Fourteenth and in the larger, ad hoc, pragmatic approach to "takings" jurisprudence such as we have described. Absent a persuasive theory of natural property rights, however, this may be the most reasonable approach that does not squander use values for the sake of market value—that does not ruin the environment to make speculators rich.

Notes

Acknowledgements: This essay is a revised version of a paper read at a conference, "Upstream/Downstream: Issues in Environmental Ethics," at Bowling Green State University, Bowling Green, Ohio, September 10, 1988. Portions of the paper will also appear in a book review of *Private Property and Eminent Domain* to be published in *Environmental Ethics*.

1. Alexis de Tocqueville, *Democracy in America* (New York: Random House, 1981), chap. 6.
2. See, e.g., *Penn Central Transportation Co.* v. *New York City*, 438 U.S. 104, 107 (1978) (holding that the city

could operate a "comprehensive program to preserve historic landmarks" without "effecting a 'taking' requiring the payment of 'just compensation'"); *Steel Hill Developers, Inc.,* v. *Town of Sanbornton,* 469 F.2d 956, 959 (1st Cir. 1972) ("preserving [the] 'charm [of] a New England small town'"); and *County Commissioners* v. *Miles,* 246 Md. 355, 372, 228, A.2d 450, 459 (1967) (allowing "the preservation, in some manner, of existing conditions").

3. *Just v. Marinette County,* 56 Wis. 2d 7, 201 N.W.2d, 761 (1972); *Sibson* v. *State of New Hampshire,* 115 N.H. 124, 336 A.2d 239 (1975). In dozens of similar court challenges to state prohibitions on filling or otherwise changing wetland and coastal environments, plaintiffs generally succeed in winning compensation under the "takings" clause of the Fifth Amendment (or under analogous provisions in state constitutions) only if they are able to show that they are deprived of all reasonable and viable economic use of their land. For an exhaustive survey showing a "trend" toward upholding the validity of wetland regulations, see Daniel R. Mandeleker, "Land Use Takings, the Compensation Issue," *Hastings Constitutional Law Quarterly* 8 (1981): 491, esp. 495–502; and Sarah E. Redfield, *Vanishing Farmland: A Legal Solution for the States* (Lexington, MA.: D. C. Heath, 1984), chap. 2.

4. *Agins* v. *City of Tiburon,* 447 U.S. 255, 261 (quoting from the Cal. Gov't. Code Ann. sec. 65561(b) (West, 1983) (recognizing the legitimacy of open space plans to "discourage the 'premature and unnecessary conversion of open-space land to urban uses'").

5. *Hodel* v. *Virginia Surface Mining and Reclamation Association,* 452 U.S. 264 (1981) (sustaining the Surface Mining Control and Reclamation Act).

6. The Endangered Species Act of 1973 (16 U.S.C. secs. 1531–43) (1976 & Supp. I 1977 & Supp. II 1978 & Supp. III 1979) requires (sec. 1536) that all federal departments and agencies "insure that actions authorized, funded, or carried out by them do not jeopardize the continued existence of such endangered species." The act effectively makes the preservation of habitat a condition of any federal permit for development.

7. For discussion of litigation concerning ordinances expanding public access to waterfront property, see Carol Rose, "The Comedy of the Commons: Custom, Commerce, and Inherently Public Property," *University of Chicago Law Review* 53 (1986): 711, 713–23.

8. *Keystone Bituminous Coal Association* v. *DeBenedictus,* 55 LW 4326 (March 9, 1987).

9. For a discussion of environmental zoning for ecological purposes in the context of the "takings" problem see "Developments in the Law: Zoning," *Harvard Law Review* 91 (1978), 1427, 1618–24.

10. A landowner who proceeds against the government in this way is said to assert a theory of "inverse condemnation" of his land because he, rather than the government, initiates the action. See *San Diego Gas and Electric Co.* v. *City of San Diego,* 450 U.S. 621, 638 n. 2 (1981) (Brennan, J., dissenting).

11. The Fifth Amendment to the Constitution of the United States. This provision is now applicable to the states through the Fourteenth Amendment. *Chicago, B. & O. R.R.* v. *City of Chicago,* 166 U.S. 226, 235–41 (1897). Almost all the states have analogous clauses in their constitutions. For documentation, see "Developments in the Law," 1463.

12. Thus, in the leading case, *Pennsylvania Coal Co.* v. *Mahon* (260 U.S. 393, 415), Justice Holmes stated "that while property may be regulated to a certain extent, if regulation goes too far it will be considered as a taking." It is difficult to predict how a "takings" will be decided. Ackerman notes that "recent wetlands regulation cases have divided approximately evenly on the issue of compensation." Bruce Ackerman, *Private Property and the Constitution* (New Haven: Yale University Press, 1977), 191 n. 7 and 217 n. 54.

13. *Pennsylvania Coal,* 260 U.S. 416.

14. Carol M. Rose, "*Mahon* Reconstructed: Why the Takings Issue Is Still a Muddle," *Southern California Law Review* 57 (1984): 561.

15. Allison Dunham, "*Griggs* v. *Allegheny County* in Perspective: Thirty Years of Supreme Court Expropriation Law," *Supreme Court Review* 63 (1962): 105.

16. S. Van Alstyne, "Taking or Damaging by Police Power: The Search for Inverse Condemnation Criteria," *Southern California Law Review* 44 (1971): 1, 39. ("The judicial calculus involved in the balancing process is described in a variety of unilluminating ways.")

17. W. Oakes, "'Property Rights' in Constitutional Analysis Today," *Washington Law Review* 56 (1981): 583, 602–3 (characterizing takings decisions as "ad hoc line drawing").

18. W. B. Stoebuck, "Police Power, Takings, and Due Process," *Washington and Lee Law Review* 37 (1980): 1057, 1062–63 (referring to "extreme confusion about police power takings").

19. Comment, "Regulation of Land Use: From Magna Carta to a *Just* Formulation," *UCLA Law Review* 23 (1976): 904, 904–5 (takings decisions are "bafflingly" inconsistent).

20. Thomas Hippler, "Reexamining 100 Years of Supreme Court Regulatory Taking Doctrine: The Principles of 'Noxious Use,' 'Average Reciprocity of Advantage,' and 'Bundle of Rights,' from *Mugler* to *Keystone Bituminous Coal*," *Environmental Affairs* 14 (1987): 633–725 (describing "the rather mystifying nature of regulatory takings jurisprudence").

21. Fred Bosselman, David Callies, and John Banta, *The Taking Issue* (Washington, DC: Council on Environmental Quality, GPO, 1973), 322.

22. *Nollan* v. *California Coastal Commission*, 55 LW 5145, 5156 (Stevens, I., dissenting). Here Justice Stevens echoes Justice Brennen in *Penn Central Transportation Co.* (428 U.S. 123, 124) (stating that the question "of what constitutes a 'taking' for purposes of the Fifth Amendment has proved to be a problem of considerable difficulty" susceptible to no "set formula"). Cf. Joseph Sax, "Takings and the Police Power," *Yale Law Journal* 74 (1964): 36, 37 ("the predominant characteristic of this area of law is a welter of confusing and apparently incompatible results"). Cf. *Goldblatt* v. *Town of Hempstead*, 369 U.S. 590, 594 (1962). ("There is no set formula to determine where regulation ends and taking begins.")

23. See, e.g., Ackerman, *Private Property*; Frank Michelman, "Property, Utility, and Fairness: Comments of the Ethical Foundations of 'Just Compensation' Law," *Harvard Law Review* 80 (1968), 1165–1258; and Joseph Sax, "Takings, Private Property and Public Rights," *Yale Law Journal* 81 (1971), 149–86.

24. *Just* v. *Marinette Co.*, 56 Wis. 2d 7, 201 N.W.2d 761, 768 (1972).

25. Ibid., 767.

26. Ellen Frankel Paul, *Property Rights and Eminent Domain* (New Brunswick, NJ: Transaction Books, 1987), 138. Unless otherwise noted, all quotations attributed to Paul in this article are taken from this work.

27. Richard Epstein, *Takings: Private Property and the Power of Eminent Domain* (Cambridge: Harvard University Press, 1985), 123.

28. See, for example, Paul's comments in "A Reflection on Epstein and His Critics," *Miami Law Review* 41 (1986): 235.

29. 123 U.S. 623, 669 (1887).

30. Ibid., 671–672.

31. *Lawton* v. *Steele*, 152 U.S. 133, 140 (1894).

32. See, for example, *Powell* v. *Pennsylvania*, 127 U.S. 678 (1888).

33. Ackerman, *Private Property*, 102.

34. Courts may meet their constitutional obligation as long as they apply these standards consistently in all cases. For discussion of this point, see ibid., 14.

35. C. Haar, *Land-Use Planning* (Boston: Little, Brown, 1959), 410. Justice Holmes may have had the centrality of evolving community standards in mind when he said in *Mahon* that "this is a question of degree—and therefore cannot be disposed of by general propositions." This seems to be consistent with the view sometimes attributed to Holmes that judges apply standards of good taste and reasonableness and not simply formal legal prescriptions.

36. P. Soper, "The Constitutional Framework of Environmental Law," in his *Federal Environmental Law* (St. Paul, MN.: West, 1974), 67.

37. Ibid.

38. Epstein, *Takings*, 20, endorses this analysis of property rights, citing W. Blackstone, *Commentaries* (1765), 2. Robert Goodin cites Frank Snare, "The Concept of Property," *American Philosophical Quarterly* 9 (1972), 200–206; and C. B. Macpherson, "Human Rights as Property Rights, *Dissent* 24 (1977): 72–77.

39. Robert Goodin puts the point as follows: "The right to destroy is usually not part and parcel of the central incidents of the right to property, as ordinarily understood." Robert Goodin, "Property Rights and Preservationist Duties," paper presented at the Conference Group on Political Economy, American Political Science Association Annual Conference, Chicago, September 1987, 3.

40. John Locke, *Second Treatise of Government*, chap. 5, sec. 46.

41. For discussion, see William Rogers, "Bringing People Back: Toward a Comprehensive Theory of Taking in Natural Resources Law," *Ecology Law Quarterly* 10 (1982): 205, 248–51. Rogers cites about 20 relevant cases at 2.49 nn. 214–16.

42. Locke, *Second Treatise*, chap. 5, sec. 27.

43. 56 Wis. 2d 18, 201 N.W.2d 768.

44. Ibid., 17.

45. For a discussion of the "Lockean Proviso," see Robert Nozick, *Anarchy, State, and Utopia* (New York: Basic Books, 1974), 174–82.

46. Ellen Frankel Paul, "The Just Takings Issue," *Environmental Ethics* 3 (1981): 309, 320.

The Rio Declaration (1992)

Preamble

The United Nations Conference on Environment and Development,

Having met at Rio de Janeiro from 3 to 14 June 1992,

Reaffirming the Declaration of the United Nations Conference on the Human Environment, adopted at Stockholm on 16 June 1972, and seeking to build upon it,

With the goal of establishing a new and equitable global partnership through the creation of new levels of cooperation among States, key sectors of societies and people,

Working toward international agreements which respect the interests of all and protect the integrity of the global environmental and developmental system,

Recognizing the integral and interdependent nature of the Earth, our home,

Proclaims that:

Principle 1

Human beings are at the centre of concerns for sustainable development. They are entitled to a healthy and productive life in harmony with nature.

Principle 2

States have, in accordance with the Charter of the United Nations and the principles of international law, the sovereign right to exploit their own resources pursuant to their own environmental and developmental policies, and the responsibility to ensure that activities within their jurisdiction or control do not cause damage to the environment of other States or of areas beyond the limits of national jurisdiction.

Principle 3

The right to development must be fulfilled so as to equitably meet developmental and environmental needs of present and future generations.

Principle 4

In order to achieve sustainable development, environmental protection shall constitute an integral part of the development process and cannot be considered in isolation from it.

Principle 5

All States and all people shall cooperate in the essential task of eradicating poverty as an indispensable requirement for sustainable development, in order to decrease the disparities in standards of living and better meet the needs of the majority of the people of the world.

Principle 6

The special situation and needs of developing countries, particularly the least developed and those most environmentally vulnerable, shall be given special priority. International actions in the field of environment and development should also address the interests and needs of all countries.

Principle 7

States shall cooperate in a spirit of global partnership to conserve, protect and restore the health and integrity of the Earth's ecosystem. In view of the different contributions to global environmental degradation, States have common but differentiated responsibilities. The developed countries acknowledge the responsibility that they bear in the international pursuit of sustainable development in view of the pressures their societies place on the global environment and of the technologies and financial resources they command.

Principle 8

To achieve sustainable development and a higher quality of life for all people, States should reduce and eliminate unsustainable patterns of production and consumption and promote appropriate demographic policies.

The Rio Declaration, approved by the United Nations Conference on Environment and Development (Rio de Janeiro, Brazil, June 3–14, 1992) and later endorsed by the 47th session of the United Nations General Assembly on December 22, 1992.

Principle 9

States should cooperate to strengthen endogenous capacity-building for sustainable development by improving scientific understanding through exchanges of scientific and technological knowledge, and by enhancing the development, adaptation, diffusion and transfer of technologies, including new and innovative technologies.

Principle 10

Environmental issues are best handled with the participation of all concerned citizens, at the relevant level. At the national level, each individual shall have appropriate access to information concerning the environment that is held by public authorities, including information on hazardous materials and activities in their communities, and the opportunity to participate in decision-making processes. States shall facilitate and encourage public awareness and participation by making information widely available. Effective access to judicial and administrative proceedings, including redress and remedy, shall be provided.

Principle 11

States shall enact effective environmental legislation. Environmental standards, management objectives and priorities should reflect the environmental and developmental context to which they apply. Standards applied by some countries may be inappropriate and of unwarranted economic and social cost to other countries, in particular developing countries.

Principle 12

States should cooperate to promote a supportive and open international economic system that would lead to economic growth and sustainable development in all countries, to better address the problems of environmental degradation. Trade policy measures for environmental purposes should not constitute a means of arbitrary or unjustifiable discrimination or a disguised restriction on international trade. Unilateral action to deal with environmental challenges outside the jurisdiction of the improving country should be avoided. Environmental measures addressing transboundary or global environmental problems should, as far as possible, be based on an international consensus.

Principle 13

States shall develop national law regarding liability and compensation for the victims of pollution and other environmental damage. States shall also cooperate in an expeditious and more determined manner to develop further international law regarding liability and compensation for adverse effects of environmental damage caused by activities within their jurisdiction or control to areas beyond their jurisdiction.

Principle 14

States should effectively cooperate to discourage or prevent the relocation and transfer to other States of any activities and substances that cause severe environmental degradation or are found to be harmful to human health.

Principle 15

In order to protect the environment, the precautionary approach shall be widely applied by States according to their capabilities. Where there are threats of serious or irreversible damage, lack of full scientific certainty shall not be used as a reason for postponing cost-effective measures to prevent environmental degradation.

Principle 16

National authorities should endeavour to promote the internalization of environmental costs and the use of economic instruments, taking into account the approach that the polluter should, in principle, bear the cost of pollution, with due regard to the public interest and without distorting international trade and investment.

Principle 17

Environmental impact assessment, as a national instrument, shall be undertaken for proposed activities that are likely to have a significant adverse impact on the environment and are subject to a decision of a competent national authority.

Principle 18

States shall immediately notify other States of any natural disasters or other emergencies that are likely to produce sudden harmful effects on the environment of those States. Every effort shall be made by the international community to help States so afflicted.

Principle 19

States shall provide prior and timely notification and relevant information to potentially affected States on activities that may have a significant adverse transboundary environmental effect and shall consult with those States at an early stage and in good faith.

Principle 20

Women have a vital role in environmental management and development. Their full participation is therefore essential to achieve sustainable development.

Principle 21

The creativity, ideals and courage of the youth of the world should be mobilized to forge a global partnership in order to achieve sustainable development and ensure a better future for all.

Principle 22

Indigenous people and their communities, and other local communities, have a vital role in environmental management and development because of their knowledge and traditional practices. States should recognize and duly support their identity, culture and interests and enable their effective participation in the achievement of sustainable development.

Principle 23

The environment and natural resources of people under oppression, domination and occupation shall be protected.

Principle 24

Warfare is inherently destructive of sustainable development. States shall therefore respect international law providing protection for the environment in times of armed conflict and cooperate in its further development, as necessary.

Principle 25

Peace, development and environmental protection are interdependent and indivisible.

Principle 26

States shall resolve all their environmental disputes peacefully and by appropriate means in accordance with the Charter of the United Nations.

Principle 27

States and people shall cooperate in good faith and in a spirit of partnership in the fulfilment of the principles embodied in this Declaration and in the further development of international law in the field of sustainable development.

C. PRESERVING BIODIVERSITY

PREVIEW

As extinction spreads, some of the lost forms prove to be keystone species, whose disappearance brings down other species and triggers a ripple effect through the demographies of the survivors. The loss of a keystone species is like a drill accidentally striking a power line. It causes the lights to go out all over.[1]

E. O. Wilson

Death is one thing; an end to birth is something else.[2]

Michael Soulé and David Wilcox

Imagine that we are about to enter a conference room in a large hotel, Hotel Gaia if one likes, the only one in the cosmos, and all living creatures live somewhere in this huge hotel. As we enter to discuss the destiny of many of these fellow beings (not to mention our own species), we note that parts of the hotel are on fire. Some of the fires were started by members of "our" group, our species. We know that we cannot put out all these fires, and stop starting new ones, without persuading others that many lives must be saved and that we must stop starting these fires. And we know that as we reflect on these matters and explore these problems, the fires will spread and many will die and in some cases the last of a certain kind will die and that group will be no more since extinction is forever. That is what is meant by the "death of birth." In that context we go into the conference room to discuss the issues; "further studies" have their costs. We must figure out how bad the fire is and what is threatened and what we can do about it. Well, at least some must do that; others go to put out a few fires.

We do not seem to mourn the extinction of certain groups of biological organisms. Some we tend to view as insignificant. Recall that talk of species includes various types of fauna (mammals, marsupials, insects, and so on) as well as flora (e.g., trees, grass). The skeptic may ask whether it matters if the earth contains one less type of horned toad or one less type of mosquito. Given its role as a carrier of disease, should we regret, or should we celebrate, the extinction of the Norwegian rat? In short, what's so bad about the disappearance of certain species (other than *Homo sapiens!*)? Alternatively, are there compelling reasons to draw the moral conclusion that we ought to make strenuous efforts to preserve species and foster a biodiverse world? One might ask as well: "What's so great about people?" "Why preserve *Homo sapiens?*" If we could imagine things from the viewpoint of a grizzly bear or a coyote, perhaps we would not mourn the extinction of those superpredators classified as *Homo sapiens*. We need to survey and reassess the reasons for and against preservation. The selections in this section will facilitate the development of a considered view on these matters. We organize our thoughts in these segments:

1. The concept of species

2. Empirical data about the rate of extinction and the effects of extinction

3. Arguments for and against preservation

4. A sketch of the essays in the section

The Concept of Species

Not everyone will recall the usual biological taxonomy: kingdom, phylum, class, order, family, genus, and species. We might ask whether the classification "species" is the relevant one with which to be concerned, but we shall set aside that question in favor of others. There are some slippery differences between considering our relations to *species* and to current *members of a species*. There is a distinction between focus on an open class (e.g., a species) and a closed one (e.g., the 1984 U.S. Supreme Court). A closed class ceases to be the class that it is if its membership changes. Ignoring this difference is likely to generate confusion. It is of interest that a given species can continue to exist at time t^{n+1} even though all the members of that species at t^n have ceased to exist at t^{n+1} (suppose that new members are on the scene at t^{n+1}).

The concept of a species, then, is unlike that of concepts designating certain groups, such as the 1984 U.S. Olympic women's volleyball team (a closed class). In contrast, the species designated as "the humpback whale" is not to be understood as the set of currently existing whales. Killing all such existing whales would be sufficient to extinguish the species (barring later reconstitution from residual genetic materials, e.g., frozen cells), but such an event is not necessary for the species to cease to exist. Even if there is a negative duty not to kill any whale and even if that duty were not (henceforth) violated, the whale might cease to exist. Another type of act, sterilization of all the members of a species, could cause the species to cease to exist (even though such an act would not violate any duty not to kill members of that species). There is, then, a certain asymmetry between considering the relations we may have toward members of a species and relations to the species as such. Further, a negative duty not to extinguish a species is not identical with a possible duty not to kill members of that species. In further contrast, a positive duty to preserve a given species, the humpback whale, for example, might be carried out (in principle) by preserving only a small number of humpbacks. Some who advocate a duty to "preserve species" no doubt have in mind something stronger—a duty to help many members of a species thrive and reproduce.

Another conceptual matter, closely related to a focus on species, concerns whether a species can have moral rights, and not merely legal rights. Even if it is clear that individuals of certain sorts (you, but not your thumb) can have rights, it is less clear that a complex entity such as a species can. Those who claim that we have duties to preserve certain species may claim (at this juncture) that moral rights intelligibly and reasonably can be attributed to entities other than individuals (e.g., corporations, governments, or families). But what sorts of complex entities can have rights? One may maintain that not all duties are correlative to rights possessed by the entity to whom the duty is owed. For example, some assert that we have certain duties to human infants, comatose humans, and even dead humans (e.g., not to deal recklessly with the corpse), even though they are not bearers of rights. The questions of whether a species conceptually can possess rights (as opposed to individual members of the species possessing them) and whether any species does are questions requiring further exploration. These distinctions are relevant to the larger moral issue of whether we are failing in any duties we might have to preserve any or all species. What is it, however, about the current situation that is thought to be deserving of great concern?

Prospective Extinction

Most in the public spotlight is the threatened extinction of certain "charismatic megafauna," e.g., the tiger, blue whale, whooping crane, giant panda, orangutan, cheetah, and northern spotted owl.[3] Less dramatic, but of equal or greater significance, is the probable current loss of a dozen species per day, and the probable loss of millions by the year 2000. What is often not recognized—in discussions of the prospective fate of different species—is the very dramatic historical turnabout that has developed in recent years and that is continuing. The data on why the current era is undergoing an extinction spasm are found in the striking essay excerpted from E. O. Wilson's book *The Diversity of Life* (see also the fine essay "Tropical Forests and Their Species: Going, Going . . ." by Norman Myers in Section VI-D). Briefly, due to human activity and intervention in natural processes, there is a radical increase in the number of members of one species, *Homo sapiens,* and a radical increase in the rate of extinction of other species (on our increase see the essay by Ronnie Zoe Hawkins in Section VI-A on human population). Whether these changes are good or bad, a reason to celebrate or mourn, is a matter of evaluation; we regard it as a largely unrecognized megatragedy of modern times. It seems fair to say that our species, numbering close to 6 billion and weighing over 200 million tons, temporarily dominates the planet (*if* we ignore the little creatures discussed earlier by E. O. Wilson). Current population projections suggest that we will number 10 to 12 billion people by the year 2025. In spite of the evident problems (say, the need for adequate food, shelter, and health care) attending large and dense populations of people, the propensity of humans to "be fruitful and multiply" has led to both the direct and indirect destruction (intentional or not; foreseen or not) of many species of plants and animals by the cramping, erosion, or elimination of their habitats or food supplies.

What is new under the sun is a significant increase in the rate of extinction caused by human activity. Between 1600 and 1900, a species became extinct about once every four years. From 1900 to 1960, the rate was about one per year. Since then, estimates have ranged from 100 per year up to 40,000 per year in the last quarter of this century. This last figure is based in part on the projected destruction of prairie land, wetlands, and tropical moist forests (some assume the latter to contain 2 to 5 million species each). Even if these estimates are seriously in error, radical changes are under way.

Sketching the Arguments

As we noted, one view of the demise of thousands, or even millions, of species, of habitats, and of ecosystems is, "So what?" Should we be concerned? Should we act differently? Why? If so, how? Or why not? The arguments in favor of our making efforts to preserve species, or certain species, tend to fall into two broad categories—as one might surmise. First are the purely anthropocentric considerations; other species should be preserved because they are valuable to us human beings. Some argue that we should, for purely prudential reasons, protect or promote our human interests now. Some urge that we have duties to other, indeed nonexistent, humans (is it not wrong to turn the earth into a garbage dump for future generations of humans?); recall Brian Barry's essay in Section VI-A.

Second, as we noted in Part III, powerful arguments can be marshalled on behalf of the view that members of at least some other species have moral standing (or are intrinsically valuable). If so, we have duties not to harm them—duties not derivative from, or dependent on, contingent facts about whether the preservation of animals in the long or short run promotes human interests.

As noted in the Preview to "The Other Animals" (Part III), the criteria for possession of moral standing such as sentience, possession of consciousness, or self-consciousness will not "confer" moral standing on all animals. Furthermore, on the widely held assumption that plants lack these traits, such

grounds provide no basis for concluding that we owe direct duties to plants or many animals (for example, thousands of insect species). Thus, according to such views, there is no *direct* duty to preserve thousands of plants and animal species. Some defenders of the "land ethic" and some biocentric egalitarians (of both an *individualist* and *holist* bent; see Section IV-A) take a contrary view. This type of dispute is often alluded to in terms of a conflict between animal liberationists and defenders of "the land ethic" (or, in somewhat misleading terminology, defenders of an *"environmental* ethic"). A closer examination of this matter is found in Part IV. If it is true that individual animals (or some) have rights, or intrinsic value, or moral standing (as the case may be), is it also the case that any species (or ecosystem) has rights, intrinsic value, or moral standing? In her essay, Lilly-Marlene Russow defends a negative answer to this question.

Even if (but we are *not* assuming this) there are no direct duties to individual animals, to individual plants, to species, or to ecosystems, there are evident advantages to humans' preserving many species, other things being equal. The advantages accruing to humans from having certain animals and plants around to exploit are enormous. Much of this exploitation (recall the essays in Part III) may be morally justifiable, but it is reasonable to believe that much human "use" of plants and animals is (virtually) uncontroversially permissible, e.g., shearing sheep for wool, keeping dogs and cats for pets, making valuable drugs from plants, and harvesting trees from farms (not to be confused with the National Forests). There is, then, a *consequentialist* line of argument for preserving certain species.[4] Sometimes, doing so may maximize utility (whether the utilities accruing to sentient animals are weighed in here—as in classic utilitarianism—is, of course, an important matter). In some cases the benefit of preserving a species cannot be "cashed" readily in terms of the value of experimenting on, eating, or making products from its members. Sometimes, the value of preservation seems to be mainly, or solely, of an aesthetic sort. The question arises as to whether this is a rational basis for urging the preservation of the giant panda, the blue whale, the Florida cougar, or old forests. Even if the appeal to the preservation of aesthetic values succeeds in the just mentioned cases, it is less likely to provide a plausible ground for preserving ugly, or very small, nocturnal creatures (or species). Indeed, it is hard, and perhaps impossible, to defend the preservation or conservation of certain species on the ground that they themselves are valuable as economic resources. At least some species seem to be useless as aesthetic, economic, or ecological resources. On the latter point, compare Russow's query about the ecological role of a species all of whose members are in zoos—or all of which were bred to live briefly only in a laboratory (such as lab rats). Still, some species or other entities are part of an ecosystem or habitat that is itself valuable. If we are to preserve a certain species, then we cannot blithely, or ruthlessly, continue to destroy their habitats. Analogously, it would be absurd to maintain that we cared about whooping cranes and then allowed their nesting places to be turned into yet another shopping mall or condominium complex. We have already discussed the conflict between so acting and maintaining the "licence-to-kill" conception of property rights that is popular in the United States.

An obvious difficulty is inherent in trying to measure the aesthetic value of experiences. A standard "measuring rod," of course, is the "cash value" of a thing. How many dollars, for example, is it worth to preserve a blue whale (or heighten the probability of its preservation) so that our grandchildren might see it—and not just a film or a photograph? Economists have suggestions, of course, about how to assign a monetary value to things whose value we find hard to measure, or even regard

as incommensurable—not measurable in terms of alien stuff (e.g., human life in terms of dollars). What one would be willing to pay to lower the probability of premature death (e.g., accepting a lower income to have a safer job) is often suggested as a useful measure of the cash value of "life" (or enhanced likelihood of a longer life). These matters were explored somewhat in Part V but are examined in the context of the problem of assigning value to biodiversity in the later essay by Alan Randall.

As we noted earlier, some maintain that certain species have intrinsic value. There are, however, various obscurities surrounding the concept of intrinsic value. Generally, it seems that when it is claimed that "X has intrinsic value" what is meant is that "X is valuable in itself and apart from whatever valuation of X is made by others" (e.g., people). But sometimes an alternative interpretation is employed. To say that "X is intrinsically valuable" means that "X is valued by others for X's own sake" (in contrast with what philosophers often mean when they claim that pleasure is intrinsically good or valuable). This latter interpretation, unlike the former, requires valuers to be around. Would the Grand Canyon or the giant panda lack intrinsic value if people (valuers) did not exist? Or if possession of the capacity to live a meaningful life (one in which how things went was not a matter of indifference to the possessor) is necessary for something to possess intrinsic value, it would seem that only sentient, or perhaps only conscious, entities could have intrinsic value. This would include most people (but not the brain-dead or anencephalic infants) and many animals, but little else would have intrinsic value based on this criterion.

If we allow that all tigers have intrinsic value and that that consideration is the only basis for concluding that we owe them certain direct duties, say, not to cause them premature death or foster their living under certain circumstances, then there is no obvious nonanthropocentric basis for saying that we have special duties to preserve those kinds of tigers which may be on an endangered species list as opposed to those which are not. This consideration is surely one motivation for examining whether some sort of intrinsic value can sensibly be ascribed to species as such.

In short there is no easy path to finding common ground for the conclusion that many or all species ought to be preserved—indeed for identifying a rational justification for the somewhat powerful preservationist instincts many of us share. One final item for reflection: If it is argued that X (a dog, say) has intrinsic value and Y (a very valuable diamond ring, for example) does not, should we automatically preserve X instead of Y if for some reason we have to choose one or the other (imagine that a house is on fire and that we can save only the dog or the ring? Consider another example. Suppose that instead of a diamond ring, what might be saved is the only accessible antidote for a poison that a child has just ingested. Many practical environmental problems involve a similar kind of conflict; that is, we must sacrifice one thing of value (or some sort) to preserve something else of value (of some sort). Just how to resolve the trade-offs in a nonarbitrary manner is a recalcitrant matter; recall once more the discussions in Section IV-B on conflict resolution.

A Sketch of the Other Essays

We already noted the focus of Lilly-Marlene Russow's essay on whether species as such matter, as well as some of the appalling data on the severe decline in biodiversity noted by E. O. Wilson. A major attempt to try to halt the loss of species in the United States was the passage of the Endangered Species Act (ESA) of 1973. The act sought to protect, evidently, those species thought to be endangered. It has been criticized by some for focusing only on species, instead of on all animals or all sentient animals (criticisms, in different

ways, of some defenders of animal rights and some biocentrists). The ESA requires that federal agencies ensure that their actions are not likely to jeopardize the continued existence of threatened or endangered species or adversely modify or destroy their habitats. Many who support the intent of the act suggest that what is needed is an "endangered habitat act" since it is foolish to continue to destroy the places where animals live and then go to sometimes very expensive and desperate lengths to rescue some species whose prognosis for recovery may be a guarded one. In part, the suggestion is that we must engage in more *preventive* action (including the stopping of our regular, deliberate destruction of habitats), and not just in rescue efforts. Restraint imposes costs—the costs of foregone opportunities—but it is by no means obvious that the costs outweigh the benefits to humans, even on a purely anthropocentric basis. They may, however, depending on modes of accounting and limited time frames. It is clear that many defenders of logging the old-growth forests in the northwest United States assign no intrinsic value to the preservation of the northern spotted owl or other species of fauna in that habitat and that they see great 100- to 300-year-old trees as only so many board feet, as a mere commodity whose value is utterly wasted when the trees finally fall to the ground and rot (the rotting trees, themselves, however, provide habitat for many creatures).

Between 1979 and 1991, there were 120,000 "consultations" between federal agencies and appropriate reviewers, often the U.S. Fish and Wildlife Service, over whether species would be jeopardized by proposed activities. The findings in 99 percent of those cases were one of no jeopardy, and only 34 projects were canceled in that period.[5] All this suggests that industrial complaints over constraints imposed by the ESA are misplaced. One might also infer, given all that we know about federal deregulation and the probusiness attitude that prevailed during that period, that the ESA was not strongly enforced by a largely antienvironmental federal administration. Still, of the 600 or so species listed in the U.S. (1100 worldwide) as threatened or endangered, 238 are said to be stable or improving.[6] It is worth noting that the ESA's restraints have little effect on uses of "private property" that result in habitat destruction or similar situations in areas over which no nation has full sovereignty, e.g., the oceans.

It is natural to wonder what sort of entity is a species, and are we not arbitrarily picking out some collection of creatures when we employ the notion of species. Alternatively, do species correspond to eternal essences in the mind of God as some insist? Should concern about preservation not focus on subspecies or genera or some other grouping? The selection from Stephen Jay Gould, "What Is a Species?" addresses the question of the reality of species, and he defends the view that what we call species are almost always objective entities in nature. Holmes Rolston, in an excerpt which we have entitled "Why Species Matter," suggests reasons for valuing the continued existence of species beyond those for preserving the existence of individual plants and animals.[7] Indeed, he claims that it is difficult to separate the value of individuals from the ecostemic pyramid which is the matrix of the existence of individuals. In a detailed examination of the question of the moral standing of ecosystems and species, Lawrence Johnson defends the view that they are living entities with morally significant interests in their own right. He addresses the interesting question of how such entities can be said to possess interests even though they do not seem to be goal-oriented, or to "have goals," in the way that individual animals or plants might. Of further interest is the fact that sometimes what seems conducive to the survival of the genotype (one kind of construal of species identity) may be destructive to the individual animal whose genotype is in question.

In "What Mainstream Economists Have to Say About the Value of Biodiversity," Allan Randall spells out how a mainstream economic approach (MEA) would address some questions before us. Before reading Randall, the reader might find it useful to review "Utilitarianism and Economic Theory" in "An Introduction to Ethical Theory." The MEA tends to be anthropocentric in taking human want-satisfaction as the good or welfare to be promoted; hence, the value of the lives of other species is viewed as only *instrumental* in nature. Once more, two radically contrasting viewpoints confront the reader.

We have discussed the difficulties of defending a conception of moral standing to which the mainstream view is committed. We have also noted the counterintuitive quality of the assumption that the fulfillment of *any* human preference is a good, e.g., the desire of a child abuser to fulfill his or her desires; nevertheless, the MEA persists in being, as Randall notes, "persistently nonjudgmental about people's preferences" as if this were a theoretical virtue.[8] We will explore the issue no further, but once more ponder the assumption that *whatever* someone values (wants) is valuable and ought to be promoted.[9]

Randall allows that the MEA is "anthropocentric" in that "humans are assigning values." This use of 'anthropocentric' is at odds with its use in moral philosophy; as it is used technically in moral philosophy, the term concerns *what* has moral standing and not *who* is "assigning values." So a biocentrist view is not "anthropocentric" in the philosophical usage of the term even though a human (who else?) makes the judgment. The MEA is anthropocentric in both senses. Aside from questions about how economists interpret (intrinsic) value, first as want-fulfillment, then as the wanter's willingness to pay (WTP) for something or willingness to accept (WTA) something, Randall notes that market prices reflect *economic value* only under rather special conditions which are generally not satisfied in the case of determining the value of biodiversity. Even if market values (prices) are unreliable, conceptualization of kinds of value by economists (see Randall on *use, existence, option value*) is useful; we may want to know whether the case for preserving certain flora or fauna or habitats can rest *solely* on the value assigned by an MEA. In *some* cases, those who deny that certain forms of life have moral standing, as well as their opponents, may agree on preservation policies.

A key step in MEA is the discounting of the value (positive or negative) of states of affairs in the distant future. Randall notes that "by discounting at standard rates, the inevitable collapse of living systems on this planet several hundred years from now could be counterbalanced by relatively trivial economic gains in the immediate future." Given this implication, why should any rational person rely on such discounting as a means to determine present value? To invoke an analogy, if a mathematical shortcut yielded the right answer only 95 percent of the time, why rely on it in *all* cases, e.g., even when it implies radically counterintuitive results? These difficulties aside, governments do not have unlimited resources, and hard choices must be made about how to allocate resources in efforts to maintain and preserve biodiversity. Such choices are not avoided even if one approaches these matters from a nonanthropocentric, nonutilitarian, and nonindividualist point of view.

For reasons discussed throughout this volume (see also the later excerpt from *The Diversity of Life,* by E. O. Wilson), it seems reasonable to believe that the preservation of any, or virtually all, species is a good in itself. Randall discusses another approach which assumes as much, the safe minimal standard (SMS). This standard says that we should maintain a safe minimal standard (the minimal level of preservation which ensures survival) unless the opportunity costs (those goods humans would have to forego if resources went to maintaining preservation) are intolerably high. This proposal sounds tautologous, but it is nevertheless of some interest. If not tautologous, it seems straightforwardly

moral in nature, and one wonders whether it is to be thought of as derivative from some other principle or basic (i.e., nonderivative) in nature. We leave the question for the reader. One advocate of this view, Richard C. Bishop, defends the principle, in part, on the basis of considerations from game theory, and in particular the consideration that in situations like this one in which one cannot ascertain the expected cost or expected benefit of preservation or nonpreservation (due to uncertainties and the inability to estimate certain probabilities of harm or benefit), one ought to *minimize maximum losses* (i.e., choose the alternative [preservation]) whose worst outcome is better than the worst outcome of any other available alternative (irreversible loss of that which is of great value).[10] What is lost now *may* be a loss only to this generation; what is lost via extinction is a loss for all future generations. Should we, or should we not, mourn the permanent loss of the last remaining smallpox virus?[11]

The mainstream economic approach aside, David Ehrenfeld in "Why Put a Value on Biodiversity?" forcefully emphasizes the danger (indeed the impossibility) of trying to put a "dollar value" on biodiversity and the perhaps concurrent assumption that "doing so the right way" will lead to the appropriate preservation of biodiversity. As he observes, market incentives may lead some corporations to act so as to preserve species on some occasions but not others. There is little reason to believe that the so-called Invisible Hand will invariably connect profit maximization to preservation of biodiversity. Economists tend to agree that the Invisible Hand (markets) will not lead to the right level of diversity; in their view, the key question is whether one will arrive there after externalities are corrected.[12] Still, in Ehrenfeld's view it is both dangerous and wrong to deny the inherent value of biodiversity and to try to gauge its value solely in terms of economic benefit.

In standard economic theory, as we have noted, the ultimate state of affairs thought to be constitutive of the good, or that state of affairs thought to be good for its own sake, is the fulfillment of human wants or preferences. And economists tend to take these preferences as "given," that is, not to criticize them or to sort them into categories and assume that only some should be fulfilled. On this view, the only value that trees, animals, or ecosystems might have is in the fulfillment of existing human preferences. In "Transformative Values," Bryan Norton observes that nonhuman nature, the existence of other species, also serves to transform our preferences. Indeed, many people, e.g., John Muir, Ralph Waldo Emerson, Thoreau and Native Americans, have written of the value of sacred places, of the wilderness and of its special peace-inducing or inspiring qualities. If the nonhuman world has value in this way, then the assumption that all value is to be equated with the fulfillment of human wants cannot be correct. In any case, this is a distinct argument for the preservation of biodiversity and of wild places which diverges from the usual tendency in modern economic theory to take preferences as given.

The task of learning the relevant facts, gaining perspective, and weighing matters in an all-things-considered manner is not quickly accomplished. Our selection by E. O. Wilson helps us to understand the extent to which the loss of species diversity is "irreversible." Our *time frame* is important here. Suppose that someone took your car or bike and told you, "Don't worry, I'll have it back shortly . . . a few days before you are 100 years old." For your purposes the loss would be complete and irreversible. How long will it take for comparable biodiversity to return after the massive extinctions currently under way and increasing? Wilson considers the record after the explosion at Krakatau in 1883, a volcanic eruption equivalent to 100–150 tons of TNT, which left an island without life on it. Other evidence is derived from the five major extinctions that have occurred in the history of our planet. The five mass extinctions, according to

E. O. Wilson, are, in terms of geological period and time before the present: Ordovician, 440 million years; Devonian, 365 million years; Permian, 245 million years; Triassic, 210 million years; and Cretaceous, 66 million years. Of what relevance is it that life in some forms and some degree of diversity has returned or continued? Wilson reviews some of the data on the rate at which many species are disappearing, especially due to the destruction of those habitats that are the richest of all in species diversity, the tropical forests.[13] As difficult as it may be to formulate the most reasonable view as to what should be done to halt or slow "the silent hemorrhage," we are forced to pause and reflect deeply when Wilson observes:

> The creation of that diversity came slow and hard: 3 billion years of evolution to start the profusion of animals that occupy the seas, another 350 million years to assemble the rain forests in which half or more of the species on earth now live. . . . Young or old, all living species are direct descendants of the organisms that lived 3.8 billion years ago.[14]

On the face of it, collective human behavior sustained over decades poses greater risks of harm to the diversity of life than does what many of us were raised to think of as the greatest danger of all, nuclear war. Yet a certain ignorant and mindless cynicism continues to ridicule those who think beyond their own lives and beyond the present. One wonders who merits a widely invoked label, "prolife."

If we agreed that there is a powerful presumption in favor of preserving biodiversity, we would still be faced with some difficult choices between different policies. Roger Paden addresses how we are to understand the idea of preserving nature for its own sake. After reviewing one distinction between conservationist and preservationist views, Paden examines a distinction between two understandings of the preservationist notion that we ought to preserve nature for its own sake, a notion which calls for preserving natural *processes* and *products,* e.g., species of flora and fauna. Paden contends that these prescriptions can lead to opposing policies and illustrates the point by reference to the requirements of the Endangered Species Act and the U.S. Park Service's policy of letting forest fires burn themselves out. In his essay, he promises, in brief, to force us to confront an unnoticed ambiguity, to decide to which policy we are indeed committed (barring some manner of reconciling them), and to set forth more clearly the moral grounds for choosing one over the other or trying to formulate a middle view.

NOTES

1. Edward O. Wilson, *The Diversity of Live* (Cambridge, MA: Harvard University Press, 1992).

2. Attributed to Michael Soulé and David Wilcox by Norman Myers in "Tropical Forests and Their Species," in *Biodiversity,* edited by E. O. Wilson and Frances M. Peter (Washington: National Academy Press, 1988), p. 32.

3. The expression "charismatic megafauna" is attributed to Dennis Murphy of the Center of Conservation Biology at Stanford in the essay "The Butterfly Problem," by Charles Mann and Mark Plummer in the *Atlantic Monthly* (January 1992), 49.

4. On the notion of consequentialism, see "An Introduction to Ethical Theory," Section I-B-4.

5. The figures are from the "Endangered Species Act: Bulwark Against the Tide of Extinction," distributed by the National Wildlife Federation.

6. Ibid.

7. The Rolston selection here is the latter portion of his essay "Environmental Ethics: Values in and Duties to the Natural World" the first part of which we have reprinted in Part III under the title "Beyond Ethics by Extension."

8. A great deal of work has been done in philosophy in the two decades on the question of when it is justifiable to intervene on paternalistic grounds with the choices or behavior of others, e.g., Donald VanDeVeer, *Paternalistic Intervention* (Princeton, NJ: Princeton University Press, 1986); Joel Feinberg, *Harm to Self* (New York: Oxford University Press, 1986); Gerald Dworkin, "Paternalism," in *Morality and the Law,* edited by Richard Wasserstrom (Belmont, CA: Wadsworth Publishing, 1971).

9. We have no doubt that few *utilitarians* would *want* to be saddled with this assumption. The key question is how the *theory* of utilitarianism can be remedied to yield the implication that the fulfillment of some preferences (which ones?) receive no weight in the utilitarian calculus.

10. The rule of rational choice under situations of uncertainty, noted in the text, is also called the "maximin rule." It is also relevant to choices we confront in policy decisions about global warming; on this see the discussion in VI-E. See also Richard C. Bishop, "Endangered Species and Uncertainty: The Economics of a Safe Minimal Standard," *American Journal of Agricultural Economics,* Vol. 60, No. 1 (February 1978), 10–18.

11. This interesting question was posed by one of our reviewers.

12. This point would have been overlooked but for a reminder by Talbott Page.

13. On this topic see the essay by Norman Myers in the following section.

14. E. O. Wilson, *The Diversity of Life* (Cambridge, MA: Harvard University Press, 1992).

What Is a Species? _____

Stephen Jay Gould

I had visited every state but Idaho. A few months ago, I finally got my opportunity to complete the roster of 50 by driving east from Spokane, Washington, into western Idaho. As I crossed the state line, I made the same feeble attempt at humor that so many of us try in similar situations: "Gee, it doesn't look a bit different from easternmost Washington." We make such comments because we feel the discomfort of discord between our mental needs and the world's reality. Much of nature (including terrestrial real estate) is continuous, but both our mental and political structures require divisions and categories. We need to break large and continuous items into manageable units.

Many people feel the same way about species as I do about Idaho—but this feeling is wrong. Many people suppose that species must be arbitrary divisions of an evolutionary continuum in the same way that state boundaries are conventional divisions of unbroken land. Moreover, this is not merely an abstract issue of scientific theory but a pressing concern of political reality. The Endangered Species Act, for example, sets policy (with substantial teeth) for the preservation of species. But if species are only arbitrary divisions in nature's continuity, then what are we trying to preserve and how shall we define it? I write this article to argue that such a reading of evolutionary theory is wrong and that species are almost always objective entities in nature.

Let us start with something uncontroversial: the bugs in your backyard. If you go out to make a complete collection of all the kinds of insects living in this small discrete space, you will collect easily definable "packages," not intergrading continua. You might find a kind of bee, three kinds of ants, a butterfly or two, several beetles, and a cicada. You have simply validated the commonsense notion known to all: in any small space during any given moment, the animals we see belong to separate and definable groups—and we call these groups species.

In the eighteenth century this commonsense observation was translated, improperly as we now know, into the creationist taxonomy of Linnaeus. The great Swedish naturalist regarded species as God's created entities, and he gathered them together into genera, genera into orders, and orders into classes, to form the taxonomic hierarchy that we all learned in high school (several more categories, families and phyla, for example, have been added since Linnaeus's time). The creationist version reached its apogee in the writings of America's greatest nineteenth-century naturalist (and last truly scientific creationist), Louis Agassiz. Agassiz argued that species are incarnations of separate ideas in God's mind, and that higher categories (genera, orders, and so forth) are therefore maps of the interrelationships among divine thoughts. Therefore, taxonomy is the most important of all sciences because it gives us direct insight into the structure of God's mind.

Darwin changed this reverie forever by proving that species are related by the physical connection of genealogical descent. But this immensely satisfying resolution for the great puzzle of nature's order engendered a subsidiary problem that Darwin never fully resolved: If all life is interconnected as a genealogical continuum, then what reality can species have? Are they not just arbitrary divisions of evolving lineages? And if so, how can the bugs in my backyard be ordered in separate units? In fact, the two greatest evolutionists of the nineteenth century, Lamarck and Darwin, both questioned the reality of species on the basis of their evolutionary convictions. Lamarck wrote, "In vain do naturalists consume their time in describing new species"; while Darwin lamented: "we shall have to treat species as . . . merely artificial combinations made for convenience. This may not be a cheering prospect; but we shall at least be freed from the vain search for the undiscovered and undiscoverable essence of the term *species*" (from the *Origin of Species*).

But when we examine the technical writings of both Lamarck and Darwin, our sense of paradox is heightened. Darwin produced four long volumes on the taxonomy of barnacles, using conventional species for his divisions. Lamarck spent seven years (1815–1822) publishing his generation's standard, multivolume compendium on the diversity of animal life—*Histoire naturelle des animaux sans vertèbres*, or *Natural History of Invertebrate Animals*—all divided into species, many of which he named for the first time himself. How can these two great evolutionists have denied a concept in theory and then used it so centrally and extensively in practice? To ask the question more generally: If the species is still a useful and necessary concept, how can we define and justify it as evolutionists?

The solution to this question requires a preamble and two steps. For the preamble, let us acknowledge that the conceptual problem arises when we extend the "bugs in my backyard" example into time and space. A momentary slice of any continuum looks tolerably discrete; a slice of salami or a cross section of a tree trunk freezes a complexly changing structure into an apparently stable entity. Modern horses are discrete and separate from all other existing species, but how can we call the horse (*Equus caballus*) a real and definable entity if we can trace an unbroken genealogical series back through time to a dog-size creature with several toes on each foot? Where did this "dawn horse," or "eohippus," stop and the next stage begin; at what moment did the penultimate stage become *Equus caballus?* I now come to the two steps of an answer. First, if each evolutionary line were like a long salami, then species would not be real and definable in time and space. But in almost all cases large-scale evolution is a story of branching, not of transformation in a single line—bushes, not ladders, in my usual formulation. A branch on a bush is an objective division. One species rarely turns into another by total transformation over its entire geographic range. Rather, a small population becomes geographically isolated from the rest of the species—and this fragment changes to become a new species while the bulk of the parental population does not alter. "Dawn horse" is a misnomer because rhinoceroses evolved from the same parental lineage. The lineage split at an objective branching point into two lines that became (after further events of splitting) the great modern groups of horses (eight species, including asses and zebras) and rhinos (a sadly depleted group of formerly successful species).

Failure to recognize that evolution is a bush and not a ladder leads to one of the most common vernacular misconceptions about human biology. People often challenge me: "If humans evolved from apes, why are apes still around?" To anyone who understands the principle of bushes, there simply is no problem: the human lineage emerged as a branch, while the rest of the trunk continued as apes (and branched several more times to yield modern chimps, gorillas, and so on). But if you think that evolution is a ladder or a salami, then an emergence of humans from apes should mean the elimination of apes by transformation.

Second, you might grasp the principle of bushes and branching but still say: Yes, the ultimate products of a branch become objectively separate, but early on, while the branch is forming, no clear division can be made, and the precursors of the two species that will emerge must blend indefinably. And if evolution is gradual and continuous, and if most of a species' duration is spent in this state of incipient formation, then species will not be objectively definable during most of their geologic lifetimes.

Fair enough as an argument, but the premise is wrong. New species do (and must) have this period of initial ambiguity. But species emerge relatively quickly, compared with their period of later stability, and then live for long periods—often millions of years—with minimal change. Now, suppose that on average (and this is probably a fair estimate), species spend one percent of their geologic lifetimes in this initial state of imperfect separation. Then, on average, about one species in a hundred will encounter problems in definition, while the other 99 will be discrete and objectively separate—cross sections of branches showing no confluence with others. Thus, the principle of bushes, and the speed of branching, resolve the supposed paradox: continuous evolution can and does yield a world in which the vast majority of species are separate from all others and clearly definable at any moment in time. Species are nature's objective packages.

I have given a historical definition of species—as unique and separate branches on nature's bush. We also need a functional definition, if only because historical evidence (in the form of a complete fossil record) is usually unavailable. The standard criterion, in use at least since the days of the great French naturalist Georges de Buffon (a contemporary of Linnaeus), invokes the capacity for interbreeding. Members of a species can breed with others in the same species but not with individuals belonging to different species.

This functional criterion is a consequence of the historical definition: distinct separateness of a branch emerges only with the attainment of sufficient evolutionary distance to preclude interbreeding, for otherwise the branch is not an irrevocably separate entity and can amalgamate with the parental population. Exceptions exist, but the reproductive criterion generally works well and gives rise to the standard one-liner for a textbook definition of a species: "a population of actually or potentially reproducing organisms sharing a common gene pool."

Much of the ordinary activity of evolutionary biologists is devoted to learning whether or not the groups they study are separate species by this criterion of "reproductive isolation." Such separateness can be based on a variety of factors, collectively termed "isolating mechanisms": for example, genetic programs so different that an embryo cannot form even if egg and sperm unite; behaviors that lead members of one species to shun individuals from other populations; even something so mundane as breeding at different times of the year, or in different parts of the habitat—for example, on apple trees rather than on plum trees—so that contact can never take place. (We exclude simple geographic separation—living on different continents, for example—because an isolating mechanism must work when actively challenged by a potential for interbreeding through spatial contact. I do not belong to a separate species from my brethren in Brazil just because I have never been there. Similarly, reproductive isolation must be assessed by ordinary behavior in a state of nature. Some truly separate species can be induced to interbreed in zoos and laboratories. The fact that zoos can make tiglons—tiger-lion hybrids—does not challenge the separate status of the two populations as species in nature.)

Modern humans (species *Homo sapiens*) fit these criteria admirably. We are now spread all over the world in great numbers, but we began as a little twig in Africa (the historical criterion). We may look quite different from one another in a few superficially striking aspects of size, skin color, and hair form, but there is astonishingly little overall genetic difference among our so-called races. Above all (the functional criterion), we can all interbreed with one another (and do so with avidity, always, and all over the world), but not with any member of another species (movies about flies notwithstanding). We are often reminded, quite correctly, that we are very similar in overall genetic program to our nearest cousin, the chimpanzee—but no one would mistake a single individual of either species, and we do not hybridize (again, various science fictions notwithstanding).

I do not say that these criteria are free from exceptions; nature is nothing if not a domain of exceptions, where an example against any clean generality can always be found. Some distinct populations of plants, for example, can and frequently do interbreed with others that ought to be separate species by all other standards. (This is why the classification of certain groups—the rhododendrons for example—is such a mess.) But the criteria work in the vast majority of cases, including humans.

Species are not arbitrary units, constructed for human convenience, in dividing continua. Species are the real and objective items of nature's morphology. They are "out there" in the world as historically distinct and functionally separate populations "with their own historical role and tendency" (as the other textbook one-liner proclaims).

Species are unique in the Linnaean hierarchy as the only category with such objectivity. All higher units—genera, families, phyla, et cetera—are human conventions in the following important respect. The evolutionary tree itself is objective; the branches (species) emerge, grow, and form clusters by subsequent branching. The clusters are clearly discernible. But the status we award to these so-called higher taxa (clusters of branches with a single root of common evolutionary ancestry) is partly a matter of human decision. Clusters A and B in the figure are groups of species with a common parent. Each branch in each cluster is an objective species. But what are the clusters themselves? Are they two genera or two families? Our decision on this question is partly a matter of human preference constrained by the rules of logic and the facts of nature. (For example, we cannot take one species from cluster A and one from cluster B and put them together as a single genus—for this would violate the rule that all members of a higher taxon must share a common ancestor without excluding other species that are more closely related to the common ancestor. We cannot put domestic cats and dogs in one family while classifying lions and wolves in another.)

The taxonomic hierarchy recognizes only one unit below species—the subspecies. Like higher taxa, subspecies are also partly objective but partly based on human decision. Subspecies are defined as distinctive subpopulations that live in a definite geographic subsection of the entire range of the species. I cannot, for example, pluck out all tall members of a species, or all red individuals, wherever they occur over the full geographic range, and establish them as subspecies. A subspecies must be a distinct geographic subpopulation—not yet evolved far enough to become a separate species in its own right but different enough from other subpopulations (in terms of anatomy, genetic structure, physiology, or behavior) that a taxonomist chooses to memorialize the distinction with a name. Yet subspecies cannot be irrevocably unique natural populations (like full species) for two reasons: First, the decision to name them rests with human taxonomists, and isn't solely dictated by nature. Second, they are, by definition, still capable of interbreeding with other subpopulations of the species and are, therefore, impermanent and subject to reamalgamation.

This difference between species and subspecies becomes important in practice because our Endangered Species Act currently mandates the protection of subspecies as well. I do not dispute the act's intention or its teeth, for many subspecies do manifest distinctly evolved properties of great value and wonder (even if these properties do not render them reproductively isolated from other populations of the species). We would not, after all, condone the genocide of all Caucasian human beings because members of other races would still exist; human races, if formally recognized at all, are subspecies based on our original geographic separations. But since subspecies do not have the same objective status as species (and since not all distinct local populations bear separate names), argument over what does and does not merit protection is inevitable. Most of the major ecological wrangles of recent years—rows over the Mount Graham red squirrel or the northern spotted owl—involve subspecies, not species.

The taxonomic issues were once abstract, however important. They are now immediate and vital—and all educated people must understand them in the midst of our current crisis in biodiversity and extinction. I therefore close with two observations.

By grasping the objective status of species as real units in nature (and by understanding why they are not arbitrary divisions for human convenience), we may better comprehend the moral rationale for their preservation. You can expunge an arbitrary idea by rearranging your conceptual world. But when a species dies, an item of natural uniqueness is gone forever. Each species is a remarkably complex product of evolution—a branch on a tree that is billions of years old. All the king's horses and men faced an easy problem compared with what we would encounter if we tried to reconstitute a lost species. Reassembling Humpty-Dumpty is just an exceedingly complex jigsaw puzzle, for the pieces lie at the base of the wall. There are no pieces left when the last dodo dies.

But all species eventually die in the fullness of geologic time, so why should we worry? In the words of Tennyson (who died exactly 100 years ago, so the fact is no secret):

> From scarped cliff and quarried stone
> She cries, "A thousand types are gone:
> I care for nothing. All shall go."

(From *In Memoriam*.)

The argument is true, but the time scale is wrong for our ethical concerns. We live our lives within geologic instants, and we should make our moral decisions at this proper scale—not at the micromoment of thoughtless exploitation for personal profit and public harm; but not at Earth's time scale of billions of years either (a grand irrelevancy for our species' potential tenure of thousands or, at most, a few million years).

We do not let children succumb to easily curable infections just because we know that all people must die eventually. Neither should we condone our current massive wipeout of species because all eventually become extinct. The mass extinctions of our geologic past may have cleared space and created new evolutionary opportunity—but it takes up to 10 million years to reestablish an interesting new world, and what can such an interval mean to us? Mass extinctions may have geologically distant benefits, but life in the midst of such an event is maximally unpleasant—and that, friends, is where we now reside, I fear.

Species are living, breathing items of nature. We lose a bit of our collective soul when we drive species (and their entire lineages with them), prematurely and in large numbers, to oblivion. Tennyson, paraphrasing Goethe, hoped that we could transcend such errors when he wrote, in the same poem:

> I held it truth, with him who sings
> To one clear harp in divers tones
> That men may rise on stepping-stones
> Of their dead selves to higher things.

Why Do Species Matter?

Lilly-Marlene Russow

I. Introduction

Consider the following extension of the standard sort of objection to treating animals differently just because they are not humans: the fact that a being is or is not a member of species *S* is not a morally relevant fact, and does not justify treating that being differently from members of other species. If so, we cannot treat a bird differently *just* because it is a California condor rather than a turkey vulture. The problem, then, becomes one of determining what special obligations, if any, a person might have toward California condors, and what might account for those obligations in a way that is generally consistent with the condemnation of speciesism. Since it will turn out that the solution I offer does not admit of a direct and tidy proof, what follows comprises three sections which approach this issue from different directions. The resulting triangulation should serve as justification and motivation for the conclusion sketched in the final section.

II. Species and Individuals

Much of the discussion in the general area of ethics and animals has dealt with the rights of animals, or obligations and duties toward individual animals. The first thing to note is that some, but not all, of the actions normally thought of as obligatory with respect to the protection of vanishing species can be recast as possible duties to individual members of that species. Thus, if it could be shown that we have a *prima facie* duty not to kill a sentient being, it would follow that it would be wrong, other things being equal, to kill a blue whale or a California condor. But it would be wrong for the same reason, and to the same degree, that it would be wrong to kill a turkey vulture or a pilot whale. Similarly, if it is wrong (something which I do not think can be shown) to deprive an individual animal of its natural habitat, it would be wrong, for the same

reasons and to the same degree, to do that to a member of an endangered species. And so on. Thus, an appeal to our duties toward individual animals may provide some protection, but they do not justify the claim that we should treat members of a vanishing species with *more* care than members of other species.

More importantly, duties toward individual beings (or the rights of those individuals) will not always account for all the actions that people feel obligated to do for endangered species—e.g., bring into the world as many individuals of that species as possible, protect them from natural predation, or establish separate breeding colonies. In fact, the protection of a species might involve actions that are demonstrably contrary to the interests of some or all of the individual animals: this seems true in cases where we remove all the animals we can from their natural environment and raise them in zoos, or where we severely restrict the range of a species by hunting all those outside a certain area, as is done in Minnesota to protect the timber wolf. If such efforts are morally correct, our duties to preserve a species cannot be grounded in obligations that we have toward individual animals.

Nor will it be fruitful to treat our obligations to a species as duties toward, or as arising out of the rights of, a species thought of as some special superentity. It is simply not clear that we can make sense of talk about the interests of a species in the absence of beliefs, desires, purposeful actions, etc.[1] Since having interests is generally accepted as at least a necessary condition for having rights,[2] and since many of the duties we have toward animals arise directly out of the animals' interests, arguments which show that animals have rights, or that we have duties towards them, will not apply to species. Since arguments which proceed from interests to rights or from interests to obligations make up a majority of the literature on ethics and animals, it is unlikely that these arguments will serve as a key to possible obligations toward species.

Environmental Ethics, Vol. 3, No. 2 (Summer 1981) 101–12. Reprinted by permission of the publisher and author.

Having eliminated the possibility that our obligations toward species are somehow parallel to, or similar to, our obligations not to cause unwarranted pain to an animal, there seem to be only a few possibilities left. We may find that our duties toward species arise not out of the interests of the species, but are rooted in the general obligation to preserve things of value. Alternatively, our obligations to species may in fact be obligations to individuals (either members of the species or other individuals), but obligations that differ from the ones just discussed in that they are not determined simply by the interests of the individual.

III. Some Test Cases

If we are to find some intuitively acceptable foundation for claims about our obligations to protect species, we must start afresh. In order to get clear about what, precisely, we are looking for in this context, what obligations we might think we have toward species, what moral claims we are seeking a foundation for, I turn now to a description of some test cases. An examination of these cases illustrates why the object of our search is not something as straightforward as "Do whatever is possible or necessary to preserve the existence of the species"; a consideration of some of the differences between cases will guide our search for the nature of our obligations and the underlying reasons for those obligations.

Case 1. The snail darter is known to exist only in one part of one river. This stretch of river would be destroyed by the building of the Tellico dam. Defenders of the dam have successfully argued that the dam is nonetheless necessary for the economic development and well-being of the area's population. To my knowledge, no serious or large-scale attempt has been made to breed large numbers of snail darters in captivity (for any reason other than research).

Case 2. The Pére David deer was first discovered by a Western naturalist in 1865, when Pére Armand David found herds of the deer in the Imperial Gardens in Peking: even at that time, they were only known to exist in captivity. Pére David brought several animals back to Europe, where they bred readily enough so that now there are healthy populations in several major zoos.[3] There is no reasonable hope of reintroducing the Pére David deer to its natural habitat; indeed, it is not even definitely known what its natural habitat was.

Case 3. The red wolf (*Canis rufus*) formerly ranged over the southeastern and southcentral United States. As with most wolves, they were threatened, and their range curtailed, by trapping, hunting, and the destruction of habitat. However, a more immediate threat to the continued existence of the red wolf is that these changes extended the range of the more adaptable coyote, with whom the red wolf interbreeds very readily; as a result, there are very few "pure" red wolves left. An attempt has been made to capture some pure breeding stock and raise wolves on preserves.[4]

Case 4. The Baltimore oriole and the Bullock's oriole were long recognized and classified as two separate species of birds. As a result of extensive interbreeding between the two species in areas where their ranges overlapped, the American Ornithologists' Union recently declared that there were no longer two separate species; both ex-species are now called "northern orioles."

Case 5. The Appaloosa is a breed of horse with a distinctively spotted coat; the Lewis and Clark expedition discovered that the breed was associated with the Nez Percé Indians. When the Nez Percé tribe was defeated by the U.S. Cavalry in 1877 and forced to move, their horses were scattered and interbred with other horses. The distinctive coat pattern was almost lost; not until the middle of the twentieth century was a concerted effort made to gather together the few remaining specimens and reestablish the breed.

Case 6. Many strains of laboratory rats are bred specifically for a certain type of research. Once the need for a particular variety ceases—once the type of research is completed—the rats are usually killed, with the result that the variety becomes extinct.

Case 7. It is commonly known that several diseases such as sleeping sickness, malaria, and human encephalitis are carried by one variety of mosquito but not by others. Much of the disease control in these cases is aimed at exterminating the disease-carrying insect; most people do not find it morally wrong to wipe out the whole species.

Case 8. Suppose that zebras were threatened solely because they were hunted for their distinctive striped coats. Suppose, too, that we could remove this threat by selectively breeding zebras that are not striped, that look exactly like mules, although they are still pure zebras. Have we preserved all that we ought to have preserved?

What does an examination of these test cases reveal? First, that our concept of what a species *is* is not at all unambiguous; at least in part, what counts as a species is a matter of current fashions in taxonomy. Furthermore, it seems that it is not the sheer diversity or number of species that matters: if that were what is valued, moral preference would be given to taxonomic schemes that separated individuals into a larger number of species, a suggestion which seems absurd. The case of the orioles suggests that the decision as to whether to call these things one species or two is not a moral issue at all.[5] Since we are not evidently concerned with the existence or diversity of species in *this* sense, there must be something more at issue than the simple question of whether we have today the same number of species represented as we had yesterday. Confusion sets in, however, when we try to specify another sense in which it is possible to speak of the "existence" of a species. This only serves to emphasize the basic murkiness of our intuitions about what the object of our concern really is.

This murkiness is further revealed by the fact that it is not at all obvious what we are trying to preserve in some of the test cases. Sometimes, as in the case of the Appaloosa or attempts to save a subspecies like the Arctic wolf or the Mexican wolf, it is not a whole species that is in question. But not all genetic subgroups are of interest—witness the case of the laboratory rat—and sometimes the preservation of the species at the cost of one of its externally obvious features (the stripes on a zebra) is not our only concern. This is not a minor puzzle which can be resolved by changing our question from "why do species matter?" to "why do species and/or subspecies matter?" It is rather a serious issue of what makes a group of animals "special" enough or "unique" enough to warrant concern. And, of course, the test cases reveal that our intuitions are not always consistent: although the cases of the red wolf and the northern oriole are parallel in important respects, we are more uneasy about simply reclassifying the red wolf and allowing things to continue along their present path.

The final point to be established is that whatever moral weight is finally attached to the preservation of a species (or subspecies), it can be over-

ridden. We apparently have no compunction about wiping out a species of mosquito if the benefits gained by such action are sufficiently important, although many people were unconvinced by similar arguments in favor of the Tellico dam.

The lesson to be drawn from this section can be stated in a somewhat simplistic form: it is not simply the case that we can solve our problems by arguing that there is some value attached to the mere existence of a species. Our final analysis must take account of various features or properties of certain kinds or groups of animals, and it has to recognize that our concern is with the continued existence of individuals that may or may not have some distinctive characteristics.

IV. Some Traditional Answers

There are, of course, some standard replies to the question "Why do species matter?" or, more particularly, to the question "Why do we have at least a *prima facie* duty not to cause a species to become extinct, and in some cases, a duty to try actively to preserve species?" With some tolerance for borderline cases, these replies generally fall into three groups: (1) those that appeal to our role as "stewards" or "caretakers," (2) those that claim that species have some extrinsic value (I include in this group those that argue that the species is valuable as part of the ecosystem or as a link in the evolutionary scheme of things), and (3) those that appeal to some intrinsic or inherent value that is supposed to make a species worth preserving. In this section, with the help of the test cases just discussed, I indicate some serious flaws with each of these responses.

The first type of view has been put forward in the philosophical literature by Joel Feinberg, who states that our duty to preserve whole species may be more important than any rights had by individual animals.[6] He argues, first, that this duty does not arise from a right or claim that can properly be attributed to the species as a whole (his reasons are much the same as the ones I cited in Section II of this paper), and second, while we have some duty to unborn generations that directs us to preserve species, that duty is much weaker than the actual duty we have to preserve species. The fact that our actual duty extends beyond our duties to future generations is explained by the claim that we have duties of "stewardship" with respect to the world as a whole. Thus, Feinberg notes that his "inclination is to seek an explanation in terms of the requirements of our unique station as rational custodians of the planet we temporarily occupy."[7]

The main objection to this appeal to our role as stewards or caretakers is that it begs the question. The job of a custodian is to protect that which is deserving of protection, that which has some value or worth.[8] But the issue before us now is precisely *whether* species have value, and why. If we justify our obligations of stewardship by reference to the value of that which is cared for, we cannot also explain the value by pointing to the duties of stewardship.

The second type of argument is the one which establishes the value of a species by locating it in the "larger scheme of things." That is, one might try to argue that species matter because they contribute to, or form an essential part of, some other good. This line of defense has several variations.

The first version is completely anthropocentric: it is claimed that vanishing species are of concern to us because their difficulties serve as a warning that we have polluted or altered the environment in a way that is potentially dangerous or undesirable for us. Thus, the California condor, whose eggshells are weakened due to the absorption of DDT, indicates that something is wrong: presumably we are being affected in subtle ways by the absorption of DDT, and that is bad for us. Alternatively, diminishing numbers of game animals may signal overhunting which, if left unchecked, would leave the sportsman with fewer things to hunt. And, as we become more aware of the benefits that might be obtained from rare varieties of plants and animals (drugs, substitutes for other natural resources, tools for research), we may become reluctant to risk the disappearance of a species that might be of practical use to us in the future.

This line of argument does not carry us very far. In the case of a subspecies, most benefits could be derived from other varieties of the same species. More important, when faced with the loss of a unique variety or species, we may simply decide that, even taking into account the possibility of error, there is not enough reason to think that the species will ever be of use; we may take a calculated risk and decide that it is not worth it. Finally, the use of a species as a danger signal may apply to

species whose decline is due to some subtle and unforeseen change in the environment, but will not justify concern for a species threatened by a known and foreseen event like the building of a dam.

Other attempts to ascribe extrinsic value to a species do not limit themselves to potential human and practical goods. Thus, it is often argued that each species occupies a unique niche in a rich and complex, but delicately balanced, ecosystem. By destroying a single species, we upset the balance of the whole system. On the assumption that the system as a whole should be preserved, the value of a species is determined, at least in part, by its contribution to the whole.[9]

In assessing this argument, it is important to realize that such a justification (a) may lead to odd conclusions about some of the test cases, and (b) allows for changes which do not affect the system, or which result in the substitution of a richer, more complex system for one that is more primitive or less evolved. With regard to the first of these points, species that exist only in zoos would seem to have no special value. In terms of our test cases, the David deer does not exist as part of a system, but only in isolation. Similarly, the Appaloosa horse, a domesticated variety which is neither better suited nor worse than any other sort of horse, would not have any special value. In contrast, the whole cycle of mosquitoes, disease organisms adapted to these hosts, and other beings susceptible to those diseases is quite a complex and marvelous bit of systematic adaption. Thus, it would seem to be wrong to wipe out the encephalitis-bearing mosquito.

With regard to the second point, we might consider changes effected by white settlers in previously isolated areas such as New Zealand and Australia. The introduction of new species has resulted in a whole new ecosystem, with many of the former indigenous species being replaced by introduced varieties. As long as the new system works, there seems to be no grounds for objections.

The third version of an appeal to extrinsic value is sometimes presented in Darwinian terms: species are important as links in the evolutionary chain. This will get us nowhere, however, because the extinction of one species, the replacement of one by another, is as much a part of evolution as is the development of a new species.

One should also consider a more general concern about all versions of the argument which focus on the species' role in the natural order of things: all of these arguments presuppose that "the natural order of things" is, in itself, good. As William Blackstone pointed out, this is by no means obvious: "Unless one adheres dogmatically to a position of a 'reverence for all life,' the extinction of some species or forms of life may be seen as quite desirable. (This is parallel to the point often made by philosophers that not all 'customary' or 'natural' behavior is necessarily good)."[10] Unless we have some other way of ascribing value to a system, and to the animals which actually fulfill a certain function in that system (as opposed to possible replacements), the argument will not get off the ground.

Finally, then, the process of elimination leads us to the set of arguments which point to some *intrinsic value* that a species is supposed to have. The notion that species have an intrinsic value, if established, would allow us to defend much stronger claims about human obligations toward threatened species. Thus, if a species is intrinsically valuable, we should try to preserve it even when it no longer has a place in the natural ecosystem, or when it could be replaced by another species that would occupy the same niche. Most important, we should not ignore a species just because it serves no useful purpose.

Unsurprisingly, the stumbling block is what this intrinsic value might be grounded in. Without an explanation of that, we have no nonarbitrary way of deciding whether subspecies as well as species have intrinsic value or how much intrinsic value a species might have. The last question is meant to bring out issues that will arise in cases of conflict of interests: is the intrinsic value of a species of mosquito sufficient to outweigh the benefits to be gained by eradicating the means of spreading a disease like encephalitis? Is the intrinsic value of the snail darter sufficient to outweigh the economic hardship that might be alleviated by the construction of a dam? In short, to say that something has intrinsic value does not tell us *how much* value it has, nor does it allow us to make the sorts of judgments that are often called for in considering the fate of an endangered species.

The attempt to sidestep the difficulties raised by subspecies by broadening the ascription of value to include subspecies opens a whole Pandora's box. It would follow that any genetic variation within a species that results in distinctive charac-

teristics would need separate protection. In the case of forms developed through selective breeding, it is not clear whether we have a situation analogous to natural subspecies, or whether no special value is attached to different breeds.

In order to speak to either of these issues, and in order to lend plausibility to the whole enterprise, it would seem necessary to consider first the justification for ascribing value to whichever groups have such value. If intrinsic value does not spring from anything, if it becomes merely another way of saying that we should protect species, we are going around in circles, without explaining anything.[11] Some further explanation is needed.

Some appeals to intrinsic value are grounded in the intuition that diversity itself is a virtue. If so, it would seem incumbent upon us to create new species wherever possible, even bizarre ones that would have no purpose other than to be different. Something other than diversity must therefore be valued.

The comparison that is often made between species and natural wonders, spectacular landscapes, or even works of art, suggest that species might have some aesthetic value. This seems to accord well with our naive intuitions, provided that *aesthetic value* is interpreted rather loosely; most of us believe that the world would be a poorer place for the loss of bald eagles in the same way that it would be poorer for the loss of the Grand Canyon or a great work of art. In all cases, the experience of seeing these things is an inherently worthwhile experience. And since diversity in some cases is a component in aesthetic appreciation, part of the previous intuition would be preserved. There is also room for degrees of selectivity and concern with superficial changes: the variety of rat that is allowed to become extinct may have no special aesthetic value, and a bird is neither more nor less aesthetically pleasing when we change its name.

There are some drawbacks to this line of argument: there are some species which, by no stretch of the imagination, are aesthetically significant. But aesthetic value can cover a surprising range of things: a tiger may be simply beautiful; a blue whale is awe-inspiring; a bird might be decorative; an Appaloosa is of interest because of its historical significance; and even a drab little plant may inspire admiration for the marvelous way it has been adapted to a special environment. Even so, there may be species such as the snail darter that simply have no aesthetic value. In these cases, lacking any alternative, we may be forced to the conclusion that such species are not worth preserving.

Seen from other angles, once again the appeal to the aesthetic value of species is illuminating. Things that have an aesthetic value are compared and ranked in some cases, and commitment of resources may be made accordingly. We believe that diminishing the aesthetic value of a thing for mere economic benefit is immoral, but that aesthetic value is not absolute—that the fact that something has aesthetic value may be overridden by the fact that harming that thing, or destroying it, may result in some greater good. That is, someone who agrees to destroy a piece of Greek statuary for personal gain would be condemned as having done something immoral, but someone who is faced with a choice between saving his children and saving a "priceless" painting would be said to have skewed values if he chose to save the painting. Applying these observations to species, we can see that an appeal to aesthetic value would justify putting more effort into the preservation of one species than the preservation of another; indeed, just as we think that the doodling of a would-be artist may have no merit at all, we may think that the accidental and unfortunate mutation of a species is not worth preserving. Following the analogy, allowing a species to become extinct for *mere* economic gain might be seen as immoral, while the possibility remains open that other (human?) good might outweigh the goods achieved by the preservation of a species.

Although the appeal to aesthetic values has much to recommend it—even when we have taken account of the fact that it does not guarantee that all species matter—there seems to be a fundamental confusion that still affects the cogency of the whole argument and its application to the question of special obligations to endangered species, for if the value of a species is based on its aesthetic value, it is impossible to explain why an endangered species should be more valuable, or more worthy of preservation, than an unendangered species. The appeal to "rarity" will not help, if what we are talking about is species: each species is unique, no more or less rare than any other species: there is in each case one and only one species that we are talking about.[12]

This problem of application seems to arise because the object of aesthetic appreciation, and, hence, of aesthetic value, has been misidentified, for it is not the case that we perceive, admire, and appreciate a *species*—species construed either as a group or set of similar animals or as a name that we attach to certain kinds of animals in virtue of some classification scheme. What we value is the existence of individuals with certain characteristics. If this is correct, then the whole attempt to explain why species matter by arguing that *they* have aesthetic value needs to be redirected. This is what I try to do in the final section of this paper.

V. Valuing the Individual

What I propose is that the intuition behind the argument from aesthetic value is correct, but misdirected. The reasons that were given for the value of a species are, in fact, reasons for saying that an individual has value. We do not admire the grace and beauty of the species *Panthera tigris*; rather, we admire the grace and beauty of the individual Bengal tigers that we may encounter. What we value then is the existence of that individual and the existence (present or future) of individuals like that. The ways in which other individuals should be "like that" will depend on why we value that particular sort of individual: the stripes on a zebra do not matter if we value zebras primarily for the way they are adapted to a certain environment, their unique fitness for a certain sort of life. If, on the other hand, we value zebras because their stripes are aesthetically pleasing, the stripes do matter. Since our attitudes toward zebras probably include both of these features, it is not surprising to find that my hypothetical test case produces conflicting intuitions.

The shift of emphasis from species to individuals allows us to make sense of the stronger feelings we have about endangered species in two ways. First, the fact that there are very few members of a species—the fact that we rarely encounter one—itself increases the value of those encounters. I can see turkey vultures almost every day, and I can eat apples almost every day, but seeing a bald eagle or eating wild strawberries are experiences that are much less common, more delightful just for their rarity and unexpectedness. Even snail darters, which, if we encountered them every day would be drab and uninteresting, become more interesting just because we don't—or may not—see them every day. Second, part of our interest in an individual carries over to a desire that there be future opportunities to see these things again (just as when, upon finding a new and beautiful work of art, I will wish to go back and see it again). In the case of animals, unlike works of art, I know that this animal will not live forever, but that other animals like this one will have similar aesthetic value. Thus, because I value possible future encounters, I will also want to do what is needed to ensure the possibility of such encounters—i.e., make sure that enough presently existing individuals of this type will be able to reproduce and survive. This is rather like the duty that we have to support and contribute to museums, or to other efforts to preserve works of art.

To sum up, then: individual animals can have, to a greater or lesser degree, aesthetic value: they are valued for their simple beauty, for their awesomeness, for their intriguing adaptations, for their rarity, and for many other reasons. We have moral obligations to protect things of aesthetic value, and to ensure (in an odd sense) their continued existence; thus, we have a duty to protect individual animals (the duty may be weaker or stronger depending on the value of the individual), and to ensure that there will continue to be animals of this sort (this duty will also be weaker or stronger, depending on value).

I began this paper by suggesting that our obligations to vanishing species might appear inconsistent with a general condemnation of speciesism. My proposal is not inconsistent: we value and protect animals because of their aesthetic value, not because they are members of a given species.

Notes

1. Cf. Joel Feinberg, "The Rights of Animals and Future Generations," in *Philosophy and Environmental Crisis*, ed. William Blackstone (Athens: University of Georgia Press, 1974), pp. 55–57.

2. There are some exceptions to this: for example, Tom Regan argues that some rights are grounded in the intrinsic value of a thing in "Do Animals Have a Right to Life?" in *Animal Rights and Human Obligations*, eds. Tom Regan and Peter Singer (Englewood Cliffs, NJ: Prentice-Hall, 1975), pp. 198–203. These and similar cases will be dealt with by examining the proposed foundations of rights; thus, the claim that species have intrinsic value will be considered in Section III.

3. The deer in China were all killed during the Boxer rebellion; recently, several pairs were sent to Chinese zoos.

4. *Predator 7*, no. 2 (1980). Further complications occur in this case because a few scientists have tried to argue that all red wolves are the result of interbreeding between grey wolves (*Canis lupus*) and coyotes (*C. latans*). For more information, see L. David Mech, *The Wolf* (Garden City, NY: Natural History Press, 1970), pp. 22–25.

5. Sometimes there are moral questions about the practical consequences of such a move. The recent decision to combine two endangered species—the seaside sparrow and the dusky seaside sparrow—aggravates the difficulties faced by attempts to protect these birds.

6. Joel Feinberg, "Human Duties and Animal Rights," in *On the Fifth Day: Animal Rights and Human Ethics*, Richard Knowles Morris and Michael W. Fox, eds. (Washington: Acropolis Books, 1978), p. 67.

7. Ibid, p. 68.

8. Cf. Feinberg's discussion of custodial duties in "The Rights of Animals and Future Generations," *Philosophy and Environmental Crisis*, pp. 49–50.

9. A similar view has been defended by Tom Auxter, "The Right Not to Be Eaten," *Inquiry* 22 (1979): 222–23.

10. William Blackstone, "Ethics and Ecology," *Philosophy and Environmental Crisis*, p. 25.

11. This objection parallels Regan's attack on ungrounded appeals to the intrinsic value of human life as a way of trying to establish a human right to life. Cf. Thomas Regan, "Do Animals Have a Right to Life?" *Animal Rights and Human Obligations*, p. 199.

12. There is one further attempt that might be made to avoid this difficulty: one might argue that species do not increase in value due to scarcity, but that our duties to protect a valuable species involve more when the species is more in need of protection. This goes part of the way toward solving the problem, but does not yet capture our intuition that rarity does affect the value in some way.

Why Species Matter*

Holmes Rolston III

Sensitivity to the wonder of life . . . can sometimes make an environmental ethicist seem callous. On San Clemente Island, the U.S. Fish and Wildlife Service and the Natural Resource Office of the U.S. Navy planned to shoot two thousand feral goats to save three endangered plant species (*Malacothamnus clementinus, Castilleja grisea,* and *Delphinium kinkiense*), of which the surviving individuals numbered only a few dozen. After a protest, some goats were trapped and relocated. But trapping all of them was impossible, and many thousands were killed. In this instance, the survival of plant species was counted more than the lives of individual mammals; a few plants counted more than many thousands of goats.

Those who wish to restore rare species of big cats to the wild have asked about killing genetically inbred, inferior cats presently held in zoos, in order to make space available for the cats needed to reconstruct and maintain a population that is genetically more likely to survive upon release. All the Siberian tigers in zoos in North America are descendants of seven animals; if these tigers were replaced by others nearer to the wild type and with more genetic variability, the species might be saved in the wild. When we move to the level of species, sometimes we decide to kill individuals for the good of their kind.

Or we might now refuse to let nature take its course. The Yellowstone ethicists let the bison drown, in spite of its suffering; they let the blinded bighorns die. But in the spring of 1984 a sow grizzly and her three cubs walked across the ice of Yellowstone Lake to Frank Island, two miles from shore. They stayed several days to feast on two elk carcasses, and the ice bridge melted. Soon afterward, they were starving on an island too small to support them. This time the Yellowstone ethicists

promptly rescued the grizzlies and released them on the mainland, in order to protect an endangered species. They were not rescuing individual bears so much as saving the species.

Coloradans have declined to build the Two Forks Dam to supply urban Denver with water. Building the dam would require destroying a canyon and altering the Platte River flow, with many negative environmental consequences, including further endangering the whooping crane and endangering a butterfly, the Pawnee montane skipper. Elsewhere in the state, water development threatens several fish species, including the humpback chub, which requires the turbulent spring runoff stopped by dams. Environmental ethics doubts whether the good of humans who wish more water for development, both for industry and for bluegrass lawns, warrants endangering species of cranes, butterflies, and fish.

A species exists; a species ought to exist. An environmental ethic must make these assertions and move from biology to ethics with care. Species exist only instantiated in individuals, yet they are as real as individual plants or animals. The assertion that there are specific forms of life historically maintained in their environments over time seems as certain as anything else we believe about the empirical world. At times biologists revise the theories and taxa with which they map these forms, but species are not so much like lines of latitude and longitude as like mountains and rivers, phenomena objectively there to be mapped. The edges of these natural kinds will sometimes be fuzzy, to some extent discretionary. One species will slide into another over evolutionary time. But it does not follow from the fact that speciation is sometimes in progress that species are merely made up and not found as evolutionary lines with identity in time as well as space.

A consideration of species is revealing and challenging because it offers a biologically based counterexample to the focus on individuals—typi-

---

*This selection is the latter portion of Rolston's essay "Environmental Ethics: Values in and Duties to the Natural World," the first part of which we have reprinted in Part III under the title "Beyond Ethics by Extension."

"Environmental Ethics: Values in and Duties to the Natural World," by Holmes Rolston III, in *Ecology, Economics, Ethics: The Broken Circle,* edited by F. Herbert Bormann and Stephen R. Kellert (New Haven: Yale University Press, 1991), pp. 82–96. Reprinted by permission.

cally sentient and usually persons—so characteristic in classical ethics. In an evolutionary ecosystem, it is not mere individuality that counts; the species is also significant because it is a dynamic life-form maintained over time. The individual represents (re-presents) a species in each new generation. It is a token of a type, and the type is more important than the token.

A species lacks moral agency, reflective self-awareness, sentience, or organic individuality. The older, conservative ethic will be tempted to say that specific-level processes cannot count morally. Duties must attach to singular lives, most evidently those with a self, or some analogue to self. In an individual organism, the organs report to a center; the good of a whole is defended. The members of a species report to no center. A species has no self. It is not a bounded singular. There is no analogue to the nervous hookups or circulatory flows that characterize the organism.

But singularity, centeredness, selfhood, and individuality are not the only processes to which duty attaches. A more radically conservative ethic knows that having a biological identity reasserted genetically over time is as true of the species as of the individual. Identity need not attach solely to the centered organism; it can persist as a discrete pattern over time. From this way of thinking, it follows that the life the individual has is something passing through the individual as much as something it intrinsically possesses. The individual is subordinate to the species, not the other way around. The genetic set, in which is coded the telos, is as evidently the property of the species as of the individual through which it passes. A consideration of species strains any ethic fixed on individual organisms, much less on sentience or persons. But the result can be biologically sounder, though it revises what was formerly thought logically permissible or ethically binding. When ethics is informed by this kind of biology, it is appropriate to attach duty dynamically to the specific form of life.

The species line is the vital living system, the whole, of which individual organisms are the essential parts. The species too has its integrity, its individuality, its right to life (if we must use the rhetoric of rights); and it is more important to protect this vitality than to protect individual integrity. The right to life, biologically speaking, is an adaptive fit that is right for life, that survives over millennia. This idea generates at least a presumption that species in a niche are good right where they are, and therefore that it is right for humans to let them be, to let them evolve.

Processes of value that we earlier found in an organic individual appear at the specific level: defending a particular form of life, pursuing a pathway through the world, resisting death (extinction), regenerating, maintaining a normative identity over time, expressing creative resilience by discovering survival skills. It is as logical to say that the individual is the species' way of propagating itself as to say that the embryo or egg is the individual's way of propagating itself. The dignity resides in the dynamic form; the individual inherits this form, exemplifies it, and passes it on. If, at the specific level, these processes are just as evident, or even more so, what prevents duties from arising at that level? The appropriate survival unit is the appropriate level of moral concern.

A shutdown of the life stream is the most destructive event possible. The wrong that humans are doing, or allowing to happen through carelessness, is stopping the historical vitality of life, the flow of natural kinds. Every extinction is an incremental decay in this stopping of life, no small thing. Every extinction is a kind of superkilling. It kills forms (species) beyond individuals. It kills essences beyond existences, the soul as well as the body. It kills collectively, not just distributively. It kills birth as well as death. Afterward nothing of that kind either lives or dies.

Ought species x to exist? is a distributive increment in the collective question, ought life on Earth to exist? Life on Earth cannot exist without its individuals, but a lost individual is always reproducible; a lost species is never reproducible. The answer to the species question is not always the same as the answer to the collective question, but because life on Earth is an aggregate of many species, the two are sufficiently related that the burden of proof lies with those who wish deliberately to extinguish a species and simultaneously to care for life on Earth.

One form of life has never endangered so many others. Never before has this level of question—superkilling by a superkiller—been deliberately faced. Humans have more understanding than ever of the natural world they inhabit and of the speciating processes, more predictive power to foresee the intended and unintended results of their actions, and more power to reverse the undesirable consequences. The duties that such power and vision generate no longer attach simply to individuals or persons but are emerging duties to specific forms of life. What is ethically callous is the maelstrom of killing and insensitivity to forms of life and the sources producing them. What is required is principled responsibility to the biospheric Earth.

Human activities seem misfit in the system. Although humans are maximizing their own species interests, and in this respect behaving as does each of the other species, they do not have any adaptive fitness. They are not really fitting into the evolutionary processes of ongoing biological conservation and elaboration. Their cultures are not really dynamically stable in their ecosystems. Such behavior is therefore not right. Yet humanistic ethical systems limp when they try to prescribe right conduct here. They seem misfits in the roles most recently demanded of them.

If, in this world of uncertain moral convictions, it makes any sense to assert that one ought not to kill individuals without justification, it makes more sense to assert that one ought not to superkill the species without superjustification. Several billion years' worth of creative toil, several million species of teeming life, have been handed over to the care of this late-coming species in which mind has flowered and morals have emerged. Ought not this sole moral species do something less self-interested than count all the produce of an evolutionary ecosystem as nothing but human resources? Such an attitude hardly seems biologically informed, much less ethically adequate. It is too provincial for intelligent humanity. Life on Earth is a many-splendored thing; extinction dims its luster. An ethics of respect for life is urgent at the level of species.

Ecosystems

A species is what it is where it is. No environmental ethics has found its way on Earth until it finds an ethic for the biotic communities in which all destinies are entwined. "A thing is right," urged Aldo Leopold (1968 [1949]), "when it tends to preserve the integrity, stability, and beauty of the biotic community. It is wrong when it tends otherwise." Again, we have two parts to the ethic: first, that eco-

systems exist, both in the wild and in support of culture; second, that ecosystems ought to exist, both for what they are in themselves and as modified by culture. Again, we must move with care from the biological assertions to the ethical assertions.

Giant forest fires raged over Yellowstone National Park in the summer of 1988, consuming nearly a million acres despite the efforts of a thousand fire fighters. By far the largest ever known in the park, the fires seemed a disaster. But the Yellowstone land ethic enjoined: "Let nature take its course; let it burn." So the fires were not fought at first, but in midsummer, national authorities overrode that policy and ordered the fires put out. Even then, weeks later, fires continued to burn, partly because they were too big to control but partly too because Yellowstone personnel did not really want the fires put out. Despite the evident destruction of trees, shrubs, and wildlife, they believe that fires are a good thing—even when the elk and bison leave the park in search of food and are shot by hunters. Fires reset succession, release nutrients, recycle materials, and renew the biotic community. (Nearby, in the Teton wilderness, a storm blew down fifteen thousand acres of trees, and some people proposed that the area be disclassified from wilderness to allow commercial salvage of the timber. But a similar environmental ethic said, "No, let it rot.")

Aspen are important in the Yellowstone ecosystem. Although some aspen stands are climax and self-renewing, many are seral and give way to conifers. Aspen groves support many birds and much wildlife, especially beavers, whose activities maintain the riparian zones. Aspen are rejuvenated after fires, and the Yellowstone land ethic wants the aspen for their critical role in the biotic community. Elk browse the young aspen stems. To a degree this is a good thing, because it provides the elk with critical nitrogen, but in excess it is a bad thing. The elk have no predators, because the wolves are gone, and as a result the elk overpopulate. Excess elk also destroy the willows, and that destruction in turn destroys the beavers. So, in addition to letting fires burn, rejuvenating the aspen might require park managers to cull hundreds of elk—all for the sake of a healthy ecosystem.

The Yellowstone ethic wishes to restore wolves to the greater Yellowstone ecosystem. At the level of species, this change is desired because of what the wolf is in itself, but it is also desired because the greater Yellowstone ecosystem does not have its full integrity, stability, and beauty without this majestic animal at the top of the trophic pyramid. Restoring the wolf as a top predator would mean suffering and death for many elk, but that would be a good thing for the aspen and willows, the beavers, and the riparian habitat and would have mixed benefits for the bighorns and mule deer (the overpopulating elk consume their food, but the sheep and deer would also be consumed by the wolves). Restoration of wolves would be done over the protests of ranchers who worry about wolves eating their cattle; many of them also believe that the wolf is a bloodthirsty killer, a bad kind. Nevertheless, the Yellowstone ethic demands wolves, as it does fires, in appropriate respect for life in its ecosystem.

Letting nature take its ecosystemic course is why the Yellowstone ethic forbade rescuing the drowning bison but required rescuing the sow grizzly and her cubs, the latter case to insure that the big predators remain. After the bison drowned, coyotes, foxes, magpies, and ravens fed on the carcass. Later, even a grizzly bear fed on it. All this is a good thing because the system cycles on. On that account, rescuing the whales trapped in the winter ice seems less of a good thing, when we note that rescuers had to drive away polar bears that attempted to eat the dying whales.

Classical, humanistic ethics finds ecosystems to be unfamiliar territory. It is difficult to get the biology right and, superimposed on the biology, to get the ethics right. Fortunately, it is often evident that human welfare depends on ecosystemic support, and in this sense all our legislation about clean air, clean water, soil conservation, national and state forest policies, pollution controls, renewable resources, and so forth is concerned about ecosystem-level processes. Furthermore, humans find much of value preserving wild ecosystems, and our wilderness and park system is impressive.

Still, a comprehensive environmental ethics needs the best, naturalistic reasons, as well as the good, humanistic ones, for respecting ecosystems. Ecosystems generate and support life, keep selection pressures high, enrich situated fitness, and allow congruent kinds to evolve in their places with sufficient containment. The ecologist finds that eco-systems are objectively satisfactory communities in the sense that organismic needs are sufficiently met for species to survive and flourish, and the critical ethicist finds (in a subjective judgment matching the objective process) that such ecosystems are satisfactory communities to which to attach duty. Our concern must be for the fundamental unit of survival.

An ecosystem, the conservative ethicist will say, is too low a level of organization to be respected intrinsically. Ecosystems can seem little more than random, statistical processes. A forest can seem a loose collection of externally related parts, the collection of fauna and flora a jumble, hardly a community. The plants and animals within an ecosystem have needs, but their interplay can seem simply a matter of distribution and abundance, birth rates and death rates, population densities, parasitism and predation, dispersion, checks and balances, and stochastic process. Much is not organic at all (rain, groundwater, rocks, soil particles, air), and some organic material is dead and decaying debris (fallen trees, scat, humus). These things have no organized needs. There is only catch-as-catch-can scrimmage for nutrients and energy, not really enough of an integrated process to call the whole a community.

Unlike higher animals, ecosystems have no experiences; they do not and cannot care. Unlike plants, an ecosystem has no organized center, no genome. It does not defend itself against injury or death. Unlike a species, there is no ongoing telos, no biological identity reinstantiated over time. The organismic parts are more complex than the community whole. More troublesome still, an ecosystem can seem a jungle where the fittest survive, a place of contest and conflict, beside which the organism is a model of cooperation. In animals the heart, liver, muscles, and brain are tightly integrated, as are the leaves, cambium, and roots in plants. But the so-called ecosystem community is pushing and shoving between rivals, each aggrandizing itself, or else seems to be all indifference and haphazard juxtaposition—nothing to call forth our admiration.

Environmental ethics must break through the boundary posted by disoriented ontological conservatives, who hold that only organisms are real, actually existing as entities, whereas ecosystems are nominal—just interacting individuals. Oak trees are real, but forests are nothing but collections of trees. But any level is real if it shapes behavior on the level below it. Thus, the cell is real because that pattern shapes the behavior of amino acids; the organism, because that pattern coordinates the behavior of hearts and lungs. The biotic community is real because the niche shapes the morphology of the oak trees within it. Being real at the level of community requires only an organization that shapes the behavior of its members.

The challenge is to find a clear model of community and to discover an ethics for it: better biology for better ethics. Even before the rise of ecology, biologists began to conclude that the combative survival of the fittest distorts the truth. The more perceptive model is coaction in adapted fit. Predator and prey, parasite and host, grazer and grazed, are contending forces in dynamic process in which the well-being of each is bound up with the other—coordinated as much as heart and liver are coordinated organically. The ecosystem supplies the coordinates through which each organism moves, outside which the species cannot really be located.

The community connections are looser than the organism's internal interconnections but are not less significant. Admiring organic unity in organisms and stumbling over environmental looseness is like valuing mountains and despising valleys. The matrix that the organism requires to survive is the open, pluralistic ecological system. Internal complexity—heart, liver, muscles, brain—arises as a way of dealing with a complex, tricky environment. The skin-out processes are not just the support; they are the subtle source of the skin-in processes. In the complete picture, the outside is as vital as the inside. Had there been either simplicity or lockstep concentrated unity in the environment, no organismic unity could have evolved. Nor would it remain. There would be less elegance in life.

To look at one level for what is appropriate at another makes a mistake in categories. One should not look for a single center or program in ecosystems, much less for subjective experiences. Instead, one should look for a matrix, for interconnections between centers (individual plants and animals, dynamic lines of speciation), for creative stimulus and open-ended potential. Everything will be connected to many other things, sometimes by obligate associations but more often by partial and pliable dependencies, and, among other things, there will be no significant interactions. There will be functions in a communal sense: shunts and crisscrossing pathways, cybernetic subsystems and feedback loops. An order arises spontaneously and systematically when many self-concerned units jostle and seek to fulfill their own programs, each doing its own thing and forced into informed interaction.

An ecosystem is a productive, projective system. Organisms defend only their selves, with individuals defending their continuing survival and with species increasing the numbers of kinds. But the evolutionary ecosystem spins a bigger story, limiting each kind, locking it into the welfare of others, promoting new arrivals, increasing kinds and the integration of kinds. Species increase their kind, but ecosystems increase kinds, superposing the latter increase onto the former. Ecosystems are selective systems, as surely as organisms are selective systems. The natural selection comes out of the system and is imposed on the individual. The individual is programmed to make more of its kind, but more is going on systemically than that; the system is making more kinds.

Communal processes—the competition between organisms, statistically probable interactions, plant and animal successions, speciation over historical time—generate an ever-richer community. Hence the evolutionary toil, elaborating and diversifying the biota, that once began with no species and results today in five million species, increasing over time the quality of lives in the upper rungs of the trophic pyramids. One-celled organisms evolved into many-celled, highly integrated organisms. Photosynthesis evolved and came to support locomotion—swimming, walking, running, flight. Stimulus-response mechanisms became complex instinctive acts. Warm-blooded animals followed cold-blooded ones. Complex nervous systems, conditioned behavior, and learning emerged. Sentience appeared—sight, hearing, smell, taste, pleasure, pain. Brains coupled with hands. Consciousness and self-consciousness arose. Culture was superposed on nature.

These developments do not take place in all ecosystems or at every level. Microbes, plants, and lower animals remain, good of their kinds and, serving continuing roles, good for other kinds. The understories remain occupied. As a result, the quantity of life and its diverse qualities continue— from protozoans to primates to people. There is a push-up, lock-up ratchet effect that conserves the upstrokes and the outreaches. The later we go in time, the more accelerated are the forms at the top of the trophic pyramids, the more elaborated are the multiple trophic pyramids of Earth. There are upward arrows over evolutionary time.

The system is a game with loaded dice, but the loading is a pro-life tendency, not mere stochastic process. Though there is no Nature in the singular, the system has a nature, a loading that pluralizes, putting natures into diverse kinds: nature$_1$, nature$_2$, nature$_3$ ... nature$_n$. It does so using random elements (in both organisms and communities), but this is a secret of its fertility, producing steadily intensified interdependencies and options. An ecosystem has no head, but it heads toward species diversification, support, and richness. Though not a superorganism, it is a kind of vital field.

Instrumental value uses something as a means to an end; intrinsic value is worthwhile in itself. No warbler eats insects to become food for a falcon; the warbler defends its own life as an end in itself and makes more warblers as it can. A life is defended intrinsically, without further contributory reference. But neither of these traditional terms is satisfactory at the level of the ecosystem. Though it has value *in* itself, the system does not have any value *for* itself. Though it is a value producer, it is not a value owner. We are no longer confronting instrumental value, as though the system were of value instrumentally as a fountain of life. Nor is the question one of intrinsic value, as though the system defended some unified form of life for itself. We have reached something for which we need a third term: systemic value. Duties arise in encounters with the system that projects and protects these member components in biotic community.

Ethical conservatives, in the humanistic sense, will say that ecosystems are of value only because they contribute to human experiences. But that mistakes the last chapter for the whole story, one fruit for the whole plant. Humans count enough to have the right to flourish in ecosystems, but not so much that they have the right to degrade or shut down ecosystems, not at least without a burden of proof that there is an overriding cultural gain. Those who have traveled partway into environmental ethics will say that ecosystems are of value be-cause they contribute to animal experiences or to organismic life. But the really conservative, radical view sees that the stability, integrity, and beauty of biotic communities are what are most fundamentally to be conserved. In a comprehensive ethics of respect for life, we ought to set ethics at the level of ecosystems alongside classical, humanistic ethics.

Value Theory

In practice the ultimate challenge of environmental ethics is the conservation of life on Earth. In principle the ultimate challenge is a value theory profound enough to support that ethics. In nature there is negentropic construction in dialectic with entropic teardown, a process for which we hardly yet have an adequate scientific theory, much less a valuational theory. Yet this is nature's most striking feature, one that ultimately must be valued and of value. In one sense, nature is indifferent to mountains, rivers, fauna, flora, forests, and grasslands. But in another sense, nature has bent toward making and remaking these projects, millions of kinds, for several billion years.

These performances are worth noticing, are remarkable and memorable—and not just because of their tendencies to produce something else; certainly not merely because of their tendency to produce this noticing in certain recent subjects, our human selves. These events are loci of value as products of systemic nature in its formative processes. The splendors of Earth do not simply lie in their roles as human resources, supports of culture, or stimulators of experience. The most plausible account will find some programmatic evolution toward value, and not because it ignores Darwin but because it heeds his principle of natural selection and deploys it into a selection exploring new niches and elaborating kinds, even a selection upslope toward higher values, at least along some trends within some ecosystems. How do we humans come to be charged up with values, if there was and is nothing in nature charging us up so? A systematic environmental ethics does not wish to believe in the special creation of values or in their dumbfounding epigenesis. Let them evolve. Let nature carry value.

The notion that nature is a value carrier is ambiguous. Much depends on a thing's being more or less structurally congenial for the carriage. We value a thing and discover that we are under the sway of its valence, inducing our behavior. It has among its strengths (Latin: *valeo*, "be strong") this capacity to carry value. This potential cannot always be of the empty sort that a glass has for carrying water. It is often pregnant fullness. Some of the values that nature carries are up to us, our assignment. But fundamentally there are powers in nature that move to us and through us.

No value exists without an evaluator. So runs a well-entrenched dogma. Humans clearly evaluate their world; sentient animals may also. But plants cannot evaluate their environment; they have no options and make no choices. A fortiori, species and ecosystems, Earth and Nature, cannot be bona fide evaluators. One can always hang on to the assertion that value, like a tickle or remorse, must be felt to be there. Its *esse* is *percipi*. To be, it must be perceived. Nonsensed value is nonsense. There are no thoughts without a thinker, no percepts without a perceiver, no deeds without a doer, no targets without an aimer.

Such resolute subjectivists cannot be defeated by argument, although they can be driven toward analyticity. That theirs is a retreat to definition is difficult to expose, because they seem to cling so closely to inner experience. They are reporting, on this hand, how values always excite us. They are giving, on that hand, a stipulative definition. That is how they choose to use the word *value*.

If value arrives only with consciousness, experiences in which humans find value have to be dealt with as appearances of various sorts. The value has to be relocated in the valuing subject's creativity as a person meets a valueless world, or even a valuable one—one able to be valued but one that before the human bringing of valuableness contains only possibility and not any actual value. Value can only be extrinsic to nature, never intrinsic to it.

But the valuing subject in any otherwise valueless world is an insufficient premise for the experienced conclusions of those who respect all life. Conversion to a biological view seems truer to world experience and more logically compelling. Something from a world beyond the human mind, beyond human experience, is received into our mind, our experience, and the value of that something does not always arise with our evaluation of it. Here the order of knowing reverses, and also enhances, the order of being. This too is a perspective

but is ecologically better-informed. Science has been steadily showing how the consequents (life, mind) are built on their precedents (energy, matter), however much they overleap them. Life and mind appear where they did not before exist, and with them levels of value emerge that did not before exist. But that gives no reason to say that all value is an irreducible emergent at the human (or upper-animal) level. A comprehensive environmental ethics reallocates value across the whole continuum. Value increases in the emergent climax but is continuously present in the composing precedents. The system is value-able, able to produce value. Human evaluators are among its products.

Some value depends on subjectivity, yet all value is generated within the geosystemic and ecosystemic pyramid. Systemically, value fades from subjective to objective value but also fans out from the individual to its role and matrix. Things do not have their separate natures merely in and for themselves, but they face outward and co-fit into broader natures. Value-in-itself is smeared out to become value-in-togetherness. Value seeps out into the system, and we lose our capacity to identify the individual as the sole locus of value.

Intrinsic value, the value of an individual for what it is in itself, becomes problematic in a holistic web. True, the system produces such values more and more with its evolution of individuality and freedom. Yet to decouple this value from the biotic, communal system is to make value too internal and elementary; this decoupling forgets relatedness and externality. Every intrinsic value has leading and trailing *and*'s. Such value is coupled with value from which it comes and toward which it moves. Adapted fitness makes individualistic value too system-independent. Intrinsic value is a part in a whole and is not to be fragmented by valuing it in isolation.

Everything is good in a role, in a whole, although we can speak of objective intrinsic goodness wherever a point-event—a trillium, for example—defends a good (its life) in itself. We can speak of subjective intrinsic goodness when such an event registers as a point-experience, at which point humans pronounce both their experience and what it is to be good without need to enlarge their focus. Neither the trilliums nor the human judges of it require for their respective valuings any further contributory reference.

When eaten by foragers or in death resorbed into humus, the trillium has its value destroyed, transformed into instrumentality. The system is a value transformer where form and being, process and reality, fact and value, are inseparably joined. Intrinsic and instrumental values shuttle back and forth, parts-in-wholes and wholes-in-parts, local details of value embedded in global structures, gems in their settings, and their setting-situation a corporation where value cannot stand alone. Every good is in community.

In environmental ethics one's beliefs about nature, which are based upon but exceed science, have everything to do with beliefs about duty. The way the world is informs the way it ought to be. We always shape our values in significant measure in accord with our notion of the kind of universe that we live in, and this process drives our sense of duty. Our model of reality implies a model of conduct. Differing models sometimes imply similar conduct, but often they do not. A model in which nature has no value apart from human preferences will imply different conduct from one in which nature projects fundamental values, some objective and others that further require human subjectivity superimposed on objective nature.

This evaluation is not scientific description; hence it is not ecology per se but metaecology. No amount of research can verify that, environmentally, the right is the optimum biotic community. Yet ecological description generates this valuing of nature, endorsing the systemic rightness. The transition from *is* to *good* and thence to *ought* occurs here; we leave science to enter the domain of evaluation, from which an ethics follows.

What is ethically puzzling and exciting is that an *ought* is not so much derived from an *is* as discovered simultaneously with it. As we progress from descriptions of fauna and flora, of cycles and pyramids, of autotrophs coordinated with heterotrophs, of stability and dynamism, on to intricacy, planetary opulence and interdependence, unity and harmony with oppositions in counterpoint and synthesis, organisms evolved within and satisfactorily fitting their communities, and we arrive at length at beauty and goodness, we find that it is difficult to say where the natural facts leave off and where the natural values appear. For some people at least, the sharp *is-ought* dichotomy is gone; the values seem to be there as soon as the facts are fully in, and both values and facts seem to be alike properties of the system.

There is something overspecialized about an ethic, held by the dominant class of *Homo sapiens*, that regards the welfare of only one of several million species as an object and beneficiary of duty. If the remedy requires a paradigm change about the sorts of things to which duty can attach, so much the worse for those humanistic ethics no longer functioning in, or suited to, their changing environment. The anthropocentrism associated with them was fiction anyway. There is something Newtonian, not yet Einsteinian, besides something morally naive, about living in a reference frame in which one species takes itself as absolute and values everything else relative to its utility. If true to its specific epithet, which means wise, ought not *Homo sapiens* value this host of life as something that lays on us a claim to care for life in its own right?

Only the human species contains moral agents, but perhaps conscience on such an Earth ought not to be used to exempt every other form of life from consideration, with the resulting paradox that the sole moral species acts only in its collective self-interest toward all the rest. Is not the ultimate philosophical task the discovery of a whole great ethic that knows the human place under the sun?

Toward the Moral Considerability of Species and Ecosystems _____

Lawrence E. Johnson*

Introduction

Of considerable importance to our environmental ethics, and a matter of much debate, is the moral status of species and ecosystems, and perhaps that of certain other wholes. Of related importance is the question of what such things *are*. I take a fairly strong line on these matters. I maintain that species and ecosystems (and certain other things, for that matter) are entities, that they have interests—and, moreover, that those interests and all interests, are morally significant. I do not discuss this last claim here, though I do argue for it elsewhere.[1] Here I concentrate on the claims that they are entities and that they have interests. I have also argued in favor of those claims elsewhere, in connection with species.[2] Here I propose to develop these claims further, and to extend them to include ecosystems as well. I defend these claims against objections that such beings cannot have identity or interests because evolution does not proceed on that level. My purpose, however, is not primarily to refute these objections, but rather, more positively, to try to clarify what my claims mean and what their truth amounts to. To do this adequately, I examine not only what species and ecosystems are, but also what it means to say that such things count as entities and have interests. These questions cannot be fully separated. To ask what a species or an ecosystem is, we must ask whether they are entities of some sort. Yet we cannot begin by first asking what an entity is. That would be impossibly general. Rather we must ask what it might mean to say that a species, or an ecosystem, is an entity, and then determine whether it is possible for things of that sort to have interests.

*Philosophy Discipline, School of Humanities, The Flinders University of South Australia, P.O. Box 2100, Adelaide, South Australia 5001. Johnson is the author of *A Morally Deep World: An Essay in Moral Considerability and Environmental Ethics* (New York: Cambridge University Press, 1991).

Species as Entities

Let us begin by asking what it is for a species to be an entity. While doing so, we glance sideways at such questions as what it means for an individual organism, a lichen, a slime mold, an ecosystem, or Gaia to be an entity. In a sense, such questions can easily be answered: everything is a thing. While obvious, and indeed true, such an answer is trivial. There are lots of ways of being something. For each thing, we must ask what sort of thing is *that* thing. In particular, we must sharpen the focus on what it is we are trying to figure out, and what problems we are trying to solve, when we try to figure out whether species are entities.

Presumably we can all agree that individual organisms are unproblematically entities. The standard view has been that species are collections of individual organisms. But collections of what sort? Traditionally, it was held to be a class of relevantly similar organisms. One problem with this position, however, is that it is not always easy (or even possible) to find some feature which they all have in common and which distinguishes them from members of other species. If we are dealing with a species that is distinct and fairly uniform, it may be possible to define a class of relevantly similar individuals—though it does not thereby follow that this would be the best approach to understanding such a species. If we are dealing with a species that has a wide degree of variation, or even different forms or life stages, there may be no feature whatever that they all have in common.

The closest alternative is to try to conceive of a species as being a class tied together by some scheme of so-called "family resemblances." This approach can be made to work, to a point, and it works better than the preceding scheme. Nevertheless, we no longer have *the* characteristic of a species. Moreover, one has a sense that the family-resemblance scheme for the species is stitched together after the fact. Instead of the species being

Environmental Ethics, Vol. 14, No. 2 (Summer 1992), 145–157. Reprinted by permission.

what it is because it has certain characteristics, a scheme of characteristics is settled upon describing what the species happens to be. What, then, if anything at all, is a species?

The problem is further complicated by the fact that unlike most classes we cannot just give a particular species an ostensive definition. We cannot just say that it is a class composed of that, that, . . . and that, for the simple reason that the membership of the species is continuously changing. The species *Homo sapiens*, for example, has a differing membership every time someone is born or dies. Classes aren't supposed to change membership like that. Indeed, if a class is defined by what its membership is, it *cannot* change membership at all while still being that class. Yet a species may, over the years, come to have an entirely different membership while remaining, at least pretty much, the same species. Some species may remain the same, as much as we can tell, for thousands or even millions of years. Others may change much more rapidly. All species, nevertheless, do change over time, and this fact is another problem for the claim that species are classes of some sort. Species change. They evolve. They sometimes branch into two or more species. Most eventually become extinct. Classes don't do things like that. Actually, classes don't *do* anything. Thus, whatever species are, they evidently aren't classes, at least not according to anything like the standard conception of what a class is. Anyone who wanted to insist that they are classes would have to invent some radically new conception.

What species are, or are not, is currently a matter of considerable debate among biologists and those concerned with the philosophy of biology. These days, most thinking about species is in terms of their evolutionary role, shaped by their environment and formed on the basis of—indeed, formed as articulations of—their evolving genetic lineages. In a sense, a limited one, of course, organisms are viewed as DNA's way of making more DNA. Perhaps the boldest suggestion is the proposal that species are entities in their own right, that they are, in a manner of speaking, "super organisms." The idea is that a species is a genetic lineage, a whole ongoing biological life process. Unlike a great many other entities, though not unlike all of them, a species-entity spans a number of spatially separate individuals. Still, through internal and external

factors, this genetic lineage maintains itself in its environment as a fairly cohesive entity. When a species branches off from its ancestral species, it assumes its own identity as a separate entity.

Conceptions of species as entities—there is more than one such conception—have historically been associated with "punctuated-equilibria" views about evolution, and the first major expression of a species as entity was put forward in association with such a theory. According to the punctuated-equilibrium theory, species stay more or less the same until, relatively suddenly (by evolutionary time scales), a new one springs up, one having its own identity.

Theories toward the sudden-leaps end of the spectrum tend to be more receptive to the species-as-entities conception because they often view species as having separate identities. Most gradualistic theories portray species as blending into one another, creating a host of messy questions about where to draw the line, thereby discouraging the idea that species are entities in their own right. This difficulty is summarized as follows by Richard Dawkins, a gradualist who denies that species are entities:

> [T]he punctuationists . . . make a big point of treating 'the species' as a real 'entity'. To a non-punctuationist, 'the species' is definable only because the awkward intermediates are dead. An extreme anti-punctuationist, taking a long view of the entirety of evolution history, cannot see 'the species' as a discrete entity at all. He can see only a smeary continuum. On his view a species never has a clearly defined beginning, and it only sometimes has a clearly defined end (extinction); often a species does not end decisively but turns gradually into a new species. A punctuationist, on the other hand, sees a species as coming into existence at a particular time (strictly there is a transition period with a duration of tens of thousands of years, but this duration is short by geological standards). Moreover, he sees a species as having a definite, or at least rapidly accomplished, end, not a gradual fading into a new species. Since most of the life of a species, on the punctuationist view, is spent in unchanging stasis, and since a species has a discrete beginning and end, it follows that, to a punctuationist, a species can be said to have a definite, measurable 'life span'. The non-punctuationist would not see a species as hav-

ing a 'life span' like an individual organism. The extreme punctuationist sees 'the species' as a discrete entity that really deserves its own name. The extreme anti-punctuationist sees 'the species' as an arbitrary stretch of continuously flowing river, with no particular reason to draw lines delimiting its beginning and end.[3]

The problem of where to draw the line is not the only difficulty that can be raised against the idea that species are entities, and we shall consider others in due course. It is, nonetheless, a problem of considerable importance, a problem which must be faced up to, and one which gives us a good place to start.

Where Do You Draw the Line?

If the difficulty—more like impossibility—of drawing precise lines *did* exclude the possibility of species being viewed as entities, then we would just have to abandon the idea. This would be so even if we adopted a punctuationist account, for on any form of punctuationism (short of a theory of special creation) there would still be a transitional period when the nature and boundaries of the species were indeterminate. That it was a relatively short period of indeterminacy would logically be beside the point. To the very limited extent to which I am entitled to have a view on such a subject, I am inclined toward gradualism. Nevertheless, I maintain that a resolution of that issue does not mandate or preclude any conclusion on the issue of whether species are entities.

I argue that it is possible to get around the line-drawing problem while still maintaining that species are entities in a meaningful and worthwhile sense. Whether they truly are entities is a further question, independent of the question of boundaries. First, however, we must attend to the conceptual problem of whether entities need precise boundary lines. I argue that sharp boundaries for entities are only conceptual conveniences, and not ontological necessities.

The easiest way to demonstrate that determinate boundaries are not necessary in order to be an entity is to take a look at a counterexample. Consider the planet Jupiter. We cannot use its surface as a boundary for the simple reason that it doesn't have one. Although the core of the planet is surrounded by liquids and gases, which are part of the

planet, they do not have any precise boundaries or termination. They just get thinner as they get farther from the center, until eventually there is not quite empty space. We can define some boundary to suit ourselves, but that is one which we have formulated, not one which is inherently real. Yet Jupiter undoubtedly is an entity.

Jupiter, however, is not an entity that is very similar to a living being. Let us turn to an example which is closer at hand, individual organisms. Although it's easy to think that an organism is a determinate entity—one with a definite beginning and end in time, filling a particular volume of space, and having its own particular identity, it is not really all that clear-cut. Individual organisms are a bit fuzzy around the edges, with a fuzziness that may be instructive as we think about species. To start with, the conception of an individual does not take place at a specific moment, but is a process that goes on for as much as twenty-four hours, without having an exact beginning. Neither is death something which happens at a precise moment, as current controversies make clear. Some vital functions continue longer than others. (Indeed, certain life processes, such as the growth of hair, continue for a very long time after other life processes have ceased.) Finding boundaries becomes even more difficult, and arbitrary, when we take into account the fact that the zygotes sometimes split into twins, or when we stop to think about cloning. Even spatial location is somewhat imprecise, given that our life processes do not precisely begin and end with our skin (which itself is not a precise boundary). Moreover, our location, size, shape, and just about everything about us undergoes radical changes during our lifetime. Even so, an organism undeniably is something. But what, if anything, gives that something its identity?

It might be suggested that there is something to which we can point as giving identity to individual organisms: genes—or, more accurately, genotypes. A genotype persists whatever changes an organism undergoes. Still, while there is something fairly definite to which we can point in the case of an individual organism, it is less than clear that what we are thereby pointing to is the organism's identity. What an organism *is* is not entirely determined by its genes, as genes may be manifested in different ways (or not at all) according to environmental circumstances. Genetically identical individuals may differ quite markedly. (In the case of a person, we might at least raise the further complication of whether the person's genotype plus phenotype define his or her identity. A person, after all, is formed through experiences, decisions, value choices, etc. For our example we would do better to stick to less developed organisms, where the idea of a determinate *thing* is less obviously out of place.)

What an organism is is consistent with its genes, obviously, and with its environment, but it is not entirely determined by either. Its identity is shaped by its genes and its history in that environment—and certainly its identity is not just the sum of its physical characteristics at a particular moment in time. A living being is better thought of as a process, a life process, than as a thing. In that respect it is like a wave moving across water—which is not just an object made out of water, having a particular shape, position, volume, and mass—and is understood as an ongoing process, with a past as well as a present, moving through time into the future. Characteristically, a living being is a process which hangs together. It maintains itself in a fluctuating environment which, unless countered, would soon terminate it. This is generally true of living entities, and it is true of species and ecosystems.

Living things are peculiar in that they go against the universal long-term trend toward increased entropy—doing so through systematic means of self-maintenance. As Sayre puts it: "The typifying mark of a living system ... appears to be its persistent state of low entropy, sustained by metabolic processes for accumulating energy, and maintained in equilibrium with its environment by homeostatic feedback processes."[4] That is not all there is to it, however, not by any means, for a refrigerator with a thermostat meets Sayre's characterization; yet it is not alive. What is it about life that makes the difference? Of critical importance, I think, is the fact that a living being, unlike other beings, has its own integrated wholeness. It has *organic unity,* by which I mean that its character is an integrated expression of its subsidiary systems. The various means by which your body controls its temperature—via the sweat glands and respiratory and circulatory systems, etc.—are integral features of your system (you) as a whole. In contrast, the

thermostat is really an add-on to the rest of the refrigerator, not essentially a feature of it. Neither is the preferred temperature range an essential feature. The right temperature for your refrigerator is determined not by the inherent character of the refrigerator, but by your own objectives. Indeed, a refrigerator is given its identity as a *refrigerator* only through our interests in it. In contrast, the right body temperature for you is not determined from the outside, nor even by your own choices, but, literally, by every fibre of your being. A living being has *self-identity* in that what it is and what serves to maintain it are determined by its own nature. All of a living being defines its favored states, what its central range of homeostasis is, and the life processes of the being as a whole are integrated toward maintaining them. Accordingly, that which serves to maintain its viability is in the interests of a living being.

Species and Interests

Species and ecosystems, I suggest, must be understood as living entities in their own right. Not only do they meet Sayre's characterization, but they also have organic unity and self-identity. They are integrated beings, determining their own character and acting so as to maintain it. Species and ecosystems thereby not only have character but interests in their own right. A species or ecosystem has an interest in whatever contributes to its ongoing viability—to whatever contributes to that living system maintaining itself. These are claims that I must defend in the face of challenges.

It has been claimed to the contrary that species and ecosystems do not have character or interests at all—*not in their own right.* In this section, I consider this counterclaim in connection with species in response to a particular objection raised by Dawkins. In the next section, I go on to an examination of ecosystems.

Dawkins argues that species cannot have traits in their own right, and therefore cannot have interests in their own right, because traits cannot be selected for at the species level. Evolution proceeds on the level of individuals, not on the level of species. He writes:

> Species don't have eyes and hearts; the individuals in them do. If a species goes extinct be-

cause of poor eyesight, this presumably means that every individual in the species died because of poor eyesight. Quality of eyesight is a property of individual animals. What kinds of traits can *species* be said to have? The answer must be traits that affect the survival and reproduction of the species, in ways that cannot be reduced to the sum of their effects on individual survival and reproduction. . . . But this is pretty unconvincing. It is hard to think of reasons why species survivability should be decoupled from the sum of the survivabilities of the individual members of the species.[5]

Of course, neither Dawkins nor anyone else denies that species have characteristics. They clearly do in some sense—but Dawkins holds that they do only in a sense which defines the characteristics of a species directly in terms of the characteristics of its individual species members. The duckbilled platypus species is characterized by its famous facial feature because its individual species members each possess one. According to Dawkins, it is impossible for a characteristic to pertain to a species in its own right unless evolution proceeds on the species level. He argues at some length that it does not and cannot. Whether or not evolution proceeds on the level of species, however, is not an issue which needs to be debated in this connection. Even if we agree with Dawkins that evolution cannot proceed on that level—and it might well be that it cannot—it may still be that a species can have characteristics, in particular, interests, in its own right. After some preliminary remarks, I provide examples of such characteristics.

Dawkins tells us that a trait on the species level must be one that affects the survival and reproduction of the species, but cannot be reduced to its effects on individual survival and reproduction. He maintains that these things cannot be decoupled, and draws the conclusion that there are no traits on the species level. I deny the soundness of this argument, for it is by no means necessary to deny that positive effects for the species can be reduced to positive effects for the individual. Genes are manifested in individual organisms and it is through them that selection takes place. A trait on the species level would be manifested through individual organisms, but would not be the sum of the traits of the individual organisms. Presumably (unless there were selection on the species level) a

trait would have to be selected for because its manifestation in an individual organism tended to be beneficial to that organism's reproduction, the means by which the genes for that trait are proliferated. Though selected for through individuals, it could still be a trait of a species as a whole, and not just a summation of the traits of individual organisms. By way of comparison, the properties of a glacier or river are not the summed properties of individual water molecules, much less atoms, although glacial or riverine properties might theoretically be reducible to those of molecules or atoms. Whether or not their properties are reducible—I remain neutral on the question of emergent properties—glaciers have properties of a different sort which are not just those of individual molecules multiplied by large numbers.

There are examples of traits of species as wholes that are not the summation of the traits of individuals. The trait of having genetic diversity provides a case in point. It would be absurd to say that individual organisms have genetic diversity in the sense that species do, though individual organisms might instantiate that diversity. Genetic diversity is important to the long-term welfare of many bisexual species, which accordingly have an interest in maintaining it. In their breeding arrangements and in their internal chemistry, bisexual species go to quite some lengths to maintain their genetic diversity. In the past it has been in the interests of individual organisms to have the traits by means of which genetic diversity is maintained, although on the level of individuals the interests were different interests in different traits. While genetic diversity is manifested through and selected for through individual organisms, the diversity that is beneficial to the species as a whole is by no means a matter of the aggregated interests of individual organisms. Once we recognize that a species is not a collection of individuals but a living system, an ongoing life process in its own right, it is easier to see it as having character and interests in its own right.

Still, it could be asked persistently, how can selection for traits on the individual level yield traits on the species level? As Dawkins and all other biologists are quite well aware, natural selection is not just a matter of some genes beating other genes in competition. Things are much more complex. All of the surrounding environment, genetic and non-genetic, has to be considered. Fundamentally, evolutionary selection takes place at the level of the gene. Yet is is through the manifestation of the gene that selection takes place, and genes are manifested in individual organisms *interacting with their environment.*

Genes evolve in the presence of other genes and are frequently influenced by the presence of other genes, often mutually. Genes are selected for the most part according to how well they get along with (the manifestations of) other genes—be they other genes in the same organism, or in other organisms of the same species, or elsewhere in the environment. Species and ecosystems are loaded with genes which manifest themselves in such a way as to fit in with other genes in other beings of various sorts. If not precisely cooperation, it is still a matter of interacting so as to maintain a viable balance. Genes—or, more accurately, genotypes—are selected positively when their manifestation in the organism is such as to lend itself to the replication of genes of that sort, and they are selected against when the opposite is true. The sort of manifestation that is favorable to the genotype may or may not be conducive to the further existence of the organism. It may save the organism's life or, as in the case of the stinging response of bees, it may cost the organism its life. Again, manifestations that are very favorable for genotypes, such as those for sexually attractive characteristics, may not affect the organism's continued existence one way or another. Genotypes manifest themselves in individual organisms in particular environments and it is what happens here that determines what gets selected for or against. Genotypes tend to be selected for, and so to proliferate, when they tend toward manifestation in viable individuals, viable species, and viable ecosystems.

Other examples of genes interacting, and species having interests, are to be found in cases in which certain species have an interest in being preyed upon. In the absence of predators removing the old, the ill, the defective, and the supernumerary, things can go quite badly for some species. Among many examples, that of the Kaibab deer and the mountain lions is a famous case in point. It proved to be a major disaster for the deer species when its perennial predator was removed. It is not in the interest of any individual deer to be killed

by a mountain lion. At most, it might be in the interests of one deer for some other deer to be removed from competition. Nevertheless, the good of the species is not to be determined by adding up how much certain individual deer are benefited and others injured. Indeed, often the individuals most affected are those indeterminate beings who do not yet exist—which certainly turned out to be the case on the Kaibab plateau. Computing the effects on individual existent deer (or other organisms) would be difficult if not impossible, but the disastrous effect on the deer species and on the whole ecosystem on the Kaibab plateau was quite unambiguous.

Ecosystems and Interests

Distinct from the question of whether species are entities, with interests, though not entirely independent of it, is the question of whether ecosystems are entities and have interests. I maintain that ecosystems are not just aggregations of plants and animals occurring in the same area. Rather, they are living systems with their own organic unity and self-identity, having and acting so as to maintain their own character. Accordingly, I maintain that they have an interest in whatever is conducive to their viability. It seems evident to me that the entire ecosystem of the Kaibab plateau, and not just the deer, had an interest in those mountain lions, and that the interest was not just the summed interest of the individual organisms. We might also note that analogous to the interest that the deer had in being preyed upon is the interest certain ecosystems have in being subject to periodic fires, an interest that is also distinct from those of individual organisms.

This line of reasoning is resisted by Harley Cahen, who tells us:

> The goal-directedness of living things gives us a plausible and nonarbitrary standard upon which to "base assignments of interests." If ecosystems, though not sentient, are goal-directed, then we may (without absurdity) attribute interests to them, too. . . . I concede that the heralded stability and resilience of some ecological systems make them prima facie goal-directed. When such an ecosystem is perturbed in any one of various ways, it bounces back. The members of the ecosystem do just what is necessary (within limits) to re-

store the system to equilibrium. But are they cooperating in order to restore equilibrium? That is surely imaginable. One the other hand, each creature might instead be "doing its own thing," with the fortunate but incidental result that the ecosystem remains stable. If this is correct, then we are dealing with a behavioral byproduct, not a systematic goal.[6]

Following Larry Wright,[7] he goes on to take the line that "G can be a goal of behavior B only if B occurs *because* it tends to bring about G. If G plays no explanatory role it cannot be a genuine goal."[8] I feel more than a little apprehensive about the term *goal*, as I suspect that things which I would wish to avoid might be packed into it. Instead of using such a term, I prefer to discuss these matters in terms of a living system maintaining its identity, unity, or center of homeostasis, or something along those lines. However, let us ask whether an ecosystem's tendency to maintain itself in the face of disruptive influences or fluctuations in its environment is to be understood as being, so to speak, goal-directed. Do some things go on in an ecosystem *because* their going on serves to maintain the ecosystem?

Cahen argues that the tendency of an ecosystem to maintain itself is to be understood as the incidental effect, or byproduct of the system's component parts. He writes:

> . . . the tendency of an ecosystem to bounce back after a disturbance is merely the net result of self-serving responses by individual organisms. We need not view stability as a system "goal." . . . Certain forms of trophic structure typically enhance community stability, . . . but trophic structure does not take on particular form because that form enhances stability.
>
> Someone might be tempted to conclude that my own argument undermines the moral considerability of organisms. Organisms, after all, consist of cells. The cells have goals of their own. Does my individualism require us to regard the behavior of organisms as merely a byproduct of the selfish behavior of cells? It does not. Cells do have their own goals, but these goals are largely subordinated to the organism's goals, because natural selection selects *bodies,* not cells. If the cells do not cooperate for the body's sake, the body dies and the cells die, too. . . .
>
> So much for organisms. A familiar process—ordinary, individualistic natural selec-

tion—ensures that they are goal-directed. Is there a process that could account for goal-directedness in ecosystems? The only candidate I know of for this job is group selection operating at the community level.[9]

He then goes on to discuss group selection and community selection, arguing that because evolution does not work in this way, ecosystems are not goal-directed, and therefore do not have interests. Given that moral considerability is tied to interests, it is supposed to follow that ecosystems are not morally considerable in their own right.

Cahen's argument that ecosystems lack interests (in their own right) is somewhat different from Dawkins' argument that species lack interests (in their own right). He does not base his argument on any claim that they lack interests (on that level) because they lack characteristics (on that level). Rather, he claims that ecosystems lack interests because they are not goal-directed. Like Dawkins, nevertheless, he maintains that they lack the necessary prerequisite for having interests because they could not have been evolutionarily selected to have the prerequisite. Both Dawkins and Cahen argue for their respective conclusions on the grounds that natural selection does not proceed on the level at which they deny there are interests or the prerequisites of interests. Concerning this point, accordingly, my response to Cahen is in large part similar to my response to Dawkins.

Of course, I quite agree with Cahen that moral considerability is tied to interests, and that to be morally considerable in their own right, ecosystems must have interests in their own right. I maintain, however, that ecosystems do have interests. They do have—if not goals—at least centers of homeostasis around which their lives fluctuate, and which are central to their identity. It is in their interests to maintain their life processes within at least a broad equilibrium around those centers of homeostasis, thereby maintaining their viability. It is not because they are *goals* that maintaining these centers of homeostasis is important. That way of putting it is much too anthropocentric, or at least anthropomorphic, in its inspiration (and in my view it is mistaken even in the case of humans). Maintaining these centers of homeostasis is important to the ecosystem, is in its interest, because doing so serves to maintain its viability.

That an ecosystem maintains itself is not, I be-

lieve, just a happy accident resulting from individual organisms doing their own thing. Although they certainly do do their own thing, it does not at all follow that the contribution which they thereby make to the ecosystem's maintaining itself is not a reason why those individual organisms do as they do. That it is characteristic of them to do as they do—indeed, that they are there and so able to do it—cannot just be dismissed as an extraneous by-product. It may well be that they are there, and are as they are, as a result of natural selection because they contribute to the well-being of the ecosystem. It may be that conditions are such that individuals, or, more properly, genotypes, are favored because their contributions to the well-being of the ecosystem contribute to their own selective advantage. There is no need at all to invoke group or community selection.

Individuals can contribute, non-accidentally, to the well-being of ecosystems analogously as cells contribute, non-accidentally, to the well-being of whole organisms. This point, as Cahen notes, is the basis for an objection to his own position. Unfortunately, however, his handling of this objection is quite seriously misdirected. He dismisses the objection on the grounds that evolutionary selection proceeds on the level of individuals. That being so, he argues, cells will be constituted so as to contribute to the well-being of the organism. Since evolution proceeds on the level of the individual, he argues, there is no reason for individuals to contribute, except accidentally, to the well-being of anything else. The fundamental flaw in Cahen's argument is that evolution, as we have already noted, does not—except derivatively—proceed on the level of the individual organism. Rather, it proceeds directly on the genotypic level. Genotypes,

nevertheless, find expression on many levels, including those of cells, individual organisms, species, and ecosystems. If a genotype is to have any but a brief future, it had better fit in with other genotypes that make those things viable.

As Cahen notes, if the individual organism is to survive it has to have cells that can function and cooperate for the sake of the individual. To this requirement we might add that the cells, to survive, had better form a viable organism (if they are to form an organism at all). It is also true that in order to survive cells and individual organisms need to be in an environment that can maintain the conditions for their survival. For all these reasons, there is evolutionary pressure for genotypes to fit in functionally with other genotypes around them— be they in the same organism, or elsewhere in their environment. Examples of genotypes responding to and cooperating with genotypes in other organisms, including organisms of very different kinds, are too numerous to mention and are familiar to anyone aware that bees pollinate flowers. By the same token, ecosystems need viable cells, viable organisms, and, for that matter, viable species in order to carry on. Neither genes nor genotypes have any of these things as *goals*, of course. Nevertheless, genotypes are selected to mesh with a lot of other genotypes and the world in general, maintaining viable cells, organisms, species, and ecosystems, and thereby themselves.

In this paper, I have argued that the interaction of genes or genotypes with the environment and the manifestation of this interaction at all higher levels makes it possible not only for individual organisms, but also species and ecosystems properly to be considered living entities in their own right, which therefore can also have interests in their own right. This status is not affected by the fact that evolutionary selection does not directly proceed on those levels. Though indirectly, species and ecosystems have evolved in such a way that their life processes tend to maintain the viability of the whole. Their interests suffer to the extent that their life processes are unable to do so. Because of these interests, it is possible for species and ecosystems meaningfully to be said to have moral standing.

Notes

1. In Lawrence E. Johnson, *A Morally Deep World* (Canberra: Australian National University, 1987), and in the later and much improved *A Morally Deep World: An Essay in Moral Considerability and Environmental Ethics* (New York: Cambridge University Press, 1991).

2. Lawrence E. Johnson, "Humanity, Holism, and Environmental Ethics," *Environmental Ethics* 5 (1983): 345–54.

3. Richard Dawkins, *The Blind Watchmaker* (Harlow, England: Longmans, 1986), p. 264.

4. Kenneth M. Sayre, *Cybernetics and the Philosophy of Mind* (New York: Humanities, 1976), p. 71.

5. Dawkins, *Blind Watchmaker,* pp. 266–67.

6. Harley Cahen, "Against the Moral Considerability of Ecosystems," *Environmental Ethics* 10 (1988): 203, 207.

7. Larry Wright, "Explanation and Teleology," *Philosophy of Science* 29 (1972): 204–18.

8. Cahen, "Against the Moral Considerability of Ecosystems," pp. 207–08.

9. Ibid., pp. 210–11.

What Mainstream Economists Have to Say About the Value of Biodiversity

Alan Randall

A wide variety of methodological and ideological perspectives has informed and directed economic inquiry. Nevertheless, in each of the topical areas where economists specialize, it seems that one or, at most, a few approaches are now recognized as mainstream. For evaluating proposed policies to influence the way resources are allocated, the welfare change measurement approach (which includes benefit-cost analysis, BCA) currently enjoys mainstream status. My purpose here is to explain what this approach can contribute to understanding the value of biodiversity. I will distill the basic message into a few simple propositions, stating them one by one and offering a few paragraphs of elaboration on each.

Welfare Change Measurement Implements an Explicit Ethical Framework

Each human being is assumed to have a well-defined set of preferences. While the way these preferences are ordered should satisfy certain logical requirements, preferences may be *about* literally anything in the range of human concerns. Mainstream economists argue that preferences are seldom whimsical or capricious. Rather, people come by their preferences consciously, in a process that involves learning, acquisition of information, and introspection. The mainstream economic approach is doggedly nonjudgmental about people's preferences: what the individual wants is presumed to be good for that individual.

The ethical framework built on this foundation is *utilitarian, anthropocentric,* and *instrumentalist* in the way that it treats biodiversity. It is utilitarian, in that things count to the extent that people want them; anthropocentric, in that humans are assigning the values; and instrumentalist, in that biota is regarded as an instrument for human satisfaction.

There may be other views of the role of nonhuman life forms. For example, animals and plants may be seen as having a good of their own, possessing rights, or being the beneficiaries of duties and obligations arising from ethical principles incumbent on humans. Some people, including some economists, may subscribe to some of these views. Nevertheless, my purpose here is to confine myself to one particular instrumental, utilitarian, and anthropocentric formulation, exploring its implications for valuation. Implications of other approaches will, on their own merits, provide perspectives in addition to those offered here.

Having established preferences as a basis for valuation, any utilitarian formulation must come to grips with two additional issues: resource scarcity and interpersonal conflicts. The mainstream economic approach recognizes the role of ethical presumptions in resolving these conflicts and asserts two explicit ethical propositions. First, at the level of the individual, value emerges from the process in which each person maximizes satisfaction by choosing, on the bases of preference and relative cost, within a set of opportunities bounded by his or her own endowments (i.e., income, wealth, and rights). Thus, individuals with more expansive endowments have more to say about what is valued by society. Second, societal valuations are determined by simple algebraic summation of individual valuations. This means that from society's perspective, a harm to one person is cancelled by an equal-size benefit to someone else. By way of comparison with the ethics of welfare change measurement, note that individualism, as an ethic, accepts the first of these propositions, but explicitly rejects the second and instead, argues for protections against individual harm for the benefit of society as a whole. The classical market, in which all exchange is voluntary, institutionalizes (in principle) the individualist ethic.

Many economists are to some extent uncomfortable with the propositions that underlie welfare change measurement—and they are sympathetic with the discomfort of noneconomists—but these propositions have the virtue of explicitness: at least, one knows where mainstream economics stands.

The Economic Approach Is Not Limited to the Commercial Domain

The explicit ethical framework of mainstream economics leads to the following definitions of value. To the individual, the value of gain (i.e., a change to a preferred state) is the amount he or she is willing to pay (WTP) for it, and the value of a loss is the amount he or she would be willing to

accept (WTA) as sufficient compensation for the loss. For society, the net value of a proposed change in resource allocation is the interpersonal sum of WTP for those who stand to gain minus the interpersonal sum of WTA for those who stand to lose as a result of the change.

Because most laypersons have encountered the ideas that economics is concerned with markets and that since Adam Smith economists have believed that an invisible hand drives market behavior in socially useful directions, it is important for me to be precise about the relationship between economic values (WTP and WTA) and market prices. If everything people care about were private (in technical terms, rival and exclusive) and exchanged in small quantities in competitive markets, prices would reveal WTP and WTA for small changes. Conversely, prices are uninformative or positively misleading where any of the following is true: where people are concerned about goods and amenities that are in some sense public (i.e., nonexclusive or nonrival); where impediments to competitive markets are imposed (by governments or by private cartels and monopolies); and where the proposed change involves a big chunk rather than a marginal nibble of some good, amenity, or resource. The point is that market prices reveal value (in the mainstream economic sense of that term) not in general but only in a rather special and limiting case.

Most issues involved with biodiversity violate the special case where market price is a valid indicator of economic value. Nevertheless, the general theory of economic value encompasses these broader concerns. Here lies the distinction between economic values and commercial values; the essential premises for economic valuation are utility, function, and scarcity; organized markets are essential only to commerce. It is a fundamental mistake to assume that economics is concerned only with the commercial.

There Is an (Almost) Adequate Conceptual Basis for Economic Valuation of Biodiversity

The total value of a proposed reduction in biodiversity is the interpersonal sum of WTA. This total value has components that arise from *current use, expected future use,* and *existence.* Use values derive from any form of use, commercial or noncommercial, and including use as a source of raw materials, medicinal products, scientific and educational materials, aesthetic satisfaction, and adventure, personally experienced or vicarious. Future use values must take into account the aversion of humans to risks (e.g., the risk that the resource may no longer be available when some future demand arises) and the asymmetry between preservation and some kinds of uses (preservation now permits later conversion to other uses, whereas conversion now eliminates preservation as a later option). The concerns have encouraged the conceptualization of various kinds of option values, which are adjustments to total value to account for risk aversion and the irreversibility of some forms of development.

To keep the value of existence separate and distinct from the value of use, existence value must emerge independently of any kind of use, even vicarious use. That is a stringent requirement. Nevertheless, valid existence values can arise from human preference for the proper scheme of things. If some people derive satisfaction from just knowing that some particular ecosystem exists in a relatively undisturbed state, the resultant value of its existence is just as real as any other economic value.

For evaluating proposals that would have long-term effects, it is a fairly standard practice in economics to calculate present values by discounting future gains and losses. This procedure seems reasonable when evaluating alternative investments expected to last no more than one generation. When it is applied to potential disasters in the more distant future, it makes many people, including quite a few economists, uneasy. By discounting at standard rates, the inevitable collapse of the living systems on this planet several hundred years from now could be counterbalanced by relatively trivial economic gains in the immediate future. This unresolved issue of how to deal with long-range future impacts is what led me to insert the caveat "almost" in the heading of this section.

Techniques for Empirical Valuation Exist and Are Applicable to Many Biodiversity Issues, but Lack of Information Can Be Daunting

When price information is available and is informative about value, the analytics are relatively simple and familiar to most economists. The challenges in valuation arise where direct price information is unavailable and when price is not a valid indicator of value. For those situations, the valuation methods that have been developed and are considered reputable by economists fall into two broad classes: implicit pricing methods and contingent valuation.

The *implicit pricing methods* are applicable when the unpriced amenity of interest can be purchased as a complement to, or a characteristic of, some ordinary marketed goods. For example, travel services are purchased as a complement to outdoor recreation amenities, which permits valuation of outdoor recreation amenities by the travel cost method (Clawson and Knetsch, 1966). Hedonic analysis of the housing market may be used, for example, to estimate the value of such nonmarketed amenities as access that housing provides to open space or to a shoreline (Brown and Pollakowski, 1977).

Contingent valuation methods are implemented in survey or experimental situations (Cummings et al., 1986). Alternative policy scenarios are introduced and the choices made by citizen participants reveal WTP or WTA, directly or indirectly. Like other survey or experimental methods, the results may be sensitive to the design and conduct of the research. Nevertheless, there is growing theoretical and empirical evidence that contingent valuation yields results that are replicable and accurate within broad limits. The major advantage of this type of valuation is its broad applicability: it can determine WTP or WTA for any plausible scenario that can be effectively communicated to the sample of citizens. For estimating existence values, for instance, it may be the only feasible method.

With respect to biodiversity, the experts (i.e., ecologists and paleontologists) often have little confidence in their estimates of the impacts of ecosystem encroachment or disturbance. All too often the experts disagree. In these areas, contingent valuation cannot compensate for ignorance. If the experts cannot construct credible scenarios describing the effects of alternative policies on biodiversity, the WTP or WTA of citizens reacting to these scenarios will reflect that uncertainty and misinformation as well as any additional uncertainty they may have about their own preferences concerning biodiversity. More generally, the accuracy of any measure of value based on the preferences of ordinary citizens is limited by the reliability of citizen knowledge about the consequences of alternative actions for biodiversity. Some may regard this as an argument that policy should be based on the judgments of experts rather than of citizens. I disagree. It seems that public opinion quite rapidly reflects expert opinion when the latter is confidently held and expressed with convincing argument. On the other hand, confusion, ignorance, and apathy among the laity typically reflect incomplete and dissonant signals from the specialists.

Policy Decision Criteria Have Been Proposed

Mainstream economists have proposed two alternative criteria for deciding preservation issues. The *modified BCA* (benefit-cost analysis) approach attempts to implement the conceptual framework of welfare change measurement by identifying and measuring (insofar as possible) the benefits and costs of the alternative courses of action. This approach requires major efforts to measure the noncommercial components of economic value, including amenity, option, and existence values. The benefit-cost decision criterion itself is modified, however, by assigning any benefits of doubt to the preservation side of the ledger. The logic for this is that more is often known and can be documented about the benefits obtainable from commercial uses than is known about the benefits of preservation.

In another approach, the *safe minimum standard* (SMS) is defined as the level of preservation that ensures survival. Proponents of the SMS approach argue that although measuring the benefits of diversity in every instance is a daunting task, there is ample evidence that biodiversity is (in broad and general terms) massively beneficial to humanity.

Whereas the modified BCA approach starts each case with a clean slate and painstakingly builds from the ground up a body of evidence about the benefits and costs of preservation, the SMS approach starts with a presumption that the maintenance of the SMS for any species is a positive good. The empirical economic question is, "Can we afford it?" Or, more technically, "How high are the opportunity costs of satisfying the SMS?" The SMS decision rule is to maintain the SMS unless the opportunity costs of so doing are

intolerably high. In other words, the SMS approach asks, how much will we lose in other domains of human concern by achieving a safe minimum standard of biodiversity? The burden of proof is assigned to the case against maintaining the SMS.

The SMS approach avoids some of the pitfalls of formal BCA, e.g., the treatment of gross uncertainty as mere risk, the false appearance of precision in benefit estimation, and the problem of discounting. In contrast to the procedure of discounting, the SMS approach simply accepts that the costs of preservation may fall disproportionately on present generations and the benefits on future generations. Its weakness is that it redefines the question rather than providing the answers. Nevertheless, an appealing argument can be made that "can we afford it?", with a presumption in favor of the SMS unless the answer is a resounding NO, is the proper question.

The Empirical Cupboard Is Not Bare

It is customary to draw attention to the scarcity of hard information about the economic value of biodiversity. But for each of the valuation methods discussed above, there has been a smattering of apparently successful empirical application. Fisher and Hanemann (1984) have used ordinary market data to estimate the potential value of the plant breeding that recently resulted in the discovery of perennial grass related to corn. Literally dozens of economists have used implicit pricing methods to estimate the values of various environmental amenities. Stoll and Johnson (1984) used the contingent valuation method (CVM) to estimate the existence values for whooping cranes. Bishop (in press) used CVM to estimate the existence values for Wisconsin's bald eagles and striped shiners (a rather obscure freshwater fish). Bennett (1984) used CVM to estimate the existence value of a unique ecosystem that survives in a remote part of the coastline of southeastern Australia. Bishop (1980) has also completed some empirical analyses based on the SMS criterion. For several cases in the United States (the California condor, snail darter, and leopard lizard) and for mountain gorillas in low-income tropical Ruanda, he found the opportunity costs of preservation to be reasonably low. In such cases, preservation decisions are not difficult.

Clearly, the empirical evidence is spotty at this stage, but these examples serve to counter the impression that high-quality empirical work on the value of diversity is not feasible.

Further Comments on the Mainstream Economics Approach

The mainstream economic approach has a built-in tendency to express the issues in terms of trade-offs. In that respect, it has much in common with the common law notion of balancing the interests. This makes the mainstream economic approach potentially helpful in the resolution of conflicts. Perhaps it also makes the economic approach anathema to those who would brook no compromise.

Important problems in making decisions concerning biodiversity are seldom of the all-or-none variety. It is easy to provide the mainstream economic answer to the question, What is the value of all the nonhuman biota on the planet Earth? Its value is infinite based on the following logic: elimination of all nonhuman biota would lead to the elimination of human life, and a life-loving human would not voluntarily accept any finite amount of compensation for having his or her own life terminated. Earth's human population surely includes at least one such person. Thus, across the total population, the sum of WTA for elimination of all nonhuman biota is clearly infinite. Nonetheless, the question posed is not very useful. The meaningful questions concern the value lost by the disappearance of a chip of biodiversity here and a chunk there. For this smaller question, it is often possible to provide an economic answer that is useful and reasonably reliable.

The goal of the mainstream economic approach is to complete a particular form of utilitarian calculation. This calculation is expressed in money values and includes (in raw or modified form) the commercial values that are expressed in markets. However, it expands the account to include things that enter human preference structures but are not exchanged in organized markets. This extension and completion of a utilitarian account, where preservation of biodiversity is at issue, is useful because it shows that commercial interests do not always prevail over economic arguments.

The claim that it is useful to complete this utilitarian account does not depend on any prior claim that the utilitarian framework is itself the preferred ethical system. Environmental goals that may be served by arguments that the biota has rights that should be considered, or that it is the beneficiary of duties and obligations deriving from ethical principles incumbent on humans, may also be served by completing a utilitarian account that demonstrates the value implications of human preferences that extend beyond commercial goods to include biodiversity. Some people would argue that a complete discussion of the value of biodiversity should extend beyond utilitarian concerns. Even these people would, presumably, prefer a reasonably complete and balanced utilitarian analysis to the truncated and distorted utilitarian analysis that emerges from commercial accounts.

References

Bennett, J. 1984. Using direct questioning to value the existence benefits of preserved national areas. Aust. J. Agric. Econ. 28:136–152.

Bishop, R. 1980. Endangered species: An economic perspective. Trans. North Am. Wildl. Nat. Resour. Conf. 45:208–218.

Bishop, R. In press. Uncertainty and resource valuation: Theoretical principles for empirical research. In G. Peterson and C. Sorg, eds. Toward the Measurement of Total Value. USDA Forest Service, Rocky Mountain Forest and Range Experiment Station General Technical Report, Fort Collins, CO.

Brown, G., and H. Pollakowski. 1977. Economic value of shoreline. Rev. Econ. Stat. 69:273–278.

Clawson, M., and J. Knetsch. 1966. Economics of Outdoor Recreation. Johns Hopkins University Press, Baltimore. 327 pp.

Cummings, R., D. Brookshire, and W. Schulze. 1986. Valuing Environmental Goods: A State of the Art Assessment of the Contingent Valuation Method. Rowman and Allenheld, Totowa, NJ. 270 pp.

Fisher, A., and M. Hanemann. 1984. Option Values and the Extinction of Species. Working Paper No. 269. Giannini Foundation of Agricultural Economics, Berkeley, CA. 39 pp.

Stoll, J., and L. Johnson. 1984. Concepts of value, nonmarket valuation, and the case of the whooping crane. Trans. North Am. Wildl. Nat. Resour. Conf. 49:382–393.

Why Put a Value on Biodiversity?

David Ehrenfeld

In this chapter, I express a point of view in absolute terms to make it more vivid and understandable. There are exceptions to what I have written, but I will let others find them.

That it was considered necessary to have a section in this volume devoted to the value of biological diversity tells us a great deal about why biological diversity is in trouble. Two to three decades ago, the topic would not have been thought worth discussing, because few scientists and fewer laymen believed that biological diversity was—or could be—endangered in its totality. Three or four decades before that, a discussion of the value of biological diversity would probably have been scorned for a different reason. In the early part of this century, that value would have been taken for granted; the diversity of life was considered an integral part of life, and one of the nicest parts at that. Valuing diversity would, I suspect, have been thought both presumptuous and a terrible waste of time.

Now, in the last part of the twentieth century, we have meetings, papers, and entire books devoted to the subject of the value of biological diversity. It has become a kind of academic cottage industry, with dozens of us sitting at home at our word processors churning out economic, philosophical, and scientific reasons for or against keeping diversity. Why?

There are probably many explanations of why we feel compelled to place a value on diversity. One, for example, is that our ability to destroy diversity appears to place us on a plane above it, obliging us to judge and evaluate that which is in our power. A more straightforward explanation is that the dominant economic realities of our time—technological development, consumerism, the increasing size of governmental, industrial, and agricultural enterprises, and the growth of human populations—are responsible for most of the loss of biological diversity. Our lives and futures are dominated by the economic manifestations of these often hidden processes, and survival itself is viewed as a matter of economics (we speak of tax shelters and safety nets), so it is hardly surprising that even we conservationists have begun to justify our efforts on behalf of diversity in economic terms.

It does not occur to us that nothing forces us to confront the process of destruction by using its own uncouth and self-destructive premises and terminology. It does not occur to us that by assigning value to diversity we merely legitimize the process that is wiping it out, the process that says, "The first thing that matters in any important decision is the tangible magnitude of the dollar costs and benefits." People are afraid that if they do not express their fears and concerns in this language they will be laughed at, they will not be listened to. This may be true (although having philosophies that differ from the established ones is not necessarily inconsistent with political power). But true or not, it is certain that if we persist in this crusade to determine value where value ought to be evident, we will be left with nothing but our greed when the dust finally settles. I should make it clear that I am referring not just to the effort to put an actual price on biological diversity but also to the attempt to rephrase the price in terms of a nebulous survival value.

Two concrete examples that call into question this evaluating process come immediately to mind. The first is one that I first noticed a number of years ago: it was a paper written in the *Journal of Political Economy* by Clark (1973)—an applied mathematician at the University of British Columbia. That paper, which everyone who seeks to put a dollar value on biological diversity ought to read, is about the economics of killing blue whales. The question was whether it was economically advisable to halt the Japanese whaling of this species in order to give blue whales time to recover to the point where they could become a sustained economic resource. Clark demonstrated that in fact it was economically preferable to kill every blue whale left in the oceans as fast as possible and reinvest the profits in growth industries rather than to wait for the species to recover to the point where it could sustain an annual catch. He was not recommending this course—just pointing out a danger of relying heavily on economic justifications for conservation in that case.

Another example concerns the pharmaceutical industry. It used to be said, and to some extent still is, that the myriad plants and animals of the world's remaining tropical moist forests may well contain a great many chemical compounds of potential benefit to human health—everything from safe contraceptives to cures for cancer. I think this is true, and for all I know, the pharmaceutical companies think it is true also, but the point is that this has become irrelevant..Pharmaceutical researchers now believe, rightly or wrongly, that they can get new drugs faster and cheaper by computer modeling of the molecular structures they find promising on theoretical grounds, followed by organic synthesis in the laboratory using a host of new technologies, including genetic engineering. There is no need, they claim, to waste time and money slogging around in the jungle. In a few short years, this so-called value of the tropical rain forest has fallen to the level of used computer printout.

In the long run, basing our conservation strategy on the economic value of diversity will only make things worse, because it keeps us from coping with the root cause of the loss of diversity. It makes us accept as givens the technological/socioeconomic premises that make biological impoverishment of the world inevitable. If I were one of the many exploiters and destroyers of biological diversity, I would like nothing better than for my opponents, the conservationists, to be bogged down over the issue of valuing. As shown by the example of the faltering search for new drugs in the tropics, economic criteria of value are shifting, fluid, and utterly opportunistic in their practical application. This is the opposite of the value system needed to conserve biological diversity over the course of decades and centuries.

Value is an intrinsic part of diversity; it does not depend on the properties of the species in question, the uses to which particular species may or may not be put, or their alleged role in the balance of global ecosystems. For biological diversity, value *is*. Nothing more and nothing less. No cottage in-

dustry of expert evaluators is needed to assess this kind of value.

Having said this, I should stop, but I won't, because I would like to say it in a different way.

There are two practical problems with assigning value to biological diversity. The first is a problem for economists: it is not possible to figure out the true economic value of any piece of biological diversity, let alone the value of diversity in the aggregate. We do not know enough about any gene, species, or ecosystem to be able to calculate its ecological and economic worth in the larger scheme of things. Even in relatively closed systems (or in systems that they pretend are closed), economists are poor at describing what is happening and terrible at making even short-term predictions based on available data. How then should ecologists and economists, dealing with huge, open systems, decide on the net present or future worth of any part of diversity? There is not even a way to assign numbers to many of the admittedly most important sources of value in the calculation. For example, we can figure out, more or less, the value of lost revenue in terms of lost fisherman-days when trout streams are destroyed by acid mine drainage, but what sort of value do we assign to the loss to the community when a whole generation of its children can never experience the streams in their environment as amenities or can never experience home as a place where one would like to stay, even after it becomes possible to leave.

Moreover, how do we deal with values of organisms whose very existence escapes our notice? Before we fully appreciated the vital role that mycorrhizal symbiosis plays in the lives of many plants, what kind of value would we have assigned to the tiny, threadlike fungi in the soil that make those relationships possible? Given these realities of life on this infinitely complex planet, it is no wonder that contemporary efforts to assign value to a species or ecosystem so often appear like clumsy rewrites of "The Emperor's New Clothes."

The second practical problem with assigning value to biological diversity is one for conservationists. In a chapter called "The Conservation Dilemma" in my book *The Arrogance of Humanism*, I discussed the problem of what I call nonresources (Ehrenfeld, 1981). The sad fact that few conservationists care to face is that many species, perhaps most, do not seem to have any conventional value at all, even hidden conventional value. True, we can not be sure which particular species fall into this category, but it is hard to deny that there must be a great many of them. And unfortunately, the species whose members are the fewest in number, the rarest, the most narrowly distributed—in short, the ones most likely to become extinct—are obviously the ones least likely to be missed by the biosphere. Many of these species were never common or ecologically influential; by no stretch of the imagination can we make them out to be vital cogs in the ecological machine. If the California condor disappears forever from the California hills, it will be a tragedy: but don't expect the chaparral to die, the redwoods to wither, the San Andreas fault to open up, or even the California tourist industry to suffer—they won't.

So it is with plants (Ehrenfeld, 1986). We do not know how many species are needed to keep the planet green and healthy, but it seems very unlikely to be anywhere near the more than quarter of a million we have now. Even a mighty dominant like the American chestnut, extending over half a continent, all but disappeared without bringing the eastern deciduous forest down with it. And if we turn to the invertebrates, the source of nearly all biological diversity, what biologist is willing to find a value—conventional or ecological—for all 600,000-plus species of beetles?

I am not trying to deny the very real ecological dangers the world is facing; rather, I am pointing out that the danger of declining diversity is in great measure a separate danger, a danger in its own right. Nor am I trying to undermine conservation; in fact, I would like to see it find a sound footing outside the slick terrain of the economists and their philosophical allies.

If conservation is to succeed, the public must come to understand the inherent wrongness of the destruction of biological diversity. This notion of wrongness is a powerful argument with great breadth of appeal to all manner of personal philosophies.

Those who do not believe in God, for example, can still accept the fact that it is wrong to destroy biological diversity. The very existence of diversity is its own warrant for survival. As in law, long-established existence confers a powerful right to a continued existence. And if more human-centered values are still deemed necessary, there are plenty available—for example, the value of the wonder, excitement, and challenge of so many species arising from a few dozen elements of the periodic table.

And to countenance the destruction of diversity is equally wrong for those who believe in God, because it was God who, by whatever mechanism, caused this diversity to appear here in the first place. Diversity is God's property, and we, who bear the relationship to it of strangers and sojourners, have no right to destroy it (Berry, 1981; Lamm, 1971). There is a much-told story (Hutchinson, 1959) about the great biologist, J. B. S. Haldane, who was not exactly an apostle of religion. Haldane was asked what his years of studying biology had taught him about the Creator. His rather snide reply was that God seems to have an "inordinate fondness for beetles." Well why not? As God answered Job from the whirlwind in the section of the Bible that is perhaps most relevant to biological diversity, "Where were you when I laid the foundations of the earth?" (Job 38:4). Assigning value to that which we do not own and whose purpose we can not understand except in the most superficial ways is the ultimate in presumptuous folly.

The great biochemist Erwin Chargaff, one of the founders of modern molecular biology, remarked not too many years ago, "I cannot help thinking of the deplorable fact that when the child has found out how its mechanical toy operates, there is no mechanical toy left" (Chargaff, 1978, p. 121). He was referring to the direction taken by modern scientific research, but the problem is a general one, and we can apply it to conservation as well. I cannot help thinking that when we finish assigning values to biological diversity, we will find that we don't have very much biological diversity left.

References

Berry, W. 1981. The gift of good land. Pp. 267–281 in The Gift of Good Land. North Point Press, San Francisco.

Chargaff, E. 1978. Heraclitean Fire: Sketches from a Life Before Nature. Rockefeller University Press, New York. 252 pp.

Clark, C. W. 1973. Profit maximization and the extinction of animal species. J. Pol. Econ. 81:950–961.

Ehrenfeld, D. 1981. The Arrogance of Humanism. Oxford University Press, New York. 286 pp.

Ehrenfeld, D. 1986. Thirty million cheers for diversity. New Sci. 110:38–43.

Hutchinson, G. E. 1959. Homage to Santa Rosalia, or Why are there so many kinds of animals? Am. Nat. 93:145–159.

Lamm, N. 1971. Ecology in Jewish law and theology. Pp. 161–185 in Faith and Doubt. Ktav Publishing House, New York.

Transformative Values

Bryan Norton

I began by defining four categories of reasons for protecting species. These categories, defined in terms of the values to which they appeal, were formed by the intersection of two dichotomies, one distinguishing values according to who or what is served by them and the other according to the type of value involved. Anthropocentric arguments comprehend all reasons that ultimately appeal to the intrinsic value located in human beings, while nonanthropocentric arguments appeal to intrinsic value located in nonhuman species. Cutting across this dichotomy is another one: the value of an experience can lie either in its fulfilling an existing, prior preference of some individual (demand value) or in its altering or transforming such preferences.

Arguments available to support species protection can then be classified as appealing to (a) human demand values; (b) human transformative values; (c) nonhuman demand values; or (d) nonhuman transformative values. To countenance arguments based on (d) would require an assault on a very widely accepted metaphysical dichotomy, which singles out humans as the only known species whose members can rationally consider and reject value commitments. I have chosen not to give serious consideration to values in this category, as my purpose is to examine and then establish viable bases for policy formation.

Serious consideration is being given, then, to values in three categories. No one, including those who place no special stock in species preservation, seriously denies that nonhuman species satisfy human demand values. [An earlier part of *Why Preserve Natural Variety?*], while not attempting to exhaust sources of such satisfactions, emphasizes some easily overlooked instances, concluding that nonhuman species and the ecosystems they compose serve human demand values in many not readily understood or quantified ways. Yet species protectionists are justifiably uneasy with resting their case wholly on the positive manner in which nonhuman species satisfy human demand values.

Most preservationists who have gone beyond human demand values in their pleas for enlightened policies have appealed to values entirely independent of human objectives. This nonanthropocentric alternative is ethically radical, espousing as it does new moral demands on policy formation—demands originating outside of and capable of competing with human demands and yet it has attracted numerous and vocal proponents. It expresses in moral terms the outrage of environmentalists at human destruction of other organisms and attempts to show the inherent limits of human exploitation of nature.

But the initial attraction of this approach proved . . . illusive. The greater portion of the attraction derives from the promise to annex the well-developed and largely uncontroversial system of ethical rules governing treatment of human individuals to the cause of species preservation. But attempts to move, by analogy, from moral concern for human individuals to a corresponding moral concern capable of supporting a policy of species preservation face two serious disadvantages. First, species preservationists require a basis for protecting a wide range of species spread throughout the phylogenetic scale. To attain this comprehensive basis, they must extend the analogy from human individuals to all individual organisms. This cannot but weaken the analogy, as it taxes credibility to deny any difference, morally, between "mistreating" plants and mistreating humans.

Second, even leaving aside these problems of scope, concern for individual specimens of nonhuman species supports policies often at odds with the best strategy for preserving species. A species is a composite of individuals surviving beyond the death of any of its individual members, and there is no necessary connection between the protection of individual interests and the preservation of species into indefinite time.

Locating intrinsic value in species themselves or in ecosystems holds some promise of providing nonanthropocentric reasons for preserving species, reasons not dependent upon individual concerns. But these approaches go beyond the simple annexation of standard ethical rules and principles; they require the development of an axiology clarifying and justifying their claims. No uncontroversial bases for analogy are available here, and the task of nonindividualistic nonanthropocentrists is an arduous one. They must define a nonindividualistic conception of intrinsic value and then state some positive characteristic standing as the mark of such value. Only then can they begin to argue that nonhuman species and ecosystems have the relevant characteristic and to derive policies from those values.

Thus, while no arguments rule out appeals to nonindividualistic intrinsic value, the development of an adequate ethic based upon such a foundation is surely a long way off. Even if promising alternatives were being suggested at this point, it is dubious that they could receive the necessary clarification and support to inform environmental policy in time to avoid the cataclysmic reduction in biological diversity feared by scientific experts.

Here, then, is the dilemma: Ought species preservationists to continue espousing nonanthropocentric reasons for species preservation, knowing full well that these reasons cannot yet be supported by a clear and rationally defensible axiology, or should they fall back on unquestioned human demand values as the full basis for the policies they recommend? The first alternative supports obligations sufficiently strong to limit human destruction of other species but at the cost of leaving preservationists open to the charge that their arguments are based on unclear and unsupported value premises. The second alternative avoids this charge but only at the cost of putting the goals of species preservationists on a par with other human demands. How can preservationists argue that the long-term demand value of species should receive high priority in a world faced on every hand with pressing and immediate human demands for food, shelter, and other basic needs?

It is the central thesis of this book that this excruciating dilemma is a false one because it unnecessarily contracts the range of human values to those founded on demands for given preferences. However important are the ways species serve human demands, there exists an entirely different category of important human values that cannot themselves be reduced to these demands. To assume that policies favoring species preservation must either be based on intrinsic value of nonhumans or else that these policies must rest on no sounder basis than the shifting, contingent preferences humans express for material goods and services is to ignore the role of other species and varied ecosystems in forming and transforming values. The next subject requiring extensive discussion is, then, transformative values.

The way out of the preservationist's perplexing dilemma is to refuse to accept the view that all felt preferences are on a par. Some can survive a rigorous process of examination and emerge as considered preferences; others cannot. In this way species preservationists can give importance to some demand values while criticizing and rejecting others as less worthy of concern. They can accept the prima facie value of satisfying individual human preferences while reserving the right to criticize some of these preferences as overly consumptive, materialistic, and unworthy of satisfaction.

This crucial distinction between worthy and unworthy preferences requires that we recognize an ambiguity in the concept of rationality as applied to human ends and objectives. To say that someone is a rational seeker of ends is sometimes to say no more than that she is *capable of* countenancing reasons in deciding what ends to pursue. At other times it is to say that she has *correctly identified and weighted* the factors that justify pursuing a chosen goal or goals. Only demand values that are rational in the second, stronger sense have an unquestioned claim in policy formation, and only those need be invoked to support species preservation for its benefits to human consumers. And at the same time this structure provides a role for a new category of values—those that I have called transformative.

A value system that includes transformative as well as demand values can limit and sort demand views according to their legitimacy within a rational world view. To the extent that one values having a rational set of felt preferences, experiences that contribute to the formation of a rational world view and an attendant adjustment of felt preferences have transformative value.

This more complex, though still anthropocentric, value system is doubly congenial to the goals of environmental preservationists. It allows them to express their legitimate concern that runaway expansion of human demand values, especially overly materialistic and consumptive ones, constitutes much of the problem of species endangerment. It also highlights the value of wild species and undisturbed ecosystems as occasions for experiences that alter those very felt preferences. Occasions such as these have value of a different order, although value still couched in human terms. Insofar as environmentalists believe that experience of nature is a necessary condition for developing a consistent and rational world view, one that fully recognizes man's place as a highly evolved animal whose existence depends upon other species and functioning ecosystems, they also believe that such experiences have transformative value. Experience of nature can promote questioning and rejection of overly materialistic and consumptive felt preferences. Appeals to the transformative value of wild species and undisturbed ecosystems thereby provide the means to criticize and limit demand values that threaten to destroy those species and ecosystems while at the same time introducing an important value that humans should place upon them.

An illustration may prove helpful here. Suppose an adult comes upon a child playing in the woods. The child is gleefully destroying eggs from the nests of groundbirds. The adult gently explains to the child that eggs are necessary to hatch baby birds and shows the child baby birds in another nest. The child is fascinated, watches the baby birds being fed by the mother, and loses interest in his destructive game. Now he begins to show solicitous concern for the welfare of birds and asks many questions. Eventually, he grows up to be an amateur ornithologist, deriving untold pleasure from a lifetime interest in birds. The initial appeal of the destructive felt preference and the demand value represented has now been transformed. To the extent that one believes the child's posteducational preferences are more rational and less open to criticism, one also believes that the encounter with the birds has value: it has transformed irrational and indefensible felt preferences into more defensible considered preferences.

This example stands as a microcosm of the power of nature to transform values across society. When the initial felt preferences of a whole society are askew, the need for transformative value is correspondingly more urgent, as Joseph Sax explains in his compelling book, *Mountains without Handrails*:

> The preservationist is not an elitist who wants to exclude others, notwithstanding popular opinion to the contrary; he is a moralist who wants to convert them. He is concerned about what other people do in the parks not because he is unaware of the diversity of taste in the society, but because he views certain kinds of activity as calculated to undermine the attitudes he believes the parks can, and should, encourage. He sees mountain climbing as promoting self-reliance, for example, whereas "climbing" in an electrified tramway is perceived as a passive and dependent activity.[1]

Sax perceives that preservationists are moralists: they attempt to transform values. He also sees that the preservationists' moralism extends to the whole society. They are extolling the virtues of a society that protects natural places and the values they stand for:

> The preservationists do not merely aspire to persuade individuals how to conduct their personal lives. . . . The parks are, after all, public institutions which belong to everyone, not just to wilderness hikers. The weight of the preservationist view, therefore, turns not only on its persuasiveness for the individual as such, but also on its ability to garner the support—or at least the tolerance—of citizens in a democratic society to bring the preservationist vision into operation as official policy.[2]

The case being made extends to social values: What type of society shall we have? An answer to this question requires, Sax believes, appeals to values that can only be found in, and protected in, nature. This is the transformative value of nature. . . .

*

When environmentalists in general and species preservationists in particular criticize the over-materialistic and overconsumptive nature of contemporary values, they do not intend merely to say that those values are inconsistent with one tradition in American intellectual history. Nor did the founders of that tradition see themselves as creating a subjective set of values incapable of general application. While Thoreau and, especially, Emerson emphasize the new possibilities for a distinctive culture to emerge in the new world, they leave no doubt that such a culture would attain an objective, universal truth:

> We must trust the perfection of the creation so far as we believe that whatever curiosity the order of things has awakened in our minds, the order of things can satisfy. Every man's condition is a solution in hieroglyphic to those inquiries he would put. He acts it as life, before he apprehends it as truth. In like manner, nature is already, in its forms and tendencies, describing its own design. . . . Let us inquire, to what end is nature?
>
> All science has one aim, namely, to find a theory of nature. . . . To a sound judgment, the most abstract truth is the most practical. Whenever a true theory appears, it will be its own evidence. Its test is, that it will explain all phenomena.[3]

These are not the words of a relativist. Emerson is extolling the virtues of a fresh start in the new world not because he seeks a distinctive philosophy valid only in a new context but because he believes the old ways have concealed the path to a complete, consistent, and correct view of nature. What is to be abandoned is not the old objective of universal truth but the old way toward that objective, littered with the encrustations of worn-out cultures. The new start is noteworthy because truths imperceptible in the corrupt societies of the old world lie open to the understanding of unspoiled humans more in touch with nature's harmonies.

When environmentalists represent themselves as the harbingers of a new world view and a new set of values, they may intend to create a new path but toward a universal and objective destination. They believe that it would be a good thing—an un-

qualifiedly and nonrelativistically good thing—if the human species were to adopt a world view and set of values that placed them in harmony with the workings of nature. To the extent that our current culture has failed to achieve such harmony, they believe it has taken a wrong road and not just a road wrong "for us"—an objectively wrong road.

They believe that the values this culture now seeks are inconsistent with a rational and realistic world view. If humans would see the world aright, if they would see themselves and their activities in proper perspective, they would reject current felt preferences and strive toward the adoption of higher, less materialistic, and less consumptive values—a set of considered preferences appropriate to a modern, rationally defensible world view.

Now, critics have every right to be skeptical here. My argument so far has been generated from, first, listening to what species preservationists are saying and, second, developing concepts and principles that they could use to support those statements. It is a far more difficult task to support such a framework, a task that cannot fully be undertaken here. In the remainder of this chapter, I will show, in a preliminary manner, how species preservationists might make their case. My goal will be to show which premises are essential and how they might be made plausible rather than to produce knockdown arguments. I offer a blueprint rather than a finished building.

The conceptual apparatus outlined in this book, the distinction between felt and considered preferences and the attendant disjunction of demand and transformative values, provides the scaffolding for building the edifice. But it provides no firm foundation. For that, substantive premises concerning the nature of what is real and what is valuable must be supported. Only given these can the critique of felt preferences and the promulgation of considered ones proceed.

First, species preservationists, and environmentalists more generally, believe that the human species has evolved as other species have, within complex and interrelated ecosystems. While modern technology may often obscure this fact, *Homo sapiens* remains dependent upon biotic and abiotic environments in countless ways. Our present needs and characteristics and the very evolutionary necessities embodied in our genes are the result of past adaptations to environmental conditions. Further, the future possibilities among which we will choose are likewise determined by the interaction of current genes and future environmental conditions. Two great ideas come together here: Darwinian biology has taught us that humans are, basically, evolved animals; ecology has taught that evolution works within almost unbelievably complex and interrelated organic systems on interlocking levels ranging through molecules, cells, organs, organisms, habitats, ecological systems, the biota as a whole and, ultimately, the abiotic system. All levels of life interact within the parameters set by the abiotic conditions that at once determine and are determined by them. In a sense these two great ideas, once combined, provide an ontology for the ecological world view, a recognition of certain things as most basic and determinative.

If the first principle of the ecological world view sets down an ontology, the second principle provides an epistemology of sorts. As was just noted, preservationists believe that the natural world is extraordinarily complex. The levels of interrelationships are multifarious, and minute alterations in the smallest elements making up a system initiate further alterations cascading throughout the system, and these affect again the elements themselves. An epistemology appropriate to this belief is cautious and skeptical in its particular claims to knowledge and in its assessment of knowledge generally. The more we understand, the more we realize how little we understand. Where every fact, no matter how specific, causally depends upon alterations in a system that it in turn alters, dogmatism is not a virtue. The ecological world view and its attendant skepticism represent the final undermining of Cartesian epistemology. The search for unquestioned and unquestionable premises, for "first truths," for certainty, is at an end. Theories, however grand, become models to help us to understand how change courses through systems. First principles are heuristic starting points, as open to alteration as are the effects they hypothetically predict. While one need not doubt that change takes place according to some coherent principles, the principles are best seen as means to understanding reality rather than as constituting it. From quantum mechanics to ecological theory the epistemological lesson is the same: each action, even if it is a measuring action, changes the system in which it intervenes. Human knowledge alters

the nature of the systems known, and this fact follows (at least loosely) from the ontology of the preservationist: human knowledge occurs within and affects the system of nature.

Third, preservationists believe that the ecological world view, embodying these ontological and epistemological principles, lends credence to a generally ecological approach to values and objectives.[4] The approach is one of humility. The variety and intricacy of nature are so far beyond our current comprehension that, while more knowledge usually helps, so much more is needed that wisdom implies the pursuit of cautious goals. Action based upon knowledge of a single relationship abstracted from a complexly interrelated system is dangerous. Manipulation of single variables produces unforeseen results. This is what environmentalists mean when they caution that "you can never do just one thing." But humility need not imply despair. If humans are highly evolved animals, then the species has succeeded, through the ages, in developing a viable relationship with its biotic and abiotic environment. The natural history of *Homo sapiens,* viewed as a highly evolved and highly intelligent but physically dependent being that has survived in a hostile world, can stand as a guide to human behavior.

Does this philosophy imply quiescence, a paralysis of human will in the face of looming human problems? No. The human species would never have survived had it not used its intelligence to alter the world in which it lived. Even lacking complete understanding of the components and interrelationships of the system on which we depend, ther are bases for determining wise human action. Nature's system works because of harmonies and balances within the system. Natural systems are geared for change by component parts: systems are dynamic, not static. But they are more geared for some types of change than others. Incremental changes that mimic natural processes, such as taking older and weaker organisms to fulfill human needs, or controlling an outbreak of a pest species by encouraging its natural enemies, work within the established patterns of the system of nature. These changes set off compensating mechanisms already in place; information flows through the system, allowing other organisms to react.

Abrupt changes, changes with no parallels in normal biological or climatological processes, scramble the feedback messages and leave the system in disarray.[5] Ecosystems have few mechanisms for adapting to expanses of concrete, and these act too slowly to protect the system paved over from simplification and collapse. A bulldozer's clearing of a small patch can be remedied in a few seasons; it is similar enough to the clearing caused by the fall of a large tree, which is subsequently filled through processes of colonization and succession. But if a whole area is defoliated, even the colonizers are beaten back from their frontiers. The process of recovery is slow and incomplete; opportunists take and hold possession for a longer time, making it more difficult for full regeneration to take place.

Thus, the ontology and epistemology of the ecological world view give rise to a positive value—that of harmony with nature and nature's way. It is good, in this view, to do things in a way that mimics nature's patterns; it is good to promote the natural processes that, if not interrupted, produce greater diversity; it is good to introduce alterations slowly enough to allow nature to react. And it is bad to thwart those natural processes, to interrupt well-established patterns, to introduce irreversible changes.

*

Besides objecting that these are vague platitudes, the skeptic may argue that this system only replaces short-term selfish motives with a more enlightened sense of self-interest. In one sense this skepticism is justified. Transformative values are human (anthropocentric) values. These values are not limited by intrinsic values discovered in, or attributed to, nonhuman nature. But the distinction between felt preferences and the considered preferences that replace them leads to an important qualification of the skeptic's point.

A considered preference is one that survives after a complex process of analysis and self-criticism. Such a process might take a number of forms, but it will be useful to sketch one of these. For concreteness let us consider Jane, a young woman who lives near home and helps her parents with the family business. Her parents are generous, and she is able to afford many luxuries, including expensive clothes, a comfortable apartment, and a sports car. But she is vaguely dissatisfied.

One evening, more from boredom than any other motive, Jane accompanies a friend to a meeting of a conservation group. Jane has always liked birds and is inspired by slides of whooping cranes.

It is disturbing to her that human activities have brought this species to the brink of extinction, and she is angered by a government plan to further compromise its remaining habitat. Jane makes a considerable donation to the conservation group and hardly misses the amenities she might have purchased instead. Soon she becomes an enthusiastic volunteer and spends all of her free time in conservationist activities.

Finally Jane decides to attend a distant university that has a special program in wildlife protection. To her surprise Jane's parents adamantly oppose the plan and refuse both emotional and financial support. When they learn that she is still considering the move, her father asks, "You mean a few birds mean more to you than your own parents?"

Faced with that question, Jane begins some real soul-searching. Does she value endangered wildlife more than she values her parents? She remembers that one speaker at the conservation meetings said that all living things have intrinsic value. She had been puzzled and had asked what that meant. He had answered that all living things have the same kind of value that humans do. That didn't help much, and it certainly doesn't convince her that birds are more valuable than her parents.

Jane has reached an impasse. On the one side are her parents and the comfortable life style that working for them guarantees. On the other are her newly developed ideals to protect wild animals and the environment. Eventually she realizes that she will never resolve the issue framed in terms of whether the animals she hopes to protect have sufficient intrinsic value to counterbalance her love for her parents.

Then she begins to see the question in quite different terms. She realizes that, since her first attendance at the conservation meetings, *she* has changed. She had begun studying ecology texts and now finds a walk in the woods stimulating and satisfying. She also notices that she feels more comfortable in her "Save the Animals" sweatshirt than in an expensive new dress. A day of shopping, once her favorite activity, leaves her less satisfied than a day working as a volunteer for a conservation cause. Without really thinking about it, she has realized that there are more important things than material possessions.

In the end she concludes that, however much she loves her parents, the decision is hers. And, while the discussions she's had about intrinsic value in nature do not help her to make her decision, she knows that her ideals have changed. The process began when she saw the slides of whooping cranes. It continued when she read ecology texts that talked about the interdependencies of all living things, and when she did volunteer work. At the same time her tastes and preferences changed. And she believes that she is a better person for these changes.

Jane decides to sell her sports car to cover the first year's tuition. With a small scholarship, a small loan, and a part-time job, she is able to cover her surprisingly modest material needs, and she eventually graduates. While her parents remain incredulous and often remark that she'd be welcome to return to the business, Jane knows she won't accept their offer.

It is important not to suggest that every person faces exactly the same self-examination in exactly the same way, but Jane's example allows us to focus on some key aspects of the processes of considering preferences. First, the process often begins with a new experience, or with a new orientation toward a common experience. Attending the conservation meeting and seeing slides of whooping cranes planted a seed that grew and flowered in Jane's consciousness. Second, Jane began to alter her behavior by donating money and by volunteering to work for preservation goals before any radical reexamination took place. Some people may begin by reconsidering their deepest values and principles, but Jane's concrete approach is more common. Third, when Jane discovered that her shifting interests brought new meaning to her life, she began to feel uncomfortable with her previous life goals and the satisfactions she had sought. Finally, Jane came to the realization that the new goals and ideals that had taken shape were objectively better than the old ones. It was not crucial that Jane determine that wild animals have intrinsic value—it was only necessary that she conclude that her new values, which avoid unnecessary consumption, are better than her old, materialistic ones. She is especially happy to realize that pursuing her new values also protects species, both because she no longer wears a fur coat and because her new career will make a positive contribution to the cause of species preservation.

Species preservationists view their activities similarly. If they believe that the ecological world view represents a more accurate picture of the world and that the value system suggested by it is objectively better than the value system of materialism and conspicuous consumption, then they will value endangered species and natural ecosystems for their role in transforming human world views and human value systems. Jane's story began with an encounter with an endangered species. If the story of her individual transformation is plausible, species preservationists can hope that a parallel transformation might occur in our entire society. But it will not occur if nature is so altered that encounters with wild species become unlikely. Species preservationists should emphasize the value of wild species, especially endangered ones, as catalysts for the reconsideration of currently consumptive felt preferences.

As long as species preservationists agree that a nonmaterialistic value system is objectively better than one based upon unlimited consumption, it does not matter whether they also agree that nature has intrinsic value. The transformative value of wild species and natural ecosystems provides adequate reason to preserve them, quite independent of whether nature has intrinsic value.

In one sense, then, the skeptic is correct. Jane rejects her consumptive life style for self-oriented reasons. She does not rely on attributions of intrinsic value to nonhuman species to force a change in herself. Nor does she sacrifice her interests for the competing interests of other species. Has she, then, merely substituted a somewhat enlightened self-interest for an unenlightened self-interest? By a complex process impossible to separate into sharply defined stages, Jane's preferences, if spread throughout the entire population, would no doubt improve the long-term survivability of the species. But this realization was not determinative in Jane's story, nor is this realization the "justification" for the changes in her attitudes. Jane concluded, after her process of change, that her new values were objectively better than the consumptive ones she gave up, meaning that she had a better and richer life as a result of the transformation. The value of the change is measured in human terms, but that conclusion is merely a restatement of the original premise, that transformative values are anthropocentric.

Environmentalists accept the "ecological world view" as sketched. . . . They also believe that encounters with wild species can precipitate changes in human consciousness, alterations in world views sufficient to create a new ontology, a new epistemology, and a new approach to value. If they also believe that the new, less materialistic values that are thereby created are objectively better than the materialistic, consumptive values they replace, they should value all wild species, including endangered ones, for their transformative value. On this anthropocentric basis they can argue that species should be preserved, regardless of whether they also believe that species have intrinsic value.

This, then, is a coherent and complete argument for protecting species. It recognizes the demand value that species have, while also insisting that experience of wild species can enlighten demand values by initiating a process of reexamination. Such experiences interact with, and support, ideals that undermine a materialistic, consumptive style of life. Attributions of intrinsic value to nonhuman species might be included in those new ideals but need not be.

Species preservationists can argue that their world view—its ontology, its epistemology, and its value of harmony with nature—is a rational response to the world as it is encountered one hundred years after Darwin's formative discoveries. In this way they can offer a framework within which felt preferences can be criticized and demand values transformed by a process that shares essential features with the alterations in Jane's consciousness. Species preservationists can argue that overly consumptive demand values are less rational because their fulfillment threatens the system within which the human species has evolved and must continue to exist.

But the caution against destroying that system, the advocacy of harmony as a better course than hubris, is not understandable solely in terms of demand values, even when the demand is for survival. The risks to survival taken by the human species when it flouts natural constraints are only symptomatic of a deeper crisis, according to those who fully accept the ecological world view. They are symptomatic of a rejection of a deep truth about ourselves—that we differ from other living things only in the nature of our adaptations. To destroy other species and the ecosystems in which they evolve is to treat our own past with contempt. It is to forget who we are. If we do not know who we are, it is unlikely that we will adopt a rationally justifiable value system.

According to the ecological world view, then, the human species faces constraints imposed by its dependence upon natural ecosystems. Some demand values are consistent with a recognition of this fact and others are not. Those that are not must be subjected to rational criticism. But the sort of ecological world view within which these values can be criticized cannot be articulated a priori. It can only be worked out by deepening our understanding of ecological relationships—how species function in natural ecosystems. If species are destroyed and ecosystems degraded, the human race cannot gain the knowledge necessary to formulate the details of such a world view. Wild species and pristine ecosystems teach us about ecological relationships and provide analogies and metaphors that give us self-knowledge. They also provide the occasions for forming and criticizing our values, as felt preferences are measured against the evolving world view. In this way they have transformative value.

The Diversity of Life

E. O. Wilson

... [D]iversity, the property that makes resilience possible, is vulnerable to blows that are greater than natural perturbations. It can be eroded away fragment by fragment, and irreversibly so if the abnormal stress is unrelieved. This vulnerability stems from life's composition as swarms of species

The Diversity of Life, by Edward O. Wilson (Cambridge, MA: Harvard University Press, 1992), pp. 14–17, 19, 24, 25, 29, 31, 344–48, 351. Reprinted by permission of the publishers. ©1992 by Edward O. Wilson.

of limited geographical distribution. Every habitat, from Brazilian rain forest to Antarctic bay to thermal vent, harbors a unique combination of plants and animals. Each kind of plant and animal living there is linked in the food web to only a small part of the other species. Eliminate one species, and another increases in number to take its place. Eliminate a great many species, and the local ecosystem starts to decay visibly. Productivity drops as the channels of the nutrient cycles are clogged. More of the biomass is sequestered in the form of dead vegetation and slowly metabolizing, oxygen-starved mud, or is simply washed away. Less competent pollinators take over as the best-adapted bees, moths, birds, bats, and other specialists drop out. Fewer seeds fall, fewer seedlings sprout. Herbivores decline, and their predators die away in close concert.

In an eroding ecosystem life goes on, and it may look superficially the same. There are always species able to recolonize the impoverished area and exploit the stagnant resources, however clumsily accomplished. Given enough time, a new combination of species—a reconstituted fauna and flora—will reinvest the habitat in a way that transports energy and materials somewhat more efficiently. The atmosphere they generate and the composition of the soil they enrich will resemble those found in comparable habitats in other parts of the world, since the species are adapted to penetrate and reinvigorate just such degenerate systems. They do so because they gain more energy and materials and leave more offspring. But the restorative power of the fauna and flora of the world as a whole depends on the existence of enough species to play that special role. They too can slide into the red zone of endangered species.

Biological diversity—"biodiversity" in the new parlance—is the key to the maintenance of the world as we know it. Life in a local site struck down by a passing storm springs back quickly because enough diversity still exists. Opportunistic species evolved for just such an occasion rush in to fill the spaces. They entrain the succession that circles back to something resembling the original state of the environment.

This is the assembly of life that took a billion years to evolve. It has eaten the storms—folded them into its genes—and created the world that created us. It holds the world steady. When I rose

at dawn the next morning, Fazenda Dimona had not changed in any obvious way from the day before.* The same high trees stood like a fortress along the forest's edge; the same profusion of birds and insects foraged through the canopy and understory in precise individual timetables. All this seemed timeless, immutable, and its very strength posed the question: how much force does it take to break the crucible of evolution?

*

Krakatau, earlier misnamed Krakatoa, an island the size of Manhattan located midway in the Sunda Strait between Sumatra and Java, came to an end on Monday morning, August 27, 1883. It was dismembered by a series of powerful volcanic eruptions. The most violent occurred at 10:02 A.M., blowing upward like the shaped explosion of a large nuclear bomb, with an estimated force equivalent to 100–150 megatons of TNT. The airwave it created traveled at the speed of sound around the world, reaching the opposite end of the earth near Bogotá, Colombia, nineteen hours later, whereupon it bounced back to Krakatau and then back and forth for seven recorded passages over the earth's surface. The audible sounds, resembling the distant cannonade of a ship in distress, carried southward across Australia to Perth, northward to Singapore, and westward 4,600 kilometers to Rodriguez Island in the Indian Ocean, the longest distance traveled by any airborne sound in recorded history.

As the island collapsed into the subterranean chamber emptied by the eruption, the sea rushed in to fill the newly formed caldera. A column of magma, rock, and ash rose 5 kilometers into the air, then fell earthward, thrusting the sea outward in a tsunami 40 meters in height. The great tidal waves, resembling black hills when first sighted on the horizon, fell upon the shores of Java and Sumatra, washing away entire towns and killing 40,000 people. The segments traversing the channels and reaching the open sea continued on as spreading waves around the world. The waves were still a meter high when they came ashore in Ceylon, now Sri Lanka, where they drowned one person, their last casualty. Thirty-two hours after the explosion, they rolled in to Le Havre, France, reduced at last to centimeter-high swells.

*Fazenda Dimona is a place on the edge of a rain forest in Brazil, one of the locations of E. O. Wilson's research.

The eruptions lifted more than 18 cubic kilometers of rock and other material into the air. Most of this tephra, as it is called by geologists, quickly rained back down onto the surface, but a residue of sulfuric-acid aerosol and dust boiled upward as high as 50 kilometers and diffused through the stratosphere around the world, where for several years it created brilliant red sunsets and "Bishop's rings," opalescent coronas surrounding the sun.

Back on Krakatau the scene was apocalyptic. Throughout the daylight hours the whole world seemed about to end for those close enough to witness the explosions. At the climactic moment of 10:02 the American barque *W. H. Besse* was proceeding toward the straits 84 kilometers east northeast of Krakatau. The first officer jotted in his logbook that "terrific reports" were heard, followed by

a heavy black cloud rising up from the direction of Krakatoa Island, the barometer fell an inch at one jump, suddenly rising and falling an inch at a time, called all hands, furled all sails securely, which was scarcely done before the squall struck the ship with terrific force; let go port anchor and all the chain in the locker, wind increasing to a hurricane; let go starboard anchor, it had gradually been growing dark since 9 A.M., and by the time the squall struck us, it was darker than any night I ever saw; this was midnight at noon, a heavy shower of ashes came with the squall, the air being so thick it was difficult to breathe, also noticed a strong smell of sulfur, all hands expecting to be suffocated; the terrible noises from the volcano, the sky filled with forked lightning, running in all directions and making the darkness more intense than ever; the howling of the wind through the rigging formed one of the wildest and most awful scenes imaginable, one that will never be forgotten by any one on board, all expecting the last days of the earth had come; the water was running by us in the direction of the volcano at the rate of 12 miles per hour, at 4 P.M. wind moderating, the explosions had nearly ceased, the shower of ashes was not so heavy; so was enabled to see our way around the decks; the ship was covered with tons of fine ashes resembling pumice stone, it stuck to the sails, rigging and masts like glue.

In the following weeks, the Sunda Strait returned to outward normality, but with an altered geography. The center of Krakatau had been re-

placed by an undersea crater 7 kilometers long and 270 meters deep. Only a remnant at the southern end still rose from the sea. It was covered by a layer of obsidian-laced pumice 40 meters or more thick and heated to somewhere between 300° and 850°C, enough at the upper range to melt lead. All traces of life had, of course, been extinguished.

Rakata, the ash-covered mountain of old Krakatau, survived as a sterile island. But life quickly enveloped it again. In a sense, the spinning reel of biological history halted, then reversed, like a motion picture run backward, as living organisms began to return to Rakata. Biologists quickly grasped the unique opportunity that Rakata afforded: to watch the assembly of a tropical ecosystem from the very beginning. Would the organisms be different from those that had existed before? Would a rain forest eventually cover the island again?

The first search for life on Rakata was conducted by a French expedition in May 1884, nine months after the explosions. The main cliff was eroding rapidly, and rocks still rolled down the sides incessantly, stirring clouds of dust and emitting a continuous noise "like the rattling of distant musketry." Some of the stones whirled through the air, ricocheting down the sides of the ravines and splashing into the sea. What appeared to be mist in the distance turned close up into clouds of dust stirred by the falling debris. The crew and expedition members eventually found a safe landing site and fanned out to learn what they could. After searching for organisms in particular, the ship's naturalist wrote that "notwithstanding all my researches, I was not able to observe any symptom of animal life. I only discovered one microscopic spider—only one; this strange pioneer of the renovation was busy spinning its web." . . .

*

What was the greatest blow ever suffered by life through all time? Not the 1883 explosions at Krakatau, which were not even the worst in recorded history. An 1815 eruption at Tambora, 1,400 kilometers to the east of Krakatau on the Indonesian island of Sumbawa, lifted five times as much rock and ash as Krakatau. It inflicted more environmental destruction and killed tens of thousands of people. About 75,000 years ago a still greater eruption occurred in the center of northern Sumatra. It blew out a phenomenal 1,000 cubic kilometers of solid material, creating an oval depression 65 kilometers long that filled with fresh water and persists to this day as Lake Toba. Paleolithic people lived on the island then. We can only imagine what they felt in the presence of an eruption one hundred times the magnitude of Krakatau, and what stories of gods and apocalypse proliferated in the culture afterward.

Great eruptions are likely to have occurred repeatedly across long stretches of geological time. A simple form of statistical reasoning leads to this conclusion. The frequency curve of the intensity of volcanic eruptions around the world, like so many chance phenomena, peaks near the low end and tapers off for a long distance toward the high end. This means that most eruptions are relatively minor perturbations, consisting of a plume of vapor from a fumarole here, a minor lava flow there. Lava fountains and big flows, the next step up, are less common but still occur on a yearly basis somewhere in the world. An event the size of the Krakatau explosion happens once or twice a century. An eruption as big as the one at Toba is far rarer but, over millions of years, probably inevitable.

The same statistical reasoning applies to the fall of meteorites. A large number ranging in size from dust particles to pebbles reach the earth's surface each year, streaking in at 15 to 75 kilometers a second. A much smaller number range in size from baseballs to soccer balls. They account for the majority of the thirty or so meteorites worldwide that can be seen traveling all the way down and are then located by searchers on foot. A very few are much more massive. The largest ever observed in the United States was a 5,000-kilogram meteorite that fell in Norton County, Kansas, on February 18, 1948. Over millions of years only a few truly gigantic meteorites reach the earth's surface. One with a diameter of 1,250 meters gouged out Canyon Diablo in Arizona. Another monster, 3,200 meters in diameter, created the Chubb Depression at Ungava, Quebec.

By extrapolation upward along the scale of violence, it is conceivable and even likely that a volcanic eruption or a meteorite strike occurs once every 10 million or 100 million years so great as to literally shake the earth, drastically change its atmosphere, and as a result extinguish a substantial portion of the species then living. Something of that kind might have happened at the end of the Mesozoic era 66 million years ago, when dinosaurs and a few other prevailing groups of animals were set back or extinguished altogether. . . .

[T]he Cretaceous extinction was only one of five such catastrophes that occurred over the last half-billion years, and it was not the most severe. Furthermore, the earlier spasms appear not to have been associated with meteorite strikes or unusually heavy volcanism. The five mass extinctions occurred in this order, according to geological period and time before the present: Ordovician, 440 million years; Devonian, 365 million years; Permian, 245 million years; Triassic, 210 million years; and Cretaceous, 66 million years. There have been a great many second- and third-order dips and rises, but these five are at the far end of the curve of violence, and they stand out. They are to other episodes as a catastrophe is to a misfortune, a hurricane to a summer squall. . . .

To summarize: life was impoverished in five major events, and to lesser degree here and there around the world in countless other episodes. After each downturn it recovered to at least the original level of diversity. How long did it take for evolution to restore the losses after the first-order spasms? The number of families of animals living in the sea is as reliable a measure as we have been able to obtain from the existing fossil evidence. In general, five million years were enough only for a strong start. A complete recovery from each of the five major extinctions required tens of millions of years. In particular the Ordovician dip needed 25 million years, the Devonian 30 million years, the Permian and Triassic (combined because they were so close together in time) 100 million years, and the Cretaceous 20 million years. These figures should give pause to anyone who believes that what *Homo sapiens* destroys, Nature will redeem. Maybe so, but not within any length of time that has meaning for contemporary humanity. . . .

For the green prehuman earth is the mystery we were chosen to solve, a guide to the birthplace of our spirit, but it is slipping away. The way back seems harder every year. If there is danger in the human trajectory, it is not so much in the survival of our own species as in the fulfillment of the ultimate irony of organic evolution: that in the instant of achieving self-understanding through the mind of man, life has doomed its most beautiful creations. And thus humanity closes the door to its past.

The creation of that diversity came slow and hard: 3 billion years of evolution to start the profusion of animals that occupy the seas, another 350 million years to assemble the rain forests in which half or more of the species on earth now live. There was a succession of dynasties. Some species split into two or several daughter species, and their daughters split yet again to create swarms of descendants that deployed as plant feeders, carnivores, free swimmers, gliders, sprinters, and burrowers, in countless motley combinations. These ensembles then gave way by partial or total extinction to newer dynasties, and so on to form a gentle upward swell that carried biodiversity to a peak—just before the arrival of humans. Life had stalled on plateaus along the way, and on five occasions it suffered extinction spasms that took 10 million years to repair. But the thrust was upward. Today the diversity of life is greater than it was 100 million years ago—and far greater than 500 million years before that.

Most dynasties contained a few species that expanded disproportionately to create satrapies of lesser rank. Each species and its descendants, a sliver of the whole, lived an average of hundreds of thousands to millions of years. Longevity varied according to taxonomic group. Echinoderm lineages, for example, persisted longer than those of flowering plants, and both endured longer than those of mammals.

Ninety-nine percent of all the species that ever lived are now extinct. The modern fauna and flora are composed of survivors that somehow managed to dodge and weave through all the radiations and extinctions of geological history. Many contemporary world-dominant groups, such as rats, ranid frogs, nymphalid butterflies, and plants of the aster family Compositae, attained their status not long before the Age of Man. Young or old, all living species are direct descendants of the organisms that lived 3.8 billion years ago. They are living genetic libraries, composed of nucleotide sequences, the equivalent of words and sentences, which record evolutionary events all across that immense span of time. Organisms more complex than bacteria—protists, fungi, plants, animals—contain between 1 and 10 billion nucleotide letters, more than enough in pure information to compose an equivalent of the *Encyclopaedia Britannica*. Each species is the product of mutations and recombinations too complex to be grasped by unaided intuition. It was sculpted and burnished by an astronomical number of events in natural selection, which killed off or otherwise blocked from reproduction the vast majority of its member organisms before they completed their life spans. Viewed from the perspective of evolutionary time, all other species are our distant kin because we share a remote ancestry. We still use a common vocabulary, the nucleic-acid code, even though it has been sorted into radically different hereditary languages. . . .

Organisms are all the more remarkable in combination. Pull out the flower from its crannied retreat, shake the soil from the roots into the cupped hand, magnify it for close examination. The black earth is alive with a riot of algae, fungi, nematodes, mites, springtails, enchytraeid worms, thousands of species of bacteria. The handful may be only a tiny fragment of one ecosystem, but because of the genetic codes of its residents it holds more order than can be found on the surfaces of all the planets combined. It is a sample of the living force that runs the earth—and will continue to do so with or without us.

We may think that the world has been completely explored. Almost all the mountains and rivers, it is true, have been named, the coast and geodetic surveys completed, the ocean floor mapped to the deepest trenches, the atmosphere transected and chemically analyzed. The planet is now continuously monitored from space by satellites; and, not least, Antarctica, the last virgin continent, has become a research station and expensive tourist stop. The biosphere, however, remains obscure. Even though some 1.4 million species of organisms have been discovered (in the minimal sense of having specimens collected and formal scientific names attached), the total number alive on earth is somewhere between 10 and 100 million. No one can say with confidence which of these figures is the closer. Of the species given scientific names, fewer than 10 percent have been studied at a level deeper than gross anatomy. The revolution in molecular biology and medicine was achieved with a still smaller fraction, including colon bacteria, corn, fruit flies, Norway rats, rhesus monkeys, and human beings, altogether comprising no more than a hundred species.

Enchanted by the continuous emergence of new technologies and supported by generous funding for medical research, biologists have probed deeply along a narrow sector of the front. Now it is time to expand laterally, to get on with the great Linnean enterprise and finish mapping the biosphere. The most compelling reason for the broadening of goals is that, unlike the rest of science, the study of biodiversity has a time limit. Species are disappearing at an accelerating rate through human action, primarily habitat destruction but also pollution and the introduction of exotic species into residual natural environments. I have said that a fifth or more of the species of plants and animals could vanish or be doomed to early extinction by the year 2020 unless better efforts are made to save them. This estimate comes from the known quantitative relation between the area of habitats and the diversity that habitats can sustain. These area-biodiversity curves are supported by the general but not universal principle that when certain groups of organisms are studied closely, such as snails and fishes and flowering plants, extinction is determined to be widespread. And the corollary: among plant and animal remains in archaeological deposits, we usually find extinct species and races. As the last forests are felled in forest strongholds like the Philippines and Ecuador, the decline of species will accelerate even more. In the world as a whole, extinction rates are already hundreds or thousands of times higher than before the coming of man. They cannot be balanced by new evolution in any period of time that has meaning for the human race.

Why should we care? What difference does it make if some species are extinguished, if even half of all the species on earth disappear? Let me count the ways. New sources of scientific information will be lost. Vast potential biological wealth will be destroyed. Still undeveloped medicines, crops, pharmaceuticals, timber, fibers, pulp, soil-restoring vegetation, petroleum substitutes, and other products and amenities will never come to light. It is fashionable in some quarters to wave aside the small and obscure, the bugs and weeds, forgetting that an obscure moth from Latin America saved Australia's pastureland from overgrowth by cactus, that the rosy periwinkle provided the cure for Hodgkin's disease and childhood lymphocytic leukemia, that the bark of the Pacific yew offers hope for victims of ovarian and breast cancer, that a chemical from the saliva of leeches dissolves blood clots during surgery, and so on down a roster already grown long and illustrious despite the limited research addressed to it.

In amnesiac revery it is also easy to overlook the services that ecosystems provide humanity. They enrich the soil and create the very air we breathe. Without these amenities, the remaining tenure of the human race would be nasty and brief. The life-sustaining matrix is built of green plants with legions of microorganisms and mostly small, obscure animals—in other words, weeds and bugs. Such organisms support the world with efficiency because they are so diverse, allowing them to divide labor and swarm over every square meter of the earth's surface. They run the world precisely as we would wish it to be run, because humanity evolved within living communities and our bodily functions are finely adjusted to the idiosyncratic environment already created. Mother Earth, lately called Gaia, is no more than the commonality of organisms and the physical environment they maintain with each passing moment, an environment that will destabilize and turn lethal if the organisms are disturbed too much. A near infinity of other mother planets can be envisioned, each with its own fauna and flora, all producing physical environments uncongenial to human life. To disregard the diversity of life is to risk catapulting ourselves into an alien environment. We will have become like the pilot whales that inexplicably beach themselves on New England shores.

Humanity coevolved with the rest of life on this particular planet; other worlds are not in our genes. Because scientists have yet to put names on most kinds of organisms, and because they entertain only a vague idea of how ecosystems work, it is reckless to suppose that biodiversity can be diminished indefinitely without threatening humanity itself. Field studies show that as biodiversity is reduced, so is the quality of the services provided by ecosystems. Records of stressed ecosystems also demonstrate that the descent can be unpredictably abrupt. As extinction spreads, some of the lost forms prove to be keystone species, whose disappearance brings down other species and triggers a ripple effect through the demographics of the survivors. The loss of a keystone species is like a drill accidentally striking a powerline. It causes lights to go out all over.

These services are important to human welfare. But they cannot form the whole foundation of an enduring environmental ethic. If a price can be put on something, that something can be devalued, sold, and discarded. It is also possible for some to dream that people will go on living comfortably in a biologically impoverished world. They suppose that a prosthetic environment is within the power of technology, that human life can still flourish in a completely humanized world, where medicines would all be synthesized from chemicals off the shelf, food grown from a few dozen domestic crop species, the atmosphere and climate regulated by computer-driven fusion energy, and the earth made over until it becomes a literal spaceship rather than a metaphorical one, with people reading displays and touching buttons on the bridge. Such is the terminus of the philosophy of exemptionalism: do not weep for the past, humanity is a new order of life, let species die if they block progress, scientific and technological genius will find another way. Look up and see the stars awaiting us.

But consider: human advance is determined not by reason alone but by emotions peculiar to our species, aided and tempered by reason. What makes us people and not computers is emotion. We have little grasp of our true nature, of what it is to be human and therefore where our descendants might someday wish we had directed Spaceship Earth. Our troubles, as Vercors said in *You Shall Know Them*, arise from the fact that we do not know what we are and cannot agree on what we want to be. The primary cause of this intellectual failure is ignorance of our origins. We did not arrive on this planet as aliens. Humanity is part of nature, a species that evolved among other species. The more closely we identify ourselves with the rest of life, the more quickly we will be able to discover the sources of human sensibility and acquire the knowledge on which an enduring ethic, a sense of preferred direction, can be built.

The human heritage does not go back only for the conventionally recognized 8,000 years or so of recorded history, but for a least 2 million years, to the appearance of the first "true" human beings, the earliest species composing the genus *Homo*. Across thousands of generations, the emergence of culture must have been profoundly influenced by simultaneous events in genetic evolution, especially those occurring in the anatomy and physiology of the brain. Conversely, genetic evolution must

have been guided forcefully by the kinds of selection rising within culture.

Only in the last moment of human history has the delusion arisen that people can flourish apart from the rest of the living world. Preliterate societies were in intimate contact with a bewildering array of life forms. Their minds could only partly adapt to that challenge. But they struggled to understand the most relevant parts, aware that the right responses gave life and fulfillment, the wrong ones sickness, hunger, and death. The imprint of that effort cannot have been erased in a few generations of urban existence. I suggest that it is to be found among the particularities of human nature, among which are these:

- People acquire phobias, abrupt and intractable aversions, to the objects and circumstances that threaten humanity in natural environments: heights, closed spaces, open spaces, running water, wolves, spiders, snakes. They rarely form phobias to the recently invented contrivances that are far more dangerous, such as guns, knives, automobiles, and electric sockets.

- People are both repelled and fascinated by snakes, even when they have never seen one in nature. In most cultures the serpent is the dominant wild animal of mythical and religious symbolism. Manhattanites dream of them with the same frequency as Zulus. This response appears to be Darwinian in origin. Poisonous snakes have been an important cause of mortality almost everywhere, from Finland to Tasmania, Canada to Patagonia; an untutored alertness in their presence saves lives. We note a kindred response in many primates, including Old World monkeys and chimpanzees: the animals pull back, alert others, watch closely, and follow each potentially dangerous snake until it moves away. . . .

Wilderness is a metaphor of unlimited opportunity, rising from the tribal memory of a time when humanity spread across the world, valley to valley, island to island, godstruck, firm in the belief that virgin land went on forever past the horizon.

I cite these common preferences of mind not as proof of an innate human nature but rather to suggest that we think more carefully and turn philosophy to the central questions of human origins in the wild environment. We do not understand ourselves yet and descend farther from heaven's air if we forget how much the natural world means to us. Signals abound that the loss of life's diversity endangers not just the body but the spirit. If that much is true, the changes occurring now will visit harm on all generations to come.

The ethical imperative should therefore be, first of all, prudence. We should judge every scrap of biodiversity as priceless while we learn to use it and come to understand what it means to humanity. We should not knowingly allow any species or race to go extinct. And let us go beyond mere salvage to begin the restoration of natural environments, in order to enlarge wild populations and stanch the hemorrhaging of biological wealth. There can be no purpose more enspiriting than to begin the age of restoration, reweaving the wondrous diversity of life that still surrounds us.

The evidence of swift environmental change calls for an ethic uncoupled from other systems of belief. Those committed by religion to believe that life was put on earth in one divine stroke will recognize that we are destroying the Creation, and those who perceive biodiversity to be the product of blind evolution will agree. Across the other great philosophical divide, it does not matter whether species have independent rights or, conversely, that moral reasoning is uniquely a human concern. Defenders of both premises seem destined to gravitate toward the same position on conservation.

The stewardship of environment is a domain on the near side of metaphysics where all reflective persons can surely find common ground. For what, in the final analysis, is morality but the command of conscience seasoned by a rational examination of consequences? And what is a fundamental precept but one that serves all generations? An enduring environmental ethic will aim to preserve not only the health and freedom of our species, but access to the world in which the human spirit was born.

Two Types of Preservation Policies*

Roger Paden

Debates within the field of environmental ethics have been decisively shaped by two related distinctions. The first is a distinction between two supposedly radically dissimilar and opposing ethical positions, the traditional Western "anthropocentric" ethic and a new environmentalist "biocentric ethic." Although these ethics are generally considered to be polar opposites, in fact, I believe, both often make use of the same moral theory, namely, preference or "interest" utilitarianism.[1] According to the interpretation of this theory, most common among anthropocentrists, the only thing that has "intrinsic" value is the satisfaction of human interests. Other things may have instrumental value to the degree that they are useful in helping to satisfy those interests, but the only "final goods," to use Aristotle's phrase, are those satisfactions. A biocen-

tric theory, on the other hand, typically holds that the satisfaction of the interests of nonhumans, such as animals and, perhaps, plants, is also intrinsically valuable, is also a final good. On this view, actions that result in the satisfaction of those interests are also morally commendable, *ceteris paribus*, independently of their effect on human interest satisfaction.

This distinction gives rise to another distinction between two kinds of positions concerned with the protection of the environment. One position, "conservationism," seeks to protect the environment in order to guarantee the long-term availability for humans of scarce natural resources. As the goal of this policy is to maximize total (present and future) human interest-satisfaction, conservationism is taken to be based on traditional anthropocentric concerns. The other position, "preservationism," is usually thought to be based on the newer biocentric ethic because it holds that nature must be protected and preserved in a pristine state

*I would like to thank Gary Varner for his careful and helpful criticisms of an earlier version of this essay.

"for its own sake" in order to guard its interests, independently of any potential instrumental value that protection may have in satisfying human interests.[2]

Given these distinctions, two general approaches to environmental protection follow. Environmental ethicists have typically taken the articulation and defense of one or the other of these positions to be the central task of their field. However, I believe that these neat distinctions will not withstand careful investigation. Moreover, I think that they obscure the moral foundations of our duties to natural entities and may prevent us from fully grasping and acting on those duties. In part, these distinctions are misleading because they obscure another distinction, one between two types of preservationist policies. I believe that an understanding of that distinction is essential to the development and defense of any truly adequate preservationist position.

I

Unless we have a clear idea of what we mean by the term "nature," any claim that we have a direct duty to nature to protect it will be open to multiple and perhaps conflicting interpretations. In our society, as I will outline below, "nature" generally has been understood in two ways. These two interpretations of nature, I believe, can be associated with two radically different approaches to environmental preservation. Unfortunately, these two interpretations and the approaches to environmental preservation that they support entail opposing kinds of policies. Let us look at two important examples.

In 1973, Congress passed the first Endangered Species Act. Arguably, this act, together with its successors, has done more to preserve wilderness areas than any other law. Oddly enough, however, the original purpose of the act was not to protect wilderness areas, but to protect endangered species, by protecting individual members of those species from hunters, developers, and polluting industries. However, as the law was written, it not only forbid the direct killing of those animals but also required the preservation of their "critical habitats." As the Supreme Court interpreted this law, this must be done "without exception" and at "whatever cost." Unfortunately, as the act was writ-

ten and later amended, it contained several loopholes, such as the possibility of administrative review of controversial applications. In these reviews, economic considerations would be allowed to play a significant role, possibly resulting in reduced protection. Nevertheless, endangered species legislation still provides significant protection to the environment, and is a paradigm example of this type of preservationist policy.[3]

In 1964 the U.S. Park Service adopted a controversial fire management policy that best exemplifies another kind of preservationist program. This policy, recognizing that naturally occurring forest fires play an important role in maintaining a viable ecosystem, forbids Park Service employees from fighting naturally occurring forest fires unless the fires threaten famous landmarks or tourist areas. Instead, these fires were to be left to burn themselves out.[4] This policy clearly represents a different kind of preservation policy, one that seeks not to preserve specific species or other parts of nature, but instead to isolate nature from human interference or, in the words of the policy itself, to "neutralize the unnatural influences of man, thus permitting the natural environment to be maintained essentially by nature."[5]

These two examples represent two vastly different approaches to environmental preservation. The Endangered Species Act is a paradigm example of what I will call a "product preservation policy." It tries to preserve specific parts or products of nature, in this case specific endangered species. It assumes that our direct duty to nature is a duty to protect those products. On the other hand, the Park Service's fire management policy is a paradigm example of what I will call a "process preservation policy." It does not seek to protect specific parts of nature, but instead requires us to preserve natural systems—the dynamic processes of nature. Obviously, these two general kinds of policies differ in several ways.

First, these polices entail contradictory programs. Product preservation policies, such as those aimed at the preservation of species, as recent attempts to preserve the California condor have demonstrated, will often require humans to interfere with ongoing natural processes. For example, to prevent an extinction, people might have to manipulate an endangered species' habitat by controlling predators and diseases or by ensuring an adequate food supply. As a result, the adoption of such a policy would probably require a high level of intervention in natural systems. Moreover, it is important to understand that such a policy would require these interventions even if the extinctions could be traced to natural causes.[6] In these cases, policies that aim at the preservation of species would require people to halt or control the natural developmental processes that are the cause of the extinctions. Because these policies are based on the assumption that all species have intrinsic value and, therefore, deserve to be preserved, they cannot, in principle, distinguish between extinctions based on their causes. On the other hand, the Park Service's fire management policy, if taken to its logical conclusion, would forbid such interference, even if interference were necessary to preserve valuable parts of nature, for on this view, it is essential to preserve intrinsically valuable natural processes. As a result, it is probable that, if the environmental movement continues to influence federal legislation, these two kinds of policies will come increasingly into conflict. While process preservation policies would require us, with some exceptions, to let naturally occurring, but destructive, processes continue without interference, even if this threatens intrinsically valuable natural products, product preservation policies would require us to protect those products, even if doing so necessitated the creation of largely "artificial" environments.

Second, these two kinds of policies are based on two different ideas of nature. Product preservation policies assume that nature consists of a collection of discrete parts or products, each with its own interests that, *ceteris paribus*, should be satisfied. Process preservation policies, on the other hand, assume that nature is a dynamic system. Unfortunately, these two conceptions are often confused in environmentalist declarations. For example, when Aldo Leopold declares that we must protect the "integrity, stability, and beauty" of the "biotic community,"[7] it is unclear what he intends us to do. Leopold's principle, that is to say, cannot support a consistent preservation policy because it inconsistently requires us to protect both the "stability" and the "integrity" of ecosystems. To see that this principle is inconsistent, it is necessary to understand its fundamental terms. "Stability," I believe, simply implies a lack of change.[8] A thing is stable if its internal structure remains the same and if its constituent parts do not change. For example, a society is stable if it maintains an unchanging institutional structure and as long as the nature of its members does not undergo any radical changes as one generation replaces another. "Integrity," however, has an entirely different meaning. People have integrity, I believe, if they are not easily influenced by outside events; for example, if they do not allow considerations of temporary political gain to alter their fundamental principles. Indeed, integrity can even lead people to change, as when a more complex understanding of moral principles leads a person to abandon a previously held policy position. Thus, a person has integrity to the degree that he or she is self-determining. Similarly, a natural system could be said to possess integrity to the degree that it is self-determining, that is, to the degree to which it is free from significant human interference. Because Leopold's principle is cast in terms of these two very different terms, it entails inconsistent duties. If we have a duty to protect the stability of a biotic community, we would, on occasion, have to intervene in the biotic community. However, if we have a duty to respect that community's integrity, we would have to refrain from interfering with that community.

The fundamental reason that Leopold's principle is ambiguous, however, is not because he failed to appreciate the distinction between stability and integrity, but rather because he held an ambiguous conception of the "biotic community." In using that phrase, no doubt, Leopold wanted to draw our attention to the similarities between the biotic and human "communities." Perhaps the best way to explain the source of Leopold's problem is to point out that human communities can be understood on two different models. While "libertarians" understand human communities to consist of essentially independent, intrinsically valuable persons, "communitarians" understand them in terms of developing traditions. Unfortunately Leopold, in effect, adopted both these views, despite the fact that they are incompatible. When stressing stability, Leopold adopted the libertarian model which emphasizes the intrinsic value of the parts, but when stressing integrity, he adopted the communitarian model, which emphasizes the importance of the whole. Thus, implicit in Leopold's principle are two contradictory conceptions of nature. One conception is essentially individualistic, in which nature is thought of as a set of relatively independent parts. The other is essentially holistic, in which nature is thought of as a dynamic whole. Unfortunately, from these differing conceptions, different programs follow.

II

Product and process preservation approaches to environmental preservation can be distinguished on practical and conceptual grounds, but they *must* also be distinguished on moral grounds. These two approaches can only be defended through appeals to fundamentally different kinds of moral arguments. Unfortunately, this has not been generally recognized.

The reason for this is that environmental ethics has been dominated by a particular moral paradigm which understands value solely in terms of the satisfaction of interests. Work in environmental ethics typically falls within the utilitarian tradition of moral philosophy, broadly construed.[9] In particular, most justifications of preservationist policies have been constructed within this paradigm. There is nothing necessarily wrong with this, if what is to be justified is a product preservation policy—at least in those cases in which the product in question can conceivably have some kind of interest. If natural products do have interests, then it might be possible to justify a product preservation policy within this paradigm.

However, justifications of process preservation policies could only be constructed within this paradigm, if it is plausible to attribute interests to natural processes or natural wholes—for example, to ecosystems. Of course, many environmentalists have claimed—citing as evidence the striking stability and resilience of ecosystems, especially their ability to maintain a dynamic equilibrium—that ecosystems are goal-directed.[10] Moreover, because there is a conceptual connection between being goal-directed and having interests, such that to be directed at a goal is to have an interest, many environmentalists have argued that if nature is goal-directed, it must have morally significant interests.[11] I would argue, however, that nature is not goal-directed and, therefore, that it can have no interests. If this is true, then it would be impossible to justify process preservation policies by appealing to the interests of nature.

If a thing is to be said to have a goal, it must not only pursue that goal through a variety of flexible, but persistent, behaviors but also engage in those behaviors *because* they will lead to that goal. That is, a system is goal-directed only if its actions tend to bring about a goal *and* its actions occur *because* they tend to bring about that goal.[12] It is clear that animals and plants qualify as goal-directed according to this definition. As a result, it may be possible to attribute morally significant interests to them. Given this definition, it might even be possible to attribute morally significant interests to some robots and sophisticated guided missiles. However, even given this definition, it is not possible to attribute morally significant interests to ecosystems. The fact that ecosystems can maintain complex dynamic equilibriums does not, as many environmental ethicists believe, show that they are goal-directed. This is the case because stability is not the "goal" of ecosystems; it is instead a "by-product" of the goal-directed behavior of their constituent organisms.[13]

To illustrate this point, a direct analogy could be drawn between ecosystems and economies. Although the people participating in an economy are goal-directed and, therefore, have interests, this does not imply that the economy is goal-directed. This is the case despite the fact that the economy, through a variety of mechanisms, maintains a dynamic equilibrium. The economy does not aim at equilibrium, nor does it have an interest in maintaining equilibrium. Therefore, although various political actions may affect the economy, and possibly hurt the interests of the people participating in it, no such action can negatively affect the interests of the economy itself, as it has none. Similarly, with ecosystems. Because ecosystems are not goal-directed, they have no interests. If this is the case, however, it is a mistake to attribute interests to them.

If ecosystems have no interests, then we can have no obligation to protect their interests. However, if this is true, the moral justification of product preservation policies, which can be based on appeals to the interests of those products, must be very different from the moral justification of process preservation policies, which cannot be based on an appeal to the interests of those processes. While product preservation policies can be based on principles requiring the equal protection of interests, process preservation policies must be based on wholly different considerations.

III

The realization that there are two distinct kinds of preservationist positions indicates that the simple division of "ethics" into traditional anthropocentric and modern biocentric ethics may be mistaken. Indeed, recognition of the unique character of process preservation policies puts that distinction in a new light: Anthropocentrism and biocentrism, as they are usually conceived, actually differ very little. Both are typically constructed within a moral paradigm that understands morality to be a matter of the satisfaction of interests. They disagree only on the range of entities that can be said to have interests. Thus, whereas conservationism seeks to maximize only human interests, product preservationism seeks to include nonhuman interests into the moral calculus. However, if process preservation policies can be morally justified on biocentric grounds and if my argument that ecosystems do not have interests is correct, then that paradigm is, at the very least, incomplete. Given my arguments, therefore, it might seem to be a good idea for environmental ethicists to abandon the project of developing teleological accounts of nature in order to explore the possibility of developing a new moral paradigm that could better justify process preservation policies.[14] Such work, however, would face two immediate problems.

The first problem is conceptual. Process preservation policies entail that a distinction can be drawn between natural processes and artificial processes ("human interference"). In practice this distinction is relatively easy to make. In theory, however, it is open to the objection that human beings are merely another part of nature. If so, then this distinction is clearly a spurious one; the residue, it might be thought, of an older "dualistic" anthropocentric metaphysics that in other contexts preservationists have rejected. Still, it might be possible to maintain this distinction without reverting to a dualistic metaphysics. Indeed, one way to maintain this distinction has already been suggested in this paper: We are beings with interests and goals, while nature is not.[15]

The second problem is more "practical." If process preservation policies cannot be justified within the paradigm that has dominated environmental ethics, then it would seem that a new moral paradigm, a new ethic, must be developed. This would, however, in all probability be an impossible task, for, as John Passmore has put it, "an ethic . . . is not the sort of thing one can simply decide to have; 'needing an ethic' is not the least like 'needing a new coat.' A 'new ethic' will arise out of existing attitudes or not at all."[16] Luckily, as several environmental ethicists, most notably perhaps, Sagoff[17] and Hargrove,[18] have pointed out, there is no need to develop a "new" ethic, for a close examination of Western—and particularly American—attitudes toward nature will reveal an existing, but often overlooked, ethic sufficient to ground preservationist policies.

This older ethic is based on a variety of "attitudes" or judgments about nature, such as that nature is beautiful, or intensely interesting, or connected with or essential to our humanity. Unfortunately, modern philosophers, who, like Passmore, have adopted the interest-satisfaction model of morality, have tended either to ignore these attitudes, believing them to be irrelevant to moral theory, or they have understood them in terms of that model. For example, they have understood the moral significance of the statement that something is beautiful to be that it is "aesthetically satisfying." They have tended, that is to say, to cash out the moral value of a beautiful object in terms of its ability to satisfy an aesthetic interest. It then follows that our duty to preserve beautiful objects is, in fact, a duty to ourselves to maximize the satisfaction of our aesthetic interests. Given this view, together with the fact that our desires for aesthetic experiences are typically relatively weak, it follows that it will be difficult to justify any process preservation policy on these grounds. It is for this reason, in fact, that I believe, that some environmentalists have been driven to attribute strong countervailing interests to nature. However, a better approach, one more in line with our moral intuitions, would be to resist the reduction of beauty to interest-satisfaction and to argue that we have a direct duty to protect beautiful things simply because they are beautiful. This duty is not only independent of any duty we might have to ensure future interest-satisfaction; it is also, at least arguably, more important.[19]

Modern philosophers typically feel uncomfortable with these kinds of claims. We are not used to dealing with such "thick" moral concepts, and we lack a developed theory within which they can be deployed. Therefore, we are worried about the proper response to their inevitable conflict. Finally, that those philosophers who adopt this view often also seem to adopt forms of intuitionism and relativism worries us even more.[20] But, given the problems with the attempt to attribute interests to nature, if a process preservation policy is to be defended on biocentric grounds, it may, in the end, be better to defend it through an appeal to such thick moral concepts as beauty.

Beyond the discomfort engendered by the use of these thick concepts, two objections have been raised to this kind of defense of preservation policies. First, it has been argued that, as it is human beings who judge things to be beautiful, beauty must itself be anthropocentric, and anthropocentrism fails to do justice to the intrinsic value of nature. This, however, is misleading. Although judging something to be beautiful, like believing something to be important, is a subjective—perhaps uniquely human—state, as Kant pointed out, such judgments, like all beliefs, have objective content. We claim that nature is beautiful, understanding ourselves to be making an objective claim. The beauty is *for* us, but it is *in* nature. Our duty to preserve nature is a duty to it, based on the fact that it is beautiful. It is not a duty to our subjective experience, although that experience may inform us of our duty.

Second, it might be objected that, because our ability to recognize, appreciate, and respond to beauty is so fragile, beauty is not a strong foundation for preservationist policies. It is, of course, true that we will be motivated to protect nature's beauty only if we recognize that beauty, and that our ability to recognize beauty depends on our subjective, perhaps socially determined, constitution. Moreover, it might be added that we are becoming, seemingly, a society of people who do not respond (as a society) to beauty nor value it. As noted above, our aesthetic interests—and, therefore, our aesthetic motivations—are notoriously weak. Because of these factors, it might be argued, it is imperative that we develop preservationist arguments based on some other ground, such as the assumption that nature has interests.

This argument, however, rests on a confusion between the justification of a moral claim and our motivation to act morally, and it will lead us to give bad reasons for good policies. Even worse, such an argument will be counterproductive, partly because, as I have argued, it will be impossible to sustain the claim that nature has morally significant interests. More importantly, such an argument will be counterproductive because it will tend to undercut all arguments for the preservation of nature, such as Leopold's appeal to natural beauty, that are grounded in its aesthetic value. This is so for the following reason. A good case can be made, I believe, for the claim that our increasing social inability to respond to beauty is, at least in part, a consequence of our rigid adherence to the interest-satisfaction paradigm of morality. If this is the case, then our dependence on that paradigm may be self-fulfilling, in that it may ultimately diminish our ability to respond to arguments based on thick moral concepts and, thereby, undercut all preservationist policies.

The adoption of an aesthetically grounded approach to preservationism would allow us to dispense with the simple distinction between anthropocentric and biocentric ethics, as it relieves us of the burden of discovering and evaluating interests "centered" in ourselves or nature. As a result, we would not have to pretend that nature is intrinsically valuable solely because it has interests, nor would we have to pretend that beauty is valuable solely because it satisfies our interests in having aesthetic experiences. Giving up this view would be liberating. It would allow us to abandon the attempt to reconstruct a teleological conception of nature. It would allow us to adopt a more plausible explanation of the value of beauty. Most importantly, it would help us overcome the idea that the relationship between humans and nature is necessarily antagonistic that lies implicit in the distinction between anthropocentrism and biocentrism. Abandoning this distinction would not only lead to a healthy reexamination of our relations to nature but also might allow us to fully understand the foundation of our duties to nature.

Notes

1. In what follows, I will focus my remarks on those biocentric philosophers who use this moral theory. Some biocentrists do not use this theory, but instead appeal to "the rights of nature," e.g., see Roderick Nash, *The Rights of Nature: A History of Environmental Ethics* (Madison: University of Wisconsin

Press, 1989). I believe that my criticisms would also apply to them, but I will not develop that line here.

2. For a more detailed discussion of the history of conservationism and preservationism in U.S. history, see my "Wilderness Management" forthcoming in *Environmental Rights in Conflict,* Joseph Pappin, ed., Temple University Press.

3. For an excellent history of this legislation, see, Nash, *The Rights of Nature,* pp. 174–78.

4. USDA, *Final Report on Fire Management Policy, May 5, 1989* (Washington, DC: U.S. Government Printing Office, 1989), p. 2.

5. A. S. Leopold, et al., "Resource Management Policy," in National Park Service, *Compilation of Administrative Policies for the National Parks and National Monuments of Scientific Significance (Natural Area Category),* rev. ed. (Washington, DC: U.S. Government Printing Office, 1970), p. 106, quoted in Eugene Hargrove, *Foundations of Environmental Ethics* (Englewood Cliffs, NJ: Prentice-Hall, 1989), pp. 139–40.

6. Indeed, section 1533 of the Endangered Species Act explicitly protects all endangered species, no matter the cause of their endangerment.

7. Aldo Leopold, *A Sand County Almanac: With Essays on Conservation from Round River* (New York: Ballantine Books, 1968), p. 262.

8. For example, see Bryan Norton, "Agricultural Development and Environmental Policy: The Conceptual Issues," *Agriculture and Human Values* 2 (1985), 62–63, for a discussion of the meaning of "stability" as it applies to environmental issues.

9. Of course, many environmentalists, unlike some utilitarians, believe that animals and plants have interests.

10. For example, see J. E. Lovelock, *Gaia: A New Look at Life on Earth* (Oxford: Oxford University Press, 1979), or Holmes Rolston, *Environmental Ethics: Duties to and Values in the Natural World* (Philadelphia: Temple University Press, 1988).

11. Harley Cahen, "Against the Moral Considerability of Ecosystems," *Environmental Ethics* 10 (1988): 195–216.

12. Larry Wright, "Explanation and Teleology," *Philosophy of Science* 19 (1972): 211–23.

13. Cahen, "Against the Moral Considerability of Nature."

14. Another possibility, of course, would be to develop purely anthropocentric arguments for process preservation policies. An example of this kind of argument can be found in Bryan Norton, *Why Preserve Natural Variety?* (Princeton, NJ: Princeton University Press, 1987). Of course, one problem with these kinds of arguments is that they are not "biocentric," that is, they do not support our intuition that nature is valuable in itself. This may not be a serious problem, however.

15. Of course, to draw a distinction between humans and nature in this way undercuts any claim that nature is morally significant *because* it has interests. In any case, however, more work would have to be done on this issue to show the moral significance of this distinction.

16. John Passmore, *Man's Responsibility for Nature: Ecological Problems and Western Traditions,* 2nd ed. (London: Duckworth, 1980), p. 56.

17. Mark Sagoff, *The Economy of the Earth* (Cambridge: Cambridge University Press, 1988), pp. 124–145.

18. Hargrove, *Foundations,* pp. 77–136.

19. See Sagoff, *The Economy of the Earth,* pp. 101–106, for such an argument.

20. For examples of this tendency toward intuitionism, see Hargrove, *Foundations,* pp. 1–13, and Sagoff, *Economy of the Earth,* pp. 146–170.

D. FORESTS AND WILDERNESS

PREVIEW

I'm the Lorax who speaks for the trees
which you seem to be chopping
as fast as you please.

Dr. Seuss, The Lorax[1]

Even on the eve of the end of the world,
plant a tree.

The Koran

The term "wilderness" is not easy to define, but a useful working definition is: an area of the earth substantially untrammeled or unmodified by human beings. Virtually no one suggests that an area must be entirely untouched by humans in order to qualify as wilderness. For example, in defining the context of wilderness, the Wilderness Act of 1964 recognized human beings as visitors who do not remain.[2] Val Routley [now Val Plumwood], in her comment on John Passmore's remark that the presence of recreationists converts wilderness into "man-made landscape," maintains: "The occasional human presence and evidence of human activity around trails do not convert an area to a 'man-made landscape,'—anymore than the presence of a wombat trail creates a wombat-made landscape."[3]

What is it that is so especially valuable about wilderness? Does its existence fill a need in the human psyche? Is there some value in just knowing that it is there to go into if we should want to do that? Must its existence be good for us at all? Is there a moral obligation to preserve wilderness and wildness?

Many of the arguments that are given in defense of preserving the wild are labelled utilitarian. Here "utilitarian" carries one of its traditional meanings, that of identifying as good those things that are useful or "of utility" to human beings (consider "utility companies"). For example, the scientific, recreational, aesthetic, and spiritual arguments are all utilitarian in this sense. Perhaps, according to a utilitarian view, there is an optimal amount of wilderness.

One argument related to scientific concerns maintains that wilderness should be preserved because it contains a reservoir of genetic diversity. Norman Myers in his "Tropical Forests and Their Species: Going, Going . . . ?" explains in rich detail a mass extinction episode that we are witnessing now due to worldwide deforestation.

Recreational, aesthetic, and spiritual arguments for wilderness preservation center on the importance of wilderness experience. Wilderness often evokes responses of awe, wonder, even terror. For much of human history, wilderness denoted a harsh environment "cursed by God, and commonly occupied by foul creatures."[4] The same scenes that once elicited fear, contempt, and alienation are at other times touted as the source of inspiration, spiritual catharsis, and therapy from the stress

and strain of civilized life. For example, the Derbyshire peak region in England was once considered unfit for viewing. "Travelers . . . were advised to keep their coach blinds drawn while traversing the region so as not to be shocked by its ugliness and wildness. Within a few decades, however, the very same region came to be regarded as so attractive that it inspired lines of extravagant praise by nineteenth-century poets."[5]

Aesthetic considerations can be powerful, but they have their limitations. For example, John Rodman points out that aesthetic arguments are particularly plausible in arguing for the preservation of the Sierra and the Grand Canyons, but not with respect to saving the marshes and brushlands.[6] He further asserts that some, but not all, sacred spaces are informed by an aesthetic of the sublime and the beautiful. Thus, if we rely on aesthetic considerations, what we save depends in part on our conception of what is beautiful or ugly, awe-inspiring or threatening, clarifying or puzzling.

Wilderness, it is claimed, has a positive influence on human character: "Wilderness can teach us moral lessons; we can learn humility and gratitude, but we also can gain self-reliance, independence, and courage in facing the challenge of the wild. Wilderness has molded us as a nation; Daniel Boone, the Oregon Trail, and the Western frontier are all part of our national heritage."[7] The loss of wilderness may mean the loss of freedom in a sense quite different from freedom as a cultural symbol. Freedom will be lost in that our choices among environments will be limited to those we create ourselves.[8]

Bryan G. Norton, as the title of his book—*Toward Unity Among Environmentalists*—indicates, sees general agreement and accord among contemporary environmentalists in their policy proposals for preserving forests or wilderness. In his short section on Forest Service policy, he says that both the Forest Service and organizations such as The Wilderness Society and the Sierra Club now recognize that managing national forests is "a balancing act."[9] He means by this that both have accepted that national forests will have a "productive" use (the Pinchot influence) and both accept the importance of aesthetic and amenity values (the Muir influence). Preservation organizations, he says, ". . . [argue] for wilderness whenever possible as a counterforce against a perceived bias of foresters toward timber production over other aesthetic and moral goals."[10]

Perri Knize, in his "The Mismanagement of the National Forests," does not sanction a balancing act. He thinks the Forest Service should get out of the timber industry altogether. Grinding up our ancient trees into pulp ". . . to make disposable diapers and cellophane for cigarette packs"[11] is inexcusable when, among other considerations, ". . . we don't need the lumber, . . . the timber program loses money . . . the program is used to prop up faltering local economies artificially, and . . . we have a biological stake in an end to logging our national forests."[12] Knize would replace the funds the Forest Service now receives from timber sales with recreation fees. He says, "Without fees, all taxpayers are paying for the destruction of the national forests. With fees, those who used the national forests would be paying to preserve their integrity."[13]

It is easy to assume after amassing all these reasons for wilderness preservation that the case we have made applies globally. The work of Ramachandra Guha, however, makes clear that in exporting our valuing of wilderness preservation to third-world countries as in our supporting tiger preserves, Americans fail to recognize how culture-bound their values are. America, as a large and rich country, can afford to preserve wilderness. As Guha sees it, doing so is just one more consumer luxury and one that third-world countries cannot afford. They must give higher priority

to the ". . . integration of ecological concerns with livelihood and work."[14] Here and in his concern for equity and social justice, Guha is in agreement with Vandana Shiva. Guha would in all likelihood agree with Ian Barbour's statement that "wilderness has molded [the United States] as a nation." Perhaps Guha would even agree that wilderness has taught Americans some virtues, but social justice and moderation in consumption have not been among them.

NOTES

1. Dr. Seuss, *The Lorax* (New York: Random House, 1971).

2. Public Law 88-577 in U.S., *Statutes At Large*, 78, pp. 890–96.

3. Val Routley [now Val Plumwood], "Critical Notice of John Passmore's *Man's Responsibility for Nature*," *Australasian Journal of Philosophy*, 53 (1975), 182.

4. René Dubos, *The Wooing of the Earth* (New York: Charles Scribner's Sons, 1980), p. 10.

5. René Dubos, *The Wooing of the Earth*, p. 14.

6. John Rodman, "Four Forms of Ecological Consciousness Reconsidered," *Ethics and the Environment*, edited by Donald Scherer and Thomas Attig (Englewood Cliffs, NJ: Prentice-Hall, 1983), p. 86.

7. Ian Barbour, *Technology, Environment, and Human Values* (New York: Praeger, 1980), p. 83.

8. See Edward B. Swain for a defense of freedom in this sense, "Wilderness and the Maintenance of Freedom, *The Humanist* (March/April 1983).

9. Bryan G. Norton, *Toward Unity Among Environmentalists* (New York: Oxford University Press, 1991), p. 106.

10. Bryan G. Norton, *Toward Unity Among Environmentalists*, p. 106.

11. Perri Knize, "The Mismanagement of the National Forests," *The Atlantic Monthly* (October 1991), 100.

12. Perri Knize, "The Mismanagement of the National Forests," p. 108.

13. Perri Knize, "The Mismanagement of the National Forests," p. 112.

14. Ramachandra Guha, "Radical American Environmentalism and Wilderness Preservation: A Third World Critique," *Environmental Ethics*, Vol. 11, No. 1 (Spring 1989), 81.

Tropical Forests and Their Species: Going, Going . . . ?

Norman Myers

There is strong evidence that we are into the opening stages of an extinction spasm. That is, we are witnessing a mass extinction episode, in the sense of a sudden and pronounced decline worldwide in the abundance and diversity of ecologically disparate groups of organisms.

Of course extinction has been a fact of life since the emergence of species almost 4 billion years ago. Of all species that have ever existed, possibly half a billion or more, there now remain only a few million. But the natural background rate of extinction during the past 600 million years, the period of major life, has been on the order of only one species every year or so (Raup and Sepkoski, 1984). Today the rate is surely hundreds of times higher, possibly thousands of times higher (Ehrlich and Ehrlich, 1981; Myers, 1986; Raven, 1987; Soulé, 1986; Western and Pearl, in press; Wilson, 1987). Moreover, whereas past extinctions have occurred by virtue of natural processes, today the virtually exclusive cause is *Homo sapiens*, who eliminates entire habitats and complete communities of species in super-short order. It is all happening in the twinkling of an evolutionary eye.

To help us get a handle on the situation, let us take a lengthy look at tropical forests. These forests cover only 7% of Earth's land surface, yet they are estimated to contain at least 50% of all species (conceivably a much higher proportion). Equally important, they are being depleted faster than any other ecological zone.

Tropical Forests

There is general agreement that remaining primary forests cover rather less than 9 million square kilometers, out of the 15 million or so that may once have existed according to bioclimatic data. There is also general agreement that between 76,000 and 92,000 square kilometers are eliminated outright each year, and that at least a further 100,000 square

kilometers are grossly disrupted each year (FAO and UNEP, 1982; Hadley and Lanley, 1983; Melillo et al., 1985; Molofsky et al., 1986; Myers, 1980, 1984). These figures for deforestation rates derive from a data base of the late 1970s; the rates have increased somewhat since then. This means, roughly speaking, that 1% of the biome is being deforested each year and that more than another 1% is being significantly degraded.

The main source of information lies with remote-sensing surveys, which constitute a thoroughly objective and systematic mode of inquiry. By 1980 there were remote-sensing data for approximately 65% of the biome, a figure that has risen today to 82%. In all countries where remote-sensing information has been available in only the past few years—notably Indonesia, Burma, India, Nigeria, Cameroon, Guatemala, Honduras, and Peru—we find there is greater deforestation than had been supposed by government agencies in question.

Tropical deforestation is by no means an even process. Some areas are being affected harder than others; some will survive longer than others. By the end of the century or shortly thereafter, there could be little left of the biome in primary status with a full complement of species, except for two large remnant blocs, one in the Zaire basin and the other in the western half of Brazilian Amazonia, plus two much smaller blocs, in Papua New Guinea and in the Guyana Shield of northern South America. These relict sectors of the biome may well endure for several decades further, but they are little likely to last beyond the middle of next century, if only because of sheer expansion in the numbers of small-scale cultivators.

Rapid population growth among communities of small-scale cultivators occurs mainly through immigration rather than natural increase, i.e., through the phenomenon of the shifted cultivator. As a measure of what ultrarapid growth rates can already impose on tropical forests, consider the situation in Rondonia, a state in the southern sector of Brazilian Amazonia. Between 1975 and 1986, the population grew from 111,000 to well over 1 million, i.e., a 10-times increase in little more than 10 years. In 1975, almost 1,250 square kilometers of forest were cleared. By 1982, this amount had grown to more than 10,000 square kilometers, and by late 1985, to around 17,000 square kilometers (Fearnside, 1986).

It is this broad-scale clearing and degradation of forest habitats that is far and away the main cause of species extinctions. Regrettably, we have no way to know the actual current rate of extinction, nor can we even come close with accurate estimates. But we can make substantive assessments by looking at species numbers before deforestation and then applying the analytic techniques of island biogeography. To help us gain an insight into the scope and scale of present extinctions, let us briefly consider three particular areas: the forested tracts of western Ecuador, Atlantic-coast Brazil, and Madagascar. Each of these areas features, or rather featured, exceptional concentrations of species with high levels of endemism. Western Ecuador is reputed to have once contained between 8,000 and 10,000 plant species with an endemism rate somewhere between 40 and 60% (Gentry, 1986). If we suppose, as we reasonably can by drawing on detailed inventories in sample plots, that there are at least 10 to 30 animal species for every one plant species, the species complement in western Ecuador must have amounted to 200,000 or more in all. Since 1960, at least 95% of the forest cover has been destroyed to make way for banana plantations, oil exploiters, and human settlements of various sorts. According to the theory of island biogeography, which is supported by abundant and diversified evidence, we can realistically expect that when a habitat has lost 90% of its extent, it will eventually lose half its species. Precisely how many species have actually been eliminated, or are on the point of extinction, in western Ecuador is impossible to say. But ultimate accuracy is surely irrelevant, insofar as the number must total tens of thousands at least, conceivably 50,000—all eliminated or at least doomed in the space of just 25 years.

Very similar baseline figures for species totals and endemism levels, and a similar story of forest depletion (albeit for different reasons and over a longer time period), apply to the Atlantic-coastal forest of Brazil, where the original 1 million square kilometers of forest cover have been reduced to less than 50,000 square kilometers (Mori et al., 1981). Parallel data apply also to Madagascar, where only 5% of the island's primary vegetation remains undisturbed—and where the endemism levels are rather high (Rauh, 1979).

So in these three tropical forest areas alone, with their roughly 600,000 species, the recent past must have witnessed a sizeable fallout of species. Some may not have disappeared as yet, due to the time lag in equilibration, i.e., delayed fallout effects stemming from habitat depletion. But whereas the ultimate total of extinctions in these areas in the wake of deforestation to date will presumably amount to some 150,000 species, we may realistically assume that already half, some 75,000 species, have been eliminated or doomed.

Deforestation in Brazil's Atlantic-coastal forest and Madagascar has been going on for several centuries, but the main damage has occurred during this century, especially since 1950, i.e., since the spread of broad-scale industrialization and plantation agriculture in Brazil and since the onset of rapid population growth in Madagascar. This all means that as many as 50,000 species have been eliminated or doomed in these areas alone during the last 35 years. This works out to a crude average of almost 1,500 species per year—a figure consistent with the independent assessment of Wilson (1987), who postulates an extinction rate in all tropical forests of perhaps 10,000 species per year. Of course many reservations attend these calculations. More species than postulated may remain until a new equilibrium is established and causes their disappearance. Conversely, more species will presumably have disappeared during the later stages of the 35-year period than during the opening stage. Whatever the details of the outcome, we can judiciously use the figures and conclusions to form a working appraisal of the extent that an extinction spasm is already under way.

Extinction Rates: Future

The outlook for the future seems all the more adverse, though its detailed dimensions are even less clear than those of the present. Let us look again at tropical forests. We have seen what is happening to three critical areas. We can identify a good number of other sectors of the biome that feature exceptional concentrations of species with exceptional levels of endemism and that face exceptional threat of depletion, whether quantitative or qualitative. They include the Choco forest of Colombia; the Napo center of diversity in Peruvian Amazonia, plus seven other centers (out of 20-plus centers of diversity in Amazonia) that lie around the fringes of the basin and hence are unusually threatened by settlement programs and various other forms of development; the Tai Forest of Ivory Coast; the montane forests of East Africa; the relict wet forest of Sri Lanka; the monsoon forests of the Himalayan foothills; northwestern Borneo; certain lowland areas of the Philippines; and several islands of the South Pacific (New Caledonia, for instance, is 16,100 square kilometers, almost the size of New Jersey, and contains 3,000 plant species, 80% of them endemic).

These various sectors of the tropical forest biome amount to roughly 1 million square kilometers (2.5 times the size of California), or slightly more than one-tenth of the remaining undisturbed forests. As far as we can best judge from their documented numbers of plant species, and by making substantiated assumptions about the numbers of associated animal species, we can estimate that these areas surely harbor 1 million species (could be many more)—and in many of the areas, there is marked endemism. If present land-use patterns and exploitation trends persist (and they show every sign of accelerating), there will be little left of these forest tracts, except in the form of degraded remnants, by the end of this century or shortly thereafter. Thus forest depletion in these areas alone could well eliminate large numbers of species, surely hundreds of thousands, within the next 25 years at most.

Looking at the situation another way, we can estimate, on the basis of what we know about plant numbers and distribution together with what we can surmise about their associated animal communities, that almost 20% of all species occur in forests of Latin America outside of Amazonia and that another 20% are present in forests of Asia and Africa outside the Zaire basin (Raven, 1987). That is, these forests contain some 1 million species altogether, even if we estimate that the planetary total is only 5 million. All the primary forests in which these species occur may well disappear by the end of this century or early in the next. If only half the species in these forests disappear, this will amount to several hundred thousand species.

What is the prognosis for the longer-term future? Could we eventually lose at least one-quarter, possibly one-third, or conceivably an even larger share of all extant species? Let us take a quick look at Amazonia (Simberloff, 1986), If deforestation continues at present rates until the year 2000, but then comes to a complete halt, we could anticipate an ultimate loss of about 15% of the plant species and a similar percentage of animal species. If Amazonia's forest cover were to be ultimately reduced to those areas now set aide as parks and reserves, we could anticipate that 66% of the plant species will eventually disappear together with almost 69% of bird species and similar proportions of all other major categories of species.

Of course we may learn how to manipulate habitats to enhance survival prospects. We may learn how to propagate threatened species in captivity. We may be able to apply other emergent conservation techniques, all of which could help to relieve the adverse repercussions of broad-scale deforestation. But in the main, the damage will have been done. For reasons of island biogeography and equilibration, some extinctions in Amazonia will not occur until well into the twenty-second century, or even further into the future. So a major extinction spasm in Amazonia is entirely possible, indeed plausible if not probable.

Tropical Forest and Climatic Change

Protected areas are not likely to provide a sufficient answer for reasons that reflect climatic factors. In Amazonia, for instance, it is becoming apparent that if as much as half the forest were to be safeguarded in some way or another (e.g., through multiple-use conservation units as well as protected areas), but the other half of the forest were to be developed out of existence, there could soon be at work a hydrologic feedback mechanism that would allow a good part of Amazonia's moisture to be lost to the ecosystem (Salati and Vose, 1984). The remaining forest would likely be subjected to a steady desiccatory process, until the moist forest became more like a dry forest, even a woodland—with all that would mean for the species communities that are adapted to moist forest habitats. Even with a set of forest safeguards of exemplary type and scope, Amazonia's biotas would be more threatened than ever.

Still more widespread climatic changes with yet more marked impact are likely to occur within the foreseeable future. By the first quarter of the next century, we may well be experiencing the climatic dislocations of a planetary warming, stemming from a buildup of carbon dioxide and other so-called greenhouse gases in the global atmosphere (Bolin and Doos, 1986; DoE, 1985). The consequences for protected areas will be pervasive and profound. The present network of protected areas, grossly inadequate as it is, has been established in accord with present-day needs. Yet its ultimate viability will be severely threatened in the wake of a greenhouse effect as vegetation zones start to migrate away from the equator with all manner of disruptive repercussions for natural environments (Peters and Darling, 1985).

These, then, are some dimensions of the extinction spasm that we can reasonably assume will overtake the planet's biotas within the next few decades (unless of course we do a massively better job of conservation). In effect we are conducting an irreversible experiment on a global scale with Earth's stock of species.

Repercussions for the Future of Evolution

The foreseeable fallout of species, together with their subunits, is far from the entire story. A longer-term and ultimately more serious repercussion could lie in a disruption of the course of evolution, insofar as speciation processes will have to work with a greatly reduced pool of species and their genetic materials. We are probably being optimistic when we call it a disruption; a more likely outcome is that certain evolutionary processes will be suspended or even terminated. In the graphic phrasing of Soulé and Wilcox (1980), "Death is one thing; an end to birth is something else."

From what little we can discern from the geologic record, a normal recovery time may require millions of years. After the dinosaur crash, for instance, between 50,000 and 100,000 years elapsed before there started to emerge a set of diversified and specialized biotas, and another 5 to 10 million

years went by before there were bats in the skies and whales in the seas (Jablonski, 1986). Following the crash during the late Permian Period, when marine invertebrates lost about half their families, as many as 20 million years elapsed before the survivors could establish even half as many families as they had lost (Raup, 1986).

The evolutionary outcome this time around could prove even more drastic. The critical factor lies with the likely loss of key environments. Not only do we appear ready to lose most if not virtually all tropical forests, but there is also progressive depletion of coral reefs, wetlands, estuaries, and other biotopes with exceptional biodiversity. These environments have served in the past as preeminent power-houses of evolution, in that they have supported the emergence of more species than have other environments. Virtually every major group of vertebrates and many other large categories of animals have originated in spacious zones with warm, equable climates, notably tropical forests. In addition, the rate of evolutionary diversification—whether through proliferation of species or through the emergence of major new adaptations—has been greatest in the tropics, again most notably in tropical forests.

Of course tropical forests have been severely depleted in the past. During drier phases of the recent Ice Ages (Pleistocene Epoch), they have been repeatedly reduced to only a small fraction, occasionally as little as one-tenth, of their former expanse. Moreover, tropical biotas seem to have been unduly prone to extinction. But the remnant forest refugia usually contained sufficient stocks of surviving species to recolonize suitable territories when moister conditions returned (Prance, 1982). Within the foreseeable future, by contrast, it seems all too possible that most tropical forests will be reduced to much less than one-tenth of their former expanse, and their pockets of holdout species will be much less stocked with potential colonizers.

Furthermore, the species depletion will surely apply across most if not all major categories of species. This is almost axiomatic, if extensive environments are eliminated wholesale. The result will contrast sharply with the end of the Cretaceous Period, when not only placental mammals survived (leading to the adaptive radiation of mammals, eventually including humans), but also birds, amphibians, and crocodiles, among other nondinosaurian reptiles. In addition, the present extinction spasm looks likely to eliminate a sizeable share of terrestrial plant species, at least one-fifth within the next half century and a good many more within the following half century. By contrast, during most mass-extinction episodes of the prehistoric past, terrestrial plants have survived with relatively few losses (Knoll, 1984). They have thus supplied a resource base on which evolutionary processes could start to generate replacement animal species forthwith. If this biotic substrate is markedly depleted within the foreseeable future, the restorative capacities of evolution will be all the more reduced.

In sum, the evolutionary impoverishment of the impending extinction spasm, plus the numbers of species involved and the telescoped time scale of the phenomenon, may result in the greatest single setback to life's abundance and diversity since the first flickerings of life almost 4 billion years ago.

References

Bolin, B., and B. R. Doos, eds. 1986. The Greenhouse Effect: Climatic Change and Ecosystems. Wiley, New York. 541 pp.

DoE (U.S. Department of Energy). 1985. Direct Effects of Increasing Carbon Dioxide on Vegetation. U.S. Department of Energy, Washington, DC.

Ehrlich, P. R., and A. H. Ehrlich. 1981. Extinction: The Causes and Consequences of the Disappearance of Species. Random House, New York. 305 pp.

FAO and UNEP (Food and Agriculture Organization and United Nations Environment Programme). 1982. Tropical Forest Resources. Food and Agriculture Organization of the United Nations, Rome, Italy, and United Nations Environment Programme, Nairobi, Kenya. 106 pp.

Fearnside, P. M. 1986. Human Carrying Capacity of the Brazilian Rain Forest. Columbia University Press, New York. 293 pp.

Gentry, A. H. 1986. Endemism in tropical versus temperate plant communities. Pp. 153–181 in M. E. Soul, ed. Conservation Biology: The Science of Scarcity and Diversity. Sinauer Associates, Sunderland, MA. 584 pp.

Hadley, M., and J. P. Lanley. 1983. Tropical forest ecosystems: Identifying differences, seeing similarities. Nat. Resour. 19:2–19.

Jablonski, D. 1986. Causes and consequences of mass extinction: A comparative approach. Pp. 183–230 in D. K. Elliot, ed. Dynamics of Extinction. Wiley Interscience, New York.

Knoll, A. H. 1984. Patterns of extinction in the fossil record of vascular plants. Pp. 21–68 in M. H. Nitecki, ed. Extinctions. University of Chicago Press, Chicago.

Melillo, J. M., C. A. Palm, R. A. Houghton, G. M. Woodwell, and N. Myers. 1985. A comparison of recent estimates of disturbance in tropical forests. Environ. Conserv. 12(1):37–40.

Molofsky, J., C. A. S. Hall, and N. Myers. 1986. A Comparison of Tropical Forest Surveys. U.S. Department of Energy, Washington, DC.

Mori, S. A., B. M. Boom, and G. T. Prance. 1981. Distribution patterns and conservation of eastern Brazilian coastal forest tree species. Brittonia 33(2):233–245.

Myers, N. 1980. Conservation of Tropical Moist Forests. A report prepared for the Committee on Research Priorities in Tropical Biology of the National Research Council. National Academy of Sciences, Washington, DC. 205 pp.

Myers, N. 1984. The Primary Source: Tropical Forests and Our Future. W. W. Norton, New York. 399 pp.

Myers, N. 1986. Tackling Mass Extinction of Species: A Great Creative Challenge. Albright Lecture, University of California, Berkeley. 40 pp.

Peters, R. L., and J. D. S. Darling. 1985. The greenhouse effect and nature reserves. BioScience 35(11):707–717.

Prance, G. T., ed. 1982. Biological Diversification in the Tropics. Proceedings of the Fifth International Symposium of the Association for Tropical Biology, held at Macuto Beach, Caracas, Venezuela, February 8–13, 1979. Columbia University Press, New York. 714 pp.

Rauh, W. 1979. Problems of biological conservation in Madagascar. Pp. 405–421 in D. Bramwell, ed. Plants and Islands. Academic Press, London, U.K.

Raup, D. M. 1986. Biological extinction in earth history. Science 231:1528–1533.

Raup, D. M., and J. J. Sepkoski. 1984. Periodicity of extinction in the geologic past. Proc. Natl. Acad. Sci. USA 81:801–805.

Raven, P. H. 1987. We're Killing Our World. Keynote paper presented to Annual Conference of the American Association for the Advancement of Science, Chicago, February 1987. Missouri Botanical Garden, St. Louis.

Salati, E., and P. B. Vose. 1984. Amazon basin: A system in equilibrium. Science 225:129–138.

Simberloff, D. 1986. Are we on the verge of a mass extinction in tropical rain forests? Pp. 165–180 in D. K. Elliot, ed. Dynamics of Extinction. Wiley, New York.

Soul, M. E. 1986. Conservation Biology, The Science of Scarcity and Diversity. Sinauer Associates, Sunderland, MA.

Soul, M. E., and B. A. Wilcox, eds. 1980. Conservation Biology: An Evolutionary-Ecological Perspective. Sinauer Associates, Sunderland, MA. 395 pp.

Western, D., and M. Pearl, eds. In press. Conservation 2100. Proceedings of International Conference on

Threatened Wildlife and Species, Manhattan, October 1986, organized by the New York Zoological Society. Oxford University Press, New York.

Wilson, E. O. 1987. Biological diversity as a scientific and ethical issue. Pp. 29–48 in Papers Read at a Joint Meeting of the Royal Society and the American Philosophical Society. Volume 1. Meeting held April 24, 1986, in Philadelphia. American Philosophical Society, Philadelphia.

The Mismanagement of the National Forests

By Perri Knize

There once was a time when if a tree was felled in the forest, nobody saw, and business went on as usual. But now a tree can't be felled anywhere in the national forests without causing violent tremors all the way to Washington, D.C. There the bureaucrats at the once-proud and formerly revered U.S. Forest Service, the administrators of the national forests, are losing credibility as forty years of forest devastation come to light.

While our government supports schemes to trade Third World debt for intact Third World rain forests and dispatches American foresters to Ecuador and Honduras to aid those countries in proper forest management, the Forest Service is deforesting our national timberlands at a rate that rivals Brazil's. What remains of America's original virgin forests is being clipped away daily in our public lands, lands that contain the most biomass per acre of any forests on the planet. We are losing intact ecosystems, watersheds, fish habitat, wildlife habitat, recreation lands, and native-species diversity to a degree that may be irreparable.

Once, the land could accommodate this "management" without attracting much notice. The national forests, unlike national parks, have traditionally provided wood, grass, and minerals to the private sector. But population growth, shifting demographics, and reduced resources mean that foresters are increasingly hard-pressed to find forest areas where nobody will see the clear-cuts.

When I joined the U.S. Forest Service as a volunteer wilderness guard, in the summer of 1983, I, like most Americans, thought the Forest Service was a conservation organization dedicated to preserving the nation's wild lands. I was vaguely aware that the Forest Service sold trees, but was unprepared for the extensive logging roads and cutting I saw on the Beaverhead and Bitterroot national forests, in southwest Montana. Entire mountain-sides were shorn of cover, and rough roads crisscrossed their faces, creating terraces that bled topsoil into the rivers when the snows melted in spring. Since that summer I've traveled to national forests all over the United States, from the Carolinas to Alaska, and seen the same and worse: Entire mountain ranges have their faces shaved in swaths of forty to a hundred acres which from the air resemble mange. From the ground these forests, charred and smoking from slash burning, look like battlefields.

I was shocked: the Forest Service seemed more concerned about selling trees than about the vitality of the public's forests. Yet I met many dedicated Forest Service employees at all levels of the agency who were terribly unhappy about the emphasis on timber, and I felt compelled to learn as much as I could about why the Forest Service was pursuing such an apparently destructive policy.

After all, the national forests supply only about 15 percent of the nation's wood, and Forest Service research shows that if that timber were removed from the market, half of the loss would be replaced by wood from private industrial tree farms and half by wood substitutes that are already on the market. Seventy-two percent of all the timberland in the United States is privately owned. This land is far better suited to tree farming than federal land—it is fertile, low-elevation, accessible, and for the most part does not have the intact ecosystems found on public land. Our national forests, although they are richer in biological diversity, have comparatively little value as tree farms. They are

The Atlantic Monthly, Vol. 268, No. 4 (October 1991), 98–100, 103–104, 107–108, and 111–112. Reprinted by permission of International Creative Management, Inc. Copyright 1991 by Perri Knize.

for the most part thin-soiled, steep, high-elevation, less accessible lands that produce low-quality timber. They are the lands nobody would take, even for nothing, when the government was divvying up the West.

Despite the abundance of merchantable private timber and the relatively low value of public timber, no one has seriously considered ending national-forest logging. With the exception of a tiny minority of passionate nature lovers who are considered extremist, virtually everyone I've interviewed over the past eight years says that ending national-forest logging is impractical if not impossible.

A thoughtful look at the condition of our forests, the needs of our communities, and the national demand for wood products reveals that ending national-forest logging is not only possible but also highly pragmatic. In fact, we can end logging on the national forests and at the same time improve the future economic stability of small communities now dependent on timber dollars, stabilize our wood supply, save and spend more wisely the billions now pouring out of the federal Treasury, and preserve the health of our virgin forests— if we decide to. We can do it because, contrary to conventional wisdom, we don't need national-forest timber—not for jobs, certainly not for the income, and not for the nation's wood supply. Most commercial-timber owners would actually benefit if the government were no longer competing with them: as prices rose, long-term forest planning would become more feasible and profitable. The Forest Service itself would benefit, as it escaped the endless and expensive forest-management planning with an emphasis on timber which inevitably lands it in court. Forest Service employees could begin to inventory and study the national forests, as they were mandated to do in the National Forest Management Act of 1976, though without adequate funding for the job. They could begin repairing the damage of the past forty years, instead of trying to produce board feet that can no longer be cut in an environmentally responsible fashion.

Timber Mythology

In view of these benefits, why isn't the Forest Service eager to end national-forest logging? Why is it adamant that that cannot or should not be done? The Forest Service rebuffs all such suggestions with three arguments that I call collectively the Great Federal Timber Mythology.

Myth No. 1: Federal timber is needed to meet an ever-escalating demand for wood fiber.

Myth No. 2: Timber sales overall make a profit for the federal Treasury.

Myth No. 3: Federal timber, even if sold at a loss, aids timber-dependent communities.

Last year the Forest Service once again predicted, as it has since its founding, in 1905, that demand for national-forest timber would continue to rise and that timber would remain in short supply. In fact the demand for timber has declined since the invention of the internal-combustion engine and since we began using electricity and fuel oil instead of wood for our energy needs. Many privately held forests logged in the nineteenth century are now regrown. Horse pasture and farmland have returned to forest. We actually have more standing trees today than we did ninety years ago. So whereas the old-growth trees that provide the softwood lumber used for products like fine furniture and musical instruments are indeed in short supply, particularly in the Pacific Northwest, we have plenty of wood fiber that can be made into less-refined products. Most of our ancient trees are not made into pianos and armoires anyway, but are ground into pulp to make disposable diapers and cellophane for cigarette packs. Obviously, small-diameter trees from tree farms would serve that purpose just as well. As for building materials, we can also create them from small-diameter trees. Oriented-strand board, chipboard, finger-joint board, and particle board—made from chips or small pieces of wood—are already available; they are stronger than regular wood and can be made from very young trees grown in rows like a corn crop.

"Crop forests are where our timber supply really comes from," says a former logging manager at Weyerhauser Corporation, who asked not to be named. He explains that the industry wants the old timber on the national forests only because with minimal processing these logs bring a premium price overseas. "As to old growth, everyone has gored that fatted calf long enough. Weyerhauser made a fortune from old growth, but you can't cut the last one and say, 'Gee, that was nice. What do we do now?'"

One sign that we have a glut of wood fiber in the United States is that although we exported 4.2 billion board feet of raw logs last year, we can still find plentiful, cheap toilet paper in the supermarket. Timber has such a low market value in this country that owners of private timberland often find that growing trees doesn't pay—the rate of return isn't high enough. Many are selling off their forests and using the profits to reduce their debt. If timber were scarce—and valuable—this would be a poor business practice.

The Forest Service exacerbates the situation by flooding the market with cheap national-forest timber, driving prices down. One could argue reasonably that the national-forest timber program, by competing with the private sector, is destroying the environmental quality of our private timberlands as well.

It also empties the federal purse. "If we simply gave the loggers fourteen thousand dollars a year not to cut the trees, we'd be a lot better off," says K. J. Metcalf, a retired Forest Service planner in Alaska, about his review of the Tongass forest plan in 1978. He echoed the sentiments of many of the agency's critics. The Forest Service has long claimed that the government makes money on timber sales, but an analysis performed at the request of the House Government Operations Subcommittee on the Environment, Energy, and Natural Resources shows that the Forest Service timber program has lost $5.6 billion over the past decade. Robert Wolf, a retired staffer at the Congressional Research Service, a forester, and a road engineer, analyzed the Forest Service's timber-income accounting system at the request of Representative Mike Synar, the chairman of the subcommittee. At the time this was written, Wolf expected to submit his testimony in September. He says his original intention was to show that sales of national-forest timber were profitable and beneficial. Instead, he found that most of the 122 national forests have never earned a dime on timber, and only fifteen showed a profit last year. The Forest Service claims that it made $630 million on its timber program last year; that claim, Wolf says, stems from inflated revenues and discounted costs.

The "net" revenue figure doesn't make allowances for the 25 percent of gross receipts ($327 million last year) that must be paid to counties from which timber has been removed, as compensation for property taxes lost because those lands aren't privately owned. Nor does it take into consideration road-maintenance expenses—another $80 million. Land-line location (surveying to confirm national-forest boundaries) cost another $24 million. The Forest Service also overlooked some $60 million spent on protection against insects and disease, maintenance of staff buildings, map-making, and fire protection.

Another $575 million—funds earmarked for reforestation, brush disposal, timber salvage sales, roads built to accommodate timber buyers, and other programs—was depreciated over more years than appropriate for accounting purposes. The Forest Service has used a number of creative accounting gimmicks, including amortizing roads over 240 years. (One year roads on the Chugach National Forest, in Alaska, were amortized over 1,800 years.) The typical life of a logging road, however, is twenty-five years; that's why 60 percent of each year's road-building budget is earmarked for reconstruction. Last year the Forest Service received appropriations of $700 million for the timber program from the federal Treasury, yet spent more than $1 billion. According to Wolf's calculations, after a realistic amortization of costs, the timber program actually generated a net *loss* to the federal Treasury of $186 million last year.

One reason timber sales don't make money is that most national-forest timber is virtually worthless. Short growing seasons and poor, unstable soils mean that a national-forest tree may need 120 years to reach maturity. "No one in his right mind would pay what it costs to grow it," says Wolf, who now calls the Forest Service timber program "a fraud." Since the Forest Service was founded on the promise that the timber program would make money, to admit losses after so many years of false claims would threaten not only the agency's timber program, and therefore about a third of its 45,000 jobs, but quite probably the existence of the Forest Service itself.

Even in the face of evidence that the timber market is glutted, and that its operations run at a net loss, the Forest Service will justify selling trees as a way to provide small communities with jobs. But national-forest timber isn't keeping people employed; although timber production and logging on federal lands have increased, industry employment has declined. Automation, exports of raw lumber, and competition for foreign labor are the causes. As for small community sawmills wholly dependent on old-growth national-forest timber, their timber supply is limited. The small family mill is destined to go the way of the small family farm, and leveling the national forests won't save it.

The loggers and mill workers who depend on national-forest timber are, like the forests, victims of federal policy. Since the end of the Second World War the Forest Service has fostered in their communities an expectation that federal timber would be available indefinitely, and a way of life has evolved around that expectation. If the Forest Service and the loggers' elected representatives had been honest with their constituents even ten years ago, and warned them that the supply of trees could not support their industry forever, mill owners and loggers might not have invested further in lumber operations that are doomed, national-forest timber or no. These communities were misled, and they deserve aid in adjusting to what is for them a catastrophe.

But aiding those affected by an end to national-forest logging is less problematic than it seems. The jobs that would be lost are not irreplaceable, nor are they as numerous as claimed by the timber industry, which wants to maintain the flow of cheap national-forest old-growth lumber. A study funded by the timber industry predicted that 100,000 jobs would be lost in the Pacific Northwest as a consequence of restrictions to protect the spotted owl. But according to a Forest Service assessment written for other purposes, the true number is closer to 6,000. The industry study counted jobs projected for the year 2000 if logging continued to increase as was once planned, and it included a loss of secondary jobs, such as pumping gas and waiting tables, though the relatively healthy economy of the Pacific Northwest is creating new jobs in many other sectors.

The Forest Service says that only 106,000 jobs nationwide—including approximately 15,000 in the agency itself—are related to national-forest timber. An agency report speculated that these jobs would be replaced in part by new logging jobs when wood production shifted to private industrial lands. And in communities without nearby industrial timberland new jobs could be created, including jobs rehabilitating the national forests, with federal funds saved when national-forest timber was no longer being sold at a loss.

Inevitably, the small communities dependent on national-forest logging must diversify their economies or die. But if we do not end logging before their timber supply is exhausted, the clear-cuts that surround these communities will bankrupt their future. Once the forests are gone, they will have neither the timber industry nor property values nor the recreation potential that could help them build a stable economic future. Logging the national forests results in the loss, rather than the strengthening, of community stability.

So if jobs are being lost despite increased logging, and the U.S. government loses millions a year on that logging, and we don't even need the lumber, why does the Forest Service persist in logging the national forests? When environmentalists, economists, forest planners, and policy-makers say it is not practical to end national-forest logging, they mean it is not practical *politically*.

Political Realities

The National Forest Management Act of 1976 stipulates that those who are most intimate with the national forests—the public and the local Forest Service team—should work together to decide how they are to be managed. But in practice the forests are ruled by competing and complementary agendas in Washington, D.C. Forest Service administrators are concerned with maximizing their budgets, holding on to their jobs, and preserving the status quo. Congressmen want jobs in their districts and continued timber-industry support for their re-election campaigns. And the White House wants to take care of its friends. All use national-forest timber as a means to achieve their aims.

More than a quarter of the money the Forest Service spends comes from selling timber— whether the sales make money or not—through a little-known law called the Knutson-Vandenberg Act of 1930. The K-V Act allows the Forest Service to retain virtually all its gross timber receipts in order to fund projects like tree-planting, wildlife-habitat improvement, and trail-building, and to buy equipment like computers, refrigerators, and so on. It is a back-door way of funding the agency without going through the appropriations process. Last year K-V money and similar timber funds added $475 million to the Forest Service budget, above and beyond congressional appropriations. Because Congress has limited its funding to timber-sales development, fire fighting, and road-building on the national forests, and has resisted the agency's requests for support of other programs, K-V money is often the only resource on which the Forest Service can rely to finance many of its non-timber activities. Erosion control, campground improvements, and plant and animal inventory, for example, are all funded by timber sales.

For this reason the K-V Act has led to absolutely perverse management. According to Randal O'Toole, a natural-resource economist and the author of a tendentious book titled *Reforming the Forest Service*, mismanagement in the pursuit of K-V money is rampant. O'Toole has analyzed the management of more than half the national forests. He found, for example, that when Gallatin National Forest, in Montana, needed funds to close roads to protect grizzly-bear habitat, its managers held timber sales and built roads in other prime grizzly habitat. When the Medicine Bow National Forest, in Wyoming, needed funds to inventory ancient Indian archaeological sites, it sold timber on those very sites, destroying them in the process. And in the Sequoia National Forest, in California, when foresters needed funds for a prescribed burn to protect giant-sequoia groves from wildfire, à la Yellowstone National Park, they sold timber in the groves to get the money they needed to pay for the prescribed burn. But the clear-cuts left only a few giant trees, surrounded by devastation. Instead of burning, the foresters had to replant the area, at a cost of $1,000 an acre. The point of these seemingly pointless exercises was to get and spend money. Like most bureaucracies, the Forest Service is deeply concerned with keeping overhead accounts full and maximizing its budget.

Since a third of all K-V money is spent on administrative overhead for every level of the Forest Service, from the Washington office down to the local districts, the promise of K-V funds encourages everyone in the Forest Service, including wildlife biologists and recreation specialists, to support timber sales, even if those sales damage the resources they are charged with protecting.

Because the Forest Service is so heavily dependent on timber sales, ensuring the future of the timber program is critical to the agency. That future depends on a vast network of access roads. In addition to the annual budget appropriation and the K-V money, the Forest Service has a capital-investment fund—known as hard money—set aside by Congress just for building and reconstructing roads. Last year this fund was $270 million. In addition to the 360,000 miles of roads already on the national forests—nearly one mile of road for every square mile of forest, or a system about eight times the length of the U.S. interstate highway system—the Forest Service has ambitious plans to build another 43,000 miles of roads over the next fifty years. Depending on the type of road and terrain, building these roads can cost as little as $5,000 or as much as $500,000 a mile. The agency is anxious to get roads into even marginally productive areas, critics say, because a roadless area can become a designated wilderness, off limits to logging forever.

Another way the Forest Service hopes to protect the timber program is by rewarding forest managers with promotions for meeting their timber quotas. Congress sets these quotas as a means of accounting for the money it has given the Forest Service. If the agency has said it will sell 11 billion board feet of timber in return for its $700 million congressional appropriation, at the close of the fiscal year Congress will want to know that in fact the agency has sold the trees. To make sure they are sold, the Forest Service assigns sales targets to the nine national-forest regions, according to their capacity. Each regional forester's performance rating depends in part on coming within five percent of his target.

Congress's concern about jobs is of a different nature. To get votes, a public servant needs to get jobs and money for his or her district, and in small communities in the West timber sales mean jobs, and money in the county coffers for roads and schools. Counties are entitled to 25 percent of gross receipts from the national forests within their boundaries, so county commissioners are deeply interested in national-forest programs that generate receipts, and many cannot meet their budgets without them. These officials exert tremendous pressure on members of Congress and agency officials to keep the volume of timber cut in the national forests as high as possible. Congressmen from states with lots of national forest are usually zealous about complying if they want to stay in office.

They are also ready to express gratitude to the timber industry for its campaign contributions. The industry contributes to the campaigns of several key congressmen on the appropriations committees who go to bat for timber interests every year when the timber and roads budget comes up for review. Last fall, for example, the soon-to-be retired Senator James McClure, of Idaho, added to the 1991 appropriations bill a promise of a five percent funding bonus for wildlife and recreation to any Forest Service region that meets or exceeds its timber targets—this at a time when regional foresters throughout the West were insisting that they could no longer meet federally mandated targets without damaging the land and violating environmental laws.

The 9.5 billion board feet of timber scheduled for sale on the national forests this year, and the more than 2,000 miles of timber roads scheduled to be built, will continue to make following environmental standards and guidelines difficult. Former Forest Service officials have admitted to overcutting in the past, and timber targets remain high, causing some in the agency to protest that not enough trees are left to meet them. On a day I spent on the Willamette National Forest last year, no one was in the Blue River Ranger District office. The district had three days left to meet its timber target, and the rangers were out on the ground, scrambling to find trees that met specifications for cutting.

"Anybody—on the back of an envelope—could have figured out that the rate of [timber] harvest cannot be sustained," said Max Peterson, a former Forest Service chief, when he met with agency employees at the Wenatchee National Forest in 1989. He said the cut should go down at least 25 percent; some forest planners, knowing the Forest Service to be extremely conservative on such matters, understood that to mean the cut should go down at least 75 percent.

Heavy cutting in much of the Pacific Northwest over the past decade was caused in part by congressional orders to the Forest Service which resulted in a cut far larger than the agency itself recommended. Last year Oregon's congressional delegation attached a rider to the federal appropriations bill allowing the Forest Service to sell more timber than existing laws allowed, and greatly reducing the possibilities of judicial review. A federal appeals court recently declared the rider unconstitutional.

But the impact of Congress on national-forest management is mild compared with the negative influence of the White House. My season with the Forest Service coincided with the era of John

Crowell, Jr., a former timber-industry attorney and lobbyist appointed by President Reagan, as assistant secretary of commerce for natural resources and the environment—the official who oversees the Forest Service. Crowell, who had worked for Louisiana-Pacific Corporation, one of the largest buyers of federal timber, dedicated his term in office to doubling the amount of timber cut on the national forests, and he ordered the Forest Service to ignore federal court orders and national environmental laws to meet that goal.

Logging and road-building in forbidden areas was a familiar occurrence in the national-forest system during the Crowell era, and it continues to this day. Logging in a designated wilderness has been discovered several times on the Willamette National Forest. Crowell's successor, George Dunlop, another Reagan appointee, refused to approve any national-forest plan in the Pacific Northwest that didn't increase logging. As a result, Forest Service Region Six is now under such pressure to meet its targets that some districts have wandered into areas off limits to timber sales.

The President's influence on timber management can be far more direct. In June of last year the Forest Service was about to endorse the Jack Ward Thomas report, a study prepared by a team of scientists from the Forest Service and other natural-resource agencies. The Thomas report spelled out which lands should be spared from logging in the Pacific Northwest in order to save the northern spotted owl from extinction. The week before Dale Robertson, the chief of the Forest Service, was to announce the agency's endorsement of the report, timber-industry representatives paid a visit to the White House. Shortly thereafter the Bush Administration announced that it was ordering its own special task force, chaired by Clayton Yuetter, the Secretary of Agriculture, to study the spotted-owl situation further and to come up with more options. Months later Bush's task force announced its conclusions: the Thomas report's recommendations should be accepted in principle, and the cut should be reduced, but less old-growth forest should be protected than the Thomas report implied. The delay meant that timber sales in spotted-owl habitat continued unrestricted by either report all summer; by the time Bush's task force made its announcement, the logging season was just about over.

The stalling continues. The Forest Service says

it may need another two or three years to come up with a management plan for the spotted owl. And last May a court ordered the agency to withdraw sales planned for 66,000 acres of prime spotted-owl habitat. Those acres would have been in addition to the 400,000 acres of owl habitat already logged since 1984, when the agency began preparing guidelines for the spotted owl. William L. Dwyer, the U.S. district judge presiding over the case in Seattle (also, ironically, a Reagan appointee), wrote a stunning denunciation of the White House in his decision:

> More is involved here than a simple failure by an agency to comply with its governing stature. The most recent violation of the National Forest Management Act exemplifies a deliberate and systematic refusal by the Forest Service and the Fish and Wildlife Service to comply with the laws protecting wildlife. This is not the doing of the scientists, foresters, rangers, and others at the working levels of these agencies. It reflects decisions made by higher authorities in the executive branch of government.

Biological Costs

Judge Dwyer's decision underscores the fundamental reason why we should not be harvesting the national forests. Aside from the facts that we don't need the lumber, that the timber program loses money, that the program is used to prop up faltering local economies artificially, and that the real reasons for timber cutting continue to be unacknowledged, we have a biological stake in an end to logging on our national forests.

The greatest threat represented by our current national-forest policy is that it will destroy biological diversity on public lands. Forest scientists say that the national forest are most valuable to us as founts of life. Our native and old-growth forests are intricate, fragile webs encompassing everything from bacteria, fungi, and insects to grizzly bears, wolves, and ancient sequoias. They constitute a complex, interdependent plant and animal community that is the foundation upon which we human beings eat and breathe. Scientists say they understand little about forest biological systems, but they do know that the fresh air and clean water our forests produce are essential to our survival, because they are basic components of the food chains that keep all species alive. As species die off, the ecosystem is simplified, and the more simplified it becomes, the less life it is capable of supporting.

We are learning more about the value of the national forests every day. For example, scientists have recently concluded that forests play a major role in the absorption and storage of carbon dioxide. When very old trees, those more than 200 years old, are cut down, vast stores of carbon are released, owing to soil disturbance, decay, and the burning that accompanies tree harvesting. The resulting climatic changes are called global warming.

With global warming, habitats that will nurture biological diversity become an even more pressing need. When climates change, species must migrate if they are to survive, and land-based species must have connecting corridors of undisturbed forest through which to move unmolested. The burden of protecting habitat that can nurture diversity must fall on the public natural-resource agencies, because virtually all the original, intact ecosystems remaining in the United States are on our public lands.

Our national forests also embody other important values. A national forest is a place where you might awaken to find a bull elk staring you down, startled from his drink at a glacier-fed lake. Snow-tipped crags and rocky cirques reflect in pools and creeks and waterfalls of penetrating clarity; the water is so clear that to look at it is to be mesmerized and merged with it. Sometimes the only sound is the wind, roaring through the giant firs like a locomotive. At other times the silence is so deep and inviolate that you can hear, seemingly, to infinity. To visit a national forest is to let a bit of the harmony lacking in our contemporary lives seep in. A lifelong New Yorker visiting a Montana national forest last summer said that camping there was like staying in a five-star hotel—a city-dweller's ultimate compliment, and a measure of how claustrophobic and diminished our everyday surroundings have become. The wildness, solitude, and silence of the national forests are now among our country's greatest luxuries.

The Forest Service's predominant logging method, clear-cutting, destroys the visual beauty of the national forests. But the threat to biological diversity is more subtle. By law, clear-cuts must be reforested, and they are usually replanted with one favored tree species. These plantings then grow into even-aged monocultures—they are tree farms, not forests. Diversity is reduced, and wildlife is stressed as nesting sites, dens, and cover from predators are lost. Although the young grasses growing in clear-cuts do provide food for deer and elk, the loss of cover drives away bear, turkey, squirrels, and other species. Clear-cutting is also dangerous where rains are heavy and terrain is steep, as in southeast Alaska, on the western slope of the Cascade Mountains, and in the northwest corner of the Rockies. Flooding, soil erosion, water contamination, and loss of fisheries as sediment flushes into spawning streams are often the result. In some areas washouts and mud slides occur, and soil is removed down to bedrock. Clear-cutting changes the flow of streams, causing flooding during rains and drought during dry periods. It also interferes with recreation: no one wants to go hiking or camping in a clear-cut, and clear-cutting often obliterates recreation trails.

We know that clear-cutting destroys the complexity of forest ecology because we have the example of Europe, which was essentially deforested more than 300 years ago. Foresters there are still trying to figure out how to bring the forests back. Modern forestry techniques have evolved from the attempts, beginning in eighteenth-century Germany, to regenerate old-growth forests like the ones that we are logging here. The forests that European foresters so painstakingly tend are sterile: birds don't sing in them; sticks, not logs, are harvested from them; and now Europeans are worried about the long-term fertility of their soil. "Look to Europe for what the future holds," says Paul Alaback, a research biologist for the Forest Service in Juneau, Alaska. "Is it really necessary to cut all the forests down before we learn from others' mistakes?"

The Forest Service is now experimenting with an alternative to clear-cutting called new forestry. New forestry is an attempt to protect diversity by simulating natural events like windstorms and fires. As I've seen it practiced at the Andrews Experimental Forest, in Oregon, new forestry looks like a messy version of clear-cutting. Instead of clearing the land of all timber and burning the remaining debris, the foresters leave dead and living trees standing in clusters, slash unburned, and dead trees and debris on the ground and in streams. This new method can be just as ugly as a clear-cut and more expensive, because it requires being more careful and yields fewer board feet per acre. And no one knows for sure if it helps preserve long-term biological diversity, the purpose for which it was created by Jerry Franklin, a Forest Service scientist. It may not be biologically destructive, but new forestry is almost always aesthetically destructive, and if it is adopted in place of clear-cutting, more timber will be sold below cost and net returns will be reduced on those forests that do earn money. We'll lose more money on the national forests than ever.

All of this points toward the conclusion that the Forest Service shouldn't be in the timber business. Managing the land to sustain its ecology is inherently incompatible with managing it to turn a profit. The time frame allowed under today's shortsighted economic system is far too limited to take biological diversity into account, and alternatives to clear-cutting will only increase deficit timber sales. Without regulation or financial incentives, most private industry will never manage its land to enhance biological diversity—long rotations (the number of years trees grow before harvest) don't help short-term profit margins—so this role must fall to the Forest Service. But as long as the Forest Service is in the timber business, its time horizon, too, will be far too short.

A Proposal

We need to reconsider the purpose of the national forests. Most people agree that public lands should exist to benefit the public, with private use permitted only when it does not reduce that public benefit. Yet the Forest Service's timber program is beneficial chiefly to politicians in Washington, to a small segment of the timber industry, and to the Forest Service's administrators. Taxpayers, small communities, recreationists, the owners of private timberland—and the land itself—all lose. The national forests without logging would not be the same as the national parks: hunting, grazing, mining, irrigation, and other private uses that don't interfere with the public's right to enjoy its land would continue. But without the logging program the Forest Service could, like the National Park Service, emphasize a stronger conservation ethic.

Such a shift in management cannot be achieved without confronting the political realities. That is why any legislation to reform national-forest management must change the incentives that motivate the Forest Service and private users of the forests. If the Forest Service gets funds for its programs by selling timber, and timber management is destroying the national forests for other uses, then we must find a means other than timber to fund the national forests. The most logical approach would be to charge recreation fees.

In its 1990 planning paper the Forest Service estimated that if it were allowed to charge fees for recreation, the income to the agency could be more than $5 billion a year, or three times what it earns in gross timber receipts. The estimate is based on fees that national-forest users have said they would be willing to pay, ranging from a few dollars for picnicking to nearly thirty dollars a day for big-game hunting. As Randal O'Toole has pointed out, this income, combined with the money saved by ending logging on the national forests, would fund the agency entirely from its own receipts; tax dollars would no longer be needed to support the Forest Service. Instead, only those who used the national forests would pay, and their fees would ensure that the forests were managed in the best interests of recreationists.

When the agency's funding no longer came from Congress, pork-barrel politics would no longer dictate how the forests were managed. County commissioners would stop putting pressure on their congressmen to appropriate funds for timber sales, because counties that depend on timber receipts for their roads and schools would get even more money from recreation than they did from timber. Private industry and landowners would benefit, because the value of their land and their timber would increase, and they, too, could charge recreation fees. With part of the billions of taxpayer dollars we were no longer investing in the Forest Service, we could

easily create programs to help communities dependent on national-forest timber make the transition to a more diverse local economy, one that would serve them for the long term.

Without fees, all taxpayers are paying for the destruction of the national forests. With fees, those who used the national forests would be paying to preserve their integrity. Hikers, hunters, fishermen, backpackers, and skiers would begin to get the resources and management they need to enjoy the national forests, instead of getting leftovers after the interests of the timber industry have been served. With this new emphasis we could fund an inventory of, research on, and monitoring of national-forest species and ecosystems to help us repair the damage done by forty years of overcutting.

To accomplish this revolution in national-forest management, Congress must be persuaded that recreation fees and an end to national-forest logging are a sensible and practical way to ensure a healthy future for our national forests. Environmental groups should endorse these recommendations as a means to preservation. County governments should support this plan because it would more than double their revenues from national-forest use. Large industrial timber farmers like Weyerhauser and International Paper should favor it because it would increase the value of their lands and their timber. Fiscal conservatives and those worried about the national debt should support this plan because it would save taxpayers the yearly cost of managing the national forests. An unprecedented coalition of these interests would stop national-forest logging in its tracks. Congress and the White House would have to comply.

Forest Service Policy

Bryan G. Norton

Pinchot conflated his own career goal, to institute and lead an active, effective, and productive forestry profession, with the public goals of resource conservation. Following Pinchot's lead, the wise-use wing of the environmental movement initially excluded aesthetic and other "noneconomic" goals

from its category of uses. Concern for fair and farsighted resource use, as it was institutionalized under Pinchot's influence in the governmental bureaucracies, centered on narrow commodity-oriented values. The bureaucracies therefore failed to develop a conception of "resources" broad enough to comprehend [John] Muir's aesthetic/spiritual concerns.

Muir had equal difficulty explaining how wise use of forests for productivity fit into his more preservationist approach—he discussed these matters less and less as his opposition to Pinchot's narrow utilitarianism grew. Muir's followers and Pinchot's followers increasingly talked past each other, unable to comprehend the other's viewpoint within their own worldview. In the early environmental movement, no positive program of environmental policy emerged beyond shared opposition to unrestrained exploitation; no common moral and aesthetic vocabulary evolved, much less a shared vision of what it would be like for humans to live *in* true harmony with the world of nature, even while living *on* nature's resources. [Aldo] Leopold made bold steps toward a unification of these approaches but, even today, the environmentalists' dilemma, reflected as a lack of common vocabulary and common positive vision, affects discourse on resource policy.

In the intervening years, however, the lines of separation between the policies of the two traditions have blurred. For example, during the 1920s the Park Service—created as a counterforce against the orientation toward productivity in the Forest Service—succumbed to boosterism and emphasized development and road-building. Meanwhile the Forest Service, under the influence of Leopold and Arthur Cathart (who was hired as a consulting "recreational engineer"), set aside wilderness and roadless areas in the National Forests. Preservationists, therefore, allied themselves for a time with the Forest Service in opposition to the Park Service. By the end of World War II, however, Pinchot's emphasis on productivity had reasserted itself in the Forest Service, and the process of designating Forest Service lands as wilderness virtually ended. The Forest Service once again pursued a policy of unrestrained road-building and cheap timber sales through the 1940s and 1950s, until the revolution in consumer tastes, especially a rapidly growing demand for outdoor recreation, once again altered the Forest Service approach.[1]

John McGuire, whose career in the Forest Service began before World War II and who served as Chief of the Forest Service from 1972 until his retirement in 1979, says: "A major change in the goals of forestry during my time in the Forest Service has been a growing acceptance of valuing nonmarket resources. These still cannot be readily analyzed in the benefit-cost sense, but these values are much more likely to be recognized by people in general today."

Furthermore, he believes, these changes affect policy:

> Now, if the American people want more of something such as timber or forage from the National Forests, the Forests Service goes to budget-makers and Congressmen and says: "Here are some of the costs that will be incurred." We then insist on funds to support recreation, to mitigate effects on wildlife, and to protect other values that may be threatened. If we get the added funds, we can probably offset the costs to these other values.

McGuire sees these changes as intimately tied with the important changes in public attitudes that occurred during the 1960s and 1970s: "The growth in the public perception of nonmarket values has in a way both led to, and supported, the growth of the second environmental movement that occurred during the 60s and 70s. And these changes have had a profound effect on Forestry."[2]

As Samuel Hays argues, concern had shifted from production to consumption, and consumer interest in amenities pushed conservationists in the government resource agencies toward a broader conception of the public good. For example, in 1960, Congress approved the Multiple Use–Sustained Yield Act, which mandated the Forest Service to consider recreational uses as well as timber production in the National Forests; four years later Congress extended the idea of multiple use to Bureau of Land Management lands as well. In that same year it also passed the Wilderness Bill, committing the government to "managing" wilderness areas without concern for productivity.[3]

Today, resource managers are forced to make every decision with an eye on the effects it will have on broader social values. Foresters who think of their profession simply as timber production are badly out of step—forestry has instead become a balancing act, a balancing of timber production against recreation, of forest management against wilderness values, of productivity of single-stand forestry against the goals of ecological diversity.[4] Foresters have therefore abandoned the assumption that they can manage forests for a particular purpose such as timber production while paying no heed to other social values.

Especially important is acceptance of responsibility among forest managers to protect biological diversity. Throughout the Forest Service there are popping up small cadres of researchers and managers who specialize in protecting biological diversity. By accepting this responsibility, the Forest Service opens itself to criticism of its methods from outside the forestry profession. While foresters can claim to be experts on timber production, they cannot claim overriding expertise in protecting biological diversity. Whereas Pinchot's Forest Service could ignore outside criticism, insisting that their expertise gave them the right to manage forests without outside interference, today's forester is liable to be shown wrong by an academic biologist or a restoration ecologist if a management plan causes serious disruption in the composition of species in the forest.

This new responsibility for protecting biological diversity also forces forest managers to transcend single-species management. The early forays of foresters into wildlife management mostly involved attempts, such as Leopold's, to maximize one or a few game species, each with its own management plan. Over the decades, foresters have recognized the futility of atomistic, single-species management and have gradually accepted whole-habitat management as essential in most cases. Management for protecting biological diversity completes this trend—a forest manager, in the final analysis, is responsible for managing every species in the forest. This implies that the manager must be a forest ecologist as well as a timber manager.

Nor do I mean to suggest that all of the movement toward a consensus has been from the conservationist side. Preservationists, who once thought they could preserve natural systems by isolating them, have been forced to admit that even the largest parks do not constitute whole ecosystems, so wildlife management must range over park boundaries. But this quickly implies that the mix of uses around the park will determine the qualities of the park. This in turn implies that the parks must be seen as one element of the larger pattern of land use and that they can be protected only if that larger pattern is devised with an eye toward their protection from spillover of the activities surrounding the park.[5] Preservationists have therefore been drawn into debates about the proper complex of land uses around park boundaries and into society-wide debates about clean air and clean wa-

ter. The preservationists, like the timber managers, have been driven toward management of whole ecosystems rather than isolated portions of those systems.

It is important not to paper over real differences. Attacks on the Forest Service by modern preservationists for below-value timber sales, for superfluous road-building, and for short-selling recreational values have never been more intense. Further, wildlife- and wilderness-oriented organizations fault the service for doing a miserable job of protecting diversity on the lands they manage. But the differences, however rancorous, are no longer all-or-nothing disputes. The Forest Service has clearly and explicitly accepted the legislative mandate that makes its management a balancing act. Likewise, preservation organizations such as the Wilderness Society and the Sierra Club have accepted the same formulation of the problem, accepting that the national forests will have some productive use, but arguing for wilderness wherever possible as a counterforce against a perceived bias of foresters toward timber production over other, aesthetic and moral goals.

The arguments now represent disagreements of degree and, as in the early days of conservation, these policy disagreements play themselves out as disputes regarding the appropriateness of particular uses for particular lands: What is the proper mix of economic management and contribution to noncommercial values for a public agency? While these issues are not easy, they are now discussed in a context of both sides accepting that management will involve finding a balance, and that the Forest Service will be held accountable for the effects of its activities on the whole range of social values. Essential to this consensus is the agreement that contextual management must supersede atomistic management—that management must take into account the important role of health and stability of the larger landscape in which productive and recreational units are embedded.

While this shift in values can be considered a victory of Muir over Pinchot, the victory is by no means complete. First of all, once a narrow worldview is entrenched in a bureaucracy, new legislation and broader leadership from the top will at best alter it slowly. On a deeper level, however, the methodological innovations of hypothetical market techniques for measuring amenity values represent a response to only one aspect of Muir's and Leopold's disagreement with the early resource managers. The Axiom of Usefulness performed two key functions in the early conservationists' worldview: It focused their efforts on commodity production, but reliance on the unquestioned value of maximizing sustainable production also encouraged resource managers to believe that their enterprise of "scientific resource management" was a value-free discipline. Since scientific resource managers merely maximized measurable outputs of desirable products, their professional tasks seemed to them to involve no value judgments.

The acceptance of aesthetic and amenity values has broadened the mission of resource managers, but many of them never questioned the underlying assumption that social preferences can be measured scientifically and can be used to determine what values public agencies should pursue. The broadening of values that took place in the post-Pinchot resource agencies therefore involved no attack on the assumption that economics, perhaps supplemented by questionnaires to determine nonmarket preferences, could scientifically determine the goals of the profession.

One might say that the Axiom of Usefulness was replaced with the Axiom of Consumer Value in their minds and in their management approach. The Axiom of Consumer Value, unlike its predecessor, countenances a broad conception of human value—a product or experience is valuable to the public if some members of the public desire it. But the Axiom of Consumer Value shares with its predecessor the implication that the task of resource managers is to maximize public satisfactions, and it views those satisfactions as "givens." Wide acceptance of the Axiom of Consumer Value among resource managers, therefore, represents a broadening of management goals to include aesthetic, recreational, and amenity values, but does not represent an acceptance of science as ecstatic and normative. Nor does it represent an acceptance of Leopold's conception of conservation biology and environmental management as a value-laden search for a culturally adequate conception of man's ethical relation to land. . . .

Notes

1. See T. H. Watkins, "Untrammeled by Man," *Audubon*, November 1989, pp. 78ff., for a history of this episode in Forest Service history.

2. Interview with author, Washington, DC, May 21, 1986; also see Hays, *Beauty, Health.*

3. William K. Wyant, *Westward in Eden: The Public Lands and the Conservation Movement* (Berkeley: University of California Press, 1982), pp. 279–81.

4. See Hays, *Beauty, Health,* chap. 4, especially pp. 123–28, for a more detailed account of how the Forest Service, although showing bureaucratic resistance, has gradually accepted that its task is one of "a broker among conflicting demands" (p. 128).

5. See Alston Chase, *Playing God in Yellowstone* (Boston: Atlantic Monthly Press, 1986), for a detailed account of the problems caused when the Park Service designed management plans on the (false) assumption that Yellowstone National Park could be managed as a self-sufficient ecosystem.

Radical American Environmentalism and Wilderness Preservation: A Third World Critique

Ramachandra Guha*

I. Introduction

The respected radical journalist Kirkpatrick Sale recently celebrated "the passion of a new and growing movement that has become disenchanted with the environmental establishment and has in recent years mounted a serious and sweeping at-

*Centre for Ecological Sciences, Indian Institute of Science, Bangalore 560 012, India. This essay was written while the author was a visiting lecturer at the Yale School of Forestry and Environmental Studies. He is grateful to Mike Bell, Tom Birch, Bill Burch, Bill Cronon, Diane Mayerfeld, David Rothenberg, Kirkpatrick Sale, Joel Seton, Tim Weiskel, and Don Worster for helpful comments.

Environmental Ethics, Vol. 11, No. 1 (Spring 1989), 71–83. Reprinted by permission.

tack on it—style, substance, systems, sensibilities and all."[1] The vision of those whom Sale calls the "New Ecologists"—and what I refer to in this article as deep ecology—is a compelling one. Decrying the narrowly economic goals of mainstream environmentalism, this new movement aims at nothing less than a philosophical and cultural revolution in human attitudes toward nature. In contrast to the conventional lobbying efforts of environmental professionals based in Washington, it proposes a militant defence of "Mother Earth," an unflinching opposition to human attacks on undisturbed wilderness. With their goals ranging from the spiritual to the political, the adherents of deep ecology span a wide spectrum of the American environmental movement. As Sale correctly notes, this emerging strand has in a matter of a few years made its presence felt in a number of fields: from academic philosophy (as in the journal *Environmental Ethics*) to popular environmentalism (for example, the group Earth First!).

In this article I develop a critique of deep ecology from the perspective of a sympathetic outsider. I critique deep ecology not as a general (or even a foot soldier) in the continuing struggle between the ghosts of Gifford Pinchot and John Muir over control of the U.S. environmental movement, but as an outsider to these battles. I speak admittedly as a partisan, but of the environmental movement in India, a country with an ecological diversity comparable to the U.S., but with a radically dissimilar cultural and social history.

My treatment of deep ecology is primarily historical and sociological, rather than philosophical, in nature. Specifically, I examine the cultural rootedness of a philosophy that likes to present itself in universalistic terms. I make two main arguments: first, that deep ecology is uniquely American, and despite superficial similarities in rhetorical style, the social and political goals of radical environmentalism in other cultural contexts (e.g., West Germany and India) are quite different; second, that the social consequences of putting deep ecology into practice on a worldwide basis (what its practitioners are aiming for) are very grave indeed.

II. The Tenets of Deep Ecology

While I am aware that the term *deep ecology* was coined by the Norwegian philosopher Arne Naess,

this article refers specifically to the American variant.[2] Adherents of the deep ecological perspective in this country, while arguing intensely among themselves over its political and philosophical implications, share some fundamental premises about human-nature interactions. As I see it, the defining characteristics of deep ecology are fourfold.

First, deep ecology argues that the environmental movement must shift from an "anthropocentric" to a "biocentric" perspective. In many respects, an acceptance of the primacy of this distinction constitutes the litmus test of deep ecology. A considerable effort is expended by deep ecologists in showing that the dominant motif in Western philosophy has been anthropocentric—i.e., the belief that man and his works are the center of the universe—and conversely, in identifying those lonely thinkers (Leopold, Thoreau, Muir, Aldous Huxley, Santayana, etc.) who, in assigning man a more humble place in the natural order, anticipated deep ecological thinking. In the political realm, meanwhile, establishment environmentalism (shallow ecology) is chided for casting its arguments in human-centered terms. Preserving nature, the deep ecologists say, has an intrinsic worth quite apart from any benefits preservation may convey to future human generations. The anthropocentric-biocentric distinction is accepted as axiomatic by deep ecologists, it structures their discourse, and much of the present discussions remains mired within it.

The second characteristic of deep ecology is its focus on the preservation of unspoilt wilderness—and the restoration of degraded areas to a more pristine condition—to the relative (and sometimes absolute) neglect of other issues on the environmental agenda. I later identify the cultural roots and portentous consequences of this obsession with wilderness. For the moment, let me indicate three distinct sources from which it springs. Historically, it represents a playing out of the preservationist (read *radical*) and utilitarian (read *reformist*) dichotomy that has plagued American environmentalism since the turn of the century. Morally, it is an imperative that follows from the biocentric perspective; other species of plants and animals, and nature itself, have an intrinsic right to exist. And finally, the preservation of wilderness also turns on a scientific argument—viz., the value of biological diversity in stabilizing ecological regimes and in retaining a gene pool for future generations. Truly radical policy proposals have been put forward by deep ecologists on the basis of these arguments. The influential poet Gary Snyder, for example, would like to see a 90 percent reduction in human populations to allow a restoration of pristine environments, while others have argued forcefully that a large portion of the globe must be immediately cordoned off from human beings.[3]

Third, there is a widespread invocation of Eastern spiritual traditions as forerunners of deep ecology. Deep ecology, it is suggested, was practiced both by major religious traditions and at a more popular level by "primal" peoples in non-Western settings. This complements the search for an authentic lineage in Western thought. At one level, the task is to recover those dissenting voices within the Judeo-Christian tradition; at another, to suggest that religious traditions in other cultures are, in contrast, dominantly if not exclusively "biocentric" in their orientation. This coupling of (ancient) Eastern and (modern) ecological wisdom seemingly helps consolidate the claim that deep ecology is a philosophy of universal significance.

Fourth, deep ecologists, whatever their internal differences, share the belief that they are the "leading edge" of the environmental movement. As the polarity of the shallow/deep and anthropocentric/biocentric distinctions makes clear, they see themselves as the spiritual, philosophical, and political vanguard of American and world environmentalism.

III. Toward a Critique

Although I analyze each of these tenets independently, it is important to recognize, as deep ecologists are fond of remarking in reference to nature, the interconnectedness and unity of these individual themes.

(1) Insofar as it has begun to act as a check on man's arrogance and ecological hubris, the transition from an anthropocentric (human-centered) to a biocentric (humans as only one element in the ecosystem) view in both religious and scientific traditions is only to be welcomed.[4] What is unacceptable are the radical conclusions drawn by deep ecology, in particular, that intervention in nature should be guided primarily by the need to preserve biotic integrity rather than by the needs of humans. The latter for deep ecologists is anthropocentric,

the former biocentric. This dichotomy is, however, of very little use in understanding the dynamics of environmental degradation. The two fundamental ecological problems facing the globe are (i) overconsumption by the industrialized world and by urban elites in the Third World and (ii) growing militarization, both in a short-term sense (i.e., ongoing regional wars) and in a long-term sense (i.e., the arms race and the prospect of nuclear annihilation). Neither of these problems has any tangible connection to the anthropocentric-biocentric distinction. Indeed, the agents of these processes would barely comprehend this philosophical dichotomy. The proximate causes of the ecologically wasteful characteristics of industrial society and of militarization are far more mundane: at an aggregate level, the dialectic of economic and political structures, and at a micro-level, the life-style choices of individuals. These causes cannot be reduced, whatever the level of analysis, to a deeper anthropocentric attitude toward nature; on the contrary, by constituting a grave threat to human survival, the ecological degradation they cause does not even serve the best interests of human beings! If my identification of the major dangers to the integrity of the natural world is correct, invoking the bogy of anthropocentrism is at best irrelevant and at worst a dangerous obfuscation.

(2) If the above dichotomy is irrelevant, the emphasis on wilderness is positively harmful when applied to the Third World. If in the U.S. the preservationist/utilitarian division is seen as mirroring the conflict between "people" and "interests," in countries such as India the situation is very nearly the reverse. Because India is a long settled and densely populated country in which agrarian populations have a finely balanced relationship with nature, the setting aside of wilderness areas has resulted in a direct transfer of resources from the poor to the rich. Thus, Project Tiger, a network of parks hailed by the international conservation community as an outstanding success, sharply posits the interests of the tiger against those of poor peasants living in and around the reserve. The designation of tiger reserves was made possible only by the physical displacement of existing villages and their inhabitants; their management requires the continuing exclusion of peasants and livestock. The initial impetus for setting up parks for the tiger and other large mammals such as the rhinoceros

and elephant came from two social groups, first, a class of ex-hunters turned conservationists belonging mostly to the declining Indian feudal elite and second, representatives of international agencies, such as the World Wildlife Fund (WWF) and the International Union for the Conservation of Nature and Natural Resources (IUCN), seeking to transplant the American system of national parks onto Indian soil. In no case have the needs of the local population been taken into account, and as in many parts of Africa, the designated wildlands are managed primarily for the benefit of rich tourists. Until very recently, wildlands preservation has been identified with environmentalism by the state and the conservation elite; in consequence, environmental problems that impinge far more directly on the lives of the poor—e.g., fuel, fodder, water shortages, soil erosion, and air and water pollution—have not been adequately addressed.[5]

Deep ecology provides, perhaps unwittingly, a justification for the continuation of such narrow and inequitable conservation practices under a newly acquired radical guise. Increasingly, the international conservation elite is using the philosophical, moral, and scientific arguments used by deep ecologists in advancing their wilderness crusade. A striking but by no means atypical example is the recent plea by a prominent American biologist for the takeover of large portions of the globe by the author and his scientific colleagues. Writing in a prestigious scientific forum, the *Annual Review of Ecology and Systematics,* Daniel Janzen argues that only biologists have the competence to decide how the tropical landscape should be used. As "the representatives of the natural world," biologists are "in charge of the future of tropical ecology," and only they have the expertise and mandate to "determine whether the tropical agroscape is to be populated only by humans, their mutualists, commensals, and parasites, or whether it will also contain some islands of the greater nature—the nature that spawned humans, yet has been vanquished by them." Janzen exhorts his colleagues to advance their territorial claims on the tropical world more forcefully, warning that the very existence of these areas is at stake: "if biologists want a tropics in which to biologize, they are going to have to buy it with care, energy, effort, strategy, tactics, time, and cash."[6]

This frankly imperialist manifesto highlights the multiple dangers of the preoccupation with wilderness preservation that is characteristic of deep ecology. As I have suggested, it seriously compounds the neglect by the American movement of far more pressing environmental problems within the Third World. But perhaps more importantly, and in a more insidious fashion, it also provides an impetus to the imperialist yearning of Western biologists and their financial sponsors, organizations such as the WWF and IUCN. The wholesale transfer of a movement culturally rooted in American conservation history can only result in the social uprooting of human populations in other parts of the globe.

(3) I come now to the persistent invocation of Eastern philosophies as antecedent in point of time but convergent in their structure with deep ecology. Complex and internally differentiated religious traditions—Hinduism, Buddhism, and Taoism—are lumped together as holding a view of nature believed to be quintessentially biocentric. Individual philosophers such as the Taoist Lao Tzu are identified as being forerunners of deep ecology. Even an intensely political, pragmatic, and Christian-influenced thinker such as Gandhi has been accorded a wholly undeserved place in the deep ecological pantheon. Thus the Zen teacher Robert Aitken Roshi makes the strange claim that Gandhi's thought was not human-centered and that he practiced an embryonic form of deep ecology which is "traditionally Eastern and is found with differing emphasis in Hinduism, Taoism and in Theravada and Mahayana Buddhism."[7] Moving away from the realm of high philosophy and scriptural religion, deep ecologists make the further claim that at the level of material and spiritual practice "primal" peoples subordinated themselves to the integrity of the biotic universe they inhabited.

I have indicated that this appropriation of Eastern traditions is in part dictated by the need to construct an authentic lineage and in part a desire to present deep ecology as a universalistic philosophy. Indeed, in his substantial and quixotic biography of John Muir, Michael Cohen goes so far as to suggest that Muir was the "Taoist of the [American] West."[8] This reading of Eastern traditions is selective and does not bother to differentiate between alternate (and changing) religious and cultural traditions; as it stands, it does considerable violence to the historical record. Throughout most recorded history the characteristic form of human activity in the "East" has been a finely tuned but nonetheless conscious and dynamic manipulation of nature. Although mystics such as Lao Tzu did reflect on the spiritual essence of human relations with nature, it must be recognized that such ascetics and their reflections were supported by a society of cultivators whose relationship with nature was a far more *active* one. Many agricultural communities do have a sophisticated knowledge of the natural environment that may equal (and sometimes surpass) codified "scientific" knowledge; yet, the elaboration of such traditional ecological knowledge (in both material and spiritual contexts) can hardly be said to rest on a mystical affinity with nature of a deep ecological kind. Nor is such knowledge infallible; as the archaeological record powerfully suggests, modern Western man has no monopoly on ecological disasters.

In a brilliant article, the Chicago historian Ronald Inden points out that this romantic and essentially positive view of the East is a mirror image of the scientific and essentially pejorative view normally upheld by Western scholars of the Orient. In either case, the East constitutes the Other, a body wholly separate and alien from the West; it is defined by a uniquely spiritual and nonrational "essence," even if this essence is valorized quite differently by the two schools. Eastern man exhibits a spiritual dependence with respect to nature—on the one hand, this is symptomatic of his prescientific and backward self, on the other, of his ecological wisdom and deep ecological consciousness. Both views are monolithic, simplistic, and have the characteristic effect—intended in one case, perhaps unintended in the other—of denying agency and reason to the East and making it the privileged orbit of Western thinkers.

The two apparently opposed perspectives have then a common underlying structure of discourse in which the East merely serves as a vehicle for Western projections. Varying images of the East are raw material for political and cultural battles being played out in the West; they tell us far more about the Western commentator and his desires than about the "East." Inden's remarks apply not merely to Western scholarship on India, but to Orientalist constructions of China and Japan as well:

> Although these two views appear to be
> strongly opposed, they often combine to-

gether. Both have a similar interest in sustaining the Otherness of India. The holders of the dominant view, best exemplified in the past in imperial administrative discourse (and today probably by that of 'development economics'), would place a traditional, superstition-ridden India in a position of perpetual tutelage to a modern, rational West. The adherents of the romantic view, best exemplified academically in the discourses of Christian liberalism and analytic psychology, concede the realm of the public and impersonal to the positivist. Taking their succour not from governments and big business, but from a plethora of religious foundations and self-help institutes, and from allies in the 'consciousness industry,' not to mention the important industry of tourism, the romantics insist that India embodies a private realm of the imagination and the religious which modern, western man lacks but needs. They, therefore, like the positivists, but for just the opposite reason, have a vested interest in seeing that the Orientalist view of India as 'spiritual,' 'mysterious,' and 'exotic' is perpetuated.[9]

(4) How radical, finally, are the deep ecologists? Notwithstanding their self-image and strident rhetoric (in which the label "shallow ecology" has an opprobrium similar to that reserved for "social democratic" by Marxist-Leninists), even within the American context their radicalism is limited and it manifests itself quite differently elsewhere.

To my mind, deep ecology is best viewed as a radical trend within the wilderness preservation movement. Although advancing philosophical rather than aesthetic arguments and encouraging political militancy rather than negotiation, its practical emphasis—viz., preservation of unspoilt nature—is virtually identical. For the mainstream movement, the function of wilderness is to provide a temporary antidote to modern civilization. As a special institution within an industrialized society, the national park "provides an opportunity for respite, contrast, contemplation, and affirmation of values for those who live most of their lives in the workaday world."[10] Indeed, the rapid increase in visitations to the national parks in postwar America is a direct consequence of economic expansion. The emergence of a popular interest in wilderness sites, the historian Samuel Hays points out, was "not a throwback to the primitive, but an integral part of the modern standard of living as people sought to add new 'amenity' and 'aesthetic' goals and desires to their earlier preoccupation with necessities and conveniences." [11]

Here, the enjoyment of nature is an integral part of the consumer society. The private automobile (and the life style it has spawned) is in many respects the ultimate ecological villain, and an untouched wilderness the prototype of ecological harmony; yet, for most Americans it is perfectly consistent to drive a thousand miles to spend a holiday in a national park. They possess a vast, beautiful, and sparsely populated continent and are also able to draw upon the natural resources of large portions of the globe by virtue of their economic and political dominance. In consequence, America can simultaneously enjoy the material benefits of an expanding economy and the aesthetic benefits of unspoilt nature. The two poles of "wilderness" and "civilization" mutually coexist in an internally coherent whole, and philosophers of both poles are assigned a prominent place in this culture. Paradoxically as it may seem, it is no accident that Star Wars technology and deep ecology both find their fullest expression in that leading sector of Western civilization, California.

Deep ecology runs parallel to the consumer society without seriously questioning its ecological and socio-political basis. In its celebration of American wilderness, it also displays an uncomfortable convergence with the prevailing climate of nationalism in the American wilderness movement. For spokesmen such as the historian Roderick Nash, the national park system is America's distinctive cultural contribution to the world, reflective not merely of its economic but of its philosophical and ecological maturity as well. In what Walter Lippman called the American century, the "American invention of national parks" must be exported worldwide. Betraying an economic determinism that would make even a Marxist shudder, Nash believes that environmental preservation is a "full stomach" phenomenon that is confined to the rich, urban, and sophisticated. Nonetheless, he hopes that "the less developed nations may eventually evolve economically and intellectually to the point where nature preservation is more than a business." [12]

The error which Nash makes (and which deep ecology in some respects encourages) is to equate environmental protection with the protection of wilderness. This is a distinctively American notion, borne out of a unique social and environmental history. The archetypal concerns of radical environmentalists in other cultural contexts are in fact quite different. The German Greens, for example, have elaborated a devastating critique of industrial society which turns on the acceptance of environmental limits to growth. Pointing to the intimate links between industrialization, militarization, and conquest, the Greens argue that economic growth in the West has historically rested on the economic and ecological exploitation of the Third World. Rudolf Bahro is characteristically blunt:

> The working class here [in the West] is the richest lower class in the world. And if I look at the problem from the point of view of the whole of humanity, not just from that of Europe, then I must say that the metropolitan working class is the worst exploiting class in history.... What made poverty bearable in eighteenth- or nineteenth-century Europe was the prospect of escaping it through exploitation of the periphery. But this is no longer a possibility, and continued industrialism in the Third World will mean poverty for whole generations and hunger for millions. [13]

Here the roots of global ecological problems lie in the disproportionate share of resources consumed by the industrialized countries as a whole *and* the urban elite within the Third World. Since it is impossible to reproduce an industrial monoculture worldwide, the ecological movement in the West must begin by cleaning up its own act. The Greens advocate the creation of a "no growth" economy, to be achieved by scaling down current (and clearly unsustainable) consumption levels. [14] This radical shift in consumption and production patterns requires the creation of alternate economic and political structures—smaller in scale and more amenable to social participation—but it rests equally on a shift in cultural values. The expansionist character of modern Western man will have to give way to an ethic of renunciation and self-limitation, in which spiritual and communal values play an increasing role in sustaining social life. This revolution in cultural values, however, has as its point of departure an understanding of environmental processes quite different from deep ecology.

Many elements of the Green program find a strong resonance in countries such as India, where a history of Western colonialism and industrial development has benefited only a tiny elite while exacting tremendous social and environmental costs. The ecological battles presently being fought in India have as their epicenter the conflict over nature between the subsistence and largely rural sector and the vastly more powerful commercial-industrial sector. Perhaps the most celebrated of these battles concerns the Chipko (Hug the Tree) movement, a peasant movement against deforestation in the Himalayan foothills. Chipko is only one of several movements that have sharply questioned the nonsustainable demand being placed on the land and vegetative base by urban centers and industry. These include opposition to large dams by displaced peasants, the conflict between small artisan fishing and large-scale trawler fishing for export, the countrywide movements against commercial forest operations, and opposition to industrial pollution among downstream agricultural and fishing communities.[15]

Two features distinguish these environmental movements from their Western counterparts. First, for the sections of society most critically affected by environmental degradation—poor and landless peasants, women, and tribals—it is a question of sheer survival, not of enhancing the quality of life. Second, and as a consequence, the environmental solutions they articulate deeply involve questions of equity as well as economic and political redistribution. Highlighting these differences, a leading Indian environmentalist stresses that "environmental protection per se is of least concern to most of these groups. Their main concern is about the use of the environment and who should benefit from it."[16] They seek to wrest control of nature away from the state and the industrial sector and place it in the hands of rural communities who live within that environment but are increasingly denied access to it. These communities have far more basic needs, their demands on the environment are far less intense, and they can draw upon a reservoir of cooperative social institutions and local ecological knowledge in managing the "commons"—forests, grasslands, and the waters—on a sustainable basis. If colonial and capitalist expansion has both accentuated social inequalities and signaled a precipitous fall in ecological wisdom, an alternate ecology must rest on an alternate society and polity as well.

This brief overview of German and Indian environmentalism has some major implications for deep ecology. Both German and Indian environmental traditions allow for a greater integration of ecological concerns with livelihood and work. They also place a greater emphasis on equity and social justice (both within individual countries and on a global scale) on the grounds that in the absence of social regeneration environmental regeneration has very little chance of succeeding. Finally, and perhaps most significantly, they have escaped the preoccupation with wilderness preservation so characteristic of American cultural and environmental history.[17]

IV. A Homily

In 1958, the economist J. K. Galbraith referred to overconsumption as the unasked question of the American conservation movement. There is a marked selectivity, he wrote, "in the conservationist's approach to materials consumption. If we are concerned about our great appetite for materials, it is plausible to seek to increase the supply, to decrease waste, to make better use of the stocks available, and to develop substitutes. But what of the appetite itself? Surely this is the ultimate source of the problem. If it continues its geometric course, will it not one day have to be restrained? Yet in the literature of the resource problem this is the forbidden question. Over it hangs a nearly total silence."[18]

The consumer economy and society have expanded tremendously in the three decades since Galbraith penned these words; yet his criticisms are nearly as valid today. I have said "nearly," for there are some hopeful signs. Within the environmental movement several dispersed groups are working to develop ecologically benign technologies and to encourage less wasteful life styles. Moreover, outside the self-defined boundaries of American environmentalism, opposition to the permanent war economy is being carried on by a peace movement that has a distinguished history and impeccable moral and political credentials.

It is precisely these (to my mind, most hopeful) components of the American social scene that are missing from deep ecology. In their widely noticed book, Bill Devall and George Sessions make no mention of militarization or the movements for peace, while activists whose practical focus is on developing ecologically responsible life styles (e.g., Wendell Berry) are derided as "falling short of deep ecological awareness."[19] A truly radical ecology in the American context ought to work toward a synthesis of the appropriate technology, alternate life style, and peace movements.[20] By making the (largely spurious) anthropocentric-biocentric distinction central to the debate, deep ecologists may have appropriated the moral high ground, but they are at the same time doing a serious disservice to American and global environmentalism.[21]

Notes

1. Kirkpatrick Sale, "The Forest for the Trees: Can Today's Environmentalists Tell the Difference," *Mother Jones* 11, no. 8 (November 1986): 26.

2. One of the major criticisms I make in this essay concerns deep ecology's lack of concern with inequalities *within* human society. In the article in which he coined the term *deep ecology,* Naess himself expresses concerns about inequalities between and within nations. However, his concern with social cleavages and their impact on resource utilization patterns and ecological destruction is not very visible in the later writings of deep ecologists. See Arne Naess, "The Shallow and the Deep, Long-Range Ecology Movement: A Summary," *Inquiry* 16 (1973): 96 (I am grateful to Tom Birch for this reference).

3. Gary Snyder, quoted in Sale, "The Forest for the Trees," p. 32. See also Dave Foreman, "A Modest Proposal for a Wilderness System," *Whole Earth Review,* no. 53 (Winter 1986–87): 42–45.

4. See, for example, Donald Worster, *Nature's Economy: The Roots of Ecology* (San Francisco: Sierra Club Books, 1977).

5. See Centre for Science and Environment, *India: The State of the Environment 1982: A Citizens Report* (New Delhi: Centre for Science and Environment, 1982); R. Sukumar, "Elephant-Man Conflict in Karnataka," in Cecil Saldanha, ed., *The State of Karnataka's Environment* (Bangalore: Centre for Taxonomic Studies, 1985). For Africa, see the brilliant analysis by Helge Kjekshus, *Ecology Control and Economic Development in East African History* (Berkeley: University of California Press, 1977).

6. Daniel Janzen, "The Future of Tropical Ecology," *Annual Review of Ecology and Systematics* 17 (1986): 305–06; emphasis added.

7. Robert Aitken Roshi, "Gandhi, Dogen, and Deep Ecology," reprinted as appendix C in Bill Devall and George Sessions, *Deep Ecology: Living as if Nature Mattered* (Salt Lake City: Peregrine Smith Books, 1985). For Gandhi's own views on social re-

construction, see the excellent three-volume collection edited by Raghavan Iyer, *The Moral and Political Writings of Mahatma Gandhi* (Oxford: Clarendon Press, 1986–87).

8. Michael Cohen, *The Pathless Way* (Madison: University of Wisconsin Press, 1984), p. 120.

9. Ronald Inden, "Orientalist Constructions of India," *Modern Asian Studies* 20 (1986): 442. Inden draws inspiration from Edward Said's forceful polemic, *Orientalism* (New York: Basic Books, 1980). It must be noted, however, that there is a salient difference between Western perceptions of Middle Eastern and Far Eastern cultures, respectively. Due perhaps to the long history of Christian conflict with Islam, Middle Eastern cultures (as Said documents) are consistently presented in pejorative terms. The juxtaposition of hostile and worshiping attitudes that Inden talks of applies only to Western attitudes toward Buddhist and Hindu societies.

10. Joseph Sax, *Mountains Without Handrails: Reflections on the National Parks* (Ann Arbor: University of Michigan Press, 1980), p. 42. Cf. also Peter Schmitt, *Back to Nature: The Arcadian Myth in Urban America* (New York: Oxford University Press, 1969), and Alfred Runte, *National Parks: The American Experience* (Lincoln: University of Nebraska Press, 1979).

11. Samuel Hays, "From Conservation to Environment: Environmental Politics in the United States since World War Two," *Environmental Review* 6 (1982): 21. See also the same author's book entitled *Beauty, Health and Permanence: Environmental Politics in the United States, 1955–85* (New York: Cambridge University Press, 1987).

12. Roderick Nash, *Wilderness and the American Mind,* 3rd ed. (New Haven: Yale University Press, 1982).

13. Rudolf Bahro, *From Red to Green* (London: Verso Books, 1984).

14. From time to time, American scholars have themselves criticized these imbalances in consumption patterns. In the 1950s, William Vogt made the charge that the United States, with one-sixteenth of the world's population, was utilizing one-third of the globe's resources. (Vogt, cited in E. F. Murphy, *Nature, Bureaucracy and the Rule of Property* [Amsterdam: North Holland, 1977, p. 29]). More recently, Zero Population Growth has estimated that each American consumes thirty-nine times as many resources as an Indian. See *Christian Science Monitor,* 2 March 1987.

15. For an excellent review, see Anil Agarwal and Sunita Narain, eds., *India: The State of the Environment 1984–85: A Citizens Report* (New Delhi: Centre for Science and Environment, 1985). Cf. also Ramachan-

dra Guha, *The Unquiet Woods: Ecological Change and Peasant Resistance in the Indian Himalaya* (Berkeley: University of California Press, forthcoming).

16. Anil Agarwal, "Human-Nature Interactions in a Third World Country," *The Environmentalist* 6, no. 3 (1986): 167.

17. One strand in radical American environmentalism, the bioregional movement, by emphasizing a greater involvement with the bioregion people inhabit, does indirectly challenge consumerism. However, as yet bioregionalism has hardly raised the questions of equity and social justice (international, intranational, and intergenerational) which I argue must be a central plank of radical environmentalism. Moreover, its stress on (individual) *experience* as the key to involvement with nature is also somewhat at odds with the integration of nature with livelihood and work that I talk of in this paper. Cf. Kirkpatrick Sale, *Dwellers in the Land: The Bioregional Vision* (San Francisco: Sierra Club Books, 1985).

18. John Kenneth Galbraith, "How Much Should a Country Consume?" in Henry Jarrett, ed., *Perspectives on Conservation* (Baltimore: Johns Hopkins Press, 1958), pp. 91–92.

19. Devall and Sessions, *Deep Ecology*, p. 122. For Wendell Berry's own assessment of deep ecology, see

his "Amplications: Preserving Wildness," *Wilderness* 50 (Spring 1987): 39–40, 50–54.

20. See the interesting recent contribution by one of the most influential spokesmen of appropriate technology—Barry Commoner, "A Reporter at Large: The Environment," *New Yorker*, 15 June 1987. While Commoner makes a forceful plea for the convergence of the environmental movement (viewed by him primarily as the opposition to air and water pollution and to the institutions that generate such pollution) and the peace movement, he significantly does not mention consumption patterns, implying that "limits to growth" do not exist.

21. In this sense, my critique of deep ecology, although that of an outsider, may facilitate the reassertion of those elements in the American environmental tradition for which there is a profound sympathy in other parts of the globe. A global perspective may also lead to a critical reassessment of figures such as Aldo Leopold and John Muir, the two patron saints of deep ecology. As Donald Worster has pointed out, the message of Muir (and, I would argue, of Leopold as well) makes sense only in an American context; he has very little to say to other cultures. See Worster's review of Stephen Fox's *John Muir and His Legacy*, in *Environmental Ethics* 5 (1983): 277–81.

E. DEGRADING THE PLANET

PREVIEW

[I] thought she was a spinster. What's she so worried about genetics for?

Member of the Federal Pest Control Review Board (about Rachel Carson)[1]

. . . what the computer models are suggesting is that children born today may see a climate change approximately the size of an Ice Age.[2]

Jonathan Weiner, *The Next 100 Years*

Which environmental problems matter the most? Deep ecologists and urban advocates appear to disagree. Gary Snyder, a poet and deep ecologist, asks, "How much room for nature is there in the environmental movement? In the Earth Day speeches last spring there was little talk about trees or animals or wil-

derness; the discussion largely centered on air pollution, on solid waste, on global threats like ozone destruction."[3] In contrast, Karl Grossman, in his essay, "Environmental Racism," complains about just the opposite state of affairs. He quotes a leader of a Harlem environmental group: "We get so used to the stereotype that what environmentalism means is wildlife and the preservation of open space. There [has] not been sufficient movement on urban environmental problems: incinerators, sewage treatment plants, factories polluting the air, devastating occupational exposure."[4] This section focuses on the latter: environmental threats such as hazardous wastes, pollution, poisoning of the earth with pesticides, our trash problem, and ozone depletion and the risks of global warming.

Warwick Fox dates "[t]he birth of the environmental movement . . . to the virtual explosion of interest that attended the 1962 publication of Rachel Carson's *Silent Spring*."[5] A best seller and much celebrated in the cartoons of the day, *Silent Spring* is about the contamination of the environment with chemical poisons, especially the widespread practice of aerial spraying with toxic pesticides such as DDT. Poisons used to kill certain insects, Carson argued, become embedded in the food chain. Notably, birds eat the contaminated insects and die. Eventually, no birds sing; hence, the title, *Silent Spring.*

Silent Spring begins with a fable warning us of what could happen if we fill our world with poisonous chemicals. Interestingly, H. Patricia Hynes, in her book, *The Recurring Silent Spring*, says, "Since . . . 1985 there have been at least three publicized 'silent springs,' in Bhopal, Chernobyl, and the Rhine River, two of which involved pesticides. Many of the major ecological disasters of the past two decades have occurred in the manufacture, storage, use, and disposal of pesticides or chemical compounds with deadly biocidal components."[6] Carson ends her book by admonishing scientists not to take the disastrous road of the chemical control of insects, but instead to take the road of "biological solutions, based on understanding of the living organisms they seek to control, and of the whole fabric of life to which these organisms belong."[7]

In his foreword to the 25th-anniversary edition of *Silent Spring*, Paul Brooks points out that the reception of Carson's book was "as bitter and unscrupulous as anything of the sort since the publication of Charles Darwin's *Origin of Species* a century before."[8] A review from *Time* magazine from September 28, 1962, for example, calls the book "unfair, one-sided, and hysterically overemphatic" and argues that Carson's "emotional and inaccurate outburst . . . may do harm by alarming the nontechnical public."[9]

It is in this heated response to the book

that its most significant message to the reader of the 1990s lies, for surely the virulent reactions of Carson's critics speak of more than a difference of opinion on chemicals. Her claim that neither scientists nor government officials nor the public understood the dangers of pesticides and agricultural chemicals obviously touched some raw nerves. Again quoting Paul Brooks, "It was not simply that she was opposing indiscriminate use of poisons but—more fundamentally—that she had made clear the basic irresponsibility of an industrialized technological society toward the natural world."[10] Carson concluded, says H. Patricia Hynes, ". . . that the arrogant control of nature by science and technology was at the root of pollution and the silencing of spring."[11]

Paul Brooks concludes his foreword with the following: "*Silent Spring* will continue to remind us that in our overorganized and overmechanized age, individual initiative and courage still count: change can be brought about . . . by altering the direction of our thinking about the world we live in."[12] After completing her manuscript, Carson herself said in a letter to Dorothy Freeman:[13]

> . . . I took Jeffie [her cat] into the study and played the Beethoven violin concerto—one of my favorites, you know. And suddenly the tension of four years was broken and I let the tears come. I think I let you see last summer what my deeper feelings are about this when I said I could never again listen happily to a thrush song if I had not done all I could. And last night the thoughts of all the birds and other creatures and all the loveliness that is in nature came to me with such a surge of happiness, that now I had done what I could—I had been able to complete it—now it had its own life. . . . [14]

Looking at Carson's work through the commentators' eyes, one can see the parallel between Carson and Lynn White, Jr., deep ecologists, Native American writers, and others who call for a fundamental change in attitude toward the environment, an openness to the voices of birds and the land that would make possible some reciprocal relationship between human beings and the earth which is precluded, indeed, silenced by an attitude of arrogance and domination.[15]

President John F. Kennedy's Science Advisory Committee was critical of pesticide use in industry and government, acknowledging its debt to *Silent Spring*.[16] As a consequence, DDT was taken off the U.S. market. However, as Hynes and others point out, the continued manufacture of DDT in the United States for export to foreign countries comes home to roost. "Nearly 50 million pounds of DDT have been manufactured in the U.S. each year and exported to foreign countries since the chemical was suspended here. It is then imported back on fruits and vegetables in what has been labeled a 'circle of poison'".[17]

We could benefit, Hynes says, from a fresh reading of *Silent Spring* in light of the work of a relatively new U.S. industry—biotechnology. An ecology-centered agriculture, as advanced in *Silent Spring*, is arguably not part of a biotech future. "Developing herbicide-tolerant plant lines—that is, plants genetically modified to survive being sprayed with a herbicide—constitutes about 40 percent of the U.S. biotechnology research in agriculture."[18] Hence, chemical solutions are still viewed with approval. In passing, we note that fear of harming the biotechnology industry was the main reason former president George Bush gave for the United States not signing the "biodiversity agreement" at the Earth Summit.

Pesticides are problems that quite literally will not go away, but other forms of pollution are more visible and perhaps more compelling. In December, 1992, a 28-foot sperm whale beached itself on the North Carolina coast, starving because of garbage clogging its digestive system. "We found a couple of plastic bottles, a chunk of rubber the size of a foot-

ball and a Styrofoam float—the ones as big as basketballs—with 30 feet of rope attached,"[19] said David Webster, a professor of marine biology at the University of North Carolina at Wilmington.

Plastics have longer life spans in nature than almost any pesticide, but luckily they are tremendously malleable. As *The New York Times* reported in 1992, some countries are taking advantage of plastic's potential for reuse:

> In 1992, Germany passed a law that makes manufacturers and retailers responsible for taking back and recycling parts when a car is discarded. As a result, car companies like BMW and Volkswagen are producing cars whose plastic parts can be dismantled into parts that are recyclable. Traditionally, companies remove batteries and fuel tanks from a car and then shred what remains. The metals are removed from the shredded material and the plastics go into landfills. But these plastics are "semi-hazardous" waste, contaminated with oil, automotive fluids and lead.[20]

The German plan to encourage manufacturers to recycle plastic products could keep those products from turning into ocean-borne trash such as that which killed the whale.

Paul Connett, in a following essay, "The Disposable Society," challenges us to deal with "... the trash crisis ... in North America" and to "... start handling our discarded materials as if the future mattered."[21] Connett begins by analyzing the dimensions of the problem in terms of, first, overconsumption, and, second, throwing much away. He assesses many competing practical solutions to the trash crisis. One interesting example is what to do about the fact that our landfills are full. One seemingly easy answer is trash incinerators. Why bother with dreary recycling when we can just burn it? Here's the catch: "For every three tons of trash that is burned, one ton of ash is produced."[22] The ash, it turns out, is toxic—hazardous waste. As Connett says:

> It doesn't make economic or environmental sense to convert three tons of trash into one ton of toxic ash. Ash landfills are proving as difficult to site as raw-waste landfills. People don't want the ash in their backyard any more than they wanted the trash. Nor will future generations thank us for these acres of toxic ash. We have to question the ethics of leaving future generations with the problems of containing, guarding, and monitoring our permanent toxics for eternity.[23]

Acknowledging that no one wants the trash in his or her backyard, the topic of "environmental racism" turns our attention to where the trash is going and has gone. There has been, says Benjamin F. Chavis, Jr., a "deliberate targeting of people of color communities for toxic waste facilities" and an "official sanctioning of the life-threatening presence of poisons and pollutants in our communities."[24] "... [M]inorities bear a greater burden from lead poisoning, airborne toxins and contaminated drinking water ...," says Deeohn Ferris, an attorney for the National Wildlife Federation. "The condition is called 'environmental racism.'"[25] Explaining further, environmental researcher Hope Taylor says, "Small dirty industries have a tendency to locate in minority communities for two reasons: One, cheap labor. And two, their relative lack of knowledge about environmental concerns."[26]

> Several studies indicate a discriminatory pattern of pollution:
> - In a study of blacks and whites making less than $15,000 a year, twice as many blacks had dangerous levels of lead in their bloodstreams, according to the Centers for Disease Control.
> - A National Law Journal study [in 1992] of 1,177 Superfund waste dumps found that the EPA began cleanups 20 percent quicker in white neighborhoods than in black neighborhoods. The same study found that EPA penalties against polluters averaged $335,566 in white neighborhoods compared to $55,318 in black areas.
> - An estimated 300,000 farm workers—90 percent of whom are minorities—suffer each year from pesticide-related illnesses, according to the EPA.[27]

Karl Grossman, in his essay, "Environmental Racism," analyzes the pattern of placing hazardous facilities in black and native American communities in the United States; he also makes the connection between this phenomenon and the dumping of hazardous wastes in third-world countries.[28] One striking example is found in an internal memo written by Lawrence Summers, chief economist of the World Bank. Leaked to the press, the December 12, 1991, memo begins, "Just between you and me, shouldn't the World Bank be encouraging *more* migration of the dirty industries to the LDCs [less developed countries]?"[29]

Characterizing pollution as a problem of justice and fairness, says Bryan G. Norton, is "... in the tradition of Rachel Carson's moralism."[30] In support of his claim, Norton quotes Carson on pollution and the Bill of Rights:

> We have subjected enormous numbers of people to contact with these poisons, without their consent and often without their knowledge. If the Bill of Rights contains no guarantee that a citizen shall be secure against lethal poisons distributed either by private individuals or by public officials, it is surely only because our forefathers, despite their considerable wisdom and foresight, could conceive of no such problem.[31]

According to Norton, Richard Ayers, senior staff attorney at the National Resources Defense Council and chair of the National Clean Air Coalition, is speaking in this tradition when he says, "Pollution is somebody's garbage, somebody's unwanted material and polluters have no right to impose, involuntarily on me, an exposure to those materials for their profit." [32] To pass on unconsented to, nontrivial costs to others is to violate what many philosophers refer to as the "Harm Principle." A crude version of the Harm Principle is that it is wrong to harm others (on balance) without their voluntary, informed consent. [33] So if by "pollution" we understand such passing on of costs, then doing so is morally problematic to say the least, and there is a parallel between so polluting and cases of burglary, embezzlement, assault, or rape. [34] As was discussed in An Introduction to Ethical Theory, paradigmatic harms such as theft typically happen in a short span of time, have a single, readily identifiable causal agent and a single, readily identifiable recipient or victim. In contrast, much pollution imposes harms over a long period of time on many recipients, and sometimes the occurrence of a bad outcome is not certain—it occurs only after a long period of deterioration and sometimes only in conjunction with other similar forms of pollution. Recall the slow effects of exposure to nuclear radiation, toxic chemicals, or asbestos particles.

It is important to note that the main types of pollution we have been discussing—poisons and toxic waste—do not represent everything that could be classified as pollution. Arguably, all factories, most food production, and all cars pollute. Broadening the conception of what counts as pollution increases the plausibility that some pollution is acceptable and that what we need is an optimal amount of pollution. For example, some people point out that there is a cost of not polluting. One moral question concerns under what conditions it is permissible to generate wastes, what kinds, and at what rate.

U.S. Senators Tim Wirth and John Heinz, in the following excerpt from their public policy study, *Project 88: Harnessing Market Forces to Protect Our Environment*, suggested in 1988 that pollutants threatening the ozone layer be reduced and that some potential ozone de-

pleters can be phased out altogether. They advocate a market-based approach—issuing permits to corporations and allowing them to trade permits among themselves. This proposed solution is similar to allowing companies to buy "polluting rights" from one another, a practice already under way and discussed by William Ruckelshaus in Section V-C. (See also A. Myrick Freeman's ideas on charging for pollution in Section V-A.)

Different types of pollution pose different kinds of threats. It is not for nothing that people do not want toxic dumps in their backyard. Moreover, it is fairly uncontroversial that the depletion of the ozone layer by pollutants such as chlorofluorocarbons (CFCs) used for refrigeration and aerosol products will lead to a higher incidence of skin cancers, cataracts, and impaired immune systems.

If Socrates or Aristotle were alive today, we are confident that neither would be surprised by talk of "ethics and climate." We expect the expression to become more familiar as it becomes clear that humans' actions are powerfully affecting the world's climate, and we can no longer think of the earth as some fixed, unalterable stage on which lives come and go and on which human activities have only a negligible effect. Arguably, one of the greatest threats to humankind and much of the biota is the threat of global warming. "What is this alleged threat?" one might ask, for many deny that there is *any* such threat and claim that the warnings of environmentalists amount only to the same old doomsday talk, a mere device to place new restrictions on "free" enterprise.

The situation is this. Due to the emission of certain gases, "greenhouse gases," such as methane, carbon dioxide, and nitrous oxide, many of the warming rays of the sun which would otherwise bounce off the earth and be reradiated back into the stratosphere are "trapped" in the earth's atmosphere by the layer of these gases accumulating there. [35] That is the "greenhouse effect." There is no significant controversy about whether it occurs. The phenomenon is millions of years old, and without the greenhouse effect the oceans would be solid ice.[36] The phenomenon makes most, if not all, life on earth possible. It is also widely agreed that the data show that the earth warmed about 1 degree Fahrenheit or 1/2 degree Celsius (or centigrade) between 1860 and the 1980s. The year 1981 was the warmest in 100 years (remember, we speak of average global surface temperature and not local extremes). And 1983 was even warmer.[37] The hottest year prior to 1993 was 1988. It is this latter increase in average global surface temperature which people today are commonly referring to when they speak of "global warming." Some degree of global warming is, then, noncontroversial. It does *not* follow that these warm years were *caused* by an *intensification* of the greenhouse effect; they *could* just be random occurrences.

What is clear is that *a warming trend has occurred over the last 130 years.* That is not controversial. What is a matter of some dispute is why this phenomenon has occurred. Is an intensification of the greenhouse effect the correct explanation of that increase?[38] Is there a more plausible explanation, or only some reluctance to embrace the greenhouse explanation? Corporations, major emitters of the most important greenhouse gases, have powerful vested interests in denying that they are imposing a cosmic-sized risk on humankind, and they would rather not engage in costly procedural changes. Also having vested interests are those politicians who profit from the support of those interests; it is predictable, then that *whatever the facts are,* such voices will deny that there is a problem, will insist that only "further study" is called for, or will insist that the costs of change are too great.

To speak of a trend is sometimes to suggest not just that there has been a trend *in the past* but that forces at work will bring about a certain stream of events in the future. So, there is not only a dispute about the explanation for past occurrences but also what is going to happen in, say, the next 100 years. This source of disagreement is evidently connected with the view that the evident warming trend of 130+ years is due to recent human industrial activities and growing population which have intensified the greenhouse effect. If that is the explanation, then we can only expect that trend to continue until and unless unexpected natural events alter that trend or humans collectively alter their behavior so significantly as to cease contributing to those factors causing an increase in global warming.

The average global temperature of the planet has waxed and waned radically over the eons. At one time sea creatures swam in the waters which once existed in what are now hot and dry African deserts. In Mecca, Indiana fossil remains of 13-foot-long sharks have been found.[39] In Greenland there are fossils of alligators that once roamed there.[40] On the top of Mt. Everest, now 5 miles above sea level, and usually covered in snow, is a layer of limestone which resulted from the fossils of plantlike animals which lived in shallow seas some 300 million years ago.[41] The Finger Lakes of New York State were formed by giant glaciers as they receded during the end of the last Ice Age.[42] At the peak of that period, about 20,000 years ago, the earth was, of course, comparatively colder. At the end of that period, about 16,000 years ago, the ice on Manhattan Island (e.g., New York City) was one-half mile deep.[43] The ice covered 11,000,000 square miles of land on the globe that is today free of ice; a concomitant of that was that sea levels fell 350 feet. The striking fact is that at the depth of that Ice Age, the average global temperature was *5 degrees Celsius colder than today.*[44] No hominid but *Homo sapiens* came to exist (again, that's us, "man, the Doubly Wise") about 50,000 years ago, but only a *1.5 degree* Celsius increase in the global average would make the earth warmer than it has been in 100,000 years.[45] As we noted, the increase in the last 130 years has been 1/2 degree Celsius. If the five billion tons of carbon (to take one example) we humans collectively emit into the atmosphere each year significantly contributes to the increase in warming, then we are playing a kind of global Russian roulette, that is, we are engaged collectively in behavior which seriously increases the risks to life on earth.[46] Luxembourg has a ratio of about two persons per car. Imagine what might happen if the one billion Chinese, for example, came to own one automobile for every two persons. Yet people who live in affluent societies cannot readily say "do as we preach, but not as we do." Once again we need to ask whether our lifestyle is ecologically sustainable.

A series of important questions must be dealt with, the leading ones of which are the following:

1. Will the increase in global warming continue?

2. If so, for how long and at what rate?

3. Is the recent trend caused mainly by an increase in the emission of greenhouse gases?

4. If so, what are the benefits of taking steps to avoid contributing to, or halting, this trend?

5. What will be the costs of so *acting?* The costs of *not* acting?

6. What is a reasonable and morally acceptable choice to make under the circumstances?

So, we confront questions concerning the *magnitude of the benefits and harms* which increased warming might bring. In addition, there are evidently questions concerning the *probability* that warming will intensify and, if so, at what rate. Omitting details, the *magnitude* of harm associated with a rise of 3 degrees Celsius (Centigrade) by late the next century would probably be catastrophic for large parts of the planet. In exploring the question of what we ought to do, one might consider what one should do personally, e.g., what should one do about the *possibility* of

one's house burning down, getting tetanus, smallpox, or polio, or sustaining serious injury in an automobile accident? There may be low-cost ways of avoiding a serious harm; in some of the cases just mentioned, one might simply get a vaccination. Analogously there are some low-cost ways of reducing carbon emissions and alternatively there are high-cost ways of avoiding serious harms; for example, one might undergo a series of rather painful shots to ensure that one will not suffer the worst effects of being bitten by a possibly rabid dog. Analogously, the extremely high cost of having a powerful military is a price the United States has chosen to pay as a means of warding off attack, and so on.

In many if not all cases in which one faces the possibility of being subjected to a serious harm of unclear probability, it is prudent to hedge one's bets, and to do so in some cases by undertaking activities which are, in fact, quite costly—all depending on the magnitude of the threat. Recall once again the military example or the case of purchasing expensive health insurance to avoid financial disaster. Contemporary decision theory distinguishes two kinds of decision-making scenarios. In one, *"decision-making under risk,"* the probabilities of certain outcomes are known; here the rule of rationality to be followed is said to be: *maximize expected utility.* What is crucial if this rule is to be followed is to estimate accurately the benefits and costs of the different paths we can pursue (to emphasize a point: including the costs of *not* acting to slow or halt human-generated increases in global warming). The other decision-making scenario (often called *decision-making under uncertainty*) is that in which it is not possible to estimate the probabilities of the different outcomes associated with a choice of one path or another. Here many people think (the point is controversial) that the rational choice is to choose the alternative whose worst outcome is better than the worst outcome of any other available alternative, that is, *"maximin"* or maximize the minimum. Here again an enormous nest of empirical "economic" (broadly understood) questions arise, for one must compare, roughly, the costs and benefits of choosing the path of (1) doing little to halt increases in warming, the benefits of such inaction, and the costs of future increased warming if it occurs, and (2) doing a lot to prevent future increases in warming, the costs of such action, and the benefits of halting or diminishing the warming if one succeeds in doing so. Again, all this is oversimplified, but we hope to have identified the extremes between which one can choose. The later essay by Stephen Schneider surveys the situation from the standpoint of a scientist.

In his excellent volume *The Next 100 Years*, Jonathan Weiner observes that, "We do not respond to emergencies that unfold in slow motion. We do not respond adequately to the invisible."[47] Again, it may be worth comparing the horror of the Holocaust, the fury it evoked, the massive effort to fight the Nazis, and the slower, more passive reaction to the threat of HIV, which almost certainly will kill more people in the next two or three decades than died in the Holocaust. There is good reason to believe that we humans collectively are engaged in a massive transformation of the planet and are flirting with a human and ecological disaster of horrendous proportions. Yet we cannot point to it. We do not hear it. We cannot film it. We do not see the blood in the streets. We do not see the torn bodies of little children as in a war. It is not on television. We have powerful incentives to deny the very existence of a problem. As noted, wealthy corporate and political interests will use their enormous influence to control what people will think and what they will do.

NOTES

1. H. Patricia Hynes, *The Recurring Silent Spring* (New York: Pergamon Press, 1989), pp. 18–19.

2. Jonathan Weiner. *The Next 100 Years* (New York: Bantam Books, 1991), p. 103.

3. Gary Snyder, *The Practice of the Wild*, North Point,

1990, reviewed by Bill McKibben, "The Moutain Hedonist," *The New York Review of Books* (April 11, 1991), p. 29.

4. Peggy Shepard quoted in "Environmental Racism," by Karl Grossman, *The Crisis* (April 1991), p. 31.

5. Warwick Fox, *Toward a Transpersonal Ecology.* (Boston: Shambhala, 1990), p. 4.

6. H. Patricia Hynes, *The Recurring Silent Spring*, p. 13.

7. Rachel Carson, *Silent Spring* (Boston: Houghton Mifflin Company, 1962), p. 278.

8. Paul Brooks, Foreword to *Silent Spring.* (Boston: Houghton Mifflin Company, 1962), p. xii.

9. *Time*, Vol. 80, No. 13 (September 28, 1962), pp. 45 and 48.

10. Paul Brooks, Foreword to *Silent Spring*, p. xii.

11. H. Patricia Hynes, *Recurring Silent Spring*, p. 24.

12. Paul Brooks, Foreword to *Silent Spring*, pp. xiii–xiv.

13. Rachel Carson and Dorothy Freeman spent ten consecutive summers together in Maine where "they met for beach picnics, found wild haunts, lay on the rocks and in sunny, grassy enclaves where they watched migrating birds, read to each other, and discussed Carson's [work]." (Hynes, p. 30) Carson's letters to Freeman, to whom, according to Paul Brooks, Carson "gave herself completely," are held by Freeman and are unavailable to the public. (Hynes, p. 2)

14. Paul Brooks, *The House of Life: Rachel Carson at Work.* (Boston: Houghton Mifflin Company, 1972), pp. 271–272.

15. Thanks to Anthony Weston for our conversations about attitudes toward the environment, if not about Rachel Carson. Note Warwick Fox's remarks on the similarities between Rachel Carson and Lynn White, Jr., vis-a-vis the Western attitude of arrogance toward the environment in *Toward a Transpersonal Ecology*, pp. 4–5.

16. Paul Brooks, *The House of Life: Rachel Carson at Work*, p. 305.

17. H. Patricia Hynes, "'Spring' Lessons Timeless and Ignored," *The News and Observer*, Raleigh, NC, September 14, 1992. See also R. Repetto, "Paying the Price: Pesticide Subsidies in Developing Countries," Research Report No. 2; World Resources Institue, Washington, 1985, and Kristin Shrader-Frechette, *Risk and Ratio*, Berkeley: University of California Press, 1991, for more factual material on U.S. pesticide exports and their dangers here and abroad.

18. H. Patricia Hynes, "'Spring' Lessons Timeless and Ignored."

19. "Whale Starved Because Garbage Clogged Stomach," *The News and Observer*, Raleigh, NC, December 13, 1992, p. 10C.

20. "Manufacturers Urged to Make Environmentalism a Goal," *The New York Times*, September 29, 1992, p. B7.

21. Paul Connett, "The Disposable Society," *Ecology, Economics, Ethics: The Broken Circle*, edited by F. Herbert Bormann and Stephen R. Kellert (New Haven: Yale University Press, 1991), pp. 101 and 122.

22. Paul Connett, "The Disposable Society," p. 104.

23. Paul Connett, "The Disposable Society," p. 105.

24. Benjamin F. Chavis, Jr., quoted in "Black and Green," by William Rees, *The New Republic*, March 2, 1991, p. 15.

25. "Some See Racism in Waste Decisions," *The News and Observer*, Raleigh, NC, November 12, 1992, p. 1A.

26. "Some See Racism in Waste Decisions," p. 12A.

27. "Some See Racism in Waste Decisions," p. 12A.

28. Karl Grossman, "Environmental Racism," *The Crisis*, p. 17.

29. "Let Them Eat Pollution," *The Economist*, February 8, 1992, p. 66.

30. Bryan G. Norton, *Toward Unity Among Environmentalists* (New York: Oxford University Press, 1992), p. 123.

31. Rachel Carson, *Silent Spring*, pp. 12–13.

32. Bryan G. Norton, *Toward Unity Among Environmentalists*, p. 123.

33. Another "rights variant" on the Harm Principle would be that it is wrong to infringe the rights of others without their voluntary, informed consent. The latter version requires the elaboration of a theory of rights specifying what rights the "others" have. The perceptive reader will note that who or what counts as a *relevant other* raises the absolutely fundamental question of what sorts of things have moral standing. Traditional ethical theorizing, with the notable exception of J. S. Mill and Jeremy Bentham, often has assumed that the relevant other was a human, often an adult, perhaps a property owner, head of household, and in some cases a male. Any essential reference to the relevance of consent requires a good deal of elaboration as well, that is, an addressing of some questions about who is capable of giving or withholding voluntarily informed consent, what counts as voluntary consent, what counts as informed, and so on. We note that both plants and some humans are incapable of consent, e.g., babies or comatose editors. In part we are suggesting that the widespread supposition, shared by most economists and most people, that at least many forms of the passing on of the costs of pollution are

wrong rests on a number of moral suppositions which may constitute a kind of hidden moral theory on which much economic reasoning tacitly relies. The complexities of the Harm Principle are discussed in Joel Feinberg's outstanding volume *Harm to Others* and in the series of volumes of which it is a part (New York: Oxford University Press, 1984).

34. In contrast, one might "fowl one's own nest," that is, pollute it and, hence, not pass on costs to others.

35. The amount of methane has doubled in the last 150 years, due in large part to cattle production and humans' consumption of beef. There are over one billion cows on the planet according to one estimate. Their contribution to the emission of methane is not trivial. See Weiner, *Planet Earth*, p. 139.

36. Weiner, *Planet Earth*, p. 139.

37. Ibid., p. 74.

38. As the editors use the terms 'hypothesis' and 'theory,' we do *not* mean to imply that that which receives such a label is not true or is not known to be true; we take, for example, Darwin's theory and the theory of continental drift to be true in their basic outlines.

39. See Louise B. Young's wonderfully written book, *The Blue Planet* (Boston: Little, Brown and Company, 1983), p. 169.

40. Jonathan Weiner, *Planet Earth* (Toronto: Bantam Books, 1986), p. 128.

41. Brown, op. cit., p. 13.

42. That was the most recent of five identified major glacial epochs. Ibid., p. 141.

43. In the 1960s, French archaeologists found glacier-scarred rocks in southern Algeria which are dated 400 million years ago. See Louise B. Young, *The Blue Planet* (Boston: Little, Brown and Company, 1983), p. 138.

44. Weiner, *The Next Hundred Years*, pp. 102–103. Weiner relies in part on John Imbrie, *Ice Ages*.

45. Ibid., p. 103. The expression "man, the double wise" is Weiner's.

46. Global warming even in worst-case scenarios may pose no threat at all to the continuation of *life* on earth, in that life of *some* sort would survive it. But if biodiversity is radically altered (and opportunist creatures reign, e.g., lice, fleas, and tics) and tens of millions of humans suffer and prematurely die, then it would be of little solace that life would go on. Thus, the central threat is not to life *as such*.

47. Weiner, *The Next Hundred Years*, p. 241.

1. TRASHING THE EARTH'S CRUST

Silent Spring

Rachel Carson

A Fable for Tomorrow

There was once a town in the heart of America where all life seemed to live in harmony with its surroundings. The town lay in the midst of a checkerboard of prosperous farms, with fields of grain and hillsides of orchards where, in spring, white clouds of bloom drifted above the green fields. In autumn, oak and maple and birch set up a blaze of color that flamed and flickered across a backdrop of pines. Then foxes barked in the hills and deer silently crossed the fields, half hidden in the mists of the fall mornings.

Along the roads, laurel, viburnum and alder, great ferns and wildflowers delighted the traveler's eye through much of the year. Even in winter the roadsides were places of beauty, where countless birds came to feed on the berries and on the seed heads of the dried weeds rising above the snow. The countryside was, in fact, famous for the abundance and variety of its bird life, and when the flood of migrants was pouring through in spring and fall people traveled from great distances to observe them. Others came to fish the streams, which flowed clear and cold out of the hills and contained shady pools where trout lay. So it had been from the days many years ago when the first settlers raised their houses, sank their wells, and built their barns.

Then a strange blight crept over the area and everything began to change. Some evil spell had settled on the community: mysterious maladies swept the flocks of chickens; the cattle and sheep sickened and died. Everywhere was a shadow of death. The farmers spoke of much illness among their families. In the town the doctors had become more and more puzzled by new kinds of sickness appearing among their patients. There had been several sudden and unexplained deaths, not only among adults but even among children, who would be stricken suddenly while at play and die within a few hours.

There was a strange stillness. The birds, for example—where had they gone? Many people spoke of them, puzzled and disturbed. The feeding stations in the backyards were deserted. The few birds seen anywhere were moribund; they trembled violently and could not fly. It was a spring without voices. On the mornings that had once throbbed with the dawn chorus of robins, catbirds, doves, jays, wrens, and scores of other bird voices there was now no sound; only silence lay over the fields and woods and marsh.

On the farms the hens brooded, but no chicks hatched. The farmers complained that they were unable to raise any pigs—the litters were small and the young survived only a few days. The apple trees were coming into bloom but no bees droned among the blossoms, so there was no pollination and there would be no fruit.

The roadsides, once so attractive, were now lined with browned and withered vegetation as though swept by fire. These, too, were silent, deserted by all living things. Even the streams were now lifeless. Anglers no longer visited them, for all the fish had died.

In the gutters under the eaves and between the shingles of the roofs, a white granular powder still showed a few patches; some weeks before it had fallen like snow upon the roofs and the lawns, the fields and streams.

No witchcraft, no enemy action had silenced the rebirth of new life in this stricken world. The people had done it themselves.

This town does not actually exist, but it might easily have a thousand counterparts in America or elsewhere in the world. I know of no community that has experienced all the misfortunes I describe. Yet every one of these disasters has actually happened somewhere, and many real communities have already suffered a substantial number of them. A grim specter has crept upon us almost unnoticed, and this imagined tragedy may easily become a stark reality we all shall know. . . .

The Obligation to Endure

The history of life on earth has been a history of interaction between living things and their surroundings. To a large extent, the physical form and the habits of the earth's vegetation and its animal life have been molded by the environment. Considering the whole span of earthly time, the opposite effect, in which life actually modifies its surroundings, has been relatively slight. Only within the moment of time represented by the present century has one species—man—acquired significant power to alter the nature of his world.

During the past quarter century this power has not only increased to one of disturbing magnitude but it has changed in character. The most alarming of all man's assaults upon the environment is the contamination of air, earth, rivers, and sea with dangerous and even lethal materials. This pollution is for the most part irrecoverable; the chain of evil it initiates not only in the world that must support life but in living tissues is for the most part irreversible. In this now universal contamination of the environment, chemicals are the sinister and little-recognized partners of radiation in changing the very nature of the world—the very nature of its life. Strontium 90, released through nuclear explosions into the air, comes to earth in rain or drifts down as fallout, lodges in soil, enters into the grass or corn or wheat grown there, and in time takes up its abode in the bones of a human being, there to remain until his death. Similarly, chemicals sprayed on croplands or forests or gardens lie long in soil, entering into living organisms, passing from one to another in a chain of poisoning and death. Or they pass mysteriously by underground streams until they emerge and, through the alchemy of air and sunlight, combine into new forms that kill vegetation, sicken cattle, and work unknown harm on those who drink from once pure wells. As Albert Schweitzer has said, "Man can hardly even recognize the devils of his own creation."

It took hundreds of millions of years to produce the life that now inhabits the earth—eons of time in which that developing and evolving and diversifying life reached a state of adjustment and balance with its surroundings. The environment, rigorously shaping and directing the life it supported, contained elements that were hostile as well as supporting. Certain rocks gave out dangerous radiation; even within the light of the sun, from which all life draws its energy, there were short-wave radiations with power to injure. Given time—time not in years but in millennia—life adjusts, and a balance has been reached. For time is the essential ingredient; but in the modern world there is no time.

The rapidity of change and the speed with which new situations are created follow the impetuous and heedless pace of man rather than the deliberate pace of nature. Radiation is no longer merely the background radiation of rocks, the bombardment of cosmic rays, the ultraviolet of the sun that have existed before there was any life on earth; radiation is now the unnatural creation of man's tampering with the atom. The chemicals to which life is asked to make its adjustment are no longer merely the calcium and silica and copper and all the rest of the minerals washed out of the rocks and carried in rivers to the sea; they are the synthetic creations of man's inventive mind, brewed in his laboratories, and having no counterparts in nature.

To adjust to these chemicals would require time on the scale that is nature's; it would require not merely the years of a man's life but the life of generations. And even this, were it by some miracle possible, would be futile, for the new chemicals come from our laboratories in an endless stream; almost five hundred annually find their way into actual use in the United States alone. The figure is staggering and its implications are not easily grasped—500 new chemicals to which the bodies of men and animals are required somehow to adapt each year, chemicals totally outside the limits of biologic experience.

Among them are many that are used in man's war against nature. Since the mid-1940's over 200 basic chemicals have been created for use in killing insects, weeds, rodents, and other organisms described in the modern vernacular as "pests"; and they are sold under several thousand different brand names.

These sprays, dusts, and aerosols are now applied almost universally to farms, gardens, forests, and homes—nonselective chemicals that have the power to kill every insect, the "good" and the "bad," to still the song of birds and the leaping of fish in the streams, to coat the leaves with a deadly film, and to linger on in soil—all this though the intended target may be only a few weeds or insects. Can anyone believe it is possible to lay down such a barrage of poisons on the surface of the earth without making it unfit for all life? They should not be called "insecticides," but "biocides."

The whole process of spraying seems caught up in an endless spiral. Since DDT was released for civilian use, a process of escalation has been going on in which ever more toxic materials must be found. This has happened because insects, in a triumphant vindication of Darwin's principle of the survival of the fittest, have evolved super races immune to the particular insecticide used, hence a deadlier one has always to be developed—and then a deadlier one than that. It has happened also because destructive insects often undergo a "flareback," or resurgence, after spraying, in numbers greater than before. Thus the chemical war is never won, and all life is caught in its violent crossfire.

Along with the possibility of the extinction of mankind by nuclear war, the central problem of our age has therefore become the contamination of man's total environment with such substances of incredible potential for harm—substances that accumulate in the tissues of plants and animals and even penetrate the germ cells to shatter or alter the very material of heredity upon which the shape of the future depends.

Some would-be architects of our future look toward a time when it will be possible to alter the human germ plasm by design. But we may easily be doing so now by inadvertence, for many chemicals, like radiation, bring about gene mutations. It is ironic to think that man might determine his own future by something so seemingly trivial as the choice of an insect spray.

All this has been risked—for what? Future historians may well be amazed by our distorted sense of proportion. How could intelligent beings seek to control a few unwanted species by a method that contaminated the entire environment and brought the threat of disease and death even to their own kind? Yet this is precisely what we have done. . . .

The Other Road

We stand now where two roads diverge. But unlike the roads in Robert Frost's familiar poem, they are not equally fair. The road we have long been traveling is deceptively easy, a smooth superhighway on which we progress with great speed, but at its end lies disaster. The other fork of the road—the one "less traveled by"—offers our last, our only chance to reach a destination that assures the preservation of our earth.

The choice, after all, is ours to make. If, having endured much, we have at last asserted our "right to know," and if, knowing, we have concluded that we are being asked to take senseless and frightening risks, then we should no longer accept the counsel of those who tell us that we must fill our world with poisonous chemicals; we should look about and see what other course is open to us.

A truly extraordinary variety of alternatives to the chemical control of insects is available. Some are already in use and have achieved brilliant success. Others are in the stage of laboratory testing. Still others are little more than ideas in the minds of imaginative scientists, waiting for the opportunity to put them to the test. All have this in common: they are *biological* solutions, based on understanding of the living organisms they seek to control, and of the whole fabric of life to which these organisms belong. Specialists representing various areas of the vast field of biology are contributing—entomologists, pathologists, geneticists, physiologists, biochemists, ecologists—all pouring their knowledge and their creative inspirations into the formation of a new science of biotic controls. . . .

Through all these new, imaginative, and creative approaches to the problem of sharing our earth with other creatures there runs a constant theme, the awareness that we are dealing with life—with living populations and all their pressures and counterpressures, their surges and recessions. Only by taking account of such life forces and by cautiously seeking to guide them into channels favorable to ourselves can we hope to achieve a reasonable accommodation between the insect hordes and ourselves.

The current vogue for poisons has failed utterly to take into account these most fundamental considerations. As crude a weapon as the cave man's club, the chemical barrage has been hurled against the fabric of life—a fabric on the one hand delicate and destructible, on the other miraculously tough and resilient, and capable of striking back in unexpected ways. These extraordinary capacities of life have been ignored by the practitioners of chemical control who have brought to their task no "high-minded orientation," no humility before the vast forces with which they tamper.

The "control of nature" is a phrase conceived in arrogance, born of the Neanderthal age of biology and philosophy, when it was supposed that nature exists for the convenience of man. The concepts and practices of applied entomology for the most part date from that Stone Age of science. It is our alarming misfortune that so primitive a science has armed itself with the most modern and terrible weapons, and that in turning them against the insects it has also turned them against the earth.

Principal Sources

"Report on Environmental Health Problems," *Hearings*, 86th Congress, Subcom. of Com. on Appropriations, March 1960, p. 170.

Swanson, Carl P., *Cytology and Cytogenetics*. Englewood Cliffs, NJ: Prentice-Hall, 1957.

SIDELIGHT: If Earth Could Speak

It surprises me no end that you members of *Homo sapiens* can get so fascinated with your own family histories and yet tend to remain so abysmally ignorant of Me, the Home Planet, the sustainer of life; after all, to quote some human, your time living on my surface doesn't amount to a hill of beans. Lend me your 12 billion ears for a minute.

You finally came to recognize that I am not flat and that I do not have four corners. You came to understand rather noteworthy events such as continental drift only in the last 40 years. Now virtually all of you have learned that I am a little older than 4004 B.C. If you wish to be "geologically correct" I am about 4.5 billion years old, and I am using "billion" as the Americans do to mean "1000 million." So, you hominids have only been around, as some of you say, for a "twinkling of the geological eye," namely about 4 million years. Life itself took quite a while to get up and running, about one and a half billion years since my birthday; that is, it began quite simply in my oceans about 3.5 billion years ago, as your scientists, in the 1950s, inferred from the stromatolite fossils found on one of my favorite continents, Australia. You "hyper-recent types," i.e., members of the species *Homo sapiens sapiens*, have been stirring things up for about 50,000 to 100,000 years. Of course your records only tend to go back about 5000 years at best; you've really got to learn how to take care of your past better, and I'm not even going to mention the future you seem to be, rather literally, cooking up—what some of

you used to call a "witches' brew," I believe. You are causing things to get out of hand, and even beyond my attempts to balance things out. That newcomer you call Aristotle was on to something when he said "moderation in all things." You were not such a problem when there were only a half-billion of you back about 1650, or when there were a billion of you back about 1800 or so, but you are about as bad as the rabbits; you're pushing six billion and now doubling in number in 40 years or so. Do you not see the collision course that you are on, or is it that you just do not give a damn about your grandchildren? You finally invented a means of preventing conception and yet many of you prefer to ravage each other and use up my resources rather than use one of your more intelligent devices. Some of you still treat every fertilized human egg as if it were a rare phenomenon. Let me tell you something; eggs are cheap and human sperm are in plentiful supply. The average male's ejaculation could quickly repopulate the planet. What is *not* in plentiful supply, what is not so readily replaceable is the delicate balance of clean air, unfouled water (why do you keep moving humongous quantities of my oil through my nice oceans in gigantic single-hulled supertankers?), the balance of ecosystems, the protection of my ozone layer, and those factors that keep the climate in such gradual flux as to keep morbidity and premature mortality within the limits that allow for a healthy and biodiverse, sustainable planet.

Unlike some of my more successful species, such as the dinosaurs, who lasted over 150 million years, the "smart money" among planetary gamblers is that you people will not be around for a fraction of the time; was it not that foolish philosopher Protagoras who said that "man is the measure of all things"? And your "economists" and "utilitarians" seem to keep recommending ways to maximize fulfillment of the desires (however silly and contrary to my maintaining a healthy biosphere) of just one of millions of the species to whom I offer sustenance.

Of course, not all the hard times are to be blamed on your "high-rolling" practices. I must admit that a while back, about 245 million years ago, my Siberian volcanoes acted up considerably and about 95 percent of all species came to a bad end. I believe your scientists speak of it as the "great dying" or the Permian extinction. Most tragic. For your records, it was much worse than the other four Big Ones (namely, the Ordivician, 440 million years ago; the Late Devonian, 365 million years ago; the Late Triassic, 210 million years ago; or the one most familiar to you, the Final Cretaceous, 66 million years ago). Indeed, I much prefer having lively and biodiverse, ongoing (i.e., sustainable) activity.

Furthermore, some of you have ridiculous appetites—including many of your thinner members. For example, the average American is using 40 times as much energy as an average person in developing countries. Do you have any idea how many millions of years it took Me to store up those fossil fuels? You Americans seem to think that you are smart to charge a pittance for gasoline when other nations ration it out at $4 a gallon. Do you know that one of your "solutions," namely, nuclear power, yields deadly radioactivity for thousands of years, not long to me, of course, but perilous to human life and many other forms?

By the way, the next Ice Age is only about 10,000 years from now. Do you know that I have had many others during my history? I remember the last one, a real doozy—back around 20,000 B.C.E.—why, it seems like only yesterday! The average temperature on my surface was only about 1.5 to 2 degrees Celsius cooler than today, but the ice over that "beehive" of humans that you call New York City was about a half-mile high, of little interest to Me, of course, but more than a little trouble for you. Of course, it might put a needed dent in your numbers. Or are you rehearsing for that by overheating everything in the meantime? It's "no skin off my surface," so to speak, but you have warmed the surface about one-half a degree Celsius in the last moment, I mean what you call "a century," with all your carbon dioxide and other emissions. If you double those CO_2 levels again, the average temperature on my surface is going to be hotter than it has been in a *million* years (about 4 degrees Fahrenheit). Do you Youngsters on my surface really think that you can survive beyond the next century without catastrophe when, of course, you members of *Homo sapiens sapiens* have been around, I note once more, only about 50,000 years? I suppose that you have figured out what happens to my glaciers when you do that, and you might surmise where all that water goes, and what then happens to my land surface that is only a few feet above sea level—and what happens to large numbers of members of your species when you are under water for very long.

The Disposable Society

Paul H. Connett

When some people look into a trash bag, they see things like plastic, paper, metal, and food waste. I see our whole world being thrown away.

It is an astonishing and disturbing fact that since World War II, we have consumed more of the world's finite energy resources than had been con-

Ecology, Economics, Ethics: The Broken Circle, edited by F. Herbert Bormann and Stephen R. Kellert (New Haven: Yale University Press, 1991), pp. 99–122. Reprinted by permission of the publisher.

sumed by the whole of human history up to World War II (Hubert, 1971). Some people would blame this increase on the growing world population, but when we note that the average U.S. citizen consumes 50 times more steel, 56 times more energy, 170 times more newsprint, 250 times more motor fuel, and 300 times more plastic than the average Indian citizen (Miller, 1988), it is clear that we are looking at overconsumption, as well as overpopulation. Although overpopulation will certainly exacerbate the problem, one could argue that a preoccupation with overpopulation is a convenient way of shifting the ethical issue overseas.

Taken as a whole, the United States, with 4.8 percent of the world's population, consumes about 33 percent of the world's processed energy and mineral resources (Miller, 1988). If we include other industrial powers, 24 percent of the world's population consumes about 80 percent of those resources. Other people have raised the ethical issue of this inequitable use of resources across our globe, but here I would like to raise the ethical issue of the inequitable use of resources across time. A few generations are using up resources that should be spread thin across centuries, if not millennia. It is almost as if we are colonizing the future. Although we can be moved to tears by plays written more than two thousand years ago and symphonies composed two hundred years ago, we hardly blink at depriving future generations of the resources they will need to survive.

Not only do we overconsume, but we also compound the crime by throwing much away. In America, each year we throw away 1.6 billion pens, 2 billion disposable razors, 16 billion diapers, 22 billion plastic grocery bags, and enough office paper to build a twelve-foot-high wall from New York City to Los Angeles (Environmental Defense Fund, 1988; Lichiello and Snyder, 1988; Environmental Protection Agency, 1989). But that's not all we are throwing away to serve our insatiable thirst for consumption. Thousands of animal and plant species are being lost as the rain forests are cut and converted to pasture. Our topsoil is being thrown away through unsound tillage and overreliance on synthetic fertilizers and pesticides. Our small farmers are being thrown away as our chemical manufacturers take over American farming. Our sense of community has been lost to the isolationism of hours and hours in front of the television screen,

and our sense of reality is being thrown away to the advertising industry as it sells us a set of dreams and fantasies attached to an endless stream of objects we do not need.

Fortunately, planet earth functions via feedback mechanisms: We can push things only so far before it complains. The complaints ensuing from overconsumption of our resources are coming to us at both the global level and the local level. At the global level the complaints, or warning signals, are taking the form of global warming; damage to the ozone layer; and the buildup of man-made toxic residues in the biota, in our food chains, in our fatty tissues, and in mothers' breast milk. Right now in Germany breast-fed children get one hundred times their so-called allowable daily intake of dioxins and furans (Fürst et al., 1989, and references within; Bailey and Connett, 1990). We can only hope that the safety margins for these standards are sufficiently large for there to be no subtle damage to a child's immune system or other developing tissues.

At the local level, the warning signal is the trash crisis. We are running out of places to dispose of the disposables of our disposable society.

At both the global level and the local level, these warning signals are delivering the same message: We can't run a throwaway society on a finite planet. We were foolish ever to believe that we could. The ethical imperative is clear. We have to stop living as if future generations had another planet to go to. With this ethical imperative in mind, I will discuss the trash crisis that is currently affecting many communities in North America. I will be discussing waste management as if the future mattered.

Making Waste

If the future really mattered to us, we wouldn't be talking about waste management. We would be talking about resource management. Nature makes no waste. We make waste; nature makes soil. One creature's waste is another creature's nutrients. Nature recycles everything, or rather it did until we started to put our synthetic materials into the environment.

We make waste in several ways. Our manufacturers make waste by overusing some materials and misusing others. We, as consumers, make waste by mixing all our discarded materials together. When we mix the smelly with the nonsmelly, everything becomes smelly. When we mix the toxic with the nontoxic, we have to treat the whole mixture as if it were all toxic. And if we mix the useless with the useful, the whole lot becomes practically useless. Moreover, this act of mixing all our discarded materials together creates something else: a very negative attitude toward the mixture, an attitude that is betrayed by the words we use to describe it—*waste, trash, refuse, garbage, rubbish*. This negative attitude predisposes us to want this material out of our lives as quickly as possible, and as far away from us as possible. But as environmentalists have pointed out, there is no "away." The "away" we are using for most of our trash in the United States is landfills. About 80 percent of our household trash is currently going to landfills (Environmental Protection Agency, 1989). But these landfills are causing many problems.

Landfills

Five main types of problems are associated with the disposal of raw waste in landfills. First, we are running out of space to site new landfills, especially near major urban centers. Second, toxic chemicals from households and from industry are leaking out of landfills and getting into surface water and groundwater. Third, many problems are created by putting organic matter such as food and yard waste and other biodegradable materials into landfills. Undesirable animals like rats and gulls feed on this material and multiply. The organic materials are broken down by anaerobic microorganisms into a variety of substances, including the gas methane, some very smelly compounds, and a mixture of organic acids. It is these organic acids that help to leach out the toxics from the rest of the waste. Fourth, raw-waste disposal in landfills presents an ethical problem. Currently, many objects and materials that could be used again are thrown into landfills, thus depriving future generations of these resources. Finally, a political problem is created. People don't want to live near landfills. They don't like the smell, the rats, the dangers, or the traffic. Politicians know that siting new landfills in their district is tantamount to committing political suicide.

Because no strategy of waste management eliminates landfills completely, we must find ways to site new ones or expand old ones. The traditional approach to siting new landfills is to attempt to convince the public that a particular strategy will control what comes out of them. Promoters talk of plastic liners, clay liners, leachate collection and treatment, daily cover, final cover, and capping. The problem is that no one, including the Environmental Protection Agency (*Federal Register*, 1981, 1982), believes that a landfill can be made leakproof. A better approach is to control what goes into the landfill. The most controversial debate in waste management today is the form that such control should take.

Currently, a debate rages over two possible strategies for controlling what goes into a landfill. The high-tech approach is to burn unseparated trash in massive incinerators and bury only the ash residue and noncombustibles in a landfill. The low-tech approach is to separate the trash and bury only what remains after intensive efforts to remove toxics, reuse objects, recycle materials, and compost biodegradables.

Incineration

A complication in the decision-making process in the United States is that the building of trash incinerators has become the biggest boost to construction engineering since the building of nuclear power plants. Indeed, a number of major engineering companies that were building nuclear power plants are currently engaged in building trash incinerators.

Trash incineration is also embraced by municipal officials who are daunted by the task of getting people to separate and recycle their trash. Building trash incinerators seems advantageous because it requires no change in the habits of citizens, waste haulers, or manufacturers. Therein lies the problem with incineration, from an ethical point of view. It represents business as usual, a prop for the disposable society.

Despite the formidable forces promoting incinerators, they have excited intense public opposition. From 1986 through 1990, more than a hundred incinerator projects have been either canceled or put on hold (Lipsett and Farrell, 1990). Citizens have opposed incinerators for many reasons, including concerns about huge financial costs and about the health and environmental impacts of air

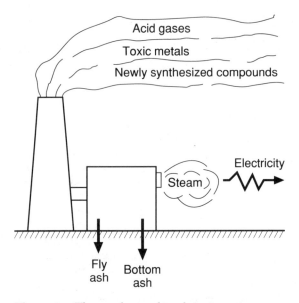

Figure 1   The products of trash incineration.

emissions (fig. 1). As the industry has moved to reduce air emissions by a combination of better devices to control combustion and air pollution, it has gotten itself into a catch-22. The better the air pollution control devices, the more toxic the ash that is produced and the more difficult to site the ash landfill that must be developed along with the incinerator.

For every three tons of trash that is burned in an incinerator, one ton of ash is produced. Approximately 10 percent is fly ash and 90 percent bottom ash. Under the Resource Conservation and Recovery Act, large generators of solid waste are required to ascertain if the material is toxic before dispatching it to a landfill. The Environmental Protection Agency devised a test that attempts to simulate the leaching conditions of a regular landfill: the Extraction Procedure Toxicity Test, or EP Tox Test (Environmental Protection Agency, 1986). Material that fails this test must be sent to a designated hazardous waste facility; material that passes can be sent to a regular landfill. The Environmental Defense Fund (1987) compiled a list of EP Tox Test results for ash from U.S. incinerators. According to the report, 100 percent of all fly ash samples, 38 percent of all bottom ash samples, and 47 percent of all combined ash samples failed the test for lead, cadmium, or both. Those test results have brought

cries of protest from the industry, its proponents in Washington, and various state regulatory agencies. As David Sussman, vice president of the major incinerator company Ogden Martin, stated, "It means *finito, morte,* the end, for the resource recovery industry if ash is treated as hazardous waste" (*Waste-to-Energy Report,* 1986). Anxious to avoid shutting down the industry, several states, including New York, have reclassified the ash as "special waste," even when it fails the toxicity test (*New York Times,* 1987).

More than any other factor, the ash presents us with concrete evidence that incineration is not the answer to the trash crisis. It doesn't make economic or environmental sense to convert three tons of trash into one ton of toxic ash. Ash landfills are proving as difficult to site as raw-waste landfills. People don't want the ash in their backyard any more than they wanted the trash. Nor will future generations thank us for these acres of toxic ash. We have to question the ethics of leaving future generations with the problems of containing, guarding, and monitoring our permanent toxics for eternity.

Source Separation

Household trash is made by mixing all our discarded materials together. Clearly, the key step to unmaking it is to separate it, or rather to keep it separate, because most of the materials are used separately.

The Components of Trash

Our classification system for sorting trash will be influenced by what we want to do with the materials. The classification system described below has several important goals: reducing waste, conserving resources, conserving topsoil, removing toxics from the waste stream, minimizing our dependence on landfills, and changing the nature of what goes into landfills. Our trash can be divided into six categories: avoidables, reuseables, recyclables, compostables, toxics, and the rest.

Avoidables. We have been persuaded that many of the items we use add to the convenience of our daily lives. Whether disposable razors, flashlights, lighters, cameras, pens, plastic bags, and many other disposable items really make our lives significantly more convenient is highly debatable.* But whether they do or not, we have to question their continued use if they compound our waste and pollution problems and threaten to deprive future generations of a fair share of the planet's finite resources. At this point, we are talking about changing personal purchasing habits, but if the problems get more acute, then we may be talking about legislation or taxation to require manufacturers to share in the costs of disposal of the materials they use.

Reusables. When someone throws out an object like a couch or a refrigerator, it probably means that the owner no longer wants the object in his or her living space. It probably does not mean that the object is entirely useless, fit only for the garbage heap or to be burned. Objects with a useful life left in them should not be compounding our trash problem or our resource problem. We already have many common mechanisms for handling such objects. We can give or sell them to a friend, we can have a yard sale, or we can give them to a thrift shop run by a voluntary organization such as the Salvation Army or Goodwill Industries. Such mechanisms are seldom comprehensive, however, and an important community task is to set up a comprehensive system, such as a community reuse-and-repair center. Such a center, in conjunction with voluntary organizations and voluntary help, can maximize the reclamation and reuse of useful objects, as well as stimulate job training opportunities and other positive community developments.

Recyclables. If we cannot recover and reuse the object, then the next best thing is to recover the material from which it is made. Many materials in our waste stream can be recycled, although their marketability varies with location in the United States. Such materials include newspaper, office paper, mixed paper, corrugated cardboard, clear glass, colored glass, aluminum, other metals, and several plastics. Of these, the most problematic component is mixed paper, for which the market is very unstable.

*According to figures cited in the original essay from which this version derives, the typical breakdown of discarded materials in an American household is: paper 42%, yard waste 16%, food waste 7%, metal 9%, glass 9%, plastic 7%, and other 10%.

Compostables. Compostables are all the materials that will biodegrade in a landfill and are not otherwise recyclable, such as food waste, yard waste, tissues, food-contaminated paper, and kitty litter. In a landfill this biodegradable material causes a whole host of problems, but if composted (biodegraded by microorganisms that use oxygen), it can be converted into a more stable product that can be used for a variety of purposes, depending upon its final quality. These uses include landfill cover; landscaping material for parks, roadsides, and golf courses; topsoil for strip-mine reclamation and for forest management. For households with the requisite space, composting can be done in the backyard. For others, it can be done at a central facility. The simple act of keeping this smelly material out of the trash accomplishes two things: It makes the business of recycling and upgrading more palatable, more profitable, and far easier, and it makes the residue after recycling more benign in a landfill.

Toxics. One German study indicates that about 1 percent by weight of the materials that we use in the household is toxic, and that about 50 percent of this toxic material is in household and car batteries (Koch et al., 1986). Other household toxics are contained in substances like paint, paint thinners, paint strippers, cleaners, solvents, and pesticides. Three conclusions become apparent if we wish to minimize the pollution caused by the toxics in our waste: We should look for ways to clean and protect our homes that do not involve toxics (Greenpeace, 1988); we should try to use up those toxics that we do use, rather than throw them away; and we should keep the remaining unavoidable toxics separate from the rest of the trash and put them aside for special handling.

The Rest. After we have removed the above items from our trash, the remainder is what we might call the new trash: the stuff that we couldn't reuse, recycle, or compost and that isn't toxic. A lot of this material will be junk mail; packaging that blends two or more materials such as plastic paper and foil (small fruit juice containers, for example), and plastics that can't be readily recycled (expanded polystyrene containers, for example). In the short term we should try to avoid purchasing such materials. In the long term we should try to legislate or tax them out of existence. One of the valuable results of source separation is that it educates people to the massive waste of resources this sixth category of trash represents, and it thereby leads to growing political pressure on the manufacturing industry to use less packaging and more recyclable materials in its products. Put simply, when you burn three tons of trash, you convert it into one ton of ash that no one wants, but when you separate three tons of trash, you can convert it into one ton of recyclables, one ton of compostables, and one ton of education. Ultimately, the education reduces to one irresistible message to manufacturers: If you can't recycle it, don't make it.

Many communities in the United States either have passed or are considering legislation to ban expanded polystyrene and other disposable plastic containers (Nancy Skinner, pers. com., 1989). These efforts have been so successful that a recent memorandum from the Society of the Plastics Industry complained, "The image of plastics among consumers is deteriorating at an alarmingly fast pace. Opinion research experts tell us that it has plummeted so far and so fast, that we are approaching a point of no return." The Society estimated that the effort to combat the decline would cost more than $50 million a year for the next three years (Thomas, 1989).

Household Handling of Separated Materials

Figure 2 is a rough schematic of a simple and convenient system combining household separation of trash with community collection and handling. In this system all the compostables are put into one container, all the recyclables into another, and the rest (minus the toxics, reusables, and avoidables) into a third. These three categories, which represent the bulk of the discards, are collected on the regular trash day, using a variety of modified garbage trucks, and are taken to a recycling and composting facility. The reusables are either collected by a voluntary organization or delivered by the householder to the reuse-and-repair center. The toxics are either collected intermittently or delivered by the householder to the toxic waste exchange (which could be part of the reuse-and-repair center), where materials like paints and paint thinners and strippers can be used by other members of the community. Special plastic containers

can also be given to householders for the collection of such items as waste oil and household batteries. This approach is currently operating successfully in Hamburg, New York (Kroll, 1985), and Neunkirchen, Austria (Work on Waste, 1988).

The three-container system for compostables, recyclables, and the rest is currently operating in Heidelberg and a number of other communities in Germany (Bailey and Connett, 1986). Pilot projects are also operating in the United States with considerable success (Commoner et al., 1989).

Materials Recovery Facilities

The modules that could be included in a materials recovery facility are a reuse-and-repair section; a waste exchange for household toxics; a composting section; a section for separating, upgrading, and marketing the mixed recyclables; a section for screening mixed residue before putting it in a landfill; a section for handling commercial waste; and a section for handling landscaping and building debris. The more ambitious centers might also include sections to process some of the recovered materials into marketable products. The Belgian ET-1 system, for example, can convert comingled plastics into a variety of objects like fence posts, lumber sections, traffic signs, and park benches (Brewer, 1987).

Although no single community in the United States has yet to put all these modules together, working examples of each module, and several combinations of them, are operating successfully in both Europe and the United States (Bailey and Connett, 1986, 1987a, b, c, d, 1988a, b, 1989a, b).

Reuse and Repair.   Several U.S. communities have excellent examples of reuse-and-repair centers, including Wellesley, Massachusetts; Berkeley, California; Portage, Michigan; and Wilton, New Hampshire. The Wellesley center is affectionately called the dump, but it is a dump that no one wants to get rid of. It is built around an old defunct incinerator in attractive parklike surroundings. The usual drop-off containers for separated recyclables are conveniently placed adjacent to adequate parking arrangements. Next to the drop-off containers is a trailer owned by Goodwill Industries, which accepts used clothing and small appliances. In the basement of the old incinerator is an area set aside for waste oil, car batteries, and tires. At the rear of

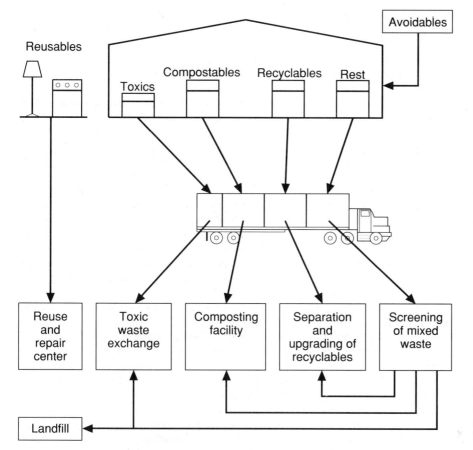

Reusables

Avoidables

Toxics   Compostables   Recyclables   Rest

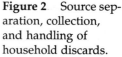

| Reuse and repair center | Toxic waste exchange | Composting facility | Separation and upgrading of recyclables | Screening of mixed waste |

Landfill

Figure 2 Source separation, collection, and handling of household discards.

the building is an area where residents can drop off leaves and lawn clippings and can help themselves to compost. There is also a "take it or leave it" section where residents can drop off their old appliances and help themselves to other people's bric-a-brac. Finally, residents can leave books on a large bookshelf, help themselves to other books, and even order books. In Wellesley, parents keep their kids in line by threatening not to take them to the dump, and politicians, looking for votes during a campaign, know where to find people on a Saturday morning (Pat Berdau, pers. com., 1988; Bailey and Connett, 1989b).

In Berkeley several voluntary organizations and small businesses operate several materials recovery modules in conjunction with the city's transfer station. These modules include a curbside collection program, a drop-off center, a buy-back center, and a large reuse section. The reuse section, which is run by a small business called Urban Ore, looks like a huge flea market. It grosses seventeen thousand dollars a month and provides a number of good jobs. Urban Ore grosses another twenty-five thousand dollars by selling reusable building items like doors, windows, and bathtubs. The company lives up to the motto of its owner, Dan Knapp, who is a former sociology professor: It's not waste until it is wasted (Knapp, pers. com., 1988; Bailey and Connett, 1989b).

An excellent example of a recycling center that does extensive repair work is the one run by Jay Eaton in Portage, Michigan (Eaton, pers. com., 1988; Bailey and Connett, 1989b). Eaton says that if you stay in his recycling center long enough, anything you want will come through the door. It is an inspiration to see the quantity and variety of objects that Eaton is able to get back into useful service. He has a particular affection for handtools, and after replacing the handles and removing the rust, he puts the finishing touch on with discarded paint.

Many of the features discussed above are also incorporated in a small rural recycling center in Wilton, New Hampshire. This facility was set up by five towns in August 1979. According to the operators, the people who use the facility have willingly cooperated with the extensive separation demanded. In addition to recycling more materials than any other comparable recycling facility in New Hampshire, the center offers many reuse opportunities. In addition to selling reclaimed clothing, it offers reclaimed books, bric-a-brac, and furniture for a small fee to people who can afford it and at no charge to those who cannot (Pat Johannesen, pers. com., 1991).

At its best, a reuse-and-repair center could become the nucleus of an exciting community resource park (fig. 3). Were an enlightened municipality to provide the buildings and area needed to set up such a facility, it could generate enormous dividends in the form of community education, motivation, and development; involvement of senior-citizen and youth groups; job training; exchange and reuse of toxic wastes, such as paints; and the demonstration of backyard composting. Such a facility could become self-supporting, and once the creativity and enthusiasm of the local community had been unleashed, many kinds of positive and exciting components could be incorporated, such as a trash museum; a competition for the most valuable object recovered or the most creative use found for junk; a natural history museum tied to the composting section and featuring recycling in nature; and a community garden that uses some of the compost. I can think of no better way to take us away from the negative image of disposing of trash and toward the positive notion of conserving both human and material resources.

Separation of Mixed Recyclables

Many facilities—ranging from the modest shed built by volunteer labor in the village of Rodman, New York, to Joe Garbarino's three-acre, $10 million building in San Rafael, California—separate, upgrade, and market recyclable materials (Bailey and Connett, 1987a, 1988a, 1989b; Garbarino, pers. com., 1987; Charles Valentine, pers. com., 1988). Such facilities are labor-intensive, and they use fairly modest equipment: conveyor belts, glass crushers, magnetic separators, balers, and shredders, and a variety of forklift trucks. Some of the most elegant aids to separation have been developed by the Bezner Corporation in Germany and are being imported into the United States by New England Container Recycling, Inc., a company that recently built a materials recovery facility in Johnston, Rhode Island (Bailey and Connett, 1986, 1989b; Richard Kattar, pers. com., 1989).

As communities begin to rely on large private companies to streamline the separation of mixed recyclables, it's important that we don't eliminate the small operations and voluntary organizations that have traditionally earned money by collecting separated recyclables like aluminum cans and corrugated cardboard. They can be protected by making sure that the separation facility offers a buyback option for already separated materials.

Separation of Commercial Waste. People have been so preoccupied with the waste produced by households that they sometimes forget to consider commercial waste in waste management scenarios, even though commercial waste can be a significant contributor to the landfill problem. Fortunately, from the point of view of materials recovery, commercial waste is much easier to handle than household waste because it is more homogeneous, being dominated by corrugated cardboard and office paper. Commercial waste is also easier to separate because it is less contaminated with smelly material.

An excellent example of a facility that handles a large quantity of commercial waste is in Burbank, California (Bailey and Connett, 1989b). The facility, which processes nine hundred tons of waste per day, separates out the usual bottles, cans, newspaper, office paper, and corrugated cardboard. It has also taken the innovative step of bringing in equipment from the paper industry to convert the mixed-paper fraction to a gray paper pulp, because the pulp is much easier to sell to the paper industry on a regular basis than mixed paper, which is so vulnerable to market conditions.

Composting. The weakest module in the United States is the composting section. Composting is underused by many communities and is oversold by companies asserting that the entire

COMMUNITY RESOURCE PARK

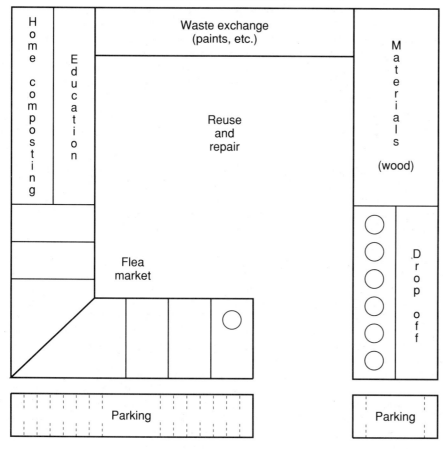

Figure 3 A community resource park can be the center of a variety of voluntary activities, job-training possibilities, and community development.

waste stream can be composted. That argument doesn't make biological or economic sense, because microbes cannot destroy heavy metals or many of the synthetic organic materials in the waste stream. If communities wish to use or sell the compost, it is critical that they carefully select clean, organic material. On the other hand, communities are far too timid when they compost only yard waste such as leaves and lawn clippings.

A variety of equipment and strategies, from the low-tech windrow approach and the intermediate indoor-trough method to high-tech in-vessel systems, can successfully compost a wide range of organic material (BioCycle, 1989). The windrow system simply involves putting the material out in long rows that are regularly turned by a front loader or by a specially designed windrow turner

that can turn a whole row in one sweep (Bailey and Connett, 1989a, b). The drawbacks to this system are that it needs a lot of space, is vulnerable to the weather, and takes longer to produce finished compost than the other systems.

The trough method is like an internal windrow system. A good example of this method is currently operating in Lebanon, Connecticut, by a company called International Processing Systems (Bailey and Connett, 1989b). It handles a variety of organic waste, including animal manures, sawdust from a gun factory, apple pumice, mycelium waste from a pharmaceutical company, mushroom waste, sewage sludge, and wood chips. The waste is placed in concrete troughs that are 6 feet wide, 6 feet high, and 180 feet long. Rails along the top of the troughs carry a machine that mixes the material and shifts it 10 feet each day, so that after eighteen days it has moved the length of the trough and is ready for curing. The troughs are situated in sheds, four troughs to a shed. Air is blown through the material from vents underneath the troughs and is removed from the system by suction vans in the roof. This air can be cleaned by pushing it through soil filters, or Boden filters (Bailey and Connett, 1986, 1989b). This elegant system can process different materials in separate troughs to produce various grades of compost.

In-vessel systems come in two major types: horizontal cylinders that are rotated, and vertical cylinders containing paddles that rotate inside the system (Bailey and Connett, 1986, 1989b). Such systems allow the operating parameters to be tightly controlled. Of particular concern is the control of air and temperature. An adequate supply of air is necessary to keep the system aerobic, because anaerobic organisms take over the biodegradation in the absence of air (as in landfills) and produce smelly compounds. Temperature is important because, left to itself, the compost pile will overheat, destroying many of the microorganisms that do the work and rendering the process inefficient and anaerobic (Feinstein et al., 1987).

I recommend that communities use composting for two distinct purposes: to produce a salable product (topsoil) and to keep biodegradable organic material out of landfills. To achieve the first purpose, good source separation is essential, so that contamination from household toxics is kept to a minimum. The better this control, the better the overall economics of the operation becomes. After obtaining a high-grade compost in this fashion, a second composting operation can be used as part of the screening process at the landfill.

Screening Materials at the Landfill. In a comprehensive materials recovery program, no unscreened waste would be allowed into the landfill. In fact, no waste truck would be allowed direct access to the landfill. Instead, the residue from the source separation program, and any other mixed waste, would be dumped on conveyor belts where well-paid and well-protected workers would remove any toxics or recyclables missed in source separation programs, as well as other nonrecyclable and nonbiodegradable materials, such as certain plastics, synthetic textiles, and rubberized ma-

terials. These latter materials would be baled to conserve space and buried in the landfill. Their nature would also be carefully studied, because a more resource-conscious future will demand either that ways be found for these materials to be recycled or that their manufacture be curtailed. In a well-organized screening facility, the material left on the conveyor belts would be essentially nontoxic, nonrecyclable, and biodegradable. Consisting largely of mixed-paper products, food waste, and other organic materials, it would be shredded and composted, perhaps with sewage sludge, to produce a low-grade compost suitable for landfill cover and possibly other nonagricultural purposes, such as road shoulders, strip-mine reclamation, and reforestation. The uses will hinge upon careful analysis for heavy-metal content. The closest I have seen to such a screening-composting operation is in Fillmore County, Minnesota (Bailey and Connett, 1989a).

Not only does such a screening facility offer a community the maximum diversion of material from a landfill, but it also offers the decision makers their most likely strategy for successfully siting a landfill. The siting process could be further facilitated if the community is given the opportunity to define precisely what material is acceptable in the landfill and is given a contract in which community representatives are allowed inspection rights to both the screening facility and the landfill, and the right to close the landfill if unlawful material is found entering it.

It is important to remember that although reuse and recycling can reduce the quantity of material going into landfills, composting and the removal of toxics are what dramatically change a landfill's character. Moreover, community inspection rights and the landfill screening facility are more likely to win a community's acceptance than leachate control devices and governmental monitoring.

Practical Considerations
How Much Will Materials Recovery Cost?
Although some of the objects and materials recovered using source separation will provide a net income (after collection, upgrading, and transport to market), it would be a mistake to see the whole program as a profit-making venture. Just as we do not expect landfills to make a profit for a commu-

nity, we should not expect recycling scenarios to make a net profit. We should see recycling as providing a service to both the local community and the environment as a whole. The economics of the system will be driven by avoided disposal costs— the money saved by not putting the materials into an expensive landfill. In this respect, we should welcome the increased costs of landfills, because those costs will put taxpayers and environmentalists on the same side.

Three recent major studies—conducted for Buffalo, New York (Commoner et al., 1988); North Hempstead, New York (Latham et al., 1988); and Seattle, Washington (Seattle Solid Waste Utility, 1988)—indicated that source separation, coupled with intensive materials recovery, is cheaper than incineration. Although avoided disposal costs will be the key economic driving force behind our proposed scenario at the local level, further stimulus could be provided at the state and federal level. Both state and federal authorities could stimulate markets for the reclaimed materials, especially with government procurement policies. The federal government could further reward communities with what could be called conserved-resource credits for each ton of material recycled or composted. Such a reward system would recognize the improvement to the national economy by conserving energy and finite resources, as well as the reduction in global pollution that will ensue. Such federal recognition would be a critical step in the paradigm shift from waste management to resource management.

Can Materials Recovery Make a Big Difference?   As far as extending the life of landfills is concerned, the volume reduction achieved by a waste-handling strategy is of key importance. Unfortunately, recycling results are usually recorded by weight because recyclable materials are sold by weight. Many items that are currently recycled are light in weight, such as corrugated cardboard and plastics, or they contain a lot of air, such as bottles and cans. A rudimentary recycling program often achieves a far more impressive volume reduction than weight reduction. After two years of a mandatory recycling program in North Stonington, Connecticut, for example, consulting engineers recorded a 65 percent reduction in landfill space requirements (Bailey and Connett, 1987c). After

four months of a mandatory recycling program, Rodman, New York, a small rural community with a population of 850, recorded a 71 percent volume reduction in the material sent to the landfill (Bailey and Connett, 1988a; Charles Valentine, pers. com., 1988).

The town of Neunkirchen, Austria, achieved 65 percent and 67 percent reductions (by weight) in 1986 and 1987, respectively, via a combination of source separation, recycling, and composting (Work on Waste, 1988). A pilot study conducted by the Center for the Biology of Natural Systems for the town of East Hampton, Long Island, showed that one hundred households using a four-container system (two for recyclables, one for compostables, and one for the rest) achieved a massive 84 percent reduction by weight (Commoner et al., 1989). Critics have pointed out that this project used committed volunteers and cannot be considered indicative of potential achievements in other communities. But if an 84 percent reduction can be achieved when the necessary commitment is available, shouldn't we be putting our efforts into getting that kind of commitment from the average citizen?

Will People Participate?   Several factors can maximize citizen participation. First, source separation needs to be as convenient as possible, and no program is more convenient than having recyclables picked up on the same day as the regular trash. The actual separation need not take more than a few minutes a day, because what we are talking about is only a new set of habits. Second, the urgency and value of such an effort, for the community and for the environment, need to be conveyed. With the growing awareness of global environmental problems, that should not be difficult. Third, there is no point in stressing the urgency of a situation and then allowing people to take part on a voluntary basis. With few exceptions, mandatory programs achieve far greater participation than voluntary ones.

The enforcement need not be extremely punitive to be effective. The curbside separation program in Hamburg, New York, achieves a 98 percent participation rate by not picking up unseparated waste (Kroll, 1985). Nor need the program be grim. In Rockford, Illinois, a humorous note is added by having a colorful "trashman," in a gaudy outfit and a polka-dotted truck, inspect the trash of one household each week. If he finds no recyclables in the trash, the householder wins a thousand dollars. If the householder doesn't win, someone the following week could win two thousand dollars, and so on—a garbage lottery. Since the program started, the participation rate has increased fourfold (Bailey and Connett, 1987b, 1989b).

In High Bridge, New Jersey, another financial incentive has proved successful. Citizens are required to purchase trash coupons. Each time a garbage bag is put out, a coupon must be used, but material put out for recycling and composting requires no coupon. Large objects are also assessed. For example, a couch requires six trash coupons for municipal disposal. As a result, people are becoming more imaginative about getting reusable objects to places where some extra life can be extracted from them. Officials estimate that the waste stream has been reduced by 25 percent with this approach (*New York Times*, 1988).

According to the Institute for Local Self Reliance, at least ten U.S. communities now achieve a recycling and composting rate greater than 40 percent (Platt et al., 1990). A 40 percent rate was considered impossible by many analysts in the early 1980s.

Do Markets Exist for Recyclables? Trash separation alone does not make recycling successful. To be truly recycled, materials have to be reused. That means someone has to want the materials enough to pay for them. The three factors for maximizing the recyclability of materials are quality, quantity, and regularity.

Will the Markets Be Flooded? As recycling gets more and more popular across North America, some people fear that markets for certain materials, particularly the lower grades of paper, will become flooded. Most analysts believe, however, that this phenomenon will be only temporary, as industries adjust to a large and dependable supply of cheap material. Indeed, in February 1990, Red Cavaney, the president of the American Paper Institute, announced that the paper industry was increasing its recycling goal from 25 percent to 40 percent of its total production (*Kalamazoo Gazette*, 1990). The plastics industry is also expected to increase its recycling commitment dramatically, in part because of

the efforts of many communities to ban a number of disposable plastic products. Meanwhile, state and federal agencies could sustain this momentum by adjusting their own procurement policies to stimulate the markets for secondary materials and look for other incentives to encourage their use. In the long run, the national economy, the global environment, and future generations will benefit as we decrease our dependence on the extraction of virgin resources. The economic, ecological, and ethical imperatives are clear: We must make recycling work.

Do Markets for Compost Exist? The better the control on the organic inputs to compost, the more likely the product can be used and sold. The most important market for compost is probably landscaping. One only has to check the price of topsoil in the local horticulture supply store to verify this point. Lower-grade composts can be used for landfill cover and the reclamation of strip mines and deforested areas. Such areas could use every ounce of compost the United States could produce. From the most pessimistic view, even if the compost ends up in a landfill, the community is still much better off because composting produces a significant volume reduction and the landfill will be far more benign.

Will Incineration Still Be Necessary? I believe that if the strategy outlined is pursued, an incinerator will be unnecessary. But one does not have to accept this position to recognize the wisdom of postponing the decision to build an incinerator until the community has seen what it can do with a more beneficial strategy of source separation and materials recovery. From an economic point of view, it is important to note that the only materials that can be burned and that cannot be composted are synthetic materials like plastic. Not only is composting technology much cheaper (in terms of initial capital and the costs of maintenance and replacement) and safer than incineration, but the remaining unrecycled plastics can also be far more safely and cheaply placed in a landfill than the residual ash from an incinerator can.

Over the last year or so the catchphrase of incinerator promoters has been *integrated waste management*. What that term means in practice is a combined program of recycling and incineration. This seemingly even-handed approach, however, is actually the promotion of incineration by other means, a fact that can be confirmed by comparing the funds budgeted for the two components. Moreover, one has to know only that 80 percent of the waste stream is both recyclable and combustible to realize the difficulty of marrying these incompatible components in one program. Our best shot at an integrated program is to integrate expensive landfills (with the major expense going to the screening facility at the landfill) with source separation and materials recovery. In short, if an expensive trash incinerator is built, its use must be maximized to pay back the bonds that are issued to cover its enormous cost. If, on the other hand, an expensive landfill is established, the minimization of its use is in everyone's interest.

Is Materials Recovery Realistic? Fortunately, we have an interesting and recent historical example in the energy crisis in the 1970s. The high-tech approach was labeled as the practical, realistic solution and the low-tech approach was labeled as pie in the sky. Some people said that massive nuclear power stations must be built, but others suggested that the more practical solution was to conserve energy via the use of more-efficient appliances, home insulation, and smaller cars. The response was deafening: The American people would never drive smaller cars. History has shown, however, that since 1973 the United States has saved more energy through conservation measures than it has generated in new power plants (Flavin and Durning, 1988). I believe that as more evidence comes in, it will become clear that in both the short term and the long term, the simpler strategy of source separation and materials recovery is the more *practical* way of reducing our dependence on unacceptable landfills.

A Commitment to the Future

The landfill crisis has been a blessing in disguise. It is a timely reminder at the local level that a throwaway society cannot succeed on a finite planet. It is a clear indicator that we have broken the circle that binds the ecology, economics, and ethics of wise resource management.

The modern state-of-the-art waste-to-energy trash incinerator is a sophisticated answer to the wrong question. Our task is not to find a new place to put trash but to find ways to unmake trash. Incineration merely burns the embarrassing evidence of the throwaway ethic. We have to challenge the ethic. Instead of spending millions of dollars perfecting the art of destruction of throwaway objects, we must stop making objects we have to throw away.

The trash crisis will not be solved with magic machines and costly consultants but by mobilizing our citizens' common sense, creativity, and need for community. Although some materials can be recycled and composted for a net profit, the main economic driving force for the materials recovery approach will be the avoided costs of expensive landfills and modern trash incinerators. Most local officials will recognize this benefit, but they might not fully consider the larger benefits for future generations and the national economy that can be gained by reducing our demand for raw materials.

Some people have seen the solving of the trash crisis as a rather grim and boring task. Others have seen it as an exciting and challenging opportunity. Of all the environmental problems with which we are confronted, this is the one with which every citizen is intimately involved. Every day that we make trash exacerbates the problem. When we learn to source separate and recycle we can be part of the solution. Moreover, many communities have also shown that when they go about maximizing material recovery, it can also be a source of considerable community pride and community development.

No one can pretend that any solution to the trash crisis is going to be simple or cheap. What is important is that we choose a solution that takes us in the right direction. Any problems with source separation and materials recovery are worth overcoming because this strategy is the only one that offers a genuine long-term solution on a finite planet. More than any other single demand, the strategy of source separation and materials recovery requires that local decision makers put their faith back in the people rather than in magic machines.

In wartime, societies recycle. Our task is to convince our people and our leaders that the way we are currently handling our raw materials and our waste is a war on the future. The economic, ecological, and ethical imperatives are clear: We must make recycling work. It is not a question of *if* but *how,* not a question of *when* but *now.* We must start handling our discarded materials as if the future mattered.

References

Bailey, R., and P. Connett. 1986. *Recycling in Germany.* Canton, NY: Video Active Productions. Videotape.

Bailey, R., and P. Connett. 1987a. *Joe Garbarino: The Only Way to Go.* Canton, NY: Video Active Productions. Videotape.

Bailey, R., and P. Connett. 1987b. *Millie Zantow: Recycling Pioneer.* Canton, NY: Video Active Productions. Videotape.

Bailey, R., and P. Connett. 1987c. *Recycling in the USA: Don't Take No for an Answer.* Canton, NY: Video Active Productions. Videotape.

Bailey, R., and P. Connett. 1987d. *Skamania County, Washington: A Materials Recovery Center.* Canton, NY: Video Active Productions. Videotape.

Bailey, R., and P. Connett. 1988a. *How Rodman Recycles.* Canton, NY: Video Active Productions. Videotape.

Bailey, R., and P. Connett. 1988b. *Zoo Doo and You Can Too.* Canton, NY: Video Active Productions. Videotape.

Bailey, R., and P. Connett. 1989a. *Recycling's Missing Link: Fillmore County, Minnesota.* Canton, NY: Video Active Productions. Videotape.

Bailey, R., and P. Connett. 1989b. *Waste Management as if the Future Mattered.* Canton, NY: Video Active Productions. Videotape.

Bailey, R., and P. Connett. 1990. *Europeans Mobilizing Against Trash Incineration.* Canton, NY: Video Active Productions. Videotape.

BioCycle staff, ed. 1989. *The BioCycle Guide to Composting Municipal Wastes.* Emmaus, PA: J. G. Press.

Brewer, G. 1987. "European Plastics Recycling, Part 1," *Resource Recycling* (May/June).

Commoner, B., M. Frisch, J. Quigley, A. Stege, D. Wallace, T. Webster, and T. Luppino. 1988. *Final Report: Intensive Recycling Feasibility Study for the City of Buffalo.* Flushing, NY: Center for the Biology of Natural Systems, Queens College.

Commoner, B., M. Frisch, H. A. Pilot, J. Quigley, A. Stege, D. Wallace, and T. Webster. 1989. *Intensive Recycling Pilot Project in East Hampton, N.Y.* Flushing, NY: Center for the Biology of Natural Systems, Queens College.

Environmental Defense Fund. 1987. *Summary of All Available EP Toxicity Testing Data on Incinerator Ash.* Washington, DC.

Environmental Defense Fund. 1988. *If You Are Not Recycling You Are Throwing It All Away.* Washington, DC.

Environmental Protection Agency. 1986. *Test Methods for Evaluation Solid Waste: Physical/Chemical Methods,* 3rd ed. EPA/SW846. Washington, DC.

Environmental Protection Agency. 1989. *The Solid Waste Dilemma: An Agenda for Action.* EPA/530-SW-89–019. Washington, DC: Office of Solid Waste.

Federal Register. 1981. February 5, 11, 128.

Federal Register. 1982. March 26, 32, 284–32, 285.

Feinstein, M. S., F. C. Miller, J. A. Hogan, and P. F. Strom. 1987. "Analysis of EPA Guidance on Composting Sludge, Parts 1–4. *BioCycle,* January–April.

Flavin, C., and A. B. Durning. 1988. *Building on Success: The Age of Energy Efficiency.* World Watch paper no. 82. Washington, DC: World Watch Institute.

Franklin Associates, 1986. *Characterization of Municipal Solid Waste in the United States, 1960–2000.* Prairie Village, KA.

Fürst, P., C. Krüger, H. A. Meemken, and W. Groebel. 1989. "PCDD and PCDF Levels in Human Milk: Dependence on the Period of Lactation." *Chemosphere* 18:439–444.

Greenpeace. 1988. *Stepping Lightly on the Earth: Everyone's Guide to Toxics in the Home.* Vancouver, British Columbia.

Hubert, M. K. 1971. Energy Resources. In *Environment, Resources, Pollution and Society,* ed. W. W. Murdock. Stamford, CN: Sinauer Associates.

Kalamazoo (Mich.) *Gazette.* 1990. "Paper Industry Sets Recycling Goal." February 14.

Koch, T. C., J. Seeberger, and H. Petrik. 1986. *The Ecological Handling of Trash: A Handbook for Optimized Concepts for Waste Handling.* Karlsruhe: C. F. Muller.

Kroll, G. 1985. "Mandatory Recycling in the Village of Hamburg, New York." *Journal of Resource Management and Technology* 14:4.

Latham, S. B., J. W. Allen, T. Goldfarb, J. Morris, and W. M. Vukoder. 1988. *A Non-Incineration Solid Waste Management and Recycling Plan for the Town of North Hempstead, New York.* Sea Cliff, NY: New York Coalition to Save Hempstead Harbor.

Lichiello, P., and L. Synder. 1988. *Plastics: The Risks and Consequences of Its Production and Use.* Los Angeles: School of Architecture and Urban Planning, University of California.

Lipsett, B., and D. Farrell. 1990. *Solid Waste Incineration Status Report.* Arlington, VA: Citizen's Clearinghouse for Hazardous Wastes.

Miller, J. T. 1988. *Living in the Environment.* Belmont, CA: Wadsworth.

New York Times. 1987. "Incinerators Held to Pose Ash Hazard." September 30.

New York Times. 1988. "Pay-by-Bag Trash Disposal Pays, New Jersey Town Discovers." November 24.

Platt, B., C. Doherty, A. Broughton, and D. Morris. 1990. *Beyond 40%: Record Setting Recycling and Composting Programs.* Washington, DC: Institute of Local Self Reliance.

Seattle Solid Waste Utility. 1988. *Recycling Potential Assessment and Waste Stream Forecast.* Seattle, WA.

Skinner, N. 1989. Berkeley City Council, 2180 Milvia Street, Berkeley, CA 94704.

Thomas, L. 1989. Memorandum from the Society of the Plastics Industry to its members. December 22. Washington, DC.

Waste-to-Energy Report. 1986. "Industry Concern Growing over EPA Proposal to Classify Ash as Hazardous." September 16.

Work on Waste, USA, staff. 1988. "In Austria a County of 100,000 Recycles 67% of Its Waste." *Waste Not*, no. 9, 1. Canton, NY.

Environmental Racism

Karl Grossman

"We're sitting in a center of a donut surrounded by a hazardous waste incinerator that gives off PCB's, seven landfills that are constantly growing—they look like mountains," Hazel Johnson was saying. "There are chemical plants, a paint factory, two steel mills which give off odors, and lagoons filled with all kinds of contaminants that emit 30,000 tons of poison into the air each year. And there's a water reclamation district where they dry sludge out in the open. The smell is horrible, like bodies decomposing."

Mrs. Johnson was describing Atgeld Gardens, a housing project in which 10,000 people, nearly all African-Americans, reside on the Southeast Side of Chicago, surrounded on every side by sources of pollution.

The result: environmental diseases and death.

"We have lots of cancer, respiratory problems, birth deformities," Mrs. Johnson went on. "Just the other day, there were three cancer deaths. Then more. We've been having babies born with brain tumors. One baby was born with her brain protruding from her head. She's two now, blind and she can't walk. My daughter was five months pregnant. She took ultra-sound and the doctors found the baby had no behind, no head," said Mrs. Johnson, the mother of seven. "The baby had to be aborted."

Mrs. Johnson has no doubt that "the terrible health problems we have in our community are related to the pollution," the product of trying to live amid one of the most concentrated areas of environmental contamination in the U.S.

And she is clear about why her area gets dumped on because it is largely inhabited by African-Americans and Hispanics. "In Chicago, everything is mostly dumped out in this area where we are. They figure that we're not going to come out and protest and disagree." But Mrs. Johnson has, for 10 years now, as the head of People for Community Recovery, been fighting back.

"Atgeld Gardens symbolizes environmental racism," the Rev. Benjamin Chavis, Jr., the noted civil rights leader and executive director of the United Church of Christ's Commission for Racial Justice, declared. "The community is surrounded on all four sides by pollution and has one of the highest cancer rates in the nation. The public officials in Chicago are well aware of the circumstances that these people are forced to live in, yet, because of their race, the city has no priority in stopping this type of environmental injustice."

Rev. Chavis was the first to use the term "environmental racism" in 1987 with the release of what has become a landmark study by the commission, "Toxic Wastes and Race in the United States." It has taken several years for the import of the report, notes Rev. Chavis, to take hold.

But now that has well begun. There have been a series of important events, including a week long tour by the Rev. Jesse Jackson, shortly before Earth Day 1990 of low-income minority communities struck by pollution. He stressed the "relationship between environment and empowerment" and declared it "a new day and a new way. No longer will corporations be allowed to use job blackmail to poison poor people be they black, brown, yellow, red, or white. We are demanding that all corporate poisoners sign agreements to stop the poisoning of our communities."

The Crisis, Vol. 98, No. 4 (April 1991), 14–17, 31–32. Reprinted by permission of the publisher.

Rev. Jackson was accompanied by Dennis Hayes, a principal organizer of both the original Earth Day, in 1970, and last year's event, and John O'Connor, executive director of the National Toxics Campaign who emphasized that "for the environmental movement to be successful in saving the planet, it must include all races, ethnic groups, rich and poor, black and white, and young and old. When our movement to clean up the nation is truly a reflection of all people in the country, it is at that point that we will succeed in stopping the poisoning of America."

Issuing a report in 1990, at a National Minority Health Conference in Washington on environmental contamination, describing how "a marriage of the movement for social justice with environmentalism" was taking place was the Panos Institute. "Organizing for environmental justice among people of color has grown from a small group of activists in the 1970s to a movement involving thousands of people in neighborhoods throughout the U.S.," said Dana A. Alston, director of the Environment, Community Development and Race Project of Panos, an international group that works for "sustainable development." She added in the report, "We Speak for Ourselves: Social Justice, Race and Environment," that "communities of color have often taken a more holistic approach than the mainstream environmental movement, integrating 'environmental' concerns into a broader agenda that emphasizes social, racial, and economic justice."

In Atlanta in 1990, at a conference on environmental problems in minority areas sponsored by the federal Agency for Toxic Substances and Disease Registry and others, attended by 300 community leaders, doctors and governmental officials, Dr. Aubrey F. Manley, deputy assistant secretary of the Department of Health and Human Services, stated, "Poor and minority organizations charged eight major national environmental groups with racism in their hiring practices and demanded that they substantially increase the number of people of color on their staffs. The environmental groups acknowledged the problem—"The truth is that environmental groups have done a miserable job of reaching out to minorities," said Frederick D. Krupp, executive director of the Environmental Defense Fund—and set up an Environmental Consortium for Minority Outreach.

And last year, too, the Commission for Racial Justice organized a workshop on racism and the environment for the Congressional Black Caucus, whose members, unbeknownst to many, are rated as having among the best pro environmental voting records in Congress by the League of Conservation Voters, which scores Congressional representatives on their environmental records.

A key event to be held this year will be the first National Minority Environmental Leadership Summit in Washington, D.C. in October. "We want to bring together leaders of community groups, environmental groups, civil rights organizations and academic, scientific, governmental and corporate organizations to participate in this three-day corporate meeting," says Charles Lee, research director of the Commission for Racial Justice, which is organizing the gathering. "The purpose of this summit is to develop a comprehensive and tangible national agenda of action that will help reshape and redirect environmental policy-making in the United States to fully embrace the concerns of minority Americans."

People of color have been the worst victim of environmental pollution for a long time. Lee tells of the building of the Gauley Bridge in West Virginia in the 1930s: "Hundreds of African-American workers from the Deep South were brought in by the New Kanawha Power Company, a subsidiary of the Union Carbide Corporation, to dig the Hawks Nest tunnel. Over a two year period, approximately 500 workers died and 1,500 were disabled from silicosis, a lung disease similar to Black Lung. Men literally dropped on their feet breathing air so thick with microscopic silica that they could not see more than a yard in front of them. Those who came out for air were beaten back into the tunnel with ax handles. At subsequent Congressional hearings, New Kanawha's contractor revealed, "I knew I was going to kill these niggers, but I didn't know it was going to be this soon."

Lee relates how "an undertaker was hired to bury dead workers in unmarked graves" and of his agreeing "to perform the service for an extremely low rate because the company assured him there would be a large number of deaths."

But it was not until recent years that this and other horror stories of environmental racism started to be examined in their systematic context.

It was in 1982 that residents of predominantly African-American Warren County, North Carolina asked the Commission for Racial Justice for help in their protests against the siting of a dump for

PCB's—the acronym for polychlorinated biphenyls, a carcinogen. In a campaign of civil disobedience that ensued, there were more than 500 arrests, including the commission's Rev. Chavis, Dr. Joseph Lowery of the Southern Christian Leadership Conference, and Congressman Walter Fauntroy of Washington.

It was during that effort that Rev. Chavis began considering the connection between the dumping in Warren County and the federal government's Savannah River nuclear facility, long a source of radioactive leaks and located in a heavily African-American area of South Carolina, and the "largest landfill in the nation" in the mainly black community of Emelle, Alabama. "We began to see evidence of a systematic pattern which led us to a national study," recounted Rev. Chavis.

That study—"Toxic Wastes and Race in the United States"—clearly shows what Rev. Chavis suspected: communities of color are where most of America's places of poison are located. In detail, the analysis looked at a cross-section of the thousands of U.S. "commercial hazardous water facilities" (defined by the U.S. Environmental Protection Agency as places licensed for "treating, storing or disposing of hazardous wastes") and "uncontrolled toxic waste sites" (defined by EPA as closed and abandoned sites), and correlated them with the ethnicity of the communities in which they are located.

Some of the study's major findings:

- "Race proved to be the most influential among variables tested in association with the location of commercial hazardous waste facilities. This represented a consistent national pattern."

- "Communities with the greatest number of commercial hazardous wastes facilities had the highest composition of ethnic residents."

- "Although socio-economic status appeared to play an important role in the location of commercial hazardous waste facilities, race still proved to be more significant."

- "Three out of every five black and Hispanic Americans lived in communities with uncontrolled toxic waste sites."

- "Blacks were heavily overrepresented in the populations of metropolitan areas with the largest number of uncontrolled toxic waste

sites."—Memphis, St. Louis, Houston, Cleveland, Chicago, and Atlanta.

- "Approximately half of all Asian/Pacific Islanders and American Indians lived in communities with uncontrolled toxic waste sites."

The analysis called for change. "This report firmly concludes that hazardous wastes in black, Hispanic and other racial and ethnic communities should be made a priority issue at all levels of government. This issue is not currently at the forefront of the nation's attention. Therefore, concerned citizens and policy-makers, who are cognizant of this growing national problem, must make this a priority concern."

It called for: the U.S. president "to issue an executive order mandating federal agencies to consider the impact of current policies and regulations on racial and ethnic communities"; state governments "to evaluate and make appropriate revisions in their criteria for the siting of new hazardous waste facilities to adequately take into account the racial and socio-economic characteristics of potential host communities"; the U.S. Conference of Mayors, the National Conference of Black Mayors and the National League of Cities "to convene a national conference to address these issues from a municipal perspective"; and "civil rights and political organizations to gear up voter registration campaigns as a means to further empower racial and ethnic communities to effectively respond to hazardous wastes in racial and ethnic communities at the top of state and national legislative agendas."

Environmentalist Barry Commoner commented that the report showed the "functional relationship between poverty, racism and powerlessness and the chemical industry's assault on the environment."

It was in 1978 that sociologist Robert Bullard first began exploring environmental racism. He was asked by Linda McKeever Bullard, his wife, to conduct a study on the siting of municipal landfills and incinerators in Houston for a class-action lawsuit challenging a plan to site a new landfill in the "solid middle class" mostly African-American Houston neighborhood of Northwood Manor, notes Bullard. Just out of graduate school, a new professor at Texas Southern University, he found that from the 1920s to that time, all five of Houston's landfills and six out of eight of its incinerators were sited in black neighborhoods. That led to wider studies by Dr. Bullard on how "black communities, because of their economic and political vulnerability, have been routinely targeted for the siting of noxious facilities, locally unwanted land uses and environmental hazards."

He wrote several papers and, last year, his book, *Dumping in Dixie: Race, Class, and Environmental Quality*, came out. Black communities are consistently the ones getting dumped on "because of racism, plain and simple," says Dr. Bullard, now a professor at the University of California at Riverside.

Often it is a promise of "jobs, jobs, and jobs that are held out as a savior" for these communities although, in fact, "these are not labor-intensive industries." The companies involved, meanwhile, figure they can "minimize their investment" by avoiding the sort of lawsuit more likely to be brought by a white community faced with having a toxic dump, an incinerator, a paper mill, a slaughterhouse, a lead smelter, a pesticide plant, "you name it," said Dr. Bullard. Also, with planning and zoning boards commonly having "excluded people of color," the skids are further greased. And to top it off, "because of housing patterns and limited mobility, middle-income and lower-income blacks," unlike whites, often cannot "vote with their feet" and move out when a polluting facility arrives. "Targeting certain communities for poison is another form of discrimination," charged Dr. Bullard.

He tells in *Dumping in Dixie* of how African-Americans in Houston and Dallas; in Alsen, Louisiana; Institute, West Virginia, and Emelle, Alabama "have taken on corporate giants who would turn their areas into toxic wastelands." He is enthused by the existence of how "literally hundreds of environmental justice groups are made up of people of color."

One of the many organizations is the Gulf Coast Tenants Association. "We have not only the dumping here, but we get the up-front stuff; this is where much of the petrochemical industry is centered, and where they produce a lot of the stuff," says Darryl Malek-Wiley, the New Orleans-based group's director of research. "Cancer Alley is the nickname for this area," speaking of the 75-mile swath along the Mississippi from Baton Rouge to New Orleans. The group offers courses in environmental education and assists people to fight environmental hazards in their communities and block

the siting of new ones. The placement of hazardous facilities in black communities in the South follows a pattern of subjugation going back "hundreds of years," notes Malek, with "the industrial age" giving this a new translation. And, he says, it should be viewed in connection with the dumping of hazardous waste in Third World countries.

Up North, in the middle of America's biggest city, New York—Peggy Shepard has been challenging environmental racism as a leader of West Harlem Environmental Action (WHE ACT). Obnoxious, "exploitive" facilities placed in our area in recent years, she notes, have included a huge sewage treatment plant, a "marine transfer station" for garbage, and yet another bus storage depot. "We organized around a series of issues in our community that turned out to be all environmental [in] nature." WHE ACT has been "networking with organizations around" New York City and found that what had happened to West Harlem is typical of what has occurred to other African-American and Hispanic neighborhoods. "We get so used to the stereotype that what environmentalism means is wildlife and the preservation of open space. There had not been sufficient movement on urban environmental problems: incinerators, sewage treatment plants, factories polluting the air, devastating occupational exposure."

Sulalman Mahdi is southeast regional director of the Center for Environment, Commerce and Energy in Atlanta. "Our work involves educating the African-American community around the whole question of the environment. I am particularly interested in bridging the civil rights movement and the environmental justice movement," says Mahdi.

He became involved in the "green" movement while working in the campaign for reparations in land for African-Americans for the injustices committed against them. Living in southern Georgia, near Brunswick, "a papermill town and smelling the sulfur all the time" from the papermill lands, he concluded as he choked on the putrid air, that "we need to fight for environmental protection or the land we seek might not be of any real value once it's returned."

He takes the African-American perspective on nature right back to Africa, and indeed is writing a book on African ecology. The African approach to nature "is very similar to that of the Native Americans," says Mahdi. He speaks of the "founder of agriculture, the founder of botany" both ancient Egyptians. He sees a solid "relationship between our freedom struggle" and battling the environmental abuse subjected on African-Americans, what he terms "environmental genocide."

Genocide is also the word used by Lance Hughes of Native Americans for a Clean Environment. "As states and various municipalities have been closing down a lot of dumps because of public opposition, the companies have been descending on the reservations across the country," says Hughes. Indian reservations are seen as good dump sites by their firms because they are considered sovereign entities not subject to local or state environmental restrictions.

The group of which he is director was formed six years ago because of radioactive contamination caused by a twin set of nuclear production facilities run by Kerr-McGee in northeast Oklahoma amid a large concentration of Native Americans. One produces nuclear fuel for weaponry, the other for nuclear power plants. Further, some of the nuclear waste generated at them is put in fertilizer throughout the state, and also by Kerr-McGee on 10,000 acres surrounding the nuclear facilities.

"The hay and cattle from that land is sold on the open market," says Hughes. The Native Americans who live in the area have many "unusual cancers" and a high rate of birth defects from "genetic mutation. It gets pretty sad," says Hughes, "with babies born without eyes, babies born with brain cancers."

Wildlife is also born deformed. "We found a nine-legged frog and a two-headed fish. And there was a four-legged chicken." Hughes emphasizes that the subjugation of Native Americans "is still going on. The name of the game has been changed, but I would call it the same—genocide, because that is exactly what the result is."

The Southwest Organizing Project (SWOP) is a multi-ethnic, multi-issue organization which began a decade ago in a predominantly Chicano area of Albuquerque, New Mexico. "We have a municipal landfill, the largest pig farm in the city of Albuquerque, a dogfood plant, Texaco, Chevron, General Electric, a sewage plant," says Richard Moore, SWOP co-director. This, he said, is typical of Hispanic and African-American communities in the Southwest.

"Wherever you find working class, ethnic communities you find environmental injustice," says Moore, whose group has grown to fight environmental racism throughout New Mexico. "We have been organizing door-to-door, building strong organizations, going up against pretty major organizations." Non-partisan voter registration has been a key tool. The group was also the founding organization of the Southwest Network of Environmental and Economic Justice, which Moore co-chairs, that brings together people in seven Southwest states also on a multi-ethnic, multi-issue basis.

Moore was one of the signatories of the letter sent to eight major environmental organizations protesting their lack of minority representation (example: of the 315 staff members of the Audubon Society, only three were black).

Importantly, not scored in that letter were three prominent national environmental groups: Greenpeace, the National Toxics Campaign, and Earth Island Institute. In a breakthrough, in contradiction to the pattern elsewhere, the president of Earth Island Institute is an African-American.

Carl Anthony is not only president of Earth Island Institute, headquartered in San Francisco, but director of its Urban Habitat program. "We're very interested in issues at two ends of the spectrum: global warming, the ozone layer, depletion of global resources—and the negative environmental impacts on communities of poor people and people of color. In order to bring these two concerns together," says Anthony, "we have to develop a new kind of thrust and a new kind of leadership in communities of color to address the needs of our communities and also the larger urban community in making a transaction to more sustainable urban patterns." Urban Habitat is "basically a clearinghouse for a lot of people all over the country who want to work on these issues. And it helps alert people from our community to the issues that concern them: toxics, energy issues, air quality, water quality."

Anthony, an architect who says he has "always been aware of environmental issues," is a designer of buildings and a professor of architecture at the University of California at Berkeley, where he is now teaching a new course for the school, Race, Poverty, and the Environment. He speaks with great pleasure of his involvement with Earth Island Institute, but is dubious about whether some of the other national environmental groups will become fully multi-ethnic. They have long taken an "elitist perspective. I doubt that Audubon, for instance, will ever make a big push in this direction."

Chicago's Hazel Johnson has worked closely with Greenpeace, the national environmental group most committed to direct action. "I have a very good working relationship with Greenpeace. It is more than an action group. I have gone with Greenpeace to many places and they have come out to assist us." She spoke of one recent demonstration carried on by her People for Community Recovery against yet one more incinerator planned for her community in which, with Greenpeace, "we chained ourselves to trucks."

"Unequivocally," says Lee, of the Commission for Racial Justice, "minority communities are the communities most at risk to environmental pollution." He paints in words the panorama of pollution. There is the heavy exposure to pesticides of Hispanic farmworkers, including those in Delano, California, where "there is an estimated 300,000 pesticide-related cancers among farmworkers each year."

There are the effects of radioactive contamination on Native Americans, especially the Navajos, the nation's primary work force in the mining of uranium—who have extreme cancer rates as a result. "There is lead poisoning of children in urban areas—with an estimated 55 percent of the victims being African-Americans," says Lee. There is the mess in Puerto Rico, "one of the most heavily polluted areas in the world," with U.S. petrochemical and pharmaceutical companies long having discharged toxics on a massive scale. All the people in the island's town of La Ciudad Cristiana were forced to be relocated due to mercury poisoning. The terrible stories go on and on. Says Lee: "We still have a long way to go in truly addressing this issue."

"To understand the causes of these injustices, it is important to view them in a historical context," he notes. "Two threads of history help to explain the disproportionate impact of toxic pollution on racial and ethnic communities. The first is the long history of oppression and exploitation of African-Americans, Hispanic Americans, Asian-Americans, Pacific Islanders, and Native Americans. This has taken the form of genocide, chattel slavery, indentured servitude, and racial discrimination in employment, housing and practically all aspects of life in the United States. We suffer today from the remnant of this sordid history, as well as from new and institutionalized forms of racism. The other thread of history is the massive expansion of the petrochemical industry since World War II."

"Environmental racism is racial discrimination in environmental policy-making," says Rev. Chavis. "Wherever you find non-white people, that's where they want to dump stuff. And it's spreading all over the world. A lot of toxic chemicals have been going for dumping in the Pacific Islands, and Africa; it recently was revealed that Kenya has been allowing us to dump nuclear wastes." (The Organization of African Unity has denounced the dumping by the U.S. and European countries of hazardous waste in Africa as "toxic terrorism" and "a crime against Africa and the African people.")

"I think when we define the freedom movement, it now includes the environmental issues," says Rev. Chavis. "We now understand the insidious nature of racism. Fighting it does not just involve getting civil rights laws on the books. It goes beyond that. Racism has so permeated all facets of American society. We see the struggle against environmental racism as being an ongoing part of the civil rights and freedom movement in this country, something we are going to make part of our agenda, not a side issue but a primary issue. We must be just as vigilant in attacking environmental racism as racism in health care, housing, and schools."

2. TRASHING THE STRATOSPHERE

Ozone Depletion

A Public Policy Study sponsored by Senator Timothy E. Wirth, Colorado,
and Senator John Heinz, Pennsylvania

Recent assessments confirm what many have feared for some time—that chlorofluorocarbons (CFCs) and related chemicals are depleting stratospheric ozone.[1] This loss is of concern because stratospheric ozone screens out ultraviolet (UV) radiation before it reaches the earth's surface. Ozone depletion will thus increase UV radiation, potentially increasing human skin-cancer incidence, promoting cataracts, suppressing immune responses, and causing other adverse effects to animals, plants, and materials [see Figure 1].

The Nature of the Problem

The most important potential ozone depletors (PODs) are CFC-11, 12, and 113, carbon tetrachloride, methyl chloroform, and Halon 1301 and 1211.[2] All are artificially synthesized compounds used in a wide variety of industrial processes and consumer products. Annual worldwide sales of CFCs alone are currently on the order of $2.2 billion,[3] and are continuing to grow at more than 5% annually. Ironically, PODs' chemical stability, which makes them generally nonflammable, non-toxic, and among the safest of industrial chemicals, is also the characteristic which allows them to survive long enough in the atmosphere to reach the stratosphere, where they are decomposed by intense UV radiation.[4]

The CFCs of concern are used to produce rigid insulating foams and flexible cushioning foams; as refrigerants in industrial, mobile, and home air-conditioning systems and refrigerators; as aerosol propellants except in the few countries (including the United States) which have prohibited all but "essential" aerosol applications;[5] for degreasing, metal cleaning, and other industrial applications; and in dry cleaning. Additionally, Halons are used as fire extinguishants.

The possibility that CFCs could deplete ozone was first recognized in 1974;[6] but recent assessments of trends in satellite and ground-station measurements suggest that depletion is occurring more rapidly than previously anticipated. The discovery that ozone has been severely and increasingly depleted (since the late 1970s) in the Antarctic springtime has heightened international concern. The consequences of stratospheric ozone depletion are even more uncertain than its extent, but they could be dramatic. UV exposure has been linked to non-melanoma skin cancers, a relatively easily treated, rarely lethal condition; and increased UV doses could also increase lethal melanoma skin cancer incidence, suppress immune responses, contribute to cataract formation and other ocular damage, and damage plants, aquatic organisms, outdoor plastics, and protective coatings (paints).

Federal Policy

Like the greenhouse effect, stratospheric ozone depletion is a true global commons problem: POD emissions from any nation eventually affect the ozone layer everywhere. International cooperation in limiting ozone depletion is therefore essential. Since the United States accounts for about one-third of current POD emissions—more than any other nation—it must play an important role in limiting ozone depletion.

Significant progress has been made in the last few years. The Vienna Convention for the Protection of the Ozone Layer, negotiated in 1985, provides a framework for international negotiations and cooperative research; the Montreal Protocol to the Convention was signed by 31 countries in September, 1987. If a sufficient number of countries ratify it, signatories will be committed to freezing and subsequently reducing production and consumption of most of the major PODs. The Protocol calls for periodic assessments of the current understand-

Project 88 (Harnessing Market Forces to Protect Our Environment: Initiatives for the New President),
Washington, DC, December 1988.

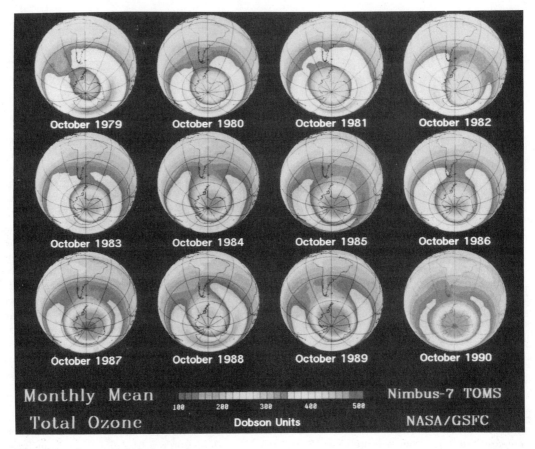

Figure 1   Ozone depletion.

ing of scientific and economic factors. There are exemptions allowing increased POD production for export to developing countries which consume less than a specified per capita level; and, if offset by reductions in another country, to "rationalize" production and thus lower costs. The Protocol establishes a flexible, effective framework for worldwide reduction of POD emissions. It allows countries significant flexibility to accommodate national needs while limiting each country's contribution to ozone depletion (in proportion to its 1986 contribution).

The United States has ratified the Protocol, and EPA has proposed regulations to implement its restrictions. EPA envisions a system of production and import permits allowing permit holders to produce and/or import a specified quantity of PODs in a twelve-month period.[7] As the quantities of PODs available are restricted, prices are expected to rise, providing an incentive for POD users to: (1) develop non-POD-dependent products or manufacturing processes and substitute chemicals; (2) reduce the quantity of PODs required per unit product; and (3) recover PODs from the production process and reuse them. Permits will be allocated to producers and importers in accordance with their 1986 levels of these activities, but can be freely traded among firms; market forces will determine not only the applications in which PODs are used, but also the division of the allowed quantity among specific PODs.[8]

Recommendation 7: Phase-Out POD Emissions through EPA's Tradeable Permit System

A number of factors must be considered when designing a strategy for addressing ozone depletion. Although annual production and import permits now proposed allow for adjustments, a conservative bias (erring on the side of preserving stratospheric ozone) is appropriate for setting control levels. Because PODs survive in the atmosphere for 75 years or more, today's emissions will affect ozone levels a century from now. The most recent evidence demonstrates that an 85% reduction in POD production is needed just to stabilize ozone at present levels.[9] We propose moving to a 100% phase-out of selected PODs.

Either a conventional regulatory approach or the tradeable permit approach could be used to move toward that zero level. The advantage of the incentive-based approach is that it is likely to be more effective (for any given level of aggregate control) and should certainly be less costly. Given the extensive variety of commercial POD applications and the wide-ranging nature of potential alternatives, conventional command-and-control regulatory approaches would be difficult for the government to implement and unnecessarily expensive for industry. Developing specific requirements for the hundreds of POD applications and enforcing these requirements on the thousands of firms which use PODs would be an administrative nightmare. In contrast, market-based approaches like EPA's marketable permits will provide economic incentives for firms to reserve PODs for their most valued uses, thereby minimizing the costs of reducing POD use.

The market-based approach offers several additional benefits over command-and-control regulations. First, it is likely to be far more effective in stimulating firms to adopt measures which require changed work practices, such as recovering PODs from a production line or when servicing refrigeration equipment. Although conventional regulations can require firms to pursue technological solutions, like installing emission-control equipment, it is difficult to ensure that the equipment is properly maintained and operated, and even more difficult to enforce restrictions on the shop floor. Second, this approach provides industry with incentives to develop substitute chemicals, industrial processes, and consumer products. . . . Command-and-control regulations provide little incentive for innovation. Such rules give firms little incentive to develop methods to reduce emissions more than needed to meet requirements.

One potential difficulty with the marketable-permit approach is that PODs represent a very small cost share in many applications. For example, in refrigeration and air-conditioning equipment, the cost of the refrigerant is only a few dollars out of a total price of hundreds or thousands of dollars. In these cases, firms may have less incentive to develop substitute products, since consumers may not be sensitive to the proportionately small price increase which would be needed to pay the increased cost of the refrigerant. To offset this possible effect, EPA may wish to impose engineering controls or product bans in a limited number of cases. Finally, consideration should be given to the auctioning of initial permits, an idea which is consistent with EPA's request for comments on August 25, 1988.

In summary, EPA's proposed use of marketable permits is an admirable use of market mechanisms to achieve environmental goals at minimum economic cost. Preventing further stratospheric ozone depletion may well be the first environmental-policy context in which such an approach is adopted on a wide scale. Several additional and complementary approaches may also be valuable. . . .

Notes

1. National Aeronautics and Space Administration. *Executive Summary, Ozone Trends Panel.* Washington, DC, March 15, 1988.

2. Although the term "CFC" is often used to indicate the class of potential ozone-depleting substances, it is misleading. Only three of the seven most important PODs are CFCs, and several of the proposed POD substitutes are CFCs, e.g., CFCs 134a, 141b, 142b, 143a, and 152a.

3. Shabecoff, Philip. "The Race to Find CFC Substitutes." *The New York Times,* March 31, 1988, p. 25.

4. Most of these chemicals are expected to survive in the atmosphere for 75 years or more.

5. In 1978, the U.S. government banned all "nonessential" aerosol uses of CFC-11 and CFC-12, at that time the major application of these compounds. Canada, Sweden, and Norway enacted similar controls; and in the early 1980s, the European Economic Community capped CFC production at current capacity, a level well in excess of current production.

6. Molina, M. J., and F. S. Rowland. "Stratospheric Sink for Chlorofluoromethanes: Chlorine Catalyzed Destruction of Ozone." *Nature* 249 (1974): 810–812.

7. U.S. Environmental Protection Agency. "Protection

of Stratospheric Ozone." *Federal Register* 52 (239), 47486–47523, December 14, 1987.

8. Permits apply to specific PODs, weighted by their relative ozone-depletion efficiencies. For example, the same permit may allow a firm to use either 1 kg of CFC-11 or 0.8 kg of CFC-113. This feature permits efficient substitution among PODs at no cost

to the environment. A similar scheme may be appropriate for control of greenhouse gases, acid-rain precursors, and other pollutants.

9. Hoffman, John S., and Michael J. Gibbs. *Future Concentrations of Stratospheric Chlorine and Bromine.* EPA 400/1–88/005. Washington, DC: U.S. Environmental Protection Agency, August 1988.

Doing Something About the Weather

Stephen H. Schneider

In 1988 "the environment" became a media event, rivaling politics and baseball for the big American stories of the year. The covers of Time and Newsweek, as well as top news pieces on local and national television and radio, were filled with the summer's drought, heat, hurricane winds, fire, and smoke. Leading the list of problems that have revitalized the environmental movement this year is one described by a century-old theory: that the globe is steadily warming from the so-called "greenhouse effect."

Did the heat wave of 1988 finally demonstrate that the crescendo of warnings by many scientists over the past decade had been too long ignored? Or, rather, was it just a random act by a perverse and fickle Nature requiring no action from human beings other than cleaning up the damage and trying to be less vulnerable next time?

In July alone I had probably 100 phone calls from journalists, many of whom said, in effect, "Okay, you've been carrying a banner about global warming for the past 15 years. Are you finally ready to give us an I-told-you-so?" Before I let on how I answer such a question, we need some background on just what the greenhouse effect is, what kind of scientific consensus exists over its likelihood, what it might mean for the environment and society, and, ultimately, what we can or should do about it.

In the familiar sense of a building made of glass, a greenhouse can be a pleasant place to grow tropical plants in cold winter climates. It also can be like an overheated car with windows closed, parked in the sun on a summer's day. The metaphor works both ways. One diplomat friend has urged

me for years to drop the "greenhouse" label altogether, since it doesn't convey sufficient unpleasantness to motivate action by the public. Call it the "global heat trap," he recommended, and maybe more people would pay attention to the warning. The last time I heard that advice was in May 1988—just before the infamous Summer of '88.

The way a greenhouse works is that the glass allows sunlight to heat the inside of the house; then the panes block the air on the inside from mixing with the cooler air outside the greenhouse. The glass also, but to a much lesser extent, forms a trap inside the greenhouse for another form of energy, so-called infrared radiant energy.

All objects with heat give off radiation with different amounts of energy and at different wavelengths. The very hot sun gives off high-energy, short-wavelength radiation, whereas Earth's cooler surface gives off longer-wavelength, lower-energy radiation. The gases in Earth's atmosphere, and in the atmospheres of Mars and Venus also, have the property of greenhouse glass: They are more "transparent" to incoming solar energy than they are to outgoing infrared energy. The gases tend to trap radiant heat near a planet's surface—the more the gases, the more the trapping of heat.

Thus Mars—a planet with a *thin*, predominantly carbon dioxide atmosphere—has a mean temperature well below that of most deep freezers. Venus—with a very *thick*, largely carbon dioxide atmosphere—has a temperature hotter than an oven. Earth—with a *moderate* amount of atmosphere—contains liquid water, equable temperatures, and abundant life. Mars is too cold, Venus is too hot, and Earth is just right—what some planetary cli-

World Monitor, Vol. 1, No. 3 (December 1988), 28–37. Reprinted by permission.

matologists call the Goldilocks Phenomenon, which is well understood to be a result of the greenhouse effect.

So far, there is little controversy, except perhaps over terminology—whether to call it a greenhouse effect or a heat trap. Indeed, the greenhouse effect is one of the most accepted and best documented theories in the atmospheric sciences.

The controversy begins to build, though, when we have to translate extra heating of Earth's surface into future scenarios of climate changes. To do that, we have to project how much the greenhouse gases will increase in the future. The primary culprit for the buildup of greenhouse gases in Earth's atmosphere is the burning of fossil fuels: coal, oil, and gas. The hydrocarbon molecules contained in these fuels started out as dead, buried plant matter hundreds of millions of years ago. Burning them for heat simply means combining their hydrocarbon molecules with oxygen. An inevitable by-product is carbon dioxide (CO_2). CO_2 is a very effective greenhouse gas. Right now there is incontrovertible evidence that there is about 25% more CO_2 in the atmosphere than there was a century ago, the buildup coming largely from the burning of fossil fuels but also from deforestation. Deforestation contributes to the greenhouse effect in two ways: (1) The burning of trees puts CO_2 into the air; (2) the elimination of trees leaves in the air some of the CO_2 that would have been removed by their intake of that gas to help manufacture the plants' growth.

How much CO_2 will be injected into the atmosphere in the future depends upon three factors: technology, standard of living, and population size. In order to project the global emissions of carbon dioxide, we need to project the emissions per fuel technology (coal is the worst, natural gas half as bad, solar and nuclear virtually CO_2 free). We also need to project the global standard of living; that is, the per capita consumption of each of these technologies. Finally, we need to forecast the total population size using each of the technologies. Total emissions is the product of these three factors. Each of the factors is difficult to project, and thus there is controversy over just how much CO_2 might build up into the future.

Most estimates suggest that CO_2 will double sometime around the middle of the next century. But CO_2 is only part of the greenhouse story. There are other gases such as chlorofluorocarbons (the very culprits in stratospheric ozone reduction and the headline-making ozone hole that permits an increase in damaging rays from the sun), methane (produced by animals, in rice paddies, and in other decaying plant matter), and a host of other minor "trace" gases.

These other trace greenhouse gases, taken together, add about as much to the enhanced greenhouse effect as increases in CO_2.

During a recent Senate Energy Committee hearing, Sen. Tim Wirth of Colorado introduced a bill to curb the emissions of greenhouse gases, especially CO_2. Some pointed conflicts arose among witnesses from the Department of Energy (DOE) and other scientists, including me. The DOE argued that there is so much uncertainty associated with the details of how the climate will change that it would be folly to invest present resources to hedge against a problem whose dimensions are not clear. I countered that platitudes about scientific uncertainty had for too long been used as an excuse to avoid action.

When I first started in climatology in 1971, I recall a government official telling us we had ten years more to study without risk. Then, at a congressional hearing in 1981, a Department of Energy official said essentially the same thing. It would not be surprising to hear this advice again in 1991.

Indeed, how long we should study "before" we act is not a scientific judgment but a value judgment, weighing the costs of any present investments to slow down the future climate change versus the costs of that change descending on us unchecked. There is no "right" or "wrong" here, simply a philosophical difference over how to weigh environmental and financial costs.

At Senator Wirth's hearing, Sen. Bill Bradley of New Jersey began to press the scientists on the panel. He wanted some very specific reasons why constituents in his state, for example, should worry about a degree or two change in the average temperature or, more important, why they should be willing to pay extra money to insulate their homes or drive cars that are smaller and get better mileage—and thus use less CO_2-producing fuel. Finally, he homed in on a critical question: Was there *anything* that we were sure about?

I responded that it was indeed true that we can't be certain that the very warm and dry summer of 1988 was directly a result of the greenhouse effect. Nor could we directly attribute the unusual summer heat in the southeast in 1986 to the greenhouse effect, nor the devastation from hot weather in the Corn Belt in August 1983, nor the temperatures that killed not only crops but people in the late spring and early summer of 1980 in Texas, Oklahoma, Arkansas, and Missouri. It is quite possible that any of these events was simply a random occurrence. But the fact is that the three hottest years of the 20th century all occurred in the 1980s—in '81, '83, and '87. The summer of '88 is likely to be counted among those, too.

In fact, it is no easier to determine whether these kinds of events are connected to the observed one-half to one degree F. of warming that we think the world has undergone in the past 100 years than it is to determine whether rolling snake eyes three times in a row proves a pair of dice is loaded. It's the mathematics of probability not some Las Vegas tout that assures us that the more rolls we make, the surer we are of the true odds. The longer we wait to establish scientific certainty that the greenhouse effect has descended, the greater the dose of climate change we and the rest of the living things on this planet will have to adapt to over the next several generations.

One could think of a summer's climate as a giant game of dice. In this probability metaphor the pair of climatic dice have not simply 12 faces but 1,200, including warm ones and wet ones and dry ones and so forth. Most climate scientists think that the world will warm up, and will warm up dramatically in the next century. If so, the climate would in effect erase some of the colder faces and replace them with an increasing number of warmer ones. And, as a number of climate theories suggest, there could be some drier ones, too.

Therefore, no honest scientist can claim that 1988 or any of the heat waves in the 1980s were absolutely, certainly attributable to the greenhouse effect. In fact, there are a number of suggestions that the unusual drought pattern in 1988 was the result of an out-of-position jet stream caused by unusually cold water in the equatorial Pacific Ocean. However, even if this theory proves true, increased global temperatures increase evaporation of water from farm fields and make extreme heat waves more intense.

How important is a degree or two of temperature change? Senator Bradley asked. Let's go back 18,000 years to the height of the last ice age, when mile-high ice sheets covered most of Canada and went as far south as the Great Lakes, across New England, and into New York State and the northern half of Long Island. This age ended about 10,000 years ago, giving way to the present interglacial period in which civilization has grown and flourished in warm conditions.

Many people are surprised to find out that the ice age was only about 9 degrees F. colder than the present average Earth temperature. It took some 10,000 years for the planet to recover from that ice age. It was an event that literally revamped the ecological face of the world, radically altering what could grow where.

The world's sea level rose by hundreds of feet, species went extinct, others evolved.

All of this took place with some average rate of a few degrees F. temperature change per *thousand* years. But now, if we continue to burn fossil fuels and to deforest at the current rate (or at expanded rates as favored by some politicians, businesses, or economists), then it is quite plausible that we will change the climate something like 2 degrees to 10 degrees in a *century*. This is some 10 to 50 times faster than the average natural rates of change following Earth's recovery from the last ice age.

What is scary about that scenario is not that we have a detailed description of who "wins" and who "loses" and precisely what changes where, but that we are virtually certain that this magnitude and rate of change is bound to cause major surprises.

When this point came up at the Wirth hearing, Senator Bradley asked: "I presume that you can tell me what some of those surprises are that might be lurking."

"A surprise," I replied somewhat sheepishly, "is by definition something that you doubt is going to happen."

However, I was delighted he asked, and added that we could speculate on some major changes in the distribution of forest species, unusual changes in ocean temperature patterns, shifts in growing season, new agricultural zones, major changes in the likelihood of forest fires—an event made emotionally tangible by this summer's disasters in North America and last year's in China—and the fear that tropical diseases could expand out of their present regions.

Of course, most surprises are just that, unforeseen. Already we have an example of a nasty surprise from human pollution of the atmosphere: the Antarctic ozone hole. I am sure that constituents in New Jersey (or Texas) would have no difficulty relating to damages caused by storms that have passed along their coast from time to time, pushing water against the shore in what is known as a storm surge. In such surges the sea level can rise five, 10, or perhaps as much as 18 feet, temporarily inundating coastal areas, causing tens of millions (and sometimes billions) of dollars in damage.

How far each storm surge penetrates inland, and how much damage it does, depends on the height of the sea level when the storm hits. If the storm hits at high tide, it is much more likely to do damage than if it hits at low tide.

Similarly, if the world average sea level increases by several feet—as many climatologists project is likely over the next 100 years—then the probability of any particular storm surge damaging some part of a coastline every, say, 25 years, might change to that level of damage occurring, say, every 15 years. This could totally alter permissible land uses. We know that sea level is now about five inches or so higher around the world than it was a century ago. It is currently rising roughly one-half inch per decade. This is consistent with the fact that the world has warmed up by something as much as 1 degree F. in the last century—quite possibly, but not certainly, as a result of the buildup of greenhouse gases.

Another way that people can understand why a few degrees warming deserves our concern is to focus on the unpleasant issue of intense heat waves. The year 1988 saw such conditions in most sections of the United States. Certainly it seems logical that, if the average temperature of the world is rising, heat waves will be more frequent or more intense.

Indeed, two of my colleagues and I calculated just how we might be loading the climatic dice.

For example, in Washington, D.C., the probability of five or more days in a row in July with afternoon temperatures greater than 95 degrees F. is now about one in six—the odds of getting one face of an unloaded die. If the temperature increased by "only" 3 degrees F., and nothing else in the climate changed, then the odds of that unpleasant heat wave go up to nearly one in two—three faces of the die loaded by our actions.

In Des Moines, the equivalent odds go from one in 17 to one in five.

And in Dallas, the odds of five or more 100-plus degrees F. days in a row goes from one in three to two in three if July average temperatures go up by 3 degrees F.

One doesn't need a graduate course in atmospheric science to fathom those kinds of probability shifts.

Also, when it is hotter and drier, there is a greater chance of forest fires, particularly in the western US. Moreover, adequate moisture is essential to the US maintaining its position as the chief grain-exporting nation in the world. Noted environmental scientist Roger Revelle has suggested that one plausible scenario for the US from greenhouse warming is that it would lose its comparative advantage as an agricultural exporter, since the warming of high-latitude regions in Canada and the Soviet Union could very well open new farming lands, while the yields of grain in the U.S.'s greenhouse-warmed plains could be lowered somewhat relative to yields under present climatic conditions.

Climatic models differ in their detailed predictions of regional climate changes that might occur in different parts of the world. But they all agree that major fluctuations in the accustomed patterns of growing seasons, precipitation, and solar radiation will be experienced. The models also suggest that warming of the oceans will force the sea water to expand, just as liquid in a thermometer expands when heated, thereby causing some coastal inundation.

The Netherlands is the most obvious place to expect that a rise in sea level could be devastating. However, the Dutch have already invested billions of dollars in dikes and are actually less vulnerable to sea-level rise than many other places in the world, such as Indonesia, Bangladesh, Venice, or Florida. The Dutch do worry that they will have to deliberately flood some of their reclaimed land, not because the ocean will breach the dikes but because the increased sea level will cause saltwater incursion into their ground water. To prevent this may require them to flood some of their now agricultural or suburban land with Rhine River water.

Climatic models differ about what happens to monsoon-dependent lands such as Africa or India. But there are strong suggestions that monsoon rainfall in India might increase. At first blush, that might seem like an advantage, since drought frequently raises havoc with this monsoon-dependent area. On the other hand, 1988 saw disastrous flooding in Bangladesh. Farmlands, animal habitats, and residences were destroyed.

Therefore, an increase in the reliability or intensity of monsoon rainfall would indeed be a major benefit in India and Bangladesh, for example—but only if these countries had made the investment of the hundreds of billions of dollars required to build massive public works projects to control floods and store water for later irrigation. But, if those climate changes occurred very rapidly before such investments were made, then the advantage of more intense or reliable rainfall could well be turned into the disaster of increased frequency of flooding.

In essence, while the details of regional changes are still debated it seems quite likely that there will be substantial redistribution of climatic resources around the world. The more rapidly the change evolves the more likely it is that the negative impacts of unaccustomed climate will dominate the potential benefits. The latter might accrue if the changes occurred more slowly and we thus had enough advance warning to adopt remedies or even take advantage of the change.

Therefore, we come back to the question posed to me at the outset: Can I say, "I told you so"? I think the most accurate answer is, "I told you so—almost." To be absolutely sure scientifically, we need to have more warmer years.

The problem scientists face in trying to communicate complex and controversial issues with governmental policy implications is formidable. On the one hand, our loyalty to the scientific method requires that we tell "the truth, the whole truth, and nothing but the truth"—meaning all the caveats, ifs, ands, and buts. On the other hand, as human beings, we would like to see the world a better place, which to many of us means reducing the risk of unprecedentedly rapid climatic change. That means offering up scary scenarios, inserting few caveats, and getting lots of media coverage.

This "double ethical bind" we frequently find ourselves in cannot be solved by any formula. Each scientist has to decide for himself or herself what the right balance is between being effective and being honest. I hope that means being both. To me, the prospect of global warming has been sufficiently compelling to deserve everyone's attention, even with the uncertainties admitted up front.

That philosophy hasn't worked so well over the past 15 years, I must admit, at least until the Summer of '88 made global warming appear credible. The irony is that a solid case of good physics had been given vastly too little credibility for 15 years, whereas one, essentially random, hot event in 1988 has perhaps given us climatologists too much credibility.

Not that I want people to ignore the Summer of '88, for it reminds human beings we still must cope with our vulnerability to nature. It is also the kind of event that could become more common with global warming. Therefore, I think the heightened public consciousness about the greenhouse effect at the close of business in 1988 has brought us to about the right level of concern, but unfortunately for the wrong reasons. I hope the inevitable cold and wet season anomalies that the climatic probabilities will roll us sometime soon won't be equally overinterpreted in the other direction.

Finally, let's turn to the question about whether we should act to do something about the prospect of unprecedentedly rapid environmental change. How do we know our forecasts are right? I recall a number of years ago discussing with a congressional committee that our mathematical computer models were projecting major changes in climate and that, to me, this called for government action on improving energy efficiency standards—among other concrete actions.

How do you verify these models? I was asked. One way is to check their performance in a seasonal cycle test. Winter is something like 25 degrees F. colder than summer across the Northern Hemisphere, I said, and the models do extremely well at reproducing this much larger climate change than anything we project in the next century from human pollution.

"You mean to tell me," one representative said after the hearing, "that you guys have spent a billion dollars of the taxpayers' money proving that the winter is cold and the summer is hot?"

"Yes, sir," I replied, "and we are very proud of it—for if we couldn't reproduce that very large seasonal climate signal in our models, then I wouldn't have the nerve to stand before you and suggest that there is a good likelihood of major climate change from human pollution."

In fact, this piece of evidence, taken together with the fact that the world is one-half to one degree or so F. warmer than it was a century ago (while at the same time there is 25% more CO_2)—and adding in the Goldilocks Phenomenon, too—makes a strong circumstantial case for the plausibility of most climatologists' warnings. So what do we do about them? is the obvious next question.

In my value system, a prudent society hedges against potentially dangerous future outcomes, just as a prudent person installs insulating glass, repairs a roof, waterproofs a cellar, or buys insurance. Of course, if one spent all one's resources investing to protect against every conceivable future risk, there would be nothing left to live on today. Thus we need a priority system for determining what are the prudent investments to help us cope with the greenhouse effect.

It is my opinion that the best kinds of policies to deal with the greenhouse effect fall in the category of "tie-in strategies." Quite simply, a tie-in strategy would involve making an investment in some activity that reduces the amount of greenhouses gases that otherwise would have gone into the atmosphere but *at the same time* also provides other benefits having nothing to do with climate.

Such high-leverage investments are the goals of efficient business enterprises. The most obvious category of tie-in strategy investments is the more efficient use of energy. Fuel not burned produces no CO_2, as well as no acid rain, no negative health effects from acute air pollution, and no further dependence on imported energy supplies—hence, an argument against wasteful burning. Also, the more energy efficient a manufacturing process is—that is, the less energy it takes to manufacture some product—the cheaper it will be to sell that product, particularly if the price of energy increases as many expect it will over the next several decades as oil supplies diminish.

Currently, Japan, Germany, Italy, and other economic competitors of the United States are more than twice as efficient as the US in terms of the amount of energy used to make manufactured products. Thus energy efficiency not only reduces the magnitude of climate change but also reduces acid rain, negative health effects of air pollution in cities, and dependence on imported energy supplies—and increases a nation's competitiveness over the long term.

The strategic investment of several tens of billions of dollars a year to make America more energy efficient and ultimately more economically competitive seems a valuable policy regardless of whether environmental change materializes as forecast. With all the benefits taken together, the case for action now is compelling.

However, such policies often run into the ideological opposition of those who claim that such decisions should be made by private investment. Indeed, private investment has over the past ten years substantially improved the energy efficiency of American transportation, power production, space heating, and appliances. But there is still a long way to go, and in the past few years the rate of gain in energy efficiency has radically dropped off.

Detroit is now arguing, with Washington tending to capitulate, that the government should lower automobile gasoline-mileage standards. This is exactly the wrong way to go. It is a view dominated by short-term considerations, next year's profit and loss, without adequate regard to the protection of long-term environmental resources such as a stable climate or the reliability of energy supplies in the future.

Another tie-in strategy deals with the development of nonfossil-fuel energy supplies, such as solar photovoltaic generators, or a new generation of inherently safer nuclear power plants. I have not personally been a fan of nuclear power—and certainly would not advocate easing the licensing of existing power plants of the designs that failed at Chernobyl or Three Mile Island. But there are many designs now on the drawing board that could satisfy a number of the legitimate concerns that people have had about nuclear power. Environmentalists shouldn't dismiss the nuclear option outright simply because of the dread N-word. But nuclear advocates must first prove that their new designs are essentially free of meltdown risk and waste disposal hazard and can be cost effective in relation to the alternatives, including energy conservation.

The bottom line of the global warming, greenhouse effect issue is that we insult the environment at a faster rate than we understand the consequences. Simple prudence suggests that modifying the global climate at 10 to 50 times the average natural rates of change in the past is not a planetary experiment that we should casually allow, particularly since there are many measures available that could substantially slow down our impact on Earth and at the same time buy many other benefits.

How Climatic Models Work

Our climatic theories suggest that the future will see global average temperatures some 2 degrees to 10 degrees F. warmer over the next century than at present.

How are these estimates of 2 to 10 degrees F. temperature increases made? Given some scenario of increasing trace greenhouse gases, we turn next to the primary tool used by climatologists in making quantitative estimation of how much global warming will take place: mathematical models of climate run on the best available supercomputers.

Since no laboratory experiment can be built that remotely captures the complexity of Earth's climate system, scientists instead build mathematical models. Equations are written down to represent the basic physical laws that govern the motions of the atmosphere, oceans, and ice. These include the conservation of mass, the conservation of momentum, the conservation of energy, and thermodynamics laws about the state of gases. However, the equations cannot be solved exactly, so techniques are developed that involve creating a discrete number of points or "grids" around the globe at which solutions to the equations are approximated.

Everything that occurs on smaller scales than these roughly 300-by-300-mile grid boxes is not explicitly treated in the model. Rather, we have to invent statistical rules to associate, for example, the average relative humidity at the four corners of the grid box with the average amount of cloudiness within that grid box. Winds, temperatures, precipitation, sunlight, relative humidity are all then predicted internally at each of the model's grid points. The model at my lab uses a global grid with spacing of 4.5 degrees latitude by 7.5 degrees longitude and nine vertical levels. In this example, we divide Earth's surface into a grid of 1,920 squares, with nine levels, which makes 17,280 boxes—with all these weather variables calculated every 30 minutes. It takes 10 hours of time on a Cray Supercomputer to compute a year's weather.

The detailed predictions of different models at different institutions around the world agree roughly that a doubling of CO_2 would eventually increase global temperatures something like 5 to 9 degrees F.; they disagree markedly as to the specific regional distribution of climatic changes and their time evolution. Nevertheless, these models do a credible job of predicting the very large difference in temperature between winter and summer, Mars and Venus, and some climatic aspects of ancient Earth, so that it is a good bet that their global scale temperature predictions are accurate to about 50%.

The United States alone cannot prevent ozone depletion or the greenhouse effect. But Americans will have no moral persuasion over the one billion Chinese, for example, who are rapidly developing polluting coal resources, unless Americans themselves lead the way with substantial increases in energy efficiency. Furthermore, if the US wants developing countries to pollute less, the US will have to help them to deploy alternative technologies that can provide economic development opportunities with less ultimate pollution. At the same time, Americans will get dual benefits—less total global pollution and new potential markets for their wares.

In 1975 I attended a meeting called by anthropologist Margaret Mead which she entitled "The Atmosphere: Endangered and Endangering." I wondered why an anthropologist was getting involved in such controversial questions of physics. "Quite simple," she told me. "The atmosphere is the last symbol of global interdependence we have. If we can't solve some of our problems in the face of threats to this global commons, then I can't be very optimistic about the future of the world."

The weather of 1988 has lifted the debate about climate change from ivy-covered halls and stone and glass government offices into the public consciousness. I hope that a cold, wet winter or normal summer or two won't deter humanity from undertaking the important steps needed first to slow down and eventually to reverse the radical changes we are inflicting on our own world.

To be sure, there are many uncertainties yet to be resolved. But we purchase insurance as individuals and defense forces as a society on strategic grounds, even though there is great uncertainty about our personal futures or how our nation may need to defend itself. Protecting the planet should also be a strategic goal, but of humanity; slowing down our pollution of the atmosphere is international insurance against the uncomfortable risks of future grim surprises.

To delay action is to commit Earth and its inhabitants to larger amounts of more rapidly occurring environmental change than there would be if we act now. The dilemma rests, metaphorically, in our gazing into a very dirty crystal ball. The tough problem is how long we clean the glass before we act on what we think we see inside.

VII

Varieties of Activism

PREVIEW

> Monkeywrenching is a proud American tradition . . . going all the way back to the Boston Tea Party in 1773.[1]
>
> *Dave Foreman*

> Henry David Thoreau [was] sent to jail for refusing to pay his poll tax to protest the U.S. war against Mexico. When Ralph Waldo Emerson came to bail him out, Emerson called through an open window and said, "Henry, what are you doing in there?" Thoreau quietly replied, "Ralph, what are you doing out there?"[2]
>
> *Dave Foreman*

Radical forms of environmental activism can be found in groups such as Earth First! and the Sea Shepherds. Earth First! is often associated with its founder, Dave Foreman, as well as with tactics called "monkeywrenching." Monkeywrenching or ecological sabotage (alternatively called ecotage or "night-work") is a name, as Foreman explains, "for the destruction of machines or property that are used to destroy the natural world."[3] It includes wrecking heavy equipment, spiking trees (driving nails into trees in order to damage saw blades), and sinking holes in whaling ships as the Sea Shepherds do.

Although Earth First!ers engage in many nondestructive protests, such as chaining themselves to a bulldozer or sitting in a tree scheduled to be cut down, the events publicized in the name of Earth First! center on property destruction. Foreman is perhaps best known for his 1987 book *Ecodefense: A Field Guide to Monkeywrenching*. A how-to-do-it book, it contains, as Rik Scarce nicely summarizes, "detailed instructions for destroying

just about anything used to ruin wild places, including heavy equipment, power and seismographic lines, and snowmobiles. Jamming locks, making smoke bombs, engaging in sabotage in an urban environment, and protecting oneself against discovery are among the other topics exhaustively discussed."[4]

Both Earth First! and the Sea Shepherds claim to be committed to nonviolence, although they condone limited property destruction. Neither group considers destruction of property to be violence. In contrast, a more mainstream environmental organization such as Greenpeace, originally known as the "Don't Make a Wave Committee,"[5] is committed to the principle of no property destruction. Scarce, in his recent book on the radical environmental movement, illustrates the difference: ". . . Greenpeace led an ultimately successful boycott against Icelandic fish products to protest that nation's whaling policy, and some of its activists even stalled the offloading of Icelandic fish from a freighter to publicize the issue; the Sea Shepherd's approach was to sink half of the Icelandic whaling fleet."[6]

Greenpeace is a large, well-organized, hierarchical structure with chapters capable of generating a direct mailing on a national and an international scale. Earth First!, on the other hand, is made up of little clumps of people in different locations with no central organization. As Scarce points out, anyone can act in name of Earth First![7] Although Greenpeace has been in the forefront of guerrilla theater—going to the site of a seal clubbing or a whaling ship to get media attention—the organization expelled Board of Directors member Paul Watson for throwing a wooden club and pelts into the water during a protest of the killing of baby harp seals.[8] Watson, who went on to found the Sea Shepherds, calls Greenpeace "the Avon ladies of the environmental movement." In a more temperate statement about the relationship between radical and more mainstream groups, Dave Foreman recently said, ". . . I think we have allowed the Sierra Club and other groups to actually take stronger positions than they would have before and yet appear to be more moderate than ever."[9]

People disagree about the appropriate description of the activities of radical environmentalists. For example, *Newsweek,* in a 1982 piece on Earth First!, described the actions of the group as "pranks."[10] Michael Martin sees ecological sabotage as at least close to (fitting an expanded version of) civil disobedience. Ecotage, he says, is markedly different from the standard case of civil disobedience in that the illegal actions performed are not public. As Edward Abbey, author of *The Monkey Wrench Gang,* said, "I'm not advocating illegal activity . . . [except] at night."[11] However, as Martin points out, the underground railroad is thought by some to be an example of civil disobedience, and this effort to free slaves was not, indeed, could not be, conducted in public. Nor would anyone likely call the activities of the underground railroad "pranks" for they were not amusing, playful, or malicious in intent. Eugene C. Hargrove, editor of *Environmental Ethics,* condemned monkeywrenching as "paramilitary operations . . . closer to terrorism than civil disobedience. . . ."[12] The charge of terrorism is heard fairly often. Ecowarriors reject the label of terrorist, as Rik Scarce says, because of "the precautions they take to avoid injuring others."[13]

There are many accounts of terrorism, but looking at just one contemporary example— Bat-Ami Bar On's "Why Terrorism Is Morally Problematic"—is helpful in determining whether it makes sense or is stretching a point to call monkeywrenchers eco-terrorists. Bar On says that "terrorism produces people who

are afraid . . . [it] places its victims in a life threatening situation in which one feels both a need to do something to save oneself and a helplessness."[14] Having in mind the context of state terrorism and such actions as bombing a city, shooting indiscriminately in an airport, and abducting and killing people, Bar On compares terrorism to seasoning (the process used by pimps to form prostitutes) and torture as practices that "involve the intentional erosion of selves and the intentional breaking of wills. . . ."[15] She speaks of the "daily fears for . . . survival and physical well-being. . . ."[16] We must ask ourselves whether these consequences seem an apt description of the results of ecosabotage. In his book, *Green Rage,* Christopher Manes reports that "President of Louisiana-Pacific Harry Merlo remarks, 'Terrorism is the name of the game for radical environmental goals . . .' [Mike] Roselle . . . [replies], 'Real terrorists would not be spiking trees . . . but spiking Merlo.'"[17]

When the Greenpeace ship *Rainbow Warrior* was bombed and sunk by the French government and a member of the crew drowned, nobody described the incident as terrorism.[18] When a member of the British Parliament said to the then Prime Minister Margaret Thatcher, "' . . . it's a British ship with a British flag and a British captain and a British crew in a British Commonwealth harbor sunk by the French government,' she said, 'It's none of our concern. . . .'"[19] Unsurprisingly, Paul Watson, who told this story, finds Margaret Thatcher's remark hypocritical.[20] Certainly, the choice to describe people as terrorists may depend in part on the ends they are trying to accomplish. Conor Cruise O'Brien sums up this point nicely: "We reserve the use [of the words 'terrorism' and 'terrorist'] in practice for politically motivated violence of which we disapprove. The words imply a judgment about the political context in which those who we decide to call terrorists operate, and above all about the nature of the regime under which and against which they operate. We imply that the regime itself is legitimate. If we call them 'freedom fighters' we imply that the regime is illegitimate."[21]

Needless to say, little, if any, controversy surrounds the recommendations of legal ways to help the environment such as those suggested by Paul and Anne Ehrlich and those done by Rachel L. Bagby's mother.

"Daughters of Growing Things" was written by Rachel L. Bagby about the work of her mother, Rachel E. Bagby, in Philadelphia. Written in interview style, the material is taken from phone conversations between mother and daughter over a period of three years. In a low- and no-income neighborhood in Philadelphia, Rachel E. Bagby helps folks—especially teenagers—grow huge vegetable gardens in what used to be vacant lots where purse snatchers and other criminals would hide in the tall weeds. As Rachel E. Bagby says, ". . . you have weeds taller than I am. People be afraid to go by Twenty-first street. That's where we had to go to go to the store. . . ."[22] Now proud teenagers gain confidence in themselves and their first work experience in the gardens.

As Paul and Anne Ehrlich point out, there are many things professionals can do to protect the environment. The things they have in mind are specific to professions, e.g., there are actions that can be done and positions that can be taken by engineers because they are engineers, by entomologists because they are entomologists, by economists because they are economists. We have noted and tried to analyze some of the activities of radical environmentalists, and we have documented extraordinary things that ordinary folks like Rachel E. Bagby can do if they have the imagination, the determination, and the good will.

NOTES

1. Dave Foreman, *Confessions of an Eco-Warrior* (New York: Harmony Books, 1991), pp. 118–119.

2. Dave Foreman, *Defending the Earth: A Dialogue Between Murray Bookchin and Dave Foreman*, edited by

Steve Chase (Boston: South End Press, 1991), pp. 70–71.

3. Dave Foreman, *Confessions of an Eco-Warrior*, p. 118.

4. Rik Scarce, *Eco-Warriors: Understanding the Radical Environmental Movement* (Chicago: The Noble Press, Inc., 1990).

5. Scarce, p. 47.

6. Scarce, pp. 103–104.

7. Scarce, p. 71.

8. Doing so was a crime under Canadian law, and Greenpeace lost its tax exempt status as a result. See Scarce, p. 101.

9. Dave Foreman, *Defending the Earth: A Dialogue Between Murray Bookchin and Dave Foreman*, p. 39.

10. See *Newsweek*, July 19, 1982, 26–27.

11. *Denver Post*, July 5, 1982, quoted in *Green Rage: Radical Environmentalism and the Unmaking of Civilization* (Boston: Little, Brown and Company, 1990), p. 81.

12. Eugene C. Hargrove, "Ecological Sabotage: Pranks or Terrorism?" *Environmental Ethics*, Vol. 4 (1982), 292.

13. Scarce, p. 77.

14. Bat-Ami Bar On, "Why Terrorism Is Morally Problematic," *Feminist Ethics*, edited by Claudia Card (Lawrence: University of Kansas Press, 1991), pp. 111, 112.

15. Bar On, p. 116.

16. Bar On, p. 122.

17. Christopher Manes, *Green Rage: Radical Environmentalism and the Unmaking of Civilization* (Boston: Little, Brown and Company, 1990), p. 177. The Louisiana-Pacific Corporation is the largest purchaser of timber from the national forests. Mike Roselle is co-founder of Earth First!

18. See Scarce, p. 112, and Roderick Frazier Nash, *The Rights of Nature: A History of Environmental Ethics* (Madison: University of Wisconsin Press, 1989), p. 180.

19. Scarce reported this statement from an interview with Paul Watson, p. 113.

20. Scarce, p. 113.

21. Bar On, p. 109, quoting Conor Cruise O'Brien, "Terrorism Under Democratic Conditions: The Case of the IRA," in *Terrorism, Legitimacy, and Power: The Consequences of Political Violence*, ed. Martha Creshnaw (Middletown, CT: Wesleyan University Press, 1983), p. 91.

22. Rachel L. Bagby, "Daughters of Growing Things," in *Reweaving the World: The Emergence of Ecofeminism*, ed. Irene Diamond and Gloria Feman Orenstein (San Francisco: Sierra Club Books, 1990), p. 237.

Strategic Monkeywrenching

Dave Foreman

. . . Only one hundred and fifty years ago, the Great Plains were a vast, waving sea of grass stretching from the Chihuahuan Desert of Mexico to the boreal forest of Canada, from the oak-hickory forests of the Ozarks to the Rocky Mountains. Bison blanketed the plains—it has been estimated that 60 million of the huge, shaggy beasts moved across the grass. Great herds of pronghorn and elk also filled this Pleistocene landscape. Packs of wolves and numerous grizzly bears followed the immense herds.

One hundred and fifty years ago, John James Audubon estimated that there were several *billion* birds in a flock of passenger pigeons that flew past him for several days on the Ohio River. It has been said that a squirrel could travel from the Atlantic seaboard to the Mississippi River without touching the ground, so dense was the deciduous forest of the East.

At the time of the Lewis and Clark Expedition, an estimated 100,000 grizzlies roamed the western half of what is now the United States. The howl of the wolf was ubiquitous. The condor dominated the sky from the Pacific Coast to the Great Plains. Salmon and sturgeon filled the rivers. Ocelots, jaguars, margay cats and jaguarundis roamed the Texas brush and Southwestern deserts and mesas. Bighorn sheep in great numbers ranged the mountains of the Rockies, Great Basin, Southwest and Pacific Coast. Ivory-billed woodpeckers and Carolina parakeets filled the steamy forests of the Deep South. The land was alive.

East of the Mississippi, giant tulip poplars, chestnuts, oaks, hickories and other trees formed the most diverse temperate deciduous forest in the world. On the Pacific Coast, redwood, hemlock, Douglas fir, spruce, cedar, fir and pine formed the grandest forest on Earth.

In the space of a few generations we have laid waste to paradise. The tall grass prairie has been transformed into a corn factory where wildlife means the exotic pheasant. The short grass prairie is a grid of carefully fenced cow pastures and wheat fields. The passenger pigeon is no more. The

last died in the Cincinnati Zoo in 1914. The endless forests of the East are tame woodlots. The only virgin deciduous forest there is in tiny museum pieces of hundreds of acres. Six hundred grizzlies remain and they are going fast. There are only three condors left in the wild and they are scheduled for capture and imprisonment in the Los Angeles Zoo. Except in northern Minnesota and Isle Royale, wolves are known merely as scattered individuals drifting across the Canadian and Mexican borders (a pack has recently formed in Glacier National Park). Four percent of the peerless Redwood Forest remains and the monumental old growth forest cathedrals of Oregon are all but gone. The tropical cats have been shot and poisoned from our southwestern borderlands. The subtropical Eden of Florida has been transformed into hotels and citrus orchards. Domestic cattle have grazed bare and radically altered the composition of the grassland communities of the West, displacing elk, moose, bighorn sheep and pronghorn and leading to the virtual extermination of grizzly, wolf, cougar, bobcat and other "varmints." Dams choke the rivers and streams of the land.

Nonetheless, wildness and natural diversity remain. There are a few scattered grasslands ungrazed, stretches of free-flowing river undammed and undiverted, thousand-year-old forests, Eastern woodlands growing back to forest and reclaiming past roads, grizzlies and wolves and lions and wolverines and bighorn and moose roaming the backcountry; hundreds of square miles that have never known the imprint of a tire, the bite of a drill, the rip of a 'dozer, the cut of a saw, the smell of gasoline.

These are the places that hold North America together, that contain the genetic information of life, that represent sanity in a whirlwind of madness.

In January of 1979, the Forest Service announced the results of RARE II [its Roadless Area Review and Evaluation]: of the 80 million acres of undeveloped lands on the National Forests, only

Ecodefense: A Field Guide to Monkeywrenching, by Dave Foreman (Tucson, AZ: Ned Ludd, 1987), pp. 10–17. Reprinted by permission of the author.

15 million acres were recommended for protection against logging, road building and other "developments." In the big tree state of Oregon, for example, only 370,000 acres were proposed for Wilderness protection out of 4.5 million acres of roadless, uncut forest lands. Of the areas nationally slated for protection, most were too high, too dry, too cold, too steep to offer much in the way of "resources" to the loggers, miners and graziers. Those roadless areas with critical old growth forest values were allocated for the sawmill. Important grizzly habitat in the Northern Rockies was tossed to the oil industry and the loggers. Off-road-vehicle fanatics and the landed gentry of the livestock industry won out in the Southwest and Great Basin. . . .

The BLM [Bureau of Land Management] wilderness review has been a similar process of attrition. It is unlikely that more than 9 million acres will be recommended for Wilderness out of the 60 million with which the review began. Again, it is the more spectacular but biologically less rich areas that will be proposed for protection.

During 1984, Congress passed legislation designating minimal National Forest Wilderness acreages for most states (generally only slightly larger than the pitiful RARE II recommendations and concentrating on "rocks and ice" instead of crucial forested lands). In the next few years, similar picayune legislation for National Forest Wilderness in the remaining states and for BLM Wilderness will probably be enacted. The other roadless areas will be eliminated from consideration. National Forest Management Plans emphasizing industrial logging, grazing, mineral and energy development, road building, and motorized recreation will be implemented. Conventional means of protecting these millions of acres of wild country will largely dissipate. Judicial and administrative appeals for their protection will be closed off. Congress will turn a deaf ear to requests for additional Wildernesses so soon after disposing of the thorny issue. The effectiveness of conventional political lobbying by conservation groups to protect endangered wild lands will evaporate. And in half a decade, the saw, 'dozer and drill will devastate most of what is unprotected. The battle for wilderness will be over. Perhaps 3% of the United States will be more or less protected and it will be open season on the rest. Unless . . .

Many of the projects that will destroy roadless areas are economically marginal. It is costly for the Forest Service, BLM, timber companies, oil companies, mining companies and others to scratch out the "resources" in these last wild areas. It is expensive to maintain the necessary infrastructure of roads for the exploitation of wild lands. The cost of repairs, the hassle, the delay, the down-time may just be too much for the bureaucrats and exploiters to accept if there is a widely-dispersed, unorganized, *strategic* movement of resistance across the land.

It is time for women and men, individually and in small groups, to act heroically and admittedly illegally in defense of the wild, to put a monkeywrench into the gears of the machine destroying natural diversity. This strategic monkeywrenching can be safe, it can be easy, it can be fun, and—most importantly—it can be effective in stopping timber cutting, road building, overgrazing, oil and gas exploration, mining, dam building, powerline construction, off-road-vehicle use, trapping, ski area development and other forms of destruction of the wilderness, as well as cancerous suburban sprawl.

But it must be strategic, it must be thoughtful, it must be deliberate in order to succeed. Such a campaign of resistance would follow these principles:

Monkeywrenching Is Non-Violent

Monkeywrenching is non-violent resistance to the destruction of natural diversity and wilderness. It is not directed toward harming human beings or other forms of life. It is aimed at inanimate machines and tools. Care is always taken to minimize any possible threat to other people (and to the monkeywrenchers themselves).

Monkeywrenching Is Not Organized

There can be no central direction or organization to monkeywrenching. Any type of network would invite infiltration, *agents provocateurs* and repression. It is truly individual action. Because of this, communication among monkeywrenchers is difficult and dangerous. Anonymous discussion through this book and its future editions, and through the Dear Ned Ludd section of the *Earth First! Journal,* seems to be the safest avenue of communication to refine techniques, security procedures and strategy.

Monkeywrenching Is Individual

Monkeywrenching is done by individuals or very small groups of people who have known each other for years. There is trust and a good working relationship in such groups. The more people involved, the greater are the dangers of infiltration or a loose mouth. Earth defenders avoid working with people they haven't known for a long time, those who can't keep their mouths closed, and those with grandiose or violent ideas (they may be police agents or dangerous crackpots).

Monkeywrenching Is Targeted

Ecodefenders pick their targets. Mindless, erratic vandalism is counterproductive. Monkeywrenchers know that they do not stop a specific logging sale by destroying any piece of logging equipment which they come across. They make sure it belongs to the proper culprit. They ask themselves what is the most vulnerable point of a wilderness-destroying project and strike there. Senseless vandalism leads to loss of popular sympathy.

Monkeywrenching Is Timely

There is a proper time and place for monkeywrenching. There are also times when monkeywrenching may be counterproductive. Monkeywrenchers generally should not act when there is a non-violent civil disobedience action (a blockade, etc.) taking place against the opposed project. Monkeywrenching may cloud the issue of direct action and the blockaders could be blamed for the ecotage and be put in danger from the work crew or police. Blockades and monkeywrenching usually do not mix. Monkeywrenching may also not be appropriate when delicate political negotiations are taking place for the protection of a certain area. There are, of course, exceptions to this rule. The Earth warrior always thinks: Will monkeywrenching help or hinder the protection of this place?

Monkeywrenching Is Dispersed

Monkeywrenching is a wide-spread movement across the United States. Government agencies and wilderness despoilers from Maine to Hawaii know that their destruction of natural diversity may be met with resistance. Nation-wide monkeywrenching is what will hasten overall industrial retreat from wild areas.

Monkeywrenching Is Diverse

All kinds of people in all kinds of situations can be monkeywrenchers. Some pick a large area of wild country, declare it wilderness in their own minds, and resist any intrusion against it. Others specialize against logging or ORV's [off-road vehicles] in a variety of areas. Certain monkeywrenchers may target a specific project, such as a giant powerline, construction of a road, or an oil operation. Some operate in their backyards, others lie low at home and plan their ecotage a thousand miles away. Some are loners, others operate in small groups.

Monkeywrenching Is Fun

Although it is serious and potentially dangerous activity, monkeywrenching is also fun. There is a rush of excitement, a sense of accomplishment, and unparalleled camaraderie from creeping about in the night resisting those "alien forces from Houston, Tokyo, Washington, DC, and the Pentagon." As Ed Abbey says, "Enjoy, shipmates, enjoy."

Monkeywrenching Is Not Revolutionary

It does *not* aim to overthrow any social, political or economic system. It is merely non-violent self-defense of the wild. It is aimed at keeping industrial "civilization" out of natural areas and causing its retreat from areas that should be wild. It is not major industrial sabotage. Explosives, firearms and other dangerous tools are usually avoided. They invite greater scrutiny from law enforcement agencies, repression and loss of public support. (The Direct Action group in Canada is a good example of what monkeywrenching is *not*.) Even Republicans monkeywrench.

Monkeywrenching Is Simple

The simplest possible tool is used. The safest tactic is employed. Except when necessary, elaborate commando operations are avoided. The most effective means for stopping the destruction of the wild are generally the simplest: spiking trees and spiking roads. There are obviously times when more detailed and complicated operations are called for. But the monkeywrencher thinks: What is the simplest way to do this?

Monkeywrenching Is Deliberate and Ethical

Monkeywrenching is not something to do cavalierly. Monkeywrenchers are very conscious of the gravity of what they do. They are deliberate about taking such a serious step. They are thoughtful. Monkeywrenchers—although non-violent—are warriors. They are exposing themselves to possible arrest or injury. It is not a casual or flippant affair. They keep a pure heart and mind about it. They remember that they are engaged in the most moral of all actions: protecting life, defending the Earth.

A movement based on these principles could protect millions of acres of wilderness more stringently than any Congressional act, could insure the propagation of the grizzly and other threatened life forms better than an army of game wardens, and could lead to the retreat of industrial civilization from large areas of forest, mountain, desert, plain, seashore, swamp, tundra and woodland that are better suited to the maintenance of natural diversity than to the production of raw materials for overconsumptive technological human society.

If loggers know that a timber sale is spiked, they won't bid on the timber. If a Forest Supervisor knows that a road will be continually destroyed, he won't try to build it. If seismographers know that they will be constantly harassed in an area, they'll go elsewhere. If ORVers know that they'll get flat tires miles from nowhere, they won't drive in such areas.

John Muir said that if it ever came to a war between the races, he would side with the bears. That day has arrived.

The Sea Shepherds: Bringing Justice to the High Seas

Rik Scarce

Paul Watson says he doesn't remember when he first heard of the *Sierra*, an infamous pirate whaling ship that prowled the waters of the Atlantic for nearly twenty years. It was like an archetypal specter that was always *out there*, menacing the waves in the collective consciousness of anti-whaling activists. In the summer of 1979, with little more than a "gut feeling" to go on, Watson set out to change all that by tracking down and destroying the 678-ton killer/factory ship that haunted him. His bond with whales was strong, having been cemented by a vision in an Oglala Sioux sweat lodge when he was initiated into the tribe following the Indian uprising at Wounded Knee in 1973. A bison appeared to Watson, who was made a member of the tribe after he snuck into the besieged encampment during the seventy-one day rebellion and worked as a medic. The buffalo told him that he should "concentrate on the mammals of the sea, especially whales."[1]

It was a profound visitation, Watson says, especially because of the messenger. "The Plains Indians were the first people to ever fight a war to save something other than themselves—the buffalo."[2]

In this parable of the high seas, the *Sierra* was a seagoing version of the rapacious foreigners who wiped out Indians and bison in their relentless drive to "conquer the west." Like Buffalo Bill, the *Sierra* was a terrorist practicing genocide, bound by no written or moral law. In one three-year period the *Sierra* slaughtered 1,676 whales, selling the meat to Japan for 138,000 yen per metric ton. At a time of increasing international pressure to halt all whaling, the *Sierra* operated with impunity toward the unenforceable strictures and quotas established by the International Whaling Commission (IWC).[3] Watson felt that such lawlessness could be stopped only by taking the fight to the high seas. Only months before, he had convinced Cleveland Amory, a philanthropist and president of the Fund for Animals, to put up the money for a ship that

Eco-Warriors: Understanding the Radical Environmental Movement, by Rik Scarce (Chicago: The Noble Press, 1990), pp. 97–100. Reprinted by permission of the author.

Watson re-christened the *Sea Shepherd*. Amory had an abiding love for all animals and a strong urge to protect them through whatever non-violent means were available. As he wrote in the introduction to Watson's book, *Sea Shepherd*, "I wanted a tough team able to take on—head-on, if need be—the major cruelties to which so many animals are regularly and ruthlessly subjected."[4] In Watson, Amory saw an ideal warrior for the animals of the sea. During a June 1979 meeting, Amory asked his captain to take the ship to the Aleutians and block a fur seal kill there. But the barrel-chested, baby-faced, blunt-spoken Watson felt the *Sierra* gnawing at his bones. His ship was ready to go. "Give me a month," Watson pleaded with his benefactor. He wanted to search out the *Sierra* and send it to the depths to avenge the gentle leviathans who had met their end at the point of the pirate's harpoon. Amory relented, and the desperate chase soon was on.[5]

The *Sea Shepherd* began life in 1960 as a 779-ton, 206-foot-long deep-water trawler, a cod fishing ship that Watson purchased with Amory's money in December 1978 for $120,000. Its time on the ocean ended barely a year later at the bottom of the harbor at Leixoes, Portugal, scuttled by order of its own Captain Watson to avoid having it turned over to the pirate whalers. But that is the denouement to the hunt for the *Sierra*. The story begins on July 15, 1978, when Watson discovered the whaling vessel off the Portuguese coast. The twenty-eight-year-old commander found his adversary after a cross-ocean hunt lasting twelve days, guided only by some vague information that the *Sierra* would be somewhere off the Iberian peninsula. The excitement over the imminent end of the chase must have been tremendous, but the ships were too far from shore for Watson to act. His strict code of non-violence prevented him from smashing into his antagonist then and there, on a cold and frothy sea far from port, risking the lives of the *Sierra*'s crew and his own. Watson figured he would soon enough have his opportunity.

The next day that chance came, but was nearly lost. After following the outlaw ship all night as it slowly made for shore, Watson was tricked into port by the Portuguese authorities around noon. They had him believe that the *Sierra* was heading in as well, when in reality it was soon to leave. Watson, more determined than ever to get the pirates,

dashed the *Sea Shepherd* out of the harbor without permission. He had been docked for one hour, which was long enough to discharge nearly all of his twenty-person crew—only two chose to stand with him and risk the uncertain punishment that would befall them. Then it was onward after the *Sierra*.

Watson sailed out of the mouth of the port to find the pirate whaler sitting languidly at anchor a quarter-mile from shore, biding its time until the appointed hour to steam out and meet a Japanese cargo ship into which it would disgorge its whale flesh. Watson wasted no time in heading straight for the *Sierra*, whose crew was sunbathing on deck. On the first attack he used the *Sea Shepherd*'s concrete-reinforced bow to smash into the *Sierra*'s leading edge in the hope of severing the pendent harpoon platform; the collision left major damage to the whaler but failed to take off the executioner's stand. Watson banked his ship hard and took aim amidships of the *Sierra*. Its crew ran about frantically. They must have been trying to start the engines, but no wake could be seen. Sitting there idle, the *Sierra* was an easy target. "When you ram another ship and you can control it in calm waters," Watson explains, "it's not like two cars hitting each other. You've got 750 tons of metal hitting 680 tons of metal. That's a lot of steel to absorb the shock of the impact."[6] Gentle though it might have felt, the second charge was devastating, the combination of speed and mass as powerful as a bomb. The collision ripped open a hole in the hull six feet wide by eight feet long. Whale meat could be seen hanging inside. As Watson turned to administer the *coup de gras*, his adversary finally got underway and limped the short distance to the harbor.

Suddenly, it was Watson's turn to play the outlaw. He and his tiny crew ran the *Sea Shepherd* at full speed up the coast in hopes of reaching Spanish territorial waters, thereby avoiding any penalties which the Portuguese might levy. Their desperate dash ended eight miles short of the mark, when a Portuguese naval destroyer demanded that Watson turn his ship around or be fired upon. The *Sea Shepherd* was escorted back to Leixoes and docked at the far end of the harbor from the critically damaged, listing *Sierra*.

The *Sea Shepherd* sat there for four and a half months while the Portuguese debated what to do. Maritime law dictated that the ship, not the captain or the crew, was to blame for certain high seas crimes, so Watson was released. He spent much of his time on television and radio shows telling of his exploit. Then in December, Watson was finally given the terms, or term, under which the *Sea Shepherd* would be returned to him: pay $750,000 in damages and fines. Refusal to pay would mean the *Sea Shepherd* would be forfeited to the *Sierra*'s owners. Watson flew to Portugal to inspect his ship and found that many vital components had been stripped by thieves, including the port police, who had stolen the ship's radio.

Even if he had been able to raise three-quarters of a million dollars to get his $120,000 ship back, the repair expenses would be enormous. Giving up the ship to the whalers was out of the question. Watson's way was clear. As close to heartbroken as the tough merchant marine could ever be, Watson realized that his only choice was to scuttle his pride and joy, sending it to the bottom of the harbor and then running like hell.

Amidst the pandemonium of New Year's Eve, *Sea Shepherd* Chief Engineer Peter Woof crept aboard the vessel at night, stealing into the engine room. There he opened a valve that, when closed, kept sea water from entering the engine. Brine gushed into the ship. Woof escaped from the vessel before it sank. He immediately left the country; Watson, however, wanted one last look at his ves-

sel. The day after the scuttling, he drove by the port. Police were everywhere; it was obvious the job was well-done. Watson avoided extraordinary security measures by the incensed Portuguese authorities and escaped to London.[7]

On February 6, 1980, a bomb tore open the hull of the fully-refitted *Sierra* as it sat in Lisbon's harbor, ready to sail and kill once more. It sank in 10 minutes. An anonymous caller to United Press International said, "The *Sierra* will kill no more whales! We did it for the *Sea Shepherd*." Within weeks, two of Spain's five whalers were sunk by the same three saboteurs who did-in the *Sierra*. Watson was an ocean away at the time of all three bombings. No one was injured, and the perpetrators were never caught.[8] . . .

Notes

1. Paul Watson, *Sea Shepherd* (New York: W. W. Norton, 1982), p. 70.
2. Interview with Paul Watson, Poulsbo, Washington, November 26, 1989.
3. Watson, *Sea Shepherd*, pp. 214–215.
4. Ibid., p. 11.
5. Ibid., p. 212.
6. Watson interview.
7. Watson, *Sea Shepherd*, pp. 225–251.
8. Ibid., p. 250.

Ecosabotage and Civil Disobedience

Michael Martin

Introduction

The recent arrest by the FBI of Dave Foreman, founder of the radical environmental group Earth First!, for conspiracy to sabotage two nuclear power plants and a facility that manufactures triggers for nuclear bombs[1] raises anew the issue of the morality of breaking the law for ethical purposes. In this paper I explore a number of analytic and moral questions connected with what has been called ecosabotage: sabotage for the purpose of ecological protection. What is ecosabotage? Is it a form of civil disobedience? Can it be morally justi-

fied? Have advocates of ecosabotage such as Foreman in fact provided an ethically acceptable justification for what they sometimes advocate? Although ecosabotage has received wide coverage in popular magazines[2] and other periodicals,[3] these important and difficult questions have been in large part neglected by environmental ethicists.[4]

Ecosabotage Defined

Sabotage in the name of environmental protection not only has occurred in real life but has also

Environmental Ethics, Vol. 12, No. 4 (Winter 1990), 291–310. Reprinted by permission of the author and publisher.

been detailed in field guides and in fiction. In their book, *Ecodefense: A Field Guide to Monkey Wrenching,* Dave Foreman and Bill Haywood describe a number of techniques that can be used to stop, or at least slow down, the destruction of the environment by lumber companies, land developers, and similar organizations.[5] These include how to spike trees with nails in order to break saw blades, use cutting torches on power lines, puncture tires of road construction equipment, disable bulldozers, and burn billboards. Edward Abbey's novel, *The Monkey Wrench Gang,* which influenced the leaders of Earth First!,[6] tells the story of a small group of environmental activists in the southwestern United States who, among other things, blow up railroad bridges, destroy construction machinery, and pull up survey stakes to frustrate land development and road construction.[7] Field guides and fictional accounts aside, environmental activists such as Margaret K. Millet, Mark L. Davis, and Marc A. Baker have reportedly actually tried to cut down a tower that carries power to pump water to the Central Arizona Project, a massive irrigation canal. Earth First! cofounder Howie Wolke is reported to have spent six months in jail for pulling up survey stakes that marked a road into a site where an oil well was being drilled,[8] Paul Watson, leader of the radical environment group the Sea Shepherds has claimed responsibility for sinking two of Iceland's four whaling ships by opening key valves in the ships,[9] and the Sea Shepherds also reportedly sank two Spanish whalers and one Cypriot whaling ship by attaching mines to the hulls.[10]

Can this great variety of acts of ecosabotage be subsumed under one definition? Perhaps, but the construction of such a definition is not easy. I approach the analytic task by first considering some of the elements that such a definition must include. First, any definition of ecosabotage must distinguish it from legal protests concerning environmental issues. Clearly this cannot be done merely in terms of the goals of the two kinds of activities, since an act of ecosabotage and a lawful ecological demonstration can have the same long-range goal, viz., the protection of the environment. Second, a definition of ecosabotage must distinguish it from sabotage for nonecological purposes, for example, wartime sabotage. This distinction cannot be made on purely behavioral grounds, since externally considered, some wartime sabotage might be indistinguishable from ecosabotage. For example, sabotaging a nuclear munitions plant might be either an act of wartime sabotage or an act of ecosabotage depending on what the act is supposed to achieve. Third, the definition must not restrict ecosabotage to the destruction of property. Even some acts of wartime sabotage do not involve this, for example, the removal of essential parts of machinery in a munitions factory. In ecosabotage, the removal of survey stakes from road construction sites might more appropriately be called obstruction rather than destruction.[11] Fourth, ecosabotage should be distinguished from the typical acts of civil disobedience that have been adapted by environmental organizations such as Greenpeace.[12] Fifth, ecosabotage must be distinguished from vandalism, the destruction of property or other mischief that is motivated by malice or spite.

It is also important to recognize that an adequate definition of ecosabotage must be as ethically neutral as possible—that is, the moral justification of ecosabotage must not be built into its definition. In other words, the question of what ecosabotage *means* must be separated as much as possible from the question of whether ecosabotage is *morally justified.* To be sure, these two questions are difficult to separate when, for example, it is unclear whether some criteria are relevant to the definitional or the moral issues. For example, it could be argued that part of the definition of ecosabotage is that it does not aim at harming human beings or other animal forms. On the other hand, it could be maintained that this is not part of the definition of ecosabotage and that an act of ecosabotage that aims at harming human or animal forms is simply not morally justified. An adequate definition of ecosabotage must decide such issues in a principled way.

Taking these elements into account, I suggest the following definition:

> Person *P*'s act *A* is an act of ecosabotage iff (if and only if) (1) in doing *A, P* has as *P*'s aim to stop, frustrate, or slow down some process or act that *P* believes will harm or damage the environment, (2) *P*'s act *A* is motivated by a sense of religious or moral concern, (3) *A* is illegal, and (4) *A* is not a public act.

Condition (1) seems essential if ecosabotage is to be distinguished from other forms of sabotage. Condition (2) also appears essential because it distinguishes ecosabotage from vandalism. Foreman, for example, argues that destroying the technology that is polluting the Earth is a moral responsibility. He also goes so far as to claim that "it's a form of worship toward the Earth. It's really a very spiritual thing to go out and do."[13] These remarks suggest that ecosaboteurs can be motivated by religious as well as moral considerations. Thus, we need not claim that an act of ecosabotage *must* be morally motivated, for it can be religiously inspired. Condition (3) also seems essential for any definition of ecosabotage. Without it, a private act of prayer aimed at petitioning the deity to stop the destruction of the environment would be an act of ecosabotage because such an act would otherwise meet conditions (1), (2), and (4). Condition (4) is the most controversial condition in the definition, for it is certainly not clear that it needs to be part of the definition and the vagueness of ordinary language makes it uncertain whether it should be a necessary condition for the correct application of the term.[14] However, I see no other way to distinguish a typical act of civil disobedience used by environmental activists, for example, placing one's body in front of road construction equipment, from an act of ecosabotage, such as pulling up survey stakes. As I have already noted, the crucial difference between these two acts is not that the latter destroys property and the former does not. The difference can best be seen when one compares the typical acts of civil disobedience practiced by organizations such as Greenpeace and the acts of ecosabotage that are allegedly practiced by members of Earth First!.[15] In a typical Greenpeace action, arrests are expected. Indeed, Greenpeace activists may want to be arrested as a way of advertising their cause. This is not to say that Greenpeace always publicizes its plans in advance. Surprise is essential for some of its actions. Nevertheless, once an action is completed—once the entrance to the incinerator is blocked or the whalers are frustrated—Greenpeace activists do not try to escape; they stay and accept their arrest, hoping that it will be reported in the media. On the other hand, an act of ecosabotage is done in secret. Even when ecosaboteurs do not destroy property but merely disturb operations, they do not intend to be caught. Indeed, part of Foreman and Haywood's field guide to monkey wrenching is devoted to instructing potential ecosaboteurs on how not to get arrested.[16] This is not to say that if ecosaboteurs are caught, they will not

use their own arrests to their own advantage in the media, but getting caught is not typically part of their plan.

This definition is value neutral in the sense that it does not assume that act A is either religiously or morally justified or unjustified. Although it can be assumed that the ecosaboteur *believes* that his or her act is justified either morally or religiously, the ecosaboteur could be mistaken. Moreover, the definition is neutral about whether A is effective or not in stopping, frustrating, or slowing down some process that is believed to be damaging the environment. The ecosaboteur believes that the act will be effective, but, again, he or she could be mistaken.

I have chosen not to include the condition that P believes that A will not injure any human beings or living things in the *definition* of ecosabotage. To be sure, ecosaboteurs typically maintain that they intend no such injury. Foreman is reported to have said that his philosophy "is nonviolent because it is directed toward inanimate machinery."[17] Paul Watson, the leader of the Sea Shepherds, waited until after the crew had left to sink the Icelandic whaling ships. Doc Sarvis, the philosophical spokesperson for "the monkey wrench gang" in Abbey's novel, is also opposed to violence against human beings. However, it is doubtful that this condition should be part of the definition of ecosabotage. Consider the analogous case of wartime sabotage. A worker who, in order to help the enemy, intentionally caused damage to a munitions plant although he or she knew other workers would be injured, would not for that reason alone have failed to perform an act of sabotage. On analogy with this example, I am inclined to maintain that although considerations of intentional noninjury to human beings or other animals are relevant in determining the morality of an act of ecosabotage, they are irrelevant when we are simply considering whether some act is or is not one of ecosabotage.

Ecosabotage and Civil Disobedience

Is ecosabotage as defined above a type of civil disobedience? On the standard account of civil disobedience, the answer seems to be "No." Consider these typical definitions of civil disobedience taken from discussions of the topic by leading contemporary philosophical theorists.[18] According to Hugo Bedau, an act A is an act of civil disobedience iff A is illegal, done publicly, nonviolently and conscientiously with the intent to frustrate (one of) the laws, policies or decisions of the government.[19] According to Jeffrie Murphy, an act A is an act of civil disobedience iff (i) there is some law L according to which A is illegal, (ii) L is believed by the agent to be immoral or unconstitutional or irreligious or ideologically objectionable, and (iii) this belief motivates or explains A.[20] According to Christian Bay, an act is an act of civil disobedience iff A is an act or process of public defiance of a law or policy enforced by established government authorities insofar as the action is premeditated, understood by the actor(s) to be illegal or contested legally, carried out and persisted in for limited public ends and by way of carefully chosen and limited means.[21] Finally, according to Carl Cohen, an act A is an act of civil disobedience iff A is an act of protest, deliberately unlawful, and conscientiously and publicly performed.[22]

On three of these definitions, an act of ecosabotage is clearly not an act of civil disobedience. For Bedau, Bay, and Cohen, it is a necessary condition of civil disobedience that it be publicly performed. Ecosabotage, however, by the definition proposed above is not publicly performed. In addition, Bedau's definition rules out many acts of ecosabotage as acts of civil disobedience by requiring that an act of civil disobedience be nonviolent. Furthermore, Bedau's and Bay's definitions rule out many acts of ecosabotage as acts of civil disobedience because acts of ecosabotage are often aimed at frustrating the actions or policies of private companies and not the government.

Murphy's definition does not seem to apply to the typical act of ecosabotage for a different reason. An ecosaboteur who breaks some law L by destroying construction equipment probably does not object on either moral or constitutional or religious grounds to the law L insofar as it states that it is illegal to knowingly destroy someone else's property. What he or she objects to is the use to which the construction equipment is being put. Murphy, however, in a footnote qualifies his definition by saying that "the agent may have no objection to L per se but may violate L because he views it as symbolic for or instrumentally involved with some

other law L' . . . to which he does object. In my view, such a person (Thoreau, for example) is also to be regarded as civilly disobedient."[23] Taken by itself this seems to allow a typical act of ecosabotage to be an act of civil disobedience because, for example, the ecosaboteur objects to some law L' that allows the timber company to clear-cut the forest. Law L, the law that the ecosaboteur is breaking, is in some sense "instrumentally involved with L'." However, later on in the same footnote Murphy adds: "What is most important is that motives of this sort be distinguished from the typical criminal motive: self-interest. We do not think of a criminal act as a *public* act of *protest:* but these features *do* typically characterize acts of civil disobedience."[24] If we take this qualification seriously, then ecosabotage is not civil disobedience for it is certainly not a *public* act of protest. In the end, then, these four definitions of civil disobedience exclude ecosabotage because of the requirement that acts of civil disobedience must be done publicly.

Some general category is surely needed that includes both morally and religiously motivated illegal acts whether they are done publicly or not. One could accomplish this by expanding the concept of civil disobedience to include nonpublic acts. This, in fact, is the approach taken by Howard Zinn when he defines an act of civil disobedience "broadly" as a deliberate violation of the law for a vital social purpose.[25] Interestingly enough, from the standpoint of ordinary usage, Zinn's definition seems to be more correct than the others so far considered. Certainly people who ran the underground railroad before the Civil War were said to have engaged in acts of civil disobedience, but these acts were not publicly performed.[26] In accordance with Zinn's definition, an act of ecosabotage *could* be an act of civil disobedience on the grounds that by definition ecosaboteurs are motivated by a sense of religious or moral duty and that at least some ecosaboteurs do deliberately violate the law for a vital social, i.e., moral, purpose. However, it is unclear if all acts of ecosabotage fall under Zinn's definition. Would an ecosaboteur who pulled up survey stakes or destroyed construction equipment because of a mystical-religious feeling of unity with nature be described as breaking the law for a vital *social* purpose?

I suggest taking a different approach. Let us allow that civil disobedience must be public, or at least that it must be done for a social purpose, and introduce the concept of *conscientious wrongdoing* to cover either public *or* nonpublic law breaking for either religious *or* moral purposes. In this context, we can then specify that an act *A* is an act of conscientious wrongdoing iff it is an act of breaking a law for some moral or religious purpose. In this way, acts of civil disobedience on both the standard account and Zinn's expanded version as well as acts of ecosabotage can be considered special cases of conscientious wrongdoing.

Can Ecosabotage Be Given a Consequentialist Justification?

As I have just shown, without an expanded analysis of civil disobedience, ecosabotage cannot be viewed as a form of civil disobedience. Nevertheless, the civil disobedience literature can still provide insight into ecosabotage's possible justification. Most theorists of civil disobedience maintain that because acts of civil disobedience break the law and conflict with accepted modes of social conduct, they require some special justification to overcome what seems to be their prima facie wrongness. The same could be said about acts of ecosabotage.

If one follows this line of argument, the burden of justification is clearly on the civil disobedient person or the ecosaboteur. This burden is thought to be especially difficult to meet in a democracy because when laws are made by the people's representatives, they seem to have a legitimate claim to the obedience of all citizens. Yet this claim is never absolute. Democratic processes do not work perfectly: unjust and evil laws can be enacted; short-sighted and destructive policies can be pursued; it can either be impossible or can take too much time to change laws by lawful means. Thus, concerned citizens may sometimes legitimately entertain illegal means of changing the status quo and educating and arousing their fellow citizens. Before they become civil disobedients or ecosaboteurs, however, they need to have a clear rational justification for their action.[27]

Carl Cohen, in his comprehensive study of civil disobedience, reports that historically there have been two basic ways to justify civil disobedience: the appeal to higher law and the appeal to teleological or consequentialist considerations.[28]

Although both approaches are relevant to the justification of ecosabotage, I focus on the consequentialist justification in detail in this essay.[29] This emphasis is in no way intended to suggest, however, that there are no limits to consequentialist justification.[30]

As Cohen maintains, a consequentialist justification need not be restricted to a specific calculus of goods or evils:

> It simply indicates that the justification will rely upon some intelligent weighing of consequences of the disobedient act. The protester here argues, in effect, that his particular disobedience of a particular law, at a particular time, under given circumstances, . . . is likely to lead in the long run to a better or more just society than would his compliance, under those circumstances, with the law in question.[31]

According to Cohen, the disobedient person appeals to two sorts of factors to justify his or her actions: moral principles that specify the goal of the disobedient act and factual considerations that specify the means to achieving this goal. The goals of the disobedient act, Cohen argues, are usually not in question but are shared by the vast majority of the citizens of the community. In the rare cases that they are not in harmony with the community, their justification "is almost certain to fail."[32] On the other hand, the means of achieving the goals are controversial and their justification involves a delicate and often inconclusive balancing of conflicting considerations. The person who is contemplating a disobedient act must consider the *background* of the case at hand and ask questions such as: "How serious is the injustice whose remedy is the aim of disobedient protest? How pressing is the need for that remedy? . . . Have extraordinary but lawful means—assemblies of protests, letter-writing campaigns, etc.—been given full trial?"[33] The potentially disobedient person must also consider the *negative* effects of the disobedience and ask questions such as:

> How great is the expense incurred by the community as a consequence of the disobedience? . . . Is any violence entailed or threatened by the disobedient act? And if so, to property or to persons? . . . Has a bad example been set, a spirit of defiance or hooliganism been encouraged? Has respect for law been decreased in

the community, or the fundamental order to society disturbed?[34]

Finally, the potential disobedient must estimate the *positive* results from the contemplated action and ask questions such as: how much influence will the disobedient act have in accomplishing change? Will it bring significant pressure to bear on legislatures that can bring about change? Can it attract public attention to some wrong or evil? Will the public put pressure on lawmakers? Or will the action of the disobedient be misunderstood and cause resentment? Will there be a backlash against the protesters?

These considerations are surely relevant to any consequentialist justification of acts of ecosabotage. Further, there seems to be no reason why a successful justification could not be given for at least some such acts. On a general level, the environmental goal of the public seems to be very similar to the goal of the ecosaboteurs: saving the environment from destruction and pollution. Recent polls indicate that the public is extremely concerned about environmental problems and is willing to go far in affording it protection.[35] Whether the more specific goals of radical environmental groups would be approved by the public is less clear; for example, Earth First!'s goal of saving the grizzly bears or the Sea Shepherds' goal of saving the whales. Nevertheless, it is not implausible to suppose that most people are sympathetic with these specific goals to some degree.

Whether members of environmental groups who use ecosabotage can justify their means in relation to the goal of saving the environment is, of course, the crucial issue. Unless strong general arguments can be raised against *any* use of ecosabotage, the justification of each proposed act of ecosabotage must be decided individually. A consideration of some of the most obvious general arguments against ecosabotage suggests that such arguments are in fact weak and cannot therefore be used to undermine all ecosabotage.

First, it may be objected that ecosabotage is beyond the pale of moral legitimacy because it involves violence. However, since there is no plausible general argument against the use of violence in civil disobedience, it hardly seems likely that ecosabotage can be faulted simply on this ground. Even Thoreau[36] and Gandhi[37] allowed that violence is sometimes an appropriate action and history

points to cases in which violence in civil disobedience has had a beneficial effect. As Zinn points out:

> Violent labor struggles of the 1930's brought significant gains for labor. Not until Negro demonstrations resulted in violence did the national government begin to work seriously on civil rights legislation. No public statement on race relations has had as much impact as the Kerner Commission report, the direct result of outbreaks of violence in the ghettos.[38]

In any case, the distinction between violence against people and violence against property that both Zinn[39] and Cohen[40] stress in the context of justifying civil disobedience is relevant here. Violence directed against property is much less difficult to justify than violence against people.[41] Zinn has emphasized that violence in the context of civil disobedience should "be guarded, limited, aimed carefully at the source of injustice."[42] Advocates of ecosabotage in Earth First! say that violence should be directed only against property: they advocate destroying only equipment and facilities that are themselves used to destroy, deface, and pollute the environment.[43] Ecosaboteurs in the Sea Shepherds also attempt to limit and focus their violence: they wreck equipment that is used to destroy whales.

A second possible objection to ecosabotage is that it erodes respect for the law, thus deteriorating the social fabric of civilized society. However, as a general argument against ecosabotage, this has no greater weight than it does against traditional civil disobedience. As Cohen notes, the allegation that civil disobedience erodes the social fabric is "essentially factual, not philosophical, but the facts are exceedingly complex and difficult to determine accurately. . . . The evidence available from the American experience of the 1950s and 1960s does not seem to support the allegation."[44] The same counterargument applies to ecosabotage. To be sure, there is a great amount of disrespect for the law in our country and in the world: murder, massacre, terrorism, rape, governmental corruption, and white collar crimes are rife. But it is pure conjecture to suppose that ecosabotage with its carefully circumscribed scope and targets has contributed or will significantly contribute to this disrespect.

In any case, one might argue that respect for the law is not the highest value. As Cohen points out: "It is possible, of course, that the wrong against which the civil disobedient protests is more serious than the alleged deleterious consequence to the social fabric."[45] Foreman and others would surely argue that what they are fighting for is more important than respect for the law. Indeed, they might maintain that respect for the law will be of little importance in a world with polluted air and water, devoid of natural wildernesses, and depleted of most of its natural variety. This value assessment is controversial, but it is not obviously wrong or absurd.

One important difference between civil disobedience and ecosabotage provides the basis for another objection. It could be argued that although civil disobedients disobey the law on one level, they show respect for it on another level by acting publicly—thus inviting arrest—and by accepting the result of the punishment. Ecosaboteurs, on the other hand, show their contempt for the law by acting secretly, thus attempting to avoid arrest and punishment. Although the standard accounts of civil disobedience that require publicly performed acts would not allow secret acts to be acts of civil disobedience, these same accounts provide a rationale for such secret acts. As Cohen argues in defense of the operation that helped runaway slaves escape to Canada, "To continue this practice in the interests of other, later runaways, it was essential for the managers of the underground railways to conceal their repeated violations of the fugitive slave laws. Concealment in such cases is a pressing tactical need, stemming from concern for the welfare of specific human beings, not from shame or remorse for the disobedient conduct."[46] Surely the same sort of argument could be used to defend ecosaboteurs: to continue protecting the environment, they must conceal their identity.[47] Concealment in such cases is a pressing tactical need, stemming from concern for the welfare of the environment, not from shame or remorse for unlawful conduct. There is no a priori reason to suppose that ecosaboteurs have less personal integrity than the managers of the underground railroad or that they consider their cause less morally significant than the managers of the underground railway considered theirs.

There are, of course, other general arguments that can be used against ecosabotage, but because they parallel the general ones that have been raised

against civil disobedience and can be answered in a similar way, we need not consider them here.[48]

Have Advocates of Ecosabotage Successfully Justified Ecosabotage?

One might reasonably conclude from the above that although ecosabotage can be morally justified on consequentialist grounds in some contexts and although there are no general arguments standing in the way of such justification, the case for particular acts of ecosabotage has yet to be made. Although it is beyond the scope of this paper to provide such a justification, I consider critically how in fact advocates of ecosabotage such as Foreman have attempted to justify ecosabotage. In some cases where there is a gap in the justification, I fill in what I believe is a reasonable extrapolation or reconstruction of what a rational ecosaboteur might say. I show that the rationales given by advocates of ecosabotage follow in outline the sort of argument that, according to Cohen, a consequentialist justification of civil disobedience should take.

In a consequentialist justification, the moral goals of the civil disobedient are usually shared by the community. When they are not, they are likely to fail to persuade the community and not succeed politically. I have argued above that the general goals of ecosabotage are probably shared by most members of the community and that even the particular ones may be. However, Foreman explicitly interprets these goals in a nonanthropocentric way. Advocating the environmental philosophy of deep ecology, he argues:

> Deep ecology says that *every* living thing in the ecosystem has intrinsic worth and a nature-given right to be there. The grizzly bear, for example, has a right to exist for its *own* sake—not just for material or entertainment value to human beings. Wilderness has a right to exist for its *own* sake, and for the sake of the diversity of life-forms it shelters; we shouldn't have to justify the existence of the wilderness area by saying, "Well, it protects the watershed, and it's a nice place to backpack and hunt, and it's pretty. . . ." Furthermore, deep ecology goes beyond the individual and says that it's the *species* that's

important. And more important yet is the *community of species* that makes up a given biosystem. And ultimately, our concern should be with the community of *communities*—the ecosystem.[49]

Whether Foreman's biocentrism and holism is philosophically justified, we cannot decide here.[50] But what does seem likely is that these points of view are not widely shared by the vast majority of the moral community and would be considered by the majority of the community to be rather eccentric. Given his biocentric and holistic interpretation of the goals of Earth First!, therefore, the means as well as the goals of the organization become controversial. As Cohen points out: "Even if the community is wrong [about the goals], and the eccentrics right, deliberate disobedient pursuit of their special objectives, as long as they are in the moral minority, is not likely to advance the protesters' goals and not likely to be defensible on utilitarian grounds."[51] However, the ecosaboteur need not pursue what the moral community will perceive as eccentric goals. There are good anthropocentric reasons why natural diversity should be preserved,[52] why tropical forest should be safeguarded,[53] why whales should be saved,[54] and so on.

According to Cohen, a civil disobedient must consider the background of the case at hand and evaluate both the importance of the goals and whether legal means have been given a fair trial. Foreman's statement certainly suggests that he advocates deliberating on the background of acts of ecosabotage very carefully and has considered the importance of the goals of ecosabotage and legal alternatives to it. Thus, he maintains:

> Species are going under every day. Old-growth forests are disappearing. Overgrazing continues to ruin our western public lands. Off-road vehicles are cutting up the countryside everywhere. Poisons are continually and increasingly being injected into the environment. Rain forests are being clear-cut. In short, the environment is *losing* . . . everywhere. And to try to fight such an essential battle with less than every weapon we have available to us is foolish and, in the long run, suicidal.[55]

One need not just take Foreman's word for this bleak picture of environmental devastation. Many environmentalists have painted a similar picture, albeit in more scholarly and less colorful tones.[56]

But are there not legal means of stopping the destruction? Foreman at one time certainly thought there were. At the beginning of his environmental career he was a Washington lobbyist for the conventional environmental group, the Wilderness Society. However, personal experience quickly led to his disillusionment with the effectiveness of such groups in bringing about change and stopping the devastation.[57] Now as a member of Earth First! he has had personal experience of illegal actions being effective. He cites one example in which the legal action of the Sierra Club, a conventional environmental organization, failed to stop the destruction of a wilderness while Earth First!'s blockage of road construction by civil disobedience provided enough public awareness to be successful.[58]

One wonders, of course, if Foreman's experience is typical and if he has reported the facts accurately. Are there cases not mentioned by Foreman where legal means have succeeded and where illegal ones have not? To give a more adequate justification, one would have to consider in a systematic way a wider range of cases than Foreman considers in which legal and illegal methods have been tried in order to see their relative effectiveness. His anecdotal evidence at most makes a prima facie case that illegal means are sometimes more effective than legal means for affording environmental protection.[59]

Cohen also suggests that in any utilitarian justification of civil disobedience it is important to consider the possible negative consequences of one's action. Foreman gives evidence of having done this. When asked whether monkey wrenching—his term for ecosabotage—is counterproductive to the environmental cause and serves only to make environmentalists look bad, Foreman had this to say:

> On the surface, this argument seems worth considering. But the fact is, there's *already* an awful lot of monkey wrenching going on, and such a backlash hasn't come about. The Forest Service tries to keep it quiet, industry tries to keep it quiet, and I think that there has even been an effort in the media to downplay the extent and effectiveness of monkey wrenching in America today. . . . It's easy to be cowed into compromising and being overly moderate by

the charge that you are going to cause a negative reaction, going to tarnish the whole environmental movement. But in my opinion, the *argument itself* is a more fearsome anti-environmental weapon than any actual backlash could ever hope to be, because it keeps many of us from using all the tools we have available to slow down the destruction.[60]

Again independent evidence for a negative reaction should be sought. For example, do Greenpeace's door-to-door canvassers find it harder than a few years ago to obtain contributions because of the negative publicity occasioned by Earth First!? Do polls show that the public is becoming less sympathetic to environmental causes than it was before news of ecosabotage? Until evidence such as this is obtained we will not know if ecosabotage is having a negative impact. But Foreman is certainly justified in remaining skeptical about the purported negative impact until such evidence is produced.

Another possible negative consequence of ecosabotage is the unintentional injury to human beings. This problem is considered to be especially worrisome in the case of tree spiking. The main danger is that a saw blade can break and cause injury to the saw operator or to other people involved in the milling process. Ecosaboteurs respond to this problem in at least three different ways. Some tree spikers mark the trees they have spiked. For example, it is reported that after Mike Roselle, a member of Earth First!, spiked trees in Cathedral Forest, he painted a large *S* on them.[61] Thus, the recommended procedure is the notification of all parties who would be involved in cutting and milling trees. Consequently, only those who defied the warning were in jeopardy.[62] Other spikers, however, try to keep their spikes from being detected,[63] arguing that automation places most mill operators in control booths out of danger.[64] Although this might be true, it would not protect the sawyers cutting down the tree. The chain on the sawyer's chain saw can break upon hitting a spike, whip back into the sawyer and cause serious injuries. Moreover, some ecosaboteurs may argue that although they should take care not to injure people, "nothing is more dangerous to the long-term health of the people of this planet than the largescale destruction of the environment, and we have to stop that."[65] Consequently, any potential danger to the mill workers must be weighed against the greater danger to the world's population through environmental damage. Whether these answers are completely adequate is a difficult issue that we cannot pursue here.[66]

Cohen also maintains that a potential civil disobedient must estimate the positive results from the contemplated action. Does ecosabotage have positive results? For example, does it accomplish the goal of slowing or stopping the destruction of the environment? Foreman says:

> I'm convinced that monkey wrenching can be one of the most effective ways of protecting our few remaining wild places. If a sufficient number of sincere individuals and small groups around the country were to launch a serious campaign of strategic monkey wrenching—a totally defensive effort to halt the continued destruction of wilderness—it would in fact cause the retreat of industrial civilization from millions of acres of wildlands.
>
> For example, if a logging company knows that the trees are going to be consistently spiked with large nails—which plays hell with expensive saw blades at the mills—or that roads will be repeatedly blocked by having rocks dumped onto them, it quickly becomes impractical to try to maintain a profitable operation . . . so industrialization will retreat, leaving more land for the grizzly bear, for elk, for old-growth forests. . . .
>
> For these reasons, along with the fact that conventional efforts to save the environment *are not working,* I believe that monkey wrenching is probably the single most effective thing that can be done to save natural diversity.[67]

It is important to notice that in this quotation Foreman argues only that ecosabotage *could* work, not that it *has* worked or *will* work. However, Foreman does cite actual cases in which conventional civil disobedience methods, for example, blockage of a road by human beings, have been successful in getting public sympathy and attention. An ecosaboteur might argue by analogy: because conventional methods of civil disobedience have worked, it is likely that methods of ecosabotage will work as well. However, this analogy is far from perfect. Human beings blocking a road may make good press and create favorable publicity whereas tree spiking and rock dumping may not. Foreman's argument, in any case, is not based on the favorable publicity that monkey wrenching will cause. He maintains that ecosabotage will make it economically unfeasible for industry to continue to destroy the wilderness. In principle, this may be true. But does the use of ecosabotage in fact work in this way? Until evidence is cited of industrialization *actually* retreating, "leaving more land for the grizzly bear, for elk, for old-growth forest" as a result of tree spiking and other acts of ecosabotage, one should leave as an open question whether ecosabotage is justified in terms of Cohen's utilitarian model of justification.

It is also important to note that in the passage just cited Foreman argues that ecosabotage can be effective if "a sufficient number" of individuals and groups engage in it. If it is not successful now, Foreman might argue, it is because not enough people are trained and devoted ecosaboteurs. This may or may not be true, but a similar argument could be invoked by environmentalists who are opposed to ecosabotage. After all, it might be argued, if enough people marched on Washington, wrote letters to their government representatives, and performed public acts of conscientious wrongdoing, that is, engaged in conventional civil disobedience, it would "cause the retreat of industrial civilization from millions of acres of wildlands." The number of people needed is unclear. But it is plausible to suppose that public outrage would have to be extensive—as, for example, it ultimately was in relation to the Vietnam War—to have the sort of impact that Foreman desires.

Foreman argues simultaneously that ecosabotage is already widespread, but that its presence is being covered up by government, industry, and the media, that the environment is losing, and that a sufficient number of ecosaboteurs would save the environment. Although there is no inconsistency in these remarks, they do raise the question of just how much more ecosabotage would have to occur to prevent the environment from losing and to save the environment from destruction. In response, it might be argued that the number of ecosaboteurs that would be necessary for making a significant impact on environmental protection is several orders of magnitude less than the number of legal protesters, letter writers, public acts of civil disobedience, and so on that would produce the same impact. For this reason at least, it may be said, ecosabotage is to be recommended over conventional

strategies. On the other hand, the training and dedication that is involved in leading the life of an ecosaboteur would surely limit the number of potential candidates. Indeed, it is not clear that there are enough potential ecosaboteurs to make the difference that Foreman wants. Furthermore, in view of probable arrests it would seem that their ranks would have to be constantly replenished. There are then indirect considerations suggesting that ecosabotage is not likely in practice to have the impact that Foreman anticipates in theory.

Although Foreman does not cite evidence that ecosabotage actually works, a very recent article by C.M. does.[68] C.M. maintains that monkey wrenching is probably costing the government and industry about 20 to 25 million dollars per year in terms of damaged equipment, lost time, and legislative and law enforcement expenses. "This represents money industry is not able to use to deforest public lands, sink oil wells in the backcountry, invest in more destructive equipment, influence politicians with campaign contributions. . . ."[69] Even if corporations pass on these costs to their customers, according to C.M., monkey wrenching will cause the price of wood products to increase and thus indirectly decrease their consumption.

C.M. supplements this theoretical argument by citing actual cases in which ecosabotage has worked. For example, C.M. claims that there have been two cases in which the Forest Service withdrew timber sales after learning that trees were spiked. Moreover, C.M. argues that the firebombing of a $250,000 wood chipper in Hawaii, which "was grinding rainforest into fuel for sugar mills (without a permit and in violation of a court order)," left the company bankrupt. Finally, he or she argues that the controversial nature of ecosabotage has publicity value by taking "seemingly obscure environmental issues out the dark of scientific calculations into the limelight of individual passion and commitment."[70]

C.M.'s arguments for ecosabotage, nevertheless, are not enough to justify its use on utilitarian grounds. For this, C.M. would also have to show that typical acts of civil disobedience, that is, public acts of conscientious wrongdoing, were ineffective, for surely these are more desirable otherwise on utilitarian grounds than acts of ecosabotage if only because they are less likely to be interpreted as showing contempt for the law. In general, nonpublic acts of conscientious wrongdoing can be justified only when public nonviolent acts of conscientious wrongdoing cannot be utilized. Presumably there was no public way to help runaway slaves.[71] In the case of ecosabotage, however, public illegal means seem to be available. Road construction can be halted, for example, by lying down in front of the equipment, as well as by monkey wrenching the engines that run the equipment; trees can be protected by climbing them as well as by spiking. These nonviolent acts of conscientious wrongdoing also cost the government and industry a large amount of money, and have publicity value. In order to make their case, ecosaboteurs must show that public nonviolent acts of conscientious wrongdoing cannot work *and* that acts of ecosabotage can. To my knowledge they have not done so.[72]

Conclusion

In this paper I have defined ecosabotage and related this definition to several well-known analyses of civil disobedience. The comparison shows that ecosabotage cannot be assimilated to civil disobedience unless one expands the definition of the latter. The standard analyses of civil disobedience simply exclude it. I have suggested that ecosabotage and civil disobedience be considered special cases of the more general concept of conscientious wrongdoing. I have argued that although ecosabotage cannot be considered a form of civil disobedience on the standard analysis of this concept, the civil disobedience literature can provide important insights into the justification of ecosabotage.

Although other types of justification are possible, only a consequentialist one was considered in this paper. At present, there is no reason to suppose that some acts of ecosabotage could not be justified on consequentialist grounds, but I have concluded that advocates of ecosabotage such as Dave Foreman have not provided a full consequentialist justification of its use in concrete cases.

Evidence has been cited by C.M. showing that it does actually work in practice, but evidence is lacking that acts of civil disobedience would not be preferable. Nevertheless, Foreman and other advocates of ecosaboteurs such as C.M. have come further along in giving an adequate consequentialist justification of ecosabotage than is often realized

and they have also met many of the objections against its use.

Notes

1. Jim Robbins, "For Environmentalist, Illegal Acts Are Acts of Love," *Boston Globe,* 2 June 1989, p. 3.

2. See, for example, John J. Berger, "Tree Shakers," *Omni* 9 (1987): 20–22; Jamie Malanowski, "Monkey-Wrenching Around," *The Nation,* 2 May 1987, pp. 568–70; Joe Kane, "Mother Nature's Army," *Esquire,* February 1987, pp. 98–106.

3. J. A. Savage, "Radical Environmentalists: Sabotage in the Name of Ecology," *Business and Society Review* 56–59 (Summer 1986): 35–37; David Peterson, "The Plowboy Interview: Dave Foreman: No Compromise in Defense of Mother Earth," *Mother Earth News,* January–February 1985, pp. 16–22.

4. Two notable exceptions are Eugene C. Hargrove, "Ecological Sabotage: Pranks or Terrorism" *Environmental Ethics* 4 (1982): 291–92, and Roderick Nash, *The Rights of Nature: A History of Environmental Ethics* (Madison: University of Wisconsin Press, 1989), pp. 189–98.

5. Dave Foreman and Bill Haywood, eds., *Ecodefense: A Field Guide to Monkeywrenching,* 2d ed. (Tucson, AZ: A Ned Ludd Book, 1987).

6. See Kane, "Mother Nature's Army," p. 100.

7. Edward Abbey, *The Monkey Wrench Gang* (New York: Avon Books, 1975).

8. Robbins, "For Environmentalists, Illegal Acts Are Acts of Love," p. 3.

9. *New York Times,* 10 November 1986, p. A1; November 13, p. A21. Cited by Sissela Bok. *A Strategy for Peace* (New York: Pantheon Press, 1989), pp. 179–80, n. 12.

10. *New York Times,* 10 November 1986, p. A10. Cited by Bok, *A Strategy for Peace,* pp. 179–80, n. 12.

11. The point here is not whether the parts of the machinery or the survey stakes are property, but that no property needs to be destroyed. Of course, survey stakes might be destroyed by being burned, but this need not happen in order for an act of ecosabotage to occur. One might, of course, argue that a survey itself is a type of property, because it costs money to construct, and that pulling up the stakes destroys it, because it costs money to do the survey again. Nevertheless, in this broad sense of property, acts of civil disobediece, e.g., sit-ins and blockades, also destroy property in this sense because they cost money. On grounds of clarity I do not use property in this broad sense.

12. See Jan Knippers Black, "Greenpeace: The Ecologi-

cal Warriors," *USA Today,* November 1986, pp.
26–29; Michael Harwood, "Daredevils for the Environment," *New York Times Magazine,* 2 October 1988,
pp. 72–75.

13. Robbins, "For Environmentalist, Illegal Acts Are
Acts of Love," p. 3.

14. It may be objected that this definition has a mistaken implication, namely, that a public act cannot
be an act of ecosabotage. Suppose that as members
of the road construction crew watch in amazement
an environmental activist disables a bulldozer in order to prevent road construction and suppose this
act was motivated by a moral concern for the environment. Surely, it may be said, this would be a
case of ecosabotage. However, the concept of sabotage is vague and in some cases people's linguistic
intuitions may differ over what is a correct application of the term. I personally would hesitate to call
this an act of sabotage. At the very least, most
people would agree that it is a marginal or borderline case. My definition can be understood as an *explication* of the concept of ecosabotage–that is, as an
attempt to reconstruct the meaning of ecosabotage
by eliminating vagueness and thus exclude certain
borderline cases. For an account of explication see
Michael Martin, *Concepts of Science Education* (Glenview, IL: Scott, Foresman and Company, 1972),
pp. 77–79.

15. It should be noted that Earth First! does not *officially* advocate ecosabotage, but unlike Greenpeace
it does not reject it.

16. Foreman and Haywood, *Ecodefense,* chap. 9.

17. Robbins, "For Environmentalist, Illegal Acts Are
Acts of Love," p. 3; see also Dave Foreman, "Strate-
gic Monkeywrenching," in Foreman and Haywood,
Ecodefense, p. 14.

18. It should be noted that except for Bedau's, these
definitions do not include nonviolence as part of
the *meaning* of civil disobedience. However, one
should recall that nonviolent methods have been a
crucial part of civil disobedience practice from Gandhi to King. See Gene Sharp, *The Politics of Nonviolent Action,* part 3, *The Dynamics of Nonviolent Action*
(Boston: Porter Sargent Publisher, 1973), p. 608. Nevertheless, it is doubtful that nonviolent methods
should be built into the meaning of civil disobedience. One may imagine circumstances in which a
person honestly believes that he or she is justified
in using violence to make his or her protest effective. To say that such a person's act could not be an
act of civil disobedience seems arbitrary. See Carl
Cohen, *Civil Disobedience, Conscience, Tactics, and the
Law* (New York: Columbia University Press, 1971),
pp. 22–36.

19. H. A. Bedau, "On Civil Disobedience," *Journal of
Philosophy,* 53 (1961): 661. Quoted in Hugo Adam
Bedau, ed., *Civil Disobedience: Theory and Practice*
(New York: Pegasus, 1969), p. 218.

20. Jeffrie Murphy, "Introduction," *Civil Disobedience
and Violence,* ed. Jeffrie Murphy (Belmont, CA:
Wadsworth Publishing Co., 1971), p. 1.

21. Christian Bay, "Civil Disobedience: Prerequisite for
Democracy in Mass Sociey," in *Civil Disobedience
and Violence,* p. 76.

22. Cohen, *Civil Disobedience,* p. 39.

23. Murphy, "Introduction," *Civil Disobedience and Violence,* p. 1, n. 1.

24. Ibid.

25. Howard Zinn, "A Fallacy on Law and Order: That
Disobedience Must Be Absolutely Nonviolent," in
Civil Disobedience and Violence, p. 103.

26. See Cohen, *Civil Disobedience,* p. 18, who claims that
such examples constitute "a marginal category."

27. In order to apply this argument to ecosabotage in
the United States, certain assumptions must be
made that might well be challenged. For example,
it must be assumed that the laws that facilitate environmental destruction are democratically established and that it is a prima facie wrong to disobey
a democratically established law.

28. Cohen, *Civil Disobedience,* chap. 5.

29. According to Cohen, civil disobedients have often attempted to justify their conduct by appeals to a law
higher than human law. This higher law justification
has taken two major forms: an appeal to commands
of God that are revealed to human beings in the Bible
or other allegedly divinely inspired works or an appeal to nontheological higher laws that are discerned
by the light of natural reason. There are three serious
problems with both types of justifications. First, there
seems to be no objective way to decide what these
higher laws are. Second, principles of higher law are
usually stated vaguely and abstractly. Consequently,
it seems impossible to reach any objective decision
on how they apply to concrete cases. Third, such justification would at best justify *direct* civil disobedience, that is, the breaking of a law that is itself morally objectionable in terms of higher law principles.
But many acts of civil disobedience are indirect—
that is, the civil disobedient disobeys some law that
he or she has no objection to because the disobedience is a means to eliminate some serious injustice in
a related area. It could be argued that these same
problems are found in any attempt to justify ecosabotage by appeal to higher law principles. However, Cohen is mistaken in limiting nonconsequentialist justifications of civil disobedience to the higher

law tradition. A complete account of nonconsequentialist justifications of civil disobedience would also
have to take into account deontological theories of
justification ranging from Kant to Rawls.

30. For a review of some recent literature see Hugo
Bedau, "The Limits of Utilitarianism and Beyond,"
Ethics 95 (1985): 333–41. For a standard criticism of
utilitarianism see William Frankena, *Ethics*, 2d. ed.
(Englewood Cliffs, NJ: Prentice-Hall, 1973), chap. 3.
See also G. E. Moore, *Principa Ethica* (Cambridge:
Cambridge University Press, 1903), chap. 5, secs.
91–93.

31. Cohen, *Civil Disobedience*, p. 120. If Cohen means
that the goal must be shared by the vast majority to
be *morally* justified, he is mistaken. I do not interpret him in this way, however. It is correct, nevertheless, that unless the goal is shared by the majority,
the civil disobedient will not be practically successful—that is, the disobedient will have failed to justify his or her action to the community, and thus
the disobedient will not be politically effective.

32. Ibid., p. 123.

33. Ibid., p. 125.

34. Ibid., p. 125–26.

35. A recent national opinion survey indicates that
eighty percent of Americans agree with the following statement: "Protecting the environment is so important that requirements and standards cannot be
too high, and continuing environmental improvement must be made regardless of cost." Cited by
Martin and Kathleen Feldstein, "In Defense of Pollution," *Boston Globe*, 1 August 1989, p. 24.

36. Thoreau defended John Brown in "A Plea for Captain John Brown," delivered in Concord and Boston
a month before his execution. See Zinn, "A Fallacy
on Law and Order," p. 105.

37. Gandhi wrote in *Young India*, "No rules can tell us
how this disobedience may be done and by whom,
when and where, nor can they tell us which laws
foster untruth. It is only experience that can guide
us." And "I do believe that where there is only
a choice between cowardice and violence I would
advise violence." See Zinn, "A Fallacy on Law and
Order," p. 105.

38. Zinn, "A Fallacy on Law and Order," p. 110.

39. Ibid., p. 106.

40. Cohen, *Civil Disobedience*, p. 125.

41. Hargrove calls our attention to the fact that our sociey is "dedicated to the protection of property (including construction equipment and bridges)." See
Hargrove, "Ecological Sabotage," p. 291. Even so
there is a clear moral distinction to be drawn between violence against people and violence against
property.

42. Zinn, "A Fallacy on Law and Order," p. 109.

43. See Foreman, "Strategic Monkeywrenching," *Ecodefense*, p. 15.

44. Cohen, *Civil Disobedience*, pp. 150–51.

45. Ibid., p. 150.

46. Ibid., pp. 19–20. On Cohen's own definition the
managers of underground railways did not perform
acts of civil disobedience. Cohen (p. 39) defines
civil disobedience in terms of acts that are publicly
performed.

47. T. O. Hellenbach, "The Future of Monkeywrenching," in Foreman and Haywood, *Ecodefense*,
p. 19.

48. See Cohen, *Civil Disobedience*, chap. 6.

49. Peterson, "The Plowboy Interview," p. 18.

50. For a recent critique of these points of view see
Bryan G. Norton, *Why Preserve Natural Variety?*
(Princeton, NJ: Princeton University Press, 1989),
chaps. 8 and 9.

51. Cohen, *Civil Disobedience*, p. 123.

52. See Norton, *Why Preserve Natural Variety?* chap. 11.

53. Norman Myers, *The Primary Source: Tropical Forests
and Our Future* (New York: W. W. Norton & Company, 1985), chaps. 10–15.

54. Peter M. Dora, "Cetaceans: A Litany of Cain,"
People, Penguins, and Plastic Trees, ed. Donald
VanDeVeer and Christine Pierce (Belmont, CA:
Wadsworth Publishing Co. 1986), pp. 127–34.

55. Peterson, "The Plowboy Interview," p. 22; see also
Foreman, "Strategic Monkeywrenching," *Ecodefense*,
pp. 10–14.

56. See, for example, Lester R. Brown, Christopher Flavin, and Sandra Postel, "A World at Risk," *The State
of the World: 1989*, ed. L. Brown et al. (New York: W.
W. Norton & Company,1989), pp. 3–20; Myers, *The
Primary Source*, chaps. 5–9; Norman Myers, "The
Sinking Ark," *People, Penguins, and Plastic Trees*,
pp. 111–119.

57. Kane, "Mother Nature's Army," p. 100.

58. Peterson, "The Plowboy Interview," p. 19. It should
be noted that this was not an act of ecosabotage.

59. However, the independent evidence provided by
the effectiveness of the illegal actions of
Greenpeace in protecting whales and seals con-
firms Foreman's contention. See Black,
"Greenpeace: The Ecological Warriors," p. 29.

60. Peterson, "The Plowboy Interview," pp. 21–22.

61. Kane, "Mother Nature's Army," p. 98.

62. Savage, "Radical Environmentalists," p. 35.

63. See Foreman and Haywood, *Ecodefense*, pp. 24–51.

64. Malanowski, "Monkey-Wrenching Around," p. 569. But whether all employees of the mills, for example, the head rig offbearers who guide the logs, are safe is another question.

65. Ibid.

66. It should be noted that according to defenders of ecosabotage there has never been a documented case of anyone being seriously injured from its practice. See C.M., "An Appraisal of Monkeywrenching," Earth First!, 2 February 1990.

67. Peterson, "The Plowboy Interview," p. 21.

68. See C.M., "An Appraisal of Monkeywrenching." According to *Earth First!* C.M. "is a widely published

69. Ibid.

70. Ibid.

71. See Lester Rhodes, "Carrying on a Venerable Tradition," *Earth First!*, 2 February 1990. Rhodes compares ecosaboteurs to those who ran the underground railroad.

72. To be sure, Foreman has argued that monkey wrenching should not be used when there is a nonviolent civil disobedience action such as blockages taking place. But what must be shown is that blockages and the like cannot bring about the same results as ecosabotage. See Foreman, "Strategic Monkeywrenching," *Ecodefense*, p. 15.

writer and scholar whose career dictates anonymity."

Influencing Policy

Paul R. Ehrlich and Anne H. Ehrlich

When people consider what they can do personally to help extricate humanity from its predicament, actions like bicycling, recycling, and eating less meat inevitably come to mind. And well they might. After all, those are exactly the sorts of things recommended in the dozens of books published for Earth Day, such as *50 Simple Things You Can Do to Save The Earth*.[1] Yet few of those books mentioned the single most important direct action a person can take: limit oneself to one or two children. The reason for the latter should now be clear to you, and the other direct steps are abundantly covered in other sources. Instead of reviewing them, we will concentrate on what people can do to improve the human prospect *in*directly, by influencing the policies of large organizations, be they governments, political parties, corporations, environmental action groups, or the World Bank.

This indirect action is crucial, since the proportion of people who are motivated and able to take individual action is still too small to have much influence on such things as deforestation and society's use of fossil fuels—and those on the wrong side of the battle have both economic clout and social inertia on their side. What you can do to influence policy will naturally depend on your personal preferences and who you are. One of us (guess which) likes to work quietly to shape the policies of environmental organizations; the other prefers to cajole decision makers publicly to mend their ways. Some of our friends and colleagues do things as diverse as work within government or corporations as "moles" to effect change, picket the World Bank to speed its conversion from a world-wrecking to a world-saving organization, write letters to public officials telling them to shape up, or simply support good causes financially. Many of the actions that are available to all citizens are detailed in our earlier book, *The Population Explosion*.[2] There is no "right way" to work for a better future—*chacun à son goût*. Each action is a contribution to a growing global movement.

Who You Are

Obviously, who you are to a large degree shapes your opportunities. Not everyone can work within the government; an economist can potentially have more influence on government policy than a biologist can, if only because politicians are more accustomed to listening to the advice of economists, even though they may not always follow it.

Politicians themselves and corporate executives are often in especially powerful positions. But the good news is that *anyone* can have an important influence—concern, effort, and readiness to use an opportunity are all that are required.

Our discussion is divided somewhat according to opportunity—starting at home with a relatively small but potentially influential group, scientists. Scientists have a special responsibility to contribute to getting humanity out of its predicament. First of all, it was science that provided the mechanisms for the lowering of the death rate that was largely responsible for the post–World War II population explosion. High birth rates in poor countries would not have led to enormous population increases if antibiotics and the control of malarial mosquitoes with synthetic pesticides had not dramatically reduced mortality among the young. Even earlier, science provided improved agricultural techniques and basic public-health measures that accelerated population growth in what are now the rich countries. And science provided the other tools that made humanity a global force. Second, *Homo sapiens* is now far too abundant to be able to support itself with prescientific technologies. Neither hunting and gathering nor subsistence farming could supply enough food for even today's 5.4 billion people, let alone the additional 4 to 9 billion increase in population size to which humanity is committed. Great efforts by the scientific community will be required to provide an adequate (let alone abundant) living for 9 to 14 billion people. Since achieving even that is problematic, the scientific community as a whole should be mobilized to alert society to its peril.

So far, the performance of scientists in addressing the predicament has been far from sterling; and many, if not most, scientists remain essentially unengaged. In part, the lack of involvement probably arises from the narrow reductionist approach of most science, an approach that has been both a blessing and a curse of the entire scientific enterprise. Scientists are career-oriented, and their principal rewards come from focusing closely on interesting but limited questions: How do chemical reactions on surfaces affect the chemistry of air pollutants? How can a superhot plasma be contained in a magnetic bottle? How does genetic information interact with the environment to produce an individual organism? Indeed, many scientists were trained to bore in on the "truth," ignore the possible implications of their work for society, and stay out of politics.

This situation has been changing, inspired originally by physicists' moral qualms generated by the use of nuclear energy in weapons. Ecologists and evolutionists increasingly have been matching their research with action. The Ecological Society of America and the American Institute of Biological Sciences are both involved in trying to save biodiversity. Academic biologists at the Rocky Mountain Biological Laboratory raised $20,000 to help buy a critical tract of rainforest in Argentina that was in jeopardy and add it to a preserve. But the change is still not sufficiently fast and widespread. Curiously, even most molecular biologists seem, at the moment, relatively uninterested in doing their share to stem the tide of biotic destruction.

That the crucial problem of the decline of organic diversity is receiving so little attention from scientists is doubtless due to the low status of the sciences that deal with biodiversity and its functions: taxonomy (the science of classification), evolutionary biology, and ecology. The central importance of these disciplines, not just in biology but in all science,[3] has been eclipsed by rapid progress in more reductionist disciplines and in a gentlemanly consent to the current misallocation of resources devoted to research. For instance, funding for biomedical research, aimed largely at curing heart disease and cancer (and, most recently, AIDS), has been roughly 100 times that available to support ecosystem health. While substantial success in the direct battles with the diseases of adults could extend life expectancy a few years in rich nations, failure to protect ecosystem health could lead to a shortening of life expectancy by decades—to hundreds of millions or more dead children.[4]

So, if you are a scientist, one of the first things you might wish to do personally is to start lobbying your colleagues and the federal government for more support of the disciplines that deal most directly with environmental issues; and if at all possible, direct your own efforts toward them, even if you are not working in an area normally thought of as environmental. The problems are so broad and pervasive that almost any scientific discipline can be applied to them.[5]

Basically, the scientific community must organize itself to deal with the most pressing set of issues it has ever faced. Especially important are people trained in environmental sciences, and the changes in their professional lives are, or soon will be, more profound than those of other disciplines. Ecologists will find the demand for their expertise increasing rapidly, even though they now struggle to find funds to allow them to carry on research or find jobs where they can employ their knowledge and pass it on to students. Systematists (those who study the classification and evolutionary relationships of organisms) will have to change their entire approach to their discipline.[6] In large degree, they must switch away from attempting to describe organic diversity gradually and thoroughly, and working out the patterns in which it has evolved, toward finding ways instead to evaluate quickly the geography of diversity and to help conservation biologists save the objects of systematists' study. A second important task is to make extensive sample collections for preservation by methods (such as very-low-temperature freezers) that will make them available for detailed biochemical examination in the future.[7] Techniques of molecular systematics are shedding new light on the history of life,[8] and the creation of an artificial fossil record (in the sample collections) could clearly be a boon to future scientists working to salvage ecosystem services on a biotically impoverished planet.

Evolutionists also have their work cut out for them putting the human predicament into an appropriate biological and historical context for laypeople. They can help explain the legacy of genetic and cultural evolution that makes it so difficult for people to recognize the predicament and take action to solve it.[9] They can explain why repeated widespread use of synthetic pesticides and antibiotics is a losing tactic in the war against the organisms that eat or compete with our crops, carry disease to us, or cause disease. Evolutionists can make people aware that dreaded diseases such as AIDS are caused by organisms that themselves are products of evolution and will be subject to further evolution—perhaps to the great detriment of our species. Above all, evolutionists can explain how *Homo sapiens* fits into nearly 4 billion years of evolution. They can put people in touch with their own humanity and their place in the universe, and in the process stimulate thought on the purposes of the entire human enterprise and its relationship to our planet, to our only known companions in the universe, and to our descendants.

Great challenges also face individuals in management sciences. For example, much of the eco-

logical destruction in the world's forests, especially in rich nations such as the United States, Canada, Australia, and Sweden, can be laid at the feet of forestry scientists who have been narrowly trained and generally believe that the only good forests consist of even-aged stands of identical trees, preferably exotic pines or eucalyptus, planted in straight rows and harvested regularly as a crop. They are not taught that such stands are, by comparison to mixed stands of native trees, biological deserts that support little biodiversity and, as a result, may be difficult to maintain in the long run. Many apparently are even unaware of the benefits of old-growth stands, not just for the preservation of other organisms and recreational value, but as reservoirs of genetic diversity that may be essential to the long-term health of the local timbering industry. Things are gradually changing in the better forestry schools, but we cannot afford to wait until they are all modernized and an entire new generation of foresters is trained. Enlightened working foresters themselves must initiate many changes in policy, even at the risk of strong opposition from their conservative colleagues and the timber industries that in many nations have strong influence over forestry practices. Some are already doing it.

Entomologists (scientists who study insects, spiders, and mites) have a special double role to play in the human predicament. Since their domain covers the vast majority of biodiversity, their first task is to educate the public about the importance of the "little things that run the world."[10] The second role derives from the still much-too-prevalent misuse of powerful poisons in insect-control programs. This misuse is due both to a long history of deficient training in ecology and evolutionary biology in many entomology departments, and pressure from the petrochemical industry to maximize insecticide use (and long acquiescence from the United States Department of Agriculture and land-grant universities).[11] The situation is changing, though. Entomologists have, happily, been at the forefront of designing systems of integrated pest management (IPM) that work with the natural pest-control functions of ecosystems. These systems have been enormously successful, even in poor nations.[12] Much greater efforts are needed, however, for a universal conversion to systems that employ insecticides sparingly when needed, as a scalpel rather than as a sledgehammer at all times. Individual entomologists need to speak out strongly on these issues within their institutions and professional organizations, even at the risk of some professional penalties such as have plagued others who attempted to rationalize the pest-control system, from Rachel Carson to Robert van den Bosch.

No challenge is likely to be greater in coming decades than producing and distributing adequate food supplies for the fast-growing human population. Not only entomologists, but all agricultural scientists will be deeply interested in increasing production. Here again ecological-evolutionary knowledge must be applied to avoid a substantial lowering of Earth's carrying capacity for humanity by long-term damage from an inappropriate intensification of agriculture. Climate change, loss of biodiversity (including genetically distinct varieties of crops and livestock), evolution of pesticide-resistant pests and disease vectors are among the consequences of pushing to maximize production without adequate attention to ecological side effects. The loss of carrying capacity, combined with the increased need for resources generated by population growth alone, eventually may cause more misery than increased food supplies can alleviate.

The future of increased food production will lie in new directions taken by agricultural scientists. While there still is room for increasing yields of many crops—the traditional strategy—the most fruitful next steps are likely to emphasize an ecological approach. Agricultural scientists, long largely isolated from ecology and evolutionary biology, need to establish more collaborative partnerships with scientists in those fields and begin developing new cultivation systems for different soil-climate regimes.

Biologists from many disciplines will necessarily become involved in a global effort to rehabilitate degraded natural ecosystems. So much of the planet is occupied by ecosystems that are mere shadows of their former selves that restoration (as opposed to simple preservation) is bound to become increasingly important. Efforts will range from large-scale operations such as Dan Janzen's attempt to restore the Guanacaste dry forest in Costa Rica to restoring small habitats in urban areas to make them once again capable of supporting certain butterflies—signs of returning environmental health.[13]

The world has long since passed the point where even 5.4 billion people could be supported at a reasonable standard of living, even for a few decades, without the support of new, environmentally benign technologies—and those technologies must rest on a foundation of sound basic science. The needs are endless, and society's support of science should increase once they are understood. Physicists, for instance, are needed to seek ecologically safer ways of mobilizing energy, help develop better public understanding of the dynamics of the atmosphere and oceans, and explore such potential bonanzas as high-temperature superconductivity. Earth scientists are needed to help with that chore, to find better ways of dealing with changes in sea level, and to continue uncovering the ways in which valuable substances are concentrated in Earth's crust.

The struggle to understand the sources, sinks, and interactions of substances in the atmosphere that contribute to global warming as well as cause other dangerous problems such as ozone depletion and acid deposition, will require collaboration among atmospheric chemists, climatologists, geologists, and biologists, among others. Chemists are needed to design new industrial and agricultural compounds that are less toxic, shorter-lived, or both. Molecular biologists, properly supported, can contribute by producing crops that need less water or fertilizer, tolerate high-salt or low-nutrient conditions, and are more resistant to pests. Perhaps more important, they may be able to develop mechanisms to protect humanity from AIDS and its inevitable successors, and they can contribute to the search for safer, more dependable and effective contraceptives.

While we have often been critical of the allocation of resources in science and the performance of scientists in dealing with the human predicament,[14] the baby must not be thrown out with the bathwater. Scientific expertise will be needed in the coming decades as it has never been needed before, and the scientific community will need unprecedented support for its research. Some of that research will necessarily be targeted to solve immediate social problems, as has been the research support going into the battle against AIDS. But basic scientific advances, which usually flow from the creative insights of individual minds, will be essential to lay groundwork for meeting the challenges of a difficult future and must be strongly supported.

The science-society interface is bound to remain fraught with misunderstanding until the majority of scientists recognize the need to explain their work to the general public. Even those working on the most esoteric "pure" research problems should be able to make the case that understanding the complexities of the universe has intrinsic benefits for humanity. At the same time, the public must accept a responsibility to see that everyone gets an appreciation of science as part of his or her basic education. A scientifically illiterate public cannot even sensibly exercise broad control over the scientific community it supports, let alone understand the scientific aspects of everyday life and society's problems. Science, mathematics, and technology now compose perhaps half of our culture—that is, of the body of nongenetic information that *Homo sapiens* builds, stores, and transmits. That those subjects are often neglected or poorly taught is a central problem of education, especially in the United States.

Engineers, a group usually counted on to apply the advances of the scientific community for the good of society, could be at the cutting edge of solving the human predicament. Some already are, working on problems as diverse as designing solar energy systems or better constructed, more durable and energy-efficient buildings, light bulbs, and appliances, to finding ways to remove toxic substances from aquifers.

However, like many scientists, engineers often have a tendency to focus narrowly that has served them well professionally, but is no longer adaptive for themselves or for society. All too often they practice "suboptimization"—doing in the best way possible something that should never be done at all. Examples of suboptimization are myriad. One is designing new roads to carry an expected increase in automobiles in places like England and California where motor vehicles are already strangling societies, or designing better "muscle cars" to run on those roads, or, worse yet, off-road vehicles to run off them. Others are improving the design of throwaway plastic products, whether "biodegradable" or not, or designing ever more clever and destructive weapons.

On the other hand, many engineers are already helping to heal Earth. They design sewage-treatment plants and other waste-disposal facilities, design earthquake-resistant and energy-efficient buildings, and help biologists with the physical aspects of environmental restoration proj-

ects.[15] The scope for engineering contributions to the global restoration effort is enormous. One example is the development of soil "imprinters," motorized devices that force angular teeth into the soil surface of desertified areas to change the soil structure, forming "funnels" that allow rainwater to infiltrate rapidly during intense storms rather than to simply run off the hardened surface.[16] The funnels also collect seeds, litter, and topsoil, and provide protected sites for seedlings, aiding revegetation.[17] Considering the scale of the desertification problem, such engineering innovations clearly could be vastly beneficial. Restoration engineering is a profession whose time is coming.[18]

Like scientists, all engineers must consider the ecological and social consequences of their own acts and those of their profession. Some may be willing to help make their fields obsolete or even to change fields. Petroleum engineers could proclaim the temporary nature of society's dependence on oil, emphasize the need for energy efficiency and for exploring solar options, and even switch to solar engineering themselves. There will be plenty of jobs for engineers in putting together a sustainable world; they would have everything to gain by helping to push society to move in that direction.

One of the most cheering trends today is the growing interest of the medical community in ecosystem health. In 1988 the World Health Organization (WHO) acknowledged for the first time the problem of a burgeoning human population destroying its own life-support systems.[19] A British physician, Maurice King, writing in *The Lancet*, pointed out that the WHO report "neglects . . . the contribution to planetary ill health made by the industrial one-fifth of the world, which makes greater demands on the global ecosystem than do the remaining four-fifths."[20] King discussed the thorny moral problems confronting those trying to develop public-health policies for poor nations where attempts to reduce infant mortality without complementary efforts toward family planning and developing sustainable agriculture "increase the man years of human misery." We hope King's provocative views, and similar ones voiced by R. Gordon Booth ("It all comes back to one plain fact; *there are too many people*"),[21] will stimulate new dialogue within the medical community and help that community lead the way in tying together in the public mind human and ecosystem health.

That the medical community has special responsibilities in this area has been made explicit by two American internists, Michael McCally and Christine Cassel: "Concern for the health of the general public has been an important responsibility of the profession since the industrial revolution."[22] They point out that "global environmental change will cause illness on a massive scale," and urge physicians to inject their health expertise into the debate on global change. They urge that more physicians join environmental organizations to become informed on the issues and then support appropriate environmental legislation.

Physicians hold a special place in American culture, and are thus in an ideal position to educate people on the risks of environmental degradation and to counsel them on how to protect their own environmental health (including counseling them on how to avoid having more than two children). The organization Physicians for Social Responsibility, which was founded in response to the threat of nuclear war, can be expected to press for programs in environmental health. Even the rather conservative American Medical Association has urged that the role of physicians in environmental education be expanded.[23] So the groundwork has already been laid for the full-scale participation of a key group of professionals in healing Earth.

It is the social scientists, though, whose personal efforts are going to be most essential if civilization is to endure. At center stage will be the economists, some of whom are beginning to grasp both the depth of the crisis facing humanity and the crucial role that their discipline and expertise must play in solving it. Economists are burdened with a set of models derived from an era when the scale of the human enterprise was small enough relative to the biosphere that relegating environmental impacts to the realm of "externalities" was not a major problem. The problem is that in the context of present-day reality, these externalities represent, as one economist put it, "the capacity of the earth to support life."[24] Yet because they are external to the models (and because appreciation of their severity requires some knowledge of other sciences) these externalities are rarely given the weight they deserve.

At the same time, economists know more than do people in other disciplines about how to build models of the world that fit the realities of the late twentieth century. As the discussion of a carbon tax and tradable pollution permits demonstrated,

economists can come up with good ideas for internalizing at least some of the environmental externalities that are amenable to inclusion in the market system. They have also explored difficult issues such as how to deal with irreversibility,[25] the depletion of natural capital,[26] the optimal use of renewable resources,[27] pollution control in the presence of uncertainty,[28] and limiting the total throughput of the economy.[29]

Recent work by Robert Repetto of the World Resources Institute on how national accounts deal with natural-resource depletion is especially interesting. Repetto recalculated the growth of the Indonesian economy from 1970 to 1984, taking into account loss of forests, erosion of soils, and pumping of oil. He found that instead of growing 7.1 percent annually, as suggested by standard economic indicators, net growth was only 4.0 percent. In addition, if depreciation of other natural capital such as fossil fuels, metals, and fisheries had been taken into consideration, the real growth rate would be even lower. Repetto concluded that nations like Indonesia that are deeply dependent on the exploitation of nonrenewable natural resources (as are most poor nations) must diversify their economies if they are to develop successfully. In his words, "important measures of economic performance such as income and productivity growth, capital formation, and savings can be badly distorted by not recognizing natural resource assets as a form of capital."

Much more new thinking is required, however. So much of current macroeconomic thought is based implicitly on notions of perpetual growth and infinite substitution that vast opportunities exist for economists to rework their discipline into one that could make enormous contributions to the design of a sustainable society. No other social science has so great an opportunity, is as well prepared with analytic tools to take advantage of it, and is as likely to be listened to by decision makers.

Economists must also begin to go public on issues that they understand very well but that politicians and the general public often ignore or fail to grasp. A good example is the utter inadequacy of GNP as an indicator of the state of society. Economists should start holding public forums on the complexities of defining growth, what actually is growing, and issues relative to an end of growth (as normally defined). When distinguished economists start saying in public that growth in GNP (or in the physical aspects of the economy) is not necessarily a desirable goal in rich countries, and when they start pointing out repeatedly that a sound economy is utterly dependent on sound ecosystems to support it, they will help legitimate the changes that politicians need to start making.

Economists must also do more to inform the public about the value-neutrality that pervades their discipline (and other sciences). They are specialists at analyzing what *will* happen under given circumstances, but generally eschew voicing opinions on what *should* happen. They must carefully explain that economics generally does not speak to that.

A mission for psychologists would be educating the public on how the human nervous system evolved and how the outcome of that process shapes everyone's perceptions in ways that make it difficult to come to grips with the human predicament.[30] Being aware of our natural handicaps should make it easier to get around them and deal with the real problems. The variety of contributions that psychologists can make will be obvious to them, from helping to negotiate some of the necessary social dislocations to finding methods to ease the psychological traumas that may be caused by them—for example, by designing retraining programs for people phased out of coal mining, logging, or automobile manufacturing.

Other social scientists have major contributions to make as well, since the better society is understood, the better are the chances that it can be changed so as to make it sustainable over the long haul. The breakup of the communist empire and the dismal failure of the Soviet regime to satisfy human wants *or* to protect the environment suggest that one type of political/social organization can be dismissed as a path to a sustainable world. Uncritical faith in the market to solve all problems, however, in light of the global externalities that must be dealt with, is alarming to environmentalists—even those who recognize that market mechanisms accomplish more social good in many, if not most, situations than central control. A new discussion is very much in order about how human societies can reasonably be organized to preserve democracy, provide opportunities for individual expression and achieving success (but perhaps not with conspicuous consumption as the ultimate criterion), while maintaining sustainability as the central goal of society. It would be very interesting to conduct this discussion with Soviet and Eastern European social scientists participating. Such a discussion has yet to be broached, though, let alone reach the spotlight.

A critical role must be played by journalists, especially those connected with the electronic media. It would be nice if the world had the luxury of waiting for a generation to be educated in school systems to grasp the changes that are needed. But we do not; unless society changes course sharply in the next decade, we see very little chance of a satisfactory denouement to the human predicament. A great deal of public education must be done through newspapers, magazines, radio, and television. A start has been made, from *Time* magazine's recently improved coverage of environmental issues to the introduction of these issues into the story lines of TV shows. Increasing numbers of people in the entertainment business are following Robert Redford's lead and making working for environmental sanity a major commitment.[31]

Business executives, government bureaucrats, judges, and politicians are, more than most, on the front lines of environmental issues—whether they want to be or not. Business executives who inform themselves (and those in their employ) of the dimensions of the human predicament will be doing themselves and their firms a great service.[32] Leaders are needed for such difficult tasks as designing global institutions that can assure that market economies operate so as to internalize major externalities and provide for some reasonable level of equity in the distribution of goods. Discussion of the nature of such institutions has occurred sporadically for a long time, but has begun to take on new urgency as the realities of global change start to sink in.[33]

In our view, in the near future, global institutions (such as the UN and many of its agencies) could usefully provide a forum for discussing how to modify the market system to deal properly with externalities and how to adjust the terms of international trade. Both of these are central issues to growth management and sustainable development in poor nations. These discussions most likely will occur against a backdrop of global political change, of which the recent ethnic struggles in newly liberated eastern Europe are only the latest prominent manifestation. There is a worldwide trend toward separatism and local control by relatively small ethnic and religious (or "tribal" or "peasant") groups.[34] Whether they be Native Americans, Soviet Lithuanians or Georgians, Sikhs in India, Kurds in Iraq, Catholics in Northern Ireland, French Canadians in Quebec, the Basques in Spain, or the Flemish in Belgium, people are demanding more local control over their lives and resources. This could be a useful trend if politicians can steer it into a system in which environmental costs and benefits are more equitably distributed; it could be an utter disaster if it led to isolationism and trade barriers that prevented the cooperation among groups that will be necessary for solving global environmental and economic problems.

We could continue the litany of tasks for those with special expertise or position, but obviously almost anyone with motivation and virtually any kind of expertise can do something, even if the connection between what they know and the human predicament may seem tenuous at first. Attorneys can educate themselves on population-environment issues and then donate some of their time to efforts such as protecting the access of women to abortions or finding new ways of using the law to protect biodiversity.[35] English teachers can assign readings by Garrett Hardin, Aldo Leopold, Ed McGaa, Wallace Stegner, Peter Steinhart, or other writers knowledgeable on environmental issues to classes for analysis (many already are using examples from environmental literature). Social studies teachers can point out why rich nations must be considered overpopulated and emphasize the importance of the poor and minorities getting involved in environmental issues—since they will suffer most from rising food prices and generally are forced to live in the most polluted areas. Physicians can join Physicians for Social Responsibility, become more deeply involved in issues of the allocation of health care and the protection of society against novel epidemics, and follow the lead of pioneering colleagues in using their unique position in society to encourage people to tackle the problems of ecosystem health. Airline pilots can tell their passengers about the overdraft on the Ogallala aquifer as they fly their passengers over the characteristic circular irrigation patterns on the Great Plains. TV weatherpersons could explain that regional record hot spells or cold snaps do not speak for or against the question of global warming—which is an average phenomenon of worldwide climate, not an attribute of local weather. Parents can work through their local PTA and

school board to get more coverage in curricula of the human predicament. And everyone can contribute mightily by becoming determined letter writers. Politicians are much more susceptible to the pressures generated by thoughtful letters, and by persistent demands for replies and action, than most citizens realize.

When writing to a legislator or other government official, be brief and specific, and if possible use professional or business letterhead. Don't say something like "Senator Sloe, I want you to work harder to protect biodiversity." Instead, make a specific request such as "I want you to become a cosponsor and active supporter of Senator Smart's bill S. 10XX, which greatly strengthens the Endangered Ecosystems Act, and to let me know what initiatives you are promoting to deal with the erosion of biodiversity outside the United States." If Senator Sloe's staff writes you a letter for him to sign that basically says, "Thank you for your views," write back and say, "Senator, I'm not satisfied with your vacuous response—I want to know what you are doing about one of the most critical elements of our national security."

If you don't get a satisfactory reply after a few letters, try calling Senator Sloe's office and asking to speak to the member of his staff who deals with environmental issues. If you want to be a real wise-ass, ask for the staffer who deals with security issues and then act surprised when he or she claims that biodiversity isn't in his or her bailiwick. As a last resort, write Sloe and explain the steps you and your friends are going to take to return him to his private law practice if he doesn't get moving fast on the biodiversity issue—or whatever critical environmental issue you are writing about. Generally, such tactics will be most effective if you address your questions to legislators who are on the committee appropriate to solving the problems involved.

If possible, get to know your representative and senators personally. They all hold regular meetings in their districts, and they usually are willing to meet with you at least briefly if you travel to Washington. Write or phone in advance for an appointment and have a specific agenda to discuss; go with a few other constituents if possible. Don't expect a great deal of time; congresspeople are busy.

Finally, everyone can do those things that

we've largely ignored [here] because they are so well covered in others.[36] Those include recycling, eating less meat, biking or walking instead of driving, conserving water and electricity, and all the other things that help each of us tread more lightly on the planet. And, of course, all parents should see to it that their one or two children are thoroughly educated on environmental issues, if not in school, then at home.

Whatever your role in society, your contributions are needed. Having read this far you obviously are willing to spend part of your time becoming informed about the human predicament. Once you are informed, the pervasiveness of the predicament puts you in a position to do something about it. We think everyone should donate at least 10 percent of his or her time to learning about the world and acting on the knowledge—to "tithe" their time to society. Politicians and other "leaders" aren't going to get the job done for us—especially if we don't communicate clear instructions. We have to take responsibility ourselves for a far-reaching transformation of our society. We wish you luck; all of us will need it.

Notes

1. The Earthworks Group, 1990, Earthworks Press, Berkeley, CA.
2. Simon & Schuster, New York, 1990.
3. Scientists themselves, after all, are the outcome of an evolutionary process.
4. Life expectancies, unless otherwise stated, are life expectancies at birth. Most of the variation in life expectancy in the past, and we suspect in the future, will be governed by death rates in the first few years of life; stating that life expectancies will be dramatically lower means that many more infants and young children will be dying prematurely.
5. Environmental sciences are not just the domain of biologists. Chemists like Sherwood Rowland, Mario Molina, and Susan Solomon, physicists like John Holdren and Steve Schneider, and many other physical scientists have already made extremely important contributions. Prominent scientists of all disciplines can call public attention to various aspects of the dilemma, as biologist Garrett Hardin, botanists Peter Raven and Hugh Iltis, plant physiologist Harold Mooney, earth scientists Preston Cloud and Earl Cook, behaviorists Thomas Eisner and E. O. Wilson, entomologist Richard South-

wood, ornithologists Thomas Lovejoy and Peter Myers, ecosystem scientists Gene Likens, George Woodwell, and Peter Vitousek, physicists John Fremlin and John Harte, geophysicist Harrison Brown, climatologists Thomas Malone and Walter Orr Roberts, astronomer Carl Sagan, and innumerable others have done.

6. See P. Ehrlich, 1964, "Some Axioms of Taxonomy," *Systematic Zoology,* Vol. 13, pp. 109–143; M. Soulé, 1990, "The Real Work of Systematics," *Annals of the Missouri Botanical Garden,* vol. 77, pp. 4–12.
7. Such changes were suggested to taxonomists three decades ago (Ehrlich, 1964), but the museums of the world have yet to undertake a systematic sampling program, and the time available is becoming very short.
8. C. Woese, O. Kandler, and M. Wheelis, "Towards a Natural System of Organisms: Proposal for the Domains Archaea, Bacteria, and Eucarya," 1990, *Proceedings of the National Academy of Sciences,* vol. 87, pp. 4576–4579.
9. R. Ornstein and P. Ehrlich, 1989, *New World/New Mind,* Doubleday, New York.
10. E. Wilson, 1987, "The Little Things That Run the World (the Importance and Conservation of Invertebrates)," *Conservation Biology,* vol. 1, pp. 344–346.
11. R. van den Bosch, 1978, *The Pesticide Conspiracy,* Doubleday, New York.
12. K. Holl, G. Daily, and P. Ehrlich, 1990, "Integrated Pest Management in Latin America," *Environmental Conservation,* vol. 17, no. 4, pp. 341–350.
13. S. Weiss and D. Murphy, 1990, "Thermal Microenvironments and the Restoration of Rare Butterfly Habitat," in J. Berger (ed.), *Environmental Restoration: Science and Strategies for Restoring the Earth,* Island Press, Washington, DC, pp. 50–60.
14. P. Ehrlich, 1986, *The Machinery of Nature,* Simon & Schuster, New York; P. Ehrlich and E. Wilson, 1991, "Biodiversity Studies: Science and Policy" (in press), *Science.*
15. Berger, 1990.
16. R. Dixon, 1979, *Land Imprinter, Vegetative Rehabilitation and Equipment Workshop, 33rd Annual Report,* USDA/Forest Service, Casper, WY.
17. R. Dixon, 1990, "Land Imprinting for Dryland Revegetation and Restoration," and R. Virginia, 1990, "Desert Restoration: The Role of Woody Legumes," pp. 14–22 and 22–30 in Berger, 1990.
18. For example, see J. Cairns, 1988, *Rehabilitating Damaged Ecosystems,* vols. I and II, CRC Press, Boca Raton, FL.
19. World Health Organization, 1988, *From Alma Ata to*

the Year 2000: Reflections at the Midpoint, WHO, Geneva.

20. M. King, 1990, "Health Is a Sustainable State," *The Lancet* (15 September), vol. 336, pp. 664–667.

21. R. Booth, 1990, "*Homo sapiens*—A Species Too Successful," *Journal of the Royal Society of Medicine,* vol. 83, pp. 757–759.

22. M. McCally and C. Cassel, 1990, "Medical Responsibility and the Global Environment," *Annals of Internal Medicine* vol. 113, 15 September, pp. 467–473.

23. American Medical Association Council on Scientific Affairs, 1989, "Stewardship of the Environment," *AMA House of Delegates Report: G (I-89),* American Medical Association, Chicago.

24. H. Daly and J. Cobb, 1989, *For the Common Good,* Beacon Press, Boston, p. 37.

25. K. Arrow and A. Fisher, 1974, "Environmental Preservation, Uncertainty, and Irreversibility," *Quarterly Journal of Economics,* vol. 88, pp. 313–319.

26. R. Repetto, 1989, "Balance-Sheet Erosion: How to Account for the Loss of Natural Resources," *International Environmental Affairs,* vol. 1, pp. 103–137.

27. H. Hotelling, 1931, "The Economics of Renewable Resources," *Journal of Political Economy,* vol. 39, pp. 137–175; R. Stavins, 1990, "Alternative Renewable Resource Strategies: A Simulation of Optimal Use," *Journal of Environmental Economics and Management,* vol. 19, pp. 143–159.

28. P. Dasgupta, P. Hammond, and E. Maskin, 1980, "On Imperfect Information and Optimal Pollution Control," *Review of Economic Studies,* vol. 47, no. 4, pp. 857–860.

29. H. Daly, 1977, *Steady-State Economics,* Freeman, San Francisco.

30. Ornstein and Ehrlich, 1989.

31. A new organization of actors, performers, and production workers in television and recording, dedicated to "creating environmental awareness," was formed in 1990: Earth Communications Office, or ECO. It gives us particular pleasure that one of the most dedicated environmentalists in Hollywood and an ECO board member is Ed Begley, Jr., who became famous for his fine portrayal of a Dr. Ehrlich on the TV show "St. Elsewhere."

32. For instance, Esprit Corps of San Francisco sponsors regular seminars for its employees on important public issues, including environmental issues.

33. See J. Harris, 1991, "Global Institutions and Ecological Crisis," *World Development,* 19 (in press).

34. See W. McNeill, 1991, "The Peasantry's Awakening All over the World," *Washington Post National Weekly Edition,* 7–13 January.

35. An example of such an attempt was C. Stone, 1974, *Should Trees Have Standing? Towards Legal Rights for Natural Objects,* Kaufmann, Los Altos, CA.

36. Some examples in addition to *50 Simple Things* are B. Anderson (ed.), 1990, *Ecologue,* Prentice-Hall, New York; D. MacEachern, 1990, *Save Our Planet: 750 Everyday Ways You Can Help Clean Up the Earth,* Dell, New York; and W. Steger and J. Bowermaster, 1990, *Saving the Earth: A Citizen's Guide to Environmental Action,* Knopf, New York.

Daughters of Growing Things

Rachel L. Bagby

I am a farmer's daughter

daughter
of daughter
of daughter
of women
who
knew
what to plant
during which growing moon

I am a grandchild
of harpist

music
of growing things

Rachel L. Bagby,
"Bringings Up and Comings Round"

This essay tells of an ongoing effort to maintain mutually nuturing relationships with nature, human

Reweaving the World: The Emergence of Ecofeminism, edited by Irene Diamond and Gloria Feman Orenstein (San Francisco: Sierra Club Books, 1990), pp. 231–248. Reprinted by permission of the publisher.

and elemental, in the midst of a low- and no-income urban village community of about 5,000 people. *Webster's New World Dictionary* reserves the use of the word *village* for certain types of living units located in the country. Yet, despite its location within the city of Philadelphia, the area on which this essay focuses meets every other qualification listed under "village community" in that it is comprised of a group of houses, is larger than a hamlet, functions as a self-governing political unit, and has several half-acre plots that are worked by the community.

Philadelphia Community Rehabilitation Corporation (PCRC) is the institution through which this work is accomplished. Momma—Rachel Edna Samiella Rebecca Jones Bagby—is the woman who founded it. PCRC's operating budget is financed from the $4,000 in rents collected each month, a yearly bazaar (complete with prizes for the best sweet potato pie), and a seemingly infinite number of chicken dinners, plant sales, and bus trips to Atlantic City. It employs a regular staff of three to five and numerous independent contractors. Every summer a handful of teenagers get their first work experience there. Its "repeopling" program has renovated and rented more than fifty formerly vacant homes and created a twelve-unit shared-house.

And then there are the gardens, the focus of this essay.

The material was culled from more than forty cassette recordings of phone conversations between me and Momma—between Northern California and North Philadelphia, Pa.—over the past 3 years. It is essential to have Momma tell her stories in her own, inimitable voice. While the interview format comes close, we are still working on a hybrid form of prose and musical notation that will do the rhythms and melodies of her speech justice. What may seem to be misspellings and grammatical errors are intentional, ways of honoring Momma's voice. Much of her power in the community comes from her *way* with people. Much of that way is communicated in her manner of speaking.

DAUGHTER: How much land do you have?

MOTHER: I think it's about 5 acres. I imagine if you measured it, it would be about 5 acres. All the different lots we have.

DAUGHTER: And how do you choose your lots for the gardens?

MOTHER: We didn't choose the lots. We just got the lot that we could get. These were empty lots, in other words. Rather than to grow weeds, we just begged the city to let us have them. And we paid for some of them, too. [At a cost of about $500 per half acre.] Some of them are really ours; we own.

DAUGHTER: So these were empty lots?

MOTHER: They were all empty lots, yes, and we just got them, we asked for them in order to make the place look better than growing a whole lot of weeds. We just grow something that's more useful—food and flowers. Make it beautiful. And the food is outta sight. Rather than to grow weeds. Why sit and grow weeds when you can do something with it? So this is what we did, and it's working, and it's spreading. We have a meeting now every month.

DAUGHTER: We'll come back to the meetings. First tell me how much food you get from the garden.

MOTHER: Out of that garden? We made more tomatoes than we could use and still have tomatoes coming out of our ears. Green peppers, too. And we still have them.

DAUGHTER: So what did you do? Can them?

MOTHER: Yeah, we canned them. And the tomatoes are canned. Remember I told you? Tomatoes are canned, the peppers are canned, and I have a lot of the greens canned. Vegetables we don't buy. Peas we dried. We still got dried peas. California black eyes. And it yields a lot because, see, what you do is as fast as one crop get through, you plant another one until the frost falls. In the winter, we can't plant; before then we plant winter greens. We plant okra, then we plant potatoes; we plant cucumber; and then we plant carrots. You know, so we just put different things in as food. We just keep things going until the frost falls.

DAUGHTER: So you rotate the crops?

MOTHER: We rotate the crops. That's how you yield more. Right now, we're planting some seeds, as soon as, next week we'll be planting seeds so we can set them outdoors when the weather breaks.

DAUGHTER: How did you have to prepare the land? And what was the original shape? Wasn't there glass and bottles and all that?

MOTHER: We just took hoes and rakes and stuff and raked it. Dug it as deep as the plants will grow, and raked all that stuff and put it out.

DAUGHTER: What?

MOTHER: We dug with something called a grub hoe and just paid some boys for just going in and digging it up. Tole them, "Just dig it as deep as the food will grow."

DAUGHTER: How deep is that?

MOTHER: About as deep as my leg.

DAUGHTER: So that if you stood up, your waist would be at the cement?

MOTHER: My knee would be in the ground.

DAUGHTER: So we're talking maybe 2 feet?

MOTHER: Yeah, 2 or 3 feet. What we did, we did that and then we asked for top soil and had folks go out in the park and get the horse manure from the park.

DAUGHTER: What park?

MOTHER: Woodside Park, right here. You remember Woodside Park! The stables—the drippings from the horses. Stable compost, they call it. Stable manure. It's one of the largest parks in the United States! That's right! See, when you come, you're in such a hurry you forgot all the good parts. All you see is these raggedy places. But there are some good parts.

DAUGHTER: I know Momma. The best part in Philadelphia is *you*!

MOTHER: Well . . . There are some good parts. Anyway, that's where we get the compost. We go out there and get it and it don't cost anything. Just go out there and haul it.

DAUGHTER: It's free.

MOTHER: Yeah. You don't pay for that! It's there for the getting. It makes such good dirt. You heap it up, all that stuff. That's how your crop grows.

DAUGHTER: Now, you said you paid some boys to do it.

MOTHER: We had two or three boys and we paid the men to dig it up for us. We didn't have a plow. I know how we used to do it in the South, turn it with the turnplow and two horses. But we didn't have the turnplow here, so we just paid the men to dig it up and dig it deep and they had to dig it right.

DAUGHTER: How long did they work on this?

MOTHER: It didn't take them long. Took 'em like 2 days.

DAUGHTER: And you paid some young boys to work on it, too?

MOTHER: Yes, about $3 an hour even.

DAUGHTER: So they were employed for that little bit. How old were they?

MOTHER: One was—I think the best worker was 14. His name was Joey, I think. I can't remember his name. I called him Joey.

DAUGHTER: So after they turned it, they plowed it up and then hauled out all that they dug up?

MOTHER: No, we took the rake and raked up what wasn't too good. Raked up as much as we could. They, you set it out and they picked it up, then you paid them to get rid of it is what we did.

DAUGHTER: There's still glass and stuff down there, but the food just grows around it?

MOTHER: That's what I'm saying. That's what we did.

DAUGHTER: Then you got the horse drippings?

MOTHER: We got that from the horse stables before we raked up the place and had it all chopped up in there together.

DAUGHTER: Oh, I see. So first you turned it by digging it up, then you put the drippings down and turned it all up together?

MOTHER: Right. Then chop it up again.

DAUGHTER: Who did the planting?

MOTHER: Well, I supervised the planting.

DAUGHTER: Who helped you?

MOTHER: Most everybody helped.

DAUGHTER: Women, men, about how many people?

MOTHER: Six of us.

DAUGHTER: Do you plant from seeds?

MOTHER: You plant from seeds, some of them were planted from seeds and some of them were plants we bought. The ones that we couldn't get enough plants up from seeds we bought.

DAUGHTER: What did you buy?

MOTHER: Red cabbage and carrots, more or less we bought those seeds. And all the herbs, I bought those seeds. But see, once you plant them, you don't plant them the next year.

DAUGHTER: They just come back?

MOTHER: Yes. Now I did say *all*. I'm wrong, because thyme you don't plant anymore, the peppermint you don't plant, so many of the stuff you don't plant anymore. You just plant it one time and it comes back every year.

DAUGHTER: And you timed it all based on the moon?

MOTHER: Yes. I always plant according to the moon. According to that, I plant. According to the light I know when to plant.

DAUGHTER: So how much did it cost for . . . ?

MOTHER: Oh! I forgot!

DAUGHTER: I know Momma, just try to estimate for seeds and . . .

MOTHER: I think the tools were quite expensive.

DAUGHTER: Let me ask you the full question, all right? The whole question is, how much did it cost for the seeds, the plants, the hoes, the other equipment that you got, paying the boys? How much do you think all that cost?

MOTHER: Well, the land was about $1,000 for the land. And we put the fence up. I think that wire fence was $1,300—cyclone fence. Then we used the boys 2 days and I paid them, that was $3 an hour. There was two boys, $3 an hour for 16 hours. The seeds run you less than a dollar a pack, you know, and I didn't get but one pack each because I had about five or six different herbs, so that's what the seeds are.

DAUGHTER: But you got other plants.

MOTHER: The plants will run you about $1.50 to $2.00. Say, about $10 worth of plants. That's not the seeds, though. The seeds were about $5 for all the seeds, say, $10 for the seeds. That's just an estimate, now.

DAUGHTER: And the equipment?

MOTHER: Well, we bought . . . We don't have to buy equipment every year. We bought about $200 worth of equipment, but we don't buy that every year.

DAUGHTER: Well, you don't buy the land or the fence every year either. It looks like your yearly cost is $20 for the seeds and plants.

MOTHER: Yes, you can put about $20 or $25 for the year. For the seeds themselves, and the plants. They just use the equipment over and over again.

DAUGHTER: That $25 feeds how many people for how long?

MOTHER: About twelve households for one season. When spring comes, you start all over again.

DAUGHTER: So it feeds you for the fall and the winter, doesn't it?

MOTHER: Yeah, that's one season. During the summer we eat a lot out of there. We don't have to can it.

DAUGHTER: So it feeds you year round? Vegetables.

MOTHER: Yeah. Vegetables year round. I told you. Vegetables we don't buy.

DAUGHTER: That's a big savings, Momma.

MOTHER: I'm trying to get these folks to realize that.

DAUGHTER: What happens at your meetings? You said the meetings have been growing.

MOTHER: We trying to get them to realize how much they save by doing this. And spread it. Because the city has so many vacant lots so they can plant these things. This is what we're trying to get them to do and show them the value of having, of doing this. We see so many of them lazy, they say they can't do, but you *can* do it.

DAUGHTER: You say the meetings have been getting bigger?

MOTHER: Yes. I think the meetings have been getting larger and more valuable.

DAUGHTER: How many people come to the meetings?

MOTHER: We had forty-nine last week.

DAUGHTER: And you're meeting once a week?

MOTHER: Once a month.

DAUGHTER: Who comes to these meetings?

MOTHER: Just people that're interested in planting gardens. Neighborhood people. And now we're letting them see how the food looks canned.

DAUGHTER: That's what you do in your meetings? What else do you do? It sounds like a real educational program.

MOTHER: That's what it is! See how it look canned, and also how it tastes.

DAUGHTER: You give them samples?

MOTHER: Yes. I just thought of that out of my head, you know, but it's a lot of work.

DAUGHTER: How many meetings have you had?

MOTHER: We had one last month. And this month we'll have another one. We plan to have one every month.

DAUGHTER: You're building up to planting season? How did you get people interested before, since you've just started the meetings? This is the first time you've had them, right?

MOTHER: This is the first time I started the meetings.

DAUGHTER: You just go around and talk to people?

MOTHER: Like door-to-door campaigning. Door-to-door education.

DAUGHTER: You are such a jewel on this planet, Momma. You are wonderful!

MOTHER: *(Quietly)* What do you mean?

DAUGHTER: What do you mean what do I mean? You really are. I don't know. It's real unusual what you're doing and you're helping people and you're keeping that connection between the Earth and people and . . .

MOTHER: You know what? *(Laughs)* We help ourselves when we help others. You can't help yourself unless you, you have to help somebody, too.

DAUGHTER: Tell me a little about your background. *I* know it. *You* know it, but tell me again so I can get it on this tape.

MOTHER: See, what give me the idea to do this, is I just got sick and tired of walking by weeds. Absolutely a disgrace to me. Instead of growing weeds, if weeds can grow where there's nothing but cement and bricks and stuff, if weeds can grow in there, something else can grow also. And you have the weeds taller than I am. People be afraid to go by Twenty-first Street. That's where we had to go to go to the store, and people would snatch pocketbooks and run over you, and you couldn't find them in the weeds. So that's how we got started with that. Now, when I was home, I came up on the farm . . .

DAUGHTER: Home where?

MOTHER: South Carolina. I came up on a farm. My father was a farmer. And I loved it. We grew our stuff there. I really loved it. To sit there and get in a field of watermelon and walk on watermelons from one end to the other. I thought it was fun.

DAUGHTER: To walk on them? And they wouldn't bust?

MOTHER: When they were smaller, you know. When they get ripe, they get tender.

DAUGHTER: You mean when they're smaller, they're harder?

MOTHER: Yes. And I was little, too. Anyway, what I'm trying to say is he would grow so many watermelons that you could hardly see the ground. That's just how [many] there were. Sweet taters, peanuts, all kinds of beans, white potatoes. So, I learned that he would plant his stuff at a certain time. Some I have forgotten, but he would get the *Farmer's Almanac*. . . .

I plant things in the ground when the sign of the moon . . . you plant the fish. In that *Farmer's Almanac*. Like the carrots. I won't plant carrots from the corner of the moon. I plant like beans and those kind of things that go on top of the ground. Anything underneath, you plant the fish. And peas, you plant them on the twins and your leaves will be hanging with beans and stuff. I'll never forget that, because I used to have to drop that stuff. I used to love to do that, too; drop the seeds in the ground.

I knew how to drop them. I knew how to take my hand and put it in so it won't spread out. I put it in right down and I could bend then, you know, when you're young you can bend, you can buckle. And I would take my hand and put it right down in the ground. I would do an acre or so a day and wouldn't think nothing of it. And I loved it. It's just in me. That's all.

I like to see things grow instead of wasting. And all these vacant lots you can't, you don't have the money to put houses on all them, but you can buy a little dollar worth of seeds and put on them. Can't put houses on them, but you sit and eat that stuff that comes from them. Look at the flowers that are so pretty. That sort of thing. So this is what started. And everybody, it's spreading, you know.

DAUGHTER: It's really wonderful Momma. I'm wondering about how Philadelphia Green [a horticultural society devoted to assisting neighborhood revitalization efforts] and how the city [of Philadelphia] got involved. You approached the city, right? The city wasn't doing it at first, right?

MOTHER: No, but then we approached the city to help us, because I found out they could help us do a lot. That's how I got in with them. Anything that I think can give us a hand, because we need a lot of help out here. Anybody that can give us a hand we approach them. The Philadelphia Green can have a lot of things; they can help with the tools, they can send out people to help, now like we don't have those tapes and stuff. They have that and they bring it out and show these different gardens on these tapes and tell you what it's all about.

DAUGHTER: You mean video tapes?

MOTHER: Video tape. They have that, so then they bring it out for us. But if you don't ever ask for it, you won't get it.

DAUGHTER: Philadelphia Green has existed for a while, hasn't it?

MOTHER: See, that started when you were here, because when I was over at ACDC [Advocate

Community Development Corporation], I planted the first garden over there. You were in high school and I was there working ACDC.

DAUGHTER: It was 1970?

MOTHER: Yes, something like that. I planted the first garden over there.

DAUGHTER: And Philadelphia Green existed then?

MOTHER: They existed then and I got involved when we first got the plants, the little pots to put flowers on the steps. That was Philadelphia Green. Ever since then. That's how I got started. That's why I worked there as long as I did because I was glad to be involved with people, you know. And these gardens and stuff. Now we have it ourselves. So it's a joy. It's work, but it's a joy, and we're opening a park.

DAUGHTER: What else are you planning?

MOTHER: Well, we're planning to do more gardening. We're trying hard not to slide backward. We're trying to go forwards. Add a little bit more each year.

DAUGHTER: What else are you doing?

MOTHER: Gardening, shared housing, and regular housing. We're also getting tutoring for literacy, starting to teach some people how to read and get jobs. We just started that. That's the tutoring I been wanted. I want to get that going in a big way.

DAUGHTER: Do you still have training programs for kids to get employment?

MOTHER: Yes, we still have that job bank, that's what we call that. So people can get a job. So that's it. And it keeps you going, too, just like those different directions on the *Farmer's Almanac*.

DAUGHTER: Keeps you out of trouble, too.

MOTHER: Well, I never get in too much trouble no way. I have a whole lot I can do. See, I've always been able to keep myself busy. I've never been able to not have anything to do. See, I can sit and crochet. I want to sew. I piece quilts. There's so much you can do. My goodness! If I wasn't doing that [work with PCRC] I'd stay in this house here a month and don't even go to the door and work the whole time.

DAUGHTER: How do you think what you do relates to ecology, relates to the Earth? How do you talk about that?

MOTHER: Well, I talk about it like I always do, 'cause this is where you see the real nature of the universe. The real one, without . . . before it's transformed into different things. Because even children don't have the least idea of the food they eat. What grows in the ground, what grows on top, what good for blood, what good for different things. A lot of adults don't have any idea. So that's how I relate it to everyday living.

You get firsthand . . . everybody get a firsthand look at real nature. That's how I see it. That's how I love it. You can see it come up, you can see it grow and you see how it grows, and see it dies if you don't take care of it. That tells you something.

DAUGHTER: What does it tell you?

MOTHER: It tells you that if you're not taken care of, tells you, you got to take care of whatever you have. If you don't it will die then, or grow wild like the things in the fields, out in the woods. God has created things to stay alive without being taken care of but you can't try to, like to say, try to tame them. If you try to tame them you have to give them some of that that they get ordinarily. But the Earth is created so that everything should be taken care of.

DAUGHTER: By somebody or something?

MOTHER: By nature, and then if you interfere with it . . .

DAUGHTER: Say that again, the Earth was created . . .

MOTHER: To take care of everything on Earth. It's supposed to be taken care of. That's why, man, they say, has been made the highest of all things, because we're supposed to take care of the things that we cultivate. We're supposed to take care of them. And if we're not going to take care of it let it grow wild, the Earth will take care of it.

DAUGHTER: But if you interfere . . .

MOTHER: Right. If you interfere with it, and we must if we can survive. See, we must interfere because we need these things *to* survive. And it goes around and around. See, we need these things to survive therefore when you plant something you hafta take care of it. If you don't, it'll die. Either you take care of it or leave it alone.

DAUGHTER: What kind of resistance have you met?

MOTHER: People not wantin' to work. They don't want to get their hands dirty. They don't want to, not want to work, what I mean is, you take a lot of mothers don't want to wash the greens, they don't wanna dig down and get the carrots from the ground, they don't want to get the turnips from the ground. That's dirt. When they get it it's in the store and they clean, so to speak. So a lot of them rather go to the store and get it. I say, "How long it's been in that store? You can get it right from here and clean it, put it right in your pot or eat it like it is. Put it in your salad and you get the real, all the vitamins."

So you have resistance, people say, I can't bend down, can't bend over, or my fingernails too long. They don't tell you that but you look at the fingernails and know they're too long to do any work. So that's the resistance you get. You get a lot of that, 'cause we are uneducated to the facts. And not just that, but in a lot of things. We just don't seem to understand.

But I feel as though our children would better understand how to take care of things and would have a better feeling of the things around them, you know. It begins when you're, you know, small really.

DAUGHTER: Do you work with children a lot in the garden?

MOTHER: I love to, yes. I generally have them in there and showing them the grass from the weeds and from the plants and how it looks and how they grow, too. The grass grows, too. The weeds grow, too. That's part of nature. They say, "What good are they?" This can be a fertilizer for next year. "What!? Weeds!?" You let them sit there and rot and that replenish the Earth. See, everything has a cycle. See, those the kinda things.

DAUGHTER: How do you get the children in there?

MOTHER: All you have to do is open the gate and say "Come on children." If I had more strength I'd have all the kids in there, but I don't have the strength anymore and I can't get anyone interested in the children. The mothers say, yeh, take the children so they can sit down and look at television. But all the kids that I have met want to get out there in the garden and they beg you to let them come in and help. It takes a lot of time with children. And I don't have that much time trying to do all these other things. But I

would just have someone to just go with them. I don't have that. The mothers not interested anymore. "I gotta look at my soap opera." And they are their children. "Here, you can take 'em, I gotta look at my soap opera. I'll give you money. Take 'em to such and such a thing. You take 'em while I sit and watch my soap opera, or do anything else." So those opposition you get now.

DAUGHTER: And what kind of hope do you have? Even with that opposition, how do you keep on going?

MOTHER: Faith. I know out of all of that, it may be one or two that you'll get through to. Even with one, I'll be thankful. You know. Faith. Just keep on going. You do that with children, all of them will not end up in jail. Some of 'em come out all right. But you don't look for a whole lot. You don't expect a whole lot.

DAUGHTER: Why do you think that if you show them the living things that will help them straighten up?

MOTHER: It help, it helps them to . . . I think it will help them to appreciate the beauty of the Earth, and of nature; we call it mother nature.

DAUGHTER: Do you think it helps them appreciate the beauty of each other and their abilities?

MOTHER: This is the thing. If you can appreciate the Earth, you can appreciate the beauty of yourself. Even if this has beauty, I, too, have beauty. The same creator created both. And if I learned to take care of that I'll also take care of myself and help take care of others. See, taking care of yourself and appreciating yourself is the first step. But you can't go with a child and say that. You know, you show 'em this and they'll say, "ummmm," you know, some of these other things'll come to them themselves, or "if this is it, then I, look at me." Then they won't feel so let down all the time. Sometime we fail in trying to do that.

DAUGHTER: What do you mean you may fail?

MOTHER: Sometime you may fail, the children may not get it. They may not. Like I say, you may get one or two. That's what I mean. I am who I am whether I'm black, blue, or brown. I'm a human being. Therefore, I stand for just as much right as you stand for although my color is different, you see. I'm no less than you are regardless of my color.

DAUGHTER: You see the children move past some of that as a result of working?

MOTHER: Yes. Yes. They compare sometimes so you let them see pictures of other children working, say, "Well, I can do it as well as he can do it."

DAUGHTER: You show them pictures of other children working?

MOTHER: Right. And then see that's giving them confidence in themselves that they can do things, too, other than throw a ball and bat a ball. Other than break out people's windows and curse in the street. "If they can stop and make things, make a beautiful plant, so can I." Some of them will stop and say that. And they'll tell you, "Let's do our garden."

DAUGHTER: Do you have special meetings for children?

MOTHER: Special meetings, special workshops. They don't have the same workshops as the adults. Yes.

DAUGHTER: The organization has special meetings?

MOTHER: For children. We have to.

DAUGHTER: What age groups?

MOTHER: We have all ages.

DAUGHTER: From what? Starting where?

MOTHER: Acch! We have some small 'cause the, uh, the 8-year-old wanna bring the 2-year-old. Some of 'em so little, but we don't turn them away. Long as they can walk and talk, they come. From 3 up. But we don't limit the age group.

DAUGHTER: What's the oldest?

MOTHER: Well, the teenagers get so . . . but we have some teenagers help us with the others though. We have some as long as they in school and don't have a job.

DAUGHTER: And how many children are you working with?

MOTHER: Oh! I don't know.

DAUGHTER: Give me an estimate.

MOTHER: (Sigh) Look like to me it's 'bout fifty or more. Because of the fact—uh, it's more than that. But I can't work with the children like I want to. That's the only thing. I want to work with them on a regular basis. Like I would like to work with those children every week. Have just 2 hours or 3 hours every week working with the kids. You'd be surprised to see the difference. With all this stuff going on you have

to create agencies that's going to work with the children to help, because in every state of the universe—I don't know 'bout, I haven't read much about the foreign states—there're abandoned children. Because of crack, because of alcohol, or because of this or because of that, you name it.

We gon' have to learn to set up something to work with these kids because outta that, one of those abandoned children you get one or two children, one or two kids that will carry on, that will not use and will not do the stuff that they were abused by. See, because a lot of people think that if you don't beat a child it's not abuse, but there're other ways to abuse children. And more damaging, or just as damaging. It's a whole lotta ways to abuse children. I know.

DAUGHTER: How often do you meet with the children?

MOTHER: Well, see, it depends. Like right now I'm not meeting with them because I'm with this housing. Usually it's during the summer. But see that isn't the way it's supposed to . . . not like I would like to have it. I would like to have a year-round program for the children. You gotta have a place, you gotta have money, you gotta have those things to do this with. We have a meeting like at Christmas. Last week was a Christmas workshop. Then we have a fall workshop.

DAUGHTER: Special workshops.

MOTHER: Yes. That isn't enough for them.

DAUGHTER: What did you do during the fall workshop?

MOTHER: Fall workshop we had making pumpkins and Thanksgiving. That was the fall workshop. Making pumpkins and playing in the hay. Things like the old folks do, like they did before. Some children had never seen a bundle of hay and had something like a hay ride, you know, put it up and let you slide down on the hay.

DAUGHTER: Where did you have that?

MOTHER: In the yard, in the garden.

DAUGHTER: As part of the composting?

MOTHER: Right. So see, that was fall, that's just one time. Then we had a workshop for Christmas, how you make decorations, that's another time. . . . During the winter, you work from the proceeds of the fall. But it isn't enough to get through. I feel as though if we could work constantly with the children we could reach more of them. Now it takes a smart child to remember from this workshop to that workshop how it connects. But see, the majority of them can't get it.

DAUGHTER: What do you mean, "how it connects"?

MOTHER: Okay, we get the pinecones, we only can get the pinecones certain time of year. And we tell them that this pinecone has matured, it's grown, and now we can do this with it. But now how many children gonna remember that when we make them for Christmas. So then see, it's too big a gap to reach most children now. It's too big a gap between them.

DAUGHTER: So, you want them to see the process, to see the stages?

MOTHER: That's it. It's very sad to me, 'cause they missing so much. It's really sad. Go around, you see all these children in the street, you see all these babies having babies, it's sad. Sad times.

DAUGHTER: So, how do you maintain what you *are* doing with the adults, through all that resistance? I know you said you have those door-to-door campaigns sometimes. But how do you pass their resistance?

MOTHER: Just keep on talking to them and showing them different things.

DAUGHTER: Do you work one-on-one with them?

MOTHER: You have . . . it's better. A lot of times it's better. You get better results to work one-on-one because everyone is different.

DAUGHTER: And what kind of articles do you read?

MOTHER: Well, like I was reading the article we had in the paper couple Sundays ago 'bout abandoned children and how many children in this state, I was talking about this state, that has been abandoned. And how they were talking about they didn't have enough workers to work closely with these children and how these crack mothers and drunken fathers and crack fathers just put the children out in the street. And just last week, last week?, this week, the mother stole a car and was renting them out to people and sending her son out to make sure the car came back and one 16-year-old find it out and killed the boy. Those kind of things. . . .

DAUGHTER: So, when you're working with the folks you read them articles like that and . . .

MOTHER: And I say, "Now, this is the type of mother you don't wanna be. You had these children and you have a responsibility whether you take or accept it or not." I say not just mothers have responsibility, fathers, too, but, where the fathers? If you know where the fathers are, you love them so much you won't turn them in. Then if you won't turn them in, you work for your child, that's all. You work and do it.

DAUGHTER: What age group are you talking about?

MOTHER: All these mothers now are having children. Most of 'em are teenagers. Most of 'em are young children. Most of them are babies themselves.

DAUGHTER: And these are the same mothers whose children you get and take to the garden?

MOTHER: Yes, a lot of them. And a lot of these mothers we take to the garden are young. Most of 'em young. I don't think I have an old person with a child that we take to the garden. Most of 'em these young mothers. I can't think of a one.

DAUGHTER: What do you do? How do you get to them? You just go up to their house or what do you do?

MOTHER: And ask them would you like for your child to join, and then the children come and ask you. A lot of them come and ask you.

DAUGHTER: The children do?

MOTHER: Right. Then we go to the house. So I got Helen working with me now and another lady to head up that project. I hope it'll work well. Get the children involved. Went in the block and took every name of a child that wanted to work. And asked to work. You didn't have to ask them. And then went to the mothers and had the mothers to agree and asked them to come and help us. Only two came out. The others had something else to do. They didn't have time to come. "I give you some money but I don't have time." You know. Those kinda things.

DAUGHTER: And how many children were there?

MOTHER: Oh Jesus, we had about twenty-some-odd. 'Round thirty-three or thirty-four children and two parents.

DAUGHTER: And how about the old folks that you

do have working on the garden. You go door to door with them, too?

MOTHER: Yeh, some of them like to work in the garden. The older folks.

DAUGHTER: And what do you call older? What age group?

MOTHER: Well, the ones without children mostly. 'Cause I have one lady . . .

DAUGHTER: That's over 40 or how old?

MOTHER: Over 40, yeh. Over 40. They come to the garden because they love it. And they never done it before and they say they learning. So they enjoy it. Over 40, I got over 40 up to how old? I think we had a 90-year-old man working in the garden, but he not able to come anymore. But he worked 'til he was 90-something years old. We give him a plaque for being the oldest gardener that we had. And he had the prettiest garden we had.

DAUGHTER: He did now? Was he from the South?

MOTHER: Yep.

DAUGHTER: Do you have a bunch of folks from the South working?

MOTHER: Yes. He couldn't read, but he'd have you to read it to him and he would catch it as you read it and go do just what you say.

DAUGHTER: Read what now?

MOTHER: Like the directions on the paper how you plant? You read it out to him, he won't miss a thing. He go right on and do it.

DAUGHTER: So everybody has a place?

MOTHER: Right. That's it. So that's how it's done, but it takes a lot of time and a lot of . . . When everybody says it's hard because it takes a lot of time. It takes a lot of time with these people to counsel them. It's a lot of time. And you can't do it in a hurry and you can't do it one time and you can't limit the times that you hafta do it. You have to do it until it gets done. That's all.

DAUGHTER: But you do see some results?

MOTHER: Well, yes, you see a good bit of results. I saw a good bit of results this summer when we plant those, were putting those plants out. They said the plants were not gonna stay. The children themselves didn't destroy any of the plants. They watched out for the plants. And they enjoyed the street. They played ball but none of the ball broke those plants. They watched out for it. Close as it is. They watched out for it and that was marvelous.

When you have your vision, that's one step, as you go through one it'll go to the next step. And you follow it, nothing gonna be unturned, everything will work in place.

DAUGHTER: But if you follow it?

MOTHER: Yeh, and keep on praying. Can't stop. Can't stop 'cause too much out here. And a lot of times you may have to change sometimes. Who knows? You know what I mean?

DAUGHTER: You may have to change directions a little bit.

MOTHER: Right. May have to change your directions. So you have to keep in touch always. You have to, have to constantly think it over and . . . you know . . . pray for guidance 'cause you don't know when you have to change. So when time come to change you know to change. 'Cause I pray for my strength and my health and guidance so that I can go 'head. 'Cause I have to pray for the words to be right to go talk to some of these parents 'cause some of them may get insulted. You have to pray for that patience. I pray for that patience and understanding.

DAUGHTER: It takes a lot of patience?

MOTHER: Oh, yeh. Ha! Don't start without patience, honey.

BIBLIOGRAPHY

Note: We wish to call special attention to the journal *Environmental Ethics*, a pioneering periodical from the early days of an emerging field of study. The founding editor, Eugene Hargrove, as of 1993 was in the Department of Philosophy at the University of North Texas in Denton, Texas. We also wish to call attention to these periodicals: *Environmental Values, Between the Species*, the *Trumpeter*, the *Journal of the Society for Conservation Biology*, and *Ecological Economics*. Other journals which occasionally focus on environmental issues are *Inquiry*, the *Monist*, the *American Philosophical Quarterly*, *Ethics*, the *Journal of Value Inquiry*, and *Philosophy and Public Affairs*. Bibliographies are springboards from which to jump; the materials cited here, notoriously "incomplete" in many respects, will lead the reader to other important works. Those interested will find the two annotated bibliographies drawn up by Eric Katz to be of great assistance: (1) "Environmental Ethics: A Select Annotated Bibliography, 1983–1987," in *Research in Philosophy & Technology*, Vol. 9, pp. 251–285; and (2) "Environmental Ethics: A Select Annotated Bibliography: II: 1987–1990, in *Research in Philosophy & Technology*, Vol. 12, pp. 287–324. In 1993 Katz was at the New Jersey Institute of Technology, University Heights, Newark, NJ 07102, and was preparing a third bibliography. For current bibliographic references, videotape information, and current announcements about conferences on, or related to, environmental ethics, see the lively and thorough *International Society for Environmental Ethics Newsletter*, which is now available from Professor Laura Westra, Department of Philosophy, University of Windsor, Windsor, Ontario N9B 3P4, Canada. On a broad variety of topics in ethics, the excellent two-volume *Encyclopedia of Ethics*, edited by Lawrence Becker and Charlotte Becker (New York: Garland Publishing Co., 1992), will prove extremely useful.

I. An Introduction to Ethical Theory

Feldman, Fred. *Introductory Ethics* (Englewood Cliffs, NJ: Prentice-Hall, 1978).

Hargrove, Eugene. *Foundations of Environmental Ethics* (Englewood Cliffs, NJ: Prentice-Hall, 1989).

Miller, Harlan B., and William H. Williams, eds. *The Limits of Utilitarianism* (Minneapolis: University of Minnesota Press, 1982).

Nash, Roderick, F. *The Rights of Nature: A History of Environmental Ethics* (Madison: University of Wisconsin Press, 1989).

Rachels, James, ed. *The Elements of Moral Philosophy* (New York: McGraw-Hill, 1993).

———. *The Right Thing to Do* (New York: Random House, 1989).

Regan, Tom, and Donald VanDeVeer, eds. *And Justice for All* (Totowa, NJ: Rowman and Littlefield, 1982).

Ruggiers, Vincent. *Thinking Critically About Ethical Issues* (Mountain View, CA: Mayfield Publishing, 1992).

Sen, Amartya, and Bernard Williams, eds. *Utilitarianism and Beyond* (Cambridge: Cambridge University Press, 1982).

Sher, George, ed. *Moral Philosophy* (San Diego: Harcourt Brace Jovanovich, Publishers, 1987).

Singer, Peter. *Applied Ethics* (Oxford: Oxford University Press, 1988).

———. *Practical Ethics* (Cambridge: Cambridge University Press, 1979).

Sterba, James. *Morality in Practice* (Belmont, CA: Wadsworth Publishing Company, 1988).

Taylor, Paul. *Problems of Moral Philosophy* (Belmont, CA: Dickenson Publishing Co., 1967).

II. Western Religions and Environmental Attitudes

Aquinas, Thomas. *Summa Contra Gentiles*, trans. Anton Pegis et al. (5 Vols.) (Garden City, NY: Image Books, 1955–57).

———. *Summa Theologica* (60 Vols.) (London: Eyre and Spottiswoode; and New York: McGraw-Hill, 1964).

Attfield, Robin. *The Ethics of Environmental Concern* (Athens: The University of Georgia Press, 2nd edition, 1991).

———. *God and the Secular: A Philosophical Assessment of Secular Reasoning from Bacon to Kant* (Cardiff: University College Cardiff Press, 1978).

Berry, Thomas. *The Dream of the Earth* (San Francisco: Sierra Club Books, 1988).

Dombrowski, Daniel. *Hartshorne and the Metaphysics of Animal Rights* (Albany: State University of New York Press, 1981).

Ehrenfeld, D. *The Arrogance of Humanism* (New York: Oxford University Press, 1981).

Hume, C. W. *The Status of Animals in the Christian Religion* (London: Universities Federation for Animal Welfare, 1957).

Karrer, Otto. ed. *St. Francis of Assisi, The Legends and the Lauds*, trans. N. Wydenbruck (London: Sheed & Ward, 1977).

Linzey, Andrew. *Animal Rights: A Christian Assessment of Man's Treatment of Animals* (London: SCM Press, 1976).

———. *Christianity and the Rights of Animals* (New York: Crossroads, 1987).

Passmore, John. *Man's Responsibility for Nature* [*MRN*] (London: Duckworth, 1974; 2nd edition, 1980).

Peacocke, A. R. *Creation and the World of Science* (Oxford: Oxford University Press, 1979).

Rachels, James. *Created from Animals: The Moral Implications of Darwinism* (New York: Oxford University Press, 1990).

Regan, Tom, ed. *Animal Sacrifices: Religious Perspectives on the Use of Animals in Science* (Philadelphia: Temple University Press, 1986).

Rockefeller, Steven C., and John C. Elder, eds. *Spirit and Nature: Why the Environment Is a Religious Issue* (Boston: Beacon Press, 1992).

Rolston, Holmes, III. *Science and Religion: A Critical Survey* (New York: Random House, 1987).

Schweitzer, Albert. *Reverence for Life*, edited by R. H. Fuller (London: SPCK, 1970).

Spring, David, and Eileen Spring, eds. *Ecology and Religion in History* (New York: Harper & Row, 1974).

White, Lynn, Jr. *Medieval Technology and Social Change* (Oxford: Clarendon Press, 1962).

III. The Other Animals

Adams, Carol J. *The Sexual Politics of Meat: A Feminist-Vegetarian Critical Theory* (New York: Continuum, 1990).

The Animals' Agenda: The International Magazine of Animal Rights and Ecology. P. O. Box 6809, Syracuse, NY 13217.

Between the Species. P. O. Box 254, Berkeley, CA 94701.

Clark, Stephen. *The Moral Status of Animals* (Oxford: Clarendon Press, 1977).

Crosby, Alfred W. *Ecological Imperialism* (New York: Cambridge University Press, 1986).

Dawkins, Marian. *Animal Suffering: The Science of Animal Welfare* (New York: Routledge, Chapman, and Hall, 1980).

Ehrenfeld, D. *The Arrogance of Humanism* (New York: Oxford University Press, 1981).

Fox, M. W. *Returning to Eden: Animal Rights and Human Responsibility* (New York: Viking Press, 1980).

Fox, Michael, and Nancy Wiswall. *The Hidden Costs of Beef* (Washington, DC: Humane Society of the United States, 1989).

Frey, R. G. *Interests and Rights: The Case Against Animals* (Oxford: Clarendon Press, 1980).

———. *Rights, Animals and Suffering* (Oxford: Basil Blackwell Ltd., 1983).

Godlovitch, Stanley, Roslind Godlovitch, and John Harris, eds. *Animals, Men, and Morals* (New York: Taplinger Pub. Co., 1972).

Hargrove, Eugene. *The Animal Rights/Environmental Ethics Debate: The Environmental Perspective* (Albany: State University of New York Press, 1992).

Harrison, Ruth. *Animal Machines: The New Factory Farming Industry* (London: Stuart, 1964).

Inquiry, Vol. 22, No. 1–2 (Summer 1979). Includes a useful bibliography; the entire issue is about animals.

Johnson, Edward. *Species and Morality*, Ph.D. Dissertation in Philosophy at Princeton University (1976); see University Microfilms International, 1977: Ann Arbor, Michigan.

Kroc, Ray. *Grinding It Out: The Making of McDonald's* (Chicago: Henry Regnery, 1977).

Lappé, Frances Moore. *Diet for a Small Planet* (New York: Ballantine Books, 1982).

Lappé, Frances Moore, and Joseph Collins. *Food First: Beyond the Myth of Scarcity* (New York: Ballantine Books, 1978).

Lovejoy, Arthur O. *The Great Chain of Being: A Study of the History of an Idea.* (Cambridge, MA: Harvard University Press, 1936).

Magell, Charles. *A Bibliography on Animal Rights and Related Matters* (Washington, DC: University Press of America, 1981).

Mason, Jim, and Peter Singer. *Animal Factories* (New York: Crown, 1980).

Midgley, Mary. *Animals and Why They Matter* (Harmondsworth, England: Penguin Books Ltd., 1983).

———. *Beast and Man* (Ithaca, NY: Cornell University Press, 1979).

Rachels, James. *Created from Animals: The Moral Implications of Darwinism* (New York: Oxford University Press, 1990).

Regan, Tom. *All That Dwell Therein: Animal Rights and Environmental Ethics* (Berkeley: University of California Press, 1982).

———. *The Case for Animal Rights* (Berkeley: University of California Press, 1983).

———. *The Thee Generation: Reflections on the Coming Revolution* (Philadelphia: Temple University Press, 1991).

Regan, Tom, and Peter Singer, eds. *Animal Rights and Human Obligations* (Englewood Cliffs, NJ: Prentice-Hall, 1976).

Rifkin, Jeremy. *Beyond Beef: The Rise and Fall of the Cattle Culture* (New York: Dutton, 1992).

Rollin, Bernard. *Animal Rights and Human Morality*, revised edition (Buffalo: Prometheus Press, 1992).

———. *The Unheeded Cry: Animal Consciousness, Animal Pain and Science* (Oxford: Oxford University Press, 1989).

Rosenfield, Lenora. *From Beast-Machine to Man-Machine* (New York: Columbia University Press, 1968).

Ryder, Richard. *Speciesism: The Ethics of Vivisections* (Edinburgh: Scottish Society for the Prevention of Vivisection, 1974).

———. *Victims of Science: The Use of Animals in Research* (London: Davis-Poynter, 1975).

Serpell, James. *In the Company of Animals: Study of Human-Animal Relationships* (Oxford: Basil Blackwell, 1986).

Singer, Peter. *Animal Liberation* (New York: A New York Review Book, distributed by Random House, 1975).

———. *The Expanding Circle* (New York: Farrar, Straus, and Firoux, 1981).

———. *Practical Ethics* (Cambridge: Cambridge University Press, 1979).

———, ed. *In Defense of Animals* (New York: Basil Blackwell, 1987).

IV-A. The Broader, Biotic Community

Callicott, J. Baird, ed. *Companion to a Sand County Almanac: Interpretive and Critical Essays* (Madison: University of Wisconsin Press, 1987).

Engberg, Robert, and Donald Wesling, eds. *John Muir: To Yosemite and Beyond: Writings from the Years 1863 to 1875* (Madison: University of Wisconsin Press, 1980).

Flader, Susan L. *Thinking Like a Mountain: Aldo Leopold and the Evolution of an Ecological Attitude Toward Deer, Wolves, and Forests* (Columbia: University of Missouri Press, 1974).

Hays, Samuel P. *Conservation and the Gospel of Efficiency: The Progressive Conservation Movement, 1890–1920* (Cambridge, MA: Harvard University Press, 1959).

Lovelock, James. *Gaia: A New Look at Life on Earth* (New York: Oxford University Press, 1981).

Marsh, George Perkins. *Man and Nature* (Cambridge, MA: Harvard University Press, 1965).

The Monist, Vol. 75, No. 2 (April 1992); special issue on The Intrinsic Value of Nature.

Pinchot, Gifford. *The Fight for Conservation* (Seattle: University of Washington Press, 1910).

Schultz, Robert C., and J. Donald Hughes, eds. *Ecological Consciousness: Essays from the Earthday X Colloquium, University of Denver, April 21–24, 1980* (Washington, DC: University Press of America, 1981).

Wright, Larry. *Teleological Explanation* (Berkeley: University of California Press, 1976).

IV-B. Approaches to Conflict Resolutions

Broome, John. *Weighing Goods* (Cambridge, MA: Basil Blackwell, 1991).

IV-C. Deep Ecology and Social Ecology

Bookchin, Murray. *The Ecology of Freedom: The Emergence and Dissolution of Hierarchy* (Palo Alto: Cheshire Books, 1982).

———. *The Philosophy of Social Ecology: Essays on Dialectical Naturalism* (Toronto: Black Rose Books, 1990).

———. *Post-Scarcity Anarchism* (San Francisco: Ramparts Press, 1971).

———. *Remaking Society: Pathways to a Green Future* (Boston: South End Press, 1990).

———. *Toward an Ecological Society* (Montreal: Black Rose Books, 1980).

Bradford, George. *How Deep Is Deep Ecology? A Challenge to Radical Environmentalists* (Ojai, CA: Times Change Press, 1989).

Clark, John, ed. *The Anarchist Moment: Reflections on Culture, Nature, and Power* (Toronto: Black Rose Books, 1984).

———. *Renewing the Earth: The Promise of Social Ecology* (London: Green Print, 1990).

Devall, Bill. *Simple in Means, Rich in Ends, Practicing Deep Ecology* (Salt Lake City: Peregrine Smith Books, 1988).

Devall, Bill, and George Sessions. *Deep Ecology, Living as if*

Nature Mattered (Salt Lake City: Peregrine Smith Books, 1985).

Drengson, Alan R. *Beyond Environmental Crisis: From Technocratic to Planetary Person* (New York: Peter Lang, 1989).

Evernden, Neil. *The Natural Alien* (Toronto: University of Toronto Press, 1985).

Fox, Warwick. *Toward a Transpersonal Ecology: Developing New Foundations for Environmentalism* (Boston: Shambhala, 1990).

Harbinger: The Journal of Social Ecology. P. O. Box 89, Plainfield, VT 05667.

LaChapelle, Delorse. *Earth Wisdom* (Silverton, CO: Way of the Mountain Center, 1978).

Naess, Arne. *Ecology, Community, and Lifestyle* (Cambridge: Cambridge University Press, 1989).

Sale, Kirkpatrick. *Dwellers in the Land, The Bioregional Vision* (San Francisco: Sierra Club Books, 1985).

Seed, John, Joanna Macy, Pat Fleming, and Arne Naess. *Thinking Like a Mountain, Towards a Council of All Beings* (Philadelphia: New Society Publishers, 1988).

Snyder, Gary. *The Old Ways* (San Francisco: City Lights Books, 1977).

———. *The Practice of the Wild.* (San Francisco: North Point Press, 1990).

———. *Turtle Island* (New York: New Directions Books, 1977).

Spretnak, Charlene, and Fritjof Capra. *Green Politics,* rev. ed. (Santa Fe: Bear and Company, 1986).

Tobias, Michael, ed. *Deep Ecology* (San Diego: Avant Books, 1977).

The Trumpeter. LightStar, P. O. Box 5853. Victoria, BC, Canada V8R-6S8.

IV-D. Ecofeminism

Adams, Carol J., ed. *Ecofeminism and the Sacred* (Orbis Books, 1992).

Allen, Paula Gunn. *The Sacred Hoop: Recovering the Feminine in American Indian Tradition* (Boston: Beacon Press, 1986).

Biehl, Janet. *Rethinking Ecofeminist Politics* (Boston: South End Press, 1991).

Brown, Wilmette. *Roots: Black Ghetto Ecology* (London: Housewives in Dialogue, 1986).

Caldecott, Leonie, and Stephanie Leland, eds. *Reclaim the Earth: Women Speak Out for Life on Earth* (London: The Women's Press, 1983).

Diamond, Irene, and Gloria Feman Orenstein, eds. *Reweaving the World, The Emergence of Ecofeminism* (San Francisco: Sierra Club Books, 1990).

Easlea, Brian. *Science and Sexual Oppression: Patriarchy's Confrontation with Women and Nature* (London: Weidenfeld and Nicholson, 1981).

The Ecofeminist Newsletter, A publication of the National Women Studies Association (NWSA) Ecofeminist Task Force, ed. Noel Sturgeon, Middletown, CT: Center for the Humanities, Wesleyan University.

Environmental Review. Special issue on Women and Environmental History, guest editor, Carolyn Merchant, 8(1), 1984.

Gaard, Greta, ed. *Ecofeminism: Women, Animals, Nature* (Philadelphia: Temple University Press, 1993).

Gray, Elizabeth Dodson. *Green Paradise Lost* (Wellesley, MA: Roundtable Press, 1979).

Griffin, Susan. *Women and Nature: The Roaring Inside Her* (New York: Harper and Row Publishers, Inc., 1978).

Heresies #13: Feminism and Ecology 4 (1981).

Hypatia. Special issue on Ecological Feminism 6 (Spring 1991).

Kolodny, Annette. *The Lay of the Land: Metaphor as Experience and History in American Life and Letters* (Chapel Hill: University of North Carolina Press, 1975).

List, Peter C., ed. *Radical Environmentalism: Philosophy and Tactics* (Belmont, CA: Wadsworth Publishing Co., 1993).

Merchant, Carolyn. *The Death of Nature: Women, Ecology, and the Scientific Revolution* (New York: Harper and Row Publishers, Inc., 1983).

———. *Ecological Revolution: Nature, Gender, and Science in New England* (Chapel Hill: University of North Carolina Press, 1990).

———. *Radical Ecology: The Search for a Livable World* (New York: Routledge, 1992).

The New Catalyst #10. 1987–88. Special issue on Women/Earth Speaking: Feminism and Ecology (Winter).

Plant, Judith, ed. *Healing the Wounds: The Promise of Ecofeminism* (Santa Cruz, CA: New Society Publishers, 1989).

Reuther, Rosemary Radford. *New Women, New Earth: Sexist Ideologies and Human Liberation* (New York: The Seabury Press, 1975).

Studies in the Humanities 15, No. 2 (1988). Special issue on Feminism, Ecology, and the Future of the Humanities. Edited by Patrick Murphy.

V. Economics, Ethics, and Ecology

Arthur, John, and William H. Shaw, eds. *Justice and Economic Distribution* (Englewood Cliffs, NJ: Prentice-Hall, Inc., 1978).

Berry, Wendell. *Home Economics* (San Francisco: North Point Press, 1987).

Bormann, F. H., and Stephen R. Kellert, eds. *Ecology, Economics, and Ethics: The Broken Circle* (New Haven: Yale University Press, 1991).

Brundtland, G. *Our Common Future* (New York: Oxford University Press, 1987).

Costanza, Robert. *Ecological Economics* (New York: Columbia University Press, 1991).

Daly, Herman E. *Steady-State Economics: The Economics of Biophysical Equilibrium and Moral Growth* (San Francisco: W. H. Freeman, 1977).

Daly, Herman, and John Cobb. *For the Common Good: Redirecting the Economy Toward Community, the Environment, and a Sustainable Future* (Boston: Beacon Press, 1989).

de la Court, Thijs. *Beyond Brundtland: Green Development in the 1990s* (New York: New Horizons Press, 1990).

Douglas, Mary, and Baron Isherwood. *The World of Goods* (New York: Basic Books, 1979).

Dryzek, John S. *Rational Ecology: Environment and Political Economy* (New York: Basil Blackwell, 1987).

Elkington, John, and Jonathan Shopley. *The Shrinking Planet: U.S. Information Technology and Sustainable Development* (Holmes, PA: World Resources Institute, 1988).

Elkins, Paul. *Green Economics* (New York: Doubleday, 1992).

Elster, J. and E. Hylland, eds. *Foundations of Social Choice Theory* (Cambridge: Cambridge University Press, 1983).

Freeman, A. Myrick, III, Robert Haveman, and Allen Kneese. *The Economics of Environmental Policy* (New York: Wiley, 1973).

Fusfield, Daniel. *The Age of the Economist* (Glenview, IL: Scott Foresman and Company, 1986).

Goodland, Robert, ed. *Race to Save the Tropics: Ecology and Economics for a Sustainable Future* (Covelo, CA: Island Press, 1990).

Gupta, Avijit. *Ecology and Development in the Third World* (New York: Routledge, 1988).

Kneese, A., S. Ben-David, and W. D. Shulze, eds. *The Ethical Foundations of Benefit-Cost Analysis* (Washington, DC: Resources for the Future, 1983).

Krutilla, John, and Anthony Fisher. *The Economics of Natural Environments* (Washington, DC: Resources for the Future, 1985).

Leonard, H. Jeffrey, et al. *Environment and the Poor: Development Strategies for a Common Agenda* (New Brunswick, NJ: Transaction Publishers, 1989).

MacLean, Douglas, ed. *Values at Risk* (Totowa, NJ: Rowman and Littlefield, 1986).

MacNeil, Jim, Pieter Winsemius, and Taizo Yakushiju. *Beyond Interdependence* (New York: Oxford University Press, 1991).

Milbrath, Lester. *Envisioning a Sustainable Society* (Albany, NY: SUNY Press, 1989).

Mishan, Edward J. *The Cost of Economic Growth* (Harmondsworth: Penguin Books, 1969).

Okun, Arthur M. *Equality and Efficiency: The Big Tradeoff* (Washington, DC: Brookings Institution, 1975).

Orr, David W. *Ecological Literacy: Education and the Transition to an Environmental Postmodern World* (Albany: State University of New York Press, 1992).

Pearce, David, Edward Barbier, and Anil Markandya. *Blueprint for a Green Economy* (London: Earthscan Publications, 1989).

———. *Sustainable Development: Economics and Environment in the Third World* (Brookfield, VT: Gower, 1990).

Perrings, Charles. *Economy and Environment* (Cambridge: Cambridge University Press, 1987).

Posner, Richard. *The Economics of Justice* (Cambridge, MA: Harvard University Press, 1981).

Rawls, J. *A Theory of Justice* (Cambridge, MA: Harvard University Press, 1971).

Sagoff, Mark. *The Economy of the Earth* (Cambridge: Cambridge University Press, 1988).

Schelling, Thomas. *Micromotives and Macrobehavior* (New York: Norton, 1978).

Schumacher, E. F. *Small Is Beautiful* (New York: Harper and Row, 1973).

Sen, A. K. *Collective Choice and Social Welfare* (San Francisco: Holden-Day, 1970).

———. *On Ethics and Economics* (New York: Basil Blackwell, 1987).

Seneca, Joseph, and Michael Taussig. *The Environmental Economics* (Englewood Cliffs, NJ: Prentice-Hall, 1979).

Shrader-Frechette, K. S. *Risk and Rationality* (Berkeley: University of California Press, 1991).

Stokey, Edith, and Richard Zeckhauser. *A Primer for Policy Analysis* (New York: Norton & Company, 1978).

Tribe, Laurence H., Corrine S. Schelling, and John Voss, eds. *When Values Conflict: Essays on Environmental Analysis, Discourse, and Decision* (Cambridge, MA: Ballinger Publishing Co., 1976).

Waring, Marilyn. *If Women Counted: A New Feminist Economics* (San Francisco: HarperCollins, 1988).

VI-A. Human Population and Pressure on Resources

Bayles, Michael D., ed. *Ethics and Population* (Cambridge, MA: Schenkman, 1976).

Cole, H. et al. *Thinking About the Future: A Critique of the Limits to Growth* (London: Chatto & Windus and Sussex University Press, 1973).

Donaldson, Peter J. *Nature Against Us: The United States*

and the World Population Crisis (Chapel Hill: University of North Carolina Press, 1990).

Ehrlich, Paul R. *The Population Bomb* (London: Pan Books/ Ballantine, 1971).

Ehrlich, Paul R., and Anne H. Ehrlich. *The Population Explosion* (New York: Simon & Schuster, 1990).

———. *Population, Resources, Environment: Issues in Human Ecology* (San Francisco: W. H. Freeman, 2nd ed., 1972).

Hardin, Garrett. *Exploring New Ethics for Survival: The Voyage of the Spaceship Beagle* (New York: Viking Press, 1972).

Hartman, Betsy. *Reproductive Rights and Wrongs: The Global Politics of Population Control and Contraceptive Choice* (New York: Harper and Row, 1987).

Lappé, Frances Moore, and Joseph Collins. *World Hunger: Twelve Myths* (New York: Grove Press, 1986).

Malthus, Thomas Robert. *Population: The First Essay* (Ann Arbor: Ann Arbor Paperbacks, University of Michigan Press, 1959).

Orr, David, and Marvin S. Soroos. *The Global Predicament* (Chapel Hill, NC: University of North Carolina Press, 1979).

Partridge, Ernest, ed. *Responsibilities to Future Generations* (New York: Prometheus Books, 1981).

Sen, Amartya. *Poverty and Famines* (New York: Oxford University Press, 1981).

Simon, Julian L. *The Ultimate Resource* (Princeton, NJ: Princeton University Press, 1981).

Simon, Julian, and Herman Kahn, eds. *The Resourceful Earth* (Oxford: Basil Blackwell, 1984).

VI-B. From the Commons to Property

Ackerman, Bruce A. ed. *Economic Foundations of Property Law* (Boston: Little, Brown and Company, 1975).

———. *Private Property and the Constitution* (New Haven, Yale University Press, 1977).

Becker, Lawrence C. *Property Rights: Philosophical Foundations* (London, Routledge and Kegan Paul, 1977).

Blumenfeld, Samuel L. *Property in a Humane Economy* (La Salle, IL: Open Court, 1974).

Gewirth, Alan. *Human Rights: Essays in Justification and Application* (Chicago: University of Chicago Press, 1982).

Hardin, Garrett, and John Baden, eds. *Managing the Commons* (San Francisco: W. H. Freeman, 1977).

MacPherson, C. B. *The Political Theory of Possessive Individualism: Hobbes to Locke* (Oxford: Oxford University Press, 1962).

Nozick, Robert. *Anarchy, State, and Utopia* (New York: Basic Books, 1974).

Pennock, J. R., and J. W. Chapman, eds. *Property* (New York: New York University Press, 1980).

Waldron, Jeremy. *The Right to Private Property* (Oxford: Clarendon Press, 1988).

VI-C. Preserving Biodiversity

Barbier, Edward, Joanne Burgess, Timothy Swanson, and David Pearce. *Elephants, Ivory and Economics* (London: Earthscan Publications, 1990).

Colinvaux, Paul. *Why Big Fierce Animals Are Rare* (Princeton, NJ: Princeton University Press, 1978).

Ehrenfeld, David W. *The Arrogance of Humanism* (New York: Oxford University Press, 1978).

———. *Conserving Life on Earth* (New York: Oxford University Press, 1972).

Ehrlich, Paul, and Anne Ehrlich. *Extinction* (New York: Random House, 1981).

McNeely, J. A. *Economics and Biological Diversity* (Gland, Switzerland: International Union for the Conservation of Nature and Natural Resources, 1988).

McNeely, Jeffrey A., Kenton R. Miller, Walter V. Reid, Russell Mittermeier, and Timothy B. Werner. *Conserving the World's Biological Diversity* (Washington, DC: WRI, 1990).

Myers, Norman. *A Wealth of Wild Species: Storehouse for Human Welfare* (Boulder, CO: Westview Press, 1983).

Norton, Bryan, ed. *The Preservation of the Species* (Princeton, NJ: Princeton University Press, 1985).

———. *Why Preserve Natural Variety?* (Princeton, NJ: Princeton University Press, 1987).

Regenstein, Lewis. *The Politics of Extinction* (New York: Macmillan and Company, 1975).

Wilson, E. O., ed. *Biodiversity* (Washington, DC: National Academy Press, 1986).

———. *Biophilia* (Cambridge, MA: Harvard University Press, 1984).

———. *The Diversity of Life* (Cambridge, MA: Harvard University Press, 1992).

VI-D. Forests and Wilderness

Agarwal, Bina. *Cold Hearths and Barren Slopes: The World Fuel Crisis in the Third World* (New Delhi: Allied Publishers Private Limited, 1986).

Barney, Daniel R. *The Last Stand, Ralph Nader's Study Group Report on the National Forests* (New York: Grossman Publishers, 1974).

Dietrich, William. *The Final Forest: The Battle for the Last Great Trees of the Pacific Northwest* (New York: Simon and Schuster, 1992).

Frome, Michael. *Battle for the Wilderness* (New York: Praeger Publishers, 1974).

Gillis, M. D., and R. Repetto. *Public Policies and the Misuse of Forest Resources* (New York: Cambridge University Press, 1988).

Gradwohl, Judith, and Russell Greenberg. *Saving the Tropical Forests* (Washington, DC: Island Press, 1988).

Gregersen, Hans, Sydney Draper, and Dieter Elz, eds. *People and Trees: The Role of Social Forestry in Sustainable Development* (Washington, DC: World Bank Publications, 1989).

Guha, Ramachandra. *The Unquiet Woods: Ecological Change and Peasant Resistance in the Himalaya* (Berkeley: University of California Press, 1990).

Hurst, Philip. *Rainforest Politics: Ecological Destruction in South-East Asia* (London: Zed Books, 1990).

Mahar, Dennis J. *Government Policies and Deforestation in Brazil's Amazon Region* (Washington, DC: World Bank, 1989).

Myers, Norman. *The Primary Source: Tropical Forests and Our Future* (New York: Norton Publishing, 1984).

Nash, Roderick, ed. *American Environmentalism: Readings in Conservation History,* 3rd ed. (New York: McGraw-Hill, 1990).

———. *Wilderness and the American Mind* (New Haven: Yale University Press, 1973).

Nations, James D. *Tropical Rainforests, Endangered Environment* (New York: Franklin Watts, 1988).

Norse, Elliot A. *Ancient Forests of the Pacific Northwest* (Washington, DC: Island Press, 1990).

Repetto, R., and M. Gillis, eds. *Public Policies and the Misuse of Forest Resources* (New York: Cambridge University Press, 1988).

Routley, Richard, and Val Routley. *The Fight for the Forests* (Canberra: Australian National University Press, 1974).

Schwartz, William, ed. *Voices for the Wilderness* (New York: Ballantine Books, Inc., 1969).

Shiva, Vandana. *Forestry Crisis and Forestry Myths: A Critical Review of Tropical Forests: A Call for Action.* (*Tropical Forests: A Call for Action* is a joint report of The World Bank, UNDP, and World Resources Institute.) (Malaysia: World Rainforest Movement, 1987).

Suess, Dr. *The Lorax* (New York: Random House, 1971).

VI-E. Degrading the Planet

Abrahamson, D. *The Challenge of Global Warming* (Washington, DC: Island Press, 1989).

Benedick, Richard E., et al. *Greenhouse Warming: Negotiating a Global Regime* (Washington, DC: World Resources Institute, 1991).

———. *Ozone Diplomacy: New Directions in Safeguarding the Planet* (Cambridge, MA: Harvard University Press, 1991).

Brown, Michael H. *Toxic Cloud: The Poisoning of America's Air* (New York: Harper Collins, 1988).

Brown, Wilmette. *Roots: Black Ghetto Ecology* (London: Housewives in Dialogue, 1986).

Dotto, Lydia. *The Ozone War* (Garden City, NY: Doubleday, 1978).

Fisher, David E. *Fire and Ice: The Greenhouse Effect, Ozone Depletion, and Nuclear Winter* (New York: Harper & Row, 1990).

Gibson, Mary, ed. *To Breathe Freely: Risk, Consent, and Air* (Totowa, NJ: Rowman & Allanheld, 1985).

Hynes, H. Patricia. *The Recurring Silent Spring* (New York: Pergamon Press, 1989).

Leggett, Jeremy. *Global Warming: The Greenpeace Report* (New York: Oxford University Press, 1990).

MacLean, Doug, ed. *Energy and the Future* (Totowa, NJ: Rowman and Littlefield, 1983).

Oppenheimer, M., and R. Boyle. *Dead Heat* (New York: Basic Books, 1990).

Reid, Walter V. *Drowning the National Heritage: Climate Change and the U.S. Coastal Biodiversity* (Washington, DC: World Resources Institute, 1991).

———. *Keeping Options Alive: The Scientific Basis for Conserving Biodiversity* (Washington, DC: World Resources Institute, 1989).

Schneider, Stephen H. *Global Warming: Are We Entering the Greenhouse Century?* (San Francisco: Sierra Club Books, 1989).

Shrader-Frechette, K. S. *Nuclear Power and Public Policy* (Dordrecht, Holland: Reidel, 1989).

VII. Varieties of Activism

Abbey, Edward. *Abbey's Road* (New York: E. P. Dutton, 1979).

———. *Hayduke Lives!* (Boston: Little, Brown and Company, 1990).

———. *The Monkey Wrench Gang* (New York: Avon Books, 1976).

Arnold, Ron. *Ecology Wars, Environmentalism As If People Mattered* (Bellevue, WA: The Free Enterprise Press, 1987).

Brown, Michael, and John May. *The Greenpeace Story* (New York: Dorling Kindersley, Inc., 1991).

Chase, Steve, ed. *Defending the Earth, A Dialogue Between Murray Bookchin and Dave Foreman* (Boston: South End Press, 1991).

Davis, John, and Dave Foreman, eds. *The Earth First! Reader, Ten Years of Radical Environmentalism* (Salt Lake City: Peregrine Smith, 1991).

Day, David. *The Environmental Wars* (New York: St. Martin's Press, 1989).

———. *The Whale War* (San Francisco: Sierra Club Books, 1987).

Editors of *Ramparts*. *Eco-Catastrophe* (San Francisco: Canfield Press, 1970).

Foreman, Dave. *Confessions of an Eco-Warrior* (New York: Harmony Books, 1991).

Hepworth, James, and Gregory McNamee, eds. *Resist Much, Obey Little, Some Notes on Edward Abbey* (Salt Lake City: Dream Garden Press, 1985).

Hunter, Robert. *Warriors of the Rainbow, A Chronicle of the Greenpeace Movement* (New York: Holt, Rinehart and Winston, 1979).

Hunter, Robert, and Paul Watson. *Cry Wolf!* (Vancouver, Canada: Shepherds of the Earth, 1985).

Kerrick, Michael. *Ecotage from Our Perspective, An Explanation of the Willamette National Forest's Policy on Environmental Sabotage Known as Ecotage*. A Report for Civil Leaders (Eugene, OR: Willamette National Forest, 1985).

Lewis, Martin W. *Green Delusions: An Environmentalist Critique of Radical Environmentalism* (Durham, NC: Duke University Press, 1992).

Love, Sam, ed. *Earth Tool Kit, A Field Manual for Citizen Activists* (New York: Pocket Books, 1971).

Love, Sam, and David Obst, eds. *Ecotage!* (New York: Pocket Books, 1972).

Manes, Christopher. *Green Rage* (Boston: Little, Brown and Company, 1990).

Mitchell, John G., with Constance L. Stallings. *Ecotactics: The Sierra Club Handbook for Environment Activists* (New York: Pocket Books, 1970).

Paehlke, Robert. *Environmentalism and the Future of Progressive Politics* (New Haven: Yale University Press, 1989).

Ritter, Don. *Ecolinking: Everyone's Guide to Online Environmental Information* (Berkeley, CA: Peachpit Press, 1992).

Scarce, Rik. *Eco-Warriors: Understanding the Radical Environmental Movement* (Chicago: The Noble Press, Inc., 1990).

Sea Shepherd Log. Newsletter of the Sea Shepherd Conservation Society, 1314 2nd St., Santa Monica, CA 90401.

The Student Environmental Action Guide: 25 Simple Things We Can Do, by the Student Action Coalition (Berkeley: Earth Works Press, 1991).

Tokar, Brian. *The Green Alternative, Creating an Ecological Future* (San Pedro, CA: R. & E. Miles, 1987).

Watson, Paul, and Warren Rogers. *Sea Shepherd: My Fight for Whales and Seals* (New York: W. W. Norton, 1982).

About the Planet

Ehrlich, Paul R., and Anne H. Ehrlich. *Healing the Planet* (Reading, MA: Addison-Wesley Publishing, 1991).

Ehrlich, Paul R., Anne H. Ehrlich, and J. P. Holdren. *Ecoscience: Population, Resources, Environment* (San Francisco: W. H. Freeman, 1977).

Ehrlich, P. R., and J. Roughgarden. *The Science of Ecology* (New York: Macmillan, 1987).

Hull, David. *Darwin and His Critics* (Cambridge, MA: Harvard University Press, 1973).

Imbrie, John, and Katherine Imbrie. *Ice Ages: Solving the Mystery* (Short Hulls, NJ: Enslow Publishers, 1979).

Kohn, David. *The Darwinian Heritage* (Princeton, NJ: Princeton University Press, 1985).

Lappé, Francis Moore. *Diet for a Small Planet* (New York: Ballantine Books, 10th anniversary edition, 1985).

Meadows, Dennis. *Beyond the Limits* (Post Mills, VT: Chelsea Green Publishing, 1992).

Miller, J. T. *Living in the Environment* (Belmont, CA: Wadsworth Publishing, 1988).

Odum, E. P. *Fundamentals of Ecology* (Philadelphia: Saunders Publishing, 1969).

Schmidt, Victor A. *Planet Earth and the New Geoscience* (Dubuque, IA: Kendall-Hunt, 1985).

Shepard, Paul. *Subversive Science* (Boston: Houghton Mifflin, 1969).

Weiner. *The Next 100 Years* (New York: Bantam Books, 1990).

———. *Planet Earth* (New York: Bantam Books, 1986).

Woodwall, George. *The Earth in Transition* (Cambridge: Cambridge University Press, 1990).

Young, Louise. *The Blue Planet* (Boston: Little, Brown and Co., 1983).

General Works by Single Authors and Collections

Armstrong, Susan J., and Richard G. Botzler, eds. *Environmental Ethics: Divergence and Convergence* (New York: McGraw-Hill, 1992).

Attfield, Robin. *The Ethics of Environmental Concern* (Athens: The University of Georgia Press, 2nd edition, 1991).

Barbour, Ian. *Technology, Environment, and Human Values* (New York: Praeger, 1980).

Blackstone, William T., ed. *Philosophy and Environmental Crisis* (Athens: University of Georgia Press, 1974).

Brennan, Andrew. *Thinking About Nature: An Investigation of Nature, Value and Ecology* (London: Routledge; and Athens: University of Georgia Press, 1988).

Callicott, J. Baird. *In Defense of the Land Ethic* (Albany: State University of New York Press, 1989).

Cooper, David E., and Joy A. Palmer, eds. *The Environment in Question* (London: Routledge, 1992).

Des Jardins, Joseph R. *Environmental Ethics: An Introduction to Environmental Philosophy* (Belmont, CA: Wadsworth, 1993).

Drengson, Alan R. *Beyond Environmental Crisis: From Technocrat to Planetary Person* (New York: Peter Lang Publishing Co., 1989).

Eckersley, Robyn. *Environmentalism and Political Theory: Toward an Ecocentric Approach* (Albany: State University of New York Press, 1992).

Elliot, Robert, and Arran Gare, eds. *Environmental Philosophy: A Collection of Readings* (University Park: Pennsylvania State University Press, 1983).

Gunn, Alastair S., and Aarne Vesilind, eds. *Environmental Ethics for Engineers* (Chelsea, MI: Lewis Publishers, 1986).

Hanson, Philip P., ed. *Environmental Ethics: Philosophical and Policy Perspective*, Vol. I (Burnaby, BC: Simon Fraser University, 1986).

Hart, Richard E., ed. *Ethics and the Environment* (Lanham, MD: University Press of America, 1992).

Johnson, Lawrence E. *A Morally Deep World: An Essay on Moral Significance and Environmental Ethics* (Cambridge: Cambridge University Press, 1991).

McCloskey, H. J. *Ecological Ethics and Politics* (Totowa, NJ: Rowman and Littlefield, 1983).

Miller, Alan S. *Gaia Connections: An Introduction to Ecology, Ecoethics, and Economics* (Totowa, NJ: Rowman and Littlefield, 1991).

Norton, Bryan G. *Toward Unity Among Environmentalists* (New York: Oxford University Press, 1991).

Passmore, John. *Man's Responsibility for Nature: Ecological Problems and Western Traditions* (New York: Charles Scribner's Sons, 1974).

Potter, Van Rensselaer. *Global Bioethics: Building on the Leopold Legacy* (Lansing: Michigan State University Press, 1989).

Regan, Tom, ed. *Earthbound: New Introductory Essays in Environmental Ethics* (New York: Random House, 1984).

Rolston, Holmes, III. *Environmental Ethics* (Philadelphia: Temple University Press, 1988).

———. *Philosophy Gone Wild: Essays in Environmental Ethics* (Buffalo, NY: Prometheus Books, 1986).

Scherer, Donald. *Upstream/Downstream: Issues in Environmental Ethics* (Philadelphia: Temple University Press, 1990).

Scherer, Donald, and Thomas Attig, eds. *Ethics and the Environment* (Englewood Cliffs, NJ: Prentice-Hall, 1983).

Shrader-Frechette, K. S., ed. *Environmental Ethics* (Pacific Grove, CA: The Boxwood Press, 1981).

Stone, Christopher F. *Earth and Other Ethics: The Case for Moral Pluralism* (New York: Harper and Row, 1987).

VanDeVeer, Donald, and Christine Pierce. *People, Penguins and Plastic Trees: Basic Issues in Environmental Ethics* (Belmont, CA: Wadsworth Publishing Co., 1986).

Wenz, Peter S. *Environmental Justice* (Albany: State University of New York Press, 1988).

Weston, Anthony. *Toward Better Problems: New Perspectives on Abortion, Animal Rights, the Environment, and Justice* (Philadelphia: Temple University Press, 1992).

Zimmerman, Michael, J. Baird Callicott, George Sessions, Karen J. Warren, and John P. Clark, eds. *Environmental Philosophy: From Animal Rights to Radical Ecology* (Englewood Cliffs, NJ: Prentice-Hall, 1993).